ACKNOWLEDGME

Grateful acknowledgment is made to the following publisher for permission to quote from their works:

Butterworths: *The All England Law Reports* have been reproduced by the kind permission of LexisNexis Butterworths Tolley a division of Reed Elsevier (UK) Limited.

Incorporated Council for Law Reporting for England & Wales: *The Law Reports; The Weekly Law Reports.*

While every care has been taken to establish and acknowledge copyright, and contact the copyright owners, the publishers tender their apologies for any accidental infringement. They would be pleased to come to a suitable arrangement with the rightful owners in each case.

Trinity College Library Dublin
University of Dublin

Superseded item withdrawn from stock.
Not to be lent or resold if found please
return to TCD Library, Dublin 2, Ireland

Date of withdrawal: 8/1/07

Authorised by: JL

PREFACE

This sourcebook continues to provide legislative texts and extracts from case decisions for those who need a handy compendium of primary material on the intellectual property law of the United Kingdom. It is intended as a complement to William Cornish and David Llewelyn, *Intellectual Property: Patents, Copyright, Trade Marks and Allied Rights*, which is appearing in a Fifth Edition in 2003. There is accordingly no editorial commentary here.

Much of United Kingdom IP law derives directly or by incorporation from regulations and directives of the European Union. Of all the areas of private law, intellectual property is now the most Europeanised. Since the previous edition the law of registered designs has been subjected to the twin process previously meted out to registered trade marks. A Community Registered Design has been introduced (together with a short-term unregistered right). National registered rights continue as an alternative but subject to harmonisation measures which secure standard legislative provisions across member states. Despite the efforts of the states which have successively presided over the EU, the Community Patent Convention has lain on the shelf since 1975. Member States have been intransigent over the issue of translating patent specifications into all EU languages and over the creation of a Community jurisdiction to try Community Patent actions. However, as this edition goes to press the EU Council has indicated a new determination to introduce this unitary right as soon as it can be achieved.

The EU trade marks regime continues to provoke an unending stream of issues about the scope and operation of the new law. The drafting of that law left fundamental questions obscure. A flood of case-law strives to settle differences of approach. It used to be thought that such differences derived from national attitudes. Inevitably they have some influence. Equally it now seems that any trade mark system provokes a range of attitudes. Some judges favour an ever-broadening approach that is considered to reflect "modern" business practices. Others show more concern for allowing a reasonable degree of freedom among competitors to emulate developments stemming from others. As ever, individual judges are affected by the positions of the particular parties to litigation, so that their decisions appear to swivel between the two poles. All in all, the experience has provided one of the most intense trials of EU harmonisation of laws.

As to copyright, the desperate attempts to adapt it so as to give meaning to proprietary rights on the Internet has resulted in the EU's Information Society Directive of 2001, which is difficult to transpose into the national context, in the UK as elsewhere. At the stage of going to press, it has been possible only to refer to the UK Government's proposed amendments to the Copyright, Designs and Patents Act 1988 and not to the final form of the eagerly awaited Regulations. This is one point at which fully international law is being transposed into our law, since the Directive develops upon obligations laid down in the WIPO Treaties on Copyright and on Performers and Phonograms, both of 1996. Otherwise there are few novel points at which international conventions have given rise to changes in domestic law.

W.R.C.
Cambridge,
March, 2003

CONTENTS

Contents

TABLE OF CASES

TABLE OF STATUTES

Foreign Statutes

TABLE OF STATUTORY INSTRUMENTS

TABLE OF EUROPEAN LEGISLATION

Regulations

TABLE OF INTERNATIONAL TREATIES AND CONVENTIONS

1 PATENTS FOR INVENTIONS

1.1 Granting and Maintenance of Patents

1.1.1 International Connections

1.1.1.1 Patents Act 1977, s.130(7): Interpretation of 1977 Act

S.130(7) Whereas by a resolution made on the signature of the Community Patent Convention the governments of the member states of the European Economic Community resolved to adjust their laws relating to patents so as (among other things) to bring those laws into conformity with the corresponding provisions of the European Patent Convention, the Community Patent Convention and the Patent Cooperation Treaty, it is hereby declared that the following provisions of this Act, this is to say, sections 1(1) to (4), 2 to 6, 14(3), (5) and (6), 37(5), 54, 60, 69, 72(1) and (2), 74(4), 82, 83, 88(6) and (7), 100 and 125, are so framed as to have, as nearly as practicable, the same effects in the United Kingdom as the corresponding provisions of the European Patent Convention, the Community Patent Convention and the Patent Cooperation Treaty have in the territories to which those Conventions apply.

1.1.1.2 Patents Act 1977, s.5: Priority under the Paris Industrial Property Convention

S.5(1) For the purposes of this Act the priority date of an invention to which an application for a patent relates and also of any matter (whether or not the same as the invention) contained in any such application is, except as provided by the following provisions of this Act, the date of filing the application.

(2) If in or in connection with an application for a patent (the application in suit) a declaration is made, whether by the applicant or any predecessor in title of his, complying with the relevant requirements of rules and specifying one or more earlier relevant applications for the purposes of this section made by the applicant or a predecessor in title of his and each having a date of filing during the period of twelve months immediately preceding the date of filing the application in suit, then—

(a) if an invention to which the application in suit relates is supported by matter disclosed in the earlier relevant application or applications, the priority date of that invention shall instead of being the date of filing the application in suit be the date of filing the relevant application in which that matter was disclosed or, if it was disclosed in more than one relevant application, the earliest of them;

(b) the priority date of any matter contained in the application in suit which was also disclosed in the earlier relevant application or applications shall be the date of filing the relevant application in which that matter was disclosed or, if it was disclosed in more than one relevant application, the earliest of them.

(3) Where an invention or other matter contained in the application in suit is also disclosed in two earlier relevant applications filed by the same applicant as in the case of the application in suit of a predecessor in title of his and the second of those relevant applications was specified in or in connection with the application in suit, the second of those relevant applications shall, so far as concerns that invention or matter, be disregarded unless—

(a) it was filed in or in respect of the same country as the first; and

(b) not later than the date of filing the second, the first (whether or not so specified) was unconditionally withdrawn, or was abandoned or refused, without—

(i) having been made available to the public (whether in the United Kingdom or elsewhere);
(ii) leaving any rights outstanding; and
(iii) having served to establish a priority date in relation to another application, wherever made.

(4) The foregoing provisions of this section shall apply for determining the priority date of an invention for which a patent has been granted as they apply for determining the priority date of an invention to which an application for that patent relates.

(5) In this section "relevant application" means any of the following applications which has a date of filing, namely—

(a) an application for a patent under this Act;

(b) an application in or for a convention country (specified under section 90 below) for protection in respect of an invention or an application which, in accordance with the law of a convention country or a treaty or international convention to which a convention country is a party, is equivalent to such an application.

(6) References in subsection (5) above to a convention country include references to a country, other than the United Kingdom, which is a member of the World Trade Organisation.

For the equivalent provision in the European Patent Convention, see Article 88. Note also: Patents Act 1977, s.6—Disclosure of matter between earlier and later applications.

1.1.1.3   *Asahi Kasei Kogyo's Application* [1991] R.P.C. 485, HL

A patent claimed the protein known as Human Tissue Necrosis Factor (HTNF), produced by recombinant DNA technology. Its use is in reducing tumours in humans. Against it, under s.2(3), was cited a European patent application, filed at a later date but claiming an earlier priority from a Japanese application. This last described the genetic structure of HTNF, but gave no information about how it was obtained. The House of Lords faced arguments based on conflicting decisions. One line of authorities held that priority could be based on an earlier statement that a specific substance had been made; the other required that there be an "enabling disclosure" in the earlier document, describing to the ordinary skilled technician how it could be made. The latter view was preferred and was held to apply equally—

(i) *to the question whether there was anticipation under s.2(2) and 2(3);*

(ii) *to the question whether priority could be claimed from an earlier Convention, British or European application; and*

(iii) *to the question whether a patent specification adequately disclosed the invention under ss.14(3) and 72.*

Lord Oliver (with whom other members of the House agreed):

Section 5 of the Act shows a distinction between the invention to which an application relates and "matter" contained in the application and contemplates that there may be different priority dates for the two. The priority date of the invention under subsection 2(a) is to be the date of filing of an earlier relevant application which contains matter "supporting" the invention, whereas the priority date of "matter contained in the application in suit" is to be the date of filing of the earliest relevant application in which "that matter" was disclosed. The Act does not contain any definition of the word "supported" but some assistance can be obtained from the provisions of section 14(5) which require the claim in an application to be "supported" by the description. That must, I think, involve the conclusion that if that which is contained in the description of the specification does not enable the claim to be established, it cannot be said to "support" it, for the Act can hardly have contemplated a complete application for a patent lacking some of the material necessary to sustain the claims made. Since, therefore, subsection (3) of section 14 requires in terms that the specification disclose the invention in a way which will enable it to be performed by a person skilled in the art (*i.e.* it must contain an "enabling disclosure") it follows that a description in an earlier application which contains no enabling disclosure will not "support" the invention so as to enable it, as an invention, to claim priority from the date of that application under section 5(2)(a), although the description will be entitled to a priority as "matter contained" in the application in suit under section 5(2)(b).

The question can, perhaps, best be tested by an example which assumes an initial application containing no more than a rudimentary description, but an extensive claim going well beyond what is described. If that is followed by a further application containing the same claim but a substantially different description, albeit incorporating part of the description in the earlier application, it could not be seriously argued that the invention claimed in the second application was "supported" by matter in the first. The original description was inadequate to support the claim and the claim, which is the same in both applications, can hardly "support" itself.

In a case in 1958 before Lloyd-Jacob J. in the Patents Appeal Tribunal, conveniently referred to by the abbreviated title of *G.K.I.'s Application* [1958] R.P.C. 51, an application was made for a patent for chemical compounds described as metal borohydrides, one of which was calcium borohydride. On the examination under section 7(2) of the Act the examiner cited an article in a chemical encyclopaedia which referred to various borohydrides, including that of calcium, stating that "they have been prepared but their properties have not been reported as yet". The superintending examiner required deletion from the claim of the reference to calcium borohydride on the ground that the claim could not be sustained in the face of "a clear statement ... that this same compound has already been made". The broad claim for calcium borohydride "as new compound" carried an assumption that the invention lay in the compound itself and not in a process of manufacture, and if that were so, the invention was sufficiently disclosed if the cited document

3

"specifies in clear terms the compound claimed, and states, explicitly or implicitly, that the compound has been made". Lloyd-Jacob J. in a very short judgment, upheld the decision of the superintending examiner on the ground that:

> "it is not accurate to suggest that at the date of this application ... (calcium bor- ohydride) ... was a new compound in the sense that its existence had not been indicated in the literature."

That is the full extent of the relevant exegesis, but it was subsequently explained by the same judge in *Smith Kline & French Laboratories' Application* [1968] R.P.C. 415, on grounds which, for my part, I am bound to say I find less than satisfactory. These were that a claim to a product is appropriate only where it results from a development in art of manufacture. A product could be "new" only if its mere existence evidenced the novelty of the art or process and that condition could not be satisfied if the existence of the product had already been disclosed in some prior publication. Whether or not that was valid reasoning, *G.K.I.'s Application* has, I understand, regulated the Patent Office practice ever since, at any rate so far as concerns applications under the Act of 1949.

On the other side of the line there are more recent decisions of Falconer J. in *Genentech Inc's (Human Growth Hormone) Patent* [1989] R.P.C. 613, *Pall Corp v Commercial Hydraulics* [1990] F.S.R. 329, and *Quantel (Bedford) Ltd v Spaceward Microsystems Ltd* [1990] R.P.C. 83. The test for determining whether a prior publication has anticipated a claimed invention must, I think, be the same as that for determining whether an existing patent ought to be revoked for want of novelty under section 72 of the Act or section 32 of the Patents Act 1949. In the *Genentech* case the petitioner sought revocation of Genentech's patent on grounds (*inter alia*) of anticipation. Falconer J. reviewed a number of decisions of high authority relating to the test for determining whether an invention is anticipated by an antecedent statement or publication all of which pointed to the conclusion that a dis- closure, in order to constitute an anticipation, required to be an enabling disclosure. The principle applicable, he held, was that stated by Lord Westbury L.C. in *Hills v Evans* (1862) L.J. Ch. 457, 463:

> "... the antecedent statement must be such that a person of ordinary knowledge of the subject would at once perceive, understand and be able practically to apply the dis- covery without the necessity for making further experiments ..."

Posing the question "What is the nature and extent of the information ... necessary to disprove the novelty of the subsequent patent?" Lord Westbury answered:

> "... the information ... given by the prior publication must ... be equal to that given by the subsequent patent. ... If specific details are necessary for the practical working and real utility of the alleged invention, they must be found substantially in the prior publication."

Applying this to the case before him, Falconer J. concluded that "to constitute anticipation of a claim to a new chemical compound by a prior document the disclosure in that prior document must be an enabling disclosure in the sense I have indicated". In reaching this conclusion he necessarily disapproved, although he did not say so in terms, of the decision of the Patent Appeals Tribunal in *G.K.I.'s Application*, unless it can be said that there is some valid distinction to be drawn between "publication" for the purposes of the Act of 1949 and making something "available to the public" for the purposes of the Act. Section 101 of the Act of 1949 effectively precludes such an argument.

It should be added that the same approach as that adopted by Falconer J. in the *Genentech* case has been adopted in the European Patent Office in *Imperial Chemical Industries PLC's*

(Herbicides) Application (Decision T206/83), (1986) 5 E.P.O.R. 232, [1987] O.J. EPO 5, and *Collaborative Research Inc (Preprorennin) Application (Decision T81/87)* [1990] O.J. EPO 250. The headnote of the latter case reads:

"In accordance with EPC Article 87 a European patent application is only entitled to priority in respect of the same invention as was disclosed in the previous application. This means that the subject matter of the claims of the European application must be clearly identifiable in the previous application as a whole. Identical wording is not required.

In order to give rise to priority the disclosure of all the essential elements, *i.e.* features of the invention in the priority document must either be express or be directly and unambiguously implied by the text as filed. Missing elements which are to be recognised as essential only later on are thus not part of the disclosure."

1.1.1.4 Patents Act 1977, s.77: Effect of European Patent (UK)

S.77(1) Subject to the provisions of this Act, a European patent (UK) shall, as from the publication of the mention of its grant in the European Patent Bulletin, be treated for the purposes of Parts I and III of this Act as if it were a patent under this Act granted in pursuance of an application made under this Act and as if notice of the grant of the patent had, on the date of that publication, been published under section 24 above in the journal; and—

(a) **the proprietor of a European patent (UK) shall accordingly as respects the United Kingdom have the same rights and remedies, subject to the same conditions, as the proprietor of a patent under this Act;**

(b) **references in Parts I and III of this Act to a patent shall be construed accordingly; and**

(c) **any statement made and any certificate filed for the purposes of the provision of the convention corresponding to section 2(4)(c) above shall be respectively treated as a statement made and written evidence filed for the purposes of the said paragraph (c).**

(2) Subsection (1) above shall not affect the operation in relation to a European patent (UK) of any provisions for the European Patent Convention relating to the amendment or revocation of such a patent in proceedings before the European Patent Office.

(3) Where in the case of a European patent (UK)—

(a) **proceedings for infringement, or proceedings under section 58 above, have been commenced before the court or the comptroller and have not been finally disposed of, and**

(b) **it is established in proceedings before the European Patent Office that the patent is only partially valid,**

the provisions of section 63 or, as the case may be, of subsections (7) to (9) of section 58 apply as they apply to proceedings in which the validity of a patent is put in issue and in which it is found that the patent is only partially valid.

(4) Where a European patent (UK) is amended in accordance with the European Patent Convention, the amendment shall have effect for the purposes of Parts I and III of this Act as if the specification of the patent had been amended under this Act; but subject to subsection (6)(b) below.

(4A) Where a European patent (UK) is revoked in accordance with the European Patent

Convention, the patent shall be treated for the purposes of Parts I and III of this Act as having been revoked under this Act.

(5) Where—

(a) under the European Patent Convention a European patent (UK) is revoked for failure to observe a time limit and is subsequently restored; and

(b) between the revocation and publication of the fact that it has been restored a person begins in good faith to do an act which would, apart from section 55 above, constitute an infringement of the patent or makes in good faith effective and serious preparations to do such an act;

he shall have the rights conferred by section 28(6) above, and subsections (8) and (9) of that section shall apply accordingly. Section 28A(4) and (5) above, and subsection (6) and (7) of that section shall apply accordingly.

(6) While this subsection is in force—

(a) subsection (1) above shall not apply to a European patent (UK) the specification of which was published in French or German, unless a translation into English of the specification as amended is filed at the Patent Office and the prescribed fee is paid before the end of the prescribed period;

(b) subsection (4) above shall not apply to an amendment made in French or German unless a translation of the amendment into English is filed at the Patent Office and the prescribed fee is paid before the end of the prescribed period.

(7) Where a translation of a specification or amendment into English is not filed in accordance with subsection 6(a) or (b) above, the patent shall be treated as always having been void.

Note: for the effects of international applications under the PCT, see PA 1977, ss.89, 89A, 89B.

(8) The comptroller shall publish any translation filed at the Patent Office under subsection (6) above.

(9) Subsection (6) above shall come into force on a day appointed for the purpose by rules and shall cease to have effect on a day so appointed, without prejudice, however, to the power to bring it into force again.

Note also: s.78—European patent (UK) applications.

1.1.1.5   Patents Act 1977, s.89: International Application under the Patent Cooperation Treaty

S. 89.(1) An international application for a patent (UK) for which a date of filing has been accorded under the Patent Co-operation Treaty shall, subject to—

section 89A (international and national phases of application), and
section 89B (adaptation of provisions in relation to international application),

be treated for the purposes of Parts I and III of this Act as an application for a patent under this Act.

(2) If the application, or the designation of the United Kingdom in it, is withdrawn or (except as mentioned in subsection (3)) deemed to be withdrawn under the Treaty, it shall be treated as withdrawn under this Act.

(3) An application shall not be treated as withdrawn under this Act if it, or the designation of the United Kingdom in it, is deemed to be withdrawn under the Treaty—

    (a) because of an error or omission in an institution having functions under the Treaty, or

    (b) because, owing to circumstances outside the applicant's control, a copy of the application was not received by the International Bureau before the end of the time limited for that purpose under the Treaty,

or in such other circumstances as may be prescribed.

(4) For the purposes of the above provisions an application shall not be treated as an international application for a patent (UK) by reason only of its containing an indication that the applicant wishes to obtain a European patent (UK), but an application shall be so treated if it also separately designates the United Kingdom.

(5) If an international application for a patent which designates the United Kingdom is refused a filing date under the Treaty and the comptroller determines that the refusal was caused by an error or omission in an institution having functions under the Treaty, he may direct that the application shall be treated as an application under this Act, having such date of filing as he may direct.

Note: Article 89A specifies that Patent Cooperation Treaty provisions apply until the period for international application expires, and deals with various consequences. Article 89B deals with matters concerning priority and publication.

1.1.2   Patent Granting Procedure: Basic Provisions of UK Act

1.1.2.1   Patents Act 1977, s.14: Making of Application

S.14(1) Every application for a patent—

    (a) shall be made in the prescribed form and shall be filed at the Patent Office in the prescribed manner; and

    (b) shall be accompanied by the fee prescribed for the purposes of this subsection (hereafter in this Act referred to as the filing fee).

(2) Every application for a patent shall contain—

    (a) a request for the grant of a patent;

    (b) a specification containing a description of the invention, a claim or claims and any drawing referred to in the description of any claim; and

    (c) an abstract;

but the foregoing provision shall not prevent an application being initiated by documents complying with section 15(1) below.

(3) The specification of an application shall disclose the invention in a manner which is clear enough and complete enough for the invention to be performed by a person skilled in the art.

(4) Without prejudice to subsection (3) above, rules may prescribe the circumstances in which the specification of an application which requires for its performance the use of a micro-organism is to be treated for the purposes of this Act as complying with that subsection.

(5) The claim or claims shall—

    (a) define the matter for which the applicant seeks protection;

    (b) be clear and concise;

    (c) be supported by the description; and

    (d) relate to one invention or to a group of inventions which are so linked as to form a single inventive concept.

(6) Without prejudice to the generality of subsection (5)(d) above, rules may provide for treating two or more inventions as being so linked as to form a single inventive concept for the purposes of this Act.

(7) The purpose of the abstract is to give technical information and on publication it shall not form part of the state of the art by virtue of section 2(3) above, and the comptroller may determine whether the abstract adequately fulfils its purpose and, if it does not, may reframe it so that it does.

(8) Rules may require a person who has made an application for a patent for an invention which requires for its performance the use of a micro-organism not to impose or maintain in the prescribed circumstances any restrictions on the availability to the public of samples of the micro-organism and the uses to which they may be put, subject, however, to any prescribed exceptions, and rules may provide that in the event of a contravention of any provision

included in the rules by virtue of this subsection the specification shall be treated for the purposes of this Act as not disclosing the invention in a manner required by subsection (3) above.

(9) An application for a patent may be withdrawn at any time before the patent is granted and any withdrawal of such an application may not be revoked.

Note also: s.13—Mention of inventor; s.15—Date of filing application; s.16— Early publication of application; s.17—Preliminary examination. For the equivalent steps in applying for a European patent through the European Patent Office, see EPC Arts.75–86 and EPC Rules 13–19, 24–36.

For international applications, see Patent Cooperation Treaty, Chapter I and PCT Rules 3–52.

1.1.2.2 Patents Act 1977, s.18: Substantive examination and grant or refusal of patent

S.18(1) Where the conditions imposed by section 17(1) above for the comptroller to refer an application to an examiner for a preliminary examination and search are satisfied and at the time of the request under that subsection or within the prescribed period—

(a) a request is made by the applicant to the Patent Office in the prescribed form for a substantive examination; and

(b) the prescribed fee is paid for the examination;

the comptroller shall refer the application to an examiner for a substantive examination; and if no such request is made or the prescribed fee is not paid within that period, the application shall be treated as having been withdrawn at the end of that period.

(1A) If the examiner forms the view that a supplementary search under section 17 above is required for which a fee is payable, he shall inform the comptroller, who may decide that the substantive examination should not proceed until the fee is paid; and if he so decides, then unless within such period as he may allow—

(a) the fee is paid, or

(b) the application is amended so as to render the supplementary search unnecessary,

he may refuse the application.

(2) On a substantive examination of an application the examiner shall investigate, to such extent as he considers necessary in view of any examination and search carried out under section 17 above, whether the application complies with the requirements of this Act and the rules and shall determine that question and report his determination to the comptroller.

(3) If the examiner reports that any of those requirements are not complied with, the comptroller shall give the applicant an opportunity within a specified period to make observations on the report and to amend the application so as to comply with those requirements (subject, however, to section 76 below), and if the applicant fails to satisfy the comptroller that those requirements are complied with, or to amend the application so as to comply with them, the comptroller may refuse the application.

(4) If the examiner reports that the application, whether as originally filed or as amended in pursuance of section 17 above, this section or section 19 below, complies with those requirements at any time before the end of the prescribed period, the comptroller shall notify the applicant of that fact and, subject to subsection (5) and sections 19 and 22 below and on payment within the prescribed period of any fee prescribed for the grant, grant him a patent.

(5) Where two or more applications for a patent for the same invention having the same priority date are filed by the same applicant or his successor in title, the comptroller may on that ground refuse to grant a patent in pursuance of more than one of the applications.

Note also: s.20—Failure of application; s.21—Observations by third party on patentability; s.22—National security and public safety; s.23—Restrictions on UK residents making applications abroad. For the equivalent steps in European Patent Office procedure, see EPC Arts.90–98 and EPC Rules 39–54.

For international preliminary examination, PCT Chapter II and PCT Rules 53–75.

1.1.3   Grant and Term

1.1.3.1   Patents Act 1977, s.24: Publication and certificate of grant

S.24(1) As soon as practicable after a patent has been granted under this Act the comptroller shall publish in the journal a notice that it has been granted.

(2) The comptroller shall, as soon as practicable after he publishes a notice under subsection (1) above, send the proprietor of the patent a certificate in the prescribed form that the patent has been granted to the proprietor.

(3) The comptroller shall, at the same time as he publishes a notice under subsection (1) above in relation to a patent publish the specification of the patent, the names of the proprietor and (if different) the inventor and any other matters constituting or relating to the patent which in the comptroller's opinion it is desirable to publish.

1.1.3.2   Patents Act 1977, s.25: Term of patent

S.25(1) A patent granted under this Act shall be treated for the purposes of the following provisions of this Act as having been granted, and shall take effect, on the date on which notice of its grant is published in the journal and, subject to subsection (3) below, shall continue in force until the end of the period of 20 years beginning with the date of filing the application for the patent or with such other date as may be prescribed.

(2) A rule prescribing any such other date under this section shall not be made unless a draft of the rule has been laid before, and approved by resolution of, each House of Parliament.

(3) A patent shall cease to have effect at the end of the period prescribed for the payment of any renewal fee if it is not paid within that period.

(4) If during the period of six months immediately following the end of the prescribed period the renewal fee and any prescribed additional fee are paid, the patent shall be treated for the purposes of this Act as if it had never expired, and accordingly—

   (a) anything done under or in relation to it during that further period shall be valid;

   (b) an act which would constitute an infringement of it if it had not expired shall constitute such an infringement; and

   (c) an act which would constitute the use of the patented invention for the services of the Crown if the patent had not expired shall constitute that use.

(5) Rules shall include provision requiring the comptroller to notify the registered proprietor of a patent that a renewal fee has not been received from him in the Patent Office before the end of the prescribed period and before the framing of the notification.

Note also: s.26—Patent not to be impugned for lack of unity; s.28—Restoration of lapsed patents; s.29—Surrender of patents.

EC law now provides for the granting of Supplementary Protection Certificates (SPC), which in effect extend the terms of Member State patents in the fields of medicines and plant protection products. The object of these SPCs is to compensate for delays in exploiting the protected inventions which follow from testing procedures for safety and like considerations: see Regs 1768/92 and 1610/96.

1.1.4   Amendment

1.1.4.1   Patents Act 1977, s.19: General power to amend application before grant

S.19(1) At any time before a patent is granted in pursuance of an application the applicant may, in accordance with the prescribed conditions and subject to section 76 below, amend the application of his own volition.

(2) The comptroller may, without an application being made to him for the purpose, amend the specification and abstract contained in an application for a patent so as to acknowledge a registered trade mark.

1.1.4.2   Patents Act 1977, s.27: General power to amend specification after grant

S.27(1) Subject to the following provisions of this section and to section 76 below, the comptroller may, on an application made by the proprietor of a patent, allow the specification of the patent to be amended subject to such conditions, if any, as he thinks fit.

(2) No such amendment shall be allowed under this section where there are pending before the court or the comptroller proceedings in which the validity of the patent may be put in issue.

(3) An amendment of a specification of a patent under this section shall have effect and be deemed always to have had effect from the grant of the patent.

(4) The comptroller may, without an application being made to him for the purpose, amend the specification of a patent so as to acknowledge a registered trade mark.

(5) A person may give notice to the comptroller of his opposition to an application under this section by the proprietor of a patent, and if he does so the comptroller shall notify the proprietor and consider the opposition in deciding whether to grant the application.

1.1.4.3   Patents Act 1977, s.75: Amendment of patent in infringement or revocation proceedings

S.75(1) In any proceedings before the court or the comptroller in which the validity of a patent is put in issue the court or, as the case may be, the comptroller may, subject to section 76 below, allow the proprietor of the patent to amend the specification of the patent in such manner, and subject to such terms as to advertising the proposed amendment and as to costs, expenses or otherwise, as the court or comptroller thinks fit.

(2) A person may give notice to the court or the comptroller of his opposition to an amendment proposed by the proprietor of the patent under this section, and if he does so the court or the comptroller shall notify the proprietor and consider the opposition in deciding whether the amendment or any amendment should be allowed.

(3) An amendment of a specification of a patent under this section shall have effect and be deemed always to have had effect from the grant of the patent.

(4) Where an application for an order under this section is made to the court, the applicant shall notify the comptroller, who shall be entitled to appear and be heard and shall appear if so directed by the court.

1.1.4.4   Patents Act 1977, s.76: Amendments of applications and patents not to include added matter

S.76(1) An application for a patent which—

(a) is made in respect of matter disclosed in an earlier application, or in the specification of a patent which has been granted, and

(b) discloses additional matter, that is, matter extending beyond that disclosed in the earlier application, as filed, or the application for the patent, as filed,

may be filed under sections 8(3), 12 or 37(4) above, or as mentioned in section 15(4) above, but shall not be allowed to proceed unless it is amended so as to exclude the additional matter.

(2) No amendment of an application for a patent shall be allowed under sections 17(3), 18(3) or 19(1) if it results in the application disclosing matter extending beyond that disclosed in the application as filed.

(3) No amendment of the specification of a patent shall be allowed under sections 27(1), 73 or 75 if it—

(a) results in the specification disclosing additional matter, or

(b) extends the protection conferred by the patent.

S.76A Biotechnological inventions
(1) Any provision of, or made under, this Act is to have effect in relation to a patent or an application for a patent which concerns a biotechnological invention, subject to the provisions of Schedule A2.

(2) Nothing in this section or Schedule A2 is to be read as affecting the application of any provision in relation to any other kind of patent or application for a patent.

For Sch. A2, see paras 1.2.3.1 and 1.2.5.1 below.

For amendment in EPO procedure, see EPC Art.123.

1.1.5   Revocation and Opposition

1.1.5.1   Patents Act 1977, s.72: Power to revoke patents on application

S.72(1) Subject to the following provisions of this Act, the court or the comptroller may on the application of any person by order revoke a patent for an invention on (but only on) any of the following grounds, that is to say—

(a) the invention is not a patentable invention;

(b) that the patent was granted to a person who was not entitled to be granted that patent;

(c) the specification of the patent does not disclose the invention clearly enough and completely enough for it to be performed by a person skilled in the art;

(d) the matter disclosed in the specification of the patent extends beyond that disclosed in the application for the patent, as filed, or, if the patent was granted on a new application filed under sections 8(3), 12 or 37(4) above or as mentioned in section 15(4) above, in the earlier application, as filed;

(e) the protection conferred by the patent has been extended by an amendment which should not have been allowed.

(2) An application for the revocation of a patent on the ground mentioned in subsection (1)(b) above—

(a) may only be made by a person found by the court in an action for a declaration or declarator, or found by the court or the comptroller on a reference under section 37 above, to be entitled to be granted that patent or to be granted a patent for part of the matter comprised in the specification of the patent sought to be revoked; and

(b) may not be made if that action was commenced or that reference was made after the end of the period of two years beginning with the date of the grant of the patent sought to be revoked, unless it is shown that any person registered as a proprietor of the patent knew at the time of the grant or of the transfer of the patent to him that he was not entitled to the patent.

(3) Rules under section 14(4) and (8) above shall, with any necessary modifications, apply for the purposes of subsection (1)(c) above as they apply for the purposes of section 14(3) above.

(4) An order under this section may be an order for the unconditional revocation of the patent or, where the court or the comptroller determines that one of the grounds mentioned in subsection (1) above has been established, but only so as to invalidate the patent to a limited extent, an order that the patent should be revoked unless within a specified time the specification is amended under section 75 below to the satisfaction of the court or the comptroller, as the case may be.

(5) A decision of the comptroller or on appeal from the comptroller shall not estop any party to civil proceedings in which infringement of a patent is in issue from alleging invalidity of the patent on any of the grounds referred to in subsection (1) above, whether or not any of the issues involved were decided in the said decision.

(6) Where the comptroller refuses to grant an application made to him by any person under this section, no application (otherwise than by way of appeal or by way of putting validity in issue in proceedings for infringement) may be made to the court by that person under this section in relation to the patent concerned, without the leave of the court.

(7) Where the comptroller has not disposed of an application made to him under this section, the applicant may not apply to the court under this section in respect of the patent concerned unless either—

    (a) the proprietor of the patent agrees that the applicant may so apply, or

    (b) the comptroller certifies in writing that it appears to him that the question whether the patent should be revoked is one which would more properly be determined by the court.

Note also: s.73—Comptroller's power to revoke patents of his own initiative; s.74—Proceedings in which validity of patent may be put in issue.

1.1.5.2   European Patent Convention, Arts 99, 100: Opposition

Art. 99(1) Within nine months from the publication of the mention of the grant of the European patent, any person may give notice to the European Patent Office of opposition to the European patent granted. Notice of opposition shall be filed in a written reasoned statement. It shall not be deemed to have been filed until the opposition fee has been paid.

(2) The opposition shall apply to the European patent in all the Contracting States in which that patent has effect.

(3) An opposition may be filed even if the European patent has been surrendered or has lapsed for all the designated States.

(4) Opponents shall be parties to the opposition proceedings as well as the proprietor of the patent.

(5) Where a person provides evidence that in a Contracting State, following a final decision, he has been entered in the patent register of such State instead of the previous proprietor, such person shall, at his request, replace the previous proprietor in respect of such State. By derogation from Article 118, the previous proprietor and the person making the request shall not be deemed to be joint proprietors unless both so request.

Art. 100 Opposition may only be filed on the grounds that:

    (a) the subject-matter of the European patent is not patentable within the terms of Articles 52 to 57;

    (b) the European patent does not disclose the invention in a manner sufficiently clear and complete for it to be carried out by a person skilled in the art;

    (c) the subject-matter of the European patent extends beyond the content of the application as filed, or, if the patent was granted on a divisional application or on a new application filed in accordance with Article 61, beyond the content of the earlier application as filed.

Note also: EPC Arts.101–105 and EPC Rules 55–63 on opposition proceedings; and EPC Arts.106–112 and EPC Rules 64–67 on appeals from decisions of EPO Divisions.

1.2 Validity

1.2.1 Novelty

1.2.1.1 Patents Act 1977, ss.1(1), 2: Statutory provisions

S.1(1) A patent may be granted only for an invention in respect of which the following conditions are satisfied, that is to say—

    (a) the invention is new;

    (b) it involves an inventive step;

    (c) it is capable of industrial application;

    (d) the grant of a patent for it is not excluded by subsections (2) and (3) below; and references in this Act to a patentable invention shall be construed accordingly.

For s.1(2)–(5), see below, 1.2.3.1. Section 1(1) corresponds in large measure to EPC Art.52(1).

S.2(1) An invention shall be taken to be new if it does not form part of the state of the art.

(2) The state of the art in the case of an invention shall be taken to comprise all matter (whether a product, a process, information about either, or anything else) which has at any time before the priority date of that invention been made available to the public (whether in the United Kingdom or elsewhere) by written or oral description, by use or in any other way.

(3) The state of the art in the case of an invention to which an application for a patent or a patent relates shall be taken also to comprise matter contained in an application for another patent which was published on or after the priority date of that invention, if the following conditions are satisfied, that is to say—

    (a) that matter was contained in the application for that other patent both as filed and as published; and

    (b) the priority date of that matter is earlier than that of the invention.

(4) For the purposes of this section the disclosure of matter constituting an invention shall be disregarded in the case of a patent or an application for a patent if occurring later than the beginning of the period of six months immediately preceding the date of filing the application for the patent and either—

    (a) the disclosure was due to, or made in consequence of, the matter having been obtained unlawfully or in breach of confidence by any person—

        (i) from the inventor or from any other person to whom the matter was made

available in confidence by the inventor or who obtained it from the inventor because he or the inventor believed that he was entitled to obtain it; or

    (ii) from any other person to whom the matter was made available in confidence by any person mentioned in sub-paragraph (i) above or in this sub-paragraph or who obtained it from any person so mentioned because he or the person from whom he obtained it believed that he was entitled to obtain it;

(b) the disclosure was made in breach of confidence by any person who obtained the matter in confidence from the inventor or from any other person to whom it was made available, or who obtained it, from the inventor; or

(c) the disclosure was due to, or made in consequence of the inventor displaying the invention at an international exhibition and the applicant states, on filing the application, that the invention has been so displayed and also, within the prescribed period, files written evidence in support of the statement complying with any prescribed conditions.

(5) In this section references to the inventor include references to any proprietor of the invention for the time being.

(6) In the case of an invention consisting of a substance or composition for use in a method of treatment of the human or animal body by surgery or therapy or of diagnosis practised on the human or animal body, the fact that the substance or composition forms part of the state of the art shall not prevent the invention from being taken to be new if the use of the substance or composition in any such method does not form part of the state of the art.

Section 2 corresponds broadly to EPC Arts.54, 55. But compare, in particular, EPC Arts.54(2), 55(1):

The state of the art shall be held to comprise everything made available to the public by means of a written or oral description, by use, or in any other way, before the date of filing of the European patent application. EPC, Art. 55(1): For the application of Article 54 a disclosure of the invention shall not be taken into consideration if it occurred no earlier than six months preceding the filing of the European patent application and if it was due to, or in consequence of:

    (a) an evident abuse in relation to the applicant or his legal predecessor, or

    (b) the fact that the applicant or his legal predecessor has displayed the invention at an official, or officially recognised, international exhibition falling within the terms of the Convention on international exhibitions signed at Paris on 22 November 1928 and last revised on 30 November 1972.

1.2.1.2   *Fomento v Mentmore* [1956] R.P.C. 87, CA

The plaintiff's patent, No. 609,817, was for an improvement to the nib of a ball-point pen designed to make the flow of ink continuous and uniform. The essence of the invention can best be appreciated by imagining a ball sitting on a rather wide golf-tee; round the side of the ball is placed a metal housing, but between the housing and the tee is a gap forming a horizontal ring. In terms of the specification, the tee is the base seat through which the supply of ink from the reservoir is fed. The housing is the lateral seat. The crux of the invention was said to be the discovery that if the ring-gap between lateral and base seat comes below the equator of the ball the ink flows better.

The attack on the validity of the patent arose from the claim that the patentees themselves had both published a description of making ball-point pens which would mean performing the invention, and that they had made pens embodying the invention available to the public before the priority date of the patent.

The common technique for inserting the ball in a ball-point nib, and then closing the housing around it so that it was kept in at the top, was called peining. The housing was formed into a cylinder at the top end, the ball was dropped into it and the housing was then hit with a peining tool shaped to close the cylinder up. The force of this last step had the effect of deforming the housing so as to produce a ring gap. The defendants alleged that the ring gap would occur below the equatorial line and that the plaintiffs had been peining in this way before they appreciated that the ring gave them a better flow of ink.

The plaintiff's activities were said to amount to an anticipation by virtue of (1) publication and (2) use.

Publication: This was alleged to have been made in a prior UK Patent No. 564,172. The patent was concerned with improvements to the base-seat and made no mention of the ring-gap as such, nor did it give explicit instructions as to how a nib would be made embodying its special base-seat.

Of this Jenkins L.J. said:

Mr Mould for the defendants submitted that, even if none of the specific instances of publication by prior user was held to have been made out, the defendants would, nevertheless, still be entitled to succeed on the following grounds. Firstly, he propounded the general proposition that, when a man publishes a specification describing an article but containing no directions as to how it is to be made, and the article when made by a normal method will necessarily possess a particular characteristic not mentioned in the specification, a man entering the field thereafter cannot validly claim a patent in respect of that same article on the strength of its possession of that particular characteristic, for in such a case the second comer has invented nothing; he has merely discovered that the article already described will, when made in a normal way, possess that particular characteristic, and a mere discovery is not an invention within the meaning of the Act, because it is not a manner of new manufacture within the meaning of the Statute of Monopolies. (See section 32(1)(d) of the Act and the definition of "invention" by reference to the Statute of Monopolies contained in section 101(1).) Mr Mould contended that this proposition applied to the present case so as to invalidate the patent in suit, because peining was a normal, and indeed obvious, method of performing an operation such as the closing of the ball housing of the pen described in the prior specification No. 564,172 and peining would necessarily produce the particular characteristic of a lower lateral seat separated from the base seat by an annular space. ...

As to Mr Mould's first proposition, Mr Shelley submitted, firstly, that peining was not a normal or obvious method of closing the ball housing, and, secondly, that, even if it was, it would not necessarily produce the relevant characteristic of a lower lateral seat separated from the base seat by an annular space. I agree with the Judge and with my Lord that peining must be taken to have been a normal, and indeed obvious, method of closing the ball housing, in view of the evidence of Dr Aitchison and the assumption to this effect clearly made in the specification of the patent in suit. On the other hand, I also agree with the learned Judge and my Lord that the evidence of Dr Aitchison and the experimental peining operations of Messrs Moss and Leistikow fall short, having regard to the evidence of Mr Wicks of establishing that peining must necessarily produce the relevant characteristic, though, as the learned Judge said, it "might well" do so if the operator was merely seeking to make a pen that would write, without any intention one way or the other on the question of lateral seating.

Mr Mould submitted that, if peining "might well" produce a lower lateral seat, that was enough for his purpose: and he relied on the case of *British Thomson-Houston v Charlesworth, Peebles & Co* (1925) 42 R.P.C. 180, and particularly on the speech of Lord Shaw at 206. With respect, that seems to me to have been an entirely different case. The earlier patent there related to treating tungsten so as to make it ductile when hot, while the later patent related to the subjecting of tungsten to a similar but somewhat more protracted treatment so as to make it ductile when cold; and Lord Shaw held that the later patent involved no inventive step. Here, the alleged invention resides in a particular characteristic in a given article, which characteristic is a new departure in the sense that it has never before been described or claimed. If in fact the article has never been made so as to possess that characteristic, and the characteristic is a useful or potentially useful one, I do not think that the plaintiffs' patent is to be held invalid because a person working a prior specification in which, so far from being described or claimed, the relevant characteristic seems inferentially to have been excluded, might unwittingly produce it.

Lord Evershed, in arriving at the same conclusion, remarked:

I think therefore notwithstanding the passage to which Mr Mould referred, that it is necessary, if he is to establish his first and broadest proposition, to show not only that peining was at the relevant date a normal method of manufacture to employ, but that if peining were employed it would, save in exceptional cases (as one might say, in 99 cases out of 100) produce the lower lateral seat.

Use: *This was alleged to have occurred by manufacture and sale of peined pens having annular spaces below the equator before the priority date. Proof was also proffered of particular instances in which such pens had been given away before that date.*

The law on this aspect of the case was discussed only by Evershed M.R.:

Of the various attacks in the way of prior publication made upon the patent in the Court below, the learned Judge, Lloyd-Jacob J., rejected all the attacks but one. But he came to the conclusion that there had been proved publication by prior user in certain very few specific cases: in the case of two pens supplied to a Mr Hogan and in the case of two pens supplied one each to a Mrs MacLean and a Mr Hulme.

Now, there is, I apprehend, no dispute about the law; and indeed Mr Shelley has not, as I have followed him, contended otherwise than that, if the Judge came to a right conclusion as to the facts or inferences of fact in regard to these cases of supply to Hogan, MacLean and Hulme, then indeed there had been prior publication by user and the patent failed in validity.

The matter is dealt with in the case of *Humpherson v Syer* (1887) 4 R.P.C. 407. I will read a short passage from the judgment of Bowen L.J., and another short passage from the judgment of Fry L.J. The case, I should say, was one which concerned a device for preventing water waste, and the passage I am about to read related to the effect of the patentee having asked a gentleman named Widner to make one of the devices. Bowen L.J. at 413 said: "Was Widner a person to whom this communication had been made in a manner which left him free both in law and equity to do what he like with the information? If so, the information, of course, had been given to a member of the public, and there was nothing further to serve as consideration for any patent."

To the same purpose Fry L.J., at 414 referred to the language of Lindley L.J., and Cotton L.J., in an earlier case. In that case, Lindley L.J., delivering the judgment both of himself and of Cotton L.J., said: " 'On the present occasion it is unnecessary to decide this'—that is another point—'and without going so far as to say that the judge ought to give such a direction, I am clearly of opinion that the judge ought at least to tell the jury to find for the defendant on the issue that the patentee was the first and true inventor if they thought that the German specification had been so published in this country as to have become known to any one here' ". Therefore, in the view of the Lords Justices, the knowledge of any one here was enough to give the public the possession of the invention.

It may seem at first sight a hard result for the patentee; but in light of that authority it is I think clear that if the cases of these few pens were proved, pens having the necessary characteristics so as to bring them with scope of 609,817—if those few pens came to the hand of Hogan, MacLean and Hulme in circumstances which left them free at law and equity to do whatever they liked with them and what they discovered from them (subject only, of course, to the effect of Patent 564,172) then it would appear to follow that the plaintiffs must in this case fail.

The Court of Appeal placed no reliance on the case of Hulme, but each member gave substantially similar reasons for agreeing with the trial judge that there had been prior publication through use in the cases of MacLean and Hogan.

Jenkins L.J.:

As to Mrs MacLean, it will be remembered that her story was that a Canadian Air Force man came into her shop and asked her if he could write on the counter. She gave him permission, and he did his writing, and went away, leaving his pen behind. When he returned some time later, she gave him his pen and said that it was a nice one, or something of the sort, and the Canadian then said, "I will get you one for your birthday". This, according to Mrs MacLean, took place on October 1944, her birthday being on the 28th of that month. In November 1944, according to Mrs MacLean, she removed to another shop, and the Canadian redeemed his promise as to the pen by coming to the new shop and presenting her with one. That was some time in November, and she fixed it by the fact that she had moved from one shop to another in November 1944. There was no doubt as to the provenance of the pen or that it embodied the relevant features of the lower lateral seat and the annular space. The contest centred round the actual date of acquisition. The learned Judge assessed Mrs MacLean's evidence in these words: "The evidence of Mrs MacLean completely satisfied me that the Exhibit V.A.T.B. was acquired by her as and when she asserted".

1.2.1.3   *Bayer's Application* (G 6/88) [1990] O.J. EPO 114, Enlarged Bd. App., EPO

This case referred to the Enlarged Board the question whether it was permissible to seek claims in the form "use of compound X for a stated purpose", in order to protect the discovery that the compound, already known for one use, has a further useful characteristic that previously was unknown.

1. Having regard to the purpose for which questions are referred to the Enlarged Board as set out in EPC Article 112, it is appropriate that the Enlarged Board should not take too narrow a view of the question which has been referred but should consider and answer it in such a way as to clarify the points of law which lie behind it.

2. Prior to the entry into force of the European Patent Convention in 1978, the role of patent claims in determining the protection conferred by a patent had developed differently within the national patent systems of the countries that are now Contracting States. Such different developments reflected somewhat different national philosophies underlying the concept of patent protection.

In particular, the extent to which the wording of the claims determined the scope of protection varied considerably from country to country, and this factor significantly affected drafting practice.

In some countries, in particular Germany, in practice the protection conferred by a patent depended more upon what was perceived to be the inventor's contribution to the art, as disclosed in the patent, by way of the general inventive concept, than upon the wording of the claims. In other countries, in particular the United Kingdom, the precise wording of the claims was regarded as crucial, because the claims were required to define the boundary between what was protected and what was not, for purposes of legal certainty.

2.1 The manner in which claims were drafted naturally developed differently in the different countries, depending upon the relative importance of their function. Clearly in a country such as the United Kingdom, the wording of a claim had to provide a much more precise definition of what was sought to be protected than in countries such as Germany, where a statement of the essence of the inventive concept was more appropriate.

2.2. There are basically two different types of claim, namely a claim to a physical entity (*e.g.* product, apparatus) and a claim to a physical activity (*e.g.* method, process, use).

Various sub-classes are possible (*e.g.* a compound, a composition, a machine; or a manufacturing method, a process of producing a compound, a method of testing, etc.). Furthermore, claims including both features relating to physical activities and features relating to physical entities are also possible. There are no rigid lines of demarcation between the various possible forms of claim.

2.3 The question which has been referred to the Enlarged Board is concerned with "use" claims: that is, with claims defining a "use of compound X for a particular purpose", or similar wording.

The recognition or discovery of a previously unknown property of a known compound, such property providing a new technical effect, can clearly involve a valuable and inventive contribution to the art.

In countries such as Germany, such inventions have for many years commonly been sought to be protected by means of "use" claims.

In countries such as the United Kingdom, prior to 1978 such "use" claims were rarely found in patent applications and patents; a claim to an invention of such a character would normally have been defined in terms of the essential physical steps comprising the "activity" to be protected.

2.4 Despite the entry into force of the European Patent Convention, European patent applications originating in the different Contracting States have continued commonly to include claims drafted in accordance with the traditional practices of such Contracting States discussed above.

However, the requirements for drafting claims in respect of inventions which are the subject of European patent applications and patents, and the patentability of such inventions, are all matters which must be decided upon the basis of the law under the European Patent Convention. The function of the claims is central to the operation of the European patent system.

2.5 EPC Article 84 provides that the claims of a European patent application "shall define the matter for which protection is sought". EPC Rule 29(1) further requires that the claims "shall define the matter for which protection is sought in terms of the technical features of the invention". The primary aim of the wording used in a claim must therefore be to satisfy such requirements, having regard to the particular nature of the subject invention, and having regard also to the purpose of such claims.

The purpose of claims under the EPC is to enable the protection conferred by the patent (or patent application) to be determined (EPC Article 69), and thus the rights of the patent owner within the designated Contracting States (EPC Article 64), having regard to the patentability requirements of EPC Articles 52 to 57. It follows that the technical features of the invention are the physical features which are essential to it.

When considering the two basic types of claim referred to in paragraph 2.2 above the technical features of a claim to a physical entity are the physical parameters of the entity, and the technical features of a claim to an activity are the physical steps which define such activity. A number of decisions of the Boards of Appeal have held that in appropriate cases technical features may be defined functionally (see, *e.g.* Decision T–68/85 [1987] O.J. EPO 228; Decision T–139/85 [1987] E.P.O.R. 229).

3. For the purpose of determining their technical features, the claims must be interpreted in accordance with EPC Article 69(1) and its protocol. The protocol was adopted by the Contracting States as an integral part of the European Patent Convention in order to provide a mechanism for harmonisation of the various national approaches to the drafting and interpretation of claims discussed in paragraph 2.1 above. The central role of the claims under the European Patent Convention would clearly be undermined if the protection and consequently the rights conferred within individual designated Contracting States varied widely as a result of purely national traditions of claim interpretation: and the protocol was added to the European Patent Convention as a supplement primarily directed to providing an intermediate method of interpretation of claims of European patents throughout their life, as a compromise between the various national approaches to interpretation and determination of the protection conferred ("... so as to combine a fair protection for the patentee with a reasonable degree of certainty for third parties").

The object of the protocol is clearly to avoid too much emphasis on the literal wording of the claims when considered in isolation from the remainder of the text of the patent in which they appear; and also to avoid too much emphasis upon the general inventive concept disclosed in the text of the patent as compared to the relevant prior art, without sufficient regard also to the wording of the claims as a means of definition.

4. The legal problems associated with the patentability of claims to the new use of a known compound provided the subject-matter for the first seven decisions to be issued by the Enlarged Board of Appeal, namely G 1–7/83 (three of which, G 1/83, G 5/83 and G 6/83 in German, English and French respectively, are published in [1985] O.J. EPO 60, 64, 67). Such decisions were all concerned with the patentability of further medical uses for a substance already known to have one medical use; and with the appropriate form of claim

in respect of such an invention. All such decisions have essentially the same content. In this decision, it is only necessary to refer to the relevant German language decision, G 1/83.

The present Enlarged Board has considered how far the reasoning there set out bears upon the point of law to be decided in the present case.

The question of law which was referred to the Enlarged Board in G 5/83 arose essentially because of the particular exclusion from patentability in relation to "methods of treatment of the human or animal body" set out in the first sentence of EPC Article 52(4), and the exception to that exclusion set out in EPC Article 54(5). The reasoning in G 5/83 is therefore primarily directed to answering a question of law concerning the allowability of claims whose subject-matter is a particular kind of medical or veterinary invention. The *ratio decidendi* of that decision is essentially confined to the proper interpretation of EPC Articles 52(4) and 54(5) in their context.

In that field of technology, the normal type of use claim is prohibited by EPC Article 52(4), but EPC Article 54(5) expressly provides for an exception to the general rules for novelty (EPC Article 54(1) to (5)) in respect of the first medical or veterinary use of a substance or composition, by allowing a claim to the substances or compositions for that use. G 1/83 applied this to cases of second and subsequent therapeutic use, but expressly indicated that such a special approach to the derivation of novelty could only be applied to claims to the use of substances or compositions intended for use in a method referred to in EPC Article 52(4). The present Enlarged Board of Appeal endorses that view.

G 1/83 has the effect of giving to the inventor of a new use for a known medicament a protection analogous to but restricted in comparison with the protection normally allowable for a new non-medical use. The patentability of a second non-medical new and non-obvious use of a product is clearly recognised in principle (see Reasons para. 21). The patentability of "the (second or subsequent) use of a substance or composition for the manufacture of a medicament for a specified new and inventive therapeutic application" was accepted, because although the exclusion of therapeutic methods from patentability provided in Article 52(4) (on the ground that then these are not susceptible of industrial application) has the effect of excluding from patentability a claim directed to the use of a substance for therapy (see Reasons para. 13), this type of claim would be clearly allowable (as susceptible of industrial application) for a non-medical use. Compare: "The use of X for treating disease A in mammals" (not allowed), with "The use of X for treating disease B in cereal drops" (allowed).

In contrast, the question of law which has been referred to the Enlarged Board in the present case is not related to medical inventions but is of a general nature, being primarily concerned with the question of interpretation of EPC Article 54(1) and (2).

5. The question referred assumes that the only novel feature in the claim under consideration is the purpose for which the compound is to be used. However, insofar as the question of interpretation of EPC Article 54(1) and (2) and the question of the allowable scope of protection (if any) of inventions concerning a further non-medical use are matters of general importance, it will be appropriate for this Board to consider the question raised more generally, and in particular to consider other possible constructions for such use claims.

6. As discussed at paragraphs 2 to 2.5 above, the claims of a European patent should clearly define the technical features of the subject invention and thus its technical subject-matter, in order that the protection conferred by the patent can be determined and a comparison can be made with the state of the art to ensure that the claimed invention is

inter alia novel. A claimed invention lacks novelty unless it includes at least one essential technical feature which distinguishes it from the state of the art.

When deciding upon the novelty of a claim, a basic initial consideration is therefore to construe the claim in order to determine its technical features.

7. In relation to a claim whose wording clearly defines a new use of a known compound, depending upon its particular wording in the context of the remainder of the patent, the proper interpretation of the claim will normally be such that the attaining of a new technical effect which underlies the new use is a technical feature of the claimed invention. In this connection, and with reference to the discussion in paragraphs 2.1 and 2.2 above, it is necessary to bear in mind the protocol to EPC Article 69, as discussed in paragraph 4 above. Thus with such a claim, where a particular technical effect which underlies such use is described in the patent, having regard to the protocol, the proper interpretation of the claim will require that a functional feature should be implied into the claim, as a technical feature; for example, that the compound actually achieves the particular effect.

7.1 An example of such a claim which should be so interpreted can be given by reference to the facts in Decision T–231/85 ([1989] O.J. EPO 74). The claims in question define "Use of (certain compounds) ... for controlling fungi and for preventive fungus control"—and the application contained teaching as to how to carry this out so as to achieve this effect. Prior published document (1) described the use of the same compounds for influencing plant growth. In both application T–231/85 and document (1), the respective treatments were carried out in the same way (so the means of realisation was the same).

The Examining Division held that the claimed invention lacked novelty, apparently on the basis that the means of realisation was the same in document (1), and so the claimed effect underlying the use for fungus control must have been achieved in the treatment described in document (1). The Board of Appeal on the other hand held that the claimed invention was novel, on the basis that the technical teaching ("Lehre") in the application was different from that in document (1), and that the use was hitherto unknown, even though the means of realisation was the same.

In the view of the Enlarged Board, with reference to the discussion concerning the interpretation of claims in paragraph 7, the claim in question should properly be construed, having regard to the protocol to EPC Article 69, as implicitly including the following functional technical feature: that the named compounds, when used in accordance with the described means of realisation, in fact achieve the effect (*i.e.* perform the function) of controlling fungus. Such a functional feature is a technical feature which qualifies the invention: and the use claim is properly to be considered as a claim containing technical features both to the physical entity (the compound and its nature), and to a physical activity (the means of realisation). In other words, when following the method of interpretation of claims set out in the protocol, what is required in the context of a claim to the "use of a compound A for purpose B" is that such a claim should not be interpreted literally, as only including by way of technical features "the compound" and "the means of realisation of purpose B"; it should be interpreted (in appropriate cases) as also including as a technical feature the function of achieving purpose B (because this is the technical result). Such a method of interpretation, in the view of the Enlarged Board, is in accordance with the object and intention of the protocol to EPC Article 69.

If the proper construction of such a claim in the context of a particular patent is such as to include such a functional technical feature, the question which remains to be considered is whether such claimed invention is novel.

8. EPC Article 54(2) defines the state of the art as comprising "everything made available to

the public by means of a written or oral description, by use, or in any other way". Thus, whatever the physical means by which information is made available to the public (*e.g.* written description, oral description, use, pictorial description on a film or in a photograph, etc., or a combination of such means), the question of what has been made available to the public is one of fact in each case.

The word "available" carries with it the idea that, for lack of novelty to be found, all the technical features of the claimed invention in combination must have been communicated to the public, or laid open for inspection.

In the case of a "written description" which is open for inspection, what is made available in particular is the information content of the written description. Furthermore, in some cases, the information which the written description actually contains, teaching the carrying out of a process for example, also makes available further information which is the inevitable result of carrying out such teaching (see in this respect Decision T–12/81, Diastereomers [1982] O.J. EPO 296, Reasons paras 7 to 10; Decision T–124/87, Copolymers [1989] E.P.O.R. 33; and Decision T–303/86 Flavour concentrates [1989] E.P.O.R. 95 for example).

In each such case, however, a line must be drawn between what is in fact made available, and what remains hidden or otherwise has not been made available. In this connection the distinction should also be emphasised between lack of novelty and lack of inventive step: information equivalent to a claimed invention may be "made available" (lack of novelty), or may not have been made available but obvious (novel, but lack of inventive step), or not made available and not obvious (novel and inventive). Thus, in particular, what is hidden may still be obvious.

8.1 In cases where, for example, a compound has previously been described as having been used, but for a different purpose from the claimed use, and the previously described use had inherently had the same technical effect as the claimed use, the question arises as to whether there is a lack of novelty. In this connection problems in relation to infringement can also arise if there is no finding of lack of novelty in such circumstances, since a user of the previously described use would risk infringement of a later filed patent.

In respect of this submission, the Enlarged Board would emphasise that under EPC Article 54(2) the question to be decided is what has been "made available" to the public: the question is not what may have been "inherent" in what was made available (by a prior written description, or in what has previously been used (prior use), for example). Under the European Patent Convention, a hidden or secret use, because it has not been made available to the public, is not a ground of objection to validity of a European patent. In this respect, the provisions of the European Patent Convention may differ from the previous national laws of some Contracting States, and even from the current national laws of some non-Contracting States. Thus, the question of "inherency" does not arise as such under EPC Article 54. Any vested right derived from prior use of an invention is a matter for national law (see, in this connection, *e.g.* Article 38 of the Community Patent Convention, not yet in force). Furthermore, as to the suggested problems concerning infringement referred to above, it is to be noted that analogous problems would result from G 1/83 in the medical area.

8.2 This point may be illustrated by a further reference to the facts of Decision T–231/85. If the claims are interpreted as discussed in paragraph 7.1, the question in relation to novelty is whether document (1) made available to the public the technical feature that the compounds, when used as described, achieved the effect of controlling fungus.

The Board of Appeal there referred in its decision to the "hitherto unknown" use of such compounds for controlling fungi and the "unnoticed protective effect" (even though the means of application of such compounds to plants (the "technical realisation") was the same). Thus, although document (1) described a method of treating plants with compounds in order to regulate their growth which, when carried out, would inevitably have been inherently a use of such compounds for controlling fungi, nevertheless it appears that the technical feature of the claim set out above and underlying such use was not "made available" to the public by the prior written description in document (1).

9. The answer to the question referred may therefore be summarised as follows: with respect to a claim to a new use of a known compound, such new use may reflect a newly discovered technical effect described in the patent. The attaining of such a technical effect should then be considered as a functional technical feature of the claim (*e.g.* the achievement in a particular context of that technical effect). If that technical feature has not been previously made available to the public by any of the means as set out in EPC Article 54(2), then the claimed invention is novel, even though such technical effect may have inherently taken place in the course of carrying out what has previously been made available to the public.

1.2.1.4   *Catnic Components v C. Evans & Co* [1983] F.S.R. 401, Falconer J.

The action concerned the lintels that were the subject of Catnic v Hill & Smith *(below, 1.3.1.6), Evans having bought them from Hill & Smith. Evans attacked the validity of the patent (under the Patents Act 1949, s.32(1)) on the basis of prior discovery of the invention by an architect, Edmonds. Some years before the priority date of the patent, Edmonds made a drawing in cross-section for such a lintel and had arranged for a portion of it (not long enough for use) to be made up.*

Falconer J. found that all persons to whom Edmonds had shown his drawings and section were bound by implied obligations of confidence, so that the invention had not been made available to the public. Equally there had been no prior use, since the model did not itself constitute a lintel. The defendant, however, argued that, under the 1949 Act, prior invention was of itself a ground of invalidity, provided that the inventor was himself free in law and equity to use it as he pleased. Reliance was placed particularly on Bristol-Myers' Application *[1969] R.P.C. 146.*

Falconer J.:

That was a case in which the Queen's Bench Divisional Court considered an application for certiorari to set aside a decision of the Patent Appeal Tribunal in an appeal in an opposition to a patent application. The matter in issue was whether a particular prior document, admittedly relevant to its contents, had been published before the priority date of the patent application so as to be available as a prior publication under section 14(1)(e) of the 1949 Act. The document in question was a South African patent specification which had been received from South Africa but in this country by an employee of Boots Pure Drug Company in his capacity as such employee.

I should point out that "published" in the 1949 Act is defined as meaning "made available to the public". Lord Parker C.J., giving the judgment of the court, referred to the decision of the Court of Appeal in the *Fomento* case (above, 1.2.1.2) and, after pointing out (at 155) that in the *Fomento* case the Court of Appeal had treated the question of prior user as equivalent to the question whether the giving of the pens had been a publication which made available to the public the means of knowledge of the invention, continued:

> "It seems to us that we are bound by this authority to reject the contention that publication depends either upon anything in the nature of a dedication to the public or upon the degree of dissemination of the information alleged to have been published. On the contrary, if the information, whether in documentary form or in the form of the invention itself, has been communicated to a single member of the public without inhibiting fetter, that is enough to amount to a making available to the public and we do not think it is open to us to construe the words 'made available to the public' in section 101 in a sense which conflicts with this decision."

It will be noted that the Divisional Court in that case was dealing with a communication to the Boots Pure Drug Company in this country as making available to the public the contents of the document in question, but was not considering any question as to the knowledge of the communicator.

Both those cases derive the principle applied from the early case of *Humpherson v Syer*; but reference to that case shows that it is no authority for the proposition that Mr Jacob seeks to establish in this case, namely, that the knowledge of Mr Edmonds, whom he refers to, and I think rightly, as a "prior inventor", is knowledge which is available to anticipate the plaintiffs' patent. In that case (which is reported in (1887) 4 R.P.C. 184 at first instance and in the same volume at 407 in the Court of Appeal) the case concerned a device called a "waste-water preventer". The plaintiff's patent which the defendant was alleged to infringe was for a waste-water preventer without an air valve. The defendant, himself an inventor, had a patent earlier in date for a waste-water preventer with an air valve. Some time before the date of the plaintiff's patent the defendant had given instructions to one Widmer to make up a waste-water preventer and this was made up and the model made was without an air valve, that is to say, was the same as the plaintiff's patented device. One question was whether the disclosure in the instructions to Widmer constituted a publication of the plaintiff's invention or whether it was made in confidence and the passage cited by the Master of the Rolls in the *Fomento* case as the test from the *Humpherson v Syer* case is dealing with that question. In fact, the model in question was apparently also exhibited in the defendant's shop and seen by several people, and that was held to be a prior use which invalidated the plaintiff's patent.

But it is important to notice that it was nowhere suggested either in the case at first instance or in the Court of Appeal, so far as any indication in the two reports goes, that the knowledge of the defendant of the device which anticipated the plaintiff's patent was itself sufficient to invalidate the plaintiff's patent. It seems to me that it must follow that the authority relied upon in the *Fomento* and *Bristol-Myers'* cases, cannot go to the extent of supporting Mr Jacob's proposition that Mr Edmonds' knowledge alone is sufficient to anticipate the plaintiffs' patent in the present case.

However that may be, Mr Bateson for the plaintiffs submits that the defendants are not entitled to rely on Mr Edmonds' own knowledge of his concept and his model. Apart from pointing out that Mr Edmonds' knowledge was confidential to himself, Mr Bateson referred me to a number of authorities, some of which I must refer to now, although I do not propose to refer to all of them. Before I go to them, however, I must state that I apprehend that it has long been well-settled law that a patent is not invalidated for anticipation by reason of the prior knowledge of a third person who, prior to the date of the patent, has himself invented the same invention but has kept it to himself, not making any non-confidential disclosure of it and not attempting to patent it himself, so that the public has had no way of learning of it from him.

As further support, Falconer J. referred to a number of early authorities relied on by counsel for the plaintiff. The first was *Dollond's Case* (1776) 1 W.P.C. 43, of which Buller J. remarked in *Boulton & Watt v Bull* (1795) 2 Hy.Bl. 463:

"The objection to Dollond's Patent was that he was not the inventor of the new method of making object glasses, but that Dr Hall had made the same discovery before him. But it was holden that, as Dr Hall had confined it to his closet and the public were not acquainted with it, Dollond was to be considered as the inventor."

Mr Bateson also referred to the notes on that case in Webster at 44.

"The preceding would appear to be the first decision on the meaning of the statute in the case of two rival inventors within the realm; the case of *Edgebury v Stephens* (1693) 1 W.P.C. 35, *ante* at 35, had decided that the introducer from foreign parts of an invention within the realm is the true and first inventor within the meaning of the statute, and this case decides that publication is essential to the acquiring that character; that user in private, without some publication, will not defeat the claim of the subsequent independent inventor and publisher of his invention under letters patent for the benefit of the public; the question then arises, what user is such a publication as will defeat a patent, and two cases of user present themselves; first, by the patentee; second, by a stranger.

The words of the statute are 'The working or making of any manner of new manufactures, which others, at the time of making such letters patent and grant, shall not use; the words of the letters patent are "new invention as to the public use and exercise thereof"'."

I point out that the statute there referred to is, of course, section 6 of the Statute of Monopolies. ...

After references to a number of cases, the note in Webster continues with a citation from the direction to the jury of Sir N. Tindal C.J.—I think in the Court of Common Pleas—in the case of *Cornish v Keene*, and I should read it. Sir N. Tindal said:

"It will be for the jury to say whether the invention was or was not in public use and operation at the time the patent was granted. There are certain limits to this question. A man may make experiments in his own closet; if he never communicates these experiments to the world, and lays them by, and another person has made the same experiments, and, being satisfied, takes a patent, it would be no answer to say that another person had made the same experiments: there may be several rivals starting at the same time; the first who comes and takes a patent, it not being generally known to the public, that man has a right to clothe himself with the authority of the patent, and enjoys the benefit of it. If the evidence, when properly considered, classes itself under the description of experiment only, that would be no answer. On the other hand, the use of an article might be so general as to be almost universal; then you can hardly suppose anybody would take a patent. Between these two limits most cases will range themselves; and it must be for the jury to say whether the evidence convinces their understanding that the subject of the patent was in public use and operation at the time when the patent was granted."...

The next case cited by Mr Bateson to which I wish to refer is that of *Gadd v Mayor of Manchester* (1892) 9 R.P.C. 516. In that case the plaintiffs' patent related to a construction of gas-holder and the defendants who were sued for infringement attacked its validity on a number of grounds, one of which was that the invention had been prior published by one

Terrace, who had invented the same device, and the question was whether Terrace had prior published the invention. ...

On this issue the decision of the court was unanimous. It is important to note the criterion applied by Lindley L.J. ...:

> "Terrace's invention was never used in public, nor indeed at all; and such knowledge of it as the persons to whom it was communicated really had, cannot be regarded as knowledge acquired by or open to the public in any sense whatever. The public had no access to Mr Terrace's description of his invention. No one had access to that who was not confidentially consulted respecting it."...

In my judgment, *Dollond's* case, *Cornish v Keene* and *Gadd's* case, as well as, indeed, *Humpherson v Syer* are sufficient authorities (although that list is not exhaustive) to establish the principles which I stated earlier that I apprehend to have long been well-settled law, namely, that a patent is not invalid by reason of the fact that, before the inventor applied for the patent, another person had independently made the same invention if that earlier inventor has kept his knowledge of it to himself. (I am, of course, considering in this case a patent under the Patents Act 1949, and I say nothing about a patent under the Act of 1977.) The later inventor, who applies for the patent for the invention and thus is the first to publish the invention, is the "true and first inventor" in patent law.

It was argued for the defendant that, since the grounds of invalidity had been entirely codified by the Act of 1949 (American Cyanamid's (Dann) Patent [1971] R.P.C. 425, HL), the need to show consideration for a patent grant had disappeared and the case law just referred to was no longer applicable. Falconer J. rejected this, relying upon views expressed by Lords Wilberforce, Guest and Diplock in the Dann case and Lord Diplock in Bristol-Myers' (Johnson) Application [1975] R.P.C. 127 that the concept of consideration for the grant underlay several of the statutory grounds of invalidity, including the requirements of novelty and lack of obviousness.

1.2.1.5 *Du Pont's (Witsiepe) Application* **[1982] F.S.R. 303, HL**

The application in suit concerned the discovery of a plastic co-polymer which, because of its rapid hardening rate, was specially suited to injection moulding and high-speed extrusion. The co-polymer comprised:

(a) terephthalic acid (TPA)

(b) 1, 4-butanediol

(c) a poly (alkylene oxide) glycol

The opponent asserted that (under the Patents Act 1949, s.14(1)(b)) the claimed invention had been published in a prior British specification, an ICI patent (No. 682,866). This related to a co-polymer for textile fibre with an improved absorption of water, making for easier dyeing. It consisted of elements (a) and (c) in the Du Pont specification together with one of nine glycols, (five of which were specifically named). Among these five was tetramethylene glycol, another name for (b) 1, 4-butanediol. All the examples given in the specification, however, made use of another of the glycols—ethylene glycol. Accordingly the alleged anticipation was a purely paper suggestion.

Lord Wilberforce:

The opponents' case is simply put. The ICI specification gave sufficient directions to enable a chemist to make any of the indicated nine copolyesters. Each and all of these was therefore available to the public. All that is required by the law is that a person of ordinary knowledge and skill in the subject would be able to make the product without the necessity of making further experiments and without taking any new inventive step. This requirement, they claim, was amply satisfied by the ICI specification.

In order to consider whether this argument is correct, or whether it is too simplistic, it is necessary to look more closely at the process by which an invention is disclosed in a document, and the nature of the identification required. There are several principles here involved. First, it may be true to say as a general rule that where an invention for a substance is specifically disclosed, with a claim for particular advantages, or where a substance is already known, a discovery that the disclosed or known substance has some advantage or useful quality not previously recognised does not give a right to a patent. The difficulty arises when disclosure is made of a group or class of substances for which some advantage is claimed, and later it is found that one or more of this group or class possesses special advantages not belonging to the rest of the group or class, and not previously identified. This situation arises particularly in relation to inventions in the chemical field, particularly where molecular combinations are involved. In many fields, of which those concerned with polymeric chains are a good example, the number of combinations of chains, sub-chains, rings, individual molecules, may be very large. When a researcher is able to discover that a particular combination produces advantageous results he will most probably be able to assert, and will assert in the specification of his invention, that the same qualities will be produced by a number of variants or homologues described by a formula, or formulae. Moreover, having described how to produce the particular combination, he may well be able to assert, with truth, that productions of any of the combinations can be made by any skilled chemist, following the indications he has given. Is, then, the mere fact that he has disclosed or published in general terms the possibility of these combinations, in such a way that they can be made, a disclosure or publication of unrecognised advantages which may be found to be possessed by one or some of them?

The law regarding selection patents has been developed to deal with this problem. It has done so in the direction of recognising two objectives, first to protect the original inventor, as regards the invention which he has made, but secondly, to encourage other researchers in the field to use their inventive powers so as to discover fresh advantages and to treat the discovery of such advantages as inherent in selected members of the group or class as a patentable invention. The modern statement of this part of the law as regards chemical patents is the judgment of Maugham J. in *I.G. Farbenindustrie AG's Patents* (1930) 47 R.P.C. 289, a case concerned with chemical combinations for the production of dyes. It has been approved and carried forward in cases concerned with the production of synthetic penicillins, where again the number of possible molecular variations is very large. The present position was compendiously stated by Lord Diplock:

"The patents at any rate to the extent that they claim the products para-hydroxy-penicillin and Amoxycillin respectively, are selection patents.

The inventive step in a selection patent lies in the discovery that one or more members of a previously known class of products possess some special advantage for a particular purpose, which could not be predicted before the discovery was made (in *Re I.G.*

Farbenindustrie AG's Patents (1930) 47 R.P.C. 283 *per* Maugham J. at 322–323). The *quid pro quo* for the monopoly granted to the inventor is the public disclosure by him in his specification of the special advantages that the selected members of the class possess." (*Beecham Group Ltd v Bristol Laboratories International SA* [1978] R.P.C. 521 at 579).

My own opinion contains observations to a similar effect—*loc. cit., p.* 568.

That case was concerned not with any question as to validity, but with one arising under a contract, but it has been applied to a validity issue by the New Zealand Court of Appeal in a judgment dated December 22, 1981. The general principle is now securely part of the law and needs no fresh discussion in the present case. I confine myself to such aspects as are necessary for our decision.

In the first place, in order to leave open a field for selection by a subsequent inventor, it does not matter whether the original field is described by formula or by enumeration. A skilled chemist could, in most cases, quite easily transform the one into the other and the rights of the subsequent inventor cannot depend upon the notation used. In the present case, the ICI specification uses both a formula, and, to some extent, an enumeration: it does not matter to which one directs attention.

Secondly, the size of the initial group or class is not in itself decisive as to a question of prior publication of an invention related to a selected member or members. A selection patent might be claimed for one or several out of a class of 10 million (*cf. I.G. Farbenindustrie AG's Patents* at 321) or for one out of two (*cf.* the selection of one of two epimers of a synthetic penicillin combination). The size of the class may be relevant to a question of obviousness, and that question in turn may depend, in part, upon whether the later invention relates to the same field as that occupied by the prior invention, or to a different field. If an ordinary uninventive man would not be likely to look for the advantages he desires to produce in the area occupied by the prior invention, a decision to do so may well amount to the beginning of an inventive step. Here, to look for a product possessing special thermoplastic and elastomeric qualities in a 20-year-old patent concerned with producing dyeable fibres involves, prima facie, an inventive approach.

Thirdly, disclosing a prior invention does not amount to prior publication of a later invention if the former merely points the way which might lead to the latter. A much quoted and useful passage is that from the judgment of the Court of Appeal in *General Tire & Rubber Co v Firestone Tyre & Rubber Co* [1972] R.P.C. 456 at 486. There Sachs L.J. said:

"A signpost, however clear, upon the road to the patentee's invention will not suffice. The prior inventor must be clearly shown to have planted his flag at the precise destination before the patentee."

Attractive metaphors may be dangerous for those in search of precision, but the passage illustrates the necessity that the alleged prior disclosure must clearly indicate that use of the relevant material (*i.e.* that ultimately selected) does result in a product having the advantages predicted for the class. The point is well put by the New Zealand Court of Appeal. Dealing with semi-synthetic penicillin, the court (*per* Cooke J.) said:

"If such a compound has not been made before, its properties often cannot be predicted with any confidence: and where that is the case we do not consider that the invention claimed can fairly or accurately be described as 'published', even if a skilled chemist would realise that to make the compound by routine means would be practicable. A making of the compound and a discovery of its properties is necessary before the 'invention' has occurred and can be published." (My emphasis.)

This is in line with, but adds a useful precision to what was said by Maugham J.:

> "It must be remembered, of course, that the selected compounds have not been made before, or the patent would fail for want of novelty." (*I.G. Farbenindustrie AG's Patents*, at 321.)

In *Kaye v Chubb & Sons Ltd* (1887) 4 R.P.C. 289, Lord Esher M.R., too, had referred to "any clear conclusion . . . either as to the result or as to the means" (my emphasis) at 298.

I do not think that there is any inconsistency between the principle so stated and those authorities which are concerned with the degree of information necessary to enable a product to be made (see *Gillette Safety Razor Co v Anglo-American Trading Co Ltd* (1913) 30 R.P.C. 465 at 480; *C. Van Der Lely NV v Bamfords Ltd* [1963] R.P.C. 61; *Ransburg Co v Aerostyle Ltd* [1968] R.P.C. 287). When one is dealing with this question, the fact that the product has not been made or tested may well be irrelevant, but different considerations arise when the issue is as to the field left open for subsequent researchers.

It is the absence of the discovery of the special advantages, as well as the fact of non-making, that makes it possible for such persons to make an invention related to a member of the class.

Applying the law as I have endeavoured to state it, I have no doubt that the invention made by Du Pont was not disclosed or published by ICI. The latter merely indicated that the use, with other ingredients, of one preferred glycol would produce a compound with particular qualities, suggesting at the same time that use of any one of the other eight glycols would produce the same result. There was no statement that any of these others had in fact been used or that the product resulting therefrom had been found to have any particular advantages. That left it open to Du Pont to select one of them, to exercise upon it inventive research, and to discover that the product so made had valuable properties in a different field. I do not therefore understand how it can be claimed that this product, with its advantages, had been anticipated by ICI.

It is said by the opponents that it is wrong for Du Pont to seek to monopolise one of the products envisaged by ICI which has now passed into the public domain through expiry of the ICI patent. If the Du Pont invention had been made during the currency of the ICI patent, Du Pont, though entitled to exploit its invention, would have had to obtain a licence from ICI to make a product covered by ICI's patent. Now that ICI's invention is in the public domain, there is no need for such a licence and there is no basis in law on which Du Pont's monopoly can be cut down. That Du Pont is able to carve out a new monopoly out of the area claimed by ICI is an inevitable consequence of the doctrine of selection patents. In spite of this, ICI would have been able during the currency of its patent to exploit its preferred product, and variants of it, by use of any of the other diols (other than 1, 4-butanediol). And similarly such use remains available to the public. There is no reason why either ICI or the public should be able to prevent Du Pont from using its own invention: so to prevent it would remove the possibility of selection patents.

For these reasons I agree with the judgments of Whitford J. and the Court of Appeal and would dismiss the appeal.

Lord Simon of Glaisdale *after referring,* inter alia, *to the doctrine of selection patents as formulated by Maugham J. in* I.G. Farbenindustrie *and Evershed J. in* Dreyfus' Application *(1945) 62 R.P.C. 125 at 133, continued:*

These citations suggest what is the meaning of "class" for the purpose of the law of selection patents. It is a group of products or processes from all of which some particular result or results may be predicted. So, too, products or processes are "related" or "homologous" if some similar result may be predicted of them as may be predicted of other members of the class, and especially of any product or process (also a member of the class) for which a given result has been claimed. If from such a class of related or homologous products or processes a property, quality or use is discovered which could not have been predicted by anyone ordinarily skilled in the art in question, that discovery may be an invention giving rise to a valid selection patent.

If such is the nature of the "class" for the purpose of selection patent law, "specific" must for the purpose of that law stand in contradistinction. The product or process will be specifically patented and as such published in priority, so as to be effectively monopolised and unavailable for any later patent, if it is identified in the earlier specification but is not in that specification a member of a "class" (in the sense suggested above). Even then it will not bar a later patent if it is no more than a starting point on the road to a new invention—is merely what counsel for the appellants called an "enabling disclosure".

In *Hill v Evans* (1862) 4 De G.F. & J. 288, Lord Westbury said at 307, 308:

> "I cannot find in any of those [earlier] patents a clear, distinct and definite indication of the admittedly beneficial discovery that was afterwards made by the plaintiff."

And in *General Tire & Rubber Co v Firestone Tyre & Rubber Co Ltd* [1972] R.P.C. 457 at 486, Sachs L.J. said:

> "A signpost, however clear, upon the road to the patentee's invention will not suffice. The prior inventor must be clearly shown to have planted his flag at the precise destination before the patentee."

It is not necessary to decide what is the consequence of a new quality or property or use being found in or for a product or process part of a class given in a previous specification but therein also made the subject matter of a formal example. Counsel for the respondents was prepared to concede that the product or process would thereby be so successfully monopolised as to be unavailable as the subject of a valid selection patent. It seemed to Buckley L.J. in the Court of Appeal (at 495) that such a concession might be necessary, though he refrained from expressing a concluded view. I would myself prefer to leave the point open.

Counsel for the appellants urged powerfully that, if the respondents' general contention was correct, then the polyester using 1, 4-butanediol would be effectively monopolised for all purposes; so that it could be taken out of the public domain at the end of the monopoly period—in the instant case, for example, remonopolised to be used by Du Pont even for dyeing purposes. This point may to some extent be bound up with the question whether the concession I have just referred to had to be made. You cannot obtain a valid patent generally for the discovery of a new quality in or use of a known product or process. But, as Lord Wilberforce pointed out, this does not apply when the new quality or use is discovered in or for a product or process which is merely a member of a class (in the sense used in selection patent law). The subject of the selection patent is the inventive step as described by Lord Diplock. I am not convinced that this necessarily involves that the different inventive step the subject matter of the earlier patent is subsumed. But, if it were, that would be something inherent in the very concept of selection patents, which inevitably involve the taking over by a later patent of part of an area previously claimed in an earlier one for a "class".

Applying the foregoing to the instant appeal, the compound of TPA and 1, 4-butanediol was a member of a class of nine glycol compounds in the ICI patent. It could not have predicted that this class of nine glycols, singly or *seriatim*, named or innominate, would have any property or quality giving novel utility in injection moulding etc. The compound in the ICI patent was not "specific" within the meaning of selection patent law. Du Pont's discovery that the compound of TPA and 1, 4-butanediol had the said unpredictable property or quality meant that the discovery was an inventive step such as would give rise to a valid selection patent. Until it had been made and tested for such property or quality it was not "known or used" within the meaning of section 32(1)(e) of the Patents Act 1949.

It follows that I respectfully agree with the judgments of the courts below; and I would dismiss the appeal.

Lord Keith of Kinkel:

I have had the benefit of reading in draft the speeches prepared by my noble and learned friends Lord Wilberforce and Lord Simon of Glaisdale, and I am in agreement with the reasoning therein contained. I share the doubts expressed by my noble and learned friend Lord Simon of Glaisdale as to whether upholding the validity of the respondents' patent necessarily involves that the use of their compound for producing fibres capable of being readily dyed will be included in their monopoly, and I do not consider it necessary or appropriate that any concluded opinion on that matter should be expressed.

My Lords, I too would dismiss the appeal.

Lord Russell of Killowen and Lord Bridge of Harwich concurred in both these speeches.

1.2.1.6   *MOBIL/Friction-reducing Additive* G 2/88 [1990] E.P.O.R. 73, Enlarged Bd. App., EPO

The claim, which the patentee sought to insert by amendment, was for: "use of at least one per cent by weight based on the total composition of [defined compounds] as a friction reducing additive in a lubricant composition comprising a major proportion of a lubricating oil". Oil containing these additives in that proportion were already known for the purpose of inhibiting the formation of rust on ferrous metal.

The Enlarged Board of Appeal, after finding the amendment otherwise allowable, addressed the permissibility of a claim to a use where the only novelty lay in the purpose for which the use was being carried out: in this case the reduction of friction as distinct from the inhibition of rust.

The Board referred to EISAI's Application [1985] O.J. EPO 64, and the special interpretation of EPC, Art.54(5), which treated claims to compositions for the manufacture of medicaments as novel if based upon the discovery of a second non-obvious medical use for them. Since this followed from the exclusion from patentability of methods of medical treatment, it was distinct from the question now before the Board, which was answered thus:

9. In relation to a claim whose wording clearly defines a new use of a known compound, depending upon its particular wording in the context of the remainder of the patent, the

proper interpretation of the claim will normally be such that the attaining of a new technical effect which underlies the new use is a technical feature of the claimed invention. In this connection ... it is necessary to bear in mind the protocol to EPC Article 69. ... Thus with such a claim, where a particular technical effect which underlies such use is described in the patent, having regard to the protocol, the proper interpretation of the claim will require that a functional feature should be implied into the claim, as a technical feature; for example, that the compound actually achieves the particular effect.

9.1. An example of such a claim which should be so interpreted can be given by reference to the facts in Decision T–231/85 [*BASF/Triazole derivatives* [1989] E.P.O.R. 293]. The claims in question define "Use of (certain compounds) ... for controlling fungi and for preventative fungus control"—and the application contained teaching as to how to carry this out so as to achieve this effect. Prior published document (1) described the use of the same compounds for influencing plant growth. In both the application in suit and document (1), the respective treatments were carried out in the same way (so the means of realisation was the same).

The Examining Division held that the claimed invention lacked novelty, apparently on the basis that the means of realisation was the same in document (1), and so the claimed effect underlying the use for fungus control must have been achieved in the treatment described in document (1). The Board of Appeal on the other hand held that the claimed invention was novel, on the basis that the technical teaching ("Lehre") in the application was different from that in document (1), and that the use was hitherto unknown, even though the means of realisation was the same.

In the view of the Enlarged Board [in the *BASF* case], with reference to the discussion concerning the interpretation of claims in paragraph 9 above, the claim in question should properly be construed, having regard to the protocol to EPC Article 69, as implicitly including the following functional technical feature: that the named compounds, when used in accordance with the described means of realisation, in fact achieve the effect (that is, perform the function) of controlling fungus. ...

If the proper construction of such a claim in the context of a particular patent is such as to include such a functional technical feature, the question which remains to be considered is whether such claimed invention is novel. ...

10.1 [T]he respondent submitted that in cases where, for example, a compound has previously been described as having been used, but for a different purpose from the claimed use, and the previously described use had inherently had the same technical effect as the claimed use, on this basis there was lack of novelty (a so-called "doctrine of inherency"). In this connection, he also relied upon the problems involved in relation to infringement if there was no finding of lack of novelty in such circumstances: in particular, a user of the previously described use would risk infringement of a later filed patent.

In respect of this submission, the Enlarged Board would emphasise that under EPC Article 54(2) the question to be decided is what has been "made available" to the public: the question is not what may have been "inherent" in what was made available (by a prior written description, or in what has previously been used (prior use), for example). Under the European Patent Convention, a hidden or secret use, because it has not been made available to the public, is not a ground of objection to validity of a European patent. In this respect, the provisions of the European Patent Convention may differ from the previous national laws of some Contracting States, and even from the current national laws of some non-Contracting States. Thus, the question of "inherency" does not arise as such under EPC Article 54. Any vested right derived from prior use of an invention is a matter for national law (see, in this connection, for example, Article 38 of the Community Patent Convention, not yet in force).

Furthermore, as to the suggested problems concerning infringement referred to above, it is to be noted that analogous problems would result from G 05/83 [*EISA/Second medical indication* [1985] EPO O.J. 3/64] in the medical area. ...

10.3 The answer ... may therefore be summarised as follows: with respect to a claim to a new use of a known compound, such new use may reflect a newly discovered technical effect described in the patent. The attaining of such a technical effect should then be considered as a functional technical feature of the claim (for example, the achievement in a particular context of that technical effect). If that technical feature has not been previously made available to the public by any of the means as set out in EPC Article 54(2), then the claimed invention is novel, even though such technical effect may have inherently taken place in the course of carrying out what has previously been made available to the public.

1.2.1.7   *Merrell Dow v Norton* [1996] R.P.C. 76, HL

Merrell Dow had held a patent on the drug terfenadine, which had been highly successful as an antihistamine treatment. In the body terfenadine was in fact metabolised into an acid metabolite and it was this substance that was almost exclusively responsible for its effectiveness. Nine years before the end of the terfenadine patent, Merrell Dow patented the acid metabolite.

After the first patent expired, the respondents sold terfenadine. Merrell Dow alleged that they were infringing the acid metabolite patent by supplying consumers with the essential means of making the acid metabolite within the human body. The respondents argued that the making of the acid metabolite within the human body by the ingestion of terfenadine formed part of the state of the art prior to the grant of the patent, and therefore the invention was not "new" within the meaning of s.2 of the Patents Act 1977. They argued that the invention had previously been made available to the public, first, through its use (by persons taking terfenadine) and, secondly, through disclosure in the specification for the terfenadine patent.

Lord Hoffmann (with whom the other Law Lords agreed) held that there was no anticipation through use, but found anticipation by disclosure.

Anticipation by use

It is important to notice that anticipation by use relies solely upon the fact that the volunteers in the clinical trials took terfenadine and therefore made the acid metabolite. There is no suggestion in the Agreed Statement of Facts and Issues that the volunteers were also at liberty to analyse the terfenadine to discover its composition. If it was open to them to have done so, they would have been in the same position as if they had read the terfenadine specification and the arguments for anticipation by use would have been the same as for anticipation by disclosure. If anticipation by use is to be treated as a separate argument, it must be assumed that the volunteers were given terfenadine capsules by employees of Merrell Dow for the sole purpose of swallowing them. They took them without knowing their composition and produced within themselves a substance which was not then readily capable of being identified but is now known to have been the acid metabolite.

(a) *The Old Law*

I think that there can be no doubt that under the Patents Act 1949, uninformative use of the kind I have described would have invalidated the patent. One of the grounds for revocation in section 32(1) was (e): "the invention ... is not new having regard to what was *known or used*, before the priority date of the claim, in the United Kingdom." (Emphasis added) Ground 32(1)(i) was that before the priority date the invention was "secretly used" in the United Kingdom. In *Bristol-Myers Co (Johnson's) Application* [1975] R.P.C. 127 this House decided that use included secret or otherwise uninformative use. (I distinguish between secret and uninformative use because the House decided by a majority that "secret" meant that information about the invention had been deliberately concealed. It did not include a case in which the manufacturer was also unaware of the relevant facts.) Bristol-Myers had applied for a patent with a product claim for an ampicillin compound which was found to be more stable than alternative forms. Beechams were able to show, from samples providentially retained, that before the priority date they had made some quantities of that particular compound, although at the time they did not know or care which ampicillin compound it was and were unaware of the advantages discovered by Bristol-Myers. Furthermore, they had marketed the ampicillin in a form which made it impossible to discover what the original compound had been. Thus the anticipation upon which Beechams relied conveyed no relevant information about the product to the general public. The compound in the hands of the reasonably skilled member of the public told him nothing about its distinctive chemical form or how he could make it or what the advantages of that form would be. Nevertheless, the compound was anticipated by use.

The reasoning of the House was founded upon two principles of the old United Kingdom patent law. The first, to which I have already referred, was that the Crown could not grant a patent which would enable the patentee to stop another trader from doing what he had done before. It did not matter that he had been doing it secretly or otherwise uninformatively. The second was that the test for anticipation before the priority date was in this respect co-extensive with the test for infringement afterwards. If the use would have been an infringement afterwards, it must have been an anticipation before. For the purpose of infringement, it was not necessary that the defendant should have realised that he was doing an infringing act. Such knowledge was therefore equally unnecessary for anticipation.

(b) *The New Law*

Mr Floyd submitted that *Bristol-Myers Co (Johnson's) Application* was still good law. In section 2(2), the state of the art comprised "all matter," which could be "a product, a process, information about either, or anything else" which had been "made available to the public" in any way, including by "use." Mr Floyd said that "all matter" must include products or processes which conveyed no information about themselves. Otherwise, why make separate mention of "information about either"? The product itself therefore counted as part of the state of the art and could be made available to the public by use. Thus the acid metabolite had been made available to the public by use, even though such use conveyed no information to the public about the nature of the product or how to make it.

I think that this argument, which in any event depends upon a rather refined *inclusio unius* construction of the parenthetical expansion of the words "all matter", dissolves completely when one looks, as one must, at Article 54. This provision makes it clear that to be part of the state of the art, *the invention* must have been made available to the public. An invention is a piece of information. Making matter available to the public within the meaning of section 2(2) therefore requires the communication of information. The use of a product makes the invention part of the state of the art only so far as that use makes available the necessary information.

The 1977 Act therefore introduced a substantial qualification into the old principle that a patent cannot be used to stop someone doing what he has done before. If the previous use was secret or uninformative, then subject to section 64, it can. Likewise, a gap has opened between the tests for infringement and anticipation. Acts done secretly or without knowledge of the relevant facts, which would amount to infringements after the grant of the patent, will not count as anticipations before.

This construction of section 2(2) is supported by a number of authorities both in the courts of this country and the EPO. I shall refer to only two. In *PLG Research Ltd v Ardon International Ltd* [1993] F.S.R. 197 at 225, Aldous J. said:

> "Mr Thorley submitted that if a product had been made available to the public, it was not possible thereafter to patent the product whether claimed as a product claim or a product-by-process claim. That submission is too broad. Under the 1977 Act, patents may be granted for an invention covering a product that has been put on the market provided the product does not provide an enabling disclosure of the invention claimed. In most cases, prior sale of the product will make available information as to its contents and its method of manufacture, but it is possible to imagine circumstances where that will not happen. In such cases a subsequent patent may be obtained and the only safeguard given to the public is section 64 of the Act."

And in *MOBIL/Friction reducing additive Decision G 02/88* [1990] E.P.O.R. 73 the Enlarged Board of Appeal of the EPO said (at 88):

> "[T]he Enlarged Board would emphasise that under Article 54(2) EPC the question to be decided is what has been 'made available' to the public: the question is not what may have been 'inherent' in what was made available (by a prior written description, or in what has previously been used (prior use), for example). Under the EPC, a hidden or secret use, because it has not been made available to the public, is not a ground of objection to [the] validity of a European patent. In this respect, the provisions of the EPC may differ from the previous national laws of some Contracting States, and even from the current national laws of some non-Contracting States. Thus, the question of 'inherency' does not arise as such under Article 54. Any vested right derived from prior use of an invention is a matter for national law..."

Mr Thorley is therefore right in saying that his claim cannot be dismissed simply on the ground that making the acid metabolite is something which has been done before. To that extent, the intuitive response is wrong.

Anticipation by disclosure

I turn therefore to the ground upon which the respondents succeeded before Aldous J. and the Court of Appeal, namely that the disclosure in the terfenadine specification had made the invention part of the state of the art. This is different from the argument on anticipation by use because it relies not upon the mere use of the product by members of the public but upon the communication of information. The question is whether the specification conveyed sufficient information to enable the skilled reader to work the invention.

Mr Thorley [counsel for Merrell Dow] says that no one can know about something which he does not know exists. It follows that if he does not know that the product exists, he cannot know how to work an invention for making that product in any form. The prior art contained in the terfenadine specification gave no indication that it would have the effect of creating the acid metabolite in the human body. Therefore it did not contain sufficient information to enable the skilled reader to make the substance in that or any other form. It did not make the acid metabolite available to the public.

What does Mr Thorley mean when he says that no one knew that the acid metabolite existed? There is an infinite variety of descriptions under which the same thing may be known. Things may be described according to what they look like, how they are made, what they do and in many other ways. Under what description must it be known in order to justify the statement that one knows that it exists? This depends entirely upon the purpose for which the question is being asked. Let me elaborate upon an example which was mentioned in argument. The Amazonian Indians have known for centuries that cinchona bark can be used to treat malarial and other fevers. They used it in the form of powdered bark. In 1820, French scientists discovered that the active ingredient, an alkaloid called quinine, could be extracted and used more effectively in the form of sulphate of quinine. In 1944, the structure of the alkaloid molecule ($C^{20}H^{24}N^2O^2$) was discovered. This meant that the substance could be synthesised.

Imagine a scientist telling an Amazonian Indian about the discoveries of 1820 and 1944. He says: "We have found that the reason why the bark is good for fevers is that it contains an alkaloid with a rather complicated chemical structure which reacts with the red corpuscles in the bloodstream. It is called quinine." The Indian replies: "That is very interesting. In my tribe, we call it the magic spirit of the bark." Does the Indian know about quinine? My Lords, under the description of a quality of the bark which makes it useful for treating fevers, he obviously does. I do not think it matters that he chooses to label it in animistic rather than chemical terms. He knows that the bark has a quality which makes it good for fever and that is one description of quinine.

On the other hand, in a different context, the Amazonian Indian would not know about quinine. If shown pills of quinine sulphate, he would not associate them with the cinchona bark. He does not know quinine under the description of a substance in the form of pills. And he certainly would not know about the artificially synthesised alkaloid.

I recognise that there is a distinction between cinchona bark and terfenadine. The former is a substance occurring in nature and the latter is an artificial product. But the distinction is not material to the present question, which is essentially an epistemological one: what does it mean to know something, so that it can be part of the state of the art? The quinine example shows that there are descriptions under which something may in a relevant sense be known without anyone being aware of its chemical composition or even that it has an identifiable molecular structure. This proposition is unaffected by whether the substance is natural or artificial.

So far I have been considering what it means to know about something in ordinary everyday life. Do the same principles apply in the law of patents? Or does patent law have a specialised epistemology of its own? Mr Thorley argues that it does. He says that for a substance to be known so as to be part of the state of the art within the meaning of section 2, it must be known (or be readily capable of being known) by its chemical composition. No other description will do. He says that by 1977 the science of chemistry had advanced so far that the chemical composition of virtually everything was either known or readily ascertainable by analysis. Therefore the legislature assumed that knowledge that something existed could safely be equated with knowledge of its chemical composition. Section 64 would provide a safety net for people like Amazonian Indians who were doing things with substances which did not readily yield to analysis.

My Lords, I think that on this point the Patents Act 1977 is perfectly clear. Section 2(2) does not purport to confine the state of the art about products to knowledge of their chemical composition. It is the *invention* which must be new and which must therefore not be part of the state of the art. It is therefore part of the state of the art if the information which has been disclosed enables the public to know the product under a description sufficient to work the invention.

In this case, knowledge of the acid metabolite was in my view made available to the public by the terfenadine specification under the description "a part of the chemical reaction in the human body produced by the ingestion of terfenadine and having an anti-histamine effect". Was this description sufficient to make the product part of the state of the art? For many purposes, obviously not. It would not enable anyone to work the invention in the form of isolating or synthesising the acid metabolite. But for the purpose of working the invention by making the acid metabolite in the body by ingesting terfenadine, I think it plainly was. It enabled the public to work the invention by making the acid metabolite in their livers. The fact that they would not have been able to describe the chemical reaction in these terms does not mean that they were not working the invention. Whether or not a person is working a product invention is an objective fact independent of what he knows or thinks about what he is doing. ... The Amazonian Indian who treats himself with powdered bark for fever is using quinine, even if he thinks that the reason why the treatment is effective is that the tree is favoured by the Gods. The teachings of his traditional medicine contain enough information to enable him to do exactly what a scientist in the forest would have done if he wanted to treat a fever but had no supplies of quinine sulphate. The volunteers in the clinical trials who took terfenadine were doing exactly what they would have done if they had attended Merrell Dow's Strasbourg symposium and decided to try making the acid metabolite in their livers by ingesting terfenadine.

It may be helpful at this point to highlight the similarities and the distinctions between the case for anticipation by use, which I have rejected, and the case for anticipation by disclosure, which I have accepted. In both cases no one was aware that the acid metabolite was being made. In the case of anticipation by use, however, the acts relied upon conveyed no information which would have enabled anyone to work the invention, *i.e.* to make the acid metabolite. The anticipation in this form relies solely upon the fact that the acid metabolite was made, as the anticipation in *Bristol-Myers Co (Johnson's) Application* [1975] R.P.C. 127 relied solely upon the fact that ampicillin trihydrate had been made and sold to the public. It disavows any reliance upon extraneous information, such as the formula for making terfenadine and the instructions to take it for its anti-histamine effect. Anticipation by disclosure, on the other hand, relies upon the communication to the public of information which enables it to do an act having the inevitable consequence of making the acid metabolite. The terfenadine specification teaches that the ingestion of terfenadine will produce a chemical reaction in the body and for the purposes of working the invention in this form, this is a sufficient description of the making of the acid metabolite. Under that description the acid metabolite was part of the state of the art.

1.2.1.8 *Evans Medical's Patent* **[1998] R.P.C. 517, Laddie J.**

The patent was for pertactin, a surface antigen of the whooping cough bacterium, Bordatella pertussis. For various reasons, the earlier patent application from which priority was claimed, was held not to make an "enabling disclosure" and was therefore invalid for lack of novelty. It was also successfully attacked for anticipation by use. At the priority date there was already on the market Takeda's vaccine, which must have contained pertactin though no one appreciated this. Counsel for the patentee (Howe) relied upon the finding of non-anticipation by use in Merrell Dow v Norton *(above, 1.2.1.7).*

Laddie J:

Mr Howe argues that in the light of *Merrell Dow* to invalidate a patent it is not enough to demonstrate that the invention is inherent in the prior art. He says that the invention is only part of the state of the art and invalid "if the information which has been disclosed enables the public to know the invention under a description sufficient to work the invention". He is prepared to concede that that something far less than a chemical structure would suffice to make a substance known so as to destroy the novelty of a later claim to that substance. But he says that the present case involves no recognition of the existence of the substance, pertactin, in the art at all and therefore falls within category of cases where there may be inherency but no invalidity. He argues that, as happened in *Merrell Dow* itself, a "few passing words" may be enough to amount to invalidating disclosure, even if they do not characterise what is being disclosed but this was not such a case. I put to him a hypothetical example in which an encyclopedia, readily available before the priority date, contained an entry describing with precision how to make a whooping cough vaccine. If followed, the instructions would always produce a vaccine containing significant amounts of pertactin. However, the presence of that particular antigen was not known or obvious. He agrees that a vaccine so made would infringe, but he says that it is a necessary consequence of his interpretaton of *Merrell Dow* that, as long as nobody knew that it contained this particular antigen, the patent is not bad for obviousness or anticipation. Mr Howe agrees that his argument is unpalatable but he says that is what the House of Lords has decided is the law. Furthermore, he says that if he is right in relation to anticipation, the same must follow in relation to obviousness.

Mr Kitchin put an entirely different construction on *Merrell Dow*. He said that the House of Lords confirmed that one could not obtain a valid patent for characterising or analysing a known product. What you cannot do is get a patent for an old product merely because you have discovered a little bit more about its chemical make-up and structure. He says that all that has been done, in terms of disclosure by this patent, is to say, "A part of what was previously known is provided by this component"—perhaps. The component produces a response, but precisely what that contribution is and what it is doing is, even now, very much an open question. But in terms of the information relevant to the invention, there is no more now than there was before. . . .

Mr Howe puts particular emphasis on Lord Hoffmann's reasoning in relation to prior use. Evans' case is that even if following the prior art would inevitably produce a vaccine which falls within the claims of the patent in suit, it does not invalidate the latter because no one before the relevant priority date knew that such a vaccine contained pertactin. However, anyone following the prior art now would infringe, whether or not he knew that the vaccine he made contained pertactin. As I have noted above, Mr Howe readily accepts that this argument seems unpalatable but he points out that Lord Hoffmann warned against coming to an "intuitive response" or from being too swayed by "the extraordinary consequences" of or "one's initial incredulity" at a finding of validity. Adopting Lord Hoffmann's words, he says that Evans' arguments are serious and "cannot be dismissed simply on the grounds that they produce results which seem contrary to common sense" [1996] R.P.C. 79 at 84 line 30. However, at times it appeared to me that Mr Howe's argument turned Lord Hoffmann's words of caution on their head. It seemed that any reading of *Merrell Dow* or the Patents Act which gave rise to a conclusion consistent with common sense was suspect.

Laddie J. described Lord Hoffmann's approach to anticipation by disclosure in Merrell Dow, *stressing that for an anticipation what is needed is clear instruc-*

tions to carry out the invention, not instructions in any particular form or including any particular description of what occurs during execution. He continued by quoting the first passage from Lord Hoffmann's speech set out above, at p. 33. Then he referred to the final passage there quoted, above, p. 36, and continued:

Therefore not only were the users, *i.e.* the patients, ignorant of the creation of the metabolite but the case was not put forward on the basis that they had been told to take the pills for the antihistamine effect. Under the pre-1977 law this would have been called secret prior use. As Lord Hoffmann explains such uninformative use is no longer invalidating. But this does not affect the well established principle that prior art directions or information which will inevitably result in the use of a patented process or creation of the patented product invalidates by anticipation.

With this in mind, it is possible to assess the impact of the prior art in this case. First, however, one must be clear as to what the invention in issue is. Claim 1 includes a wide range of partially purified protein mixtures containing pertactin. For the reasons set out above, I have come to the conclusion that a number of pieces of the prior art teach or render it obvious to manufacture such mixtures. The claim is therefore invalid. Similar considerations apply to the other claims said to have independent validity. The only hesitation I have arises in relation to the prior art Takeda vaccine. It could be said that since the pertactin content of that product was unknown there is no difference between this case and *Merrell Dow*. I have come to the conclusion that even that argument is incorrect. In *Merrell Dow*, the patients were never in possession of a product containing the metabolite. The metabolite only came into existence inside their livers. But here the Takeda vaccine itself is a product within the claims. It was open to anyone to analyse it. It is as invalidating as the other prior art.

1.2.2 Inventive Step

1.2.2.1 Patents Act 1977, s.3 Inventive step

S.3 An invention shall be taken to involve an inventive step if it is not obvious to a person skilled in the art, having regard to any matter which forms part of the state of the art by virtue only of section 2(2) above (and disregarding section 2(3) above).

1.2.2.2 *Williams v Nye* **(1890) 7 R.P.C. 62, CA**

The plaintiff patented a machine for making sausages which was in effect a combination of a mincing machine and a filling machine, both of which were old. He brought an action for infringement against the defendant who put in issue the validity of the patent on the ground that the alleged invention consisted simply in joining two well-known machines, and therefore lacked subject-matter.

Lindley L.J.:

I also think that, having regard to Gilbert and Nye's patent, the present appeal cannot be supported. Gilbert and Nye's patent consisted of two things: first of all there was the cutting part: and then there was the filling part, that filling part being a screw which operated upon the cut meat and forced it along into the skin which had to be filled. Donald improved the cutting part. He did nothing to the filling part, but left it out. Therefore what has the plaintiff done? He has simply taken, so far as I can see, Gilbert and Nye's invention, and has substituted Donald's cutter for Gilbert's cutter. That is the whole of what he has done. I do not think a patent can be granted for that considering that the object was perfectly well known; that the utility of the forcing nozzle was known; that the object of it had been attained before, and there is nothing which amounts to what is understood by an invention. I think in principle the decision in *Harwood v The Great Northern Ry* (1864) 11 H.L. at 654 governs this case, and that the patent must be held invalid.

Cotton L.J. delivered a longer judgment to similar effect and Lopes L.J. agreed.

1.2.2.3 *Windsurfing International v Tabur Marine* **[1985] R.P.C. 59, CA**

The plaintiff held a patent for a windsurfer, which claimed the following combination of features:

- *an unstayed spar (i.e. a mast without lines to hold it in position) seated in a universal joint (allowing it to move in all directions above the board);*
- *a Bermuda rig (i.e. a triangular sail) held taut between a pair of arcuate booms, themselves mounted on the spar, so as to be able to move laterally around it and fixed together at the other end.*

The second of these groups of features was well-known at the priority date. What was novel was its combination with the unstayed spar in a universal joint. This enabled the windsurfer to be steered by manipulation of the sail and

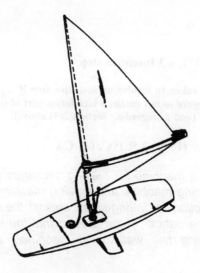

allowed the user to escape from too high winds by capsizing the sail into the water, both crucial features of the craft.

The patent was attacked as obvious using two pieces of prior art:

  (i)   An article by Darby in a sailing magazine describing the same concept, save that the board had been fitted with a square sail.

  (ii) Use by Chilvers of a home-built craft for two summers at Hayling Island, which embodied the same concept, save that the booms were straight, at least when not in use.

As to the general principle, Oliver L.J. (for the Court of Appeal) said:

There are, we think, four steps which require to be taken in answering the jury question. The first is to identify the inventive concept embodied in the patent in suit. Thereafter, the court has to assume the mantle of the normally skilled but unimaginative addressee in the art at the priority date and to impute to him what was, at that date, common general knowledge in the art in question. The third step is to identify what, if any, differences exist between the matter cited as being "known or used" and the alleged invention. Finally, the court has to ask itself whether, viewed without any knowledge of the alleged invention, those differences constitute steps which would have been obvious to the skilled man or whether they require any degree of invention.

As to the Darby article:

As regards the first step, we respectfully agree with the learned judge that the inventive concept of the patent is the free-sail concept. It is that which constitutes the essential difference between the patent in suit and other conventional vehicles propelled by sail. Going back, then, to the priority date, anyone familiar with sailing and sailing craft would then have known, as part of his general knowledge, the difference between square sail and Bermuda rigs and the disadvantages as regards manoeuvrability presented by the former. He would also have been familiar with twin booms arcuate in shape known as "wishbone" booms which, though not in wide use in the 1960s, were well known to anyone interested in constructing light craft. Darby's article was addressed initially to the knowledgeable handyman for whom the American journal *Popular Science Monthly* (in which it first appeared) was designed and, so far as the publication in this country was concerned, was directed to members of a society dedicated to amateur research into yachts. It in fact disclosed, and disclosed to persons knowledgeable in the art, the self-same inventive step claimed by the patent in suit, the only difference of any substance being the use of the kite rig held by the crossed spar and boom instead of a Bermuda rig with a wishbone boom. We agree, of course, that one must not assume that the skilled man, casting his experienced eye over Darby, would at once be fired with the knowledge that here was something which had a great commercial future which he must bend every effort to develop and improve, but he must at least be assumed to appreciate and understand the free-sail concept taught by Darby and to consider, in the light of his knowledge and experience, whether it will work and how it will work. In the light of the evidence, it seems to us inescapable that anyone skilled in the art and contemplating Darby's article in 1966 would immediately recognise, as the witnesses did, that the kite rig suggested for this very simple and elementary device would suffer from the disadvantages that it would perform poorly upwind and would require to be manipulated from the lee side of the sail.

As to the Chilvers craft:

If Peter Chilvers had adopted, as part of his device, the conventional wishbone boom in place of the more primitive straight split boom which he in fact used, it would, we should have thought, have been quite unarguable that this would not have been an anticipation under [the Patents Act 1949, s.32(1)] sub-paragraph (e), for the notion behind anticipation is, as we understand it, that it would be wrong to enable the patentee to prevent a man from doing what he has lawfully done before the patent was granted. No doubt, the philosophy behind sub-paragraph (f) is different to this extent, that a patent is granted only for an invention and that which is obvious is not inventive, but it also must, we think, take into account the same concept as anticipation, namely that it would be wrong to prevent a man from doing something which is merely an obvious extension of what he has been doing or of what was known in the art before the priority date of the patent granted.

Oliver L.J. drew support from the speech of Lord Moulton in Gillette Safety Razor v Anglo-American Trading *(1913) 30 R.P.C. 465 at 480, and from Lords Reid, Morris and Diplock in* Bristol Myers' (Johnson) Application *[1975] R.P.C. 127 at 141, 144–145, 159. He concluded that neither the relatively short usage, nor the limited audience, were grounds for ignoring it.*

1.2.2.4   *Hallen v Brabantia* [1991] R.P.C. 195, CA

The invention in issue was for a corkscrew of the "self-pulling type" (as illustrated). This type had been known since the nineteenth century, but in the 1970s had been largely replaced on the market, in particular by the "twin-lever" type, an Italian invader. The principal claim was for a self-pulling corkscrew in which the screw is coated with a friction-reducing material. The specification described the use of the well-known non-stick polymer, PTFE, as the coating and asserted that this not only improved the penetration of the screw but considerably—and surprisingly—improved withdrawal of the cork. The defendant attacked the validity of the patent principally for obviousness under the Patents Act 1977, s.3.

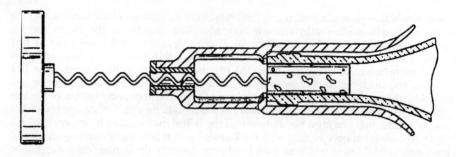

Slade L.J. (for the Court of Appeal):

The judge held that on the evidence it was obvious to apply PTFE to any corkscrew. We agree. As [counsel for the defendant] submitted, once the idea of coating a corkscrew with PTFE was known to improve the penetration of the cork by one type of corkscrew, it was self-evident that it would improve the penetration by *any* corkscrew, as indeed it was self-evident to Mr Tabard, Mr Halsey and the patentees themselves.

Given that the self-puller was in 1978 still both a known and marketable device, and given that the improved ease of penetration, as demonstrated and known from Sanbri (1973) [cited prior art], made the use of PTFE on any marketable corkscrew worthwhile, it must, in our judgment, be deemed to have been obvious to the hypothetical, albeit unimaginative, skilled man to apply it to the self-puller, even for that limited purpose. This is, in our judgment, the insuperable obstacle facing the plaintiffs on this appeal.

True it is that, as the judge found, it was not obvious that coating a self-puller with PTFE would have the dramatic effect that it did in extracting the cork, and indeed that probably without the intervention of the patent in suit such a corkscrew would not have been marketed for many years. However, as he rightly appreciated, these were in law irrelevant considerations. The dramatic improvement in extraction was for the plaintiffs a golden bonus; but it is common ground that an added benefit, however great, will not found a valid patent if the claimed innovation is obvious for another purpose: *Morgan & Co v Windover & Co*, (1890) 7 R.P.C. 131 at 134; *Drysdale v Davey Paxman & Co (Colchester) Ltd* (1937) 55 R.P.C. 95 at 113; *Parks-Cramer Co v G. W. Thornton & Sons Ltd* [1969] R.P.C. 112 at 127–128. This is a critically important principle for the purpose of this appeal. It was not, in our judgment, incumbent on the defendants to adduce expert evidence or evidence from the trade affirmatively to support their case as to "obviousness" or to explain why no self-puller with a helix coated with friction-reducing material had ever appeared on the market before 1978. ...

[Counsel for the plaintiff] has argued that ... the plaintiffs' invention can still be upheld as a selection patent. Even if it was obvious to coat all or any types of corkscrew (including self-pullers) to improve their performance during insertion, nevertheless the plaintiffs' invention was not obvious because, from the wide class of all such coated corkscrews, the inventor selected one particular type which has surprising and non-obvious advantages over the others.

The concept of selection patents has been supported by the decision of the House of Lords in *E. I. Du Pont de Nemours & Co (Witsiepe's) Application* [1982] F.S.R. 303, where earlier authorities were reviewed. The leading case on the subject perhaps remains the decision of Maugham J. in *I. G. Farbenindustrie AG's Patents*, (1930) 47 R.P.C. 289. There he stated (322–323) that to be valid a selection patent must fulfil three conditions:

(1) The selection must be based on some substantial advantage to be secured by the use of the selected members (or avoiding some substantial disadvantage).

(2) All members of the selected class must possess the advantage in question.

(3) The selection must be in respect of a quality of a special character which can fairly be said to be peculiar to the selected group. "In a selection patent the condition that there must be a substantial advantage attributable to the use of the selected members is inherent in the so-called invention." . . .

[T]he well-known parts of Maugham J.'s judgment referred to above were directed to a chemical patent and care must be taken when applying them to a mechanical patent. Nevertheless, in the case of chemical selection patents, it might not be necessary for all the compounds in the broad class actually to have been made (they could be very numerous) so long as their formulae and common properties were ascertained. Thus, though being merely "notional" compounds, they might still qualify as a broad class from which a selection patent stemmed. By analogy, we are not wholly persuaded that in the case of a mechanical patent a broad identifiable combination of known mechanical parts and substances commonly used therewith (*e.g.* oil) might never constitute a broad class from which a selection patent might stem, even though that combination did not yet physically exist.

[Counsel for the defendant] submitted that to establish a selection patent, the advantage claimed must be spelt out with particularity in the patent specification and that it was not so spelt out here. We agree with both these points. As to the first, Maugham J. in the *I. G. Farbenindustrie* case stressed the need for such particularity in the drafting of the specification of a patent, saying (47 R.P.C. 289 at 323):

"It should be obvious, after what I have said as to the essence of the inventive step, that it is necessary for the patentee to define in clear terms the nature of the characteristic which he alleges to be possessed by the selection for which he claims a monopoly. He has in truth disclosed no invention whatever if he merely says that the selected group possesses advantages. Apart altogether from the question of what is called sufficiency, he must disclose an invention; he fails to do this in the case of a selection for special characteristics, if he does not adequately define them. The cautions repeatedly expressed in the House of Lords as regards ambiguity have, I think, special weight in relation to selection patents. (*Natural Colour etc. Ltd v Bioschemes Ltd* (1915) 32 R.P.C. 256 at 266; and see *British Ore etc. Ltd v Minerals Separation Ltd* (1910) 27 R.P.C. 33 at 47.)

I will summarise the conclusion at which I have arrived by saying that in a selection patent the inventive step lies in the selection for a useful and special property or characteristic adequately defined; and this is the proposition which has to be kept in mind in considering the application to amend and the Petition for revocation."

Although [counsel for the plaintiff] sought to assert that the patentees in the present case had by the selection fulfilled these requirements, we cannot agree. It is in our judgment clear that the draftsman of the specification did not have a selection patent in mind. If he had done so, one would have expected express and clear assertions to the effect (a) that the Screwpull turned the use of PTFE to special advantage over other corkscrews in the extraction stage, and (b) that it had therefore overcome the problem with which all previous self-pullers had been afflicted. The extracts from the specification which we have set out at some length earlier in this judgment with this point in mind, in our opinion, demonstrate the absence of any such clear assertions. No one reading it would readily appreciate that the special useful improvement achieved by the addition of a coating of PTFE to the helix of a self-puller manifests itself during the process of extraction of the cork. On these short grounds, we reject the argument for a selection patent.

1.2.2.5 *Bayer's (Baatz—Carbonless Copying Paper) Application* [1982] O.J. EPO 206, Tech. Bd. App.

The application concerned a carbonless copying paper. The material on the surface of the paper which would act in place of a carbon sheet was a dye contained in micro-capsules. An earlier published specification (German application, No. 2,251,381) revealed that the walls of the capsules could be made of a particular class of polyisocyanates. The claimed invention was said to lie in the selection of a sub-group of this class. The Examining Division held the selection obvious. But on appeal, the applicant produced evidence of comparative tests showing, as the advantage of the selection, that the paper did not so rapidly lose its copying capacity.

Referring to this prior art, the Board of Appeal stated:

6. The indisputably *novel* carbonless copying papers according to the application differ from these in that a more precisely presented oxadiazinetrione diisocyanate is employed as polyisocyanate. To this extent the problem could be seen as the mere preparation of another carbonless copying paper ...

8. As shown in comparative experiments 20–22, the applicant had defined the *problem, vis-à-vis* the nearest prior art as not just preparing other copying papers but *improved* copying papers.

Referring to the prior art already mentioned, the Board stated:

11. But from the point of view of the problem of preparing copying paper having improved storage stability, the prior art cited by the Examining Division did not give any indication for selection of the more precisely prescribed oxadiazinetrione diisocyanate according to the claim from the enormous number of possible polyisocyanates for the micro-encapsulation of dyestuff-intermediates.

Referring to another similar prior specification, the Board said:

12. The document does not furnish any inducement to employ the oxadiazinetrione diisocyanates for the production of *improved* copying papers: since this special class of compounds is merely mentioned incidentally and not emphasised by an example. Mere mention of a group of substances amongst numerous other groups of substances permits at best a surmise of comparable suitability and effectiveness for the purpose in hand if these groups of substances are interchanged.

A further prior specification covered, inter alia, polyisocyanates within the current application for use as coatings for wood, metal and the like and for mouldings and foam. The Board commented:

13. Even with knowledge of this prior art the person skilled in the art could at the most expect that if he were to use these oxadiazinetrione diisocyanates to produce wall material for micro-capsules he would get only qualitatively and quantitatively similar results as in German unexamined application 2,251,381. Thus the person skilled in the art who—as in this case—had tried to improve the copying papers specified in German unexamined application 2,251,381 would, on the basis of the prior art cited, not have arrived at the solution claimed in the application. The

teaching of the present application, that the employment of the oxadiazinetrione diisocyanates as claimed leads to significantly improved copying papers must—independently of whether it is expressed in the form of the product claim 1 or the use claim 2—be regarded as surprising, and hence involving an inventive step within the meaning of EPC Article 56.

1.2.2.6 *Fives-Cail Babcock's Application* [1982] O.J. EPO 225, Tech. Bd. App.

The applicant for a European patent claimed to have discovered that scrapers for cleaning an endless conveyor belt could be effectively supported by rods made of plastic reinforced by glass fibre. In the prior art, these rods were made of metal and had a tendency to break. Claim 1 was in the following form:

1. Cleaning apparatus for endless conveyor belt, comprising a set of independent scrapers connected to a support by means of elastic elements, characterised in that each elastic element is composed of a glass-fibre-reinforced plastics rod.

The main issue on appeal to the European Patent Office Technical Board of Appeal was whether this involved an inventive step over the prior art:

4.1 According to what the applicant says in his submission received on December 30, 1981, there are disadvantages in using elastic elements made of metal as a means of supporting the scrapers, because such metal components often break.

Considering that the rod-shaped design of elastic elements in an apparatus possessing the features indicated in the first part of Claim 1 was already known (see the drawing in patent specification DT 58900, particularly reference symbol 5), the problem to be solved in connection with the apparatus according to Claim 1 consists in discovering a rod-shaped elastic element which is less prone to breakage.

4.2 This problem undeniably confronts the conveying equipment specialist: however, it prompts him at the same time to seek its solution in the field of materials science. Consequently, the skilled person qualified to solve the problem cannot be a conveying equipment specialist, but has to be a materials specialist alone. Therefore, the assessment of whether the problem's solution (which, according to Claim 1, consists in replacing metal by a synthetic resin reinforced with glass fibres) involves an inventive step must be made by reference to the knowledge and ability of a materials specialist, not a conveying equipment specialist.

4.3 A materials specialist customarily uses plastics in place of traditional materials, particularly in cases where traditional materials would not function satisfactorily, in the present case. The skilled person knows that the only suitable possibility is a synthetic material of sufficient elasticity and fatigue strength. He also knows that synthetic resins reinforced with glass fibres meet those requirements. It thus immediately occurs to him to suggest using a synthetic resin reinforced with glass fibres as the material for rod-shaped elastic elements.

If the skilled person is unsure whether glass fibre rods break less easily than the known springy strips or rods, he can simply conduct an experiment.

4.4 For the foregoing reasons, the Board cannot agree with the applicant that the skilled person relevant in the assessment whether the invention involves an inventive step is the specialist in the technical field indicated in the preamble of the claim.

4.5 Thus, the subject-matter of Claim 1 does not involve an inventive step (EPC Article 56).

Claim 1 is therefore not allowable under EPC Article 52(1).

1.2.2.7 *Mobey Chemical's Application* [1982] O.J. EPO 394, Tech. Bd. App.

The applicant claimed a process for producing MBP (methylene bisphenyl isocyanate) which was liquid and stable in storage by heating the substance in the presence of catalyst (P.O.—phosopholine acid) to a temperature of 180° to 300°C and then quenching it to 100°C or less. This was said to be an improvement over the prior art in which quenching was not used and the catalyst had to be removed by the use of a poison which itself had undesirable consequences. Alternatively higher temperatures had to be used.

6. In summary it is clear that, given the problem to be solved, neither the methods of the prior art individually, nor their respective combination with the generally available specialist knowledge, would make the solution according to the invention with the advantageous effects achieved foreseeable. While it is inadmissible to combine unrelated or conflicting documents in order to deny inventive step, it is indeed permissible to consider various documents together mosaically in order to prove a prejudice or a general trend pointing away from the invention. The idea of departing from the catalyst poison regarded as indispensable, in conjunction with the teaching that the P.O. catalysts decompose at higher temperature, represents a valuable simplification of the state of the art which could not have been found without an inventive step.

1.2.2.8 *American Cyanamid Co (Dann's) Patent* [1971] R.P.C. 425 at 451 *per* Lord Diplock:

Since the original discovery of the therapeutic uses of antibiotics and of the methods of aerobic fermentation by which they can be produced from micro-organisms to be found in nature, further advances in this field of medicine have been achieved by searching for and finding hitherto unidentified strains of micro-organisms existing in the natural state from which useful new antibiotics can be prepared by what is now a well-known standard process. The task of finding such a strain of micro-organism, calls for the exercise of technical proficiency and is laborious and very costly, for the odds against success are large. It is not easy to see what inventive step, as distinct from the mere exercise of proficiency and practice, is involved in this kind of research, but the result of success in it is a new product useful to humanity which does not exist in nature. If such research is to be encouraged in a competitive society, the monetary rewards of success must be assured to those who undertake the expense; and the means of doing so in this and in most other countries with comparable social systems is by according to the successful discoverer of the new product the controlled and limited monopoly granted for inventions under the national patent laws.

1.2.2.9 *Johns-Manville's Patent* [1967] R.P.C. 479, CA

Asbestos cement (a mixture of asbestos, cement and silica) was prepared from a slurry—a concentrated aqueous suspension of finely divided particles—of these ingredients. The process of producing shaped asbestos cement articles, such as pipes, from this slurry was well known and widely used at the priority date of the patent. The first step was to pick up from a cylinder rotating in the wet mixing vat a thin skin of the slurry on a moving belt made of felt which acted as a filter through which the water was drained from the solids until the mixture had reached the right consistency to enable the skin of asbestos cement on the felt to be transferred mechanically to a revolving cylinder upon which it built up in spiral layers or laminations.

The use of flocculating agents to aid filtration was well known. But the flocculating agents previously available had not been found effective for use in the production of shaped asbestos cement articles. The alleged invention in the patent in suit consisted simply of adding to the mixture of suspended solids to be filtered in the process of manufacturing asbestos cement pipes the known, but recently developed, flocculating agent, polyacrylamide, in the proportions recommended by the manufacturers of that product. The respondents claimed that the patent was invalid for obviousness.

Diplock L.J. (for the court):

The successful use of this flocculating agent in the process called for some adjustment in the operation of the manufacturing plant such as increasing the speed of movement of the felt filter, or adding more water to the slurry. Those adjustments are not referred to in the specification, and it is now common ground that it was unnecessary to do so, for the need for adjustments and the nature of those required would be obvious to anyone skilled in the industry. Their introduction would accordingly involve no inventive step.

If there is any inventive step involved in the appellants' claim, it is in the idea of using a known, but recently developed, flocculating agent in a known filtration process in which it had not been used before. This idea, when put into practice as indicated in the specification, with the necessary but unspecified adjustments to the plant, does produce substantial economies of manufacture. If the idea was not obvious, the invention claimed is patentable.

The respondents' case was simply that "a person versed in the art" of manufacturing asbestos cement pipes (which nowadays means a hypothetical and highly qualified technologist in the research department of asbestos cement pipe manufacturers) would be likely to read the two publications referred to, and that if he did so the information which they contained about polyacrylamides would make him realise that here was a flocculating agent which was well worth trying out in the filtration process used in his own industry in order to see whether it would have beneficial results. If that had been established, the respondents in my view have made out their case that the idea of using polyacrylamides as flocculating agents in the manufacture of cement asbestos pipes was, at the priority date, "obvious and clearly did not involve any inventive step".

I have endeavoured to refrain from coining a definition of "obviousness" which counsel may be tempted to cite in subsequent cases relating to different types of claims. Patent law can too easily be bedevilled by linguistics, and the citation of a plethora of cases about other inventions of different kinds. The correctness of a decision upon an issue of obviousness does not depend upon whether or not the decider has paraphrased the words of the Act in some particular verbal formula. I doubt whether there is any verbal formula which is appropriate to all classes of claims. The superintending examiner used the expression "alerted to the possibilities" of using polyacrylamides in improving the filterability of asbestos cement slurries. I find no fault with this phrase in the context of the claim in the appellants' specification. The learned judge preferred the expression "see without difficulty that these newly-introduced polymers would be of advantage in his filtration step". I think that "would be" puts it too high if it postulates prior certainty of success before actually testing the polymers in the filtration process; it is enough that the person versed in the art would assess the likelihood of success as sufficient to warrant actual trial. I do not, however, understand that the learned judge meant more than this, for he did not consider that there was any genuine difference between his phrase and that used by the superintending examiner.

The publications relied upon are a sales pamphlet entitled "Aerofloc Reagents", which contains the manufacturers' particulars of polyacrylamide flocculating agents, and directions for their use. It does not refer specifically to their potential value in asbestos cement manufacturing, but deals primarily with their commercial application in various kinds of mining industries in which the flocculation of mineral particles in aqueous solution can be of advantage. Asbestos, cement and silica are, all three, minerals. The second document, an article by Mr A. M. Swift in a technical journal of the pulp and paper industries, refers specifically to the flocculating effect of polyacrylamides upon, *inter alia*, cement and clay particles. The polyacrylamides were stated to be effective in very small quantities. As compared with other flocculating agents they would thus be present in minute quantities only in the filtered product. The superintending examiner and the Patents Appeal Tribunal were both of opinion that, filtration processes being common to many industries, these documents, although addressed primarily to the mining and paper industries respectively, were likely to be read by those concerned with the asbestos cement industry, and that such readers would have realised that here was a newly introduced flocculating agent which it was well worth trying out in their own filtration process. I can see no grounds which would justify this court in reversing this concurrent finding by two expert tribunals. And there, but for an argument to which I must now advert, is an end of this appeal.

It has been contended with protracted vigour in this court, as it was before both tribunals below, that the action which was in fact taken by a particular witness, who was an actual research worker in the asbestos cement manufacturing industry, when polyacrylamides were first drawn to his attention, demonstrates that these concurrent findings were wrong. The individual was the manager of the respondents' own research department, who made a statutory declaration in support of their application. His evidence discloses that when he first heard of polyacrylamides (which was before the documents relied upon were published) he sought to obtain samples in order to see whether they would be effective flocculating agents for use in the filtration process involved in the manufacture of asbestos cement pipes. As a result of his inquiries he obtained trial quantities of polyacrylamide from the manufacturers, and subsequently received from them the documents relied on when they were published in 1957. In 1956 he carried out experiments with a polyacrylamide and asbestos cement slurry. He "found that it improved the filtration of the slurry, but that this resulted in the formation of a thicker skin of asbestos cement being transferred from the felt filter belt to the revolving cylinder, and a corresponding reduction in the number of laminations for a given thickness in the final product. This had an adverse effect upon its quality." He accordingly abandoned his experiments in 1957, and did not resume them until 1960 (that is, after the priority date of the applicants' specification). He then found out for himself that by speeding up the rate of travel of the belt, the thickness of the skin of asbestos cement upon the felt could be reduced, and the number of laminations correspondingly increased so that the quality of the final product was unimpaired.

In so far as this witness obtained literature about flocculating agents used in other industries, and realised, as soon as he heard of them, that polyacrylamides were well worth trying out as flocculating agents in his own industry of manufacturing asbestos cement pipes, his evidence confirms the opinion of the superintending examiner and the Patents Appeal Tribunal that the idea of trying out these newly introduced flocculating agents in the filtration process in that industry would be obvious to persons "versed in the art". His failure to persevere with his experiments, when he found that the skin of asbestos cement upon the felt filter was too thick, would be cogent evidence for the appellants if the invention claimed in their specification included an adjustment to the speed of the filter belt. But there is not a word about this in their specification. If, appreciating the necessity for such an adjustment involved any inventive step, the specification could be attacked upon the alternative ground set out in section 14(1)(g), namely, that it "does not sufficiently and fairly describe the invention or the method by which it is to be performed". But it is (and so far as the appellants are concerned, it has to be) common ground that, once the idea of adding polyacrylamides to the asbestos cement slurry used in the manufacture of asbestos cement pipes has been tried out, and the thicker skin of asbestos resulting from the improved filtration observed, the necessary adjustment to the speed of the filter belt to obviate any deleterious effect upon the quality of the final product would be obvious, notwithstanding that the respondents' own research manager did not find it so.

All that this evidence shows is that this particular witness's glimpse of the obvious was spasmodic. To this extent he was atypical of the hypothetical person "versed in the art" of manufacturing asbestos cement pipes, whom the superintending examiner, the Patents Appeal Tribunal and this court must postulate as reading the publications relied upon, and drawing from them those conclusions about the likelihood of polyacrylamides being useful in that manufacture, to which his skill, his knowledge and his experience would lead him. Like the learned judge, I see nothing in this evidence to throw doubt upon the conclusions reached by the superintending examiner and by the Patents Appeal Tribunal itself that the idea of adding a polyacrylamide to the asbestos cement slurry in the manufacture of shaped asbestos cement articles was obvious having regard to the information published in the two documents relied upon.

I would dismiss the appeal.

Russell and Willmer L.JJ. delivered brief concurring judgments.

1.2.2.10 *Olin Mathieson Chemical v Biorex Laboratories* **[1970] R.P.C. 157, Graham J.**

The phenothiazines are a vast group of organic substances with a basically similar chemical structure. Certain members of the class were first known as useful dyes and then as anti-malarial drugs. One sub-class, having as its principal characteristic a chlorine radical, was later found to contain a member that was useful as a tranquilliser: chlorpromazine. The plaintiffs experimented upon another sub-class, in which the chlorine radical ($-Cl$) was replaced by a trifluoromethyl radical ($-CF3$). They too found that one member, tri-fluoroperazine, was a useful tranquilliser and they could predict that other members of the sub-class (which was itself very large) would have a similar characteristic. (The basic chemistry of the whole group is outlined in an Appendix to the judgment: [1970] R.P.C. at 197–200).

In relation to the legal test of obviousness, Graham J. said:

It is, however, most important, in my judgment, to remember that during the years covered by this history a very large number of patents and proposals, the vast majority of which came to nothing, were made in this general field in the endeavour to find really useful drugs. This can probably best be appreciated from a study of documents prepared by Dr Margaret Simkins, the head of the Research Information Department at Smith, Kline & French. She gave evidence, the effect of which was that, if asked at the relevant date to provide information to a research team faced with the problem of producing an alternative for or better drug than chlorpromazine, she would produce all the information on phenothialzines and methods of making them which she could find had been recorded to date, together with any other useful information on the subject such as which other companies had patents in the field and for what drugs. This would result in extracts and tabulations such as M.A.S. 7 and other documents.

That this was what she would have done was not really disputed, and I accept her evidence in this respect. This would have meant that the research group would have information about, *inter alia*, all the Rhone-Poulenc patents and work in this field, the Smith papers and a great number of other patents and papers covering a very wide variety of suggestions for substitutions in the side chains and in the phenothiazyl ring and at the "2", "3", and "4" positions. If interest was shown by the research group in the use of (–CF), for substitution, and this would be one possibility brought to their attention by the first search, and asked for further information on this topic, then it seems certain that papers mentioning this substituent, such as Caldwell, Lindenstruth, Nes and Burger, and Walborsky, would be found and brought to their attention. For the purposes of answering the question of obviousness, I have assumed that such papers would be so produced.

In testing the validity of claim 1, and this, of course, is the most vulnerable claim, the vital question which must then be answered, in my judgment, can perhaps best be expressed as follows:

"Would the notional research group at the relevant date, in all the circumstances, which include a knowledge of all the relevant prior art and of the facts of the nature and success of chlorpromazine, directly be led as a matter of course to try the –CF, substitution in the '2' position in place of the –Cl atom in chlorpromazine or in any other body which, apart from the –CF, substitution, has the other characteristics of the formula of claim 1, in the expectation that it might well produce a useful alternative to or better drug than chlorpromazine or a body useful for any other purpose?"

This question is in fact a sort of jury question, and must be decided objectively, and the judge cannot surrender his decision to the witnesses, though their evidence may be of assistance in placing him in a better position to come to the right answer.

1.2.3 Patentable Subject-matter

1.2.3.1 Patents Act 1977, s.1(2)–(5), s.4 Sch.A2, paras 1–6, 11: Excluded Subject-matter; Industrial Application

S.1(2) It is hereby declared that the following (among other things) are not inventions for the purposes of this Act, that is to say, anything which consists of—

(a) a discovery, scientific theory or mathematical method;

(b) a literary, dramatic, musical or artistic work or any other aesthetic creation whatsoever;

(c) a scheme, rule or method for performing a mental act, playing a game or doing business, or a program for a computer;

(d) the presentation of information;

but the foregoing provision shall prevent anything from being treated as an invention for the purposes of this Act only to the extent that a patent or application for a patent relates to that thing as such.

(3) A patent shall not be granted for an invention the commercial exploitation of which would be contrary to public policy or morality.

(4) For the purposes of subsection (3) above, exploitation shall not be regarded as contrary to public policy or morality only because it is prohibited by any law in force in the United Kingdom or any part of it.

(5) The Secretary of State may by order vary the provisions of subsection (2) above for the purpose of maintaining them in conformity with developments in science and technology; and no such order shall be made unless a draft of the order has been laid before, and approved by resolution of, each House of Parliament.

S.4(1) Subject to subsection (2) below, an invention shall be taken to be capable of industrial application if it can be made or used in any kind of industry, including agriculture.

(2) An invention of a method of treatment of the human or animal body by surgery or therapy or of diagnosis practised on the human or animal body shall not be taken to be capable of industrial application.

(3) Subsection (2) above shall not prevent a product consisting of a substance or composition being treated as capable of industrial application merely because it is invented for use in any such method.

Section 1(2) corresponds in general to EPC Art.52(2), (3); s.1(3) to Art.53(a); s.4(1) to Art.57; and s.4(2) and (3) to Art.52(4).

Sch.A2, paras 1–6, 11, (implementing Biotechnology Directive (98/40/EC), Arts. 1–6; for paras 7–10, see below, para. 1.3.2.1).

1. An invention shall not be considered unpatentable solely on the ground that it concerns—

(a) a product consisting of or containing biological material; or

(b) a process by which biological material is produced, processed or used.

2. Biological material which is isolated from its natural environment or produced by means of a technical process may be the subject of an invention even if it previously occurred in nature.

3. The following are not patentable inventions—

(a) the human body, at the various stages of its formation and development, and the simple discovery of one of its elements, including the sequence or partial sequence of a gene;

(b) processes for cloning human beings;

(c) processes for modifying the germ line genetic identity of human beings;

(d) uses of human embryos for industrial or commercial purposes;

(e) processes for modifying the genetic identity of animals which are likely to cause them suffering without any substantial medical benefit to man or animal, and also animals resulting from such processes;

(f) any variety of animal or plant or any essentially biological process for the production of animals or plants, not being a micro-biological or other technical process or the product of such a process.

4. Inventions which concern plants or animals may be patentable if the technical feasibility of the invention is not confined to a particular plant or animal variety.

5. An element isolated from the human body or otherwise produced by means of a technical process, including the sequence or partial sequence of a gene, may constitute a patentable invention, even if the structure of that element is identical to that of a natural element.

6. The industrial application of a sequence or partial sequence of a gene must be disclosed in the patent application as filed.

11. In this Schedule:

"essentially biological process" means a process for the production of animals and plants which consists entirely of natural phenomena such as crossing and selection;
"microbiological process" means any process involving or performed upon or resulting in microbiological material;
"plant variety" means a plant grouping within a single botanical taxon of the lowest known rank, which grouping can be:

(a) defined by the expression of the characteristics that results from a given genotype or combination of genotypes; and

(b) distinguished from any other plant grouping by the expression of at least one of the said characteristics; and

(c) considered as a unit with regard to its suitability for being propagated unchanged.

1.2.3.2   *Biogen v Medeva* [1997] R.P.C. 1, HL

This leading decision will be considered more fully considered (below, 1.2.4.2), in relation to adequate disclosure. One issue was whether, in the Patents Act

1977, s.1(1), a court has to consider whether it is dealing with an "invention" before turning to whether the invention is patentable.

Lord Hoffmann (for the House), after quoting s.1(1), continued:

The Act thus lays down various conditions, both positive (in paragraphs (a) to (c)) and negative (in paragraph (d)) which an invention must satisfy in order to be a "patentable invention". This scheme might suggest that logically one should first decide whether the claimed invention can properly be described as an invention at all. Only if this question receives an affirmative answer would it be necessary to go on to consider whether the invention satisfies the prescribed conditions for being "patentable". In practice, however, I have no doubt that in most cases this would be a mistake and cause unnecessary difficulty.

The Act does not define the concept of an invention. Section 1(1) was intended to reflect, "as nearly as practicable", Article 52 of the European Patent Convention ("EPC"): see section 130(7) of the 1977 Act. Article 52 also has no definition of an invention. It seems that the parties to the EPC were unable to agree upon one: see Singer and Singer, *The European Patent Convention* (English ed. 1995 by Ralph Lunzer), paragraph 52.04). But the reason why the parties were content to do without a definition was that they recognised that the question would almost invariably be academic. The four conditions in section 1(1) do a great deal more than restrict the class of "inventions" which may be patented. They probably also contain every element of the concept of an invention in ordinary speech. I say probably, because in the absence of a definition one cannot say with certainty that one might not come across something which satisfied all the conditions but could not be described as an invention. But the draftsmen of the Convention and the Act, as well as counsel at the bar, were unable to think of any examples. Just in case one should appear, section 1(5) gives the Secretary of State power to vary the list of matters excluded by paragraph (d) "for the purpose of maintaining them in conformity with developments in science and technology".

As the four conditions are relatively familiar ground, elucidated by definitions in the Act and the jurisprudence of the courts and the E.P.O., it will normally be more convenient to start by deciding whether they are satisfied. In virtually every case this will be the end of the inquiry. There may one day be a case in which it is necessary to decide whether something which satisfies the conditions can be called an invention, but that question can wait until it arises.

One can of course imagine cases in which the alleged subject-matter is so obviously not an invention that it is tempting to take an axe to the problem by dismissing the claim without inquiring too closely into which of the conditions has not been satisfied. So in *Genentech Inc's Patent* [1989] R.P.C. 147 at 264 Mustill L.J. said, by reference to the ordinary speech meaning of "invention":

> "You cannot invent water, although you certainly can invent ways in which it may be distilled or synthesised."

This is obviously right and in such a case it may seem pedantic to say that water fails the condition in paragraph (a) of section 1(1) because it is not new. Unfortunately, most cases which come before the courts are more difficult. Judges would therefore be well advised to put on one side their intuitive sense of what constitutes an invention until they have considered the questions of novelty, inventiveness and so forth. In the present case, I think that Medeva's counsel was right to resist the invitation of the Court of Appeal to make submissions on whether the claims constituted an invention.

1.2.3.3 *Vicom's Application* [1987] O.J. EPO 14, Tech. Bd. App.

An applicant sought in particular to procure the following amended claims:

1. A method of digitally processing images in the form of a two-dimensional data array having elements arranged in rows and columns in which an operator matrix of a size substantially smaller than the size of the data array is convolved with the data array, including sequentially scanning the elements of the data array with the operator matrix, characterised in that the method includes repeated cycles of sequentially scanning the entire data array with a small generating kernel operator matrix to generate a convolved array and then replacing the data array as a new data array; the small generating kernel remaining the same for any single scan of the entire data array and although comprising at least a multiplicity of elements, nevertheless being of a size substantially smaller than is required of a conventional operator matrix in which the operator matrix is convolved with the data array only once, and the cycle being repeated for each previous new data array by selecting the small generating kernel operator matrices and the number of cycles according to conventional error minimisation techniques until the last new data array generated is substantially the required convolution of the original data array with the conventional operator matrix.

8. Apparatus for carrying out the method in Claim 1 including data input means (10) for receiving said data array, and said data array to generate an operator matrix for scanning said data array to generate the required convolution of the operator matrix and the data array, characterised in that there are provided feedback means (50) for transferring the output of the mask means (20) to the data input means, and control means (30) for causing the scanning and transferring of the output of the mask means (20) to the data input means to be repeated a predetermined number of times.

The Examining Division rejected these as constituting a mathematical method which did not define new technical subject-matter in terms of technical features. The Technical Board of Appeal disagreed.

After holding that the claimed invention was susceptible of industrial application (Art.57), it considered both whether the claims were excluded as being for a mathematical method as such and a computer program as such:

5. There can be little doubt that any processing operation on an electric signal can be described in mathematical terms. The characteristic of a filter, for example, can be expressed in terms of a mathematical formula. A basic difference between a mathematical method and a technical process can be seen, however, in the fact that a mathematical method or a mathematical algorithm is carried out on numbers (whatever these numbers may represent) and provides a result also in numerical form, the mathematical method or algorithm being only an abstract concept prescribing how to operate on the numbers. No direct technical result is produced by the method as such. In contrast thereto, if a mathematical method is used in a technical process, that process is carried out on a physical

entity (which may be a material object but equally an image stored as an electric signal) by some technical means implementing the method and provides as its result a certain change in that entity. The technical means might include a computer comprising suitable hardware or an appropriately programmed general purpose computer.

6. The Board, therefore, is of the opinion that even if the idea underlying an invention may be considered to reside in a mathematical method a claim directed to a technical process in which the method is used does not seek protection for the mathematical method *as such*.

7. In contrast, a "method for digitally filtering data" remains an abstract notion not distinguished from a mathematical method so long as it is not specified what physical entity is represented by the data and forms the subject of a technical process, *i.e.* a process which is susceptible of industrial application. ...

11. The appellants have stressed that the application discloses new hardware for carrying out the claimed methods but admit on the other hand that at least in principle it is possible to implement the method and apparatus according to the application by a suitably programmed conventional computer although such a computer may not be optimised for carrying out digital image processing (*cf.* p.A–2 of the Statement of Grounds).

12. The Board is of the opinion that a claim directed to a technical process which process is carried out under the control of a program (be this implemented in hardware or in software, cannot be regarded as relating to a computer programme *as such* within the meaning of EPC Article 52(3), as it is the application of the program for determining the sequence of steps in the process for which in effect protection is sought. Consequently, such a claim is allowable under EPC Article 52(2)(c) and (3).

13. Concerning the apparatus Claim 8, the Examining Division has held that it is not acceptable because a new apparatus is not clearly disclosed. According to the decision under appeal, the claim when interpreted in the light of the description and the drawings seems to imply only the use of a conventional computer which could not provide the basis of an acceptable product claim in view of EPC Articles 52(1) and 54. The Board understands this as meaning that the Examining Division was of the opinion that a conventional computer programmed so as to carry out a method according to one or more of the method claims is not novel.

14. In the view of the Board, however, EPC Article 54 leaves no room for such an interpretation. A computer of known type set up to operate according to a new program cannot be considered as forming part of the state of the art as defined by EPC Article 54(2).

This is particularly apparent in the present case as Claims 8–11 clearly embrace also the use of special hardware, for which some indications are given in the description and also mixed solutions combining some special hardware with an appropriate program.

15. In view of certain considerations by the Examining Division which appear to apply to the apparatus claims as well (*cf.* para. 10 above) it remains to be examined if the present apparatus Claim 8 would be objectionable under EPC Article 52(2)(c) as qualified by (3). For reasons analogous to these given in paragraph 12 above, the Board holds that this is not the case and the same applies to the other apparatus Claims 9–11. Generally claims which can be considered as being directed to a computer set up to operate in accordance with a specified program (whether by means of hardware or software) for controlling or carrying out a technical process cannot be regarded as relating to a computer program *as such* and thus are not objectionable under EPC Article 52(2)(c) and (3).

16. In arriving at this conclusion the Board has additionally considered that making a

distinction between embodiments of the same invention carried out in hardware or in software is inappropriate as it can fairly be said that the choice between these two possibilities is not of an essential nature but is based on technical and economical considerations which bear no relationship to the inventive concept as such.

Generally speaking, an invention which would be patentable in accordance with conventional patentability criteria should not be excluded from protection by the mere fact that for its implementation modern technical means in the form of a computer program are used. Decisive is what technical contribution the invention is defined in the claim when considered as a whole makes to the known art.

Finally, it would seem illogical to grant protection for a technical process controlled by a suitably programmed computer but not for the computer itself when set up to execute the control.

1.2.3.4 *Merrill Lynch's Application* [1989] R.P.C. 561, CA

The application concerned a data processing system for making a trading market in securities, which deployed a known computer system programmed in a standard language. Claim 1 was as follows:

> *In combination in a data processing system for making a trading market in at least one security in which the system proprietor is acting as principal; said system including means for receiving trade orders for said at least one security from system customers, said trade orders including fields identifying the stock to be traded and characterisation of the trade as a customer purchase or sale, and the number of shares for the transaction; means for retrieving and for storing operative bid and asked prices for said at least one security; means for entering and for storing order qualification parameters, said parameters and said stored prices determining which received orders and qualified for execution; means for storing data characterising position, cost and profit for said at least one security; qualifying means responsive to said received trade orders and said stored prices and order qualification parameters for qualifying a trade order for execution when the received trade order fields do not violate the stored prices and qualification parameters; means for executing each trade order qualified by said qualification means; and post-execution updating means for updating said position and at least one of said stored parameters upon execution of a trade order.*

At first instance, Falconer J. rejected the claim as being for a computer program as such (s.1(2)(c)) and in doing so placed emphasis on the phrase "to the extent that" which introduces the whole of s.1(2):

It seems to me that the words "to the extent that" contemplate that the subsection is also to be applicable to cases where the invention involves one of the excluding matters (specified in paras (a), (b), (c) and (d)), but does not relate to it only. Using the exemplification of an invention involving a computer program, Mr Thorley submitted that the wording "only to the extent that" means that there cannot be a patentable invention in so far as the invention resides in the computer program itself, but if some practical (*i.e.* technical) effect is achieved by the computer or machine operating according to the instructions contained in the program and such effect is novel and inventive (*i.e.* not obvious), a claim directed to that practical effect will be patentable, notwithstanding it is defined by that computer program. In my judgment, Mr Thorley was right in that submission.

In Genentech's Patent *[1989] R.P.C. 147, Whitford J., at first instance, took a different view, holding that the prohibition in s.1(2) was limited to inventions which related to the matters there specified and did not include modes of using these matters in a process or in relation to an artefact. In* Genentech, *the Court of Appeal preferred this view and refused to accept Falconer J.'s reasoning above, while being careful to cast no doubt on the actual result reached by Falconer J. in the present case which was then also taken on appeal. The Court of Appeal followed its view in* Genentech. *Fox L.J. (for the court) proceeded to quote from* Vicom's Application *(above, 1.2.3.3). He concluded:*

The position seems to me to be this, *Genentech* decides that the reasoning of Falconer J. is wrong. On the other hand, it seems to me to be clear, for the reasons indicated by Dillon L.J., that it cannot be permissible to patent an item excluded by section 1(2) under the guise of an article which contains that item—that is to say, in the case of a computer program, the patenting of a conventional computer containing that program. Something further is necessary. The nature of that addition is, I think, to be found in the *Vicom* case where it is stated: "Decisive is what technical contribution the invention makes to the known art". There must, I think, be some technical advance on the prior art in the form of a new result (*e.g.* a substantial increase in processing speed as in *Vicom*).

Now let it be supposed that claim 1 can be regarded as producing a new result in the form of a technical contribution to the prior art. That result, whatever the technical advance may be, is simply the production of a trading system. It is a data-processing system for doing a specific business, that is to say, making a trading market in securities. The end result, therefore, is simply "a method ... of doing business", and is excluded by section 1(2)(c). The fact that the method of doing business may be an improvement on previous methods of doing business does not seem to me to be material. The prohibition in section 1(2)(c) is generic; qualitative considerations do not enter into the matter. The section draws no distinction between the method by which the mode of doing business is achieved. If what is produced in the end is itself an item excluded from patentability by section 1(2), the matter can go no further. Claim 1, after all, is directed to "a data processing system for making a trading market". That is simply a method of doing business. A data processing system operating to produce a novel technical result would normally be patentable. But it cannot, it seems to me, be patentable if the result itself is a prohibited item under section 1(2). In the present case it is such a prohibited item.

We were referred to *International Business Machines Corp's Application* [1980] F.S.R. 564, as being on all fours with the present case, but it was decided under the 1949 Act, which is not in the same form as the 1977 Act.

In the end, therefore, for the reasons which I have indicated, I reach the same result as Falconer J., namely that there is not a patentable invention here. I would dismiss the appeal.

1.2.3.5   *Fujitsu Limited's Application* [1997] R.P.C. 608, CA

The patent application related to a method and apparatus for modelling a synthetic crystal structure for designing inorganic materials. The apparatus in question involved a computer program so that an operator could select an atom, a lattice vector and a crystal face in each of two crystal structures displayed by the computer. The computer then converted data representing the physical layouts of the two crystal structures into data representing the crystal structure that would have been obtained by combining the original two structures in that way. The resulting data was then displayed to give an image of the resulting combined structure.

Claims 9 and 10 read as follows:

9. A method of manufacturing a structure which is a crystalline combination of two crystal structures, the method comprising an investigation of the effects of combining the two crystal structures using a method according to any one of the preceding claims.

10. A computer apparatus for creating a computer image of a synthetic crystal structure formed of a first crystal structure having a plurality of atoms and lattices and a second crystal structure having a plurality of atoms and lattices, said apparatus comprising:

computer storage means for ...

selection means for selecting from ...

specifying means, coupled to said selecting means, for specifying ...

transformation means for transforming said ...

computer display means for displaying ...

The applicant argued that these claims related to a method of manufacture and an apparatus respectively, and so could not be claims consisting of a method for performing a mental act. The defined steps taken by the apparatus were not determined by the skill and assessment of the operator. Moreover, it was argued that the invention as claimed was patentable because it provided a technical contribution, in the form of processing images of real objects or providing a labour-saving and error-free tool.

Aldous L.J. (for the Court).

Computer programs as such—technical contribution

[I] have difficulty in identifying clearly the boundary line between what is and what is not a technical contribution. In *Vicom* it seems that the Board concluded that the enhancement of the images produced amounted to technical contribution. No such contribution existed in *Gale's Application* ([1991] R.P.C. 305) which related to a ROM programmed to enable a computer to carry out a mathematical calculation or in *Merrill Lynch* which had claims to a data processing system for making a trading market in securities. Each case has to be decided upon its own facts . . . .

There is only one invention. The fact that it is claimed as a method, a way of manufacture or an apparatus having appropriate features is irrelevant. Further there is no dispute as to what the invention is. In summary it uses a computer program so that an operator can select an atom, lattice vector and a crystal face in each of two crystal structures displayed. The computer, upon instruction and using the program, then converts data representing the physical layouts of the two crystal structures into data representing the physical layout of the structure that is obtained by combining the original two structures in such a way that the selected atoms, the selected lattice vectors and the selected faces are superposed. The resulting data are then displayed to give a picture of the resulting combined structure. Clearly the whole operation revolves around the computer program and the question for decision is whether there is a technical contribution so that it cannot be said that the invention consists of a computer program as such.

Mr Birss put forward two grounds for concluding that the application included a technical contribution. First, relying on *Vicom*, he submitted that the technical contribution was provided by the processing of real images or structures. I have already concluded that *Vicom* does not support so rigid a view. Thus this submission must be rejected. Second, he submitted, that the application provided a new tool for modelling crystal structure combinations which relieved the chemist of the laborious task of building a model. It provided a solution to the problem of providing a quick and error free way of creating real images of two crystal structures joined together.

Mr Birss is right that a computer set up according to the teaching in the patent application provides a new "tool" for modelling crystal structure combinations which avoids labour and error. But those are just the sort of advantages that are obtained by use of a computer program. Thus the fact that the patent application provides a new tool does not solve the question of whether the application consists of a program for a computer as such or whether it is a program for a computer with a technical contribution.

I believe that the application is for a computer program as such. In *Vicom* the technical contribution was provided by the generation of the enhanced display. In the present case the combined structure is the result of the directions given by the operator and use of the program. The computer is conventional as is the display unit. The two displays of crystal structures are produced by the operator. The operator then provides the appropriate way of superposition and the program does the rest. The resulting display is the combined structure shown pictorially in a form that would in the past have been produced as a model. The only advance is the computer program which enables the combined displays to be portrayed quicker.

Method of performing a mental act

After reviewing a passage from his earlier decision in Wang Laboratories Inc's Application *[1991] R.P.C. 463 at 472, Aldous L.J. continued:*

Mr Birss submitted that the reasoning in my judgment in *Wang* was flawed. He submitted that it was not possible to perform a mental act using a computer and a claim to a method of using a computer could not be a claim to a method of performing a mental act. As a matter of semantics that may be right, but as has been made clear in *Merrill Lynch* and *Gale*, it is necessary to look at the substance of the application when dealing with the question of whether it is patentable. A claim to a computer operating in a particular way is no more patentable than a claim to a computer program. A claim to a method of carrying out a calculation (a method of performing a mental act) is no more patentable when claimed as being done by a computer than when done on a piece of paper. Methods of performing mental acts, which means methods of the type performed mentally, are unpatentable, unless some concept of technical contribution is present.

1.2.3.6   *IBM'S Application/Computer Program* [1999] R.P.C. 861; [1999] E.P.O.R. 301, Tech. Bd. App.

A program was claimed which caused information from a first window on a computer screen to be displayed in another part of that window when obscured by a second window. The Technical Board of Appeal found this to be patentable subject-matter in that the software provided a technical solution in the functioning of the computer. The program could moreover be claimed not just as a computer so programmed, but as a computer program product on any medium which made it readable by a computer. This made sale of the program for installation an act of direct infringement:

Technical character of programs for computers

6.1. For the purpose of interpreting the exclusion from patentablilty of programs for computers under Article 52 (2) and (3) EPC, it is assumed that programs for computers cannot be considered as having a technical character for the very reason that they are programs for computers.

6.2. This means that physical modifications of the hardware (causing, for instance, electrical currents) driving from the execution of the instructions given by programs for computers cannot *per se* constitute the technical character required for avoiding the exclusion of those programs.

6.3. Although such modifications may be considered to be technical, they are a common feature of all those programs for computers which have been made suitable for being run on a computer, and therefore cannot be used to distinguish programs for computers with a technical character from programs for computers as such.

6.4. It is thus necessary to look elsewhere for technical character in the above sense: it could be found in the further effects deriving from the execution (by the hardware) of the instructions given by the computer program. Where the said further effects have a technical character or where they cause the software to solve a technical problem, an invention which brings about such an effect may be considered an invention, which can, in principle, be the subject-matter of a patent.

6.5. Consequently a patent may be granted not only in the case of an invention where a piece of software manages, by means of a computer, an industrial process or the working of a piece of machinery, but in every case where a program for a computer is the only means, or one of the necessary means, of obtaining a technical effect within the meaning specified above, where, for instance, a technical effect of that kind is achieved by the internal functioning of a computer itself under the influence of the said program.

In other words, on condition that they are able to produce a technical effect in the above sense, all computer programs must be considered as inventions within the meaning of Article 52 (1) EPC, and may be the subject-matter of a patent if the other requirements provided for by the EPC are satisfied.

6.6. As already indicated in the previous paragraph, the said technical effect may also be caused by the functioning of the computer itself on which the program is being run, i.e. by the functioning of the hardware of that computer. It is clear that also in this situation the physical modifications of the hardware deriving from the execution of the instructions given by the program within the meaning indicated under points 6.2 and 6.3 above cannot *per se* constitute the technical character required for avoiding exclusion.

In this case it is only the said further technical effect which matters when considering the patentability requirements, and no importance should be attached to the specific further use of the system as a whole. The expression "the system as a whole" means that the hardware plus the software, that is the system consisting of the hardware as programmed in accordance with the program concerned (hardware + software).

7. *Case law of the Boards of Appeal of the EPO*

7.1. The considerations contained in Reasons 4,5 and 6 above are in line with the main stream in the case law of the Boards of Appeal of the EPO.

As far as patentability is concerned, the Boards have so far required inventions to possess technical character. To the present Board's knowledge there are no decisions in which a Board of Appeal has attributed a technical character to a computer program for the sole reason that the program is destined to be used in a technical apparatus, namely a computer.

This can be illustrated by one of the early decisions of the Boards in this field, T–208/84 (*Vicom* O.J. 1987, 14), as cited above. This invention concerned "A method of digitally processing images in the form of a two-dimensional data array ...", which made use of a mathematical method incorporated in a computer program run on an appropriate computer to do the said processing.

In this case it was held that the method according to the invention was not excluded from patentability, because it constituted a technical process which was carried out on a physical entity. This entity might be a material object but equally an image stored as an electric signal. Thus the said method was neither a mathematical method as such nor a computer program as such.

7.2. The fact that the physical modifications of the hardware deriving from the execution of the instructions of a computer program cannot *per se* constitute the technical character of the programs for computers as required for the purpose of avoiding their exclusion from patentability under Article 52(2)(c) and (3) EPC is demonstrated for example by Decision T–22/85 (*IBM* O.J. 1990, 12), according to which the said physical modifications of the hardware cause electrical currents.

7.3. A typical example of an invention which concerns the internal functioning of a computer caused by the programs running on it was the subject of Decision T–769/92 (*Sohei* O.J. 1995, 525), according to which the fact that technical considerations were required in order to arrive at the invention was considered to lend sufficient technical character to the invention as claimed for it to avoid exclusion from patentability under Article 52(2)(c) and (3), whereas no importance was attributed to the specific use of the system as a whole.

7.4. The basic idea of the invention resides in the computer program.

Of particular importance to the present case is the fact that, according to the case law of the Boards of Appeal, a claim directed to the use of a computer program for the solution of a technical problem cannot be regarded as seeking protection for the program as such within the meaning of Article 52 (2)(c) and (3) EPC, even if the basic idea underlying the invention may be considered to reside in the computer program itself, as illustrated for example by Decisions T–208/84 (O.J. 1987, 14), as cited above, and T–115/85 (*IBM* O.J. 1990, 30).

The case law thus allows an invention to be patentable when the basic idea underlying the invention resides in the computer program itself.

8. The Board takes this opportunity to remark that, for the purpose of determining the extent of the exclusion under Article 52 (2) and (3) EPC, the said "further" technical effect may, in its opinion, be known in the prior art.

Determining the technical contribution an invention achieves with respect to the prior art is therefore more appropriate for the purpose of examining novelty and inventive step than for deciding on possible exclusion under Article 52(2) and (3).

9. *Claim for a computer program product*

9.1. As already pointed out under Reason 1, the only question to be decided in this appeal is whether the subject-matter of Claims 7 to 10 is excluded form patentability under Article 52 (2) and (3) EPC. These claims are directed to a computer program product and have to be examined from the point of view of what may be called "the further technical effect", which, if present, may lead to the subject-matter not being excluded under Article 52(2) and (3) EPC.

9.2. Such products normally comprise a set of instructions which, when the program is loaded, makes the hardware execute a specific procedure producing a particular result.

9.3. It is self-evident that in this instance the basic idea underlying the invention resides in the computer program. It is also clear that, in such a case, the hardware on which the program is intended to run is outside the invention, *i.e.* the hardware is not part of the invention. It is the material object on which the physical changes carried out by running the program take place.

Furthermore, it is clear that if, for instance, the computer program product comprises a computer-readable medium on which the program is stored, this medium only constitutes the physical support on which the program is saved, and thus constitutes hardware.

9.4. Every computer program product produces an effect when the program concerned is made to run on a computer. The effect only shows in physical reality when the program is being run. Thus the computer program product itself does not directly disclose the said effect in physical reality. It only discloses the effect when being run and consequently only possesses the "potential" to produce the said effect.

This effect may also be technical in the sense explained under Reason 6, in which case it constitutes the "further technical effect" mentioned there. This means that a computer program product may possess the potential to produce a "further" technical effect.

Once it has been clearly established that a specific computer program product, when run on a computer, brings about a technical effect in the above sense, the Board sees no good reason for distinguishing between a direct technical effect on the one hand and the potential to produce a technical effect, which may be considered as an indirect technical effect, on the other hand.

A computer program product may therefore possess a technical character because it has the potential to cause a predetermined further technical effect in the above sense. According to the above, having technical character means not being excluded from patentability under the "as such" provision pursuant to Article 52 (3) EPC.

This means that a computer program product having the potential to cause a pre-determined further technical effect is, in principle, not excluded from patentability under Article 52 (2) and (3). Consequently, computer program products are not excluded from patentability under all circumstances.

9.5. In contrast to the reasons given in the decision under appeal, the Board has derived the technical character of the computer program product from the potential effect the program possess, which effect is set free and may reveal itself when the program is made to run on a computer.

1.2.3.7 *PBS Partnership/Pensions benefits system* [2001] O.J. EPO 441, Tech. Bd. App.

The application concerned a scheme for organising an employer's pension system by processing data relating to the employee, to the whole group of insured employees, to life assurance for them and to administrative costs, in order to produce specified information; this included the employer's con-tributions in consequence to be made to a master trust, the face amount of the life policy on each employee and the benefits to be paid to pensioners. A first group of claims were to the scheme simply as a method of organising com-puterised calculations. A second group of claims were to apparatus (i.e. a computer) programmed to carry out the scheme. In a decision that is not easily penetrated by a non-specialist, the Technical Board of Appeal distinguished, on the one hand, the question whether a computerised procedure was excluded from patentability—either as a business method "as such" or a computer program "as such"; and, on the other, the question whether it constituted an inventive step.

As regards the method claims it drew attention to the continuing requirement of EPC Art.52(2) and (3) that the invention must have a technical character if it is not to be excluded as a program or business method "as such", and pro-ceeded:

Claim 1 of the main request is, apart from various computing means mentioned in that claim, directed to a "method for controlling a pension benefits program by administering at least one subscriber employer account". All the features of this claim are steps of processing and producing information having purely administrative, actuarial and/or financial char-acter. Processing and producing such information are typical steps of business and economic methods.

Thus the invention as claimed does not go beyond a method of doing business as such and, therefore, is excluded from patentability under Article 52(2)(c) in combination with Article 52(3) EPC; the claim does not define an invention within the meaning of Article 52(1) EPC.

However, as regards the apparatus claims, it concluded the opposite:

In the board's view a computer system suitably programmed for use in a particular field, even if that is the field of business and economy, has the character of a concrete apparatus in the sense of a physical entity, man-made for a utilitarian purpose and is thus an invention within the meaning of Article 52(1) EPC.

This distinction with regard to patentability between a method for doing business and an apparatus suited to perform such a method is justified in the light of the wording of Article 52(2)(c) EPC, according to which "schemes, rules and methods" are non-patentable categories in the field of economy and business, but the category of "apparatus" in the sense of "physical entity" or "product" is not mentioned in Article 52(2) EPC.

This means that, if a claim is directed to such an entity, the formal category of such a claim does in fact imply physical features of the claimed subject-matter which may qualify as technical features of the invention concerned and thus be relevant for its patentability.

As part of its conclusion it rejects the "contribution" approach which had been included in the EPO Guidelines to Examiners as follows:

"the examiner should disregard the form or kind of claim and concentrate on its content in order to identify the real contribution which the subject-matter claimed, considered as a whole, adds to the known art. If this contribution is not of a technical character, there is no invention within the meaning of Article 52(1)". This confuses the requirement of "invention" with the requirements of "novelty" and "inventive step."

The Board's conclusion is:

There is no basis in the EPC for distinguishing between "new features" of an invention and features of that invention which are known from the prior art when examining whether the invention concerned may be considered to be an invention within the meaning of Article 52(1) EPC. Thus there is no basis in the EPC for applying this so-called contribution approach for this purpose.

However the apparatus claims had in any case to pass the test of inventive step and at that juncture it became necessary to consider what technical element could supply this requirement. The Board's conclusion was against even the apparatus claims.

1.2.3.8 *Ciba-Geigy's Propagating Material Application* **[1984] O.J. EPO 112, Tech. Bd. App.**

An applicant sought to procure the following (amended) claims:

"Claim 13: Propagating material for cultivated plants, treated with an oxime derivative according to formula 1 in claim 1.

Claim 14: Propagating material according to claim 13, characterised in that it consists of seed".

The Examining Division rejected them as debarred by EPC Art.53(b); but the Technical Board of Appeal disagreed:

2. No general exclusion of inventions in the sphere of animate nature can be inferred from

the European Patent Convention (*cf.* EPC Article 52(1) in conjunction with Article 53(b) after the semi-colon, and Rules 28 and 28a). However, EPC Article 53(b) before the semi-colon prohibits the granting of patents for certain biological inventions. This provision, which needs to be examined more closely in the present case, says that patents shall not be granted in respect of plant varieties or essentially biological processes for the production of plants. The skilled person understands the term "plant varieties" to mean a multiplicity of plants which are largely the same in their characteristics and remain the same within specific tolerances after every propagation or every propagation cycle. This definition is reflected in the International Convention for the Protection of New Varieties of Plants of December 2, 1961, which is intended to give the breeder of a new plant variety a protective right (Article 1(1)) extending both to the reproductive or vegetative propagating material and also to the whole plant (Article 5(1)). Plant varieties in this sense are all cultivated varieties, clones, lines, strains and hybrids which can be grown in such a way that they are clearly distinguishable from other varieties, sufficiently homogeneous, and stable in their essential characteristics (Article 2(2) in conjunction with Article 6(1)(a), (c) and (d)). The legislator did not wish to afford patent protection under the European Patent Convention to plant varieties of this kind, whether in the form of propagating material or of the plant itself.

3. Claims 13 and 14, whose maintenance resulted in the refusal of the present application, concern propagating material, in particular seeds of cultivated plants, treated with a sulphurous oxime derivative which is characterised in greater detail in claim 1. A definition of cultivated plants in the description (*cf.* p.9, para. 3) shows that this includes all plants which yield substances in any form. Examples of known plants are listed. Propagating material from such cultivated plants comprises all reproductive plant components, including plants and plantlings which have begun to be germinated, but particularly seeds (*cf.* p.10, para. 2, of the description).

Even if certain known varieties of wheat, millet and barley are mentioned in the examples in connection with oxime treatment (*cf.* pp.35 and 36 of the description), the subject-matter of claims 13 and 14 is not an individual variety of plant distinguishable from any other variety, but the claims relate to any cultivated plants in the form of their propagating material which have been chemically treated in a certain way. However, EPC Article 53(b) prohibits only the patenting of plants or their propagating material in the genetically fixed form of the plant variety.

4. The very wording of EPC Article 53(b) before the semi-colon precludes the equation of plants and plant varieties, which would also be at variance with the general sense of the provision. Plant varieties were excluded from European patent protection mainly because several of the signatory States to the European Patent Convention have developed special protection for plant breeding at national and international level (R. Singer, *The New European Patent System*, Seminar Services International, p.22, para. 6).

In EPC Article 53(b) before the semi-colon the authors adhered strictly to the wording of Article 2(b) of the Strasbourg Patent Convention of November 27, 1963, in which the Contracting States to that Convention were given the opportunity to exclude plant varieties, amongst other things, from patent protection. Even at that time the majority of the States represented on the Council of Europe were already of the opinion that plant varieties should be protected not by patents but by a special industrial property right (Pfanner, *Vereinheitlichung des materiellen Patentrechts im Rahmen des Europarats*, [1962] G.R.U.R. Int. 545, 547).

By contrast, the innovation claimed here does not lie within the sphere of plant breeding, which is concerned with the genetic modification of plants. Rather, it acts on the propagating material by means of chemical agents in order to make it resistant to agricultural chemicals. The new parameter for the propagating material, namely treatment with an oxime derivative, is not a criterion which can be characteristic of a plant variety as far as the protection of varieties is concerned. There is therefore no conflict between the protection of varieties or the patent as different forms of protection for propagating material treated in this way. In fact, patent protection is the only possibility.

Technologically, the treatment with an oxime derivative is a plant protection measure which, in contrast to other cases, is carried out on a marketable object, namely the propagating material. It is not necessary for the object of the treatment always to be a plant variety, since the treatment can also be carried out on propagating material which does not meet the essential criteria of homogeneity or stability characteristic of a plant variety. Conversely, it is immaterial to the question of patentability that the propagating material which is treated can also be, or is primarily, a plant variety. If plant varieties have been excluded from patent protection because specifically the achievement involved in breeding a new variety is to have its own form of protection, it is perfectly sufficient for the exclusion to be left restricted, in conformity with its wording, to cases in which plants are characterised precisely by the genetically determined peculiarities of their natural phenotype. In this respect there is no conflict between areas reserved for national protection of varieties and the field of application of the European Patent Convention. On the other hand, innovations which cannot be given the protection afforded to varieties are still patentable if the general prerequisites are met.

5. Moreover, the propagating material claimed is not the result of an essentially biological process for the breeding of plants—which would be excluded from patent protection—but the result of treatment with chemical agents (*e.g.* dressing agents, seed-dressing processes, immersion of the plantling in an oxime solution, *cf.* p.6, line 23; p.9, line 8; and p.10, lines 17–20). To summarise, therefore, EPC Article 53(b) is not an obstacle to the patenting of the propagating material claimed in the present case.

1.2.3.9   *Harvard Onco-Mouse* T–19/90 [1990] O.J. EPO 476, Tech. Bd. App.; [1991] E.P.O.R. 525, Ex. D.

The application had as its principal claims the following:

1. *A method for producing a transgenic non-human mammalian animal having an increased probability of developing neoplasms, said method comprising introducing an activated oncogene sequence into a non-human mammalian animal at a stage no later than the eight-cell stage.*

2. *A transgenic non-human mammalian animal whose germ cells and somatic cells contain an activated oncogene sequence introduced into said animal, or an ancestor of said animal, at a stage no later than the eight-cell stage, said oncogene optionally being further defined according to any one of Claims 3 to 10.*

The Technical Board of Appeal overruled the Examining Division's refusal to grant the patent on various grounds, but required the Division to consider further whether exploitation of the invention would be contrary to "ordre public" or morality (EPC Art.53(a)).

3. Sufficiency of Disclosure (EPC Article 83)

3.2. As the Examining Division pointed out in the contested decision, the claimed invention refers to all non-human mammalian animals, whereas the invention described in the examples has been performed only on mice. In these circumstances the Division was not convinced that a skilled person would be able to carry out successfully on all other kinds of non-human mammals the invention as performed on mice. The Examining Division, therefore, refused the application, *inter alia*, on the ground that the claims were unrealistically broad.

3.3 However, the mere fact that a claim is broad is not in itself a ground for considering the application as not complying with the requirement for sufficient disclosure under EPC Article 83. Only if there are serious doubts, substantiated by verifiable facts, may an application be objected to for lack of sufficient disclosure.

Although the Examining Division was right in saying that certain non-human mammals other than mice have very different numbers of genes and different immune systems, it does not necessarily follow that the invention cannot be carried out on such animals. On the contrary, at least one source (Palmiter & Brinster, (1986) 20 Ann. Rev. Genet. 465–499) suggests that those skilled in the art might very well be able to carry out the invention on non-human mammals other than mice. Nor is the Board itself aware of any verifiable facts which could cast serious doubt on the possibility for a skilled person to carry out the invention as claimed. ...

3.7 The Examining Division ... took the view that the decision in case T 292/85 (see above)—referred to by the appellants—was irrelevant to the present case. That decision concerned a genetic engineering invention involving polypeptide expression. Objections of insufficient disclosure had been raised to the broad term "bacteria" which, it was felt, could include unsuitable species or variants. There, the Board took the view that the unsuitability of unspecified variants was immaterial as long as suitable variants were known to the skilled person through the disclosure or on the basis of his common general knowledge. A biological invention was thus considered sufficiently disclosed if it clearly indicated at least one way in which the skilled person could carry it out.

3.8 The Board, in contrast to the Examining Division, considers that the above ruling can also be applied to the present case. The invention clearly indicates how the skilled person can achieve chromosomal incorporation of an activated oncogene sequence into the genome of a non-human mammal, disclosing as it does an activated mouse myc gene introduced into a suitable plasmid and then micro-injected into mouse eggs at a given stage of cellular development. First, this ensures that the invention can be reproduced on mice. Secondly, it may be assumed that the skilled person is aware—in the same way as in case T –292/85—of other suitable mammals on which the invention can likewise be successfully performed. There is thus no reason why the application should be refused on the ground that it involves an extrapolation from mice—as particularly featured in the application—to mammals in general. ...

4. Exceptions to patentability under EPC Article 53(b)

4.1. The present patent application concerns, *inter alia*, genetically manipulated non-human mammals. The first half-sentence of EPC Article 53(b) reads as follows in English, French and German:

"European patents shall not be granted in respect of:

(a) ...

(b) plant or animal varieties or essentially biological processes for the production of plants or animals";

"*Les brevets européens ne sont pas délivrés pour:*

(a) ...

(b) les variétés végétales ou les races animales ainsi que les procédés essentiellement biologiques d'obtention de végétaux ou d'animaux";

"*Europäische Patente werden nicht erteilt für:*

(a) ...

(b) Pflanzensorten oder Tierarten sowie für im wesentlichen biologische Verfahren zur Züchtung von Pflanzen oder Tieren".

4.2 As pointed out by the Examining Division, the three texts of EPC Article 53(b) differ in terminology as to the non-patentable area. In particular, the German term "*Tierarten*" is broader than the English "animal varieties" and the French "*races animales*".

4.3 EPC Article 177(1) lays down that the English, French and German texts of the European Patent Convention are all equally authentic. In the present case, there is obviously a need to establish their common meaning through interpretation of the Convention in order to determine to what extent animals are excluded from patentability under EPC Article 53(b), first half-sentence.

4.4 In the decision under appeal the Examining Division interpreted EPC Article 53(b) as excluding not only certain groups of animals from patentability but, in fact, animals as such. The Board is unable to accept this interpretation.

4.5 First, the Examining Division did not take duly into account that EPC Article 53(b) is an exception, for certain kinds of inventions, to the general rule under EPC Article 52(1) that European patents "shall be" granted for all inventions which are susceptible of industrial application, which are new and which involve an inventive step. Any such exception must, as repeatedly pointed out by the Boards of Appeal, be narrowly construed (*cf.* in particular T–320/87 point 6, [1990] O.J. EPO, 76). The Examining Division has given no convincing reasons for deviating in this particular case from this principle of interpretation, nor are any such reasons apparent to the Board.

4.6 The possibility that the reference to certain categories of animals rather than to animals as such was simply a mistake by the legislators can be ruled out. Nothing in the legislative history of either the European Patent Convention or the Strasbourg Convention of November 27, 1963 on the Unification of Certain Points of Substantive Law on Patents for Invention, whose Article 2(b) was taken over and incorporated into EPC Article 53(b), supports such an assumption. On the contrary, a clear indication that the terms "animal varieties", "*races animales*" and "*Tierarten*" were not intended to cover animals as such is the wording of EPC Article 53(b) itself. The very same provision also contains, as appears from paragraph 4.1 above, a reference to "animals" (in general). In using the different terms "*animal varieties*" ("*races animales*", "*Tierarten*") and "*animals*" ("*animaux*", "*Tiere*") in this way, the legislators cannot have meant "animals" in both cases.

4.7 In contrast to the exclusion of "plant varieties" from patentability under EPC Article 53(b) (*cf.* T 320/87—see above), the preparatory documents to this provision are completely silent as to the purpose of excluding "animal varieties" from patentability. However, the purpose of a law (*ratio legis*) is not merely a matter of the actual intention of the legislators at the time when the law was adopted, but also of their presumed intention in the light of changes in circumstances which have taken place since then. It is now the task of the European Patent Office to find a solution to the problem of the interpretation of EPC Article 53(b) with regard to the concept of "animal varieties", providing a proper balance between the interest of inventors in this field in obtaining reasonable protection for their efforts and society's interest in excluding certain categories of animals from patent protection. In this context it should, *inter alia*, be borne in mind that for animals—unlike plant varieties—no other industrial property right is available for the time being.

4.8 To sum up, the Board concludes that the Examining Division was wrong in refusing the present application on the ground that EPC Article 53(b) excludes the patenting of animals as such. The proper issue to be considered is, therefore, whether or not the subject-matter of the application is an "animal variety" ("*race animale*", "*Tierart*") within the meaning of EPC Article 53(b). On this point the contested decision is for obvious reasons entirely silent. In view of the importance of this matter and the desirability of having it considered by at least two instances, the Board will exercise its powers under EPC Article 111(1) to remit the case to the department of first instance for further prosecution. It should also be noted that a number of questions outlined below and not yet dealt with by the Examining Division now need to be considered.

In its resumed examination with regard to EPC Article 53(b), the Examining Division must, as indicated above, first consider whether the subject-matter of the present application constitutes an "animal variety", "*race animale*" or "*Tierart*" within the meaning of that provision. If it comes to the conclusion that the subject-matter is not covered by any of these three terms, then EPC Article 53(b) constitutes no bar to patentability. If, however, it considers that any of these terms applies, then refusal of the application would only be justified if that specific term represents the proper interpretation of Article 53(b) (see point 4.3 above). This would also presuppose that EPC Article 53(b) can be applied at all in respect of animals which are genetically manipulated, given that neither the drafters of the Strasbourg Convention nor those of the European Patent Convention could envisage this possibility.

4.9 Essentially biological processes (EPC Article 53(b), first half-sentence, second alternative).

4.9.1 Process claims
Under EPC Article 53(b), first half-sentence, European patents are not granted for essentially biological processes for the production of animals. The present invention contains process claims for the production of transgenic, non-human mammals with an increased propensity to develop neoplasms through chromosomal incorporation of an activated oncogene sequence into the genome of the non-human mammal. The oncogene is inserted by technical means into a vector (*e.g.* a plasmid), which is then micro-injected at an early embryonic stage. In the Board's view, the Examining Division correctly concluded that this is not an "essentially biological process" within the meaning of EPC Article 53(b).

4.9.2 Product claims
Claim 19 under the main request relates to a transgenic non-human mammalian animal whose germ cells and somatic cells contain an activated oncogene sequence as a result of chromosomal incorporation into the genome of the animal itself or into the genome of one of its ancestors. It thus covers both transgenic animals produced according to the process claims, making use of micro-injection, and the descendants of such animals. While the former are the result of a non-biological process, their descendants can be the outcome of a biological process based on sexual reproduction.

The Examining Division took the view that by artificially combining a non-biological and a breeding process the applicant was seeking to circumvent the exclusion under EPC Article 53(b), first half-sentence, particularly since the two processes would give rise to two different products. The Board doubts whether the latter point is legally correct as the products of the two processes, at least from the point of view of patent law, cannot be distinguished from each other in respect of the transferred gene. However, this question may be left open for the time being since the basic assertion in the contested decision—that Claim 19 circumvents EPC Article 53(b), and thus precludes the grant of a patent—is wrong in any case. As the Examining Division has noted, Claim 19 is a product claim. In the absence of any other definition, the product claimed is defined in terms of the process by which it is produced. Claim 19 is thus a "product-by-process" claim. But a product-by-process claim remains a product claim irrespective of the process it refers to. So a successful Claim 19 would result in a product patent, not a process patent. Since, however, EPC Article 53(b) excludes only processes for the production of animals, with which Claim 19 is not concerned, this provision *per se* is no bar to patenting the product.

It may also be added that a reproductive process could conceivably be other than sexual, *i.e.* other than essentially biological, for example if an animal which has received the oncogene sequence by the first process were then to be cloned by asexual, technical means.

4.10 Microbiological processes and the products thereof (EPC Article 53(b), second half-sentence)
EPC Article 53(b), second half-sentence, provides that EPC Article 53(b), first half-sentence, does not apply to microbiological processes or the products thereof. The Examining Division did not decide whether the present invention involves a microbiological process, taking the view that EPC Article 53(b), second half-sentence, does not apply if the product (in this case the animal) is excluded under the first half-sentence on the grounds that the second part of the provision cannot be interpreted in a manner which would set aside the first part. The Board does not share this view. As indicated above, EPC Article 53(b), first half-sentence, is an exception to the general principle of patentability contained in EPC Article 52(1). The second half-sentence is an exception to this exception, ensuring that the patentability bar does not cover microbiological processes or the products thereof. In other words, the general principle of patentability under EPC Article 52(1) is restored for inventions involving microbiological processes and the products of such processes. Consequently, patents are grantable for animals produced by a microbiological process. The Examining Division must therefore consider, should the case arise, whether the claimed processes constitute microbiological processes within the meaning of EPC Article 53(b).

5. Exception to patentability under EPC Article 53(a)

Under the heading "Considerations under EPC Article 53(a)" in the contested decision, the Examining Division argued that patent law is not the right legislative tool for regulating problems arising in connection with genetic manipulation of animals. The Board considers, however, that precisely in a case of this kind there are compelling reasons to consider the implications of EPC Article 53(a) in relation to the question of patentability. The genetic manipulation of mammalian animals is undeniably problematical in various respects, particularly where activated oncogenes are inserted to make an animal abnormally sensitive to carcinogenic substances and stimuli and consequently prone to develop tumours, which necessarily cause suffering. There is also a danger that genetically manipulated animals, if released into the environment, might entail unforeseeable and irreversible adverse effects. Misgivings and fears of this kind have been expressed by a number of persons who have filed observations with the Board under EPC Article 115. Considerations of precisely this kind have also led a number of Contracting States to impose legislative control on genetic engineering. The decision as to whether or not EPC Article 53(a) is a bar to patenting the present invention would seem to depend mainly on a careful weighing up of the suffering of animals and possible risks to the environment on the one hand, and the invention's usefulness to mankind on the other. It is the task of the department of first instance to consider these matters in the context of its resumed examination of the case.

On the reference back, the Examining Division stated:

3. In considering whether the claimed invention is contrary to "*ordre public*" or morality the following principles of patent law are to be noted:

- A patent does not give a positive right to its proprietor to use the invention but rather only confers the right to exclude others from using the invention for a limited period of time. If the legislator is of the opinion that certain technical knowledge should be used under limited conditions only it is up to him to enact appropriate legislation.

- EPC Article 52(1) contains a general principle of patentability which can only be denied if other provisions in the law exclude certain subject-matter from the access to a patent. Such exclusions are to be interpreted narrowly.

- The development of new technologies is normally afflicted with new risks; this is an experience mankind has made many times in the past. The experience has also shown that these risks should not generally lead to a negative attitude *vis-à-vis* new technologies but rather to a careful weighing up of the risks on the one hand and the positive aspects on the other and that the result of this consideration should be the determining factor in whether a new technology should be used or not. If higher life forms are involved in the new technology it is not only the risk which must be considered but also the possible harm which is done to such higher life forms. This leads one to the question of morality. Inventions which are made in connection with a new technology and which are to be patented under the European Patent Convention have to satisfy the requirements of EPC Article 53(a). This means that for each individual invention the question of morality has to be examined and possible detrimental effects and risks have to be weighed and balanced against the merits and advantages aimed at.

- From the previous item it follows that biotechnological inventions and particularly inventions relating to genetic engineering are not in general excluded from patent protection.

4. In the case at hand three different interests are involved and require balancing: there is a basic interest of mankind to remedy widespread and dangerous diseases, but on the other hand the environment has to be protected against the uncontrolled dissemination of unwanted genes and, moreover, cruelty to animals has to be avoided. The latter two aspects may well justify regarding an invention as immoral and therefore unacceptable unless the advantages, that is the benefit to mankind, outweigh the negative aspects. The following considerations particularly apply:

(i) The present invention's usefulness to mankind cannot be denied. Cancer is one of the most frequent causes of death in many countries of the world and also causes severe suffering. Any contribution to the development of new and improved human anti-cancer treatments is therefore a benefit to mankind and must be regarded as valuable and highly welcome by everybody. Legislation in Contracting States allows animal testing under certain restrictions and subject to administrative approval.

(ii) The applicant has pointed out that the use of the animals according to the invention gives rise to a smaller number of animals being required when compared to the number of animals needed in corresponding conventional testing. Accordingly, the present invention contributes to a reduction of the overall extent of animal suffering.

(iii) Another question to be considered in this connection is whether there exist alternatives to animal testing in the given context which are as reliable as the animal tests and which are therefore accepted by health authorities. In this respect it is noteworthy to take into account what the scientific community thinks about animal testing procedures in cancer research and this is well reflected in an overview article by A. Berns, (1991) 1 *Current Biology* 28, who concludes that onco-mice are a powerful tool with which co-operating genes in tumorigenesis can be identified. Thus it is clear that in cancer research animal test models are at present considered indispensable.

(iv) In respect of "possible risks to the environment" the Division has considered the purpose of the present invention and the risk which may be associated by practising the invention in the purpose-limited way. Obviously, the purpose of the present invention is to provide animal test models which are to be used exclusively in the laboratory under controlled conditions by qualified staff. No release is intended into the general environment. Therefore the risk of an uncontrolled release is practically limited to intentional misuse or blatant ignorance on the part of the laboratory personnel carrying out the tests. The mere fact that such uncontrollable acts are conceivable cannot be a major determinant for deciding whether a patent should be granted or not.

Exclusion from patentability cannot be justified merely because a technology is dangerous. There are many examples of inventions, the patentability of which has never been questioned, which cannot be used without severe security measures. For example work with certain pathogens is allowed under very limited conditions only and release of the material into the environment must be excluded by appropriate measures; patentable inventions may nevertheless arise from such work.

The regulation of the handling of dangerous material is not the task of the European Patent Office but is rather the business of specialised governmental authorities.

(v) In the overall balance the Examining Division concludes that the present invention cannot be considered immoral or contrary to public order. The provision of a type of test animal useful in cancer research and giving rise to a reduction in the amount of testing on animals together with a low risk connected with the handling of the animals by qualified staff can generally be regarded as beneficial to mankind. A patent should therefore not be denied for the present invention on the grounds of EPC Article 53(a).

(vi) It should be stressed that the above considerations apply *solely* to the present case and that other cases of transgenic animals are conceivable for which a different conclusion might be reached in applying EPC Article 53(a).

NOTE: On the interpretation of EPC, Art. 53(b), see also PA 1977, Sch. A2, para. 4, above, para. 1.2.3.1.

1.2.3.10   *Plant Genetic Systems/Glutamine Synthetase Inhibitors* [1995] E.P.O.R. 357, Tech. Bd. App.

The invention related to the genetic engineering of plants and seeds in order to make them herbicide resistant. The Board described it as follows:

The aim of the present invention is essentially to develop plants and seeds which are resistant to a particular class of herbicides, namely glutamine synthetase inhibitors (GSIs), and which are thereby selectively protected against weeds and fungal diseases. It should be noted that GSI-resistant plants or seeds could also be obtained by traditional plant selection methods, since some plants may be naturally resistant or may develop such a resistance. The patent in suit discloses the use of modern biotechnological techniques for the production of GSI-resistant plants and seeds which contain, integrated into their genome in a stable manner, heterologous DNA encoding a protein capable of inactivating or neutralising the above-mentioned herbicides. In that way, a new trait is added to the genetic material of a plant of interest, which allows the plant to grow in the presence of GSIs.

The opponents (appellants) argued that the invention was not patentable by reason of Art.53(a) and (b) of the European Patent Convention (equivalent to s.1(3)(a) and (b) of the Patents Act 1977; see above, 1.2.3.1 for the amended form of these provisions). On Art.53(a) the Board said:

5. It is generally accepted that the concept of "*ordre public*" covers the protection of public security and the physical integrity of individuals as part of society. This concept encompasses also the protection of the environment. Accordingly, under EPC Article 53(a), inventions the exploitation of which is likely to breach public peace or social order (for example, through acts of terrorism) or seriously to prejudice the environment are to be excluded from patentability as being contrary to "*ordre public*".

6. The concept of morality is related to the belief that some behaviour is right and acceptable whereas other behaviour is wrong, this belief being founded on the totality of the accepted norms which are deeply rooted in a particular culture. For the purposes of the European Patent Convention, the culture in question is the culture inherent in European society and civilisation. Accordingly, under EPC Article 53(a), inventions the exploitation of which is *not* in conformity with the conventionally-accepted standards of conduct pertaining to this culture are to be excluded from patentability as being contrary to morality.

7. The second half-sentence of EPC Article 53(a) contains the qualification "that the exploitation shall not be deemed to be so contrary merely because it is prohibited by law or regulation in some or all of the Contracting States". This qualification makes clear that the assessment of whether or not a particular subject-matter is to be considered contrary to either "*ordre public*" or morality is not dependent on any national laws or regulations. Conversely and by the same token, the Board is of the opinion that a particular subject-matter shall not automatically be regarded as complying with the requirements of EPC Article 53(a) merely because its exploitation is permitted in some or all of the Contracting States. Thus, approval or disapproval of the exploitation by national law(s) or regulation(s) does not constitute *per se* a sufficient criterion for the purposes of examination under EPC Article 53(a).

8. From the historical documentation relating to the European Patent Convention it appears that the view according to which "the concept of patentability in the European patent law must be as wide as possible" predominated (see document IV/2071/61–E, at p.5,

point 2, first para.). Accordingly, the exceptions to patentability have been narrowly construed, in particular in respect of plant and animal varieties (see, for example, Decisions T–320/87 *Lubrizol/Hybrid plants* [1990] E.P.O.R. 173 and T–19/90 *Harvard/Onco-Mouse* para. 1.2.3.9). In the Board's view, this approach applies equally in respect of the provisions of EPC Article 53(a). ...

10. The Board notes that both the historical documentation and the above-quoted case law recognise that, in principle, patents may be granted in respect of inventions concerning plants or animals (excluding plant or animal varieties) as well as inventions relating to processes of a technical nature for their production (see, in particular, Decision T–19/90 (above, 1.2.3.8), point 4.10 of the Reasons as well as document IV/2071/61–E, at p.6 of the European Patent Convention Working Party). Thus, in the Board's judgment, it can be inferred from the above that seeds and plants *per se* shall not constitute an exception to patentability under EPC Article 53(a) merely because they represent "living" matter or, as submitted by the appellants, on the ground that plant genetic resources should remain the "common heritage of mankind". In respect of the latter point, the Board observes that the patenting of wild-type plant resources which may be used as starting material is not at issue in the present case. That such resources should belong to the "common heritage of mankind" is therefore not in jeopardy.

11. Thus, under EPC Article 53(a), the relevant question is not whether living organisms are excluded as such, but rather whether or not the publication or exploitation of an invention related to a particular living organism is to be considered contrary to "*ordre public*" or morality. ...

15. In order to establish that the subject-matter claimed in the patent in suit is objectionable under EPC Article 53(a), the appellants rely, *inter alia*, on:

    (i) a survey conducted among Swedish farmers on questions relating to genetic engineering and "super crops", according to which the large majority (82 per cent) is against genetic engineering, and, in particular, against "super crops" (for example, herbicide-resistant plants); and

    (ii) an opinion poll carried out in Switzerland on the patentability of animals and plants, according to which the majority (69 per cent) is opposed thereto.

They submit that both survey and opinion poll are probative of public opinion to the effect that patents should not be granted for these kinds of inventions. The Board does not agree with this conclusion. The results of surveys or opinion polls can scarcely be considered decisive *per se* when assessing patentability of a given subject-matter with regard to the requirements of EPC Article 53(a), for the following reasons:

    – Surveys and opinion polls do not necessarily reflect "*ordre public*" concerns or moral norms that are deeply rooted in European culture.

    – The results of surveys and opinion polls can fluctuate in an unforeseeable manner within short time periods and can be very easily influenced and controlled, depending on a number of factors, including the type of questions posed, the choice and the size of the representative sample, and so on.

    – Surveys of particular groups of people (for example, farmers) tend to reflect their specific interests and/or their biased beliefs.

    – As stated above, the question whether EPC Article 53(a) constitutes a bar to patentability is to be considered in each particular case on its merits. Consequently, if surveys and opinion polls were to be relied on, they would have to be made *ad hoc* on the basis of specific questions in relation to the particular subject-matter claimed. For obvious reasons, such a procedure is scarcely feasible.

– Like national law(s) and regulation(s) approving or disapproving the exploitation of an invention (see point 7 above), a survey or an opinion poll showing that a particular group of people or the majority of the population of some or all of the Contracting States opposes the granting of a patent for a specified subject-matter, cannot serve as a sufficient criterion for establishing that the said subject-matter is contrary to "*ordre public*" or morality. . . .

17.1 The appellants have expressed concerns about the dominion that was sought to be exercised by man over the natural world by the use of plant genetic engineering techniques. In this respect, it has to be considered that plant biotechnology is a technology which aims at accomplishing practical improvements or advances in the area of plants by using modern scientific knowledge. The development of this technology inevitably allows a better understanding and control of the natural phenomena linked to plants. However, in the Board's view, this does not render activities in this technical field intrinsically wrong. Indeed, in the Board's judgment, plant biotechnology *per se* cannot be regarded as being more contrary to morality than traditional selective breeding because both traditional breeders and molecular biologists are guided by the same motivation, namely to change the property of a plant by introducing novel genetic material into it in order to obtain a new and, possibly, improved plant. However, compared with traditional breeding techniques, genetic engineering techniques applied to plants allow a more powerful and accurate control of genetic modifications. Plant biotechnology allows punctual gene modifications as well as the introduction into a given plant of genetic material from unrelated species of plants and from organisms other than plants. These techniques are an important tool to assist in plant breeding, which enables the performance of manipulations that would simply not be feasible by means of traditional breeding techniques. The impressive potential of these techniques is at the origin of the concerns and apprehensions expressed by public opinion and generates considerable disagreement and controversy. This factual situation forms the basis of the appellants' objection to the dominion gained by man over the natural world. These concerns are understandable because the power of science for good and evil has always troubled man's mind. Like any other tool, plant genetic engineering techniques can be used for constructive or destructive purposes. It would undoubtedly be against "*ordre public*" or morality to propose a misuse or a destructive use of these techniques. Thus, under EPC Article 53(a), no patent may be granted in respect of an invention directed to such a use. Consequently, it has to be established in the present case whether or not the claimed subject-matter relates to a misuse or to a destructive use of plant biotechnology. . . .

17.3 In the Board's judgment, none of the claims of the patent in suit refer to subject-matter which relates to a misuse or destructive use of plant biotechnological techniques because they concern activities (production of plants and seeds, protection of plants from weeds or fungal diseases) and products (plant cells, plants, seeds) which cannot be considered to be wrong as such in the light of conventionally accepted standards of conduct of European culture. Alleged environmental consequences due to these activities will have to be considered against the background of the "*ordre public*" issue (see point 18 below). . . .

18.3 The function of a patent office is to grant patents, that is, exclusive rights to make use of inventions claimed in said patents for a limited geographical area and for a specified time. The Board agrees with the appellants' submission that patent offices are placed at the crossroads between science and public policy. However, at this crossroads patent offices are not alone, but find themselves side-by-side with an increasing number of other authorities and bodies, in particular regulatory authorities and bodies, whose function is, *inter alia*, to ensure that the exploitation of a given technology, regardless of whether it is protected by a patent or not, takes place within the regulatory framework provided by laws, international treaties, administrative provisions, and so on (see, for example, the list of competent authorities responsible for the implementation of the EEC Directive 90/220, Exhibit A submitted by the respondents). The assessment of the hazards stemming from the exploitation of a given technology is one of the important duties of such regulatory authorities and bodies.

18.4 In most cases, potential risks in relation to the exploitation of a given invention for which a patent has been granted cannot be anticipated merely on the basis of the disclosure of the invention in the patent specification. Typical examples are patents granted for chemical compounds with a pharmaceutical use. In this particular technical field, patents are generally granted on the basis of preliminary *in vitro* or animal data before any human clinical data become available. In fact, the actual approval (or disapproval) by the competent authorities of the exploitation of pharmaceutical products is often obtained only after the grant of the patent. This is because a realistic assessment of therapeutical operability requires a comprehensive and time-consuming programme of testing and evaluation of the products. The results of such tests are usually not available to patent offices during the prosecution of a case. During this time, the exploitation of the claimed products is most likely to be in the initial phase when risk and safety assessment by the competent authorities or bodies has either not yet taken place or not yet been completed. The same holds true for many other products the exploitation of which is subject to an approval by the competent authorities or bodies, such as herbicides, insecticides, and so on. These specialised authorities and bodies are in a position to carry out a realistic assessment of risks or even hazards on the basis of the regulations in force, of objective criteria and of scientifically valid parameters. Also, transgenic plants normally require regulatory approval in the majority of the countries where biotechnological developments are taking place before even initial small-scale field testing can be performed (see, for example, EEC Directives 90/219 and 90/220).

The Board referred to the evidence presented by the appellants that the exploitation of the invention was likely seriously to prejudice the environment and continued:

18.7 These documents provide fundamental evidence of possible hazards from the application of genetic engineering techniques to plants, in particular regarding the production of herbicide-resistant plants. This is done in order to increase the readers' awareness of the need to exploit this technology with caution. On the one hand, scientists are invited to minimise the risks by applying sensible design to experiments. On the other hand, administrators, in particular regulatory authorities and bodies, are invited to carry out their task of trying to detect even rare hazards and to assess all the risks involved in the exploitation of this technology. The Board observes that the mere fact that, as deplored by Beaumont [one of the appellants' expert witnesses], there may be inadequacies in the existing regulatory framework does not vest the European Patent Office with authority to carry out tasks which should properly be the duty of a special regulatory authority or body constituted to that effect. However, in the Board's view, the quoted documents do not lead to the definite conclusion that the exploitation of any of the claimed subject-matter would seriously prejudice the environment and is, therefore, contrary to *"ordre public"*. It would be unjustified to deny a patent under EPC Article 53(a) merely on the basis of possible, not yet conclusively-documented hazards. As already pointed out (see points 18.2 and 18.3 above), a patent does not amount *per se* to an authorisation to exploit the invention claimed in the patent. For the latter regulatory approval must be obtained. Should the competent authorities and bodies, after having definitively assessed the risks involved, prohibit the exploitation of the invention, the patented subject-matter could not be exploited anyhow. If, however, regulatory approval is given based on the finding that no risks or minimal risks are involved, then patent protection should be available.

18.8 in the present case, since no sufficient evidence of actual disadvantages has been adduced, the assessment of patentability with regard to EPC Article 53(a) may not be based on the so-called "balancing exercise" of benefits and disadvantages, as submitted by the appellants. The Board observes that such a "balancing exercise" is not the only way of assessing patentability with regard to EPC Article 53(a), but just one possible way, perhaps useful in situations in which an actual damage and/or disadvantage (for example, suffering of animals as in the case of Decision T 19/90 above) exists.

1.2.3.11 *American Cyanamid v Berk* [1976] R.P.C. 231, Whitford J.

The plaintiffs had isolated strains of the micro-organism, Streptomyces aureofaciens, which could be used to produce the antibiotic, tetracycline, with almost no admixture of chlortetracycline. The form of S. aureofaciens (A–377) had produced the two substances together and it was by experimentation with mutations of this isolate that the plaintiff's invention had been reached. Claim 1 of its patent read: "The process of producing tetracycline which comprises cultivating a strain of S. aureofaciens" having the ability to produce the drug to the virtual exclusion of chlortetracycline and have certain colour patterns in their reflectant spectra.

The defendants, when sued for infringement, counter-claimed, inter alia, *that the invention was not patentable under the Patents Act 1949. On this issue, Whitford J. said:*

In support of his proposition that a biochemical process is outside the scope of the Patents Act, counsel for the defendants made reference to the fact that Parliament thought it necessary to pass a special Act—I quote from the words of the preamble—

"to provide for the granting of proprietary rights to persons who breed or discover plant varieties and for the issue of compulsory licences in respect thereof".

This Act was the Plant Varieties and Seeds Act 1964. It provided for plant breeders' rights, and certain conditions were laid down which had to be fulfilled by those who wished to take advantage of the statute. Only certain persons were entitled to make application for protection, and it was a specific provision of the Act that varieties which were to be the subject of protection under the Act should comply with certain rules. The rules provided that the variety must be clearly distinguishable by one or more important morphological, physiological or other characteristics from any other variety whose existence was a matter of common knowledge at the date of the application. If the applicant was able to satisfy the registering authority that he had in fact a new variety, he could secure protection for a specified period; but specific provision was made in the Act that the holder of rights under the Act should ensure that, throughout the period during which the rights were exercisable, he would be in a position to produce to the authority reproductive material capable of producing the variety to which the rights related.

The submission of counsel was that in substance the type of process with which I am now concerned is really one which is very akin in many respects, so far as relevant protection is concerned, to plants and new varieties of plants. These micro-organisms, it was said, are merely carrying out a natural function; they are found by the investigator in nature; they are subject to mutation so that new varieties are derived, as may be the case with plants. When these new varieties have been derived by mutation, they may be found to have particularly desirable properties, as may be the case with new plants producing blooms of particular colours or of especial fragrance or improved fruit. What was suggested was that the Patents Act is really not of sufficient breadth to cover a process using a micro-organism growing in the natural way; and that, if protection is to be given for processes based on the use of micro-organisms of this kind, it can only be through the passage of some legislation comparable with the Plant Varieties and Seeds Act 1964.

I decline so to hold. These Streptomyces, to take merely the example of the micro-organisms with which I am particularly concerned, do not, so far as is known, produce antibiotics in nature at all. They have to be transferred to some appropriate medium, selected, mutated, re-selected and so on, before they produce any, still less any appreciable, quantity of antibiotic. Production of the required antibiotic may, indeed will, require a whole series of selection and mutation steps, and the whole process is one which at the end, before the antibiotic which goes on the market is produced, will involve a great variety of manufacturing techniques. Such a process is, to my mind, in no way analogous to the production by selective breeding of, for example a better tomato, an example chosen by counsel for the plaintiffs. It appears to me to use the present case as an example, that the work of Dr Growich and his assistant, Mr Deduck, in the production of mutant strains which produce nearly 100 per cent tetracycline—the four T-strains and the two S-strains—was as much, and the use of the specific strains in a process such as is claimed by the subsidiary claims of the Growich patent can be considered as much, a method for producing a new and salutary effect intimately connected with trade and manufacture as was the method involving the operation of James Watt's condenser. I reject this attack.

1.2.3.12 *Schering's Application* [1971] R.P.C. 337, Patents Appeal Tribunal in banc

The applicant sought to patent its discovery that a known type of oral contraceptive, a particular gestagen, could effectively be administered in much smaller doses than had previously been given. This reduced undesirable side-effects.

Claim 1 read:
"A method of contraception without suppression of ovulation, wherein there is administered to a human female parenterally or by implantation a gestagen as hereinbefore defined, the gestagen being free from oestrogens and being administered in a dose as hereinbefore defined".

Whitford J. (for the Tribunal) reviewed the authorities under the pre-1977 law which precluded methods of medical treatment from the scope of the patent system and held them to be good law. He continued:

On a narrower line of defence the applicants say that a process for contraception is not a process for "medical treatment" in the sense of treatment to cure or prevent disease and that the established practice relates only to medical treatment. In the broader sense this does not, of course, meet the point that in the *C and W* case the Solicitor-General, while endorsing the Patent Office refusal of the application on the ground that it related to medical treatment, in fact rejected the application because it was not directed to the making of an object of commercial value.

Reference has, however, already been made to the fact that today it is recognised that the vendible product "test", though sometimes useful, is not conclusive. The numerous authorities touching this question have been recently reviewed most comprehensively and lucidly in the decision of the High Court of Australia in *N.R.D.C.'s Application* [1961] R.P.C. 134 (HC Australia) and it is unnecessary to go through them again in detail. We agree fully with the reasons and conclusions in that case on this point and note that the desirability of having a homogeneous development of the law in all countries which have adopted our system of patent legislation was emphasised by Lord Parker L.C.J., in the *Swift* case [1962] R.P.C. 47.

In *Cementation Co's Application* (1945) 62 R.P.C. 151 claims to a method of treating subterranean formations by the injection of chemicals so as to avoid or suppress underground combustion were allowed in this Tribunal. The present claim is to a process involving a chemical treatment which will avoid or suppress conception. Unless any treatment of the human body, as opposed to medical treatment to cure or prevent disease, is to be considered as being outside the scope of patent protection, there seems to be no reason why such a claim should not be allowed. The process is in the field of the useful as opposed to the fine arts. It is of commercial significance because it will produce a result which people are going to be prepared to pay for and which is widely considered desirable in the present climate of public opinion. It ought to be protected if it is, as must be accepted for the present purposes, of inventive merit and because it is a process which others no doubt would be only too anxious to adopt, if they could, without paying tribute to anyone.

The application was accordingly permitted to proceed to grant.

1.2.3.13 *Unilever's (Davis) Application* [1983] R.P.C. 219, Falconer J.

Under the Patents Act 1977, an application was lodged of which Claim 1 was as follows:

> *"A method for immunising poultry against coccidiosis, wherein the poultry are reared on a diet comprising nutrient feed material containing added viable sporulated oocysts of at least one species of coccidia to which the poultry are susceptible, the oocysts being present in a concentration sufficient only to induce sub-clinical infection in the poultry."*

The Patent Office objected that this could not be taken to be capable of industrial application, since (under s.4(2)) it was "an invention of a method of treatment of the human or animal body by surgery or therapy or of diagnosis practised on the human or animal body". The applicant, relying on medical works, argued that "therapy" related only to curative and not to prophylactic treatment. After reviewing the arguments in detail, Falconer J. concluded:

Thus far I am firmly of the view that the word "therapy" in section 4(2) is to be construed in its wider sense as meaning the medical treatment of disease, including preventive treatment, as well as curative treatment, and it is not to be construed in the narrower sense of meaning curative treatment only.

Mr Watson [for the Applicant] relied strongly on the principle of construction that, where the wording of a statute is prima facie ambiguous, there is a presumption against any change in the existing law. The principle is stated in *Maxwell* (12th ed.), p.116 thus:

"It is presumed that the legislature does not intend to make any change in the existing law beyond that which is expressly stated in, or follows by implication from, the language in the statute in question. It is thought to be in the highest degree improbable that Parliament would depart from the general system of law without expressing its intention with irresistible clearness, and to give any such effect to general words merely because this would be their widest, usual, natural or literal meaning would be to place on them a construction other than that which Parliament must be supposed to have intended. If the arguments on a question of interpretation are 'fairly evenly balanced, that interpretation should be chosen which involves the least alteration of the existing law'."

That is a quotation from Lord Reid in *George Wimpey & Co Ltd v British Overseas Airways Corp* [1955] A.C. 169 at 191.

Under that principle Mr Watson submitted that, if the word "therapy" can be regarded as having either the wider or the narrower meaning in section 4(2) and there is no other guidance, as he submits, in the Act to which one can refer, the court should construe it in a way which would least prevent a person from obtaining a patent. He pointed out that in the prior art the medical treatment of persons, not only curative but prophylactic or preventive, was not patentable. He referred to *Schering AG's Application* [1971] R.P.C. 337 and the dictum in the decision therein the passage bridging 343 and 344, where it was authoritatively stated that methods for the medical treatment of human beings to cure or prevent disease were not patentable. Although this was so stated in that case, which was a case in the Patents Appeal Tribunal where both patent judges Graham J. and Whitford J. were sitting, the principle had long been established before that case.

Mr Watson submitted further that, in contradistinction to the position with regard to medical treatment for human beings, up to 1977 there had been many patents accepted and many granted for methods of medical treatment of animals. Mr Watson referred me to the decision in *Swift & Co's Application* [1962] R.P.C. 37, a case in which the invention was a method of improving the tenderness of meat by injecting an enzyme solution into the live animal shortly before slaughter, in which the Divisional Court quashed the decision of the Patents Appeal Tribunal which had upheld the Comptroller in refusing the application. It is correct, as Mr Watson submitted, that, as far as animals are concerned, such patents for the treatment of animals have been allowed to proceed to grant, and in particular following the decision of the Patent Office, given in the light of the *Swift* case, in *United States Rubber Co's Application* [1964] R.P.C. 104, which related to a method of medically treating an animal where it was stated it would be acceptable, though not acceptable in respect of human beings. That being the position with regard to patent applications in respect of methods of treatment of animals as distinct from human beings, Mr Watson submitted that the principle under which he brought this argument should be applied, namely, that in the absence of clear wording the legislature must be presumed not to have intended to change the law, in particular the law he is referring to as to the patentability of methods of treatment in respect of animals.

I do not see how the argument can begin to run in this particular case. It seems to be that there is no basis for the operation of that principle which Mr Watson invoked because Parliament made it abundantly clear in the long title to the Act which I have read that the old law of patents is being swept away. I have already read the title of the statute. Right at the beginning of that long title, the Act is described as "An Act to establish a new law of patents applicable to future patents". And again as I have already pointed out, this application is an application under the 1977 Act. I have already referred to section 130(7) which includes within its terms the very section with which we are now concerned, namely, section 4. One of the striking changes in the 1977 Act was to include for the first time in our patent law in section 1, as qualified by section 4, a statutory definition of what constituted a patentable invention.

But apart from that there is another difficulty inherent in this argument advanced by Mr Watson. Section 4(2) draws no distinction between the treatment of the human body and the treatment of the animal body. If "therapy" were to be read narrowly so as to include prophylactic treatment as the applicants contend it should, at least in relation to the treatment of animals, that narrow construction of "therapy" would apply equally to the treatment of human beings, or, as it is put in the section, to the human body, thus rendering patentable methods of prophylactic treatment of diseases of human beings. That would be a change in the law as it is stated in *Schering's* case which, as I have pointed out already, although stated clearly in that state, it had been a long-established principle before that case was decided.

Realising that difficulty, I think, Mr Watson submitted, as I understood him, that in section 4(2) the word "therapy" in relation to the treatment of human beings could have a different meaning from that which it bore in relation to the treatment of animals. I cannot think that Parliament intended the word "therapy" to be used in two different senses in section 4(2), one in relation to the treatment of the human and another in relation to the treatment of the animal body. The very language of the subsection it seems to me negates such a dual construction. I think there is much force in the observation of the principal examiner in the last sentence of the second complete paragraph of p.3 of his decision, where he says:

"Similarly if prophylactic treatments in the veterinary field were to be regarded as an exception, then section 4(2) would surely have made this clear."

In my judgment the word "therapy" in section 4(2) is to be construed in its wide meaning as including preventive, that is to say, prophylactic, treatment as well as curative treatment of disease of the human body and the animal body. Accordingly under the terms of section 4(2) the applicants' invention is not to be taken as being capable of industrial application, and is therefore not a patentable invention. Accordingly the appeal falls to be dismissed.

1.2.3.14 *Siemens/Flow Measurement* [1989] O.J. EPO 171, Tech. Bd. App.

The applicant sought a patent for a method of measuring the flow of small quantities of liquid through a tube by injecting a bubble into the liquid and then measuring its rate of progression between two points on the tube. The technique could be applied in particular in a device planted in the human or animal body for the administration of a drug such as insulin. Claims 1–3 claimed the device without requiring that means be provided for linking the flow time thus ascertained to a control signal in order to control a device for conveying the liquid. Claim 4 covered this additional element.

The European Patent Office Examining Division rejected all the claims by reference to EPC Art.52(4). Allowing the appeal, the Appeal Board offered the following comments:

In the Board's opinion the introduction of a drug into the human body by means of a device for controlled drug administration that has already been implanted is clearly unconnected with either a surgical or a diagnostic method.

The check on the operation of the device therefore requires no medical knowledge whatsoever as regards the behaviour of the body into which the device is introduced. For this reason the Board is satisfied that the problem objectively inferable from the application documents is addressed solely to the engineer designing the device for controlled drug administration and not to the doctor using the finished product.

Of Claims 1–3 the Appeal Board stated:

3.2.2. The Board regards such a method as solely matter for the apparatus designer. The operating parameters measured according to the method claimed allow the doctor complete liberty to plan the operating timetable of the pump—and thus the drug intake required for treatment—with medical discretion. Hence, even if under Claim 1 protection is granted for a method of measurement carried out in relation to an implanted device for controlled drug administration, the doctor is in no way hindered in exercising his professional skills, *i.e.* preventing, curing or alleviating illness; *cf.* also the definition of therapeutic action in point 3 of Decision T–144/83 of European Patent Office Technical Board of Appeal 3.3.1 dated March 27, 1986 ([1986] O.J. EPO 301, 304). Non-commercial and non-industrial medical and veterinary activities are therefore not restricted by patent rights in this case; *cf.* in this connection point 22 of Decision G 1/83 of the European Patent Office Enlarged Board of Appeal dated December 5, 1984 ([1985] O.J. EPO 60–63).

3.2.3 A method therefore does not fall within the scope of the first sentence of EPC Article 52(4) if there is no functional link and hence no physical causality between its constituent steps carried out in relation to a therapy device and the therapeutic effect produced on the body by that device.

Of Claim 4 the Appeal Board stated:

5.2 In the Board's opinion, a finding that a claim seeks protection, *inter alia*, for a therapeutic method covered by EPC Article 52(4) is not warranted unless the said claim defines a control mechanism in full technical detail which, when embodied in an implanted device for controlled drug administration, clearly determines when what volume of which drug fluid is fed to the body within what period of time. Only then would the controlling action claimed, when featured in an implanted device for controlled drug administration, have any functional connection with the quality and quantity of the drug dose and a direct causal influence on the therapeutic effect produced, thus hindering the doctor in the exercise of his professional skill. The derivation and use of the control signal as specified in Claim 4, however, merely enhances the technical capabilities of the device and does not cause any such hindrance.

1.2.3.15 *Wellcome—Pigs I* [1989] O.J. EPO 13, Tech. Bd. App.

Pig mange is caused by an infestation of ectoparasites. The applicants for a European patent claimed a method of controlling such an infestation by applying a pesticide (admixed with an aliphatic hydrocarbon oil, in order to prevent the pesticide from being absorbed) to areas of a pig's body. The European Patent Office refused the claim, relying upon EPC Art.52(4).

The Technical Board of Appeal upheld this view, but on a somewhat different basis. It reviewed Arts.52–57 and concluded:

However, the scheme of Articles 52 to 57 as set out above makes it quite clear that even though agricultural methods in general are potentially patentable subject-matter, the particular methods defined in EPC Article 52(4) are excluded from patentability. In other words, for the particular methods defined in EPC Article 52(4), EPC Article 52(4) takes precedence over EPC Article 57.

3.6 The excluded methods are:

(i) methods for treatment of the human or animal body by surgery or therapy;

(ii) diagnostic methods practised on the human or animal body.

3.7 The exclusion of such methods from patentability is not a new provision under the European Patent Convention. Prior to the coming into force of the European Patent Convention, such methods were excluded from patentability under the national laws of many European countries. The policy behind the exclusion of such methods is clearly in order to ensure that those who carry out such methods as part of the medical treatment of humans or the veterinary treatment of animals should not be inhibited by patents.

3.8 The Board has considered the relevant preparatory documents which led to the European Patent Convention. The interpretation of the EPC Articles 52 and 57 set out above appears to be fully consistent with such documents, in that the object of the provision of EPC Article 52(4) was to exclude from patentability "treatment intended to cure or alleviate the suffering of animals" (see in particular Conference document BR/219/72, para. 27). ...

In relation to the particular claim, the Board held:

4.3 Therefore, to summarise, if a claimed method requires the treatment of an animal body by therapy, it is a method which falls within the prohibition on patentability set out in EPC Article 52(4). It is not possible as a matter of law to draw a distinction between such a method as carried out by a farmer and the same method as carried out by a veterinarian, and to say that the method when carried out by a farmer is an industrial activity and therefore patentable under Article 57, and when carried out by a veterinarian is a therapeutic treatment not patentable under Article 52(4). Nor is it possible as a matter of law to distinguish between the use of such a method for the treatment of ectoparasites and endoparasites.

4.4 A further question to be decided in this appeal is whether, as a matter of fact, the treatment of pigs infested with pig mange is treatment of a disease. The appellant has submitted that mange is not a disease. However, in the Board's view it is clear that, contrary to the submission of the appellant, mange is a disease of the skin which is caused by the presence of parasites. Thus the *Shorter Oxford English Dictionary* defines mange as "A cutaneous disease occurring in many ... animals, caused by an arachnidan parasite". Furthermore, effective treatment of this disease is only possible by treatment of the infected body so as to eradicate the ectoparasites which caused it.

The Examples in the descriptive part of the application in suit are all concerned with the treatment of pigs infested with pig mange (sarcoptes scabei). It is noted that the reference cited by the appellant—Monnig's *Veterinary Helminthology and Entomology* (London, 1962—p.516) states that "Sarcoptic mange is a scheduled disease in most countries".

As a matter of fact, the Board therefore considers that the examples in the application in suit are each carrying out a method of treatment of diseased pigs' bodies, and that such a method is a method for treatment of the animal body by therapy.

The Board refused to reach the opposite conclusion on the basis of Stafford-Miller's Application [1984] F.S.R. 258, which it distinguished on two grounds:

6.2 As to (i), the Board's finding set out in paragraph 4.4 above that the treatment of pigs infected with a pig mange as a therapeutic treatment of a disease is made on the basis of the evidence before it. The finding of the UK Patents Court to the effect that an infestation of lice on human beings is not a disease was based on different evidence, and is therefore not persuasive to the Board.

As to (ii) the legal framework in which the *Stafford-Miller* case was decided must be distinguished from that of the present appeal on the following basis. ... Thus the function of the Patents Court in the *Stafford-Miller* case was only to decide whether the claimed invention in that case was possibly patentable: not whether it was actually patentable. The court's conclusion in the penultimate sentence on 261 reflects this function: "... I am not sufficiently satisfied that these claims fall on the wrong side of the line as to justify saying at this stage in their life that these patents are incapable of providing a good basis for a sound claim". The court thus gave the applicants the benefit of the doubt.

In contrast to the function of the UK Patents Court in the *Stafford-Miller* case, in the present case the function of this Board is to decide the question of actual patentability of the claims having regard to EPC Article 52(4). Thus the decision in the present case would not cause any lack of uniformity in the law of the European Patent Convention countries.

The Board also held that there was no justification for taking a "special view" of the relation between Art.52(4) and Art.57, similar to that taken of "second medical applications" in the Eisai case [1985] O.J. EPO 64, below, 1.2.3.18.

1.2.3.16   *T–58/87 (Salminen—Pigs III)* [1989] E.P.O.R. 125, Tech. Bd. App.

The patentee claimed a method and apparatus for preventing piglets from suffocating under the dam in a brooding pen, in which a sensor, such as a photo-electric cell, was placed to detect when the dam stood up; hot air could then be blown beneath her so as to discourage the piglets from going to her.

The Opposition Division and the Board of Appeal were united in upholding the claims, despite the opponent's objection that they fell within EPC Art.52(4). The Board of Appeal stated:

The Board agrees in that the word "therapy"

- covers any non-surgical treatment which is designed to cure, alleviate, remove or lessen the symptoms of, or prevent or reduce the possibility of contracting any malfunction of the animal body (*cf. Patent Law of Europe and the United Kingdom* by A. M. Walton, H. I. L. Laddie, J. P. Baldwin and D. J. T. Kitchin (1983), p.II [684]); and also

- relates to the treatment of a disease in general or to a curative treatment in the narrow sense as well as the alleviation of the symptoms of pain and suffering (*cf. Chambers Twentieth Century Dictionary*, 1399, "Therapy"; *The Oxford English Dictionary*, Vol. XI, 280, "Therapy"; and, for example, Decision T–144/83, point 3, [1986] O.J. EPO 301).

The behaviour of newborn piglets to creep under the dam standing up to eat and drink either during or after farrowing cannot be fairly regarded as a malfunction of piglets whose instinct is not adequately developed. Furthermore, as far as the language of Claim 1 is concerned, it clearly covers a method for protection of piglets from the disadvantageous consequences of this behaviour, such as suffocating under the dam, by blowing air under the standing dam thus creating unpleasant conditions for the piglets. This cannot reasonably be called a treatment by therapy, which is practised on the bodies of piglets, within the meaning of EPC Article 52(4). As the Opposition Division rightly considered, the invention is concerned with preventing accidents, analogous to a method of preventing a worker from trapping his hand in machinery.

1.2.3.17 *Organon Laboratories' Application* [1970] R.P.C. 574, Graham J.

These proceedings tested the validity of a "pack claim" for the administration of a drug, as oral contraceptive for women. The claim read:

> *A pack of between 20 and 27 discrete dosage units such as tablets, pills or capsules for human oral administration at the rate of one unit per day over a period of between 20 and 27 successive days in order to stimulate anovulatory cycles, comprising a tube, box or chart in or on which units of two different kinds are packed in a particular order together with written or printed indications or directions, the indications or directions and the manner of packing being such as to provide guidance in relation to and to facilitate the taking at the said rate first of 6 to 13 units containing an oestrogenic compound only as a hormonal substance and consequently 14 to 16 units containing a combination of an oestrogenic compound and a progestative compound.*

Graham J.:

The applicants claim to have discovered an improvement in the so-called and known "sequential" treatment to prevent conception. This known treatment involves the taking of an oestrogenic compound from the second to fifth day after the beginning of the menstrual period until the 20th day and then taking a combination of oestrogenic and progestative compounds from the 20th to the 25th day. The applicants' improvement, which they have christened the "Normophasic" method, involves also two successive phases and preferably lasts for 22 days, beginning not later than the fifth day after the onset of the last menstruation, the first period during which an oestrogenic compound is taken lasting seven days, and the second phase during which a combined oestrogenic and progestative compound is taken lasting 15 days. The Normophasic method is claimed to be "fully reliable", and if it turns out to be so it will no doubt be recognised as a valuable new weapon in the armoury of our female population. For present purposes, it will be assumed to be a novel discovery.

The invention claimed, however, is not the discovery of the Normophasic method, but is the box or card in or on which the pills suitable for taking during one menstrual period are arranged in no doubt a convenient order for following the accompanying instructions, and the question for decision is whether such a box or card with the pills so arranged is a manner of new manufacture within the section. ...

The discovery of a new method of treatment, which may itself be very meritorious even though not patentable, may it seems to me give subject matter to a pack or card of pills suitable for the carrying out of that method if, first, there is something novel in the constitution of the pack or card itself. Thus there might be something novel and not obvious in the particular physical form or structure of the pack or card, such as for example in the method of attachment of the pills to the card in order to ensure that they cannot be taken in the wrong order or in the physical structure of the parts or construction of the pack, which has the same effect. Secondly, however, even though, as in the case here, the general public are in possession of the idea that pills can usefully be arranged on a card or in a pack with suitable instructions to enable any particular course of treatment to be carried out, there may also be room for an invention or manner of new manufacture within the section consisting of the mere idea of a new card with the particular pills arranged in the new order suitable for the newly discovered method of treatment if there is no reason why anyone would be likely to want to arrange those pills in that order, unless and until they had learned of the new method. Though the truth may be that the basic discovery lies in the method of treatment and not in the arrangement of the pills on the card and though the arrangement itself is not in any way a guarantee that the treatment must or will be followed, the card itself cannot unequivocally be said to be obvious if no-one would be likely to want to make it except for the treatment in question.

1.2.3.18   *Ciba-Geigy (Dürr's) Application* **[1977] R.P.C. 83, CA**

The plaintiff discovered that a known chemical could be used as a selective weed-killer to kill monocotyledinous weeds (such as grasses) occurring in a monocotyledinous crop. In order to secure effective protection against competitors it sought a "pack claim" in the following terms:

> *12. A compound of the formula defined in claim 1 in a container which bears instructions for use in selectively combating weeds at a locus comprising wheat, barley, rye, oats, rice, maize, cotton or soya.*

Russell L.J. (for the Court of Appeal):

At the outset of the argument we were startled by the proposition that it can be an invention to state in writing that which has been discovered; that is to say, that the known material can be used to combat selectively weeds in the loci described. It is however clear that if the claim can be sustained so that rival manufacturers of the substance cannot without infringement or licence sell in containers bearing the information in question, it will contribute greatly to the solution of the policing problem. Graham J. after discussing the cases of *L'Oreal* [1970] R.P.C. 565 and *Organon* [1970] R.P.C. 574 and *Dow Corning* [1974] R.P.C. 235 and after referring to a passage from the opinion of Lord Roche in the *Mullard* case [1936] R.P.C. 323 with a comment thereon with which we agree, summarised his decision as follows:

> "Applying the principles of those cases ... it seems quite impossible to say that by the claim (claim 12) ... the applicants here are doing any more than claiming any package of any shape or size which will not in any way be modified by any instructions also included, that pack containing only a well-known and admittedly old material ... they have not by the words used in any way modified their pack or qualified it so that it has a particular shape or construction or is particularly suitable for the purpose for which the material is intended to be used. It is really in effect only claiming the old material as such."

We find ourselves entirely in agreement with the decision of the Patents Appeal Tribunal. We cannot see that it can sensibly be said that there is any invention involved in claim 12, any manner of new manufacture. The invention is the discovery that this known substance

90

may be used without harm to the stated crops for the purpose of selectively combating weeds. There seems to us to be nothing inventive about parcelling up the known material in any and every convenient package or container having written thereon the information that it can be used for the stated purpose in the stated loci. There is no interaction between the container with its contents and the writing thereon. The mere writing cannot make the contents in the container a manner of new manufacture. There is nothing novel in the mere presentation of information by ordinary writing or printing on a container.

1.2.3.19 *Schering's and Wyeth's Applications* [1985] R.P.C. L545, Patents Court: Whitford and Falconer JJ.

The decision considered the patentability and novelty of claims involving the discovery of a second medical use for a known substance. The proposed claims were in two main forms: (i) use of the substance for the new purpose; and (ii) use of the substance for manufacturing a medicament for the new purpose (the "Swiss form", since its recognition by the Swiss Patent Office). The Patents Court rejected the claims of the first type, but allowed those of the second.

(i) Substance-for-new-use claims
Claim 1 of Wyeth's Application *read: "The use of a guanidine of [given formula] or a pharmaceutically acceptable acid addition salt thereof in treating diarrhoea in mammals or poultry". The substances were already known to be effective for lowering blood pressure, as hyperglycaemic agents and for anti-ulcer treatment. The UK Patent Office had already rejected similar claims in the "Hydropyridine" decision (*Bayer's Application *[1984] R.P.C. 11). But the German Supreme Court had allowed them in the equivalent German application ([1983] O.J. EPO at 26). The Enlarged Board of Appeal of the European Patent Office, in* Eisai's Application *([1985] O.J. EPO 64), had chosen to pronounce it "unfortunate" that in consequence Bayer had not appealed to the Patents Court in the U.K., because "the decisions of the national courts of two Contracting States tending in the same direction might have had great weight".*

In the present application, Falconer J. stated:

While, of course, this court will desire at all times to pay respect to the decisions of the Federal Court of Justice of the Federal Republic of Germany, the Federal Court's Hydropyridine decision appears to be based on earlier German national case law whereas this court (as also the Comptroller) has to apply the United Kingdom statute, the relevant provisions of which, as already indicated, we think have been correctly applied by the Principal Examiner in refusing to allow claims worded in the form of Wyeth claims 1 and 2.

(ii) Swiss form of claim
Claim 3 of Wyeth's Application read: "The use of guanadine of [given formula] or a pharmaceutically acceptable acid salt thereof in the preparation of an antidiarrhoeal agent in ready-to-use drug form for treating or preventing diarrhoea in mammals or poultry". The Schering application contained equivalent claims. In rejecting them, the Hearing Officer relied upon Ciba-Geigy's (Dürr) Application *[1977] R.P.C. 83 and* Adhesive Dry Mounting v Trapp *(1910) 27*

R.P.C. 341. Falconer J. held that such an invention was capable of industrial application (Patents Act 1977, ss.1(1)(c), 4) and was not merely the presentation of information (s.1(2)); but that, if the matter were one purely of interpreting ss.1–4 of that Act (and especially s.2(6)), it would be difficult to conclude that the invention was novel. However he continued:

But the matter is not to be considered without regard to the position, as it has developed, under the corresponding provisions of the European Patent Convention. As pointed out earlier, by section 130(7) of the 1977 Act, it is declared that certain sections, including, *inter alia*, section 4(2), 4(3) and 2(6), of the Act are so framed as to have the same effects in the United Kingdom as the corresponding provisions of the European Patent Convention (respectively Articles 52(4) and 54(5)) have in the territories to which the European Patent Convention applies, which territories include the United Kingdom. It is, therefore, convenient at this point to consider the decision of the Enlarged Board of Appeal of the European Patent Office in the *Eisai* case in respect of the Swiss form of claim.

In paragraph 21 the Board states:

"... EPC Article 52(1) expresses a general principle of patentability for inventions which are industrially applicable, new and inventive and it is clear that in all fields of industrial activity other than those of making products for use in surgery, therapy and diagnostic methods, a new use for a known product can be fully protected as such by claims directed to that use.

"This is in fact the appropriate form of protection in such cases as the new and non-obvious use of the known product constitutes the invention and it is the clear intention of the European Patent Convention that a patent be granted for the invention to which a European patent application relates (compare EPC Articles 52(1), 69, 84 and Rule 29 read together). EPC Article 54(5) provides an exception to this general rule, however, so far as the first use of medicaments is concerned, in respect of which the normal type of use claim is prohibited by EPC Article 52(4). In effect, in this case the required novelty for the medicament which forms the subject-matter of the claim is derived from the new pharmaceutical use."

"It seems justifiable by analogy to derive the novelty for the process which forms the subject-matter of the type of use claim now being considered from the new therapeutic use of the medicament and this irrespective of the fact whether any pharmaceutical use of the medicament was already known or not. It is to be clearly understood that the application of this special approach to the derivation of novelty can only be applied to claims to the use of substances or compositions intended for use in a method referred to in EPC Article 52(4)."

"The intention of EPC Article 52(4), ... is only to free from restraint non-commercial and non-industrial medical and veterinary activities. To prevent the exclusion from going beyond its proper limits, it seems appropriate to take a special view of the concept of the 'state of the art' defined in EPC Article 54(2). EPC Article 54(5) alone provides only a partial compensation for the restriction on patent rights in the industrial and commercial field resulting from EPC Article 52(4), first sentence. It should be added that the Enlarged Board does not deduce from the special provision of EPC Article 54(5) that there was any intention to exclude second (and further) medical indications from patent protection other than by a purpose-limited product claim. ... No intention to exclude second (and further) medical indications generally from patent protection can be deduced from the terms of the European Patent Convention; nor can it be deduced from the legislative history of the articles in question."

"For these reasons, the Enlarged Board considers that it is legitimate in principle to allow claims directed to the use of a substance or composition for the manufacture of a medicament for a specified new and inventive therapeutic application, even in a case in which the process of manufacture as such does not differ from known processes using the same active ingredient."....

That approach to the novelty of the Swiss type of use claim directed to a second, or subsequent, therapeutic use if equally possible under the corresponding provisions of the 1977 Act and, notwithstanding the opinion expressed earlier as to the better view of the patentability of such a Swiss type claim under the material provisions of the Act considered without regard to the position, as it has developed, under the corresponding provisions of the European Patent Convention, having regard to the desirability of achieving conformity the same approach should be adopted to the novelty of the Swiss type of claim now under consideration under the material provisions of the Act.

1.2.3.20   *Chiron Corporation v Murex Diagnostics Ltd* [1997] R.P.C. 535, CA

The plaintiffs owned patents which included claims to polypeptides, immunoassays, polynucleotides, antibodies, vaccines, methods of in vitro propagation, of the Hepatitis-C Virus ("HCV"). The defendants manufactured and sold kits to test for the presence of HCV, and were sued for patent infringement. On appeal the defendants unsuccessfully argued, inter alia, *that the plaintiff's patent was invalid since it claimed a discovery as such. However, they successfully argued that the second part of claim 11 of the plaintiff's patent included polypeptides that were not capable of industrial application.*

Morritt L.J. (for the Court):

Discovery as such:

This issue arises under section 1(2) (above, para. 1.2.3.1).

The relevant article in the European Patent Convention is Article 52(2), which, as far as relevant, provides:

> (2) The following in particular shall not be regarded as inventions within the meaning of paragraph (1):
>
>   (a) discoveries...

Neither the Act nor the Convention contains a definition of the words "discovery" or "invention". The Act gives no indication as to the content of any further disqualification from patentability referred to by the words "(amongst other things)". It is noteworthy that the Convention contains a different emphasis in this respect...

The parties were agreed that the discovery in this case comprised three features, namely that HCV infection provokes a detectable antibody response, that the agent which causes HCV is a single positive stranded RNA virus and the determination of the genetic sequence of an isolate of HCV.

For the appellants, it was submitted that all the claims ... covered a discovery as such because although all the claims were to physical products (or methods of using those products) they were not defined by reference to their physical or chemical structure. Thus, as it was argued, the claims covered a discovery as such because they foreclosed the use of the discovery in making other inventions.

The scope of the subsection was considered by this Court in *Genentech Inc's Patent* [1989] R.P.C. 147 and *Gale's Application* [1991] R.P.C. 305.

Morritt L.J. referred to passages in the latter set out in para. 1.2.3.5. He continued:

There is nothing in either of these cases to suggest that the physical structure or chemical formula of the product resulting from the discovery must be disclosed. It would be inconsistent with both of them that that should be so if the useful application does not itself have to be inventive or novel. In reality the objection of the appellants is not that Chiron have patented a discovery as such but that the invention has been insufficiently disclosed. . . .

In our judgment all the claims in this case cover inventions properly so called and not discoveries as such ... the claim is to a polypeptide which is the physical expression in conjunction with further physical attributes to constitute immunoassays and so forth.

For completeness we should make plain that we do not consider that the words "(among other things)" open up a new range of objections to the conclusion that something new is an invention. Rather it is recognition that that subsection is not exhaustive and has therefore not changed the law any further than the subsection expressly provides. It seems to us that any other conclusion would be inconsistent with the different emphasis apparent in the European Patent Convention.

Industrial Application:

The objection under this head was to the second part of claim 11 (and other claims dependent on it) which encompasses:

"a polypeptide in substantially isolated form ... whose sequence is encoded in a polynucleotide selectively hybridisable with the polynucleotide as shown in any one of Figures 1, 3–32, 36, 46 or 47."

It is claimed that it cannot be patentable invention as it is not capable of industrial application as required by section 1(1)(c). That phrase is defined in section 4 by reference to whether the invention "can be made or used in any kind of industry, including agriculture". These provisions were new in 1977, having been introduced in consequence of the European Patent Convention, and are required by section 130(7) to be construed and applied so far as possible to produce uniformity. The corresponding Articles are Articles 52(1) and 57. The former requires the invention to be "susceptible of industrial application" and the latter defines such susceptibility by reference to whether the invention "can be made or used in any kind of industry, including agriculture".

It was demonstrated at the trial that the polypeptide resulting from the second part of claim 11 might have nothing to do with HCV, as a polynucleotide may selectively hybridise with the polynucleotide as shown in the specified figures without encoding either the virus protein or more importantly the antigenic determinant to the antibodies produced by exposure to HCV. Thus the claim covers an almost infinite number of polypeptides which are useless for any known purpose. The appellants claimed that section 4 was not satisfied as there is no industry for the making of useless products. The judge dealt with this submission ... in these terms.

"It is important to remember that the old law which provided for revocation if the claims were not fairly based on the description or lacked utility was swept away by the 1977 Act. The law is not that set out in the 1977 Act. Section 4(1) states that inventions shall be taken to be capable of industrial application 'if it can be made . . . in any kind of industry'. Although the range of polypeptides falling within the claims, and in particular claim 11, may be large, there is no evidence to suggest that once the sequence is known they could not be made by industry. I therefore reject the submission of the defendants."

. . . We accept that the polypeptides claimed in the second part of claim 11 can be made, . . . it is a routine task to see whether one polynucleotide will hybridise with another. But the sections require that the invention can be made or used "in any industry" so as to be "capable" or "susceptible of industrial application". The connotation is that of trade or manufacture in its widest sense and whether or not for profit. But industry does not exist in that sense to make or use that which is useless for any known purpose.

On this point we prefer the submissions for the appellants. We think that they more accurately reflect the true meaning of sections 1(1)(c) and 4 and the manifest intention of the Patents Act 1977 and the European Patent Convention that monopoly rights should be confined to that which has some useful purpose. We think that the judge fell into error by giving the sections too literal a construction and in considering what can be made and used by industry rather than what can be made and used in any kind of industry.

Accordingly we would allow the appeal to the extent of declaring the invalidity of the second half of claim 11 and of other claims dependent on it.

1.2.4   Adequate Disclosure

1.2.4.1   *No Fume v Pitchford* (1935) 52 R.P.C. 231, CA

The plaintiff claimed a "smokeless" ashtray in the following terms:

"An ash receptacle which, without the use of moveable parts, retains the smoke rising from objects thrown into it, characterised by the fact that it consists of a closed container into which extends a shaft of substantially constant cross section, the sides of which, with the sides of the receptacle, form a trapped space closed above, whilst wholly beneath the shaft is provided a deflecting member, which deflects objects thrown in wholly to one side of the lower mouth of the shaft".

Romer L.J.:

Let me deal with the question of sufficiency first. Be it observed from the very words I have used, that the patentee fulfils his duty if in his complete specification he describes and ascertains the nature of the invention, and the manner in which the invention is to be performed, sufficiently and fairly. It is not necessary that he should describe in his specification the manner in which the invention is to be performed, with that wealth of detail with which the specification of the manufacturer of something is usually put before the workman who is engaged to manufacture it. Specifications very frequently contain mistakes; they also have omissions. But if a man skilled in the art can easily rectify the mistakes and can readily supply the omissions, the patent will not be held to be invalid. The test to be applied for the purpose of ascertaining whether a man skilled in the art can readily correct the mistakes or readily supply the omissions, has been stated to be this: Can he rectify the mistakes and supply the omissions without the exercise of any inventive faculty? If he can, then the description of the specification is sufficient. If he cannot, the patent will be void for insufficiency.

That principle was laid down—I do not know whether for the first time or not in a reported case—in the case of *R. v Arkwright* reported in the first volume of *Webster's Patent Cases* at p.64. There Buller J., in summing up to the jury, said this: "It has been truly said by the counsel, that if the specification be such that mechanical men of common understanding can comprehend it, to make a machine by it, it is sufficient; but then it must be such that the mechanics may be able to make the machine by following the directions of the specification, without any new inventions or additions of their own." It is plain, I think, that by the word "additions" the learned judge meant inventive additions. That principle has been applied in numerous cases, to which Mr Whitehead called our attention in his opening and to which the Master of the Rolls has already referred. In those circumstances, I should only desire to refer to a short passage in the judgment of Sir George Jessel in *Otto v Linford*, (46 Law Times N.S. 35). That was a case relating to the Otto gas engine; and it had been alleged, among other things, that the patent was void for insufficiency, inasmuch as the specification did not show the proportions in which the air was to be put in as regards the combustible mixture. Sir George Jessel said this, on 41:

"The first thing to be remembered, in specifications of patents, is that they are addressed to those who know something about the matter. A specification for improvements in gas motor engines is addressed to gas-motor engine-makers and workers, not to the public outside. Consequently you do not require the same amount of minute information that you would in the case of a totally new invention, applicable to a totally new kind of manufacture. In this case the inventor says this: 'I am going to turn that which was a sudden explosion of gas into a gradual explosion of gas, and I am going to do that by the introduction of a cushion of air in one place between the piston and the combustible mixture'. If a man is left without any more information he asks: 'How much air am I to let in?' He lets in a little air, and he finds that the thing explodes as before; and he lets in some more, and he finds directly, on the mere regulation of his stop-cock, how much is required; and he finds very soon that he has let in enough, and now there is a gradual expansion, and no longer a sudden and explosive expansion. It does not appear to me that that requires invention. It requires a little care and watching, and that is all."

That being the principle to be applied, we turn to the specification of the patent in suit. I am not going to read it again; but the patentee tells us that he has discovered that, if an ash-tray be made so that it consists of "a closed container, into which extends an inlet shaft of substantially constant cross section, the sides of which, with the sides of the container form a trapped space completely closed above, whilst wholly beneath the shaft is provided a deflecting member which deflects everything that is thrown into the container away from and to one side of the lower mouth of the shaft", the smoke of a cigarette thrown into the shaft will not come out through the shaft but will be retained in the receptacle: subject, however, to this, that you must not make the container too large or too small, or the other integers he has mentioned too large or too small. You will not get the result of the smoke being contained, if you do. But once given the fact that, if the thing be made in the way mentioned, the desired result will be obtained if the various integers bear one to another the proper relative proportion, it requires no invention or inventive study further to discover within what limits those proportions should lie. That can be done easily enough by a series of experiments similar to the experiment Sir George Jessel referred to as necessarily being made by a workman who wanted to find, in the case of the Otto gas-engine, how much air he should let in to produce the result that the patentee said would be produced.

The specification as has been pointed out by the Master of the Rolls, expressly says this:

> "The dimensions of the shaft and of the deflecting member, relatively to one another and to the sides of the closed container, being so selected that the smoke rising from objects thrown into the container is collected entirely in the enclosed space, and upon cooling is again thrown down without, however, during its movement being able to pass the lower mouth of the shaft."

In other words, the patentee does not tell the world within what limits the relative proportions of the integers he has mentioned must be kept to produce the desired result. If, however, a workman skilled in the art can by trial and error readily discover for himself what the proportions should be in order to give the desired result, then, inasmuch as I have already pointed out, that to discover those proportions requires the exercise of no inventive faculty at all, the patentee has complied with his obligation.

It is further to be observed in this case that the patentee does show a drawing illustrating, as he says, one construction of the ash-tray by way of example. So the workman has not only the common knowledge of his trade to help him, but he has also the example shown by the figure attached by the patentee to the specification. Further, Mr Gill stated in his evidence that he found no difficulty whatsoever, by following the directions contained in the specification, in making an ash-tray which had the desired result. On p.7 of the first day of the evidence, he was asked this. Reading from the defence, this question is put to him:

> "It is impossible to discover from the specification what relative dimensions of the shaft, deflecting member and closed container, will satisfy the requirements of the invention".

That is from the particulars of objection. He was asked: "Do you find any such impossibility? (A.) No; I find no difficulty, following the specification, in arriving at suitable dimensions, and nothing which I have done in attempting to carry out the invention has led me to any such difficulty as is suggested in this paragraph." It is established by the authorities that the question of sufficiency or non-sufficiency is a question of fact. That is the only evidence that has been given in this case upon this question. For that reason and for the other reasons which I have mentioned, I am of opinion that this patent is not void for want of sufficiency.

Romer L.J. proceeded to hold the claims not unnecessarily ambiguous. Lord Hanworth M.R. and Maugham L.J. delivered judgments upholding the validity of the patent.

1.2.4.2   *Biogen v Medeva* [1997] R.P.C. 1, HL

The European patent (UK) allegedly infringed by the defendant needed to derive priority from an earlier British application ("Biogen 1"). At its own date of application it had become obvious. The crucial claims in "Biogen 1" were to genetically engineered DNA molecules containing an insert needed to produce a crucial protein for a vaccine against the Hepatitis B virus. The virus itself consisted of an outer protein envelope (the surface antigen), an inner protein core (the core antigen) and DNA genome within the core. Because of this, DNA molecules had to be constructed with inserts for the surface antigen and for the core antigen; and these were necessarily different.

Biogen's appeal to the House of Lords was dismissed, their Lordships forming the view that the earlier British application did not support the EPO patent as claimed, denying it the priority of "Biogen 1". At the application date of Biogen 1, the only available DNA source was the Hepatitis Virus itself ("Dane particle"). Owing to a lack of information about coding sequences, fragments of the DNA of the Dane particle were made with restriction enzymes chosen simply on the basis that they would cleave the particle into the largest fragments. Using a standard plasmid, a recombinant DNA molecule had been made from these large fragments. It was then expressed in a host bacterium. The European patent claimed any recombinant DNA molecule which expressed the genes of any Hepatitis B Virus antigen in any host cell, and any method of manufacture that would achieve the necessary expression.

On the concept of "enabling disclosure" in the law of patents, after considering s.5(2)(a) of the Patents Act 1977 and Asahi Kasei Kogyo KK's Application [1991] R.P.C. 485 (see para. 1.1.1.3), Lord Hoffmann explained:

The concept of an enabling disclosure is central to the law of patents. For present purposes it touches the matters in issue at three different points. First, as we have seen, it forms part of the requirement of "support" in section 5(2)(a). Secondly, it is one of the requirements of a valid application in section 14. And thirdly, it is essential to one of the grounds for the revocation of a patent in section 72. I shall start with section 14. Subsection (3) says:

"The specification of an application shall disclose the invention in a manner which is clear enough and complete enough for the invention to be performed by a person skilled in the art."

This is plainly a requirement of an "enabling disclosure". In addition, subsection (5)(c) says that the claim or claims shall be "supported by description". It was by reference to subsection (3) that Lord Oliver of Aylmerton, who gave the leading speech in *Asahi*, reasoned at page 536 that a description would not "support" the claims for the purpose of subsection (5)(c) unless it contained sufficient material to enable the specification to constitute the enabling disclosure which subsection (3) required: "the Act can hardly have contemplated a complete application for a patent lacking some of the material necessary to sustain the claims made." By parity of reason, he said that "support must have the same meaning in section 5(2)(a)."

The absence of an enabling disclosure is likewise one of the grounds for the revocation of a patent specified in section 72(1). Paragraph (c) says that one such ground is that—

"the specification of the patent does not disclose the invention clearly enough and completely enough for it to be performed by a person skilled in the art."

This is entirely in accordance with what one would expect. The requirement of an enabling disclosure in a patent application is a matter of substance and not form. Its absence should therefore be a ground not only for refusal of the application but also for revocation of the patent after grant. Similarly, the same concept is involved in the question of whether the patent is entitled to priority from an earlier application. This is not to say that the question in each case is the same. The purposes for which the question is being asked are different. But the underlying concept is the same. . . .

The need for an enabling disclosure to satisfy the requirements of support under section 5(2)(a), valid application under section 14 and sufficiency under section 72(1)(c) has, I think, been plain and undisputed since the decision in *Asahi*. What has been less clear is what the concept of an enabling disclosure means. Part of the difficulty has been caused by a misinterpretation of what the Technical Board of Appeal of the EPO said in *Genentech I/ Polypeptide expression* (T–292/85) [1989] O.J. EPO 275). This was a patent for a plasmid suitable for transforming a bacterial host which included an expression control sequence or "regulon" which could enable the expression of foreign DNA as a recoverable polypeptide. The Examining Division was willing to grant a patent only in respect of the plasmids, bacteria and polypeptides known at the date of application. The Technical Board of Appeal allowed the appeal, saying that the Examining Division had taken too narrow a view of the requirement of enabling disclosure:

"What is also important in the present case is the irrelevancy of the particular choice of a variant within the functional terms 'bacteria', 'regulon' or 'plasmid'. It is not just that *some* result within the range of polypeptides is obtained in each case but it is the *same* polypeptide which is expressed, independent of the choice of these means. Unless variants of components are also embraced in the claims, which are, now or later on, equally suitable to achieve the same effect in a manner which could not have been envisaged without the invention, the protection provided by the patent would be ineffectual . . . The character of the invention this time is one of general methodology which is fully applicable with any starting material, and is, as it was already stated, also independent from the known, trivial, or inventive character of the end-products."

In other words, the applicants had invented a general principle for enabling plasmids to control the expression of polypeptides in bacteria and there was no reason to believe that it would not work equally well with any plasmid, bacterium or polypeptide. The patent was therefore granted in general terms. . . .

In fact the Board in *Genentech I/Polypeptide expression* was doing no more than apply a principle of patent law which has long been established in the United Kingdom, namely that the specification must enable the invention to be performed to the full extent of the monopoly claimed. If the invention discloses a principle capable of general application, the claims may be in correspondingly general terms. The patentee need not show that he has proved its application in every individual instance. On the other hand, if the claims include a number of discrete methods or products, the patentee must enable the invention to be performed in respect of each of them.

Thus if the patentee has hit upon a new product which has a beneficial effect but cannot demonstrate that there is a common principle by which that effect will be shared by other products of the same class, he will be entitled to a patent for that product but not for the class, even though some may subsequently turn out to have the same beneficial effect: see *May & Baker Ltd v Boots Pure Drug Co Ltd* (1950) 67 R.P.C. 23 at 50. On the other hand, if he has disclosed a beneficial property which is common to the class, he will be entitled to a patent for all products of that class (assuming them to be new) even though he has not himself made more than one or two of them.

Since *Genentech I/Polypeptide expression* the EPO has several times reasserted the well established principles for what amounts to sufficiency of disclosure. In particular, in *Exxon/Fuel Oils* (T/409/91) [1994] O.J. EPO 653, paragraph 3.3, the Technical Board of Appeal said of the provision in the European Patent Convention equivalent to section 14(5)(c) of the Act:

> "Furthermore, Article 84 EPC also requires that the claims must be supported by the description, in other words, it is the definition of the invention in the claim that needs support. In the Board's judgment, this requirement reflects the general legal principle that the extent of the patent monopoly, as defined by the claims, should correspond to the *technical contribution* to the art in order for it to be supported, or justified."

After considering the "excessive claim" cases of O'Reilly v Morse *56 U.S. (15 How.) 62 (1854) and* British United Shoe Machinery v Simon Collier *(1908) 26 R.P.C. 21 at 49–50 (Parker J.), Lord Hoffmann said:*

I return ... to consider the technical contribution to the art which Professor Murray made in 1978 and disclosed in Biogen 1. As it seems to me, it consisted in showing that despite the uncertainties which then existed over the DNA of the Dane particle—in particular, whether it included the antigen genes and whether it had introns—known recombinant techniques could nevertheless be used to make the antigens in a prokaryotic host cell ... I accept the judge's findings that the method was shown to be capable of making both antigens and I am willing to accept that it would work in any otherwise suitable host cell. Does this contribution justify a claim to a monopoly of *any* recombinant method of making the antigens? In my view it does not. The claimed invention is too broad. Its excessive breadth is due, not to the inability of the teaching to produce all the promised results, but to the fact that the same results could be produced by different means ...

I would therefore hold that Biogen 1 did not support the invention as claimed in the European Patent and that it is therefore not entitled to the priority date of Biogen 1. As it is conceded that the invention was obvious when the patent application was filed it is invalid.

Concerning the claim of "insufficiency" under s.72(1)(c), Lord Hoffmann held that the above reasoning leads to the conclusion that the patent was also invalid for insufficiency. He went on to address the question of the date on which the specification must "disclose the invention clearly enough and completely enough for it to be performed by a person skilled in the art", and agreed with the Court of Appeal that the relevant date of compliance is the date of application, as opposed to the date of publication of the application:

... It would be illogical if a patent, which ought to have been rejected under section 14(3), is rendered immune from revocation under section 72(1)(c) by advances in the art between the date of application and the publication of the specification ...

On the question of obviousness, Lord Hoffmann stated:

Aldous J. identified the inventive concept as "the idea or decision to express a polypeptide displaying HBV antigen specificity in a suitable host"... I can only observe that as formulated by Aldous J., the inventive concept means, in effect, having the idea of making HBV antigens by recombinant DNA technology. But that seems to me to be putting the matter far too wide. The idea of making HBV antigens by recombinant DNA technology was shared by everyone at the Geneva meeting of Biogen in February 1978 and no doubt by others working in the field, just as the idea of flying in an heavier-than-air machine had existed for centuries before the Wright brothers. The problem which required invention was to find a way of doing it. . . .

... I would agree with Hobhouse L.J. that, so stated, the concept was obvious. It is, however, clear from the reasoning of Aldous J. that in order to explain why he regarded the decision as involving an inventive step it is necessary to describe it with rather more particularity. A proper statement of the inventive concept needs to include some express or implied reference to the problem which it required the invention to overcome . . . It seems to me, therefore that a more accurate way of stating the inventive concept as it appeared to Aldous J. is to say that it was the idea of trying to express unsequenced eukaryotic DNA in a prokaryotic host. . . .

... [I]f the concept is reformulated in accordance with the judge's reasoning as I have suggested, the argument for the existence of an inventive step is much stronger. If no question of principle were involved, I think it would be wrong to interfere with the judge's assessment. But the inventiveness alleged in this case is of a very unusual kind. It is said to consist in attempting something which a man less skilled in the art might have regarded as obvious, but which the expert would have thought so beset by obstacles as not to be worth trying. In *Raleigh Cycle Co Ltd v H. Miller & Co Ltd* (1946) 63 R.P.C. 113 the Court of Appeal was prepared to assume that it could be inventive to realise that a bicycle hub dynamo of conventional design could function satisfactorily even though it rotated at a lower speed than was previously thought essential. There may be a question of principle here but, like the Court of Appeal in that case, I shall not pursue the question of whether this amounts to an inventive step for the purposes of patent law because I am content to assume, without deciding, that what Professor Murray did was not obvious.

1.3   Infringement

1.3.1   Scope of Monopoly

1.3.1.1   European Patent Convention, Art. 69 and Protocol; Patents Act 1977, ss.125, 130(7): Extent of protection

European Patent Convention
Art. 69(1) The extent of the protection conferred by a European patent or a European patent application shall be determined by the terms of the claims. Nevertheless, the description and drawings shall be used to interpret the claims.

(2) For the period up to grant of the European patent, the extent of the protection conferred by the European patent application shall be determined by the latest filed claims contained in the publication under Article 93. However, the European patent as granted or as amended in opposition proceedings shall determine retroactively the protection conferred by the European patent application, in so far as such protection is not thereby extended.

Protocol on the Interpretation of Article 69
Article 69 should not be interpreted in the sense that the extent of the protection conferred by a European patent is to be understood as that defined by the strict, literal meaning of the wordings used in the claims, the description and drawings being employed only for the purpose of resolving an ambiguity found in the claims. Neither should it be interpreted in the sense that the claims serve only as a guideline and that the actual protection conferred may extend to what, from a consideration of the description and drawings by a person skilled in the art, the patentee has contemplated. On the contrary, it is to be interpreted as defining a position between these extremes which combines a fair protection for the patentee with a reasonable degree of certainty for third parties.

Patents Act 1977
S.125(1) For the purposes of this Act an invention for a patent for which an application has been made or for which a patent has been granted shall, unless the context otherwise requires, be taken to be that specified in a claim of the specification of the application or patent, as the case may be, as interpreted by the description and any drawings contained in that specification, and the extent of the protection conferred by a patent or application for a patent shall be determined accordingly.

(2) It is hereby declared for the avoidance of doubt that where more than one invention is specified in any such claim, each invention may have a different priority date under section 5 above.

(3) The Protocol on the Interpretation of Article 69 of the European Patent Convention (which Article contains a provision corresponding to subsection (1) above) shall, as for the time being in force, apply for the purposes of subsection (1) above as it applies for the purposes of that Article.

S.130(7) Whereas by a resolution made on the signature of the Community Patent Convention the governments of the member states of the European Economic Community resolved to adjust their laws relating to patents so as (among other things) to bring those laws into conformity with the corresponding provisions of the European Patent Convention, the Community Patent Convention and the Patent Cooperation Treaty, it is hereby declared that the following provisions of this Act, this is to say, sections 1(1) to (4), 2 to 6, 14(3), (5) and (6), 37(5), 54, 60, 69, 72(1) and (2), 74(4), 82, 83, 88(6) and (7), 100 and 125, are so framed as to have, as nearly as practicable, the same effects in the United Kingdom as the corresponding provisions of the European Patent Convention, the Community Patent Convention and the Patent Cooperation Treaty have in the territories to which those Conventions apply.

1.3.1.2 *Electrical and Musical Industries Ltd v Lissen* [1939] 56 R.P.C. 23 at 39–42, HL

Lord Russell:

The Court of Appeal have stated that in their opinion no special rules are applicable to the construction of a specification, that it must be read as a whole and in the light of surrounding circumstances; that it may be gathered from the specification that particular words bear an unusual meaning; and that, if possible, a specification should be construed so as not to lead to a foolish result or one which the patentee could not have contemplated. They further have pointed out that the claims have a particular function to discharge. With every word of this I agree; but I desire to add something further in regard to the claim in a specification.

The function of the claims is to define clearly and with precision the monopoly claimed, so that others may know the exact boundaries of the area within which they will be trespassers. Their primary object is to limit and not to extend the monopoly. What is not claimed is disclaimed. The claims must undoubtedly be read as part of the entire document, and not as a separate document; but the forbidden field must be found in the language of the claims and not elsewhere. It is not permissible, in my opinion, by reference to some language used in the earlier part of the specification, to change a claim which by its own language is a claim for one subject-matter, which is what you do when you alter the boundaries of the forbidden territory. A patentee who describes an invention in the body of a specification obtains no monopoly unless it is claimed in the claims. As Lord Cairns said, there is no such thing as infringement of the equity of a patent, *Dudgeon v Thomson* (1877) 3 App.C. at 34. ...

I would point out that there is no question here of words in Claim 1 bearing any special or unusual meaning by reason either of a dictionary found elsewhere in the specification or of technical knowledge possessed by persons skilled in the art. The prima facie meaning of words used in a claim may not be their true meaning when read in the light of such a dictionary or of such technical knowledge; and in those circumstances a claim, when so construed, may bear a meaning different from that which it would have borne had no such assisting light been available. That is construing a document in accordance with the recognised canons of construction. But I know of no canon or principle which will justify one in departing from the unambiguous and grammatical meaning of a claim and narrowing or extending its scope by reading into it words which are not in it; or will justify one in using stray phrases in the body of a specification for the purpose of narrowing or widening the boundaries of the monopoly fixed by the plain words of a claim.

A claim is a portion of the specification which fulfils a separate and distinct function. It, and it alone, defines the monopoly; and the patentee is under a statutory obligation to state in the claims clearly and distinctly what is the invention which he desires to protect. As

Lord Chelmsford said in this House many years ago: 'The office of a claim is to define and limit with precision what it is which is claimed to have been invented and therefore patented.' (*Harrison v Anderston Foundry Co* (1876) 1 App. (at 574). If the patentee has done this in a claim the language of which is plain and unambiguous, it is not open to your lordships to restrict or expand or qualify its scope by reference to the body of the speci- fication. Lord Loreburn emphasised this when he said: 'The idea of allowing a patentee to use perfectly general language in the claim and subsequently to restrict or expand or qualify what is therein expressed by borrowing this or that gloss from other parts of the specifi- cation is wholly inadmissible.' *Ingersoll Sergeant Drill Co v Consolidated Pneumatic Tool Co* (1907) 25 R.P.C. 61 at 83. Sir Mark Romer expressed the same view in the following felicitous language: 'One may and one ought to refer to the body of the specification for the purpose of ascertaining the meaning of words and phrases used in the claims, or for the purpose of resolving difficulties of construction occasioned by the claims when read by themselves. But where the construction of a claim when read by itself is plain, it is not in my opinion, legitimate to diminish the ambit of the monopoly claimed merely because in the body of the specification the patentee has described his invention is more restricted terms than in the claim itself.'

1.3.1.3   *Van der Lely v Bamfords* [1963] R.P.C. 61, HL

The plaintiff company developed a mechanised hay-rake whose rake wheels, instead of being driven round mechanically, were moved by contact with the ground. This was the principal feature of the invention as patented, but it was found to have been anticipated by a photograph of an American hay-rake having the same characteristic. Claims 1–10, which referred to this feature, were accordingly invalid.

A second inventive feature claimed in the plaintiff's specification allowed the rake to be converted for the purpose of turning swathes of crop (as distinct from raking the crop together). In the embodiment first described, the rake wheels were ranged down the side of the mechanism, so that they were parallel and slightly overlapping. To convert to a swathe-turner, the hindmost wheels were moved forward to a position, side by side with the foremost wheels. Claim 11 read:

'A device as claimed in claim 10 wherein of the row or each row one or more of the rake wheels situated hindmost in the direction of motion of the vehicular frame is/are separately or jointly dismountable from the said row, and means is provided to carry the dismounted wheels in one or more groups adjacent the foremost rake wheels of the original row and parallel thereto'.

This claim was held valid. The defendant company, however, produced a rake in which the three foremost wheels were dismounted, and remounted beside the hindmost wheels.

Viscount Radcliffe:

I do not say that what is called in legal jargon the "pith and marrow" principle has no longer any status in patent law. To the extent I disagree with the argument put before us by Sir Lionel Heald on behalf of the respondents and, with all respect to that argument, I think that he attributes a general significance to the decision of this House in *EMI v Lissen* (above, 1.3.1.2) which is greater than it is capable of sustaining. On the other hand, the application of this principle is from first to last directed to the prevention of abuse of patent rights by colourable evasion: it is not a special or "benevolent" method of construing an uncertain claim; and I think that he is right to remind us that the basic duty of the patentee to state clearly what is the invention for which he seeks protection and the modern practice of building up patent claims by a meticulous accumulation of separate or combined elements has left a good deal less room for a patentee to complain of abuse, where there is no textual infringement, than may have been allowed to him at some periods in the past.

When, therefore, one speaks of theft or piracy of another's invention or says that it has been "taken" by an alleged infringer and this "pith and marrow" principle is invoked to support the accusation, I think that one must be very careful to see that the inventor has not by the actual form of his claim left open to the world the appropriation of just that property that he says has been filched from him by piracy or theft. After all, it is he who has committed himself to the unequivocal description of what he claims to have invented, and he must submit in the first place to be judged by his own action and words.

If he is so judged, I cannot for my part see what inventive idea is claimed by claim 11, regarded as a separate claim, except the idea of dismounting the hindmost wheels and bringing them forwards to a position adjacent to and parallel with the foremost wheels. Without that claim 11 adds nothing material to what is contained in claim 10; and claim 10, it is agreed, fails because it is only a statement of a general principle and is too wide and vague for enforceability. I cannot, therefore, embark upon an enquiry whether the dismountability of the hindmost wheels is an essential or unessential element of the invention claimed, because it seems to me that the patentee himself has told us by the way that he has drawn up claim 11 that this dismountability of the hindmost wheels is the very element of his idea that makes it an invention. When one says, then, as has been said by the majority of the Court of Appeal, that the appellants have "deliberately chosen to make it an essential feature of the claim that the hindmost wheels should be detachable," what one means is not merely that the wording of this claim has been carefully selected, as has all the rest of the patent document, to put the appellants in as strong a position as their expert advisers thought attainable or desirable, but also that the appellants have stated clearly and without equivocation that the point of their invention lies in its application to the hindmost wheels. The case has not revealed why they decided to concentrate on this aspect. It may be, as the trial judge thought, that they simply had not realised that the required vehicular frame could be devised which allowed for the retention in position of the hindmost wheels. If so, it does not seem to me unfair to say that the respondents' device of bringing the foremost wheels back contains an element of inventive ingenuity. But however that may be, I think that, as the Court of Appeal thought, "why they so confined the claim is not for us to speculate." The fact is that they did; and it is not open to them to complain if others are found to have occupied the ground that they so deliberately refrained from enclosing.

Lord Jenkins, Hodson and Devlin concurred, Lord Reid dissented.

1.3.1.4 *Rodi & Wienenberger v Showell* [1969] R.P.C. 367, HL

The plaintiff company held a patent for an expandable watch-strap made up of two layers of sleeves. Each sleeve was connected to two sleeves in the layer above or below by "U-shaped connecting bows" As Claim 1 described them. These bows were inserted along each side of the strap and were themselves held in place by means of springs within each sleeve. The rotation of the bows allowed the strap to expand. The defendants' straps replaced each pair of U-

*shaped bows (one on each side) with a single C-shaped bow which ran right
across the sleeve.*

Lord Upjohn:

First, the question is whether the relevant claim has been infringed. This is purely a
question of construction of the claim read as a matter of ordinary language, in the light of
the complete specification taken as a whole, but the claim must be construed as a document
without having in mind the alleged infringement. What is not claimed is disclaimed. The
claim must be read through the eyes of the notional addressee, the man who is going to
carry out the invention described. There are many authorities on this, but it is unnecessary
to review them, for I have already said enough to show that, in my view, this document
must be read through the eyes of the common man at his bench.

In considering the claim the court must ascertain what are the essential integers of the
claim: this remains a question of construction and no general principles can be laid down
(see my observations in *Van der Lely v Bamfords Ltd* [1961] R.P.C. 296 at 313 approved on
appeal to this House).

Secondly, the essential integers having been ascertained the infringing article must be
considered. To constitute infringement the article must take each and every one of the
essential integers of the claim. Non-essential integers may be omitted or replaced by
mechanical equivalents; there will still be infringement. I believe that this states the whole
substance of the "pith and marrow" theory of infringement. Furthermore, where the
invention as in this case, resides in a new combination of known integers but also merely in
a new arrangement and interaction of ordinary working parts it is not sufficient to show
that the same result is reached; the working parts must act on one another in the way
claimed in the claim of this patent. This is well illustrated by *Birmingham Sound Reproduce
Ltd v Collaro Ltd* [1956] R.P.C. 232 where Lord Evershed M.R. delivering the judgment of
the court said at 245:

> "Thus the essence of the invention resides wholly in the selection and arrangement of
> the parts and the manner in which they interact when arranged in accordance with the
> invention. It is therefore essential to the invention that it should consist of the par-
> ticular parts described in the claim arranged and acting upon each other in the way
> described in the claim."

The question therefore appears to be whether the allegedly infringing apparatus consists of
substantially the same parts acting upon each other in substantially the same way as the
apparatus claimed as constituting the invention. It is not enough to find that the parts
comprised in the respondents' apparatus individually or collectively perform substantially
similar functions to those performed individually or collectively by the parts comprised in
the apparatus claimed as the appellants' invention, or that the respondents' apparatus
produces the same result as the appellants' apparatus. It must be shown that the respondents' selection and arrangements of parts is substantially the same as the appellants'
selection and arrangement of parts, for it is in such selection and arrangement that the
appellants' invention resides.

So if the patentee has in his specification limited the essential features of his claim in a
manner that may appear to be unnecessary, it may be that the copier can escape infringement by adopting some simple mechanical equivalents so that it cannot be said that every
essential integer of the claim has been taken: the *Van der Lely* case (above, 1.3.1.3)
(admittedly a borderline case which led to a conflict of judicial opinion upon its facts)
affords a very good example. But it must be remembered that unlike a conveyance or

commercial document which is normally *inter partes* and must be interpreted, frequently very broadly, so far as possible to give effect to what appears to have been the intentions of the parties, a patent is a grant of a monopoly forbidding others to enter a part of the general commercial territory open to all of her Majesty's subjects and so in the interests of those subjects that territory must be marked out with reasonable clarity by the claim, construing it fairly in the light of the relevant art.

Together with Lords Morris of Borth-y-Gest, Hodson and Guest, Lord Upjohn found that U-shaped bows were essential integers and that accordingly there was no infringement.

Lords Reid and Pearce dissented, Lord Pearce saying:

It is not enough to say that the U-shaped bow was an essential integer and that the respondents have not got two U-shaped bows but only one C-shaped connector. For the question is whether the essential part of the essential integer is taken although the inessential parts of it have been omitted. Neither the individual U-shape (as opposed to any other alphabetical shape) nor its lack of attachment to the connector at the other end is its essential quality. Its essential feature lies in that it connects two adjacent sleeves by a bridge between two parallel limbs that lie in the sleeves and pivots on the spring. The C-shaped connector has this feature too, since it has at each end a U-shape which performs the functions of the plaintiffs' U-shaped bows and it pivots on the spring in precisely the same way. In all essential respects, therefore it is the same.

1.3.1.5 *Beecham v Bristol* [1978] R.P.C. 153, HL

The plaintiff owned four patents relating to a new class of semi-synthetic penicillins and to methods for their manufacture. One such penicillin was known as Ampicillin and proved to be a valuable antibiotic. The patentee owned similar patents in the US where the second defendants were licensees. The first defendant, a wholly-owned subsidiary of the second defendant, imported and sold in the UK an antibiotic known as Hetacillin which was an acetone derivative of Ampicillin. It was not disputed that the clinical effectiveness of Hetacillin was due entirely to the Ampicillin into which it reverted in the presence of water. Whenever it was administered as an antibiotic it accordingly reverted to Ampicillin in the bloodstream. In response to this importation, the plaintiff sued the defendants for infringement of various claims of the four patents and by earlier proceedings had secured interim relief preventing further importation. One basis of claim was a "pith and marrow" infringement of the claim to Ampicillin. This succeeded and the extract here given relates to this.

It was also alleged that manufacture of intermediate substances in the US and subsequent importation of Hetacillin derived from them infringed claims to those intermediate substances by virtue of the doctrine of infringing importation in Saccharin Corp v Anglo-Continental Chemical (1900) 17 R.P.C. 307. Infringement on this ground was also found, but it is not clear whether, by virtue of the Patents Act 1977, s.60(1)(c), the decision is still applicable in any respect on this question.

Lord Diplock (for the House of Lords):

Contemporaneously with the rise of the doctrine of infringing importation there was developing another doctrine known by the phrase adopted by Lords Cairns L.C. in *Clark v Adie* (1877) 2 App.Cas. 315 as that of "pith and marrow." It first arose in connection with mechanical patents for machines or processes which made use of novel combinations of known mechanical principles. Regarded separately each element or integer in the machine or process might not be new; the novelty and accordingly the invention lay in the particular combination of them. When *Clark v Adie* was in the Court of Appeal (1875) L.R. 10 Ch. 667) James L.J. was able to say: "In fact, every, or almost every, patent is a patent for a new combination." The doctrine which, in the case of mechanical patents to which it has principally been applied, is also known as the doctrine of "equivalents", was lucidly stated by Lord Parker, then Parker J., in *Marconi v British Radio Telegraph and Telephone Co Ltd* (1911) 28 R.P.C. 181 at 217, where he said: "Where ... the combination or process, besides being itself new, produces new and useful results, everyone who produces the same results by using the essential parts of the combination or process is an infringer, even though he has, in fact, altered the combination or process by omitting some unessential part or step and substituting another part or step which is equivalent to the part or step that he has omitted."

The increasing particularity with which the claims are drafted and multiplied in modern specifications may have reduced the scope of application of the doctrine of "pith and marrow", but I am unable to accept the argument advanced by Bristol that this has made the doctrine obsolete. It still remains a part of patent law as is acknowledged in speeches delivered in this House as recently as *C. Van der Lely NV v Bamfords Ltd* [1963] R.P.C. 61; *Rodi & Weinberger AG v Henry Showell Ltd* [1969] R.P.C. 367. Directed as it is against colourable evasion of a patent it is not in my view confined to mechanical inventions or to claims for new combinations of integers, but in appropriate cases, though they may be rare, is applicable to claims for new products. ...

I turn first to the contention by Beechams that under the pith and marrow doctrine the product Hetacillin was an infringement of their claim to Ampicillin as a product. At the hearing before Mr Falconer this contention was much more extensive and covered all claims in the patents to all products made from 6-APA by acylation and to the product 6-APA itself. This may account for his rejection of it. The Court of Appeal in their judgment dealt only with the application of the doctrine to the claim to Ampicillin itself. This they held to be infringed under the pith and marrow doctrine.

I have already expressed my opinion that the pith and marrow doctrine is applicable to claims for new products as well as to new processes; and I agree with the Court of Appeal that the relationship of Hetacillin to Ampicillin provides a clear case for its application. It was argued that what is claimed in the patents as an essential feature of the class of products to which Ampicillin belongs is the presence of an amino group in the alpha position, and that this feature is absent in Hetacillin. This is literally true at the time of importation and sale but it ceases to be true as soon as Hetacillin is put to use for the only purpose for which it is intended. The substitution for the postulated amino group of the variant incorporated in Hetacillin is evanescent and reversible and for all practical purposes of use can be regarded as the equivalent of the amino group in Ampicillin. In the apt phrase used by the Court of Appeal, it is the reproduction of the substance Ampicillin, albeit temporarily masked.

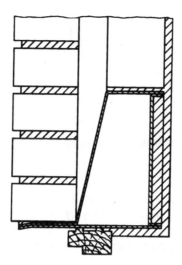

Figure 1

1.3.1.6 *Catnic Components v Hill & Smith* [1982] R.P.C. 183, HL

The plaintiff's patented invention concerned galvanised steel lintels for doors and windows for use in cavity walls. It was a breakthrough in the industry and a considerable commercial success, providing a substitute for solid, much heavier lintels. It depended for its resilience upon the particular formation of steel plates, which in cross-section appeared as in Figure 1.

The element chiefly in dispute in the infringement proceedings (italicised in Claim 1) is marked "105" on the drawing, which is Figure 1 in the plaintiff's specification. Claim 1 read:

"A lintel for use over apertures in cavity walls having an inner and outer skin comprising a first horizontal plate or part adapted to support a course or a plurality of superimposed units forming part of the inner skin and a second horizontal plate or part substantially parallel to the first and spaced therefrom in a downward vertical direction and adapted to span the cavity in the cavity wall and be supported at least at each end thereof upon courses forming parts of the outer and inner skins respectively of the cavity wall adjacent an aperture, and a first rigid inclined support member extending downwardly and forwardly from or near the front edge adjacent the cavity of the first horizontal plate or part and joining with the second plate or part at an intermediate position which lies between the front and rear edge of the second plate or part and adapted to extend across the cavity, and a second rigid support member extending vertically from or from near the rear edge of the first horizontal plate or part to join with the second plate or part adjacent its rear edge." (Emphasis added).

The variation which the defendant introduced into its lintel with a view to

Figure 2

avoiding infringement of this claim appeared as follows (for a lintel three bricks high—if of two bricks, the angle is increased to 8°): see Figure 2.

Lord Diplock (in whose speech Lords Keith of Kinkel, Scarman, Lowry and Roskill concurred):

My Lords, in their closely reasoned written cases in this House and in the oral argument, both parties to this appeal have tended to treat "textual infringement" and infringement of the "pith and marrow" of an invention as if they were separate causes of action, the existence of the former to be determined as a matter of construction only and of the latter upon some broader principle of colourable evasion. There is, in my view, no such dichotomy; there is but a single cause of action and to treat it otherwise, particularly in cases like that which is the subject of the instant appeal, is liable to lead to confusion.

The expression "no textual infringement" has been borrowed from the speeches in this House in the hay-rake case, *Van der Lely v Bamfords* (above, 1.3.1.3) where it was used by several of their Lordships as a convenient way of saying that the word "hindmost" as descriptive of rake wheels to be dismounted could not as a matter of linguistics mean "foremost": but this did not exhaust the question of construction of the specification that was determinative of whether there had been an infringement of the claim or not. It left open the question whether the patentee had made his reference to the "hindmost" (rather than any other wheels) as those to be dismounted, an essential feature of the monopoly that he claimed. It was on this question that there was a division of opinion in this House and in the Court of Appeal in the hay-rake case.

My Lords, a patent specification is a unilateral statement by the patentee, in words of his own choosing, addressed to those likely to have a practical interest in the subject matter of his invention (*i.e.* "skilled in the art"), by which he informs them what he claims to be the essential features of the new product or process for which the letters patent grant him a monopoly. It is those novel features only that he claims to be essential that constitute the so-called "pith and marrow" of the claim. A patent specification should be given a pur-posive construction rather than a purely literal one derived from applying to it the kind of meticulous verbal analysis in which lawyers are too often tempted by their training to indulge. The question in each case is: whether persons with practical knowledge and experience of the kind of work in which the invention was intended to be used, would understand that strict compliance with a particular descriptive word or phrase appearing in a claim was intended by the patentee to be an essential requirement of the invention so that any variant would fall outside the monopoly claimed, even though it could have no material effect upon the way the invention worked.

The question, of course, does not arise where the variant would in fact have a material effect upon the way the invention worked. Nor does it arise unless at the date of publication of the specification it would be obvious to the informed reader that this was so. Where it is not obvious, in the light of then existing knowledge, the reader is entitled to assume that the patentee thought at the time of the specification that he had good reason for limiting his monopoly so strictly and had intended to do so, even though subsequent work by him or others in the field of the invention might show the limitation to have been unnecessary. It is to be answered in the negative only when it would be apparent to any reader skilled in the art that a particular descriptive word or phrase used in a claim cannot have been intended by a patentee, who was also skilled in the art, to exclude minor variants which, to the knowledge of both him and the readers to whom the patent was addressed, could have no material effect upon the way in which the invention worked.

My Lords, upon analysis of the speeches in this House in *Van Der Lely v Bamfords* the division of opinion between Lord Reid and the remainder of their Lordships appears to have been due to his thinking that it would be obvious to the informed reader that dismounting the "foremost" rather than the "hindmost" wheels was an immaterial variant, whereas the majority were not satisfied that this was even the fact, let alone that it was obviously so. In the bracelet case, *Rodi and Wienenberger AG v Henry Showell Ltd* where this House was more evenly divided, the difference between the majority and the minority appears to have turned upon their respective views as to whether the particular variant alleged to be an infringement, had a material effect upon what were claimed to be the advantages obtained by the patented invention—as to which they differed. In the third of the trilogy of leading cases in this House upon this topic, the Ampicillin case, *Beecham Group Ltd v Bristol Laboratories Ltd* [1977] F.S.R. 215; [1978] R.P.C. 153, the descriptive phrase was "an amino group in the alpha position." In the alleged infringing antibiotic, Hetacillin, this amino group had been temporarily converted by a further chemical reaction into a molecular structure that was no longer an amino group, but the reaction was reversible and upon being put to use as an antibiotic, (which necessitated contact with water) it reverted to its original form as an amino group and in that form produced its prophylactic effects. This House unanimously held that this temporary masking of the amino group amounted to an immaterial variant. It would be obvious to anyone skilled in the specialised art of selecting and synthesising polymers for use as antibiotics that the essential feature of the invention was that when put to use for its intended purpose, the product should have an amino group in the alpha position; and that, accordingly, the patentee's reference to this feature of his claim cannot have been intended by him to exclude products in which the amino group in that position was temporarily displaced during a period before the product was put to any prophylactic use.

The essential features of the invention that is the subject of claim 1 of the patent in suit in the instant appeal are much easier to understand than those of any of the three patents to which I have just referred; and this makes the question of its construction simpler. Put in a nutshell the question to be answered is: Would the specification make it obvious to a builder familiar with ordinary building operations that the description of a lintel in the form of a weight-bearing box girder of which the back plate was referred to as "extending vertically" from one of the two horizontal plates to join the other, could not have been intended to exclude lintels, in which the back plate although not positioned at precisely 90° to both horizontal plates was close enough to 90° to make no material difference to the way the lintel worked when used in building operations? No plausible reason has been advanced why any rational patentee should want to place so narrow a limitation on his invention. On the contrary, to do so would render his monopoly for practical purposes worthless, since any imitator could avoid it and take all the benefit of the invention by the simple expedient of positioning the back plate a degree or two from the exact vertical.

It may be that when used by a geometer addressing himself to fellow geometers, such expressions descriptive of relative position as "horizontal", "parallel", "vertical" and "vertically" are to be understood as words of precision only; but when used in a description of a manufactured product intended to perform the practical function of a weight-bearing box girder in supporting courses of brickwork over window and door spaces in buildings, it seems to me that the expression "extending vertically" as descriptive of the position of what in use will be the upright member of a trapezoid-shaped box girder, is perfectly capable of meaning positioned near enough to the exact geometrical vertical to enable it in actual use to perform satisfactorily all the functions that it could perform if it were precisely vertical; and having regard to those considerations to which I have just referred that is the sense in which in my opinion "extending vertically" would be understood by a builder familiar with ordinary building operation. Or, putting the same thing in another way, it would be obvious to him that the patentee did not intend to make exact verticality in the positioning of the back plate an essential feature of the invention claimed.

My Lords, if one analyses line by line the ways in which the various expressions are used in the specification, one can find pointers either way as to whether in particular lines various adjectives and adverbs descriptive of relative position are used as words of precision or not. Some of these are discussed in the judgments of the majority of the Court of Appeal who found the pointers in favour of precision stronger than those to the contrary, of which one example is the description of the two "horizontal" plates as being only "substantially parallel". For my part I find the result of such analysis inconclusive and of little weight as compared with the broad considerations to which I have referred and which are a consequence of giving as I think one should, a purposive construction to the specification. It follows that I have reached the same conclusion as the trial judge and Sir David Cairns, although not by the route of drawing a distinction between "textual infringement" and infringement of the "pith and marrow" of the invention. Accordingly I would allow the appeal.

1.3.1.7 *Improver Corp v Remington Consumer Products Ltd* [1990] F.S.R. 181, Hoffmann J.

The plaintiffs' European patent (UK) was for an electrical device for plucking hairs from the body. Its principal element consisted of a helical spring bent to form an arc which was rotated at a high speed. Because of the arcuate form, on the convex side the spring would open out, while on the concave side it would close together. Hairs would accordingly be captured and then plucked with the rotation of the spring. The result was less painful than waxing, and more longlasting than shaving. The plaintiffs' own device, "Epilady", was a great commercial success.

The claims in the patent were defined by reference to a "helical spring". Because the principle of the invention could be embodied in springs in many configurations, the description ended with an "equivalents clause":

"It will be evident to those skilled in the art that the invention is not limited to the details of the foregoing illustrative embodiments, and that the present invention may be embodied in other specific forms without departing from the essential attributes thereof, and it is therefore desired that the present embodiments be considered in all respects as illustrative and not restrictive, reference being made to the appended claims, rather than to the foregoing description, and all variations which come within the meaning and range of equivalency of the claims are therefore intended to be embraced therein".

The defendants' device was designed as a less painful alternative to "Epilady". In place of a helical spring it had a tube of synthetic rubber, partly cut through by slits. When rotated, hair was drawn into the slits and then plucked, as the slits squeezed together. For this variant, a US patent had been secured. It was marketed as "Smooth & Silky", with additional tubes for replacement after some seven hours' use.

Hoffmann J. introduced the issue of infringement thus:

The question of infringement turns upon a short but undoubtedly difficult point of construction, namely whether the rubber rod is a "helical spring" as that expression is used in the claims of the patent in suit. In the Court of Appeal at the interlocutory injunction stage of this action Dillon L.J. said that a more attractive way of putting the question, from the plaintiff's point of view, was to ask whether the rod was a "mechanical equivalent" for a helical spring. But I think with respect, for reasons which I shall explain, that these are different ways of saying the same thing.

The proper approach to the interpretation of English patents registered under the Patents Act 1949 was explained by Lord Diplock in *Catnic Components Ltd v Hill & Smith Ltd.* The language should be given a "purposive" and not necessarily a literal construction. If the issue was whether a feature embodied in an alleged infringement which fell outside the primary, literal or a contextual meaning of a descriptive word or phrase in the claim ("a variant") was nevertheless within its language as properly interpreted, the court should ask itself the following three questions:

(1) Does the variant have a material effect upon the way the invention works? If yes, the variant is outside the claim. If no—

(2) Would this (*i.e.* that the variant had no material effect) have been obvious at the date of publication of the patent to a reader skilled in the art. If no, the variant is outside the claim. If yes—

(3) Would the reader skilled in the art nevertheless have understood from the language of the claim that the patentee intended that strict compliance with the primary meaning was an essential requirement of the invention. If yes, the variant is outside the claim.

On the other hand, a negative answer to the last question would lead to the conclusion that the patentee was intending the word or phrase to have not a literal but a figurative meaning (the figure being a form of synecdoche or metonymy) denoting a class of things which included the variant and the literal meaning, the latter being perhaps the most perfect, best-known or striking example of the class.

After further observations on the law, he examined the evidence of the rival experts in relation to the first and second questions, and found that the defendants' variant had no material effect on the way the invention worked, and that this would have been obvious to the skilled reader. On the latter issue, he remarked:

Mr Young [for the defendants] interpreted this question to mean that the variant must be one which would have suggested itself to the skilled man as an obvious alternative to the thing denoted by the literal meaning. In this case, he said, the term "helical spring" did not suggest a rubber rod as an obvious alternative. On the contrary, it was an inventive step.

He relied upon the evidence of Dr Laming who said that mention of a helical spring would not have made him think of a rubber rob and that the choice of the latter was innovative.

I do not think that this is what Lord Diplock meant by the question and I think that Mr Young has been misled by Lord Diplock's use of the word "obvious" into thinking that he must have been intending to refer to the rule that an obvious improvement is not an inventive step. In my view the question supposes that the skilled man is told of both the invention and the variant and asked whether the variant would obviously work in the same way. An affirmative answer would not be inconsistent with the variant being an inventive step. For example, the choice of some material for the bendy rod which was *a priori* improbable (*e.g.* on account of its expense) but had been discovered to give some additional advantage (*e.g.* painless extraction) might be a variant which obviously worked in the same way as the invention and yet be an inventive step. Nor would it matter that the material in question, being improbable, would not have suggested itself to the skilled man as an obvious alternative. Questions such as these may be relevant to the question of construction (Lord Diplock's third question) but not at this stage of the inquiry.

On the third question, Hoffmann J. referred in detail to the views of the experts—Dr Sharpe for the plaintiffs and Dr Laming for the defendants. He concluded:

In my judgment the difference between the experts depends upon how one construes the equivalents clause. The first part of the clause merely says that the description should not be used to restrict the meaning of the language used in the claims. That is not the question here. What matters is the final words: "and all variations which come within the meaning and range of equivalency of the claims are therefore intended to be embraced therein". If this means: "whatever contrary impression the skilled man may be given by the language of the claims read in the context of the rest of the description, all references in the claims to hardware are deemed to include any other hardware which would in any circumstances function in the same way" then I think Dr Sharpe must be right. In my judgment, however, the clause does not have so wide an effect. The words I have quoted say that the variation must still come within the meaning of the claims and the reference to "range of equivalency" means in my judgment no more than "don't forget that the claims must be interpreted in accordance with *Catnic* and the protocol".

Thus interpreted, I do not think that "helical spring" can reasonably be given a wide generic construction and I accept Dr Laming's reasons for thinking that a skilled man would not understand it in this sense. This is not a case like *Catnic* in which the angle of the support member can be regarded as an approximation to the vertical. The rubber rod is not an approximation to a helical spring. It is a different thing which can in limited circumstances work in the same way. Nor can the spring be regarded as an "inessential" or the change from metal spring to rubber rod as a minor variant. In *Catnic* Lord Diplock asked rhetorically whether there was any reason why the patentee should wish to restrict his invention to a support angled at precisely 90°, thereby making avoidance easy. In this case I think that a similar question would receive a ready answer. It would be obvious that the rubber had problems of hysteresis which might be very difficult to overcome. The plaintiff's inventors had done no work on rubber rods. Certainly the rubber rod cannot be used in the loop configuration which is the plaintiff's preferred embodiment. On the other hand, drafting the claim in wide generic terms to cover alternatives like the rubber rod might be unacceptable to the patent office. I do not think that the hypothetical skilled man is also assumed to be skilled in patent law and he would in my judgment be entitled to think that patentee had good reasons for limiting himself, as he obviously appeared to have done, to a helical coil. To derive a different meaning solely from the equivalents clause would in my view be denying third parties that reasonable degree of certainty to which they are entitled under the protocol.

The German Decisions

The patent in suit is being litigated in a number of countries but the only one in which the action has come to trial is in Germany, where the Landgericht of Düsseldorf found in favour of the plaintiff. This naturally causes me concern because the Landgericht was interpreting the same patent according to the same protocol and came to a different conclusion. It seems to me that the reason for the difference between me and my colleagues in Düsseldorf is that, having answered what I have labelled as Lord Diplock's first two questions in the same way as I have, they treated those answers as concluding the matter in favour of the plaintiff and did not find it necessary to ask the third question at all. The specification, they said, conveyed to the expert "the understanding that the configuration of the hair engaging portion as helical spring has to be understood functionally" and that the expert to whom the patent was directed would have "no difficulties in perceiving and understanding this meaning of the teaching of the invention". This does seem to me with respect to be a interpretation closer to treating the language of the claims as a "guideline" than the median course required by the protocol. I also detect some difference in approach between the Landgericht and the Oberlandesgericht (Court of Appeal) which had previously discharged an interlocutory injunction granted by the Landgericht. The Court of Appeal placed much more emphasis upon the language of the specification. Its view on the primary meaning of a helical spring was as follows:

> "A spiral or helical shape is characterised by curved lines such as those showing on the level a spiral and, three-dimensionally, more or less the rising turns of a screw. Nothing else is meant by the theory of the [plaintiff's] patent and this is made clear to a person skilled in the art by the state of the art to which the patent refers and on which its proposition is undoubtedly based. A solid roller-shaped hair-engaging part with vertical incisions at a distance from each other can therefore at the most constitute an equivalent means of replacement for the helical spring".

The court went on to say that the rubber rod undoubtedly worked in the same way as the helical spring (*i.e.* it answered Lord Diplock's first question in the same way as I have). Although it does not specifically say so, I think it may be assumed that it would have regarded this as equally obvious to anyone skilled in the art. But when dealing with the question of whether this would affect the question of construction, *i.e.* whether the skilled man would have regarded the rubber rod as included in the claims of the patent, the Court of Appeal expressed considerable doubt. He could have done so if he had analysed the function of the spring in the invention and then set about thinking of equivalents to perform the same function. But the court doubted whether—

> "the average person skilled in the art thinks in such a theoretical way. This applies particularly to the present case because there appeared to be no need for theorising in view of the fact that a normal helical spring was known as a perfectly suitable means for plucking".

It may be said that the expert evidence before the Landgericht at the trial was different, but I doubt whether this could have been so. There was no real difference between the views of Dr Sharpe and Dr Laming on questions of engineering: the difference lay in the approach to construction, which is really a question of law.

1.3.1.8   *PLG Research v Ardon International* [1995] F.S.R. 116, CA

The plaintiffs owned two patents for methods of producing stretched plastic nets, each of which required starting material that was "substantially uniplanar". One of the defendant's products was alleged to infringe both patents, and another product, one of them. Neither of the defendant's products used starting material which in a strict sense was uniplanar. But the Court of Appeal in the end found that for one product only, the departure from uniplanarity would have no significant effect on the behaviour of the starting material and that this would be obvious to a skilled addressee.

Neill L.J. (for the Court of Appeal) considered the test of "non-literal" infringement in Catnic *and its reformulation by Hoffmann J. in* Improver v Remington *in the light of the comments upon the latter by the Oberlandesgericht Düsseldorf in the equivalent German litigation. He said:*

The appellants invited us to hold that the English law of infringement has been radically changed by the 1977 Act, which was passed in implementation of a convention entered into for the express purpose of ensuring uniformity of approach to the construction of patents issued by the European Patents Office. Thenceforth, the appellants submitted, what may conveniently be described as "the third *Catnic* question" (although it is to be noticed that in Lord Diplock's original formulation it was the only *Catnic* question) no longer forms any part of the English law of infringement. It has, they submitted, been replaced by a doctrine of "functional equivalence" under which, save in special circumstances or to prevent a defence of anticipation, favourable answers to the first two *Catnic* questions should be conclusive in favour of the patentee.

We are unable to accept this submission, at least in its most extreme form, for two reasons. In the first place, as Hoffmann J. pointed out, the so-called third *Catnic* question is the only one which raises a question of construction. In our judgment its elimination without the substitution of some other question would fly in the face of Article 69 of the Convention, the protocol, and section 125(1), which make the language of the claim determinative of its scope. In the second place, the German courts at least have repeatedly stated that functional equivalence is not conclusive, and that the scope of the claim must be determined by its wording. In the *German Improver* case (*Improver Corp and Sicommerce AG v Remington Products Inc*) [1993] I.I.C. 838 the Oberlandesgericht stated:

> When evaluating the scope of protection of Claim 1 of the patent in suit, however, *the argument cannot be limited to identity of effect only* ... For the purpose of fairly delimiting the actual improvement of the field of technical knowledge achieved by an inventor on the basis of EPC Article 69(1) and the protocol on Interpretation, the protected invention will only be considered to be used if a person skilled in the art, *on the basis of reflections progressing from the meaning of the patent claims, i.e.* the invention described therein, could find out, with the help of his professional knowledge at the priority date, the modified means used with the disputed embodiment as a means being identical in effect for solving the problem underlying the invention. (Emphasis added).

In the *Ion Analysis* case [1991] I.I.C. 249 in 1988 the Düsseldorf Oberlandesgericht stated:

> In examining a patent infringement, it must first of all be established on the basis of the understanding of a person skilled in the art, what is the content of the claims, *i.e.*

the meaning which a person skilled in the art would give to the wording of the claim ... This means that merely establishing that an effect is the same is not sufficient to justify the conclusion that the invention which has been granted protection in the patent at issue has been used...
This means that the Court of Appeal has merely established that the two apparatuses achieve the same effect and coincide in a "decisive idea". *That is not sufficient to justify the conclusion that a patent has been infringed.* What is decisive is whether the person skilled in the art, *by studying the invention described in the patent claims,* was able to discover the altered means used in the device attacked. ... (Emphasis added).

And in the *Heavy Metal Oxidation Catalysts* case (1989) 3 G.R.U.R. 205 case in 1988 the same court stated:

... the content of the claims *to be determined by interpretation* is not just the starting point but the key criterion for determining the extent of protection conferred. As regards the utilization of the patent by equivalent means, the crucial point is whether these means will come to the person of ordinary skill in the art from his technical knowledge and recourse of the description and the drawings on the basis of the considerations *which are guided by the text of the claims.* The interpreted meaning of the claims is the starting point for examining whether or not a person of ordinary skill in the art was capable of finding the modified means used in the impugned embodiment on the basis of his technical knowledge as providing an equivalent solution to the problem underlying the invention. *Widening the extent of protection to include a process which the person skilled in the art can find in the patent description on the strength of his technical knowledge but which is not reflected in the text of the claims is not compatible with the maxim of clarity in law.* (Emphasis added).

In the *Handle Cord for Battery* case [1991] I.I.C. 104, (1989) 72 G.R.U.R. 903 in 1989 the Bundesgerichtshof (the Federal Supreme Court) stated:

Use of the invention may also exist in cases where the embodiment to be judged deviates from the meaning of the content of the patent claims but where the person skilled in the art, based on ideas deriving from the meaning of the content of the invention defined in the claims, was able, due to his technical expertise, to identify the modified means employed in the challenged embodiment as being equally effective in the solution of the problem underlying the invention ... *The determination of the scope of protection of a patent under the new Act requires that the meaning of the content of the patent claims, to be determined by interpretation, constitutes not only a point of departure but the decisive basis for the determination of the scope of protection. This must be based on the patent claims...*
The fact that the challenged embodiment deviates from the wording of the claim ... does not preclude the inclusion of the challenged embodiment into the scope of the patent at issue from the point of view of equivalency. *However, what is missing is the observation that the average person skilled in the art would have been able to discover the embodiment deviating from the wording and literal sense of the patent claim by proceeding from the invention as it is defined in the patent claim.*

In applying the protocol, therefore, the German courts, no less than ours, insist that the scope of a patent must be determined by its language; and, while the extent of protection goes beyond the literal content of the claim to cover functional equivalents, it does not go beyond functional equivalents which are deducible from the wording of the claim. In determining the extent of protection, they ask whether the variant embodied in the disputed device is one which is deducible by a person skilled in the art from the wording and drawings of the claims. This appears to us to be not quite the same as the third *Catnic* question, but to be arguably more in conformity with the requirement of the protocol that

117

the wording of the patent should be construed so as to afford a fair measure of protection for the patentee.

The correct approach in the light of the protocol

In the present case the expression to be construed is "substantially uniplanar". The word "substantially" imports a degree of flexibility which precludes an exact and literal construction, and makes it unnecessary to consider whether Lord Diplock's purposive construction was an accurate if proleptic application of the protocol. It clearly went at least part of the way towards the European position by stretching the claims to cover minor variants which obviously have no material effect on the way the invention works. It does not, however, appear to us to be useful to consider whether it went further and may be taken as indicating the proper approach to construction under the protocol. Such an exercise merely engenders a sterile debate on the precise meaning of Lord Diplock's words, a matter which should now be left to legal historians. Lord Diplock was expounding the common law to the construction of a patent. This has been replaced by the approach laid down by the Protocol. If the two approaches are the same, reference to Lord Diplock's formulation is unnecessary, while if they are different it is dangerous. In future, it is to be hoped that attention will be concentrated on the requirements of the protocol and the developing European jurisprudence and not on those of the common law before 1977.

In Assidoman Multipack v Mead Corp *[1995] R.P.C. 321 at 337, Aldous J. referred to the remarks in the* PLG *judgment consigning Lord Diplock's purposive construction to legal historians, and said:*

In that part of their judgment, the Court of Appeal are, I believe, making it clear that their observations on the applicability of "purposive" construction under the 1977 Act are *obiter*. For myself, I would be loathe to discard 14 years of case law unless it is certain that "purposive" construction is not the correct approach under the Act. If it be right that "purposive" construction should be left to legal historians, then it is necessary to put forward another means of navigation to enable the court to steer the correct course between Scylla and Charybdis. The middle ground referred to in the protocol is not clearly defined and every court within the Community has adopted a method of interpretation which it believes to be consistent with the protocol. Recourse can be made jurisprudence of other signatories to the Convention, but that requires analysis and rationalisation of the views of judges from many countries, not only Germany, but also such countries as France, Holland, Denmark and Sweden. There is no European position except that set out in the protocol.

The Court of Appeal decision in the *PLG* case has made it necessary to decide whether this court is bound to follow the guidance given by Lord Diplock in the *Catnic* case. Having reviewed the authorities in the Court of Appeal, I conclude that the correct approach to construction under the Patents Act 1977 is "purposive" construction and believe that this court is bound to follow the guidance given by Lord Diplock as developed in the cases to which I have referred. Further I have been unable to think of any better guidance which hopefully will result in consistent decisions between the courts of this country and those of other parties to the Convention. I suspect that the Court of Appeal in the *PLG* case ultimately came to the same conclusion in that, when they came to decide whether the Old and New LBO products infringed, they concluded that there was no infringement even though the starting material might have been functionally equivalent to a uniplanar material because that "would not have been obvious to the skilled man and could not be deduced from the language of the patents in suit".

1.3.1.9 *American Home Products v Novartis* [2001] R.P.C. 159, CA

The claimant owned a patent for rapamycin—a complex antibiotic molecule extractable from Streptomyces hygroscopicus by conventional means or by genetic engineering. It had a known use for its anti-fungal and anti-tumour properties, but was later found to be a valuable immuno-suppressant in transplant surgery. The main claim for this latter discovery was accordingly in "Swiss form", i.e. to a medicament incorporating rapamycin for inhibiting organ or tissue transplant rejection in a mammal. The body of the specification referred expressly to the many derivatives and pro-drugs of rapamycin which by the substitution of side-chains would alter the three-dimensional shape of the molecule and possibly improve its therapeutic performance. But the claim was restricted to the use of "rapamycin". The alleged infringement, known as SDZ RAD, was one such derivative. Its efficacy had been demonstrated by the defendant, but only after substantial further research. Laddie J. held that this derivative was an infringement of the claim within the Protocol, concluding:

I do not believe that any reasonable and objective person skilled in the art would read this patent as indicating that the inventive contribution was limited to rapamycin alone or that Professor Calne intended to restrict his monopoly simply to the use of that single chemical. ... To do that would have rendered the patent virtually valueless. It would have left out of its scope, for example, those closely similar molecules which could be derived by standard chemistry from rapamycin and which probably would have included many which those in the art would have expected to have equivalent or even better immunosuppressant properties. It would have disclosed to the art the novel seam of interrelated molecules but have claimed only one of them. In practice it was inevitable that the discovery of the activity of rapamycin would lead workers in the art to look for similar molecules derived from rapamycin which would have a better profile of properties.

In reversing that judgment, Aldous L.J (for the Court of Appeal) took particular notice of the breadth of the extended interpretation being sought, since the issue would arise equally in relation to any "variant" of rapamycin which was found to work. For the Improver *questions, the "variant" was taken to be SDZRAD and the answer to Question I was that it did work in the same way. As to Question 2 (concerning whether this was obvious), he stated:*

Upon the findings of fact by the judge, this question has to be answered "No". As the judge held, there was, at the date of the patent, a strong probability that other derivatives would work, but it was impossible to predict with certainty whether any particular one would. It may be that SDZ RAD was a good candidate to try, but it was not obvious that it would work as an immunosuppressant. To find out, the product would have to be made and tested. A similar conclusion would be reached for other derivatives. At most it was likely that one or more derivatives would work, but which would require research.

The skilled person, who read the specification, would not be able to predict how many derivatives would have the appropriate effect nor be able to predict with any certainty whether any would or which would. The inventor, as stated in the specification, had only discovered and described the second medical use of rapamycin. It was left to others to find out which derivatives, if any, worked. Also, concentration on what was the technical contribution does not reflect the true task of the Court which is construction of the claim according to the Protocol. As pointed out in *Wheatley*, it is unfair to a patentee to construe his claim in a way not intended. To ignore a limitation could render a patent invalid contrary to the wishes of the patentee. In any case it would be unfair to third parties to construe a claim in a way that the patentee had indicated by language that it should not be construed.

Aldous L. J. proceeded to answer Question 3 by finding that the patentee must be understood from the specification to have been intending "rapamycin" to refer only to that substance alone. Because that was so, the specification was found not to be lacking in sufficiency of description. Had it be construed so as to cover effective derivatives, it would have been invalid for this reason. By way of final comment he said:

For my part I do not agree that a patent limited to the second use of rapamycin is virtually valueless. The patent protects the second medical use and the long and expensive work that has been carried out to obtain regulatory approval. Thus a person who wishes to market a derivative has to make the derivative and then carry out the long and expensive work needed to get it on the market. Without the patent, other manufacturers could use the work of the patentees. In any case, I do not believe that the patent system should be used to enable a person to monopolise more than that which he has described in sufficient detail to amount to an enabling disclosure. If it was, it would in this case stifle research to find a derivative of rapamycin which was a substantially better immunosuppressant than rapamycin itself.

1.3.2 Acts Constituting Infringement

1.3.2.1 Patents Act 1977, s.60; Sch.A2, paras 7–10

Meaning of infringement

S.60(1) Subject to the provisions of this section, a person infringes a patent for an invention if, but only if, while the patent is in force, he does any of the following things in the United Kingdom in relation to the invention without the consent of the proprietor of the patent, that is to say—

    (a) where the invention is a product, he makes, disposes of, offers to dispose of, uses or imports the product or keeps it whether for disposal of otherwise;

    (b) where the invention is a process, he uses the process or he offers it for use in the United Kingdom when he knows, or it is obvious to a reasonable person in the circumstances, that its use there without the consent of the proprietor would be an infringement of the patent;

    (c) where the invention is a process, he disposes of, offers to dispose of, uses or imports any product obtained directly by means of that process or keeps any such product whether for disposal or otherwise.

(2) Subject to the following provisions of this section, a person (other than the proprietor of the patent) also infringes a patent for an invention if, while the patent is in force and without the consent of the proprietor, he supplies or offers to supply in the United Kingdom a person other than a licensee or other person entitled to work the invention with any of the means, relating to an essential element of the invention, for putting the invention into effect when he knows, or it is obvious to a reasonable person in the circumstances, that those means are suitable for putting, and are intended to put, the invention into effect in the United Kingdom.

(3) Subsection (2) above shall not apply to the supply or offer of a staple commercial product unless the supply or the offer is made for the purpose of inducing the person supplied or, as the case may be, the person to whom the offer is made to do an act which constitutes an infringement of the patent by virtue of subsection (1) above.

(4) Without prejudice to section 86 below, subsections (1) and (2) above shall not apply to any act which, under any provision of the Community Patent Convention relating to the exhaustion of the rights of the proprietor of a patent, as that provision applies by virtue of that section, cannot be prevented by the proprietor of the patent.

(5) An act which, apart from this subsection, would constitute an infringement of a patent for an invention shall not do so if—

    (a) it is done privately and for purposes which are not commercial;

    (b) it is done for experimental purposes relating to the subject-matter of the invention;

    (c) it consists of the extemporaneous preparation in a pharmacy of a medicine for an individual in accordance with a prescription given by a registered medical or dental practitioner or consists of dealing with a medicine so prepared;

    (d) it consists of the use, exclusively for the needs of a relevant ship, of a product or process in the body of such a ship or in its machinery, tackle, apparatus or other accessories, in a case where the ship has temporarily or accidentally entered the internal or territorial waters of the United Kingdom;

(e) it consists of the use of a product or process in the body or operation of a relevant aircraft, hovercraft or vehicle which has temporarily or accidentally entered or is crossing the United Kingdom (including the air space above it and its territorial waters) or the use of accessories for such a relevant aircraft, hovercraft or vehicle;

(f) it consists of the use of an exempted aircraft which has lawfully entered or is lawfully crossing the United Kingdom as aforesaid or of the importation into the United Kingdom, or the use or storage there, of any part or accessory for such an aircraft.

(g) it consists of the use by a farmer of the product of his harvest for propagation or multiplication by him on his own holding, where there has been a sale of plant propagating material to the farmer by the proprietor of the patent or with his consent for agricultural use;

(h) it consists of the use of an animal or animal reproductive material by a farmer for an agricultural purpose following a sale to the farmer by the proprietor of the patent or with his consent, of breeding stock or other animal reproductive material which constitutes or contains the patented invention.

(6) For the purposes of subsection (2) above a person who does an act in relation to an invention which is prevented only by virtue of paragraph (a), (b) or (c) of subsection (5) above from constituting an infringement of a patent for the invention shall not be treated as a person entitled to work the invention, but—

(a) the reference in that subsection to a person entitled to work an invention includes a reference to a person so entitled by virtue of section 55 above; and

(b) a person who by virtue of section 28A(4) or (5) above or section 64 below is entitled to do an act in relation to the invention without it constituting such an infringement shall, so far as concerns that act, be treated as a person entitled to work the invention.

(6A) Schedule A1 contains—

(a) provisions restricting the circumstances in which subsection (5)(g) applies: and

(b) provisions which apply where an act would constitute an infringement of a patent but for subsection (5)(g).

(6B) For the purposes of subsection (5)(h), use for an agricultural purpose—

(a) includes making an animal or animal reproductive material available for the purposes of pursuing the farmer's agricultural activity; but

(b) does not include sale within the framework, or for the purposes, of a commercial reproduction activity.

(6C) In paragraphs (g) and (h) of subsection (5) "sale" includes any other form of commercialisation.

(7) In this section—

"relevant ship" and "relevant aircraft, hovercraft or vehicle" mean respectively a ship and an aircraft, hovercraft or vehicle registered in, or belonging to, any country, other than the United Kingdom, which is a party to the Convention for the Protection of Industrial Property signed at Paris on 20th March 1883, or which is a member of the World Trade Organisation; and "exempted aircraft" means an aircraft to which section 89 of the Civil Aviation Act 1982 (aircraft exempted from seizure in respect of patent claims) applies.

Section 60(1) is derived from Community Patent Convention, Art. 25; s.60(2) and (4) from Art. 26; and s.60(5)–(7) from Art. 27; s.60(4) provides machinery for giving effect to the exhaustion principle prescribed in Arts 28 and 76.

Sch. A2, paras 7–10 (implementing Biotechnology Directive (98/440/EC)) Arts. 8–10.

7. The protection conferred by a patent on a biological material possessing specific characteristics as a result of the invention shall extent to any biological material derived from that biological material through propagation or multiplication in an identical or divergent form and possessing those same characteristics.

8. The protection conferred by a patent on a process that enables a biological material to be produced possessing specific characteristics as a result of the invention shall extend to the biological material directly obtained through that process and to any other biological material derived from the directly obtained biological material through propagation or multiplication in an identical or divergent form and possessing those same characteristics.

9. The protection conferred by a patent on a product containing or consisting of genetic information shall extend to all material, save as provided for in paragraph 3(a) above, in which the product is incorporated and in which the genetic information is contained and performs its function.

10. The protection referred to in paragraphs 7, 8 and 9 above shall not extend to biological material obtained from the propagation or multiplication of biological material placed on the market by the proprietor of the patent or with his consent, where the multiplication or propagation necessarily results from the application for which the biological material was marketed, provided that the material obtained is not subsequently used for other propagation or multiplication.

1.3.2.2   *Smith Kline and French v Harbottle* **[1980] R.P.C. 363, Oliver J.**

The first defendant, Harbottle, ordered a drug, Cimetidine, patented by the plaintiff in the UK, from Italy. It arranged for its importation into England with the intention of re-exporting it. It was carried to Heathrow by British Airways and stored there in their bonded warehouse to the order of Harbottle. The plaintiff alleged that, under the Patents Act 1977, s.60(1), British Airways thereby infringed the patent as a person who "keeps" the product "whether for disposal or otherwise." It was argued on the plaintiff's behalf that this expression was deliberately meant to be wider than the equivalent provisions in the Community Patent Convention.

Oliver J.:

Article 25 of the Community Patent Convention is in these terms:

> "A community patent shall confer on its proprietor the right to prevent all third parties not having his consent: (a) from making, offering, putting on the market, or using a product which is the subject matter of the patent, or importing or stocking the product for these purposes; (b) from using a process which is the subject-matter of the patent or when the third party knows or it is obvious in the circumstances that the use of the process is prohibited without the consent of the proprietor of the patent, from offering the process for use within the territories of the contracting states, and (c) from

offering, putting on the market, using, importing or stocking for these purposes the product obtained directly by a process which is the subject-matter of the patent."

Article 27 is in terms which are very similar to those which appear in subsection 5 of section 60. That article provides:

"The rights conferred by a community patent shall not extend to (a) acts done privately and for non-commercial purposes; (b) acts done for experimental purposes relating to the subject-matter of the patented invention," and then it goes on with similar provisions with regard to exempted aircraft and that sort of thing.

It is I think obvious from a comparison of the provisions of Article 27 and the provisions of section 60(5) that the intention of the framers of the statute was to give effect to the provisions of the convention, and indeed, as I have pointed out, section 130(7) states not only that that was the intention but that it is indeed being achieved.

"Keep" is a word with many meanings. Indeed in its transitive sense the *Shorter Oxford English Dictionary* records no less than 26 different nuances. Literally an attendant in the left luggage office at Euston "keeps" a suitcase committed to his charge. If it contained a patented article I suppose he thus "keeps" the article. But it would be surprising if he thereby became an infringer and liable to an injunction. Mr Prescott does not—at least I do not think he does—so contend. But beyond this point at what point does a person "keep" property within the meaning of the section? In my judgment, clearly what the draftsman had in mind was "keeping" in the sense of "keeping in stock" so as to give effect to the words of the Convention "stocking the product for these purposes." Indeed it is worth noting that in the *Shorter Oxford English Dictionary* one of the meanings of the verb "to stock" is "(b) esp"—which I presume means "especially"—"to keep goods in stock for sale." Mr Gratwick therefore submits that, whatever else the word may mean in the section, the word "keep" in the context of this Act connotes a keeping in some capacity and for a purpose other than that of a mere custodian or warehouseman. He submits that there is at least an ambiguity here, and he referred me to the following passage from *Gartside v Inland Revenue Commissioners* [1968] A.C. 553, 612 where Lord Reid says: "It is always proper to construe an ambiguous word or phrase in light of the mischief which the provision is obviously designed to prevent, and in light of the reasonableness of the consequences which follow from giving it a particular construction.

I find this argument persuasive. If it had really been intended to effect a revolutionary change, such as Mr Prescott suggests, I would have expected it to be done by much stronger and more positive language than this. Indeed, as Mr Gratwick has pointed out, where the legislature did intend to make an alteration in the existing law or at least to clarify it, as in subsection 2 of section 60, it did so quite expressly.

It is not, I think, necessary for me to seek to arrive at a definitive meaning of the statutory provision on this application, and I do not intend to do so. It is sufficient for the purposes of this case to say merely that I remain wholly unpersuaded that anything that British Airways have done in relation to the goods in carrying them or warehousing them in this case constitutes an infringement within the meaning of section 60. It follows from that, first, that the plaintiffs' motion for judgment against British Airways must fail and, secondly, that British Airways are entitled to succeed on their interpleader motion.

1.3.2.3 *Kalman v PCL Packaging* [1982] F.S.R. 406, Falconer J.

The plaintiffs owned a patent for filters that were used in processes for extruding plastics; the patent claimed both the filters and their use in plastics production. The first defendant, PCL, obtained two filters within the scope of the patent from the second defendant, Berlyn, a corporation which traded only in the US. These were consigned f.o.b. in Boston, Massachusetts to British Airways for shipment to PCL, the purchase price having been previously paid. Under the Uniform Commercial Code of the US, Art. 2–401, Berlyn accordingly parted with all possession, actual and constructive, at this shipping point and the buyer assumed all risk of loss and liability for carriage charges. Shortly after delivery, PCL were notified by the plaintiffs of their patent, and Berlyn undertook to indemnify PCL against any consequent loss. In an action for infringement of the British patent, Berlyn sought to strike out the statement of claim and to set aside service upon them out of the jurisdiction on the ground that they had committed no tort in the jurisdiction.

Counsel for the plaintiff sought to make out his case against Berlyn upon a number of provisions of the Patents Act 1977, s.60 and associated principles of common law.

Falconer J.:

(i) Offering to dispose within the jurisdiction and disposing within the jurisdiction (section 60(1)(a)).

(It is convenient under this paragraph to deal with the second of the ways in which Mr Hobbs put his cause of action under this paragraph, first of all, that is to say the allegation that Berlyn Corporation had disposed of the apparatus, the filters in question, within the jurisdiction. This involves considering the meaning to be given to the phrase "dispose of" in paragraph (a) of the subsection. It is a term which is new to our patent jurisprudence, at least in relation to infringement. Referring to the long title to the Patents Act 1977, Mr Hobbs submitted that the Act had established a whole new system of law and in particular, so he submitted, the concept of vending as an infringing act had gone having been deliberately left out of the acts specified in paragraph (a) of the subsection, so that cases such as *Badische Anilin und Soda Fabrik v H Johnson & Co* (1897) 14 R.P.C. 919, were no longer good law. He submitted that if that case had had to be decided on the law as it is under section 60 of the 1977 Act it would have been decided differently and, so he submitted, on the lines of the dissenting judgment of Rigby L.J. in that case in the Court of Appeal, whose judgment is to be found in 14 R.P.C. at 416.

I do not accept this submission. In the first place, one way of disposing of an article is to sell it.

Falconer J. cited dictionary definitions in support and noted that s.60(1) was intended to correspond to the Community Patent Convention Art. 25(a):

"A Community patent shall confer on its proprietor the right to prevent all third parties not having his consent: (a) From making, offering, putting on the market or using a product which is the subject-matter of the patent, or importing or stocking the product for these purposes."

He continued:

Mr Hobbs agreed that the expression in that paragraph of that Article "putting on the market" is equivalent to the phrase "dispose of" in the statute. "Putting on the market," perhaps a somewhat colloquial expression, surely in its usually accepted sense connotes offering for sale and selling. Nowadays it may also I think embrace other forms of marketing a product, such as leasing, but I do not have to consider that possibility here. Certainly it seems to me that, bearing in mind the express provisions of section 130(7) and that wording of Article 25 of the Community Patent Convention, "dispose of" in paragraph (a) of section 60 must at least include selling, that a sale of an article must be a disposal of it within the meaning of paragraph (a) in the subsection.

It seems to me also that had the legislature intended to effect such a radical change in the law as to infringement as Mr Hobbs submits, one would have expected that to have been made clearer and stronger with more positive language, as was done for instance in section 60(2), which altered the previous law as to contributory infringement.

In the present case the sales of the two filters in question had been effected in the United States outside the jurisdiction, had been completed so that the property had passed to the buyer while the article was still in the United States and Berlyn Corporation had parted with possession, both actual and constructive, and had no further rights of any kind in either of the filters after delivery to the shipping point in the United States Berlyn Corporation had disposed of the filters in the United States and, having no further property in them or possession of them or any right of any kind in them, could not effect any further disposal of them whatsoever.

Mr Hobbs submitted that the Berlyn Corporation had disposed of the filters in the United Kingdom by delivering them to PCL. He said the act of disposal by Berlyn Corporation was delivery into the possession of PCL and that act was completed, so he said, in the United Kingdom when the carrier delivered to PCL. He referred to the acts of the intervening parties, such as the forwarding agents and carriers as—and I quote—"mere ministerial acts," an expression I think he borrowed from the dissenting judgment of Rigby L.J. in the *Badische Anilin* case to which I have referred.

For the reasons I have already stated, I reject this argument. Once Berlyn Corporation delivered to the shipping point in the United States they had no further property in, possession of, or any rights in or any control of the goods, which were PCL's, and Berlyn Corporation could not effect any further act of disposing the goods.

Alternatively, still under this head of cause of action, Mr Hobbs submitted that Berlyn Corporation were liable for disposal of the goods in the United Kingdom on the footing that the carriers were agents of Berlyn Corporation and the carriers had disposed of the goods in the United Kingdom by delivery to PCL. I reject this argument also. It necessarily presupposes that the carriers in delivering to PCL in the United Kingdom had committed an act of infringement under section 60(1)(a) by so doing. As to that, I would refer to the judgment of Oliver J., as he then was, in the case of *Smith, Kline & French Laboratories Limited v R.D. Harbottle (Mercantile) Limited and Others* [1980] R.P.C. 363.

I now go back to consider Mr Hobbs' first way of putting the plaintiffs' case, namely, that Berlyn Corporation have infringed in that they have offered to dispose of within the jurisdiction apparatus within the claims of the patent in suit, namely, at least one of the two filters in question. In section 60(1)(a), which I have read, of the enumerated acts which if performed in the United Kingdom would be infringing, the one immediately preceding the words "offers to dispose of" is the one I have just considered, "disposes of". To be an infringement, that immediately preceding act, "disposes of" must of course be an act within the United Kingdom. In my view, the legislature was intending in the expression "offers to dispose of" to prohibit offering in the United Kingdom to do the immediately preceding prohibited act, that is, disposing of the product in the United Kingdom.

Falconer J. referred to a telex from Berlyn to PCL which stated "We can ship your machine on Monday via British Airways ... Please advise the airport to ship to ...". He continued:

Mr Hobbs says that that telex is an offer to dispose of the filter in question in the United Kingdom using British Airways as a carrier, as agents he says of Berlyn Corporation, to bring into the United Kingdom and hand over to PCL in this country, and that he says would be a disposal in the United Kingdom. He says that this telex, since it arrived in this country and was received in this country, is an offer in the jurisdiction, on the strength of the decision of the House of Lords in *Brinkibon Ltd v Stahag Stahl und Stahlwarenhandelgesellschaft mbH* [1982] 1 All E.R. 239.

Assuming for present purposes without deciding, that it was an offer in the United Kingdom and assuming that British Airways as carrier were to be such as the agents of Berlyn Corporation, which I am not to be taken as deciding, I have already held that British Airways in carrying into and delivering the filters to PCL in this country did not dispose of the goods in the jurisdiction within the meaning of section 60(1)(a), so that there was no offer, whether made within or without the jurisdiction, of a disposal of the filters in the United Kingdom by reason of the action of British Airways in carrying in and handing over to PCL within the jurisdiction. So that, in my judgment, the plaintiffs have not shown a cause of action within the jurisdiction on this ground.

(ii) Offering a process for use within the jurisdiction (section 60(1)(b)).

With all respect to Mr Hobbs, it seems to me that this argument is a complete non-starter. Section 60(1)(b) requires the offer of a process for use in the United Kingdom. In my judgment, on no reasonable or sensible view of the facts in this case could Berlyn be said to have offered to PCL the use of a process in the United Kingdom. What was offered to PCL was the sale of the filters in question in the United States of America, to PCL in the case of the first filter and of course to the hire purchase company in the case of the second one, with delivery f.o.b. to the shipping point in the United States of America and I cannot see how either of those transactions could have amounted to an offer to PCL of the use of a process in the United Kingdom.

(iii) Supplying essential means for putting the invention into effect (section 60(2)).

This sub-section requires the supply in the United Kingdom, or the offer to supply in the United Kingdom, of the means in question for putting the patented invention into effect in the United Kingdom. There was no supply in the United Kingdom to PCL or offer to supply in the United Kingdom to PCL by Berlyn Corporation of the filters in question. They were supplied to PCL in the United States of America pursuant to sales in the United States of America, f.o.b. the shipping point in the United States of America and, in my judgment, the plaintiffs cannot have any cause of action against Berlyn Corporation under this head.

(iv) Joint tort committed by Berlyn and PCL.

As I understand the law, to be a joint tortfeasor a person must have acted in concert with another pursuant to a common design in the commission of the tort, that is to say, it has got to be a joint tort. . . .

What Mr Hobbs says is that Berlyn Corporation, with knowledge of the plaintiffs' British patent, have since at least July 23, 1981, which is the date of the indemnity, collaborated with PCL in an arrangement whereby PCL continued to use the filters in their process in the United Kingdom while Berlyn Corporation, to use Mr Hobbs' own expression, "have stood guard over the arrangement," which I understood to mean by reason of the indemnity and the submission is that all that amounts to a common design between Berlyn Corporation and PCL to infringe the plaintiffs' patent.

As I have said, I cannot accept that argument. On the facts as I have stated them, I do not consider that Berlyn Corporation were guilty of acting in concert to infringe the plaintiffs' patent at all. Moreover, it is quite clear that at common law, on the facts as I have stated them, Berlyn Corporation would not be infringers of the plaintiffs' patent either as joint tortfeasors or as procuring infringement by PCL.

The principle of law applicable was settled by the decisions of the Court of Appeal in *Townsend v Haworth* (1875) 48 L.J. (N.S.) 770, and in *Dunlop Pneumatic Tyre Co Ltd v D Moseley & Sons Limited* (1904) 21 R.P.C. 274. Those authorities were followed recently by the Court of Appeal in *Belegging en Exploitatiemaatschappij Lavender BV v Witten Industrial Diamonds Limited* [1979] F.S.R. 59. Referring to those two old authorities Buckley L.J. with whose judgment the other lords justices agreed, Goff L.J. and Eveleigh L.J. at 64 after giving the references to the two cases, *Townsend v Haworth* and *Dunlop Pneumatic Tyre Co Ltd v D Moseley & Sons Ltd* said:

"In the former of these two cases"—that is *Townsend v Haworth*—"Mellish L.J. stated the principle tersely and forcefully as follows: 'Selling materials for the purpose of infringing a patent to the man who is going to infringe it, even although the party who sells it knows that he is going to infringe it and indemnifies him, does not by itself make the person who so sells an infringer. He must be a party with the man who so infringes and actually infringe'."

"In the latter case"—that is *Dunlop Pneumatic Tyre Co Ltd v D Moseley & Sons Ltd*—"Vaughan Williams L.J. said (at 278):

'The real question which was intended to be raised by the plaintiffs was this—whether the selling of an article intended to be used for the purpose of infringing a patent is an infringement of the patent. In my judgment it is not.' In the same case Stirling C.J. said (at 281) that *Townsend v Haworth* was authority that the sale of an article does not become an infringement merely because the vendor knows that the purchaser intends to use the article when sold for the purposes of infringing the patent, and Cozens Hardy L.J. said (at 282) that *Townsend v Haworth* was a decision that there is no infringement by defendants, even though they sell to persons with the intent that those persons should afterwards use the article sold for infringing purposes, or even if they took an indemnity in the case of any infringement being made". . . .

"In *Dunlop v Moseley* Vaughan Williams L.J. *obiter* (at 280) expressed the opinion that that action would have failed even though the plaintiffs were able to substantiate the proposition that the goods manufactured and sold by the defendants could not be used for any purpose other than an infringing purpose. I would agree with this, for goods which cannot be used otherwise than in an infringing manner may nevertheless be disposed of without any infringement. They may, for example, be exported."

No doubt the law so stated in those authorities has been altered by section 60(2) in the 1977

Act, to which provision I have already referred, but the alteration to the common law principle so effected, in my view, is strictly limited in that, as I have already pointed out, under section 60(2) a person who supplies any of the means relating to an essential element of the patented invention for putting the invention into effect only infringes within the subsection if he supplies in the United Kingdom.

Had it been the intention of the legislature to abrogate the principle of *Townsend v Haworth* and *Dunlop Pneumatic Tyre Co Ltd v D Moseley & Sons Ltd*, where the sale and supply was outside the United Kingdom, one would have expected clear language to that effect. On the contrary, the language restricts the alteration of the law to the case of supply in the United Kingdom. If that be right, so that the common law principle enunciated in those authorities still obtains in respect of supply outside the United Kingdom, as a matter of law Mr Hobbs' submission on joint tortfeasance must fail. But however that may be, in my judgment, on the facts there has been no common design between Berlyn Corporation and PCL to infringe the plaintiffs' patent in the United Kingdom.

Falconer J. proceeded to distinguish Morton-Norwich Products v Intercen *[1978] R.P.C. 501 as a case in which there had been a common design to infringe on the part of a foreign manufacturer and an English importer. He quoted from Graham J.'s judgment in that case:*

> "If however I am wrong and the proper view is that Intercen have themselves done no acts here contributing to the actual commission of the tort, I still hold the view that by virtue of such common design they have no defence to the claim of joint tortfeasance. A person may be liable as a joint tortfeasor provided he has such common design although he has not himself done anything within the jurisdiction which taken by itself would amount to an actionable tort. See *The Koursk* [1924] at 140, and *Brook v Bool* [1928] 2 K.B. 578 at 586. I therefore hold here that the defendants are guilty of infringement of the English patent by reason of their acts of joint tortfeasance with the Easter companies, who in fact sold the material in question here."

I have read enough of that case to point the distinction on the facts of that case from the present one. There was in fact, as it was held, a common design to sell in this country and that was quite different to the facts in this case.

(v) Procuring commission of a tort within the jurisdiction.

Falconer J. quoted from Buckley L.J.'s judgment in Lavender v Witten *(above):*

> "Facilitating the doing of an act is obviously different from procuring the doing of the act. In *Townsend v Haworth* the sale of an ingredient necessary for an infringing manufacture must have facilitated the infringement, but was held not to amount to an infringement, even though the vendor knew how the ingredient was to be used and indemnified the purchaser against any infringement claim. Mr Young says that this was because the purchaser approached the vendor and was not persuaded by the vendor to make the purchase or to infringe. But in the present case there is no allegation that the defendants persuaded Edel to make the purchase or even that they sought his custom in any way."

In this case there is no question of Berlyn Corporation persuading PCL to purchase the filters, less still to use them, or that Berlyn Corporation actually sought PCL's custom, that is to say, the United Kingdom PCL. The position was quite different. It was Mr Holmes of

PCL who sought the filters from Berlyn Corporation, who persuaded both PCL Canada and PCL U.S. to release one of the two filters already destined for PCL U.S. that was only allowed by Berlyn Corporation on payment terms much more stringent than had been asked of PCL U.S. A filter was to be released, and was indeed released, only after payment of the whole of the purchase price in the U.S. prior to release to the shipping point. As to the second filter, it was again Mr Holmes who wrote to Berlyn Corporation and sought it. There was no question of persuading by Berlyn Corporation. That did not arise at all. I reject this contention of procuring as a possible cause of action against Berlyn Corporation on the facts.

1.3.3   Defence of Prior User

1.3.3.1   Patents Act 1977, s.64 (amended by CDPA 1988, Sch. 5, para. 17)

S.64(1) Where a patent is granted for an invention, a person who in the United Kingdom before the priority date of the invention—

- (a) does in good faith an act which would constitute an infringement of the patent if it were in force, or
- (b) makes in good faith effective and serious preparations to do such an act,

has the right to continue to do the act or, as the case may be, to do the act, notwithstanding the grant of the patent; but this right does not extend to granting a licence to another person to do the act.

(2) If the act was done, or the preparations were made, in the course of a business, the person entitled to the right conferred by subsection (1) may—

- (a) authorise the doing of that act by any partners of his for the time being in that business, and
- (b) assign that right, or transmit it on death (or in the case of a body corporate on its dissolution), to any person who acquires that part of the business in the course of which the act was done or the preparations were made.

(3) Where a product is disposed of to another in exercise of the rights conferred by subsection (1) or (2), that other and any person claiming through him may deal with the product in the same way as if it had been disposed of by the registered proprietor of the patent.

1.3.4   Procedure and Remedies

1.3.4.1   Patents Act 1977, s.61(1), (2): Proceedings for infringement of patent

S.61(1) Subject to the following provisions of this Part of this Act, civil proceedings may be brought in the court by the proprietor of a patent in respect of any act alleged to infringe the patent and (without prejudice to any other jurisdiction of the court) in those proceedings a claim may be made—

(a) for an injunction or interdict restraining the defendant or defender from any appre-hended act of infringement;

(b) for an order for him to deliver up or destroy any patented product in relation to which the patent is infringed or any article in which that product is inextricably comprised;

(c) for damages in respect of the infringement;

(d) for an account of the profits derived by him from the infringement;

(e) for a declaration or declarator that the patent is valid and has been infringed by him.

(2) The court shall not, in respect of the same infringement, both award the proprietor of a patent damages and order that he shall be given an account of the profits.

1.3.4.2   *Watson Laidlaw v Potts Cassels and Williamson* (1914) 31 R.P.C. 104, HL

The plaintiff company's patent was for a device which reduced oscillation of the spindle in washing machines. The defendant was found to have infringed the patent by incorporating the invention in its washing machines. The plaintiff was awarded £1,500 as a "jury estimate" by the Lord Ordinary, which was increased to £3,000 by the Second Division of the Inner House. The number of machines sold by the defendant was 252, of which 130 were sold to the Java trade. There was evidence that the plaintiff would not have made these sales.

Lord Shaw:

In my opinion, the case does raise sharply an important question as to the assessment of damages in patent cases, and with that question I proceed to deal. It is probably a mistake in language to treat the methods usually adopted in ascertaining the measure of damages in patent cases as principles. They are the practical working rules which have seemed helpful to judges in arriving at a true estimate of the compensation which ought to be awarded against an infringer to a patentee. In the case of damages in general, there is one principle which does underlie the assessment. It is what may be called that of restoration. The idea is to restore the person who has sustained injury and loss to the condition in which he would have been had he not so sustained it. In the cases of financial loss, injury to trade, and the like, caused either by breach of contract or by tort, the loss is capable of correct appre-ciation in stated figures. In a second class of cases, restoration being in point of fact difficult, as in the case of loss of reputation, or impossible, as in the case of loss of life, faculty, or limb, the task of restoration under the name of compensation calls into play inference, conjecture, and the like. This is necessarily accompanied by those deficiencies which attach to the conversion into money of certain elements which are very real, which go to make up the happiness and usefulness of life, but which were never so converted or measured. The restoration by way of compensation is therefore accomplished to a large extent by the exercise of a sound imagination and the practice of the broad axe. It is in such cases, my Lords, whether the result has been attained by the verdict of a jury or the finding of a single judge, that the greatest weight attaches to the decision of the Court of First Instance. The reasons for this are not far to seek—such as the value of testimony at first hand, down to even the nuances of its expression, and they include, of course, the attitude and demeanour of the witnesses themselves. In all these cases, however, the attempt which justice makes is to get back to the *status quo ante* in fact, or to reach imaginatively, by the process of compensation, a result in which the same principle is followed. In patent cases the principle of restoration is in all instances to some extent, and in many instances to the entire extent dependent upon the same principle of restoration. The patentee may show that the trade done by the infringer would have been his (the patentee's) trade, and he is entitled in such cases to be restored against the action of the infringer; and he may adopt, in liquidating that principle in money, an alternative course. He may say, "I shall accept the profits which have been made by the infringer in this trade which ought to have been my trade;" or he may take the other head of the alternative and say, "The illicit opposition to, and interference with, my own trade caused me damage. I lost profit which I would have otherwise made in it; I lost business connexion; the development of my business on its natural lines was interrupted by my being driven by these acts of piracy out of sections of my own trade." These and other things may be heads of damage ... In the course, however, of deciding cases, certain expressions have been used by learned judges, which, according to the contention, are to the effect, or truly mean, that if the patentee chooses the latter course, namely, to reckon up his claim under heads of damage, he is limited, so to speak, by the principle of restoration. Phrases, for instance, have been used, which it is said imply that the entire measure of his damage is the loss which has incurred of the trade done in the pirated articles. ...

It is at this stage of the case, however, my Lords, that a second principle comes into play. It is not exactly the principle of restoration, either directly or expressed through compensation, but it is the principle underlying price or hire. It plainly extends—and I am inclined to think not infrequently extends to patent cases. But, indeed, it is not confined to them. For wherever an abstraction or invasion of property has occurred, then, unless such abstraction or invasion were to be sanctioned by law, the law ought to yield a recompense under the category or principle, as I say, either of price or of hire. If A, being a liveryman, keeps his horse standing idle in the stable, and B, against his wish or without his knowledge, rides or drives it out, it is no answer to A for B to say: "Against what loss do you want to be restored? I restore the horse. There is no loss. The horse is none the worse; it is the better for the exercise." ... [I will] assume that the respondents would not have done the Java trade in the 130 machines sold in that island by the infringers, and containing the patented part. The argument is—for indeed this instance covers sufficiently the whole ground—the argument is: Here it is demonstrated that the respondents have lost no trade which they could have obtained; and under the cover of certain judicial dicta the infringers are entitled to say that the entire measure of the respondents' damage is exhausted when restoration of the *status quo ante* has been obtained ... [S]uppose the respondents had chosen to ask for an account of the profits made by the infringers upon the infringing machines, they would have been entitled to obtain it, and a decree for the amount, and it would have been no answer to say: "The account shall be given, but there shall be excluded from it places which we shall establish your trade would never have reached." ...

[I]n such cases it appears to me that the correct and full measure is only reached by adding that a patentee is also entitled, on the principle of price or hire, to a royalty for the unauthorised sale or use of every one of the infringing machines in a market which the infringer, if left to himself, might not have reached. Otherwise, that property which consists in the monopoly of the patented articles granted to the patentee has been invaded, and indeed abstracted, and the law, when appealed to, would be standing by and allowing the invader or abstractor to go free. In such cases a royalty is an excellent key to unlock the difficulty, and I am in entire accord with the principle laid down by Lord Moulton in *Meters Ltd v Metropolitan Gas Meters Ltd* (1911) 28 R.P.C. 163. Each of the infringements was an actionable wrong, and although it may have been committed in a range of business or of territory which the patentee might not have reached, he is entitled to hire or royalty in respect of each unauthorised use of his property. Otherwise, the remedy might fall unjustly short of the wrong.

1.3.4.3 Patents Act 1977, ss.62, 63: Remedies, Limitation upon Relief

S.62(1) In proceedings for infringement of a patent damages shall not be awarded, and no order shall be made for an account of profits, against a defendant or defender who proves that at the date of the infringement he was not aware, and had no reasonable grounds for supposing, that the patent existed; and a person shall not be taken to have been so aware or to have had reasonable grounds for so supposing by reason only of the application to a product of the word "patent" or "patented", or any word or words expressing or implying that a patent has been obtained for the product, unless the number of the patent accompanied the word or words in question.

(2) In proceedings for infringement of a patent the court or the comptroller may, if it or he thinks fit, refuse to award any damages or make any such order in respect of an infringement committed during any further period specified under section 25(4) above, but before the payment of the renewal fee and any additional fee prescribed for the purposes of that subsection.

(3) Where an amendment of the specification of a patent has been allowed under any of the provisions of this Act, no damages shall be awarded in proceedings for an infringement of the patent committed before the decision to allow the amendment unless the court or the comptroller is satisfied that the specification of the patent as published was framed in good faith and with reasonable skill and knowledge.

S.63(1) If the validity of a patent is put in issue in proceedings for infringement of the patent and it is found that the patent is only partially valid, the court or the comptroller may, subject to subsection (2) below, grant relief in respect of that part of the patent which if found to be valid and infringed.

(2) Where in any such proceedings it is found that a patent is only partially valid, the court or the comptroller shall not grant relief by way of damages, costs or expenses, except where the plaintiff or pursuer proves that the specification for the patent was framed in good faith and with reasonable skill and knowledge, and in that event the court or the comptroller may grant relief in respect of that part of the patent which is valid and infringed, subject to the discretion of the court or the comptroller as to costs or expenses and as to the date from which damages should be reckoned.

(3) As a condition of relief under this section the court or the comptroller may direct that the specification of the patent shall be amended to its or his satisfaction upon an application made for that purpose under section 75 below, and an application may be so made accordingly, whether or not all other issues in the proceedings have been determined.

Note also: s.65—Certificate of contested validity; ss.66, 67—Proceedings for infringement by a co-owner, and by an exclusive licensee; s.68—Effect of non-registration of a transaction, etc., on infringement proceedings; s.69—Infringement of rights, conferred by publication of application; s.71—Declaration of non-infringement. For threats proceedings under s.70, see below, 7.1.3.1.

1.4 Ownership and Dealings

1.4.1 Ownership: General

1.4.1.1 Patents Act 1977, s.7: Right to apply for and obtain a patent

S.7(1) Any person may make an application for a patent either alone or jointly with another.

(2) A patent for an invention may be granted—

    (a) primarily to the inventor or joint inventors;

    (b) in preference to the foregoing, to any person or persons who, by virtue of any enactment or rule of law, or any foreign law or treaty or international convention, or by virtue of an enforceable term of any agreement entered into with the inventor before the making of the invention, was or were at the time of the making of the invention entitled to the whole of the property in it (other than equitable interests) in the United Kingdom;

    (c) in any event, to the successor or successors in title of any person or persons mentioned in paragraph (a) or (b) above or any person so mentioned and the successor or successors in title of another person so mentioned;

and to no other person.

(3) In this Act "inventor" in relation to an invention means the actual deviser of the invention and "joint inventor" shall be construed accordingly.

(4) Except so far as the contrary is established, a person who makes an application for a patent shall be taken to be the person who is entitled under subsection (2) above to be granted a patent and two or more persons who make such an application jointly shall be taken to be the persons so entitled.

Note also: s.8—Determination before grant of questions about entitlement; s.9—Determination after grant of questions referred before grant; s.10—Handling of application by joint applicants; s.11—Effect of transfer of application under s.8 or 10; s.12—Determination of questions about entitlements to foreign and convention patents, etc; s.37—Determination of right to patent after grant; s.38—Effect of transfer under s.37.

1.4.2 Transactions

1.4.2.1 Patents Act 1977, ss.30, 33: Transactions; Registration

S.30(1) Any patent or application for a patent is personal property (without being a thing in action), and any patent or any such application and rights in or under it may be transferred, created or granted in accordance with subsections (2) to (7) below.

(2) Subject to section 36(3) below, any patent or any such application, or any right in it, may be assigned or mortgaged.

(3) Any patent or any such application or right shall vest by operation of law in the same way as any other personal property and may be vested by an assent of personal representatives.

(4) Subject to section 36(3) below, a licence may be granted under any patent or any such application for working the invention which is the subject of the patent or the application; and—

    (a) to the extent that the licence so provides, a sub-licence may be granted under any such licence and any such licence or sub-licence may be assigned or mortgaged; and

    (b) any such licence or sub-licence shall vest by operation of law in the same way as any other personal property and may be vested by an assent of personal representatives.

(5) Subsections (2) to (4) above shall have effect subject to the following provisions of this Act.

(6) Any of the following transactions, that is to say—

    (a) any assignment or mortgage of a patent or any such application, or any right in a patent or any such application;

    (b) any assent relating to any patent or any such application or right;

shall be void unless it is in writing and is signed by or on behalf of the parties to the transaction (or, in the case of an assent or other transaction by a personal representative, by or on behalf of the personal representative) or in the case of a body corporate is so signed or is under the seal of that body.

(7) An assignment of a patent or any such application or a share in it, and an exclusive licence granted under any patent or any such application, may confer on the assignee or licensee the right of the assignor or licensor to bring proceedings by virtue of section 61 or 69 below for a previous infringement or to bring proceedings under section 58 below for a previous act.

Note: s.32 (amended 1986) creating Register of Patents.

S.33 Effect of registration, etc., on rights in patents
(1) Any person who claims to have acquired the property in a patent or application for a patent by virtue of any transaction, instrument or event to which this section applies shall be entitled as against any other person who claims to have acquired that property by virtue of an earlier transaction, instrument or event to which this section applies if, at the time of the later transaction, instrument or event—

    (a) the earlier transaction, instrument or event was not registered, or

    (b) in the case of any application which has not been published, notice of the earlier transaction, instrument or event had not been given to the comptroller, and (c) in any case, the person claiming under the later transaction, instrument or event, did not know of the earlier transaction, instrument or event.

(2) Subsection (1) above shall apply equally to the case where any person claims to have acquired any right in or under a patent or application for a patent, by virtue of a transaction, instrument or event to which this section applies, and that right is incompatible with any such right acquired by virtue of an earlier transaction, instrument or event to which this section applies.

(3) This section applies to the following transactions, instruments and events:

(a) The assignment or assignation of a patent or application for a patent, or a right in it;

(b) the mortgage of a patent or application or the granting of security over it;

(c) the grant, assignment or assignation of a licence or sub-licence, or mortgage of a licence or sub-licence, under a patent or application;

(d) the death of the proprietor or one of the proprietors of any such patent or application of any person having a right in or under a patent or application and the vesting by an assent of personal representatives of a patent, application or any such right; and

(e) any order or directions of a court or other competent authority—

    (i) transferring a patent or application or any right in or under it to any person; or

    (ii) that an application should proceed in the name of any person; and in either case the event by virtue of which the court or authority had power to make any such order or give any such directions.

(4) Where an application for the registration of a transaction, instrument or event has been made, but the transaction, instrument or event has not been registered, then, for the purposes of subsection (1)(a) above, registration of the application shall be treated as registration of the transaction, instrument or event.

1.4.3 Co-ownership

1.4.3.1 Patents Act 1977, s.36: Joint Ownership

S.36(1) Where a patent is granted to two or more persons, each of them shall, subject to any agreement to the contrary, be entitled to an equal undivided share in the patent.

(2) Where two or more persons are proprietors of a patent, then, subject to the provisions of this section and subject to any agreement to the contrary—

(a) each of them shall be entitled, by himself or his agents, to do in respect of the invention concerned, for his own benefit and without the consent of or the need to account to the other or others, any act which would apart from this subsection and section 55 below, amount to an infringement of the patent concerned; and

(b) any such act shall not amount to an infringement of the patent concerned.

(3) Subject to the provisions of section 8 and 12 above and section 37 below and to any agreement for the time being in force, where two or more persons are proprietors of a patent one of them shall not without the consent of the other or others grant a licence under the patent or assign or mortgage a share in the patent or in Scotland cause or permit security to be granted over it.

(4) Subject to the provisions of those sections, where two or more persons are proprietors of a patent, anyone else may supply one of those persons with the means, relating to an essential element of the invention, for putting the invention into effect, and the supply of those means by virtue of this subsection shall not amount to an infringement of the patent.

(5) Where a patented product is disposed of by any of two or more proprietors to any person, that person and any other person claiming through him shall be entitled to deal with the product in the same way as if it had been disposed of by a sole registered proprietor.

(6) Nothing in subsection (1) or (2) above shall affect the mutual rights or obligations of trustees or of the personal representatives of a deceased person, or their rights or obligations as such.

(7) The foregoing provisions of this section shall have effect in relation to an application for a patent which is filed as they have effect in relation to a patent and—

(a) references to a patent and a patent being granted shall accordingly include references respectively to any such application and to the application being filed; and

(b) the reference in subsection (5) above to a patented product shall be construed accordingly.

1.4.4 Employees' Inventions

1.4.4.1 European Patent Convention, Art. 60(1): Right to a European patent

Art. 60(1) The right to a European patent shall belong to the inventor or his successor in title. If the inventor is an employee the right to the European patent shall be determined in accordance with the law of the State in which the employee is mainly employed; if the State in which the employee is mainly employed cannot be determined, the law to be applied shall be that of the State in which the employer has his place of business to which the employee is attached.

1.4.4.2 Patents Act 1977, s.39 (as amended by the Copyright, Designs and Patents Act 1988, Sch. 5, para. 11(1): Right to employees' inventions)

S.39(1) Notwithstanding anything in any rule of law, an invention made by an employee shall, as between him and his employer, be taken to belong to his employer for the purposes of this Act and all other purposes if—

  (a) it was made in the course of normal duties of the employee or in the course of duties falling outside his normal duties, but specifically assigned to him, and the circumstances in either case were such that an invention might reasonably be expected to result from the carrying out of his duties; or

  (b) the invention was made in the course of the duties of the employee and, at the time of making the invention, because of the nature of his duties and the particular responsibilities arising from the nature of his duties he had a special obligation to further the interests of the employer's undertaking.

(2) Any other invention made by an employee shall, as between him and his employer, be taken for those purposes to belong to the employee.

(3) Where by virtue of this section an invention belongs, as between him and his employer, to an employee, nothing done—

  (a) by or on behalf of the employee or any person claiming under him for the purposes of pursuing an application for a patent, or

  (b) by any person for the purpose of performing or working the invention,

shall be taken to infringe any copyright or design right to which, as between him and his employer, his employer is entitled in any model or document relating to the invention.

1.4.4.3 *Worthington Pumping Engine v Moore* (1903) 20 R.P.C. 41, Byrne J.

Moore acted as general manager for the foreign business of the plaintiff, an American pump corporation. He was employed at a high salary and was in effect the alter ego of the plaintiff corporation outside the US He developed improvements in the plaintiff's pumps which resulted in his making two patent applications in his own name.

Byrne J.:

Both patents were taken out by the defendant without communication of his intention to do so to the plaintiff corporation, and they remained in ignorance of the fact that the patents existed until a short time before the defendant's dismissal, and the defendant acted, during the whole of the time of his service subsequent to taking out the patents by advertising, giving orders for pumps made in accordance with the patents, and otherwise, in a manner only consistent with good faith if he recognised that the plaintiff corporation were entitled to treat the subject-matter of the patents as their own. A great amount of evidence was adduced, and a large number of sketches, drawings, and copies of drawings called "blue prints", which are reproductions, by process, of drawings, were put in and dealt with in much detail in the course of the case.

In the result I think it is proved that everything in both patents disclaimed, and also the cross-over ports and the independent passage in Patent No. 4302 were represented in drawings belonging to the plaintiff corporation prior to instructions being given for taking out the patents. There is no reasonable colour for any claim for a patent on the part of the defendant for anything in these patents unless it be in respect of the piston valves having two heads at each end of the piston rod, and the concentric arrangement of valves in one plane. As to these, though I think that the idea of getting rid of stuffing boxes and of substituting the introduction of steam between two heads of the piston rod at each end were due to the defendant, yet the realisation of the idea and bringing it to a practical result belongs, if the evidence adduced by the defendant is to be relied on, to Marichal, another servant of the plaintiff corporation, working as a servant in the ordinary course of his employment, under the direction of the defendant. As to the other matter, I think that the idea of the detail of construction so far as putting concentric rings in one plane is concerned, is probably due to the defendant. It appears to me that every drawing supplied to Mr Marks, the patent agent acting in the matter of preparing the Specifications, Provisional and Complete, were documents which were brought into existence for the purposes of the corporation and by their servants, except such as are due to J. Simpson & Co Ltd, in the ordinary course of their duty at the expense of the corporation and without a notion of securing a patent for the defendant at the expense of the corporation.

I propose now to deal with the principles of law applicable to the case; and, first, I desire to say that I recognise and quite appreciate the principle of those cases which have established that the mere existence of a contract of service does not *per se* disqualify a servant from taking out a patent for an invention made by him during his term of service, even though the invention may relate to subject-matter germane to and useful for his employers in their business, and that, even though the servant may have made use of his employer's time and servants and materials in bringing his invention to completion, and may have allowed his employers to use the invention while in their employment; but, on the other hand, without repeating what has been so fully and admirably expressed by the Court of Appeal in the two cases of *Lamb v Evans*, L.R. [1893] 1 Ch. 218, and *Robb v Green*, L.R. [1895] 2 Q.B. 315 it is clear that all the circumstances must be considered in each case. I consider that, bearing in mind the principles laid down in the authorities to which I have referred, it is impossible to say in the present case that the defendant has established the right he claims, having regard to the obligations to be implied arising from his contract of service, and I am of opinion that his case is inconsistent with an observance of that good faith which ought properly to be inferred or implied as an obligation arising from his contract.

Having regard to the nature and scope of the defendant's employment, to the obligations and duties arising from such employment, to the trust reposed in him, to his own conduct in endeavouring to establish a trade for his employers in the very articles he, in the action brought by him against them, sought to preclude them from using, I think I should be wrong in holding that he is entitled to continue to hold his patents as against the plaintiff corporation, even with the belated undertakings which his counsel offered to give on his behalf.

1.4.4.4   *British Syphon v Homewood* **[1956] R.P.C. 225, Roxburgh J.**

The defendant was employed by the plaintiff company as chief technician, advising on all technical matters relating to their business and in charge of design and development. He invented a novel method of dispensing soda water that kept the remaining contents in better condition than any prior device. Shortly before leaving the plaintiff's employ for a rival firm, he applied to patent the device. The plaintiff sought an assignment of this application.

Roxburgh J. first considered whether the defendant made the invention only after a date on which his terms of employment were so changed as to leave him free to keep it. The judge concluded that the invention was made before this date and that the defendant had given false evidence on the matter.

Now that, to my mind, leads to the difficult and unexplored point of law. It is common ground that the defendant had not been expressly asked to design any new method of dispensing soda water by a low-pressure system or any other system, and that he had not been asked to give any advice in relation to any such problem. This is the circumstance which, as far as I can see, differentiates this case from all that have gone before. I cannot find even an oblique discussion of this problem anywhere in the many authorities which the industry of counsel has disclosed. I revert, then, to the defendant's position. He was employed to give the plaintiffs technical advice in relation to the design or development of anything connected with any part of the plaintiffs' business. No particular problem had been put before him, but if, and as often has, any problem of that kind was put before him, it was his duty to be ready to tender his advice and to assist in any matter of design or development. He was, as I put it during the argument, standing by, and paid to stand by, in that respect. He had other functions, but those are not material to the present case.

Now, would it be consistent with good faith, as between master and servant, that he should in that position be entitled to make some invention in relation to a matter concerning a part of the plaintiffs' business and either keep it from his employer, if and when asked about the problem, or even sell it to a rival and say: "Well, yes, I know the answer to your problem, but I have already sold it to your rival"?

In my judgment, that cannot be consistent with a relationship of good faith between a master and a technical adviser. It seems to me that he has a duty not to put himself in a position in which he may have personal reasons for not giving his employer the best advice which it is his duty to give if and when asked to give it. Of course, what I am saying only relates to matters concerning the business of his employer. That, of course, is quite clear; but, in matters of that type, it seems to me that he has a duty to be free from any personal reason for not giving his employer the best possible advice. *A fortiori*, it seems to me that he is not entitled to put himself into the position of being able to say: "Well, you retained me to advise you, and I will tell you what I advise you. Do it this way, but you will have to buy the method from your rival, because I have just sold it to him, having invented it yesterday".

That seems to me to be reasoning which, in the absence of authority, makes it right and proper for me to decide that this invention (which, in my judgment, plainly relates to and concerns the business of the plaintiff company, namely, the distribution of soda water to the public in containers of a satisfactory character), if made during a time during which the chief technician is standing by under the terms of his employment, must be held to be in equity the property of the employer. Accordingly, my decision is for the plaintiffs.

The plaintiffs were given relief as follows: An order that the defendant assign to the plaintiffs the patent when granted: an order that the defendant execute any additional necessary documents relating to the invention; and an injunction against disclosure of the invention. The defendant was ordered to pay the costs of the action.

1.4.4.5 *Harris's Patent* [1985] R.P.C. 19, Falconer J.

Wey valves are used to control the flow of coal dust and similar material through chutes and ducts. Reiss Engineering manufactured Wey valves under licence from a Swiss company, Sistag. Harris was employed (at a salary of £6,900 in 1978) as manager of Reiss's Wey valve division. In August 1978 he was notified of redundancy and left in December 1978. In between he invented an improved valve which he subsequently applied to patent. Reiss Engineering sought, by reference under the Patents Act 1977, ss.8 and 37, to establish its ownership of the right to apply and patent as Harris's employer.

Falconer J. referred to the 1977 Act, s.39 as the source of substantive principle concerning employees' inventions. He continued:

Mr Pumfrey, for the appellants, submitted that it was common ground that paragraphs (a) and (b) of section 39(1) reflected the prior law; and Miss Vitoria, for Mr Harris, submitted that section 39 was declaratory of the common law position. No doubt it is true that subsection (1) of section 39 reflects, at least to a considerable degree, the prior law developed in the authorities as to the rights, as between employer and employee, in inventions made by employees, but I wish to make it clear that I am not to be taken as holding that section 39 is declaratory of the previous common law position in that regard, for, as at present advised, I entertain some doubt as to whether section 39 is so declaratory of the common law position. It is not necessary to decide that point for the purposes of this appeal, and I leave it open.

However, it seems to me to be quite clear from the language of section 39—see the opening six words and the wording of subsection (2)—that the intention of the legislature was that rights, as between employer and employee, in any employee's invention made after the appointed day are to be governed by, and only by, the provisions of section 39, and that is reinforced by the provisions of section 42(1) and (2), which render unenforceable against an employee any contractual provision which diminishes his rights under section 39.

I have referred to this aspect because I have had cited to me, as did the superintending examiner, a number of the well-known cases concerning employees' inventions decided under the law as developed in the earlier authorities. No doubt, guidance may be obtained from such previous cases as to how courts have assessed the duties of the employee in a particular case and particular circumstances; but, having regard to the clear opening words of section 39, it is the provisions of section 39 to which regard must be had for the law governing any employee's invention made after the appointed day.

Falconer J. noted the submission that this invention belonged to the employer, under s.39(1)(a), as (i) having been made in the course of normal duties and (ii) the circumstances were such that an invention might reasonably be expected to result from the carrying out of the duties. He continued:

As to the second requirement in the paragraph, that is to say, whether the circumstances were such that an invention might reasonably be expected to result from his carrying out those duties, Miss Vitoria submitted that the circumstances referred to in paragraph (a) must be the circumstances in which the invention was made: and it seems to me that submission might be right. Mr Pumfrey, in the course of his argument, pointed out that the wording of the paragraph was "an invention might reasonably be expected to result" and not "the invention might" and so on. But plainly, the wording "an invention" cannot mean any invention whatsoever; it is governed by the qualification that it has to be an invention that "might reasonably be expected to result from the carrying out of his duties" by the employee. That wording applies equally to the second alternative in paragraph (a), that of "specifically assigned" duties falling outside the employee's normal duties; and, therefore, in my judgment the wording "an invention might reasonably be expected to result from the carrying out of his duties" must be referring to an invention which achieves, or contributes to achieving, whatever was the aim or object to which the employee's efforts in carrying out his duties were directed, in the case of alternative (i) of paragraph (a) his normal duties being performed at the time; in the case of alternative (ii) of paragraph (a) the specifically assigned duties, that is to say, such an invention as that made, though not necessarily the precise invention actually made and in question. The circumstances to be taken into account for the purposes of paragraph (a) of section 39(1) will, of course, depend on the particular case, but clearly a circumstance which must always loom large will be the nature of the employee's duties, either his normal duties or the specifically assigned duties, as the case may be. The nature of Mr Harris's normal duties have to be examined, therefore, from this aspect also.

Falconer J. proceeded to find that Harris's duties as manager were confined to selling Wey valves and dealing in the first instance with the difficulties of customers. If these difficulties were technical he was expected to refer them to Sistag for solution. Reiss Engineering conducted no research and on one occasion when Harris suggested a technical improvement, Reiss's managing director indicated that he had no interest in it. In consequence, it was held to be no part of his employment to perform duties that might result in invention. Accordingly, the patent properly belonged to Harris under s.39(2).

1.4.4.6 *Electrolux v Hudson* **[1977] F.S.R. 312, Whitford J.**

The first defendant, Hudson, was employed as a senior storekeeper by the plaintiff company, which manufactured vacuum cleaners. In collaboration at home with his wife (second defendant), Hudson devised an adaptor for connecting a dust-bag to a vacuum cleaner. Together they applied to patent it, but the plaintiff claimed to be entitled to it by virtue of the terms, express and implied, of Hudson's employment. The plaintiff contended that the following standard term was a condition of that employment:

(a) If at any time during the period of your employment, you shall invent, discover or ascertain any process, invention or improvement (whether patentable or not) relating to any articles manufactured and/or marketed by the company or its associated companies or undertakings or firms in the United Kingdom or elsewhere, you shall forthwith, at the expense of the company, disclose to the company or any agent appointed by it, a full and complete description of the nature of the said process, invention, discovery or improvement and the mode of performing it, and the said process, invention, discovery or improvement shall remain the sole and absolute property of the company; and you shall, if and when required by the company, at the expense of the company, join with the company in applying for letters patent for the said process, invention, discovery or improvement (if patentable) and/or other similar protection in any part of the world and shall on the request by, and at the cost of, the company, execute and do all such instruments and things necessary to test the said process, invention, discovery or improvement, and any letters patent and/or other similar protection that may be obtained relating thereto, in the company or otherwise as the company may direct.

(b) Should the company consider the said process, discovery, invention, or improvement, to be of such importance that your usual remuneration is inadequate compensation for it, the company will make you an allowance and in fixing such allowance, special consideration will be given to the fact of whether the said process, discovery, invention or improvement is outside the scope of your normal duties and has not been invented, discovered, or ascertained as a result of the experience you have gained in the employment of the company. The company's decision as to making the said allowance and as to the amount thereof is final and is binding on you.

Whitford J. referred to Schroeder v Macaulay *[1974] 3 All E.R. 616:*

Lord Diplock says that what you have got to consider when you have to come to a conclusion as to whether a particular restraint is enforceable is whether the bargain in question was a fair bargain, whether the restrictions imposed were reasonably necessary for the protection of the legitimate interests of the person imposing the restrictions, and also whether they were commensurate with the benefit secured by the person on whom the restriction was imposed.

Of course, if you employ somebody to make inventions or do research you pay them at a rather different rate than the rate at which Mr Hudson was employed as a storeman. His salary in 1971 was £1,302 per annum. It may no doubt have been subsequently increased, though nobody bothered to lead any evidence about it. But one can take it that this was just the sort of salary that was paid to a storeman; it is not the sort of salary that is paid to a research worker. He was not employed to do research or to make inventions, and it is to my mind absurd to suggest that it could reasonably have been necessary in the protection of the interests of the plaintiffs to impose upon Mr Hudson a restraint in respect of any processes, inventions or improvements relating not only to articles manufactured by the plaintiffs, and which might be in store at the depot where he was a storeman, but also relating to articles manufactured or marketed by any of the associated undertakings, companies or firms, the diversity of whose activities I have already briefly made reference to. This clause is much too wide to be enforceable as against Mr Hudson.

His Lordship proceeded to find that there was no basis on which to separate out a more limited obligation to disclose any invention that the plaintiff had made. Nor could he find any implied undertaking upon Hudson to hold the invention for the plaintiff, since he was not employed to invent and he had made the invention outside working hours without using his employers' materials.

1.4.4.7   Patents Act 1977, ss.40–43: Compensation of employees for certain inventions

S.40(1) Where it appears to the court or the comptroller on an application made by an employee within the prescribed period that the employee has made an invention belonging to the employer for which a patent has been granted, that the patent is (having regard among other things to the size and nature of the employer's undertaking) of outstanding benefit to the employer and that by reason of those facts it is just that the employee should be awarded

compensation to be paid by the employer, the court or the comptroller may award him such compensation of an amount determined under section 41 below.

(2) Where it appears to the court or the comptroller on an application made by an employee within the prescribed period that—

(a) a patent has been granted for an invention made by and belonging to the employee;

(b) his rights in the invention, or in any patent or application for a patent for the invention, have since the appointed day been assigned to the employer or an exclusive licence under the patent or application has since the appointed day been granted to the employer;

(c) the benefit derived by the employee from the contract of assignment assignation or grant or any ancillary contract ("the relevant contract") is inadequate in relation to the benefit derived by the employer from the patent; and

(d) by reason of those facts it is just that the employee should be awarded compensation to be paid by the employer in addition to the benefit derived from the relevant contract;

the court or the comptroller may award him such compensation of an amount determined under section 41 below.

(3) Subsections (1) and (2) above shall not apply to the invention of an employee where a relevant collective agreement provides for the payment of compensation in respect of inventions of the same description as that invention to employees of the same description as that invention to employees of the same description as that employee.

(4) Subsection (2) above shall have effect notwithstanding anything in the relevant contract or any agreement applicable to the invention (other than any such collective agreement).

(5) If it appears to the comptroller on an application under this section that the application involves matters which would more properly be determined by the court, he may decline to deal with it.

(6) In this section—

"the prescribed period", in relation to proceedings before the court, means the period prescribed by rules of court, and "relevant collective agreement" means a collective agreement within the meaning of the Trade Union and Labour Relations (Consolidation) Act 1992, made by or on behalf of a trade union to which the employee belongs, and by the employer or an employers' association to which the employer belongs which is in force at the time of the making of the invention.

(7) References in this section to an invention belonging to an employer or employee are references to it so belonging as between the employer and the employee.

S.41 Amount of compensation
(1) An award of compensation to an employee under section 41(1) or (2) above in relation to a patent for an invention shall be such as will secure for the employee a fair share (having regard to all the circumstances) of the benefit which the employer has derived, or may reasonably be expected to derive, from the patent or from the assignment, assignation or grant to a person connected with the employer of the property or any right in the invention or the property in, or any right in or under, an application for that patent.

(2) For the purposes of subsection (1) above the amount of any benefit derived or expected to be derived by an employer from the assignment, assignation or grant of—

    (a) the property in, or any right in or under, a patent for the invention or an application for such a patent; or

    (b) the property or any right in the invention;

to a person connected with him shall be taken to be the amount which could reasonably be expected to be so derived by the employer if that person had not been connected with him.

(3) Where the Crown or a Research Council in its capacity as employer assigns or grants the property in, or any right in or under, an invention, patent or application for a patent to a body having among its functions that of developing or exploiting inventions resulting from public research and does so for no consideration or only a nominal consideration, any benefit derived from the invention, patent or application by that body shall be treated for the purposes of the foregoing provisions of this section as so derived by the Crown or, as the case may be, Research Council.

In this subsection "Research Council" means a body which is a Research Council for the purposes of the Science and Technology Act 1965.

(4) In determining the fair share of the benefit to be secured for an employee in respect of a patent for an invention which has always belonged to an employer, the court or the comptroller shall, among other things, take the following matters into account, that is to say—

    (a) the nature of the employee's duties, his remuneration and the other advantages he derives or has derived from his employment or has derived in relation to the invention under this Act;

    (b) the effort and skill which the employee has devoted to making the invention;

    (c) the effort and skill which any other person has devoted to making the invention jointly with the employee concerned, and the advice and other assistance contributed by any other employee who is not a joint inventor of the invention; and

    (d) the contribution made by the employer to the making, developing and working of the invention by the provision of advice, facilities and other assistance, by the provision of opportunities and by his managerial and commercial skill and activities.

(5) In determining the fair share of the benefit to be secured for an employee in respect of a patent for an invention which originally belonged to him, the court or the comptroller shall, among other things, take the following matters into account, that is to say—

    (a) any conditions in a licence or licences granted under this Act or otherwise in respect of the invention or the patent;

    (b) the extent to which the invention was made jointly by the employee with any other person; and

    (c) the contribution made by the employer to the making, developing and working of the invention as mentioned in subsection (4)(d) above.

Section 41(6) provides for lump sum or periodic payments, s.41(7) for further applications, s.41(8) for variation, discharge or suspension of orders and s.41(9)–(11) for execution.

S.42 Enforceability of contracts relating to employee's inventions
(1) This section applies to any contract (whenever made) relating to inventions made by an employee, being a contract entered into by him—

(a) with the employer (alone or with another); or

(b) with some other person at the request of the employer or in pursuance of the employee's contract of employment.

(2) Any term in a contract to which this section applies which diminishes the employee's rights in inventions of any description made by him after the appointed day and the date of the contract, or in or under patents for those inventions or applications for such patents, shall be unenforceable against him to the extent that it diminishes his rights in an invention of that description so made, or in or under a patent for such an invention or an application for any such patent.

(3) Subsection (2) above shall not be construed as derogating from any duty of confidentiality owed to his employer by an employee by virtue of any rule of law or otherwise.

(4) This section applies to any arrangement made with a Crown employee by or on behalf of the Crown as his employer as it applies to any contract made between an employee and an employer other than the Crown, and for the purposes of this section "Crown employee" means a person employed under or for the purposes of a government department or any officer or body exercising on behalf of the Crown functions conferred by any enactment or a person serving in the naval, military or air forces of the Crown.

S.43 Supplementary
(1) Sections 39 to 42 above shall not apply to any invention made before the appointed day.

(2) Sections 39 to 42 above shall not apply to an invention made by an employee unless at the time he made the invention one of the following conditions was satisfied in his case, that is to say—

(a) he was mainly employed in the United Kingdom; or

(b) he was not mainly employed anywhere or his place of employment could not be determined, but his employer had a place of business in the United Kingdom to which the employee was attached, whether or not he was also attached elsewhere.

(3) In sections 39 to 42 above and this section, except so far as the context otherwise requires, references to the making of an invention by an employee are references to his making it alone or jointly with any other person, but do not include references to his merely contributing advice or other assistance in the making of an invention by another employee.

(4) Any references in sections 40 to 42 above to a patent and to a patent being granted are respectively references to a patent or other protection and to its being granted whether under the law of the United Kingdom or the law in force in any other country or under any treaty or international convention.

(5) For the purposes of sections 40 and 41 above the benefit derived or expected to be derived by an employer from a patent shall, where he dies before any award is made under section 40 above in respect of the patent, include any benefit derived or expected to be derived from the patent by his personal representatives or by any person in whom it was vested by their assent.

(6) Where an employee dies before an award is made under section 40 above in respect of a patented invention made by him, his personal representatives or their successors in title may

exercise his right to make or proceed with an application for compensation under subsection (1) or (2) of that section.

(7) In sections 40 and 41 above and this section "benefit" means benefit in money or money's worth.

(8) Section 533 of the Income and Corporation Taxes Act 1970 (definition of connected persons) shall apply for determining for the purposes of section 41(2) above whether one person is connected with another as it applies for determining that question for the purposes of the Tax Acts.

1.4.4.8   *Memco-Med Ltd's Patent* [1992] R.P.C. 403, Aldous J.

The applicant had assisted his employer, Memco-Med Ltd, to develop an improved model ("the R model") of door detector unit for lift doors, for which a patent had been obtained. After leaving his employment the applicant claimed that this invention was of outstanding benefit to Memco-Med Ltd and sought compensation from them pursuant to s.40(1) of the Patents Act 1977. Aldous J. said:

Section 40 draws a distinction between the patent and the invention; thus the task of the court is to ascertain whether the patent, not the invention, is of outstanding benefit to the employer, that benefit being a benefit in money or money's worth.

The benefit from the patent may be readily recognisable where the patent is licensed and royalties are paid. However, the task of the court will be more difficult in cases where an employer exploits the patent by manufacturing articles in accordance with the invention of the patent. In such cases, the court will need to differentiate between the benefit from using the inventive advance and that from the patent. It is also possible to imagine a case where the patent is not licensed and the invention is never put into practice, but the patent is of great benefit to the patentee to prevent activities which would compete with those carried on by the patentee.

Whether or not a patent is of outstanding benefit will depend on all the surrounding facts and in every case the court must ascertain whether the patent, as opposed to the invention, has been of outstanding benefit. In so doing it is apt to answer two questions:

(1) Has the patent been of benefit to the employer? To answer that question it is likely to be useful to assume that the patent was never granted due to some failure by the patent agents and thereafter to decide what would have been the position of the employer. It will then be possible to ascertain the benefit from the patent by comparing the actual position of the employer with the position he would have been in if the patent had not been granted, bearing in mind the benefit must be in money or money's worth.

(2) Is the benefit outstanding? The superintending examiner in this case quoted from the decision in *Ellis's Application* [*GEC Avionics Ltd's Patent*] [1992] R.P.C. 107 to the effect that the rationale being the requirement for outstanding benefit was that the employee had already received compensation for the invention through remuneration for his employment.

As was said in *Ellis's Application*:

"It is for this reason that the section (section 40 that is) uses the word 'outstanding' to qualify the benefit which would make it just that the employee should receive compensation. Moreover, it is noted that the word 'outstanding' is used rather than 'significant' or 'substantial' or other such term. It must be something out of the ordinary and not such as one would normally expect to arise from the results of the duties that the employee is paid for. It is, I think, for this reason that reference is made to the size and nature of the employer's undertaking, and that the benefit (to the employer) must be looked at in the total context of the activities of the employer concerned to see whether it is outstanding."

Dr Ferdinando in *Monks' Application [British Steel plc's Patent]* [1992] R.P.C. 117 said, at p.5 of the transcript:

"Thirdly, subsection (1) makes clear that the patent must be of 'outstanding' benefit if the application is to succeed. Mr Tritton submitted that, taken at face value, this indicated that the patent must stand out from the rest. In *Ellis*, the hearing officer noted that the statute did not use the words such as 'significant' or 'substantial', and opined that 'something out of the ordinary was required'. While Mr Tritton was plainly correct in describing 'outstanding' as a comparative term, I would regard it as going further than that, implying a superlative. The test I must apply in reaching my decision as to whether an award is warranted must be correspondingly stiff."

I do not disagree with the approaches of those superintending examiners. The word "outstanding" denotes something special and requires the benefit to be more than substantial or good. I believe that it is unwise to try to redefine the word "outstanding". Courts will recognise an outstanding benefit when it occurs.

The section requires the court to assess whether the benefit is outstanding, having regard among other things to the size and nature of the employer's undertaking. Thus the court must look at the employer's undertaking, which may be the whole or a division of the employer's business, and ascertain the benefit to the employer taking into account the size and nature of that business and all the surrounding circumstances.

The court accepted that over a period of five years the sales of the "R" model, which were all to a single customer (Otis), were of "great if not vital" importance to Memco-Med Ltd, but nevertheless held that the patent was not of outstanding benefit to it:

The fact that the sales of the "R" model were vital is a relevant consideration to decide whether the patent is of outstanding benefit but cannot be determinative. The existence of those sales is consistent with the case of Memco-Med, namely that all the sales were to Otis, that the sales resulted from the price and quality of the product and the good relationship Memco-Med had with Otis, and that the patent played no part in obtaining sales, let alone the profit from those sales. . . .

I have found it helpful when considering the evidence filed by the parties to look for indications as to whether Memco-Med would have sold any fewer detectors if the patent had not been granted. Although Mr Trett [the applicant] did suggest in his reply evidence that the patent had some effect upon other manufacturers and himself, I did not find that evidence convincing. The evidence does not establish that the patent has been of substantial benefit to Memco-Med, let alone of outstanding benefit.

The patent is not what is called a master patent, namely one which controls a particular type of product. Further, the sales of the "R" model were all to Otis, thus the patent could not have benefited Memco-Med unless it helped to secure sales to Otis. There is no evidence remote from Otis but the history of the relationship between Otis and Memco-Med supports the conclusion that their business relationship would have been the same whether or not a patent had been granted. . . .

1.4.5   Compulsory Licences and Crown Use

1.4.5.1   Patents Act 1977, ss.48, 48A: Compulsory licences

Compulsory licences: general

S.48(1) At any time after the expiration of three years, or of such other period as may be prescribed, from the date of the grant of a patent, any person may apply to the comptroller on one or more of the relevant grounds—

  (a) for a licence under the patent;

  (b) for an entry to be made in the register to the effect that licences under the patent are to be available as of right; or

  (c) where the applicant is a government department, for the grant to any person specified in the application of a licence under the patent.

(2) Subject to sections 48A and 48B below, if he is satisfied that any of the relevant grounds are established, the comptroller may—

  (a) where the application is under subsection (1)(a) above, order the grant of a licence to the applicant on such terms as the comptroller thinks fit;

  (b) where the application is under subsection (1)(b) above, make such an entry as is there mentioned;

  (c) where the application is under subsection (1)(c) above, order the grant of a licence to the person specified in the application on such terms as the comptroller sees fit.

(3) An application may be made under this section in respect of a patent event though the applicant is already the holder of a licence under the patent; and no person shall be estopped or barred from alleging any of the matters specified in the relevant grounds by reason of any admission made by him, whether in such a licence or otherwise, or by reason of his having accepted a licence.

(4) In this section "the relevant grounds" means—

  (a) in the case of an application made in respect of a patent whose proprietor is a WTO proprietor, the grounds set out in section 48A(1) below;

  (b) in any other case, the grounds set out in section 48B(1) below.

(5) A proprietor is a WTO proprietor for the purposes of this section and sections 48A, 48B, 50 and 52 below if—

  (a) he is a national of, or is domiciled in, a country which is a member of the World Trade Organisation; or

  (b) he has a real and effective industrial or commercial establishment in such a country.

(6) A rule prescribing any such other period under subsection (1) above shall not be made unless a draft of the rule has been laid before, and approved by resolution of, each House of Parliament.

Compulsory licences: WTO proprietors

S.48A(1) In the case of an application made under section 48 above in respect of a patent whose proprietor is a WTO proprietor, the relevant grounds are—

(a) where the patented invention is a product, that a demand in the United Kingdom for that product is not being met on reasonable terms;

(b) that by the reason of the refusal of the proprietor of the patent concerned to grant a licence or licences on reasonable terms-

   (i) the exploitation in the United Kingdom of any other patented invention which involves an important technical advance of considerable economic significance in relation to the invention for which the patent concerned was granted is prevented or hindered, or

   (ii) the establishment or development of commercial or industrial activities in the United Kingdom is unfairly prejudiced;

(c) that by reason of conditions imposed by the proprietor of the patent concerned on the grant of licences under the patent, or on the disposal or use of the patented product or on the use of the patented process, the manufacture, use or disposal of materials not protected by the patent, or the establishment or development of commercial or industrial activities in the United Kingdom, is unfairly prejudiced.

(2) No order or entry shall be made under section 48 above in respect of a patent whose proprietor is a WTO proprietor unless—

(a) the applicant has made efforts to obtain a licence from the proprietor on reasonable commercial terms and conditions; and

(b) his efforts have not been successful within a reasonable period.

(3) No order or entry shall be so made if the patented invention is in the field of semi-conductor technology.

(4) No order of entry shall be made under section 48 above in respect of a patent on the ground mentioned in subsection (1)(b)(i) above unless the comptroller is satisfied that the proprietor of the patent for the other invention is able and willing to grant the proprietor of the patent concerned and his licensees a licence under the patent for the other invention on reasonable terms.

(5) A licence granted in pursuance of an order or entry so made shall not be assigned except to a person to whom the patent for the other invention is also assigned.

(6) A licence granted in pursuance of an order or entry made under section 48 above in respect of a patent whose proprietor is a WTO proprietor—

(a) shall not be exclusive;

(b) shall not be assigned except to a person to whom there is also assigned the part of the enterprise that enjoys the use of the patented invention, or the part of the goodwill that belongs to that part;

(c) shall be predominantly for the supply of the market in the United Kingdom;

(d) shall include conditions entitling the proprietor of the patent concerned to remuneration adequate in the circumstances of the case, taking into account the economic value of the licence; and

(e) shall be limited in scope and in duration to the purpose for which the licence was granted.

Note: s.48B deals with cases where the proprietor is not a WTO proprietor.

Section 51 gives government the power, after an unfavourable report from the Competition Commission, to apply to the Comptroller for various forms of relief, including endorsement of the patent, "Licences of Right". For licences of right in general, see ss.46, 47.

Section 52 provides for opposition, appeal and arbitration in respect of compulsory licences; and ss.53 and 54 contain supplementary provisions.

1.4.5.2   Patents Act 1977, ss.55, 56: Crown Use

S.55(1) Notwithstanding anything in this Act, any government department and any person authorised in writing by a government department may, for the services of the Crown and in accordance with this section, do any of the following acts in the United Kingdom in relation to a patented invention without the consent of the proprietor of the patent, that is to say—

(a) where the invention is a product, may—

    (i) make, use, import or keep the product, or sell or offer to sell it whether to do so would be incidental or ancillary to making, using, importing or keeping it; or

    (ii) in any event, sell or offer to sell it for foreign defence purposes or for the production or supply of specified drugs and medicines, or dispose or offer to dispose of it (otherwise than by selling it) for any purpose whatever;

(b) where the invention is a process, may use it or do in relation to any product obtained directly by means of the process anything mentioned in paragraph (a) above;

(c) without prejudice to the foregoing, where the invention or any product obtained directly by means of the invention is a specified drug or medicine, may sell or offer to sell the drug or medicine;

(d) may supply or offer to supply to any person any of the means, relating to an essential element of the invention, for putting the invention into effect;

(e) may dispose or offer to dispose of anything which was made, used, imported or kept in the exercise of the powers conferred by this section and which is no longer required for the purpose for which it was made, used, imported or kept (as the case may be),

and anything done by virtue of this subsection shall not amount to an infringement of the patent concerned.

(2) Any act done in relation to an invention by virtue of this section is in the following provisions of this section referred to as use of the invention; and "use", in relation to an invention, in sections 56 to 58 below shall be construed accordingly.

Section 55(3) provides for royalty-free use of certain prior inventions, recorded and tried.

(4) So far as the invention has not been so recorded or tried, any use of it made by virtue of this section at any time either—

(a) after the publication of the application for the patent for the invention; or

(b) without prejudice to paragraph (a) above, in consequence of a relevant communication made after the priority date of the invention otherwise than in confidence;

shall be made on such terms as may be agreed either before or after the user by the government department and the proprietor of the patent with the approval of the Treasury or as may in default of agreement be determined by the court on a reference under section 58 below.

Section 55(5)–(7) deal with royalties for use after publication of the patent application, the timing of the government department's authorisation and notification of use to the patentee.

(8) A person acquiring anything disposed of in the exercise of powers conferred by this section, and any person claiming through him, may deal with it in the same manner as if the patent were held on behalf of the Crown.

Section 55(9) defines "relevant communication".

(10) Subsection (4) above is without prejudice to any rule of law relating to the confidentiality of information.

S.56(1) Any reference in section 55 above to a patented invention, in relation to any time, is a reference to an invention for which a patent has before that time been, or is subsequently, granted.

(2) In this Act, except so far as the context otherwise requires, "the services of the Crown" includes—

(a) the supply of anything for foreign defence purposes;

(b) the production or supply of specified drugs and medicines; and

(c) such purposes relating to the production or use of atomic energy or research into matters connected therewith as the Secretary of State thinks necessary or expedient;

and "use for the services of the Crown" shall be construed accordingly.

Section 56(3) further defines the case under section 56(2)(a).

(4) For the purposes of section 55(1)(a) and (c) above and subsection (2)(b) above, specified drugs and medicines are drugs and medicines which are both—

(a) required for the provision of pharmaceutical services, general medical services or general dental services, that is to say, services of those respective kinds under Part II of the National Health Service Act 1977, Part II of the National Health Service (Scotland) Act 1978, or the corresponding provisions of the law in force in Northern Ireland or the Isle of Man, and

(b) specified for the purposes of this subsection in regulations made by the Secretary of State.

Section 57 relates to the position of exclusive and similar licensees under a patent where there is Crown use.

Section 57A (added in 1988) reverses Patchett's Patent *[1967] R.P.C. 237, by permitting compensation to be awarded in respect of lost production for which the patentee or exclusive licensee had spare capacity.*

Section 58 confers on the court jurisdiction to award compensation under these provisions. Section 59 makes special provision for Crown use during a period of emergency.

2 CONFIDENTIAL INFORMATION

2.1 Nature of Obligation

2.1.1 *Prince Albert v Strange* (1849) 1 Mac. & G. 25, LC

Queen Victoria and her consort had executed a private collection of etchings of which impressions had been printed and carefully guarded. By his amended bill, the Prince asserted that Strange, together with two other defendants, both called Judge, and their confederates, had in some manner obtained impressions, which had been surreptitiously taken from the plates. The defendants were restrained by injunction from exhibiting, publishing, parting with or disposing of the etchings, and from printing a descriptive catalogue of the etchings.

The defendant, Strange, while protesting his loyalty as a subject, maintained that as a matter of strict right, he was free to publish both etchings and catalogue and would surrender the copies in his possession only if indemnified as to costs. He then applied to have the injunction dissolved so far as it related to the catalogue. The defendant appealed from Knight Bruce V.C.'s refusal to grant this application.

Lord Cottenham L.C.:

The property of an author or composer of any work, whether of literature, art, or science, in such work unpublished and kept for his private use or pleasure, cannot be disputed, after the many decisions in which that proposition has been affirmed or assumed. I say assumed, because in most of the cases which have been decided, the question was not as to the original right of the author, but whether what had taken place did not amount to a waiver of such right; as in the case of letters, how far the sending the letter; in the case of dramatic compositions, how far the oral delivery of the lecture had deprived the author of any part of his original right and property; questions which could not have arisen if there had not been such original right of property. It would be a waste of time to refer in detail to the cases upon this subject. If, then, such right and property exist in the author of such works, it must so exist exclusively of all other persons: can any stranger have any right or title to, or interest in, that which belongs exclusively to another, and yet this is precisely what the defendant claims, although by a strange inconsistency he does not dispute the general proposition as to the plaintiff's right and property in the etchings in question, and as incident to it, the right to prevent the exhibition or publication of any copies of them, yet he insists that some person, having had access to certain copies, how obtained I will presently consider, and having from such copies composed a description and list of the originals, he,

155

the defendant, is entitled to publish such list and description; that is, that he is entitled, against the will of the owner, to make such use of his exclusive property. It being admitted that the defendant does not publish a copy, that is an impression of the etching, how in principle does a catalogue, list, or description differ? A copy or impression of the etching would only be a means of communicating knowledge and information of the original, and does not a list and description do the same? The means are different, but the object and effect are similar; for, in both, the object and effect is to make known to the public more or less of the unpublished work and composition of the author, which he is entitled to keep wholly for his private use and pleasure, and to withhold altogether, or so far as he may please, from the knowledge of others. Cases upon abridgements, translations, extracts, and criticisms of published works, have no reference whatever to the present question; they all depend upon the extent of right under the acts respecting copyright, and have no analogy to the exclusive rights in the author of unpublished compositions, which depend entirely upon the common law right of property. A clerk of Sir John Strange having, whilst in his employ, made an abridgment of such of his MS cases as related to evidence, was restrained by Lord Hardwicke in 1754, from publishing it, the cases being then unpublished. Upon the first question, therefore, that of property, I am clearly of opinion that the exclusive right and interest of the plaintiff in the composition or work in question being established, and there being no right or interest whatever in the defendant, the plaintiff is entitled to the injunction of this court to protect him against the invasion of such right and interest by the defendant, which the publication of any catalogue would undoubtedly be; but this case by no means depends solely upon the question of property, for a breach of trust, confidence, or contract, would of itself entitle the plaintiff to an injunction. The plaintiff's affidavits state the private character of the work or composition, and negative any licence or authority for publication, the gifts of some of the etchings to private friends certainly not implying any such licence or authority and state distinctly the belief of the plaintiff, that the catalogue and the descriptive and other remarks therein contained, could not have been compiled or made, except by means of the possession of the several impressions of the said etchings surreptitiously and improperly obtained. To this case no answer is made, the defendant saying only that he did not, at the time, believe that the etchings had been improperly obtained, but not suggesting any mode by which they could have been properly obtained, so as to entitle the possessor to use them for publication. If, then, these compositions were kept private, except as to some given to private friends, possession of the defendant, or of his intended partner Judge, must have originated in a breach of trust, confidence, or contract, in Brown or some person in his employ taking more impressions than were ordered, and retaining the extra number, or in some person to whom copies were given, which is not to be supposed, but which, if the origin of the possession of the defendant or Judge, *Duke of Queensberry v Shebbeare* ((1758) 2 Eden. 329); and upon the evidence on behalf of the plaintiff, and in the absence of any explanation on the part of the defendant, I am bound to assume that the possession of the etchings by the defendant or Judge has its foundation in a breach of trust, confidence, or contract, as Lord Eldon did in the case of Mr Abernethy's lectures (3 Law J. Chanc. 209); and upon this ground also I think the plaintiff's title to the injunction sought to be discharged, fully established. The observations of Vice-Chancellor Wigram in *Tipping v Clarke* ((1843) 2 Hare 393) are applicable to this part of the case. He says: "Every clerk employed in a merchant's counting-house is under an implied contract that he will not make public that which he learns in the execution of his duty as clerk. If the defendant has obtained copies of books, it would very probably be by means of some clerk or agent of the plaintiff; and if he availed himself surreptitiously of the information which he could not have had except from a person guilty of a breach of contract in communicating it, I think he could not be permitted to avail himself of that breach of contract." In this opinion, I fully concur, and think that the case supposed by Sir J Wigram has actually arisen, or must from the evidence be assumed to have arisen in the present, and that the consequences must be what Sir J Wigram thought would follow. Could it be contended that the clerk, though not justified in communicating copies of the accounts, might yet be permitted to publish the substance and effect of them? In that, as in this case, the matter or thing of which the party has obtained knowledge, being the exclusive property of the owner, he has a right to the interposition of this court to prevent any use being made of it, that is to say, he is entitled to be protected in the exclusive use and enjoyment of that which is exclusively his. This was the opinion of Lord Eldon, expressed in the case of *Wyatt v Wilson* in 1820 (unreported), respecting an engraving of George the Third during his illness, in which, according to a note with which I have been favoured by Mr Cooper, he said, "If one of the late king's physicians had kept a diary of what he heard and saw, this court would not, in the king's lifetime, have permitted him to print and publish it." The case of Sir J. Strange's MSS is applicable upon this point also.

2.1.2   *Saltman Engineering v Campbell Engineering* (1948) 65 R.P.C. 203, CA

Saltmans or Ferotec, associated companies, owned copyright in drawings for a leather punch. On their behalf, a third plaintiff, Monarch, arranged for the defendant to manufacture punches for them. It was alleged that, in implied breach of confidence, the defendant used the designs to manufacture and sell its own punches (claims in copyright and contract were not the subject of the judgments given in the Court of Appeal):

Lord Greene M.R.:

Vaisey J. dealt with the case in this way. He, first of all, declined to find that any contract was made between Monarch and the defendants. There was no question of any contractual relationship between the defendants and either of the other two plaintiffs and accordingly, so far as contract was concerned, it was essential to find a contract between Monarch and the defendants. That the learned judge refused to find.

The main part of the claim is based on breach of confidence, in respect of which a right may be infringed without the necessity of there being any contractual relationship. I will explain what I mean. If two parties make a contract, under which one of them obtains for the purpose of the contract or in connexion with it some confidential matter, then, even though the contract is silent on the matter of confidence, the law will imply an obligation to treat that confidential matter in a confidential way, as one of the implied terms of the contract: but the obligation to respect confidence is not limited to cases where the parties are in contractual relationship. The learned judge, having declined to find any contract between Monarch and the defendants, went on, if I understand his judgment correctly, to hold that for that reason there could be no relationship of confidence between any of the plaintiffs and the defendants. In my opinion, the learned judge erred in law in coming to that conclusion. He did not deal with the really substantial point in the case, namely, whether or not the defendants had committed a breach of confidence which infringed the rights of Saltmans, who owned the confidential matter. Into that question he did not go and the consequence is, from our point of view, that we have not the advantage of any findings of his own matters of fact which are relevant to the issue of breach of confidence as between Saltmans and the defendants.

Without going further into the matter it seems to me that the existence of a confidential obligation in relation to these drawings, as between Saltmans and the defendants, is abundantly proved; in fact it is not disputed.

His Lordship referred to certain passages in the evidence of the defendants' works manager and continued:

I need not go into the law, which I think is correctly stated in a formula which leading counsel for the defendants himself accepted. I will read it:

> "If a defendant is proved to have used confidential information, directly or indirectly obtained from a plaintiff, without the consent, express or implied of the plaintiff, he will be guilty of an infringement of the plaintiff's rights."

There are several cases which deal with this (*Morison v Moat* (1851) 8 Hare 241, is one of the better known of them) and I need not examine them further. The principle is established and is not disputed; and it is perfectly clear that an obligation, based on confidence, existed and bound the conscience of the defendants down to November 22, 1945. I think that I shall not be stating the principle wrongly, if I say this with regard to the use of confidential information. The information, to be confidential, must, I apprehend, apart from contract, have the necessary quality of confidence about it, namely, it must not be something which is public property and public knowledge. On the other hand, it is perfectly possible to have a confidential document, be it a formula, a plan, a sketch, or something of that kind, which is the result of work done by the maker on materials which may be available for the use of anybody; but what makes it confidential is the fact that the maker of the document has used his brain and this produced a result which can only be produced by somebody who goes through the same process.

What the defendants did in this case was to dispense in certain respects with the necessity of going through the process which had been gone through in compiling these drawings, and thereby to save themselves a great deal of labour and calculation and careful draughts-manship. No doubt, if they had taken a finished article, namely, the leather punch, which they might have bought in a shop, and given it to an expert draughtsman, that draughtsman could have produced the necessary drawings for the manufacture of machine tools required for making that particular finished article. In at any rate a very material respect they saved themselves that trouble by obtaining the necessary information either from the original drawings or from the tools made in accordance with them. That, in my opinion, was a breach of confidence. In the view that I take this case is a simple one: there has been a breach of confidence, the duty of confidence owed in the circumstances of this case by the defendants to Saltmans. It is not necessary to go into the question whether there was an implied obligation of confidence as between the two contracting parties, Monarch and the defendants. I need say nothing about that, because quite obviously in the circumstances, if Monarch obtained any relief based on that, they could hold it only for the benefit of the Saltmans, who are the owners of this confidential matter.

Somervell and Cohen L.JJ. delivered concurring judgments.

2.1.3　*Seager v Copydex (No. 1)* [1967] 2 All E.R. 415, CA

The plaintiff invented and patented one carpet-grip, the "Klent", which he was seeking to exploit. While discussing with two of the defendant's managers the possibility of the defendant marketing the "Klent", the plaintiff revealed to them in confidence the crucial idea for another grip, whose characteristics were a V-tang and a strong point. The managers stated that they were not interested in the idea. However, after negotiations over the "Klent" came to nothing, the defendant developed their own carpet grip which turned out to embody the very idea of the plaintiff's alternative and to be called the "Invisigrip"—a name which the plaintiff said he had suggested. At the trial allegations of fraud against the defendant were rejected. On appeal, the Court of Appeal found that the man-

agers must have been responsible for unconsciously making use of the plaintiff's information, thus engaging in an honest breach of confidence.

Lord Denning M.R.:

The Law: I start with one sentence in the judgment of Lord Greene M.R.: in *Saltman Engineering Co Ltd v Campbell Engineering Co Ltd* [1963] 3 All E.R. 423n.

> "If a defendant is proved to have used confidential information, directly or indirectly obtained from the plaintiff, without the consent, express or implied, of the plaintiff, he will be guilty of an infringement of the plaintiff's rights."

To this I add a sentence from the judgment of Roxburgh J. in *Terrapin Ltd v Builders' Supply Co (Hayes) Ltd, Taylor Woodrow Ltd & Swiftplan Ltd* [1960] R.P.C. 128, which was quoted and adopted as correct by Roskill J. in *Cranleigh Precision Engineering Co Ltd v Bryant* [1966] R.P.C. 81:

> "As I understand it, the essence of this branch of the law, whatever the origin of it may be, is that a person who has obtained information in confidence is not allowed to use it as a springboard for activities detrimental to the person who made the confidential communication, and springboard it remains even when all the features have been published or can be ascertained by actual inspection by any member of the public."

The law on this subject does not depend on any implied contract. It depends on the broad principle of equity that he who has received information in confidence shall not take unfair advantage of it. He must not make use of it to the prejudice of him who gave it without obtaining his consent. The principle is clear enough when the whole of the information is private. The difficulty arises when the information is in part public and in part private. As for instance in this case. A good deal of the information which the plaintiff gave to the defendant company was available to the public, such as the patent specification in the Patent Office, or the "Klent" grip, which he sold to anyone who asked. But there was a good deal of other information which was private, such as, the difficulties which had to be overcome in making a satisfactory grip; the necessity for a strong, sharp tooth; the alternative forms of tooth; and the like. When the information is mixed, being partly public and partly private, then the recipient must take special care to use only the material which is in the public domain. He should go to the public source and get it: or, at any rate, not be in a better position than if he had gone to the public source. He should not get a start over others by using the information which he received in confidence. At any rate, he should not get a start without paying for it. It may not be a case for injunction but only for damages, depending on the worth of the confidential information to him in saving him time and trouble.

Conclusion: Applying these principles, I think that the plaintiff should succeed. On the facts which I have stated, he told the defendant company a lot about the making of a satisfactory carpet grip which was not in the public domain. They would not have got going so quickly except for what they had learned in their discussions with him. They got to know in particular that it was possible to make an alternative grip in the form of a "V-tang", provided the tooth was sharp enough and strong enough, and they were told about the special shape required. The judge thought that the information was not significant. But I think it was. It was the springboard which enabled them to go on to devise the "Invisigrip" and to apply for a patent for it. They were quite innocent of any intention to take advantage of him. They thought that, as long as they did not infringe his patent, they were exempt. In this they were in error. There were not aware of the law as to confidential information.

I would allow the appeal and give judgment to the plaintiff for damages to be assessed.

Salmon L.J.:

... the germ of the idea and the broad principle of the domed v-shaped prong was I am certain implanted in their minds by the plaintiff at the interview of March 13, 1962, and afterwards subconsciously reproduced and used, if only as a springboard, to forestall the plaintiff with "Invisigrip". This is no reflection on their honesty, but it infringes the plaintiff's rights. I would accordingly allow the appeal.

Winn L.J.:

To my own mind it appears that the proper conclusion to be drawn from all the material before the court, not by any means primarily from the direct evidence, is that the plaintiff did explain his "Invisigrip" idea to Mr Boon and Mr Preston; that they absorbed what he told them; and were able to recall enough from their memories to indicate to Mr Sudbury and Mr Turl what they wanted them to produce.

In doing so they did not, I think, realise that they were infringing a duty of confidence: I think that they did infringe it. In so holding I do not imply any condemnation of Mr Boon or Mr Preston as dishonest men. Mr Preston made a most revealing statement in evidence in the court below where he said "... action for breach of confidence. I did not know such a thing existed ... the only problem was that we might infringe his patent". In my view the appeal succeeds.

Lord Denning M.R.:

The court grants neither an account of profits, nor an injunction, but only damages to be assessed by the master. Damages should be assessed on the basis of reasonable compensation for the use of the confidential information which was given to the defendant company.

For subsequent proceedings on the quantification of damages, see below,
2.4.1.

2.1.4   *Fraser v Evans* [1969] 1 All E.R. 8, CA

The plaintiff, a public relations consultant, was employed by the Greek Government to make a report. The plaintiff expressly agreed never to "reveal to any person or organisation any information related to the work in the areas where it was operating, or information which comes to the knowledge during the course of [the] contract"; but there was no corresponding undertaking by the Greek Government.

The report subsequently fell into the hands of a journalist for The Sunday Times *(defendant) who then obtained an interview with the plaintiff. At the interview the defendant's English translation of the report was compared with the plaintiff's original English version and some discrepancies were noted. Following the interview, the plaintiff became concerned that* The Sunday Times *might publish an article on the report which might be damaging to him. He succeeded in obtaining an injunction against* The Sunday Times *from which the newspaper appealed.*

The plaintiff's claim alleged libel, breach of confidence and infringement of copyright. The Sunday Times *admitted that the article would be defamatory of the plaintiff but argued that the facts alleged were true and that any comments on the extracts from the report were fairly and honestly made on a matter of public interest.*

Lord Denning M.R.:

First, *Libel.* In so far as the article will be defamatory of the plaintiff, it is clear he cannot get an injunction. The court will not restrain the publication of an article, even though it is defamatory, when the defendant says that he intends to justify it or to make fair comment on a matter of public interest. That has been established for many years ever since *Bonnard v Perryman* [1891] 2 Ch. 269. The reason sometimes given is that the defences of justification and fair comment are for the jury, which is the constitutional tribunal, and not for a judge; but a better reason is the importance in the public interest that the truth should out. As the court said in that case (at 284):

> "The right of free speech is one which it is for the public interest that individuals should possess, and, indeed, that they should exercise without impediment, so long as no wrongful act is done."

There is no wrong act done if it is true, or if it is fair comment on a matter of public interest. The court will not prejudice the issue by granting an injunction in advance of publication.

Secondly, *Breach of confidence.* The plaintiff says that the report was a confidential document and that the publication of it should be restrained on the principles enunciated in the cases from *Prince Albert v Strange* (1849) 1 Mac. & G. 25; to *Margaret Duchess of Argyll (Femme Sole) v Duke of Argyll* [1967] Ch. 302. These cases show that the court will, in a proper case, restrain the publication of confidential information. The jurisdiction is based, not so much on property or on contract, but rather on the duty to be of good faith. No person is permitted to divulge to the world information which he has received in confidence, unless he has just cause or excuse for doing so. Even if he comes by it innocently, nevertheless, once he gets to know that it was originally given in confidence, he can be restrained from breaking that confidence. For the party complaining must be the person who is entitled to the confidence and to have it respected. He must be a person to whom the duty of good faith is owed. It is at this point that I think that the plaintiff's claim breaks down. There is no doubt that the plaintiff himself was under an obligation of confidence to the Greek government. The contract says so in terms; but there is nothing in the contract which expressly puts the Greek government under any obligation of confidence. Nor, so far as I can see, is there any implied obligation. The Greek government entered into no contract with the plaintiff to keep it secret. We have seen affidavits—one of them as late as this morning—which say that it was not the policy of the Greek government to publish, or allow the publication of any documents prepared by the plaintiff or his firm, and that they would, as a matter of practice, keep them confidential. But that policy still leaves them free, in point of law, to circulate the documents or their contents to anyone whom they please. The information was obtained for them by the plaintiff under a contract with them. They paid for it. They were the people entitled to the information. They were the people to say aye or no whether it should be communicated elsewhere, or be published generally. It follows that they alone have any standing to complain if anyone obtains the information surreptitiously or proposes to publish it. And they did not complain of the publication now proposed. At any rate, they have not come to the court to complain. On this short point it seems to me that the plaintiff himself cannot proceed on breach of confidence in his own behalf, to prevent *The Sunday Times* publishing the article.

Even if the plaintiff had any standing to complain, *The Sunday Times* say that, in any event, they have just cause or excuse for publishing. They rely on the line of authority from *Gartside v Outram* (1856) 26 L.J. Ch. 113, to the latest case, *Initial Services Ltd v Putterill* [1968] 1 Q.B. 396. They quote the words of Wood V.C. in *Gartside v Outram* at 114, that "... there is no confidence as to the disclosure of iniquity." I do not look on the word "iniquity" as expressing a principle. It is merely an instance of just cause or excuse for breaking confidence. There are some things which may be required to be disclosed in the public interest, in which event no confidence can be prayed in aid to keep them secret. I feel that it might be difficult for *The Sunday Times* to make out that case here. We have the plaintiff's report before us, and on a reading of it, I doubt whether it is such as to enable them to make out this ground for publication.

Thirdly, *It was said*: Seeing that no injunction should be granted in respect of the defamatory aspect of the article, likewise no injunction should be granted in respect of the breach of confidence. The plaintiff should not be able to avoid the salutary rule of law in libel by framing the case in breach of confidence. Reliance was placed on *Sim v H.J. Heinz Co Ltd* [1959] R.P.C. 75. I do not think it necessary to rule on this point today. I can well see that there may be cases where it would be wrong to grant an injunction on breach of confidence when it would not be granted on libel; but I can equally well see that there are some cases of breach of confidence which are defamatory, where the court might intervene, even though the defendant says that he intends to justify.

The final point is on *copyright*. There is no doubt that the plaintiff was the author of this report and is entitled to the literary copyright in it. But copyright does not subsist in the information contained in the report. It exists only in the literary form in which the information is dressed. If *The Sunday Times* were going to print this report in full, thus taking the entire literary form, it might well be a case for an injunction to restrain the infringement of copyright. But *The Sunday Times* say that they are going to do no such thing. They say that they are only going to print short extracts from it, followed up with some of the statements which the plaintiff made to them and their comments on it. They say that that would be a "fair dealing" such as is permitted by section 6(3)(a) of the Copyright Act 1956, which provides that:

> "No fair dealing with a literary ... work shall constitute an infringement of the copyright in the work if it is for the purpose of reporting current events—(a) in a newspaper ..."

We have not seen what is going to be published. We cannot pre-judge the matter. We cannot say that there is going to be an unfair dealing when *The Sunday Times* say that it is to be fair dealing. So no injunction should be granted to prevent them publishing.

It all comes back to this. There are some things which are of such public concern that the newspapers, the Press, and, indeed, everyone is entitled to make known the truth and to make fair comment on it. This is an integral part of the right of free speech and expression. It must not be whittled away. *The Sunday Times* assert that, in this case, there is a matter of public concern. They admit that they are going to injure the plaintiff's reputation, but they say that they can justify it; that they are only making fair comment on a matter of public interest; and, therefore, that they ought not to be restrained. We cannot pre-judge this defence by granting an injunction against them. I think that the injunction which has been granted should be removed. *The Sunday Times* should be allowed to publish the article at their risk. If they are guilty of libel or breach of confidence, or breach of copyright, that can be determined by an action hereafter and damages awarded against them. But we should not grant an interim injunction in advance of an article when we do not know in the least what it will contain. I would allow the appeal accordingly and discharge the injunction.

Davies and Widgery L.JJ. concurred.

2.1.5 *Coco v A.N. Clark (Engineers) Ltd* [1969] R.P.C. 41, Megarry J.

The plaintiff had developed the "Coco" moped which featured, inter alia, *some special engine parts. He entered into negotiations with the defendants with a view to them ultimately manufacturing it. After approximately four months of discussions the defendants broke off negotiations, alleging difficulties with the transmission design. The defendants then wrote to the plaintiff offering him a royalty of 5 shillings per engine on the first 50,000 engines made, but this was not accepted.*

The defendants subsequently manufactured and sold their own "Scamp" moped. They admitted that the piston and carburettor were of the same type as the plaintiff's.

The plaintiff sought an injunction against the manufacture and sale of any machines in which the defendants had made use, directly or indirectly, of any confidential information the property of the plaintiff.

Megarry J.:

The equitable jurisdiction in cases of breach of confidence is ancient: confidence is the cousin of trust. The Statute of Uses, 1535, is framed in terms of "use, confidence or trust;" and a couplet, attributed to Sir Thomas More Lord Chancellor, avers that

> "Three things are to be helpt in Conscience;
> Fraud, Accident and things of Confidence."

See 1 Rolle's Abridgement 374. In the middle of the last century, the great case of *Prince Albert v Strange* (1849) 1 Mac. & G. 25 reasserted the doctrine. In the case before me, it is common ground that there is no question of any breach of contract, for no contract ever came into existence. Accordingly, what I have to consider is the pure equitable doctrine of confidence, unaffected by contract. Furthermore, I am here in the realms of commerce, and there is no question of any marital relationship such as arose in *Duchess of Argyll v Duke of Argyll* [1967] Ch. 302. Thus limited, what are the essentials of the doctrine?

Of the various authorities cited to me, I have found *Saltman Engineering Co Ltd v Campbell Engineering Co Ltd* [1948] 65 R.P.C. 203; *Terrapin Ltd v Builders' Supply Co (Hayes) Ltd* [1960] R.P.C. 128, and *Seager v Copydex Ltd* [1967] 1 W.L.R. 923; [1967] R.P.C. 349, of the most assistance. All are decisions of the Court of Appeal. I think it is quite plain from the *Saltman* case that the obligation of confidence may exist where, as in this case, there is no contractual relationship between the parties. In cases of contract, the primary question is no doubt that of construing the contract and any terms implied in it. Where there is no contract, however, the question must be one of what it is that suffices to bring the obligation into being; and there is the further question of what amounts to a breach of that obligation.

In my judgment, three elements are normally required if, apart from contract, a case of breach of confidence is to succeed. First, the information itself, in the words of Lord Greene M.R. in the *Saltman* case at 215, must "have the necessary quality of confidence about it." Secondly, that information must have been imparted in circumstances importing an obligation of confidence. Thirdly, there must be an unauthorised use of that information to the detriment of the party communicating it. I must briefly examine each of these requirements in turn.

First, the information must be of a confidential nature. As Lord Greene said in the *Saltman* case at 215, "something which is public property and public knowledge" cannot *per se* provide any foundation for proceedings for breach of confidence. However confidential the circumstances of communication, there can be no breach of confidence in revealing to others something which is already common knowledge. But this must not be taken too far. Something that has been constructed solely from materials in the public domain may possess the necessary quality of confidentiality: for something new and confidential may have been brought into being by the application of the skill and ingenuity of the human being. Novelty depends on the thing itself, and not upon the quality of its component parts. Indeed, often the more striking the novelty, the more commonplace its components. Mr Mowbray demurs to the concept that some degree of originality is requisite. But whether it is described as originality or novelty or ingenuity or otherwise, I think there must be some product of the human brain which suffices to confer a confidential nature upon the information: and, expressed in those terms, I think that Mr Mowbray accepts the concept.

The difficulty comes, as Lord Denning M.R. pointed out in the *Seager* case at 931, when the information used is partly public and partly private; for then the recipient must somehow segregate the two and, although free to use the former, must take no advantage of the communication of the latter. To this subject I must in due course return. I must also return to a further point, namely, that where confidential information is communicated in circumstances of confidence the obligation thus created endures, perhaps in a modified form, even after all the information has been published or is ascertainable by the public; for the receipt must not use the communication as a springboard (see the *Seager* case, at 931 and 933). I should add that, as shown by *Cranleigh Precision Engineering Ltd v Bryant* [1965] 1 W.L.R. 1293; [1966] R.P.C. 81, the mere simplicity of an idea does not prevent it being confidential (see 1309 and 1310). Indeed, the simpler an idea, the more likely it is to need protection.

The second requirement is that the information must have been communicated in circumstances importing an obligation of confidence. However secret and confidential the information, there can be no binding obligation of confidence if that information is blurted out in public or is communicated in other circumstances which negative any duty of holding it confidential. From the authorities cited to me, I have not been able to derive, any very precise idea of what test is to be applied in determining whether the circumstances import an obligation of confidence. In the *Argyll* case at 330, Ungoed-Thomas J. concluded his decision of the circumstances in which the publication of marital communications should be restrained, as being confidential by saying, "If this was a well-developed jurisdiction doubtless there would be guides and tests to aid in exercising it." In the absence of such guides or tests he then in effect concluded that part of the communications there in question would on any reasonable test emerge as confidential. It may be that that hard-worked creature, the reasonable man, may be pressed into service once more: for I do not see why he should not labour in equity as well as at law. It seems to me that if the circumstances are such that any reasonable man standing in the shoes of the recipient of the information would have realised that upon reasonable grounds the information was being given to him in confidence, then this should suffice to impose upon him the equitable obligation of confidence. In particular, where information of commercial or industrial value is given on a business-like basis and with some avowed common object in mind, such as a joint venture or the manufacture of articles by one party for the other, I would regard the recipient as carrying a heavy burden if he seeks to repel a contention that he was bound by an obligation of confidence: see the *Saltman* case at 216. On that footing, for reasons that will appear, I do not think I need explore this head further. I merely add that I doubt whether equity would intervene unless the circumstances are of sufficient gravity; equity ought not to be invoked merely to protect trivial tittle-tattle, however confidential.

Thirdly, there must be an unauthorised use of the information to the detriment of the person communicating it. Some of the statements of principle in the cases omit any mention of detriment; others include it. At first sight, it seems that detriment ought to be present if equity is to be induced to intervene; but I can conceive of cases where a plaintiff might have substantial motives for seeking the aid of equity and yet suffer nothing which could fairly be called detriment to him, as when the confidential information shows him in a favourable light but gravely injures some relation or friend of his whom he wishes to produce. The point does not arise for decision in this case, for detriment to the plaintiff plainly exists. I need therefore say no more than that although for the purposes of this case I have stated the proposition in the stricter form I wish to keep open the possibility of the true proposition being in the wider form.

Before I turn to the second main head, that of interlocutory relief, I should mention one point on the substantive law that causes me some difficulty during the argument. This is what may be called the "spring-board" doctrine. In the *Seager* case at 931, Lord Denning quoted a sentence from the judgment of Roxburgh J. in the *Terrapin* case, which was quoted and adopted as correct by Roskill J. in the *Cranleigh* case. It runs as follows:

> "As I understand it, the essence of this branch of the law, whatever the origin of it may be, is that a person who has obtained information in confidence is not allowed to use it as a spring-board for activities detrimental to the person who made the confidential communication, and spring-board it remains even when all the features have been published or can be ascertained by actual inspection by any member of the public."

Salmon L.J. in the *Seager* case at 933 also states:

> "The law does not allow the use of such information even as a spring-board for activities detrimental to the plaintiff."

Quite apart from authority I would recognise the principle enshrined in those words as being salutary. Nevertheless, I am not entirely clear how it is to be put into practical effect in every case. Suppose a case where there is a confidential communication of information which is partly public and partly private; suppose that the recipient of the information adds in confidence ideas of his own, improving the initial scheme; and suppose that the parties then part, with no agreement concluded between them. How is a conscientious recipient of the ideas to comply with the requirements that equity lays upon him? For in the words of Lord Denning at 931 in the *Seager* case, he

> "must take special care to use only the material which is in the public domain. He should go to the public source and get it: or, at any rate, not be in a better position than if he had gone to the public source. He should not get a start over others by using the information which he received in confidence."

Suppose that the only confidential information communicated is that some important component should be made of aluminium instead of steel and with significant variations in its design and dimensions. The recipient knows that this change will transform a failure into success. He knows that, if he had persevered himself, he might have come upon the solution in a week or in a year. Yet he is under a duty not to use the confidential information as a spring-board or as giving him a start.

What puzzles me is how, as a law-abiding citizen, he is to perform that duty. He could, I suppose, commission someone else to make the discovery anew, carefully abstaining from saying anything to him about aluminium or the design and dimensions which will achieve success; but this seems to me to be artificial in the extreme. Yet until this step is taken and the discovery made anew, he cannot make use of his own added ideas for the further improvement of the design which he had already communicated in confidence to the original communicator, ideas which would perhaps make a success into a triumph. He cannot build his superstructure as long as he is forbidden to use the foundations. Nor is the original communicator in a much better case. He is free to use his own original idea, which converted failure into success; but he cannot take advantage of the original recipient's further ideas, of which he knows, until such time as he or someone commissioned by him would, unaided by any coincidence, have discovered them.

For those who are not law-abiding and conscientious citizens there is, I suppose, a simple answer; ignore the duty, use the information, and then pay damages. This may be the course which Lord Denning envisaged in the *Seager* case: for after stating that the recipient should not get a start over others by using the confidential information, he continued at 932: "At any rate, he should not get a start without paying for it. It may not be a case for injunction or even for an account, but only for damages, depending on the worth of the confidential information to him in saving time and trouble." I also recognise that a conscientious and law-abiding citizen, having received confidential information in confidence, may accept that when negotiations break down the only honourable course is to withdraw altogether from the field in question until his informant or someone else has put the information into the public domain and he can no longer be said to have any start. Communication thus imposes upon him a unique disability. He alone of all men must for an uncertain time abjure this field of endeavour, however great his interest. I find this scarcely more reasonable than the artificiality and uncertainty of postponing the use of the information until others would have discovered it.

The relevance of the point, I think, is this. If the duty is a duty not to use the information without consent, then it may be the proper subject of an injunction restraining its use, even if there is an offer to pay a reasonable sum for that use. If, on the other hand, the duty is merely a duty not to use the information without paying a reasonable sum for it, then no such injunction should be granted. Despite the assistance of counsel, I feel far from assured that I have got to the bottom of this matter. But I do feel considerable hesitation in expressing a doctrine of equity in terms that include a duty which law-abiding citizens cannot reasonably be expected to perform. In other words, the essence of the duty seems more likely to be that of not using without paying, rather than of not using at all. It may be that in fields other than industry and commerce (and I have in mind the *Argyll* case) the duty may exist in the more stringent form; but in the circumstances present in this case I think that the less stringent form is the more reasonable. No doubt this matter may be canvassed and resolved at the trial; but on motion, in a case where both the probabilities and the evidence support the view that the fruits of any confidential communication were to sound in monetary compensation to the communicator, I should be slow to hold that it was right to enjoin the defendant company from making any use of the information.

Megarry J. then considered whether under the circumstances this was an appropriate case for granting an interlocutory injunction. Given the conflict between the defendant's letter offering a royalty and the plaintiff's allegation of fraud based on his conviction that the defendant was out to get his engine "without paying for it", and the fact that at this interlocutory stage no cross-

examination had taken place, he refused the grant and adjourned the matter to trial. The Terrapin case was distinguished on its facts. The defendants gave an undertaking to keep an account of a royalty of 5 shillings per "Scamp" engine manufactured. This was to be paid into a special trust account which would protect the plaintiff in the event of any financial disaster to the defendant pending the outcome of the trial.

2.1.6   *Thomas Marshall v Guinle* **[1979] 1 Ch. 227, Megarry V.C.**

The defendant was appointed managing director of the plaintiff company for a period of 10 years. His service agreement provided that he was not to engage in any other business without the company's consent while he was employed as managing director; that during and after his employment, he was not "to disclose" confidential information in relation to the affairs, customers or trade secrets of the company and its group; and that after ceasing to be managing director he was not, inter alia, "to use or disclose" confidential information about the suppliers and customers of the group. Without the company's knowledge, the defendant began to trade on his own account and on behalf of his two companies in competition with the company and, in doing so, he bought from the company's suppliers and sold to the company's customers. The defendant purported to resign as managing director at a time when his contract had another four-and-a-half years to run. The company applied for interim injunctions to restrain the defendant, inter alia, from disclosing or using any confidential information or trade secret of the company during or after his employment.

Megarry V.C., in granting the application held that in view of the contractual limitation of obligation concerning confidential information to "disclosing", the breaches of confidence could not themselves justify an injunction against using the information, but the defendant's breaches of fiduciary duty did so. On the meaning of "confidential information" to be covered by the injunction, he said:

It is far from easy to state in general terms what is confidential information or a trade secret. Certain authorities were cited, but they did not carry matters very far. Plainly "something which is public property and public knowledge" is not confidential: see *Saltman Engineering Co Ltd v Campbell Engineering Co Ltd* (1948) 65 R.P.C. 203 at 215, per Lord Greene M.R. On the other hand, "something that has been constructed solely from materials in the public domain may possess the necessary quality of confidentiality: for something new and confidential may have been brought into being by the application of the skill and ingenuity of the human brain. Novelty depends on the thing itself, and not upon the quality of its constituent parts": *Coco v A.N. Clark (Engineers) Ltd* [1969] R.P.C. 41 at 47, a case that was not cited, but in part draws on the *Saltman* case, which was. Costs and prices which are not generally known may well constitute trade secrets or confidential information: see *Herbert Morris Ltd v Saxelby* [1916] 1 A.C. 688 at 705, referring to prices.

If one turns from the authorities and looks at the matter as a question of principle, I think (and I say this very tentatively, because the principle has not been argued out) that four elements may be discerned which may be of some assistance in identifying confidential information or trade secrets which the court will protect. I speak of such information or secrets only in an industrial or trade setting. First, I think that the information must be information the release of which the owner believes would be injurious to him or of advantage to his rivals or others. Second, I think the owner must believe that the information is confidential or secret, *i.e.* that it is not already in the public domain. It may be that some or all of his rivals already have the information: but as long as the owner believes it to be confidential I think he is entitled to try and protect it. Third, I think that the owner's belief under the two previous heads must be reasonable. Fourth, I think that the information must be judged in the light of the usage and practices of the particular industry or trade concerned. It may be that information which does not satisfy all these requirements may be entitled to protection as confidential information or trade secrets: but I think that any information which does satisfy them must be of a type which is entitled to protection.

2.1.7   *Smith Kline & French Laboratories (Australia) Ltd v Secretary to the Department of Community Services and Health* [1990] F.S.R. 617, Gummow J., Federal Ct of Australia

Smith Kline & French Laboratories (Australia) Ltd ("SK&F") imported the drug Cimetidine into Australia, and sold it under the trade marks "Tagamet" and "Duractin". The importation into Australia of a therapeutic substance such as Cimetidine was controlled by the Customs (Prohibited Imports) Regulations ("the regulations") administered by the Secretary to the Department of Community Services and Health ("the department"). In order to obtain approval under the regulations to import Cimetidine SK&F delivered to the department at various dates between 1975 and 1987 information relating to the chemistry and the quality control of Cimetidine called the "B1 data".

In July 1988 Alphapharm, an Australian importer and manufacturer of generic drugs, sought approval to import Cimetidine into Australia to be sold under the trade mark "Cimet". It was the practice of the department in evaluating applications by generic manufacturers to have regard to the B1 data held by the department in respect of the innovator's applications (in this case the SK&F group of companies) or related applications in respect of the same class of drugs. This practice was intended to ensure the quality, safety and efficacy of the generic product. The judge found that it would be bad scientific practice, and could be dangerous, to ignore the innovator's B1 data in evaluating a generic application.

SK&F claimed ("the SK&F proceedings") that its B1 data was confidential information supplied to the department for the sole purpose of evaluating SK&F's applications. It sought an injunction to prohibit the department from using its B1 data for any other purpose, including the evaluation of the Alphapharm application. In separate proceedings heard at the same time ("the Alphapharm proceedings") Alphapharm sought various orders including a declaration that the alleged confidential information in the SK&F B1 data might be used by the department in dealing with the Alphapharm application. Gummow J. began his analysis of the law by discussing the general nature of confidential information and identifying the issues in the case:

The alleged obligation of confidence

In *The Commonwealth v John Fairfax & Sons Ltd* (1980) 147 C.L.R. 39 at 50, Mason J. adopted the statement of principle by Swinfen Eady L.J. in *Lord Ashburton v Pape* [1913] 2 Ch. 469 at 475, that a court of equity will "restrain the publication of confidential information improperly or surreptitiously obtained or of information imparted in confidence which ought not to be divulged." It will be observed that in that formulation, confidential information improperly or surreptitiously obtained, on the one hand and information imparted in confidence, on the other, are treated as two species of the same genus. This accommodates, within the general rubric of the equitable jurisdiction, cases of eavesdropping or theft, for example, *Franklin v Giddings* [1978] Qd. R. 72. The present case is put as one of the second species, namely of information "imparted in confidence."

Where the information has passed between parties already linked by a pre-existing fiduciary relationship, special considerations may apply, which determine the extent of the duty of fidelity owed by one party to the other. These considerations will flow from the nature and content of the fiduciary relationship in question. This aspect of the law of confidence is discussed by Mr Dean in *The Law of Trade Secrets* (1990), pp.179–181; see also the treatment of confidential information in *Boardman v Phipps* [1967] 2 A.C. 46 at 89–92, 102–103, 106–107, 115–118, 127–129 and *Consul Development Pty Ltd v D.P.C. Estates Pty Ltd* (1975) 132 C.L.R. 373 at 399–400, 414. These were both cases of alleged breach of fiduciary duty involving failure to observe an obligation of fidelity, and may be compared with *Pacifica Shipping Co Ltd v Andersen* [1986] 2 N.Z.L.R. 328, and *Lac Minerals Ltd v International Corona Resources Ltd* (1989) 16 I.P.R. 27, which were cases where the plaintiff sought to found liability both in breach of fiduciary duty and breach of confidence, as distinct subject matters. The present case is not alleged to involve the imparting of confidential information in the course of a subsisting fiduciary relationship.

Nor is the present case propounded as one of contract. It would be unfortunate if the broad question whether in a particular case information had been imparted in confidence, so as to bind the conscience of the defendant in a particular way, was to be approached as if the issue was one of formation of contract, involving notions of offer and acceptance and *animus contrahendi*. The question as McPherson J. pointed out in *Fractionated Cane Technology Ltd v Ruiz-Avila* [1988] 1 Qd. R. 51 at 67 (affirmed 13 I.P.R. 609), is whether, independently of contract, the circumstances are such as to attract the intervention of equity. Equity will only intervene if the information has been communicated in circumstances importing an obligation of confidence. That was how Megarry J. put it in *Coco v A. N. Clark (Engineers) Ltd* [1969] R.P.C. 41 at 47–48, thereby directing attention to the issue of what in the whole of the relevant circumstances would suffice to impose upon the defendant an equitable obligation of confidence. The Supreme Court of Canada recently approached the matter in a similar fashion: *Lac Minerals Ltd v International Corona Resources Ltd*, *supra*, at 33, 74–77.

The B1 data for which protection is sought are identified with specificity in exhibits 6A and 6B. But counsel for Alphapharm and for the Secretary pointed to alleged deficiencies in the case made against them by denying that the B1 data identified in exhibits 6A and 6B had about it the necessary character of quality of confidence within the sense of the well known passage in the judgment of Megarry J. in *Coco v A. N. Clark (Engineers) Ltd*, above, at 47; see also Dean, *The Law of Trade Secrets* (1990), pp.105–107.

The task of segregating the B1 data, for which the applicants in the SK&F proceedings seek protection, fell upon Dr Brennan. He is the author of the documents which, after some amendments, became exhibits 6A and 6B. He joined SK&F in July 1985. Counsel for Alphapharm and for the Secretary submitted there had been insufficiently thorough efforts in the applicants' case, both to establish that all of the information identified in exhibits 6A and 6B had been confidential in character and to show that none of it had now entered the public domain. The evidence presented for the applicants in the SK&F proceedings by Mr Perrin, Mr Pickford, Dr Davies and Dr Seville, in addition to that of Dr Brennan, satisfies me that the applicants have made out their case both as to the initial subsistence of confidentiality in the B1 data identified in exhibits 6A and 6B, and as to the continued existence of confidentiality in relation to that material. It is the product of detailed and costly work, is inherently valuable and has been kept secret. As the hearing developed, it became apparent that the real issues lay elsewhere.

A general formulation apt for the present case of an equitable obligation of confidence has four elements: (i) the plaintiff must be able to identify with specificity, and not merely in global terms, that which is said to be the information in question, and must be able to show that (ii) information has the necessary quality of confidentiality (and is not, for example, common or public knowledge), (iii) the information was received by the defendant in such circumstances as to import an obligation of confidence, and (iv) there is actual or threatened misuse of that information, without the consent of the plaintiff. The authorities from which these elements are drawn are collected in *Corrs Pavey Whiting & Byrne v Collector of Customs (Vic.)* (1987) 14 F.C.R. 434 at 443. In addition, it has been suggested that the breach must inflict or be likely to inflict "detriment," a matter to which I will return later in these reasons. As I have indicated, I am satisfied that the applicants in the SK&F proceedings have made out their case as to elements (i) and (ii). The central issue concerns element (iii). If the applicants succeed also as to element (iii), then what the Secretary on his own case wishes to be at liberty to do would amount to a sufficient threat for element (iv).

The central issue is whether the Secretary and those involved in evaluating the Alphapharm application for the Cimet product are bound by an obligation of confidence owed to the applicants in the SK&F proceedings not to use for the purpose of the evaluation of the Alphapharm application, and in the particular manner I have described, the B1 data disclosed on various occasions since June 17, 1975 in relation to various applications for SK&F ... cimetidine products.

The Secretary's principal submission was that engagement in the conduct which the applicants in the SK&F proceedings seek to have the court restrain would not breach any obligation of confidence. The applicants plead ... that the B1 data was provided to the department for the sole purpose of enabling consideration and decision upon applications made by SK&F for permission to conduct clinical trials with Tagamet products, or for permission for SK&F ... to market Tagamet or Duractin products. The content of the alleged obligation of confidence is said to be not to use the information other than for that sole purpose. It is alleged that the department "well knew" of that limited purpose. Alternatively, it is submitted that the department "ought to have known" of it.

The Secretary and Alphapharm submit that while SK&F's officers considered at relevant times that the B1 data were confidential in a general sense, no-one in the applicant's camp turned his mind to the question of use by the department for the purposes the subject of this case, until Mr Perrin, the then managing director, turned his mind to the question late in 1986. Further, it is submitted that the applicants have failed to establish a knowledge or acceptance on the part of the department of the "sole purpose" as pleaded by the applicants in the SK&F proceedings. It is then submitted that it has not been shown that the department ought to have had that knowledge.

Gummow J. found that SK&F had supplied its B1 data to the department on the common understanding that it was confidential in the sense that it would not be disclosed to other pharmaceutical companies. However, until shortly before the SK&F proceedings commenced in 1987, SK&F had not turned its attention to the use of its B1 data to evaluate generic applications; so it could not claim that this data was in fact furnished for the sole purpose of evaluating its own applications. SK&F argued that the Department ought nevertheless to have "known" that its B1 data was supplied for this sole purpose. Gummow J. considered that the evidence on this question and continued:

The considerations relied upon by the applicants in the SK&F proceedings do not make good their submission that the department ought to have had the alleged "knowledge." Further, one would be cautious in attributing to one party a belief as to the purposes of another when that other party could not show that it had turned its mind to the crucial element in those alleged purposes, here, use as against disclosure.

Moreover, and this is a significant point, in assessing whether the department ought to have had the "knowledge" alleged, one should have regard to the effect of the legal framework within which the parties were dealing. One would be slow to attribute to a regulatory authority knowledge that a party dealing with it expected it to act in a manner which would inhibit it in the exercise of its legal powers and obligations. One would be slow also to attribute to that party a purpose which if fulfilled would inhibit the regulatory authority in this way. Such conduct would not readily be regarded in accord with equity and good conscience.

It is necessary at this stage to turn to the authorities and then to the terms of the regulation.

"Knew or ought to have known"—the law

The Secretary submits, in my view correctly, that the circumstance that the person who imparted the information in question intended to do so for a limited purpose will not necessarily of itself be sufficient to bind the conscience of the party to whom the information was imparted. The Secretary submits that the conscience of the other party will be bound if, by the combined effect of the confidential nature of the relevant information and the circumstances in which it was communicated, there appears an equity which answers the description of an obligation of confidence; see *Moorgate Tobacco Co Ltd v Philip Morris Ltd (No. 2)* (1984) 156 C.L.R. 414 at 437–438, *per* Deane J.

No doubt it is not necessary that the defendant should have known of the limited purpose of the disclosure to him. However, where the defendant neither knew nor ought to have known of the alleged limited purpose of the disclosure, it is difficult to see on what footing equity should intervene to bind his conscience.

The judge rejected an argument by SK&F's counsel based upon Interfirm Comparison (Australia) Pty Ltd v Law Society of New South Wales *(1975) 2 N.S.W.L.R. at 104 and continued:*

In his paper "Breach of Confidence" reprinted in *Essays in Equity* (Finn ed., 1985) p.110 at 118, Mr Gurry says (omitting footnotes):

"While the test for determining the existence of an obligation is clear, it is less clear whether the court constructs from the circumstances an objective inference that the disclosure between the parties was for a limited purpose, or whether it requires evidence that the confidant actually knew that the purpose of the disclosure was limited. There is relatively little direct authority on the point, largely because in most cases it has been clear from the circumstances that the confidant did know of the limited purpose of the disclosure. Despite the paucity of authority it would seem beyond doubt that an obligation should be imposed on a confidant where the circumstances are such as to indicate that the confidant either knew or ought to have known that information was being imparted for a limited purpose. If it were otherwise, there would be little room for any jurisdiction to enforce confidences outside express contract or express non-contractual understandings."

The learned author then passes on to consider cases of thieves and eavesdroppers where there has been no disclosure between the parties to which a limited purpose can be attached. But in such cases it can be said of the defendant that he knew or ought to have known that he should not have had the information at all, let alone for a limited purpose. See also Gurry, *Breach of Confidence* (1984) pp.115–120; the selection of authorities in these passages was shown by counsel for the Secretary to have led to inclusion of some which are inapt. Nevertheless, I accept the general thesis of the learned author that equity may impose an obligation of confidence upon a defendant having regard not only to what the defendant knew, but to what he ought to have known in all the relevant circumstances.

As I have indicated, another dimension is added to the present case by the circumstance that the disputants are not private parties, and that one of them is an officer of the Commonwealth who acts in the discharge of responsibilities placed upon him by the regulations. The special considerations that apply in such a case appear from the following passage in the judgment of McHugh J.A. in *Attorney-General for the United Kingdom v Heinemann Publishers Australia Pty Ltd* (1987) 10 N.S.W.L.R. 86 at 191. After stating that equity courts will protect the confidentiality of information imparted in confidence by governments to citizens, His Honour continued:

"Courts of Equity will also protect the confidentiality of information given by citizens to governments and their departments and agencies: *Castrol Australian Pty Ltd v EmTech Associates Pty Ltd* (1980)´51 F.L.R. 184, 33 A.L.R. 31 and *Norwich Pharmacal Co v Commissioners of Customs and Excise* [1974] A.C. 113 at 189 *per* Viscount Dilhorne. But the relationship between the modern State and its citizens is so different in kind from that which exists between private citizens that rules worked out to govern the contractual, property, commercial and private confidences of citizens are not fully applicable where the plaintiff is a government or one of its agencies. Private citizens are entitled to protect or further their own interests, no matter how selfish they are in doing so. Consequently, the publication of confidential information which is detrimental to the private interest of a citizen is a legitimate concern of a court of Equity. But governments act, or at all events are constitutionally required to act, in the public interest. Information is held, received and imparted by governments, their departments and agencies to further the public interest. Public and not private interest, therefore, must be the criterion by which Equity determines whether it will protect information which a government or governmental body claims is confidential."

The public interest to which McHugh J.A. referred as an aspect of government in this case is represented by the considerations to which, on a proper construction of the regulations, the Secretary may or must have regard in exercising the discretions given him as the relevant decision maker.

I should refer to the decision of Rath J. in *Castrol Australia Pty Ltd v EmTech Associates Pty Ltd* (1980) 51 F.L.R. 184 ... where it is apparent (and this is significant for the present case) that the assumption of an obligation of confidence of this description was within the proper discharge of the statutory functions of the [Trade Practices] Commission. This appears from the following passage (51 F.L.R. at 203):

"Although the Commission has statutory duties in regard to consumer protection, it seems obvious from the circumstances of this case that one of its means of carrying out its duties is to assist persons in the position of the plaintiff to determine whether proposed advertising will contravene the Trade Practices Act. I think that this is a legitimate procedure, and that, in following that procedure the Commission is entitled to assume an obligation of confidence in regard to information given to it. There is nothing in the Act which expressly prevents the Commission from assuming the obligation. If it does, the obligation will have its usual incidents (compare section 4M (a): *Melbourne Home of Ford Pty Ltd v Trade Practices Commission (No. 2)* (1979) 40 F.L.R. 428)."

Section 4M of the Trade Practices Act 1974 provides that whilst that statute does not affect the operation of "the law relating to breaches of confidence" nothing in that law affects the interpretation of the statute. After referring to section 4M, Rath J. then referred to the express assumption of an obligation of confidence by officers of the Commission. ...

In the present dispute, the court looks at the objective circumstances to ascertain whether the Secretary ought to have known that the B1 data were imparted on the restricted basis alleged by the applicants in the SK&F proceedings. The court must further ask whether one would attribute to the Secretary knowledge that SK&F was imparting the B1 data on those terms, if they clashed or might clash with the performance of the Secretary's functions under the regulations.

In this regard, the Secretary submitted that he ought not to be taken to have known that he was under a duty to the applicants in the SK&F proceedings not to use the B1 data in evaluating generic applications if the assumption of such a duty would or could at some future time put him in conflict with the proper discharge of his functions in respect of such generic applications.

The Secretary submits that in exercising the relevant discretions under the regulations, he is obliged to have regard to issues concerning the quality, safety and efficacy of the therapeutic substance in question, within the sense of authorities such as *Minister for Aboriginal Affairs v Peko-Wallsend Ltd* (1986) 162 C.L.R. 24 especially at 39, 61. In that case, at 61, Brennan J. said:

"A decision-maker who is bound to have regard to a particular matter is not bound to bring to mind all the minutiae within his knowledge relating to the matter. The facts to be brought to mind are the salient facts which give shape and substance to the matter: the facts of such importance that, if they are not considered, it could not be said that the matter has been properly considered."

The Secretary further submits that the use of innovator B1 data in the course of evaluating generic applications answers this description. Reference was made also to what was said by the Full Court in *Luu v Renevier* (1989) 91 A.L.R. 39 at 50, concerning the consequences of failure by a decision maker to obtain information which ought to have been obtained; the Secretary contended that the reasoning of the Full Court applied *a fortiori* to the present case, where the information was already held by the decision maker.

Then, and alternatively, it was submitted that if not bound to take into account matters of safety, quality and efficacy, the Secretary was at liberty to do so and would act properly in doing so when exercising any relevant discretion under the regulations for approval of a generic product: *R. v Australian Broadcasting Tribunal Ex p. 2HD Pty Ltd* (1979) 144 C.L.R. 45 at 49; *O'Sullivan v Farrer* (1989) 89 A.L.R. 71 at 75.

The exercise of the powers which the regulations entrust to the Secretary undoubtedly may have considerable impact upon the commercial activities of pharmaceutical companies such as SK&F. But the regulations are directed to the concern of government in matters of public health and safety, a subject quite different in character from the trading and commercial aspects of the activities of modern government.

In *Ansett Transport Industries (Operations) Pty Ltd v The Commonwealth* (1977) 139 C.L.R. 54 at 113, Aickin J. said that the distinction sought to be drawn, *inter alia*, in *Commissioners of Crown Lands v Page* [1960] 2 Q.B. 274 at 291, between "discretionary powers of the Crown to be exercised for the public good" and the exercise by the Crown of its executive power to enter into "commercial contracts" was not one which leaps to the eye. Nevertheless, since that was said, the House of Lords has endorsed a similar distinction in the law of foreign state immunity. A foreign state has no absolute immunity as regards commercial or trading transactions and the so-called "restrictive" theory of sovereign immunity now prevails at common law: *I Congreso del Partido* [1983] 1 A.C. 244. See now in Australia the Foreign States Immunities Act 1985, s.11.

The Secretary stresses, and I accept, that (a) his functions under the regulations are concerned with a matter of high government interest, public health and safety, not with commercial dealings of the type conducted in general by citizens rather than governments and (b) there was no express assurance given to SK&F as to the use to which the B1 data would not be put within the department, nor was there any consensus upon that subject.

The Secretary and Alphapharm submit that in such a setting, and in the absence of express words, the court should not impute an undertaking that would restrict or inhibit the exercise of discretionary powers. Reliance is placed upon what was said by Mason J. in *Ansett Transport Industries (Operations) Pty Ltd v The Commonwealth*, above, at 78. See also *Minister for Immigration and Ethnic Affairs v Kurtovic* (Full Court, February 7, 1990, *per* Gummow J., unreported); de Smith's *Judicial Review of Administrative Action* (4th ed., 1980), p.319; Wade, *Administrative Law* (6th ed., 1988), pp.377–378; Craig, *Administrative Law* (1983), at pp.597–600; Rogerson, "On the Fettering of Public Powers" [1971] P.L. 288 pp.296–299. Mason J.'s remarks in the *Ansett Case*, *supra*, were concerned with implied contractual terms. But, it was submitted in my view correctly, that the reasoning of His Honour was applicable also to the issue here. This is whether equity will treat the Secretary as bound, in all the circumstances, but in the absence of any express assurance or consensus by an obligation of confidence to the applicants not to use their B1 data in evaluating any generic application.

Gummow J. considered the Customs (Prohibited Imports) Regulation in detail, with particular attention to the provisions relating to approvals to import therapeutic substances in reg.5 and then concluded:

Conclusions as to obligations of confidence

I accept the submissions by the Secretary and Alphapharm that the SK&F B1 data concerning cimetidine should be regarded as having been furnished pursuant to regulation 5E so as to enable the Secretary to perform his functions under the regulations and that the applicants in the SK&F proceedings should be regarded as parties who knew or who ought to have known that this was the position. I also accept that in exercising his powers under regulation 5E and in relaxing any equivalent condition imposed upon a non-licensed importer under sub-regulation 5A(4)(a) the Secretary is bound to have regard to matters going to the quality, safety and efficacy of the therapeutic substance in question. Where he acts directly under regulation 5E, these matters are spelled out by sub-regulation 5E(3A).

In paying regard to such matters when dealing with an application in respect of a generic product, such as Cimet, the Secretary may properly have regard to B1 innovator data held by him in the manner in which he proposes to use the SK&F B1 cimetidine data when evaluating the Alphapharm application. Further, equity would not attribute to the

Secretary any obligation to the applicants in the SK&F proceedings not to use the B1 data in this way at a later stage when he had before him for evaluation a generic cimetidine product. When furnishing the B1 data in the period 1975–1987, SK&F was concerned to obtain the necessary approvals under the regulations. It did not direct its attention to what else might be done subsequently with the information by the Secretary in discharge of his functions under the regulations. There was an implicit understanding common to SK&F and the Secretary concerning non-disclosure to third parties. That understanding would have required qualification to deal with the extraordinary circumstances recognised by Mr Perrin in his evidence. But that understanding would not interfere with the proper exercise of the functions of the Secretary under the regulations. A court of equity would not impute to any relevant party the placing or acceptance of an obligation whereby in the subsequent discharge of his functions under the regulations the Secretary was restricted in the way the applicants in the SK&F proceedings contend.

The "public interest" defence

Thus it is not a question whether there is some "public interest" defence to the alleged breach of an obligation by the Secretary, but rather one of the content of any such obligation in its inception. I should note that this was the preferred approach of Scott J. to the issues in *Attorney General v Guardian Newspapers Ltd (No. 2)* [1988] 3 All E.R. 545 at 582–584, and that the judge had earlier in his reasons (at 573) set out the passage from *Moorgate Tobacco Co Ltd v Philip Morris Ltd (No. 2)*, above, in which Deane J. propounded the basis for the equitable jurisdiction in matters of confidence.

My views upon the wisdom of adopting in Australia the English authorities in which the "public interest" defence has been constructed in recent years, from what may be thought inadequate historical and doctrinal materials, have been expressed in *Corrs Pavey Whiting & Byrne v Collector of Customs (Vic.)*, above, at 451–458. Those views are consistent with what was said by Rath J. in *Castrol Australia Pty Ltd v EmTech Associates Pty Ltd*, above, at 210–216, and by Hutley A.P. in *David Syme & Co Ltd v General Motors-Holden's Ltd* [1984] 2 N.S.W.L.R. 294 at 305–306. They are reinforced by a reading of the latest English decision on the subject, *W v Egdell* [1990] 2 W.L.R. 471 at 488–489. There, concepts drawn from the law as to discovery, contempt, contract, fiduciary duty, and undue influence, as well as from the equitable obligations of confidence owed to government and between citizens, are mixed to produce a curious melange, without an indication of the significance of what was being done.

No doubt the terms "confidence" and "confidential" appear in authorities in all these fields, but it by no means follows that they are used in the same sense across the legal spectrum. One is reminded of similar confusion of thought engendered by the use of "waiver" and "rescind" in various senses; see *Beatty v Guggenheim Exploration Co* 122 N.E. 378 at 381 (1919); *Wolf Mountain Coal Limited Partnership v Netherlands Pacific Mining Co Inc* (1988) 31 B.C.L.R. (2d) 16 at 28; *Johnson v Agnew* [1980] A.C. 367 at 394–398.

Further, I would accept the submissions by counsel for the applicants in the SK&F proceedings that (i) an examination of the recent English decisions shows that the so-called "public interest" defence is not so much a rule of law as an invitation to judicial idiosyncrasy by deciding each case on an ad hoc basis as to whether, on the facts overall, it is better to respect or to override the obligation of confidence, and (ii) equitable principles are best developed by reference to what conscionable behaviour demands of the defendant not by "balancing" and then overriding those demands by reference to matters of social or political opinion.

"Detriment"

The conclusion I have reached makes it unnecessary to decide whether the applicants in the

SK&F proceedings would have failed in any event because they had not established that they would suffer detriment from the apprehended breach of confidence. But if it had been necessary to rely upon them, my conclusions would have been as follows.

If a claim rests in contract and an injunction is sought to restrain breach of a negative stipulation to respect a confidence, then no question of the inadequacy of damages should arise, although in the court's discretion an injunction might be refused on other grounds: *Dalgety Wine Estates Pty Ltd v Rizzon* (1979) 141 C.L.R. 552 at 560, 573–574.

I then turn to cases of equitable obligations of confidence. I accept what was said in *The Commonwealth v John Fairfax & Sons Ltd*, above, at 52, as authority that where a government seeks in equity to protect its secrets something more, which may be described as detriment to the public interest is required of it than of other plaintiffs in these cases. As to other cases in equity, I note that in *Coco v A. N. Clark (Engineers) Ltd*, above, at 48, Megarry J. in fact left open the question of "detriment." Differing views were expressed in the House of Lords in *Attorney-General v Guardian Newspapers Ltd (No. 2)*, above, at 639–640, 650–651, 660, 668.

The authorities have been recently assembled and discussed by Mr Dean in his work *The Law of Trade Secrets* (1990), pp.177–178. They disclose that the question remains an open one in this country. I share the view of this learned author, and of Professor Birks in his note "A Lifelong Obligation of Confidence" (1989) 105 L.Q.R. 501, that equity intervenes to uphold an obligation and not necessarily to prevent or to recover loss; see also Gurry, *Breach of Confidence* (1984) pp.407–408. The cases dealing with recovery from errant fiduciaries of profits which their principles could not have made illustrate a similar point. The basis of the equitable jurisdiction to protect obligations of confidence lies, as the present case illustrates, in an obligation of conscience arising from the circumstances in or through which the information, the subject of the obligation, was communicated or obtained: *Moorgate Tobacco Co Ltd v Philip Morris Ltd (No. 2)*, above, at 438. The obligation of conscience is to respect the confidence, not merely to refrain from causing detriment to the plaintiff. The plaintiff comes to equity to vindicate his right to observance of the obligation, not necessarily to recover loss or to restrain infliction of apprehended loss. To look into a related field, when has equity said that the only breaches of trust to be restrained are those that would prove detrimental to the beneficiaries?

In any event, I would have accepted as sufficient "detriment" the apprehended prejudice to SK&F from the presence on the market of a rival (and cheaper) cimetidine product the evaluation of which may have reached a higher standard by the apprehended use of the innovator B1 data in the manner foreshadowed by the department's witnesses.

Gummow J. dismissed the SK&F proceedings. In the Alphapharm proceedings he made a declaration that the department was and remained at liberty to use SK&F's B1 data to evaluate Alphapharm's application to market a cimetidine product in Australia.

2.1.8   *Hoechst UK Ltd v Chemiculture Ltd* [1993] F.S.R. 270, Morritt J.

The plaintiffs Hoechst made and sold agro-chemicals, including a pesticide called fenoxaprop-ethyl ("FPE") which was marketed in France and Belgium under the name PUMA and in the UK under the registered trademark CHEETAH. The defendant acquired PUMA FPE in Belgium and sold it in the UK as CHEETAH.

Pesticides such as FPE and their containers had to be approved under the Food and Environmental Protection Act. In August 1991 officers of the Health and Safety Executive of the National Agriculture Centre, acting pursuant to powers under the Act, raided the defendant's premises. One of the officers passed information obtained during the raid to the plaintiffs, who used it to support a successful ex parte *application for an* Anton Piller *search order against the defendant based upon allegations of passing off and trademark infringement. The defendant, relying upon the case of* Marcel v Commissioner of Police of the Metropolis *[1992] 1 W.L.R. 50, applied to have the* Anton Piller *order discharged on the ground that information obtained during the raid was confidential and its disclosure to a competitor like Hoechst was a breach of confidence. Morritt J. considered* Marcel *in some detail before concluding:*

The principles I extract from this authority are:

(1) Information obtained pursuant to statutory powers can only be disclosed by the recipient to such persons and for such purposes as are envisaged by the statute conferring the powers or pursuant to a court order.

(2) The remedy of the person who provided the information to ensure compliance by the recipient with his obligation is an action for breach of confidence.

(3) If the recipient discloses information in breach of duty a third party proposing to use it will not be restrained unless he is aware of the confidentiality of the information at the time of the proposed use.

In relation to the third principle, if the third party is aware of the confidentiality of the information he can be restrained from using it even if he came by it innocently: compare *Goddard v Nationwide Building Society* [1986] 3 W.L.R. 734 at 745, and *English & American Insurance Co Ltd v Herbert Smith* [1988] F.S.R. 232 at 237.

The Food and Environmental Protection Act 1985 deals in Part III with the control of pesticides. Its purpose is set out in section 16(1) in the following terms:

The provisions of this Part of this Act shall have effect

(a) with a view to the continuous development of means

(i) to protect the health of human beings, creatures and plants;
(ii) to safeguard the environment; and
(iii) to secure safe, efficient and humane methods of controlling pests; and

(b) with a view to making information about pesticides available to the public.

Subsection (2) confers wide powers to implement those purposes by regulations. Such regulations include the Control of Pesticides Regulations 1986 (SI 1986/1510). Those regulations require a pesticide to be approved by the Ministry of Agriculture, Fisheries and Food. Such approval includes the form of the container and directions for use. The approval number must be shown on the container. The FPE sold under the name of PUMA and its container do not comply with these regulations. FPE sold by Hoechst in the name CHEETAH and in its container are so approved.

For the purposes of enforcing the provisions of the Act powers of entry, search and seizure are conferred on authorised persons by section 19 and Schedule II. A justice's warrant is only necessary if entry is required to a dwelling-house.

Given the purposes of the Act and the mutual interest of both Hoechst and the Ministry and through the Ministry the Health and Safety Executive in ensuring that FPE sold as CHEETAH should be confined to FPE in a container duly approved and properly sold under the name CHEETAH, I do not think that there is any impediment to the disclosure of information by the Ministry or the Health and Safety Executive to Hoechst which is relevant to that mutual interest and concern.

Morritt J. found on the evidence that the information disclosed by the Health and Safety Executive to Hoechst was relevant to this mutual interest so that there was no breach of confidence.

2.2   Protectable Secrets

2.2.1   *Fraser v Thames Television* **[1983] 2 All E.R. 101, Hirst J.**

Three actresses and a composer (who acted as manager) conceived a television series concerned with the formation of a female rock group and its subsequent adventures. The events and personalities would be based upon the actual lives of the three actresses, who had already formed a rock group. These ideas were disclosed to the defendant television company, together with a script-writer and script-editor who were also defendants.

The four plaintiffs granted Thames an option on the ideas, it being held to be a term of this that Thames would, if it made the series, offer the three actresses first refusal of the three parts in the rock group. Thames decided to make the series. It subsequently had a dispute with the actresses over the availability of one of them for filming and it used this as a reason for engaging other actresses for the parts. This was held by Hirst J. to amount to an unreasonable repudiation of contractual obligations amounting to breach.

In addition the plaintiffs claimed damages for the breach of confidence involved in using the ideas for the series in the programme actually made without permission (the series "Rock Follies"). On this aspect Hirst J. said:

The basic principles of the law of confidence are conveniently set out in *Copinger and Skone James on Copyright* (12th ed., 1980), para. 711 as follows:

> "There is broad and developing equitable doctrine that he who has received information in confidence shall not take unfair advantage of it or profit from the wrongful use or publication of it. He must not make any use of it to the prejudice of him who gave it, without paying him for it ... If, therefore, a defendant is proved to have used confidential information, directly or indirectly obtained from a plaintiff, without his consent, express or implied, he will be guilty of an infringement of the plaintiff's rights."

It is well settled that the obligation of confidence rests not only on the original recipient, but also on any person who received the information with knowledge acquired at the time or subsequently that it was originally given in confidence: see *Copinger and Skone James on Copyright*, para. 731.

Counsel for the defendants accepted that as a matter of principle the law of confidence is capable of protecting the confidential communication of an idea. But he argued that a literary or dramatic idea cannot be protected unless it is fully developed in the form of a synopsis or treatment and embodied in permanent form (*i.e.* in writing or on film or tape). His argument relied substantially on analogies with the law of copyright.

He further submitted that considerations of legal policy require that anything so ephemeral and so subject to contradictory recollection as an oral idea should not be protected; that such protection would unduly stultify an author's freedom to develop ideas; and that such protection would be unfair to third parties confronted with rival claims to the origination of an idea, since he says it would be impossible for them to decide which claimant was right in the absence of any written formulation of the idea in question.

Counsel for the defendants further argued that where an idea is capable of development in more than one format (*e.g.* situation comedy or drama) it is not entitled to protection.

I consider first the argument by analogy with the law of copyright, which may be summarised as follows. (1) It is trite law that there is no copyright in an idea as such. How anomalous would it be, argued counsel for the defendants, if the originator of an idea was in a better position under the law of confidence than under the law of copyright with its strict time limits and carefully defended limitations. (2) The authorities on the law of copyright clearly establish that a plaintiff can only succeed if his work is in a developed written form. The same, argued counsel for the defendants, should apply in confidence. (3) Decided copyright cases in relation to dramatic works, with particular reference to section 1(2) of the Copyright Act 1911 (now incorporated in section 2 of the Copyright Act 1956) establish that mere reproduction of a plot (*i.e.* an idea) is not an infringement. Infringement only arises if there is substantial reproduction of actual dramatic incidents or situations (*Copinger and Skone James on Copyright*, paras 539–540).

On these issues, Hirst J. referred to a number of authorities and concluded:

It is therefore an essential ingredient of every copyright action that the plaintiff should start with a work in permanent form.

On the other hand, under the general law of confidence the confidential communication relied on may be either written or oral (see, *e.g. Seager v Copydex Ltd* ([1967] 2 All E.R. 415, [1967] 1 W.L.R. 923).

Copyright is good against the world generally, whereas confidence only protects against those who receive information or ideas in confidence. Although copyright has a fixed (albeit extensive) statutory time limit, and confidence, at all events in theory, no time limit, in practice the obligation in confidence ceases the moment information or idea becomes public knowledge.

Furthermore, although the law of copyright protects unpublished as well as published works, it is no part of its purpose to protect confidentiality as such. Indeed section 46(4) of the 1956 Act expressly provides that "nothing in this Act shall affect the operation of any rule of equity relating to breaches of ... confidence".

Of much more assistance are the cases cited by counsel for the defendants which deal directly with breaches of confidence in the field under consideration. In *Gilbert v Star Newspapers Co Ltd* (1894) 11 T.L.R. 4 Chitty J. granted an *ex parte* injunction restraining the defendants from publishing the plot of Mr W.S. Gilbert's comic opera "His Excellency", which was due to open a few days later. It was argued that an actor or employee at the theatre must have communicated the information to the newspaper contrary to an established custom in the theatrical profession that such information was confidential. Chitty J. based his decision on the principles of the law of confidence as enunciated in *Prince Albert v Strange* (1849) 1 Mac & G 25, 41 E.R. 1171. Counsel for the defendants submitted that this case supported his argument that there must be a written libretto in existence before the law of confidence can apply to such a situation; but there is no indication in the report that the libretto as such was ever passed to the newspaper, and Chitty J. did not base his decision on any such consideration. It is, however, noteworthy that the confidential information in *Gilbert's* case related to the plot of the opera, which (as the copyright authorities cited above show) would not be protected as such under the law of copyright. This case therefore seems to establish a wider protection under the law of confidence than under the law of copyright.

In *Fraser v Edwards* [1905–10] MacG. Cop. Cas. 10 the defendant was held liable for breach of confidence by appropriation of the character, plot and idea from a scenario which had earlier been submitted by the plaintiff to the defendant's theatre manager. Counsel for the defendants pointed out that this case concerned a fully developed written scenario.

Finally in this group of cases, counsel for the defendants cited the very recent Australian decision of *Talbot v General Television Corp Pty Ltd* [1981] R.P.C. 1, a case which on the facts has some remarkable similarities with the present case. The judgment reported is that of Harris J. at first instance in the Supreme Court of Victoria. The decision was affirmed by the Full Court, but the appellate decision is not reported, so I am informed, either here or in Australia. In this case the plaintiff, a film producer, developed an idea for a television series, which he submitted in the form of a written submission to the defendants. He heard no more about his proposal. The defendants subsequently broadcast the first segment of a series of programmes which they claimed were their own idea, but which the plaintiff claimed were derived from his. The plaintiff sought an injunction on the ground of breach of confidence, and the hearing of the application was treated as the trial of the action. The learned judge found in favour of the plaintiff. He said (at 8–9):

> "It is clear that an obligation of confidence may exist where there is no contractual relationship between the parties. Where a plaintiff sues, relying upon breach of confidence, he must establish three elements. These are: (1) that the information was of a confidential nature; (2) that the information was communicated in circumstances importing an obligation of confidence; and (3) that there has been an unauthorised use of the information to the detriment of the person communicating it (*i.e.* the plaintiff). Those statements of law are taken from the judgment of Megarry J. in *Coco v A.N. Clark Engineers Ltd* [1969] R.P.C. 41 at 47–48: see also *Ansell Rubber Co Pty Ltd v Allied Rubber Industries Pty Ltd* [1967] V.R. 37; *Mense and Ampere Electrical Manufacturing Co Pty Ltd v Milenkovic* [1973] V.R. 784 at 800–801; and *Deta Nominees Pty Ltd v Viscount Plastic Products Pty Ltd* [1979] V.R. 167. Both counsel agreed that the three elements that I have referred to were the relevant principles to be applied in this case. Mr Gillard (counsel for the defendant) submitted that none of those elements had been established by the plaintiff, and further submitted that, even if they were, there were two other reasons why the plaintiff's claim should be dismissed. Mr Archibald (counsel for the plaintiff) submitted that the plaintiff had made out his case for relief and that none of the matters raised by Mr Gillard afforded any reason why relief should be denied to the plaintiff. Mr Gillard began by submitting that the information which the plaintiff alleged had been misused by the defendant did not have the necessary quality of confidence. He put it that the plaintiff was seeking to protect an idea for a programme about millionaires, how they succeeded and what viewers could learn from them, and that this was not original. He pointed to evidence that there had been programmes before on the careers of successful men and that it was a usual practice for interviewers to ask such people the secret of their success. He also put it that there was authority for the proposition that there is "no property in an idea" (or in knowledge) and that as all the plaintiff had conveyed to the network was an idea, it was not susceptible of protection. The authorities he referred to were *F.C. of T. v United Aircraft Corp* (1943) 68 C.L.R. 525 at 534 *per* Latham C.J. and *Halsbury*, (4th ed.), Vol. 9, para. 829. But the passages referred to deal with the point in different contexts (those of the construction of the word "idea" in a statute and in copyright

law) and do not support Mr Gillard's submission in this case. What Mr Archibald said was that this abstract proposition could only divert one from the real problem, and he referred to what Lord Upjohn said in *Boardman v Phipps* [1966] 3 All E.R. 721 at 759, [1967] 2 A.C. 46 at 127, where his Lordship pointed out that "the real truth is that it [*i.e.* information] is not property in any normal sense but equity will restrain its transmission to another if in breach of some confidential relationship". The real problem, Mr Archibald said, was to decide whether the idea, or concept, had been sufficiently developed. Where it had been developed to the point of setting out a format in which it could be presented, so that it was apparent that the concept could be carried into effect, then, said Mr Archibald, it was something that was capable of being the subject of a confidence. Without deciding that it is always necessary for a plaintiff to go that far, I am satisfied that where a concept or idea has been developed to the stage where the plaintiff had developed his concept, it is capable of being the subject of a confidential communication. The plaintiff had developed his concept so that it would be seen to be a concept which had at least some attractiveness as a television programme and to be something which was capable of being realised as an actuality."

Counsel for the defendants accepted, indeed contended, that the case was rightly decided, and, though not binding on me, I find it of great assistance. He submitted that the decision rested essentially on the fact that the material submitted by the plaintiff included a substantial written submission (see [1981] R.P.C. 1 at 5). However, it is clear that the judge expressly refrained from deciding that any less elaborately worked idea would not quality for protection.

Counsel for the plaintiffs also accepted the correctness of *Talbot's* case. He drew attention to the twist or slant which was held to be original (at 9); and he submitted that this twist or slant was the kernel of the idea to which, he submitted, the written submission added nothing of substance. He also drew attention to the fact that this kernel may have been communicated orally (at 10).

Counsel for the plaintiffs submitted that, as a matter of general principle, an obligation of confidence is implied in law if the communication is made in circumstances where the parties understand the recipient will treat it as confidential. He argued that this arises either (1) where the information or idea is given in a situation where both parties recognise an ethical obligation of confidence or (2) where information or an idea is communicated by one party to another with a view to a possible joint commercial venture or contractual relationship.

So far as ideas specifically are concerned, counsel for the plaintiffs submitted that there is no requirement that the idea must be developed to any particular degree, still less that it must be embodied in writing. He accepted that it must be specific in the sense that it must be clear and identifiable and that it must be original, at least to the extent that it is distinguishable from the ordinary run of ideas in common use. While he accepted it must have potential commercial merit, he argued that there is no requirement that it should have been developed to a state where it was ready for commercial exploitation.

On general principles of the law of confidence, Hirst J. quoted from Saltman v Campbell *(above, 2.1.2),* Seager v Copydex *(Nos 1 and 2) (above, 2.1.3; below 2.4.1),* Coco v Clark *(above, 2.1.5) and* Thomas Marshall v Guinle *(above, 2.1.6). He continued:*

In my judgment there is no reason in principle why an oral idea should not qualify for protection under the law of confidence, provided it meets the other criteria I discuss below.

Neither the originality nor the quality of an idea is in any way affected by the form in which it is expressed. No doubt both the communication and the content of an oral idea may be more difficult to prove than in the case of a written idea, but difficulties of proof should not affect the principle any more than in any other branches of the law where similar problems arise (*e.g.* contract and defamation).

I do not accept counsel for the defendants' argument that this will cause unfairness to third parties, since it is clear that, in order to be fixed with an obligation of confidence, a third party must know that the information was confidential; knowledge of a mere assertion that a breach of confidence has been committed is not sufficient: see *Carl-Zeiss-Stiftung v Herbert Smith & Co (a firm) (No. 2)* [1969] 2 All E.R. 367; [1969] 2 Ch. 276.

Nor do I accept counsel for the defendants' argument that an idea which is capable of development in more than one format is not entitled to protection. In my judgment the precise format is a matter for the writer to decide, and the fact that it is developable in more than one format in no way diminishes its intrinsic value.

I accept that to be capable of protection the idea must be sufficiently developed, so that it would be seen to be a concept which has at least some attractiveness for a television programme and which is capable of being realised as an actuality (see, *per* Harris J. in *Talbot's* case [1981] R.P.C. 1 at 9). But I do not think this requirement necessitates in every case a full synopsis. In some cases the nature of the idea may require extensive development of this kind in order to meet the criteria. But in others the criteria may be met by a short unelaborated statement of an idea. In *Talbot's* case itself I do not think the detailed submission (at 5) added very much of substance to the idea which is set out in one sentence (also at 5).

Unquestionably, of course, the idea must have some significant element of originality not already in the realm of public knowledge. The originality may consist in a significant twist or slant to a well-known concept (see *Talbot's* case). This is, I think, by analogy, consistent with the statements in *Saltman's* case and *Coco's* case that novelty in the industrial field can be derived from the application of human ingenuity to well-known concepts.

To the best of my recollection, every witness in the theatre or television business on both sides agreed that if he or she received an idea from another it would be wrong to make use of it without the consent of the communicator. They of course were expressing their views in the context of a moral usage in their profession rather than of a strict legal obligation. However, the authorities, and in particular *Saltman's* case, *per* Somervell L.J. and *Marshall's* case, strongly support counsel for the plaintiff's argument that the existence of such a usage is a factor of considerable force in deciding whether a legal obligation exists. I think the law as laid down in the authorities I have cited clearly establishes that the obligation which the witnesses saw as moral is in fact also legal in character.

This of course does not mean that every stray mention of an idea by one person to another is protected. To succeed in his claim the plaintiff must establish not only that the occasion of communication was confidential, but also that the content of the idea was clearly identifiable, original, of potential commercial attractiveness and capable of being realised in actuality. With these limitations, I consider there is no basis for the fears of counsel for the defendants that authors' freedom to develop ideas will be unduly stultified.

Hirst J. concluded on the facts that there had been an actionable breach of confidence and ordered an inquiry as to damages on this and other issues.

2.2.2   *Mustad v Allcock and Dosen* (1928) [1963] 3 All E.R. 416n, HL

Dosen was employed by a Norwegian firm, Thoring & Co, as a foreman engaged in manufacturing fish-hooks, subject to an express undertaking not to reveal confidential information. Thoring became insolvent and the business was purchased by the plaintiff company. Dosen was advised that, under Norwegian law, he owed no further duty of confidence. He joined the defendant company, Allcock, and disclosed to them details of a fish-hook manufacturing machine developed by Thoring. The plaintiff began proceedings for this breach of confidence but then applied for and obtained a patent for the very idea at issue. Upon request, its solicitors twice stated that the patent covered precisely the machine referred to in the Statement of Claim and in the Court of Appeal counsel appeared to make a similar concession.

Lord Buckmaster:

The important point about the patent is not whether it was valid or invalid, but what it was that it disclosed, because, after the disclosure had been made by the appellants to the world, it was impossible for them to get an injunction restraining the respondents from disclosing what was common knowledge. The secret, as a secret, had ceased to exist. But the appellants say—and, I think, say with considerable force—that it might well have been that, in the course of the experience which the respondent Dosen had gained in their service, he had obtained knowledge of ancillary secrets connected with the patented invention which were not in fact included in the invention but which would be of very great service to any person who proceeded to make the machine to which the invention related. Junior counsel for the appellants in his admirable argument satisfied me that it was at least probable or possible that such a set of circumstances might have existed; but, having regard to what had taken place and to the express request on the part of the respondents that they should be informed if the patented machine did in fact cover the very matter the disclosure of which was made the subject of complaints, it appears to me that there was thrown on the appellants the burden of showing that there were in fact these outside matters which were not included in the specification, that they had been or there was reasonable ground for believing they might be disclosed, and that their disclosure would be a wrong against which they were entitled to be protected by injunction. Nothing of the kind occurred. There was no attempt whatever made at the trial to distinguish between those parts of the machine which were outside the patent and those which were within. At no time was evidence led for the purpose of showing the added matter which the respondent Dosen might have learned in his former master's service and which he might disclose to the detriment of the appellants.

My lords, in those circumstances it appears to me that the appellants failed to discharge their primary duty at the hearing of this dispute, and that the Court of Appeal were quite right in dissolving the injunction which had been granted, and that, in consequence, this appeal must fail.

Viscount Dunedin and Lords Phillimore, Blanesburgh and Warrington of Clyffe concurred.

2.2.3   *Cranleigh Precision Engineering v Bryant* [1964] 3 All E.R. 289, Roskill J.

The plaintiff company, Cranleigh, manufactured above-ground swimming pools to a design invented by Bryant, its managing director. He learned, from the company's patent agent, of a British patent owned by Bischoff which covered features of the Cranleigh design. Cranleigh accordingly needed a licence under it. Instead of informing Cranleigh of this, Bryant took steps to set up a rival business and for it he purchased the Bischoff patent.

Cranleigh sued, inter alia, for an injunction against making use of confidential information obtained by Bryant as an officer of Cranleigh. To this, Bryant pleaded that the relevant information, the existence of the Bischoff patent, was in the public domain and that, in accordance with Mustad v Dosen *(above, 2.2.2), it could not be protected as confidential. On this question Roskill J. said:*

The effect of that decision clearly is that if the master had published his secret to the whole world (as had the appellants in that case) the servant is no longer bound by his promise to the master not to publish that same secret, but it is important to observe that the publication in that case was publication by the master. In the present case the publication was by Bischoff, who was never the master of Bryant. Bryant's master was the plaintiffs and the plaintiffs have never published anything, even their own specification. Counsel for the defendants sought to extract from the decision in *Mustad's* case the wider proposition that no matter by whom the publication took place, all attributes of secrecy of any kind which otherwise might have attached to the information in Bryant's possession automatically disappeared, once publication had taken place.

Roskill J. then referred to support for this view in Lord Greene's judgment in Saltman v Campbell *(above, 2.1.2) and to counsel's invitation to treat Roxburgh J.'s judgment in the* Terrapin *case [1960] R.P.C. 128, as accordingly not binding on him. He continued:*

It may be that, strictly speaking, counsel for the defendants is right in saying that in those circumstances it would be open for me to hold that the passage in Roxburgh J.'s judgment in the *Terrapin* case misstated the law. I apprehend that it would be my duty to do so if I were convinced that it conflicted with the decision in the *Mustad* case, but in my judgment there is no such conflict, because the two matters are separate and distinct. I would respectfully borrow and adopt the passage as correctly stating the law which I have to apply, and I respectfully agree with the learned judge in stating that the principle, as he stated it, is a logical consequence of the decision of the Court of Appeal in *Saltman's* case. *Mustad's* case was, as I have said, a case where the employer made the publication in question. In the present case, Bryant, as possessor of what I have held to be the plaintiff's confidential information, is seeking to free himself from his obligations of confidence, not because of what the plaintiffs have published, for they have published nothing, but because of what Bischoff published—a publication of which Bryant only became aware because of his contractual and confidential relationship with the plaintiffs.

I have dealt with this question at length, for the matter was argued at length before me. Applying the law as I conceive it to be, I have no doubt that Bryant acted in grave dereliction of his duty to the plaintiffs in concealing from the plaintiff's board the information which he received from the plaintiff's patent agents, and in taking no steps whatsoever to protect the plaintiffs against the possible consequences of the existence and publication of the Bischoff patent. I also have no doubt that Bryant acted in breach of confidence in making use, as he did as soon as he left the plaintiffs, of the information regarding the Bischoff patent which he had acquired in confidence and about its various effects on the plaintiff's position, for his own advantage and for that of the defendant company. Any other conclusion would involve putting a premium on dishonesty by managing directors. In reaching this conclusion I have not lost sight of the fact that the heads of agreements, unlike the draft service agreement which Bryant refused to sign, contained no express obligation not to divulge confidential information, but this makes no difference, for, were it necessary, I would not hesitate to imply in the contract of employment between Bryant and the plaintiffs the relevant obligation. It is both reasonable and necessary so to do. The plaintiffs relied on the decision of the Court of Appeal in *Swain v West (Butchers) Ltd* [1936] 3 All E.R. 261, in support of their argument that Bryant was under a duty to report to the plaintiff's board that of which the plaintiff's patent agents had informed him. I need only say that my conclusion on that part of the case is, I think, consistent with that decision. I reject the argument that it was a mere error of judgment on Bryant's part not to report this. It is difficult to think that as Bryant was able to buy the Bischoff specification in October-November, 1963, for a relatively trivial sum, the plaintiffs could not have done so at least as cheaply, had Bryant given them the opportunity of so doing.

2.2.4 *Interfirm Comparison v Law Society of New South Wales* [1977] R.P.C. 137, Bowen J., SC, NSW

The plaintiff conducted comparisons of costs, productivity, profitability, etc., between firms in the same business or profession. The defendant, the solicitors' professional body of New South Wales, wanted to collect certain objective data and so approached the plaintiff for that purpose.

Following a meeting between the parties, the defendant received a document described as a proposal for the survey, together with copies of a questionnaire which had previously been used and developed in 1972. The defendant decided that the proposal was unsuitable. With the assistance of the University of New England, it prepared and issued its own survey and questionnaire.

The plaintiff sought (i) to restrain the defendants from making use of confidential information and copyright material belonging to it; and (ii) an inquiry as to damages.

The defendant, by making a photostat copy of the plaintiff's questionnaire and sending the copy to the university, was held to have infringed the plaintiff's copyright in it. There was also found to be a breach of confidence in sending the plaintiff's questionnaire to the university, even though this was done by error or oversight and even though there was no evidence that the university had made any use of it. On this issue, Bowen J. said:

In my opinion, having regard to the amount of skill, judgment and labour involved in the preparation of the proposal and the 1972 questionnaire, and to the limited purpose of the negotiation between the plaintiff and the defendant in furtherance of which the material was supplied, both documents were confidential, in the sense that they could be used by the Law Society only for the purpose for which they had been given to it, that is to say, for the purpose of considering the deciding whether it would engage the services of the plaintiff for its own survey and interfirm comparison; they could not, without the plaintiff's assent, be used for other unrelated purposes—for example, for the purpose of publishing a book of precedents or writing an article in the *Law Society's Journal*.

It was argued for the defendant that much, if not all, of the material in the proposal and the questionnaire was already well-known, and should, on this ground, be denied the protection of confidentiality.

Although it is true, as I have pointed out in relation to copyright, that much of the material in the proposal and questionnaire was generally known, the particular expression and arrangement of this material found in the proposal and questionnaire was new; it was not generally known.

Then it is argued for the defendant that disclosure to any member of the public will destroy the claim to confidentiality, and that the plaintiff itself had destroyed any confidentiality in the 1972 questionnaire by the manner in which it had distributed it. In this regard counsel for the defendant relied upon patent cases dealing with disclosure which would cause an invention to be regarded as part of public knowledge in that field of the law (*R. v Patents Appeal Tribunal Ex p. Lovens Kemiske Fabriks Handelsaktieselskab* [1968] 1 W.L.R. 1727 at 1734; [1968] 3 All E.R. 536; *Fomento Industrial SA v Mentmore Manufacturing Co Ltd* [1956] R.P.C. 87 at 99).

It appears to me that decisions relating to patents are not helpful in dealing with questions of confidentiality. The Patents Act itself by its provisions raises some points of difference. But apart from that, in the case of an invention the State offers to the inventor a monopoly in return for disclosure in his specification of his invention. If an inventor has already disclosed his invention, even to one member of the public, it may be held as a matter of principle that he has no consideration to offer in return for the grant of monopoly (see *Humpherson v Syer* (1887) 4 R.P.C. 407 at 413). The law relating to confidentiality of communications appears to me to be based upon different principles—the long-standing equitable principles relating to fair-dealing with the work of another. It is closer to the law relating to copyright in unpublished works than to the law of patents. The authorities indicate that even though secrecy may be imperfect in relation to communication which is given in confidence, that communication may still be protected by the principles of confidentiality.

2.2.5 *Potters-Ballotini v Weston-Baker* [1977] R.P.C. 202, CA

The plaintiff company was the only British manufacturer of ballotini (glass beads), though it had competitors in Germany and Austria. Its general manager and works manager gave notice and, while working out the notice period, formed Bishop Auckland Glass with a leading employee of the company which had installed the plaintiff's furnace. The new company was able to set up its production assembly and factory on lines very similar to the plaintiff's so as to be in a position to start manufacturing almost before the plaintiff learned of what had happened. It accordingly sought interlocutory relief on the wide terms referred to in Lord Denning M.R.'s judgment. After reviewing the facts, he said:

All this sounds as if these three men were guilty of much wrongdoing. But it must be remembered that it is only wrong if Potters have a right to be protected. It is clear that Potters have no patent for any part of their machines, their process or their products; and that they have no claim to any copyright in any sketch, design, or drawing which was used in making the plant or any part of it. Thus, having no industrial property vested in them, Potters have sought to rely on the protection which the courts give to information imparted in confidence. It is well settled that information imparted in confidence (especially information which is imparted in confidence to servants or agents) will be protected. The courts will restrain the use of it if it is in breach of good faith. I need only quote the sentence which I have used in *Seager v Copydex Ltd* [1967] 1 W.L.R. 931: "The law on this subject does not depend on any implied contract. It depends on the broad principle of equity that he who has received information in confidence shall not take unfair advantage of it. He must not make use of it to the prejudice of him who gave it without obtaining his consent." Potters rely here on breach of confidence, and particularly in regard to Mr Weston-Baker and Mr Cramphorn.

At the outset, however, there is this point to consider. Potters had made express agreements with Mr Weston-Baker and Mr Cramphorn by which each agreed not for one year to use for himself, confidential information. What is the effect of the "one year"? Does it mean that after the year has ended, then men can use the information freely? We have been referred to passages from Lord Greene's statements in *Vokes Ltd v Heather* (1945) 62 R.P.C. 135, and his later statement in *British Celanese Ltd v Moncrieff* [1948] Ch. 578. I do not think it is necessary or desirable to give any final ruling, but I must say that these clauses seem to me designed to cover the period for which the company is seeking to protect confidential information. It can well be said that, after the men had left for one year, they were free from an obligation as to the use of confidential information. The dates are these: In February 1974 Mr Weston-Baker gave a year's notice. It was because of differences of policy. He was paid a year's salary, and worked a certain amount during the year. One year was the right period of notice. It would end in February or March 1975. In November 1974 Mr Cramphorn gave notice. He left in February 1975 and went to Messrs Boylin. So the employment of these two men certainly came to an end in March 1975. If the obligation as to confidence is governed by the contract—and was only for one year after the service ended—it would come to an end in March 1976, that is, next month. If either of them broke it in the past, there might be a remedy in damages, but there would not be a remedy by way of injunction for the future, seeing that they will soon be free to use it as they please.

The next point is: To what extent was this information to be regarded truly as confidential? Here we come up against another difficulty. As I have said, there is no patent and no copyright relied upon. There is no doubt whatever that a man, even in the course of his employment by others, may have quite a range of expertise and knowledge of his own which he is entitled to have for his own benefit. We know that Mr Cramphorn worked on these plants. He knew, I should have thought, as much as anyone about them. As I ventured to say myself in *Stephenson Jordan & Harrison Ltd v MacDonald & Evans* (1952) 69 R.P.C. 23: "A servant cannot help acquiring a great deal of knowledge of his master's method of business and of the science which his master practises. The servant when he leaves cannot be restrained from using the knowledge so acquired, so long as he does not take away trade secrets or lists of customers". I added:: "The claim for breach of confidence seemed to be an attempt to acquire a monopoly of a branch of human knowledge which the law does not permit except so far as Parliament has authorised it."

In this case it seems to me there would be great difficulty in determining to what extent the features of this plant or this process were confidential, especially when one remembers that there are other rival plants making ballotini in Germany and Austria, and have done for many years. There is a great deal of information which may be said to be in the public domain. But, apart from that, if not in the public domain, how far was it confidential to Potters—so as to belong to them—as distinct from the man's own knowledge and expertise, which he certainly is not to be prevented from using, as was pointed out, of course, in *Morris (Herbert) Ltd v Saxelby* [1916] 1 A.C. 688.

So there seems to me to be a great difficulty in defining what are the items of confidential information to which Potters would be entitled. We were given by Mr Leggatt a most useful table showing 13 items. Some of them he had to acknowledge could not be said to be confidential although they were items which had been copied. But he pointed to others which were confidential, particularly a part of the furnace and how it was made. He may succeed upon some items eventually, but it must be remembered that the injunction which is sought in is the most general terms. It is sought to restrain the defendants from using information, and so forth, obtained during their employments as to the working of any processes, as to know-how and the like. That is uncertain in the extreme. It is well established that an injunction ought to be such that the party affected can know with certainty what he is or is not allowed to do. There is no such certainty here.

Potters have even more difficulty in making a case against Mr Boylin. He was not a servant but only a contractor doing work on premises. He gave no pledge of secrecy. It would be even more difficult to find him guilty of a breach of confidential information.

Mr Leggatt said, and said forcibly, that the plaintiff's know-how and their process was such that in Japan and Australia there were firms and companies ready to pay for the information: and that the Japanese Government would not dream of paying four per cent royalty unless they were satisfied that they could not have found it out themselves. Mr Leggatt says that shows how important and confidential this information is. That is a telling point, but, nevertheless, it does not overcome to my mind, the difficulty of saying what is confidential and what is not.

Assuming that the point is overcome, there is the problem, which has been discussed, and much discussed of late, of what is called the "springboard" doctrine, whereby it is said that a servant or any other person who has got confidential information ought not to save himself the time of working it out for himself or getting it from some other people without paying for it. I need not go through all the cases. They are all well summarised by Megarry J. in his valuable judgment in *Coco v A.N. Clark (Engineers) Ltd* [1969] R.P.C. 41. Although a man must not use such information as a springboard to get a start over others, nevertheless that springboard does not last for ever. If he does use it, a time may come when so much has happened that he can no longer be restrained. That is another point of difficulty.

Accordingly, Lord Denning M.R. refused to grant the interlocutory injunction sought, applying American Cyanamid v Ethicon *[1975] A.C. 396. Scarman L.J. and Sir John Pennycuick delivered concurring judgments.*

2.2.6 *Dunford & Elliott v Johnson and Firth Brown* **[1978] F.S.R. 143, CA**

The plaintiff, a company in financial difficulties, decided to raise £3 million by way of a rights issue to their shareholders. In order to induce institutional shareholders who held 43 per cent of the shares to underwrite the rights issue they had been shown a confidential report on the company's financial and technical prospects under an obligation of confidence. The institutional shareholders were of the view that £3 million was inadequate to secure the company and therefore approached on their own initiative the defendant and one other company, suggesting that each should underwrite a further £500,000 without reference to the plaintiff. Representatives from both companies were permitted to study the confidential report in depth and make notes thereon. Soon afterwards the defendant announced that it was making a takeover bid for the plaintiffs. The plaintiffs sought an injunction to restrain the use of the con-

fidential information in the report and to restrain the takeover bid itself. In the course of refusing interlocutory relief, Lord Denning M.R. referred to Megarry J.'s three requisites (Coco v Clark, above, 2.1.5) and said:

Taking those three requisites. The first is satisfied. The information did have the quality of confidence. The second is satisfied. It was imparted in circumstances importing an obligation of confidence. That is shown by the letter which I have read by Morgan Grenfell to the consortium. It is said, also, that the third requisite is satisfied. D & E say that there was an unauthorised use of the information to their detriment; or, at any rate, to the detriment of their shareholders.

I do not think, however, that these three requisites cover the whole ground. Megarry J. drew attention to circumstances in which it would be unjust to enforce a stipulation for confidence, even though all three requisites are fulfilled. For instance when, in the course of negotiations, a confidential process is disclosed, and then the negotiations break down. His instances lead me to think there is a further principle applicable in these cases. If the stipulation for confidence was unreasonable at the time of making it; or if it was reasonable at the beginning, but afterwards, in the course of subsequent happenings, it becomes unreasonable that it should be enforced: then the courts will decline to enforce it: just as in the case of a covenant in restraint of trade.

It seems to me that that principle applies to this case. Although Dunford and Elliott (through Morgan Grenfell) stipulated that this report was confidential, it seems to me that, as events turned out, it would be quite unreasonable that the courts should enforce it. For one thing, it has since been discovered that Dunford and Elliott—or, at any rate, their directors—have made considerable use themselves of the forecasts contained in the report. We have been given figures showing that three of their directors, on October 7 and 8, bought 55,000 of the shares of Dunford and Elliott at a price of 14p—very nearly the lowest price they ever reached. I would imagine that they had some at least of the favourable forecasts—the confidential forecasts—before them at the time, and were better placed to buy the shares than outsiders. In addition, we know that Dunford and Elliott disclosed this confidential information to 43 per cent of the shareholders in the company— that is, to all the institutional shareholders; and none of the others. This widespread use of the information drives a hole into the blanket of confidence: especially when that information is being used—or, shall I say misused—for the benefit of some potential shareholders, and not for the benefit of the others. So much so that it would not be reasonable that the stipulation for confidence should be enforced.

Roskill and Lawton L.JJ. delivered concurring judgments.

2.2.7 *Hubbard v Vosper* [1972] 2 Q.B. 84, CA

The defendant had participated in a course of initiation into the cult of Scientology, undertaking at the time to use the knowledge gained only for Scientology purposes and not to reveal "Level VI" materials to outsiders. He became disillusioned and wrote a book criticising the cult and quoting from "Level VI" materials comprising the works of the cult's moving spirit, Lafayette Ronald Hubbard. In interlocutory proceedings to prevent its publication, allegations of copyright infringement and breach of confidence were made.

On the issue of copyright infringement, it was held that the defendant might have a defence of fair dealing for purposes of criticism or review even though the documents from which he was quoting had been kept private and confidential (on this issue see the summary of judgments in Beloff v Pressdram *(below, 3.6.5.3).*

On breach of confidence, Megaw L.J. said:

The law will, in a proper case, intervene to restrain a defendant from revealing information or other material obtained in confidence, such as trade secrets, and the like. This depends on the broad principle of equity that he who has received information in confidence shall not take unfair advantage of it: see *Seager v Copydex* [above, 2.1.3]. But the information must be such that it is a proper subject for protection. As I said in *Fraser v Evans* [above, 2.1.4]:

> "There are some things which may be required to be disclosed in the public interest, in which event no confidence can be prayed in aid to keep them secret."

In this case counsel for the defendants has drawn our attention to the nature of these courses for which confidence is claimed. The plaintiffs themselves say that: "the material contained in these courses can be dangerous in untrained hands." Counsel for the defendants took us through the books and said that they indicate medical quackeries of a sort which may be dangerous if practised behind closed doors. They are so dangerous, he said, that it is in the public interest that these goings-on should be made known. The closed doors should be opened for all to see. We cannot decide on it today, as this is only an interlocutory application. But, I think that, even on what we have heard so far, there is good ground for thinking that these courses contain such dangerous material that it is in the public interest that it should be known.

I turn to the question of confidentiality. Lord Denning M.R. has referred to one passage which occurred in some of the documents put before us in relation to fair game. I think it is right, in fairness to the plaintiffs, that it should be said that it would seem that that particular provision has disappeared from the latest, or 1970, edition of the book "Introduction to Scientology Ethics". It is right in these circumstances that something should be said about the history of that provision. So far as the documents before us are concerned, it appears chronologically for the first time in what is described as the "Hubbard Communications Office Policy Letter of March 1, 1965", under the heading, "Justice, Suppressive Acts, Suppression of Scientology and Scientologists. The Fair Game Law". That document defined "Potential Trouble Sources. They were persons who were active in Scientology, or persons known as "preclears", who remained "connected to a person or group that is a suppressive person or group". A "suppressive person or group" is then defined in the document as "one that actively seeks to suppress or damage Scientology or a Scientologist by Suppressive Acts". "Suppressive acts" are then defined as "acts calculated to impede or destroy Scientology or a Scientologist and which are listed at length in this policy letter". I should refer to some of these "suppressive acts", the carrying out of which turns a person, for the purpose of this document, into a "suppressive person or group". "Suppressive acts" include "proposing, advising or voting for legislation or ordinances, rules or laws directed toward the Suppression of Scientology ..." so that if a voter in this country were to have the temerity to cast a vote in a Parliamentary election for a candidate who had indicated that he was minded to propose legislation which would "suppress" Scientology, that person would be guilty in the eyes of this organisation of having committed "a suppressive act". Again, "testifying hostilely before state or public enquiries into Scientology to suppress it"; "reporting or threatening to report Scientology or Scientologists to civil authorities in an effort to suppress Scientology or Scientologists from practising or receiving standard Scientology"; "bringing civil suit against any Scientology organisation or Scientologist including the non-payment of bills or failure to refund without first calling the matter to the attention of the Chairman ..."; "writing anti-Scientology letters to the press or giving anti-Scientology or anti-Scientologist evidence to the press"; "testifying as a hostile witness against Scientology in public". If words mean anything, that meant that in the eyes of this organisation a person became "a suppressive person"—"a suppressive person" guilty of a suppressive act—if, however truthful, however much compelled by process of law, he should give evidence in a court of law hostile to the organisation of Scientology. And this is the organisation which is seeking to have its documents treated as confidential by the order of the court. It went on to include among "suppressive acts": "first degree murder, arson, disintegration of persons or belongings not guilty of suppressive acts". There can be no doubt that the last five words relate to the preceding word "persons". What does that mean? That it was, in the eyes of this organisation in 1965, "a suppressive act" to be guilty of "first degree murder", provided that the person you murdered had not been guilty of suppressive acts. The implication is obvious. Yet another "suppressive act" is, "delivering up the person of a Scientologist without defense or protest to the demands of civil or criminal law".

In the 1968 edition of "Scientology Ethics" those provisions remain substantially the same and they continue at that date to include the "fair game" provisions which I have mentioned as having been included in the "Justice policy" document of 1965. In this year's it was provided that suppressive persons or groups became "fair game":

> "... by 'fair game' is meant, without rights for self, possessions or position, and no Scientologist may be brought before a Committee of Evidence or punished for any action taken against a Suppressive Person or Group during the period that person or group is 'fair game'."

Well, it may be that there is or was some explanation of that general provision, as of the related "first degree murder" provision, which will take away from it the meaning which to any ordinary person it would carry; namely, that here was an organisation which had laid down a criminal code of its own and by that criminal code it treated and required its adherents to treat, persons as outlaws deprived of any protection or sanction so far as the Scientological organisation was concerned if they had been guilty of "suppressive acts", and no Scientologist was to be condemned, under the ethical code of Scientology, for any action—I repeat any action—which he might take against such "fair game". It is right that this should be mentioned: in the latest edition of the Scientology Ethics, which appears to have been published in the year 1970 the provisions as to "fair game" have been removed from its code of ethics.

Most of the matters which I have mentioned earlier, as being examples of "suppressive acts" will remain as "suppressive acts". They come under the heading "High Crimes (Suppressive Acts)"; but the provisions as to "fair game" have disappeared from the code. One other respect in which "suppressive acts" have changed since the original policy document is this: the last five words have disappeared from that extraordinary example of a "suppressive act": "first degree murder, arson, disintegration of persons or belongings not guilty of suppressive acts". So that the Scientology organisation has now changed its provisions, from those that previously prevailed, in such a way that "first degree murder" may now apparently be regarded as a crime within this organisation, even though the murderer is a Scientologist, and even though the victim is one who, in the eyes of the organisation, has committed a "suppressive act", such as having written a letter to a newspaper adversely criticising Scientology.

In the circumstances, the court was not prepared to grant interlocutory relief.

2.2.8 *Lion Laboratories v Evans* **[1984] 2 All E.R. 417, CA**

The plaintiff company manufactured and sold the Lion Intoximeter, an instrument for measuring intoxication from alcohol, particularly in drivers. Sixty per cent of sales of the device were in the UK, where it was one of two devices approved by the Home Office for police use in breathalysing. Despite an ex parte *injunction, The Daily Express, one of the defendants, published a report alleging that the Intoximeter was liable to serious error which could lead to wrongful conviction. This information came from two former employees of the plaintiff, who were also defendants. The Court of Appeal discharged the interlocutory injunctions granted below, save in respect of specified documents.*

Stephenson L.J.:

The problem before the judge and before this court is how best to resolve, before trial, a conflict of two competing public interests. The first public interest is the preservation of the right of organisations, as of individuals, to keep secret confidential information. The courts will restrain breaches of confidence, and breaches of copyright, unless there is just cause or excuse for breaking confidence or infringing copyright. The just cause or excuse with which this case is concerned is the public interest in admittedly confidential information. There is confidential information which the public may have a right to receive and others, in particular the press, now extended to the media, may have a right and even a duty to publish, even if the information has been unlawfully obtained in flagrant breach of confidence and irrespective of the motive of the informer. The duty of confidence, the public interest in maintaining it, is a restriction on the freedom of the press which is recognised by our law, as well as by Article 10(2) of the European Convention for the Protection of Human Rights and Fundamental Freedoms, Rome, (TS 71 (1953); Cmd. 8969; November 4, 1950); the duty to publish, the countervailing interest of the public in being kept informed of matters which are of real public concern, is an inroad on the privacy of confidential matters.

So much is settled by decisions of this court, and in particular by the illuminating judgments of Lord Denning M.R. in *Initial Services Ltd v Putterill* [1967] 3 All E.R. 145; [1968] 1 Q.B. 396, *Fraser v Evans* [1969] 1 All E.R. 8; [1969] 1 Q.B. 349, *Hubbard v Vosper* [1972] 1 All E.R. 1023; [1972] 2 Q.B. 84, *Woodward v Hutchins* [1977] 2 All E.R. 751; [1977] 1 W.L.R. 760 and (dissenting) *Schering Chemicals Ltd v Falkman Ltd* [1981] 2 All E.R. 321; [1982] Q.B. 1. I add to those the speeches of Lord Wilberforce, Lord Salmon and Lord Fraser in *British Steel Corp v Granada Television Ltd* [1981] 1 All E.R. 417; [1981] A.C. 1096.

There are four further considerations. First, "There is a wide difference between what is interesting to the public and what it is in the public interest to make known": *per* Lord Wilberforce in *British Steel Corp v Granada Television Ltd* [1981] 1 All E.R. 417 at 455; [1981] A.C. 1096 at 1168. The public are interested in many private matters which are no real concern of theirs and which the public have no pressing need to know. Secondly, the media have a private interest of their own in publishing what appeals to the public and may increase their circulation or the numbers of their viewers or listeners; and (I quote from the judgment of Sir John Donaldson M.R. in *Francome v Mirror Group Newspapers Ltd* [1984] 2 All E.R. 408 at 413) "... they are peculiarly vulnerable to the error of confusing the public interest with their own interest". Thirdly, there are cases in which the public interest is best served by an informer giving the confidential information not to the press but to the police or some other responsible body, as was suggested by Lord Denning M.R. in the

Initial Services case and by Sir John Donaldson M.R. in the *Francome* case. Fourthly, it was said by Page Wood V.C. in *Gartside v Outram* (1856) 26 L.J. Ch. 113 at 114, "there is no confidence as to the disclosure of iniquity"; and although counsel concedes on the plaintiffs' behalf that, as Salmon L.J. said in *Initial Services Ltd v Putterill* [1967] 3 All E.R. 145 at 151; [1968] 1 Q.B. 396 at 410, "what was iniquity in 1856 may be too narrow, or too wide, in 1967", and in 1984 extends to serious misdeeds or grave misconduct, he submits that misconduct of that kind is necessary to destroy the duty of confidence or excuse the breach of it, and nothing of that sort is alleged against the plaintiffs in the evidence now before the court.

Counsel for the third and fourth defendants and counsel for the first and second defendants have not been able to find any case where a defendant has been able to rely on public interest in defence of a claim for breach of confidence and the plaintiff has not also been guilty of such misconduct. And there are passages in the speeches of Lord Wilberforce and Lord Fraser in *British Steel Corp v Granada Television Ltd* in which they appear to be satisfied with describing the public interest rule as the "iniquity rule". But I nowhere find any authority for the proposition, except perhaps in the judgment of Ungoed-Thomas J. in *Beloff v Pressdram Ltd* [1973] 1 All E.R. 241 at 260, that some modern form of iniquity on the part of the plaintiffs is the only thing which can be disclosed in the public interest; and I agree with the judge in rejecting the "no iniquity, no public interest" rule and in respectfully adopting what Lord Denning M.R. said in *Fraser v Evans* [1969] 1 All E.R. 8 at 11; [1969] 1 Q.B. 349 at 362 that some things are required to be disclosed in the public interest, in which case no confidence can be prayed in aid to keep them secret, and [iniquity] is merely an instance of a just cause and excuse for breaking confidence.

Griffiths L.J. put this case in argument. Suppose the plaintiffs had informed the police that their Intoximeter was not working accurately or safe to use, and the police had replied that they were nevertheless going to continue using it as breath test evidence. Could there then be no defence of public interest if the defendants sought to publish that confidential information, simply because the plaintiffs themselves had done nothing wrong but the police had? There would be the same public interest in publication, whichever was guilty or misconduct, and I cannot think the right to break confidence would be lost, though the public interest remained the same.

Bearing this last consideration in mind, in my opinion we cannot say that the defendants must be restrained because what they want to publish does not show misconduct by the plaintiffs.

We have then, with the other three considerations in mind and remembering that confidentiality is admitted, to ask what the judge called the "sole question", namely:

"... whether the defendants have shown that they have an arguable defence to the plaintiffs' claims in respect of breach of confidentiality and breach of copyright"

and that means, as counsel for the third and fourth defendants ultimately expressed it, a serious defence of public interest which may succeed, not, of course, will succeed, at the trial. He had expressed it rather differently as a reasonable defence, taking the words from the judgment of Lord Denning M.R. in *Hubbard v Vosper* [1972] 1 All E.R. 1023; [1972] 2 Q.B. 84, where it was treated like a plea of justification or fair comment in a libel suit. And there are statements in the judgments of Lord Denning M.R. in *Fraser v Evans* [1969] 1 All E.R. 8; [1969] 1 Q.B. 349 and of Roskill L.J. in the unreported case of *Khashoggi v Smith* [1980] C.A. Transcript 58, which indicate that a plaintiff should not be better off if he claims for breach of confidence than if he claims for defamation. But I respectfully agree with Sir David Cairns in *Khashoggi's* case "that there is a fundamental distinction between the two types of action". To be allowed to publish confidential information, the defendants must do more than raise a plea of public interest: they must show "a legitimate ground for supposing it is in the public interest for it to be disclosed". The, as Lord Denning M.R. said in *Woodward v Hutchins* [1977] 2 All E.R. 751 at 755; [1977] 2 W.L.R. 760 at 764, "the courts should not restrain it by interlocutory injunction, but should leave the complainant to his remedy in damages", after (I will assume, though I am not sure that Lord Denning M.R. would have agreed) considering and weighing in the balance all relevant matters, such as whether damages would be an adequate remedy to compensate the plaintiffs if they succeeded at the trial.

We cannot of course at this stage decide whether the balance will come down on the side of confidentiality or of public interest. But, to see if there is serious defence of public interest which may succeed at the trial, we have to look at the evidence and if we decide that there is such a defence, to perform a balancing exercise, as indicated for instance in the judgment of Lord Denning M.R. in *Woodward v Hutchins* and in the speech of Lord Fraser in *British Steel Corp v Granada Television Ltd* [1981] 1 All E.R. 417 at 480; [1981] A.C. 1096 at 1202, which is so apt that I follow the judge in quoting it. In that case Lord Fraser said:

> "The answer to the question therefore seems to me to involve weighing up the public interest for and against publication. The balance does not in my opinion depend on the use made of the leaked information by the appellants in this particular case. Anyone who hands over to the press a bundle of confidential documents belonging to someone else must surely expect, and intend, that, if they contain information of topical interest, it will be published in some form. The informer's motives are, in my opinion, irrelevant. It is said, and I am willing to accept, that in this case the informant neither asked for nor received any money, or other reward, but that he acted out of a keen sense of indignation about the dealings between BSC and the government before and during the strike. No doubt there is a public interest in maintaining the free flow of information to the press, and therefore against obstructing informers. But there is also I think a very strong public interest in preserving confidentiality within any organisation, in order that it can operate efficiently, and also be free from suspicion that it is harbouring disloyal employees. There is no difference in this respect between a public corporation like BSC and an ordinary company."

Stephenson L.J. reviewed the evidence in detail and continued:

The judge never referred to the damage already done to the reputation of the plaintiffs and their Intoximeter by what had already been published and merely recorded the arguments of counsel for the plaintiffs on the damage which would be done by further publication without putting it in the scales, I think because he had already decided that they tipped in the plaintiff's favour for breach of confidence and also because the damage done by March 14 is not as great as the damage done by further publication since that date. It may be distasteful to let damage done by a newspaper weigh in support of its application to be allowed to do more damage by breaking confidence. Nevertheless, the existing damage is, in my view, a matter which the court must now take into account, and that is another factor which entitles us to differ from the judge. ...

Stephenson L.J.'s final conclusion was:

The issue raised by the defendants is a serious question concerning a matter which affects the life, and even the liberty, of an unascertainable number of Her Majesty's subjects, and though there is no proof that any of them has been wrongly convicted on the evidence of the plaintiffs' Intoximeter, and we certainly cannot decide that any has, we must not restrain the defendants from putting before the public this further information how the Lion Intoximeter 3000 has worked, and how the plaintiffs regard and discharge their responsibility for it, although the information is confidential and was unlawfully taken in breach of confidence.

O'Connor and Griffiths L.JJ. delivered concurring opinions.

2.2.9 *Stephens v Avery* [1988] 2 All E.R. 477, Browne-Wilkinson V.C.

According to the plaintiff's pleading, she told her friend, Mrs Avery (first defendant), about a lesbian relationship with a Mrs Telling, who had been killed by her husband. This revelation was expressly upon terms that it was confidential. Despite this, Mrs Avery revealed the information to The Mail on Sunday, which published it. The plaintiff sued Mrs Avery, the paper and its editor for damages for the breach of confidence. The defendants sought to strike out the action as revealing no reasonable cause of action. The master refused to do so and an appeal did not succeed.

In giving judgment, Browne-Wilkinson V.C. dealt with arguments arising under the first two requirements for liability prescribed by Megarry J. in Coco v Clark *(above, 2.1.5). As regards the requirement of confidential subject-matter, he referred to* Glyn v Weston Feature Film *[1916] 1 Ch. 261 at 269, and continued:*

I entirely accept the principle stated in that case, the principle being that a court of equity will not enforce copyright, and presumably also will not enforce a duty of confidence, relating to matters which have a grossly immoral tendency. But at the present day the difficulty is to identify what sexual conduct is to be treated as grossly immoral. In 1915 there was a code of sexual morals accepted by the overwhelming majority of society. A judge could therefore stigmatise certain sexual conduct as offending that moral code. But at the present day no such general code exists. There is no common view that sexual conduct of any kind between consenting adults is grossly immoral. I suspect the works of Elinor Glyn if published today would be widely regarded as, at the highest, very soft pornography.

The sexual conduct of the plaintiff was not so morally shocking in this case as to prevent the third defendant, a major national Sunday newspaper, from spreading the story all over its front and inside pages. The submission on behalf of these defendants that the actions of the plaintiff in this case are so grossly immoral as to produce a tendency towards immoral conduct and thereby to be without the law lies ill in their mouths, since they have themselves spread the news of such conduct nationwide for their own personal profit.

If it is right that there is now no generally accepted code of sexual morality applying to this case, it would be quite wrong in my judgment for any judge to apply his own personal moral views, however strongly held, in deciding the legal rights of the parties. The court's function is to apply the law, not personal prejudice. Only in a case where there is still a generally accepted moral code can the court refuse to enforce rights in such a way as to offend that generally accepted code.

As to the submission that there is no confidentiality in tittle-tattle gossip, counsel for the defendants relied on a passage in the *Coco* case [1969] R.P.C. 41 at 48, where Megarry J. said:

> "... I doubt whether equity would intervene unless the circumstances are of sufficient gravity; equity ought not to be invoked merely to protect trivial tittle-tattle, however confidential".

Since the *Coco* case was exclusively concerned with information which was of industrial value, those remarks were plainly *obiter dicta*. Moreover, I have the greatest doubt whether wholesale revelation of the sexual conduct of an individual can properly be described as "trivial" tittle-tattle. Again, although it is true that the passage I have quoted occurs in that part of the judgment which deals with the nature of information which can be protected, it is to be noted that the judge appeared to be considering when equity would give a remedy, not dealing with the fundamental nature of the legal right. If, as I think he was, Megarry J. was saying that the discretion to grant an injunction or to award damages would not be exercised in a case which was merely trivial, I agree. But the exercise of such a discretion can only be decided in the light of all the circumstances. Those cannot be known until there has been a trial.

The Vice-Chancellor also rejected as misconceived an argument that information relating to any type of mutual sexual conduct could not be confidential since both parties to it must be aware of the facts.

As to the requirement that the information be communicated in circumstances giving rise to a duty of confidence, he stated:

Counsel for the defendants submits that in the absence of either a legally enforceable contract or a pre-existing relationship, such as that of employer and employee, doctor and patient, or priest and penitent, it is not possible to impose a legal duty of confidence on the recipient of the information merely by saying that the information is given in confidence. In my judgment that is wrong in law. The basis of equitable intervention to protect confidentiality is that it is unconscionable for a person who has received information on the basis that it is confidential subsequently to reveal that information. Although the relationship between the parties is often important in cases where it is said there is an implied as opposed to express obligation of confidence, the relationship between the parties is not the determining factor. It is the acceptance of the information on the basis that it will be kept secret that affects the conscience of the recipient of the information. I quote again from the judgment of Bingham L.J. in the *Spycatcher* case, where he said ([1988] 2 W.L.R. 805 at 904):

> "The cases show that the duty of confidence does not depend on any contract, express or implied, between the parties. If it did, it would follow on ordinary principles that strangers to the contract would not be bound. But the duty 'depends on the broad principle of equity that he who has received information in confidence shall not take unfair advantage of it': *Seager v Copydex Ltd* [1967] 2 All E.R. 415 at 417; [1967] 1 W.L.R. 923 at 931, *per* Lord Denning M.R. 'The jurisdiction is based not so much on property or on contract as on the duty to be of good faith': *Fraser v Evans* [1969] 1 All E.R. 8 at 11; [1969] 1 Q.B. 349, 361, *per* Lord Denning M.R."

If, as is here alleged, the information was communicated and accepted expressly in confidence, the conscience of Mrs Avery is just as much affected as in any other case. In my judgment the express statement that the information is confidential is the clearest possible example of the imposition of a duty of confidence.

2.2.10   *Attorney General v Guardian Newspapers (No.2)* [1990] 1 A.C. 109, HL

The scandal surrounding the publication of Spycatcher—*the memoirs of former MI5 agent, Peter Wright*—*led to extensive litigation both in New South Wales (NSW) and England. The former proceedings had a considerable impact on the latter. The book was, however, first published in the US on July 13, 1987. This the British government did not try to stop; there were constitutional objections there to imposing any prior restraint on the publication of such material.*

The timetable of events can be set out thus:

Events outside UK

1. *1985: A.G. (UK) obtains undertaking in NSW from Wright and his publishers not to publish pending trial of actions there against them for breach of confidence.*

2. *November 1986–March 1987. Powell J. tries and dismisses NSW action, but undertakings not to publish continue pending appeal.[1]*

3. *July 13, 1987: publication of Spycatcher in US Copies begin to appear in Britain without attempts by Customs to stop them.*

Events in UK

1.(a) *June 1986: after receiving a leak, The Observer and The Guardian publish accounts of forthcoming NSW trial and mention some of revelations of MI5 activity contained in the book.*

(b) *Millett J. grants injunctions restraining further similar reports by these newspapers, subject to exceptions including the reporting of things said in open court in Australia.*

2. *April 1987: The Independent, The Evening Standard and The London Daily News publish articles repeating some of Wright's allegations. The Court of Appeal holds these articles to be capable of constituting contempt of court by undermining the Millett injunctions against The Observer and The Guardian.[2]*

3. *July 12, 1987: by secret arrangement with Wright's US publishers, an extract from Spycatcher appears in The Sunday Times. More promised but*

(i) *The Sunday Times held by the Court of Appeal to be in contempt of the Millett injunctions.*

(ii) *House of Lords (3–2) refuse to discharge those injunctions and even remove the exception*

---

[1] *(1987) 8 N.S.W.L.R. 341.*

[2] A.G. v Newspaper Publishing *[1988] Ch. 333. After this determination of the preliminary issue, the matter came to trial against several newspapers. Three were found to have committed the actus reus of a contempt and to have had the necessary mens rea, the contempt being "in respect of conduct intended to impede or prejudice the administration of justice" (Contempt of Court Act 1981, s.6(c)); see A.G. v Times Newspapers [1992] 1 A.C. 191, HL.*

4. September 1987: New South Wales Court of Appeal upholds dismissal of the action there and undertaking not to publish lapses.[4] Further appeal to High Court of Australia upholds judgments below: June 1988.[5]

concerning reports of Australian proceedings.[3]

4. November 1987–October 1988: Trial of actions for permanent injunctions against The Observer/ Guardian and The Sunday Times commences. Injunctions refused by Scott J., the Court of Appeal and the House of Lords; but The Sunday Times is held liable to account for profits of publication on July 12, 1987.

Extracts given here are from House of Lords speeches in the UK proceedings for permanent injunctions (3. right hand above).

Lord Keith of Kinkel:

The Crown's case on all the issues which arise invokes the law about confidentiality. So it is convenient to start by considering the nature and scope of that law. The law has long recognised that an obligation of confidence can arise out of particular relationships. Examples are the relationships of doctor and patient, priest and penitent, solicitor and client, banker and customer. The obligation may be imposed by an express or implied term in a contract but it may also exist independently of any contract on the basis of an independent equitable principle of confidence: see *Saltman Engineering Co Ltd v Campbell Engineering Co Ltd* (1948) [1963] 3 All E.R. 413. It is worthy of some examination whether or not detriment to the confider of confidential information is an essential ingredient of his cause of action in seeking to restrain by injunction a breach of confidence. Presumably that may be so as regards an action for damages in respect of a past breach of confidence. If the confider has suffered no detriment thereby he can hardly be in a position to recover compensatory damages. However, the true view may be that he would be entitled to nominal damages. Most of the cases have arisen in circumstances where there has been a threatened or actual breach of confidence by an employee or ex-employee of the plaintiff, or where information about the plaintiff's business affairs has been given in confidence to someone who has proceeded to exploit it for his own benefit: an example of the latter type of case is *Seager v Copydex Ltd* [1967] 2 All E.R. 415; [1967] 1 W.L.R. 923. In such cases the detriment to the confider is clear. In other cases there may be no financial detriment to the confider, since the breach of confidence involves no more than an invasion of personal privacy. Thus in *Margaret, Duchess of Argyll v Duke of Argyll* [1965] 1 All E.R. 611; [1967] Ch. 302 an injunction was granted against the revelation of marital confidences. The right to personal privacy is clearly one which the law should in this field seek to protect. If a profit has been made through the revelation in breach of confidence of details of a person's private life it is appropriate that the profit should be accounted for to that person. Further, as a general rule it is in the public interest that confidences should be respected, and the encouragement of such respect may in itself constitute a sufficient ground for recognising and enforcing the obligation of confidence even where the confider can point to no specific detriment to himself. Information about a person's private and personal affairs may be of a

---

[3] *[1987] 3 All E.R. 316; [1987] 1 W.L.R. 1248.*

[4] *(1987) 75 A.L.R. 353.*

[5] *(1988) 78 A.L.R. 449.*

nature which shows him up in a favourable light and would by no means expose him to criticism. The anonymous donor of a very large sum to a very worthy cause has his own reasons for wishing to remain anonymous, which are unlikely to be discreditable. He should surely be in a position to restrain disclosure in breach of confidence of his identity in connection with the donation. So I would think it a sufficient detriment to the confider that information given in confidence is to be disclosed to persons whom he would prefer not to know of it, even though the disclosure would not be harmful to him in any positive way.

The position of the Crown, as representing the continuing government of the country, may, however, be regarded as being special. In some instances, disclosure of confidential information entrusted to a servant of the Crown may result in a financial loss to the public. In other instances such disclosure may tend to harm the public interest by impeding the efficient attainment of proper governmental ends, and the revelation of defence or intelligence secrets certainly falls into that category. The Crown, however, as representing the nation as a whole, has no private life or personal feelings capable of being hurt by the disclosure of confidential information. In so far as the Crown acts to prevent such disclosure or to seek redress for it on confidentiality grounds, it must necessarily, in my opinion, be in a position to show that the disclosure is likely to damage or has damaged the public interest. How far the Crown has to go in order to show this must depend on the circumstances of each case. ...

There are two important cases in which the special position of a government in relation to the preservation of confidence has been considered. The first of them is *Attorney General v Jonathan Cape Ltd* [1975] 3 All E.R. 484; [1976] Q.B. 752. That was an action for injunctions to restrain publication of the political diaries of the late Richard Crossman, which contained details of Cabinet discussions held some 10 years previously, and also of advice given to ministers by civil servants. Lord Widgery C.J. said ([1975] 3 All E.R. 484 at 495; [1976] Q.B. 752 at 770–771):

> "In these actions we are concerned with the publication of diaries at a time when 11 years have expired since the first recorded events. The Attorney-General must show (a) that such publication would be in breach of confidence, (b) that the public interest requires that the publication be restrained, and (c) that there are no other facets of the public interest contradictory to and more compelling than that relied on. Moreover, the court, when asked to restrain such a publication, must closely examine the extent to which relief is necessary to ensure that restrictions are not imposed beyond the strict requirement of public need".

Lord Widgery C.J. went on to say that, while the expression of individual opinions by Cabinet ministers in the course of Cabinet discussions were matters of confidence, the publication of which could be restrained by the court when clearly necessary in the public interest, there must be a limit in time after which the confidential character of the information would lapse. Having read the whole of volume one of the diaries he did not consider that publication of anything in them, ten years after the event, would inhibit full discussion in the Cabinet at the present time or thereafter, or damage the doctrine of joint Cabinet responsibility. He also dismissed the argument that publication of advice given by senior civil servants would be likely to inhibit the frankness of advice given by such civil servants in the future. So, in the result, Lord Widgery's decision turned on his view that it had not been shown that publication of the diaries would do any harm to the public interest.

The second case is *Commonwealth of Australia v John Fairfax & Sons Ltd* (1980) 32 A.L.R. 485. That was a decision of Mason J. in the High Court of Australia, dealing with an application by the Commonwealth for an interlocutory injunction to restrain publication of a book containing the texts of government documents concerned with its relations with other countries, in particular the government of Indonesia in connection with the "East

Timor crisis". The documents appeared to have been leaked by a civil servant. Restraint of publication was claimed on the ground of breach of confidence and also on that of infringement of copyright. Mason J. granted an injunction on the latter ground but not on the former. Having mentioned an argument for the Commonwealth that the government was entitled to protect information which was not public property, even if no public interest is served by maintaining confidentiality, he continued (at 492–493):

"However the plaintiff must show, not only that the information is confidential in quality and that it was imparted so as to import an obligation of confidence, but also that there will be 'an unauthorized use of that information to the detriment of the party communicating it' (*Coco v A.N. Clark (Engineers) Ltd* [1969] R.P.C. 41 at 47). The question then, when the executive government seeks the protection given by Equity, is: What detriment does it need to show? The equitable principle has been fashioned to protect the personal, private and proprietary interests of the citizen, not to protect the very different interests of the executive government. It acts, or is supposed to act, not according to standards of private interest, but in the public interest. This is not to say that Equity will not protect information in the hands of the government, but it is to say that when Equity protects government information it will look at the matter through different spectacles. It may be a sufficient detriment to the citizen that disclosure of information relating to his affairs will expose his actions to public discussion and criticism. But it can scarcely be a relevant detriment to the government that publication of material concerning its actions will merely expose it to public discussion and criticism. It is unacceptable, in our democratic society, that there should be a restraint on the publication of information relating to government when the only vice of that information is that it enables the public to discuss, review and criticize government action. Accordingly, the court will determine the government's claim to confidentiality by reference to the public interest. Unless disclosure is likely to injure the public interest, it will not be protected. The court will not prevent the publication of information which merely throws light on the past workings of government, even if it be not public property, so long as it does not prejudice the community in other respects. Then disclosure will itself serve the public interest in keeping the community informed and in promoting discussion of public affairs. If, however, it appears that disclosure will be inimical to the public interest because national security, relations with foreign countries or the ordinary business of government will be prejudiced, disclosure will be restrained. There will be cases in which the conflicting considerations will be finely balanced, where it is difficult to decide whether the public's interest in knowing and in expressing its opinion, outweighs the need to protect confidentiality".

I find myself in broad agreement with this statement by Mason J. In particular I agree that a government is not in a position to win the assistance of the court in restraining the publication of information imparted in confidence by it or its predecessors unless it can show that publication would be harmful to the public interest.

Lord Keith then held:

(i) that, in view of the world-wide dissemination of Spycatcher, *injunctions against* The Guardian *and* The Observer *designed to prevent them from reporting and commenting on Wright's allegations could not be justified; nor could an injunction to prevent further serialisation in* The Sunday Times.

(ii) *that an injunction should be granted against the newspaper in respect of future revelations from secret service members.*

(iii) that if proceedings had been against Wright, an injunction against publication in England might have been justified "on the principle that he should not be permitted to take advantage of his own wrong-doing".

(iv) that The Sunday Times were in breach of confidence in publishing extracts from Spycatcher on the day before US publication.

On the last issue he stated:

This leads on to consideration of the question whether *The Sunday Times* should be held liable to account to the Crown for profits made from past and future serialisation of *Spycatcher.* An account of profits made through breach of confidence is a recognised form of remedy available to a claimant: see *Peter Pan Manufacturing Corp v Corsets Silhouette Ltd* [1963] 3 All E.R. 402; [1964] 1 W.L.R. 96; *cf. Reading v Attorney General* [1951] 1 All E.R. 617; [1951] A.C. 507. In cases where the information disclosed is of a commercial character an account of profits may provide some compensation to the claimant for loss which he has suffered through the disclosure, but damages are the main remedy for such loss. The remedy is, in my opinion, more satisfactorily to be attributed to the principle that no one should be permitted to gain from his own wrongdoing. Its availability may also, in general, serve a useful purpose in lessening the temptation for recipients of confidential information to misuse it for financial gain. In the present case *The Sunday Times* did misuse confidential information and it would be naive to suppose that the prospect of financial gain was not one of the reasons why it did so. I can perceive no good ground why the remedy should not be made available to the Crown in the circumstances of this case, and I would therefore hold the Crown entitled to an account of profits in respect of the publication on July 12, 1987. I would add that in my opinion *The Sunday Times,* in the taking of the account, is not entitled to deduct in computing any gain the sums paid to Mr Wright's publishers as consideration for the licence granted by the latter, since neither Mr Wright nor his publishers were or would in the future be in a position to maintain an action in England for recovery of such payments. Nor would the courts of this country enforce a claim by them to the copyright in a work the publication of which they had brought about contrary to the public interest: *cf. Glyn v Weston Feature Film Co* [1916] 1 Ch. 261 at 269. Mr Wright is powerless to prevent anyone who chooses to do so from publishing *Spycatcher* in whole or in part in this country, or to obtain any other remedy against them. There remains, of course, the question whether the Crown might successfully maintain a claim that it is in equity the owner of the copyright in the book. Such a claim has not yet been advanced, but might well succeed if it were to be.

In reaching the same conclusions, Lord Goff of Chieveley paid particular attention to one submission on behalf of the Attorney General: that, although the effect of Wright's breach of confidence was to disseminate the information widely throughout the world, nevertheless he remained under his obligation of confidence, because he could not destroy it by his own wrongful act. Of this, Lord Goff said:

As I have already indicated, it is well established that a duty of confidence can only apply in respect of information which is confidential: see *Saltman Engineering Co Ltd v Campbell Engineering Co Ltd* (1948) [1963] 3 All E.R. 413 at 415 *per* Lord Greene M.R. From this it should logically follow that, if confidential information which is the subject of a duty of confidence ceases to be confidential, then the duty of confidence should cease to bind the confidant. This was held to be so in *O. Mustad & Sons v S. Allcock & Co Ltd* (1928) [1963] 3 All E.R. 416; [1964] 1 W.L.R. 109. That was however a case in which the confidential information was disclosed by the confider himself; and stress was placed on this point in a later case where the disclosure was not by the confider but by a third party and in which *Mustad's* case was distinguished (see *Cranleigh Precision Engineering v Bryant* [1964] 3 All E.R. 289; [1965] 1 W.L.R. 1293). It was later held, on the basis of the *Cranleigh Precision Engineering* case, that, if the confidant is not released when the publication is by a third party, then he cannot be released when it is he himself who has published the information (see *Speed Seal Products Ltd v Paddington* [1986] 1 All E.R. 91; [1985] 1 W.L.R. 1327). I have to say however that, having studied the judgment of Roskill J. in the *Cranleigh Precision Engineering* case, it seems to me that the true basis of the decision was that, in reliance on the well-known judgment of Roxburgh J. in the "springboard" case, *Terrapin Ltd v Builders' Supply Co (Hayes) Ltd* (1959) [1967] R.P.C. 375, the defendant was in breach of confidence in taking advantage of his own confidential relationship with the plaintiff company to discover what a third party had published and in making use, as soon as he left the employment of the plaintiff company, of information regarding the third party's patent which he had acquired in confidence (see [1964] 3 All E.R. 289 at 302; [1965] 1 W.L.R. 1293 at 1319). The reasoning of Roskill J. in this case has itself been the subject of criticism (see, *e.g.* Gurry *Breach of Confidence* (1984), pp.246–247); but in any event it should be regarded as no more than an extension of the springboard doctrine, and I do not consider that it can support any general principle that, if it is a third party who puts the confidential information into the public domain, as opposed to the confider, the confidant will not be released from his duty of confidence. It follows that, so far as concerns publication by the confidant himself, the reasoning in the *Speed Seal* case (founded as it is on the *Cranleigh Precision Engineering* case) cannot, in my mind, be supported. I recognise that a case where the confider himself publishes the information might be distinguished from other cases on the basis that the confider, by publishing the information, may have implicitly released the confidant from his obligation. But that was not how it was put in *Mustad's* case [1963] 3 All E.R. 416 at 418; [1964] 1 W.L.R. 109 at 111, in which Lord Buckmaster stated that, once the disclosure had been made by the confider to the world, "the secret, as a secret, had ceased to exist". For my part, I cannot see how the secret can continue to exist when the publication has been made not by the confider but by a third party.

Even so, it has been held by the judge, and by all members of the Court of Appeal in the present case, that Peter Wright cannot be released from his duty of confidence by his own publication of the confidential information, apparently on the basis that he cannot be allowed to profit from his own wrong. ...

I have to say, however, that I know of no case (apart from the present) in which the maxim has been invoked in order to hold that a person under an obligation is not released from that obligation by the destruction of the subject matter of the obligation, on the ground that that destruction was the result of his own wrongful act. To take an obvious case, a bailee who by his own wrongful, even deliberately wrongful, act destroys the goods entrusted to him, is obviously relieved of his obligation as bailee, though he is of course liable in damages for his tort. Likewise, a nightwatchman who deliberately sets fire to and destroys the building he is employed to watch; and likewise also, the keeper at a zoo who turns out to be an animal rights campaigner and releases rare birds or animals which escape irretrievably into the countryside. On this approach, it is difficult to see how a confidant who publishes the relevant confidential information to the whole world can be under any further obligation not to disclose the information, simply because it was he who wrongfully destroyed its confidentiality. The information has, after all, already been so fully disclosed that it is in the public domain: how, therefore, can he thereafter be sensibly restrained from disclosing it? Is he not even to be permitted to mention in public what is now common knowledge? For his wrongful act, he may be held liable in damages, or may be required to make restitution; but, to adapt the words of Lord Buckmaster in *Mustad's* case, the confidential information, as confidential information, has ceased to exist, and with it should go, as a matter of principle, the obligation of confidence. In truth, when a person entrusts something to another, whether that thing be a physical thing such as a chattel or some intangible thing such as confidential information, he relies on that other to fulfil his obligation. If he discovers that the other is about to commit a breach, he may be able to impose an added sanction against his doing so by persuading the court to grant an injunction; but if the other simply commits a breach and destroys the thing, then the injured party is left with his remedy in damages or in restitution. The subject matter is gone; the obligation is therefore also gone; all that is left is the remedy or remedies for breach of the obligation. This approach appears to be consistent with the view expressed by the Law Commission in their Report on Breach of Confidence (Law Com. No. 110 (1981)), paragraph 4.30 (see also the Law Commission's working paper, Breach of Confidence (Working Paper No. 58 (1974)) paras 100–101). It is right to say, however, that they may have had commercial cases in mind, rather than a case such as the present. It is however also of interest that, in the *Fairfax* case (1980) 32 A.L.R. 485 at 494, Mason J. was not prepared to grant an injunction to restrain further publication of a book by the defendants on the ground of breach of confidence, because the limited publication which had taken place was sufficient to cause the detriment which the plaintiff, the Commonwealth of Australia, apprehended. If, however, the defendants had published the book in breach of confidence, it is difficult to see why, on the approach so far accepted in the present case, the defendants should not have remained under a duty of confidence despite the publication and so liable to be restrained by injunction. . . .

I have naturally been concerned by the fact that so far in this case it appears to have been accepted on all sides that Peter Wright should not be released from his obligation of confidence. I cannot help thinking that this assumption may have been induced, in part at least, by three factors: first, the fact that Peter Wright himself is not a party to the litigation, with the result that no representations have been made on his behalf; second, the wholly unacceptable nature of his conduct; and third, the fact that he appears now to be able, with impunity, to reap vast sums from his disloyalty. Certainly, the prospect of Peter Wright, safe in his Australian haven, reaping further profits from the sale of his book in this country is most unattractive. The purpose of perpetuating Peter Wright's duty of confidence appears to be, in part to deter others, and in part to ensure that a man who has committed so flagrant a breach of duty should not be enabled freely to exploit the formerly confidential information, placed by him in the public domain, with impunity. Yet the real reason why he is able to exploit it is because he has found a safe place to do so. If within the jurisdiction of the English courts, he would be held liable to account for any profits made by him from his wrongful disclosure, which might properly include profits accruing to him from any subsequent exploitation of the confidential information after its disclosure: and, in cases where damages were regarded as the appropriate remedy, the confidant would be liable to compensate the confider for any damage, present or future, suffered by him by reason of his wrong. So far as I can see, the confider must be content with remedies such as these.

I have considered whether the confidant who, in breach of duty, places confidential information in the public domain, might remain at least under a duty thereafter not to exploit the information, so disclosed, for his own benefit. Suppose that the confidant in question was a man who, unwisely, has remained in this country, and has written a book containing confidential information and has disposed of the rights to publication to an American publishing house, whose publication results in the information in the book entering the public domain. The question might at least arise whether he is free thereafter to dispose of the film rights to the book. To me however, it is doubtful whether the answer to this question lies in artificially prolonging the duty of confidence in information which is no longer confidential. Indeed, there is some ground for saying that the true answer is that the copyright in the book, including the film rights, are held by him on constructive trust for the confider, so that the remedy lies not in breach of confidence, but in restitution or in property, whichever way you care to look at it.

Lord Goff concluded that, even if this view was not correct, he would hold it contrary to the public interest to restrain publication of a book which was freely circulating in the country already.

Lords Brightman and Jauncey of Tullichettle delivered concurring speeches. Lord Griffiths dissented on two points: he found The Guardian *and* The Observer *to have been in breach of confidence in their reports; and he would have restrained* The Sunday Times *from further serialisation of* Spycatcher.

2.3 Extent of Obligation

2.3.1 Employees

2.3.1.1 *Hivac v Park Royal* [1946] 1 All E.R. 350, CA

The plaintiff company manufactured small thermionic valves for use in hearing aids, being at the end of the war the only company in Britain to do so. Five of its skilled manual workers worked on Sundays for the defendant company, which had been established to make hearing aids with valves that competed with the plaintiff's. The plaintiff was subject to the Essential Work Order and so could not dismiss the five (who by contract were subject to 24 hours' notice) without following a complex statutory procedure. It sought interlocutory relief enjoining the defendant from procuring breach by the workers of their employment contracts.

Lord Greene M.R. reviewed the facts and continued:

There is one matter which I think I can get out of the way at once. It is argued on behalf of the plaintiffs that on the evidence what may be called confidential information must have been disclosed or utilised by these five employees for the benefit of the defendant company. The judge took the view that no such case had been made out. I do not in any way differ from that view. It seems to me that, having regard particularly to the evidence of Mr Gill, confidential information has not down to the present, at any rate, been made use of by these five employees, if, indeed, they were in possession of any such information. Of course, when one gets into the area of confidential information the law is fortunately much more certain, but once that particular element is excluded, we are in an area which has not, as I have said, been sufficiently explored.

The argument on behalf of the plaintiffs with regard to confidential information was also to the effect that, even assuming no confidential information has as yet been disclosed, and assuming there is no threat to disclose it or use it for the benefit of the defendants, it will, nevertheless, be inevitable, if those employees continue to work for the defendants, that they will put at the disposal of the defendants any confidential information which, in the course of their work for the plaintiffs, they may obtain. It is said, and said with force, that employees engaged in this particular work are bound to become acquainted with any improvements or any experiments which the plaintiffs may make in the course of their business in relation to these midget valves because they would be given the task of constructing or assembling valves for the purpose of incorporating such improvements, and so forth. That is, I think, a matter which the court cannot ignore. After all, one has to be practical in these matters, and one has to consider what the practical result will be. It may very well be said that to say that people in these circumstances can, so to speak, make a division in their minds between what is confidential and what is not, and be quite careful while they are working for the defendants to keep the confidential information locked up in some secret compartment of their minds theoretically may be all very well, but from the practical point of view has a certain unreality.

Leaving that on one side for the moment, and looking at the question from another angle, it has been said on many occasions that an employee owes a duty of fidelity to his employer. As a general proposition that is indisputable. The practical difficulty in any given case is to find exactly how far that rather vague duty of fidelity extends. Prima facie it seems to me on considering the authorities and the arguments that it must be a question on the facts of each particular case. I can very well understand that the obligation of fidelity, which is an implied term of the contract, may extend very much further in the case of one class of employee than it does in others. For instance, when you are dealing, as we are dealing here, with mere manual workers whose job is to work five-and-a-half days for their employer at a specific type of work and stop their work when the hour strikes, the obligation of fidelity may be one the operation of which will have a comparatively limited scope. The law would, I think, be jealous of attempting to impose on a manual worker restrictions the real effect of which would be to prevent him utilising his spare time. He is paid for five-and-a-half days in the week. The rest of the week is his own, and to impose upon a man, in relation to the rest of the week, some kind of obligation which really would unreasonably tie his hands and prevent him adding to his weekly money during that time would, I think, be very undesirable. On the other hand, if you have employees of a different character, you may very well find that the obligation is of a different nature. A manual worker might say: "You pay me for five-and-a-half days work. I do five-and-a-half days work for you. What greater obligation have I taken upon myself? If you want in some way to limit my activities during the other day-and-a-half of the week, you must pay me for it". In many cases that may be a very good answer. In other cases it may not be a good answer because the very nature of the work may be such as to make it quite clear that the duties of the employee to his employer cannot properly be performed if in his spare time the employee engages in certain classes of activity. One example was discussed in argument, that of a solicitor's clerk who on Sundays, it was assumed, went and worked for another firm in the same town. He might find himself embarrassed because the very client for whom he had done work while working for the other firm on the Sunday night might be a client against whom clients of his main employer were conducting litigation, or something of that kind. Obviously in a case of that kind, by working for another firm he is in effect, or may be, disabling himself from performing his duties to his real employer and placing himself in an embarrassing position. I can well understand it being said: "That is a breach of the duty of fidelity to your employer because as a result of what you have done you have disabled yourself from giving to your employer that undivided attention to their business which it is your duty to do". I merely put that forward, not for the purpose of laying down the law or expressing any concluded opinion, but merely as illustrating the danger of laying down any proposition and the necessity of considering each case on its facts.

His Lordship referred in particular to Robb v Green *[1895] 2 Q.B. 315 and* Wessex Dairies v Smith *[1935] 2 K.B. 80 and continued:*

The question here is not a question of getting the customers to leave the business but a question of building up a rival in business to the prejudice of the goodwill of the employer's business.

I am not ashamed to confess that in the course of the argument my mind has fluctuated considerably on this question. As I see it, the court stands in a sense between Scylla and Charybdis, because it would be most unfortunate if anything we said, or any other court said, should place an undue restriction on the right of the workman, particularly a manual workman, to make use of his leisure for his profit. On the other hand, it would be deplorable if it were laid down that a workman could consistently with his duty to his employer, knowingly deliberately and secretly set himself to do in his spare time something which would inflict great harm on his employer's business. I have endeavoured to raise the questions in the way that they appeal to me and, on the best consideration I can give to this matter, I think that the plaintiffs are prima facie right in this case.

That being so, what is the right course for this court to pursue? Counsel for the defendants took several points, on the assumption that a prima facie case was established, to suggest that it was not a case for an injunction. He said, for instance, that in the absence of the five workpeople in question the action was not properly constituted. There is no doubt that, in a way, it is unfortunate in an action complaining of procuring breach of contract, not to have before the court the contracting party whose breach of the contract, it is said, the defendants have procured, but the circumstances of the present case are peculiar. There is a very good practical reason why these workpeople should not be joined, and I can see no reason why the court should not be able to decide the question satisfactorily and in the absence.

Then counsel said there is no case for an injunction because if the plaintiffs are right the workpeople could be dismissed for serious misconduct. That is a much more difficult thing under the Essential Work Order than would appear from that bald statement, because the plaintiffs have not the last word in the matter. It would be unreasonable to expect them, in the circumstances of the shortage of labour and the difficult procedure they would have to go through, to take any such course. The times are peculiar, and it seems to me that the plaintiffs are entitled to have the position considered in the light of the circumstances as they in fact exist, and not in the light of some circumstances, which might have existed, in more normal times, and would have given them a remedy ready to their hand which would have made it unnecessary for them to invoke the assistance of the court.

Then counsel said, in any case there is no case for an interlocutory order. I do not think myself that any of those arguments ought to be allowed to prevail.

I conclude by saying that this is a case of deliberate and secret action by these employees, deliberate and secret action by the defendants in circumstances where both the employees and the defendants must have known the exact result of what they were doing and must have realised that what they were doing was wrong, even if they did not distinguish in their minds between the question of commercial morality and legal obligation. That being so, and there being in my opinion a prima facie case and the balance of convenience and fairness being in favour of an injunction, I think the judge who took the other view came to the wrong conclusion. I should perhaps have mentioned that he did not think that, once the question of confidential information was excluded, there was sufficient left in the action of the plaintiffs' workpeople to constitute a breach of any implied obligation. It is on that point that I take a different prima facie view. The way the matter struck me was that prima facie, in the absence of direct authority on the point, he did not feel that he ought to say that the obligation of the servants in this case went as far as it was said it did. I have come to the opposite conclusion without expressing any final judgment on the matter, because we have not all the facts before us. I think that prima facie on the facts of this case, so far as they at present appear, the conclusion ought to be the opposite one. This is the extent of our difference. In my opinion, the injunction asked for should be granted.

Morton L.J. delivered a concurring judgment and Bucknill L.J. agreed.

2.3.1.2   *Printers & Finishers v Holloway* [1965] 1 W.L.R. 1, Cross J.

Holloway, manager of the plaintiff company's flock printing plant, showed a director and employee of Vita-Tex around the plant. The plant had been set up under a confidential know-how agreement and Holloway was under instructions to keep the process involved secret. He removed some secret documents and copied others; he also ordered a machine part (a cyclone) for Vita-Tex from the know-how licensors. He then left his employ and the plaintiff began proceedings against him, two Vita-Tex directors and Vita-Tex itself for various injunctions relating to breach of confidence.

Cross J. was prepared to grant an injunction respecting the documentary material. He continued:

The second part of the injunction sought against Holloway is directed to the use or disclosure by him of information in his head, and the question whether or not it should be granted involves a consideration of the principles on which the court should act in a case of this kind. The wording of the proposed injunction is based on the description of each step in their process given by the plaintiffs in general terms in their particulars dated November 5, 1959, and in detail in the evidence of their managing director given "in camera" at the trial, with the omission of a few matters in regard to which the evidence at the trial showed clearly that the managing director was wrong in thinking that what the plaintiffs did was peculiar to them. The mere fact that the confidential information is not embodied in a document but is carried away by the employee in his head is not, of course, of itself a reason against the granting of an injunction to prevent its use or disclosure by him. If the information in question can fairly be regarded as a separate part of the employee's stock of knowledge which a man of ordinary honesty and intelligence would recognise to be the property of his old employer and not his own to do as he likes with, then the court, if it thinks that there is a danger of the information being used or disclosed by the ex-employee to the detriment of the old employer, will do what it can to prevent that result by granting an injunction. Thus an ex-employee will be restrained from using or disclosing a chemical formula or a list of customers which he has committed to memory. Again, in *Reid & Sigrist Ltd v Moss & Mechanism Ltd* (1932) 49 R.P.C. at 461 the defendant was restrained from disclosing any methods of construction or features of design of turn indicators for use in aeroplanes evolved by the plaintiffs and made known to the defendant or evolved by him whilst in their employment. The salient point there was that in the course of the development of the instrument by the plaintiffs the defendant took part in confidential discussions with an outside expert called in to advise the plaintiffs as to the best method of dealing with certain problems which had arisen. It appears, indeed, that after the discussions and while he was still in the plaintiffs' employ the defendant made and later took away with him drawings embracing the various matters discussed. But even if he had not done so and relied simply on his memory of the confidential discussions I think that an injunction would still have been granted.

What is asked for here, however goes far beyond any relief granted in any case which was cited to me. The plaintiffs are saying, in effect: "True it is that other flock printers use print and machinery similar to ours and that as we did not trouble to exact any covenant from him not to do so Holloway was entitled to go and work for a trade competitor who uses such plant and machinery. Nevertheless we are entitled to prevent him from using for the benefit of his new employers his recollection of any features of our plant, machinery or process which are in fact peculiar to us".

If this is right then, as it seems to me, an ex-employee is placed in an impossible position. One naturally approaches the problem in this case with some bias in favour of the plaintiffs, because Holloway has shown himself unworthy of their trust; but to test their argument fairly one must take the case of an employee who has been guilty of no breach of contract. Suppose such a man to be told by his new employers that at this or that stage in the process they encounter this or that difficulty. He may say to himself: "Well, I remember that on the corresponding piece of machinery in the other factory such-and-such a part was set at a different angle or shaped in a different way"; or again, "When that happened we used to do this and it seemed to work", "this" being perhaps something which he had been taught when he first went to the other factory or possibly an expedient which he had found out for himself by trial and error during his previous employment.

Recalling matters of this sort is, to my mind, quite unlike memorising a formula or list of customers or what was said (obviously in confidence) at a particular meeting. The employee might well not realise that the feature or expedient in question was in fact peculiar to his late employer's process and factory; but even if he did such knowledge is not readily separable from his general knowledge of the flock printing process and his acquired skill in manipulating a flock printing plant, and I do not think that any man of average intelligence and honesty would think that there was anything improper in his putting his memory of particular features of his late employer's plant at the disposal of his new employer. The law will defeat its own object if it seeks to enforce in this field standards which would be rejected by the ordinary man. After all, this involves no hardship on the employer. Although this law will not enforce a covenant directed against competition by an ex-employee it will enforce a covenant reasonably necessary to protect trade secrets (see the recent case of *Commercial Plastics Ltd v Vincent* [1964] 3 All E.R. 546, in which the plaintiff only failed because the covenant was too widely drawn as regards area). If the managing director is right in thinking that there are features in the plaintiffs' process which can fairly be regarded as trade secrets and which their employees will inevitably carry away with them in their heads, then the proper way for the plaintiffs to protect themselves would be by exacting covenants from their employees restricting their field of activity after they have left their employment, not by asking the court to extend the general equitable doctrine to prevent breaking confidence beyond all reasonable bounds.

Accordingly, Cross J. refused the injunction sought against Holloway and equivalent injunctions against the other defendants. However, regarding the visit of Vita-Tex's electrician, James, to the plaintiff's premises he said:

But Holloway showed him the inside of the electrical testing room because he thought that James, as Vita-Tex's electrician, would be interested in seeing how the plaintiffs coped with certain electrical problems incidental to their process, and I think that James may well have gleaned much more information from his visit than he would admit. Vita-Tex was no doubt innocent in the matter but *Prince Albert v Strange* (above, 2.1.1) shows that an injunction may be granted against someone who has acquired—or may acquire—information to which he was not entitled without notice of any breach of duty on the part of the man through whom he obtained it.

I am therefore prepared to grant an injunction restraining Vita-Tex from making any use of any information relating to the electrostatic machines or electrodes of the plaintiffs obtained by James on the occasion of his visit or visits to the plaintiffs' factory particularised in paragraph (8) of the statement of claim.

Though it is a very small matter I am also prepared to grant an injunction restraining Vita-Tex from making any use, for the purpose of flock printing, of the cyclone which Holloway improperly caused to be copied for them from the plaintiffs' cyclone.

2.3.1.3 *Lancashire Fires v S.A. Lyons* **[1996] F.S.R. 629, CA**

Jim Wright established Lancashire Fires ("L.F.") as a leading manufacturer of decorative gas fires, including "shapes" (artificial coals and logs) made by a vacuum-injected moulding system with an inorganic silica binding. The process for manufacturing the shapes had been bought in from outside, but was considered confidential by the plaintiffs, Jim Wright and L.F.

Arthur Wright, Jim's brother, was employed by L. F. and came to understand the moulding process in detail. After L.F. failed to reach an agreement to supply fires to a Canadian firm, Arthur dealt with that firm privately and set up S.A. Lyons Ltd to do the required manufacturing. In this he was given financial help by Susan Magnall, who, while remaining an employee of L.F., became an initial shareholder in S.A. Lyons. The Court of Appeal held that the moulding system was a trade secret, that Arthur knew that it could fairly be so regarded and that he was in breach of confidence in revealing it to Mrs Magnall and in giving it over to S.A. Lyons. In the course of holding that these three should be enjoined from continuing the breach, Bingham M.R. (for the Court) reviewed the legal distinctions applicable to alleged abuse of trade secrets by ex-employees:

In *Faccenda Chicken Limited v Fowler* [1984] I.C.R. 589 at 598 Goulding J. identified three classes of information which an employee might acquire in the course of his service:

"First there is information which, because of its trivial character or its easy accessibility from public sources of information, cannot be regarded by reasonable persons or by the law as confidential at all. The servant is at liberty to impart it during his service or afterwards to anyone he pleases, even his master's competitor."

This class is uncontroversial. The law of confidence does not apply to it.
The second class comprises:

"Information which the servant must treat as confidential (either because he is expressly told it is confidential, or because from its character it obviously is so) but which once learned necessarily remains in the servant's head and becomes part of his own skill and knowledge applied in the course of his master's business. So long as the employment continues, he cannot otherwise use or disclose such information without infidelity and therefore breach of contract. But when he is no longer in the same service, the law allows him to use his full skill and knowledge for his own benefit in competition with his former master; ... If an employer wants to protect information of this kind, he can do so by an express stipulation restraining the servant from competing with him (within reasonable limits of time and space) after the termination if his employment."

There is in this passage an echo of what Bennett J. said in *United Indigo Chemical Co Limited v Robinson* (1932) 49 R.P.C. 178 at 187:

"In those circumstances it seems to me to be almost impossible, in justice to the servant, to restrain him when he leaves his master's employment from using—not disclosing—information which he could not help acquiring. It seems to me that to try to restrain him by injunction from using knowledge, which in that way has become his own, is to try to do something which the Court really has no power to do, or rather has no power to enforce the injunction if one could be granted. ... That is really what the plaintiffs are trying to do here in connection with *Algaloid*. They are trying to stop the defendant from using after he has left the plaintiffs' service knowledge, skill and experience which as a result of his service have become his own."

There is also an echo of what Cross J. said in *Printers & Finishers Limited v Holloway* [1965] R.P.C. 239 at 253:

> "In this connection one must bear in mind that not all information which is given to a servant in confidence and which it would be a breach of his duty for him to disclose to another person during his employment is a trade secret which he can be prevented from using for his own advantage after the employment is over, even though he has entered into no express covenant with regard to the matter in hand. For example, the printing instructions were handed to Holloway to be used by him during his employment exclusively for the plaintiffs' benefit. It would have been a breach of duty on his part to divulge any of the contents to a stranger while he was employed, but many of these instructions are not really "trade secrets" at all. Holloway was not, indeed, entitled to take a copy of the instructions away with him; but insofar as the instructions cannot be called "trade secrets" and he carried them in his head, he is entitled to use them for his own benefit or the benefit of any future employer."

In *Faccenda* Goulding J. held that the information in issue in the case fell within this second class. It was argued on appeal that no such special class existed: [1987] Ch. 117 at 122–123. The Court of Appeal rejected this argument. It held (at 135):

> "(2) In the absence of any express term, the obligations of the employee in respect of the use and disclosure of information are the subject of implied terms.

> (3) While the employee remains in the employment of the employer the obligations are included in the implied term which imposes a duty of good faith or fidelity on the employee. For the purposes of the present appeal it is not necessary to consider the precise limits of this implied term ..."

The Court of Appeal upheld the judge's decision that the information in issue in the case fell within the second class.

On one point the Court of Appeal did differ from Goulding J. At 137 it said:

> We must therefore express our respectful disagreement with the passage in Goulding J.'s judgment at [1984] I.C.R. 589 at 599E, where he suggested that an employer can protect the use of information in his second category, even though it does not include either a trade secret or its equivalent, by means of a restrictive covenant. As Lord Parker of Waddington made clear in *Herbert Morris Ltd v Saxelby* [1916] 1 A.C. 688 at 709, in a passage to which Mr Dehn drew our attention, a restrictive covenant will not be enforced unless the protection sought is reasonably necessary to protect a trade secret or to prevent some personal influence over customers being abused in order to entice them away.

> In our view the circumstances in which a restrictive convenant would be appropriate and could be successfully invoked emerge very clearly from the words used by Cross J. in *Printers & Finishers Ltd v Holloway* [1965] 1 W.L.R. 1, 6; [1965] R.P.C. 239 at 256] (in a passage quoted later in his judgment by Goulding J. [1984] I.C.R. 589 at 601):

> > "If [the managing director] is right in thinking that there are features in his process which can fairly be regarded as trade secrets and which his employees will inevitably carry away with them in their heads, then the proper way for the plaintiffs to protect themselves would be by exacting covenants from their employees restricting their field of activity after they have left their employment, not by asking the court to extend the general equitable doctrine to prevent breaking confidence beyond all reasonable bounds."

In *Balston Limited v Headline Filters Limited* [1987] F.S.R. 330 at 347–348 Scott J. questioned whether the Court of Appeal had intended, or had been right, to express disagreement with Goulding J. and in *Wright v Gasweld Pty Limited* (1991) 20 I.P.R. 481 the Court of Appeal of New South Wales expressly preferred the view of Goulding J. We would question whether there is, as the Court of Appeal judgment suggests, any difference between the reasoning of Goulding J. and that of Cross J. It seems plain that Goulding J. had in mind a convenant against working for a competitor. So, as his observations in *Printers & Finishers Ltd v Holloway* [1965] 1 W.L.R. 1 at 5–6 and [1965] R.P.C. 239 at 256 (before the passage quoted) show, did Cross J. Such a covenant, if not in unreasonable restraint of trade, is legally enforceable. In the present case, however, there is no express covenant of any kind, and accordingly no question arises on this passage in the judgment of the Court of Appeal.

The third class identified by Goulding J. (at 600) was:

> "specific trade secrets so confidential that, even though they may necessarily have been learned by heart, and even though the servant may have left the service, they cannot lawfully be used for anyone's benefit but the master's. An example is the secret process which was the subject matter of *Amber Size and Chemical Co Limited v Menzel* [1913] 2 Ch. 239.

Bingham M.R. quoted general propositions about liability for breach of confidence from the Saltman, Printers & Finishers *and* Coco *cases (above, paras 2.1.2, 2.3.1.2 and 2.1.5) and concluded:*

In *Faccenda Chicken* (at 137) the Court of Appeal drew attention to some of the matters which must be considered in determining whether any particular item of information falls within the implied term of a contract of employment so as to prevent its use or disclosure by an employee after his employment has ceased. Those matters included: the nature of the employment: the nature of the information itself; the steps (if any) taken by the employer to impress on the employee the confidentiality of the information; and the ease or difficulty of isolating the information in question from other information which the employee is free to use or disclose. We have no doubt that these are all very relevant matters to consider. In the ordinary way, the nearer an employee is to the inner counsels of an employer, the more likely he is to gain access to truly confidential information. The nature of the information itself is also important: to be capable of protection, information must be defined with some degree of precision; and an employer will have great difficulty in obtaining protection for his business methods and practices. If an employer impresses the confidentiality of certain information on his employee, that is an indication of the employer's belief that the information is confidential, a fact which is not irrelevant: *Thomas Marshall (Exports) Limited v Guinle* [1979] Ch. 227 at 248. But how much will depend on the circumstances. These may be such as to show that information is, or is being treated as, confidential; and it would be unrealistic to expect a small and informal organisation to adopt the same business disciplines as a larger and more bureaucratic concern. It is plain that if an employer is to succeed in protecting information as confidential, he must succeed in showing that it does not form part of an employee's own stock of knowledge, skill and experience. The distinction between information in Goulding J.'s class 2 and information in his class 3 may often on the facts be very hard to draw, but ultimately the court must judge whether an ex-employee has illegitimately used the confidential information which forms part of the stock-in-trade of his former employer either for his own benefit or to the detriment of the former employer, or whether he has simply used his own professional expertise, gained in whole or in part during his former employment.

Applying the law to the facts, Bingham M.R. concluded that the case fell within Goulding J.'s third category. Relief was accordingly available, even in the absence of any restrictive covenant applying to Arthur Wright, against him, S.A. Lyons and Mrs Mangall because of her part in the common design to set up the business misusing the information.

2.3.1.4   *Triplex Safety Glass v Scorah* (1938) 55 R.P.C. 21, Farwell J.

The plaintiff glass manufacturer employed the defendant chemist under a written agreement which contained an undertaking to keep secret all records, knowledge or information of value in the manufacture of safety glass; an acknowledgement that all knowledge and information gleaned or discovered was to be the property of the plaintiffs; an obligation to communicate to the company any new application of such knowledge relating to safety glass that the defendant might conceive; an obligation to assign to the plaintiff any patent taken out by the defendant; and an undertaking, within one year, of leaving the plaintiff's employ, not to act as a chemist in the manufacture of safety glass.

During the course of his employment the defendant discovered a method of producing a particular acid which he communicated to the plaintiff together with various recommendations and suggestions. The plaintiff ignored these and did not pursue the invention.

The defendant subsequently left the plaintiff's employ and set up business on his own account manufacturing laboratory glass. The defendant carried out further experiments with the acid and found it to be useful for his own glass manufacturing. He applied for and was granted a patent. The plaintiff sought inter alia to compel the defendant to assign the patent to it in accordance with the earlier contract of employment.

Farwell J. held the express covenants of the contract to be in unreasonable restraint of trade and therefore unenforceable. However he continued:

That leaves me to deal with the question how far there may be an obligation on the defendant to do that which the plaintiffs asked him to do, apart from express contract altogether. With regard to that, the first ground on which the defendant seeks to avoid that conclusion is by saying that, where there is an express contract containing terms which are not enforceable for any reason, the court will not imply terms, because the court will assume that all the terms were in the written document and that, therefore, there is no room for implication as to other terms and that, since this contract is not enforceable, there cannot be any implied term in the contract arising from the employment under which the defendant is under any obligation to do that which he is asked to do here.

No doubt to some extent the contention that an express contract excludes any implication is true, but I do not think it can be taken to the length to which Mr Willes has invited me go. As I suggested in argument, it cannot be that, because a servant covenants in his contract of service to behave properly and honestly towards his employer and that contract of service as a whole is too wide to be enforceable, he is thereby entitled to be as dishonest and to act as unfairly as he pleases towards his employer. That obviously cannot be so and that contention does not afford a good answer to the plaintiff's claim.

In a case of this kind, in my judgment it is a term of the employment apart altogether from any express covenant, that any invention or discovery made in the course of the employment of the employee, in doing that which the employee was engaged and instructed to do during the time of his employment, during working hours and using the materials of his employers, is the property of the employers and not of the employee, and that, having made such a discovery or invention, the employee becomes a trustee for the employer or it, and he is, therefore, as a trustee, bound to give the benefit of it to his employer.

Then it is said: even if that be so, this employee was permitted, having communicated this discovery to his employers, to leave the employment of the company at a time when the company had made no kind of use of this invention or discovery or, rather, had made no attempt to patent or protect it in any way; that he was allowed to remain out of the employment of the company on his own account for some two years and that, when he did patent it for his own purposes, it would be inequitable for the company to be allowed to intervene and say: Now we want the benefit of this discovery; kindly assign your patent to us.

That argument overlooks this: that it is well settled that, once a person is put into the position of a trustee, he cannot avoid the obligations attached thereto unless the beneficiaries release him either expressly or impliedly. It might be that in certain cases the court might be able to imply a release from some special circumstances, but, in my judgment, the mere fact that nothing was done in this matter for some period is wholly insufficient to suggest that there was any such release in this case.

Under those circumstances, in my judgment, by reason of the fact that the defendant made this discovery or invention while in the employ of the company, during the company's working hours, and in pursuance of the orders of the company's servants, he became a trustee of it for the company and he has not ceased and cannot have ceased to be a trustee. If that be so, the result must follow that, when the beneficiary calls upon him to assign to the beneficiary the property of which he is a trustee, he is bound to do so subject only to this: the trustee is entitled to be indemnified against the costs to which he has been put in connection with the property of the beneficiary. A trustee is not bound to spend money on the property of another and he is entitled to be protected against any expense which he has properly incurred in protecting that property; but, subject to that, the beneficiary is entitled to call upon the trustee to transfer the property to him. In this case it seems to me that, on that ground, the plaintiffs are right in this action; that the company is entitled now to call upon the defendant to assign to them the Letters Patent in question and I will make a declaration to that effect and an Order upon the defendant to assign to them the Letters Patent in question.

2.3.2 Indirect Recipients

2.3.2.1 *Morison v Moat* **(1851) 9 Hare 492, Turner V.C.**

Morison senior and Moat senior entered a partnership to exploit Morison senior's "invention" (unpatented), which was sold as "Morison's Universal Medicine". Morison senior gave the recipe of the medicine to Moat senior under a bond not to reveal it to any other person. Shortly before Moat senior's death he appointed his son, the defendant, to succeed him in the partnership, as he had power to do. Morison senior and his sons were led to believe that Moat had not told the secret recipe to the defendant, but he had. The partnership eventually terminated and Moat junior began to manufacture in accordance with the recipe of his own account. The Morisons succeeded in obtaining an injunction to restrain him (though they failed to have him enjoined from using the name "Morison's Universal Medicine").

Turner V.C.:

It was much pressed in argument, on the part of the defendant, that the effect of granting an injunction in such a case as the present would be to give the plaintiffs a better right than that of a patentee; and the case of *Canham v Jones* (1813) 2 V. & B. 218, was cited on the defendant's behalf; but what we have to deal with here is, not the right of the plaintiffs against the world, but their right against the defendant. It may well be that the plaintiffs have no title against the world in general, and may yet have a good title against this defendant; and the case of *Canham v Jones* does not appear to me to touch the question.

The defendant admits that the secret was communicated to him by Thomas Moat. His allegation that he acquired a knowledge of it by acting as partner in the concern is disproved; and it is shewn that, if he did acquire such knowledge, he did so surreptitiously. The question is whether there was an equity against him; and I am of the opinion that there was. It was clearly a breach of faith and of contract on the part of Thomas Moat to communicate the secret. The defendant derives under that breach of faith and of contract, and I think he can gain no title by it. In *Green v Folgham* (1823) 1 Sim. & St. 398, upon a trust admitted, an account was decreed against the party to whom the secret had been divulged; and it cannot, I think, make any difference whether the trust is admitted or proved; and the cases of *Tipping v Clarke* (1843) 2 Hare 393, and *Prince Albert v Strange* [above, 2.1.1] show that the equity prevails against parties deriving under the breach of contract or duty.

It might indeed be different if the defendant was a purchaser for value of the secret without notice of any obligation affecting it; and the defendant's case was attempted to be put upon this ground. It was said that, as appointee, he came in as purchaser under the deed of June 23, 1830, and that he had no notice of the bond; but I do not think that this view of the case can avail him, for, in whatever character he may stand as appointee, he has no consequential right in the secret. So far as the secret is concerned he is a mere volunteer deriving under a breach of trust or of contract.

2.3.2.2 *Stevenson Jordan & Harrison v MacDonald & Evans* **(1951) 68 R.P.C. 190, Lloyd-Jacob J.**

The case concerned a firm of "management engineers" for whom a Mr Hemming worked as "chief of staff" to the managing director. Hemming prepared a book to be published under contract by the defendant. The extract given here is from the decision of Lloyd-Jacob J. at first instance. Unlike the Court of Appeal, Lloyd-Jacob J. found that the proposed publication involved a breach of the confidence which Hemming owed to his employers, the plaintiffs. He continued:

The defendants contend that at the time they agreed to publish this work they had no knowledge or notice of the plaintiff's claims, nor were they aware that the work contained any secret or confidential information, and they claim that in consequence they cannot now be restrained. It is to be noted that the absence of any right to publish on Mr Hemming's part must safeguard the defendants from any claim for breach of contract by his estate. It would appear, therefore, to be the position that the defendants' insistence on disclosing the contents of this book to the world, and thereby causing irreparable damage to the business of the plaintiffs, is due in part to unwillingness to bear the cost already incurred in preparing for publication (although the publishing agreement (D.10) specifically safeguards them against loss in this connection) and possibly in part to a public-spirited insistence upon a supposedly legal right. It is difficult to reconcile this attitude with the evidence of Mr J.D. MacDonald, but as the claim is made and persisted in it is necessary to examine the position so created.

Counsel for the plaintiffs expressly disclaimed any suggestion that at the date of the execution of D.10 the defendants were (or should have been) aware that Mr Hemming was acting in breach of his duty to the plaintiffs. Does this circumstance frank their avowed intention to consummate Mr Hemming's wrongdoing? The original and independent jurisdiction of this court to prevent, by the grant of an injunction, any person availing himself of a title which arises out of a violation of a right or a breach of confidence, is so well established as a cardinal principle that only a binding authority to the contrary should prevent its application by this court. None of the cases cited by counsel for the defendants appears to fetter in any way the freedom of this court to protect the plaintiffs from the disclosure of their confidential information; and Lord Cottenham's judgment in *Prince Albert v Strange* (1849) 1 Mac & G 25, expressly supports the principle. The wrong to be restrained is not the entry into the contract to publish, but the act of publishing, and an innocent mind at the time of the former cannot overcome the consequences of full knowledge at or before the time of the latter.

The judgment of Kekewich J., in *Philip v Pennell* [1907] 2 Ch. 577, which was strongly urged in argument by counsel for the defendants, does not, in my view, support his contention. The learned judge there expressly excluded from the ambit of his judgment any consideration of letters obtained improperly.

Turner V.C., in *Morison v Moat* (1851) 9 Hare 241, 263 expressed the view that a purchaser for value of a secret without notice of any obligation affecting it might be in a different position from a volunteer. Such a view is not inconsistent with the power of the court to prevent disclosure by injunction if proceedings are commenced in time.

2.3.2.3   *Wheatley v Bell* [1984] F.S.R. 16, Helsham J., SC, N.S.W.

The plaintiffs developed a "Teleguide" system of information concerning local businesses whose commercial value lay in its concentration upon a suburban area of appropriate size. They exploited their idea by dividing a city into such areas and then selling the "exclusive" franchise for each area to a franchisee, who would be supplied with information about how to attract business sub-

scribers and market the operation generally. They tested the idea in Perth, Western Australia, where the first defendant learnt about the scheme by attending a session for intending franchisees. He did not take up any franchise but instead took the scheme himself to Sydney, New South Wales, where he and an associate began to market it to franchisees in advance of the plaintiffs' launch of their scheme there.

In proceedings for interlocutory injunctions against the defendants' activities, it was held by Helsham J. that these were prima facie in breach of confidence and should therefore be restrained until trial. The question arose whether injunctions could also be granted against franchisees who had unwittingly purchased the scheme without any knowledge of the plaintiff's rights.

Helsham J.:

There is a real question as to whether the injunction should go against the innocent defendants. One of them has not appeared, that is, Mr Smith, the fourth defendant, and no problem arises here because he has not established that he is innocent of any knowledge of the circumstances of the acquisition of the idea by the first defendant. Other defendants, in effect, claim that they are persons who should be likened to bona fide purchasers for value without notice. It is said that persons in that position are, in this field of confidentiality, free to make use of information which has come to them innocently; that they are in no way tainted with the breach of trust or quasi breach of trust that affects the person from whom they obtained the information, and that, therefore, there is no equity in the plaintiffs to obtain any relief of any sort against the innocent recipients of information, albeit that it comes through the hands of a person who is guilty of imparting it in breach of the duty of confidentiality that that imparter owes to the giver of the information.

I am satisfied that the analogy which has been drawn in some of the American cases and by some of the text writers, of the situation of the innocent defendants to a bona fide purchaser for value without notice, is not the correct way of approaching the question of whether the injunction should go in the present circumstances or not. The defence of bona fide purchaser for value is an equitable defence directed towards the resolution of priorities in relation to property rights. It is an attempt to sort out amongst the claimants interested in property the order in which their various interests should prevail. But I believe that there are no property rights associated with the type of equity involved here; it is equity to restrain a person from acting in breach of confidence which is owed to another, arising from all the circumstances, and I believe that this is the way in which the authorities, to which I should pay a great regard, have treated the matter. Thus the learned author of *Equity and the Law of Trusts*, Professor Pettit (3rd ed., 1974) deals directly with this situation. I have been referred by senior counsel for the plaintiffs to a passage appearing in that edition at p.422, which reads:

"In any case it is clear that an injunction can be obtained not only against the original guilty party, but against any third party who knowingly obtained the confidential information in breach of confidence or in any other fraudulent manner. Indeed, even if a man obtains the confidential information innocently, once he gets to know that it was originally given in confidence, he can be restrained from breaking that confidence".

At least two cases are referred to as authority for that proposition. One is the case of *Fraser v Evans* [1969] 1 Q.B. 349. Lord Denning M.R. said this (at 361):

"The jurisdiction is based not so much on property or on contract as on duty to be of good faith. No person is permitted to divulge to the world information which he has received in confidence, unless he has just cause or excuse for doing so. Even if he comes by it innocently, nevertheless once he gets to know that it was originally given in confidence, he can be restrained from breaking that confidence".

A similar approach was taken by Goff J. in *Butler v Board of Trade* [1971] Ch. 680 at 690 where his Lordship refers to just cause and excuse for not being responsible for divulging confidential information. It may well be, as was suggested, again by learned counsel for the plaintiffs, that he is referring to a case where the confidential information has lost its aspect or character of confidence and has passed into the domain of public knowledge. There is no suggestion that this is the case here.

In those circumstances and in spite of the very interesting and well researched argument of counsel for the fifth defendant, I am of the view that it is proper for injunctions to be granted against all defendants and I propose to grant them in a form that can be settled in due course. I believe that the undertaking for damages, which I am instructed the plaintiffs are prepared to give, will provide adequate protection for the innocent defendants in the event that my approach to this problem turns out to be incorrect. For those reasons I propose to grant injunctions against all of the defendants.

2.3.3   No Relationship of Confidence

2.3.3.1   *Franklin v Giddings* [1978] Qd. R.72, Dunn J., SC, Queensland

*The plaintiffs bred a new form of nectarine, the Franklin Early White, and were
the sole marketers of it. The male defendant stole budwood cuttings from the
plaintiff's orchard and, by grafting them onto his own root stocks, developed an
orchard of Franklin Early Whites in direct competition with the plaintiffs. The
female defendant, his wife, did not learn how he had obtained the budwood
until later. The plaintiffs claimed equitable relief, rather than damages for conversion of the budwood.*

Dunn J. referred to textbooks on breach of confidence, and said:

What has been protected by equity has been "confidential information," that is defined by
those authors as "facts, schemes or theories which the law regards as of sufficient value or
importance to afford protection against use of them by the defendant otherwise than in
accordance with the plaintiff's wishes".

Usually, the relevance of the plaintiff's wishes is that the protected "information" has been
voluntarily imparted in confidence, often being imparted by an employer to a trusted
employee. But it is clear that equity recognised a personal obligation to respect trust and
confidence which did not arise consequently upon a contractual relationship. See *Prince
Albert v Strange* 2 DeG. & Sm. 651 (64 E.R. 293), and 1 Mac. and G. 25 (41 E.R. 1171).

Dunn J. then referred to Caird v Sime *(1887) 12 A.C. 326,* Saltman Engineering
v Campbell *(above, 2.1.2) and* Argyll v Argyll *[1967] Ch. 302. He continued:*

If I have laboured the point that the jurisdiction which I am asked to exercise exists
independently of contract, it is because learned counsel for the defendants placed a good
deal of reliance upon the circumstances that the male defendant was never employed by the
plaintiffs at Pozieres, notwithstanding an allegation in the pleadings that that had been the
case.

He also argued that the budwood twigs were not "information confidentially imparted"
and that therefore no obligation of confidence deserving of protection had arisen, challenging the proposition that "it would be extraordinary if a defendant, who acquired by
eavesdropping or other improper covert means the secrets of the plaintiff because he would
not have been able to get them by consensual arrangement, could defend proceedings by
the plaintiff on the ground that no obligation of confidence could arise without communication of the information by the plaintiff." (Meagher, Gummow and Lehane, *Equity—
Doctrines and Remedies*, p.719.)

I find myself quite unable to accept that a thief who steals a trade secret, knowing it to be a
trade secret, with the intention of using it in commercial competition with its owner, to the
detriment of the latter, and so uses it, is less unconscionable than a traitorous servant. The
thief is unconscionable because he plans to use and does use his own wrong conduct to
better his position in competition with the owner, and also to place himself in a better
position than that of a person who deals consensually with the owner.

I have already expressed the opinion that, when the male defendant stole budwood from
the plaintiff's orchard, what he got as a trade secret. The secret was the technique of

propagating Franklin Early White nectarines, using budwood from the plaintiff's orchard. The technique of budding was no secret, but the budwood existed only in the plaintiff's orchard, where the plaintiff guarded it by exercising general surveillance over fruit-pickers and visitors, and by bruiting it abroad that it was theirs and theirs alone. The "information" which the genetic structure of the wood represented was of substantial commercial value, much time and effort had been expended by the male plaintiff in evolving it and it could not be duplicated by anybody whatsoever.

I hold that the male defendant has been guilty of infringements of the plaintiff's rights since he stole and used the budwood: as for the female defendant, she has since at least the middle of last year known that the Franklin Early White nectarine trees in the orchard conducted by her husband and herself are the product of a stolen trade secret, and—this being so—it is unconscionable for her to derive any benefit from the trees, and she too infringes the plaintiff's rights.

Dunn J. treated the defendants as constructive trustees of the Franklin Early White trees and fruit which they had produced and granted the order for delivery up of the trust property for destruction which the plaintiffs had sought.

2.3.3.2 *Malone v Metropolitan Police Commissioner (No.2)* [1979] 1 Ch. 344, Megarry V.C.

The Metropolitan Police, following established procedure, arranged with the Post Office to tap the plaintiff's telephone. Partly as the result of this, the plaintiff was charged with handling stolen antiques but was acquitted. He then sought a declaration that the telephone tapping was wrongful on a number of grounds.

Megarry V.C. refused him any relief and held in particular:

> *(i) that there had been no breach of the European Convention on Human Rights, Art. 8, since the matter was not justiciable in an English court (the plaintiff subsequently succeeded on the issue before the European Court of Human Rights);*
>
> *(ii) that the plaintiff had no relevant right of property in his conversation;*
>
> *(iii) that the plaintiff had no right of privacy protecting him;*
>
> *(iv) that the plaintiff had no contractual right to confidentiality, since his relations with the Post Office were entirely statutory;*
>
> *(v) that there was no general right to confidentiality in telephone conversations; or if there were, the tapping by the police had been justified. On the last issue Megarry V.C. observed:*

In the present case, the alleged misuse is not by the person to whom the information was intended to be communicated, but by someone to whom the plaintiff had no intention of communicating anything: and that, of course, introduces a somewhat different element, that of the unknown overhearer.

It seems to me that a person who utters confidential information must accept the risk of any unknown overhearing that is inherent in the circumstances of communication. Those who exchange confidences on a bus or a train run the risk of a nearby passenger with acute hearing or a more distant passenger who is adept at lip-reading. Those who speak over garden walls run the risk of the unseen neighbour in a tool-shed nearby. Office cleaners who discuss secrets in the office when they think everyone else has gone run the risk of speaking within earshot of an unseen member of the staff who is working late. Those who give confidential information over an office intercommunication system run the risk of some third party being connected to the conversation. I do not see why someone who has overheard some secret in such a way should be exposed to legal proceedings if he uses or divulges what he has heard. No doubt an honourable man would give some warning when he relates that what he is hearing is not intended for his ears; but I have to concern myself with the law, and not with moral standards. There are, of course, many moral precepts which are not legally enforceable.

When this is applied to telephone conversations, it appears to me that the speaker is taking such risks of being overheard as are inherent in the system. As I have mentioned, the Younger Report referred to users of the telephone being aware that there were several well-understood possibilities of being overheard, and stated that a realistic person would not rely on the telephone system to protect the confidence of what he says. That comment seems unanswerable. In addition, so much publicity in recent years has been given to instances (real or fictional) of the deliberate tapping of telephones that it is difficult to envisage telephone users who are genuinely unaware of this possibility. No doubt a person who uses a telephone to give confidential information to another may do so in such a way as to impose an obligation of confidence on that other: but I do not see how it could be said that any such obligation is imposed on those who overhear the conversation, whether by means of tapping or otherwise.

If certain requirements are satisfied, then I think that there will plainly be just cause or excuse for what is done by or on behalf of the police. These requirements are, first, that there should be grounds for suspecting that the tapping of the particular telephone will be of material assistance in detecting or preventing crime, or discovering the criminals, or otherwise assisting in the discharge of the functions of the police in relation to crime. Secondly, no use should be made of any material obtained except for these purposes. Thirdly, any knowledge of information which is not relevant to those purposes should be confined to the minimum number of persons reasonably required to carry out the process of tapping. If those requirements are satisfied, then it seems to me that there will be just cause or excuse for carrying out the tapping, and using information obtained for those limited purposes. I am not, of course, saying that nothing else can constitute a just cause or excuse: what I am saying is that if these requirements are satisfied, then in my judgment there will be a just cause or excuse. I am not, for instance, saying anything about matters of national security: I speak only of what is before me in the present case, concerning tapping for police purposes in relation to crime.

So far as the evidence goes, it seems to me that the process of tapping, as carried out on behalf of the police in relation to crime, fully conforms with these requirements: indeed, there are restrictions on tapping and safeguards, which go beyond these requirements. The only possible difficulty is in relation to the "strict conditions" laid down by the Home Office which have to be satisfied before the warrant of the Home Office is sought; for I do not know what these conditions are. However, Mr Kelland's affidavit states in relation to the plaintiff that if a warrant had been sought by the Metropolitan Police (and he says nothing as to whether in fact it was) "the sole purpose in seeking such a warrant would have been to obtain information of value in the detection and prevention of serious crime." This, coupled with the other evidence, makes it clear enough, I think, that the first of the three requirements that I have stated would be satisfied. Accordingly, in my judgment, if, contrary to my opinion, telephone tapping on behalf of the police is a breach of any duty of confidentiality, there is just cause or excuse for that tapping in the circumstances of this case.

2.3.3.3   *Francome v Mirror Group* **[1984] 2 All E.R. 408, CA**

John Francome, a highly successful jockey, had his telephone tapped privately and illegally by an unrevealed person. The resulting tapes, which were said to show breaches by him of Jockey Club rules and possibly the commission of criminal offences, came into the defendant newspaper's hands and they proposed to publish an exposé.

In interlocutory proceedings for an injunction to restrain publication of material obtained in contravention of the Wireless Telegraphy Act 1949, s.5, and in breach of confidence, and to require disclosure of the source from which the tapes had been obtained, the plaintiff succeeded on the first but not the second ground.

Fox L.J., after referring to Megarry V.C.'s view of the nature of telephone tapping in the Malone *case (above, 2.3.3.2), continued:*

The Vice-Chancellor went on to say ([1979] 2 All E.R. 620 at 645; [1979] Ch. 344 at 376):

> "It seems to me that a person who utters confidential information must accept the risk of any unknown overhearing that is inherent in the circumstances of communication."

It is said that this statement negatives the existence of any right to confidentiality in the present case. I do not agree. The Vice-Chancellor was only dealing with a case of authorised tapping by the police and he makes that clear (see [1979] 2 All E.R. 620 at 651; [1979] Ch. 344 at 384). Illegal tapping by private persons is quite another matter, since it must be questionable whether the user of a telephone can be regarded as accepting the risk of that in the same way as, for example, he accepts the risk that his conversation may be overheard in consequence of the accidents and imperfections of the telephone system itself. Accordingly, in my opinion, there is a serious issue to be tried on the matter of confidentiality.

The Daily Mirror states that it will rely on iniquity and public interest as a defence to any claim of confidentiality. The claim of confidentiality and the claim of iniquity raise questions of law and fact which cannot be determined on an interlocutory application. They require a full trial.

If *The Daily Mirror* is permitted to publish the tapes now, the consequent harm to Mr Francome might be such that he could not be adequately compensated in damages for any wrong thereby done to him whatever the result of subsequent proceedings. Unless Mr Francome is given protection until the trial, I think that a trial might be largely worthless from his point of view even though he succeeded.

Fox L.J. added by way of comment on an affidavit by the Editor of The Daily Mirror.

There is one further matter. Mr Molloy, in his affidavit, says that he would have to give careful consideration to the probability that publication of the tapes would be an offence under the 1949 Act. He goes on to say that he would not regard that fact as an absolute bar to publication if he considered that publication was justifiable in the public interest. This suggests that Mr Molloy has a choice in the matter even though publication would be unlawful. It must be said flatly that he has no choice. His duty is to obey the law. Parliament by section 5(b) of the 1949 Act created a criminal offence. The proposition that citizens are free to commit a criminal offence if they have formed the view that it will further what they believe to be the public interest is quite baseless in our law and inimical to parliamentary authority. I do not disregard the existence of what is called the moral imperative. But such cases are rare in the extreme. On the evidence before us, there is nothing in the present case which approaches such a situation.

I would make the orders which I have indicated.

Sir John Donaldson M.R. and Stephen Brown L.J. delivered judgments to similar effect.

2.4   Remedies

2.4.1   *Seager v Copydex (No. 2)* [1969] 2 All E.R. 718, CA

The inquiry as to damages ordered in the first proceedings (above, 2.1.3) led to a second appeal.

Lord Denning M.R.:

Now a question has arisen as to the principles on which the damages are to be assessed. They are to be assessed, as we said, at the value of the information which the defendant company took. If I may use an analogy, it is like damages for conversion. Damages for conversion are the value of the goods. Once the damages are paid, the goods become the property of the defendant. A satisfied judgment in trover transfers the property in the goods. So, here, once the damages are assessed and paid, the confidential information belongs to the defendant company.

The difficulty is to assess the value of the information taken by the defendant company. We have had a most helpful discussion about it. The value of the confidential information depends upon the nature of it. If there was nothing very special about it, that is, if it involved no particular inventive step but was the sort of information which could be obtained by employing any competent consultant, then the value of it was the fee which a consultant would charge for it; because in that case the defendant company, by taking the information, would only have saved themselves the time and trouble of employing a consultant. But, on the other hand, if the information was something special, as for instance, if it involved an inventive step or something so unusual that it could not be obtained by just going to a consultant, then the value of it is much higher. It is not merely a consultant's fee, but the price which a willing buyer—desirous of obtaining it—would pay for it. It is the value as between a willing seller and a willing buyer. In this case, the plaintiff says that the information was very special. People had been trying for years to get a carpet grip and then he hit on this idea of a dome-shaped prong. It was, he said, an inventive step. And he is supported in this issue by the fact that the defendant company themselves have applied for a patent for it. Furthermore, if he is to be regarded as a seller, it must be remembered that he had a patent for another carpet grip called "Klent": and, if he was selling the confidential information (which I will call the "Invisigrip" information) then the sales of the "Klent" might be adversely affected. The sales of the "Klent" would be reduced owing to the competition of the "Invisigrip". So he would ask for a higher price for the confidential information in order to compensate him for the reduction in the "Klent". In these circumstances, if the plaintiff is right in saying that the confidential information was very special indeed, then it may well be right for the value to be assessed on the footing that, in the usual way, it would be remunerated by a royalty. The courts, of course, cannot give a royalty by way of damages; but it could give an equivalent by a calculation based on a capitalisation of a royalty. Thus it could arrive at a lump sum. Once a lump sum is assessed and paid, then the confidential information would belong to the defendant company in the same way as if they had bought and paid for it by an agreement of sale. The property, so far as there is property in it, would vest in them. They would have the right to use that confidential information for the manufacture of carpet grips and selling of them. If it is patentable, they would be entitled to the benefit of the patent as if they had bought it. In other words, it would be regarded as a real outright purchase of the confidential information. The value should, therefore, be assessed on that basis; and damages awarded accordingly.

In these circumstances, I do not think that we should make any such declaration as the defendant company asks. It is sufficient for us to say that, on a satisfied judgment for damages, the confidential information belongs to the defendant. There is one thing more. We have been told that patent proceedings are pending by the defending company. They are applying for a patent and the plaintiff is opposing it. That cannot affect directly the matters which we have to decide today. But the matters are so linked together that I think that the damages should be assessed not by a master in the Chancery Division but by a patent judge. I hope that one patent judge will deal with the patent proceedings as well as these damages. The only order which I would make on the motion is simply to say that the damages are to be assessed in conformity with our judgments.

Salmon and Winn L.JJ. concurred.

2.4.2   *Peter Pan Manufacturing v Corsets Silhouette* **[1963] 3 All E.R. 402, Pennycuick J.**

The plaintiff established that in producing and marketing brassieres, the defendant had misused confidential information embodied in two of its own brassieres, U15 and U25. The plaintiff sought an account of profits. As to its form, Pennycuick J. quoted in particular from Lever v Goodwin *[1887] 36 Ch.D. 1, per* Cotton L.J.:

> "It is well known that, both in trade-mark cases and patent cases, the plaintiff is entitled, if he succeeds in getting an injunction, to take either of two forms of relief. He may either say 'I claim from you the damage I have sustained from your wrongful act', or 'I claim from you the profit which you have made by your wrongful act' ... The profit for which the defendants must account is the profit which they have made by the sale of soap in that fraudulent dress to the middlemen. It is immaterial how the middlemen deal with it".

I have been referred to a number of forms of order in *Seton's Judgments and Orders*, Vol. 1, in which an account of profits has been ordered. They were patent cases, trade mark cases, or otherwise.

It seems to me that on the plain terms of those orders, what a plaintiff who elects in favour of an account of profits is entitled to, is simply an account of profits in the sense which I have indicated, that is, what has the plaintiff expended on manufacturing these goods? What is the price which he has received on their sale? And the difference is profit. That is what Peter Pan claims in the order for an account as formulated by it; that is simply an account of the profits made by Silhouette in the manufacture and sale of the brassieres U15 and U25.

Counsel for Silhouette has said that that is not the true meaning of the order for an account in the various cases to which I have referred, and that the true meaning of the order, if I understand him, is an account of the amount by which the profit made by the defendant from manufacturing articles with the aid of patents, trade-marks, confidential information, or whatever it may be, which he has in fact used exceeds the amount of the profit which he would have made if he had manufactured the same article without the aid of that material. It seems to me quite impossible to construe the orders made in the various cases as bearing that meaning, and further, so far as I can see, it is perfectly impossible to take as one factor in an account the amount of profit which Silhouette would have made by manufacturing brassieres in the styles U15 and U25 without the use of confidential information, since the manufacture of brassieres of those styles necessarily and inevitably involves the use of confidential information. Indeed, counsel very aptly said that an account in the only form which he says that Peter Pan is entitled to an account would be impracticable. I am quite unsatisfied by any authorities which have been cited to me that that is the only account to which Peter Pan is entitled, or that the account to which I have held it is entitled would present any serious difficulty in its working out.

I should, I think, mention that one of the cases cited to me by counsel for Silhouette was *Siddell v Vickers* (1892) 9 R.P.C. 152. In that case on the particular facts of the case the Court of Appeal laid down that:

> "The true test of comparison was with what the defendants would probably have used instead of the invention, looking at all the circumstances of the case".

That means only this, that the defendants could have manufactured the product in question by other means, but were able to manufacture more economically by making use of a particular appliance which they were not entitled to use. The position there seems to be wholly different from that in the present case, where the manufacture of the article in question of itself involved the use of the confidential information and Silhouette could not have manufactured that article at all without the use of confidential information. So again it seems to me that the proper order for an account is in the terms which Peter Pan have put forward, which is the time-honoured form, and I do not see myself any reason why that form should not be adopted.

2.5   Human Rights, Privacy and Confidence

2.5.1   European Convention on Human Rights, Arts 8, 10

Right to respect for private and family life

1. Everyone has the right to respect for his private and family life, his home and his correspondence.

2. There shall be no interference by a public authority with the exercise of this right except such as is in accordance with the law and is necessary in a democratic society in the interests of national security, public safety or the economic well-being of the country, for the prevention of disorder or crime, for the protection of health or morals, or for the protection of the rights and freedoms of others.

Freedom of expression

1. Everyone has the right to freedom of expression. This right shall include freedom to hold opinions and to receive and impart information and ideas without interference by public authority and regardless of frontiers. This Article shall not prevent States from requiring the licensing of broadcasting, television or cinema enterprises.

2. The exercise of these freedoms, since it carries with its duties and responsibilities, may be subject to such formalities, conditions, restrictions or penalties as are prescribed by law and are necessary in a democratic society, in the interests of national security, territorial integrity or public safety, for the prevention of disorder or crime, for the protection of health or morals, for the protection of the reputation or rights of others, for preventing the disclosure of information received in confidence, or for maintaining the authority and impartiality of the judiciary.

2.5.2   Human Rights Act 1998, s.12

Freedom of expression

S.12(1) This section applies if a court is considering whether to grant any relief which, if granted, might affect the exercise of the Convention right to freedom of expression.

(2) If the person against whom the application for relief is made ("the respondent") is neither present nor represented, no such relief is to be granted unless the court is satisfied—

   (a) that the applicant has taken all practicable steps to notify the respondent; or

   (b) that there are compelling reasons why the respondent should not be notified.

(3) No such relief is to be granted so as to restrain publication before trial unless the court is satisfied that the applicant is likely to establish that publication should not be allowed.

(4) The court must have particular regard to the importance of the Convention right to freedom of expression and, where the proceedings relate to material which the respondent claims, or which appears to the court, to be journalistic, literary or artistic material (or to conduct connected with such material), to—

(a) the extent to which—

(i) the material has, or is about to, become available to the public; or

(ii) it is, or would be, in the public interest for the material to be published;

(b) any relevant privacy code.

2.5.3 *Douglas v Hello! (No.1)* [2001] Q.B. 967, CA

The film stars, Michael Douglas and Catherine Zeta-Jones, were to marry in a blaze of controlled publicity in New York. Each contracted beforehand with the British gossip magazine, OK!, that it should have exclusive photo-coverage of the event, subject to the approval of the happy pair of the photos selected. Everyone involved, guests as well as staff, was under the clearest notice of the ban on publicity by others. Guests were asked not to take photos and they were required at the entrance to give up any equipment that was spotted on them. Either because of a breach of these confidential arrangements, or because a paparazzo somehow got a long-lens look-in, pictures of the wedding were purchased by the rival magazine Hello!. The claimants secured an interim injunction to restrain Hello! from publishing its haul.

In lifting the injunction, the Court of Appeal considered the impact of the European Human Rights Convention, Art.10 and the Human Rights Act 1998, s.12 on arrangements to ensure that a publicity contract remained exclusive. Of the three judgments, the clearest commitment to a right of privacy, distinct from breach of confidence, is found in that of Sedley L.J. Dealing with the development of English law apart from Human Rights Act considerations, he first referred to the Court's acceptance in Kaye v Robertson *[1991] F.S.R. 62 of counsel's concession that there was no right of privacy at common law and compared it with the view of Laws J. in* Hellewell v Chief Constable of Derbyshire *[1995] 1 W.L.R. 804, 807:*

"I entertain no doubt that disclosure of a photograph may, in some circumstances, be actionable as a breach of confidence... If someone with a telephoto lens were to take from a distance and with no authority a picture of another engaged in some private act, his subsequent disclosure of the photograph would, in my judgment, as surely amount to a breach of confidence as if he had found or stolen a letter or diary in which the act was recounted and proceeded to publish it. In such a case, the law would protect what might reasonably be called a right of privacy, although the name accorded to the cause of action would be breach of confidence."

Sedley L.J. referred to other authority and concluded on this aspect:

125. I would conclude, at lowest, that Mr Tugendhat [for the claimant] has a powerfully arguable case to advance at trial that his two first-named clients have a right of privacy which English law will today recognise and, where appropriate, protect. To say this is in my

belief to say little, save by way of a label, that our courts have not said already over the years. It is to say, among other things, that the right, grounded as it is in the equitable doctrine of breach of confidence, is not unqualified. As Laws J. said in *Hellewell* [above]: "It is, of course, elementary that in all such cases, a defence based on the public interest would be available."

126. What a concept of privacy does, however, is accord recognition to the fact that the law has to protect not only those people whose trust has been abused but those who simply find themselves subjected to an unwanted intrusion into their personal lives. The law no longer needs to construct an artificial relationship of confidentiality between intruder and victim: it can recognise privacy itself as a legal principle drawn from the fundamental value of personal autonomy.

127. It is relevant, finally, to note that no Strasbourg jurisprudence contra-indicates, much less countermands, the establishment in national legal systems of a qualified right of privacy; and that the courts of France and Germany, to take two other signatories of the Convention, have both in recent years developed long-gestated laws for the qualified protection of privacy against both state and non-state invention: see E. Picard, "The right to privacy in French law" in *Protecting Privacy,* (ed. B. Markesinis, 1999) and Markensinis, *The German Law of Torts,* 3rd ed. (1994), pp. 63–66.

He proceeded to deal with arguments on the Human Rights Act 1998 as follows:

128. The Human Rights Act 1998 was brought into force on October 2, 2000. It requires every public authority, including the courts, to act consistently with the European Convention for the Protection of Human Rights and Fundamental Freedoms. What this means is a subject of sharp division and debate among both practising and academic lawyers: does it simply require the court's procedures to be Convention-compliant, or does it require the law applied by the courts, save where primary legislation plainly says otherwise, to give effect to the Convention principles? This is not the place, at least without much fuller argument, in which to resolve such a large question. But some attitude has to be taken to Mr Tugendhat's submission that, whatever the current state of common law and equity, we are obliged now to give some effect to Article 8, among other provisions, of the Convention.

129. It is helpful, first of all, to see how much change he is soliciting. If he is right in his primary submission then the law is today adequately configured to respect the Convention. If it is not—for example if the step from confidentiality to privacy is not simply a modern restatement of the scope of a known protection but a legal innovation—then I would accept his submission (for which there is widespread support among commentators on the Act: see in particular Murray Hunt, "The 'Horizontal Effect' of the Human Rights Act" [1998] P.L. 423) that this is precisely the kind of incremental change for which the Act is designed: one which without undermining the measure of certainty which is necessary to all law gives substance and effect to section 6.

130. Such a process would be consonant with the jurisprudence of the European Court of Human Rights, which section 2 of the Act requires us to take into account and which has pinpointed article 8 as a locus of the doctrine of positive obligation. Thus in *X and Y v The Netherlands* (1985) 8 E.H.R.R. 235, 239–240 para. 23, the court said:

"The court recalls that, although the object of article 8 is essentially that of protecting the individual against arbitrary interference by the public authorities, it does not merely compel the state to abstain from such interference: in addition to this primarily negative undertaking, there may be positive obligations inherent in an effective respect for private or family life. These obligations may involve the adoption of measures designed to secure respect for private life even in the sphere of relations of individuals between themselves."

131. More immediately to the present point is section 12 of the Act [above].

132. There is no need to look at the parliamentary genesis of this section in order to see that it, with section 13, is of a different kind from the rest of the Act. It descends from the general to the particular, singling out one Convention right and making procedural and substantive provision for litigation in which the right is directly or indirectly implicated. The Convention right in question is the right to freedom of expression contained in Article 10 of the Convention, set out in Schedule 1 to the 1998 Act [above].

133. Two initial points need to be made about section 12 of the Act. First, by subsection (4) it puts beyond question the direct applicability of at least one article of the Convention as between one private party to litigation and another—in the jargon, its horizontal effect. Whether this is an illustration of the intended mechanism of the entire Act, or whether it is a special case (and if so, why), need not detain us here. The other point, well made by Mr Tugendhat, is that it is the "Convention right" to freedom of expression which both triggers the section (see section 12(1)) and to which particular regard is to be had. That Convention right, when one turns to it, is qualified in favour of the reputation and rights of others and the protection of information received in confidence. In other words, you cannot have particular regard to Article 10 without having equally particular regard at the very least to Article 8 [above].

134. Mr Carr [for the defendant] was disposed to accept this; so far as I can see he had no choice, although it is perhaps unexpected to find a claimant relying on section 12 against a publisher rather than vice versa. But he balked at what Mr Tugendhat submitted, and I agree, was the necessary extension of the subsection's logic. A newspaper, say, intends to publish an article about an individual who learns of it and fears, on tenable grounds, that it will put his life in danger. The newspaper, also on tenable grounds, considers his fear unrealistic. First of all. It seems to me inescapable that section 12(4) makes the right to life, which is protected by Article 2 and implicitly recognised by Article 10(2), as relevant as the right of free expression to the court's decision; and in doing so it also makes Article 17 (which prohibits the abuse of rights) relevant. But this in turn has an impact on section 12(3) which, though it does not replace the received test (or tests) for prior restraint, qualifies them by requiring a probability of success at trial. The gauging of this probability, by virtue of section 12(4), will have to take into account the full range of relevant Convention rights.

135. How is the court to do this when the evidence—*viz.* that there is and that there is not an appreciable risk to life—is no more than evenly balanced? A bland application of section 12(3) could deny the claimant the court's temporary protection, even if the potential harm to him, should the risk eventuate, was of the gravest kind and that to the newspaper and the public, should publication be restrained, minimal; and a similarly bland application of section 12(4), simply prioritising the freedom to publish over other Convention rights (save possibly freedom of religion: see section 13), might give the newspaper the edge even if the claimant's evidence were strong. I agree with Mr Tugendhat that this cannot have been Parliament's design. This is not only, as he submits, because of the inherent logic of the provision but because if the court's own obligation under section 3 of the Act to construe all legislation so far as possible compatibly with the Convention rights, an obligation which must include the interpretation of the Human Rights Act itself. The European Court of Human Rights has always recognised the high importance of free media of communication in a democracy, but its jurisprudence does not—and could not consistently with the

Convention itself—give Article 10(1) the presumptive priority which is given, for example, to the First Amendment in the jurisprudence of the United States' courts. Everything will ultimately depend on the proper balance between privacy and publicity in the situation facing the court.

136. For both reasons, and in agreement with Keene L.J. and Brooke L.J., I accept that section 12 is not to be interpreted and applied in the simplistic manner for which Mr Carr contends. It will be necessary for the court, in applying the test set out in section 12(3), to bear in mind that by virtue of section 12(1)(4) the qualifications set out in Article 10(2) are as relevant as the right set out in Article 10(1). This means that, for example, the reputations and rights of others—not only but not least their Convention rights—are as material as the defendant's right of free expression. So is the prohibition on the use of one party's Convention rights to injure the Convention rights of others. Any other approach to section 12 would in my judgment violate section 3 of the Act. Correspondingly, as Mr Tugendhat submits, "likely" in section 12(3) cannot be read as requiring simply an evaluation of the relative strengths of the parties' evidence. If at trial, for the reasons I have given, a minor but real risk to like, or a wholly unjustifiable invasion of privacy, is entitled to no less regard, by virtue of Article 10(2) than is accorded to the right to publish by Article 10(1), the consequent likelihood becomes material under section 12(3). Neither element is a trump card. They will be articulated by the principles of legality and proportionality which, as always, constitute the mechanism by which the court reaches its conclusion on countervailing or qualified rights. It will be remembered that in the jurisprudence of the Convention proportionality is tested by, among other things, the standard of what is necessary in a democratic society. It should also be borne in mind that the much quoted remark of Hoffmann L.J. in *R v Central Independent Television plc* [1994] Fam. 192, 203 that freedom of speech "is a trump card which always wins" came in a passage which expressly qualified the proposition (as Lord Hoffmann has since confirmed, albeit extrajudicially, in his 1996 Goodman Lecture) as lying "outside the established exceptions, or any new ones which Parliament may enact in accordance with its obligations under the Convention". If freedom of expression is to be impeded, in other words, it must be on cogent grounds recognised by law.

The judgments of both Brooke L.J. and Keene L.J. show considerable awareness of the need to develop English law so as to provide rights against unjustifiable invasions of privacy. Keene L.J. summarised his opinion thus:

The nature of the subject matter or the circumstances of the defendant's activities may suffice in some instances to give rise to liability for breach of confidence. That approach must now be informed by the jurisprudence of the Convention in respect of Article 8. Whether the resulting liability is described as being for breach of confidence or for breach of a right to privacy may be little more than deciding what label is to be attached to the cause of the action, but there would seem to be merit in recognising that the original concept of breach of confidence has in this particular category of cases now developed into something different from the commercial and employment relationships with which confidentiality is mainly concerned.

167. Because of these developments in the common law relating to confidence and the apparent obligation on English courts now to take account of the right to respect for private and family life under Article 8 when interpreting the common law, it seems unlikely that *Kaye v Robertson* [1991] F.S.R. 62, which held that there was no actionable right of privacy in English law, would be decided the same way on that aspect today.

Brooke L.J.'s judgment is rich in historical and comparative reference. It also draws attention to the difficulties of introducing a statutory law of privacy without also codifying breach of confidence, a reflection deriving from his Chairmanship of the English Law Commission.

In deciding on balance to refuse the interim injunction, all members of the Court laid particular stress on the fact that the case concerned exclusive publicity rather than privacy.

2.5.4 *A v B* [2002] 2 All E.R. 545, CA

The applicant, a Premier League footballer, had passing sexual relations with two women (C and D), who then wished to reveal their stories through the defendant newspaper. A's wife did not know, hence all the initials. Despite the apparent breach of confidence, the Court of Appeal refused to grant an interim injunction against publication. Lord Woolf C.J. gave guidelines to courts which had to balance the right to respect for privacy against the right of expression in the press and elsewhere (under the European Human Rights Convention, Arts 8 and 10), with regard to the impact of the Human Rights Act 1998, s.12 upon interim proceedings.

(i) The consideration of this type of application should generally begin with recognition that what is being considered is an interim application for an injunction. This means that whether any injunction is granted at all is a matter of discretion for the judge, to be exercised in accordance with what are now well-established principles which include the need to establish, as we will explain later, that after a trial it is likely that an injunction would be granted after a substantive hearing, while recognising that the grant or refusal of an interim injunction could well determine the outcome of the entire proceedings.

(ii) The fact that the injunction is being sought to protect the privacy of the claimant, and that if the injunction is not granted, the claimant may be deprived of the only remedy which is of any value is a relevant consideration. However, this consideration has to be weighed against the defendant's rights of freedom of expression. Even before the 1998 Act this would have been an important consideration.

His Lordship referred to s.12 (above 2.5.2) and continued:

Its importance has been enhanced by s.12 of the 1998 Act. The relevant provisions of s.12 are:

"(1) This section applies if a court is considering whether to grant any relief which, if granted, might affect the exercise of the Convention right to freedom of expression . . .

(3) No such relief is to be granted so as to restrain publication before trial unless the court is satisfied that the applicant is likely to establish that publication should not be allowed.

(4) The court must have particular regard to the importance of the Convention right to freedom of expression and, where the proceedings relate to material which the respondent claims, or which appears to the court, to be journalistic, literary or artistic material (or to conduct connected with such material), to—(a) the extent to which—(i)

the material has, or is about to, become available to the public; or (ii) it is, or would be, in the public interest for the material to be published; (b) any relevant privacy code."

(iii) As to the word "likely" in s.12(3) useful guidance is provided by Sir Andrew Morritt V.C. in *Imutran Ltd v Uncaged Campaigns Ltd* [2001] 2 All E.R. 385. He said of s.12 (at[17]):

> "Counsel for the defendants submitted that the requirement of likelihood imposed a higher standard that that formulated in [*American Cyanamid Co v Ethicon Ltd* [1975] 1 All E.R. 504, [1975] A.C. 396]. I did not understand this to be disputed by counsel for Imutran. He submitted that whatever the standard was his case satisfied it. Theoretically and as a matter of language likelihood is slightly higher in the scale of probability than a real prospect of success. But the difference between the two is so small that I cannot believe that there will be many (if any) cases which would have succeeded under the *American Cyanamid* test but will now fail because of the terms of s.12(3) of the 1998 Act. Accordingly I propose to apply the test of likelihood without any further consideration of how much more probable that now has to be."

There is no conflict between s.12(3) and the convention. (See *Douglas v Hello! Ltd* [2001] 2 All E.R. 289 at 326–327, [2001] Q.B. 967 at 1008 (para. 150) *per* Keene LJ.)

(iv) The fact that if the injunction is granted it will interfere with the freedom of expression of others and in particular the freedom of the press is a matter of particular importance. This well-established common law principle is underlined by s.12(4). Any interference with the press has to be justified because it inevitably has some effect on the ability of the press to perform its role in society. This is the position irrespective of whether a particular publication is desirable in the public interest. The existence of a free press is in itself desirable and so any interference with it has to be justified.

Here we would endorse the approach of Hoffmann L.J. in *R v Central Independent Television plc* [1994] 3 All E.R. 641 at 652, 653; [1994] Fam. 192 at 203, 204, where he said:

> "... publication may cause needless pain, distress and damage to individuals or harm to other aspects of the public interest. But a freedom which is restricted to what judges think to be responsible or in the public interest is no freedom. Freedom means the right to publish things which government and judges, however well motivated, think should not be published. It means the right to say things which "right-thinking people" regard as dangerous or irresponsible. This freedom is subject only to clearly defined exceptions laid down by common law or statute ... The principle that the press is free from both government and judicial control is more important that the particular case."

(v) The fact that under s.12(4) the court is required to have particular regard to whether it would be in the public interest for the material to be published does not mean that the court is justified in interfering with the freedom of the press where there is no identifiable special public interest in any particular material being published. Such an approach would turn s.12(4) upside down. Regardless of the quality of the material which is intended to publish prima facie the court should not interfere with its publication. Any interference with publication must be justified.

(vi) It is most unlikely that any purpose will be served by a judge seeking to decide whether there exists a new cause of action in tort which protects privacy. In the great majority of situations, if not all situations, where the protection of privacy is justified, relating to events after the 1998 Act came into force, an action for breach of confidence now will, where this is appropriate, provide the necessary protection. This means that at first instance it can be readily accepted that it is not necessary to tackle the vexed question of whether there is a separate cause of action based upon a new tort of privacy.

(vii) Furthermore in the majority of cases the question of whether there is an interest capable of being the subject of a claim for privacy should not be allowed to be the subject of detailed argument. There must be some interest of a private nature which the claimant wishes to protect, but usually the answer to the question whether there exists a private interest worthy of protection will be obvious. In those cases in which the answer is not obvious, an answer will often be unnecessary. This is because the weaker the claim for privacy the more likely that the claim for privacy will be outweighed by the claim based on freedom of expression. The advantage of not having to distinguish between acts which are public and those which are private in a difficult case is made clear by what Gleeson C.J. had to say on the subject in *Australian Broadcasting Corp v Lenah Game Meats Pty Ltd* (2002) 185 A.L.R. 1. He explained the difficulty of distinguishing between public and private information when he said (at 13):

> "[42] There is no bright line which can be drawn between what is private and what is not. Use of the term 'public' is often a convenient method of contrast, but there is a large area in between what is necessarily public and what is necessarily private. An activity is not private simply because it is not done in public. It does not suffice to make an act private that, because it occurs on private property, it has such measure of protection from the public gaze as the characteristics of the property, the nature of the activity, the locality, and the disposition of the property owner combine to afford. Certain kinds of information about a person, such as information relating to health, personal relationships, or finances, may be easy to identify as private; as may certain kinds of activity, which a reasonable person, applying contemporary standards of morals and behaviour, would understand to be meant to be unobserved. The requirement that disclosure or observation of information or conduct would be highly offensive to a reasonable person of ordinary sensibilities is in many circumstances a useful practical test of what is private."

(viii) The same is true in cases in which the public interest in publication is relied on to oppose the grant of an injunction. We have already made clear that even where there is no public interest in a particular publication interference with freedom of expression has to be justified. However, the existence of a public interest in publication strengthens the case for not granting an injunction. Again in the majority of situations whether the public interest is involved or not will be obvious. In the grey area cases the public interest, if it exists, is unlikely to be decisive. Judges should therefore be reluctant in the difficult borderline cases to become involved in detailed argument as to whether the public interest is involved. In a borderline case the application will usually be capable of being resolved without deciding whether there is a public interest in publication. In any event, the citation of authority is unlikely to be helpful. The circumstances in any particular case under consideration can vary so much that a judgment in one case is unlikely to be decisive in another case, though it may be illustrative of an approach.

(ix) The need for the existence of a confidential relationship should not give rise to problems as to the law. The difficulty will be as to the relevant facts. A duty of confidence will arise whenever the party subject to the duty is in a situation where he either knows or ought to know that the other person can reasonably expect his privacy to be protected. (See Lord Goff of Chieveley in *Attorney General v Guardian Newspapers Ltd (No. 2)* [1988] 3 All E.R. 545 at 658; [1990] 1 A.C. 109 at 281.) The range of situations in which protection can be provided is therefore extensive.

Obviously, the necessary relationship can be expressly created. More often its existence will have to be inferred from the facts. Whether a duty if confidence does exist which courts can protect, if it is right to do so, will depend on all the circumstances of the relationship between the parties at the time of the threatened or actual breach of the alleged duty of confidence.

(x) If there is an intrusion in a situation where a person can reasonably expect his privacy to be respected then that intrusion will be capable of giving rise to liability in an action for breach of confidence unless the intrusion can be justified. (See the approach of Dame Elizabeth Butler-Sloss P. in *Venables v News Group Newspapers Ltd* [2001] 1 All E.R. 908 at 933; [2001] Fam. 430 at 462 (para. 81).) The bugging of someone's home or the use of other surveillance techniques are obvious examples of such an intrusion. But the fact that the information is obtained as a result of unlawful activities does not mean that its publication should necessarily be restrained by injunction on the grounds of breach of confidence (see the *Australian Broadcasting* case (2001) 185 A.L.R. 1). Dependent on the nature of the unlawful activity there may be other remedies. On the other hand, the fact that unlawful means have been used to obtain the information could well be a compelling factor when it comes to exercising discretion.

(xi) More difficult is the situation where the alleged intrusion into privacy is as a result of the reporting of the information to a third party by a party to the relationship which creates the privacy. This is a material factor in situations where two people have shared a sexual relationship outside marriage. If one wishes to exercise his or her Art. 10 rights that must impact on the other's right to maintain confidentiality. For example the information may relate, as in this case, to a situation where there is a sexual relationship between two parties and one of the parties informs the media about the relationship without the consent of the other party. Here the conflict between one party's right to privacy and the other party's right of freedom is especially acute. In situations where the parties are not married (when they are, special considerations may arise) the fact that the confidence was a shared confidence which only one of the parties wishes to preserve does not extinguish the other party's right to have the confidence respected, but it does undermine that right. While recognising the special status of a lawful marriage under our law, the courts, for present purposes, have to recognise and give appropriate weight to the extensive range of relationships which now exist. Obviously, the more stable the relationship the greater the significance which is attached to it.

(xii) Where an individual is a public figure he is entitled to have his privacy respected in the appropriate circumstances. A public figure is entitled to a private life. The individual, however should recognise that because of his public position he must expect and accept that his actions will be more closely scrutinised by the media. Even trivial facts relating to a public figure can be of great interest to readers and other observers of the media. Conduct which in the case of a private individual would not be the appropriate subject of comment can be the proper subject of comment in the case of a public figure. The public figure may hold a position where higher standards of conduct can be rightly expected by the public. The public figure may be a role model whose conduct could well be emulated by others. He may set the fashion. The higher the profile of the individual concerned the more likely that this will be the position. Whether you have courted publicity or not you may be a legitimate subject of public attention. If you have courted public attention then you have less ground to object to the intrusion which follows. In many of these situations it would be overstating the position to say that there is a public interest in the information being published. It would be more accurate to say that the public have an understandable and so a legitimate interest in being told the information. If this is the situation then it can be appropriately taken into account by a court when deciding on which side of the line a case falls. The courts must not ignore the fact that if newspapers do not publish information which the public are interested in, there will be fewer newspapers published, which will not be in the public interest. The same is true on relation to other parts of the media. On the difficult issue of finding the right balance, useful guidance of a general nature is provided by the Council of Europe Resolution 1165 of 1998. We set out paras 6–12 which are in these terms.

> "6. The Assembly is aware that personal privacy is often invaded, even in countries with specific legislation to protect it, as people's private lives have become a highly lucrative commodity for certain sectors of the media. The victims are essentially public figures, since details of their private lives serve as a stimulus to sales. At the same time, public figures must recognise that the special position they occupy in society—in many cases by choice—automatically entails increased pressure on their privacy.

> 7. Public figures are persons holding public office and/or using public resources and, more broadly speaking, all those who play a role in public life, whether in politics, the economy, the arts, the social sphere, sport or in any other domain.

> 8. It is often in the name of a one-sided interpretation of the right to freedom of expression, which is guaranteed in Article 10 of the European Convention of Human Rights, that the media invade people privacy, claiming that their readers are entitled to know about public figures.

> 9. Certain facts relating to the private lives of public figures, particularly politicians, may indeed be of interest to citizens, and it may therefore be legitimate for readers, who are also voters, to be informed of those facts.

> 10. It is therefore necessary to find a way of balancing the exercise of two fundamental rights, both of which are guaranteed by the European Convention on Human Rights: the right to respect for one's private life and the right to freedom of expression.

> 11. The Assembly reaffirms the importance of every person's right to privacy, and of the right to freedom of expression, as fundamental to a democratic society. These rights are neither absolute nor in any hierarchical order, since they are of equal value.

> 12. However, the Assembly points out that the right to privacy afforded by Article 8 of the European Convention on Human Rights should not only protect an individual against interference by public authorities, but also against interference by private persons or institutions, including the mass media."

(xiii) In drawing up a balance sheet between the respective interests of the parties courts should not act as censors or arbiters of taste. This is the task of others. If there is not a sufficient case for restraining publication the fact that a more lurid approach will be adopted by the publication than the court would regard as acceptable is not relevant. If the contents of the publication are untrue the law of defamation provides prohibition. Whether the publication will be attractive or unattractive should not affect the result of an application if the information is otherwise not the proper subject of restraint.

(xiv) Section 12(4) of the 1998 Act requires the court to take into account "any relevant privacy code" but it is only one of a number of factors to be taken into account. The Press Complaints Commission Code of Practice provides:

> "It is essential to the workings of an agreed code that it be honoured not only to the letter but in the full spirit. The Code should not be interpreted so

narrowly as to compromise its commitment to respect the rights of the individual, nor so broadly that it prevents publication in the public interest ...

3 Privacy

Everyone is entitled to respect for his or her private and family life, home health and correspondence. A publication will be expected to justify intrusions into any individual's private life without consent. (ii) The use of long lens photography to take pictures of people in private places without their consent is unacceptable. Note—Private places are public or private property where there is a reasonable expectation of privacy.

4 Harassment

... They must not photograph individuals in private places (as defined by the note to clause 3) without their consent; must not persist in telephoning, questioning, pursuing or photographing individuals after having been asked to desist; must nor remain on their property after having been asked to leave and must not follow them ...

The public interest

... 1. The public interest includes: (i) Detecting or exposing crime or a serious misdemeanour. (ii) Protecting public health and safety. (iii) Preventing the public from being misled by some statement or action of an individual or organisation."

Courts may well find this statement of practice of assistance. While recognising that s.12(4) was primarily concerned with preserving the freedom of the press regard should be had to the guidance given by Brooke L.J. in *Douglas v Hello! Ltd* [2001] 2 All E.R. 289 at 313–314; [2001] Q.B. 967 at 994 (para 94), where he says:

"It appears to me that the existence of these statutory provisions, coupled with the current wording of the relevant privacy code, mean that in any case where the court is concerned with issues of freedom of expression in a journalistic, literary or artistic context, it is bound to pay particular regard to any breach of the rules set out in cl. 3 of the code, especially where none of the public interest claims set out in the preamble to the code is asserted. A newspaper which flouts cl. 3 of the code is likely in those circumstances to have its claim to an entitlement to freedom of expression trumped by art 10(2) consideration of privacy. Unlike the court in *Kaye v Robertson* [1991] FSR 62, Parliament recognised that it had to acknowledge the importance of the art 8(1) respect for private life, and it was able to do so untrammelled by any concerns that the law of confidence might not stretch to protect every aspect of family life."

(xv) However, the court should discourage advocates seeking to rely on individual decisions of the Press Complaints Commission which at best are no more than illustrative of how the Press Complaints Commission performs its different responsibilities.

[12] In the above paragraphs we have attempted to assist courts as to how they should go about the task of holding the balance between the conflicting rights when hearing these applications. We are suggesting that frequently what is required is not a technical approach to the law but a balancing of the facts. The weight which should be attached to each relevant consideration will vary depending on the precise circumstances. In many situations

the balance may not point clearly in either direction. If this is the position, interim relief should be refused. We turn to deal with the present case.

In deciding to refuse interim relief, stress was laid in particular on (i) the causal nature of A's relations with C and D which were not of the sort that the court would be astute to protect; (ii) the freedom of expression entitled them to tell their stories to the media and not just to their friends; (iii) the role model for young people which footballers adopted, so that undesirable behaviour on their part could set an unfortunate example. This last point showed that there was at least some public interest in letting people know the kind of tittle-tattle which attracted them.

2.5.5 *Campbell v MGN* [2003] 1 All E.R. 224, CA

Naomi Campbell, the well-publicised fashion model, sued for damages for breach of confidence arising from the publication of articles in The Daily Mirror. *These revealed details of the therapy to end her drug addiction which she was receiving at Narcotics Anonymous and also used photographs of her taken in the street outside the premises of that organisation. She had previously denied that she had a drug problem and accepted that the media were free to set the record straight. Her action objected that the details of her treatment and the photograph were unnecessary to achieve this. The details and the lead to get the picture must have come from her entourage or someone within Narcotics Anonymous. Whoever it was owed a clear obligation not make the disclosures. Accordingly her case was argued (i) in breach of confidence, rather than upon any tort of breaching privacy, and (ii) as a claim to compensation for misuse of sensitive personal data under the Data Protection Act 1998, s.13. Both claims succeeded at first instance but were rejected by the Court of Appeal. The issues before the latter were dealt with as follows:*

Some categories of information are well recognised as confidential. These include details of a medical condition or its treatment.

48. We do not consider that the information that Miss Campbell was receiving therapy from Narcotics Anonymous was to be equated with disclosure of clinical details of medical treatment. It was not, however, simply because of the analogy he drew between her therapy and medical treatment that Morland J. held the information disclosed to be confidential. The first test of confidentiality that he purported to apply was that suggested by Gleeson C.J. in *Australian Broadcasting Corp v Lenah Game Meats Pty Ltd* at paragraph 42. That paragraph deserves citation in full:

> "There is no bright line which can be drawn between what is private and what is not. Use of the term 'public' is often a convenient method of contrast, but there is a large area in between what is necessarily public and what is necessarily private. An activity is not private simply because it is not done in public. It does not suffice to make an act private that, because it occurs on private property, it has such measure of protection from the public gaze as the characteristics of the property, the nature of the activity, the locality, and the disposition of the property owner combine to afford. Certain kinds of information about a person, such as information relating to health, personal relationships, or finances, may be easy to identify as private; as may certain kinds of

activity, which a reasonable person, applying contemporary standards of morals and behaviour, would understand to be meant to be unobserved. The requirement that disclosure or observation of information or conduct would be highly offensive to a reasonable person of ordinary sensibilities is in many circumstances a useful practical test of what is private."

52. The editor of the *Daily Mirror* was plainly indignant that complaint should be made of the additional details that the Appellants published to embellish the story that Miss Campbell was a drug addict. He explained in evidence how he rejected an approach that castigated Miss Campbell for hypocrisy in favour of one which commended her for her efforts to overcome her addiction. We have some sympathy with his reaction. Gratuitous disclosure of confidential information may be objectionable even where it shows the complainant in a good light. Some who give to charity are anxious that their generosity should remain anonymous. Here, however, Mr Morgan was making what had been accepted to have been proper disclosure of the discreditable fact that Miss Campbell was a drug addict. We think it harsh to criticise him for painting a somewhat fuller picture in order to show her in a sympathetic light.

53. Given that it was legitimate for the appellants to publish the fact that Miss Campbell was a drug addict and that she was receiving treatment, it does not seem to us that it was particularly significant to add the fact that the treatment consisted of attendance at meetings of Narcotics Anonymous. Counsel for MGN referred us to evidence as to the significance of anonymity, reflected by the name of this organisation. First and foremost it is intended to protect its members from the stigma of drug addiction. That benefit was denied to Miss Campbell in any event. Secondly anonymity was intended to support an atmosphere of equality at meetings—but it is clear, and it was inevitable, that Miss Campbell's identity was known to others who attended meetings with her. The third reason —to protect the organisation from self-appointed spokesmen, has no relevance in the present context.

54. We do not consider that a reasonable person of ordinary sensibilities, on reading that Miss Campbell was a drug addict, would find it highly offensive, or even offensive that the *Mirror* also disclosed that she was attending meetings of Narcotics Anonymous. The reader might have found it offensive that what were obviously covert photographs had been taken of her, but that, of itself, is not relied upon as ground for legal complaint.

Entitlement in the public interest to publish the peripheral details

59. Mr Browne advanced a sophisticated argument in which he drew an analogy between the reliance on public interest to justify publication of confidential material and the defence of qualified privilege to a claim for defamation. He sought to draw support for this analogy from the decision of the Appellate Division of the Supreme Court of South Africa in *Jansen Van Vuuren v Kruger* [1993] (4) S.A. 842 and from the decision of the United States Court of Appeals, Sixth Circuit, in *Bichler v Union Bank and Trust Co* (1984) 745 F. 2d 1006.

60. The object of this analogy was to enable Mr Browne to rely on the latitude that is given to a defendant on an occasion of qualified privilege to publish matter peripheral to that which is necessary to protect the interest or discharge the duty which is the foundation of the privilege. He cited the judgment of Hirst L.J. in *Watts v Times Newspapers* [1997] Q.B. 650 at 671 in support of a test that what was published should be "not unconnected" with the purpose in hand, and not "entirely irrelevant and extraneous".

61. We do not view this sophistry with enthusiasm. Both the South African and the

American authorities were addressing a tort of breach of privacy. In this jurisdiction both protection of privacy by expanding the scope of breach of confidence and the public interest defence of qualified privilege in defamation are in the course of development—as to the latter see *Reynolds v The Times* [2001] 2 A.C. 127 and *Loutchansky v The Times* [2002] 1 All E.R. 652, [2002] 2 W.L.R. 640. We do not believe that the same test of public interest applies to justify publication in these two very different torts.

After reflecting upon an argument that the defence of public interest should be equated to that of qualified privilege in the law of defamation, the Court confirmed:

62. We take a more straightforward view of the publications in this case. The primary information that had been conveyed to the appellants was that Miss Campbell was regularly attending Narcotics Anonymous. The fact that she was a drug addict was a secondary inference from this primary fact, albeit an inescapable inference. We find the suggestion that the *Mirror* should have published the secondary inference without publishing the primary fact from which this inference was drawn to be lacking in realism. What is it suggested that the *Mirror* should have published? "Naomi Campbell is a drug addict. The *Mirror* has discovered that she is receiving treatment for her addiction?" Such a story, without any background detail to support it, would have bordered on the absurd. We consider that the detail that was given, and indeed the photographs, were a legitimate, if not an essential, part of the journalistic package designed to demonstrate that Miss Campbell had been deceiving the public when she said that she did not take drugs.

63. In respect of this issue, [MGN's counsel] referred us to the decision of the Strasbourg Court in *Fressoz and Roire v France* [2001] E.H.R.R. 1. The applicants were journalists who had published an article critical of the managing director of Peugeot, accusing him of awarding himself a massive pay rise while resisting demands for pay rises from his workforce. They had illustrated this article with photocopies of his tax returns. For this they were convicted and fined for handling the fruits of a breach of professional confidence, contrary to the Criminal Code. The Strasbourg Court held that this treatment breached Article 10, stating at paragraph 54:

> "In essence, that Article leaves it for journalists to decide whether or not it is necessary to reproduce such documents to ensure credibility. It protects journalists' rights to divulge information on issues of general interest provided that they are, acting in good faith and on an accurate factual basis and provide 'reliable and precise' information in accordance with the ethics of journalism."

64. In our judgment, the information published by the appellants was justified in order to provide a factual account of Miss Campbell's drug addiction that had the detail necessary to carry credibility. Provided that publication of particular confidential information is justifiable in the public interest, the journalist must be given reasonable latitude as to the manner in which that information is conveyed to the public or his Article 10 right to freedom of expression will be unnecessarily inhibited.

Honesty

66. Where a third party receives information that has been disclosed by his informant in breach of confidence owed to the confider, the third party will come under a duty of confidence to the confider if he knows that the information has been obtained in breach of confidence. This principle is derived from the doctrine that it is equitable fraud in a third party knowingly to assist in a breach of trust, confidence or contract by another—see *Toulson & Phipps on Confidentiality* at 7–02 and the cases there cited.

67. The mental element necessary to render a defendant liable as an accessory to a breach of trust has been refined by the decisions of the House of Lords in *Royal Brunei Airlines v Tan* [1995] 2 A.C. 378 and *Twinsectra v Yardley* [2002] 2 W.L.R. 802. On this jurisprudence [MGN's counsel] constructed an ambitious submission that, in a case such as this, a defendant will only be liable for breach of confidence if (a) he knows that the information that he publishes is confidential and (b) he knows that publication cannot be justified on the ground that it is in the public interest. Thus, so he submitted, an editor who publishes material that he knows is confidential in the mistaken belief that this is in the public interest will not be guilty of breach of confidence. He will only be liable if he has acted dishonestly.

68. We consider that these submissions are misconceived. As Toulson & Phipps remark at 7–03, while dishonesty is a natural word to use in relation to misappropriation of trust property or misuse of confidential information of a commercially valuable kind, it is not an appropriate word to use in relation to the publication of information about someone's private life in circumstances which would make the publication offensive to any fair-minded person. We consider that the media can fairly be expected to identify confidential information about an individual's private life which, absent good reason, it will be offensive to publish. We also believe that the media must accept responsibility for the decision that, in the particular circumstances, publication of the material in question is justifiable in the public interest.

69. The suggestion that complex tests of the mental state of the publisher have to be satisfied before breach of confidence can be made out in respect of publication of information which violates the right of enjoyment of private or family life is not acceptable. Mr Browne has only been able to advance such a suggestion because of the shoe-horning into the tort of breach of confidence publication of information that would, more happily, be described as breach of privacy.

70. The development of the law of confidentiality since the Human Rights Act came into force has seen information described as "confidential" not where it has been confided by one person to another, but where it relates to an aspect of an individual's private life which he does not choose to make public. We consider that the unjustifiable publication of such information would better be described as breach of privacy rather than breach of confidence.

The Court of Appeal refused to uphold the claim for compensation for wrongful disclosure of sensitive personal data, provided by the Data Protection Act 1998, s.13. Section 132 of that Act gives a defence in respect of journalistic material similar to that found in the Human Rights Act 1998, s.12. It applied not only in respect of prior restraint but also to a claim for compensation after publication.

3   COPYRIGHT

3.1   Copyright and Related Rights

3.1.1   Note on Amendments to the Copyright, Designs and Patents Act 1988

The 1988 Act has been amended in particular to give effect to the following Directives of the European Community: Legal Protection of Computer Programs (91/250)—see below, 3.6.9; Term of Protection of Copyright and Certain Related Rights (93/98)—see below, 3.5; Rental Right and Lending Right and Certain Rights related to Copyright (92/100); Copyright applicable to Satellite Broadcasting and Cable Retransmission (93/83); Databases (96/9).

3.1.2   Copyright, Designs and Patents Act 1988, ss.171, 172: General Provisions

The Directive on Harmonisation of Certain Aspects of Copyright and related Rights in the Information Society (29/2001)—commonly known as the InfoSoc Directive—introduces requirements relating to copyright on the internet which have substantial effects on copyright law more generally. It is proving difficult in the UK, as in other EU states, for the Government to reach final views on implementation of this Directive in its own law. Its draft proposals were presented in a Consultation Paper from the Patent Office dated August 7, 2002. Indications of where change will soon occur are given in the material which follows by referring to the InfoSoc Directive's provisions which call for implementation.

The liabilities of Internet Service Providers (ISPs), may arise a number of fields in addition to copyright (e.g., defamation, pornography, unacceptable public speech, etc). These "horizontal cases are the subjects of the Directive on E-Commerce (31/2000). This has been given effect in the UK by the Electronic Commerce (EC Directive) Regs. (2013/2002). The relevant provisions affecting copyright liability are given in 3.6.11.1, below.

S.171(1) Nothing in this Part affects—

(a) any right or privilege of any person under any enactment (except where the enactment is expressly repealed, amended or modified by this Act);

(b) any right or privilege of the Crown subsisting otherwise than under an enactment;

(c) any right or privilege of either House of Parliament;

(d) the right of the Crown or any person deriving title from the Crown to sell, use or otherwise deal with articles forfeited under the laws relating to customs and excise;

(e) the operation of any rule of equity relating to breaches of trust or confidence.

(2) Subject to those savings, no copyright or right in the nature of copyright shall subsist otherwise than by virtue of this Part or some other enactment in that behalf.

(3) Nothing in this Part affects any rule of law preventing or restricting the enforcement of copyright, on grounds of public interest or otherwise.

(4) Nothing in this Part affects any right of action or other remedy, whether civil or criminal, available otherwise than under this Part in respect of acts infringing any of the rights conferred by Chapter IV (moral rights).

(5) The savings in subsection (1) have effect subject to section 164(4) and section 166(7) (copyright in Acts, Measures and Bills: exclusion of other rights in the nature of copyright).

S.172(1) This Part restates and amends the law of copyright, that is, the provisions of the Copyright Act 1956, as amended.

(2) A provisions of this Part which corresponds to a provision of the previous law shall not be construed as departing from the previous law merely because of a change of expression.

(3) Decisions under the previous law may be referred to for the purpose of establishing whether a provision of this Part departs from the previous law, or otherwise for establishing the true construction of this Part.

3.2 Categories of Protected Work

3.2.1 Basic Definitions

3.2.1.1 Copyright, Designs and Patents Act 1988, ss.1, 3(1), 4–8: "Works" protected

S.1(1) Copyright is a property right which subsists in accordance with this Part in the following descriptions of work—

(a) original literary, dramatic, musical or artistic works,

(b) sound recordings, films, broadcasts or cable programmes, and

(c) the typographical arrangement of published editions.

(2) In this Part "copyright work" means a work of any of those descriptions in which copyright subsists.

(3) Copyright does not subsist in a work unless the requirements of this Part with respect to qualification for copyright protection are met (see section 153 and the provisions referred to there).

S.3(1) In this Part—
"literary work" means any work, other than a dramatic or musical work, which is written, spoken or sung, and accordingly includes—

(a) a table or compilation other than a database;

(b) a computer program;

(c) preparatory design material for a computer program; and

(d) a database;

"dramatic work" includes a work of dance or mime; and
"musical work" means a work consisting of music exclusive of any words or action intended to be sung, spoken or performed with the music.

S.3A(1) In this Part "database" means a collection of independent works, data or other materials which—

(a) are arranged in a systemic or methodical way, and

(b) are individually accessible by electronic or other means.

(2) For the purpose of this Part a literary work consisting of a database is original if, and only if, by reason of the selection or arrangement of the contents of the database the database constitutes the author's own intellectual creation.

For s.3(2), (3), see below, 3.3.1

S.4(1) In this Part "artistic work" means—

    (a) a graphic work, photograph, sculpture or collage, irrespective of artistic quality,

    (b) a work of architecture being a building or a model for a building, or

    (c) a work of artistic craftsmanship.

(2) In this Part—
"building" includes any fixed structure, and a part of a building or fixed structure; "graphic work" includes—

    (a) any painting, drawing, diagram, map, chart of plan, and

    (b) any engraving, etching, lithograph, woodcut or similar work;

"photograph" means a recording of light or other radiation on any medium on which an image is produced or from which an image may by any means be produced, and which is not part of a film; "sculpture" includes a cast or model made for purposes of sculpture.

S.5A(1) In this Part—
"sound recording" means—

    (a) a recording of sounds, from which the sounds may be reproduced, or

    (b) a recording of the whole or any part of a literary, dramatic or musical work, from which sounds reproducing the work or part may be produced, regardless of the medium on which the recording is made or the method by which the sounds are reproduced or produced.

(2) Copyright does not subsist in a sound recording which is, or to the extent that it is, a copy taken from a previous sound recording.

S.5B(1) In this Part—
"film" means a recording on any medium from which a moving image may by any means be produced.

(2) The sound track accompanying a film shall be treated as part of the film for the purposes of this Part.

(3) Without prejudice to the generality of subsection (2), where that subsection applies—

    (a) references in this Part to showing a film include playing the film sound track to accompanying the film, and

    (b) references to playing a sound recording do not include playing the film sound track to accompany the film.

(4) Copyright does not subsist in a film which is, or to the extent that it is, a copy taken from a previous film.

(5) Nothing in this section affects any copyright subsisting in a film sound track as a sound recording.".

In the text still current in April 2003, s.6 contains an elaborate definition of "broadcast" and s.7 of "cable programme". In implementing the InfoSoc Directive, Art. 4, these concepts will be amalgamated into a single notion of "broadcast" which will cover both wireless and wired communication. The current definitions are accordingly omitted.

S.8(1) In this part "published edition", in the context of copyright in the typographical arrangement of a published edition, means a published edition of the whole or any part of one or more literary, dramatic or musical works.

(2) Copyright does not subsist in the typographical arrangement of a published edition if, or to the extent that, it reproduces the typographical arrangement of a previous edition.

3.2.2 Original Literary, Dramatic and Musical Works

3.2.2.1 *University of London Press v University Tutorial Press* [1916] 2 Ch. 601, Peterson J.

The University of London assigned to the plaintiff publishers copyright in examination papers set by it for school matriculation examinations. The defendants published a number of these papers without licence, together with criticisms of them and model answers, including three on mathematics set by two co-plaintiffs, Professor Lodge and Mr Jackson. An action for copyright infringement raised the issue of the existence of copyright. Peterson J. said:

Section 1, sub-section 1, of the Copyright Act of 1911 provides for copyright in "every original literary dramatic musical and artistic work", subject to certain conditions which for this purpose are immaterial and the question is, therefore, whether these examination papers are, within the meaning of this Act, original literary works. Although a literary work is not defined in the Act, section 35 states what the phrase includes: the definition is not a completely comprehensive one, but the section is intended to show what, amongst other things, is included in the description "literary work", and the words are " 'Literary work' includes maps, charts, plans, tables and compilations". It may be difficult to define "literary work" as used in this Act, but it seems to be plain that it is not confined to "literary work" in the sense in which the phrase is applied, for instance, to Meredith's novels and the writings of Robert Louis Stevenson. In speaking of such writings as literary works, one thinks of the quality, the style, and the literary finish which they exhibit. Under the Act of 1842, which protected "books", many things which had no pretensions to literary style acquired copyright; for example, a list of registered bills of sale, a list of foxhounds and hunting days, and trade catalogues; and I see no ground for coming to the conclusion that the present Act was intended to curtail the rights of authors. In my view the words "literary work" cover work which is expressed in print or writing, irrespective of the question whether the quality or style is high. The word "literary" seems to be used in a sense somewhat similar to the use of the word "literature" in political or electioneering literature and refers to written or printed matter. Papers set by examiners are, in my opinion, "literary work" within the meaning of the present Act.

Assuming that they are "literary work", the question then is whether they are original. The word "original" does not in this connection mean that the work must be the expression of original or inventive thought. Copyright Acts are not concerned with the originality of ideas, but with the expression of thought, and, in the case of "literary work", with the expression of thought in print or writing. The originality which is required relates to the expression of the thought. But the Act does not require that the expression must be in an original or novel form, but that the work must not be copied from another work—that it should originate from the author. In the present case it was not suggested that any of the papers were copies. Professor Lodge and Mr Jackson proved that they had thought out the questions which they set, and that they made notes or memoranda for future questions and drew on those notes for the purposes of the questions which they set. The papers which they prepared originated from themselves, and were, within the meaning of the Act, original. It was said, however, that they drew upon the stock of knowledge common to mathematicians, and that the time spent in producing the questions was small. These cannot be tests for determining whether copyright exists. If an author, for purposes of copyright, must not draw on the stock of knowledge which is common to himself and others who are students of the same branch of learning, only those historians who discovered fresh historical facts could acquire copyright for their works. If time expended is to be the test, the rapidity of an author like Lord Byron in producing a short poem might be an impediment in the way of acquiring copyright, and, the completer his mastery of his subject, the smaller would be the prospect of the author's success in maintaining his claim to copyright.

3.2.2.2 *Ladbroke (Football) v William Hill* [1964] 1 All E.R. 465, HL

The plaintiff-respondents ran a weekly football pool competition by sending out coupons for completion by participants. They alleged that the defendant-appellants had copied the standard forms of their coupon into a rival version. The defendants denied that the coupons were copyright works.

Lord Reid:

A coupon is a sheet of paper on which are printed various lists of forthcoming matches between well-known teams. One called "Nothing Barred" is a full list of some 50 matches. The others are shorter list of matches selected by the bookmaker from the full list. The bets offered in respect of these lists vary in character. From some the punter must pick a certain number of winners. From others he must pick so many home or away wins or draws or a combination of these. And there are other kinds of bets offered. The variety of bets offered is very great. The respondents' coupon contained 16 lists each with an appropriate name, and we were told that no less than 148 different varieties of bet were offered if one adds up all those offered under each list. Naturally the odds offered differ widely from as low as 5–2 to as high as 20,000–1. And the respondents have one list of peculiar difficulty where they offer £100,000 for two pence. It is not disputed that a vast amount of skill, judgment, experience and work has gone into the building up of the respondents' coupon. There is keen competition in this field. If the bookmaker selects matches too easy to forecast, or offers too favourable odds, he may lose very large sums. If his selections of types of bet, matches and odds do not appeal to punters they will go to rival firms. It appears that the respondents have not altered the general form of their coupon since 1951. They only occasionally alter the odds offered for each type of bet. What is new each week is the selection of matches which are to go into the lists.

When the appellants decided to enter this field they had to devise a suitable form of coupon. Their manager who was given this task was formerly employed by the respondents, but it appears that he tried to devise a form of coupon substantially different from the respondents' coupon. The coupons of some 20 other firms in the business were produced at the trial, and, while they have a general similarity, they vary very much in the nature of their lists and the variety of bets offered in respect of many of the lists. Most of them were studied by the appellants' manager, but his proposals were rejected by the appellants' managing director, who adopted a form closely similar to the respondents' coupon. The respondents had 16 lists: the appellants' coupon contains 15 of these lists, all of which appear in the same order as in the respondents' coupon. Moreover, the varieties of bets offered by the appellants in each of these 15 lists are almost identical with the offers by the respondents in their corresponding list. It is true that, with I think one exception, each of these lists is to be found in one or more of the other bookmakers' coupons and some are to be found in almost all of them. But the appellants do not suggest that the close resemblance between their coupon and the respondents' coupon is fortuitous. They admit that a good deal was simply copied from the respondents, and they say that they were entitled to do that. By no means everything was copied. For some of the lists they devised new names or headings, and the learned trial judge has found that they worked out for themselves the hundred or more different odds offered in respect of the various kinds of bets. It was impossible to copy the selections of matches: the selections must be from the

249

matches to take place in the following week, so there would not be time for one bookmaker to copy from the coupon of another matter which alters every week.

The first question to be determined is whether or to what extent copyright attaches to these coupons. The respondents say that a coupon must be regarded as a single work and that as such it is protected by copyright. The appellants seek to dissect the coupon. They would not only dissect it into the 16 lists, but they would further dissect each list into heading, selection of matches, and statement of odds offered for the various kinds of bets. They admit that there is copyright in the selection and in the statements of odds offered: they can safely do that because there they did not copy. But they deny any copyright as regards the rest of the coupon. The Copyright Act, 1956, provides, by section 2, that copyright shall subsist in every original literary work and, by section 48, that literary work includes any written table or compilation. I have no doubt that the coupon must be treated as a single compilation. The appellants' dissection theory is derived from some statements in infringement cases and I must, therefore, examine at this point the law regarding infringement. Copyright gives the exclusive right to do certain things including "reproducing the work in any material form", (section 2(5)(a)), and reproduction includes reproduction of a substantial part of the work (section 49(a)). Broadly, reproduction means copying, and does not include cases where an author or compiler produces a substantially similar result by independent work without copying. If he does copy, the question whether he has copied a substantial part depends more on the quality than on the quantity of what he has taken. One test may be whether the part which he has taken is novel or striking, or is merely a commonplace arrangement of ordinary words or well-known data. So it may sometimes be a convenient short cut to ask whether the part taken could itself be the subject of copyright. But, in my view, that is only a short cut, and the more correct approach is first to determine whether the plaintiff's work as a whole is "original" and protected by copyright, and then to inquire whether the part taken by the defendant is substantial. A wrong result can easily be reached if one begins by dissecting the plaintiff's work and asking, could section A be the subject of copyright if it stood by itself, could section B be protected if it stood by itself, and so on. To my mind, it does not follow that, because other fragments taken separately would not be copyright, therefore the whole cannot be. Indeed, it has often been recognised that if sufficient skill and judgment have been exercised in devising the arrangements of the whole work, that can be an important or even decisive element in deciding whether the work as a whole is protected by copyright.

The appellants relied on cases where it has been held that in general the title of a work is not copyright. Those cases are dealt with by Lord Wright in the judgment of the Privy Council in *Francis Day and Hunter Ltd v Twentieth Century Fox Corp Ltd* [1940] A.C. 112, and I think that he rightly expressed the principle when he said (123–124):

> "The copying which is complained of is the use of the title, and that is too unsubstantial on the facts of this case to constitute an infringement".

None of the decisions cited in argument appears to me to conflict with the view that one must first decide whether the part taken is a substantial part. The only apparent exception would seem to be a case such as *Leslie v Young & Sons* [1894] A.C. 335, where a compilation was treated as consisting of severable parts, one of which was held to be original work and copyright while the rest was not. The appellants' main argument was based on quite a different ground. They deny that the respondents' coupon is an original compilation. There is no dispute about the meaning of the term "original":

His Lordship quoted from the University of London *case, (above, 3.2.2.1). He continued:*

In the present case, if it is permissible to take into account all the skill, judgment and labour expended in producing the respondents' coupon, there can be no doubt that it is "original". But the appellants say that the coupon must be regarded as having been produced in two stages: first, the respondents had to decide what kind of business they would do—what kinds of bets they would offer to their clients—and then they had to write these out on paper. The appellants say that it is only the skill, judgment and labour involved in the latter stage that can be considered and that that part of their operation involved so little skill, judgment or labour that it cannot qualify as "original". In fact the respondents did not proceed in that way. Their business was to devise a coupon which would appeal to the betting public, and its form and arrangement were not something dictated by previous decisions about the nature of the bets to be offered. The appellants likened the coupon to a trader's catalogue of his wares, and argued that in considering whether a catalogue is entitled to copyright one must disregard the maker's skill and work in deciding what wares he will stock for sale and only consider the skill and labour involved in the actual pre-paration of the catalogue. I do not think that that is a true analogy. Even in the case of a catalogue there may be a question whether the work in deciding what to sell and the work in deciding how to sell it are not so inter-connected as to be inseparable. Copyright in a catalogue in no way prevents honest competition—any other trader can decide to stock and sell any or all of the catalogued articles, and he can thereafter make a new catalogue of his own wares. What he must not do is simply to copy the other trader's catalogue.

The other members of the House delivered concurring speeches. The defendant was held to infringe.

3.2.2.3   *Cramp v Smythson* [1944] A.C. 329, HL

The plaintiffs asserted that a series of initial tables in the defendants' "Surrey Lightweight Diary, 1942" were copied from their "Liteblue Diary 1933" so as to constitute infringement of copyright.

Viscount Simon L.C.:

The respondents base their claim to copyright on the selection of these tables to form a combination of information, and the declaration made by the Court of Appeal is "that the collection of tables comprised in the plaintiffs' Liteblue Diary for 1933" (other than the calendar), "is a copyright work", and that the infringement by the plaintiffs consists in printing and publishing in "the Surrey Lightweight Diary, 1942" this collection of tables. Granted that the appellants copied the respondents' tables (and this is not only admitted but is indicated by the almost precise similarity of language), there seems to be nothing that can properly be described as an "original literary work" in grouping together this information. A summarized statement of the most important of the postal charges, inland, imperial and foreign, is part of the ordinary contents of any pocket diary. There would, indeed, as it seems to me, be considerable difficulty in successfully contending that ordinary tables which can be got from or checked by, the postal guide or the Nautical Almanac are a subject of copyright as being original literary work. One of the essential qualities of such tables is that they should be accurate, so that there is no question of variation in what is stated. The sun does in fact rise, and the moon set, at times which have been calculated, and the utmost that a table can do on such a subject is to state the result accurately. There is so far no room for taste or judgment. There remains, I agree, the element of choice as to what information should be given, and the respondents contend that the test of originality is satisfied by the choice of the tables inserted, but the bundle of information furnished in the respondents' diary is commonplace information which is ordinarily useful and is, at any rate to a large extent, commonly found prefixed to diaries, and, looking through the respondents' collection of tables, I have difficulty in seeing how such tables in the combination in which they appear in the respondents' 1933 diary, can reasonably claim to be "original work". There was no evidence that any of these tables was composed specially for the respondents' diary. There was no feature of them which could be pointed out as novel or specially meritorious or ingenious from the point of view of the judgment or skill of the compiler. It was not suggested that there was any element of originality or skill in the order in which the tables were arranged. My own conclusion is that the selection did not constitute an original literary work.

The other members of the House agreed.

3.2.2.4   *Byrne v Statist Co* [1914] 1 K.B. 622, Bailhache J.

The plaintiff alleged infringement of copyright in translations. On the existence of copyright, Bailhache J. said:

I think the words "original literary work" mean a literary work of which the person in whom the copyright is laid, or through whom the title to the copyright is traced, is the author. A translator of the literary work has for many years been held to be the author of his translation, and the House of Lords in *Walter v Lane* [1900] A.C. 539, went so far as to hold that a shorthand writer who reported a speech verbatim was the author of his report.

3.2.2.5   *Exxon Corp v Exxon Insurance Consultants* [1982] R.P.C. 69, CA

The plaintiffs, constituent companies of the Exxon petroleum group, (formerly Standard Oil of New Jersey) objected to the use by the defendants of "Exxon" as part of their corporate name. They secured relief against passing off; but on a claim for infringement of copyright in the word, they failed before Graham J. and the Court of Appeal Stephenson L.J. delivered a substantial judgment, in concurring with which Oliver L.J. said:

But "original literary work" as used in the statute is a composite expression, and for my part I do not think that the right way to apply a composite expression is, or at any rate is necessarily, to ascertain whether a particular subject-matter falls within the meaning of each of the constituent parts, and then to say that the whole expression is merely the sum total of the constituent parts. In my judgment it is not necessary, in construing a statutory expression, to take leave of one's common-sense, and the result to which Mr Price seeks to drive us is one which, to my mind, involves doing just that.

We have been referred to a number of cases in which copyright has been successfully claimed in, for instance examination papers, football coupons and tables of ciphers; but all these—and I do not exclude the case of the telegraphic code in *Anderson v Lieber Code* [1917] 2 K.B. 469,—seem to me to fall fairly within Davey L.J.'s commonsense formulation. [For which see *Express Newspapers v Liverpool Daily Post* (below, 3.3.4).]

But that for which protection is sought in the instant case does not appear to me to have any of the qualities which commonsense would demand. It conveys no information; it provides no instruction; it gives no pleasure that I can conceive; it is simply an artificial combination of four letters of the alphabet which serves a purpose only when it is used in juxtaposition with other English words, to identify one or other of the companies in the plaintiff group.

Sir David Cairns concurred in both judgments.

3.2.2.6   *Express Newspapers v Liverpool Daily Post* [1985] F.S.R. 306, Whitford J.

The plaintiff publisher organised a competition, "Millionaire of the Month", in which contestants received a free card containing a sequence of five letters and matched it against sequences published in The Sunday Express, The Daily Express *and* The Star. *Each day or week's paper would contain a grid of five by five letters and two additional lines of five letters. Matching these with an individual card gave a claim to various prizes and further opportunities.*

The defendants copied each day's or week's grid and lines into their own newspapers. On a motion for an interlocutory injunction to restrain infringement of copyright in the varying grids and lines, the main issue was whether they amounted to literary works.

Whitford J.:

If these grids and these sequences of five letters can be said to be copyright works, I do not understand it to be argued on the defendants' side that what they have done would not be an infringement. The defendants, however, say that there is here disclosed no copyright work. The Copyright Act 1956 provides for the giving of protection under the Act in respect of a variety of works. The only relevant heading so far as the present proceedings are concerned is "literary works". By the definition section, "literary work" includes tables; and it was not suggested by Mr Jeffs, on the defendant's side, that a table could not be the subject of protection. It is of course accepted, because it is easily established by reference to one of a number of well-known authorities, that mathematical tables can acquire copyright protection as "literary work". They do so because their compilation—and compilations in themselves are by definition "literary work"—involves the exercise of skill and labour, or possibly maybe only labour.

That a great deal of skill and, indeed, a good deal of labour went into the production of the grid and the two separate sequences of five letters is, to my mind, quite plainly established from the evidence of Mr Ertel, who is with an American corporation, Amphora Enterprises Inc., who were saddled with the task of preparing these grid patterns and sequences to be used in the plaintiffs' competition. Mr Ertel's affidavit sets out in detail what he has had to do and the steps that had to be taken. He describes how participants in the competition look at the grid and see if they can match certain patterns of letters and in the same way see if they can match the sequence of five letters. He describes the difficulties that are involved in preparing these grids and five-letter sequences if you are going to arrive at a situation in which you do not get so many winning lines that the whole thing is going to become hopelessly uneconomic from the point of view of the person running the competition. He describes the constraints with which he was necessarily faced in ensuring that a sufficient number of possible winning combinations emerged to make the game attractive, without producing such a number of combinations to make the whole thing hopelessly uneconomic. He goes to some length to point out the difficulties of achieving these results. He describes also how the effort had to be made to introduce a system of some sort of check codes to avoid frauds.

Whitford J. then described how Mr Ertel achieved his result by programming a computer and rejected an argument that in consequence Mr Ertel was not the author of the grid and lines. He proceeded to address an argument that they could not constitute a literary work by virtue of the Exxon *case (above, 3.2.2.5):*

Of course, the facts in that case were very different from the facts of the present case. The earlier decision upon which Graham J. and the Court of Appeal relied, which concerned a sleeve chart—a case very well known in this field of the law—was a case in relation to which Davey L.J. speaking of the sleeve chart, said:

> "It does not add to the stock of human knowledge or give, and is not designed to give, any instruction by way of description or otherwise; and it certainly is not calculated to afford literary enjoyment or pleasure";

and he came to the conclusion that the sleeve chart in question was no more entitled to copyright as a literary work than the scale attached to a barometer in the case of *Davis v Comitti*. What the finding would be today if a claim to copyright in a sleeve chart were brought I do not need to consider.

Of this passage, Stephenson L.J. (in *Exxon Corp v Exxon Insurance Consultants International Limited*) said:

> "The words of the Lord Justice do, however, appeal to me as stating the ordinary meaning of the words 'literary work'. I would have thought, unaided or unhampered by authority, that unless there is something in the context of the Act which forbids it, a literary work would be something which was intended to afford either information and instruction, or pleasure in the form of literary enjoyment, whatever those last six words may add to the word 'pleasure'";

and counsel were unable to persuade their Lordships that this word did in fact provide information or instruction or give pleasure.

Of course, Mr Jeffs can well say that some tables—and he gave the instance of a table of logarithms—even if to some people they may give very little pleasure, do at least provide information. So, in my judgment, do the grids and the five-letter sequences. They are looked at by those who have had one of the Millionaire Club cards for the very purpose of acquiring information; they want to know whether they have won or lost. They might find out that they have won, or more probably that they have lost; but information is the whole purpose of the publication of these grids and five-letter sequences. Indeed, if they did not give information, I do not suppose the defendants would be troubling to include them in their newspapers.

3.2.2.7 *Green v Broadcasting Corp of New Zealand* [1989] R.P.C. 700, JC

In Britain, the plaintiff compered the popular television talent contest, "Opportunity Knocks". The defendant broadcast a similar show in New Zealand, using the same title. The plaintiff sued for infringement of copyright and passing off. The claims failed.

As to copyright, Lord Bridge stated:

The copyright alleged to have been infringed was claimed to subsist in the "scripts and dramatic format" of "Opportunity Knocks" as broadcast in England. The appellant's primary difficulty arises from the circumstances that no script was ever produced in evidence. Ongley J. concluded that:

"There was really no evidence that any part of the show was reduced to a written text which could properly be called a script ..."

He added later:

"No writing has been produced in evidence in this action in which, in my view, copyright could subsist".

The Court of Appeal differed from the trial judge to the extent that they accepted that the evidence established the existence of scripts. But the evidence as to the nature of the scripts and what their text contained was exiguous in the extreme. It is to be found in two short passages from the evidence given by the appellant himself. He said in the course of examination-in-chief:

"In the year 1956, I wrote the scripts of Opportunity Knocks shows, such as they were, because we would have what we would call the introductions, our stock phrases like 'For So-and-So, Opportunity Knocks', phrases such as 'This is your show, folks, and I do mean you'. The other part of the writing dealt with interviews with the people and one could not really call it writing because you were really only finding out what the artists wanted to talk about".

He said in cross-examination:

"The script of Opportunity Knocks has continuously been the same for the catch phrases, the interviews each week with the artists has differed, the script for the past 17 years and long before 1975 contained particularly the end of the show beginning with the words 'make your mind up time' using the clapometer and bringing back the five people".

On the basis of this evidence Somers J. concluded that:

"... the scripts as they are inferred to be from the description given in evidence did not themselves do more than express a general idea or concept for a talent quest and hence were not the subject of copyright".

In the absence of precise evidence as to what the scripts contained, their Lordships are quite unable to dissent from this view.

The alternative formulation of the appellant's claim relies upon the "dramatic format" of "Opportunity Knocks", by which their Lordships understand is meant those characteristic features of the show which were repeated in each performance. These features were, in addition to the title, the use of the catch phrases "for [name of competitor] opportunity knocks", "this is your show folks, and I do mean you", and "make up your mind time", the use of a device called a "clapometer" to measure audience reaction to competitors' performances and the use of sponsors to introduce competitors. It was this formulation which found favour with Gallen J.

It is stretching the original use of the word "format" a long way to use it metaphorically to describe the features of a television series such as a talent, quiz or game show which is presented in a particular way, with repeated but unconnected use of set phrases and with the aid of particular accessories. Alternative terms suggested in the course of argument were "structure" or "package". This difficulty in finding an appropriate term to describe the nature of the "work" in which the copyright subsists reflects the difficulty of the concept that a number of allegedly distinctive features of a television series can be isolated from the changing material presented in each separate performance (the acts of the performers in the talent show, the questions and answers in the quiz show, etc.) and identified as an "original dramatic work". No case was cited to their Lordships in which copyright of the kind claimed had been established.

3.2.2.8 *Wiseman v George Wiedenfeld & Nicolson* **[1985] F.S.R. 525, Whitford J.**

The second defendant, Donaldson, turned his novel, The English Way of Doing Things, *into a play with the same title. He did so on the suggestion of the plaintiff, who at various stages of the adaptation made suggestions and criticisms. The plaintiff subsequently claimed to be co-author of the play and so entitled to a share in the copyright.*

Whitford J.:

We are here concerned with a dramatic work. Both collaborators, Mr Wiseman and Mr Donaldson, must answer to the description of authors of the dramatic work. To be a joint author, a collaborator must make some contribution to the literary or dramatic form in which alone copyright can subsist.

In *Tate v Thomas* [1921] 1 Ch. 503, Eve J. said this of a Mr Peterman, who was contending that he was a joint author (at 509):

> "Mr Peterman contends that he was really the author or at least a joint author with the plaintiffs. It is not disputed that he suggested the name of the piece, and there is no doubt that in many parts of the work are introduced incidents suggested in his rough sketch or culled from works in which he has no copyright interest. One of the witnesses called for the defendants went so far as to say that the whole play was 'pinched' from other people's productions. I had the opportunity of seeing Mr Peterman in the witness box and I can well understand that he is speaking the truth when he states that he was frequently making suggestions to the authors and indicating to them how they were to do the work they had undertaken. He is a gentleman of a fertile imagination and possessed of a fluency and powers well qualifying him for communicating his views to the authors.
>
> The plaintiffs do not deny that their work embodies some ideas and a few catch lines or words for which Mr Peterman may claim credit, but they dispute altogether his claim to a share in the authorship of the work and contend (and in my opinion rightly contend) that the sum total of his contribution does not amount to anything entitled to protection under the Act. His assistance, such as it was, was confined to accessorial matters such as scenic effects, or stage 'business' not the subject matter of copyright".

I should perhaps say at this stage that Mr Donaldson conceded that there may have been a line here or there and possibly even an idea which emanated from Mr Wiseman, but he too, as in this case, contends that he and he alone was the author of the work.

At 511 of the report Eve J. said this;

> "The question whether Mr Peterman's claim to be a joint author of this work, so far as it is subject matter for protection under the Act, is one of fact; and, having heard all the evidence, I have come to the conclusion that his contributions to the matter capable of being printed and published were so insignificant and negligible as to make it quite impossible for me to hold him to have been in any sense a joint author within the Act".

In *Evans v E Hulton & Co Ltd* [1923–28] MacG. C.C. 51, Tomlin J. put the question in relation to the alleged joint author in this way:

"Did he take any part in producing the express matter which is the original literary work the subject matter of copyright?"

In *Bagge v Miller* [1917–23] MacG. C.C. 179, Russell J., speaking of the respective contributions of the plaintiff and the defendant, said this (at 182):

"As regards the plaintiff Milburn he can only succeed if he was a joint author of the sketch and so a co-owner of the copyright. He must establish that he is a joint author of the dramatic work *The Truth for an Hour*. If he does that then he would be a co-owner of the copyright which would subsist therein if it be an original dramatic work.

Mr Milburn outlined the plot verbally to Mr Bagge and suggested to him that he should write a play. Mr Bagge did so. The written sketch was entirely his, Bagge's: the dialogue is entirely his. After the sketch was written by Mr Bagge, it was discussed and Mr Milburn said that he made certain suggestions which Mr Bagge adopted. What they were I was not told. They were not apparently of sufficient importance to be told in detail. Mr Milburn had no place in composing the dramatic work beyond suggesting the idea of the sketch. He had no share in the design or execution of the work, the whole of which, so far as any character of originality belongs to it, flowed from the mind of Mr Bagge. Certainly in ordinary parlance no one would describe Mr Milburn as the author or joint author of the dramatic work. Neither is he in law an author or joint author of the dramatic work. The mere suggestion of an idea which is then embodied by another in a dramatic work written by him does not, in my opinion, constitute the originator of the idea an author or a joint author of the dramatic work. For this proposition the case of *Shepherd v Conquest*, 17 C.B. 427 is, in my opinion, a sufficient authority.

On the printed copies of the sketch Mr Milburn's name appeared (by special arrangement with Mr Bagge) as one of the authors, and Mr MacGillivray relied upon the presumption raised by section 6(3)(a) of the Act: but in my opinion the statutory presumption is displaced by the facts proved in this case".

I found Mr Donaldson a thoroughly reliable witness, very careful, very fair, and in no way prepared to overstate his case, and in complete contrast to Mr Wiseman, who was neither careful nor fair, but quite prepared to make very extravagant and unjustified claims. I am sure that Mr Wiseman is under a sense of grievance. He has no doubt persuaded himself that his pretensions are justified, and that in fact he has made a contribution to the production of this work far in excess of that which he has in fact contributed. He has, however, wholly failed to persuade me.

A good many years ago, it would seem that Mr Wiseman was likely to achieve some success in the theatre as a director; and, indeed, he referred me to certain productions in which he was concerned. He has not had any great success as an author; his promise in the field of directorial activity has not apparently been realised—at least in recent years—so far.

Mr Donaldson, of course, has basically always been a writer. As I have said, he had started to achieve some success as an author at the time when the play first came to be written. He had never really had any great experience in the theatre, and did not pretend to such experience as Mr Wiseman has in fact had. Mr Wiseman thought that *Both the Ladies and the Gentlemen* could be a success as a play. He undoubtedly saw himself as a director of a stage version, if a stage version could be produced.

When what might be described as a strict adaptation of *Both the Ladies and the Gentlemen* proved impossible, Mr Wiseman formed the view that the characters from this work could be pressed into service in a play. He urged this upon Mr Donaldson; he eventually, as I have said, managed to persuade Mr Donaldson into writing the dramatic work in which he, Mr Wiseman, now claims joint authorship.

A dramatic work involves, of course, not only dialogue but a series of incidents—dramatic situations—which in a particular order or occurrence can form the backbone of the piece. Mr Wiseman, in his evidence-in-chief and in cross-examination, however made claims extending beyond this. He claimed that he had made a significant contribution to the dialogue. "Mr Donaldson", Mr Wiseman told me, "took the lead in the dialogue, but we went over every line together". In cross-examination, again, he said: "We went over every single line inch by inch in collaboration".

I cannot accept a word of this. It was the evidence of Mr Donaldson, which I accept without reservation, that he finds himself unable to write anything other than perhaps some very simple part of a work in somebody else's presence. It was Mr Donaldson's evidence that he effectively did all the writing before Mr Wiseman, who at this stage was living at a different address, arrived at the flat occupied by Mr Donaldson around 11 o'clock in the morning or at some later stage, possibly in the evening, and at weekends.

Mr Donaldson entirely accepted that he found Mr Wiseman a most valuable critic of the lines that he had written. He accepted, indeed, that he tore up two weeks of work written while Mr Wiseman was away, as a result of criticisms by Mr Wiseman, and he re-wrote the scenes in question. It was, however, his evidence that Mr Wiseman virtually took no part in writing any single line of the dialogue; and of this I am satisfied.

3.2.2.9   *Norowzian v Arks (No 2)* [2000] F.S.R. 362, CA

Jump-cutting is a film-maker's technique which can make a human appear to act in physically impossible ways. It was a hall-mark of the Novelle Vague of the 1950s and 60s. Norowzian applied it to an advertising film, Joy, *in which the filming of a man dancing was drastically edited to give an effect of super-natural excitement. It was shown to Arks, who were advertising agents, in the hope of attracting work. Subsequently, Arks arranged the production of an advertising film for Guinness, the brewing company, called* Anticipation. *In it a man dancing was jump-cut to suggest increasing zest as he worked towards his glass of frothing stout.*

In a first case ([1988] F.S.R. 394), Norowzian, in suing for infringement, relied upon the copyright in the film (CDPA 1988, s. 5B). That action failed on the ground that the reproduction right in a film does not extend to making another film from scratch. It covers only a direct copying of the film as recorded. In this second action, Norowzian claimed copyright in his film as a dramatic work, of which he, as director of the film, was the author. At first instance, Rattee J. held that a film could not be a dramatic film since it could not be performed physically before an audience. The Court of Appeal adopted a wider view.

Nourse L.J. (with whom Brooke L.J. agreed):

Rattee J. was of the opinion that a film *per se* cannot be a dramatic work within the meaning of the 1988 Act, though it can be a recording of such a work for the purpose of section 3(2); see page 77. His view was based partly on the different categorisations adopted by paragraphs (a) and (b) of section 1(1) and partly on the express exclusion of films from the definition of dramatic work in the Copyright Act 1956; see section 48(1) of that Act. Although we were not referred to transcripts of the arguments in the court below, my strong impression is that the judge's view was influenced by the submissions of counsel then representing the claimant, who do not appear to have argued that *Joy* was itself a dramatic work. At page 77 the judge records the submission of the claimant's leading counsel as being that "*Joy* is clearly a work of dance and mime which has been recorded on film."

The argument that Joy is itself a dramatic work has been put at the forefront of the submissions of Mr Arnold, who, with Miss Reid, has appeared for the claimant in this court. That has led to an enervating dispute as to whether the point was taken below and, if it was not, whether it can be taken now. I do not believe it was distinctly taken before the judge. That has opened the way for the defendants to object that, if it had been, they might have been able to adduce evidence which would have prevented it from succeeding; *cf. Ex p. Firth* (1882) 19 Ch D 419, 429, *per* Sir George Jessel M.R. I am not persuaded that there is any substance in that objection. I see no reason why the claimant should not be allowed to take the point now.

In my judgment a film can be a dramatic work for the purpose of the 1988 Act. The definition of that expression being at large, it must be given its natural and ordinary meaning. We were referred to several dictionary and textbook definitions. My own, substantially a distilled synthesis of those which have one before, would be this: a dramatic work is a work of action, with or without words or music, which is capable of being performed before an audience. A film will often, though not always, be a work of action and it is capable of being performed before an audience. It can therefore fall within the expression "dramatic work" in section 1(1)(a) and I disagree with the judge's reason for excluding it.

As to those reasons, no mutual exclusivity between paragraphs (a) and (b) is expressed, and the absence of the requirement of originality in paragraph (b) is sufficient ground for none to be implied. Moreover, it is unsafe to base any construction of the material provisions of the 1988 Act on those of the 1956 Act. Indeed, it might be said that Parliament's omission to repeat the exclusion of films from the definition of dramatic work points rather towards their inclusion. But whether that be right or wrong, the material provisions of the 1988 Act must be construed as they stand. Where a film is both a recording of a dramatic work and a dramatic work in itself they do not exclude an overlap. In other cases there will be no overlap. Sometimes a film will simply be a recording of something which is not a dramatic work. At other times it will not be a recording of a dramatic work but a dramatic work in itself.

Once it is established that a film can be a dramatic work for the purposes of the 1988 Act it is clear that *Joy,* being a work of action capable of being performed before an audience, is such a work. Clearly, it is an original work. Two further points must be mentioned in relation to the primary question. First, in support of his argument on the 1988 Act, Mr Arnold relied on certain European materials, in particular the Berne Copyright Convention (as revised and amended up to 1979). In my view it is unnecessary to have to resort to those materials as an aid to the construction of the 1988 Act. Secondly, Mr Arnold, submitted, in the alternative, that Joy was a recording of a dramatic work. In agreeing with Rattee J. that that submission must be rejected, I need do no more than read the following passage from his judgement at page 78:

> *Joy*, unlike some films, is not a recording of a dramatic work, because, as a result of the drastic editing process adopted by Mr Norowzian, it is not a recording of anything

that was, or could be, performed or danced by anyone...It may well be, in the case of *Joy*, that the original unedited film of the actor's performance, what I believe are called "the rushes", was a recording of a dramatic work, but Mr Norowzian's claim is not in respect of copyright in them or their subject matter. His claim is in respect of the finished film.

Joy, just like many cartoon films, is, without being a recording of one, a dramatic work in itself.

Nourse L.J. nontheless upheld the trial judge's view that Anticipation *did not copy the expression of* Joy. *At most there was a striking similarity between filming and editing styles and techniques, which could not constitute infringement. In concurring, Buxton L.J. said:*

To the extent, however, that any respects in which the nature of some films (though not, for the reasons given by Nourse L.J., *Joy* that is the subject of this case) might be thought to raise questions as to the reach of the 1988 Act, I for my part would escape from any such difficulties by referring to the Berne Convention, which recognises a category of "cinematographic works" that by Article 14*bis*, signatory countries have to protect as original works: provided of course that the particular work in indeed original. Although "dramatic works" are separately referred to in the Convention, I accept that, if the 1988 Act is to be interpreted consistently with this country's international obligations under the Convention, the cinematographic works referred to in the Convention have all to be included within the Act's category of dramatic works: even in cases where the natural meaning of "dramatic work" does not or might nor embrace the particular film in question.

3.2.2.10   *Wood v Boosey* [1868] L.R. 3 Q.B. 223, Exchequer Chamber

Nicolai's opera, "Die lustigen Weiber von Windsor", was first performed in March, 1849, the composer dying two months later. Brissler then made a reduction for pianoforte of the orchestral score. Under the then existing arrangements (International Copyright Act 1844), in order for an author from a country with which there was a bi-lateral arrangement to acquire British copyright, he had to register his work giving the author's name. A registration for the Brissler arrangement of the opera was obtained in 1851, naming Nicolai as composer. The plaintiffs, claiming to be assignees of this copyright, sued the defendants for infringement. The defence denied that the registration had been properly made in Nicolai's name.

Bramwell B.:

The truth is, an opera is originally written for the voice and for different instruments. In this pianoforte score, as it is called, the parts written for the voice are identically preserved, and there can be no doubt that if a man had a copyright in the original opera, such a score would be an infringement of his copyright. But when we come to the part, not for the voices, but for the pianoforte, which is not an identical repetition of what the author wrote, it is the business of the adapter, the person who arranges it for the pianoforte, to preserve the harmony and, as far as he can, the notes and all the effects of the original composer, but he cannot produce upon the pianoforte everything that the author wrote, as he wrote it. ....

Anybody who plays any musical instrument knows it is a very common expression to say, such a piece is very well arranged, such a piece is very ill arranged; this is a very difficult arrangement, that is an easy arrangement. Those who play the German arrangements know they are more difficult than the English, because the German, with great conscientiousness, endeavours to put into the arrangement every note that the composer has put into the score as far as he can; whereas the English composer endeavours in all arrangements to make them clear for the player, and an English arrangement is by no means so laborious as the German. It is manifest, therefore, that there is some judgment and taste required on the part of the arranger for the pianoforte; and it is also certain that if it should so happen that a man should compose an opera without being able to play on the pianoforte—which is, I believe, a perfectly possible thing—he could not arrange it himself for the pianoforte. ...

It is clear, therefore, that there is something in the nature of authorship in Brissler, and his name not having been stated as the author in the register, it seems to me manifest the plaintiff has not a copyright of the pianoforte score, as it is called, and consequently cannot complain of this infringement.

Kelly C.B. delivered a judgment to the same effect; and Willes, Keating and Montague Smith JJ. and Channell B. concurred.

3.2.3   Original Artistic Works

3.2.3.1   *Kenrick v Lawrence* (1890) 25 Q.B.D. 93, Wills J.

The plaintiffs claimed copyright in the representation of a hand pointing to a square on an electoral voting paper.

Wills J.:

It was in evidence that more than a million copies of the card of the plaintiffs have been sold since the year 1885, and that they have been used at nearly every election in the kingdom. It was urged, probably with truth, that such a card was practically the only mode of instructing the illiterate voter how to record his vote, and it is obvious that if the privilege of instructing the illiterate voter how to vote, by the only vehicle by which the act of voting can be represented to the eye, and the instructions how to vote and whom to vote for can be brought home to him, be vested in the plaintiffs for seven years beyond the termination of a life which may very well subsist for half a century longer—for Mr Jefferson is now only 36 years of age—and be their monopoly, it is difficult to put an adequate value upon their property in such a right. If that period should shortly arrive, which to many politicians appears to be a kind of constitutional millennium, when all the remaining ignorance, male and female, of the three kingdoms shall be swept into the electoral fold, the amount of political power which may become vested in the plaintiffs or their assignees will be greater than it is possible to estimate, and the destinies of the country may be placed in the hands of the fortunate owner of the talisman. The mere choice of subject can rarely, if ever, confer upon the author of the drawing an exclusive right to represent the subject, and certainly where the subject chosen is merely the representation to the eye of a simple operation which must be performed by every person who records a vote there cannot possibly be an exclusive right to represent in a picture that operation. It may well be that something special in the way of artistic treatment even of this simple operation, if it existed, might be the subject of copyright; but nothing of the kind has been suggested or exists in the present case, and if it does exist without being discovered it has not been imitated, for there is nothing which in any flight of imagination can be called artistic about either the plaintiffs' or the defendants' representation of a hand making the mark of a cross. It may be also that even the coarsest, or the most commonplace, or the most mechanical representation of the commonest object is so far protected on registration that an exact reproduction of it, such as photography for instance would produce, would be an infringement of copyright. But in such a case it must surely be nothing short of an exact literal reproduction of the drawing registered that can constitute the infringement, for there seems to me to be in such a case nothing else that is not the common property of all the world. It is possible that in this case the proprietors of the drawing registered may have a right to be protected from a reproduction of their picture of a hand drawing a cross in which every line, dot, measurement, and blank space shall be rendered exactly as in the original, or in which the variations from such minute agreement shall be microscopic. But I cannot see how they can possibly make a higher claim, or say that because they have registered a drawing of a hand pencilling a cross within a square that no other person in the U.K. is at liberty to draw a hand pencilling a cross within a square for perhaps the next half century.

3.2.3.2   *Interlego v Tyco Industries* [1988] R.P.C. 343, JC

The plaintiff and its associated companies made and marketed the "Lego" toy brick system internationally. The defendants intended to manufacture a competing system in Hong Kong which, the plaintiff alleged, constituted infringement of its copyright in designs for the bricks, since the defendants had reached their designs by "reverse engineering" of the plaintiff's products.

In part, the claims related to drawings made after 1972.[1] *These were virtual copies of earlier drawings, to which were added written instructions for modifying the dimensions of the joining knobs on the bricks. The defendants accordingly denied that they attracted copyright. In giving judgment for the Judicial Committee of the Privy Council; Lord Oliver referred to Peterson J.'s remarks on the meaning of "originality" in copyright law (*University of London Press case, above, 3.2.2.1). *He proceeded:*

That statement is, of course, not complete in itself because there may clearly be original work which makes use of material obtained by the author from pre-existing sources. Perhaps the most useful exegesis is to be found in three passages from the opinion of the Board delivered by Lord Atkinson in the Privy Council case of *Macmillan & Co Ltd v Cooper* (1923) 40 T.L.R. 186, a case concerned with university textbooks consisting of abridgments of or excerpts from existing works with appropriate notes for students. Lord Atkinson observed (at 188):

"... it is the product of the labour, skill, and capital of one man which must not be appropriated by another, not the elements, the raw material, if one may use the expression, upon which the labour and skill and capital of the first have been expended. To secure copyright for this product it is necessary that labour skill, and capital should be expended sufficiently to impart to the product some quality or character which the raw material did not possess, and which differentiates the product from the raw material".

A little later, he quoted with approval the following passage from the judgment of Story J. in *Emerson v Davies* (1845) 3 Story 768 at 778–779:

"The question is not, whether the materials which are used are entirely new, and have never been used before; or even that they have never been used before for the same purpose. The true question is, whether the same plan, arrangement, and combination of materials have been used before the same purpose or for any other purpose. If they have not, then the plaintiff is entitled to a copyright, although he may have gathered hints for his plan and arrangement, or parts of his plan and arrangement, from existing and known sources. He may have borrowed much of his materials from others, but if they are combined in a different manner from what was in use before ... he is entitled to a copyright ... It is true, that he does not thereby acquire the right to appropriate to himself the materials which were common to all persons before, so as to exclude those persons from a future use of such materials; but then they have no right to use such materials with his improvements superadded, whether they consist in plan, arrangement or illustrations, or combinations; for these are strictly his own".

Lord Atkinson continued:

---

[1] From 1973, a Hong Kong Copyright Ordinance introduced the UK Copyright Act 1956 (as amended by the Design Copyright Act 1968) into the colony. The effect of this was that the post-1972 drawings were protected by artistic copyright and that copyright could be infringed by industrial reproduction (directly or indirectly) in three dimensions. In UK law this position has changed, by virtue of the Copyright Designs and Patents Act 1988, s.51: for which see below, para. 4.1.1. For an aspect of this case concerning the pre-1972 drawings, see below, 4.2.6.

"This decision is, of course, not binding on this tribunal, but it is, in the opinion of the Board, sound, able, convincing and helpful. It brings out clearly the distinction between the materials upon which one claiming copyright has worked and the product of the application of his skill, judgment, labour and learning to those materials; which product, though it may be neither novel or ingenious, is the claimant's original work in that it is originated by him, emanates from him, and is not copied".

Finally, he observed (at 190):

"What is the precise amount of the knowledge, labour, judgment or literary skill or taste which the author of any book or other compilation must bestow upon its composition in order to acquire copyright in it within the meaning of the Copyright Act of 1911 cannot be defined in precise terms. In every case it must depend largely on the special facts of that case, and must in each case be very much a question of degree".

In that context he cited with approval a passage from the judgment of Lord Kinloch in *Black v Murray* (1870) 9 M.341 at 355:

"I think it clear that it will not create copyright in a new edition of a work, of which the copyright has expired, merely to make a few emendations of the text, or to add a few unimportant notes. To create a copyright by alterations of the text, these must be extensive and substantial, practically making a new book. With regard to notes, in like manner, they must exhibit an addition to the work which is not superficial or colourable, but imparts to the book a true and real value, over and above that belonging to the text".

That case was, of course, concerned with literary copyright, but there is no distinction in principle in the case of artistic copyright, although obviously the opportunities for the creation of an original work by way of compilation of existing materials are here more limited. In *British Northrop Ltd v Texteam Blackburn Ltd* [1974] R.P.C. 57 at 68 the principle was conveniently summarised by Megarry J. as follows:

"Copyright is concerned not with any originality of ideas but with their form of expression, and it is in that expression that originality is requisite. That expression need not be original or novel in form, but it must originate with the author and not be copied from another work ... A drawing which is simply traced from another drawing is not an original artistic work: a drawing which is made without any copying from anything originates with the artist".

Lord Oliver referred to certain general remarks of Whitford J. at first instance in LB (Plastics) v Swish [1979] R.P.C. 551. He proceeded:

Originality in the context of literary copyright has been said in several well-known cases to depend on the degree of skill, labour and judgment involved in preparing a compilation. *Macmillan & Co Ltd v Cooper* (1923) 40 T.L.R. 186 was such a case. So was *G.A. Cramp & Son Ltd v F. Smythson Ltd* [1944] 2 All E.R. 92; [1944] A.C. 329. Similarly, in the speeches of Lord Reid and Lord Hodson in *Ladbroke (Football) Ltd v William Hill (Football) Ltd* [1964] 1 All E.R. 465 at 469, 475, 477; [1964] 1 W.L.R. 273 at 277, 285, 287 it is stressed that the amount of skill, judgment or labour is likely to be decisive in the case of compilations. To apply that, however, as a universal test of originality in all copyright cases is not only unwarranted by the context in which the observations were made but palpably erroneous. Take the simplest case of artistic copyright, a painting or a photograph. It takes great skill, judgment and labour to produce a good copy by painting or to produce an enlarged

264

photograph from a positive print, but no one would reasonably contend that the copy painting or enlargement was an "original" artistic work in which the copier is entitled to claim copyright. Skill, labour or judgment merely in the process of copying cannot confer originality. In this connection some reliance was placed on a passage from the judgment of Whitford J. in *L.B. (Plastics) Ltd v Swish Products Ltd* [1979] R.P.C. 551 at 568–569 where he expressed the opinion that a drawing of a three-dimensional prototype, not itself produced from the drawing and not being a work of artistic craftsmanship, would qualify as an original work. That may well be right, for there is no more reason for denying originality to the depiction of a three-dimensional prototype than there is for denying originality to the depiction in two-dimensional form of any other physical object. It by no means follows, however, that that which is an exact and literal reproduction in two-dimensional form of an existing two-dimensional work becomes an original work simply because the process of copying it involves the application of skill and labour. There must in addition be some element of material alteration or embellishment which suffices to make the totality of the work an original work. Of course, even a relatively small alteration or addition quantitatively may, if material, suffice to convert that which is substantially copied from an earlier work into an original work. Whether it does so or not is a question of degree having regard to the quality rather than the quantity of the addition. But copying, *per se*, however much skill or labour may be devoted to the process, cannot make an original work. A well-executed tracing is the result of much labour and skill but remains what it is, a tracing. Moreover, it must be borne in mind that the Copyright Act 1956 confers protection on an original work for a generous period. The prolongation of the period of statutory protection by periodic reproduction of the original work with minor alterations is an operation which requires to be scrutinised with some caution to ensure that that for which protection is claimed really is an original artistic work.

The other important consideration which has also to be borne in mind in any case of three-dimensional copying by reverse engineering is that the plaintiff's claim to protection in the case of a non-patented industrial article not registered under the Registered Designs Act 1949 rests solely on artistic copyright, that is to say on the visual image in the form of a drawing of the article from which that which is claimed to be an infringement is produced. It does not rest on the copyright owner's inventiveness or method of working, on the confidentiality of his instructions to his engineering or production staff or on his literary copyright in any written communication of those instructions. Essentially artistic copyright is concerned with visual image. This is of particular importance in the instant case, which has the unusual feature that the artistic copyright claimed stems in origin from drawings which are themselves out of copyright and therefore available for copying.

His Lordship then concluded (i) that the drawings by themselves involved alterations too insignificant to be original artistic works; but (ii) that the design information given was of technical significance and the result of considerable labour and expertise.

Reliance is ... principally placed, in this context, on the decision of the Court of Appeal in *British Leyland Motor Corp v Armstrong Patents Co Ltd* [1984] F.S.R. 591 (reversed in the House of Lords on other grounds: see [1986] 1 All E.R. 850; [1986] 1 A.C. 577). There the argument was that what had been copied was not the artistic work but the co-ordinates shown on the drawing in the form of figures. That argument was rejected. Thus, it is argued, the explanatory legend forms part of the drawing and substantial alterations to the explanatory legend are substantial alterations to the drawing.

It has, however, to be borne in mind that all these cases were concerned with a very different question from that with which this appeal is concerned. It is one thing to say that the explanatory figures and legend, because they are of value (and, indeed, perhaps essential) to an informed understanding of the drawing, cannot be ignored in considering whether copyright in the drawing has been infringed by the making of a three-dimensional article or whether the article would appear to a non-expert to be a reproduction of the drawing. It is quite another to say that explanatory material, in the form of words or figures, which are clearly the subject of literary copyright, can confer on an artistic work an originality which it does not possess in its own right. It has always to be borne in mind that infringement of copyright by three-dimensional copying is restricted to artistic copyright (section 48(1)). To produce an article by following written instructions may be a breach of confidence or an infringement of patent, but it does not infringe the author's copyright in his instructions. This is a distinction of crucial importance and it is well brought out in the following passage from the judgment of Buckley L.J. in *Catnic Components Ltd v Hill & Smith Ltd* [1982] R.P.C. 183 at 223:

"I do not question the principle that in deciding whether what has been reproduced by an alleged infringer is a substantial part of the work allegedly infringed, one must regard the quality (that is to say the importance) rather than the quantity of the part reproduced (see *Ladbroke (Football) Ltd v William Hill (Football) Ltd* ([1964] 1 All E.R. 465 at 469, 481; [1964] 1 W.L.R. 273 at 276, 293) *per* Lord Reid and Lord Pearce; but what is protected is the plaintiffs' 'artistic work' as such, not any information which it may be designed to convey. If it is said that a substantial part of it has been reproduced, whether that part can properly be described as substantial may depend upon how important that part is to the recognition and appreciation of the 'artistic work'. If an 'artistic work' is designed to convey information, the importance of some part of it may fall to be judged by how far it contributes to conveying that information, but not, in my opinion by how important the information may be which it conveys or helps to convey. What is protected is the skill and labour devoted to making the 'artistic work' itself, not the skill and labour devoted to developing some idea or invention communicated or depicted by the 'artistic work'. The protection afforded by copyright is not, in my judgment, any broader as counsel submitted, where the 'artistic work' embodies a novel or inventive idea than it is where it represents a commonplace object or theme".

The essence of an artistic work (to adopt the words of Whitford J. in *Rose Plastics GmbH v William Beckett & Co (Plastics) Ltd* (July 2, 1987, unreported, of which their Lordships have seen only an approved transcript) is that which is "visually significant"; and counsel for Tyco asks, forensically, what is there in the 1976 drawings which is visually significant and which was not contained in and directly copied from the 1968 drawings? With deference to the Court of Appeal and accepting both the importance of and the skill involved in producing the design information transmitted to the mould makers by the revised figures substituted on the drawing, their Lordships can see no alteration of any visual significance such as to entitle the drawing, as a drawing, to be described as original.

3.2.3.3   *Creation Records v News Group Newspapers* **[1997] E.M.L.R. 444, Lloyd J.**

Noel Gallagher, lead guitarist in the popgroup, Oasis, arranged with their record company for a secret publicity shoot to take place at a hotel and he in effect directed it. The photos, to be taken by Jones, were of a Rolls Royce in the hotel swimming pool, with various objects scattered around and the group among them. The Sun newspaper got wind of the shoot, arranged for a photographer, Seeburg, to stay at the hotel so as to get shots of it. One of these was then published in the paper and offered for sale as a poster. It closely resembled the photo which had been chosen for Oasis' next album.

In proceedings for interim relief, Lloyd J. found that there was an arguable case that The Sun*'s photographer had acted in breach of contract and on that basis granted an injunction against further publication of the photograph until trial. The case based on copyright, however, failed.*

Lloyd J.:

It is said, first, that the scene itself (the arrangement or composition of the members of the group, the various objects and the site) is a copyright work. I do not see how that can be so. Mr Merriman argued faintly that it was a dramatic work. Since the scene is inherently static, having no movement, story or action, I cannot accept this. Primarily, he argued that it was an artistic work, as a sculpture or collage within section 4(1)(a) of the Copyright, Designs and Patents Act 1988 or a work of artistic craftsmanship within section 4(1)(c) of that Act.

I do not regard this as seriously arguable. I do not see how the process of assembling these disparate objects together with the members of the group can be regarded as having anything in common with sculpture or with artistic craftsmanship. No element in the composition has been carved, modelled or made in any of the other ways in which sculpture is made (see *Breville (Europe) Plc v Thorn EMI Domestic Appliances Ltd* [1995] F.S.R. 77 at 94). Nor does it seem to me to be the subject or result of the exercise of any crafts-manship (see *George Hensher Ltd v Restawile Upholstery (Lancs) Ltd* [1976] A.C. 64, especially Lord Simon at 91).

I should mention in this context the case of *Shelley Films Ltd v Rex Features Ltd* [1994] E.M.L.R. 134. In this case it was held to be seriously arguable that a film set prepared for the film to be called "Mary Shelley's Frankenstein" was a work of artistic craftsmanship so that an unauthorised photograph taken of an actor on the set was a breach of copyright in the set as well, for different reasons, as of other elements in the photograph. That seems to me quite different on the facts. I can readily accept that a film set does involve crafts-manship. It is not merely an assembly of *"objets trouvés"*.

As for collage, a subject of copyright new to English law in the 1988 Act, the traditional understanding of that word is that it involves the use of glue or some other adhesive in the process of making a work of visual art, being derived from the French.

This composition was intrinsically ephemeral, or indeed less than ephemeral, in the original sense of that word of living only for one day. This existed for a few hours on the ground. Its continued existence was to be in the form of a photographic image. Accordingly, it seems to me materially different from all the particular examples put to me in this context by Mr Merriman.

Even if it were otherwise, I would not accept that it is seriously arguable that this com-position is a collage. In my view a collage does indeed involve as an essential element the sticking of two or more things together. It does not suffice to point to the collocation, whether or not with artistic intent, of such random, unrelated and unfixed elements as is seen in the photographs in question.

Next, Mr Merriman contended that Mr Seeburg's photograph was itself a copy of the official photograph taken by Mr Jones, regardless of the order in which the two were taken. I do not see how that can be argued. If the subject matter is not itself copyright, in principle two different photographers can take separate photographs of the same subject without either copying the other. Of course copyright subsists in the official photograph and if it were the only source of the scene it would be an infringement to copy that, either by a direct copying process or by the scene being recreated and a fresh photograph taken of that recreation. But it is a basic proposition of copyright law that two works created from a common source do not by reason of that fact involve copying one of the other, however similar they are. Nothing in *Bauman v Fussell* [1978] R.P.C. 485 is inconsistent with this.

As a variant on that contention Mr Merriman submitted that Mr Gallagher was the owner of the copyright in the Seeburg photograph because he was the author, the person who created it (see section 9 (1) and section 11 (1) of the 1988 Act). The basis of this is that Mr Gallagher created the subject-matter and it is therefore said that he created all photographs taken from it. It seems to me that ordinarily the creator of a photograph is the person who takes it. There may be cases where one person sets up the scene to be photographed (the position and angle of the camera and all the necessary settings) and directs a second person to press the shutter release button at a moment chosen by the first, in which case it would be the first not the second, who created the photograph. There may also be cases of collaboration between the person behind the camera and one or more others in which the actual photographer has greater input, although no complete control of the creation of the photograph, in which case it may be a work of joint creation and joint authorship (see section 10 (1)).

In the present case, however, it seems to me unarguable that anyone other than Mr Seeburg is the creator of his photograph. Mr Gallagher set up the scene and may well have chosen or approved the angle and other details of all or some of the official photographs taken by Mr Jones, in which case Mr Gallagher is the creator, or one of the creators, of the official photographs. It seems that Mr Jones does not claim to own copyright in any of these. But Mr Gallagher had nothing to do with the Seeburg photograph except to bring the subject matter into existence and of course to form part of it himself. That does not make him its creator.

3.2.4   Sound recordings

3.2.4.1   *A. & M. Records Ltd v Video Collection International Ltd* [1995] E.M.L.R. 25, Mervyn Davies J.

The second plaintiff, Inside Edge, was the service company of the well-known skaters, Torvill and Dean. Torvill and Dean wanted two tunes recorded for use with their ice dance routines, so an agent of Inside Edge, Graham Pullen, employed a conductor, Mr Ross, to produce suitable renderings of the two tunes, and Ross in turn employed a freelance arranger, Cyril Payne, to assist him.

The BBC relayed and recorded one of Torvill and Dean's performances where these two tunes were used, and licensed the defendants to sell videos of it. The second plaintiff claimed that it owned the copyright in the sound recordings of the tunes, and that the defendants' videos infringed their copyright. The defendants responded that Mr Ross and not the second plaintiff owned the copyright because he was the "author" of the "work" within the meaning of s.9(1) and 9(2)(a) of the Copyright, Patents and Designs Act 1988. The judge said:

From that basis Mr Gray for the defendants submitted that Mr Ross undertook such arrangements as are indicated in section 9(2). Mr Gray itemised the many activities in which Mr Ross engaged in the course of the production of the recording. It was common ground that Mr Ross's activities included the following:

(1) He commissioned and paid for the musical arrangements devised by Mr Payne and shown on the score made up by Mr Payne.

(2) He booked and paid for the Barnes recording studio.

(3) He arranged and paid for the attendance of 51 musicians.

(4) He engaged and paid for the scoring, a sound engineer and a fixer.

(5) He paid for all expenses attending the recording sessions such as meals, taxis and incidentals.

Thus it was submitted that Mr Ross was "the person by whom the arrangements necessary for the making of the recording were undertaken".

Mr Gray recognised that there always was an intention that Inside Edge and A&M should use the recording. It was impliedly agreed that Mr Ross would allow the plaintiffs to use the sound recordings during the skating championships and as well in the course of making and selling their compact disc. But Mr Ross had not, it was said, agreed to any more than that. Thus it was that the plaintiffs were unable to stop VCI from using the sound recording as an accompaniment to the video since the plaintiffs were not the owners of the copyright in the sound recordings. They were, it was said, only licensees of Mr Ross in respect of skating and C.D. use.

I do not accept the view that the plaintiffs were able to use the sound recordings merely because they were licensed to do so by Mr Ross. I take the view that Mr Ross did not acquire the copyright in the sound recording. The copyright was acquired by Inside Edge by the operation of section 9(2). I say that because looking at section 9(2) one can say that the "making of the recording", was the work of Mr Ross. But then one has to consider who it was who undertook the arrangements necessary for that making.

On the facts before me I take the view that Mr Pullen was the person who undertook those arrangements. He did so as the agent of Inside Edge. Having been told by Torvill and Dean what they wanted, he set about seeking a musician who was suitable for the task of making sound recordings suitable for use at the skating championships. He found Mr Ross. He made an agreement with him that Mr Ross would set up a studio and musicians at his (Mr Ross's) expense in return for a fee that would enable Mr Ross to make a profit for himself. It was known that the recordings proposed would be used not only at the skating championship but also in the course of compiling a C.D. for sale to the public. So it was, as I see it, that Mr Pullen as agent for Inside Edge undertook the arrangements for the making of the recording. Since that is so Mr Ross does not own the copyright in the recording. According to section 9(2) it is Inside Edge that owns the copyright.

The court considered other arguments and found for the plaintiffs.

3.3 Fixation

3.3.1 Copyright, Designs and Patents Act 1988, ss.3(2), 178, 58

S.3(2) Copyright does not subsist in a literary, dramatic or musical work unless and until it is recorded, in writing or otherwise; and references in this Part to the time at which such a work is made are to the time at which it is so recorded.

(3) It is immaterial for the purposes of subsection (2) whether the work is recorded by or with the permission of the author; and where it is not recorded by the author, nothing in that subsection affects the question whether copyright subsists in the record as distinct from the work recorded.

S.178 ... "writing" includes any form of notation or code, whether by hand or otherwise and regardless of the method by which or the medium in or on which, it is recorded, and "written" shall be construed accordingly.

S.58(1) Where a record of spoken words is made, in writing or otherwise, for the purpose—

(a) of reporting current events, or

(b) of broadcasting or including in a cable programme service the whole or part of the work,

it is not an infringement of any copyright in the words as a literary work to use the record or material taken from it (or to copy the record, or any such material, and use the copy) for that purpose, provided the following conditions are met.

(2) The conditions are that—

(a) the record is a direct record of the spoken words and is not taken from a previous record or from a broadcast or cable programme;

(b) the making of the record was not prohibited by the speaker and, where copyright already subsisted in the work, did not infringe copyright;

(c) the use made of the record or material taken from it is not of a kind prohibited by or on behalf of the speaker or copyright owner before the record was made; and

(d) the use is by or with the authority of a person who is lawfully in possession of the record.

3.3.2 *Walter v Lane* [1900] A.C. 539, HL

On five occasions in 1896 and 1899 the Earl of Rosebery delivered speeches on subjects of public interest to public audiences. Reporters attended on behalf of The Times *and other newspapers. The reporters for* The Times *took down the speeches in shorthand, wrote out their notes, corrected, revised and punctuated their reports for publication, and the reports were published in* The Times, *the speeches being given verbatim as delivered by Lord Rosebery.*

In 1899 the respondent published a book, incorporating these reports. Lord Rosebery made no claim, but The Times *(as assignees of the reporters' copyright) sought inter alia an injunction, damages and costs. In the Court of Appeal the parties agreed that the appeal should be treated as the trial of the action.*

Earl of Halsbury L.C.:

My Lords, I shall very much regret it if I were compelled to come to the conclusion that the state of the law permitted one man to make profit and to appropriate to himself the labour, skill, and capital of another. The law which I think restrains it is to be found in the Copyright Act, and that Act confers what it calls copyright—which means the right to multiply copies—which it confers on the author of books first published in this country.

The sole ground, as I understand the judgment of the Court of Appeal, is, that in their judgment the producer of a written speech unless he is the original speaker cannot be an "author" within the meaning of the Act. My Lords, it seems to me that this argument is based upon a too narrow and misleading use of the word "author". In my view the statute was not meant so to confine it, and I do not understand the explanation the Court of Appeal gives of the application of the word "author" to such publications as directories, red books, maps, etc.

I observe the Court of Appeal uses the word "analogy" as applicable to such questions. To my mind it is no analogy at all. If the maker of a directory, red book, or a map is an "author", one has to analyze what in such cases is the distinction between the "author" as thus referred to and the author of a spoken speech. If the producer of such a book can be an author within the meaning of the Act, I am unable to understand why the labour of reproducing spoken words into writing or print and first publishing it as a book does not make the person who has so acted as much an author as the person who writes down the names and addresses of the persons who live in a particular street.

I observe that the Court of Appeal introduces the words "original composition" as if those were the words of the statute; and at another part of the judgment it is said that "the report and the speech reported are no doubt different things, but the printer or publisher of the report is not the 'author' of the speech reported, which is the only thing which gives any value or interest to the report". The sentence is a little difficult to construe, but, as I understand it, it means to convey that the thing to which the statute gives protection must be of some value or interest. Again, I am compelled to point out that such words are not to be found in the statute.

If the question here were whether there was the right to publish at all a speech made by someone who did not himself publish it, questions like those determined in this House in *Caird v Sime* [1887] 12 App. Cas. 326, might arise. Whether the speech was delivered so as to give it to all the world and to prevent the original author of it from restricting its publication is a question with which your Lordships have here no concern. Lord Rosebery is not here complaining of the publication of it, nor claiming any proprietary right in the speeches delivered.

My Lords, I cannot help thinking that underlying the argument which has been addressed to us there is something of the contention which was boldly made nearly half a century ago in the case of *Maclean v Moody* (1858) 20 J.C. Court Sess. Cas. 1154, in the Court of Session, where, relying on the preamble, the advocate argued that the object of the statute of Victoria was to encourage literary merit, that the intellectual labour constituting authorship was alone thereby protected, and that there could be no authorship without an author. Lord Deas refused to accept such an argument, and expressed the opinion that the Act did not confine the privilege to cases in which there was a known author. But it appears to me that, although it may be true that a preamble may be a guide to the general objects of the statute, it undoubtedly is unquestioned law that it can neither restrict nor limit express enactment. And though I think in those compositions there is literary merit and intellectual labour, yet the statute seems to me to require neither, nor originality either in thought or in language.

It is admitted apparently by the Court of Appeal (and indeed insisted on as part of the reasons for their judgment) that the owner of an unpublished manuscript, although not the author of it, acquires copyright in it by first publishing it. And I observe that it is said Lord Rosebery had no copyright in his speech, and although he could have acquired copyright in it by putting it into writing and printing and publishing it, he did not do so. Here, again, the implied proposition is that the only person who could gain copyright in his speech is the person who spoke it, and that the word "original" must by construction be read into the statute—that the true analogy is the true and first inventor of the patent laws.

I think the analogy is a false one. I do not find the word "original" in the statute, or any word which imports it, as a condition precedent, or makes originality of thought or idea necessary to the right. But if the analogy were strictly pursued, I think 'it would not be favourable to the defendant. An importer of a foreign invention is for the purpose of the patent laws an inventor, and, as Lord Brougham said in *Re Berry's Patent*, there were "two species of public benefactors—the one, those who benefit the public by their ingenuity, industry, and science and invention and personal capability; the other, those who benefit the public without any ingenuity or invention of their own, by the appropriation of the results of foreign inventions. Now the latter is a benefit to the public incontestably, and therefore they render themselves entitled to be put upon somewhat, if not entirely, the same footing as inventors".

My Lords, if I have not insisted upon the skill and accuracy of those who produce in writing or print spoken words, it is not because I think the less of those qualities, but because, as I have endeavoured to point out, neither the one nor the other are conditions precedent to the right created by the statute. That right, in my view, is given by the statute to the first producer of a book, whether that book be wise or foolish, accurate or inaccurate, of literary merit or of no merit whatever.

I must notice one supposed difficulty in this view very persistently urged at the bar. It is said that in the view I have suggested there would be as many copyrights as reporters. I do not see the difficulty. Each reporter is entitled to report, and each undoubtedly would have a copyright in his own published report; but where is the difficulty?

Lords Davey, James of Hereford, Brampton and Robertson delivered concurring speeches.

3.3.3 *Roberton v Lewis* (1960) [1976] R.P.C. 169, Cross J.

The plaintiffs asserted copyright in the tune of a Scottish folk-song, "Westering Home", as arranged by Sir Hugh Roberton. Of one argument put to him, Cross J. stated:

In view of the conclusion which I have reached with regard to the verse section of the song, it is clear that the plaintiffs are not entitled to any copyright in respect of any part of the tune of "Westering Home". They argue, however, in reliance on the case of *Walter v Lane* [1900] A.C. 539, that, even if Sir Hugh had no copyright in the tune or any part of it, he nevertheless had copyright in the printed record of it which he made, and that the defendants have infringed that copyright.

Cross J. referred to the facts of Walter v Lane *(above) and continued:*

Sir Hugh's executors have this limited form of copyright which they claim but I am by no means satisfied that they have. In the first place, it is to be observed that Lord Halsbury in his speech laid considerable stress on the fact that the Copyright Act 1842, which was the Act then in force, did not provide that a work must be "original" in order to be entitled to copyright whereas the 1956 Act, reproducing in this respect the provisions of the 1911 Act, only gives copyright in "original works": see section 2(1). In view of this change it is I think at least arguable that *Walter v Lane* is no longer good law. Assuming, however, that the law is still as there laid down, the facts of this case differ very materially from those which existed in *Walter v Lane*. There the shorthand writers took down the words of speeches from the lips of a speaker who had not himself previously reduced his words into writing. In this case no one knows who the author of the tune was but in the long period of time which must have elapsed since it first came into existence it must have been sung or piped on innumerable occasions, and many of those who sung or piped it may have written down the notes, either to aid their own memories or to enable them to teach it to others. I am by no means clear that the decision in *Walter v Lane* has any application to a case where the speech or tune in question has already been accorded a material form before the record of it for which copyright is claimed came into existence. It is perhaps worth noting that counsel for the shorthandwriters in his argument in the Court of Appeal in the case of *Walter v Lane* expressly conceded that, if Lord Rosebery had written his speech out and had read it or repeated it from memory, the shorthandwriters would have no copyright in their reports of it: see [1899] 2 Ch. 766. It appears to me that this admission of counsel may well have been justified.

3.3.4   *Express Newspapers Plc v News (U.K.) Plc* [1991] F.S.R. 36, Browne-Wilkinson V.C.

The plaintiff was the proprietor of The Daily Express *and* The Daily Star *newspapers, and the defendant was the proprietor of the rival paper,* Today. *The litigation involved "tit for tat" copying of sensationalist interviews published in the two newspapers. The plaintiff published an interview with a Mrs Bordes in* The Daily Express *and the defendant used quotations from the interview without acknowledgement in its newspaper of the same day. Some months later the defendant's newspaper published an interview with a Miss Ogilvy and quotations from this story appeared in* The Daily Star *the next day. The plaintiff commenced proceedings for copyright infringement in respect of the first incident and the defendant counterclaimed in respect of the second. Browne-Wilkinson V.C., considering the counterclaim, examined the question of the copyright in quotations:*

The law as to copyright in verbatim reports of the spoken words of another was settled by the House of Lords in *Walter v Lane* [1900] A.C. 539. In that case Lord Rosebery gave a public speech. A reporter from *The Times* newspaper attended and took down that speech verbatim in shorthand. A verbatim report was published in *The Times*. Subsequently the defendant compiled a book of Lord Rosebery's speeches and, without the consent of *The Times*, included the report of Lord Rosebery's speech, the source of such report being *The Times* newspaper. The question was, did the reporter of Lord Rosebery's words have any copyright in the report? The House of Lords held that he did. Lord Halsbury at 548 said:

"Although I think in these compositions there is literary merit and intellectual labour, yet the statute seems to me to require neither, nor originality either in thought or in language."

Lord Davey at 552 said:

"It was of course open to any other reporter to compose his own report of Lord Rosebery's speech, and to any other newspaper or book to publish that report; but it is a sound principle that a man shall not avail himself of another's skills, labour, and expense by copying the written product thereof."

As a result of that House of Lords decision it was established that the mere reporting of the words of another gives rise to a reporter's copyright so long as skill and judgment have been employed in the composition of that report.

The decision was made under the Copyright Act 1842 which contains no express requirement for the work in which copyright subsists to have been an original work. From the Copyright Act 1911 onwards there has been an express statutory requirement in relation to works of this kind that the work shall be an original work (see now section 1(1)(a) of the 1988 Act). In *Roberton v Lewis* [1976] R.P.C. 169 at 174, Cross J. suggested *obiter* that the statutory requirement that the work should be an original work might mean that the decision in *Walter v Lane* was no longer good law. He was not referred to the decision of the High Court of Australia in *Sands v McDougall Proprietary Ltd & Robinson* (1917) 23 C.L.R. 49, where the court considered the impact of the introduction into the 1911 Act of the requirement for the work to be original, dealt with the matter very fully and reached the conclusion that *Walter v Lane* was still good law. They held that the word "original" in the statute does not imply inventive originality; it is enough that the work is the production of something in a new form as a result of the skill, labour and judgement of the reporter.

I prefer the view expressed by the High Court of Australia; it seems to me sound. The possibility of the continued existence of reporters' copyright is reflected in section 3(3) of the 1988 Act, which expressly refers to the possibility of the recorder of spoken words having a copyright in the record of those words as distinct from the work recorded.

Mr Burton also referred me to passages on the meaning of the word "original" in the statutes in the advice in *Interlego A.G. v Tyco Industries Inc* [1988] R.P.C. 343. It was, I think, suggested that that decision might have impliedly modified the law as laid down in *Walter v Lane*. But *Walter v Lane* was not referred to in argument, and the Privy Council were there considering quite a different point on originality which does not, in my judgment, touch on *Walter v Lane*.

I therefore approach this case on the basis that *Walter v Lane* is undeniably still good law. On that footing, if skill, labour and judgement was put into the reporting of Miss Ogilvy's words in the *Today* newspaper, copyright will subsist in the report of those words even though the words themselves are Miss Ogilvy's.

The evidence does show that there was an interview lasting over eight and a half hours with Miss Ogilvy. The skills of the reporter in this case are quite different from and much greater than those shown in the Lord Rosebery's speech case. It was not simply taken down the words of somebody who was already going public by speaking publicly. Although Miss Ogilvy had approached the reporter, the whole conduct of the interview and the selection of quotations involves at least as much (and in my view greater) skill and judgement than merely taking down the words of a speaker at a public speech.

Therefore, in my judgment, in the absence of any other defence, it has been shown that *Today* does enjoy reporter's copyright in the words of Miss Ogilvy.

The judge granted the defendant's application for summary judgment on the counterclaim. The plaintiff had previously obtained summary judgment on its claim, and as the claim and the counterclaim were legally indistinguishable the judge held that the plaintiff could not be heard to argue that there was a possible defence to the counterclaim.

3.4   Qualification and Publication

3.4.1   Copyright, Designs and Patents Act 1988, ss.157(1)–(2), 159(1), 160(1): Qualification

S.157(1) This Part extends to England and Wales, Scotland and Northern Ireland.

(2) Her Majesty may by Order in Council direct that this Part shall extend, subject to such exceptions and modifications as may be specified in the Order, to—

   (a) any of the Channel Islands,

   (b) the Isle of Man, or

   (c) any colony.

Section 157(3)–(5) add a number of ancillary powers. Section 158 deals with countries which cease to be colonies.

S.159(1) Her Majesty may by Order in Council make provision for applying in relation to a country to which this Part does not extend any of the provisions of this Part specified in the Order, so as to secure that those provisions—

   (a) apply in relation to persons who are citizens or subjects of that country or are domiciled or resident there, as they apply to persons who are British citizens or are domiciled or resident in the United Kingdom, or

   (b) apply in relation to bodies incorporated under the law of that country as they apply in relation to bodies incorporated under the law of a part of the United Kingdom, or

   (c) apply in relation to works first published in that country as they apply in relation to works first published in the United Kingdom, or

   (d) apply in relation to broadcasts made from or cable programmes sent from that country as they apply in relation to broadcasts made from or cable programmes sent from the United Kingdom.

Section 159(2) gives ancillary powers, inter alia, *to apply the Part subject to exceptions; s.159(3) requires, save in respect of Convention [countries and EEA States], reciprocity of provision as a precondition; s.159(4) defines convention country and s.159(5) allows for annulment of an Order by resolution of either House.*

S.160(1) If it appears to Her Majesty that the law of a country fails to give adequate protection to British works to which this section applies, or to one or more classes of such works, Her Majesty may make provision by Order in Council in accordance with this section restricting the rights conferred by this Part in relation to works of authors connected with that country.

Section 160(2)–(4) introduce ancillary duties and definitions.

3.4.2   Copyright, Designs and Patents Act 1988, s.175: Publication

S.175(1) In this Part "publication", in relation to a work

(a) means the issue of copies to the public, and

(b) includes, in the case of a literary, dramatic, musical or artistic work, making it available to the public by means of an electronic retrieval system;

and related expressions shall be construed accordingly.

(2) In this Part "commercial publication", in relation to a literary, dramatic, musical or artistic work means—

(a) issuing copies of the work to the public at a time when copies made in advance of the receipt of orders are generally available to the public, or

(b) making the work available to the public by means of an electronic retrieval system;

and related expressions shall be construed accordingly.

(3) In the case of a work of architecture in the form of a building, or an artistic work incorporated in a building, construction of the building shall be treated as equivalent to publication of the work.

(4) The following do not constitute publication for the purposes of this Part and references to commercial publication shall be construed accordingly—

(a) in the case of a literary, dramatic or musical work

(i) the performance of the work, or

(ii) the broadcasting of the work or its inclusion in a cable programme service (otherwise than for the purposes of an electronic retrieval system);

(b) in the case of an artistic work—

(i) the exhibition of the work,

(ii) the issue to the public of copies of a graphic work representing, or of photographs of, a work of architecture in the form of a building or a model for a building, a sculpture or a work of artistic craftsmanship,

(iii) the issue to the public of copies of a film including the work, or

(iv) the broadcasting of the work or its inclusion in a cable programme service (otherwise than for the purpose of an electronic retrieval system);

(c) in the case of a sound recording or film—

(i) the work being played or shown in public, or

(ii) the broadcasting of the work or its inclusion in a cable programme service.

(5) References in this Part to publication or commercial publication do not include publication which is merely colourable and not intended to satisfy the reasonable requirements of the public.

(6) No account shall be taken for the purposes of this section of any unauthorised act.

3.4.3 *Francis Day & Hunter v Feldman* **[1914] 2 Ch. 728, Neville J., CA**

The song, "You made me love you (I didn't want to do it)", was composed by an American in the US. It was published simultaneously in New York and London on May 5, 1913. The plaintiffs, acting for the American copyright owners, placed six copies for sale in their retail showroom in London on that date, sent one copy to the British Museum and next day four to the agent for the universities which held the deposit libraries. The song became a success the following July, whereupon the plaintiffs acquired the British Empire copyright and made large sales of the sheet music. Their action for infringement was against the publisher of a "reply song". The principal issue was whether there had been first publication in England.

Neville J.:

The first question that I have to decide is whether there has been publication in England within 14 days after May 5, 1913, within the meaning of the statute. The material words are "unless the publication in such parts of His Majesty's Dominions as aforesaid is colourable only and is not intended to satisfy the reasonable requirements of the public". There you have really a definition of what "colourable only" means. It means a case where there is no intention to satisfy the reasonable requirements of the public. In the present case I find no evidence upon which I could come to such a conclusion. It is quite true that the demand anticipated was insignificant and the supply secured to satisfy the demand was also insignificant. A dozen copies were all that were sent at the time, and it was not until some time afterwards that further copies were applied for and forwarded from America. It seems to me that the intention from the first was to satisfy the public demand in this country. In this case I think that is what the publication in England was for. I hold therefore that there was a good publication in England.

The Court of Appeal affirmed this judgment without giving reasons.

3.4.4 *British Northrop v Texteam Blackburn* **[1974] R.P.C. 57, Megarry J.**

The plaintiff's company manufactured looms and weaving machinery. The defendant's company, run by a former managing director of the plaintiff together with ex-employees, began marketing the most frequently requested of the many spare parts needed for the machines. The plaintiff alleged that all the defendant's spares infringed design copyright in drawings for the parts. In interlocutory procedures the defendants asserted inter alia that copyright by first publication in the UK or a convention country had not been proved since publication only took place when and where members of the public who had ordered them received them.

Megarry J.:

"Place of publication. In cases where the place of publication is material it would appear that it is the place where copies are received by the public, or at least capable of being so received, and not the place where copies are printed or produced".

The authority cited for this is *McFarlane v Hulton* [1899] 1 Ch. 884. That case concerned a clause in an agreement for the sale of the copyright in a sporting paper within a radius of 10 miles of the office in London. The vendors subsequently printed a sporting paper in Manchester, but in addition to offering copies for distribution or sale at their Manchester office, they sent copies to London which were offered for distribution or sale at an office within the 10 miles radius. Cozens-Hardy J. held that the paper was published both in Manchester and London; and he said at 889:

> "It seems to me that a paper is published when and where it is offered to the public by the proprietor".

I can find not a word in the case to support the proposition that publication occurs at "the place where copies are received by the public", a view which would suggest that a periodical which is offered to the public by postal subscription and has 10,000 subscribers would have 10,000 places of publication.

His Lordship derived support from Francis Day & Hunter v Feldman *(above, 3.4.3) and continued:*

Accordingly, in my judgment, under the Act of 1956 an artistic work is "issued to the public", and so published when reproductions of the work are put on offer to the public. Normally, no doubt, the reproduction will be offered for sale; but I do not see why an offer gratis should not be an offer. Again, no doubt there will usually be some process of advertisement or announcement to the public that the reproductions are on offer; but I agree with Neville J. in thinking that no such advertisement or announcement is requisite where the person concerned is prepared to supply on demand. I therefore reject Mr Mervyn Davies' contention that the plaintiffs must fail because they have not proved any positive acts of offer by the plaintiffs. Passive availability suffices, without active offering. In my judgment, subject to the 30 days' rule, the work is first published when it is first put on offer, and the place of first publication is where this occurs. In this case, it seems plain to me that, at any rate for the purposes of the motion, there is enough evidence to establish, directly or by inference, that the drawings in question were first published when parts made in accordance with the drawings were offered for sale by the plaintiffs in Blackburn. Accordingly, this ground for contending that no copyright exists in the drawings must fail. I may add that if, contrary to my opinion, the drawings are unpublished works, I should hold that it is sufficiently established for the purposes of the motion that the author was a "qualified person", when the work was made, within section 3(2), so that by this different route the defendants' attack on the subsistence of copyright in the drawings must fail. That conclusion also suffices to sustain copyright under section 3(3)(b) for drawings first published after May 1957 if the drawings, though published, were not first published in the UK or another country within the section, so that (contrary to my view) section 3(3)(a) is not satisfied.

3.4.5 *Bodley Head v Flegon* [1972] R.P.C. 587, Brightman J.

The Russian author, Alexander Solzhenitzyn, signed a Swiss power of attorney authorizing H to deal outside Russia with a novel ("August 1914"). H entered into a contract whereby a Russian edition of the work was published by the YMCA press in France in June 1971. In return for royalties, the plaintiff obtained the exclusive right to translate the work into English and publish and serialise it in inter alia the UK but not before August 1972. The defendant who had obtained a Russian copy of the work intended to publish his own English translation in December 1971. On the plaintiff's motion for an interlocutory injunction to restrain this, the defendant claimed that, since the author was a Russian (and Russia was not at that date party to the UCC) UK copyright could be acquired only by first publication in a convention country; but that first publication had taken place by "samizdat"—clandestine circulation in typed form among educated people in Russia.

On this question, Brightman J. said:

I wish to make it absolutely clear that, so far as this court is concerned, the evidence of any such publication of the novel is, at present, totally non-existent. This makes it unnecessary for me to decide whether *samizdat* circulation could, in any event, be treated as publication within the meaning of the Copyright Act 1956 so as to prevent the YMCA Press publication being treated as first publication. Section 49(2) of the Copyright Act 1956 reads in part:

> "With regard to publication, the provisions of this subsection shall have effect for the purposes of this Act, that is to say … (b) except in so far as it may constitute an infringement of copyright, or a contravention of any restriction imposed by section 43 of this Act, a publication which is merely colourable, and not intended to satisfy the reasonable requirements of the public, shall be disregarded; (c) subject to the preceding paragraphs, a literary, dramatic or musical work, or an edition of such a work, or an artistic work, shall be taken to have been published if, but only if, reproductions of the work or edition have been issued to the public".

It appears from the judgment of Neville J. in *Francis Day & Hunter v Feldman & Co* [1914] 2 Ch. 728, 732, that the words "not intended to satisfy the reasonable requirements of the public" are in effect a definition of "colourable publication". Although I do not so decide, because it is unnecessary, I would myself doubt whether *samizdat* circulation could possibly be regarded as an effort to satisfy the reasonable requirements of the Russian public. It is rather, as it seems to me, a clandestine circulation which intentionally disregards the requirements of the Russian public because such requirements cannot lawfully be voiced by potential readers or satisfied by the author.

The learned judge then refused to hold that the comity of nations would be jeopardised by granting relief, since neither publishing contract required the doing of any illegal act within Russia. He upheld the validity of the power of attorney as governed by Swiss and not by Russian law.

3.5   Duration

3.5.1   Copyright, Designs and Patents Act 1988, ss.12–15A

S.12(1) The following provisions have effect with respect to the duration of copyright in a literary, dramatic, musical or artistic work.

(2) Copyright expires at the end of the period of 70 years from the end of the calendar year in which the author dies, subject as follows.

(3) If the work is of unknown authorship, copyright expires—

    (a) at the end of the period of 70 years from the end of the calendar year in which the work was made, or

    (b) if during that period the work is made available to the public, at the end of the period of 70 years from the end of the calendar year in which it is first so made available.

subject as follows.

(4) Subsection (2) applies if the identity of the author becomes known before the end of the period specified in paragraph (a) or (b) of subsection (3).

(5) For the purposes of subsection (3) making available to the public includes—

    (a) in the case of a literary, dramatic or musical work—

        (i) performance in public, or
        (ii) being broadcast or included in a cable programme service;

    (b) in the case of an artistic work—

        (i) exhibition in public,
        (ii) a film including the work being shown in public, or
        (iii) being included in a broadcast or cable programme service;

but in determining generally for the purposes of that subsection whether a work has been made available to the public no account shall be taken of any unauthorised act.

(6) Where the country of origin of the work is not an EEA state and the author of the work is not a national of an EEA state, the duration of copyright is that to which the work is entitled in the country of origin, provided that does not exceed the period which would apply under subsections (2) to (5).

(7) If the work is computer-generated the above provisions do not apply and copyright expires at the end of the period of 50 years from the end of the calendar year in which the work was made.

(8) The provisions of this section are adapted as follows in relation to a work of joint authorship—

(a) the reference in subsection (2) to the death of the author shall be construed—

(i) if the identity of all the authors is known, as a reference to the death of the last of them to die, and

(ii) if the identity of one or more of the authors is known and the identity of one or more others is not, as a reference to the death of the last whose identity is known;

(b) the reference in subsection (4) to the identity of the author becoming known shall be construed as a reference to the identity of any of the authors becoming known;

(c) the reference in subsection (6) to the author not being a national of an EEA state shall be construed as a reference to none of the authors being a national of an EEA state.

(9) This section does not apply to Crown copyright or Parliamentary copyright (see sections 163 to 166) or to copyright which subsists by virtue of section 168 (copyright of certain international organisations).".

S.13A(1) The following provisions have effect with respect to the duration of copyright in a sound recording.

(2) Copyright expires—

(a) at the end of the period of 50 years from the end of the calendar year in which it is made, or

(b) if during that period it is released, 50 years from the end of the calendar year in which it is released;

subject as follows.

(3) For the purposes of subsection (2) a sound recording is "released" when it is first published, played in public, broadcast or included in a cable programme service; but in determining whether a sound recording has been released no account shall be taken of any unauthorised act.

(4) Where the author of a sound recording is not a national of an EEA state, the duration of copyright is that to which the sound recording is entitled in the country of which the author is a national, provided that does not exceed the period which would apply under subsections (2) and (3).

(5) If or to the extent that the application of subsection (4) would be at variance with an international obligation to which the United Kingdom became subject prior to 29th October 1993, the duration of copyright shall be as specified in subsections (2) and (3).

S.13B(1) The following provisions have effect with respect to the duration of copyright in a film.

(2) Copyright expires at the end of the period of 70 years from the end of the calendar year in which the death occurs of the last to die of the following persons—

(a) the principal director,

(b) the author of the screenplay,

(c) the author of the dialogue, or

(d) the composer of music specially created for and used in the film;

subject as follows.

(3) If the identity of one or more of the persons referred to in subsection (2)(a) to (d) is known and the identity of one or more others is not, the reference in that subsection to the death of the last of them to die shall be construed as a reference to the death of the last whose identity is known.

(4) If the identity of the persons referred to in subsection (2)(a) to (d) is unknown, copyright expires at—

(a) the end of the period of 70 years from the end of the calendar year in which the film was made, or

(b) if during that period the film is made available to the public, at the end of the period of 70 years from the end of the calendar year in which it is first so made available.

(5) Subsections (2) and (3) apply if the identity of any of those persons becomes known before the end of the period specified in paragraph (a) or (b) of subsection (4).

(6) For the purposes of subsection (4) making available to the public includes—

(a) showing in public, or

(b) being broadcast or included in a cable programme service;

but in determining generally for the purposes of that subsection whether a film has been made available to the public no account shall be taken of any unauthorised act.

(7) Where the country of origin is not an EEA state and the author of the film is not a national of an EEA state, the duration of copyright is that to which the work is entitled in the country of origin, provided that does not exceed the period which would apply under subsections (2) to (6).

(8) In relation to a film of which there are joint authors, the reference in subsection (7) to the author not being a national of an EEA state shall be construed as a reference to none of the authors being a national of an EEA state.

(9) If in any case there is no person falling within paragraphs (a) to (d) of subsection (2), the above provisions do not apply and copyright expires at the end of the period of 50 years from the end of the calendar year in which the film was made.

(10) For the purposes of this section the identity of any of the persons referred to in subsection (2)(a) to (d) shall be regarded as unknown if it is not possible for a person to ascertain his identity by reasonable inquiry; but if the identity of any such person is once known it shall not subsequently be regarded as unknown.

S.14(1) The following provisions have effect with respect to the duration of copyright in a broadcast or cable programme.

(2) Copyright in a broadcast or cable programme expires at the end of the period of 50 years from the end of the calendar year in which the broadcast was made or the programme was included in a cable programme service, subject as follows.

(3) Where the author of the broadcast or cable programme is not a national of an EEA state, the duration of copyright in the broadcast or cable programme is that to which it is entitled in the country of which the author is a national, provided that does not exceed the period which would apply under subsection (2).

(4) If or to the extent that the application of subsection (3) would be at variance with an international obligation to which the United Kingdom became subject prior to 29th October 1993, the duration of copyright shall be as specified in subsection (2).

(5) Copyright in a repeat broadcast or cable programme expires at the same time as the copyright in the original broadcast or cable programme; and accordingly no copyright arises in respect of a repeat broadcast or cable programme which is broadcast or included in a cable programme service after the expiry of the copyright in the original broadcast or cable programme.

(6) A repeat broadcast or cable programme means one which is a repeat either of a broadcast previously made or of a cable programme previously included in a cable programme service.

S.15 Copyright in the typographical arrangement of a published edition expires at the end of the period of 25 years from the end of the calendar year in which the edition was first published.

S.15A(1) For the purposes of the provisions of this Part relating to the duration of copyright the country of origin of a work shall be determined as follows.

(2) If the work is first published in a Berne Convention country and is not simultaneously published elsewhere, the country of origin is that country.

(3) If the work is first published simultaneously in two or more countries only one of which is a Berne Convention country, the country of origin is that country.

(4) If the work is first published simultaneously in two or more countries of which two or more are Berne Convention countries, then—

(a) if any of those countries is an EEA state, the country of origin is that country; and

(b) if none of those countries is an EEA state, the country of origin is the Berne Convention country which grants the shorter or shortest period of copyright protection.

(5) If the work is unpublished or is first published in a country which is not a Berne Convention country (and is not simultaneously published in a Berne Convention country), the country of origin is—

(a) if the work is a film and the maker of the film has his headquarters in, or is domiciled or resident in a Berne Convention country, that country;

(b) if the work is—

(i) a work of architecture constructed in a Berne Convention country, or
(ii) an artistic work incorporated in a building or other structure situated in a Berne Convention country,

that country;

(c) in any other case, the country of which the author of the work is a national.

(6) In this section—

(a) a "Berne Convention country" means a country which is a party to any Act of the International Convention for the Protection of Literary and Artistic Works signed at Berne on 9th September 1886; and

(b) references to simultaneous publication are to publication within 30 days of first publication.

The Duration of Copyright and Rights in Performance Regulations 1995 (SI 1995/3297) Pt III make important transitional provisions for works created before January 1, 1996. Works which are still in copyright on that date are given the extended period provided for in the revised statute and this new right is conferred in most cases on the owner at that time (paras 15–18). Where copyright is extended, licences are continued for the additional period (para. 21).

Works in which copyright had previously expired, but which, on July 1, 1995, were still in copyright in another EEA State, have their copyright revived for any remaining period of the extended term, but subject to a statutory licence for a reasonable royalty (paras 16, 17, 24, 25). Ownership is conferred in general on the owner at the date of expiry (para. 19). There is a savings clause for acts done during the "free" period between expiry and revival, and for certain consequential exploitation (para. 23) and a provision concerning moral rights (para. 22).

3.5.2 Copyright, Designs and Patents Act 1988, ss.57, 66A.

S.57 Anonymous or pseudonymous works: acts permitted on assumptions as to expiry of copyright or death of author.

(1) Copyright in a literary, dramatic, musical or artistic work is not infringed by an act done at a time, when, or in pursuance of arrangements made at a time when—

   (a) it is not possible by reasonable inquiry to ascertain the identity of the author, and
   (b) it is reasonable to assume—

      (i) that copyright has expired, or
      (ii) that the author died 70 years or more before the beginning of the calendar year in which the act is done or the arrangements are made.

(2) Subsection (1)(b)(ii) does not apply in relation to—

   (a) a work in which Crown copyright subsists, or
   (b) a work in which copyright originally vested in an international organisation by virtue of section 168 and in respect of which an Order under that section specifies a copyright period longer than 70 years.

(3) In relation to a work of joint authorship—

   (a) the reference in subsection (1) to its being possible to ascertain the identity of the author shall be construed as a reference to its being possible to ascertain the identity of any of the authors, and

(b) the reference in subsection (1)((b)(ii) to the author having died shall be construed as a reference to all the authors having died.

S.66A(1) Copyright in a film is not infringed by an act done at a time when, or in pursuance of arrangements made at a time when—

(a) it is not possible by reasonable inquiry to ascertain the identity of any of the persons referred to in section 13B(2)(a) to (d) (persons by reference to whose life the copyright period is ascertained), and

(b) it is reasonable to assume—

(i) that copyright has expired, or
(ii) that the last to die of those persons died 70 years or more before the beginning of the calendar year in which the act is done or the arrangements are made.

(2) Subsection (1)(b)(ii) does not apply in relation to—

(a) a film in which Crown copyright subsists, or

(b) a film in which copyright originally vested in an international organisation by virtue of section 168 and in respect of which an Order under that section specifies a copyright period longer than 70 years.

3.6 Infringement

3.6.1 Substantial Taking of Expression

3.6.1.1 *Plix Products v Frank M. Winstone* **[1986] F.S.R. 92, Pritchard J., SC, N.Z.**

The plaintiff company claimed copyright in drawings, moulds and models of "pocket packs" for transporting kiwi fruit. Under the New Zealand Copyright Act 1962 artistic copyright extends to industrial products in a number of ways (as to which, see Wham-O v Lincoln, *below, 4.1.4). Infringement occurred, according to the plaintiff, because the defendants gave the designer of their competing packs instructions to produce packs of the same standard dimensions as the plaintiff's. On the issue, Pritchard J., in finding for the plaintiff, observed:*

This proposition touches on the question of the idea/expression dichotomy, which is probably the most difficult concept in the law of copyright. It is no longer universally accepted that there is "no copyright in ideas".

The learned authors of *Copinger and Skone James* (12th ed., paras 2, 103, 179, 156) state unequivocally that the ideas and original thought of the author are not protected—that copyright is concerned only with the concrete forms in which ideas are expressed. There is an insistent line of authority to support this view, ranging from *Kenrick & Co v Lawrence & Co* (1890) 25 Q.B.D. 99 to *L.B. Plastics Ltd v Swish Products Ltd* [1979] R.P.C. 551, 619. In *Wham-O* [below 4.1.4], Mr Hillyer (as he then was) argued that a preliminary drawing in which the plaintiff asserted copyright was only a sketch which did no more than illustrate an idea and could not therefore be copyright material. That argument was rejected by the Court of Appeal—not on the basis that there is copyright in ideas but on the facts, because the drawing was no mere sketch but a working drawing.

The concept that copyright does not protect ideas is found unacceptable by the authors of several recent textbooks, *e.g. Laddie, Prescott & Vitoria*, pp.31 to 33, and *Lahore on Intellectual Property in Australia*, paragraphs 1121, 1151.

I think the conflict between these two philosophies is more apparent than real, and that if there is any conflict it can be resolved by an analysis of the concept of "ideas".

There are in fact two kinds of "ideas" involved in the making of any work which is susceptible of being the subject of copyright. In the first place, there is the general idea or basic concept of the work. This idea is formed (or implanted) in the mind of the author. He sets out to write a poem or a novel about unrequited love or to draw a dog listening to a gramophone or to make a kiwi fruit pocket pack—or whatever project he has in mind. While this "idea" remains as a thought in the author's mind it is, of course, not copyright. It is accepted by the proponents of the "copyright in ideas" theory that the mere act of reducing a general or basic concept of this sort to a tangible form does not result in a monopoly in the concept (*Laddie, Prescott & Vitoria*, para. 3.27).

Then there is a second phase—a second kind of "idea". The author of the work will scarcely be able to transform the basic concept into a concrete form *i.e.* "express" the idea—without furnishing it with details of form and shape. The novelist will think of characters, dialogue, details of plot and so forth. The artist will think of a certain tilt to the dog's head, to the effect of perspective, colour, light and shade. The pocket pack maker will likewise design the shapes, forms, patterns whereby he believes he can most effectively express the basic idea of pocket packs. Each author will draw on his skill, his knowledge of the subject, the results of his own researches, his own imagination in forming his idea of how he will express the basic concept. All these modes of expression have their genesis in the author's mind—these too are "ideas". When these ideas (which are essentially constructive in character) are reduced to concrete form, the forms they take are where the copyright resides.

So it is true to say (with *Laddie, Prescott & Vitoria et al.*) that copyright does extend to the protection of ideas—not to basic concepts, but to the ideas which are applied in the exercise of giving expression to basic concepts. It is equally true to say with *Copinger & Skone James* (and a formidable line of authority) that copyright subsists only in the form of expression and that infringement occurs only when such forms are copied.

The difficulty, of course, is to determine just where the general concept ends and the exercise of expressing the concept begins. It is, as Professor Cornish observes in his recent work, *Intellectual Property*, an "ill-defined boundary". There can be no general formula by which to establish the line between the general idea and the author's expression of the idea. The basic idea (or concept) is not necessarily simple—it may be complex. It may be something innovative; or it may be commonplace, utilitarian or banal. The way the author treats the subject, the forms he uses to express the basic concept, may range from the crude and simplistic to the ornate, complicated—and involving the collation and application of a great number of constructive ideas.

It is in this area that the author expends the skill and industry which (even though they may be slight) give the work its originality and entitle him to copyright. Anyone is free to use the basic idea—unless, of course, it is a novel invention which is protected by the grant of a patent. But no one can appropriate the forms or shapes evolved by the author in the process of giving expression to the basic idea. So he who seeks to make a product of the same description as that in which another owns copyright must tread with care. If he copies the details which properly belong to the expression and not the basic concept, he will infringe the copyright. That is why, when the basic idea is expressed in a crude, or simplistic form, the potential plagiarist or business competitor can, without offending, come very close to an exact reproduction of the copyright work. But where the expression is ornate, complex or detailed, then he must keep his distance: the only product he can then make without infringing may bear little resemblance to the copyright work.

While it is true that copyright law does have the effect of preventing the appropriation by a copyist of the constructive ideas of the author as to the form in which an original work is produced, this is so only because the law provides that to reproduce a substantial part of the material form (*i.e.* the shape or pattern) of the work by process of "copying" is an infringement. To hold otherwise would be to disregard the explicit terms of the Copyright Act 1962. Section 7(3) defines the restricted act as "reproducing the work in any material form". There is no copyright except by virtue of the Act (s.5(1)): the Act says nothing about taking ideas. The position is stated in clear and unambiguous terms in the following dicta from speeches delivered in the House of Lords in *L.B. Plastics Ltd v Swish Products Ltd* (above).

Lord Wilberforce at 619:

"There can be no copyright in a mere idea, so if all that the respondents had done was to take from the appellants the idea of external latching, or the 'unhanding' of components, or any other idea implicit in their work, the appellants could not complain. Nor is there infringement if a person arrives by independent work at a substantially similar result to that sought to be protected. The protection given by the law of copyright is against copying, the basis of the protection being that one man must not be permitted to appropriate the result of another's labour".

Lord Hailsham at 629:

"Of course, it is trite law that there is no copyright in ideas, and it may be that if all the respondents were shown to have copied from the appellants was the idea of some sort of external latching of the moulded corner pieces and clips to the extrusions this would have been a sound enough conclusion. But, of course, as the late Professor Joad used to observe, it all depends on what you mean by 'ideas'. What the respondents in fact copied from the appellants was no mere general idea".

3.6.1.2 *Designers Guild v Russell Williams* [2001] 1 All E.R. 700, HL

The plaintiff owned copyright in a fabric design, "Ixia", which was made up, in an Impressionistic manner, of stripes with flowers and leaves scattered over them. It alleged infringement of the work by the defendant's "Marguerite" design, in which there were both similarities and differences of detail from Ixia. At first instance, the judge found, over denials from the defendant's witnesses that there had been copying from Ixia and that the taking from that design had been substantial. On appeal the finding of copyright was not challenged, but in the Court of Appeal it was held that the taking was not substantial. The House of Lords restored the original judgment.

Lord Hoffmann:

4. Visual comparison

Mr Fysh [for the Plaintiff] was the author of the suggestion that the question of sub-stantiality could be resolved by a visual comparison between the two fabrics. He said that the question of substantiality was one of impression. That, in a sense, is true. When judges say that a question is one of impression, they generally mean that it involves taking into account a number of factors of varying degrees of importance and deciding whether they are sufficient to bring the whole within some legal description. It is often difficult to give precise reasons for arriving at a conclusion one way or the other (apart from an enu-meration of the relevant factors) and there are borderline cases over which reasonable minds may differ. But the first step in trying to answer any question (whether of impression or otherwise) is to be clear about what the question is. In the present case, it is whether the features which the judge found to have been copied from Ixia formed a substantial part of Ixia as an artistic work. That is certainly a question of judgment or impression. But why, in answering that question, should it be relevant to consider whether Ixia did or did not look like Marguerite?

The similarities between Ixia and Marguerite were of course highly relevant to the question of whether there had been copying and, if so, what features had been copied. They were the foundation upon which the judge constructed his conclusion that the features I have enumerated had been copied. But once those features have been identified, the question of whether they formed a substantial part of the plaintiff's design cannot be decided by revisiting the question of whether it looks like the defendant's. The more I listened to Mr Fysh's submissions as to why it was relevant to skilfully trying to undermine his concession that he could not challenge the judge's finding that certain features of the design had been copied. Mr Alastair Wilson [for the Defendant] met this submission on its own ground by producing two artistically draped samples of the two designs in similar colourways. I am bound to say that, at some distance, they looked remarkably similar to me. But, in a case in which there is no longer an issue over what has been copied, I do not regard this as a relevant exercise. In my respectful opinion the Court of Appeal erred in principle by allowing itself to be distracted from the statutory question, which was whether the elements found as a fact to have been copied formed a substantial part of Ixia.

5. Dissection

The exercise in dissection also, as it seems to me, involved two errors. First, it ignored substantial parts of the judge's findings on what had been copied and, secondly, it dealt with the copied features piecemeal instead of considering, as the judge had done, their cumulative effect. Thus the judge's findings on copying were by no means confined to the notion of stripes and flowers. There are many ways of depicting both stripes and flowers and the judge was obviously impressed by the fact that the defendant had been unable to find any other stripe and flower pattern which resembled Ixia or Marguerite in anything like the degree to which they resembled each other.

[. . .]

If there had been no finding that anything had been copied except the notion of flowers and stripes, the conclusion of the Court of Appeal would have been unexceptionable. But this involved ignoring the findings of fact, both in their detail and their cumulative effect.

6. Ideas and expression

It is often said, as Morritt L.J. said in this case, that copyright subsists not in ideas but in the form in which the ideas are expressed. The distinction between expression and ideas finds a place in the Agreement on Trade-Related Aspects of Intellectual Property Rights (TRIPS) (O.J. 1994 L 336, p. 213), to which the United Kingdom is a party (see Art.9.2: "Copyright protection shall extend to expressions and not to ideas. . ."). Nevertheless, it needs to be handled with care. What does it mean? As Lord Hailsham of St Marylebone said in *L.B. (Plastics) Ltd v Swish Products Ltd* [1979] R.P.C. 551, 629, "it all depends on what you mean by 'ideas' "

[. . .] if one examines the cases in which the distinction between ideas and the expression of ideas has been given effect, I think it will be found that they support two quite distinct propositions. The first is that a copyright work may express certain ideas which are not protected because they have no connection with the literary, dramatic, musical or artistic nature of the work. It is on this ground that, for example, a literary work which describes a system or invention does not entitle the author to claim protection for his system or invention as such. The same is true of an inventive concept expressed in an artistic work. However striking or original it may be, others are (in the absence of patent protection) free to express it in works of their own: see *Kleeneze Ltd v DRG (UK) Ltd* [1984] F.S.R. 399. The other proposition is that certain ideas expressed by a copyright work may not be protected because, although they are ideas of a literary, dramatic or artistic nature, they are not original, or so commonplace as not to form a substantial part of the work. *Kenrick & Co v Lawrence & Co* (1890) 25 Q.B.D. 99 is a well known example. It is on this ground that the mere notion of combining stripes and flowers would not have amounted to a substantial part of the plaintiff's work. At that level of abstraction, the idea, though expressed in the design, would not have represented sufficient of the author's skill and labour as to attract copyright protection.

Generally speaking, in cases of artistic copyright, the more abstract and simple the copied idea, the less likely it is to constitute a substantial part. Originality, in the sense of the contribution of the author's skill and labour, tends to be in the detail with which the basic idea is presented. Copyright law protects foxes better than hedgehogs. In this case, however, the elements which the judge found to have been copied went well beyond the banal and I think that the judge was amply justified in deciding that they formed a substantial part of the originality of the work.

7. The appellate function

The question of substantiality is one of mixed law and fact in the sense that it requires the judge to apply a legal standard to the facts as found. It is, as I said, one of impression in that it requires the overall evaluation of the significance of what may be a number of copied features in the plaintiff's design. I think, with respect that the Court of Appeal over-simplified the matter when they said that they were in as good a position to decide the question as the judge. I say this for two reasons.

First, although the question did not depend upon an assessment of the credibility of witnesses, there seems to me no doubt that a judge may obtain assistance from expert evidence in identifying those features of an artistic work which enable it to produce a particular visual effect ...

Secondly, because the decision involves the application of a not altogether precise legal standard to a combination of features of varying importance, I think that this falls within the class of case in which an appellate court should not reverse a judge's decision unless he has erred in principle: see *Pro Sieben Media AG v Carlton UK Television Ltd* [1999] 1 W.L.R. 605, 612–613. I agree with Buxton L.J. *Norowzian v Arks Ltd (No. 2)* [2000] F.S.R. 363, 370 when he said:

> "where it is not suggested that the judge has made any error of principle a party should not come to the Court of Appeal simply in the hope that the impression formed by the judges in this court, or at least by two of them, will be different from that of the trial judge."

Lord Bingham (with whom Lord Hope agreed), Lord Millett and Lord Scott delivered concurring judgments.

3.6.1.3   *Ravenscroft v Herbert* [1980] R.P.C. 193, Brightman J.

The plaintiff's work was a book of non-fiction. It detailed the history of the spear which forms part of the Hapsburg treasure in the Hofburg Museum, Vienna. He had traced this spear back through time and had identified it as the spear which pierced the side of Christ at the crucifixion, the spear used by many legendary historical personages, and the source of inspiration for Hitler's Germany. He had researched the history of the spear by orthodox methods and by using mystical meditation through the medium of a Dr Stein. The first defendant wrote fiction. He had read the plaintiff's book and thought it would make a good basis for a novel. He wrote a work of fiction about the post-war fate of the spear. The prologues of each section of the book recounted the story of the Hofburg spear from the Crucifixion to the end of the 1939 war. The first defendant admitted using the plaintiff's work as a source but denied copying such a substantial part as to amount to infringement of copyright.

Brightman J.:

The question which I have to decide is a question of fact, whether there has been substantial copying of "*The Spear of Destiny*" amounting to an infringement of the plaintiff's rights. This raises two issues, first whether there has been copying, and, secondly, whether such copying is substantial within the meaning of section 49. I have read both books. The plaintiff gave evidence before me during a period over four days, and the defendant for almost three days. It is absolutely plain that in writing five of the prologues that I have mentioned the defendant copied from the plaintiff's book. The next issue, therefore, is whether such copying is in relation to a substantial part of the plaintiff's book and therefore in excess of what is a legitimate degree of copying.

Mr Laddie, for the defendants, rightly says that an author has no copyright in his facts, nor in his ideas, but only in his original expression of such facts or ideas. He submitted that in deciding whether copying is substantial there are four principal matters to be taken into account. First, the volume of the material taken, bearing in mind that quality is more important than quantity; secondly, how much of such material is the subject-matter of copyright and how much is not; thirdly, whether there has been an *animus furandi* on the part of the defendant; this was treated by Page-Wood V.C. in *Jarrold v Houlston* (1857) 3 K. & J. 708, as equivalent to an intention on the part of the defendant to take for the purpose of saving himself labour; fourthly, the extent to which the plaintiff's and the defendant's books are competing works.

Copyright protects the skill and labour employed by the plaintiff in production of his work. That skill and labour embraces not only language originated and used by the plaintiff, but also such skill and labour as he has employed in selection and compilation. The principles are clear from the cases. There is a helpful summary of the authorities in *Harman Pictures NV v Osborne* [1967] 1 W.L.R. 723. For my purposes it is sufficient to cite two passages from that case which are taken from earlier authority:

"... another person may originate another work in the same general form, provided he does so from his own resources and makes the work he so originates a work of his own by his own labour and industry bestowed upon it. In determining whether an injunction should be ordered, the question, where the matter of plaintiff's work is not original, is how far an unfair or undue use has been made of the work? If, instead of searching into the common sources and obtaining your subject-matter from thence, you avail yourself of the labour of your predecessor, adopt his arrangements and questions, or adopt them with a colourable variation, it is an illegitimate use".

This appears at 730 of the report. There is also a passage:

"In the case of works not original in the proper sense of the term, but composed of, or compiled or prepared from materials which are open to all, the fact that one man has produced such a work does not take away from anyone else the right to produce another work of the same kind, and in doing so to use all the material open to him. But as the law has been precisely stated by Hall V.C. in *Hogg v Scott* (1874) L.R. 18 Eq. 444 'the true principle in all these cases is that the defendant is not at liberty to use or avail himself of the labour which the plaintiff has been at for the purpose of producing his work, that is, in fact, merely to take away the result of another man's labour or, in other words, his property' " see at 732.

In this case the judge was confronted with the well-known book by Mrs Cecil Woodham Smith entitled *"The Reason Why"* and also the script for a motion picture written by John Osborne. The question which the judge posed was this (at 736):

"... did John Osborne work independently and produce a script which, from the nature of things, has much in common with the book, or did he proceed the other way round and use the book as a basis, taking his selection of incidents and quotations therefrom, albeit omitting a number and making some alterations and additions, by reference to the common sources and by some reference to other sources?"

The main thrust of Mr Laddie's argument was that the plaintiff intended his book to be read as a factual account of historical events, that the defendant accepted it as fact and did no more than repeat certain of those facts. The plaintiff cannot claim a monopoly in historical facts. The law of copyright does not preclude another author from writing upon the same theme. It is perfectly legitimate for another person to contrive a novel about the Hofburg spear, even about its supposed ancestry and supernatural powers. Otherwise one would be driven to the conclusion that the plaintiff has a monopoly of the facts. Members of the public are entitled to use *"The Spear of Destiny"* as a historical work of reference.

I am inclined to accept that a historical work is not to be judged by precisely the same standards as a work of fiction. The purpose of a novel is usually to interest the reader and to contribute to his enjoyment of his leisure. A historical work may well have that purpose, but the author of a serious and original historical work may properly be assumed by his readers to have another purpose as well, namely to add to the knowledge possessed by the reader and perhaps in the process to increase the sum total of human experience and understanding. The author of a historical work must, I think, have attributed to him an intention that the information thereby imparted may be used by the reader, because knowledge would become sterile if it could not be applied. Therefore, it seems to me reasonable to suppose that the law of copyright will allow a wider use to be made of a historical work than of a novel so that knowledge can be built upon knowledge.

Having studied the two books and heard the evidence, I have no shadow of doubt that the defendant has copied from *"The Spear of Destiny"* to a substantial extent. In the prologues that I have mentioned he had deliberately copied the language of the plaintiff on many occasions. To a more significant extent he has adopted wholesale the identical incidents of documented and occult history which the plaintiff used in support of his theory of the ancestry and attributes of the spear, of Hitler's obsession with it and also General Patton's. He did this in order to give his novel a backbone of truth with the least possible labour to himself. In so doing he annexed for his own purposes the skill and labour of the plaintiff to an extent which is not permissible under the law of copyright. The defendant has clearly infringed the plaintiff's copyright. I am only sorry that so much time, effort and money has had to be spent on the trial of this action.

3.6.1.4 *Elanco Products v Mandops* [1980] R.P.C. 213, CA

The plaintiffs invented and patented a weed-killer, trifluralin. They marketed it with a leaflet giving extensive information on its proper use. This information was mostly also published in scientific journals.

After expiry of the patent, the defendants brought out the product, accompanied by a leaflet which, in its initial version, closely resembled the plaintiff's in format and language. On receiving objection, the defendants made a second, and then a third, version, which while still conveying the same data, were not so similar in detail.

The Court of Appeal granted an interlocutory injunction, mainly by reference to the balance of convenience. But, in finding that an arguable case had been made out, Goff L.J. considered that there was a sufficient basis for a claim that the plaintiff's leaflet constituted a literary work as a compilation; and, as to infringement, he stated:

It may well be that if the respondents had in fact at the start simply looked at the available information, including what appears in ACAS and, I think, what appears in the appellants' own literature, and from that decided what they would put in their literature and how they would express it, the appellants would at least have had considerable difficulty in bringing home any charge of infringement, even, having regard to the evidence, if the result had been extremely similar and the selection of items had been the same. But they chose, on the evidence as it stands at the moment, to proceed by making a simple and, as I think unauthorised, copy, and then they proceeded to revise it. It may well be that the result produced that way is an infringement. I say no more than that, because it will be for the trial judge to make up his mind upon all that when he has the whole of the evidence, when it has been sifted and the matter has been argued before him.

I refer again to the case of *Scott v Stamford*, where the Vice-Chancellor stated the principle thus at the end of his judgment:

"No man is entitled to avail himself of the previous labours of another for the purpose of conveying to the public the same information, although he may append additional information to that already published".

I would refer also to a passage in the judgment of the Master of the Rolls in *Moffatt & Paige Ltd v George Gill & Sons Ltd* (1902) 86 L.T. 465 at 471. This is a case having some similarity to the history in this case, since there was there a first edition to which objection was taken and which was then withdrawn, and a second edition which was compiled making use of the first, but altering it in such ways as it was thought would protect the second from any charge that it was an infringement. The learned Master of the Rolls said:

"No doubt he says: 'I am a very well-informed man; I have given, in fact, the greater part of my attention to these works, and I have no doubt I could have evolved the whole of these quotations from researches which I could have made: I know not only where those quotations come from but I know the authors and have named them as appropriate to the particular matters, and I could tell you who they were'. But, unfortunately, he did not go through the process himself; he has adopted the work of another man who may or may not have gone through it, but whether he did or did not, the defendant did not. He simply took what another man had done".

There again it seems to me plain that the appellants have an arguable case. The learned judge at the trial may decide that it was sufficient to make revisions to the offending first copy, or he may think otherwise; but in my view it plainly is an arguable case that the respondents having started off, if I may put it that way, on the wrong foot by making what I think will be found to be a deliberate copy, did not sufficiently cure the position by working from that copy instead of going to the whole of the publicly available information and starting from scratch.

3.6.1.5   *Bauman v Fussell* (1953) [1978] R.P.C. 485, CA

The plaintiff photographed two cocks fighting. The defendant, impressed by the photograph, painted a picture in which the birds were in similar positions, though the colouring was much altered. The county court judge held that the effect was entirely different and refused to find infringement. An appeal was dismissed.

Somervell L.J.:

Prima facie, the question whether the alleged infringement is a copy or reproduction within the Act is a question of fact, and unless the learned judge had misdirected himself we should not interfere. Mr Skone-James for the appellant submits that he has, and puts his case as follows. Design is a substantial part of an artistic work. The position of the birds is the main part of the design of the photograph. It has been copied or reproduced.

I think the first proposition requires some examination in relation to photographs. A man takes a photograph of a procession or the laying of a foundation stone. He, of course, has chosen when and from where the photograph should be taken. The relative position of those in the procession, or their taking part in the ceremony is not, however, his work, or his design, in the sense in which the relative position of the figures on the ceiling of the Sistine chapel was the work and design of Michelangelo. The order and arrangement of the procession has been, no doubt, carefully planned and designed by someone else. It is an individual's work that the Act is intended to protect. I do not think that a painter who was minded to make a picture of the procession, in his own style, would be committing a breach of copyright if he used the photograph to enable him to get accurately the relative positions of those taking part. What he would be taking would not be a substantial portion of the plaintiff's work. At the other end of the photographic scale one can imagine a case where the photographer has made an original arrangement of the objects animate and inanimate which he photographs in order to create a harmonious design representing, for example, Spring. Here the design would be his work. The position of the birds here is betwixt and between. It is, I think, nearer to the former than the latter category.

There is another consideration which is, I think, relevant here. It is referred to by Romer L.J. in *Brooks v Religious Tract Society* (1897) 45 W.R. 476. That was a case where part of the engraving had been copied, a collie dog, and part altered. Romer L.J. says "It was not only the dog which was taken, but also the feeling and artistic character of the plaintiff's work. They had taken the design whilst substituting cats and a tortoise for the child". This was under earlier Acts somewhat differently worded but clearly the question whether "the feeling and artistic character" have been taken is relevant to the question whether a substantial portion of the plaintiff's work has been copied or reproduced. Here the feeling and artistic character of the picture are the work of the defendant. I am not suggesting this is conclusive. I think there might well be a case where what was taken was part of the plaintiff's work in the fullest sense, there might yet be an infringement although the feeling and artistic character of the two works were different.

Birkett L.J. reached a similar conclusion; Romer L.J. dissented.

3.6.1.6   *Krisarts v Briarfine* [1977] F.S.R. 577, Whitford J.

Legendre painted a series of well-loved views of London, of which the plaintiff company owned the copyright. The defendant company first produced post-

card versions of the paintings under a licence agreement with the plaintiff. On expiry of the agreement, the defendant had Mrs Gardner paint the same scenes after showing her copies of Legendre's paintings. Her versions were not slavish copies.

Whitford J. reviewed the evidence in detail and concluded:

I think it is established, indeed I think in the end it was accepted in this case, that both artists worked in some quite considerable measure at least from view cards and photographs as well as possibly, in part, from sketches which they make individually. There is of course nothing wrong in this. It is a commonplace for artists of distinction not to paint on the spot but to prefer to make sketches or impressions or notes from which they work up their paintings at home, and it is by no means uncommon for artists to reinforce their memory by photographic representations of works which are painted in the studio. Nonetheless, at the end of the day most artists produce some distinctive contribution to a scene which may be very well known indeed, and I think, looking at the works it can be said that M. Legendre had done this and I am of the opinion that there is undoubtedly an arguable case on the plaintiffs' side that in producing the work which she in fact produced, although as I have said, it was entirely accepted that a great deal of what she did was original, Mrs Gardner has in fact made a use of the work of M. Legendre in respect of all five paintings, the subject of dispute, sufficiently substantial to base a claim of infringement of copyright. Whether at the end of the day the case will be satisfactorily made out is another matter altogether but I cannot for one moment begin to accept the submission of counsel for the defendants that this application for an interlocutory injunction must fail because there is no arguable case on the issue of infringement.

On the balance of convenience, however, Whitford J. found damages to be an adequate remedy and refused interlocutory relief.

3.6.1.7 *M.S. Associates v Power* [1988] F.S.R. 242, Falconer J.

The defendant, Power, had been employed by the plaintiff company in writing detailed code for the Library (or dictionary) Section of its "C-Gen" computer program, a program which effected translation from the computer language "Basic" into the language, "C". Subsequently the defendant had been a licensed distributor of "C-Gen" and had adapted it to the needs of a particular customer. During this period he spent eight months writing a program, "B-tran", for the same purpose which allegedly infringed copyright in the Library section of "C-Gen". On motion for an interlocutory injunction, Falconer J. said:

As to whether, on the materials now before me on the motion, it appears that the plaintiffs have a real prospect of obtaining a permanent injunction at the trial, their case is that the library section in the defendants' B-tran translator program has been derived from the library of the plaintiffs, copied to an extent that constitutes infringement of copyright. In support of their case the plaintiffs rely on what Mr Wilson referred to as "many objective similarities in structure and in detail," coupled with the fact that there had been opportunity for the first defendant to copy from the plaintiffs' Microsoft BASIC to "C," "C-Gen", program which he had access to it, first as their employee engaged on work on it and, secondly, as their distributor of that program, and particularly when as their distributor he was concerned in adapting the library section of the C-Gen program purchased by Pegasus to the particular requirements of that purchaser.

It is the first defendants' evidence that the library in his B-tran program was not copied from the plaintiffs' program. The matters relied on as similarities are set out at some length by Mr Maskell in Part D of Exhibit KRM.2 to his first affidavit and they are commented on by the first defendant, again at some length, in his Exhibit JMP.1.

I should refer briefly to the particular matters which Mr Wilson relied upon especially. The library in the plaintiffs' program, as is the defendants', is a library of "C" functions which can be called upon; to most of the functions the plaintiffs have given names beginning with "m.s.", followed by letters related to the BASIC equivalent, where there is one. In the defendants' B-tran program many of the function names are the same without the "m.s." so that many resemble the BASIC equivalent. But there is a striking line similarity in the list of functions at the beginning of the plaintiffs' program, a list which is in random order—see paragraph 3.1.5 of section D of KRM.2. It is noteworthy that in the defendants' list, as in the plaintiffs', is the function "vptrs", and, it is Mr Maskell's evidence, not apparently disputed by the first defendant, that that function is not used in the defendants' program.

Mr Hammond, an independent expert who is a lecturer in computer science at the City University and has sworn on affidavit on behalf of the defendants, regards that function list similarity as one requiring explanation. Mr Wilson regarded that as one of the closest similarities, but there are also other line similarities in section D of KRM.2—they are referred to collectively in paragraph 19 of the first defendant's affidavit and he points out that they amount to only 43 lines in a total program of 15,000 lines. (I think that total should be limited to 9,000 as that was the extent of the program made available on the second inspection).

Mr Wilson accepted that the plaintiffs have not been able to find a large number of line identities but he submitted that their case is based on similarities not just identities, although, so he argued, such identities as the lines containing the list of functions show that the similarities result from copying.

As to similarities in structure, Mr Wilson drew attention to: (i) In the defendants' program, as in the plaintiffs', the library section includes a MAP function, generating an internal reference number for an opened file—the defendants' MAP function is not identical to the plaintiffs' which includes two intermediate steps not present in the defendants' MAP function. But it is not in dispute that there is no equivalent function in BASIC—nor in BASTOC, the only competitive program for the translation of Microsoft BASIC into "C".

(ii) In the plaintiffs' program the "oct" function is arbitrarily grouped with the "hex" function following it. In the defendants' B-tran, the "oct" function similarly is grouped with the "hex" function in the source code file called "hex c". It is Mr Maskell's evidence that there is no obvious reason why it should be so grouped with the "hex" function, other than that the plaintiffs had so grouped them together, and indeed that it would have been better not to put it there but allocate it a separate source code file of its own. However, in commenting on this point, the first defendants' evidence is that the "hex" and "oct" functions are commonly grouped together and are so in Microsoft BASIC.

(iii) The plaintiffs say that the file structure itself on the library in the defendants' B-tran is logically equivalent and very similar and they point, in particular, to the "GET" function; however, Mr Power says the file structure is fundamentally different. In Exhibit JMP.2 to Mr Power's affidavit are printouts of the "GET" function and Mr Carr pointed out the defendants' takes 25 lines and the plaintiffs' takes 91. But reference to figure 4 in Exhibit JMP.3 together with the same printouts numbered and lettered as in Exhibit KRM.9 makes reasonably clear that in fact both "GET" functions follow the same routine—the only difference being that after the second stage in the routine (MAP) the plaintiffs "GET" routine offers an alternative facility (see right hand path in the left hand block diagram of figure 4 of Exhibit JMP.3). Following the routine of the left hand path in that diagram appears to show the same routine as that in the defendants' routine shown in figure 4, resulting in the same data in the same form.

Falconer J. referred to other allegations of similarity and concluded, on the materials before him, that an arguable case had been made out by the plaintiff under the first requirement of the American Cyanamid *judgment (below, 7.1.1.1). On the balance of convenience, however, he ordered a speedy trial, while refusing interlocutory relief.*

3.6.1.8 *Williamson Music v Pearson Partnership* [1987] F.S.R. 97, Judge Paul Baker Q.C.

An advertising agency produced a television advertisement for a bus company, which set out to parody the lyrics and music of "There's Nothing Like a Dame" from Rodgers and Hammerstein's musical, "South Pacific". The plaintiffs as owners of copyright in the latter sued for infringement and sought interlocutory relief.

Judge Baker:

The first issue to which I should address myself is the question as to how far a parody is an infringement of copyright. Mr Prescott observed in the course of his submissions that it is hard to see how a parody could ever be an infringement and this has been canvassed, to some extent, in the authorities. Before I look into them, I call attention to two features of parody or burlesque. First of all, it is to be observed that the parodist of the successful parody does himself do a lot of original work in parodying the first work and so can be said to create a new and original work. Of course it has necessarily to conjure up the old or it would fail as a parody, but it is commonplace in this branch of the law that copyright resides not in ideas, but in the expression of them. So the parodist may take an idea and from it a completely new and original work may be created. Another element of this is that the parodist may be indulging in literary criticism or a review of the original work. This latter point, however, does not arise in the present case, because that was not the purpose of the compilers of the advertisement, so I need not deal with any sort of defence under section 6 of the Copyright Act, that is, the fair dealing exception.

I said that there were a number of authorities and I was referred, among others, to an American authority, which I propose to take first. It is the case of *Irving Berlin v E.C. Publications Inc*, which was heard by the United States Court of Appeals, Second Circuit, in 1964, 329 Fed. 2d 541. Irving Berlin is a well known composer of songs and it seems that in this case the defendants had created and published 25 parodies of his songs. The judgment was given by Judge Kaufman of the Court of Appeals. I propose just to read two passages from his judgment, where he dealt with two precedent cases where a parody was alleged, in one of which the copyright owners had succeeded and in the other of which they had failed. Of those two cases, and I need not refer to them further, Judge Kaufman says:

> "The distinction between the two situations, Judge Carter reasoned, turned on the relative significance or 'substantiality'—in terms of both quality and quantity—of the material taken from the original motion pictures. In both cases, the court recognised in painstaking and scholarly opinions the historic importance and social value of parody and burlesque; in both, it conceded that the parodist must be permitted sufficient latitude to cause his reader or viewer to 'recall or conjure up' the original work if the

parody is to be successful. But in Benny's case, the court concluded this licence had been grossly exceeded".

I note from there the reference to quality and quantity of the material taken and in terms of substantiality.

Judge Kaufman concluded his judgment in which he rejected the claim for copyright in relation to all the 25 parodies in these terms:

"For, as a general proposition, we believe that parody and satire are deserving of substantial freedom—both as entertainment and as a form of social and literary criticism".

He makes reference to *Don Quixote* and Swift's *Gulliver's Travels* and goes on:

"At the very least, where, as here, it is clear that the parody has neither the intent nor the effect of fulfilling the demand for the original, and where the parodist does not appropriate a greater amount of the original work than is necessary to 'recall or conjure up' the object of his satire, a finding of infringement would be improper".

That is of great interest although the U.S. law on copyright is in material respects different from that here but I notice that, although the parodist is treated generously in the proceedings in the U.S., he does not in fact have a licence to appropriate the other person's work.

I suppose in England the high water mark of any liberty allowed to parodies was the judgment of Younger J., as he then was, in *Glyn v Weston Feature Film Co* [1916] 1 Ch. 261. A number of points came up in this case which are not relevant to the issues I have to decide, and I will not take time reading through the facts, beguiling as they are. The passage I had in mind came after the learned judge had concluded that there was no substantial taking by the film *Pimple's Three Weeks* of the work of Eleanor Glyn of her novel *Three Weeks*, so that the case was disposed of on that ground. What followed were some helpful observations although they are *obiter*. At 268, Younger J. says.

"Making all allowance for the fact that prior to the Act of 1911 literary copyright did not include the acting right, it certainly is remarkable that no case can be found in the books in which a burlesque even of a play has been treated as an infringement of copyright, although burlesque, frequently more distinguished than the thing burlesqued, is as old as Aristophanes, to take Mr Hartree's example".

Then he refers to certain authorities. He says why the older order had to go and then he says:

"Most probably, however, the reason is to be found involved in such observations as those of Lindley L.J. in *Hanfstaengl v Empire Palace*, or in such a decision as that of the Court of Appeal in *Francis, Day & Hunter v Feldman & Co*, or in the principle that no infringement of the plaintiff's rights takes place where a defendant has bestowed such mental labour upon what he has taken and has subjected it to such revision and alteration as to produce an original result".

He goes on to deal with another case, which perhaps qualifies that, later on in the same paragraph, because he says:

"If, in considering whether such a literary work as a novel has been infringed by such a thing as a cinematograph film, the true enquiry is, as I think it must be, whether, keeping in view the idea and general effect created by a perusal of the novel, such a degree of similarity is attained as would lead one to say that the film is a reproduction of incidents described in the novel or of a substantial part thereof, then in my opinion, the answer in the present case must be in the negative."

That case is perhaps the high water mark but there is something on the same lines in *Joy Music Limited v Sunday Pictorial Newspapers (1920) Limited* [1960] 2 Q.B. 60, a decision of McNair J. This had arisen out of a feature article in the *Sunday Pictorial* which reported the activities of H.R.H. The Duke of Edinburgh, which activities had caused raised eyebrows in some quarters. At the time there was, and still is for all I know, a form of music known as rock-and-roll and one of the then popular songs had the line: "Rock-a-Billy, Rock-a-Billy, Rock-a-Billy, Rock". It went on with that three times and ended up with some slight variation. The *Sunday Pictorial* adapted that to: "Rock-a-Philip, Rock-a-Philip, Rock-a-Philip, Rock". That was the chorus. The verses were totally different.

The complaint was that the newspaper version was an infringement of the literary copyright in the original song. There was no question of music in this case—the infringers had not used music at all. It might be said that there was no copyright as it is difficult to see how the original lines were an original literary work. They are more gibberish than anything else, but that may be too fastidious a view. That, however, is not quite the way that the learned judge disposed of the case. He found against the claim for copyright and disposed of it on these lines (at 70):

"If one had to direct a jury on this question"

—that is to say, whether a parody is an infringement

"one would clearly tell them of the various tests that have been suggested as guiding tests, and it would be proper to emphasise to them this test which Younger J. suggested as to whether the defendant had bestowed such mental labour on what he had taken and subjected it to such revision and alteration as to produce on original work. I cannot help thinking that a jury with that direction would have said that, although it is clear that the article in the *Sunday Pictorial* had its origin in 'Rock-a-Billy', it was produced by sufficient independent new work by Paul Boyle to be in itself, not a reproduction of the original 'Rock-a-Billy', but a new original work derived from 'Rock-a-Billy'. And, that being my conclusion of fact, quite shortly I sat that I am not satisfied that the article in the *Sunday Pictorial* does reproduce a substantial part of the words of the 'Rock-a-Billy' song of which the plaintiffs have the copyright".

In a case of artistic copyright, Falconer J. made some comments on that decision of McNair J. The case is *Schweppes Limited v Wellingtons Limited* [1984] F.S.R. 210, and the article in question was the bottle of Schweppes tonic water with a distinctive label. That is soft drink. The defendants were manufacturers of something known as a tonic bubble bath, which they put in a similar bottle with a very similar label, except that it had the name "Schlurppes" on it instead of "Schweppes". The design was something very similar, but it being for a totally different market there was no question of passing off. One of the points in resisting the claim of copyright infringement which was made by the defendants was that it was a parody. The learned judge deals with that in this way:

"What is said, and it has been said forcibly by Mr Tager, is that this bottle is in the nature of a parody; the article itself is meant to be sold, no doubt, as a joke, and to have the characteristics of a caricature".

Then he goes on to point out that Mr Tager relied on the decision of McNair J. in *Joy Music Limited* and he referred especially to what the headnote in that case said, which was:

"that in considering whether a parody of a literary work constituted an infringement of the copyright in that work the main test to be applied was whether the writer had bestowed such mental labour upon the material he had taken and had subjected it to such revision and alteration as to produce an original work".

Falconer J. goes on:

"and of course it is on that proposition that Mr Tager argues that there is a defence in this particular case to infringement. Put in that form, with all due respect, I do not think that a correct statement of the law. The sole test is whether the defendant's work has reproduced a substantial part of the plaintiff's *ex hypothesi* copyright work. The fact that the defendant in reproducing his work may have himself employed labour and produced something original, or some part of his work which is original, is beside the point if none the less the resulting defendant's work reproduces without the licence of the plaintiff a substantial part of the plaintiff's work. The test every time in my judgment is, as the statute makes perfectly plain: 'Has there been a reproduction in the defendant's work of a substantial part of the plaintiff's work?' "

When considering any question of parody, I accept that test of Falconer J., that the test every time is, as the statute makes perfectly plain: "Has there been a reproduction in the defendant's work or a substantial part of the plaintiff's work?"

Judge Baker examined the facts and concluded that there was no serious question to be tried in respect of the lyrics, but that there was such an issue regarding the music.

3.6.2 Proof of Copying

3.6.2.1 *Francis, Day & Hunter v Bron* [1963] Ch. 587, CA

The plaintiffs claimed that a song, "Why", composed by Mr de Angelis and published by the defendants infringed copyright in their song, "In a Spanish Town". The trial judge, Wilberforce J., found that despite various points of effective similarity, the composer had not intentionally copied and this conclusion was accepted by the Court of Appeal.

Willmer L.J.:

The composer of "Why" was called as a witness, and not only denied copying, but denied that he had ever seen the music of "Spanish Town", or even consciously heard it. He was a man of 33 years of age and had lived most of his life in the United States. He stated that he had been composing music since he was eleven, and had played various instruments in dance bands. In cross examination he admitted that at a younger age he might have heard "Spanish Town", because he had heard a lot of music, but he adhered to his statement that he had never consciously studied it, and said that he did not recall ever playing it. The judge accepted his evidence, and I do not think that we in this court could properly interfere with that finding even if we were invited to do so, which we were not. But the plaintiffs say that that is by no means the end of the case, for Mr de Angelis could well have copied from "Spanish Town" subconsciously. The song having been extensively exploited in the United States, the overwhelming probability (it is said) is that he must have heard it; and the degree of similarity between "Spanish Town" and "Why" is such that an inference of, at any rate, subconscious copying should be drawn. That, it is contended, would be enough to constitute an infringement of the plaintiffs' copyright. The judge, however, decided that there was no sufficient material to justify the inference that Mr de Angelis copied the plaintiffs' work, even subconsciously; and he accordingly dismissed the action. It is to this point that the present appeal has been mainly directed.

Counsel, in presenting his argument on behalf of the defendants, drew attention to the fact that in relation to musical copyright, under section 2 of the Act of 1956, there are only three forbidden processes, *viz.*, "reproduction", "arrangement" and "transcription". Arrangement and transcription, he submitted can be only the result of a conscious and deliberate process; a man cannot arrange or transcribe without knowing that he is doing so. The judge's acceptance of the evidence of Mr de Angelis, therefore, precludes the possibility of finding any infringement of the plaintiffs' copyright by arrangement or transcription. This submission must, I think, be accepted.

Counsel for the defendants conceded that reproduction could possibly be the result of a subconscious process. But he went on to submit that reproduction within the section could mean nothing short of identity. Reproduction, under section 49, may be of a substantial part; but there is no suggestion in the Act of 1956 of any such thing as a "substantial reproduction". In the present case it cannot be said that there is anything approaching identity between the plaintiffs' work and that of Mr de Angelis. Consequently, counsel submitted, there could be no infringement of the plaintiffs' copyright, whether conscious or unconscious, by way of reproduction.

I find myself quite unable to accept this submission, for I can find no warrant for the suggestion that reproduction, within the meaning of the section, occurs only when identity is achieved. This not only offends against common sense, but, I think, is contrary to authority. In *Austin v Columbia Gramophone Co Ltd* [1917–23] Mac. Cop. Cas. 398, the headnote reads:

> "Infringement of copyright in music is not a question of note for note comparison, but of whether the substance of the original copyright work is taken or not".

In that case, Astbury J., quoted from the earlier case of *D'Alamaine v Boosey* (1835) 1 Y & C Ex. 288, where it was laid down that "it must depend on whether the air taken is substantially the same with the original". I accept that as a correct statement of the principle.

On the other side, counsel for the plaintiffs submitted in the first place that Mr de Angelis's denial of copying was wholly irrelevant. For where, as was said to be the case here, a sufficient degree of similarity is shown, and it is further proved that the composer of the second work had access to the earlier work in the sense that he must probably have heard it, an irrebuttable presumption arises that the former has been copied from the latter. No authority was cited in support of this proposition, which, if well-founded, would eliminate the necessity for any further evidence once similarity coupled with access had been proved. In my judgment, the proposition contended for is quite untenable; the most that can be said, it seems to me, is that proof of similarity, coupled with access raises a prima facie case for the defendant to answer.

Counsel for the plaintiffs contended in the alternative that the degree of similarity found by the judge in the present case was such as to compel an inference of copying which, even if subconscious, was sufficient to give the plaintiffs a cause of action for infringement. I confess that I have found the notion of subconscious copying one of some difficulty, for at first sight it would seem to amount to a contradiction in terms, the word "copying" in its ordinary usage connoting what is essentially a conscious process. The text books on copyright make no reference to the subject, and English authority in relation to it is confined to a single dictum of Luxmoore J. in *G Ricordi & Co (London) Ltd v Clayton and Walter Ltd* [1928–35] Mac.C.C. 91. Our attention, however, was called to a number of cases in the U.S. in which the subject has been discussed, and in some of which a decision in favour of the plaintiff has been based on a finding of subconscious copying. It appears to me that the question must be considered in two stages, *viz.*, (i) whether subconscious copying is a psychological possibility; and (ii) if so, whether in a given case it is capable of amounting to an infringement of the plaintiff's copyright.

As to the first of these questions, it was suggested by counsel for the defendants that medical evidence should always be required before a finding of subconscious copying could be justified. I cannot think that this is necessary; for the psychological possibility of subconscious copying was clearly recognised by Luxmoore J. and in the various American decisions, which must be regarded as of high persuasive authority. What Luxmoore J. said in relation to the defendants before him in the *Ricordi* case [1928–35] Mac C.C. 154 was:

> "If there has been any infringement it must have been subconsciously, because the persons responsible knew the air complained of so well that they have taken it because they knew it".

Similarly, in two American cases in which the plaintiff succeeded on the ground of subconscious copying, *viz., Fred Fisher Inc v Dillingham* (1924) 298 Fed. 145, and *Edwards & Deutsch Lithographing Co v Boorman*, the decision was based on the finding of a high degree of familiarity with the plaintiffs' work. From this emerges the conclusion, which seems to me to be consonant with good sense, that, if subconscious copying is to be found, there must be proof (or at least a strong inference) of *de facto* familiarity with the work alleged to be copied. In the present case, on the findings of the judge, this element is conspicuously lacking.

On the second question, *viz.*, whether any subconscious copying proved could amount to an infringement of the plaintiffs' copyright, it seems to me that all that can be said is that at least the dictum of Luxmoore J. envisages the possibility. On this point I do not think that much help is to be derived from the American decisions which have been cited, since the American statute under which they were decided is markedly different in its terms. No evidence of American law was adduced, and in its absence it is not for us to construe the American statute. However (as was pointed out by junior counsel for the plaintiffs) it may be observed that, in order to establish an infringement of copyright, it is not necessary to prove anything in the nature of *mens rea*. The printer, for instance, may be held guilty of infringement though he has no conscious intent.

The conclusion at which I arrive on his part of the case is that subconscious copying is a possibility which, if it occurs, may amount to an infringement of copyright. But in order to establish liability on this ground, it must be shown that the composer of the offending work was in fact familiar with the work alleged to have been copied. This view, I think, is not inconsistent with the submissions put forward by Mr Skone James. In the course of an argument which I found convincing, he submitted that, in considering whether there has been reproduction, so as to constitute an infringement within the Copyright Act 1956, it is wholly irrelevant to inquire whether any copying has been conscious or subconscious. It is for this reason, he modestly suggested, that the text books are silent on the subject of subconscious copying. Mr Skone James presented his argument in four propositions which if I understood him correctly, may be summarised as follows: (i) in order to constitute reproduction, within the meaning of the Act, there must be (a) a sufficient degree of objective similarity between the two works; and (b) some causal connexion between the plaintiff's and the defendant's work. (ii) It is quite irrelevant to inquire whether the defendant was or was not consciously aware of such causal connexion. (iii) Where there is a substantial degree of objective similarity, this of itself will afford prima facie evidence to show that there is a causal connexion between the plaintiff's and the defendant's work; at least, it is a circumstance from which the inference may be drawn. (iv) The fact that the defendant denies that he consciously copied affords some evidence to rebut the inference of causal connexion arising from the objective similarity, but is in no way conclusive.

If this is the right approach (as I think it is), it becomes a simple question of fact to decide whether the degree of objective similarity proved is sufficient, in all the circumstances of the particular case, to warrant the inference that there is a causal connexion between the plaintiffs' and the defendants' work. This is the way in which, as it seems to me, the judge in the present case approached the question which he had to decide. He directed himself as follows:

"The final question to be resolved is whether the plaintiffs' work has been copied or reproduced, and it seems to me that the answer can only be reached by a judgment of fact on a number of composite elements. The degree of familiarity (if proved at all, or properly inferred) with the plaintiffs' work, the character of the work, particularly its qualities of impressing the mind and memory, the objective similarity of the defendants' work, the inherent probability that such similarity as is found could be due to coincidence, the existence of other influences on the defendant composer, and not least the quality of the defendant composer's own evidence on the presence or otherwise in his mind of the plaintiffs' work".

In my judgment that was a proper direction, against which no criticism can fairly be brought.

Willmer L.J. proceeded to accept Wilberforce J.'s conclusion that there was no sufficient material from which to infer subconscious copying.

Upjohn and Diplock L.JJ. delivered concurring judgments.

3.6.3   Acts of Infringement

3.6.3.1   Copyright, Designs and Patents Act 1988, ss.2, 16–27, 178

S.2(1) The owner of the copyright in a work of any description has the exclusive right to do the acts specified in Chapter II as the acts restricted by the copyright in a work of that description.

S.16(1) The owner of the copyright in a work has, in accordance with the following provisions of this Chapter, the exclusive right to do the following acts in the United Kingdom—

  (a) to copy the work (see section 17);

  (b) to issue copies of the work to the public (see section 18);

  (ba) to rent or lend the work to the public (see section 18A);

  (c) to perform, show or play the work in public (see section 19);

  [*(d) to communicate the work to the public (see section 20);*][1]

  (e) to make an adaptation of the work to do any of the above in relation to an adaptation (see section 21);

and those acts are referred to in this Part as the "acts restricted by the copyright".

(2) Copyright in a work is infringed by a person who without the licence of the copyright owner does, or authorises another to do, any of the acts restricted by the copyright.

(3) References in this Part to the doing of an act restricted by the copyright in a work are to the doing of it—

  (a) in relation to the work as a whole or any substantial part of it, and

  (b) either directly or indirectly;

and it is immaterial whether any intervening acts themselves infringe copyright.

(4) This Chapter has effect subject to—

  (a) the provisions of Chapter III (acts permitted in relation to copyright works), and

  (b) the provisions of Chapter VII (provisions with respect to copyright licensing).

S.17(1) The copying of the work is an act restricted by the copyright in every description of copyright work; and references in this Part to copying and copies shall be construed as follows.

(2) Copying in relation to a literary, dramatic, musical or artistic work means reproducing the work in any material form.

This includes storing the work in any medium by electronic means.

(3) In relation to an artistic work copying includes the making of a copy in three dimensions of a two-dimensional work and the making of a copy in two dimensions of a three-dimensional work.

---

[1] Likely change in implementation of the InfoSoc Directive.

(4) Copying in relation to a film or television broadcast includes making a photograph of the whole or any substantial part of any image forming part of the film or broadcast.

(5) Copying in relation to the typographical arrangement of a published edition means making a facsimile copy of the arrangement.

(6) Copying in relation to any description of work includes the making of copies which are transient or are incidental to some other use of the work.

S.18(1) The issue to the public of copies of the work is an act restricted by the copyright in every description of copyright work.

(2) References in this Part to the issue to the public of copies of a work are to the act of putting into circulation copies not previously put into circulation, in the United Kingdom or elsewhere, and not to—

   (a) any subsequent distribution, sale, hiring or loan of those copies, or

   (b) any subsequent importation of those copies into the United Kingdom;

except that in relation to sound recordings, films and computer programs the restricted act of issuing copies to the public includes any rental of copies to the public.

Section 93B imposes a non-assignable right to equitable remuneration, where an author of a literary, dramatic, musical or artistic work, or a film director, has transferred his rental right concerning a sound recording or a film to its producer. Note: s.93A which creates a presumption that such a transfer has taken place under an agreement concerning film production. If necessary the equitable remuneration will be assessed by the Copyright Tribunal (s.93C).

Infringement by rental or lending of work to the public.
18A.(1) The rental or lending of copies of the work to the public is an act restricted by the copyright in—

   (a) a literary, dramatic or musical work,

   (b) an artistic work, other than—

      (i) a work of architecture in the form of a building or a model for a building, or
      (ii) a work of applied art, or

   (c) a film or a sound recording.

(2) In this Part, subject to the following provisions of this section—

   (a) "rental" means making a copy of the work available for use, on terms that it will or may be returned, for direct or indirect economic or commercial advantage, and

   (b) "lending" means making a copy of the work available for use, on terms that it will or may be returned, otherwise than for direct or indirect economic or commercial advantage, through an establishment which is accessible to the public.

(3) The expressions "rental" and "lending" do not include—

   (a) making available for the purpose of public performance, playing or showing in public, communication to the public;

(b) making available for the purpose of exhibition in public; or

(c) making available for on-the-spot reference use.

(4) The expression "lending" does not include making available between establishments which are accessible to the public.

(5) Where lending by an establishment accessible to the public gives rise to a payment the amount of which does not go beyond what is necessary to cover the operating costs of the establishment, there is no direct or indirect economic or commercial advantage for the purposes of this section.

(6) References in this Part to the rental or lending of copies of a work include the rental or lending of the original.

S.19(1) The performance of the work in public is an act restricted by the copyright in a literary, dramatic or musical work.

(2) In this Part "performance", in relation to a work—

(a) includes delivery in the case of lectures, addresses, speeches and sermons, and

(b) in general, includes any mode of visual or acoustic presentation, including presentation by means of a sound recording, film or broadcast of the work.

(3) The playing or showing of the work in public is an act restricted by the copyright in a sound recording, film or broadcast.

(4) Where copyright in a work is infringed by its being performed, played or shown in public by means of apparatus for receiving visual images or sounds conveyed by electronic means, the person by whom the visual images or sounds are sent, and in the case of a performance the performers, shall not be regarded as responsible for the infringement.

[*S.20(1) The communication to the public of the work is an act restricted by the copyright in—*

(a) a literary, dramatic, musical or artistic work,

(b) a sound recording or film, or

(c) a broadcast.

(2) References in this Part to communication to the public are to communication to the public by electronic transmission, and in relation to a work include—

(a) the broadcasting of the work;

(b) inclusion of the work in an on-demand service or other interactive service.

(3) In this Part, "on-demand service" means an interactive service for making a work available to the public by electronic transmission in such a way that members of the public may access the work from a place and at a time individually chosen by them.][1]

---

[1] Form of amendment proposed by the UK Government in August 2002 in order to comply with the InfoSoc Directive, Art. 3.

S.21(1) The making of an adaptation of the work is an act restricted by the copyright in a literary, dramatic or musical work.

For this purpose an adaptation is made when it is recorded, in writing or otherwise.

(2) The doing of any of the acts specified in sections 17 to 20, or subsection (1) above, in relation to an adaptation of the work is also an act restricted by the copyright in a literary, dramatic or musical work.

For this purpose it is immaterial whether the adaptation has been recorded, in writing or otherwise, at the time the act is done.

(3) In this Part "adaptation"—

    (a) in relation to a literary work, other than a computer program or a database, or in relation to a dramatic work, means—

        (i) a translation of work;

        (ii) a version of a dramatic work in which it is converted into a non-dramatic work or, as the case may be, of a non-dramatic work in which it is converted into a dramatic work;

        (iii) a version of the work in which the story or action is conveyed wholly or mainly by means of pictures in a form suitable for reproduction in a book, or in a newspaper, magazine or similar periodical;

    (ab) in relation to a computer program, means an arrangement or altered version of the program or a translation of it;

    (ac) in relation to a database, means an arrangement or altered version of the database or a translation of it;

    (b) in relation to a musical work, means an arrangement or transcription of the work.

(4) In relation to a computer program a "translation" includes a version of the program in which it is converted into or out of a computer language or code or into a different computer language or code.

(5) No inference shall be drawn from this section as to what does or does not amount to copying a work.

Secondary infringement of copyright

S.22 The copyright in a work is infringed by a person who, without the licence of the copyright owner, imports into the United Kingdom, otherwise than for his private and domestic use, an article which is, and which he knows or has reason to believe is, an infringing copy of the work.

S.23 The copyright in a work is infringed by a person who, without the licence of the copyright owner—

    (a) possesses in the course of a business,

    (b) sells or lets for hire, or offers or exposes for sale or hire,

    (c) in the course of a business exhibits in public or distributes, or

    (d) distributes otherwise than in the course of a business to such an extent as to affect prejudicially the owner of the copyright, an article which is, and which he knows or has reason to believe is, an infringing copy of the work.

S.24(1) Copyright in a work is infringed by a person who, without the licence of the copyright owner—

    (a) makes,

    (b) imports into the United Kingdom,

    (c) possesses in the course of a business, or

    (d) sells or lets for hire, or offers or exposes for sale or hire,

an article specifically designed or adapted for making copies of that work, knowing or having reason to believe that it is to be used to make infringing copies.

(2) Copyright in a work is infringed by a person who without the licence of the copyright owner transmits the work by means of a telecommunications system (otherwise than by broadcasting or inclusion in a cable programme service), knowing or having reason to believe that infringing copies of the work will be made by means of the reception of the transmission in the United Kingdom or elsewhere.

S.25(1) Where the copyright in a literary, dramatic or musical work is infringed by a performance at a place of public entertainment, any person who gave permission for that place to be used for the performance is also liable for the infringement unless when he gave permission he believed on reasonable grounds that the performance would not infringe copyright.

(2) In this section "place of public entertainment" includes premises which are occupied mainly for other purposes but are from time to time made available for hire for the purposes of public entertainment.

S.26(1) Where copyright in a work is infringed by a public performance of the work, or by the playing or showing of the work in public, by means of apparatus for—

    (a) playing sound recordings,

    (b) showing films, or

    (c) receiving visual images or sounds conveyed by electronic means, the following persons are also liable for the infringement.

(2) A person who supplied the apparatus, or any substantial part of it, is liable for the infringement if when he supplied the apparatus or part—

    (a) he knew or had reason to believe that the apparatus was likely to be so used as to infringe copyright, or

    (b) in the case of apparatus whose normal use involves a public performance, playing or showing, he did not believe on reasonable grounds that it would not be so used as to infringe copyright.

(3) An occupier of premises who gave permission for the apparatus to be brought onto the premises is liable for the infringement if when he gave permission he knew or had reason to believe that the apparatus was likely to be so used as to infringe copyright.

(4) A person who supplied a copy of a sound recording or film used to infringe copyright is liable for the infringement if when he supplied it he knew or had reason to believe that what he

supplied, or a copy made directly or indirectly from it, was likely to be so used as to infringe copyright.

Infringing copies
S.27(1) In this Part "infringing copy", in relation to a copyright work, shall be construed in accordance with this section.

(2) An article is an infringing copy of its making constituted an infringement of the copyright in the work in question.

(3) Subject to subsection (3A) an article is also an infringing copy if—

(a) it has been or is proposed to be imported into the United Kingdom, and

(b) its making in the United Kingdom would have constituted an infringement of the copyright in the work in question, or a breach of an exclusive licence agreement relating to that work.

(3A) A copy of a work which has previously been sold in any other EEA State, by or with the consent of the copyright owner, is not an infringing copy for the purposes of subsection (3).

(4) Where in any proceedings the question arises whether an article is an infringing copy and it is shown—

(a) that the article is a copy of the work, and

(b) that copyright subsists in the work or has subsisted at any time,

it shall be presumed until the contrary is proved that the article was made at a time when copyright subsisted in the work.

Section 27(6) elaborates the meaning of "infringing copy" for the purposes of some specific sections.

S.178 ... "electronic" means actuated by electric, magnetic, electromagnetic, electrochemical or electromechanical energy and "in electronic form" means in a form usable only by electronic means; "facsimile copy" includes a copy which is reduced or enlarged in scale;

["rental" means any arrangement under which a copy of a work is made available for use for a limited period of time for direct or indirect economic or commercial advantage on terms that it will or may be returned, but excludes any arrangement under which a copy of a work is made available—

(a) for on the spot reference; or

(b) for the purpose of performance in public, exhibition in public, broadcasting or inclusion in a cable programme service;]

"unauthorised", as regards anything done in relation to a work, means done otherwise than—

(a) by or with the licence of the copyright owner, or

(b) if copyright does not subsist in the work, by or with the licence of the author or, in a case where section 11(2) would have applied, the author's employer or, in either case, persons lawfully claiming under him, or

(c) in pursuance of section 48 (copying etc. of certain material by the Crown).

3.6.3.2   *Turner v Performing Right Society* **[1943] Ch. 167, CA**

Two companies performed music to their employees during working hours. The performing rights in works thus used was vested in the Performing Right Society ("P.R.S.") which sought to require the companies to take a licence for the performances. The companies claimed that the performances were not in public.

Lord Greene M.R.:

In the present case the nature of the audience, when properly understood in my opinion, puts the matter beyond doubt. In each case the audience constitutes a substantial part of the working population of the district. It is collected from different households in the district. From time to time groups of work-people or individual workmen or women asked for a particular song to be played by the gramophone record. It is quite obvious, therefore, that the whole object of these performances is to supply to the workpeople something which they like. So far as regards the music, the workpeople are an audience. The fact that it assists their work appears to me to be entirely irrelevant. While the performances are being given and the workpeople are doing their work, they are doing two things at once. They are working and they are enjoying music, which normally is a thing they would enjoy in their leisure hours. Instead of having the music in their leisure hours, they have it while they are working. None the less they are, so far as the music is concerned, an audience listening to music, and the fact that they are working at the same time does not alter that, any more than it alters the fact that a housewife who turns on her radio set while she is doing her housework is listening to the music at the same time as she is doing that work.

In the present case, having regard to the character of the audience and all the relevant facts which bear upon that matter, I have no doubt that these performances were performances in public. In *Jennings v Stephens* [1936] Ch. 469, to which I have referred, I ventured to suggest that in considering the character of the audience the primary matter to consider was the relationship of the audience to the owner of the copyright, rather than the relationship of the audience to the performers. I am confirmed in that view by a consideration of the present case. When the legislature under the Copyright Act conferred upon the owner of copyright a monopoly, it no doubt intended that that monopoly should be a real and not an illusory right of property, and it is, therefore, in my opinion, important to consider whether a particular performance, the character of which is in question, is of a kind calculated to whittle down that monopoly to any substantial extent. To take a case at one end of the scale, a purely domestic performance, or what is sometimes called a quasi-domestic performance, is not a thing which is calculated to whittle down the value of the monopoly. It is a thing which can have no substantial effect in depriving the owner of the copyright of the public from whom he receives the value of the work of his brain and his imagination. If you take the other end of the scale, where there is a performance unquestionably in public, such as at a public theatre or a public concert hall, obviously if that were permitted that would whittle down the value of the monopoly. The monopoly is, of course, confined to performances in public, but in considering whether a performance is in public its effect upon the value to the owner of the copyright of his statutory monopoly is, I venture to think, a consideration to which at any rate great importance should be given.

In the present case counsel for the appellants in the second appeal invited us to pay regard not to any relationship of the audience to the owner of the copyright, but to the relationship of the audience to the performer in the present case. The performer, of course, is the proprietor of the factory who performs the music by turning on the broadcast or setting the gramophone in operation. Whatever may be the value of a consideration of the relationship of the performer to the audience in other cases, it seems to me that in the present case it affords an entirely misleading guide. It could make not the slightest difference, in my opinion, if in the present case the performances had been given not by diffusion through the factory by means of loudspeakers operated by the management, but by a neighbour who sent up a system of diffusion with loudspeakers which could be heard through the factory. The relationship of the performer to the audience in such a case would not have been the same as the relationship of the performer to the audience in the present case. The difference in the relationship could not, it seems to me, affect in the slightest degree the question whether the performance was or was not a performance in public.

Counsel for the appellants in the second appeal said that the parties in this case were all members of a community organised for work. I have already dealt to a certain extent with the work element in this case, but it seems to me impossible to do what counsel for the appellants in the second appeal asks us to do and regard everything that takes place inside the factory in regard to this music as a purely domestic concern of those taking part in it, whether as performer or as audience. The test of the relationship of the audience to the performer seems to me to break down completely in this case, whereas the test which I venture to suggest would, at any rate in a great many cases, and certainly in the present, be the most helpful one, that is, the relationship of the audience to the composer and the effect that the performance has upon his monopoly, is a consideration which does seem to me in the present case to throw a good deal of light upon the situation.

It was said that it was not legitimate to consider what the effect would be of a decision in favour of the appellants having regard to the circumstance that there are thousands of factories in the country employing, no doubt, hundreds of thousands, indeed, millions of workpeople. If these performances can be given without infringement of copyright in these two cases, they can be given in every case. It is perfectly true, of course, to say that two rights do not make a wrong; but for the purpose of discovering the real nature of the audience and the effect on the monopoly of treating these performances as private performances, it does seem to me to be relevant to consider what the result would be if performances of this kind were given in all the other factories in the country. The result would be that the employers of millions of workpeople would be giving to their workpeople without payment the fruit of the brains, skill, imagination and taste of the author, if the author be the owner of the copyright, or the property of his successors in title, without any remuneration to him or them, and would be getting the advantage of that work, taste and skill, in obtaining increased or improved output.

Luxmoore and Goddard L.JJ. delivered concurring judgments.

3.6.3.3 *Sillitoe v McGraw Hill* [1983] F.S.R. 545, Judge Mervyn Davies Q.C.

The defendant company imported and distributed a series of study notes on texts which were set books for "O" level English literature papers. They included Sillitoe's Loneliness of the Long Distance Runner, *Lee's* Cider with Rosie *and Shaw's* St Joan. *The copyright owners of these works sued for secondary infringement by importing and selling within the Copyright Act 1956, s.5(2), (3). The requirement of knowledge in those provisions was specified by the phrase, "if to his knowledge the making of the article constituted an infringement of that copyright, or (in the case of an imported article) would have constituted an infringement of that copyright if the article had been made in the place into which it was imported".*

Judge Mervyn Davies found in each case that the notes took extracts and key phrases from the texts to a degree which amounted to substantial reproduction. He had accordingly to deal with two issues: (i) the knowledge requirement for secondary infringement; (ii) the defences of fair dealing for purposes of research or private study, or for purposes of criticism or review (Copyright Act 1956, s.6(1), (2)).

(i) The knowledge requirement. The defendant's principal argument was that it was acting on the advice of counsel that the notes did not constitute infringement; and that accordingly it could not be acting with the requisite knowledge. As to this Judge Mervyn Davies said:

The onus of proving "knowledge" within section 5(2) and (3) is on the plaintiffs. The plaintiffs have to show that it was to the defendants' knowledge that the printing of the notes would have constituted an infringement, had the notes been printed in England. Mr Jeffs, for the defendants, said that the onus on the plaintiffs was heavy. I agree: see *Infabrics Ltd v Jaytex Shirt Co Ltd* [1978] F.S.R. 463. Mr Jeffs contrasted the wording of section 5(2) and (3) with sections 17(2)(b) and 18(2)(a) of the Act, and referred to *Secretary of State for Trade and Industry v Hart, The Times*, November 30, 1981 and *Laddie et al. on Copyright*, pp.385 and 386. The references to sections 17(2) and 18(2) show that the defendants having knowledge within section 5(2) is not to be read as meaning the defendants having "reasonable grounds for suspecting". . . .

Mr Mummery, for the plaintiffs, started from the basis that "knowledge" within section 5(2) means notice of fact such as would suggest to a reasonable man that a breach of copyright has been or is being committed. That submission is derived from some words of Harvey J. in the Australian case *Albert v Hoffnung & Co Ltd* [1921] S.R. (N.S.W.) 79 at 81, where the Australian equivalent of section 2(2) of the Copyright Act 1911 was under consideration. The *Albert* case was considered in *RCA Corp v Custom Cleared Sales Pty Ltd* (1978) 19 A.L.R. 123, and also reported in [1978] F.S.R. 576. In that case the Court of Appeal were dealing with an Australian provision identical with section 5(3) of the Copyright Act 1956. The judgment of the court includes these words:

> "In other words, the true position is that the court is not concerned with the knowledge of a reasonable man but is concerned with reasonable inferences to be drawn from a concrete situation as disclosed in the evidence as it affects the particular person whose knowledge is in issue".

It follows that one must consider the concrete situation disclosed by the evidence in this case and then decide what knowledge is to be attributed to the defendants, either in the way of express knowledge or knowledge that these particular defendants must have inferred.

Judge Mervyn Davies referred to authorities which did not address the question of belief in the legality of the actions. He continued:

My conclusion is that the question . . . is to be answered in the affirmative, that is that it was to the defendants' knowledge that a printing in England would constitute an infringement. I say that because in my opinion the knowledge mentioned in section 5(2) and (3) is a knowledge of the facts. Once a plaintiff fixes a defendant with notice of the facts relied on as constituting an infringement, the defendant cannot contend that he is without "knowledge" within section 5(2) because he has in good faith a belief that in law no infringement is being committed. There is here no ignorance of facts on which the defendants can rely. On the contrary, they well knew the facts, that is as to subsistence, ownership and the claim that there was a section 5(2) infringement. The defendants are in effect saying that if they are right in law, then there is no infringement and if they are wrong in law, there is no infringement either because they believe the law to be otherwise. What the defendants have done here, and knowing of the plaintiffs' complaints and the facts on which the complaints were based, was to take the risk of finding their legal advice wrong. If a person takes a deliberate risk as to whether what he is doing is wrong in law, I do not see that he can say later that he did not, at the time, know that what he was doing was wrong, if, in the event, his action is held to be wrong.

Following Van Dusen v Kritz [1936] 2 K.B. 176, Merchant Adventurers v Grew [1972] Ch. 242 and Infabrics v Jaytex [1978] F.S.R. 463, Judge Mervyn Davies held on the facts that the defendants were fixed with the requisite knowledge on receipt of the plaintiffs' letters before action and were liable once a grace period of 14 days from the date had elapsed.

(ii) Fair dealing. In regard to fair dealing for purposes of research or private study, Judge Mervyn Davies stated:

The onus of showing that an exception applies is on the defendants. Mr Jeffs contended that section 6(1) is widely drawn and not limited to the actual student, so that if a dealing is fair and for the purposes of private study the subsection applies whether the private study in mind is one's own or that of somebody else. Here, he said, the dealing was for the purpose of private study by the examinees who would acquire the notes. I do not accept that argument. To my mind section 6(1) authorises what would otherwise be an infringement if one is engaged in private study or research. The authors of the notes when writing the notes and thus "dealing" with the original work, were not engaged in private study or research. To my mind *University of London Press Ltd v University Tutorial Press Ltd* [1916] 2 Ch. 601 at 613, affords some support for this view.

In regard to fair dealing for purposes of criticism, Judge Mervyn Davies summarised the issue thus:

A reading of the notes makes plain that there are passages of criticism in all three of them. The plaintiffs accepted that, but do the notes, when reproduced in extract, show themselves to be written for the purposes of criticism only or so preponderantly for those purposes as to be regarded as works of criticism rather than anything else?

He reviewed each instance and concluded that in none did the passages of criticism justify the extensive use of extracts from the text and the summarising of storyline or plot.

In addition, he concluded that there had been no sufficient acknowledgement identifying the working in question, as required for the criticism defence. The defendants had contended that the absence of any express acknowledgement was of no consequence because the notes immediately disclosed the title of the original and the identity of its author:

At first sight this argument appears strongly attractive. But then one sees in the *Shorter Oxford Dictionary* that the dictionary meaning of "acknowledgement" includes "the act of recognising the position or claims of". There is nothing in the notes that suggests in any way that the author of the original work or anyone else has any position or claims in respect of the original work. The original work is treated, so far as appearances go, in the notes, as though it was a non-copyright work. Accordingly, on this ground too I am of the view that the defendants, as to each of the notes, failed to get within section 6(2).

3.6.3.4 *Interstate Parcel Express v Time-Life BV* (1978) 52 A.L.J.R. 9, (1977) 15 A.L.R. 35, HC, Australia

Time Inc published a series of cookery books, (of which it was copyright owner) in the US and granted its Dutch subsidiary, Time-Life BV, an exclusive licence to publish them throughout the world save the US and Canada. The defendants purchased copies of the books from distributors (Raymar) in the US and imported them into Australia, where they substantially undercut the price of the Time-Life edition.

(Sections 37 and 38 of the Australian Copyright Act 1968 are broadly equivalent to the Copyright, Designs and Patents Act 1988, ss.22–27).

Gibbs J.:

It was very properly conceded by Mr Handley on behalf of the appellant that the only issue that arises under these sections in the present case is whether the appellant, when it imported the books into Australia for the purpose of selling them, or sold them in Australia, as the case may be, did so "without the licence of the owner of the copyright".

The word "licence" in sections 37 and 38, as in the more general provisions relating to infringement that are contained in section 35 of the Act, appears to mean no more than "consent", and a licence for the purpose of those sections need not result from a formal grant, but may be given orally or be implied by conduct: see *Copinger and Skone James on Copyright*, (11th ed. 1971), para. 404. There is no suggestion that the appellant had been formally granted a licence by either of the respondents, or had received from either of them any express consent, oral or written, to import the books into Australia or to sell them in Australia. The appellant's submission was that Time Inc. had impliedly consented to the appellant doing these things. It was further submitted that the fact that this consent had been given would have constituted a defence to the action if it had been brought by Time Inc. and was therefore available to the appellant in the action brought by Time-Life, by virtue of section 121 of the Act.

The implied consent of licence was said to have been given by Time Inc. when that corporation, by itself or by Little, Brown and Co if that company was its agent first sold the books in the original course of trade, without imposing any restriction upon their resale anywhere in the world. It was said that this sale impliedly gave to the buyer of the books, and to any person claiming title through him, the consent of Time Inc. to use the books however and wherever he pleased, and therefore to import them into Australia and sell them there.

In support of the argument advanced on behalf of the appellant in favour of the view that the sale of books by or on behalf of the owner of the copyright imports a licence to sell them anywhere in the world, particular reliance was placed upon a line of cases decided in relation to patents. The effect of those cases is stated in *Blanco White: Patents for Inventions and the Protection of Industrial Designs* (11th ed. 1974), para. 3–219 as follows: "A sale of a patented article made by a patentee gives to the purchaser, in the absence of notice to the contrary, licence under the patent to exercise in relation to that article all the normal rights of an owner including the right to re-sell".

Again, at paragraph 10–101, the same learned author says: "In the absence of any express term to the contrary, when a patented article is sold by or with the consent of a patentee (or the proprietor of a registered design) the purchaser will take it together with a full licence to deal with it as if it were not patented. Further, any person into whose hands it may later come is entitled to assume that such a full licence has been given with it; it makes no difference that he may later discover that this was not so, if he was ignorant of it at the time of purchase". It was submitted on behalf of the appellant that a similar principle is applicable to the case of copyright.

This principle of patent law finds its origin in *Betts v Willmott* (1871) LR 6 Ch. App. 239 where it was held that if the owner of a patent manufactures and sells the patented article in France, the sale imports a licence to use the article in England. Lord Hatherley L.C. said, at 245: "When a man purchases an article he expects to have the control of it, and there must be some clear and explicit agreement to the contrary to justify the vendor in saying that he has not given the purchaser his licence to sell the article or to use it wherever he pleases as against himself. He cannot use it against a private assignee of the patent, but he can use it against a person who himself is proprietor of the patent, and has the power of conferring a complete right on him by the sale of the article".

The principle enunciated by Lord Hatherley L.C. is well established in patent law. However, it is not always stated by saying that the sale of the patented article confers a licence to use it. In *Société Anonyme des Manufactures de Glaces v Tilghman's Patent Sand Blast Co* (1883) 25 Ch. D.1 Cotton L.J. said, at 9: "When an article is sold without any restriction on the buyer, whether it is manufactured under one or the other patent, that, in my opinion, as against the vendor gives the purchaser an absolute right to deal with that which he so buys in any way he thinks fit, and of course that includes selling in any country where there is a patent in the possession of and owned by the vendor".

In *National Phonograph Co of Australia Ltd v Menck* [1911] A.C. 336, Lord Shaw of Dunfermline, delivering the judgment of the Judicial Committee, said, at 353: "In their Lordships' opinion, it is thus demonstrated by a clear course of authority, first, that it is open to a licensee, by virtue of his statutory monopoly, to make a sale *sub mode*, or accompanied by restrictive conditions which would not apply in the case of ordinary chattels; secondly that the imposition of these conditions in the case of a sale is not presumed, but, on the contrary, a sale having occurred, the presumption is that the full right of ownership was meant to be vested in the purchaser ...".

These statements seem to accord more with general principles than to say that a sale of an article imports a licence to use it. The sale of an article confers on the buyer all the rights of ownership including the right to use the article, but it seems a misuse of words to say that a person who sells an article consents to its being used in any way that the buyer wishes. However the statement that a patentee who sells a patented article gives the buyer his licence to use it has often been repeated by distinguished judges. In *Badische Anilin und Soda Fabrik v Isler* [1906] 1 Ch. 605 at 610 Buckley J. said: "If a patentee sells the patented article to a purchaser and the purchaser uses it, he, of course, does not infringe. But why? By reason of the fact that the law implies from the sale a licence given by the patentee to the purchaser to use that which he has bought. In the absence of condition this implied licence is a licence to use or sell or deal with the goods as the purchaser pleases ..." And although in *National Phonograph Co of Australia Ltd v Menck* Lord Shaw of Dunfermline expressed his conclusion in the words I have quoted, other passages in his judgment suggest that he accepted that the consent or licence of the patentee to use the article might be implied from the sale: see at 349, 350. The words of Buckley J. in *Badische Anilin und Soda Fabrik v Isler* must be regarded as a correct statement of the patent law. The question is, does the same principle extend to the sale of a book the subject of copyright?

One obvious difference in form between the Patents Act 1932 (Australia) (as amended) and the Copyright Act is that the former Act does not contain any provisions similar to those of sections 37 and 38 of the latter. Mr Handley submitted that this is not a valid point of distinction, because it is nevertheless an infringement of a patent to import and sell a patented article: *Pfizer Corp v Ministry of Health* [1965] A.C. 512 at 557–558, 571. However there is another important difference between the law of patent and the law of copyright. By the grant of a patent in traditional form, a patentee is granted exclusive power to "make, use, exercise and vend" the invention. The sale of a patented article, by the patentee, would be quite futile, from the point of view of the buyer, if the buyer was not entitled either to use or to resell the article which he had bought. It therefore seems necessary, in order to give business efficacy to such a sale, to imply a term that the patentee consents to the use of the patented article by the buyer and those claiming under him. The law accordingly does ordinarily imply the consent of the patentee "to an undisturbed and unrestricted use" of the patented article: *National Phonograph Co of Australia Ltd v Menck* above, at 349. To make such an implication, for the purpose only of avoiding the restrictions upon the use of the article that would otherwise be imposed by the patent, seems to be perfectly consistent with the ordinary rules governing the implication of terms in contracts. However no similar necessity exists to imply a term of this kind upon the sale of a book the subject of copyright. The owner of copyright has not the exclusive right to use or sell the work in which copyright subsists: see section 31 of the Act, and *Copinger and Skone James, op. cit.* para. 1027. The buyer of a book in which copyright subsists does not need the consent of the owner of the copyright to read, or speaking generally to resell the book. The necessity to imply a term in the contract which exists when a patented article is sold does not arise on the sale of a book, the subject of copyright. It was not, and could not be, suggested that the sale of a copy of a book is a licence to do the acts comprised in the copyright and set out in section 31 of the Act.

An owner of copyright who sells a book in which copyright subsists passes to the buyer all the rights of ownership. He does not however consent to any particular use of the book—generally speaking his consent is irrelevant. For the reasons given, the cases on patent law are distinguishable. In some circumstances when the owner of copyright sells a book his consent to a particular use may be implied. For example if the owner of copyright sold in America a commercial quantity of books for delivery to a buyer in Australia, whom he knew to be a bookseller, his consent to the importation of those books into Australia and their sale there might well be implied. In the present case it might be possible to imply the consent of Raymar Inc. to the importation of books into Australia and their resale, if the consent of Raymar Inc. were necessary before such importation and sale could lawfully be effected. However the consent of Raymar Inc. would not be material for the purposes of sections 37 and 38 of the Act. It was rightly conceded by Mr Handley that the transaction between Raymar Inc. and the appellant is irrelevant to the question whether any licence had been given by Time Inc. because Raymar Inc. was not acting as the agent of Time Inc. There is no evidence that when the books were sold by Time Inc. to Little, Brown and Co (if such a sale took place), or when they were sold by Little, Brown and Co to Raymar Inc. there was anything to indicate that the books might subsequently be imported into Australia. It is not possible to imply in the contract between Time Inc. and Little, Brown and Co, or in that between Little, Brown and Co and Raymar Inc. the term that Time Inc. consented to the importation of the books into Australia and their sale in Australia.

I have so far discussed the question with reference to the copyright law of Australia. There was no expert evidence as to the copyright law of the U.S., except as to the effect of the Sherman Act. However we were referred to sections 1 and 27 of Title 17 (Copyright) of The United States Code, which are set out in *Copinger and Skone James, op. cit.* at pp.839, 848.

Although under section 1 a person is entitled to copyright has the exclusive right "to print, reprint, publish, copy and vend the copyrighted work". It is provided by section 27 that "nothing in this title shall be deemed to forbid, prevent, or restrict the transfer of any copy of a copyrighted work the possession of which has been lawfully obtained". It has been held that "Under this provision, where there is lawful ownership transferred to a first purchaser, the copyright holder's power of control in the sale of the copy ceases": *Independent News Co v Williams* (1961) 293 F 2d 510 at 517. It would therefore appear that in the U.S., as in Australia, it is not necessary, in order to give business efficacy to the sale of a book in which copyright subsists, to imply a term that the vendor consents to the purchaser reselling it.

The appellant submitted an alternative argument, that on the sale of the books there was an implied warranty that the buyer should have and enjoy quiet possession of them, and that this warranty would be broken if the appellant was prevented by the owner of the copyright, from importing the books into Australia and selling them there. I need not consider how such a warranty, if given by Time Inc. to Little, Brown and Co or by Little, Brown and Co to Raymar Inc. could be relied upon by the appellant. Nor need I consider how such a warranty, if given by Raymar Inc. to the appellant could be set up by the appellant in an action brought by Time-Life. On any view, such a warranty would be irrelevant for the purposes of the provisions of sections 37 and 38. To warrant that the buyer shall have quiet possession of what he buys is not to warrant that the owner of the copyright consents to the importation of the purchased books into Australia and their sale there after importation, or to warrant that the buyer may import the books into Australia and resell them without the consent which these sections require.

If the arguments of the appellant were correct, sections 37 and 38 would apply only to the importation and sale of (1) articles which already infringed copyright (piratical copies) and (2) articles sold subject to an express restriction on subsequent importation and sale. To construe the sections in this way would limit their provisions in a manner which appears to be quite unwarranted by the words of the provisions themselves. The "licence of the owner of the copyright", of which the sections speak, means the consent of the owner to the importation of the articles into Australia for the purpose of selling them, or to their sale after importation, and such a licence cannot in my opinion be inferred from the mere fact that the owner of the copyright has sold the goods without any express restriction on their subsequent disposal. The provisions of section 135 of the Act, which empowers the owner of the copyright to give notice in writing to the Comptroller General of Customs, with the consequence that the importation of copies of the work in respect of which the notice was given, for the purpose of selling them is prohibited, and with the further consequence that such copies may be seized as forfeited to the Commonwealth, also appear quite inconsistent with the view that the sale of a book by itself implies a licence to import it into Australia for the purpose of resale.

For these reasons I conclude that the appellant did not have the licence of Time Inc. to import the books in question or to resell them after importation. Infringements of the kind described in sections 37 and 38 were accordingly committed. It becomes unnecessary to consider the submission made by Mr Bannon, for the first respondent, that Time Inc. could not validly have given a licence within sections 37 and 38 once it had given the exclusive licence to Time-Life and that in these circumstances section 121 would not assist the appellant, or allow the appellant to succeed, at least in relation to the second consignment of books, having regard to the knowledge with which it acted.

It seems apparent that sections 37 and 38 of the Act contemplate that the owner of copyright in a book may make regional arrangements for the distribution of copies, so as to prevent the importation into Australia for sale of books which have been sold elsewhere in the world. The appellant did not base any submission upon the provisions of the Trade Practices Act 1974 (Australia) (as amended) and no argument was addressed to us as to the possible effect of that Act on such arrangements. I accordingly express no view, one way or the other, upon that question.

The conclusion reached by Bowen C.J. in Eq. was in my opinion correct.

I would dismiss the appeal.

3.6.3.5   *L.A. Gear Inc v Hi-Tec Sports plc* [1992] F.S.R. 121, CA

An employee of the plaintiff sportswear company designed the "Fire" sports shoe for men and adapted the design to produce the "Flame" shoe for women. The plaintiff claimed copyright in "drawing 1" (the design of the Fire shoe) and "drawings 2 and 3" (the design of the Flame shoe). It considered that the "Flair" shoe that the defendant imported from Korea shortly after the "Fire" and "Flame" shoes appeared was a copy of its shoes. Its solicitors wrote a letter before action to the defendant on August 29, 1989 enclosing a copy of drawing 2 and claiming copyright therein, wrote again on September 18, and on October 4, sent the defendant a copy of drawing 1. The trial judge and the Court of Appeal found that the "Flair" shoe was an infringing copy of drawing 1, but the defendant claimed that at the date of the commencement of the pro-ceedings (October 9) it neither knew nor had any reason to believe that this was the case and so had a defence to copyright infringement under s.23 of the Act. Nourse L.J. (with whom the other members of the Court of Appeal agreed) said:

The fourth question is whether the defendant had "reason to believe" that its "Flair" shoe was an infringing copy of the "Fire" shoe within section 23.

Mr Purvis [counsel for the defendant] accepted that if the necessary reason to believe existed at the date of the issue of the writ, October 9, 1989, then the fourth question must be decided in favour of the plaintiff. Moreover, he accepted the judge's interpretation of the words "reason to believe":

> "Nevertheless, it seems to me that 'reason to believe' must involve the concept of knowledge of facts from which a reasonable man would arrive at the relevant belief. Facts from which a reasonable man might suspect the relevant conclusion cannot be enough. Moreover, as it seems to me, the phrase does connote the allowance of a period of time to enable the reasonable man to evaluate those facts so as to convert the facts into a reasonable belief."

Mr Purvis placed particular reliance on the last sentence in this passage. He emphasised that it was not until Wednesday, October 4, that the defendant received a copy of drawing 1. That left insufficient time before Monday, October 9, for the defendant to consider that drawing and make the necessary enquiries, for example from the employee in Korea, so as to bring it to a state of reasonable belief that its own shoe was an infringing copy of the plaintiff's.

This argument must ... be rejected. Here Mr Baldwin's [counsel for the plaintiff] primary submission was that the widespread promotion of the plaintiff's shoes at fairs and exhi-bitions and its widespread advertising formed a sufficient basis for an inference that both the plaintiff's shoes had come fully to the defendant's attention before the end of August 1989. Alternatively, submitted Mr Baldwin, from August 30 onwards the defendant had had a copy of drawing 2 representing a shoe which was of much the same design as the

"Fire" shoe. Moreover, in the letter of September 18 the defendant was told that the "Flame" shoe had been designed in conjunction with the "Fire" shoe and that the plaintiff's solicitors would be obtaining the early design drawings for the "Fire" shoe in order to show how the "Flame" shoe was conceived. It would in any event have been a matter of common knowledge in the trade that shoes of this kind could only be designed from drawings.

I reject Mr Baldwin's primary submission, but accept his alternative submission. I think it very clear that by October 9 at the latest the defendant had knowledge of facts from which a reasonable man would have believed that its shoe was an infringing copy of drawing 1. The key event was the defendant's receipt of the letter of September 18. There was plenty of time between then and October 9 for the facts to be evaluated and converted into a reasonable belief. Since the test is an objective one, there is no possibility of this issue being decided in favour of the defendant at a trial. I would therefore decide the fourth question, like the first three, in favour of the plaintiff.

Staughton L.J. agreed with Nourse L.J. and added this comment:

Even if the defendant had not had the knowledge required by section 23 when the writ was issued on October 9, 1989, I do not consider that this would necessarily have been an answer to the claim for an injunction. By that date the defendant had demonstrated an intention to deal in shoes which did, in fact, constitute a secondary infringement. If in the course of proceedings the defendant had acquired the relevant knowledge and had the opportunity to digest it, but still was not disposed to admit that plaintiff's right, in my opinion an injunction might well have been justified. Other remedies, however, such as delivery up or destruction, would not have been appropriate.

3.6.4   Authorising Infringement

3.6.4.1   *Moorhouse v University of New South Wales* **[1976] R.P.C. 151; [1975] A.L.R. 193, HC, Australia**

B twice copied a story from the plaintiff's book, "The Americans, Baby" on a self-service coin-in-the-slot photocopying machine in the University's library. The proceedings were in the nature of a test case to determine whether the University was thereby liable for infringement of copyright in the story. The University was alleged to have authorised the act of unlicensed copying. (Section 40 of the Australian Copyright Act 1968 is broadly equivalent to s.29 of the 1988 Act, and s.49 to section 37ff.)

Gibbs J.:

The word "Authorise", in legislation of similar intendment to section 36 of the Act, has been held judicially to have its dictionary meaning of "sanction, approve, countenance": *Falcon v Famous Players Film Co Ltd* [1926] 2 K.B. 474 at 491: *Adelaide Corp v Australasian Performing Right Association Ltd* (1928) 40 C.L.R. 481 at 489, 497; [1928] A.L.R. 127. It can also mean "permit", as in *Adelaide Corp v Australasian Performing Right Association Ltd* 40 C.L.R. at 497–8, 503. "Authorise" and "permit" appear to have been treated as synonymous. A person cannot be said to authorise an infringement of copyright unless he has some power to present it (40 C.L.R. at 497–8, 503). Express or formal permission or sanction, or active conduct indicating approval, is not essential to constitute an author- isation: "Inactivity or indifference, exhibited by acts of commission or omission, may reach a degree from which an authorisation or permission may be inferred": *Adelaide Corp v Australasian Performing Right Association Ltd* at 504. However, the word "authorise" connotes a mental element and it could not be inferred that a person had, by mere inac- tivity, authorised something to be done if he neither knew nor had reason to suspect that the act might be done, Knox C.J. and Isaacs J. referred to this mental element in their dissenting judgments in *Adelaide Corp v Australasian Performing Right Association Ltd.* Knox C.J. (p.487) held that indifference or omission is "permission" where the party charged (amongst other things) "knows or has reason to anticipate or suspect that the particular act is to be or is likely to be done". Isaacs J. apparently considered that it is enough if the person sought to be made liable "knows or has reason to know or believe" that the particular act of infringement "will or may" be done (see at 490–491). This latter statement may be too widely expressed: *cf. Sweet v Parsley* [1970] A.C. 132 at 165; [1969] 1 All E.R. 347 at 363–4. It seems to me to follow from these statements of principle that a person who has under his control the means by which an infringement of copyright may be committed—such as a photocopying machine—and who makes it available to other per- sons, knowing, or having reason to suspect, that it is likely to be used for the purpose of committing an infringement and omitting to take reasonable steps to limit its use to legitimate purposes, would authorise any infringement that resulted from its use. Cases such as *Mellor v Australian Broadcasting Commission* [1940] A.C. 491; [1940] 2 All E.R. 20, and *Winstone v Wurlitzer Automatic Phonograph Co of Australia Pty Ltd* [1946] V.L.R. 338 are consistent with this view. Although in some of the authorities it is said that the person who authorises an infringement must have knowledge or reason to suspect that the par- ticular act of infringement is likely to be done, it is clearly sufficient if there is knowledge or reason to suspect that any one of a number of particular acts is likely to be done, as for example, where the proprietor of a shop installs a gramophone and supplies a number of records any one of which may be played on it: *Winstone v Wurlitzer Automatic Phonograph Co of Australia Pty Ltd* above.

The University adopted a number of measures with a view to preventing the machines from being used to commit infringements. Each year it issued library guides and it was found by the learned trial judge that most, if not all, students commencing at the University would receive a library guide for the year of commencement and a lesser number of students would receive library guides later in their course. It thus appears that it was unlikely that all users of the library would have received any particular current library guide, and still less likely that all would have carefully read it. I find it unnecessary to consider the contents of the library guides issued in the years before 1973. The library guide for 1973 was published in a loose-leaf form and contained a bookmark on one side of which there appears, under the heading "Copyright" the following notice:

"Reader [*sic*] have a responsibility to obey the law under the Copyright Act 1968."

"A copy of the Act is available in the photocopying room and there is an extract of relevant sections on each machine."

"Photocopying may be done for the purpose of research or for private study and when a copy of the item to be copied has not previously been supplied to the person making the photocopy."

The notice did not mention that copying for the purpose of research or private study was only permissible if it amounted to a fair dealing with the work, although to have said that and no more would not have proved enlightening to most users of the library. In fact a copy of the Act was available in the photocopying room, but to provide a copy of a statute whose meaning would be obscure to the layman would not be an effective way of conveying to the users of the library advice as to how they should act to obey the law of copyright. There was, however, a notice on each machine. To place a clearly worded and accurate notice on each machine in a position where it could not be overlooked would be one measure which might be expected to have some value in informing users of the library of the limits which the University imposed on the permission which it gave them to use the machines. However, the notices in fact placed on the machines were ill adapted to that purpose. They merely set out the provisions of section 49 of the Act. Those provisions, as I have said, apply only where a copy is made by or on behalf of a librarian; they have no application where a person using the library makes a copy for himself. The notices placed on the machines were irrelevant to the position of those persons to whose attention they were intended to be directed. A further step taken by the University was to appoint attendants whose duties included the supervision of the use of the machines. The University librarian was asked to tell the court what instructions he had given to these attendants, and he replied that he had circulated the relevant provisions of the Act to all members of the staff. He continued: "I had asked those people to supervise the machines, to within their competence, in which it was with the Act, see that it was observed. In particular I asked them to watch out for people who were using the machine for an excessive time or who appeared to be copying old books." No attendant was called to give evidence as to the manner in which these duties were carried out. However, Miss Stockman, a student who had been at the University for about three years, gave evidence of her own experience in making photocopies; the only functions which she had ever observed performed by an attendant related to the maintenance of the machines.

The fatal weakness in the case for the University is the fact that no adequate notice was placed on the machines for the purpose of informing users that the machines were not to be used in a manner that would constitute an infringement of copyright. It is unnecessary to consider what the position would have been in the present case if the notices on the machines had been sufficient. The fact is that the notices actually placed on the machines, which set out section 49, were completely ineffective for the purpose for which they were apparently intended.

Jacobs and McTiernan JJ. delivered concurring judgments.

3.6.4.2 *Performing Right Society v Harlequin Record Shops* **[1979] F.S.R. 233,** Browne-Wilkinson J.

The defendants played records continuously in their shops as a known means of encouraging purchases. The plaintiff society, which owned the performing right aspect of the copyright musical works thus played claimed for infringement by performance in public. The defendant denied this and relied, in the alternative, on an implied licence from the composer or publisher to use the work in this way in order to promote sales of the record, from which they would benefit.

Browne-Wilkinson J., after reviewing the facts, said:

On this factual basis the defendants mount their first argument as follows. They say that the authorities show that in considering whether a performance is or is not in public, a most important question is whether the performance injures the composer or interferes with his proprietary rights. Moreover the authorities show that it is also important to see whether the performance is given to an audience from whom the composer would expect to receive a fee: this is what I understand Greene L.J. to have meant by the "owner's public" in *Jennings v Stephens* [1936] 1 All E.R. 409 and *Performing Right Society v Gillette Industries Ltd* [1943] 1 All E.R. 228. Then the argument goes, since restraining the performances in record shops would reduce the sale of records (causing a corresponding drop in recording royalties received by the composer) far from injuring the original owner of the copyright, performances in record shops positively benefit him. Moreover no composer would regard an audience of persons whose only common factor is that they are potential customers of records of his work as an audience for performances to which he would expect to receive a fee, *i.e.* they are not part of his public. Therefore, it is said, on the authorities the performance is not "in public".

In my judgment this first argument of the defendants is incorrect for a number of reasons. First, and to my mind decisively, its legal basis is defective. It is established that in deciding whether a performance is "in public" the character of the audience is the decisive factor. The authorities relied on by the defendants were cases in which the court had to decide whether a performance was properly called "public" when given to an audience which had certain features pointing to the performance being public and other features pointing to the performance being private: for example performances given to members of clubs and performances given by employers to employees. In such cases there is a relationship between the giver of the performance and the audience which raises the possibility of the performance being treated as being in private and the court has to decide whether the public or private features are to prevail. But in my judgment it is not a correct use of authority to lift passages from judgments dealing with performances capable of being described as being either public or private and to rely on them as authority for treating the words "in public" as not extending to a performance which on any normal meaning of the words could not be treated as anything but "public". In my judgment a performance given to an audience consisting of the persons present in a shop which the public at large are permitted, and indeed encouraged, to enter without payment or invitation with a view to increasing the shop owner's profit can only properly be described as a performance in public. I do not think the decisions relied on provide any authority for attaching to the words "in public" a special meaning which, in ordinary usage, they cannot bear.

I receive some support for this view from the decisions in *Performing Right Society v Hawthorns Hotel (Bournemouth) Ltd* [1933] Ch. 855 (in which music played in a hotel was held to be in public) and *Performing Right Society v Camelo* [1936] 3 All E.R. 557 (in which performances audible in a restaurant were treated as being "in public", though the point was not argued in that case). In this connection it was interesting that one of the witnesses, whose company runs a chain or record shops, drew a distinction between playing records to the staff of the shop (which he said was private) and to customers in the shop (which he said was public).

Even if I am wrong in this view I think there is another ground on which the defendants' first argument fails. It rests on the assumption that the court has to compare the position of the original copyright owner if records are played in record shops with his position if no records are played because the plaintiff society obtains an injunction. I am not clear how this argument works when the original owner of the copyright no longer owns the per- forming rights. But even if it is right still to treat the matter as though all the rights are still in one hand, I do not think the argument is correct. Its legal basis is that one has to look to see if, by permitting the performance without a fee, the owner of the rights will be injured. If the position is that such owner can expect that the owners of record shops, rather than suffer the loss by not playing records at all, will agree to pay a fee to the Society, the composer will be getting the best of both worlds: not only will his records continue to be sold as heretofore, but also via the Society he will get the benefit of the additional fee. I do not think it is for me to decide whether or not record shops in general will agree to pay the fee. But I am quite satisfied that the certainty of detriment by them refusing to do so has not been demonstrated in this case. Many record shop owners have already started to pay licence fees. The managing director of the defendant company and the managing director of another company running some 22 record shops (who was speaking for himself alone and not on behalf of his board) both said that rather than stop playing records in their shops, they would or would be likely to pay the fee, albeit reluctantly. The commercially prudent course would seem to be for the owner of a record shop to pay the fee rather than discontinue the playing of records. The only evidence of anyone acting against his com- mercial interest was from a gentleman who was acting on supposed principle. I think Mr Millett, for the Society, put the matter correctly when he said that it was for the owner of the performing rights to decide whether or not to try to get a fee for such performances: one of the rights which he possesses is the right to decide whether or not to charge a fee for performances to possible purchasers of records and that right is invaded by the defendant company's conduct. If a composer might take the view that a fee should be charged for performances to would-be purchasers of his work, such audiences form part of his public (in Greene L.J.'s sense) and by unauthorised performances the record shops are infringing his rights.

Browne-Wilkinson J. refused, on the evidence, to find that any licence could be implied such as was alleged to arise from the desirability of promotion.

3.6.4.3 *CBS Songs v Amstrad* [1988] R.P.C. 567, HL

Amstrad manufactured a twin-deck tape recorder. Sales literature encouraged home taping but warned that "The recording and playback of certain material may only be possible with permission. Please refer to the Copyright Act 1956, and the Performers' Protection Acts 1958–1972". The British Phonographic Industry asserted that this constituted infringement of copyright of its members, particularly in pop-song sound recordings. The litigation which was subject of consolidated appeal to the House of Lords comprised an action for a declaration of non-infringement by Amstrad and an action to restrain sale of the recorders and other relief brought in representative form on behalf of BPI. It was argued that Amstrad were liable on a number of grounds: (i) authorising infringement under the Copyright Act 1956, s.1, either by marketing the recorder or by the form of advertisement used; (ii) joint infringement with purchasers who copied unlawfully; (iii) inciting commission of tort of infringement; (iv) inciting commission of criminal offences under the 1956 Act, s.21; (v) negligence through failure to prevent, discourage or warn against infringement.

Lord Templeman (for the House of Lords):

BPI's initial submissions are that Amstrad "authorised" infringement and that Amstrad is a joint infringer together with any person who uses an Amstrad machine for the purpose of making an infringing reproduction of a recording in which copyright subsists. Section 1(1) of the 1956 Act confers on the copyright owners in a record the "exclusive right ... to authorise other persons" to copy the record. BPI submit that by selling a model which incorporates a double-speed twin-tape recorder Amstrad "authorise" the purchaser of the model to copy a record in which copyright subsists and therefore Amstrad infringe the exclusive right of the copyright owner. My Lords, twin-tape recorders, fast or slow, and single-tape recorders, in addition to their recording and playing functions, are capable of copying on to blank tape, directly or indirectly, records which are broadcast, records on discs and records on tape. Blank tapes are capable of being employed for recording or copying. Copying may be lawful or unlawful. Every tape recorder confers on the operator who acquires a blank tape the facility of copying; the double-speed twin-tape recorder provides a modern and efficient facility for continuous playing and continuous recording and for copying. No manufacturer and no machine confers on the purchaser authority to copy unlawfully. The purchaser or other operator of the recorder determines whether he shall copy and what he shall copy. By selling the recorder Amstrad may facilitate copying in breach of copyright but do not authorise it.

BPI's next submission is that Amstrad by their advertisement authorise the purchaser of an Amstrad model to copy records in which copyright subsists. Amstrad's advertisement drew attention to the advantages of their models and to the fact that the recorder incorporated in the model could be employed in the copying of modern records. But the advertisement did not authorise the unlawful copying of records; on the contrary, the footnote warned that some copying required permission and made it clear that Amstrad had no authority to grant that permission. If Amstrad had considered the interests of copyright owners, Amstrad could have declined to incorporate double-tape double-speed recorders in Amstrad's models or could have advertised the illegality of home copying. If Amstrad had deprived themselves of the advantages of offering improved recording facilities, other manufacturers would have reaped the benefit. The effect of double-tape double-speed recorders on the incidence of home copying is altogether speculative. If Amstrad had advertised the illegality of home copying the effect would have been minimal. Amstrad's advertisement was deplorable because Amstrad thereby flouted the rights of copyright owners. Amstrad's advertisement was cynical because Amstrad advertised the increased efficiency of a facility capable of being employed to break the law. But the operator of an Amstrad tape recording facility, like all other operators, can alone decide whether to record or play and what material is to be recorded. The Amstrad advertisement is open to severe criticism but no purchaser of an Amstrad model could reasonably deduce from the facilities incorporated in the model or from Amstrad's advertisement that Amstrad possessed or purported to possess the authority to grant any required permission for a record to be copied.

In *Monckton v Pathé Frères Pathephone Ltd* [1914] 1 K.B. 395 at 403 Buckley L.J. said: "The seller of a record authorizes, I conceive, the use of the record, and such use will be a performance of the musical work". In that case a performance of the musical work by the use of the record was bound to be an infringing use and the record was sold for that purpose. In *Evans v E Hulton & Co Ltd* (1924) 131 L.T. 534 at 535; [1924] All E.R. Rep 224 at 225–226 Tomlin J. said:

"... where a man sold the rights in relation to a [manuscript] to another with a view to its production, and it was in fact produced, both the English language and common sense required him to hold that this man had 'authorised' the printing and publication."

The object of the sale, namely publication, was bound to infringe. In *Falcon v Famous Players Film Co* [1926] 2 K.B. 474 the defendants hired to a cinema a film based on the plaintiff's play. It was held that the defendants infringed the plaintiff's exclusive right conferred by the Copyright Act 1911 to authorise a performance of the play. Here again, the hirer sold the use which was only capable of being an infringing use. Bankes L.J., following *Monckton v Pathé Frères Pathephone Ltd* and *Evans v E Hulton & Co Ltd*, accepted that for the purpose of the 1911 Act the expression "authorise" meant "sanction, approve, and countenance" (at 491). Atkin L.J. said (at 499):

"... to 'authorize' means to grant or purport to grant to a third person the right to do the act complained of, whether the intention is that the grantee shall do the act on his own account, or only on account of the grantor ..."

In the present case, Amstrad did not sanction, approve or countenance an infringing use of their model and I respectfully agree with Atkin L.J. and with Lawton L.J. in the present case that in the context of the Copyright Act an authorisation means a grant or purported grant, which may be express or implied, of the right to do the act complained of (see [1986] F.S.R. 159 at 207). Amstrad conferred on the purchaser the power to copy but did not grant or purport to grant the right to copy.

In *Moorhouse v University of New South Wales* [1976] R.P.C. 151 at 159, in the High Court of Australia, where the facilities of a library included a photocopying machine, Gibbs J. said:

"... a person who has under his control the means by which an infringement of copyright may be committed—such as a photocopying machine—and who makes it available to other persons, knowing, or having reason to suspect, that it is likely to be used for the purpose of committing an infringement, and omitting to take reasonable steps to limit its use to legitimate purposes, would authorise any infringement that resulted from its use."

Whatever may be said about this proposition, Amstrad have no control over the use of their models once they are sold. In this country the duties of some libraries are defined by the Copyright (Libraries) Regulations 1957 (S.I. 1957 No. 868), made under section 15 of the 1956 Act.

In *CBS Inc v Ames Records and Tapes Ltd* [1981] 2 All E.R. 812; [1982] Ch. 91 Whitford J. held that a record library which lent out records and simultaneously offered blank tapes for sale at a discount did not authorise the infringement of copyright in the records. He said ([1981] 2 All E.R. 812; at 821; [1982] Ch. 91 at 106):

"Any ordinary person would, I think, assume that an authorisation can only come from somebody having or purporting to have authority and that an act is not authorised by somebody who merely enables or possibly assists or even encourages another to do that act, but does not purport to have any authority which he can grant to justify the doing of the act."

This precisely describes Amstrad.

In *RCA Corp v John Fairfax & Sons Ltd* [1982] R.P.C. 91 at 100, in the Supreme Court of New South Wales, Kearney J. approved a passage in Laddie Prescott and Vitoria *The Modern Law of Copyright* (1980), p.403, paragraph 12.9, in these terms:

"... a person may be said to authorize another to commit an infringement if the one has some form of control over the other at the time of infringement or, if he has no such control, is responsible for placing in the other's hands materials which by their nature are almost inevitably to be used for the purpose of an infringement."

This proposition seems to me to be stated much too widely.

As Whitford J. pointed out in *CBS Inc v Ames Records and Tapes Ltd* [1981] 2 All E.R. 812 at 821; [1982] Ch. 91 at 107:

"... you can home tape from bought records, borrowed records, borrowed from friends or public libraries, from the playing of records over the radio, and indeed, at no expense, from records which can be obtained for trial periods on introductory offers from many record clubs who advertise in the papers, who are prepared to let you have up to three or four records for a limited period of trial free of any charge whatsoever."

These borrowed records together with all recording machines and blank tapes could be said to be "materials which by their nature are almost inevitably to be used for the purpose of an infringement". But lenders and sellers do not authorise infringing use.

For these reasons, which are to be found also in the judgments of the Court of Appeal ([1986] F.S.R. 159 at 207, 210, 217), I am satisfied that Amstrad did not authorise infringement.

BPI next submitted that Amstrad were joint infringers; they became joint infringers if and as soon as a purchaser decided to copy a record in which copyright subsisted; Amstrad could become a joint infringer not only with the immediate purchaser of an Amstrad model but also with anyone else who at any time in the future used the model to copy records. My Lords, Amstrad sells models which include facilities for receiving and recording broadcasts, disc records and taped records. All these facilities are lawful although the recording device is capable of being used for unlawful purposes. Once a model is sold Amstrad has no control over or interest in its use. In these circumstances the allegation that Amstrad is a joint infringer is untenable. In *Townsend v Haworth* (1875) 48 L.J. Ch. 770 the defendant sold chemicals to be used by the purchaser in infringement of patent and agreed to indemnify the purchaser if the patent should prove to be valid. Mellish L.J. said (at 773):

"Selling materials for the purposes of infringing a patent to the man who is going to infringe it, even although the party who sells it knows that he is going to infringe it and indemnifies him, does not by itself make the person who so sells an infringer. He must be a party with the man who so infringes, and actually infringe."

Counsel for BPI relied on the decision in *Innes v Short and Beal* (1898) 15 R.P.C. 449. In that case the defendant Short sold powdered zinc and gave instructions to a purchaser to enable the purchaser to infringe a process patent. Bingham J. said (at 452):

"There is no reason whatever why Mr Short should not sell powdered zinc, and he will not be in the wrong, though he may know or expect that the people who buy it from him are going to use it in such a way it will amount to an infringement of Mr Innes' patent rights. But he must not ask the people to use it in that way, and he must not ask the people to use it in that way in order to induce them to buy his powdered zinc from him."

Assuming that decision to be correct, it does not assist BPI because in the present case Amstrad did not ask anyone to use an Amstrad model in a way which would amount to an infringement.

In *Dunlop Pneumatic Tyre Co Ltd v David Moseley & Sons Ltd* [1904] 1 Ch. 612 the defendant sold tyre covers which were an essential feature of a combination patent for tyres and rims. The tyre covers were adapted for use in the manner described in the patent but not necessarily solely for use in that manner. Swinfen Eady J. said that probably most of the "covers would ultimately form part of" one or other of the patented methods but that—

"those combinations do not exhaust the purposes to which the covers may be put, and that they would be useful for other purposes in connection with other tyres ..."

(See [1904] 1 Ch. 164 at 171.) Swinfen Eady J., upheld by the Court of Appeal (see [1904] 1 Ch. 612), decided that the defendants did not infringe.

In *The Koursk* [1924] P. 140 at 156; [1924] All E.R. Rep. 168 at 175, where the question was whether the navigators of two ships had committed two separate torts or one tort in which they were both tortfeasors, Scrutton L.J. adopted the passage in *Clerk and Lindsell on Torts* (7th ed., 1921) p.59 to the effect that:

"Persons are said to be joint tortfeasors when their respective shares in the commission of the tort are done in furtherance of a common design ..."

In the present case there is no common design between Amstrad and anybody else to infringe copyright.

In *Rotocrop International Ltd v Genbourne Ltd* [1982] F.S.R. 241 Graham J. held, perhaps surprisingly, that there was novelty in a patent for a compost bin with removable panels and, less surprisingly, that a rival manufacturer who made and sold infringing bins in parts with assembly instructions was a joint tortfeasor with his customers. In that case, as in *Innes v Short and Beal* (1898) 15 R.P.C. 449, the vendor and the purchaser had a common design to carry out an infringing act.

In *Belegging- en Exploitatiemaatschappij Lavender BV v Witten Industrial Diamonds Ltd* [1979] F.S.R. 59 the defendants were alleged to have sold diamond grit for the sole purpose of making grinding tools in which it was to be embedded in a resin bond as part of a grinding material patented by the plaintiffs. Buckley L.J. held (at 66) that the defendants could not be infringers unless they—

"sold the grits in circumstances which in some way made them participants in their subsequent embodiment in resin bonded grinding wheels, or that they induced someone so to embody them ..."

My Lords, joint infringers are two or more persons who act in concert with one another pursuant to a common design in the infringement. In the present case there was no common design. Amstrad sold a machine and the purchaser or the operator of the machine decided the purpose for which the machine should from time to time be used. The machine was capable of being used for lawful or unlawful purposes. All recording machines and many other machines are capable of being used for unlawful purposes but manufacturers and retailers are not joint infringers if purchasers choose to break the law. Since Amstrad did not make or authorise other persons to make a record embodying a recording in which copyright subsisted, Amstrad did not entrench on the exclusive rights granted by the 1956 Act to copyright owners and Amstrad was not in breach of the duties imposed by the Act.

BPI submit, however, that, if the 1956 Act is defective to protect them, they are entitled to the protection of the common law. As a foundation for this submission BPI seek to elevate the quality of the rights granted by the Act. They point out that in section 17(1) of the Act the owner of copyright in any action for infringement is entitled to all such relief as is available in any corresponding proceedings in respect of infringements of other proprietary rights, that copyright is an example of intellectual property and that, in *Macmillan & Co Ltd v K & J Cooper* (1923) L.R. 51 Ind.App. 109 at 118, Lord Atkinson said that an infringer of copyright disobeyed the injunction, "Thou shalt not steal". My Lords, these considerations cannot enhance the rights of owners of copyright or extend the ambit of infringement. The rights of BPI are derived from statute and not from the Ten Commandments. Those rights are defined by Parliament, not by the clergy or the judiciary. The rights of BPI conferred by the 1956 Act are in no way superior or inferior to any other legal rights; if BPI prove that on the true construction of the Act Amstrad and Dixons have infringed the rights conferred on BPI by the Act, the court will grant appropriate and effective reliefs and remedies. But the court will not invent additional rights or impose fresh burdens.

On behalf of BPI it was submitted that even if Amstrad did not authorise infringement and were not themselves infringers, nevertheless the activities of Amstrad in the sale and advertisement of Amstrad's models constitute a common law tort. The suggested torts were three in number, namely incitement to commit a tort, incitement to commit a criminal offence and negligence.

BPI base their submission on incitement on a passage in *Lumley v Gye* (1853) 2 E. & B. 216 at 232; [1843–60] All E.R. Rep. 208 at 214 where Erle J. said:

> "It is clear that the procurement of the violation of a right is a cause of action in all instances where the violation is an actionable wrong, as in violations of a right to property, whether real or personal, or to personal security: he who procures the wrong is a joint wrong-doer, and may be sued, either alone or jointly with the agent, in the appropriate action for the wrong complained of."

In *Lumley v Gye* an opera singer and the defendant theatre owner were joint wrongdoers. They had a common design that the opera singer should break her contract with the plaintiff theatre owner, refuse to sing in the plaintiff's theatre and instead sing in the defendant's theatre. The plaintiff's cause of action against the opera singer lay in contract, and the plaintiff's cause of action against the defendant lay in tort. But both the opera singer and the defendant were joint wrongdoers participating in an unlawful common design.

BPI referred to *Belegging- en Exploitatiemaatschappij Lavender BV v Witten Industrial Diamonds Ltd* [1979] F.S.R. 59 at 66, where Buckley L.J. said:

> "The plaintiffs do not only assert infringement by the defendants. They also say that the defendants have procured, counselled and/or aided other persons to infringe. This may perhaps amount to an allegation of indirect infringement by the defendants themselves, but I am inclined to think that it is a claim in respect of a distinct suggested tort of procuring infringement by others (based upon the principle enunciated by Erle J. in *Lumley v Gye* (1853) 2 E. & B. 216 at 231; [1843–60] All E.R. Rep. 208 at 213 ..."

My Lords, I accept that a defendant who procures a breach of copyright is liable jointly and severally with the infringer for the damages suffered by the plaintiff as a result of the infringement. The defendant is a joint infringer; he intends and procures and shares a common design that infringement shall take place. A defendant may procure an infringement by inducement, incitement or persuasion. But in the present case Amstrad does not procure infringement by offering for sale a machine which may be used for lawful or unlawful copying and it does not procure infringement by advertising the attractions of its machine to any purchaser who may decide to copy unlawfully. Amstrad is not concerned to procure and cannot procure unlawful copying. The purchaser will not make unlawful copies because he has been induced or incited or persuaded to do so by Amstrad. The purchaser will make unlawful copies for his own use because he chooses to do so. Amstrad's advertisements may persuade the purchaser to buy an Amstrad machine but will not influence the purchaser's later decision to infringe copyright. Buckley L.J. observed in *Belegging- en Exploitatiemaatschappij Lavender BV v Witten Industrial Diamonds Ltd* (at 65): "Facilitating the doing of an act is obviously different from procuring the doing of an act". Sales and advertisements to the public generally of a machine which may be used for lawful or unlawful purposes, including infringement of copyright, cannot be said to "procure" all breaches of copyright thereafter by members of the public who use the machine. Generally speaking, inducement, incitement or persuasion to infringe must be by a defendant to an individual infringer and must identifiably procure a particular infringement in order to make the defendant liable as a joint infringer.

The next tort suggested by BPI was incitement to commit a criminal offence. In *Invicta Plastics Ltd v Clare* [1976] R.T.R. 251 the defendant company manufactured, advertised and sold a device to give warning of police radar speed traps. The device necessarily involved the unlawful use of apparatus for wireless telegraphy without a licence which would never have been granted. The defendants were convicted of incitement. In the present case it is submitted that Amstrad by the sale and advertisement of their models committed the tort of inciting the purchasers to commit a criminal offence. By section 21(3) of the 1956 Act it is an offence for any person to have in his possession a "plate" knowing that it is to be used for making infringing copies. By section 18(3) "plate" includes any stereotype, stone, block, mould, matrix, transfer negative or other appliance. It is said that when a purchaser of an Amstrad model has in his possession a record in which copyright subsists that record becomes a "plate" and the purchaser commits an offence under section 21(3) as soon as he forms the intention of copying that record.

There are two answers to this submission. First, as a matter of construction a record is not a plate but the product of the master recording which is a plate and from which the record is derived. Second, it is a mistake to compare crime and tort. If three persons are incited by a fourth to break into a house and cause damage each will be guilty of a crime and will receive separate punishment. The inciter will be guilty of the criminal offence of inciting others to commit crime. The other three will be guilty of the crime of breaking in. If the damage caused amounts to £5,000 then in a civil action the three who caused the damage will be jointly and severally liable for £5,000 and no more. The inciter will also be jointly and severally liable for the damage if he procures the commission of the tort and is a joint tortfeasor.

Finally, BPI submit that Amstrad committed the tort of negligence, that Amstrad owes to all owners of copyright a duty to take care not to cause or permit purchasers to infringe copyright or, alternatively, that Amstrad owes a duty to take care not to facilitate by the sale of their models or by their advertisement the infringement of copyright. My Lords, it is always easy to draft a proposition which is tailor-made to produce the desired result. Since *Anns v Merton London Borough* [1977] 2 All E.R. 492; [1978] A.C. 728 put the floodgates on the jar, a fashionable plaintiff alleges negligence. The pleading assumes that we are all neighbours now, Pharisees and Samaritans alike, that foreseeability is a reflection of hindsight and that for every mischance in an accident-prone world someone solvent must be liable in damages. In *Governors of the Peabody Donation Fund v Sir Lindsay Parkinson &*

Co Ltd [1984] 3 All E.R. 529; [1985] A.C. 210 the plaintiffs were the authors of their own misfortune but sought to make the local authority liable for the consequences. In *Yuen Kun-yeu v Attorney General of Hong Kong* [1987] 2 All E.R. 705; [1988] A.C. 175 the plaintiff chose to invest in a deposit-taking company which went into liquidation; the plaintiff sought to recover his deposit from the commissioner charged with the public duty of registering deposit-taking companies. In *Rowling v Takaro Properties Ltd* [1988] 1 All E.R. 163; [1988] 2 W.L.R. 418 a claim for damages in negligence was made against a minister of the Crown for declining in good faith to exercise in favour of the plaintiff a statutory discretion vested in the minister in the public interest. In *Hill v Chief Constable of West Yorkshire* [1988] 2 All E.R. 238; [1988] 2 W.L.R. 1049 damages against a police force were sought on behalf of the victim of a criminal. In the present proceedings damages and an injunction for negligence are sought against Amstrad for a breach of statutory duty which Amstrad did not commit and in which Amstrad did not participate. The rights of BPI are to be found in the 1956 Act and nowhere else. Under and by virtue of that Act Amstrad owed a duty not to infringe copyright and not to authorise an infringement of copyright. They did not owe a duty to prevent or discourage or warn against infringement.

Lord Templeman ended by addressing the political difficulties posed by the new technical facilities for home taping. He regarded as "lamentable" the fact that the existing law often resulted in infringement at home but could not be enforced against those who copied privately. He also mentioned the blank tape levy as a possible solution and noted its varying fortunes in British policy-making.

3.6.5 Permitted Acts: General

3.6.5.1 Note on Material included on Permitted Acts

The 1988 Act, Part I, Chap. 3, comprises nearly 40 sections of exceptions to copyright infringement. Those of particular interest are set out in this and the ensuing subsections (3.6.5–3.6.9). Those concerned with public administration (ss.45–50) have been omitted, as have the majority under the Miscellaneous heading (s.57 et seq.). Sections 51–53 (designs) are to be found at 4.1.1, s.58 (fixation) at 3.3.1.

3.6.5.2 Copyright, Designs and Patents Act 1988, ss.28–31A, 76, 178[1]

S.28(1) The provisions of this Chapter specify acts which may be done in relation to copyright works notwithstanding the subsistence of copyright; they relate only to the question of infringement of copyright and do not affect any other right or obligation restricting the doing of any of the specified acts.

(2) Where it is provided by this Chapter that an act does not infringe copyright, or may be done without infringing copyright, and no particular description of copyright work is mentioned, the act in question does not infringe the copyright in a work of any description.

(3) No inference shall be drawn from the description of any act which may by virtue of this Chapter be done without infringing copyright as to the scope of the acts restricted by the copyright in any description of work.

(4) The provisions of this Chapter are to be construed independently of each other, so that the fact that an act does not fall within one provision does not mean that it is not covered by another provision.

[*S.29(1) Fair dealing with a literary, dramatic, musical or artistic work for the purposes of research for a non-commercial purpose does not infringe any copyright in the work provided that it is accompanied by a sufficient acknowledgment.*

(1A) to be omitted

(1B) No acknowledgment is required in connection with fair dealing for the purposes mentioned in subsection (1) where this would be impossible for reasons of practicality or otherwise.

(1C) Fair dealing with a literary, dramatic, musical or artistic work for the purposes of private study does not infringe any copyright in the work.]

(2) Fair dealing with the typographical arrangement of a published edition of research or private study does not infringe any copyright in the arrangement.

(3) Copying by a person other than the researcher or student himself is not fair dealing if—

    (a) in the case of a librarian, or a person acting on behalf of a librarian, he does anything which regulations under section 40 would not permit to be done under section 38 or 39 (articles or parts of published works: restriction on multiple copies of same material), or

---

[1] Proposed amendments in implementation of the InfoSoc Directive are given in italics.

(b) in any other case, the person doing the copying knows or has reason to believe that it will result in copies of substantially the same material being provided to more than one person at substantially the same time and for substantially the same purpose.

For s.29(4), which relates to computer programs, see 3.6.9.

[*S.30(1) Fair dealing with a work for the purpose of criticism or review, of that or another work or of a performance of a work, does not infringe any copyright in the work provided that it is accompanied by a sufficient acknowledgment and provided that the work has been made available to the public.*

(1A) For the purposes of subsection (1) a work has been made available to the public if it has been made available by any means, including—

(a) *the issue of copies to the public;*

(b) *making the work available by means of an electronic retrieval system;*

(c) *the rental or lending of copies of the work to the public;*

(d) *the performance, exhibition, playing or showing of the work in public;*

(e) *the communication to the public of the work;*

but in determining generally for the purposes of that subsection whether a work has been made available to the public no account shall be taken of any unauthorised act.]

(2) Fair dealing with a work (other than a photograph) for the purpose of reporting current events does not infringe any copyright in the work provided that (subject to subsection (3)) it is accompanied by a sufficient acknowledgement.

(3) No acknowledgement is required in connection with the reporting of current events by means of a sound recording, film or broadcast where this would be impossible for reasons of practicality or otherwise.

S.31(1) Copyright in a work is not infringed by its incidental inclusion in an artistic work, sound recording, film or broadcast.

(2) Nor is the copyright infringed by the issue to the public of copies, or the playing, showing or communicating to the public of anything whose making was, by virtue of subsection (1), not an infringement of the copyright.

[*(3) A musical work, words spoken or sung with music, or so much of a sound recording or broadcast as includes a musical work or such works, shall not be regarded as incidentally included in another work if it is deliberately included.*]

[*Making of temporary copies*
S.31A Copyright in a literary work, other than a computer program or a database, or in a dramatic, musical or artistic work, the typographical arrangement of a published edition, a sound recording or a film, is not infringed by the making of a temporary copy which is transient or incidental, which is an integral and essential part of a technological process and the sole purpose of which is to enable—

(a) *a transmission of the work in a network between third parties by an intermediary, or*

(b) *a lawful use of the work;*

and which has no independent economic significance.]

S.76 Adaptations—An act which by virtue of this Chapter may be done without infringing copyright in a literary, dramatic or musical work does not, where that work is an adaptation, infringe any copyright in the work from which the adaptation was made.

S.178 "**sufficient acknowledgement**" means an acknowledgement identifying the work in question by its title or other description, and identifying the author unless—

(a) in the case of a published work, it is published anonymously;

(b) in the case of an unpublished work, it is not possible for a person to ascertain the identity of the author by reasonable inquiry.

3.6.5.3 *Beloff v Pressdram* [1973] 1 All E.R. 241, Ungoed Thomas J.

The plaintiff, an Observer *journalist, wrote a memorandum to colleagues concerning Reginald Maudling in which she revealed William Whitelaw's confidential view that Maudling was the natural successor as Conservative leader to the then Prime Minister, Edward Heath. A copy of this was given surreptitiously to a* Private Eye *journalist, Paul Foot, that magazine being in the process of publishing exposé of Maudling's connections with an off-shore financing operator, Hoffmann.* Private Eye *published the memorandum in full as part of an attack on the plaintiff for her fostering of Maudling and her own aspersions on* Private Eye's *campaign against him.*

Her action for infringement of copyright failed because of her inability to prove ownership of the copyright. The learned judge also gave his views on other issues argued before him.

Ungoed Thomas J.:

Public interest and fair dealing

In the course of this case, the defence of public interest has been interwoven with fair dealing. They are, however, separate defences and have rightly been separately pleaded. They are governed by separate considerations. Fair dealing is a statutory defence limited to infringement of copyright only. But public interest is a defence outside and independent of statutes is not limited to copyright cases and is based on a general principle of common law. I will deal first with public interest and then with fair dealing.

Public interest

The most important recent cases referred to were the Court of Appeal cases, *Initial Services Ltd v Putterill* [1967] 3 All E.R. 145, and *Hubbard v Vosper* [1972] 1 All E.R. 1023, where the claims were for infringement of copyright and also for breach of confidence.

The *Initial Services* case was on appeal to strike out certain provisions in the defence relying, in justification of disclosure of confidential information on the exposure first of breach of statutory duty to register a restrictive trade agreement and secondly that a circular issued by the plaintiffs to their customers attributing increases in their charges to the selective employment tax was misleading to the public. Lord Denning M.R. said that the exception to the obligation not to disclose confidential information:

> "extends to any misconduct of such a nature that it ought in the public interest to be disclosed to others. Wood V.C. put it in a vivid phrase: 'There is no confidence as to the disclosure of iniquity'. In *Weld-Blundell v Stephens* [1919] 1 K.B. 520, Bankes L.J. rather suggested that the exception was limited to the proposed or contemplated commission of a crime or a civil wrong; but I should have thought that that was too limited. The exception should extend to crimes, frauds and misdeeds, both those actually committed as well as those in contemplation, provided always—and this is essential—that the disclosure is justified in the public interest. The reason is because 'no private obligations can dispense with that universal one which lies on every member of the society to discover every design which may be formed, contrary to the laws of the society, to destroy the public welfare. See *Annesley v Earl of Anglesea* (1743) 17 State Tr 1139."

And Salmon L.J. said:

> "I do not think that the law would lend assistance to anyone who is proposing to commit and to continue to commit a clear breach of a statutory duty imposed in the public interest."

In that case publication, justifiable in the public interest, was considered to extend beyond exposure of what appears, at first blush, to have been meant by "contrary to the laws of the society" as stated in *Annesley v Earl of Anglesea*, although not, as I see it, beyond "disclosure of iniquity" in Wood V.C.'s phrase.

In *Hubbard v Vosper* Lord Denning M.R. treated material on scientology published in breach of confidence as susceptible to a defence of public interest on the ground that it was dangerous material, namely medical quackeries dangerous in untrained hands.

The defence of public interest clearly covers and, in the authorities does not extend beyond, disclosure, which as Lord Denning M.R. emphasised must be disclosure justified in the public interest, of matters carried out or contemplated. In breach of the country's security, or in breach of law, including statutory duty, fraud, or otherwise destructive of the country or its people, including matters medically dangerous to the public; and doubtless other misdeeds of similar gravity. Public interest, as a defence in law, operates to override the rights of the individual including copyright which would otherwise prevail and which the law is also concerned to protect. Such public interest, as now recognised by the law, does not extend beyond misdeeds of a serious nature and importance to the country and thus, in my view, clearly recognisable as such.

The learned judge proceeded to hold that the defence so conceived had not been made out.

Fair dealing

(1) The meaning of statutory "fair dealing".

After referring to the Copyright Act 1956, s.6(2), (3) and (10) and to some of the evidence the learned judge continued:

I come now to the requirement, which I specified, of fair dealing with this memorandum. Fair dealing is not defined by the Act, although subject to the requirements which I have already stated including the purpose of criticism or review or reporting current events. The references to purposes, which I have just read, differ in their wording from the reference to purposes in section 6(1) which reads:

> "No fair dealing with a literary ... work for purposes of research or private study shall constitute an infringement of the copyright in the work."

Thus "for the purpose" in subsection (1) and "if it is for the purpose" in the other subsections fundamentally have the same meaning and effect; and the difference in wording is explained by the inclusion in subsections (2) and (3) of additional provisions and requirements without parallel in subsection (1). It would, indeed, be whimsical if the relationship between fair dealing and the approved purposes were given a different significance in subsections (2) and (3) from subsection (1), in the absence of obvious reasons for making such a difference. The relevant fair dealing is thus fair dealing with the memorandum for the approved purposes. It is fair dealing directed to and consequently limited to and to be judged in relation to the approved purposes. It is dealing which is fair for the approved purposes and not dealing which might be fair for some other purpose or fair in general. Mere dealing with the work for that purpose is not enough: it must also be dealing which is fair for that purpose; whose fairness, as I have indicated, must be judged in relation to that purpose.

Thus public interest as such is outside the purpose of the section and of fair dealing. It is not of itself justification for infringement of copyright, except in so far as recognised by common law as a separate defence irrespective of the section as already mentioned.

(2) Factors in the defence of fair dealing.

I come now to the relevant factors in determining fair dealing. A number of authorities were cited, but for present purposes, at any rate, the law is most conveniently stated in *Hubbard v Vosper* by Lord Denning M.R. and by Megaw L.J. To summarise the statements: fair dealing is a question of fact and of impression, to which factors that are relevant include the extent of the quotation and its proportion to comment (which may be justifiable although the quotation is of the whole work): whether the work is unpublished; and the extent to which the work has been circularised, although not published to the public within the meaning of the Copyright Act 1956.

In our case the memorandum was unpublished. Romer J. in *British Oxygen Co Ltd v Liquid Air Ltd* in dealing with a company's letter to a trade customer as a "literary work", said that publication without the author's consent would be "manifestly unfair" as it is not a "fair dealing" with the work. Romer J.'s observations were made when the relevant statute was section 2 of the Copyright Act 1911, the precursor of section 6 of the 1956 Act. It was in wide terms into which limitations were introduced by section 6, but the differences are not material for present purposes. However, unpublished as well as published works are within the fair dealing provisions of both Acts; and what would otherwise be infringement cannot of itself, without regard to any other circumstances, be outside the exception to infringement made by those sections, so that would be to exclude from the sections what the sections in terms include. So I doubt if Romer J. ever intended that his words should be read in the sense that an unpublished work should be automatically outside the provisions of the fair dealing defence rather than a factor, although doubtless an important factor, which with other factors have to be taken into consideration in considering fair dealing. And such a conclusion seems to be in accordance with the decision and observations of the Court of Appeal in *Hubbard v Vosper*.

But receiving and using leaked information, in the sense of confidential information, which someone who has it gives to someone not entitled to it appears to be common practice in the press, and occurs in such a reputable paper as *The Observer* itself. An instance was even given in evidence of the publication by the plaintiff of such a leak. Distinctions were sought to be drawn by or on behalf of the plaintiff between different ways in which leaks occur. It was sought to distinguish between a leak by theft as contrasted with breach of confidence, and it was strongly maintained, particularly by the plaintiff in the early stages of the hearing, that the memorandum was stolen from *The Observer's* offices by someone from *Private Eye*; but Mr Foot, who knew, said that the contents of the memorandum were disclosed by someone in *The Observer* who wanted the memorandum published; and I have no hesitation in accepting the evidence of Mr Foot. A distinction was also sought to be drawn between, on the one hand, receiving and using a leak of a rival's confidential information (for example, by *Private Eye* of the confidential information of another newspaper) and on the other hand, receiving and using confidential information of some other body not a rival (for example, by *Private Eye* from a government department, an industrial company or a private firm). Mr Foot disagreed and so do I. A distinction was also suggested between a leak of information never intended by its owner to be published and a pre-empting leak in anticipation of authorised publication. The pre-empting leak might well be substantially prejudicial; and although the later such a leak takes place before authorised publication the less is apt to be the ill-consequence, yet the less too is it apt to be in the public interest, which was mostly alone relied on to justify the publication of leaked information. On all these distinctions there may well be differences of responsible views sincerely held; but for my part I am unable to make any decisive distinction between the unsought voluntary leak in this case by a person who wanted the leaked information published and other press publications of leaks which were referred to in evidence.

Ungoed Thomas J. held the publication an unfair dealing.

3.6.5.4 *Pro Sieben Media v Carlton UK Television* [1999] E.M.L.R. 109, CA

Mandy Allwood, pregnant with octuplets, secured the services of the P.R. consultant, Max Clifford, to sell exclusive rights to the media for interviews with her. In Germany, he negotiated television rights with the commercial television producer, Pro Sieben, for £30,000. After transmission of the Pro Sieben interview on the news programme, TAFF, part of it was taken by Carlton, a UK television company, and incorporated into a current affairs programme, "Selling Babies", which claimed to criticise chequebook journalism and used the Allwood case as a prime illustration of its distortive effects on the truth.

The defendants claimed that the use made of the TAFF material was fair dealing for the purposes of criticism or review and of reporting current events (CDPA 1988, s.30). At first instance, Laddie J. refused to accept either defence, mainly because of the naked animosity towards the Allwood imbroglio displayed by the Carlton producer in her oral evidence. The Court of Appeal found for the Defendants on both pleas.

Noting that both parties approached the question of what constitutes fair dealing on much the same basis, Robert Walker L.J. continued:

The position was summarised by Henry L.J. in *Time Warner Entertainments v Channel Four*

Television [1994] E.M.L.R. 1 at 14, in rejecting the submission that unrepresentative excerpts should lose the benefit of the fair dealing defence:

> "As Lord Atkin said in a different context 'The path of criticism is a public way: The wrongheaded are permitted to err therein ...' (*Ambard v Attorney General for Trinidad and Tobago* [1936] A.C. 322 at 355) 'Fair dealing' in its statutory context refers to the true purpose (that is, the good faith, the intention and the genuineness) of the critical work—is the programme incorporating the infringing material a genuine piece of criticism or review, or is it something else, such as an attempt to dress up the infringement of another's copyright in the guise of criticism, and so profit unfairly from another's work? As Lord Denning said in *Hubbard v Vosper* ([1972] 2 Q.B. 84 at 93): 'It is not fair dealing for a rival in the trade to take copyright material and use it for his own benefit.'"

This court has by contrast heard quite lengthy submissions as to whether the words "for the purpose of" in section 30(1) and section 30(2) import a subjective or objective test. The judge did not discuss this point at length, but rejected the submission made on behalf of Pro Sieben that even if the critic had the necessary purpose, the defence is not made out unless the purpose was understood by the audience.

The fact that there is no authority on the point after nearly 90 years suggests that the issue may not be of much practical importance; indeed, that it may not be a significant point of construction at all. In *Sweet v Parsley* [1970] A.C. 132 the House of Lords emphasised the importance of construing a composite phrase rather than a single word. It seems to me that in the composite phrases "for the purposes of criticism or review" and "for the purpose of reporting current events" the mental element on the part of the user is of little more importance than in such everyday composite expressions as "for the purpose of argument" or "for the purpose of comparison". The words "in the context of" or "as part of an exercise in" could be substituted for "for the purpose of" without any significant alteration of meaning.

That is not to say that the intentions and motives of the user of another's copyright material are not highly relevant for the purposes of the defences available under section 30(1) and section 30(2). But they are most highly relevant on the issue of fair dealing, so far as it can be treated as a discrete issue from the statutory purpose.

It is not necessary for the court to put itself in the shoes of the infringer of the copyright in order to decide whether the offending piece was published "for the purposes of criticism or review". This court should not in my view give any encouragement to the notion that all that is required is for the user to have the sincere belief, however misguided, that he or she is criticising a work or reporting current affairs. To do so would provide an undesirable incentive for journalists, for whom facts should be sacred, to give implausible evidence as to their intentions.

The court heard submissions on several other points of statutory construction (apart from the "sufficient acknowledgement" issue which is addressed at the end of this judgment). It is not helpful to go far into those submissions except by reference to the facts of this particular case, and the way in which the judge dealt with the evidence before him. But some general observations are called for.

"Criticism or review" and "reporting current events" are expressions of wide and indefinite scope. Any attempt to plot their precise boundaries is doomed to failure. They are expressions which should be interpreted liberally, but I derive little assistance from comparisons with other expressions such as "current affairs" or "news" (the latter word being used in the Australian statute considered in *De Garis v Neville Jeffress Pidler* (1990) 18

I.P.R. 292). However it can be said that the nearer that any particular derivative use of copyright material comes to the boundaries, unplotted though they are, the less likely it is to make good the fair dealing defence.

Criticism of a work need not be limited to criticism of style. It may also extend to the ideas to be found in a work and its social or moral implications. So in *Time Warner Entertainments v Channel Four Television* this court (in allowing an interlocutory appeal and discharging an injunction) accepted that a television programme criticising the withdrawal of the film *A Clockwork Orange* from distribution in the United Kingdom amounted to criticism of the film itself, since the content of the film and the decision to withdraw it were inseparable ([1994] E.M.L.R. 1 at 15 (Henry L.J.) and see also Neill L.J. at 13). The appellants relied on that case. Pro Sieben on the other hand pointed out that section 30(1) requires use for the purpose of criticism or review "of that or another work", and that the judge was not persuaded that criticism of the *TAFF* report, as opposed to the decision to pay for an interview, was in Ms Byrne's mind when the Carlton programme was made or broadcast.

As I have noted, the judge did not accept that the Carlton programme's use of the *TAFF* report was for the purpose of criticism or review of the *TAFF* report, and he did not consider the possibility that it might have been for the purpose of criticism or review of the *TAFF* report and the newspaper material mentioned above, taken collectively as a genre of the fruits of chequebook journalism. Instead he concluded that:

"The overriding purpose of including the TAFF extract was to show that others in the media were prepared to pay large sums for interviews but Carlton television was not."

And:

"The primary purpose was to proclaim that the defendants were above chequebook journalism and to scoff at an anonymous German broadcaster for having paid money for an interview."

Having viewed the whole of the *TAFF* report and the whole of the Carlton programme several times, I have formed a quite different impression both of the Carlton programme as a whole and of its use of the 30-second extract from the *TAFF* report. The strongest message which I derive from the Carlton programme (which is, as the judge noted, skilfully made) is that chequebook journalism is deeply inimical to truth. It divides the media into the "haves" (those who have bought an exclusive story and think that that entitles them to present it as they see fit) and the "have nots" (the rest, who resort to spoilers designed to upset their rivals, regardless of any hurt to individual feelings). Truth is likely to be an early casualty in these battles, which can be very traumatic for the "ordinary people" involved, even if they make some money out of it. The programme did however have an element of balance: one of the persons interviewed, the man who had been saved from the shark, had no complaints about his treatment at the hands of the media, and was glad that they had contributed to the cost of his treatment in hospital.

So far a concerned the need to show sufficient acknowledgment of the source, the Court of Appeal agreed with Laddie J. that the station symbol which accompanied the clips from the claimant's program satisfied the requirement.

3.6.5.5 *Ashdown v Telegraph Group* [2002] Ch. 149, CA

At a time when he was leader of the Liberal Democrat party, Paddy Ashdown had a secret discussion with the Prime Minister, Tony Blair, and three others about the possibility of formal co-operation between the Liberal Democrats and Labour. Mr Ashdown afterwards dictated a memorandum of the meeting which was highly confidential and known to be so by all who subsequently saw it. A copy nonetheless found its way by an unknown route to the political editor of the Daily Telegraph *and the paper published three pieces about the meeting, which reproduced about a quarter of the memo. In an action for an injunction to restrain further breaches of contract in the document, the defendant relied particularly on the defences of fair dealing in reporting current events (CDPA 1988, s.30(2)) and public interest (preserved by the CDPA, s.171(3)). At first instance, Morritt V.C. granted the injunction, as subsequently did the Court of Appeal. In giving the Courts judgment, Lord Phillips M.R. considered the impact of the guarantee of freedom of expression in the Human Rights Convention, Art.10, upon copyright claims which seek to curb that freedom, given the right to peaceful possession of private property, found in the First Protocol, Art.1. After characterising copyright as a negative entitlement to the protection of expression, and observing that it could be enforced by injunction, as well as by monetary compensation, he continued:*

39. We have already observed that, in most circumstances, the principle of freedom of expression will be sufficiently protected if there is a right to publish information and ideas set out in another's literary work, without copying the very words which that person has employed to convey the information or express the ideas. In such circumstances it will normally be necessary in a democratic society that the author of the work should have his property in his own creation protected. Strasbourg jurisprudence demonstrates, however, that circumstances can arise in which freedom of expression will only be fully effective if an individual is permitted to reproduce the very words spoken by another.

40. In this context, the Telegraph Group relied upon a passage in the judgment of the Strasbourg court in *Jersild v Denmark* (1994) 19 E.H.R.R. 1, 26, para 31:

"At the same time, the methods of objective and balanced reporting may vary considerably, depending among other things on the media in question. It is not for this court, nor for the national courts for that matter, to substitute their own views for those of the press as to what technique of reporting should be adopted by journalists. In this context the court recalls that article 10 protects not only the substance of the ideas and information expressed, but also the form in which they are conveyed."

41. These words do not support a general proposition that freedom of the press includes the freedom to make use of the form of words created by another in order to convey ideas and information. *Jersild v Denmark* was concerned with the right to use insulting language which was the creation of those using the language, not copied from another author.

42. More pertinent is the decision of the Strasbourg court in *Fressoz and Roire v France* (1999) 31 E.H.R.R. 28. Mr Fressoz was the publishing director of the French satirical weekly, "Le Canard Enchaîné". He published an article, written by Mr Roire, about the salary rise awarded to himself by the head of Peugeot at a time of industrial unrest. He illustrated the article by reproducing sections of the head of Peugeot's tax returns. Both men were successfully prosecuted in France for making unlawful use of these documents. Their case was referred to the Strasbourg Court, which held that Article 10 had been infringed. The court observed, at p.60, para. 54:

"If, as the government accepted, the information about Mr Calvet's annual income was lawful and its disclosure permitted, the applicants' conviction merely for having published the documents in which that information was contained, namely the tax assessments, cannot be justified under Article 10. In essence, that article leaves it for journalists to decide whether or not it is necessary to reproduce such documents to ensure credibility. It protects journalists' right to divulge information on issues of general interest provided that they are acting in good faith and on an accurate factual basis and provide 'reliable and precise' information in accordance with the ethics of journalism."

43. *Fressoz and Roire* was not a copyright case, but it illustrates a general principle. Freedom of expression protects the right both to publish information and to receive it. There will be occasions when it is in the public interest not merely that information should be published, but that the public should be told the very words used by a person, notwithstanding that the author enjoys copyright in them. On occasions, indeed, it is the form and not the content of a document which is of interest.

44. Where the subject-matter of the information is a current event, section 30(2) of the 1988 Act may permit publication of the words used. But it is possible to conceive of information of the greatest public interest relating not to a current event, but to a document produced in the past. We are not aware of any provision of the 1988 Act which would permit publication in such circumstances, unless the mere fact of publication, and any controversy created by the disclosure, is sufficient to make them "current events". This will often be a "bootstraps" argument of little merit, but on other occasions (such as disclosure by the Public Record Office under the 30-year rule) it may have a more solid basis.

45. For these reasons, we have reached the conclusion that rare circumstances can arise where the right of freedom of expression will come into conflict with the protection afforded by the 1988 Act, notwithstanding the express exceptions to be found in the Act. In these circumstances, we consider that the court is bound, in so far as it is able, to apply the Act in a manner that accommodates the right of freedom of expression. This will make it necessary for the court to look closely at the facts of individual cases (as indeed it must whenever a "fair dealing" defence is raised). We do not foresee this leading to a flood of litigation.

46. The first way in which it may be possible to do this is by declining the discretionary relief of an injunction. Usually, so it seems to us, such a step will be likely to be sufficient. If a newspaper considers it necessary to copy the exact words created by another, we can see no reason in principle why the newspaper should not indemnify the author for any loss caused to him, or alternatively account to him for any profit made as a result of copying his work. Freedom of expression should not normally carry with it the right to make free use of another's work.

In the light of this approach, Lord Phillips M.R. criticised the limits placed upon the freedom to publish copyright material in the public interest, set out by Aldous L.J. in Hyde Park Residence v Yelland, [2000] R.P.C. 604 *who confined the defence to cases where the work was (i) immoral, scandalous or contrary to family life, (ii) injurious to public life, public health and safety or the administration of justice, or (iii) where it encouraged others to act in a way referred to in (i) or (ii). This involved an unacceptably narrow reading of* Lion Laboratories v Evans. *He concluded:*

58. We prefer the conclusion of Mance L.J. [in *Yelland*] that the circumstances in which

public interest may override copyright are not capable of precise categorisation or definition. Now that the Human Rights Act 1998 is in force, there is the clearest public interest in giving effect to the right of freedom of expression in those rare cases where this right trumps the rights conferred by the 1988 Act. In such circumstances, we consider that section 171(3) of the Act permits the defence of public interest to be raised.

59. We do not consider that this conclusion will lead to a flood of cases where freedom of expression is invoked as a defence to a claim for breach of copyright. It will be very rare for the public interest to justify the copying of the form of a work to which copyright attaches. We would add that the implications of the Human Rights Act 1998 must always be considered where the discretionary relief of an injunction is sought, and this is true in the field of copyright quite apart from the ambit of the public interest defence under section 171(3).

The Court rejected the defence under s.30(1) since there was no genuine criticism or review involved in the use of the memo. As to that under s.30(2), it considered that there could be a real public interest in knowing about the meeting for its impact on party government in the UK. But it concluded that fairness did not require verbatim quotation to the extent that concurred.

3.6.6   Permitted Acts: Reprography

3.6.6.1   Copyright, Designs and Patents Act 1988, ss.37(1)–(2), 38–40, 43(3): Libraries and archives[1]

S.37(1) In sections 38 to 43 (copying by librarians and archivists)—

(a) references in any provision to a prescribed library or archive are to a library or archive of a description prescribed for the purposes of that provision by regulations made by the Secretary of State: and

(b) references in any provision to the prescribed conditions are to the conditions so prescribed.

(2) The regulations may provide that, where a librarian or archivist is required to be satisfied as to any matter before making or supplying a copy of a work—

(a) he may rely on a signed declaration as to that matter by the person requesting the copy, unless he is aware that it is false in a material particular, and

(b) in such cases as may be prescribed, he shall not make or supply a copy in the absence of a signed declaration in such form as may be prescribed.

Section 37(3) deals with false declarations, s.37(4),(5) contain additional matter on the regulations; s.37(6) extends the exception to those acting on behalf of a librarian or archivist.

S.38(1) The librarian of a prescribed library may, if the prescribed conditions are compiled with, make and supply a copy of an article in a periodical without infringing any copyright in the text, in any illustrations accompanying the text or in the typographical arrangement.

[*(2) The prescribed conditions shall include the following—*

(*a*) *that copies are supplied only to persons satisfying the librarian that they require them for the purposes of—*

(*i*) *research for a non-commercial purpose, or*
(*ii*) *private study,*

and will not use them for any other purpose;]

(b) that no person is furnished with more than one copy of the same article or with copies of more than one article contained in the same issue of a periodical: and

(c) that persons to whom copies are supplied are required to pay for them a sum not less than the cost (including a contribution to the general expenses of the library) attributable to their production.

S.39(1) The librarian of a prescribed library may, if the prescribed conditions are complied with, make and supply from a published edition a copy of part of a literary, dramatic or musical work (other than an article in a periodical) without infringing any copyright in the work, in any illustrations accompanying the work or in the typographical arrangement.

[*(2) The prescribed conditions shall include the following—*

---

[1] Passages in italics are amendments proposed in compliance with the InfoSoc Directive.

(a) *that copies are supplied only to persons satisfying the librarian that they require them for the purposes of—*

   (i) *research for a non-commercial purpose, or*
   (ii) *private study,*

   and will not use them for any other purpose;

(b) *that no person is furnished with more than one copy of the same material or with a copy of more than a reasonable proportion of any work; and*

(c) *that persons to whom copies are supplied are required to pay for them a sum not less than the cost (including a contribution to the general expenses of the library) attributable to their production.]*

S.40(1) Regulations for the purposes of sections 38 and 39 (copying by librarian of article or part of published work) shall contain provision to that effect that a copy shall be supplied only to a person satisfying the librarian that his requirement is not related to any similar requirement of another person.

(2) The regulations may provide—

   (a) that requirements shall be regarded as similar if the requirements are for copies of substantially the same material at substantially the same time and for substantially the same purpose: and

   (b) that requirements of persons shall be regarded as related if those persons receive instruction to which the material is relevant at the same time and place.

Section 41 creates an exception for the supply of copies to other libraries; s.42 for replacement copies of works; s.43 for certain copying of some unpublished works in libraries and archives; and s.44 where copying is a condition of an export licence. Section 44A provides that copyright is not infringed by the lending of copies of a work within the Public Lending Rights Scheme by a public library.

[S.43(3) The prescribed conditions shall include the following—

(a) *that copies are supplied only to persons satisfying the librarian or archivist that they require them for the purposes of—*

   (i) *research for a non-commercial purpose, or*
   (ii) *private study,*

   and will not use them for any other purpose;

(b) *that no person is furnished with more than one copy of the same material; and*

(c) *that persons to whom copies are supplied are required to pay for them a sum equivalent to but not exceeding the cost (including a contribution to the general expenses of the library or archive) attributable to their production.]*

3.6.6.2   Copyright, Designs and Patents Act 1988, ss.36, 130

S.36(1) Reprographic copies of passages from published literary, dramatic or musical works may, to the extent permitted by this section, be made by or on behalf of an educational establishment for the purposes of instruction without infringing any copyright in the work, provided that they are accompanied by a sufficient acknowledgement.

[*(1A) No acknowledgement is required in connection with the making of copies for the purposes mentioned in subsection (1) where this would be impossible for reasons of practicality or otherwise.*

(1B) Reprographic copies of passages from published editions may, to the extent permitted by this section, be made by or on behalf of an educational establishment for the purposes of instruction without infringing any copyright in the typographical arrangement of the edition.]

(2) Not more than one per cent of any work may be copied by or on behalf of an establishment by virtue of this section in any quarter, that is, in any period 1 January to 31 March, 1 April to 30 June, 1 July to 30 September or 1 October to 31 December.

(3) Copying is not authorised by this section if, or to the extent that, licences are available authorising the copying in question and the person making the copies knew or ought to have been aware of that fact.

(4) The terms of a licence granted to an educational establishment authorising the reprographic copying for the purposes of instruction of passages from published literary, dramatic or musical works are of no effect so far as they purport to restrict the proportion of a work which may be copied (whether on payment or free of charge) to less than that which would be permitted under this section.

(5) Where a copy which would otherwise be an infringing copy is made in accordance with this section but is subsequently dealt with, it shall be treated as an infringing copy for the purposes of that dealing, as if that dealing infringes copyright for all subsequent purposes.

For this purpose "dealt with" means sold or let for hire, or offered or exposed for sale or hire.

S.130 Where a reference or application is made to the Copyright Tribunal under this Chapter relating to the licensing of reprographic copying of published literary, dramatic, musical or artistic works, or the typographical arrangement of published editions, the Tribunal shall have regard to—

    (a) the extent to which published editions of the works in question are otherwise available,

    (b) the proportion of the work to be copied, and

    (c) the nature of the use to which the copies are likely to be put.

Section 136 imposes an implied indemnity in respect of schemes and licences for reprographic copying in respect of acts of infringement within the apparent scope of the permission granted.

Section 137, in relation to reprographic copying in educational establishments, gives power to the Secretary of State to extend to works that copyright owners unreasonably refuse to allow within an appropriate scheme or licence (and see also ss.138, 139). Section 140 permits, in the same field, the Secretary of State to institute an inquiry into extension of a scheme or licence to fields not covered; s.141 prescribes consequential action.

3.6.7 Permitted Acts: Education

3.6.7.1 Copyright, Designs and Patents Act 1988, ss.32(1), 34, 35(1)–(2)

[S.32(1) Copyright in a literary, dramatic, musical or artistic work is not infringed by its being copied in the course of instruction or of preparation for instruction, provided the copying—

    (a) is done by a person giving or receiving instruction,

    (b) is not by means of a reprographic process, and

    (c) is accompanied by a sufficient acknowledgement and provided that the condition in subsection (2A) is met]

Section 32(2) deals with instruction in film making; s.32(3), (4) with examinations; and s.32(5) with subsequent dealings.

Section 32(2A) requires the instruction to be in an educational or non-commercial establishment.

Section 33 creates an exception for anthologies of short passages from literary and dramatic works intended for educational use.

S.34(1) The performance of a literary, dramatic or musical work before an audience consisting of teachers and pupils at an educational establishment and other persons directly connected with the activities of the establishment—

    (a) by a teacher or pupil in the course of the activities of the establishment, or

    (b) at the establishment by any person for the purposes of instruction, is not a public performance for the purposes of infringement of copyright.

(2) The playing or showing of a sound recording, film or broadcast before such an audience at an educational establishment for the purposes of instruction is not a playing or showing of the work in public for the purposes of infringement of copyright.

(3) A person is not for this purpose directly connected with the activities of the educational establishment simply because he is the parent of a pupil at the establishment.

[*S.35(1) A recording of a broadcast, or a copy of such a recording, may be made by or on behalf of an educational establishment for the educational purposes of that establishment without thereby infringing the copyright in the broadcast, or in any work included in it, provided that it is accompanied by a sufficient acknowledgment of the broadcast.*]

(2) This section does not apply if or to the extent that there is a licensing scheme certified for the purposes of this section under section 143 providing for the grant of licences.

Section 35(3) relates to subsequent dealings.

3.6.8   Permitted Acts: Rental Right and Home Taping

3.6.8.1   Copyright, Designs and Patents Act 1988, ss.66, 70

S.66(1) The Secretary of State may by order provide that in such cases as may be specified in the order the rental to the public of copies of sound recordings, films or computer programs shall be treated as licensed by the copyright owner subject only to the payment of such reasonable royalty or other payment as may be agreed or determined in default of agreement by the Copyright Tribunal.

(2) No such order shall apply if, or to the extent that, there is a licensing scheme certified for the purposes of this section under section 143 providing for the grant of licences.

(3) An order may make different provision for different cases and may specify cases by reference to any factor relating to the work, the copies rented, the renter or the circumstances of the rental.

(4) An order shall be made by statutory instrument; and no order shall be made unless a draft of it has been laid before and approved by a resolution of each House of Parliament.

(5) Copyright in a computer program is not infringed by the rental of copies to the public after the end of the period of 50 years from the end of the calendar year in which copies of it were first issued to the public in electronic form.

(6) Nothing in this section affects any liability under section 23 (secondary infringement) in respect of the lending of infringing copies.

Section 142 regulates the jurisdiction of the Copyright Tribunal in settling sums payable under s.66.

S.70 The making for private and domestic use of a recording of a broadcast solely for the purpose of enabling it to be viewed or listened to at a more convenient time does not infringe any copyright in the broadcast or cable programme or in any work included in it.

3.6.9 Permitted Acts: Computer Material, etc.

3.6.9.1 Copyright, Designs and Patents Act 1988, ss.29(4), 50A–C, 56, 296A

S.29(4) It is not fair dealing—

(a) to convert a computer program expressed in a low level language into a version expressed in a higher level language, or

(b) incidentally in the course of so converting the program, to copy it,

(these acts being permitted if done in accordance with section 50B (decompilation)).

S.50A(1) It is not an infringement of copyright for a lawful user of a copy of a computer program to make any back up copy of it which it is necessary for him to have for the purposes of his lawful use.

(2) For the purposes of this section and sections 50B and 50C a person is a lawful user of a computer program if (whether under a licence to do any acts restricted by the copyright in the program or otherwise), he has a right to use the program.

(3) Where an act is permitted under this section, it is irrelevant whether or not there exists any term or condition in an agreement which purports to prohibit or restrict the act (such terms being, by virtue of section 296A, void).

S.50B(1) It is not an infringement of copyright for a lawful user of a copy of a computer program expressed in a low level language—

(a) to convert it into a version expressed in a higher level language, or

(b) incidentally in the course of so converting the program, to copy it, that is, to "decompile" it), provided that the conditions in subsection (2) are met.

(2) The conditions are that—

(a) it is necessary to decompile the program to obtain the information necessary to create an independent program which can be operated with the program decompiled or with another program ("the permitted objective"); and

(b) the information so obtained is not used for any purpose other than the permitted objective.

(3) In particular, the conditions in subsection (2) are not met if the lawful user—

(a) has readily available to him the information necessary to achieve the permitted objective;

(b) does not confine the decompiling to such acts as are necessary to achieve the permitted objective;

(c) supplies the information obtained by the decompiling to any person to whom it is not necessary to supply it in order to achieve the permitted objective; or

(d) uses the information to create a program which is substantially similar in its expression to the program decompiled or to do any act restricted by copyright.

(4) Where an act is permitted under this section, it is irrelevant whether or not there exists any term or condition in an agreement which purports to prohibit or restrict the act (such terms being, by virtue of section 296A, void).

S.50C(1) It is not an infringement of copyright for a lawful user of a copy of a computer program to copy or adapt it, provided that the copying or adapting—

(a) is necessary for his lawful use; and

(b) is not prohibited under any term or condition of an agreement regulating the circumstances in which his use is lawful.

(2) It may, in particular, be necessary for the lawful use of a computer program to copy it or adapt it for the purpose of correcting errors in it.

(3) This section does not apply to any copying or adapting permitted under section 50A or 50B.

S.50D(1) It is not an infringement of copyright in a database for a person who has a right to use the database or any part of the database (whether under a licence to do any of the acts restricted by the copyright in the database or otherwise) to do, in the exercise of that right, anything which is necessary for the purposes of access to and use of the contents of the database or of that part of the database.

(2) Where an act which would otherwise infringe copyright in a database is permitted under this section, it is irrelevant whether or not there exists any term or conditon in any agreement which purports to prohibit or restrict the act (such terms being, by virtue of section 296B, void).

S.56(1) This section applies where a copy of a work in electronic form has been purchased on terms which, expressly or impliedly or by virtue of any rule of law, allow the purchaser to copy the work, or to adapt it or make copies of an adaptation, in connection with his use of it.

(2) If there are no express terms—

(a) prohibiting the transfer of the copy by the purchaser, imposing obligations which continue after a transfer, prohibiting the assignment of any licence or terminating any licence on a transfer, or

(b) providing for the terms on which a transferee may do the things which the purchaser was permitted to do.

Anything which the purchaser was allowed to do may also be done without infringement of copyright by a transferee: but any copy, adaptation or copy of an adaptation made by the purchaser which is not also transferred shall be treated as an infringing copy for all purposes after the transfer.

(3) The same applies where the original purchased copy is no longer usable and what is transferred is a further copy used in its place.

(4) The above provisions also apply on a subsequent transfer, with the substitution for references in subsection (2) to the purchaser of references to the subsequent transferor.

S.296A(1) Where a person has the use of a computer program under an agreement, any term or condition in the agreement shall be void in so far as it purports to prohibit or restrict—

(a) the making of any back copy of the program which it is necessary for him to have for the purposes of the agreed use;

(b) where the conditions in section 50B(2) are met, the decompiling of the program; or

(c) the use of any device or means to observe, study or test the functioning of the program in order to understand the ideas and principles which underlie any element of the program.

(2) In this section, decompile, in relation to a computer program, has the same meaning as in section 50B.

296B. Where under an agreement a person has a right to use a database or part of a database, any term or condition in the agreement shall be void in so far as it purports to prohibit or restrict the performance of any act which would but for section 50D infringe the copyright in the database.

3.6.9.2 *John Richardson Computers Ltd v Flanders* [1993] F.S.R. 497, Ferris J.

The plaintiff claimed that its copyright in a program (for a BBC computer) for labelling and stock control in a pharmacy had been infringed by the defendants' similar program (for an IBM-compatible computer). The first defendant had worked on the plaintiff's program first as an employee and then as a consultant, but had eventually set up wholly on his own. In the course of this drawing apart, he produced the program in dispute, not working from any copy of the plaintiff's source code, but allegedly using the general scheme of the BBC program, including idiosyncratic details of certain routines.

Counsel for the plaintiff argued the issue of infringement by analogy to the taking of the plot of a book or play. Accepting this, Ferris J. referred not only to Rees v Melville *[1911–16] M.C.C. 168 at 174 and* Harman Pictures v Osborne *[1967] 1 W.L.R. 723, but also to Learned Hand J.'s judgment in* Nichols v Universal Pictures *45 F (2d) 119 (1930), from which he quoted the following well-known passage:*

"It is of course essential to any protection of literary property, whether at common law or under the statute, that the right cannot be limited literally to the text, else a plagiarist would escape by immaterial variations. That has never been the law, but, as soon as literal appropriation ceases to be the test, the whole matter is necessarily at large, so that, as was recently said by a distinguished judge, the decisions cannot help much in any new case. ... When plays are concerned the plagiarist may excise a separate scene . . .; or he may appropriate part of the dialogue. ... Then the question is whether the part so taken is 'substantial', and therefore not a 'fair use' of the copyrighted work; it is the same question as arises in the case of any other copyrighted work. ... But when the plagiarist does not take out a block *in situ*, but an abstract of the whole, decision is more troublesome. Upon any work, and especially upon a play, a great number of patterns of increasing generality will fit equally well, as more and more of the incident is left out. The last may perhaps be no more than the most general statement of what the play is about, and at times might consist only of its title; but there is a point in this series of abstractions where they are no longer protected, since otherwise the playwright could prevent the use of his 'ideas,' to which, apart from their expression, his property never extended. ... Nobody has ever been able to fix that boundary, and nobody ever can. In some cases the question has been treated as though it were analogous to lifting a proportion of the copyrighted work ...; but the analogy is not a good one, because, though the skeleton is a part of the body, it pervades and supports the whole. In such cases we are rather concerned with the line between the expression and what is expressed. As respects plays the controversy chiefly centers upon the characters and sequence of incident, these being the substance."

Ferris J. referred to further English authority and then turned to US decisions concerning the non-literal infringement of copyright in computer programs.

The United States authorities appear to place much reliance upon the principle that there is no copyright in ideas, only in the expression of ideas. This principle is now enshrined in statute in the United States. It is, of course, recognised and applied in English law too (although the dangers inherent in too extensive a reliance on it are convincingly expounded in *The Modern Law of Copyright* (Laddie, Prescott and Vitoria, 1980), paras. 2–50 to 2–55). The seminal decision in the United States appears to be *Baker v Selden* (1879) 101 U.S. 99. In that case the plaintiff had devised a new system of accounting and published a textbook describing his system and incorporating certain specimen forms. The defendant published equivalent forms for carrying out the same method and was sued for infringement of copyright. The defendant succeeded on a number of grounds, one of which was put as follows in the United States Supreme Court:

> The description of the art in a book, though entitled to the benefit of copyright, lays no foundation for an exclusive claim to the art itself. The object of the one is explanation; the object of the other is use. The former may be secured by copyright. The latter can only be secured, if it can be secured at all, by letters patent.

In *Whelan v Jaslow* [1987] F.S.R. 1 complaint was made that the defendants had infringed the plaintiffs' copyright in a computer program. The Circuit Court of Appeal for the Third Circuit attempted to formulate a rule for distinguishing idea from expression in computer programs in the following passage ([1987] F.S.R. at 19):

> Just as *Baker v Selden* focused on the end sought to be achieved by Selden's book, the line may be drawn by reference to the end sought to be achieved by the work in question. In other words the purpose or function of a utilitarian work would be the work's idea, and everything that is not necessary to that purpose or function would be part of the expression of the idea ... Where there are various means of achieving the desired purpose then the particular means chosen is not necessary to the purpose; hence there is expression not idea.

In a footnote to this part of its judgment the Circuit Court recognised that the test was necessarily difficult to state and might be difficult to understand in the abstract. It explained that the idea of the plaintiffs' program, namely the efficient management of a dental laboratory, could be accomplished in a number of different ways with a number of different program structures, with the result that the structure of the plaintiffs' program was part of the program's expression, not idea.

The approach adopted in *Whelan* has, however, not found favour in two later U.S. decisions. *Computer Associates International Inc v Altai Inc* was decided by the Court of Appeals for the Second Circuit on June 22, 1992. I was provided with a Lexis print of the decision the reference to which appears to be U.S. App Lexis 14305, 1992. The issue was whether the plaintiffs' copyright in a program called Adapter was infringed by the defendants' program called Oscar, version 3.5. Approximately 30 per cent of the code of an earlier version of Oscar, version 3.4, was found to have been copied from the code of Adapter. After the defendants realised that this had been done by the programmer employed to write version 3.4 they caused version 3.5 to be written by programmers who had no access whatever to Adapter. The plaintiffs maintained nevertheless that version 3.5 was an infringement of their copyright by virtue of the copying of the "non-literal" aspects of Adapter that is those aspects not reduced to written code. In that respect, therefore, the issue in the *Computer Associates* case was similar to the main issue in this case. The argument of the plaintiffs was that if, as illustrated by *Nichols v Universal Pictures*, to which I have referred above, and other authorities, the non-literal structures of literary works are protected by copyright and if, as the U.S. legislation like the U.K. legislation, provides computer programs are literary works, then the non-literal structures of computer programs are protected by copyright. Up to a point the Circuit Court of Appeals in the *Computer Associates* case was prepared to go along with this proposition, but it proceeded to explore its limits.

It did this by first going to *Baker v Selden*. Of the decision in that case the Circuit Court of Appeals said:

> The court concluded that those aspects of a work which "must necessarily be used as incident to" the idea system or process are also not copyrightable ... Selden's ledger sheets, therefore, enjoyed no copyright protection because they were "necessary incidents to" the system of accounting that he described. ... From this reasoning we conclude that those aspects of a computer program that are necessarily incidental to its function are similarly unprotectable.

Next the court turned to the decision in *Whelan*. After referring to criticism which that decision had received the court said:

> This criticism focuses not upon the program's ultimate purpose but on the reality of its structural design. As we have already noted, a computer program's ultimate function or purpose is the composite result of inter-acting subroutines. Since each subroutine is itself a program, and thus may be said to have its own "idea", *Whelan's* general formulation that a program's overall purpose equates with the program's idea is descriptively inadequate.

The Court of Appeals agreed with the District Judge's decision not to follow *Whelan*. It then became necessary for the Court of Appeals to formulate an alternative test. This it did by going back to what Judge Learned Hand had said in the *Nichols* case. It described this as the "abstractions test". In order to understand this label and the test itself it is necessary to read again part of the passage from *Nichols* which I have already read. As cited by the Court of Appeals in *Computer Associates* it is as follows:

> Upon any work ... a great number of patterns of increasing generality will fit equally well, as more and more of the incident is left out. The last may perhaps be no more than the most general statement of what the [work] is about, and a times might consist only of its title; but there is a point in this series of abstractions where they are no longer protected, since otherwise the [author] could prevent the use of his "ideas", to which, apart from their expression, his property never extended.

The Court of Appeals elaborated upon this process by saying that

> Initially, in a manner that resembles reverse engineering on a theoretical plane, a court should dissect the allegedly copied program's structure and isolate each level of abstraction contained within it. This process begins with the code and ends with an articulation of the program's ultimate function. Along the way, it is necessary essentially to retrace and map each of the designer's steps—in the opposite order to that in

which they were taken during the program's creation. As an anatomical guide to this procedure, the following description is helpful:

"At the lowest level of abstraction, a computer program may be thought of in its entirety as a set of individual instructions organised into a hierarchy of modules. At a higher level of abstraction, the instructions in the lowest level modules may be replaced conceptually by the functions of those modules. At progressively higher levels of abstraction, the functions of the higher-level modules conceptually replaces the implementations of those modules until, finally, one is left with nothing but the ultimate function of the program. ... A program has structure at every level of abstraction at which it is viewed. At low levels of abstraction, a program's structure may be quite complex; at the highest level it is trivial."

That description is, I think, taken from a text book which had been cited to the Court of Appeals.

In the test propounded in *Computer Associates* the discovery of a program's abstraction levels is the first step. The second step is to filter these abstractions in order to discover a "core of protectable material". In the process of filtration there are to be excluded from consideration (a) elements dictated by efficiency; (b) elements dictated by external factors and (c) elements taken from the public domain. Each of these categories is explained at some length. The essence of the "elements dictated by efficiency" is that if there is only one way to express an idea the idea and its expression are inseparable and copyright does not prevent the copying of the expression. The exclusion of "elements dictated by external factors" arises from the fact that if two persons set about the description of the same event there may be a number of particular facts which can only be described in a particular way. The Court of Appeals cited with evident approval the observation of Professor Nimmer (a well-known academic commentator on United States copyright law) that

in many instances it is impossible to write a program to perform particular functions in a specific computing environment without employing standard techniques.

As to "elements in the public domain":

plaintiffs may not claim copyright of an ... expression that is, if not standard, then commonplace in the computer software industry.

The third step in the process suggested in the *Computer Associates* case is to compare what is left of the "abstractions" made from the plaintiff's program after filtering out these elements with the program which is said to be an infringement of that program.

I have thought it right to deal at some length with the *Computer Associates* case because it explores the difficulties which arise in applying copyright law to computer programs to a greater extent than any English authority does. In the even more recent case of *Sega Enterprises Ltd v Accolade Inc* (1992) 977 F.2d 1510, the United States Court of Appeals for the Ninth Circuit approved the approach adopted by the Court of Appeals for the Second Circuit in *Computer Associates*. Not surprisingly neither of these decisions has yet been considered in an English case. There are references to *Whelan* in the judgments of Hoffmann J. in *Computer Aided Systems v Bolwell*, unreported August 23, 1989, and of Judge Paul Baker Q.C. in *Total Information Processing Systems Ltd v Daman Ltd* [1992] F.S.R. 171 but both these references are very general and neither of them can be said to indicate a preference for the *Whelan* approach over the approach which has since been adopted on two federal circuits in the United States.

There is thus nothing in any English decision which conflicts with the general approach adopted in the *Computer Associates* case. I think that in preference to seeking the "core of protectable expression" in the plaintiff's program an English court will first decide whether the plaintiff's program as a whole is entitled to copyright and then decide whether any similarity attributable to copying which is to be found in the defendant's program amounts to the copying of a substantial part of the plaintiff's program. This was the approach which was held to be correct in the *William Hill* case. But at the stage at which the substantiality of any copying falls to be assessed in an English case the question which has to be answered, in relation to the originality of the plaintiff's program and the separation of an idea from its expression, is essentially the same question as the United States court was addressing in *Computer Associates*. In my judgment it would be right to adopt a similar approach in England. This means that consideration is not restricted to the text of the code, as Mr McEwen submitted that it was when putting the defendants' case at its highest level. Moreover the argument that consideration should be limited to the "structure and organisation" of the program imports an unacceptable degree of uncertainty, because it is unclear at what level of abstraction (to use that term in the sense in which it was used in *Computer Associates*) the structure and organisation is to be discerned. Nevertheless I find difficulty in applying the abstractions test to the particular facts of this case, as will become apparent at a later stage.

Ferris J. ultimately concluded that three particular elements in the plaintiff's program had been infringed: the line editor, the amendment routines and the dose codes.

3.6.9.3 *Ibcos Computers v Barclays Mercantile* [1994] F.S.R. 297, Jacob J.

The plaintiffs owned copyright in a "suite" of accountancy programs comprising an accountancy package for computerised records in agricultural dealerships. The main programmer of these had left and developed a competing set of programs. Despite this programmer's denials of copying, Jacob J. found that many of the contributing programs had been built up from a line-by-line copy of the plaintiffs' program, a substantial quantity of which remained; and also that there had been substantial copying of structural elements. In this connection he said:

There is a danger from jumping from a conclusion that there was copying to a conclusion that a substantial part of a work has been taken. It is all too easy to say that a defendant who has lied about copying must have taken a lot. Of course it is likely in most cases that this is so. But the court must always go on to look at the further question of whether a substantial part was copied. In relation to conventional kinds of work this it can do reasonably readily. Even in the case of technical drawings it is possible to examine the parties' drawings to see whether a substantial part of the plaintiff's work is to be found in the defendant's. A good example of the right way to go about the problem is the *Billhöfer* case ([1990] F.S.R. 105). Even though there was copying (betrayed by the inessential details) there was no taking of sufficient visual features of the copyright drawing. In a computer program case, however, the court cannot so readily assess the question of substantial part unaided by expert evidence. I believe I should therefore be largely guided by such evidence.

In relation to the question of infringement, Jacob J. also set out Ferris J.'s references to Computer Associates v Altai *and remarked:*

For myself I do not find the route of going via U.S. case law particularly helpful. As I have said, U.K. copyright cannot prevent the copying of a mere general idea but can protect the copying of a detailed "idea". It is a question of degree where a good guide is the notion of overborrowing of the skill, labour and judgment which went into the copyright work. Going via the complication of the concept of a "core of protectable expression" merely complicates the matter so far as our law is concerned. It is likely to lead to overcitation of U.S. authority based on a statute different from ours. In the end the matter must be left to the value judgment of the court. Having expressed this reservation however, I thoroughly agree with what Ferris J. went on to say: "Consideration is not restricted to the text of the code . . ." That must be right: most literary copyright works involve both literal matters (the exact words of a novel or computer program) and varying levels of abstraction (plot, more or less detailed of a novel, general structure of a computer program).

I therefore think it right to have regard in this case not only to what Mr Turner called "literal similarities" but also to what he called "program structure" and "design features".

3.6.10 Remedies

3.6.10.1 Copyright, Designs and Patents Act 1988, ss.96, 97, 100, 104: Types of Remedy; Presumptions

S.96(1) An infringement of copyright is actionable by the copyright owner.

(2) In an action for infringement of copyright all such relief by way of damages, injunctions, accounts or otherwise is available to the plaintiff as is available in respect of the infringement of any other property right.

(3) This section has effect subject to the following provisions of this Chapter.

S.97(1) Where in an action for infringement of copyright it is shown that at the time of the infringement the defendant did not know, and had no reason to believe, that copyright subsisted in the work to which the action relates, the plaintiff is not entitled to damages against him, but without prejudice to any other remedy.

(2) The court may in an action for infringement of copyright having regard to all the circumstances, and in particular to—

(a) the flagrancy of the infringement, and

(b) any benefit accruing to the defendant by reason of the infringement.

award such additional damages as the justice of the case may require.

Section 98 limits the amount of damages available against a person entitled to a licence of right in consequence of a Monopolies and Mergers Commission report.

Section 99 gives the court power to order delivery up of infringing material, etc. (and see ss.113, 114).

S.100(1) An infringing copy of a work which is found exposed or otherwise immediately available for sale or hire, and in respect of which the copyright owner would be entitled to apply for an order under section 99, may be seized and detained by him or a person authorised by him.

The right to seize and detain is exercisable subject to the following conditions and is subject to any decision of the court under section 114.

(2) Before anything is seized under this section notice of the time and place of the proposed seizure must be given to a local police station.

(3) A person may for the purpose of exercising the right conferred by this section enter premises to which the public have access but may not seize anything in the possession, custody or control of a person at a permanent or regular place of business of his, and may not use any force.

(4) At the time when anything is seized under this section there shall be left at the place where it was seized a notice in the prescribed form containing the prescribed particulars as to the

person by whom or on whose authority the seizure is made and the grounds on which it is made.

(5) In this section—

"premises" includes land, buildings, movable structures, vehicles, vessels, aircraft and hovercraft; and

"prescribed" means prescribed by order of the Secretary of State.

(7) An order of the Secretary of State under this section shall be made by statutory instrument which shall be subject to annulment in pursuance of a resolution of either House of Parliament.

Sections 101, 102 deal with the rights of action of an exclusive licensee. For s.103, see below, 3.6.5.1.

Presumptions relevant to literary, dramatic, musical and artistic works

S.104(1) The following presumptions apply in proceedings brought by virtue of this Chapter with respect to a literary, dramatic, musical or artistic work.

(2) Where a name purporting to be that of the author appeared on copies of the work as published or on the work when it was made, the person whose name appeared shall be presumed, until the contrary is proved—

(a) to be the author of the work;

(b) to have made it in circumstances not falling within sections 11(2), 163, 165 or 158 (works produced in course of employment, Crown copyright, Parliamentary copyright or copyright of certain international organisations).

(3) In the case of a work alleged to be a work of joint authorship, subsection (2) applies in relation to each person alleged to be one of the authors.

(4) Where no name purporting to be that of the author appeared as mentioned in subsection (2) but—

(a) the work qualifies for copyright protection by virtue of section 155 (qualification by reference to country of first publication), and

(b) a name purporting to be that of the publisher appeared on copies of the work as first published,

the person whose name appeared shall be presumed, until the contrary is proved, to have been the owner of the copyright at the time of publication.

(5) If the author of the work is dead or the identity of the author cannot be ascertained by reasonable inquiry, it shall be presumed, in the absence of evidence to the contrary—

(a) that the work is an original work, and

(b) that the plaintiff's allegations as to what was the first publication of the work and as to the country of first publication are correct.

Section 105 creates a series of presumptions relating to sound recordings and films; and s.106 in relation to Crown copyright.

Section 107 creates a series of criminal offences relating to transactions in infringing copies. Section 108 permits orders for delivery up in criminal proceedings (and see ss.113, 114).

Section 109 makes special provision for search warrants.

Section 110 imposes criminal liability on certain corporate officers. For ss.111, 112, see below, 7.3.1.

3.6.11   Extent of Liability for Copyright Material on the Internet

3.6.11.1   Electronic Commerce (EC Directive) Regulations, 2013/2000

The following provisions, which are relevant inter alia to the liability of Internet service providers for copyright infringement, give effect to equivalent provisions in the Electronic Commerce Directive (31/2000) Arts 12–14.

Mere conduit

Article 17(1) Where an information society service is provided which consists of the transmission in a communication network of information provided by a recipient of the service or the provision of access to a communication network, the service provider (if he otherwise would) shall not be reliable for damage or for any other pecuniary remedy or for any criminal sanction as a result of that transmission where the service provider—

  (a) did not initiate the transmission;

  (b) did not select the receiver or the transmission; and

  (c) did not select or modify the information contained in the transmission.

(2) The acts of transmission and of provision of access referred to in paragraph (1) include the automatic, intermediate and transient storage of the information transmitted where:

  (a) this takes place for the sole purpose of carrying out the transmission in the communication network, and

  (b) the information is not stored for any period longer than is reasonably necessary for the transmission.

Caching

Article 18 Where an information society service is provided which consists of the transmission in a communication network of information provided by a recipient of the service, the service provider (if he otherwise would) shall not be liable for damages or for any other pecuniary remedy or for any criminal sanction as a result of that transmission where—

  (a) the information is the subject of automatic, intermediate and temporary storage where that storage is for the sole purpose of making more efficient onward transmission of the information to other recipients of the service upon their request, and

  (b) the service provider—

    (i) does not modify the information;

    (ii) complies with conditions on access to the information;

    (iii) complies with any rules regarding the updating of the information, specified in a manner widely recognised and used by industry;

    (iv) does not interfere with the lawful use of technology, widely recognised and used by industry, to obtain data on the use of the information; and

    (v) acts expeditiously to remove or to disable access to the information he has stored upon obtaining actual knowledge of the fact that the information at the initial source of the transmission has been removed from the network, or access to it has been disabled, or that a court or an administrative authority has ordered such removal or disablement.

Hosting

Article 19 Where an information society service is provided which consists of the storage of information provided by a recipient of the service, the service provider (if he otherwise would) shall not be liable for damages or for any other pecuniary remedy or for any criminal sanction as a result of that storage where—

    (a) the service provider—

        (i) does not have actual knowledge of unlawful activity or information and, where a claim for damages is made, is not aware of facts or circumstances from which it would have been apparent to the service provider that the activity of information was unlawful; or

        (ii) upon obtaining such knowledge or awareness, acts expeditiously to remove or to disable access to the information, and

    (b) the recipient of the service was not acting under the authority or the control of the service provider.

3.6.11.2 Copyright, Designs and Patents Act 1988, s. 31A (proposed)

An implementation of the InfoSoc directive, Art.5(1), exempting intermediate Internet carriers from liability for copyright infringement, the UK government has proposed the following:

Making of temporary copies

S.31A Copyright in a literary work, other than a computer program or database, or in a dramatic, musical or artistic work, the typographical arrangement of a published edition, a sound recording or a film, is not infringed by the making of a temporary copy which is transient or incidental, which is an integral and essential part of a technological process and the sole purpose of which is to enable—

    (a) a transmission of the work in a network between third parties by an intermediary; or

    (b) a lawful use of the work;

and which has no independent economic significance.

3.6.11.3 Copyright, Designs and Patents Act 1988, proposed sections

In implementation of the InfoSoc Directive, Art. 6, which requires provisions to be made against the circumvention of protection measures which limit access to Internet sites and services, the UK government has proposed to restrict the scope of the present s.296 of the 1988 Act to protection measures for computer programs (since they are not within the Directive), and otherwise to introduce the provisions that follow:

S.296(1) This section applies where copies of a computer program are issued to the public, by or with the licence of the copyright owner, in an electronic form which is copy-protected.

(2) The person issuing the copies to the public has the same rights against a person who, knowing or having reason to believe that it will be used to make infringing copies—

(a) *makes, imports, sells or lets for hire, offers or exposes for sale or hire, or advertises for sale or hire, or possesses in the course of a business any device or means specifically designed or adapted to circumvent the form of copy-protection employed, or*

(b) *publishes information intended to enable or assist persons to circumvent that form of copy-protection,*

as a copyright owner has in respect of an infringement of copyright.

(4) References in this section to copy-protection include any device or means intended to prevent or restrict copying of a computer program or to impair the quality of copies made.

(5) Expressions used in this section which are defined for the purposes of Part I of this Act (copyright) have the same meaning as in that Part.]

Section 296(3) and (6) give remedial powers equivalent to those for copyright in respect of delivery up, seizure and disposal, presumptions and withdrawal of the privilege against self-incrimination.

[Circumvention of protection measures

S.296ZA(1) This section applies where—

(a) *copies of a copyright work other than a computer program are issued or communicated to the public, by or with the licence of the copyright owner, in a form where effective technological measures have been applied; and*

(b) *a person (A) does anything which circumvents those measures knowing, or having reason to believe, that is the effect of what he is doing.*

(2) The person issuing or communicating the copies to the public has the same rights against (A) as a copyright owner has in respect of an infringement of copyright.

(3) The copyright owner, if he is not the person issuing or communicating the copies, also has the same rights against (A) as he has in respect of an infringement of copyright.

(4) The rights in subsection (2) are concurrent with those in subsection (3) and sections 101 and 102 apply to an action brought under this section except that references to an exclusive licensee shall be construed as including a person other than an exclusive licensee who issues or communicates to the public copies with the consent of the copyright owner.

(5) The following provisions apply in relation to proceedings under this section as in relation to proceedings under Part I (copyright)—

(a) *sections 104 to 106 of this Act (presumptions as to certain matters relating to copyright) and*

(b) *section 72 of the Supreme Court Act 1981, section 15 of the Law Reform (Miscellaneous Provisions) (Scotland) Act 1985 and section 94A of the Judicature (Northern Ireland) Act 1978 (withdrawal of privilege against self-incrimination in certain proceedings relating to intellectual property).*

(6) Subsections (1) to (4) and (5)(b) and any other provision of this Act as it has effect for the purposes of those subsections apply with any necessary adaptations, to rights in performances, publication right and database right.

(7) The provisions of Regulation 22 (presumptions relevant to database right) of the Copyright and Rights in Databases Regulations 1997 (SI 1997 No. 3032) apply in proceedings brought by virtue of this section in relation to database right.

Devices and services designed to circumvent technological measures

S.296ZB(1) A person commits an offence if he—

(a) makes for sale or hire, or

(b) imports otherwise than for his private and domestic use, or

(c) in the course of a business—

(i) sells or lets for hire, or
(ii) offers or exposes for sale or hire, or
(iii) advertises for sale or hire, or
(iv) possesses, or
(v) distributes, or

(d) distributes otherwise than in the course of a business to such an extent as to affect prejudicially the copyright owner any device, product or component which is primarily designed, produced, or adapted for the purpose of enabling or facilitating the circumvention of effective technological measures.

(2) A person commits an offence if he provides, promotes, advertises or markets a service in the course of a business, or otherwise than in the course of a business to such an extent as to affect prejudicially the copyright owner, the purpose of which is to enable or facilitate the circumvention of effective technological measures.

(3) A person guilty of an offence under subsections (1) or (2) is liable—

(a) on summary conviction, to imprisonment for a term not exceeding three months, or to a fine not exceeding the statutory maximum, or to both;

(b) on conviction on indictment, to imprisonment for a term not exceeding two years, or to a fine, or to both.

(4) It is a defence to any prosecution for an offence under this section for the defendant to prove that he did not know, and had no reasonable ground for believing, that—

(a) the device, product or component; or

(b) the services provided

enabled or facilitated the circumvention of effective technological measures.]

Search warrant and forfeiture provisions would also be provided analogous to those being provided in relation to offences in s.297A by the Copyright, etc. and Trade Marks (Offences and Enforcement) Act 2002.

[Rights and remedies in respect of devices and services designed to circumvent technological measures

S.296ZC(1) This section applies where—

(a) copies of a copyright work other than a computer program are issued or commu-

nicated to the public, by or with the licence of the copyright owner, in a form where effective technological measures have been applied, and

(b) *a person (B)—*

    (i) *makes for sale or hire, or*

    (ii) *imports otherwise than for his private and domestic use, or*

    (iii) *in the course of business sells or lets for hire, offers or exposes for sale or hire, advertises for sale or hire, possesses or distributes, or*

    (iv) *distributes otherwise than in the course of a business to such an extent as to affect prejudicially the copyright owner*

any device, product or component which has only a limited commercially significant purpose or use other than to circumvent, or is primarily designed, produced or adapted for the purpose of enabling or facilitating the circumvention of those measures, or

(c) *a person (C) provides, promotes, advertises or markets a service, product, device or component—*

    (i) *in the course of a business, or*

    (ii) *otherwise than in the course of a business to such an extent as to affect prejudicially the copyright owner,*

the purpose of which is to enable or facilitate the circumvention of those measures.

(2) The person issuing or communicating the copies to the public has the same rights against (B) and (C) as a copyright owner has in respect of an infringement of copyright.

(3) The copyright owner, if he is not the person issuing or communicating the copies, also has the same rights against (B) and (C) as he has in respect of an infringement of copyright.

(4) The rights in subsection (2) are concurrent with those in subsection (3) and sections 101 and 102 apply to an action brought under this section except that references to an exclusive licensee shall be construed as including a person other than an exclusive licensee who issues or communicates to the public copies with the consent of the copyright owner.

(5) Further, the copyright owner and person issuing or communicating copies to the public have the same rights under section 99 or 100 (delivery up or seizure of certain articles) in relation to any such device, product or component which a person has in his possession, custody or control with the intention that it should be used to circumvent effective technological measures, as a copyright owner has in relation to any infringing copy.

(6) The following provisions apply in relation to proceedings under this section as in relation to proceedings under Part I (copyright)—

(a) *sections 104 to 106 of this Act (presumptions as to certain matters relating to copyright), and*

(b) *section 72 of the Supreme Court Act 1981, section 15 of the Law Reform (Miscellaneous Provisions) (Scotland) Act 1985 and section 94A of the Judicature (Northern Ireland) Act 1978 (withdrawal of privilege against self-incrimination in certain proceedings relating to intellectual property)*

and section 114 of this Act applies, with the necessary modifications, in relation to the disposal of anything delivered up or seized by virtue of subsection (5).

(7) In section 97(1) (innocent infringement of copyright) as it applies to proceedings for infringement of the rights conferred by this section, the reference to the defendant not knowing

or having reason to believe that copyright subsisted in the work shall be construed as a reference to his not knowing or having reason to believe that his acts enabled or facilitated an infringement of copyright.

(8) Sub-sections (1) to (5), (6) (b) and (7) and any other provision of this Act as it has effect for the purposes of those subsections apply, with any necessary adaptations, to rights in performances, publication right and database right.

(9) The provisions of Regulation 22 (presumptions relevant to database right) of the Copyright and Rights in Databases Regulations 1997 (SI 1997 No. 3032) apply in proceedings brought by virtue of this section in relation to database right.

Interpretation of sections 296ZA to 296ZC

S.296ZD(1) In sections 296ZA to 296ZC, "technological measures" are any technology, device or component which is intended, in the normal course of its operation, to protect a copyright work other than a computer program.

(2) Such measures are "effective" if the use of the work is controlled by the copyright owner through—

(a) an access control or protection process such as encryption, scrambling or other transformation of the work, or

(b) a copy control mechanism, which achieves the intended protection.

(3) In this section, references to protection of a work are to the prevention or restriction of infringing acts in relation to the work.

(4) Expressions used in sections 296ZA to 296ZC which are defined for the purposes of Part 1 of this Act (copyright) have the same meaning as in that Part.

Rights management information

Electronic Rights Management Information

S.296ZE(1) This section applies where a person (D), knowingly and without authority, removes or alters electronic rights management information which—

(a) is associated with a copy of a copyright work, or

(b) appears in connection with the communication to the public of a copyright work, and

where (D) knows, or has reason to believe, that by so doing he is inducing, enabling, facilitating or concealing an infringement of copyright.

(2) This section also applies where a person (E), knowingly and without authority, distributes, imports for distribution or communicates to the public copies of a copyright work from which electronic rights management information—

(a) associated with the copies, or

(b) appearing in connection with the communication to the public of the work,

has been removed or altered without authority and where (E) knows, or has reason to believe, that by so doing he is inducing, enabling, facilitating or concealing an infringement of copyright.

(3) A person issuing or communicating the copies to the public has the same rights against (D) and (E) as a copyright owner has in respect of an infringement of copyright.

(4) The copyright owner, if he is not the person issuing or communicating the copies, also has the same rights against (D) and (E) as he has in respect of an infringement of copyright.

(5) The rights in subsection (3) are concurrent with those in subsection (4) and sections 101 and 102 apply to an action brought under this section except that references to an exclusive licensee shall be construed as including a person other than an exclusive licensee who issues or communicates to the public copies with the consent of the copyright owner.

(6) The following provisions apply in relation to proceedings under this section as in relation to proceedings under Part I (copyright)—

  (a) sections 104 to 106 of this Act (presumptions as to certain matters relating to copyright), and

  (b) section 72 of the Supreme Court Act 1981, section 15 of the Law Reform (Miscellaneous Provisions) (Scotland) Act 1985 and section 94A of the Judicature (Northern Ireland) Act 1978 (withdrawal of privilege against self-incrimination in certain proceedings relating to intellectual property).

(7) Subsections (1) to (5) and (6)(b), and any other provision of this Act as it has effect for the purposes of those subsections, apply, with any necessary adaptations, to rights in performances, publication right and database right.

(8) The provisions of Regulation 22 (presumptions relevant to database right) of the Copyright and Rights in Databases Regulations 1997 (SI 1997/3032) apply in proceedings brought by virtue of this section in relation to database right.

(9) Expressions used in this section which are defined for the purposes of Part I of this Act (copyright) have the same meaning as in that Part and "rights management information" means any information provided by the copyright owner which identifies the work, the author or any other right holder, or information about the terms and conditions of use of the work, and any numbers or codes that represent such information.

The following new section would be added at an appropriate place in the Act, probably in Part VII:

Remedy where effective technological measures prevent permitted acts

S.296(1) Where the application of any effective technological measure to a copyright work other than a computer program prevents a person from benefiting directly from [reference will be made here either to Articles 5.2(a), 2(b), 2(c), 2(d), 2(e), 3(a), 3(b) or 3(e) of the Directive or to provisions of the Act covering the exceptions permitted under these articles] in relation to that work then that person may issue a notice of complaint to the Secretary of State.

(2) The Secretary of State may, following receipt of a notice of complaint, give to the owner of that copyright work or an exclusive licensee such directions as appear to the Secretary of State to be requisite or expedient for the purpose of—

(a) establishing whether any voluntary measure or agreement relevant to the copyright work the subject of the complaint subsists, or

(b) (in the event it is established there is no subsisting voluntary measure or agreement) enabling the complainant to benefit from [those articles or sections] referred to in subsection (1) to which the complaint relates.

(3) The Secretary of State may also give directions—

(a) as to the form and manner in which a notice of complaint in subsection (1) may be delivered to him;

(b) as to the form and manner in which evidence of any voluntary measure or agreement may be delivered to him; and

(c) generally as to the procedure to be followed in relation to a complaint made under this section

and shall publish directions given under this subsection in such manner as in his opinion will secure adequate publicity for them.

(4) It shall be the duty of any person to whom a direction is given under this section to give effect to that direction.

(5) The obligation to comply with a direction given under subsection (2)(b) is a duty owed to the complainant; and a breach of the duty is actionable accordingly (subject to the defences and other incidents applying to actions for breach of statutory duty).

(6) Any direction under this section may be varied or revoked by a subsequent direction under this section.

(7) Any direction given under this section shall be in writing.

(8) This section does not apply—

(a) to copyright works made available by an on-demand service; or

(b) where the complainant has obtained the copyright work the subject of the complaint unlawfully.

(9) In this section—

"voluntary measure or agreement" means any measure taken voluntarily by a copyright owner or exclusive licensee or any agreement between a copyright owner or exclusive licensee and another party the purpose of which is to enable the complainant (or persons of a class to which the complainant belongs) to benefit from [those articles or sections] referred to in subsection (1) to which the complaint relates;
"effective technological measure" has the same meaning as in section 296ZD;
"exclusive licensee" means a licensee under an exclusive licence and "exclusive licence" has the same meaning as in section 92, and
"in writing" has the same meaning as in Part I this Act.

(10) Subsections (1) to (8) apply, with any necessary adaptations, to rights in performances, publication right and database right.

3.7   Moral Rights

3.7.1   Right to be Identified

3.7.1.1   Copyright, Designs and Patents Act 1988, ss.77–79

S.77(1) The author of a copyright literary, dramatic, musical or artistic work, and the director of a copyright film, has the right to be identified as the author or director of the work in the circumstances mentioned in this section; but the right is not infringed unless it has been asserted in accordance with section 78.

(2) The author of a literary work (other than words intended to be sung or spoken with music) or a dramatic work has the right to be identified whenever—

    (a) the work is published commercially, performed in public, broadcast or included in a cable programme service; or

    (b) copies of a film or sound recording including the work are issued to the public;

and that right includes the right to be identified whenever any of those events occur in relation to an adaptation of the work as the author of the work from which the adaptation was made.

(3) The author of a musical work, or a literary work consisting of words intended to be sung or spoken with music, has the right to be identified whenever—

    (a) the work is published commercially;

    (b) copies of a sound recording of the work are issued to the public; or

    (c) a film of which the sound-track includes the work is shown in public or copies of such a film are issued to the public;

and that right includes the right to be identified whenever any of those events occur in relation to an adaptation of the work as the author of the work from which the adaptation was made.

(4) The author of an artistic work has the right to be identified whenever—

    (a) the work is published commercially or exhibited in public, or a visual image of it is broadcast or included in a cable programme service;

    (b) a film including a visual image of the work is shown in public or copies of such a film are issued to the public; or

    (c) in the case of a work of architecture in the form of a building or a model for a building, a sculpture or a work of artistic craftsmanship, copies of a graphic work representing it, or of a photograph of it, are issued to the public.

(5) The author of a work of architecture in the form of a building also has the right to be

identified on the building as constructed or, where more than one building is constructed to the design, on the first to be constructed.

(6) The director of a film has the right to be identified whenever the film is shown in public, broadcast or included in a cable programme service or copies of the film are issued to the public.

(7) The right of the author or director under this section is—

    (a) in the case of commercial publication or the issue to the public of copies of a film or sound recording, to be identified in or on each copy or, if that is not appropriate, in some other manner likely to bring his identity to the notice of a person acquiring a copy.

    (b) in the case of identification on a building, to be identified by appropriate means visible to persons entering or approaching the building, and

    (c) in any other case, to be identified in a manner likely to bring his identity to the attention of a person seeing or hearing the performance, exhibition, showing, broadcast or cable programme in question;

and the identification must in each case be clear and reasonably prominent.

(8) If the author or director in asserting his right to be identified specifies a pseudonym, initials or some other particular form of identification, that form shall be used; otherwise any reasonable form of identification may be used.

(9) This section has effect subject to section 79 (exceptions to right).

S.78(1) A person does not infringe the right conferred by section 77 (right to be identified as author or director) by doing any of the acts mentioned in that section unless the right has been asserted in accordance with the following provisions so as to bind him in relation to that act.

(2) The right may be asserted generally, or in relation to any specified act or description of acts—

    (a) on an assignment of copyright in the work, by including in the instrument effecting the assignment a statement that the author or director asserts in relation to that work his right to be identified, or

    (b) by instrument in writing signed by the author or director.

(3) The right may also be asserted in relation to the public exhibition of an artistic work—

    (a) by securing that when the author or other first owner of copyright parts with possession of the original, or of a copy made by him or under his direction or control, the author is identified on the original or copy, or on a frame, mount or other thing to which it is attached, or

    (b) by including in a licence by which the author or other first owner of copyright authorises the making of copies of the work a statement signed by or on behalf of the person granting the licence that the author asserts his right to be identified in the event of the public exhibition of a copy made in pursuance of the licence.

(4) The persons bound by an assertion of the right under subsection (2) or (3) are—

(a) in the case of an assertion under subsection (2)(a), the assignee and anyone claiming through him, whether or not he has notice of the assertion;

(b) in the case of an assertion under subsection (2)(b), anyone to whose notice the assertion is brought;

(c) in the case of an assertion under subsection (3)(a), anyone into whose hands that original or copy comes, whether or not the identification is still present or visible;

(d) in the case of an assertion under subsection (3)(b), the licensee and anyone into whose hands a copy made in pursuance of the licence comes, whether or not he has notice of the assertion.

(5) In an action for infringement of the right the court shall, in considering remedies, take into account any delay in asserting the right.

S.79(1) The right conferred by section 77 (right to be identified as author or director) is subject to the following exceptions.

(2) The right does not apply in relation to the following descriptions of work—

(a) a computer program;

(b) the design of a typeface;

(c) any computer-generated work.

(3) The right does not apply to anything done by or with the authority of the copyright owner where copyright in the work originally vested—

(a) in the author's employer by virtue of section 11(2) (works produced in course of employment), or

(b) in the director's employer by virtue of section 9(2)(a) (person to be treated as author of film).

(4) The right is not infringed by an act which by virtue of any of the following provisions would not infringe copyright in the work—

(a) section 30 (fair dealing for certain purposes), so far as it relates to the reporting of current events by means of a sound recording, film, broadcast or cable programme;

(b) section 31 (incidental inclusion of work in an artistic work, sound recording, film, broadcast or cable programme);

(c) section 32(3) (examination questions);

(d) section 45 (parliamentary and judicial proceedings);

(e) section 46(1) or (2) (Royal Commissions and statutory inquiries);

(f) section 51 (use of design documents and models);

(g) section 52 (effect of exploitation of design derived from artistic work);

(h) section 57 or 66A (anonymous or pseudonymous works: acts permitted on assumptions as to expiry of copyright 8c).

(5) The right does not apply in relation to any work made for the purpose of reporting current events.

(6) The right does not apply in relation to the publication in—

(a) a newspaper, magazine or similar periodical, or

(b) an encyclopedia, dictionary, yearbook or other collective work of reference,

of a literary, dramatic, musical or artistic work made for the purposes of such publication or made available with the consent of the author for the purposes of such publication.

(7) The right does not apply in relation to—

(a) a work in which Crown copyright or Parliamentary copyright subsists, or

(b) a work in which copyright originally vested in an international organisation by virtue of section 168,

unless the author or director has previously been identified as such in or on published copies of the work.

3.7.2 Right against Derogatory Treatment

3.7.2.1 Copyright, Designs and Patents Act 1988, ss.80–82, 178

S.80(1) The author of a copyright literary, dramatic, musical or artistic work, and the director of a copyright film, has the right in the circumstances mentioned in this section not to have his work subjected to derogatory treatment.

(2) For the purposes of this section—

- (a) "treatment" of a work means any addition to, deletion from or alteration to or adaptation of the work, other than—

  - (i) a translation of a literary or dramatic work, or
  - (ii) an arrangement or transcription of a musical work involving no more than a change of key or register; and

- (b) the treatment of a work is derogatory if it amounts to distortion or mutilation of the work or is otherwise prejudicial to the honour or reputation of the author or director;

and in the following provisions of this section references to a derogatory treatment of a work shall be construed accordingly.

(3) In the case of a literary, dramatic or musical work the right is infringed by a person who—

- (a) publishes commercially, performs in public, broadcasts or includes in a cable programme service a derogatory treatment of the work; or

- (b) issues to the public copies of a film or sound recording of, or including, a derogatory treatment of the work.

(4) In the case of an artistic work the right is infringed by a person who—

- (a) publishes commercially or exhibits in public a derogatory treatment of the work, or broadcasts or includes in a cable programme service a visual image of a derogatory treatment of the work,

- (b) shows in public a film including a visual image of a derogatory treatment of the work or issues to the public copies of such a film, or

- (c) in the case of—

  - (i) a work of architecture in the form of a model for a building,
  - (ii) a sculpture, or
  - (iii) a work of artistic craftsmanship,

  issues to the public copies of a graphic work representing, or of a photograph of, a derogatory treatment of the work.

(5) Subsection (4) does not apply to a work of architecture in the form of a building; but where the author of such a work is identified on the building and it is the subject of derogatory treatment he has the right to require the identification to be removed.

(6) In the case of a film, the right is infringed by a person who—

- (a) shows in public, broadcasts or includes in a cable programme service a derogatory treatment of the film; or

- (b) issues to the public copies of a derogatory treatment of the film.

(7) The right conferred by this section extends to the treatment of parts of a work resulting from a previous treatment by a person other than the author or director, if those parts are attributed to, or are likely to be regarded as the work of, the author or director.

(8) This section has effect subject to sections 81 and 82 (exceptions to and qualifications of right).

S.81(1) The right conferred by section 80 (right to object to derogatory treatment of work) is subject to the following exceptions.

(2) The right does not apply to a computer program or to any computer-generated work.

(3) The right does not apply in relation to any work made for the purpose of reporting current events.

(4) The right does not apply in relation to the publication in—

(a) a newspaper, magazine or similar periodical, or

(b) an encyclopedia, dictionary, yearbook or other collective work of reference,

of a literary, dramatic, musical or artistic work made for the purposes of such publication or made available with the consent of the author for the purposes of such publication.

Nor does the right apply in relation to any subsequent exploitation elsewhere of such a work without any modification of the published version.

(5) The right is not infringed by an act which by virtue of section 57 (anonymous or pseudonymous works: acts permitted on assumptions as to expiry of copyright or death of author) would not infringe copyright.

(6) The right is not infringed by anything done for the purpose of—

(a) avoiding the commission of an offence,

(b) complying with a duty imposed by or under an enactment, or

(c) in the case of the British Broadcasting Corporation, avoiding the inclusion in a programme broadcast by them of anything which offends against good taste or decency or which is likely to encourage or incite to crime or to lead to disorder or to be offensive to public feeling,

provided, where the author or director is identified at the time of the relevant act or has previously been identified in or on published copies of the work, that there is a sufficient disclaimer.

S.82(1) This section applies to—

(a) works in which copyright originally vested in the author's employer by virtue of section 11(2) (works produced in course of employment) or in the director's employer by virtue of section 9(2)(a) (person to be treated as author of film),

(b) works in which Crown copyright or Parliamentary copyright subsists, and

(c) works in which copyright originally vested in an international organisation by virtue of section 168.

(2) The right conferred by section 80 (right to object to derogatory treatment of work) does not apply to anything done in relation to such a work by or with the authority of the copyright owner unless the author or director—

(a) is identified at the time of the relevant act, or

(b) has previously been identified in or on published copies of the work;

and where in such a case the right does apply; it is not infringed if there is a sufficient disclaimer.

Section 83 creates liability for secondary infringement of articles open to objection under s.80.

S.178 ... "sufficient disclaimer", in relation to an act capable of infringing the right conferred by section 80 (right to object to derogatory treatment of work), means a clear and reasonably prominent indication—

(i) given at the time of the act, and

(ii) if the author or director is then identified, appearing along with the identification,

that the work has been subjected to treatment to which the author or director has not consented.

3.7.3 False Attribution

3.7.3.1 Copyright, Designs and Patents Act 1988, s.84

S.84(1) A person has the right in the circumstances mentioned in this section—

   (a) not to have a literary, dramatic, musical or artistic work falsely attributed to him as author, and

   (b) not to have a film falsely attributed to him as director;

and in this section an "attribution", in relation to such a work, means a statement (express or implied) as to who is the author or director.

(2) The right is infringed by a person who—

   (a) issues to the public copies of a work of any of those descriptions in or on which there is a false attribution, or

   (b) exhibits in public an artistic work, or a copy of an artistic work, in or on which there is a false attribution.

(3) The right is also infringed by a person who—

   (a) in the case of a literary, dramatic or musical work, performs the work in public, broadcasts it or includes it in a cable programme service as being the work of a person, or

   (b) in the case of a film, shows it in public, broadcasts it or includes it in a cable programme service as being directed by a person.

knowing or having reason to believe that the attribution is false.

(4) The right is also infringed by the issue to the public or public display of material containing a false attribution in connection with any of the acts mentioned in subsection (2) or (3).

(5) The right is also infringed by a person who in the course of a business—

   (a) possesses or deals with a copy of a work of any of the descriptions mentioned in subsection (1) in or on which there is a false attribution, or

   (b) in the case of an artistic work, possesses or deals with the work itself when there is a false attribution in or on it,

knowing or having reason to believe that there is such an attribution and that it is false.

(6) In the case of an artistic work the right is also infringed by a person who in the course of a business—

   (a) deals with a work which has been altered after the author parted with possession of it as being the unaltered work of the author, or

   (b) deals with a copy of such a work as being a copy of the unaltered work of the author,

knowing or having reason to believe that that is not the case.

(7) References in this section to dealing are to selling or letting for hire, offering or exposing for sale or hire, exhibiting in public, or distributing.

(8) This section applies where, contrary to the fact—

> **(a)** a literary, dramatic or musical work is falsely represented as being an adaptation of the work of a person, or
>
> **(b)** a copy of an artistic work is falsely represented as being a copy made by the author of the artistic work,

as it applies where the work is falsely attributed to a person as author.

See Noah v Shuba *(below, 3.8.3.).*

3.7.4 Right of Privacy in Photographs and Films

3.7.4.1 Copyright, Designs and Patents Act 1988, s.85

S.85(1) A person who for private and domestic purposes commissions the taking of a photograph or the making of a film has, where copyright subsists in the resulting work, the right not to have—

(a) copies of the work issued to the public,

(b) the work exhibited or shown in public, or

(c) the work broadcast or included in a cable programme service;

and, except as mentioned in subsection (2), a person who does or authorises the doing of any of those acts infringes that right.

(2) The right is not infringed by an act which by virtue of any of the following provisions would not infringe copyright in the work—

(a) section 31 (incidental inclusion of work in an artistic work, film, broadcast or cable programme);

(b) section 45 (parliamentary and judicial proceedings);

(c) section 46 (Royal Commissions and statutory inquiries);

(d) section 50 (acts done under statutory authority);

(e) section 57 (anonymous or pseudonymous works: acts permitted on assumptions as to expiry of copyright or death or author).

3.7.5 General Provisions affecting Moral Rights

3.7.5.1 Copyright, Designs and Patents Act 1988, ss.86, 87, 94, 95, 103

S.86(1) The rights conferred by section 77 (right to be identified as author or director), section 80 (right to object to derogatory treatment of work) and section 85 (right to privacy of certain photographs and films) continue to subsist so long as copyright subsists in the work.

(2) The right conferred by section 84 (false attribution) continues to subsist until 20 years after a person's death.

S.87(1) It is not an infringement of any of the rights conferred by this Chapter to do any act to which the person entitled to the right has consented.

(2) Any of those rights may be waived by instrument in writing signed by the person giving up the right.

(3) A waiver—

 (a) may relate to a specific work, to works of a specified description or to works gen- erally, and may relate to existing or future works, and

 (b) may be conditional or unconditional and may be expressed to be subject to revocation;

and if made in favour of the owner or prospective owner of the copyright in the work or works to which it relates, it shall be presumed to extend to his licensees and successors in title unless a contrary intention is expressed.

(4) Nothing in this Chapter shall be construed as excluding the operation of the general law of contract or estoppel in relation to an informal waiver or other transaction in relation to any of the rights mentioned in subsection (1).

S.94 The rights conferred by Chapter IV (moral rights) are not assignable.

S.95(1) On the death of a person entitled to the right conferred by section 77 (right to identification of author or director), section 80 (right to object to derogatory treatment of work) or section 85 (right to privacy of certain photographs and films)—

 (a) the right passes to such person as he may by testamentary disposition specifically direct,

 (b) if there is no such direction but the copyright in the work in question forms part of his estate, the right passes to the person to whom the copyright passes, and

 (c) if or to the extent that the right does not pass under paragraph (a) or (b) it is exercisable by his personal representatives.

(5) Any infringement after a person's death of the right conferred by section 84 (false attri- bution) is actionable by his personal representatives.

S.95(2) deals with divided devolution of copyright, s.95(3) with multiple entitlement; s.95(4) with the continuing force of a consent or waiver; and s.95(6) with entitlement to damages recovered by personal representatives.

S.103(1) An infringement of a right conferred by Chapter IV (moral rights) is actionable as a breach of statutory duty owed to the person entitled to the right.

(2) In proceedings for infringement of the right conferred by section 80 (right to object to derogatory treatment of work) the court may, if it thinks it is an adequate remedy in the circumstances, grant an injunction on terms prohibiting the doing of any act unless a disclaimer is made, in such terms and in such manner as may be approved by the court, dissociating the author or director from the treatment of the work.

3.8 Authorship, Ownership and Dealings

3.8.1 Copyright, Designs and Patents Act 1988, ss.9, 11, 178, Copyright and Related Rights Regulations 1996, reg. 36. Authorship and ownership of copyright

S.9(1) In this Part "author", in relation to a work, means the person who creates it.

(2) That person shall be taken to be—

> (a) in the case of a sound recording [. . .] the person whom the arrangements necessary for the making of the recording [. . .] are undertaken;

> [(ab) in the case of a film, the person by whom the arrangements necessary for the making of the film are undertaken and the principal director of the film;]

> (b) in the case of a broadcast, the person making the broadcast (see section 6(3)) or, in the case of a broadcast which relays another broadcast by reception and immediate re-transmission, the person making that other broadcast;

> (c) in the case of a cable programme, the person providing the cable programme service in which the programme is included;

> (d) in the case of the typographical arrangement of a published edition, the publisher.

(3) In the case of a literary, dramatic, musical or artistic work which is computer-generated, the author shall be taken to be the person by whom the arrangements necessary for the creation of the work are undertaken.

(4) For the purposes of this Part a work is of "unknown authorship" if the identity of the author is unknown or, in the case of a work of joint authorship, if the identity of none of the authors is known.

(5) For the purposes of this Part the identity of an author shall be regarded as unknown if it is not possible for a person to ascertain his identity by reasonable inquiry; but if his identity is once known it shall be subsequently be regarded as unknown.

Among the transitional provisions contained in the Copyright and Related Rights Regulations (SI 1996/2967), note, in particular, reg.36:

36. Authorship of films

> **(1) Regulation 18 (authorship of films) applies as from commencement in relation to films made on or after 1st July 1994.**

> **(2) It is not an infringement of any right which the principal director has by virtue of these Regulations to do anything after commencement in pursuance of arrangements for the exploitation of the film made before 19th November 1992.**

This does not affect any right of his to equitable remuneration under section 93B.

S.11(1) The author of a work is the first owner of any copyright in it, subject to the following provisions.

(2) Where a literary, dramatic, musical or artistic work [or film] is made by an employee in the course of his employment, his employer is the first owner of any copyright in the work subject to any agreement to the contrary.

(3) This section does not apply to Crown copyright or Parliamentary copyright (see sections 163 and 165) or to copyright which subsists by virtue of section 168 (copyright of certain international organisations).

S.178 … "computer-generated", in relation to a work, means that the work is generated by computer in circumstances such that there is no human author of the work: "employed", "employee", "employer" and "employment" refer to employment under a contract of service or of apprenticeship.

3.8.2 *Cummins v Bond* [1927] 1 Ch. 167, Eve J.

During a seance, the plaintiff, a psychic medium, wrote down a text entitled "The Chronicles of Cleophas" about the acts and teachings of the apostles. It was in archaistic language without stops and was said to have been put down automatically by the plaintiff. The defendant took it away and edited it, then claimed the right to publish it.

Eve J.:

The issue in this action is reduced to the simple question, who, if any one, is the owner of the copyright in this work. Prima facie it is the author, and so far as this world is concerned there can be no doubt who is the author here, for it has been abundantly proved that the plaintiff is the writer of every word to be found in this bundle of original script. But the plaintiff and her witness and the defendant are all of opinion—and I do not doubt that the opinion is an honest one—that the true originator of all that is to be found in these documents is some being no longer inhabiting this world, and who has been out of it for a length of time sufficient to justify the hope that he has no reasons for wishing to return to it.

From this it would almost seem as though the individual who has been dead and buried for some 1900 odd years and the plaintiff ought to be regarded as the joint authors and owners of the copyright, but inasmuch as I do feel myself competent to make any declaration in his favour, and recognizing as I do that I have no jurisdiction extending to the sphere in which he moves, I think I ought to confine myself when inquiring who is the author to individuals who were alive when the work first came into existence and to conditions which the legislature in 1911 may reasonably be presumed to have contemplated. So doing it would seem to be clear that the ownership rests with this lady, to whose gift of extremely rapid writing coupled with a peculiar ability to reproduce in archaic English matter communicated to her in some unknown tongue we owe the production of these documents.

The learned judge found that there was no basis upon which the defendant could claim to be a co-author. He proceeded:

Alternatively, failing to establish any claim on his own behalf he submits that there is no copyright in the work at all, that it has come from a far off locality which I cannot specify, and that the plaintiff is the mere conduit pipe by which it has been conveyed to this world. I do not think that is a fair appreciation of the plaintiff's activities. They obviously involved a great deal more than mere repetition; but, apart altogether from these considerations, the conclusion which the defendant invites me to come to in this submission involves the expression of an opinion I am not prepared to make, that the authorship and copyright rest with some one already domiciled on the other side of the inevitable river. That is a matter I must leave for solution by others more competent to decide it than I am. I can only look upon the matter as a terrestrial one, of the earth earthy, and I propose to deal with it on that footing. In my opinion the plaintiff has made out her case, and the copyright rests with her.

3.8.3 *Noah v Shuba* [1991] F.S.R. 14, Mummery J.

The plaintiff, Dr Noah, was a consultant epidemiologist with the Public Health Laboratory Service (PHLS). In his own time he wrote A Guide to Hygienic Skin Piercing *which was published and distributed by the PHLS. The first defendant wrote an article for a health and beauty magazine which included substantial extracts from the* guide *without the plaintiff's permission. The defendants claimed that the plaintiff could not bring an action for copyright infringement because he had produced the* guide *in the course of his employment and therefore the PHLS owned the copyright (relying upon s.4(4) of the Copyright Act 1956, a similar provision to s.11(2) of the Copyright, Designs and Patents Act 1988). Mummery J. considered the ownership of the copyright in these terms:*

In my judgment, Dr Noah's position is very similar to that of the accountant in *Stevenson Jordan and Harrison Limited v McDonald & Evans* (1952) 1 T.L.R. 101 in relation to copyright in lectures delivered by the accountant author who was employed under a contract of service. It was held that the provisions of the Copyright Act 1911 equivalent to section 4(4) did not apply. At 111 Denning L.J. pointed out that it had to be remembered that a man employed under a contract of service may sometimes perform services outside the contract. He gave the instance of a doctor on the staff of a hospital or the master on the staff of a school employed under a contract of service giving lectures or lessons orally to students. He expressed the view that if, for his own convenience, he put the lectures into writing then his written work was not done under the contract of service. It might be a useful accessory to his contracted work, but it was not part of it and the copyright vested in him and not in his employers. Morris L.J. also pointed out at 113 that, even though the employer in that case paid the expenses of the lecturer incurred on the delivery of a lecture and was prepared to type the lectures as written by any lecturer and even though it would not have been improper for that lecturer to have prepared his lecture in the company's time and used material obtained from its library, it had not been shown that the accountant could have been ordered to write or deliver the lectures or that it was part of his duty to write or deliver them. In those circumstances the lectures were not written in the course of his employment.

I should add that, even if I had found that the guide had been written by Dr Noah in the course of his employment, I would have found on the evidence before me that there was an implied term of his contract of service excluding the operation of the statutory rule in section 4(4) vesting the copyright in the work so made in the employer PHLS. Evidence was given by Dr Noah and also by Dr Christine Miller, who was a consultant epidemiologist at PHLS from 1967 to 1987 and the author of numerous publications on vaccination, that it had for long been the practice at PHLS for employees there to retain the copyright in work written by them, usually in the form of articles, in the course of their employment there. If, for example, the articles were published in learned journals, it was the author of the article and not the PHLS who, at the insistence of most learned journals, assigned the copyright to the publishers of the journal in question. At no relevant time has the copyright in those articles been claimed by PHLS. It has acquiesced in a practice under which that copyright was retained and then assigned by the employee authors. The position of the PHLS in relation to this case is consistent with that practice. It has accepted that the copyright in the guide is vested in Dr Noah. In my judgment, this longstanding practice is sufficient material from which I can and do imply and it was a term of Dr Noah's appointment as consultant that he should be entitled to retain the copyright in works written by him in the course of his employment.

The plaintiff also sought damages for false attribution of authorship of a "work" and libel based on a small passage in the first defendant's article attributed to but not in fact written by him. The claim for false attribution was based upon the Copyright Act 1956, s.43, since replaced by Copyright, Designs and Patents Act 1988, s.84 (above, 3.7.3). (Note that under the Copyright Act 1956 there was no remedy for distortion of a work comparable with the Copyright, Designs and Patents Act 1988, s.80 (above, 3.7.2)). Mummery J. recognised that damages could be claimed for both false attribution and libel:

Thus, for example, in *Moore v News of the World Limited* [1972] 1 Q.B. 441, the claim for the statutory offence under section 43 was linked to a claim for libel. A separate award of damages could be given for the statutory offence if the other cause of action did not cover the injury caused by the false attribution of authorship. In that case the Court of Appeal upheld the jury's award to the plaintiff of £4,300 for libel and £100 for false attribution of authorship. Lord Denning M.R. observed at 450C that in most cases of false attribution of authorship there will also be a cause of action for libel or passing off and the damages for those causes of action would cover false attribution as well, so that there would be little extra award for false attribution.

The passage falsely attributed to the plaintiff consisted of 17 words appearing as the final two sentences of a longer quotation in fact taken from the guide. The defendants argued that 17 words were too short and insubstantial a matter to constitute a literary "work" within the meaning of s.43. Counsel for the plaintiff submitted that the relevant work was the quotation including both the words of which Dr Noah was the author and the words he did not write; or, alternatively, that the 17 words falsely attributed to him were on their own sufficient to constitute a "work". Mummery J. said:

In my judgment, the main submission made on behalf of Dr Noah is the correct one. Dr Noah's name was inserted on or affixed to the whole of the quoted passage so as to imply that he was the author of the whole of that passage. He was not the author of the whole of that passage. That passage has been falsely attributed to him. If Mr Shuba's argument were right, no offence would be committed under section 43 if a passage was quoted verbatim from an author's work with several key statements of the passage altered to the contrary sense simply by the insertion of the word "not". The result would be that the passage reproduced was still substantially what the author had written, but would convey to the reader the opposite meaning to what the author had written. The effect would be a violation of the author's interests protected by section 43. They are not only economic interests but also an author's interests in his reputation and in the integrity of his work.

It is not necessary for me to decide the alternative argument. I have, however, heard argument from both sides and I can say that I would have rejected Dr Noah's submission that the last two sentences on their own constituted a "work" within the meaning of section 43. Those two sentences on their own do not afford sufficient information, instruction or literary enjoyment to qualify as a work: see *Exxon Corp v Exxon Insurance Consultants International Limited* [1982] Ch. 119.

3.8.4 Copyright, Designs and Patents Act 1988, ss.90–93: Assignment, Licences, Prospective Ownership, Transmission on Death

S.90(1) Copyright is transmissible by assignment, by testamentary disposition or by operation of law, as personal or movable property.

(2) An assignment or other transmission of copyright may be partial, that is, limited so as to apply—

> **(a) to one or more, but not all, of the things the copyright owner has the exclusive right to do;**
>
> **(b) to part, but not the whole, of the period for which the copyright is to subsist.**

(3) An assignment of copyright is not effective unless it is in writing signed by or on behalf of the assignor.

(4) A licence granted by a copyright owner is binding on every successor in title to his interest in the copyright, except—

> **(a) a purchaser in good faith for valuable consideration and without notice (actual or constructive) of the licence, or**
>
> **(b) a person deriving title from such a purchaser;**

and references in this Part to doing anything with, or without, the licence of the copyright owner shall be construed accordingly.

S.91(1) Where by an agreement made in relation to future copyright, and signed by or on behalf of the prospective owner of the copyright, the prospective owner purports to assign the future copyright (wholly or partially) to another person, then if, on the copyright coming into existence, the assignee or another person claiming under him would be entitled as against all other persons to require the copyright to be vested in him, the copyright shall vest in the assignee or his successor in title by virtue of this subsection.

(2) In this Part—"future copyright" means copyright which will or may come into existence in respect of a future work or class of works or on the occurrence of a future event; and "prospective owner" shall be construed accordingly, and includes a person who is prospectively entitled to copyright by virtue of such an agreement as is mentioned in subsection (1).

(3) A licence granted by a prospective owner of copyright is binding on every successor in title to his interest (or prospective interest) in the right, except a purchaser in good faith for valuable consideration and without notice (actual or constructive) of the licence or a person deriving title from such a purchaser; and references in this Part to doing anything with, or without, the licence of the copyright owner shall be construed accordingly.

S.92(1) In this Part an "exclusive licence" means a licence in writing signed by or on behalf of the copyright owner authorising the licensee to the exclusion of all other persons, including the

person granting the licence, to exercise a right which would otherwise be exercisable exclusively by the copyright owner.

(2) The licensee under an exclusive licence has the same rights against a successor in title who is bound by the licence as he has against the person granting the licence.

S.93(1) Where under a bequest (whether specific or general) a person is entitled, beneficially or otherwise, to—

  (a) an original document or other material thing recording or embodying a literary, dramatic, musical or artistic work which was not published before the death of the testator, or

  (b) an original material thing containing a sound recording or film which was not published before the death of the testator.

The bequest shall, unless a contrary intention is indicated in the testator's will or a codicil to it, be construed as including the copyright in the work in so far as the testator was the owner of the copyright immediately before his death.

(2) In this section "right to equitable remuneration" means the author's right to be remunerated equitably in respect of any rental of any copies of the film or sound recording in which his work is included taking into account the importance of his contribution to the film or sound recording.

(3) The right to equitable remuneration may be exercised by the author—

  (a) in respect of a film, only against the film producer to whom the author's rental right is deemed to be, or is assigned, or any successor in title to the film producer in respect of that rental right; and

  (b) in respect of a sound recording, only against the producer of the sound recording to whom the author's rental right is assigned or any successor in title to the producer in respect of that rental right.

(4) Any remuneration offered or paid is not to be considered inequitable merely because it is to be paid or is paid—

  (a) by way of a single payment;

  (b) upon conclusion of the assignment.

(5) In any agreement which contains provisions dealing with an author's right to equitable remuneration, the author shall not be bound by any term or condition which purports to limit the meaning to be attributed to "equitable remuneration" by reference to actual remuneration.

Concerning the rental right, from December 1, 1996, s.93A introduces a presumption that, in a film production agreement, the rental right of an author is transferred to the producer; s.93B gives rise to a guaranteed right to equitable remuneration in respect of a transfer of rental right by an author or principal film director; and s.93 confers on the Copyright Tribunal jurisdiction to settle the amount of this remuneration.

3.8.5   *Barker v Stickney* [1919] 1 K.B. 121, CA

The plaintiff, author of "The Theory and Practice of Heating and Ventilation"
assigned copyright in it to J.F. Phillips & Sons Ltd in return for shares in the
company and a royalty. The company undertook not to assign to a third party. A
receiver was appointed for the company and the copyright was sold to the
defendant, who had full notice of the terms of the original assignment. The
plaintiff claimed from the defendant the royalty arising under that assignment.

Scrutton L.J.:

The case was considered in the court below on two lines. First, it was said the defendant has
bought a copyright with notice of a contract affecting it, and, using the copyright, must
perform the contract. Up to the year 1880 that argument might have prevailed. In *De
Mattos v Gibson* (1858 4 De G. & J. 276), Knight Bruce L.J. laid down the following rule:
"Reason and justice seem to prescribe that, at least as a general rule, where a man, by gift
or purchase, acquires property from another, with knowledge of a previous contract,
lawfully and for valuable consideration made by him with a third person, to use and
employ the property for a particular purpose in a specified manner, the acquirer shall not,
to the material damage of the third person, in opposition to the contract and inconsistently
with it, use and employ the property in a manner not allowable to the giver or seller".
Down to 1881 the cases where a purchaser of property was restricted in his use of it were
based upon the doctrine of notice, and upon that alone. Those cases will be found in the
judgment of the Court of Appeal in *London County Council v Allen* [1914] 3 K.B. 642.
About that time a change took place. In *Haywood v Brunswick Building Society* (1881) 8
Q.B.D. 403, the restriction was confined to cases where the covenant was negative. In 1882,
the year after *Werderman's Case*, 19 Ch.D. 246, was decided, Jessel M.R. himself further
limited the restriction in cases of land to negative covenants for the benefit of land, treating
them as analogous to covenants running with land which a plaintiff could not enforce
unless he had land for the benefit of which the covenant could enure. This point was
afterwards expressly decided by the Court of Appeal in *London County Council v Allen.*
Thus the doctrine was evolved as to real property. But as to personal property it was found
that the general rule of Knight Bruce L.J. was quite impracticable, and *Taddy & Co v
Sterious & Co* [1904] 1 Ch. 354; *McGruther v Pitcher* [1904] 2 Ch. 306, and *Dunlop Pneumatic Tyre Co v Selfridge & Co* [1915] A.C. 847, have settled the law that the purchaser of a
chattel is not bound by mere notice of stipulations made by his vendor unless he was
himself a party to the contract in which the stipulations were made. I see nothing to
distinguish a chose in action such as copyright from chattels or land, and I think it is clear
that a person acquiring a cause in action is not bound by mere notice of a personal
covenant by his predecessor in title. That is the effect of *Bago Pneumatic Tyre Co v Clipper
Pneumatic Tyre Co* [1902] 1 Ch. 146. *Werderman's case* was decided in the year before
London & South Western Ry Co v Gomm (1882) 20 Ch.D. 562, in which Jessel M.R. himself
greatly restricted the effect of notice, and in my view *Werderman's Case* cannot be supported on the ground that notice of a contract relating to personal property will bind a
purchaser who is not a party to that contract. So much for the first ground on which this
appeal was based.

His Lordship proceeded to hold that the plaintiff could not assert a lien or
charge as an unpaid vendor, since his entitlement to royalty did not put him in
the position of seller. Bankes and Warrington L.JJ. delivered concurring
judgments.

3.8.6   *Schroeder Music Publishing v Macaulay* [1974] 3 All E.R. 616, HL

When still an unknown 21-year-old songwriter the plaintiff agreed with the defendant music publishing company to give his services exclusively to the company for a period of five years, extending automatically to 10 years, in circumstances which afterwards materialised. Under the agreement the plaintiff assigned copyright world-wide in the songs that he composed during its term and was to receive royalties in return. The company was not obliged to publish any of the plaintiff's work; it might terminate the agreement at any time on one month's notice, and it could assign its rights. The plaintiff had no equivalent rights of termination or assignment. In the fourth year, the plaintiff sought a declaration that the agreement was void as being contrary to public policy.

Lord Reid:

The public interest requires in the interests both of the public and of the individual that everyone should be free so far as practicable to earn a livelihood and to give to the public the fruits of his particular abilities. The main question to be considered is whether and how far the operation of the terms of this agreement is likely to conflict with this objective. The respondent is bound to assign to the appellants during a long period the fruits of his musical talent. But what are the appellants bound to do with those fruits? Under the contract nothing. If they do use the songs which the respondent composes they must pay in terms of the contract. But they need not do so. As has been said they may put them in a drawer and leave them there. No doubt the expectation was that if the songs were of value they would be published to the advantage of both parties. But if for any reason the appellants chose not to publish them the respondent would get no remuneration and he could not do anything. Inevitably the respondent must take the risk of misjudgment of the merits of his work by the appellants. But that is not the only reason which might cause the appellants not to publish. There is no evidence about this so we must do the best we can with common knowledge. It does not seem fanciful and it was not argued that it is fanciful to suppose that purely commercial consideration might cause a publisher to refrain from publishing and promoting promising material. He might think it likely to be more profitable to promote work by other composers with whom he had agreements and unwise or too expensive to try to publish and popularise the respondent's work in addition. And there is always the possibility that less legitimate reasons might influence a decision not to publish the respondent's work.

It was argued that there must be read into this agreement an obligation on the publisher to act in good faith. I take that to mean that he would be in breach of contract if by reason of some oblique or malicious motive he refrained from publishing work which he would otherwise have published. I very much doubt this but even if it were so it would make little difference. Such a case would seldom occur and then would be difficult to prove.

I agree with the appellants' argument to this extent. I do not think that a publisher could reasonably be expected to enter into any positive commitment to publish future work by an unknown composer. Possibly there might be some general undertaking to use his best endeavours to promote the composer's work. But that would probably have to be in such general terms as to be of little use to the composer. But if no satisfactory positive undertaking by the publisher can be devised, it appears to me to be an unreasonable restraint to tie the composer for this period of years so that his work will be sterilised and he can earn nothing from his abilities as a composer if the publisher chooses not to publish. If there had been in clause 9 any provision entitling the composer to terminate the agreement in such an event the case might have had a very different appearance. But as the agreement stands not only is the composer tied but he cannot recover the copyright of the work which the publisher refuses to publish.

It was strenuously argued that the agreement is in standard form, that it has stood the test of time, and that there is no indication that it ever causes injustice. Reference was made to passages in the speeches of Lord Pearce and Lord Wilberforce in the *Esso Case* [1967] 1 All E.R. 699, with which I wholly agree. Lord Pearce said:

"It is important that the court, in weighing the question of reasonableness, should give full weight to commercial practices and to the generality of contracts made freely by parties bargaining on equal terms."

Later Lord Wilberforce said:

"The development of the law does seem to show, however, that judges have been able to dispense from the necessity of justification under a public policy test of reasonableness such contracts or provisions of contracts as, under contemporary conditions, may be found to have passed into the accepted and normal currency of commercial or contractual or conveyancing relations. That such contracts have done so may be taken to show with at least strong prima force that, moulded under the pressures of negotiation, competition and public opinion, they have assumed a form which satisfies the test of public policy as understood by the courts of the time, or, regarding the matter from the point of view of the trade, that the trade in question has assumed such a form that for its health or expansion it requires a degree of regulation."

But those passages refer to contracts "made freely by parties bargaining on equal terms" or "moulded under the pressures of negotiation, competition and public opinion". I do not find from any evidence in this case, nor does it seem probable, that this form of contract made between a publisher and an unknown composer has been moulded by any pressure of negotiation. Indeed, it appears that established composers who can bargain on equal terms can and do make their own contracts.

Any contract by which a person engages to give his exclusive services to another for a period necessarily involves extensive restriction during that period of the common law right to exercise any lawful activity he chooses in such manner as he thinks best. Normally the doctrine of restraint of trade has no application to such restrictions: they require no justification. But if contractual restrictions appear to be unnecessary or to be reasonably capable of enforcement in an oppressive manner, then they must be justified before they can be enforced.

In the present case the respondent assigned to the appellants "the full copyright for the whole world" in every musical composition "composed created or conceived" by him alone or in collaboration with any other person during a period of five or it might be ten years. He received no payment (apart from an initial £50) unless his work was published and the appellants need not publish unless they chose to do so. And if they did not publish he had no right to terminate the agreement or to have any copyrights re-assigned to him. I need not consider whether in any circumstances it would be possible to justify such a one-sided agreement. It is sufficient to say that such evidence as there is falls far short of justification. It must therefore follow that the agreement so far as unperformed is unenforceable.

Viscount Dilhorne concurred with Lord Reid.

Lord Diplock:

My Lords, the contract under consideration in this appeal is one whereby the respondent accepted restrictions on the way in which he would exploit his earning-power as a song-writer for the next ten years. Because this can be classified as a contract in restraint of trade the restrictions that the respondent accepted fell within one of those limited categories of contractual promises in respect of which the courts still retain the power to relieve the promisor of his legal duty to fulfil them. In order to determine whether this case is one in which that power ought to be exercised, what your Lordships have in fact been doing has been to assess the relative bargaining power of the publisher and the song-writer at the same time the contract was made and to decide whether the publisher had used his superior bargaining power to exact from the song-writer promises that were unfairly onerous to him. Your Lordships have not been concerned to enquire whether the public have in fact been deprived of the fruit of the song-writer's talents by reason of the restrictions, nor to assess the likelihood that they would be so deprived in the future if the contract were permitted to run its full course.

It is, in my view, salutary to acknowledge that in refusing to enforce provisions of a contract whereby one party agrees for the benefit of the other party to exploit or to refrain from exploiting his earning-power, the public policy which the court is implementing is not some nineteenth-century economic theory about the benefit to the general public of free-dom of trade, but the protection of those whose bargaining power is weak against being forced by those whose bargaining power is stronger to enter into bargains that are unconscionable. Under the influence of Bentham and of laissez-faire the courts in the nineteenth-century abandoned the practice of applying the public policy against uncon-scionable bargains to contracts generally, as they had formerly done to any contract considered to be usurious; but the policy survived in its application to penalty clauses and to relief against forfeiture and also to the special category of contracts in restraint of trade. If one looks at the reasoning of nineteenth-century judges in cases about contracts in restraint of trade one finds lip service paid to current economic theories but if one looks at what they said in the light of what they did, one finds that they did, one finds that they struck down a bargain if they thought it was unconscionable as between the parties to it, and upheld it if they thought that it was not.

So I would hold that the question to be answered as respects a contract in restraint of trade of the kind with which this appeal is concerned is: was the bargain fair? The test of fairness is, no doubt, whether the restrictions are both reasonably necessary for the protection of the legitimate interests of the promisee and commensurate with the benefits secured to the promisor under the contract. For the purpose of this test all the provisions of the contract must be taken into consideration.

My Lords, the provisions of the contract have already been sufficiently stated by my noble and learned friend, Lord Reid. I agree with his analysis of them and with his conclusion that the contract is unenforceable. It does not satisfy the test of fairness as I have endea-voured to state it. I will accordingly content myself with adding some observations directed to the argument that because the contract was in a "standard form" in common use between music publishers and song-writers, the restraints that it imposes on the song-writer's liberty to exploit his talents must be presumed to be fair and reasonable.

Standard forms of contracts are of two kinds. The first, of very ancient origin, are those which set out the terms on which mercantile transactions of common occurrence are to be carried out. Examples are bills of lading, charterparties, policies of insurance, contracts of sale in the commodity markets. The standard clauses in these contracts have been settled over the years by negotiations by representatives of the commercial interests involved and have been widely adopted because experience has shown that they facilitate the conduct of trade. Contracts of these kinds affect not only the actual parties to them but also others who may have a commercial interest in the transactions to which they relate, as buyers or sellers, charterers or shipowners, insurers or bankers. If fairness or reasonableness were relevant to their enforceability the fact that they are widely used by parties whose bargaining power is fairly matched would raise a strong presumption that their terms are fair and reasonable.

The same presumption, however, does not apply to the other kind of standard form of contract. This is of comparatively modern origin. It is the result of the concentration of particular kinds of business in relatively few hands. The ticket cases in the nineteenth century provide what are probably the first examples. The terms of this kind of standard form of contract have not been the subject of negotiation between the parties to it, or approved by any organisation representing the interests of the weaker party. They have been dictated by that party whose bargaining power, either exercised alone or in conjunction with other providing similar goods or services, enables him to say: "If you want these goods or services at all, these are the only terms on which they are obtainable. Take it or leave it".

To be in a position to adopt this attitude towards a party desirous of entering into a contract to obtain goods or service provides a classic instance of superior bargaining power. It is not without significance that on the evidence in the present case, music publishers in negotiating with song-writers whose success has been already established do not insist on adhering to a contract in the standard form they offered to the respondent. The fact that the appellants' bargaining power *vis-à-vis* the respondent was strong enough to enable them to adopt this "take it or leave it" attitude raises no presumption that they used it to drive an unconscionable bargain with him, but in the field of restraint of trade it calls for vigilance on the part of the court to see that they did not.

Lords Simon and Kilbrandon concurred in the speeches of Lords Reid and Diplock.

3.9 Copyright Tribunal

3.9.1 Copyright, Designs and Patents Act 1988, ss.116–119, 121, 129: Licensing Schemes and Licensing Bodies: References and Applications to Copyright Tribunal

S.116(1) In this Part a "licensing scheme" means a scheme setting out—

- (a) the classes of case in which the operator of the scheme, or the person on whose behalf he acts, is willing to grant copyright licences, and
- (b) the terms on which licences would be granted in those classes of case: and for this purpose a "scheme" includes anything in the nature of a scheme, whether described as a scheme or as a tariff or by any other name.

(2) In this [Part] a "licensing body" means a society or other organisation which has as its main object, or one of its main objects, the negotiation or granting, either as owner or prospective owner of copyright or as agent for him, of copyright licences, and whose objects include the granting of licences covering works of more than one author.

(3) In this section "copyright licences" means licences to do, or authorise the doing of, any of the acts restricted by copyright.

(4) References in this Chapter to licences or licensing schemes covering works of more than one author do not include licences or schemes covering only—

- (a) a single collective work or collective works of which the authors are the same, or
- (b) works made by, or by employees of, or commissioned by, a single individual, firm, company or group of companies.

For this purpose a group of companies means a holding company and its subsidiaries, within the meaning of section 736 of the Companies Act 1985.

S.117 Sections 118 to 123 (references and applications with respect to licensing schemes) apply to licensing schemes which are operated by licensing bodies and cover works of more than one author, so far as they relate to licences for:

- (a) copying the work,
- (b) rental or lending of copies of the work to the public,
- (c) performing, showing or playing the work in public, or
- (d) broadcasting the work or including it in a cable programme service;

and references in those sections to a licensing scheme shall be construed accordingly.

S.118(1) The terms of a licensing scheme proposed to be operated by a licensing body may be referred to the Copyright Tribunal by an organisation claiming to be representative of persons claiming that they require licences in cases of a description to which the scheme would apply, either generally or in relation to any description of case.

(2) The Tribunal shall first decide whether to entertain the reference, and may decline to do so on the ground that the reference is premature.

(3) If the Tribunal decides to entertain the reference it shall consider the matter referred and make such order, either confirming or varying the proposed scheme, either generally or so far as it relates to cases of the description to which the reference relates, as the Tribunal may determine to be reasonable in the circumstances.

(4) The order may be made so as to be in force indefinitely or for such period as the Tribunal may determine.

S.119(1) If while a licensing scheme is in operation a dispute arises between the operator of the scheme and—

  (a) a person claiming that he requires a licence in a case of description to which the scheme applies, or

  (b) an organisation claiming to be representative of such persons.

that person or organisation may refer the scheme to the Copyright Tribunal in so far as it relates to cases of that description.

(2) A scheme which has been referred to the Tribunal under this section shall remain in operation until proceedings on the reference are concluded.

(3) The Tribunal shall consider the matter in dispute and make such order, either confirming or varying the scheme so far as it relates to cases of the description to which the reference relates, as the Tribunal may determine to be reasonable in the circumstances.

(4) The order may be made so as to be in force indefinitely or for such period as the Tribunal may determine.

Section 120 provides for further reference of a scheme to the Tribunal.

S.121(1) A person who claims, in a case covered by a licensing scheme, that the operator of the scheme has refused to grant him or procure the grant to him of a licence in accordance with the scheme, or has failed to do so within a reasonable time after being asked, may apply to the Copyright Tribunal.

(2) A person who claims, in a case excluded from a licensing scheme, that the operator of the scheme either—

  (a) has refused to grant him a licence or procure the grant to him of a licence, or has failed to do so within a reasonable time of being asked, and that in the circumstances it is unreasonable that a licence should not be granted, or

  (b) proposes terms for a licence which are unreasonable, may apply to the Copyright Tribunal.

(3) A case shall be regarded as excluded from a licensing scheme for the purposes of subsection (2) if—

(a) the scheme provides for the grant of licences subject to terms excepting matters from the licence and the case falls within such an exception, or

(b) the case is so similar to those in which licences are granted under the scheme that it is unreasonable that it should not be dealt with in the same way.

(4) If the Tribunal is satisfied that the claim is well-founded, it shall make an order declaring that, in respect of the matters specified in the order, the applicant is entitled to a licence on such terms as the Tribunal may determine to be applicable in accordance with the scheme or, as the case may be, to be reasonable in the circumstances.

(5) The order may be made so as to be in force indefinitely or for such period as the Tribunal may determine.

Section 122 provides for review of an order made under s.121.

Section 123 specifies the effect of an order as to a licensing scheme.

Sections 124–128 deal with references and applications to the Tribunal concerning licensing by licensing bodies, in cases not involving a licensing scheme. The sections follow an equivalent pattern to ss.117–123, giving the Tribunal power, in the cases covered, to make orders reasonable in the circumstances.

S.129 In determining what is reasonable on a reference or application under this Chapter relating to a licensing scheme or licence, the Copyright Tribunal shall have regard to—

(a) the availability of other schemes, or the granting of other licences, to other persons in similar circumstances, and

(b) the terms of those schemes or licences,

and shall exercise its powers so as to secure that there is no unreasonable discrimination between licensees, or prospective licensees, under the scheme or licence to which the reference or application relates and licensees under other schemes operated by, or other licences granted by, the same person.

Section 130 adds further considerations to be given account in relation to reprographic copying, and ss.136–141 give special powers where such copying is in an educational establishment (see above, 3.6.6.2). Sections 131–135 deal with factors to be considered in a number of particular circumstances: educational recording of broadcasts and cable programmes (s.131), recordings, etc. of events which are subject to promoter's condition (s.132); licences of rental rights, etc. (s.133); licences concerning retransmissions (s.134). Section 135 states the Tribunal's obligation always to have regard to all relevant circumstances.

Sections 135A–H establish and regulate the statutory licence to broadcast sound recordings, so far as concerns the sound recording right in them.

3.10 Rights in Performances

Part II of the Copyright, Designs and Patents Act 1988 creates rights in performances both for performers and for those who have exclusive recording rights in the performances. In implementation of the E.C. Directive 92/100/EEC on Rental and Neighbouring Rights, the rights given to performers have been extended in various ways. The implementing instrument was the Copyright and Related Rights Regulations 1996.

3.10.1 Rights Granted

3.10.1.1 Copyright, Designs and Patents Act 1988, Part II, ss.180, 181, 185

S.180(1) This Part confers rights—

- (a) **on a performer, by requiring his consent to the exploitation of his performances (see sections 181 to 184), and**
- (b) **on a person having recording rights in relation to a performance, in relation to recordings made without his consent or that of the performer (see sections 185 to 188),**

and creates offences in relation to dealing with or using illicit recordings and certain other related acts (see sections 198 and 201).

(2) In this Part—
"performance" means—

- (a) **a dramatic performance (which includes dance and mime),**
- (b) **a musical performance,**
- (c) **a reading or recitation of a literary work, or**
- (d) **a performance of a variety act or any similar presentation,**

which is, or so far as it is, a live performance given by one or more individuals; and

"recording", in relation to a performance, means a film or sound recording—

- (a) **made directly from the live performance,**
- (b) **made from a broadcast of, or cable programme including, the performance, and**
- (c) **"copies" in relation to the issue to the public and the rental or lending of copies of a recording, includes the issue, rental or lending of the original recording.**

Section 180(3) gives rights in "pre-commencement" performances, but only in relation to acts done after commencement which were not arranged before.

Section 180(4) provides that the performance rights are independent of other intellectual property.

S.181 A performance is a qualifying performance for the purposes of the provisions of this Part relating to performers' rights if it is given by a qualifying individual (as defined in section 206) or takes place in a qualifying country (as so defined).

S.185(1) In this Part an "exclusive recording contract" means a contract between a performer and another person under which that person is entitled to the exclusion of all other persons (including the performer) to make recordings of one or more of his performances with a view to their commercial exploitation.

(2) References in this Part to a "person having recording rights", in relation to a performance, are (subject to subsection (3)) to a person—

(a) who is party to and has the benefit of an exclusive recording contract to which the performance is subject, or

(b) to whom the benefit of such a contract has been assigned, and who is a qualifying person.

(3) If a performance is subject to an exclusive recording contract but the person mentioned in subsection (2) is not a qualifying person, references in this Part to a "person having recording rights" in relation to the performance are to any person—

(a) who is licensed by such a person to make recordings of the performance with a view to their commercial exploitation, or

(b) to whom the benefit of such a licence has been assigned,

and who is a qualifying person.

(4) In this section "with a view to commercial exploitation" means with a view to the recordings being sold or let for hire, or shown or played in public.

3.10.1.2   Copyright, Designs and Patents Act 1988, ss.206, 208: Qualification for protection and extent

S.206(1) In this Part—
"qualifying country" means—

(a) the United Kingdom,

(b) another EEA State, or

(c) to the extent that an Order under section 208 so provides, a country designated under that section as enjoying reciprocal protection;

"qualifying individual" means a citizen or subject of, or an individual resident in, a qualifying country; and

"qualifying person" means a qualifying individual or a body corporate or other body having legal personality which—

(a) is formed under the law of a part of the United Kingdom or another qualifying country, and

(b) has in any qualifying country a place of business at which substantial business activity is carried on.

(2) The reference in the definition of "qualifying individual" to a person's being a citizen or subject of a qualifying country shall be construed—

(a) in relation to the United Kingdom, as a reference to his being a British citizen, and

(b) in relation to a colony of the United Kingdom, as a reference to his being a British Dependent Territories' citizen by connection with that colony.

(3) In determining for the purpose of the definition of "qualifying person" whether substantial business activity is carried on at a place of business in any country, no account shall be taken of dealings in goods which are at all material times outside that country.

S.208(1) Her Majesty may by Order in Council designate as enjoying reciprocal protection under this Part—

(a) a Convention country, or

(b) a country as to which Her Majesty is satisfied that provision has been or will be made under its law giving adequate protection for British performances.

(2) A "Convention country" means a country which is a party to a Convention relating to performers' rights to which the United Kingdom is also a party.

(3) A "British performance" means a performance—

(a) given by an individual who is a British citizen or resident in the United Kingdom, or

(b) taking place in the United Kingdom.

Section 207 applies the Part to England, Wales, Scotland and Northern Ireland. Section 208(4) provides for designation under (1)(b) to be limited in scope; s.208(5) allows designation of the Channel Islands, Isle of Man and any British colony. Sections 209, 210 extend the part to British territorial waters and British ships, aircraft and hovercraft.

3.10.2   Infringement

3.10.2.1   Copyright, Designs and Patents Act 1988, ss.181–182B

S.181 Qualifying performances

A performance is a qualifying performance for the purposes of the provisions of this Part relating to performers' rights if it is given by a qualifying individual (as defined in section 206) or takes place in a qualifying country (as so defined).

S.182 Consent required for recording, &c of live performance

(1) A performer's rights are infringed by a person who, without his consent—

  (a) makes a recording of the whole or any substantial part of a qualifying performance directly from the live performance,

  (b) broadcasts live, or includes live in a cable programme service, the whole or any substantial part of a qualifying performance,

  (c) makes a recording of the whole or any substantial part of a qualifying performance directly from a broadcast of, or cable programme including, the live performance.

(2) A performer's rights are not infringed by the making of any such recording by a person for his private and domestic use.

(3) In an action for infringement of a performer's rights brought by virtue of this section damages shall not be awarded against a defendant who shows that at the time of the infringement he believed on reasonable grounds that consent had been given.

S.182A Consent required for copying of recording

(1) A performer's rights are infringed by a person who, without his consent, makes, otherwise than for his private and domestic use, a copy of a recording of the whole or any substantial part of a qualifying performance.

(2) It is immaterial whether the copy is made directly or indirectly.

(3) The right of a performer under this section to authorise or prohibit the making of such copies is referred to in this Part as "reproduction right."

S.182B Consent required for issue of copies to the public

(1) A performer's rights are infringed by a person who, without his consent, issues to the public copies of a recording of the whole or any substantial part of a qualifying performance.

(2) References in this Part to the issue to the public of copies of a recording are to—

  (a) the act of putting into circulation in the EEA copies not previously put into circulation in the EEA by or with the consent of the performer, or

  (b) the act of putting into circulation outside the EEA copies not previously put into circulation in the EEA or elsewhere.

(3) References in this Part to the issue to the public of copies of a recording do not include—

  (a) any subsequent distribution, sale, hiring or loan of copies previously put into circulation (but see section 182C: consent required for rental or lending), or

  (b) any subsequent importation of such copies into the United Kingdom or another EEA state, except so far as paragraph (a) of subsection (2) applies to putting into circulation in the EEA copies previously put into circulation outside the EEA.

(4) References in this Part to the issue of copies of a recording of a performance include the issue of the original recording of the live performance.

(5) The right of a performer under this section to authorise or prohibit the issue to copies to the public is referred to in this Part as "distribution right".

Section 182C creates rights of rental and lending equivalent to those in copyright works (see s.18A, para. 3.6.3.1, above). Section 182D imposes a right to equitable remuneration, equivalent to that in ss.93B and 93C for copyright works, for the public performance, broadcasting and cabling of any commercially published sound recording containing the performance.

Sections 183 and 184 create "secondary" breaches of performer' rights, where the following acts are done with knowledge that a recording was illicit: showing or playing it in public; broadcasting or cable-casting it; importing, possessing or dealing with it.

Sections 186–188 define infringement of the rights of persons with exclusive recording rights. These include making an unauthorised recording otherwise than for private and domestic use (subject to a partial defence where consent was reasonably thought to exist); and secondary wrongs equivalent to those in ss.183, 184.

Sections 196–205 provide for delivery up and seizure of illicit recordings, and also for criminal proceedings, in terms equivalent to those affecting illicit copies of copyright material. See above, 3.6.10.1.

Section 189 and Sch.2 (as amended) define a set of permitted acts in relation to rights in performances. These are mostly equivalent to defences applicable to copyright claims (for which see ss.28–77; above, 3.6.5. et seq. They include: fair dealing for criticism, review and news reporting; incidental inclusion; instruction and examination; playing or showing a sound recording, film, broadcast or cable-cast at an educational establishment; lending of copies by educational establishments, libraries and archives and lending or other recordings; reception and transmission of a broadcast in a cable-cast; copying before export; various acts in public administration; copies in electronic form; recordings of spoken words in news reporting and broadcasting; recordings of folksongs; playing of sound recordings at clubs, etc.; incidental recording for broadcasts and cable-casts; supervision of broadcasts and cable-casts; free public showing of broadcasts and cable-casts immediate reception and re-transmission of broadcast in cable-cast; sub-titling for the handicapped; recording of broadcasts and cable-casts for archives.

3.10.3   Duration and Transmission of Rights

3.10.3.1   Copyright, Designs and Patents Act 1988, ss.191, 191A, 191B

S.191.(1) The following provisions have effect with respect to the duration of the rights conferred by this Part.

(2) The rights conferred by this Part in relation to a performance expire—

   (a) at the end of the period of 50 years from the end of the calendar year in which the performance takes place, or

   (b) if during that period a recording of the performance is released, 50 years from the end of the calendar year in which it is released,

subject as follows.

(3) For the purposes of subsection (2) a recording is "released" when it is first published, played or shown in public, broadcast or included in a cable programme service; but in determining whether a recording has been released no account shall be taken of any unauthorised act.

(4) Where a performer is not a national of an EEA state, the duration of the rights conferred by this Part in relation to his performance is that to which the performance is entitled in the country of which he is a national, provided that does not exceed the period which would apply under subsections (2) and (3).

(5) If or to the extent that the application of subsection (4) would be at variance with an international obligation to which the United Kingdom became subject prior to 29th October 1993, the duration of the rights conferred by this Part shall be as specified in subsections (2) and (3).

Note that the Duration of Copyright and Rights in Performances Regulations 1995 (SI 1995/3297), paras 27–35, make transitional arrangements in relation to additional terms for rights in performances which are similar in character to those affecting copyright (referred to above, 3.5.1).

S.191A Performers' property rights

(1) The following rights conferred by this Part on a performer—

   reproduction right (section 182A),
   distribution right (section 182B),
   rental right and lending right (section 182C),

are property rights ("a performer's property rights").

(2) References in this Part to the consent of the performer shall be construed in relation to a performer's property rights as references to the consent of the rights owner.

(3) Where different persons are (whether in consequence of a partial assignment or otherwise) entitled to different aspects of a performer's property rights in relation to a performance, the

rights owner for any purpose of this Part is the person who is entitled to the aspect of those rights relevant for that purpose.

(4) Where a performer's property rights (or any aspect of them) is owned by more than one person jointly, references in this Part to the rights owner are to all the owners, so that, in particular, any requirement of the licence of the rights owner requires the licence of all of them.

S.191B Assignment and licences

(1) A performer's property rights are transmissible by assignment, by testamentary disposition or by operation of law, as personal or moveable property.

(2) An assignment or other transmission or a performer's property rights may be partial, that is, limited so as to apply—

(a) to one or more, but not all, of the things requiring the consent of the rights owner;

(b) to part, but not the whole, of the period for which the rights are to subsist.

(3) An assignment of a performer's property rights is not effective unless it is in writing signed by or on behalf of the assignor.

(4) A licence granted by the owner of a performer's property rights is binding on every successor in title to his interest in the rights, except a purchaser in good faith for valuable consideration and without notice (actual or constructive) of the licence or a person deriving title from such a purchaser; and references in this Part to doing anything with, or without, the licence of the rights owner shall be construed accordingly.

The succeeding sections further characterise the performer's property rights, by analogy to provisions on copyright. These concern: agreements for future recordings (s.191C–cf. Agreements over future copyright, s.91, para. 3.8.4 above); exclusive licences (s.191D–cf. s.92. ibid.); bequest of material containing original performance (s.191E–cf. bequests of original embodiment of copyright work, s.93, ibid.); presumption of film production transfer of rental rights—cf. s.93A, noted above, 3.6.3.1); right to equitable remuneration for transfer of rental rights—cf. ss.93B, 93C, noted ibid.)

Further provisions relate to actions for infringement of the performer's property rights, and likewise lay down analogous rules to those affecting copyright. These concern: the relief available to the right owner (s.191I–cf. s.96, para. 3.6.10.1, above); limitations upon and extensions of rights to damages (s.191J—cf. s.97, ibid.); limitation of relief after a competition report (s.191K— cf. s.98, noted, ibid.); rights of an exclusive licensee (ss.191L, 191M—cf. ss.101, 102, noted, ibid.)

3.10.3.2 Copyright, Designs and Patents Act 1988, ss.192A, 192B, 193, 194

S.192A Performers' non-property rights

(1) the rights conferred on a performer by—

section 182 (consent required for recording, &c of live performance),
section 183 (infringement of performer's rights by use of recording made without consent), and
section 184 (infringement of performer's rights importing, possessing or dealing with illicit recording),

are not assignable or transmissible, except to the following extent.
They are referred to in this Part as "a performer's non-property rights".

(2) On the death of a person entitled to any such right—

(a) the right passes to such person as he may by testamentary disposition specifically direct, and

(b) if or to the extent that there is no such direction, the right is exercisable by his personal representatives.

(3) References in this Part to the performer, in the context of the person having any such right, shall be construed as references to the person for the time being entitled to exercise those rights.

(4) Where by virtue of subsection (2)(a) a right becomes exercisable by more than one person, it is exercisable by each of them independently of the other or others.

(5) Any damages recovered by personal representatives by virtue of this section in respect of an infringement after a person's death shall devolve as part of his estate as if the right of action had subsisted and been vested in him immediately before his death.

S.192B Transmissibility of rights of person having recording rights

(1) The rights conferred by this Part on a person having recording rights are not assignable or transmissible.

(2) This does not affect section 185(2)(b) or (3)(b), so far as those provisions confer rights under this Part on a person to whom the benfit of a contract or licence is assigned.

S.193 Consent

(1) Consent for the purposes of this Part [by a person having a performer's non-property rights, or by a person having recording rights,] may be given in relation to a specific performance, a specified description of performances or performances generally, and may relate to past or future performances.

(2) A person having recording rights in a performance is bound by any consent given by a person through whom he derives his rights under the exclusive recording contract or licence in question, in the same way as if the consent had been given by him.

(3) Where [a performer's non-property right] passes to another person, any consent binding on the person previously entitled binds the person to whom the right passes in the same way as if the consent had been given by him.

S.194 Infringement actionable as breach of statutory duty

An infringement of—

(a) a performer's non-property rights, or

(b) any right conferred by this Part on a person having recording rights.

is actionable by the person entitled to the right as a breach of statutory duty.

Part II continues with a series of provisions (ss.195–205) on remedies, civil and criminal, which are equivalent to those for copyright mentioned at para. 3.6.10.1, ss.105–114; and on the jurisdiction of the Copyright Tribunal in relation to rights in performances: ss.205A, 205B.

Sections 196–205 provide for delivery up and seizure of illicit recordings, and also for criminal proceedings, in terms equivalent to those affecting illicit copies of copyright material. See above, 3.6.10.1.

Section 189 and Sch.2 define a set of permitted acts in relation to rights in performances. These are mostly equivalent to defences applicable to copyright claims (for which see ss.28–77; above, 3.6.5 et seq.). They include: fair dealing for criticism, review and news reporting; incidental inclusion; instruction and examination; playing or showing a sound recording, film, broadcast or cablecast at an educational establishment; copying before export; various acts in public administration; copies in electronic form; recordings of spoken words in news reporting and broadcasting; recordings of folksongs; playing of sound recordings at clubs, etc.; incidental recording for broadcasts and cable-casts; supervision of broadcasts and cable-casts; free public showing of broadcasts and cable-casts immediate reception and re-transmission of broadcast in cable-cast; sub-titling for the handicapped; recording of broadcasts and cable-casts for archives.

3.11   Database Right

3.11.1   Copyright and Rights in Databases Regulations 1997 (No. 3032), Part III

Interpretation

12.(1) In this Part—

"database" has the meaning given by section 3A(1) of the 1988 Act [above, para. 3.2.1] ....

"extraction", in relation to any contents of a database, means the permanent or temporary transfer of those contents to another medium by any means or in any form;

"insubstantial", in relation to part of the contents of a database, shall be construed subject to Regulation 16(2);

"investment" includes any investment, whether of financial, human or technical resources;

"jointly", in relation to the making of a database, shall be construed in accordance with Regulation 14(6);

"lawful user", in relation to a database, means any person who (whether under a licence to do any of the acts restricted by any database right in the database or otherwise) has a right to use the database;

"maker", in relation to a database, shall be construed in accordance with Regulation 14;

"re-utilisation", in relation to any contents of a database, means making those contents available to the public by any means;

"substantial", in relation to any investment, extraction or re-utilisation, means substantial in terms of quantity or quality or a combination of both.

(2) The making of a copy of a database available for use, on terms that it will or may be returned, otherwise than for direct or indirect economic or commercial advantage, through an establishment which is accessible to the public shall not be taken for the purposes of this Part to constitute extraction or re-utilisation of the contents of the database.

(3) Where the making of a copy of a database available through an establishment which is accessible to the public gives rise to a payment the amount of which does not go beyond what is necessary to cover the costs of the establishment, there is no direct or indirect economic or commercial advantage for the purposes of paragraph (2).

(4) Paragraph (2) does not apply to the making of a copy of a database available for on-the-spot reference use.

(5) Where a copy of a database has been sold within the EEA by, or with the consent of, the owner of the database right in the database, the further sale within the EEA of that copy shall not be taken for the purposes of this Part to constitute extraction or re-utilisation of the contents of the database.

Database right

13.(1) A property right ("database right") subsists, in accordance with this Part, in a database

if there has been a substantial investment in obtaining, verifying or presenting the contents of the database.

(2) For the purposes of paragraph (1) it is immaterial whether or not the database or any of its contents is a copyright work, within the meaning of Part I of the 1988 Act.

(3) This Regulation has effect subject to Regulation 18.

The maker of a database

14.(1) Subject to paragraphs (2) to (4), the person who takes the initiative in obtaining, verifying or presenting the contents of a database and assumes the risk of investing in that obtaining, verification or presentation shall be regarded as the maker of, and as having made, the database.

(2) Where a database is made by an employee in the course of his employment, his employer shall be regarded as the maker of the database, subject to any agreement to the contrary.

(3) Subject to paragraph (4), where a database is made by Her Majesty or by an officer or servant of the Crown in the course of his duties, Her Majesty shall be regarded as the maker of the database.

(4) Where a database is made by or under the direction or control of the House of Commons or the House of Lords—

   (a) the House by whom, or under whose direction or control, the database is made shall be regarded as the maker of the database, and

   (b) if the database is made by or under the direction or control of both Houses, the two Houses shall be regarded as the joint makers of the database.

(5) For the purposes of this Part a database is made jointly if two or more persons acting together in collaboration take the initiative in obtaining, verifying or presenting the contents of the database and assume the risk of investing in that obtaining, verification or presentation.

(6) References in this Part to the maker of a database shall, except as otherwise provided, be construed, in relation to a database which is made jointly, as reference to all the makers of the database.

First ownership of database right

15. The maker of a database is the first owner of database right in it.

Acts infringing database right

16. (1) Subject to the provisions of this Part, a person infringes database right in a database if, without the consent of the owner of the right, he extracts or re-utilises all or a substantial part of the contents of the database.

(2) For the purposes of this Part, the repeated and systematic extraction or re-utilisation of insubstantial parts of the contents of a database may amount to the extraction or re-utilisation of a substantial part of those contents.

Term of protection

17.(1) Database right in a database expires at the end of the period of fifteen years from the end of the calendar year in which the making of the database was completed.

(2) Where a database is made available to the public before the end of the period referred to in paragraph (1), database right in the database shall expire fifteen years from the end of the calendar year in which the database was first made available to the public.

(3) Any substantial change to the contents of a database, including a substantial change resulting from the accumulation of successive additions, deletions or alterations, which would result in the database being considered to be a substantial new investment shall qualify the database resulting from that investment for its own term of protection.

(4) This Regulation has effect subject to Regulation 30.

Qualification for database right

18.(1) Database right does not subsist in a database unless, at the material time, its maker, or if it was made jointly, one or more of its makers, was—

    (a) an individual who was a national of an EEA state or habitually resident within the EEA,

    (b) a body which was incorporated under the law of an EEA state and which, at that time, satisfied one of the conditions in paragraph (2), or

    (c) a partnership or other unincorporated body which was formed under the law of an EEA state and which, at that time, satisfied the condition in paragraph (2)(a).

(2) The conditions mentioned in paragraphs (1)(b) and (c) are—

    (a) that the body has its central administration or principal place of business within the EEA, or

    (b) that the body has its registered office within the EEA and the body's operations are linked on an ongoing basis with the economy of an EEA state.

(3) Paragraph (1) does not apply in any case falling within Regulation 14(4).

(4) In this Regulation—

    (a) "EEA" and "EEA state" have the meaning given by section 172A of the 1988 Act;

    (b) "the material time" means the time when the database was made, or if the making extended over a period, a substantial part of that period.

Avoidance of certain terms affecting lawful users

19.(1) A lawful user of a database which has been made available to the public in any manner shall be entitled to extract or re-utilise insubstantial parts of the contents of the database for any purpose.

(2) Where under an agreement a person has a right to use a database, or part of a database, which has been made available to the public in any manner, any term or condition in the agreement shall be void in so far as it purports to prevent that person from extracting or re-

utilising insubstantial parts of the contents of the database, or of that part of the database, for any purpose.

Exceptions to database right

20.(1) Database right in a database which has been made available to the public in any manner is not infringed by fair dealing with a substantial part of its contents if—

    (a) that part is extracted from the database by a person who is apart from this paragraph a lawful user of the database.

    (b) it is extracted for the purpose of illustration for teaching or research and not for any commercial purpose, and

    (c) the source is indicated.

(2) The provisions of Schedule 1 specify other acts which may be done in relation to a database notwithstanding the existence of database right.

Schedule 1 creates exceptions concerning Parliamentary and judicial proceedings, Royal Commissions and statutory inquiries, material open to inspection or on an official register, material communicated to the Crown in the course of public business, public records and acts done under statutory authority.

Acts permitted on assumption as to expiry of database right

21.(1) Database right in a database is not infringed by the extraction or re-utilisation of a substantial part of the contents of the database at a time when, or in pursuance of arrangements made at a time when—

    (a) it is not possible by reasonable inquiry to ascertain the identity of the maker, and

    (b) it is reasonable to assume that database right has expired.

(2) In the case of a database alleged to have been made jointly, paragraph (1) applies in relation to each person alleged to be one of the makers.

Presumptions relevant to database right

22.(1) The following presumptions apply in proceedings brought by virtue of this Part of these Regulations with respect to a database.

(2) Where a name purporting to be that of the maker appeared on copies of the database as published, or on the database when it was made, the person whose name appeared shall be presumed, until the contrary is proved—

    (a) to be the maker of the database, and

    (b) to have made it in circumstances not falling within Regulation 14(2) to (4).

(3) Where copies of the database as published bear a label or a mark stating—

    (a) that a named person was the maker of the database, or

    (b) that the database was first published in a specified year.

the label or mark shall be admissible as evidence of the facts stated and shall be presumed to be correct until the contrary is proved.

(4) In the case of a database alleged to have been made jointly, paragraphs (2) and (3), so far as is applicable, apply in relation to each person alleged to be one of the makers.

Application of copyright provisions to database right

23. The following provisions of the 1988 Act—

> sections 90 to 93 (dealing with rights in copyright works);
> sections 96 to 98 (rights and remedies of copyright owner);
> sections 101 and 102 (rights and remedies of exclusive licensee);

apply in relation to database right and databases in which that right subsists as they apply in relation to copyright and copyright works.

Licensing of database right

24. The provisions of Schedule 2 have effect with respect to the licensing of database right.

Schedule 2 lays down extensive provisions for the reference of voluntary licensing schemes for databases to the Copyright Tribunal and s.25 formally vests the Tribunal with jurisdiction over these references.

3.11.2 Copyright and Rights in Databases Regulations 1997 (No. 3032), Part IV, regs 29, 30.

Saving for copyright in certain existing databases

29.(1) Where a database—

(a) was created on or before 27th March 1996, and

(b) is a copyright work immediately before commencement,
copyright shall continue to subsist in the database for the remainder of its copyright term.

(2) In this Regulation "copyright term" means the period of the duration of copyright under section 12 of the 1988 Act (duration of copyright in literary, dramatic, musical or artistic works).

Database right: term applicable to certain existing databases

30. Where—

(a) the making of a database was completed on or after 1st January 1983, and

(b) on commencement, database right begins to subsist in the database,

database right shall subsist in the database for the period of fifteen years beginning with 1st January 1998.

3.11.3   *British Horseracing Board v William Hill* [2002] E.C.D.R. 41, CA

The claimant, BHB, evolved from the Jockey Club in 1993, taking over important roles in the organisation and regulation of the horseracing industry. Members of the BHB comprise not only the Jockey Club but also associations of racecourse owners, racehorse owners and an industry committee. Among its functions, it establishes dates and programme content of racing fixtures, and this includes an annual list of fixtures, weight adding and handicapping, supervision of race programmes, and production of racing publications and stakebooks. The information is put together in a very large BHB Database, which is constantly being updated and verified for accuracy. It is made available to interested persons through a website which the BHB maintains with partners. On the day before a race, the declarations of runners are made available through a satellite link, SIS, for which service, the defendant and other bookmakers pay. The database costs some £4 million a year to run, but earns only £1 million from users. The defendant set up an internet booking service which relays infor-mation from SIS. For this it refused to pay any database charge and the BHB sued for breach of its sui generis *database right.*

At first instance, Laddie J. was prepared to reject a number of arguments that interpretation of the Database right should be limited in ways that would relieve the Defendant of any liability, but considered that first a number of questions about interpretation of tthe Direction should be put to the ECJ. When the Defendant appealed to the CA, it agreed that this was desirable, not least in the light of the Swedish proceedings, Fixtures Marketing v Svenska Spel, *April 11, 2000 and, on appeal, May 3, 2001; and the Dutch proceedings,* de Telegraaf v NOM, *January 30, 2001, The Hague CA, which take a narrower view. The CA summarised the questions suggested by Laddie J as follows:*

1. Whether "database-ness" is an essential quality for any "part of the contents of the database?"

2. Whether information in the form of the lists of runners created at the same time as they are published can be a relevant part of the contents of the database?

3. Does "extraction" or "reutilisation" involve having access to the database or a copy of it?

4. Does "extraction" or "reutilisation" extend to a person who is a subscriber to a service provided by a licensee of the database right owner and who thereby receives part of the contents of the database, and who makes available that part of those contents to the public in the course of his business?

5. Where there is a constantly updated database, is there a new database separate from the previous database whenever any substantial change has occurred?

The CA in effect approved of questions on these lines being put the ECJ and sought proposals from Counsel. The ECJ's answers are awaited with great interest.

4 INDUSTRIAL DESIGNS

4.1 Copyright and Industrial Design

4.1.1 Copyright Designs and Patents Act 1988, ss.51–53: Limitations on Copyright in Designs

S.51(1) It is not an infringement of any copyright in a design document or model recording or embodying a design for anything other than an artistic work or a typeface to make an article to the design or to copy an article made to the design.

(2) Nor is it an infringement of the copyright to issue to the public, or include in a film, broadcast or cable programme service, anything the making of which was, by virtue of subsection (1), not an infringement of that copyright.

(3) In this section—

"design" means the design of any aspect of the shape or configuration (whether internal or external) of the whole or part of an article, other than surface decoration; and
"design document" means any record of a design, whether in the form of a drawing, a written description, a photograph, data stored in a computer or otherwise.

S.52(1) This section applies where an artistic work has been exploited, by or with the licence of the copyright owner, by—

(a) making by an industrial process articles falling to be treated for the purposes of this Part as copies of the work, and

(b) marketing such articles, in the United Kingdom or elsewhere.

(2) After the end of the period of 25 years from the end of the calendar year in which such articles are first marketed, the work may be copied by making articles of any description, or doing anything for the purpose of making articles of any description, and anything may be done in relation to articles so made, without infringing copyright in the work.

(3) Where only part of an artistic work is exploited as mentioned in subsection (1), subsection (2) applies only in relation to that part.

(4) The Secretary of State may by order make provision—

(a) as to the circumstances in which an article, or any description of article, is to be regarded for the purposes of this section as made by an industrial process;

(b) excluding from the operation of this section such articles of a primarily literary or artistic character as he thinks fit.

(5) An order shall be made by statutory instrument which shall be subject to annulment in pursuance of a resolution of either House of Parliament.

(6) In this section—

    (a) references to articles do not include films; and

    (b) references to the marketing of an article are to its being sold or let for hire or offered or exposed for sale or hire.

S.53(1) The copyright in an artistic work is not infringed by anything done—

    (a) in pursuance of an assignment or licence made or granted by a person registered under the Registered Designs Act 1949 as the proprietor of a corresponding design, and

    (b) in good faith in reliance on the registration and without notice of any proceedings for the cancellation of the registration or for rectifying the relevant entry in the register of designs;

and this is so notwithstanding that the person registered as the proprietor was not the proprietor of the design for the purposes of the 1949 Act.

(2) In subsection (1) a "corresponding design", in relation to an artistic work, means a design within the meaning of the 1949 Act which if applied to an article would produce something which would be treated for the purposes of this Part as a copy of the artistic work.

The definition of "corresponding design" in the Registered Designs Act 1949, s.44, is in equivalent terms to those of s.53(2).

Sections 54 and 55 limit the scope of copyright in a typeface as an artistic work by excluding use of the typeface in the ordinary course of typing, printing, etc. and associated acts from the scope of infringement.

4.1.2   *Hensher v Restawile* [1976] A.C. 64, HL

The appellant-plaintiffs, manufacturers of chairs and settees, produced a temporary "mock-up" for a newly-designed suite of furniture. This mock-up was used to produce suites of furniture which sold well under the mark "The Bronx", and were imitated by the defendants, among others. The plaintiffs registered no designs but relied upon copyright in the mock-up as a "work of artistic craftsmanship" (Copyright Act 1956, s.3(1)(c), equivalent to Copyright, Designs and Patents Act 1988, s.4(1)(c)).

Lord Reid:

It is common ground that we must consider the prototype and not the furniture put on the market by the appellants. Apparently this is because the articles put on the market were not works of craftsmanship. But if there was copyright in the prototype then the furniture put on the market by the appellants was copied from it, and the respondents' products were copied from the furniture which the appellants put on the market. The respondents do not deny that this would be infringement of that copyright.

The respondents have not taken the point that such a prototype however artistic could not be a "work of artistic craftsmanship", and the point was not argued. But I feel bound to say that I have great doubt about this matter. A work of craftsmanship suggests to me a durable, useful handmade object and a work of artistic craftsmanship suggests something, whether of practical utility or not, which its owner values because of its artistic character. It appears to me to be difficult to bring within the terms or the intention of the statute an object which, however artistic it might appear to be, is only intended to be used as a step in a commercial operation and has no value in itself. I express no concluded opinion on this matter on which the decision of this case can be of no authority. This case must I think be decided on the assumption that a real chair similar to those put on the market had been made by craftsmanship.

Section 3(1) is difficult to understand unless one takes account of its origin. The Copyright Act 1911 covered artistic works. Section 35 contains a definition: "Artistic work" includes works of painting, drawing, sculpture and artistic craftsmanship, and architectural works of art and engravings and photographs. "Architectural work of art" is defined as meaning any building or structure having an artistic character or design. This brought in artistic craftsmanship and buildings for the first time. It would seem that paintings, drawings, sculpture, engravings and photographs were protected whether they had any artistic character or not, but works of craftsmanship had to be of "artistic" craftsmanship and buildings must have an "artistic" character or design. There is no further explanation of what is meant by "artistic".

The 1956 Act in section 3(1)(a) makes explicit that the works to which it refers need have no artistic quality. Section 3(1)(b) removes the need for any artistic character or design in buildings. But section 3(1)(c) preserves the limitation that there must be "artistic" craftsmanship.

The word "artistic" is not an easy word to construe or apply not only because it may have different shades of meaning but also because different people have different views about what is artistic. One may have a word which substantially everyone understands in much the same way. Recently we had to consider such a word—"insulting" (*Brutus v Cozens* [1972] 2 All E.R. 1297). Then the matter can and, indeed, must be left to the judge or jury for further explanation will confuse rather than clarify.

But here two questions must be determined. What precisely is the meaning of "artistic" in this context and who is to judge of its application to the article in question? There is a trend of authority with which I agree that a court ought not to be called on to make an aesthetic judgment. Judges have to be experts in the use of the English language but they are not experts in art or aesthetics. In such a matter my opinion is of no more value than that of anyone else. But I can and must say what in my view is the meaning of the word "artistic".

I think we must avoid philosophic or metaphysical argument about the nature of beauty, not only because there does not seem to be any consensus about this but also because those who are ignorant of philosophy are entitled to have opinions about what is artistic. I think that by common usage it is proper for a person to say that in his opinion a thing has an artistic character if he gets pleasure or satisfaction or it may be uplift from contemplating it. No doubt it is necessary to beware of those who get pleasure from looking at something which has cost them a great deal of money. But if unsophisticated people get pleasure from seeing something which they admire I do not see why we must say that it is not artistic because those who profess to be art experts think differently. After all there are great differences of opinion among those who can properly be called experts.

It is I think of importance that the maker or designer of a thing should have intended that it should have an artistic appeal but I would not regard that as either necessary or conclusive. If any substantial section of the public genuinely admires and values a thing for its appearance and gets pleasure or satisfaction, whether emotional or intellectual, from looking at it, I would accept that it is artistic although many others may think it meaningless or common or vulgar.

I think that it may be misleading to equate artistic craftsmanship with a work of art. "Work of art" is generally associated more with the fine arts than with craftsmanship and may be setting too high a standard. During the last century there was a movement to bring art to the people. I doubt whether the craftsman who set out with that intention would have regarded all their products as works of art, but they were certainly works of artistic craftsmanship whether or not they were useful as well as having an artistic appeal.

I am quite unable to agree with the view of the Court of Appeal that:

> "there must at least be expected in an object or work that its utilitarian or functional appeal should not be the primary inducement to its acquisition or retention".

The whole conception of artistic craftsmanship appears to me to be to produce things which are both useful and artistic in the belief that being artistic does not make them any less useful. A person who only wants, or has only room for, one of a particular kind of household object may be willing to pay more to get one which he regards as artistic; if a work of craftsmanship it is nonetheless of artistic craftsmanship because his primary purpose is to get something useful.

But on the other hand I cannot accept the appellants' submission or the view of Graham J. Many people—probably too many—buy things on eye appeal or because they are of a new or original design. But they would not claim that therefore they thought that their purchase had artistic merit. They might say that they were not interested in art, or that they would like to have bought an artistic object but that there was none to be had, at least at a price they could pay. It is notorious that manufacturers go to great expense in providing packaging which will catch the eye of customers. But the customer does not regard the packaging as artistic—he throws it away.

In the present case I find no evidence at all that anyone regarded the appellants' furniture as artistic. The appellants' object was to produce something which would sell. It was, as one witness said, "a winner" and they succeeded in their object. No doubt many customers bought the furniture because they thought it looked nice as well as being comfortable. But looking nice appears to me to fall considerably short of having artistic appeal. I can find no evidence that anyone felt or thought that the furniture was artistic in the sense which I have tried to explain. I am therefore of opinion that this appeal should be dismissed.

Lord Simon of Glaisdale:

The significant feature of this part of the law before 1911 was that the artistic works given copyright protection were works of fine art. This accorded with the almost universal concept current in 1862: a work of art was a product of the fine arts and primarily an easel painting. But almost from the moment of the Fine Arts Copyright Act 1862, there was a reaction, which came to be known as the Arts and Crafts movement. In 1862 itself William Morris founded "The Firm" producing a wide variety of work of decorative and applied art. In 1864 he produced his first wallpaper, hand-printed from wood blocks. In the 1880s at least five societies were founded to promote the guild ideal propagated by Ruskin and Morris. In 1883 the Arts and Crafts Exhibition Society began its work. In 1890 Morris set up the Kelmscott Press, to be followed by a number of other private presses within the decade. In 1893 came the Arts and Crafts Essay (of which eight were concerned with the design and decoration of furniture). In 1896 the Central School of Arts and Crafts was founded, with Lethaby and Frampton as joint principals. The tenth edition of the Encyclopaedia Britannica contained, for the first time, an article on "Arts and Crafts"—by Walter Crane. In 1905 Cobden-Sanderson published The Arts and Crafts Movement. In 1908 the Central School moved to its present purpose-built premises in Southampton Row. These are no more than a handful of key events: but they put beyond doubt what it was that prompted Parliament in 1911 to give copyright protection to "works of artistic craftsmanship" namely, the Arts and Crafts movement with its emphasis on the applied or decorative arts.

For the essence of the Arts and Crafts ideology was that "art" did not mean merely, or even primarily, the fine arts. Art was a way of life, standing in contrast to the prevailing life of industrialism and commercialism, which was seen as a threat to mankind's spiritual and physical well-being. "On every hand", Carlyle had written, "the living artisan is driven from his workshop, to make room for a speedier inanimate one". So the handicraftsman must be restored to his creative role in society. Moreover, his creation, wherever appropriate, should be a work of art—creation par excellence: and the artist must in turn be a craftsman. The aim of Mackmurdo's Century Guild (1882) was, on the one hand, to render all branches of art no longer "the sphere of the tradesman"; on the other, to "restore building, decoration, glass-painting, pottery, wood-carving and metal to their proper place beside painting and sculpture". The aesthetic of the movement was concerned with fitness and propriety, in contradistinction to irrelevant ornament (what Lethaby called "sham artistic twaddle"). Functional efficiency and respect for the worked material would impose its own appropriate form, showing, to quote Lethaby again, that it was "made for a human being by a human being".

But although, in my view, there can be no doubt that, when Parliament, in 1911, gave copyright protection to "works of artistic craftsmanship", it was extending to works of applied art the protection formerly restricted to works of the fine arts, and was doing so under the influence of the Arts and Crafts movement, and although the aesthetic of the Arts and Crafts movement was a handicraft aesthetic, Parliament used the words "artistic craftsmanship", not "artistic handicraft". It seems likely that this was done advisedly: I have already indicated that section 22 of the 1911 Act envisaged that an industrial design might be an artistic work. Moreover, however ideologically opposed to current industrial and commercial society, at least some of the leaders of the Arts and Crafts movement recognised that they would have to come to terms with the machine. As early as 1850 Philip Webb designed table glassware for J. Powell & Sons of Whitefriars. During the 1880s even Morris acknowledged that the machine could be useful in extinguishing all irksome and unintelligent labour, leaving us free to raise the standard of skill of hand and energy of mind of our workmen. The private presses may have used hand-made paper and designed their own typefaces, but they printed on machines. Ashbee, who went to the United States in 1900 "to tilt at the great industrial windmill", by 1911, under the influence of Frank Lloyd Wright (who had lectured on "The Art and Craft of the Machine") could no longer deny to the unpretentious machine-made object an aesthetic value; and after the failure of his Guild and School of Handicraft he himself turned to industrial design. Much of Benson's metal-work was produced by machinery on a commercial scale. The Central School of Arts and Crafts, though foremost a school of handicrafts, had as a declared aim to encourage "the industrial application of decorative design". So, although "works of artistic craftsmanship" cannot be adequately construed without bearing in mind the aims and achievements of the Arts and Crafts movement, "craftsmanship" in the statutory phrase cannot be limited to handicraft; nor is the word "artistic" incompatible with machine production (see *Britain v Hanks Brothers and Co* (1902) 86 L.T. 764).

The concession that the prototype of "The Bronx" was a work of craftsmanship has tended to distort the argument by concentrating exclusively on the meaning of the word "artistic" in the statutory phrase. But "works of artistic craftsmanship" is a composite phrase which must be construed as a whole. There is nothing to suggest that any of the words is used in other than one of its ordinary senses. A work of craftsmanship, even though it cannot be confined to handicraft, at least presupposes special training, skill and knowledge for its production: see *Cuisenaire v Reed* [1963] V.R. 719, and *Cuisenaire v South West Imports Ltd* [1968] 1 Ex.C.R. 493. "Craftsmanship", particularly when considered in its historical context, implies a manifestation of pride in sound workmanship—a rejection of the shoddy, the meretricious, the facile. But the craftsmanship—not the work itself—must, in addition, be artistic. Before turning to the various criteria which have been propounded it may be helpful to consider some examples. A cobbler is a craftsman, and those in the Arts and Crafts movement would have valued his vocation as such. But neither they, nor anyone else using the words in their common acceptation, would describe his craftsmanship as artistic, or his products as "works of artistic craftsmanship". A dental mechanic is a similar example; so is a pattern-maker, a boiler-maker, a plumber, a wheelwright, a thatcher. At the other extreme is the maker of hand-painted tiles. He too is a craftsman; but his craftsmanship would properly be described as artistic and his products as "works of artistic craftsmanship". In between lie a host of crafts some of whose practitioners can claim artistic craftsmanship, much not—or whose practitioners sometimes exercise artistic craftsmanship, sometimes not. In the former class, for example, are glaziers. The ordinary glazier is a craftsman, but he could not properly claim that his craftsmanship is artistic in the common acceptation. But the maker of stained glass windows could properly make such a claim; and indeed, the revival of stained glass work was one of the high achievements of the Arts and Crafts movement. In the latter class is the blacksmith—a craftsman in all his business, and exercising artistic craftsmanship perhaps in making wrought iron gates, but certainly not in shoeing a horse or repairing a ploughshare. In these intermediate—or rather, straddling—classes come, too, the woodworkers, ranging from carpenters to cabinet-makers: some of their work would be generally accepted as artistic craftsmanship, much not. Similarly, printers, book-binders, cutlers, needleworkers, weavers—and many others. In this straddling class also fall, in my judgment, the makers of furniture. Some of their products would be, I think, almost universally accepted as "works of artistic craftsmanship" but it would be a misuse of language to describe the bulk of their products as such. Where and how is the line to be drawn?

I think that the key passage of Graham J.'s judgment is the following:

> "My conclusion on this part of the case is therefore that these chairs and settees are 'works of artistic craftsmanship' in that they have, whether one admires them or not, distinctive characteristics of shape, form and finish, which were conceived and executed by Mr Hensher and those working with him so as to result in articles which are much more than purely utilitarian. They exhibit in my judgment distinctive features of design and skill in workmanship which the words of definition 'artistic craftsmanship' on their proper construction in their context connote."

Though this approach receives some support from *Blake v Warren* [1931] MacG. Cop. Cas. 268, a decision of an official referee on the "artistic character" of an "architectural work of art" under the 1911 Act, I respectfully agree with the comment of the Court of Appeal:

> "It seems to us that the judge has in effect come to the conclusion that in the field of furniture all that is needed to qualify as a work of artistic craftsmanship is a sufficient originality of design to qualify as a design under the Registered Designs Act 1949. Is this right in law? We do not think so. It seems to us to give no sufficient effect to the word 'artistic' in the definition in the 1956 Act. The phrase is not 'a work of craftsmanship of original design' ... Mere originality in points of design aimed at appealing to the eye as commercial selling points will not in our judgment suffice".

Although there is, as I have pointed out, an area of overlap between the Copyright Acts and the Registered Designs Acts, the two classes of statute do not give co-terminous protection as regards subject-matter: if that had been the intention, interpretative cross-reference would have been the appropriate drafting technique. Moreover, although true originality (in the way of a new sensibility or ideology or world view or technique) may be relevant aesthetically, mere novelty can hardly be so. A gimmick is almost the negation of a work of art. Its appeal, as Russell L.J. implied, is likely to be directed at satisfying other demands in the purchaser than the contemplation of beauty—desire for change, for modishness, for prestige, for example.

On the other hand, I cannot agree with the alternative criterion proposed by the Court of Appeal that:

> "... in order to qualify as a work of artistic craftsmanship, there must at least be expected in an object or work that its utilitarian or functional appeal should not be the primary inducement to its acquisition or retention".

Restawile's counsel did not attempt to support this test before your Lordships. It is, I fear, unworkable. One person may buy a chair because it is comfortable, another because it is beautiful, a third because it exactly fits the room, a fourth because it is the right price. Even without the third and fourth classes, which do not fit in the Court of Appeal's categorisation, it would be impracticable to decide on the artistic quality of the craftsmanship by a show of hands or a card vote. And in one purchaser alone the motives may be so mixed that it is impossible to say what is the primary inducement to acquisition or retention. Even more important, the whole antithesis between utility and beauty, between function and art, is a false one—especially in the context of the Arts and Crafts movement. "I never begin to be satisfied", said Philip Webb, one of the founders, "until my work looks commonplace". Lethaby's object, declared towards the end, was "to create an efficiency style". Artistic form should, they all held, be an emanation of regard for materials on the one hand and for function on the other.

Hensher's counsel put forward an argument as follows. An object is artistic if it appeals to the eye of the beholder, giving him visual pleasure. "The Bronx" proved to be more appealing than "The Denver". But, so far as utility or function was concerned, there was virtually nothing to choose between the two models. The greater appeal of "The Bronx" must, therefore, have been its "eye-appeal"—that it gave significantly greater visual pleasure. The prototype "The Bronx" was admittedly a work of craftsmanship. It inevitably follows, it was argued, that it was a work of artistic craftsmanship.

With all respect, and admitting its ingenuity, there seems to me to be much that is unacceptable in this argument. First, it is based on a hedonistic aesthetic theory (the essence of art is that it gives pleasure) which, although it has had distinguished proponents, has also been strongly disputed. Secondly, it then proceeds to stand the theory on its head—the essence of art is that it gives (visual) pleasure, therefore what gives visual pleasure is artistic. This is not only illogical, but manifestly untrue—a pretty girl or a landscape give visual pleasure without being artistic. Thirdly, this argument to is based on a contradistinction between art and function which is unsound, and particularly unsound in the instant context. Fourthly, the argument proceeds on the basis that "The Bronx" must have been bought in preference to "The Denver" for its greater utility or for its great visual appeal—and, since it was not the former, it must have been the latter. But there were many other reasons why "The Bronx" might have been bought—because the Joneses next door had just acquired such a suite, for example, or because no one in the neighbourhood had such a novelty, or because it struck the purchaser as being in the "trend" of fashion (that word was actually used in evidence to explain the common appeal of these suites), or because it seemed to be the best general value for money of the available goods, or, no doubt, for a large variety of other reasons which have nothing to do with either function or eye-appeal.

Restawile's counsel, on the other hand, propounded two alternative criteria, both reflecting another theory of aesthetics—the idealistic. The first was: an article of craftsmanship is artistic if it can be seen from the article itself or from other evidence that the author is using a utilitarian article as a vehicle to carry an expression of his idea of beauty. Counsel defined neither "idea" nor "beauty"—wisely, since philosophers have been at odds over these concepts for millennia. But without some explanation the proffered criterion is virtually tautological; since art, both in the discipline of aesthetics and in popular usage, is generally understood to be the expression or impression of beauty.

Counsel's second criterion was a variant on the first: craftsmanship is artistic if the craftsman is using a utilitarian article to give expression to an idea unassociated with the utilitarian purpose. This avoids the tautology implicit in the use of the word "beauty", but at the cost of greater vagueness. Disregarding the metaphysical implications of the use of the word "idea" in this context, this criterion would extend to the expression of ideas which would seem to be irrelevant to art—for example, novelty and gimmickry (which I have already referred to), or modishness, or obscenity, or racial prejudice. The example given by counsel was an "archetypal" fork (a work of craftsmanship) with an ornament on the handle (making it a work of artistic craftsmanship). But, as I have ventured to point out, this whole contradistinction between art and utility, between function and ornament, is entirely alien to the concepts which lie behind section 3(1)(c) of the 1956 Act. An "archetypal" spoon (assuming such a metaphysical concept can materialise) may itself be a work of artistic craftsmanship; an apostle spoon is neither more nor less likely to be so.

It is, my Lords, I confess, easier to question the criteria put forward by others than to propound one's own. The attempt must nevertheless be made. I start by re-emphasising that the statutory phrase is not "artistic work of craftsmanship", but "work of artistic craftsmanship"; and that this distinction accords with the social situation in which Parliament was providing a remedy. It is therefore misleading to ask, first, is this a work produced by a craftsman, and secondly, is it a work of art? It is more pertinent to ask, is this the work of one who was in this respect an artist-craftsman? It follows that the artistic merit of the work is irrelevant. (It is, no doubt, because section 3(1)(a), "irrespective of artistic quality", which, as comparison with the words "artistic character" in the 1911 Act demonstrates, refer to artistic merit). Not only is artistic merit irrelevant as a matter of statutory construction, evaluation of artistic merit is not a task for which judges have any training or general aptitude. Words are the tools and subject-matter of lawyers; but even in matters of literary copyright the court will not concern itself with literary merit: *Walter v Lane* [1900] A.C. 539. Since the tribunal will not attempt a personal aesthetic judgment (Stewart J. in *Hay v Sloan* (1957) 16 Fox P.C. 185) it follows again, that whether the subject-matter is or is not a work of artistic craftsmanship is a matter of evidence; and the most cogent evidence is likely to be either from those who are themselves acknowledged artist-craftsman or from those who are concerned with the training of artist-craftsmen—in other words, expert evidence. In evaluating the evidence, the court will endeavour not to be tied to a particular metaphysics of art, partly because courts are not naturally fitted to weigh such matters, partly because Parliament can hardly have intended that the construction of its statutory phrase should turn on some recondite theory of aesthetics—though the court must, of course, in its task of statutory interpretation, take cognisance of the social-aesthetic situation which lies behind the enactment, nor can counsel be prevented from probing the reasons why a witness considers the subject-matter to be or not to be a work of artistic craftsmanship. It is probably enough that common experience tells us that artists have vocationally an aim and impact which differ from those of the ordinary run of humankind. Given the craftsmanship, it is the presence of such aim and impact—what Stewart J. called "the intent of the creator and its result"—which will determine that the work is one of artistic craftsmanship.

Against this construction of the statutory phrase, the result of the instant appeal cannot be in doubt: there was no, or certainly no adequate, evidence that the prototype of the Bronx chair was a work of artistic craftsmanship. A Mrs Watney, who had been the principal furniture buyer of the Times Furnishing Co gave evidence for Henshers: some passages were quoted in the judgment of the Court of Appeal. It is sufficient here to say that she nowhere stated in her opinion any of the suites in question (or the prototype) was a work of artistic craftsmanship. Though she used the word "eye-appeal", it was in the context of commercial potentiality, selling points. Of "The Bronx" she said, "the shape ... was new. It was very flashy. It was horrible really". Of "The Denver", in respect of its common features with "The Bronx", she spoke of the "trend that was coming in". She used the word "winner"—appropriate enough in its commercial context, but hardly apt for anything more.

Mr Carter, a design consultant specialising in furniture, also gave evidence for Henshers. He did use the word "artistic"; but it was put into his mouth under the misapprehension that he had already used it. Again, the key passages are set out in the judgment of the Court of Appeal. Mr Carter agreed with Henshers' counsel that it was the intention of the designer to produce an article which appealed to the eye of the beholder: I have already ventured to indicate why this is an inadequate criterion of art or the artistic. He described "The Bronx" as "typical of the middle of the road commercial type of production furniture". He considered its design to be mediocre, although he could see that it had great appeal—slightly vulgar, though obviously quite a good commercial design, having "novelty ... quite distinct individuality".

All this is very far from establishing "The Bronx" or its prototype as a work of artistic craftsmanship. I respectfully agree with the Court of Appeal that at the most it established originality in points of design aimed at appealing to the eye as commercial selling points. I also agree that this does not suffice. If it were permissible to express a personal view, I would agree with the Court of Appeal that Henshers' suites are perfectly ordinary pieces of furniture. It would be an entire misuse of language to describe them or their prototypes as works of artistic craftsmanship.

I would, therefore, dismiss the appeal.

Lord Morris of Borth-y-Gest, Viscount Dilhorne and Lord Kilbrandon delivered concurring speeches.

4.1.3 *Merlet v Mothercare* [1986] R.P.C. 115, Walton J.

The first plaintiff, a clothes designer and maker, designed a baby's cape—the "Raincosy"—originally for her own child. Later she arranged for its manufacture by the second plaintiff. The defendant copied the cape and sold its version in its chain-stores. One of the claims was against infringement of copyright in the prototype cape (P.1) as a "work of artistic craftsmanship". On this issue, Walton J. stated:

In the leading case on the relevant subsection in the House of Lords, *George Hensher Ltd v Restawile Upholstery (Lancs) Ltd* [1975] R.P.C. 31, the question of craftsmanship was not in issue, having been, as their Lordships thought, wrongly conceded at first instance. But from their varied observations on the point, craftsmanship requires a manifestation of pride in sound workmanship, or, alternatively, as Lord Reid put it, "a durable useful handmade object". There is no doubt that P.1 was a durable—it has survived the Highland weather—extremely useful handmade object. And I think, taking into account the function it was intended to perform, the garment was sound enough, but really no more than this.

Can such workmanship be equated with craftsmanship? Unlike Hensher, the matter is not conceded and I think the case is one very much on the borderline. However, I do not think I would be justified in deciding this case simply on the basis that P.1 does not reach in its execution the standard required to amount to craftsmanship. However, "artistic craftsmanship" is a totally different matter.

The first question which arises on this point, and in many ways it is the most crucial question of all on this part of the case, is to what extent, when considering a work of artistic craftsmanship, it is permissible to consider notionally anything other than the precise work said to be a work of artistic craftsmanship itself. The reason why the matter is crucial is that Mr Fysh was in substance constrained to admit that, if regard was to be had only to the "Raincosy" itself, divorced from its use, it would be extremely difficult, if not totally impossible, to submit that any substantial section of the public would value the "Raincosy" for its appearance, or get pleasure or satisfaction, whether emotional or intellectual, from looking at it. This is the test which Lord Reid applied in the leading case already referred to of *George Hensher Ltd v Restawile Upholstery (Lancs) Ltd* at 54, lines 41 to 44, and which is a test which is otherwise the most favourable one for the plaintiffs' case.

But, says Mr Fysh, if the complex of a mother, equipped with a Kangourou or equivalent baby sling, and baby, properly protected by a "Raincosy", is observed by any mother (mothers doubtless being a substantial section of the public), they would derive immense aesthetic satisfaction from looking at the whole assemblage. Indeed, the plaintiffs' main witness on this point, Kathleen Linda Key-Scott, herself a mother, waxed lyrical, in an overtly Freudian manner, over the bundling of the baby with the mother thus effected in an alleged womb-like manner.

But how stands the law? I commence, as anybody dealing with the particular topic of garments of any nature must, with the doubts expressed by Clauson J., as he then was, in *Burke and Margot Burke Ltd v Spicers Dress Designs* [1936] Ch. 400 at 408–409. What he said was this:

"I can conceive it possible that Mrs Burke might design a frock and make it all herself, and if she did that I can well understand she might be the author of an original work of artistic craftsmanship, but that is not what has happened in this case. I do not want it to be assumed that, even so, I should feel able to hold that a lady who designed a frock and made it all herself was necessarily entitled to copyright. The point is not one which it is necessary for me to decide. It must, however, be borne in mind that the meaning of the term 'artistic' as indicated in the *Oxford English Dictionary* is that which pertains to an artist. An artist is defined in the same dictionary as: 'One who cultivates one of the fine arts in which the object is mainly to gratify the aesthetic emotions by perfection of execution whether in creation or representation'. Does a designer who herself designs and makes a frock cultivate one of the fine arts in which the object is mainly to gratify the aesthetic emotions by perfection of execution whether in creation or representation? A possible view is that what she does is merely to bring into being a garment as a mere article of commerce. If that is the right view there may be a difficulty in holding that even a lady who designs and executes a beautiful frock is necessarily the author of an original work of artistic craftsmanship. The frock when one looks at it, *qua* frock, as it might be held up on court, goes a very little way towards gratifying the aesthetic emotions. It is quite a different matter when the frock is placed upon a lady of the figure and colouring which it is designed to suit; then the frock in that connection may help to gratify the aesthetic emotions. The question whether a frock *per se* is the subject of copyright under the Act is one that can be determined only by forming a judgment upon the problem which I have thus indicated, but which in the present case it is not my duty to solve".

These observations were, of course, *obiter*; but it has been my experience, and, I think, the experience of anybody who has had anything to do with claims relating to the pirating of dress designs, that ever since that case the plaintiffs have never sought to rely upon any dress as itself being a work of artistic craftsmanship, but have always sought to rely instead upon the undoubted copyright in drawings related to the dress.

Walton J. referred to Bernstein v Sydney Murray *[1981] R.P.C. 303 and* Radley Gowns v Spirou *[1975] F.S.R. 455 and continued:*

I now return to *Hensher*. It appears to me quite clear that one thing upon which virtually all their Lordships were agreed was that the proper test was to consider whether the object under consideration had an artistic appeal in itself. Doubtless, the furniture in issue in that case was intended to be sat upon, conceivably by a united and happy family: but nobody there suggested that, as the contemplation of the furniture so filled by *paterfamilias* and *materfamilias* would give great aesthetic satisfaction, so that satisfaction could, as it were, be rubbed off on to the furniture itself.

Walton J. referred to passages in the speeches in Hensher. *He continued:*

Therefore, in my judgment I have to consider whether the "Raincosy"—or, I think, more accurately, the prototype thereof, P.1—is in itself a work of artistic craftsmanship. What, then, is the true test by which a work of artistic craftsmanship is to be judged? At first sight, all their Lordships in *Hensher* were laying down different, and apparently irreconcilable, tests; but, after having, as I freely acknowledge, originally recoiled from the test propounded by Viscount Dilhorne, namely, is the object in question a work of art?, as propounding far too stringent a test (as indeed Lord Reid said), I have finally come to the reluctant conclusion that there exists a clear majority of voices in the House of Lords for that view.

Walton J. referred to passages from the speeches of Viscount Dilhorne, Lord Simon of Glaisdale and Lord Kilbrandon. He continued:

Thus there is a clear majority of their Lordships in favour of this approach to the question, and I think that I am therefore bound to accept it. However, on reflection, I have come to the conclusion that my—and Lord Reid's—initial reluctance to accept this test, as posing too stringent a criterion, is mistaken, being based upon an instinctive value judgment as to what might constitute a work of art. But this is to do precisely what I think their Lordships regarded as impermissible—namely, to make a value judgment. At any rate in the first instance, it is not for the court to make a value judgment: the question is primarily the intention of the artist-craftsman. If his intention was to create a work of art and he has not manifestly failed in that intent, that is all that is required. It is not for the court to say that he has merely done the equivalent of flinging a paint pot in the face of the public. But, of course, he may have manifestly failed in his object, and his own *ipse dixit* cannot therefore be the sole, although it is the initial and predominant, test.

There is one further reflection. Although there must always come a first time when an artist-craftsman seeks to create a work of art, and the court may well look with just suspicion upon the first claim of this nature, it will be much easier to recognise the claim if the craftsman is already a recognised artist.

Finally, I say nothing as to the evidence which should be properly admitted as to whether the artist has succeeded in his aim of creating a work of art. There was a diversity of views in the House as to what evidence (apart of course from the intentions of the presumed artist-craftsman) was properly admissible, and especially in this last point. I do not think it would be right, since it is not required for the purposes of this case, to express any opinion thereon.

However, it appears to me clear beyond a peradventure that when creating the "Raincosy" Mme Merlet did not have in mind the creation of a work of art in any shape or form. What she had in mind, as appeared quite clearly from her evidence, was the utilitarian consideration of creating a barrier between the assumed rigours of a Highland summer and her baby in such a manner as to afford him complete protection, safely cocooned next to her warm body, in a stylish and attractive shape. It is, of course, I suppose conceivable that, although she did not set out to make a work of art, *per incuriam* she may have done so; but certainly nobody in court, whether the witnesses, counsel or the judge—or, indeed, anybody out of court who had written about the "Raincosy" and whose writing was in evidence—considered that she had done so, if one is to regard, as I have already decided, the "Raincosy" by itself. On this, the view of Mr Herbert, a witness of the greatest possible distinction in the field of designs of every nature, was terse and to the point: the "Raincosy" was, he said, a "basic commodity item". And I entirely agree.

The finding at first instance that the prototype cape did not constitute a work of artistic craftsmanship was not challenged in the proceedings before the Court of Appeal, which concerned infringement of design drawings for the cape.

4.1.4 *Wham-O Manufacturing v Lincoln* [1985] R.P.C. 127, CA, N.Z.

The first plaintiff, an American corporation, developed the well-known flying disc, the "Frisbee". It was made from plastic and was distinguished from other similar products by the addition of one or more concentric rings or ribs. These improved its aerodynamic qualities. By surreptitious collusion with the first plaintiff's Australian licensee, the defendant company produced and marketed a very similar product in New Zealand, where legislative provisions equivalent to those of the UK Copyright Act 1956, ss.3(1) and 48(1) (definitions) were in force. Inter alia, the plaintiffs succeeded in claims that the defendant's activities constituted infringement of their copyright in (i) preliminary working drawings; (ii) wooden models from which moulds were made (which were "sculptures"); (iii) moulds for production of the plastic articles (which were "engravings"); and (iv) the "Frisbees" produced by extruding liquid plastic into the moulds (which were "engravings", but not "sculptures").

On these associated issues, Davison C.J. (for the court) stated:

Copyright protection which is statutory in nature is conferred by section 7 of the Act in any "artistic work" which is defined in section 2 as follows:

"Artistic work" means a work of any of the following descriptions, that is to say—

(a) The following, irrespective of artistic quality, namely, paintings, sculptures, drawings, engravings and photographs;

(b) Works of architecture, being either buildings of models for buildings;

(c) Works of artistic craftsmanship, not falling within either of the preceding paragraphs of this definition.

"Engraving" is defined as including—"Any etching, lithograph, woodcut, print, or similar work, not being a photograph".

"Sculpture" is defined as including—"any cast or model made for purposes of sculpture".

Moller J. held that the wooden models were "sculptures"; the moulds or dies were "engravings"; and that the plastic moulded products were also "engravings". Those findings are challenged by Mr Hillyer. The question whether the plastic moulded products were also "sculptures" was posed by Moller J. but not answered in his judgment.

Before Moller J. counsel for Wham-O, in contending that the wooden model was a "sculpture" and that the moulds or dies and the finished products were "engravings" and thus proper subjects of copyright, elected to rely solely upon that part of the definition of artistic work set out in section 2(1)(a) of the Copyright Act 1962. ...

A reading of the definition of "artistic work" in section 2(1)(a) of the Act indicates that the Act when it speaks of engraving primarily has in contemplation the final prints made from an engraved plate rather than the plate itself. That was the view expressed by Paul Baker Q.C. in *James Arnold & Co Ltd v Miafern Ltd* [1980] R.P.C. 397 at 403:

> " 'Engraving' can and usually does mean an image produced from an engraved plate. The first question here is whether the engraving can mean the actual engraved plate from which the copies are taken. Looking at the sections alone, particularly the association of the word in section 3 with sculptures, drawings and photographs, it would suggest that it must be the final picture, and of course it certainly includes that".

Davison C.J. analysed further the judgment in the Miafern *case and referred to dictionary definitions of "to engrave"; he continued:*

We agree with the conclusion reached by Paul Baker Q.C. that engraving embraces not only the image made from the engraved plate but the engraved plate itself, but we prefer to reach that result by giving the word "engraving" as used in the definition of "artistic work" in section 2(1)(a) of the Act its ordinary meaning as ascertained from the sources referred to earlier. It is the purpose of copyright to protect the original skill and labour of the author and there is a large degree of that skill and labour brought to bear in making the engraved plate. We do not believe that it was the intention of Parliament to deny copyright in the plate and yet allow it in the print taken from that plate.

At this point it is necessary to consider the nature of the moulds or dies and the finished products.

The manner in which the moulds were made has been described by Mr Gillespie. A cutting tool on a lathe was used to remove metal from the die block to create the desired shape. No doubt that is the way in which the ribs or rings appearing on the finished product were formed. We see no reason why the process involved in the production of the die or mould, particularly the creation of the cuts to produce the ribs or rings, should not be regarded as the act of engraving within the provisions of section 2(1)(a) of the Act, and the mould or die so created an "engraving" just as a "print" is an engraving in terms of the extended definition in section 2 of the Act.

Moller J. in his judgment came to the view that a die or mould of the kind in question is an engraving. We agree. The purpose of the Act is to protect original artistic works. The skill and labour of the craftsman is exercised in cutting and shaping the plate—engraving it—to produce the intended design. There appears to be no reason why skill and labour so applied should not be protected from copying equally as a print made from that plate is given protection if it can properly be described as an original artistic work.

Mr Hillyer submitted that an engraving in the form of a mould or die could not be an engraving as protected by the Act because it is not meant to be appreciated visually but rather is merely a device used to create an end product, namely, the finished plastic disc. This submission cannot be upheld, particularly in view of the developing nature of the law of copyright. The requirement for works to be of artistic quality has been removed from the definition of "artistic work" in section 2 of the Act so far as the items referred to in clause (a) of that definition are concerned, and so long as the die or mould falls within the words of the definition to which we have referred then it may be the subject of copyright protection.

We next consider whether the finished product—the plastic disc created from the mould or die—is an "engraving" or a "sculpture".

The process of creating the finished product was described by Mr Gillespie in these words:

"(Q) Describe the moulding operation in which those parts operate to form the disc? (A) The injection mould is placed into a moulding machine and under very high pressure and heat plastic pellets which have been melted flow through a small opening in either the core of the cavity because it can be done from either side of the mould, that material flows into a void in between the core and the cavity. In this particular product the plastic then flows outward filling the entire cavity and then the material starts to harden. At the proper time which has been predetermined by prior testing of the mould, the moulding machine opens separating the core and the cavity from one another".

The word "print" although included in the definition "engraving" is not separately defined in the Act. The ordinary meaning of the word, however, can be readily ascertained.

Davison C.J. referred to dictionary definitions and continued:

The usual concept of a print is of something created by pressure of the plate upon a material. In the system of injection moulding used by Wham-O plastic material is forced upon the plate or into the mould. Does that method of operation prevent the finished disc so created being properly called a "print"? The result is the same although achieved by a somewhat different means. The shape of the mould is imprinted upon the plastic material forced into it.

Modern technology for creating reproductions has involved various new processes being devised and we doubt that the making of a "print" can any longer be identified with any one or more particular processes or procedures. There appears currently to be no good reason why an article produced by injection moulding from a mould which is an engraving should not be itself an engraving if it is produced from that mould.

Moller J. in his judgment after posing the question as to whether the final plastic moulded products could be brought within the definition of sculpture or engraving, simply noted that a consideration of *Arnold's* case (*James Arnold & Co Ltd v Miafern Ltd* [1980] R.P.C. 397) had brought him to the decision that each disc is an engraving in that it is "an image produced from an engraved plate" and comes within the category of a print.

We agree with Moller J. on this point.

Moller J. expressed no opinion as to whether or not the finished product was also a "sculpture". This is defined in section 2(1) of the Act simply as including: "Any cast or model made for purposes of sculpture". Being an inclusive definition, it is necessary to go to a dictionary to ascertain its comprehensive meaning. The *Shorter Oxford English Dictionary* defines "sculpture" as:

> "Originally the process or art of carving or engraving a hard material so as to produce designs or figures in relief, in intaglio, or in the round. In modern use, that branch of fine art which is concerned with producing figures in the round or in relief, either by carving, by fashioning some plastic substance, or by making a mould for casting in metal".

Although that definition refers to sculpture as a branch of fine art, for the purposes of copyright, sculpture is classed as an artistic work, irrespective of artistic quality.

Davison C.J. considered further dictionary and other definitions and continued:

One must ask in the present case, what was the original work of the author which created the article sought to be classed as a sculpture? It was not directly the creation of the final disc. It was the creation variously of drawings, wooden models and finally dies or moulds from which the finished plastic product was formed.

It would seem that where a model which is a sculpture has been created and a cast or mould is later made from that model for the purposes of reproducing the model in metal and plastic or some other form then the articles so produced may be classified as sculptures.

But it appears to us to be straining the meaning of the word "sculpture" to apply it to the discs produced by the injection moulding process used in the present case where the moulds concerned have simply been created by a process of engraving and no original model has been created.

Copyright subsists in "original works"—see section 7—but no original work in the nature of the finished disc has been created before the injection moulding process has created them. We do not overlook that the definition of sculpture in section 2 of the Act "includes any cast or model made for purposes of sculpture". But that is a different matter from a cast or model used to make the sculpture.

Furthermore it appears to me implicit in the definitions of sculpture to which we have already referred and from the article in the *New Encyclopaedia Britannica*, particularly the passage reading:

> "The art of sculpture is the branch of the visual arts that is especially concerned with the creation of expressive form in three dimensions"

that sculpture should in some way express in three-dimensional form an idea of the sculptor. It seems to us inappropriate to regard utilitarian objects such as plastic flying discs, manufactured as toys, by an injection moulding process, as items of sculpture for the purposes of the Copyright Act. They lack any expressive form of the creator and any idea which the creator seeks to convey.

In the result, we are unable to hold that the final plastic products—the discs—are sculptures in terms of the Act and entitled to copyright protection as sculptures.

Finally under this head of "sculpture" we pass to consider whether the wooden models created by Wham-O were sculptures. Moller J. held that they were sculptures within the meaning of section 2 of the Act.

We recall the definitions of "sculpture" referred to earlier in this judgment when considering whether the finished plastic products were sculptures and we note that whilst by virtue of section 7 of the Act copyright subsists in an "artistic work", an artistic work includes sculptures irrespective of artistic quality. All that is required therefore is that the work in question shall be a sculpture in the ordinary sense of that term or as included in the extended definition of sculpture contained in the Act.

We think that the wooden models of the "Frisbees", which were prepared for the various models, do fall within the definition of sculptures and are thus properly the subject of copyright protection. We agree with Moller J. on this point.

The court found sufficient originality to attract copyright, and that the defendant had substantially reproduced the various works. In consequence, there was infringement and in respect of this the judgment contains a number of further rulings. It also held the defendant not entitled to retain its registered trade mark, "Frisbee", since the application for it had not been made in good faith.

4.1.5 *Breville Europe Plc v Thorn EMI Domestic Appliances Ltd* (1985) [1995] F.S.R. 77, Falconer J.

The plaintiffs claimed that the defendants had copied the heating plates of one of their sandwich-toasters. Their claims included the allegation that certain plastic shapes made for the production of the die casting moulds for these heating plates were sculptures (and therefore artistic works pursuant to s.3 of the Copyright Act 1956; see now s.4 of the 1988 Act) and that the copyright in these sculptures would be infringed by sandwiches made on the defendants' appliances. On this question Falconer J. said:

Turning to the plaster shapes or sculptures, the defendants contended that these were not sculptures within the meaning of section 3 of the Copyright Act on the ground, as I understand Mr Young, that they were purely mechanical or functional devices and he referred me to section 1 of the definition of "sculpture" in the original statutory provision relating to copyright in sculptures, section 1 of the Sculpture Copyright Act 1814, which is to be found reproduced in Laddie, Prescott & Vitoria's *Modern Law of Copyright*, p.671. I do not see why the word "sculpture" in section 3 of the Copyright Act 1956 should not receive its ordinary dictionary meaning except in so far as the scope of the word is extended by section 48(1) which provides that " 'sculpture' includes any cast or model made for the purposes of sculpture." The *Concise Oxford Dictionary* defines sculpture as the

> Art of forming representations of objects, etc., or abstract designs in the round or in relief by chiselling stone, carving wood, modelling clay, casting metal, or similar processes; a work of sculpture,

a definition forming the basis of paragraph 3.15 on "sculptures" in the textbook just mentioned where it is suggested that:

> Since copyright may subsist irrespective of artistic quality it would seem that, for example, carved wooden patterns intended for the purpose of casting mechanical parts

in metal or plastic might well be susceptible of protection, although the point has not yet received much attention from practitioners.

In *Wham-O Manufacturing Co v Lincoln Industries Ltd* [1985] R.P.C. 127, the Court of Appeal of New Zealand held that wooden models made from preliminary drawings to enable moulds to be made for moulding plastic "Frisbee" discs fell within the definition of sculptures and were properly the subject of copyright protection: see at 157 at lines 39 to 48. In my view the plaster shapes of which P9 and P10 are reproductions were sculptures and as such attracted copyright.

On the facts Falconer J. held that the defendants had not copied the plaintiffs' heating plates, which meant that he did not have to decide the question of whether a sandwich could properly be regarded as a reproduction in a material form of a sculpture.

4.1.6 *British Leyland v Armstrong Patents* [1986] A.C. 577, HL

British Leyland claimed that Armstrong, by manufacturing exhaust pipes as replacements on British Leyland cars, infringed British Leyland's copyright in drawings for their exhaust pipes. Armstrong had necessarily reproduced the shape and configuration of these in making its own spares. The case arose under the Copyright Act 1956 and in the House of Lords it was assumed that the drawings were the subject of artistic copyright which was not the subject of any special limit on its duration. In the House of Lords it was argued by Armstrong, first, that copyright in drawings whose sole purpose was as a blueprint for a three-dimensional, functional object was not capable of being infringed by copying in three dimensions. All members of the House save Lord Griffiths rejected this argument. Both Lord Bridge and Lord Templeman gave extensive surveys of the historical development of protection for industrial designs, the latter starting from the original prohibition of monopoly in the Statute of Monopolies 1623. Both speeches laid stress on the acceptance that reproduction by indirect copying in three dimensions was infringement in King Features v Kleeman [1941] A.C. 417, and subsequent case law, and that the special exception created by the Copyright Act 1956, s.9(8) bore the implication that Parliament in 1956 thought this to be so. The confirmation of this view in L.B. (Plastics) v Swish [1979] R.P.C. 551, could not now be reversed by the House, but only by legislation. From this view Lord Griffiths delivered a strong dissent.

Secondly, it was argued (i) that the manufacturer of a car impliedly licensed the purchaser to repair it and that this licence extended to competing spare parts manufacturers; or, alternatively, (ii) that the manufacturer of a car was not entitled to derogate from his grant on sale to a purchaser by exercising his copyright so as to prevent the purchaser from effectively exercising his right to repair the car.

The extracts from the speeches of Lords Bridge, Templeman and Griffiths here given are concerned with this second line of argument.

Lord Bridge of Harwich:

The alternative argument in support of the appeal has been mainly canvassed on the basis of an implied licence. This terminology is primarily derived from the cases concerned with the repair of articles which are subject to patent protection. Letters patent, on their face, always granted to the patentee the exclusive right, "to make, use, exercise and vend" the invention. A literal application of this language would lead to the absurdity that a person who acquired the patented goods would infringe the patent if he used or resold them. To avoid this absurdity the courts had recourse to the doctrine of implied licence. In the field of repair it is clear that a person who acquires a patented article has an implied licence to keep it in repair, but must stop short of renewal: *Dunlop Pneumatic Tyre Co v Neal* [1899] 1 Ch. 807; of renewal: *Dunlop Pneumatic Tyre Co v Neal* [1899] 1 Ch. 807; *Sirdar Rubber Co Ltd v Wallington Weston & Co* [1907] R.P.C. 539. In the latter case Lord Halsbury said at 543:

> "The principle is quite clear although its application is sometimes difficult; you may prolong the life of a licensed article but you must not make a new one under the cover of repair".

His Lordship then referred to Solar Thompson v Barton *[1977] R.P.C. 537, and to Oliver L.J.'s refusal (in the Court of Appeal in* British Leyland*) to accept that any licence of copyright to repair could extend from the purchaser to a spare parts manufacturer. He continued:*

It seems to me that when one is considering machinery which is not the subject of any patent protection, it is unnecessary and may be misleading to introduce the concept of an implied licence. The owner of a car must be entitled to do whatever is necessary to keep it in running order and to effect whatever repairs may be necessary in the most economical way possible. To derive this entitlement from an implied licence granted by the original manufacturer seems to me quite artificial. It is a right inherent in the ownership of the car itself. To curtail or restrict the owner's right to repair in any way may diminish the value of the car. In the field of patent law it may be right to start from the patentee's express monopoly and see how far it is limited by exceptions. In the field of law applied to machinery which enjoys no patent protection, it seems to me appropriate to start from a consideration of the rights of the owner of the machinery and then to see how far the law will permit some conflicting legal claim to impinge upon those rights.

I can see no reason to doubt that any owner of a British Leyland car might exercise his right to repair the car, whenever the exhaust pipe needs replacement, by producing an exact copy of the original pipe in his own workshop or by instructing the local blacksmith to do the same. But in practical terms, of course, if the owner's right to repair is limited to these activities in a world of mass-produced goods, it is quite valueless. What the owner needs, if his right to repair is to be of value to him is the freedom to acquire a previously manufactured replacement exhaust system in an unrestricted market. Here then we come to the heart of the issue, where there appears to be a clear conflict of legal rights, the car owner's right to repair on the one hand, the copyright owner's right, on the other hand, to use his copyright in such a way as to maintain a monopoly in the supply of spare parts. It may be a novel, but seems to me to be an unavoidable, issue for the law to decide which of the two rights should prevail over the other.

It is, I think, conceded that in certain situations resort to copyright to starve the market of necessary spare parts for a car would be legally unacceptable. As it is put in one of the written summaries of counsel's submissions which have been such a helpful feature of the presentation of counsel's arguments in this appeal:

"The respondents recognise that the owner of a vehicle or other apparatus must be able and free to deal with that article as he or she so wishes and must be able to buy spare parts lawfully on the market for that article."

Thus, to take an extreme example, suppose a car manufacturer, to encourage early obsolescence, decided to discontinue his own supply of spare parts for every model five years after it ceased production and sought to enforce his copyright in spare parts drawings to stifle any alternative source of supply. I cannot believe that in those circumstances the law would be prepared to sustain the copyright claim, nor did I understand counsel for British Leyland to argue seriously to the contrary.

It follows that the starting point for the resolution of the conflict of competing rights to which I have referred is to recognise that in some circumstances the enforcement of the manufacturer's copyright in spare parts drawings must yield to the maintenance of a supply of spare parts to sustain the owner's right to repair. This immediately poses a problem as to where, if at all, and if so by what criteria, the law can draw a line to discriminate between acceptable and unacceptable claims to enforce copyright, which restrict the market in spare parts available to car owners for the purpose of effecting necessary repairs. The answer propounded to this problem on behalf of British Leyland is two-fold. First, it is submitted that the problem has to be resolved by reference to other legislation directed to the control of anti-competitive practices, in particular the Fair Trading Act 1973, the Competition Act 1980, and the relevant provisions of the EEC Treaty (Cmnd. 5179–11). This answer is, to my mind, unacceptable, if only for the simple reason that to accept it would imply that, had the problem arisen before 1973, no answer could have been found to it in the combined operation of the Copyright Acts and the common law. British Leyland's second answer is that the criterion for the maintenance of a supply of spare parts sufficient to meet the demands of car owners for the purposes of repair is one of necessity and that, so long as the manufacturer and his licensees are maintaining an adequate supply at reasonable prices, and more particularly if the manufacturer is willing to offer licences to all who wish to take them on reasonable terms, there can be no such necessity as to justify the subordination of the right of the copyright owner in spare parts drawings to the interest of the car owner in a free market in parts available for repair. This suggested answer to the problem seems to me both impracticable and unrealistic for two reasons. First, it would impose an impossible task on the court, whenever asked to decide whether a claim to copyright in spare parts drawings should be enforced, to have to determine without the aid of any defined criteria whether at the date of trial the manufacturer and his licensees were maintaining a supply on reasonable terms. Secondly, once the copyright owner had succeeded in his claim, he would be at liberty to vary his terms of trade to the detriment of owners of cars of his manufacture.

These considerations drive me to the conclusion that there is no such half-way house solution to the problem as has been urged upon us for British Leyland Either the court must allow the enforcement of the copyright claim to maintain a monopoly in the supply of spare parts for the copyright owner and his licensees, regardless of any adverse effect of the monopoly on car owners; or the right of car owners to a free market in spare parts necessary for economical repair should prevail and the court should accordingly decline to enforce copyright claims as against the manufacturer of spare parts intended exclusively as are Armstrong's exhaust systems, to be available as replacement parts for cars in need of repair. As I have already indicated, the first alternative would be unacceptable at one end of the spectrum of possible consequences. But, apart from this, it seems to me that there are sound reasons in principle why the second alternative should be preferred. By selling cars fitted with exhausts based on their copyright drawings British Leyland have already enjoyed the primary benefit which their copyright protects. By selling those same cars British Leyland have also created a large community of car owners who, quite independent of any contractual rights derived from British Leyland, enjoy the inherent right as owners to repair their cars by replacing the exhaust whenever necessary in the most economical way possible. To allow British Leyland to enforce their copyright to maintain a monopoly for themselves and their licensees in the supply and replacement exhausts is, to a greater or lesser extent, to detract from the owner's rights and, at least potentially, the value of their cars. There is an inconsistency between marketing cars and thereby creating whatever rights attach to their ownership on the one hand and acting to restrain the free exercise of those rights on the other. The law does not countenance such inconsistencies. It may be a novel application of the principle to preclude a plaintiff from enforcing a statutory right to which he is prima facie entitled. But, as my noble and learned friend Lord Templeman demonstrates, the application of the principle to the relationship between the mass car manufacturer and those who at any time acquire cars of his manufacture is no more than an extension to a non-contractual relationship of the considerations which underlie the classical doctrine of the law that a grantor may not derogate from his grant. Subject to two further grounds of objection canvassed on behalf of British Leyland, which I have yet to consider, it seems to me within the capacity of the common law to adapt to changing social and economic conditions to counter the belated emergence of the car manufacturer's attempt to monopolise the spare parts market in reliance on copyright in technical drawings by invoking the necessity to safeguard the position of the car owner.

A recurrent theme in the argument for British Leyland has been that they are not effectively claiming any true monopoly in exhaust pipes, since it is open to a rival manufacturer to take a British Leyland car, throw away the original exhaust system, examine the features of the underside of the car, and design a new exhaust system suitable to be fitted to it. I find no substance in this argument for two reasons. First, the evidence stops far short of establishing that a new system designed in the way suggested, which must take full account of the shape and configuration of the underside of the frame, various other parts located beneath it, and of the fixing points provided for the exhaust system, would, even if marginally different in shape from the original pipe escape the charge of reproduction by copying of a substantial part of British Leyland's drawings. Secondly, we are concerned with economic reality, and, if the British Leyland car owner is to enjoy the freedom to have his car repaired in the most economical way possible when the exhaust needs replacing, that will undoubtedly only be achieved by straight copying.

British Leyland's final objection on this aspect of the case is based on a comparison of the position under the Copyright Acts, on the one hand, and the Patents Act 1977 and the Registered Designs Act 1949 on the other. If the arguments advanced for Armstrong are permitted to defeat British Leyland's claim under the Act of 1956, then it is said, there will be nothing to prevent similar arguments being invoked to defeat the statutory monopolies conferred by the other Acts when articles protected by patents or registered designs are incorporated as parts of cars. I do not accept that this follows. The rights conferred by the Acts of 1977 and 1949 are clearly distinguishable, in that they are truly and expressly monopolistic. Moreover each Act embodies its own conditions for the grant of compulsory licences which must be taken to provide such safeguards as Parliament considered necessary against the possibility of abuse of the monopoly granted. The position seems to me to be this. Where a specific part of a car which is the subject of a patent or registered design needs repair not amounting to replacement, it will be repairable under the well-established doctrine of implied licence. Where the part requires complete replacement, it can, if practicable, be replaced by any alternative part, which will not infringe the patent or registered design. If only a new part made in accordance with the patent or registered design will provide a satisfactory replacement, the express statutory monopoly of the patentee or design proprietor will prevail. In contrast with the copyright in drawings, the monopoly conferred by the patent or registered design could be invoked not only against other manufacturers making infringing parts and offering them for sale, but also against the car owner, to prevent him making in his own workshop or commissioning from a third party a replacement part which infringed the monopoly.

Having reached a conclusion in favour of allowing the appeal, for the reasons indicated, I would find it unnecessary to hear further argument on the provisions of the EEC Treaty on which Armstrong also rely. I would allow the appeal.

Lord Templeman:

As between landlord and tenant and as between the vendor and purchaser of land, the law has long recognised that "a grantor having given a thing with one hand is not to take away the means of enjoying it with the other" *per* Bowen L.J. in *Birmingham, Dudley and District Banking Co v Ross* (1888) 38 Ch.D 295 at 313.

In *Brown v Flower* [1911] 1 Ch. 219, 225 Parker J. said that:

> "... The implications usually explained by the maxim that no one can derogate from his own grant do not stop short with easements. Under certain circumstances there will be implied on the part of the grantor a lessor obligations which restrict the user of the land retained by him further than can be explained by the implication of any easement known to the law. Thus, if the grant or demise be made for a particular purpose, the grantor or lessor comes under an obligation not to use the land retained by him in such a way as to render the land granted or demised unfit or materially less fit for the particular purpose for which the grant or demise was made."

These principles were followed in *Harmer v Jumbil (Nigeria) Tin Areas Ltd* [1921] 1 Ch. 200; *O'Cedar Ltd v Slough Trading Co Ltd* [1927] 2 K.B. 123; *Matania v The National Provincial Bank Ltd* [1936] 2 All E.R. 633 and *Kirkland* [1967] Ch. 194.

I see no reason why the principle that a grantor will not be allowed to derogate from his grant by using property retained by him in such a way as to render property granted by him unfit or materially unfit for the purpose for which the grant was made should not apply to the sale of a car. In relation to land, the principle has been said to apply

> "beyond cases in which the purpose of the grant is frustrated to cases in which that purpose can still be achieved albeit at a greater expense or with less convenience";

per Branson J. in *O'Cedar Ltd v Slough Trading Co Ltd* [1927] 2 K.B. 123 at 127. The principle applied to a motorcar manufactured in accordance with engineering drawings and sold with components which are bound to fail during the life of the car prohibits the copyright owner of the drawings from exercising his powers in such a way as to prevent the car from functioning unless the owner of the car buys replacement parts from the copyright owner or his licensee.

British Leyland own the car and the copyright in a drawing of an exhaust pipe fitted to the car. British Leyland sell the car and retain the copyright. The exercise by British Leyland of their copyright in the drawing will render the car unfit for the purpose for which the car is held. British Leyland cannot exercise their copyright so as to prevent the car being repaired by replacement of the exhaust pipe.

With this view of the second argument, Lords Scarman and Edmund-Davies agreed (the latter, after considerable doubt). Lord Griffiths dissented. On the second argument, he observed:

If, as I must for the purpose of this argument, assume that Parliament has, through copyright, given a monopolistic right to the manufacturer in the shape of his spare parts, upon what principle is the court free to refuse to enforce that right given by Parliament to the manufacturer? It is said that the manufacturer would be derogating from his grant if he enforced his copyright against another manufacturer because it would interfere with the right of the user of the car to have it repaired. The interference is said to flow from the fact that the spare parts market might be smaller if spare parts could only be produced with the licence of the original manufacturer. This is obviously a possibility but it applies equally to patented items and items protected by design copyright and is an obvious consequence of the grant of a right in the nature of monopoly.

It seems to me highly improbable that a motorcar manufacturer would exploit his copyright either to starve the spare parts market or to increase the fair price for his spare parts for I can think of nothing more damaging to his prospects of selling the car in the first place. However, if it did prove that the right Parliament had given was being abused it is, I think, for Parliament to correct the abuse and not for the courts to refuse to enforce a right that Parliament has given, particularly when it is quite obvious that the exercise of the right must impinge, to some extent, upon the rights of others.

One way in which Parliament could guard against possible abuse in the spare parts market would be to make provision for compulsory licensing as is done in the case of patents and design copyright. The fact that Parliament has not done so is, of course, yet another reason that convinces me that it never intended copyright to be used to protect the spare parts market.

Lord Griffiths was accordingly prepared to hold that the Copyright Act 1956 did not give protection to the indirect copying in three dimensions of a drawing for a purely functional object.

4.1.7   *Canon Kabushiki Kaisha v Green Cartridge* [1997] F.S.R. 817, JC

The plaintiff is a designer and manufacturer of printers and copiers which make use of toner cartridges. It commenced copyright infringement proceedings in Hong Kong against the defendant, who manufactured and sold substitute toner cartridges which were substantial copies of the plaintiff's cartridges. The defendant argued that the making and supply of its cartridges fell within the "spare parts" exception developed by the House of Lords in British Leyland v Armstrong *(above, para. 4.1.6).*

Lord Hoffmann first stated that the "spare parts" exception should be treated as the judicial expression of overriding public policy and warned that any extension of the doctrine should be approached with caution:

Their Lordships think the *British Leyland* spare parts exception cannot be regarded as truly founded upon any principle of the law of contract or property. It is instead an expression of what the House perceived as overriding public policy, namely the need to prevent a manufacturer from using copyright (as opposed to patents or design right) in order to control the aftermarket in spare parts. This appears clearly from the emphasis on the need for an "unrestricted market" as opposed to the right of the manufacturer to "use his copyright in such a way as to maintain a monopoly in the supply of spare parts" (Lord Bridge at 625) and the danger of the car owner who "sells his soul to the company store" being enmeshed in the "tentacles of copyright" (Lord Templeman at 628–629).

It is of course a strong thing (not to say constitutionally questionable) for a judicially-declared head of public policy to be treated as overriding or qualifying an express statutory right. Their Lordships therefore think that the prospect of any extension of the *British Leyland* exception should be treated with some caution. The question of whether it is contrary to the public interest for a manufacturer to be able to exercise monopoly control over his aftermarket cannot usually be answered without some inquiry into the relevant market.

The basis of the decision in *British Leyland* appears to their Lordships to rest upon two features. First, a compelling analogy with the kind of repair which the ordinary man who bought an article would unquestionably assume that he could do for himself (or commission someone else to do) without infringing any rights of the manufacturer. This is the rhetorical force of Lord Bridge's reference at 625 to the blacksmith. Secondly, an assumption that the exercise of monopoly power in the aftermarket by means of copyright would unquestionably operate against the interests of consumers. This appears from Lord Templeman's references at 628–629 to the customer selling his soul, the tentacles of copyright and his mention at 641 of the Report of the Monopolies and Mergers Commission on the refusal of the Ford Motor Company Limited to grant licences for the manufacture of certain replacement body parts (Cmnd. 9437, February 1985), which he said had "stigmatised" the company's conduct as anticompetitive.

Their Lordships consider that once one departs from the case in which the unfairness to the customer and the anticompetitive nature of the monopoly is as plain and obvious as it appeared to the House of Lords in *British Leyland*, the jurisprudential and economic basis for the doctrine becomes extremely fragile.

Applying these criteria to the present case, Lord Hoffmann concluded:

It seems plain that the analogy with repair is far weaker. The cartridge will usually be replaced at a stage when nothing whatever in the photocopier requires repair. It will simply have run out of toner. It is true that there can be said to be an element of preventive maintenance: items like the drum and wiper blade are replaced because there is a distinct possibility that they may give out at some time in the near future. But these items only form a relatively small (though important) part of the unit which is being replaced. Mr Thorley said that in *British Leyland* it was assumed that the exception permitted the manufacture of entire exhaust assemblies, even though parts (like the muffler) might still be serviceable. The point was not debated in *British Leyland* but it can be fairly assumed in Mr Thorley's favour that the House did not regard this feature as taking the product outside the repair analogy. But one cannot use this as a base from which to extend the analogy still further: there comes a point when so little of the replacement can be described as repair or even in lieu of repair that the analogy ceases to be plausible. . . .

On the competition aspect of the matter, the present case seems to their Lordships for two reasons far weaker than *British Leyland*. First, the cost of a replacement exhaust, even at two-yearly intervals during the life of the vehicle, is relatively small in relation to the capital and other running costs of the vehicle. The House of Lords appears to have assumed, with some support from contemporary reports of the Monopolies and Mergers Commission, that purchasers were unlikely to adopt "lifetime costing" in assessing the relative attractions of rival makes of vehicles and that competition in the market for the cars themselves would not therefore prevent anticompetitive practices in the aftermarket. In the present case, given the relative importance of the cost of cartridges as a proportion of the lifetime cost of the photocopier or laser printer, it would be impossible without evidence to make such an assumption. Secondly, there is already competition in the aftermarket between the plaintiff and refillers. It cannot therefore be assumed without evidence that the exercise of its intellectual property rights is giving the plaintiff a monopoly position, let alone that the position is being abused. Mr Thorley said that customers did not have a complete choice because the products of the refillers were inferior and sometimes very inferior. But even if the refill products cannot be regarded as completely substitutable for the plaintiff's products, the existence of a large refill market must inhibit the plaintiff's ability to raise prices. The other side of the coin is the fact that one of the reasons why the defendant's refilling business failed was because the plaintiff did not keep its prices sufficiently high to allow the defendant's refilled cartridges to make any substantial inroads into its market.

4.2   Registered Designs

4.2.1   Note on Registered Designs Legislation

This Section is devoted to industrial design registration in the United Kingdom under the Registered Designs Act 1949. This legislation has recently been much amended in order to conform to the rules for EC harmonisation laid down in the Designs Directive (71/1998). The particular reason for this harmonisation of national systems is the introduction of a Community Design under the Designs Regulation (6/2002). From 2003, Community Designs will be registered at the OHIM, Alicante, Spain (Office for the Harmonisation of the Internal Market (Trade Marks and Designs)). The two systems, national and Community, offer alternative forms of protection, and in large measure the same principles have been applied to both. The equivalent provisions of the ("CD Reg.") Community Designs Regulation as it affects registered designs are noted for comparison with the British law.

The Designs Regulation also provides for a short-term unregistered Community Design, about which a brief note is provided at 4.3.1.

4.2.2   Registered Designs Act 1949, as amended by the Registered Designs Regulations 2001 (SI 2001/3949), which implement Directive 98/71 ([1998] O.J. L289/28) on the protection of designs, ss.1, 1A, 1B, 1C, 1D: Registrable designs and proceedings for registration–(*cf.* CD Reg. Arts 3–8)

S.1(1) A design may, subject to the following provisions of this Act, be registered under this Act on the making of an application for registration.

(2) In this Act "design" means the appearance of the whole or a part of a product resulting from the features of, in particular, the lines, contours, colours, shape, texture or materials of the product or its ornamentation.

(3) In this Act—

"complex product" means a product which is composed of at least two replaceable component parts permitting disassembly and reassembly of the product; and
"product" means any industrial or handicraft item other than a computer program; and, in particular, includes packaging, get-up, graphic symbols, typographic type-faces and parts intended to be assembled into a complex product.

S.1A(1) The following shall be refused registration under this Act—

(a) anything which does not fulfil the requirements of section 1(2) of this Act;

(b) designs which do not fulfil the requirements of sections 1 B to 1 D of this Act;

(c) designs to which a ground of refusal mentioned in Schedule A1 to this Act applies.

(2) A design ("the later design") shall be refused registration under this Act if it is not new does not have individual character when compared with a design which—

(a) has been made available to the public on or after the relevant date; but

(b) is protected as from a date prior to the relevant date by virtue of registration under this Act or an application for such registration.

(3) In subsection (2) above "the relevant date" means the date on which the application for the registration of the later design was made or is treated by virtue of section 3B(2), (3) or (5) or 14(2) of this Act as having been made.

S.1B(1) A design shall be protected by a right in a registered design to the extent that the design is new and has individual character.

(2) For the purposes of subsection (1) above, a design is new if no identical design or no design whose features differ only in immaterial details has been made available to the public before the relevant date.

(3) For the purposes of subsection (1) above, a design has individual character if the overall impression it produces on the informed user differs from the overall impression produced on such a user by any design which has been made available to the public before the relevant date.

(4) In determining the extent to which a design has individual character, the degree of freedom of the author in creating the design shall be taken into consideration.

(5) For the purposes of this section, a design has been made available to the public before the relevant date if—

(a) it has been published (whether following registration or otherwise), exhibited, used in trade or otherwise disclosed before that date; and

(b) the disclosure does not fall within subsection (6) below.

(6) A disclosure falls within this subsection if—

(a) it could not reasonably have become known before the relevant date in the normal course of business to persons carrying on business in the European Economic Area and specialising in the sector concerned;

(b) it was made to a person other than the designer, or any successor in title of his, under conditions of confidentiality (whether express or implied);

(c) it was made by the designer, or any successor in title of his, during the period of 12 months immediately preceding the relevant date;

(d) it was made by a person other than the designer, or any successor in title of his, during the period of 12 months immediately preceding the relevant date in consequence of information provided or other action taken by the designer or any successor in title of his; or

(e) it was made during the period of 12 months immediately preceding the relevant date as a consequence of an abuse in relation to the designer or any successor in title of his.

(7) In subsections (2), (3), (5) and (6) above "the relevant date" means the date on which the

application for the registration of the design was made or is treated by virtue of section 3B(2), (3) or (5) or 14(2) of this Act as having been made.

(8) For the purposes of this section, a design applied to or incorporated in a product which constitutes a component part of a complex product shall only be considered to be new and to have individual character—

    (a) if the component part, once it has been incorporated into the complex product, remains visible during normal use of the complex product; and

    (b) to the extent that those visible features of the component part are in themselves new and have individual character.

(9) In subsection (8) above "normal use" means use by the end user; but does not include any maintenance, servicing or repair work in relation to the product.

S.1C(1) A right in a registered design shall not subsist in features of appearance of a product which are solely dictated by the product's technical function.

(2) A right in a registered design shall not subsist in features of appearance of a product which must necessarily be reproduced in their exact form and dimensions so as to permit the product in which the design is incorporated or to which it is applied to be mechanically connected to, or placed in, around or against, another product so that either product may perform its function.

(3) Subsection (2) above does not prevent a right in a registered design subsisting in a design serving the purpose of allowing multiple assembly or connection of mutually interchangeable products within a modular system.

S.1D A right in a registered design shall not subsist in a design which is contrary to public policy or to accepted principles of morality.

4.2.2.1 *Amp Inc v Utilux Proprietary Limited* [1972] R.P.C. 103, HL.

The plaintiffs alleged that the defendants had infringed two registered designs for electric terminals in a "battleaxe" shape, which had been created for use in washing machines. The trial judge held that both designs were invalid, since their allegedly novel features had been determined exclusively by the function that the article had to perform. The Court of Appeal held that this statutory objection to validity was not applicable: it had effect only when the article's function was dependent on that shape and no other for successful performance. In this case a different shape would not have affected the function of the terminals. The House of Lords refused to interpret the provision so narrowly.

Lord Reid:

In the end the case turns in my view on the proper construction of the definition of "design" in the 1949 Act. If the respondents' construction is right the appeal must be dismissed. If the appellants' construction is right the judgment of Lloyd-Jacob J. must be restored. The question in this case is whether this terminal has a design which comes within this definition.

The definition includes features of shape, configuration, pattern or ornament. We are not concerned with pattern or ornament. Configuration may have a meaning slightly different from shape: no point is made of that in this case. The first requirement is that the shape is "applied" by an industrial process. "Applied" is an appropriate word for pattern or ornament but is an awkward word with regard to shape. The idea must be that there can be two articles similar in every respect except shape, and that the novel feature of shape which is the design has been added to the article by making it in the new shape instead of in some other shape which is not novel.

Then there come the words "being features which in the finished article appeal to and are judged solely by the eye". This must be intended to be a limitation of the foregoing generality. The eye must be the eye of the customer if I am right in holding that the policy of the Act was to preserve to the owner of the design the commercial value resulting from customers preferring the appearance of articles which have the design to that of those which do not have it. So the design must be one which appeals to the eye of some customers. And the words "judged solely by the eye" must be intended to exclude cases where a customer might choose an article of that shape not because of its appearance but because he thought that the shape made it more useful to him.

... Then there come two farther limitations on the generality of the definition. We are not concerned with the first which excludes anything which though in the guise of a design is really a method or principle of construction. But the proper interpretation of the second and final limitation is the crucial question in this case.

Much of the controversy has centred around the word "dictated" which is a metaphorical word out of place in a statutory definition. Unfortunately the draftsman, instead of saying what he meant in his own words, chose to lift words from a judgment where metaphor may be useful and illustrative: it is not the function of a judge to draft definitions. In *Kestos v Kempat* (1936) 53 R.P.C. 139 Luxmoore J. said: "A mere mechanical device is a shape in which all the features are dictated solely by the function or functions which the article has to perform". I think that he probably meant that all the features served purely functional purposes and that no feature was there for any other purpose. But we are not concerned with what he meant: we are concerned with what this word "dictated" means in the context of this definition. There it is ambiguous as the draftsman would have seen if he had paused to reflect.

The respondents' argument is that a shape is only dictated by function if it is necessary to use that precise shape and no other in order to perform the function. Admittedly if that is the meaning the scope of this provision would be reduced almost to vanishing point because it is difficult to imagine any actual case where one shape and one shape alone will work. A key was suggested. Its function is to turn a particular lock, and only one shape of key will do that. But that is not quite true. In most cases at least a skeleton key of a different shape will also turn the lock. In the end no actual case was found where only one precise shape would do.

It seems improbable that the framers of this definition could have intended to insert a provision which has virtually no practical effect, so I look to see whether any other meaning produces a more reasonable result.

Again I think that a clue can be found from a consideration of what must have been the object of the provision. If the purpose of the Act was to give protection to a designer where design has added something of value to the prior art then one would expect an exclusion from protection of those cases where nothing has been added because every feature of the shape sought to be protected originated from purely functional considerations.

... There must be a blend of industrial efficiency with visual appeal. If the shape is not there to appeal to the eye but solely to make the article work then this provision excludes it from the statutory protection.

I would add to avoid misunderstanding that no doubt in the great majority of cases which the Act will protect the designer had visual appeal in mind when composing his design. But it could well be that a designer who only thought of practical efficiency in fact has produced a design which does appeal to the eye. He would not be denied protection because that was not his object when he composed the design.

I would allow this appeal.

4.2.3 Registered Designs Act 1949, s.2: Ownership, Dealings (*cf.* CD Reg. Arts 14–18)

S.2(1) The author of a design shall be treated for the purposes of this Act as the original proprietor of the design, subject to the following provisions.

(1A) Where a design is created in pursuance of a commission for money or money's worth, the person commissioning the design shall be treated as the original proprietor of the design.

(1B) Where, in a case not falling within subsection (1A), a design is created by an employee in the course of his employment, his employer shall be treated as the original proprietor of the design.

(2) Where a design becomes vested, whether by assignment, transmission or operation of law, in any person other than the original proprietor, either alone or jointly with the original proprietor, that other person, or as the case may be the original proprietor and that other person, shall be treated for the purposes of this Act as the proprietor of the design.

(3) In this Act the "author" of a design means the person who creates it.

(4) In the case of a design generated by computer in circumstances such that there is no human author, the person by whom the arrangements necessary for the creation of the design are made shall be taken to be the author.

Section 19 provides for the registration of assignments, etc. of registered designs. In particular, an interest is not to be registered unless the Registrar is satisfied that the person entitled is also entitled to the corresponding national unregistered design right (section 19(3A)). Assignment of the unregistered design right is presumed also to be an assignment of the registered design (section 19(3B)).

4.2.4 Registered Designs Act 1949, ss.3, 4, 6: Registration, Priority, Factors Affecting Novelty

S.3(1) An application for the registration of a design shall be made in the prescribed form and shall be filed at the Patent Office in the prescribed manner.

(2) An application for the registration of a design shall be made by the person claiming to be the proprietor of the design.

(3) An application for the registration of a design in which national unregistered design right subsists shall be made by the person claiming to be the design right owner.

(4) For the purpose of deciding whether, and to what extent, a design is new or has individual character, the registrar may make such searches (if any) as he thinks fit.

(5) An application for the registration of a design which, owing to any default or neglect on the part of the applicant, has not been completed so as to enable registration to be effected within such time as may be prescribed shall be deemed to be abandoned.

S.3A(1) Subject as follows, the registrar shall not refuse an application for the registration of a design.

(2) If it appears to the registrar that an application for the registration of a design has not been made in accordance with any rules made under this Act, he may refuse the application.

(3) If it appears to the registrar that an application for the registration of a design has not been made in accordance with sections 3(2) and (3) and 14(1) of this Act, he shall refuse the application.

(4) If it appears to the registrar that any ground for refusal of registration mentioned in section 1A of this Act applies in relation to an application for the registration of a design, he shall refuse the application.

S.3B(1) The registrar may, at any time before an application for the registration of a design is determined, permit the applicant to make such modifications of the application as the registrar thinks fit.

(2) Where an application for the registration of a design has been modified before it has been determined in such a way that the design has been altered significantly, the registrar may, for the purposes of deciding whether and to what extent the design is new or has individual character, direct that the application shall be treated as having been made on the date on which it was so modified.

(3) Where—

   (a) an application for the registration of a design has disclosed more than one design and has been modified before it has been determined to exclude one or more designs from the application; and

   (b) a subsequent application for the registration of a design so excluded has, within such period (if any) as has been prescribed for such applications, been made by the person who made the earlier application or his successor in title, the registrar may, for the purpose of deciding whether and to what extent the design is new or has individual character, direct that the subsequent application shall be treated as having been made on the date on which the earlier application was, or is treated as having been, made.

(4) Where an application for the registration of a design has been refused on any ground mentioned in section 1A(1)(b) or (c) of this Act, the application may be modified by the applicant if it appears to the registrar that—

   (a) the identity of the design is retained; and

   (b) the modifications have been made in accordance with any rules made under this Act.

(5) An application modified under subsection (4) above shall be treated as the original application and, in particular, as made on the date on which the original application was made or is treated as having been made.

(6) Any modification under this section may, in particular, be effected by making a partial disclaimer in relation to the application.

S.3C(1) Subject as follows, a design, when registered, shall be registered as of the date on which the application was made or is treated as having been made.

(2) Subsection (1) above shall not apply to an application which is treated as having been made on a particular date by section 14(2) of this Act or by virtue of the operation of section 3B(3) or (5) of this Act by reference to section 14(2) of this Act.

(3) A design, when registered, shall be registered as of—

    (a) in the case of an application which is treated as having been made on a particular date by section 14(2) of this Act, the date on which the application was made;

    (b) in the case of an application which is treated as having been made on a particular date by virtue of the operation of section 3B(3) of this Act by reference to section 14(2) of this Act, the date on which the earlier application was made;

    (c) in the case of an application which is treated as having been made on a particular date by virtue of the operation of section 3B(5) of this Act by reference to section 14(2) of this Act, the date on which the original application was made.

S.3D An appeal lies from any decision of the registrar under section 3A or 313 of this Act.

Sections 13–15 provide for a priority period of six months (unless extended by reciprocal agreement) to operate in respect of design applications in Paris Convention countries.

Sections 17–23, 29–30, 39–43, define powers and duties of the Registrar of Designs in maintaining the Register. The Designs Appeal Tribunal is constituted under ss.27, 28.

4.2.5 Registered Designs Act 1949, s.8: Duration (*cf.* CD Reg. Arts 12, 13)

S.8(1) The right in a registered design subsists in the first instance for a period of five years from the date of the registration of the design.

(2) The period for which the right subsists may be extended for a second, third, fourth and fifth period of five years, by applying to the registrar for an extension and paying the prescribed renewal fee.

(3) If the first, second, third or fourth period expires without such application and payment being made, the right shall cease to have effect; and the registrar shall, in accordance with rules made by the Secretary of State, notify the proprietor of that fact.

(4) If during the period of six months immediately following the end of that period an application for extension is made and the prescribed renewal fee and any prescribed additional fee is paid, the right shall be treated as if it had never expired, with the result that—

    (a) anything done under or in relation to the right during that further period shall be treated as valid,

    (b) an act which would have constituted an infringement of the right if it has not expired shall be treated as an infringement, and

(c) an act which would have constituted use of the design for the services of the Crown if the right had not expired shall be treated as such use.

Section 8A provides for restoration of a lapsed design and section 8B for the effect of an order to restore. Sections 11–11ZF permit cancellation.

4.2.6 Registered Designs Act 1949, ss.7, 7A: Infringement (*cf*. CD Reg. Arts 19(1), 20–22)

S.7(1) The registration of a design under this Act gives the registered proprietor the exclusive right to use the design and any design which does not produce on the informed user a different overall impression.

(2) For the purposes of subsection (1) above and section 7A of this Act any reference to the use of a design includes a reference to—

(a) the making, offering, putting on the market, importing, exporting or using of a product in which the design is incorporated or to which it is applied; or

(b) stocking such a product for those purposes.

(3) In determining for the purposes of subsection (1) above whether a design produces a different overall impression on the informed user, the degree of freedom of the author in creating his design shall be taken into consideration.

(4) The right conferred by subsection (1) above is subject to any limitation attaching to the registration in question (including, in particular, any partial disclaimer or any declaration by the registrar or a court of partial invalidity).

S.7A Infringements of rights in registered designs.

(1) Subject as follows, the right in a registered design is infringed by a person who, without the consent of the registered proprietor, does anything which by virtue of section 7 of this Act is the exclusive right of the registered proprietor.

(2) The right in a registered design is not infringed by—

(a) an act which is done privately and for purposes which are not commercial;

(b) an act which is done for experimental purposes;

(c) an act of reproduction for teaching purposes or for the purposes of making citations provided that the conditions mentioned in subsection (3) below are satisfied;

(d) the use of equipment on ships or aircraft which are registered in another country but which are temporarily in the United Kingdom;

(e) the importation into the United Kingdom of spare parts or accessories for the purposes of repairing such ships or aircraft; or

(f) the carrying out of repairs on such ships or aircraft.

(3) The conditions mentioned in this subsection are—

(a) the act of reproduction is compatible with fair trade practice and does not unduly prejudice the normal exploitation of the design; and

(b) mention is made of the source.

(4) The right in a registered design is not infringed by an act which relates to a product in which any design protected by the registration is incorporated or to which it is applied if the product has been put on the market in the European Economic Area by the registered proprietor or with his consent.

(5) The right in a registered design of a component part which may be used for the purpose of the repair of a complex product so as to restore its original appearance is not infringed by the use for that purpose of any design protected by the registration.

(6) No proceedings shall be taken in respect of an infringement of the right in a registered design committed before the date on which the certificate of registration of the design under this Act is granted.

S.9(1) In proceedings for the infringement of the right in a registered design damages shall not be awarded against a defendant who proves that at the date of the infringement he was not aware, and had no reasonable ground for supposing, that the design was registered; and a person shall not be deemed to have been aware or to have had reasonable grounds for supposing as aforesaid by reason only of the marking of a product with the word "registered" or any abbreviation thereof, or any word or words expressing or implying that the design applied to, or incorporated in, the product has been registered, unless the number of the design accompanied the word or words or the abbreviation in question.

The power to grant a compulsory licence of a registered design has been repealed. However, Sections 11A and 11B give consequential powers upon an unfavourable report of the Competition Commission. Section 12 and Sch.1 provide for Crown use of registered designs.

4.2.6.2 *Interlego v Tyco Industries* **[1988] R.P.C. 343, JC**

An extract from this case, concerning the originality of artistic works in copyright law, has already been given: see above, 3.2.3.2.

The claim in Hong Kong that Tyco's reverse engineering of "Lego" toy bricks involved infringement of artistic copyright in Lego production drawings turned partly on the question whether copyright existed in certain pre-1972 drawings. The relevant law was the UK Copyright Act 1911, as extended to the colony. Accordingly, the drawings would not be the subject of copyright if they were "capable of being registered" under the Registered Designs Act 1949 and were used or intended to be used as a model or pattern to be multiplied by an industrial process. This in turn raised the questions whether they were precluded from being registered designs (despite the fact that they had actually been registered) (i) because they were dictated solely by function; or (ii) because they lacked novelty, in being derived from earlier drawings that had previously been published (see Registered Designs Act 1949, s.1(3) and 1(2), above, 4.2.1).

On these issues, Lord Oliver (for the Judicial Committee) said:

Nothing is to qualify as a design at all unless it has "features ... which appeal to and are judged solely by the eye", a requirement conveniently paraphrased by saying that the finished article must have "eye-appeal". That much is clear from the definition. What is less clear is the ambit of the exclusion. There are, apart from authority, three possible constructions of the definition taken as a whole, as was pointed out by Megaw L.J. in the Court of Appeal in *Amp Inc v Utilux Pty Ltd* [1970] R.P.C. 397 at 433. It could mean that all that is registrable or is to be considered in connection with an application for registration is that part of the shape or configuration which has eye-appeal, any purely functional feature being excluded from registration. Alternatively, it could mean that any design which includes any feature which is dictated solely by function is to be excluded from registration. Or, finally, it could mean that a design which, *ex hypothesi*, has eye-appeal will be excluded from registration only if every feature of it is one which is dictated solely by function.

No one has contended for the first of these possibilities and such a construction would, indeed, make very little sense. In approaching the definition it is always to be borne in mind what is to be registered. It is a shape, configuration or pattern to be applied to a particular specified article and it is the shape or configuration of the whole article in respect of which there is to be a commercial monopoly. That necessarily involves taking the design and the article as a whole. Thus, the effective choice must be between excluding the whole shape or configuration from registration because there is a part of it that is purely functional or treating the whole shape or configuration as registrable (assuming that it has eye-appeal) unless the whole of it is dictated solely by functional considerations.

In their Lordships' view the latter construction is the one which makes better sense and it is in fact the construction which is supported by the authorities. Harking back to the 1919 Act, the evident intention is to exclude a "mere" mechanical device, that is to say an article fulfilling a mechanical function and nothing more, and there is reflected in the words "the function which the article to be made in that shape or configuration has to perform" (see section 1(3) of the 1949 Act). What is contemplated here is that an article (and that must mean the whole of the article and not simply a part of it) is to be made in a particular shape or configuration. Thus, the shape or configuration as a whole is being "applied to" the article as a whole. It then has to be asked: is that shape or configuration (*i.e.* the shape or configuration of the whole article) dictated solely by the functional purpose? Moreover, it makes no sense to exclude from registration designs for articles which have, and indeed, may be intended to have as their principal attraction, a distinctive and novel appearance merely because they contain also features, perhaps even very minor ones, which are dictated by functional requirements.

This construction accords with the original paraphrase by Luxmoore J., in *Kestos Ltd v Kempak Ltd* (1939) 53 R.P.C. 139 at 151, of the expression "mere mechanical device" as a "shape in which all the features are dictated solely by the function". He added:

"... the particular form must possess some features beyond those necessary to enable the article to fulfil the particular purpose, but the fact that some advantage is derived from the adoption of a particular shape does not exclude it from registration as a design".

It accords also with the views expressed in the House of Lords in *Stenor Ltd v Whitesides (Clitheroe) Ltd* [1947] 2 All E.R. 241; [1948] A.C. 107. There Viscount Simon (with whom Lord Macmillan agreed) expressed his concurrence with the views of Morton L.J. in the Court of Appeal that the design there in issue was excluded from registration because it possessed "no features beyond those necessary to enable the article to fulfil its function" (see [1947] 2 All E.R. 241 at 245; [1948] A.C. 107 at 122). Lord Porter expressed broadly the same view (see [1947] 2 All E.R. 241 at 249; [1948] A.C. 107 at 128). Lord Uthwatt observed ([1947] 2 All E.R. 241 at 255; [1948] A.C. 107 at 139):

"Every feature in the design was apt to serve a mechanical object and no feature had any other substantial quality. In the sum of the qualities of the design there was a mechanical device and nothing else".

Finally, it accords, on analysis, with the views expressed by the House of Lords in *Amp Inc v Utilux Pty Ltd* [1972] R.P.C. 103. That is a decision which has given rise to a little difficulty because the views expressed by the Lords who composed the committee in that case do not altogether coincide, with the result that both parties seek to avail themselves of the decision as support for different propositions. Counsel for Tyco derives from it the proposition that the mere co-existence of eye-appeal and functional efficiency is sufficient to entitle a design to registration, a proposition which appears to have been accepted in the instant case at least by Huggins V.P. in the Court of Appeal in Hong Kong. Counsel for Lego derives from it, first, the proposition that eye-appeal involves something more than mere distinctiveness of shape and, second, that given that there are features of shape which are dictated solely by function, the fact that there is also present in the shape, whether intentionally or not, an element of eye-appeal is not sufficient to confer on the shape the essential quality requisite for registrability as a design. To put it another way, a shape has to be tested by two criteria, one positive and one negative, and both must be satisfied in full before it can qualify as a design within the definition of the Act.

Accepting that there are differences of emphasis in the speeches of the various members of the committee in the *Amp* case, their Lordships are nevertheless of the view that the principles to be deducted from it are tolerably clear. First, the primary essential before a shape can be registered as a design is that it should have eye-appeal and in this context (a) the eye is that of the prospective customer and (b) the appeal is that created by a dis-tinctiveness of shape, pattern or ornamentation calculated to influence the customer's choice. This, at least, emerges from the speeches of Lord Reid (with whom Lord Donovan agreed), Lord Morris and Viscount Dilhorne (see [1972] R.P.C. 103 at 108, 112, 118). Second, the negative part of the definition does not involve, in order to demonstrate that a particular shape is "dictated solely" by function, showing that that function could not have been performed by an article in some other shape. All that has to be shown is that the relevant features of the shape were brought about only by, or are attributable only to, the function which the article in that shape is to perform, even if the same function could equally well be performed by an article of a different shape. Third, if every feature of the shape is one which is attributable solely to the function which the finished article is to perform, then the exclusion operates even though the shape may also have eye-appeal.

His Lordship considered a somewhat unclear passage in Lord Reid's speech in Amp v Utilux *and concluded that:*

Their Lordships are clearly of the opinion that the mere coincidence of eye-appeal with functional efficiency will not confer the right to protection if, in fact, every feature of the design is dictated by the function which the article is to perform. But what is the position where the shape has eye-appeal but where some only of its features are dictated solely by functional considerations? If the interpretation placed on Lord Reid's remarks is correct, then he and Lord Donovan would clearly have contemplated that in these circumstances the exclusion would not operate to deprive the shape of protection as a design. Lord Morris clearly contemplated that it would not (at 113) and Viscount Dilhorne too appears to have contemplated that any feature which went beyond those dictated solely by function and provided eye-appeal would entitle the shape as a whole to protection (at 118). This is, in their Lordships' view, clearly right in principle. The incorporation into design was evolved, at least in part, with visual appeal in mind. Exactly the same consideration applied equally to the Duplo brick, which was, as Mr Christiansen observed, evolved with the intention "to look exactly the same way as the original eight knob brick". In another part of his evidence he stressed the importance of the appearance of a toy and asserted that he had always paid particular attention to the appearance of the Lego bricks.

It has already been mentioned that, in registering their designs, Lego had to overcome objections by the registrar that there were no features of ornament on the designs. Reliance had, at that time, been placed on the knobs as ornamental features and Mr Christiansen in his evidence asserted that they fulfilled both functional and ornamental purposes. Again in relation to the tubes, which in earlier versions of the brick were castellated and were equal to the length of the skirt, Mr Christiansen's evidence was that these were replaced by an amended design in which the tubes were circular and did not go to the level of the bottom of the skirt because the castellated version was "messier" and the new version looked nicer. Thus, although the presence of knobs and tubes is no doubt attributable simply and solely to the functional purpose of providing clutch-power, the actual shape and dimensions of the particular knobs and tubes employed for that purpose were not dictated solely by their function but, in part at least, with a view to the appearance of the article as a whole. This evidence cannot be ignored and in their Lordships' view it necessarily negatives any conclusion that the shape or configuration of the Lego brick is dictated solely by the function which it has to perform. It is a shape which, in their Lordships' opinion, not only clearly has eye-appeal but has also significant features, both of outline and proportion, which are not dictated by any mechanical function which the article has to perform as part of a construction set.

It is, however, Lego's submission that, even on this hypothesis, the pre-1973 drawings are not excluded from copyright by the operation of paragraph 8(2) of Schedule 7 to the 1956 Act, because they are not designs "capable of registration under the Registered Designs Act 1949". Section 1(2) of the 1949 Act, it is argued, authorises the registration only of a design which is "new or original". These drawings reproduced, with modifications, the Page designs which had been previously published and used as the basis for manufactured articles. Thus, at the time when they were made, they ought not to have been registered and reliance is placed on a decision of the Eve J. in *Stephenson Blake & Co v Grant Legros & Co Ltd* (1916) 33 R.P.C. 406, a decision based on section 22(1) of the Copyright Act 1911, which provided that the Act should not apply to designs "capable of being registered" under the 1907 Act. In that case it had been held, on agreed preliminary issues, that the plaintiffs had, when the 1911 Act came into operation, a subsisting copyright under the Copyright Act 1842 in what was assumed to be a design which could have been registered under the Patents, Designs and Trade Marks Act 1883. One question raised was whether the effect of section 22 was to deprive them of all protection, since they could then no longer register under the 1907 Act for want of novelty. Eve J. held that, since, at the coming into operation of the 1911 Act, the plaintiffs' design was no longer new, it was then not "capable of registration" and thus was not excluded from copyright under the 1911 Act. That decision has been criticised as leading to the absurd conclusion that a person who had a design registrable under the 1907 Act but had not troubled to protect himself by registration retained his artistic copyright and was thus put in a better position than a person who had registered and who would so be deprived of his artistic copyright. Moreover, the status of the decision as an authority is open to doubt because, when the case went to the Court of Appeal, that court discharged the order on the ground that the questions raised were entirely hypothetical at the stage at which they were decided, Lord Cozens-Hardy M.R. observing that the discharge was "without prejudice to any question so that it cannot be used as a precedent" (see (1917) 34 R.P.C. 192 at 195).

The contrary conclusion was reached in the Canadian case of *Bayliner Marine Corp v Doral Boats Ltd* [1987] F.S.R. 497, where the Federal Court of Appeal of Canada, construing section 46(1) of the Canadian Copyright Act 1970 (which was in substantially the same terms as section 22(1) of the 1911 Act) held that a "design capable of being registered" did not mean "registrable" but meant only a design which complied with the criteria necessary to qualify as a "design" within the meaning of the Act. To hold the contrary would, it was pointed out, involve the absurdity that a design sufficiently novel to be entitled to registration would be excluded from copyright protection whilst one lacking novelty would be entitled to copyright for the full period of the life of the author plus 50 years. The reasoning of the Canadian court was followed by Whitford J. in *Interlego AG v Alex Folley (Vic) Pty Ltd* [1987] F.S.R. 283 at 302 and by the Court of Appeal in Hong Kong in the instant case.

Lord Oliver considered Usher v Barlow *[1952] Ch. 255, CA to lend only oblique support to Eve J.'s judgments in the* Stephenson Blake *case. Moreover, he accepted a number of contrary arguments concerning logical construction of the relevant statutory provision.*

He concluded:

In their Lordships' opinion, the Court of Appeal correctly concluded that the only sensible construction of the words "constituted a design capable of registration" in paragraph 8, having regard to the evident purpose of the statute, is that it refers to designs possessing, when they were made, those essential characteristics which qualify them as "designs". If such designs are, at that time, used or intended to be used for the purpose of industrial reproduction, they are not to qualify for copyright under the Copyright Act 1956. It follows that no copyright now subsists in Lego's pre-1973 drawings.

4.3 Unregistered Design Right (UK)

4.3.1 Note on the two types of Unregistered Design Right

The Community Design Regulation (6/2002), Arts. 11 and 19(2), creates an unregistered right but this is different in character from the UK Unregistered Design Right. It relates only to subject-matter which falls within the definition of a registrable design in the Community legislation (for which see 4.2.2 et seq., above) and it lasts for only three years from the commercialisation of the design. It is infringed only by copying.

4.3.2 Copyright, Designs and Patents Act 1988, ss.213, 258–260: Right granted, Interpretation

S.213(1) Design right is a property right which subsists in accordance with this Part in an original design.

(2) In this Part "design" means the design of any aspect of the shape or configuration (whether internal or external) of the whole or part of an article.

(3) Design right does not subsist in—

(a) a method or principle of construction.

(b) features of shape or configuration of an article which—

(i) enable the article to be connected to, or placed in, around or against, another article so that either article may perform its function, or
(ii) are dependent upon the appearance of another article of which the article is intended by a designer to form an integral part, or

(c) surface decoration.

(4) A design is not "original" for the purposes of this Part if it is commonplace in the design field in question at the time of its creation.

(5) Design right subsists in a design only if the design qualifies for design right protection by reference to—

(a) the designer or the person by whom the design was commissioned or the designer employed (see sections 218 and 219), or

(b) the person by whom and country in which articles made to the design were first marketed (see section 220),

or in accordance with any Order under section 211 (power to make further provision with respect to qualification).

(6) Design right does not subsist unless and until the design has been recorded in a design document or an article has been made to the design.

(7) Design right does not subsist in a design which was so recorded, or to which an article was made, before the commencement of this Part.

S.258(1) Where different persons are (whether in consequence of a partial assignment or otherwise) entitled to different aspects of design right in a work, the design right owner for any purpose of this Part is the person who is entitled to the right in the respect relevant for that purpose.

(2) Where design right (or any aspect of design right) is owned by more than one person jointly, references in this Part to the design right owner are at all the owners, so that, in particular, any requirement of the licence of the design right owner requires the licence of all of them.

S.259(1) In this Part a "joint design" means a design produced by the collaboration of two or more designers in which the contribution of each is not distinct from that of the other or others.

(2) References in this Part to the designer of a design shall, except as otherwise provided, be construed in relation to a joint design as references to all the designers of the design.

S.260(1) The provisions of this Part apply in relation to a kit, that is, a complete or substantially complete set of components intended to be assembled into an article, as they apply in relation to the assembled article.

(2) Subsection (1) does not affect the question whether design right subsists in any aspect of the design of the components of a kit as opposed to the design of the assembled article.

4.3.2.1 *Farmers Build Ltd v Carier Bulk Materials Handling Ltd* [1999] R.P.C. 460, CA

The defendants designed a slurry separator (Target) for the plaintiff (in accordance with the appellant's requirements) in 1991. After the collapse of their relationship in 1992, the defendants began manufacturing and selling their own slurry separator (Rotoscreen), with a different external appearance to Target, but practically identical machinery inside. It was held that unregistered design right subsisted both in the Target separator as a whole and in some of its component parts. A focal point of the appeal was whether the design was commonplace.

Mummery L.J:

(1) [The court] should compare the design of the article in which design right is claimed with the design of other articles in the same field, including the alleged infringing article, as at the time of its creation.

(2) The court must be satisfied that the design for which protection is claimed has not simply been copied (*e.g.* like a photocopy) from the design of an earlier article. It must not forget that, in the field of designs of functional articles, one design may be very similar to, or even identical with, another design and yet not be a copy: it may be an original and independent shape and configuration coincidentally the same or similar. If, however, the

court is satisfied that it has been slavishly copied from an earlier design, it is not an "original" design in the "copyright sense" and the "commonplace" issue does not arise.

(3) If the court is satisfied that the design has not been copied from an earlier design, then it is "original" in the "copyright sense". The court then has to decide whether it is "commonplace". For that purpose it is necessary to ascertain how similar that design is to the design of similar articles in the same field of design made by persons other than the parties or persons unconnected with the parties.

(4) This comparative exercise must be conducted objectively and in the light of the evidence, including evidence from experts in the relevant field pointing out the similarities and the differences, and explaining the significance of them. In the end, however, it is for the court and not for the witnesses, expert or otherwise, to decide whether the design is commonplace. That judgment must be one of fact and degree according to the evidence in each particular case. No amount of guidance given in this or in any other judgment can provide the court with the answer to the particular case. The closer the similarity of the various designs to each other, the more likely it is that the designs are commonplace, especially if there is no causal link, such as copying, which accounts for the resemblance of the compared designs. If a number of designers working independently of one another in the same field produce very similar designs by coincidence the most likely explanation of the similarities is that there is only one way of designing that article. In those circumstances the design in question can fairly and reasonably be described as "commonplace". It would be a good reason for withholding the exclusive right to prevent the copying in the case of a design that, whether it has been copied or not, it is bound to be substantially similar to other designs in the same field.

(5) If, however, there are aspects of the plaintiffs design of the article which are not to be found in any other design in the field in question, and those aspects are found in the defendant's design, the court would be entitled to conclude that the design in question was not "commonplace" and that there was good reason for treating it as protected from misappropriation during the limited period laid down in the 1988 Act. That would be so, even though the design in question would not begin to satisfy any requirement of novelty in the registered designs legislation.

On the facts, it was held that there was no design right in the individual parts of Target, but that it did subsist in the general shape and configuration of the arrangement of its parts.

4.3.3 Copyright, Designs and Patents Act 1988, ss.214, 215: Ownership, Dealings

S.214(1) In this Part the "designer", in relation to a design, means the person who creates it.

(2) In the case of a computer-generated design the person by whom the arrangements necessary for the creation of the design are undertaken shall be taken to be the designer.

S.215(1) The designer is the first owner of any design right in a design which is not created in pursuance of a commission or in the course of employment.

(2) Where a design is created in pursuance of a commission, the person commissioning the design is the first owner of any design right in it.

(3) Where, in a case not falling within subsection (2) a design is created by an employee in the course of his employment, his employer is the first owner of any design right in the design.

(4) If a design qualifies for design right protection by virtue of section 220 (qualification by reference to first marketing of articles made to the design), the above rules do not apply and the person by whom the articles in question are marketed is the first owner of the design right.

Section 222 provides for assignment, licensing, etc. of design right in equivalent terms to s.90 (above, 3.8.4) for copyright. So equally s.223 (prospective ownership) and s.225 (exclusive licences) are equivalent to ss.91 and 92. Section 224 provides that an assignment of registered design right is presumed to carry with it the (unregistered) design right.

4.3.4 Copyright, Designs and Patents Act 1988, s.216: Duration

S.216(1) Design right expires—

(a) fifteen years from the end of the calendar year in which the design was first recorded in a design document or an article was first made to the design, whichever first occurred, or

(b) if articles made to the design are made available for sale or hire within five years from the end of that calendar year, ten years from the end of the calendar year in which that first occurred.

(2) The reference in subsection (1) to articles being made available for sale or hire is to their being made so available anywhere in the world by or with the licence of the design right owner.

4.3.5 Copyright, Designs and Patents Act 1988, s.217: Qualification

S.217(1) In this Part—

"qualifying individual" means a citizen or subject of, or an individual habitually resident in, a qualifying country; and

"qualifying person" means a qualifying individual or a body corporate or other body having legal personality which—

(a) is formed under the law of a part of the United Kingdom or another qualifying country, and

(b) has in any qualifying country a place of business at which substantial business activity is carried on.

(2) References in this Part to a qualifying person include the Crown and the government of any other qualifying country.

(3) In this section "qualifying country" means—

(a) the United Kingdom,

(b) a country to which this Part extends by virtue of an Order under section 255,

(c) another member State of the European Economic Community, or

(d) to the extent that an Order under section 256 so provides, a country designated under that section as enjoying reciprocal protection.

Section 217(4) further defines "qualifying individual" in respect of UK and

British colonial citizens; s.217(5) limits "substantial business activity". Section 255 provides for the extension by Order to the Channel Islands, Isle of Man and British Colonies. Section 256 makes provision for reciprocal protection. Section 257 extends protection to British Territorial waters and continental shelf. Qualification is then secured on three bases:

    (i) Section 218: where the design is not created under commission or employment, by virtue of the designer being a qualified person;

    (ii) Section 219: where the design is created under commission or employment, by virtue of the commissioner or designer being a qualified person;

    (iii) Section 220: where neither of these gives qualifications, then by virtue of first marketing in the UK (as extended) or an EC country by an exclusive licensee for the UK who is a qualified person. Section 221 allows for further provision, with a view to fulfilling an international obligation of the UK by Order-in-Council.

4.3.6 Copyright, Designs and Patents Act 1988, ss.237, 246, 247: Licences of Right, Crown Use

S.237(1) Any person is entitled as of right to a licence to do in the last five years of the design right term anything which would otherwise infringe the design right.

(2) The terms of the licence shall, in default of agreement, be settled by the comptroller.

(3) The Secretary of State may if it appears to him necessary in order to—

    (a) comply with an international obligation of the United Kingdom, or

    (b) secure or maintain reciprocal protection for British designs in other countries,

by order exclude from the operation of subsection (1) designs of a description specified in the order or designs to articles of a description so specified.

(4) An order shall be made by statutory instrument; and no order shall be made unless a draft of it has been laid before and approved by a resolution of each House of Parliament.

Sections 238, 239 give consequential powers upon an unfavourable report of the Monopolies and Mergers Commission. Sections 240–244 provides for the Crown use of (unregistered) designs; and s.252 for reference of disputes over Crown use to the Court. Section 245 gives a similar power to that under s.237(3), in this case to exclude specified acts from the scope of infringement.

S.246(1) A party to a dispute as to any of the following matters may refer the dispute to the comptroller for his decision

    (a) the subsistence of design right,

    (b) the term of design right, or

    (c) the identity of the person in whom design right first vested;

and the comptroller's decision on the reference is binding on the parties to the dispute.

(2) No other court or tribunal shall decide any such matter except

(a) on a reference or appeal from the comptroller,

(b) in infringement or other proceedings in which the issue arises incidentally, or

(c) in proceedings brought with the agreement of the parties or the leave of the comptroller.

(3) The comptroller has jurisdiction to decide any incidental question of fact or law arising in the course of a reference under this section.

S.247(1) A person requiring a licence which is available as of right by virtue of

(a) section 237 (licences available in last five years of design right), or

(b) an order under section 238 (licences made available in the public interest)

may apply to the comptroller to settle the terms of the licence.

(2) No application for the settlement of the terms of a licence available by virtue of section 237 may be made earlier than one year before the earliest date on which the licence may take effect under that section.

(3) The terms of a licence settled by the comptroller shall authorise the licensee to do

(a) in the case of a licence available by virtue of section 237, everything which would be an infringement of the design right in the absence of a licence;

(b) in the case of a licence available by virtue of section 238, everything in respect of which a licence is so available.

(4) In settling the terms of a licence the comptroller shall have regard to such factors as may be prescribed by the Secretary of State by order made by statutory instrument.

(5) No such order shall be made unless a draft of it has been laid before and approved by a resolution of each House of Parliament.

(6) Where the terms of a licence are settled by the comptroller, the licence has effect

(a) in the case of an application in respect of a licence available by virtue of section 237 made before the earliest date on which the licence may take effect under that section, from that date:

(b) in any other case, from the date on which the application to the comptroller was made.

4.3.7 Copyright, Designs and Patents Act 1988, ss.226, 236, 229: Infringement

S.226 (*Primary infringement*) (1) The owner of design right in a design has the exclusive right to reproduce the design for commercial purposes—

(a) by making articles to that design, or

(b) by making a design document recording the design for the purpose of enabling such articles to be made.

(2) Reproduction of a design by making articles to the design means copying the design so as to produce articles exactly or substantially to that design, and references in this Part to making articles to a design shall be construed accordingly.

(3) Design right is infringed by a person who without the licence of the design right owner does, or authorises another to do, anything which by virtue of this section is the exclusive right of the design right owner.

(4) For the purposes of this section reproduction may be direct or indirect, and it is immaterial whether any intervening acts themselves infringe the design right.

(5) This section has effect subject to the provisions of Chapter III (exceptions to rights of design right owner).

Section 227 defines acts of secondary infringement equivalent to those affecting copyright under ss.22, 23(a)–(c) (above, 3.6.3.1) but in slightly different terms. Section 228 defines "infringing article" in terms equivalent to those defining "infringing copy" in relation to copyright (see s.27, above, 3.6.3.1). A design document is not an infringing article: s.228(6).

S.236 Where copyright subsists in a work which consists of or includes a design in which design right subsists, it is not an infringement of design right in the design to do anything which is an infringement of the copyright in that work.

S.229(1) An infringement of design right is actionable by the design right owner.

(2) In an action for infringement of design right all such relief by way of damages, injunctions, accounts or otherwise is available to the plaintiff as is available in respect of the infringement of any other property right.

(3) The court may in an action for infringement of design right, having regard to all the circumstances and in particular to—

(a) the flagrancy of the infringement, and

(b) any benefit accruing to the defendant by reason of the infringement,

award such additional damages as the justice of the case may require.

(4) This section has effect subject to section 233 (innocent infringement).

Sections 230, 231 give power to make orders for delivery up of infringing articles and for their disposal. Section 233 exempts a reasonably innocent primary infringer from damages and limits the remedies against such a secondary infringer to damages not exceeding a reasonable royalty. Section 234 confers a right of action on an exclusive licensee. Section 235 provides for the exercise of concurrent rights.

4.3.7.1   *C. & H. Engineering v F. Klucznik & Sons Ltd* [1992] F.S.R. 421, Aldous J.

The plaintiff and the defendant were designers and manufacturers of agricultural and animal handling equipment. Litigation between them included a

452

counterclaim by the defendant that the plaintiff had infringed its design right in a pig fender (i.e. a pen placed outside a pig house to confine piglets within a small area). The defendant's design included a metal roll bar on the top of the fender (to prevent sows trapping their teats as they stepped over it) which it claimed to have designed following a request made by a customer (Butler) to one of its employees (Jackson). Aldous J. set out ss.213, 214, and 226 of the Copyright, Designs and Patents Act 1988 (above, 4.3) and continued:

The word "original" in section 213(1) is not defined, but I believe that it should be given the same meaning as the word "original" in section 1(1)(a) of the Act, namely not copied but the independent work of the designer. It should be contrasted with novelty which is the requirement for registration of a registered design: see section 265(4) of the Act.

Section 213(4) says that the design is not original if it is commonplace in the design field in question. The word "commonplace" is not defined, but this subsection appears to introduce a consideration akin to novelty. For the design to be original it must be the work of the creator and that work must result in a design which is not commonplace in the relevant field. The designer is the creator and no design right will subsist until the design has been recorded in a document or in an article. Thus the creator is not necessarily the person who records the design but usually will be.

Section 226 appears to require the owner of a design right to establish that copying has taken place before infringement can be proved; that is similar to copyright. However the test of infringement is different. Under section 16 copyright will be infringed if the work, or a substantial part of the work, is copied. Under section 226 there will only be infringement if the design is copied so as to produce articles exactly or substantially to the design. Thus the test for infringement requires the alleged infringing article or articles be compared with the document or article embodying the design. Thereafter, the court must decide whether copying took place and, if so, whether the alleged infringing article is made exactly to the design or substantially to that design. Whether or not the alleged infringing article is made substantially to the plaintiff's design must be an objective test to be decided through the eyes of the person to whom the design is directed. Pig fenders are purchased by pig farmers and I have no doubt that they purchase them taking into account price and design. In the present case, the plaintiff's alleged infringing pig fenders do not have exactly the same design as shown in the defendant's design document. Thus it is necessary to compare the plaintiff's pig fenders with the defendant's design drawing and, looking at the differences and similarities through the eyes of a person such as a pig farmer, decide whether the design of the plaintiff's pig fender is substantially the same as the design shown in the drawing.

By 1990 pig fenders were commonplace and had been made in metal and wood. In essence Mr Butler wanted a commonplace pig fender with a metal roll bar on the top. He had seen fenders with a wooden roll bar. He gave Mr Jackson the basic measurements needed and the only part of the pig fender shown in the drawing which was not commonplace was the two inch tube on the top. Thus the design is the incorporation of the two inch pipe into a commonplace pig fender.

The first matter for decision is: who created the design? The defendant submitted that it was Mr Jackson and the plaintiff submitted it was Mr Butler; nobody submitted that they were joint creators. The creator was the person who thought of using a two inch pipe on top of a commonplace form of pig fender. I do not know whether it was Mr Jackson or Mr Butler who thought of that design and created it. As I have said, the evidence is conflicting and any conclusion as to who thought of it would be a matter of guesswork. I therefore conclude that the defendant has not established that it is the owner of the design right in its drawing of a pig fender and thus the action for infringement must fail.

Aldous J. went on to state that even if the defendant did own the design right in its drawing of the pig fender then the plaintiff had not infringed this design:

I have no doubt that the idea of having a tube as the roll bar came from the defendant's pig fender and therefore copying did take place. However, the plaintiff's pig fenders are not made exactly to the defendant's design, and I do not believe that they are made substantially to that design. Metal pig fenders must have an overall similarity due to the function they have to perform, but a person interested in their design would appreciate that the plaintiff's pig fender was of a different design to that of the defendant, although they have in common a tube as the roll bar. In that respect the two designs are substantially the same, but taken as a whole the two designs are not substantially the same. An interested man would be struck by the design features which enable the plaintiff's pig fender to be stacked. Those features not only attract the eye, but would also be seen by an interested person as being functionally significant. They contrast with the overall design features of the defendant's pig fender. The interested man looking at the plaintiff's and the defendant's pig fenders would consider the two designs to be different, but with a similar design feature—namely, the bar around the top. Therefore, the defendant's claim for infringement of a design right fails.

4.3.7.2   *Ocular Sciences Ltd v Aspect Vision Care Ltd* [1997] R.P.C. 289, Laddie J.

The plaintiffs were contact lens manufacturers, who commenced proceedings against the defendants for, inter alia, *infringing their unregistered design right in a number of lenses, covering some 200 designs (varying in power from minus to plus dioptres). The plaintiffs argued that its design comprised: (a) the front surface dimensions of the lens; (b) the rear surface dimensions; and (c) edge characteristics. The defendants argued that certain features of contact lenses, specifically the back and lens diameters, the "CN Bevel" and parallel peripheral carrier, were present to enable the contact lens to fit onto the eyeball and allow conversion of focus. Such features were argued to be excluded from design right by s.213(3)(b)(i) CDPA (see 4.3.1). The remaining features were argued to be unprotectable because they were commonplace. The plaintiffs argued that these defences did not apply. First, the eye, forming part of the human body, was not an "article" within s.213(3)(b). Secondly, the combinations of dimensions used for each lens design had not been shown to have been used before and could therefore not be regarded as commonplace.*

Laddie J. held that the plaintiffs' case on designs fell at the first hurdle: they could not prove that their individual lens designs were copied into the defendants' lens designs, under s.226(1) and (2) of the CDPA (see 4.3.6). Notwithstanding this finding, the judge went on to consider the scope of the following defences in relation to the plaintiffs' contact lens design.

The "interface" defence: s.213(3)(b)(i) CDPA:

Section 213(3)(b)(i) of the 1988 Act provides:

"Design right does not subsist in ... features of shape or configuration of an article which ... enable the article to be connected to, or placed in, around or against, another article so that either article may perform its function...."

This is sometimes referred to as the interface provision. Its original purpose was to prevent the designer of a piece of equipment from using design right to prevent others from making parts which fitted his equipment. As I read it, any features of shape or configuration of an article which meet the interface criteria must be excluded from being considered as part of the design right. Furthermore a feature which meets the interface criteria must be excluded even if it performs some other purpose, for example it is attractive. There is also nothing in the provision which requires the feature to be only one which would achieve the proper interface. If a number of designs are possible each of which enables the two articles to be fitted together in a way which allowed one or other or both to perform its function, each falls within the statutory exclusion. Mr Pumfrey argued that many of the features of the plaintiffs' lens design should be excluded from consideration by virtue of this provision.

Mr Waugh, who argued this part of the case on behalf of the plaintiffs, said that this provision could have no application to the design of contact lenses. Even if all the features of his clients' designs are there to enable the lenses to fit on the eye and under the eyelids, section 213(3)(b)(i) is irrelevant. For the latter to operate the design features of the article in suit, *i.e.* the contact lens has to be there to interface with another article. But, he said, an eye is not an "article" at all. It is part of the human body. The word "article" means something inanimate which is not and has never been alive ... I do not think that this is a matter of dictionary definition. What counts is the presumed legislative intent behind the provision. It seems to me that the subsection is drafted in wide terms to exclude all interface features. The word "article" is not intended to have a restricted meaning. It could just as well have been replaced by the word "thing". I can see no reason why it should be construed so as to exclude living or formerly living things. There is no self apparent policy consideration which justifies allowing, say, the features which enable a false hip to be fitted into the hip joint of a human to fall within the ambit of design right whereas the same features on a child's doll are excluded. I reject this submission....

Laddie J. considered, on the evidence, that the following features were excluded under the "interface" defence:

(1) *The back radius in each of the plaintiffs' lenses that enables the lens to fit against the eyeball so as to allow the lens to perform its function of correcting the focusing ability of the eye to the desired extent and to ensure that it centres over the pupil.*

(2) *The chosen lens diameters, which enable the soft lens to fit onto the eyeball and under the eyelids so as to achieve in-eye stability.*

(3) *The detailed designs of the CN Bevel and parallel peripheral carrier which enable the lens to be placed in the eye and against the conjunctiva and help the lens to perform its function of remaining in position over the cornea and under the eyelids so as to ensure that its focus correction abilities are properly employed.*

In the alternative, and for the remaining features (centre thickness, optic zone radius and front curve of each lens), the judge held that the plaintiffs' designs as a whole were "commonplace":

Section 213(4) of the 1988 Act provides that:

"A design is not 'original' for the purposes of this Part if it is commonplace in the design field in question at the time of its creation"

Mr Pumfrey argued that all of the designs in suit are commonplace and unprotectable by design right. He said that the expression "commonplace" covered designs which were ordinary, nothing more than banal, and trivial. He said it covered an unsurprising combination of well-known features even if nobody had made that precise combination before. Of course this was challenged by Mr Waugh. He said that the combinations of dimensions for each lens design was not shown to be used before. He said it was not permissible to divide up the designs into their component parts and then, by showing that each part was known in the trade, come to the conclusion that the combination was also. The combination of features which go to make-up the full design relied on must be looked at as a whole. As such, none of the designs in issue here could be called commonplace.

The expression "commonplace" can be traced back to the European Directive upon which the original 1987 Semiconductor Products (Protection of Topography) Regulations were based. There is, therefore, no domestic material which can be used as an aid to construction on the basis of *Pepper v Hart* [1993] A.C. 593 and it was not suggested by counsel that there was any European material which helped either. On the other hand, its origin does tell us something about its intended meaning. Semiconductor topographies are the detailed, highly functional, layouts of the layers of electronic connections inside an integrated circuit, or "chip". The layouts look rather like monochrome maps of the London Underground service, save that there are millions of lines and interconnections. Every semiconductor design team produces its own topographies, in the sense that the distribution of lines and connections will be their own particular choice to meet the functional requirements of the chip. In designing their layouts they will, no doubt, use certain conventional design considerations and functionally-convention circuits—that is to say circuits which operate in a well known way although the actual lines and connections will be distinguishable visually from many other embodiments of the same circuitry. This can be likened to the plumbing which connects the hot and cold water taps on a bath to the hot and cold water tanks in a house. The connections are entirely common-or-garden but the actual direction and lengths of the piping will depend on the precise locations of the tanks and the bath and the intervening obstacles. If any new combination of well-known features was intended to be the subject of a monopoly, all semiconductor topographies would be protected, and the commonplace exclusion would be no exclusion at all. The same conclusion can be reached another way. It is to be assumed that the draughtsman of the European Directive was familiar, as all intellectual property lawyers are, with the concept of originality in copyright law. There it means "originated with the author without slavish copying from some preceding work". The Directive eschews adopting that concept alone in relation to semiconductor topographies. Instead it uses the expression "commonplace" which clearly envisages some objective assessment. This follows from the provisions of Article 2(2) of the Directive:

"The topography of a semiconductor product shall be protected in so far as it satisfies the conditions that it is the result of its creator's own intellectual effort *and* is not commonplace in the semiconductor industry. Where the topography of a semiconductor product consists of elements that are commonplace in the semiconductor industry, it shall be protected only to the extent that the combination of such elements, taken as a whole, fulfils the above mentioned conditions." (My emphasis)

Essentially the same words are to be found in the 1987 Regulations.

It is always undesirable to replace one ambiguous expression by another, and for that reason it is not right to redefine the word "commonplace" in the 1988 Act, but it seems to me that the flavour of the word is much along the lines suggested by Mr Pumfrey. Any design which is trite, trivial, common-or-garden, hackneyed or of the type which would excite no peculiar attention in those in the relevant art is likely to be commonplace. This does not mean that a design made up of features which, individually, are commonplace is necessarily itself commonplace. A new and exciting design can be produced from the most trite of ingredients. But to secure protection, the combination must itself not be commonplace. That is what the European Directive and the 1987 Regulations say expressly and what is implicit in the 1988 Act. In many cases the run of the mill combination of well known features will produce a combination which is itself commonplace. With this in mind it is now possible to assess the 200 odd designs the plaintiffs rely on here. . . .

During the course of trial, most of the features of the plaintiffs' lenses was analysed in detail. It is clear that, individually, all of them are well known and that all competent designers in the field have in the past had no difficulty in working out the correct dimensions to make good workable soft lenses . . . I accept that evidence. If regard is only had to the combination of three remaining features of each lens design, they are a commonplace. Furthermore, even if I am wrong in relation to the exclusion of interface features, the plaintiffs' designs as a whole are commonplace. They do not qualify for design right protection.

4.3.8   *Electronic Techniques (Anglia) Limited v Critchley Components Limited* **[1997] F.S.R. 401, Laddie J.**

Both parties designed, manufactured and sold transformers. The plaintiff commenced proceedings against the defendant for (i) infringement of copyright in its data sheets (some of which included circuit diagrams) and (ii) infringement of the design right in its transformers. Laddie J. dismissed the plaintiff's applications for summary judgment with respect to its copyright claim, and an order to strike out certain parts of the defence relating to the applicability of the "must fit" exception: s.213(3) CDPA (see 4.3.1).

In support of its copyright claim, the plaintiff argued that infringement had taken place by insignificant takings, which over time amounted to substantial copying of the plaintiff's work following the line of authority from Cate v Devon *(1889) 40 Ch.D. 500. Laddie J. declined to order summary judgment, taking the view that in respect of some of the data sheets the defendant had a credible defence of non-substantiality. Specifically, a finding of systematic infringements required full assessment at trial of the defendant's course of conduct and motives. Moreover, the plaintiff's reliance on a literary copyright claim in relation to his circuit diagrams further reduced the scope of protection, since it excluded material which was "appreciated simply with the eye" (being the subject-matter of artistic copyright). Thus the circuit diagrams, forming a list of five or six components, were too insubstantial to qualify as original works.*

As to Design Right, the plaintiff alleged that the defendant had made its transformers to the plaintiff's design. The defendant argued that parts of the transformer fitted together to perform their function and therefore s.213(3) applied. The plaintiff argued that this part of the defence should be struck out on the basis that the "must fit" provisions applied to the whole "article" (and not parts thereof) which had to interface with other articles. Laddie J. disagreed:

The design right provisions are not concerned with protecting particular articles but with protecting certain types of designs. Section 213(2) defines those features which can form part of a protectable design. They are features of shape or configuration. The fact that the subsection says that those features are to be found inside or outside an article or part of an article does not necessarily mean that the protection afforded by the Act is restricted to those features only when applied to particular articles. On the contrary, there are reasons for thinking that this was not the legislative intention. First, reference can be made to section 213(6) which provides: "Design right does not subsist unless and until the design has been recorded in a design document or an article has been made to the design."

This appears to emphasise that what the Act is concerned with is the design itself rather than the substrate on which it is recorded or to which it is first applied. Secondly, ... the protection afforded by the Act is likely to be very limited. Since design right is presumably intended to reward and encourage design effort, it seems unlikely that that effort should only be protected and rewarded if the infringer happens to use the design on precisely the same type of article. ... For these reasons there does not appear to me to be any compelling reason for holding that the word "article" when used in the design right sections of the Act has the restricted meaning suggested by Mr Prescott. This does not mean that the article to which the designer applies the design can never be relevant to the scope or subsistence of design right. It may be that a design applied to certain articles has a different impact to the same design applied to others. In such cases it may well be that the design, in the context of other features of shape and configuration of the article itself, may be viewed differently to the same or a similar design in a different context.

If a feature of shape or configuration of one article enables that article to be connected to, or placed in, around or against another article so that either article may perform its function, the feature is excluded from protection under the design right provisions of the Act. If the policy of the Act is to prevent such interface features from qualifying for design right, I can see no reason why that policy should not apply merely because the two interfitting articles carrying the features are in fact assembled together and form the whole or part of another larger article. It follows from this that Critchley's defence under the provisions of the Act is not demurrable.

4.4   Design Right (Semiconductor Topographies) Regulations 1989

4.4.1   Definitions

These regulations introduce modifications of (unregistered) design right under the Copyright, Designs and Patents Act 1988, Part III in relation to semi-conductors. They were initially made under the European Communities Act 1972 in implementation of Council Directive 87/54. The regulations apply to products and designs defined as follows (para. 2(1)):

"semiconductor product" means an article the purpose, or one of the purposes, of which is the performance of an electronic function and which consists of two or more layers, at least one of which is composed of semiconducting material and in or upon one or more of which is fixed a pattern appertaining to that or another function; and "semiconductor topography" means a design within the meaning of section 213(2) of the Act which is a design of either of the following:

(a) the pattern fixed, or intended to be fixed, in or upon—

   (i) a layer of a semiconductor product, or
   (ii) a layer of material in the course of and for the purpose of the manufacture of a semiconductor product, or

(b) the arrangement of the patterns fixed, or intended to be fixed, in or upon the layers of a semiconductor product in relation to one another.

For semiconductors, the 1988 Act is modified as indicated in 4.4.2–4.4.6.

4.4.2   Qualification

Section 217 is altered in particular so as to allow the listing of countries with which reciprocal arrangements are established in pursuance of EC Council Directives on the matter (para. 4(2)).

Section 219 (qualification by reference to commissioner or employer) does not apply and instead s.218(2)–(4) (qualification by reference to designer) have effect (para. 4(3)).

Section 220 (qualification by reference to exclusive licensee) is altered so as to apply where the exclusive licensee for the whole EEC is a qualifying person and first marketing takes place anywhere in the EEC (para. 4(4)).

4.4.3   Ownership

Section 215, giving initial ownership to a commissioner or employer, is modified in each case by the addition, "subject to any agreement in writing to the contrary" (para. 5).

4.4.4   Duration

Section 216 is modified as follows (para. 6):

"**216. The design right in a semiconductor topography expires—**

    (a) **ten years from the end of the calendar year in which the topography or articles made to the topography were first made available for sale or hire anywhere in the world by or with the licence of the design right owner, or**

    (b) **if neither the topography nor articles made to the topography are so made available within a period of fifteen years commencing with the earlier of the time when the topography was first recorded in a design document or the time when an article was first made to the topography at the end of that period".**

4.4.5   Confidence

In relation to qualification, initial ownership and duration, para. 7 applies:

7. In determining, for the purposes of sections 215(4), 216 or 220 of the Act (as modified by these Regulations), whether there has been any marketing, or anything has been made available for sale or hire, no account shall be taken of any sale or hire, or any offer or exposure for sale or hire, which is subject to an obligation of confidence in respect of information about the semiconductor topography in question unless either—

    (a) **the article or semiconductor topography sold or hired or offered or exposed for sale or hire has been sold or hired on a previous occasion (whether or not subject to an obligation of confidence), or**

    (b) **the obligation is imposed at the behest of the Crown, or of the government of any country outside the United Kingdom, for the protection of security in connection with the production of arms, munitions or war material.**

4.4.6   Infringement

Section 226 is modified as follows (para. 8(1)):

"**226.(1) Subject to subsection (1A), the owner of design right in a design has the exclusive right to reproduce the design—**

    (a) **by making articles to that design, or**

    (b) **by making a design document recording the design for the purpose of enabling such articles to be made.**

(1A) Subsection (1) does not apply to—

    (a) **the reproduction of a design privately for non-commercial aims; or**

    (b) **the reproduction of a design for the purpose of analysing or evaluating the design or analysing, evaluating or teaching the concepts, processes, systems or techniques embodied in it**".

Paragraph 8(2)–(5) provides:

(2) Section 227 of the Act does not apply if the article in question has previously been sold or hired within—

    (a) **the United Kingdom by or with the licence of the owner of design right in the semi-conductor topography in question, or**

    (b) **the territory of any other member State of the European Economic Community or the territory of Gibraltar by or with the consent of the person for the time being entitled to import it into or sell or hire it within that territory.**

(3) Section 228(6) of the Act does not apply.

(4) It is not an infringement of design right in a semiconductor topography to—

    (a) **create another original semiconductor topography as a result of an analysis or eva-luation of the first topography or of the concepts, processes, systems or techniques embodied in it, or**

    (b) **reproduce that other topography.**

(5) Anything which would be an infringement of the design right in a semiconductor topo-graphy if done in relation to the topography as a whole is an infringement of the design right in the topography if done in relation to a substantial part of the topography.

5 TRADE MARKS AND NAMES

5.1 Liability at Common Law: Passing Off and Injurious Falsehood

5.1.1 Passing Off: General Principles

5.1.1.1 *Reddaway v Banham* [1896] A.C. 199, HL

The appellant (plaintiff) manufactured belting which, for the purpose of distinguishing it from similar products, he called "Camel-hair Belting". The yarn used was chiefly of camel hair though few people realised this. The respondent, a former employee of the appellant, began making similar belting, which he first called "Arabian" and then, in response to particular orders, "Camel-hair". Other manufacturers used almost identical yarn to make belts and sold them as "Yale", "Buffalo", etc.

The trial judge, after the jury's verdict for the plaintiff, granted an injunction restraining the defendant from continuing to use the word "Camel-hair" in such a manner as to lead purchasers into the belief that they were purchasing belting of the plaintiff's manufacture and yarn, thereby passing off their belting as and for the belting of the plaintiff's manufacture. The Court of Appeal reversed this but it was restored by the House of Lords.

Lord Herschell:

The principle which is applicable to this class of cases was, in my judgment, well laid down by Lord Kingsdown in *The Leather Cloth Co v The American Cloth Co* (1865) 11 H.L. Cas., 538. It had been previously enunciated in much the same way by Lord Langdale in the case of *Croft v Day* (1843) 7 Beav. 84. Lord Kingsdown's words were as follows:

> "The fundamental rule is that one man has no right to put off his goods for sale as the goods of a rival trader, and he cannot therefore (in the language of Lord Langdale in the case of *Perry v Truefitt* (1843) 6 Beav. 66) be allowed to use names, marks, letters, or other indicia, by which he may induce purchasers to believe that the goods which he is selling are the manufacture of another person".

It is, in my opinion, this fundamental rule which governs all cases, whatever be the particular mode adopted by any man for putting off his goods as those of a rival trader, whether it is done by the use of a mark which has become his trade mark, or in any other way. The word "property" has been sometimes applied to what has been termed a trade mark at common law. I doubt myself whether it is accurate to speak of there being property in such a trade mark, though, no doubt, some of the rights which are incident to property may attach to it. Where the trade mark is a word or device never in use before, and meaningless, except as indicating by whom the goods in connection with which it is used were made, there could be no conceivable legitimate use of it by another person. His only object in employing it in connection with goods of his manufacture must be to deceive. In circumstances such as those, the mere proof that the trade mark of one manufacturer had been thus appropriated by another, would be enough to bring the case within the rule as laid down by Lord Kingsdown, and to entitle the person aggrieved to an injunction to restrain its use. In the case of a trade mark thus identified with a particular manufacturer, the rights of the person whose trade mark it was would not, it may be, differ substantially from those which would exist if it were, strictly speaking, his property. But there are other cases which equally come within the rule that a man may not pass off his goods as those of his rival, which are not of this simple character—cases where the mere use of the particular mark or device which had been employed by another manufacturer would not of itself necessarily indicate that the person who employed it was thereby inducing purchasers to believe that the goods he was selling were the goods of another manufacturer.

The name of a person, or words forming part of the common stock of language, may become so far associated with the goods of a particular maker that it is capable of proof that the use of them by themselves, without explanation or qualification by another manufacturer, would deceive a purchaser into the belief that he was getting the goods of A, when he was really getting the goods of B. In a case of this description, the mere proof by the plaintiff that the defendant was using a name, word, or device which he had adopted to distinguish his goods would not entitle him to any relief. He could only obtain it by proving further, that the defendant was using it under such circumstances or in such manner as to put off his goods as the goods of the plaintiff. If he could succeed in proving this, I think he would, on well-established principles, be entitled to an injunction.

In my opinion, the doctrine on which the judgment of the Court of Appeal was based, that where a manufacturer has used as his trade mark a descriptive word, he is never entitled to relief against a person who so uses it as to induce in purchasers the belief that they are getting the goods of the manufacturer who has theretofore employed it as his trade mark, is not supported by authority and cannot be defended on principle. I am unable to see why a man should be allowed in this way more than in any other to deceive purchasers into the belief that they are getting what they are not, and thus to filch the business of a rival.

Lord Halsbury L.C., Lord Macnaghten and Lord Morris delivered concurring speeches.

5.1.1.2   *Spalding v Gamage* (1915) 32 R.P.C. 273, HL

The plaintiffs sold footballs. In 1910 and 1911 they used the mark "Orb" for a moulded ball calling it in some instances the "Improved Orb". In 1912, after discovering faults in some of these moulded balls, they produced a sewn ball under the mark "Improved Sewn Orb" and sold off old stock to waste rubber merchants. The defendant store, however, bought up these faulty moulded balls and advertised them in a manner imitating the announcement of the sewn balls in the plaintiffs' 1912 catalogue.

Lord Parker of Waddington:

My Lords, the action in which the Appeal arises is what is known as passing-off action, and having regard to the arguments which have been addressed to your Lordships, I think it well to say a few words as to the principle on which such actions are founded. This principle is stated by Lord Justice Turner in *Burgess v Burgess* (1843–60) 14 Ch.D. at 748, and by Lord Halsbury in *Reddaway v Banham* [1906] A.C. at 204, in the proposition that nobody has any right to represent his goods as the goods of somebody else. It is also sometimes stated in the proposition that nobody has the right to pass off his goods as the goods of somebody else. I prefer the former statement, for whatever doubts may be suggested in the earlier authorities, it has long been settled that actual passing-off of a defendant's goods for the plaintiff's need not be proved as a condition precedent to relief in Equity either by way of an injunction or of an inquiry as to profits or damages (*Edelsten v Edelsten* (1863) 1 De G., J. & S. 185, and *Iron-Ox Remedy Co Ltd v Co-operative Wholesale Society Ltd* (1907) 24 R.P.C. 425). Nor need the representation be fraudulently made. It is enough that it has in fact been made, whether fraudulently or otherwise, and that damages may probably ensue, though the complete innocence of the party making it may be a reason for limiting the account of profits to the period subsequent to the date at which he becomes aware of the true facts. The representation is in fact treated as the invasion of a right giving rise at any rate to nominal damages, the inquiry being granted at the plaintiff's risk if he might probably have suffered more than nominal damages.

The view taken by the Common Law Courts was somewhat different. The plaintiff's remedy was said to have been in the nature of an action for deceit, but it only resembled the action for deceit in the fact that the misrepresentation relied on must have been fraudulently made. In all other respects it differed from an action for deceit. For example, the plaintiff was not the party deceived, and even if it were necessary to prove that someone had been deceived, nominal damage could be obtained though no actual damage was proved. Thus in *Blofeld v Payne* (1833) 4 B. & Ad. 410 the defendants had sold their own hones in the plaintiff's wrappers as and for the plaintiff's, but there was no evidence that any purchasers had been actually deceived. Further, though special damage was alleged in the declaration, no actual damage was proved. On motion for a non-suit it was held in the King's Bench that the plaintiff was entitled to nominal damages. The action was, in fact, treated as one founded on the invasion of a right.

My Lords, the proposition that no one has a right to represent his goods as the goods of somebody else must, I think, as has been assumed in this case, involve as a corollary the further proposition, that no one, who has in his hands the goods of another of a particular class or quality, has a right to represent these goods to be the goods of that other of a different quality or belonging to a different class. Possibly, therefore, the principle ought to be re-stated as follows: A cannot, without infringing the rights of B, represent goods which are not B's goods or B's goods of a particular class or quality to be B's goods or B's goods of that particular class or quality. The wrong for which relief is sought in a passing-off action consists in every case of a representation of this nature.

My Lords, the basis of a passing-off action being a false representation by the defendant, it must be proved in each case as a fact that the false representation was made. It may, of course, have been made in express words, but cases of express misrepresentation of this sort are rare. The more common case is, where the representation is implied in the use or imitation of a mark, trade name, or get-up with which the goods of another are associated in the minds of the public, or of a particular class of the public. In such cases the point to be decided is whether, having regard to all the circumstances of the case, the use by the defendant, in connection with the goods of the mark, name, or get-up in question, impliedly represents such goods to be the goods of the plaintiff, or the goods of the plaintiff of a particular class or quality, or, as it is sometimes put, whether the defendant's use of such mark, name, or get-up is calculated to deceive. It would, however, be impossible to enumerate or classify all the possible ways in which a man may make the false representation relied on.

There appears to be considerable diversity of opinion as to the nature of the right, the invasion of which is the subject of what are known as passing-off actions. The more general opinion appears to be that the right is a right of property. This view naturally demands an answer to the question—property in what? Some authorities say property in the mark, name, or get-up improperly used by the defendant. Others say, property in the business or goodwill likely to be injured by the misrepresentation. Lord Herschell in *Reddaway v Banham* [1896] A.C. 199, expressly dissents from the former view; and if the right invaded is a right of property at all, there are, I think, strong reasons for preferring the latter view. In the first place, cases of misrepresentation by the use of a mark, name, or get-up do not exhaust all possible cases of misrepresentation. If A says falsely, "These goods I am selling are B's goods", there is no mark, name or get-up infringed unless it be B's name, and if he falsely says, "These are B's goods of a particular quality", where the goods are in fact B's goods, there is no name that is infringed at all. Further, it is extremely difficult to see how a man can be said to have property in descriptive words, such as "Camel-hair" in the case of *Reddaway v Banham* [1896] A.C. 199, where every trader is entitled to use the words, provided only he uses them in such a way as not to be calculated to deceive. Even in the case of what are sometimes referred to as Common Law Trade Marks the property, if any, of the so-called owner is in its nature transitory, and only exists so long as the mark is distinctive of his goods in the eyes of the public or a class of the public. Indeed, the necessity of proving this distinctiveness in each case as a step in the proof of the false representation relied on was one of the evils sought to be remedied by the Trade Marks Act 1875, which conferred a real right of property on the owner of a registered mark. I had to consider the matter in the case of *Burberrys v Cording* (1909) 26 R.P.C. 693 and I came to the same conclusion.

His Lordship then reviewed the evidence and concluded that there had been misrepresentation about the quality of the "Orb" balls sold by the defendant such as was likely to occasion actual damage to the plaintiffs. In particular, retailers who had purchased new "Orbs" at a price above that being charged to the public by the defendant thought that they were being unfairly treated and were likely to withdraw custom.

Lord Atkinson concurred and Lords Sumner and Parmoor gave concurring speeches.

5.1.1.3 *Samuelson v Producers Distributing* [1932] 1 Ch. 201, CA

The plaintiff wrote a revue sketch, "The New Car", which achieved fame particularly by its inclusion in a Royal Command Performance. The defendant made a film of a different sketch, "His First Car", and advertised it in a way suggesting that it was the sketch seen at the performance.

The Court of Appeal held this to constitute a form of passing off. Romer L.J. observed:

It is said that there has been no passing off. It is true there has been no passing off in fact, or indeed, perhaps, threatened, in the sense in which the word "passing-off" is used in what are popularly known as passing-off actions; that is to say, the defendants have never contended that the film which they were producing or going to produce was a film prepared or made by or on behalf of the plaintiff. But the cases in which the court has restrained passing off in the popular and usual sense, are merely instances of the application by the court of a much wider principle, the principle being that the court will always interfere by injunction to restrain irreparable injury being done to the plaintiff's property. In the present case, if, as we hold to be the case, the plaintiff was entitled to his copyright in "The New Car", he was, by virtue of the Copyright Act, entitled to the sole right of producing the sketch in film form. That was an item of his property, and how it can be said that these advertisements might not cause irreparable damage to that property of the plaintiff passes my comprehension.

5.1.1.4   *Warnink v Townend* [1979] A.C. 731, HL

The first plaintiff, a Dutch company, held 75 per cent of the English market for advocaat, a drink made of egg and spirits, and had increased its popularity by heavy advertising campaigns. Egg flip, which was also available on the English market, comprised egg and fortified wine and accordingly attracted a lower rate of excise. It was sold at a substantially cheaper price. The defendants changed the name of their egg flip to "Keeling's Old English Advocaat". Thereafter they captured an appreciable share of the advocaat market from the plaintiff and others.

Lord Diplock:

True it is that it could not be shown that any purchaser of Keeling's Old English Advocaat supposed or would be likely to suppose it to be goods supplied by Warnink or to be Dutch advocaat of any make. So Warnink had no cause of action for passing off in its classic form. Nevertheless, the learned judge was satisfied: (1) that the name "Advocaat" was understood by the public in England to denote a distinct and recognisable species of beverage; (2) that Warnink's product is genuinely indicated by that name and has gained reputation and goodwill under it; (3) that Keeling's product has no natural association with the word "Advocaat": it is an egg and wine drink properly described as an "Egg Flip", whereas Advocaat is an egg and spirit drink; these are different beverages and known as different to the public; (4) that members of the public believe and have been deliberately induced by Keeling to believe in buying their "Old English Advocaat" they are in fact buying advocaat; (5) that Keeling's deception of the public has caused and, unless prevented, will continue to cause, damage to Warnink in the trade and the goodwill of their business both directly in the loss of sales and indirectly in the debasement of the reputation attaching to the name "Advocaat" if it is permitted to be used of alcoholic egg drinks generally and not confined to those that are spirit based.

These findings, he considered, brought the case within the principle of law laid down in the Champagne *case [1961] R.P.C. 116, by Danckwerts J. and applied in the* Sherry *and* Scotch Whisky *cases [1969] R.P.C. 1 (below, 5.1.3.4); [1970] 1 W.L.R. 917. He granted Warnink an injunction restraining Keeling from selling or distributing under the name or description "Advocaat" any product which does not basically consist of eggs and spirit without any admixture of wine.*

My Lords, these findings of fact were accepted by the Court of Appeal and have not been challenged in the Lordships' House. They seem to me to disclose a case of unfair, not to say dishonest, trading of a kind for which a rational system of law ought to provide a remedy to other traders whose business or goodwill is injured by it.

Unfair trading as a wrong actionable at the suit of other traders who thereby suffer loss of business or goodwill may take a variety of forms, to some of which separate labels have become attached in English law. Conspiracy to injure a person in his trade or business is one, slander of goods another, but most protean is that which is generally and nowadays, perhaps misleading, described as "passing off". The forms that unfair trading takes will alter with the ways in which trade is carried on and business reputation and goodwill acquired. Emerson's maker of the better mousetrap if secluded in his house built in the woods would today be unlikely to find a path beaten to his door in the absence of a costly advertising campaign to acquaint the public with the excellence of his wares.

After reviewing Reddaway v Banham *and* Spalding v Gamage *(above, 5.1.1.1, 5.1.1.2), Lord Diplock continued:*

Lord Parker's explanation of the nature of the proprietary right protected by a passing off action also supplied a new and rational basis for the two nineteenth-century decisions of Page Wood V.C. in *Dent v Turpin* (1861) 2 J & H 139, and *Southorn v Reynolds* (1865) 12 L.T.(N.S.) 75, in which one of two traders, each of whom had by inheritance acquired goodwill in the use of a particular trade name, was held entitled, without joining the other, to obtain an injunction restraining a third trader from making use of the name, despite the fact that the plaintiff's right of user was not exclusive. The goodwill of his business would be damaged by the misrepresentation that the defendant's goods were the goods of a limited class of traders entitled to make use of it, of whom the plaintiff was one and the defendant was not.

My Lords, *Spalding v Gamage* and the later cases make it possible to identify five characteristics which must be present in order to create a valid cause of action for passing off: (1) a misrepresentation (2) made by a trader in the course of trade, (3) to prospective customers of his or ultimate consumers of goods or services supplied by him, (4) which is calculated to injure the business or goodwill of another trader (in the sense that this is a reasonably foreseeable consequence) and (5) which causes actual damage to a business or goodwill of the trader by whom the action is brought or (in a *quia timet* action) will probably do so.

In seeking to formulate general propositions of English law, however, one must be particularly careful to beware of the logical fallacy of the undistributed middle. It does not follow that because all passing off actions can be shown to present these characteristics, all factual situations which present these characteristics give rise to a cause of action for passing off. True it is that their presence indicates what a moral code would censure as dishonest trading, based as it is upon deception of customers and consumers of a trader's wares but in an economic system which has relied on competition to keep down prices and to improve products there may be practical reasons why it should have been the policy of the common law not to run the risk of hampering competition by providing civil remedies to every one competing in the market who has suffered damage to his business or goodwill in consequence of inaccurate statements of whatever kind that may be made by rival traders about their own wares. The market in which the action for passing off originated was no place for the mealy mouthed; advertisements are not on affidavit; exaggerated claims by a trader about the quality of his wares, assertions that they are better than those of his rivals, even though he knows this to be untrue, have been permitted by the common law as venial "puffing" which gives no cause of action to a competitor even though he can show he has suffered actual damage in his business as a result.

Parliament, however, beginning in the nineteenth century has progressively intervened in the interests of consumers to impose on traders a higher standard of commercial candour than the legal maxim *caveat emptor* calls for, by prohibiting under penal sanctions misleading descriptions of the character of quality of goods; but since the class of persons for whose protection the Merchandise Marks Acts 1887 to 1953 and even more rigorous later statutes are designed, are not competing traders but those consumers who are likely to be deceived, the Acts do not themselves give rise to any civil action for breach of statutory duty on the part of a competing trader even though he sustains actual damage as a result. *Cutler v Wandsworth Stadium* [1949] A.C. 398 and see *London Armoury Co Ltd v Ever Ready Co Ltd* [1941] 1 K.B. 742. Nevertheless the increasing recognition by Parliament of the need for more rigorous standards of commercial honesty is a factor which should not be overlooked by a judge confronted by the choice whether or not to extend by analogy to circumstances in which it has not previously been applied a principle which has been applied in previous cases where the circumstances although different had some features in common with those of the case which he has to decide. Where over a period of years there can be discerned a steady trend in legislation which reflects the view of successive Parliaments as to what the public interest demands in a particular field of law, development of the common law in that part of the same field which has been left to it ought to proceed upon a parallel rather than a diverging course.

The *Champagne* case came before Danckwerts J. in two stages: the first (reported at [1960] R.P.C. 16) on a preliminary point of law, the second (reported at [1961] R.P.C. 116) on the trial of the action. The assumptions of fact on which the legal argument at the first stage was based were stated by the judge to be:

"(1) The plaintiffs carry on business in a geographical area in France known as Champagne; (2) the plaintiffs' wine is produced in Champagne and from grapes grown in Champagne; (3) the plaintiffs' wine has been known in the trade for a long time as Champagne with a high reputation; (4) members of the public or in the trade ordering or seeing wine advertised as Champagne would expect to get wine produced in Champagne from grapes grown there and (5) the defendants are producing a wine not produced in that geographical area and are selling it under the name of 'Spanish Champagne' ".

These findings disclose a factual situation (assuming that damage was thereby caused to the plaintiffs' business) which contains each of the five characteristics which I have suggested must be present in order to create a valid cause of action for passing off. The features that distinguished it from all previous cases were (a) that the element in the goodwill of each of the individual plaintiffs that was represented by his ability to use without deception (in addition to his individual house mark) the word "Champagne" to distinguish his wines from sparkling wines not made by the champenois process from grapes produced in the Champagne district of France, was not exclusive to himself but was shared with every other shipper of sparkling wine to England whose wines could satisfy the same condition and (b) that the class of traders entitled to a proprietary right in "the attractive force that brings in custom" represented by the ability without deception to call one's wines "Champagne" was capable of continuing expansion, since it might be joined by any future shipper of wine who was able to satisfy that condition.

My Lords, in the *Champagne* case the class of traders between whom the goodwill attaching to the ability to use the word "Champagne" as descriptive of their wines was shared was a large one, 150 at least and probably considerably more, whereas in the previous English cases of shared goodwill the number of traders between whom the goodwill protected by a passing off action was shared had been two, although in the United States in 1893 there had been a case, *Pilsbury Washburn Flour Mills v Eagle*, 86 Fed. Rep. 608 in which the successful complainants to the number of seven established their several proprietary rights in the goodwill attaching to the use of a particular geographical description to distinguish their wares from those of other manufacturers.

It seems to me, however, as it seemed to Danckwerts J., that the principle must be the same whether the class of which each member is severally entitled to the goodwill which attaches to a particular term as descriptive of his goods, is large or small. The larger it is the broader must be the range and quality of products to which the descriptive term used by the members of the class has been applied, and the more difficult it must be to show that the term has acquired a public reputation and goodwill as denoting a product endowed with recognisable qualities which distinguish it from others of inferior reputation that compete with it in the same market. The larger the class the more difficult it must also be for an individual member of it to show that the goodwill of his own business has sustained more than minimal damage as a result of deceptive use by another trader of the widely shared descriptive term. As respects subsequent additions to the class, mere entry into the market would not give any right of action for passing off; the new entrant must have himself used the descriptive term long enough on the market in connection with his own goods and have traded successfully enough to have built up a goodwill for his business.

For these reasons the familiar argument that to extend the ambit of an actionable wrong beyond that to which effect has demonstrably been given in the previous cases would open the floodgates or, more ominously, a Pandora's box of litigation leaves me unmoved when it is sought to be applied to the actionable wrong of passing off.

I would hold the *Champagne* case to have been rightly decided and in doing so would adopt the words of Danckwerts J. where he said (at [1960] R.P.C. 31):

"There seems to be no reason why such licence (*ibid.* to do a deliberate act which causes damage to the property of another person) should be given to a person competing in trade, who seeks to attach to his product a name or description with which it has no natural association, so as to make use of the reputation and goodwill which has been gained by a product genuinely indicated by the name or description. In my view, it ought not to matter that the persons truly entitled to describe their goods by the name and description are a class producing goods in a certain locality, and not merely one individual. The description is part of their goodwill and a right of property. I do not believe that the law of passing off, which arose to prevent unfair trading, is so limited in scope".

In the *Champagne* case the descriptive term referred to the geographical provenance of the goods, and the class entitled to the goodwill in the term was accordingly restricted to those supplying on the English market goods produced in the locality indicated by it. Something similar was true in the *Sherry* case where the word "Sherry" as descriptive of a type of wine unless it was accompanied by some qualifying geographical adjective was held to denote wine produced by the solera method in the province of Jerez de la Frontera in Spain and the class entitled to the goodwill in the word was restricted to suppliers on the English market of wine produced in that province. In the *Scotch Whisky* case the product with which the case was primarily concerned was blended whisky and the class entitled to the goodwill in the descriptive term "Scotch Whisky" was not restricted to traders who dealt in whisky that had been blended in Scotland but extended to suppliers of blended whisky wherever the blending process took place provided that the ingredients of their product consisted exclusively of whiskies that had been distilled in Scotland. But the fact that in each of these first three cases the descriptive name under which goods of a particular type or composition were marketed by the plaintiffs among others happened to have geographical connotations is in my view without significance. If a product of a particular character or composition has been marketed under a descriptive name and under that name has gained a public reputation which distinguishes it from competing products of different composition, I can see no reason in principle or logic why the goodwill in the name of those entitled to make use of it should be protected by the law against deceptive use of the name by competitors, if it denotes a product of which the ingredients come from a particular locality, but should lose that protection if the ingredients of the product, however narrowly identified, are not restricted as to their geographic provenance. Yet in view of the findings of fact by Goulding J. to which I have already referred, this is the only way in which the instant case can be distinguished from the *Champagne, Sherry* and *Scotch Whisky* cases.

His Lordship then considered Native Guano v Sewage Manure *(1891) 8 R.P.C. 125, HL in which the plaintiff failed to prevent a competitor from calling his product "native guano" (a fertilizer made from human excreta). On this, the Court of Appeal had relied in refusing to accord protection to "advocaat". Lord Diplock considered that the case did not involve proof of a relevant mis-representation and that certain wider dicta, if still acceptable, would be in conflict with the* Champagne *case. In his view, that case could not be confined to the name of a product made by a particular class of producers. He continued:*

My Lords, the class of producers who could make "champagne" and whose right to use that word to describe their product on the English market formed a valuable part of their goodwill was a large one, much larger than the class with which the instant case is concerned, for it embraced everyone who engaged in the business of producing in the Champagne district, which is extensive, by the champenois method from grapes grown in the district and the class was capable of enlargement by the inclusion of anyone who chose to set up a new wine-producing business of that kind there. It is true that the whole process for making the finished product would have to be undertaken in the Champagne district; but this, as I have already pointed out, was not so in the *Sherry* case where bottling of the wine produced from grapes grown in the province of Jerez de la Frontera and blended by the solera method there need not take place in Spain: nor was it so in the *Scotch Whisky* case where even the blending of malt and grain whiskies provided they were distilled in Scotland need not take place in that country.

Of course it is necessary to be able to identify with reasonable precision the members of the class of traders of whose products a particular word or name has become so distinctive as to make their right to use it truthfully as descriptive of their product a valuable part of the goodwill of each of them; but it is the reputation that that type of product itself has gained in the market by reason of its recognisable and distinctive qualities that has generated the relevant goodwill. So if one can define with reasonable precision the type of product that has acquired the reputation, one can identify the members of the class entitled to share in the goodwill as being all those traders who have supplied and still supply to the English market a product which possesses those recognisable and distinctive qualities.

It cannot make any difference in principle whether the recognisable and distinctive qualities by which the reputation of the type of product has been gained are the result of its having been made in, or from ingredients produced in, a particular locality or are the result of its having been made from particular ingredients regardless of their provenance: though a geographical limitation may make it easier (a) to define the type of product; (b) to establish that it has qualities which are recognisable and distinguish it from every other type of product that competes with it in the market and which have gained for it in that market a reputation and goodwill; and (c) to establish that the plaintiff's own business will suffer more than minimal damage to its goodwill by the defendant's misrepresenting his product as being of that type.

In the instant case it is true that all but a very small portion of the alcoholic egg drink which gained for the name "Advocaat" a reputation and goodwill upon the English market, was imported from the Netherlands where, in order to bear that name, the ingredients from which it was made had to conform to the requirements of official regulations applicable to it in that country; but that is merely coincidental, for it is not suggested that an egg and spirit drink made in broad conformity with the Dutch official recipe for "Advocaat", wherever it is made or its ingredients produced, is not endowed with the same recognisable and distinctive qualities as have gained for "Advocaat" its reputation and goodwill in the English market.

So, on the findings of fact by Goulding J. to which I referred at the beginning of this speech, the type of product that has gained for the name "Advocaat" on the English market the reputation and goodwill of which Keeling's are seeking to take advantage by mis-representing that their own product is of that type, is defined by reference to the nature of its ingredients irrespective of their origin. The class of traders of whose respective businesses the right to describe their products as "Advocaat" forms a valuable part of their goodwill are those who have supplied and are supplying on the English market an egg and spirit drink in broad conformity with an identifiable recipe. The members of that class are easily identified and very much fewer in number than in the *Champagne*, *Sherry* or *Scotch Whisky* cases. Warnink with 75 per cent of the trade have a very substantial stake in the goodwill of the name "Advocaat" and their business has been shown to have suffered serious injury as a result of Keeling's putting on the English market in competition with Warnink and at a cheaper price an egg and wine based drink which they miscall "Advocaat" instead of Egg Flip which is its proper name.

My Lords, all the five characteristics that I have earlier suggested must be present to create a valid cause of action in passing off today were present in the instant case. Prima facie, as the law stands today, I think the presence of those characteristics is enough, unless there is also present in the case some exceptional feature which justifies, on grounds of public policy, withholding from a person who has suffered injury in consequence of the deception practised on prospective customers or consumers of his product a remedy in law against the deceiver. On the facts found by the judge, and I stress their importance, I can find no such exceptional feature in the instant case.

I would allow this appeal and restore the injunction granted by Goulding J.

In a concurring speech, Lord Fraser of Tullybelton stated:

It is essential for the plaintiff in a passing off action to show at least the following facts:

(1) that his business consists of, or includes, selling in England a class of goods to which the particular trade name applies;

(2) that the class of goods is clearly defined, and that in the minds of the public, or a section of the public, in England, the trade name distinguishes that class from other similar goods;

(3) that because of the reputation of the goods, there is goodwill attached to the name;

(4) that he, the plaintiff, as a member of the class of those who sell the goods, is the owner of goodwill in England which is of substantial value;

(5) that he has suffered, or is really likely to suffer, substantial damage to his property in the goodwill by reason of the defendants selling goods which are falsely described by the trade name to which the goodwill is attached.

Lords Dilhorne, Salmon and Scarman concurred in both speeches.

5.1.1.5   *Cadbury Schweppes v Pub Squash* [1981] R.P.C. 429, JC

The plaintiffs launched a lemon squash under the name "Solo" in yellow cans with a medallion that bore a general resemblance to many beer-cans. Intensive and successful television advertising suggested (i) that it resembled squash sold in pubs in former times and (ii) that it was thoroughly masculine to have as a drink. Some months later the defendant brought out a similar drink, also in yellow cans, under the name "Pub Squash" and it conducted a similar, though smaller publicity campaign. Soon afterwards, the plaintiffs' market slumped by 16 per cent. This conduct was alleged to constitute passing off.

Lord Scarman (for the Judicial Committee):

It is unnecessary to explore the law in any depth, because it is now accepted by both sides that the issue in the case is whether in promoting its product the respondent so confused or deceived the market that it passed its product off as the product of the appellants. Nevertheless the case presents one feature which is not to be found in the earlier case law. The passing off of which the appellants complain depends to a large extent on the deliberate adoption by the respondent of an advertising campaign based on themes and slogans closely related to those which the appellants had developed and made familiar to the market in the radio and television advertising of their product. Does confusion or deception, if it be shown to arise from such an advertising campaign, amount to a passing off? To answer the question it is necessary to consider the modern character of tort.

After referring to the "Advocaat" case (above, 5.1.1.4) and Hornsby Building v Sydney Building [1978] 52 A.L.J.R. 392 (High Court of Australia) at 396–97 (per Stephen J.), he continued:

The width of the principle now authoritatively recognised by the High Court of Australia and the House of Lords is, therefore, such that the tort is no longer anchored, as in its early nineteenth century formulation, to the name or trade mark of a product or business. It is wide enough to encompass other descriptive material, such as slogans or visual images, which radio, television or newspaper advertising campaigns can lead the market to associate with a plaintiff's product, provided always that such descriptive material has become part of the goodwill of the product. And the test is whether the product has derived from the advertising a distinctive character which the market recognises.

But competition must remain free; and competition is safeguarded by the necessity for the plaintiff to prove that he has built up an "intangible property right" in the advertised descriptions of his product, or, in other words, that he has succeeded by such methods in giving his product a distinctive character accepted by the market. A defendant, however, does no wrong by entering a market created by another and there competing with its creator. The line may be difficult to draw; but, unless it is drawn, competition will be stifled. The test applied by Powell J. in the instant case was to inquire whether the consuming public was confused or misled by the get-up, the formula or the advertising of the respondent's product into thinking that it was the appellants' product. And he held on the facts that the public was not deceived. Their Lordships do not think that his approach in law (save in one respect, as will later appear) to the central problem of the case can be faulted. The real question in the appeal is, therefore, one of fact, whether the judge erred in the inferences he drew from the admitted primary facts.

The appellants' alternative case of unfair trading irrespective of whether the market was deceived or confused into mistaking the respondent's product for that of the appellants' need not be considered by the Board, since the appellants now restrict themselves to a case based on such confusion. For such a case to succeed it would be necessary to show that the law of Australia has developed a tort of unfair competition along the lines suggested in the well-known decision of the United States Supreme Court, *International News Service v Associated Press*, 248 U.S. 215 (1918) at 241–242.

His Lordship quoted from the principal judgment of Pitney J. He reviewed the trial judge's findings on the evidence and refused to depart from them: there had been no significant confusion or deception at the point of sale which was not immediately corrected; it was not established that the public associated yellow cans only with "Solo", and the themes in the television advertising had not become distinctive of the plaintiff's product.

5.1.1.6   *Reckitt & Coleman v Borden* [1990] R.P.C. 341, HL at 406

For the facts of the case and a further extract, see below, para. 5.1.3.1.

Lord Oliver:

Although your Lordships were referred in the course of the argument to a large number of reported cases, this is not a branch of the law in which reference to other cases is of any real assistance except analogically. It has been observed more than once that the questions which arise are, in general, questions of fact. Neither the appellants nor respondents contend that the principles of law are in any doubt. The law of passing off can be summarised in one short general proposition—no man may pass off his goods as those of another. More specifically, it may be expressed in terms of the elements which the plaintiff in such an action has to prove in order to succeed. These are three in number. First, he must establish a goodwill or reputation attached to the goods or services which he supplies in the mind of the purchasing public by association with the identifying "get-up" (whether it consists simply of a brand name or a trade description, or the individual features of labelling or packaging) under which his particular goods or services are offered to the public, such that the get-up is recognised by the public as distinctive specifically of the plaintiff's good or services. Secondly, he must demonstrate a misrepresentation by the defendant to the public (whether or not intentional) leading or likely to lead the public to believe that goods or services offered by him are the goods or services of the plaintiff. Whether the public is aware of the plaintiff's identity as the manufacturer or supplier of the goods or services is immaterial, as long as they are identified with a particular source which is in fact the plaintiff. For example, if the public is accustomed to rely upon a particular brand name in purchasing goods or a particular description, it matters not at all that there is little or no public awareness of the identity of the proprietor of the brand name. Thirdly, he must demonstrate that he suffers or, in a *quia timet* action that he is likely to suffer, damage by reason of the erroneous belief engendered by the defendant's misrepresentation that the source of the defendant's goods or services is the same as the source of those offered by the plaintiff.

5.1.2   Passing Off: Claimant's Reputation

5.1.2.1   *Star Industrial v Yap Kwee Kor* [1975] F.S.R. 256, PC

The appellant-plaintiff, a Hong Kong company, manufactured toothbrushes which it sold in Singapore under the mark "Ace Brand" with accompanying device. This mark was not registered in Singapore. In October 1965, the Singapore Government imposed an import duty which rendered the appellant's trade unprofitable. In 1968, the respondent, a Singapore toothbrush manufacturer, changed its name to the New Star Industrial Co and adopted the appellant's mark for its brushes. These proceedings for an injunction against passing-off did not commence until 1971.

In 1968, the appellant formed a jointly-owned subsidiary in Singapore and granted it exclusive use of the mark.

Lord Diplock:

At common law this right of user of the mark or get-up in Singapore was incapable of being assigned except with the goodwill of that part of the business of the Hong Kong Company in connection with which it had previously been used. So, if despite the temporary cesser of the Hong Kong Company's business in Singapore after the import duty on toothbrushes had been imposed in 1965, it still retained—as well it might (*cf. Mouson & Co v Boehm* (1884) 26 Ch.D. 398)—a residue of goodwill capable of being revived in 1968, any right of property in that goodwill would have passed to the Singapore Company under the agreement. The Singapore Company is not a party to these proceedings and their Lordships express no view as to what rights, if any, it would have been entitled to enforce against the respondent if it had been the plaintiff in a passing-off action brought against him.

Their Lordships mention this, however, because the burden of the appellant's argument before the Board has been that the common law ought to provide the Hong Kong Company itself with a remedy against the respondent for the financial loss which it will sustain in the form of reduced dividends and royalties receivable from the Singapore Company, as a result of the respondent's piracy of the mark or get-up. ...

[One argument] is that the case of *Warwick Tyre Co Ltd v New Motor and General Rubber Co Ltd* [1910] 1 Ch. 248; (1910) 27 R.P.C. 161; 101 L.T. 889) is authority for the proposition that at common law a person who, in a business carried on by him, has used an unregistered mark or get-up to which goodwill has become attached, thereby requires a property in the mark or get-up which he may exploit by conferring for reward upon some other person the right to use the mark or get-up in his own business: and that this method of exploitation of the mark or get-up is entitled to protection at common law in an action at his suit for passing off, notwithstanding that he himself has ceased to carry on the case the business in which the mark or get-up is used. In the *Warwick* case the mark "Warwick" had originally been used by the plaintiff company upon tyres which it manufactured and sold itself. At the time when it brought a passing-off action to restrain the use of the mark by a third party it had entered into an agreement with another company ("The Dunlop Company") under which tyres bearing the mark "Warwick" were manufactured and sold for it by the Dunlop Company. It is not possible from any of the three reports of the case to discover what were the terms of the agreement between the plaintiff company and the

Dunlop Company, but from the language used by Neville J. in his judgment the inference is that the Dunlop Company had been appointed to act as selling agent for the plaintiff company for an agreed period. Whether upon the particular, but unknown, facts of the case the judge's decision in favour of the plaintiff company was right in law it is not now possible to say; but, in any event, the judge's reasoning is vitiated by the fact that it is based upon the assumption, later rejected by the House of Lords in the *Gamage* case, that what was entitled to protection by a passing-off action was a right of property in the mark itself—not a right of property in the business or goodwill in connection with which the mark was being used. In their Lordships' view the *Warwick* case cannot now be treated as authority in support of the appellant's argument.

5.1.2.2 *Ad-Lib Club v Granville* [1972] R.P.C. 673, Pennycuick V.C.

In a passing-off action the plaintiff company, which had run a successful night club called the "Ad-Lib Club" from 1964 to 1966 sought an interlocutory injunction to restrain the defendant from carrying on business as proprietor of a discotheque night club under the name or style "Ad-Lib". The plaintiff company's evidence was that it had been forced to discontinue running its own club due to noise emitting from the club's premises to those of neighbours, which had resulted in the grant of an injunction against it. Since 1966 the plaintiff company had been seeking alternative premises in order to reopen its club, but without success. The defendant, who did not file evidence or appear on the motion, had announced that a club called the "Ad-Lib Club" was opening on December 11. The plaintiff company claimed that it still possessed goodwill to which the name "Ad-Lib" attached, that members of the public would be likely to regard the new club as a continuation of the plaintiff's club, and that an interlocutory injunction should be granted.

Pennycuick V.C.:

The basis of the present action, to quote the words of Lord Parker in the case of *Spalding (A.G.) & Bros v A.W. Gamage Limited* (above, 5.1.1.2), is a proprietory right not so much in the name itself but in the goodwill established through use of the name in connection with the plaintiff's, here, establishment. I have no doubt that on the evidence the plaintiff company had by the end of 1965 established a substantial goodwill to which the name "Ad-Lib Club" was attached and that that name had become distinctive of the plaintiff company's establishment. It follows beyond a doubt that at the end of 1965 any other person had sought to use the name "Ad-Lib" in connection with a club of this character that would have been a plain invasion of the plaintiff company's goodwill. The question which is raised by the present action is simply whether by the interval of some five years which has passed since the plaintiff company's club was closed the plaintiff company must be regarded as having ceased to have any goodwill to which this name could fairly be said to be attached.

The matter is put in Halsbury's Laws of England (3rd ed.), Vol. 38, p.59, in these terms:

> "Since the right of action for passing off is based on injury to goodwill, a person who has ceased to carry on the business in which a mark or name was used, or has discontinued the use of the name or mark in his business, cannot maintain an action for passing off in respect of the name or mark, unless, it seems, he can prove that the name or mark retains a residual renown as denoting his goods".

In support of that statement there is cited the case of *Norman Kark Publications Ltd v Odhams Press Ltd* [1962] 1 All E.R. 636; [1962] R.P.C. 163 in which the first paragraph of the headnote reads:

> "In an action to restrain the use of a magazine or newspaper title on the ground of passing off the plaintiff must establish that, at the date of the user by the defendant of which the plaintiff complains, he has a proprietory right in the goodwill of the name, *viz.*, that the name remains distinctive of some product of his, so that the use of the name by the defendant is calculated to deceive: but a mere intention on the part of the plaintiff not to abandon a name is not enough".

Wilberforce J. went at length into the principles underlying proprietory right in goodwill and annexation of a name to goodwill and the laws of the right to protection of a name and on the facts of that particular case he held that the plaintiff company had lost its right in respect of the name *Today* as part of the title of a magazine.

It seems to me clear on principle and on authority that where a trader ceases to carry on his business he may nonetheless retain for at any rate some period of time the goodwill attached to that business. Indeed it is obvious. He may wish to reopen the business or he may wish to sell it. It further seems to me clear in principle and on authority that so long as he does retain the goodwill in connection with his business he must also be able to enforce his rights in respect of any name which is attached to that goodwill. It must be a question of fact and degree at what point in time a trader who has either temporarily or permanently closed down his business should be treated as no longer having any goodwill in that business or in any name attached to it which he is entitled to have protected by law.

In the present case, it is quite true that the plaintiff company has no longer carried on the business of a club, so far as I know, for five years. On the other hand, it is said that the plaintiff company on the evidence continues to be regarded as still possessing goodwill to which this name "Ad-Lib Club" is attached. It does, indeed, appear firstly that the defendant must have chosen the name "Ad-Lib Club" by reason of the reputation which the plaintiff company's "Ad-Lib" acquired. He has not filed any evidence giving any other reason for the selection of that name and the inference is overwhelming that he has only selected that name because it has a reputation. In the second place, it appears from the newspaper cuttings which have been exhibited that members of the public are likely to regard the new club as a continuation of the plaintiff company's club. The two things are linked up. That is no doubt the reason why the defendant has selected this name.

It will be observed that there is no question here of a name referring to a locality, type of activity or anything of that kind, unless one considers "Ad-Lib" as a form of activity.

I think that the proper inference to be drawn from the evidence is that the plaintiff company has indeed a residual goodwill to which this name is attached and that that goodwill is an asset of value in the hands of the plaintiff company which it is entitled to exploit, if it is so minded, in future and which it cannot be said to have abandoned. That being the position, the name is something which it is entitled to have protected by injunction.

When one comes to the balance of convenience, there is a balance which, as far as I can see—and I have only the plaintiff company's evidence before me—is wholly in favour of granting immediate interlocutory relief. It is pointed out and it is plainly right that if the defendant once opens his club under the name of "Ad-Lib Club" the plaintiff company's goodwill in that name will be gone and gone for good. On the other hand, apart from, I suppose, such promotion expenditure as had been incurred it cannot be any hardship to the defendant to be restrained from carrying on his new club under a name which he can only have selected because of the reputation in that name which resulted from the successful activities of the plaintiff company.

5.1.2.3   *Anheuser-Busch v Budejovicky Budvar* [1984] F.S.R. 413, CA

The plaintiffs had brewed and sold "Budweiser" beer in the U.S. for more than a century, taking their inspiration from the brewing techniques of the Czech town Budweis (now Ceske Budejovice). The defendants were successors to a brewing business in that town started in 1895. From 1960 they used "Budweiser" as a mark for their beer when exported from Czechoslovakia with labels in English, French and German. By a compromise agreement in 1911 between the plaintiffs and the defendants' predecessors (and with them the other brewing company of Budweis), the plaintiffs acquired exclusive rights in the mark outside Europe.

The plaintiffs had sold no significant quantity of their beer to the general public in the UK before 1974 and until 1980 sold only small quantities (thereafter it began to build a regular export trade). Well before this, however, their beer had been regularly supplied in the UK to US diplomatic and military personnel through US embassy and PX (military base) outlets. At the end of 1973, the defendants began a successful export business in the Czech beer to the UK. There was considerable evidence that as a result the public had become confused about the source of "Budweiser" beer in the UK. The plaintiffs sued the defendants for passing off.

Oliver L.J.:

The critical question, Mr Kentridge [for the plaintiffs] submits—and this must, in my judgment, be right—is what was the position when the defendants first entered the English market with their Budweiser beer in 1973/4? The learned judge's own findings establish that the plaintiffs already had by then a reputation with a substantial number of people in this country, but he regarded the plaintiffs as not themselves being in the market, and he attributed no significance to any goodwill attached to the sales of the plaintiffs' beer through the P.X. as a property which might be affected by the defendants' activities and which the plaintiffs might be entitled to protect. In this, Mr Kentridge submits, he was wrong, and it is the significance to be attached to these sales which forms the real bone of contention between the parties and which is, to my mind, the only really substantial point in the case. The question, in its simplest form, may be expressed thus: how far is it an essential ingredient of a successful claim in passing off that the plaintiff should have established in this country a business in which his goods or services are sold to the general public on the open market?

Oliver L.J. then referred to the characteristics of passing off listed by Lord Diplock and Lord Fraser in the "Advocaat" case (above, 5.1.1.4). He continued:

The substantial submission made on behalf of the defendants, however, is that the plaintiffs in this case do not satisfy Lord Fraser's first, third, fourth and fifth requirements. When the defendants first started to trade here, it is submitted, the plaintiffs had no business here and accordingly no goodwill in any relevant sense, and they could not thus suffer any damage from the defendants' activities which would ground an action here.

As mentioned above, Whitford J. found as a fact that the plaintiffs' name Budweiser was well known to a substantial number of people in this country (leaving aside for the moment US servicemen temporarily resident here) as a name associated with the beer brewed by the plaintiffs in the United States. The plaintiffs can thus legitimately claim that before the defendants' entry into the market here, they had a reputation as the brewers of a beer, Budweiser, with a substantial section of the public. The question is whether this reputation associated with a beer which, for practical purposes, nobody could buy here, constituted a goodwill in any relevant sense.

In the "*Advocaat*" case, Lord Diplock, at 744, adverted to the fact that for a trader to establish his right as plaintiff he "must have himself used the descriptive term long enough *on the market* in connection with his own goods and have traded successfully enough to have built up a goodwill for his business" (emphasis supplied). This was, of course, said in the context of a claim by a group of traders all engaged in selling goods under a particular descriptive term, but it emphasises the point that goodwill (as opposed to mere reputation) does not exist here apart from a business carried on here.

This emerges with even greater clarity from the decision of the Privy Council in *Star Industrial Co Limited v Yap Kwee Kor* (above, 5.1.2.1). In that case it was quite clear that the defendant in Singapore had quite deliberately adopted the market and get-up formerly used there by the plaintiffs in connection with their goods. But the facts were that the plaintiffs had discontinued their trade in Singapore three years before, and had no intention of resuming it. They had in fact assigned any residual goodwill that they had, and their rights, in the mark formerly used on their goods to a subsidiary company which was not a party to the action. Thus the action failed. Lord Diplock, in delivering the judgment of the Board, said:

> "A passing-off action is a remedy for the invasion of a right of property not in the mark, name or get-up improperly used, but in the business or goodwill likely to be injured by the misrepresentation made by passing off one person's goods as the goods of another. Goodwill, as the subject of proprietory rights, is incapable of subsisting by itself. It has no independent existence apart from the business to which it is attached. It is local in character and divisible; if the business is carried on in several countries a separate goodwill attaches to it in each. So when the business is abandoned in one country in which it has acquired a goodwill, the goodwill in that country perishes with it although the business may continue to be carried on in other countries".

The principle here enunciated by Lord Diplock is not, and indeed cannot very well be, disputed, but the question, to which no very clear answer emerges from the authorities, is what form of activity on the part of the plaintiff is required before it can be said that he has a "business" here to which goodwill can attach?

That the mere existence of a trading reputation in this country is insufficient in the absence of customers here is well exemplified by *The Athletes' Foot Marketing Associates Inc v Cobra Sports Ltd* [1980] R.P.C. 343, where Walton J. helpfully reviewed all the earlier cases. That case bears some similarity to the present in this respect that although the plaintiffs (these like the plaintiffs in the instant case) had expended considerable sums in advertising, all their advertising had been in the United States and was directed to the American market. There, as here, there was an awareness of the plaintiff's trade name and trading activities in a substantial section of the public in England, as a result of over-spill publicity through American journals circulating here. There were, however, no customers in England, because the plaintiffs' activities had got no further than the taking of preparatory steps for setting up business here.

The principle was expressed by Walton J. at 350 as follows:

"... as a matter of principle, no trader can complain of passing off as against him in any territory—and it will usually be defined by national boundaries, although it is well conceivable in the modern world that it will not—in which he has no customers, nobody who is in a trade relation with him. This will normally shortly be expressed by saying that he does not carry on any trade in that particular country ... but the inwardness of it will be that he has no customers in that country: no people who buy his goods or make use of his services (as the case may be) there".

This is, I think, a helpful statement, but needs, in the light of the authorities, to be approached with the caveat that "customers" must not be read restrictively as confined to persons who are in a direct contractual relationship with the plaintiff, but includes persons who buy his goods in the market.

In *Société Anonyme des Anciens Etablissements Panhard et Levassor v Panhard Levassor Motor Co Limited* (1901) 18 R.P.C. 405, the plaintiffs obtained an injunction against passing off. They had no business in England nor any agency here. Indeed their cars could not lawfully be imported into England without the licence of certain English patentees. There was, however, an English market for their cars in the sense that there was an importer (presumably with the appropriate licences) in England who bought their cars for re-sale and there were individuals who from time to time bought their cars in Paris and imported them into England. Farwell J. observed that "England was one of their markets". Thus here the sale of the plaintiffs' goods by a third party and purchase and importation by English residents was regarded as a sufficient business to support the action.

Poiret v Jules Poiret Ltd (1920) 37 R.P.C. 177 was another case in which the successful foreign plaintiff had no actual place of business in England, but he exhibited his goods here and sold to customers here either directly or through an agent.

The case of *Sheraton Corp of America v Sheraton Motels Limited* [1964] R.P.C. 202 may perhaps be said to represent the high water mark, for there the successful plaintiffs carried on no business in the United Kingdom save that bookings for their hotels abroad were effected through an office which they maintained in London and through travel agents in this country. The case is, however, a somewhat slender authority, for it was a motion for an interlocutory injunction, and the decision really proceeded on the footing that the plaintiffs might succeed at the trial in establishing a goodwill which was entitled to protection and that the balance of convenience dictated that they should be protected in the meantime.

It is, however, clear that it is not every activity in this country which might loosely be called a "business" activity that qualifies as the carry on of a business here. *Alain Bernardin et Cie v Pavilion Properties* [1967] R.P.C. 581 is a case in point. There the plaintiffs, who carried on a restaurant business in Paris under the title "The Crazy Horse Saloon" had for many years publicised their establishment by publicity material distributed to tourist organisations and hotels in the United Kingdom. They failed to restrain the carrying on by the defendants of a restaurant in London under the same name. Pennycuick J. referred to the classic statement of Lord Macnaghten in *C.I.R. v Muller & Co's Margarine Ltd* [1901] A.C. 217:

"Goodwill has no independent existence. It cannot subsist by itself. It must be attached to a business. Destroy the business and the goodwill perishes with it, though elements remain which may perhaps be gathered up and be revived again".

He also referred to the judgment of Jenkins L.J. in *Oertli AG v Bowman (London) Ltd* [1957] R.P.C. 388, in which he said:

"It is of course essential to the success of any claim in respect of passing off based on the use of a given mark or get-up that the plaintiff should be able to show that the disputed mark or get-up has become by user in this country distinctive of the plaintiff's goods so that the use in relation to any goods of the kind dealt in by the plaintiff of that mark or get-up will be understood by the trade and public in this country as meaning that the goods are the plaintiffs' goods".

Pennycuick J. observed (584):

"The statement in the judgment of Jenkins L.J. which I have just read unequivocally requires user to be in this country. That it seems to me is what one would expect: that the trader cannot acquire goodwill in this country without some sort of user in this country. His user may take many forms and in certain cases very slight activities have been held to suffice. On the other hand, I do not think that the mere sending to this country by a foreign trader of advertisements advertising his establishment abroad could fairly be treated as user in this country ... He may acquire a reputation in a wide sense in the sense of returning travellers speaking highly of that establishment, but it seems to me that those matters, although they may represent reputation in some wide sense, fall far short of user in this country and are not sufficient to establish reputation in the sense material for the purpose of a passing off action".

That case was followed by Brightman J., as he then was, in *Amway Corp v Eurway International Ltd* [1974] R.P.C. 82, where the only activity relied on by the plaintiffs apart from preliminary steps for commencing business were what were referred to as "minor trading activities". Reliance was also placed on advertisements appearing in American journals circulating in England, such as the *National Geographic Magazine*. Brightman J. held that this activity was entirely inadequate to support a passing off action based on goodwill in this country.

On the other hand, in *Globelegance BV v Sarkissian* [1974] R.P.C. 603, where an internationally known fashion designer had exhibited in England, had sold patterns here which were made up into dresses sold under his trade name, and had supplied a modest, though not insubstantial, number of ties for resale here by retailers. Templeman J. (as he then was) was prepared to hold that these activities were sufficient to constitute the carrying on of business here.

The plaintiffs in the instant case submit that they are not in any difficulty. They have proved, they submit, the existence here of a reputation with a substantial section of the public, and they have adduced evidence of sales here to such members of the public as have been admitted to bases and Embassy canteens and bars and as have attended from time to time those open days and air displays which have been organised at United States Air Force bases.

I confess that for my part I am quite unable to treat these sporadic and occasional sales as constituting in any real sense the carrying on by the plaintiffs of a business in this country. The fact is that no ordinary member of the public, whether he be indigenous or a foreign tourist, could consider himself a customer in this country for the plaintiffs' beer.

That, however, is not the end of the matter. If it is right, as I believe that it is, to regard the occasional and limited availability of the plaintiffs' beer to members of the British public in the United Kingdom as no more than a fortuitous overspill from the main area of supply, there remains the fact that the plaintiffs were in fact supplying to the P.X. for consumption in this country a rough average of 5,000,000 cans of beer ever year—a supply which had begun well before the defendants' appearance and was continuing in 1973 when the defendants first started marketing in Great Britain under the name "Budweiser". The critical question upon which this appeal hinges seems to me to be whether this supply can properly be considered as the carrying on of a business in England creating a goodwill in this country which requires to be protected from the defendants' activities. If it does, then the occasional supply to non-Service personnel adds nothing. If it does not, then it cannot, as it seems to me, be elevated by such occasional outside supply into something which it was not.

Now Mr Kentridge has, throughout his clear and helpful address to the court, repeatedly referred to goodwill in the words of Lord Macnaghten in the *Muller's Margarine* case [1901] A.C. 217 as "the attractive force which brings in custom". But one asks oneself "what custom in this country in 1973 was brought in by the knowledge of members of the indigenous British public of the plaintiffs' Budweiser beer?" And the answer must be that there was none, because however attractive they may have found the idea of drinking the plaintiffs' beer, they could not get it. In so far, therefore, as anyone was misled by the defendants' use of the name "Budweiser", the plaintiffs could suffer no damage either by loss of sales, for there were none at that time and none were contemplated, nor by loss of reputation, because if there was any such loss (which seems highly improbable) the reputation was quite unconnected with either an ability or a willingness to supply.

It may perhaps be tested in this way. Suppose an American product which is well known in America, but is and remains totally unknown to the general public in this country. It is, however, sold in the P.X. stores on American bases here but nowhere else. Is it credibly arguable that this could create a business goodwill in this country which would entitle the American manufacturer to a nationwide injunction against selling under a similar name in a market in which he does not sell and in which the name has never previously been used or heard of? It is, of course, true that some of the cases to which reference has been made above indicate that a business may be established by relatively modest acts. Nevertheless, all those cases have this feature in common, that the sales relied on were sales on the open market to the public generally. None was concerned with what we have here, namely, sales on a closed and separate market to a particular section of the public only, having the qualification of belonging to or being employed by the United States Services.

In my judgment, although for rather different reasons, the judge was right in the conclusion that he reached that both the defendants and the plaintiffs were entitled to use the name Budweiser in this country, and I would therefore dismiss the appeal.

O'Connor and Dillon L.JJ. delivered concurring judgments.

5.1.2.4   *Bristol Conservatories Ltd v Conservatories Custom Built Ltd* [1989] R.P.C. 455, CA

The plaintiffs and the defendants were competitors in the supply of ornamental windows and conservatories in Wales and the West of England. One of the plaintiffs' salesmen left to join the defendants, taking with him a portfolio of photographs of conservatories designed and built by the plaintiffs. The defendants' salesmen used copies of the portfolio to promote the defendants' business. The portfolio did not mention the plaintiffs' name or otherwise refer to them, but the plaintiffs nevertheless claimed that its use by the defendants amounted to passing off. Ralph Gibson L.J. (with whom the other members of the court agreed) relied on Samuelson v Producers Distributing Co Ltd *(1931) 48 R.P.C. 580 (above, 5.1.1.3), and* Plomien Fuel Economiser Co Ltd v National School of Salesmanship Ltd *(1943) 60 R.P.C. 209 in finding that the plaintiffs had a valid cause of action:*

I shall take first the case of *Samuelson* ... The facts were these. The plaintiff wrote a theatrical sketch. It was performed before the King and Queen at a Command Performance and received good press notices. The defendants made a film similar in some respects to the plaintiff's sketch, but it was a new composition. The defendants advertised their film by deliberate modification of the press notices so as to make them appear to refer to the film. There was no reference to the plaintiff in the advertisement. It was submitted for the defendants that the claim could not lie in passing off because that form of action required a representation whereby other persons are induced to believe that the goods or the production of the defendants are the goods or production of the plaintiff.... Lord Hanworth in *Samuelson* rejected that submission. I read from his judgment at 588, where he said:

"It appears to me quite idle to say that this is not a passing off. What was the purpose of what I have described as a moulding of the observations contained in"—and I am now altering the words to shorten them—"[the press notices] ... they were adducing the success as appropriate to and belonging to their film ... when in truth and in fact it belonged to the plaintiff and his sketch ... That seems to me to amount to a notice or invitation: 'Come and see our film and when you have seen our film you will have seen the sketch which has been spoken of in the manner which is stated in the passages which appear in the advertisement'. It appears to me quite clear that this was an attempt to pretend that the defendants' sketch was the same as the sketch which had made Her Majesty the Queen laugh ... It is a passing off action and the ground on which I think the plaintiff is entitled to complain is that, as I have said, in substance he remains the author of this sketch ... and, if he was entitled to the authorship and the copyright and to the reproduction of his sketch, then the defendants have attempted to pass off and to make use of the atmosphere which belonged to the plaintiff, in favour of their production; and therefore it was right for the plaintiff to take proceedings".

Lawrence L.J. in that case agreed but put the matter in a way closer to the classic form of the action. He said, at 592:

"It is said that there was no passing off here, because the plaintiff had not yet made a film version of his sketch and therefore he had no goods which could have been represented by the defendants as being his. The plaintiff and his licensees had the exclusive right of making a film version of the sketch, and the defendant company, in effect, by the advertisement, said that their production was a film version of the plaintiff's sketch, thereby misleading the public concerned into the belief that the defendants' production was a production which was one which the plaintiff alone could have produced; in other words, that it was the plaintiff's production. To put it in other words, they were passing off on to the public their film production as being a film production of the plaintiff's sketch".

Ralph Gibson L.J. also referred to the passage from Romer L.J.'s judgment given above (5.1.1.3). He continued:

In my judgment, the principles applied by this court in that case are well capable of application to the facts alleged by the plaintiffs here. Lord Hanworth described the substance of the defendants' misrepresentation in *Samuelson*, as set out above, that if the persons to whom the advertisement was directed went to see the defendants' film, they would see the sketch which had been spoken of favourably in the press notices, but in fact they would not. In this case the substance of the misrepresentation by the defendants, as alleged by the plaintiffs, is fairly capable of being expressed thus: "If you order a conservatory from us you will be getting a conservatory designed, manufactured and constructed by the people who have earned the goodwill and reputation that properly belongs to the party which secured the orders and designed, manufactured and constructed the conservatories shown in these photographs. The conservatories shown in the photographs indicate the skill, the experience and the reputation of the party who designed and made them. That party is Custom Built. "But, of course, it was not. Just as Lord Hanworth considered that Samuelson was entitled to take proceedings, so, if the facts alleged are proved, the plaintiffs, in my judgment, should be entitled to take proceedings for relief.

Similarly as concerns Romer L.J.'s judgment, and the protection of a right of property which was likely to be injured by the misrepresentation alleged to have been made by Custom Built, that right of property was the right the invasion of which (to quote Lord Diplock in the *Warnink* case (at 741C) is the subject of passing off actions, namely "the property in the business or goodwill likely to be injured by the misrepresentation". Lord Diplock continued:

> "The concept of goodwill is in law a broad one which is perhaps best expressed in words used by Lord Macnaghten in *I.R.C. v Muller* [1901] A.C. 217 at 223–224. 'It is the benefit and advantage of the good name, reputation and connection of a business. It is the attractive force which brings in custom'".

There can, I think, be few better ways of demonstrating the good name and reputation of a business of designing and selling conservatories specially built to fit particular houses or buildings than a collection of photographs showing the work which the owners of the business have done. Romer L.J.'s view of the extent of the principle is also, in my judgment, capable of application to the facts alleged in this case.

Next, the *Plomien Fuel Economiser* case was also a decision of this court. The facts of that case can be described as follows.

> "The plaintiffs are manufacturers of a fuel economiser which has been marketed under the name 'Plomien'. The defendants, who at one time acted as sale agents for the plaintiffs ... broke that relationship and started themselves to market an economiser which was manufactured for them. It was in respect of their transactions in connection with the marketing of that economiser that the passing off action was brought ... the defendants engaged in a deliberate attempt to deceive by putting forward their economiser as being the same as the plaintiffs' ... they represented that certain tests which had been made were tests in connection with the defendants' economiser, whereas in fact they were tests in connection with the plaintiffs' economiser. They represented that certain economisers which had been fitted for a number of purchasers, and which were in fact the plaintiffs' economiser, were the defendants' economiser".

It was argued that no passing off had been shown notwithstanding the facts to which I have referred.

Lord Greene, in a judgment with which Luxmoore L.J. and du Parcq L.J. agreed, said, at 214 of the report:

> "It is perfectly true that there is no evidence that a single person who purchased an economiser from the defendants had ever heard of the plaintiffs; but in passing off there is no necessity that the person who is deceived should have known the name of the person who complains of the passing off. In many cases the name is not known at all. It is quite sufficient, in my opinion, to constitute passing off in fact, if a person being minded to obtain goods which are identified in his mind with a definite commercial source is led by false statements to accept goods coming from a different commercial source.

Now in the present case what was it that these defendants did? They deliberately induced customers to come to their shop for the purpose of purchasing goods of the same manufacture as those supplied to the satisfied customers named on the list which they circulated. That was quite clearly their intention, because otherwise what was the use of circulating that list?"

Then I omit certain words.

"Having got them in their shop, what do they do? They do not sell those customers the goods which those customers have come to buy; they sell them goods of their own manufacture, which are quite different, in the sense that they are not the required manufacture. If that is not passing off, I really do not know what is. It is perfectly true, and I am willing to assume, that not one single customer who went to the shop (I use the word 'shop' of course metaphorically, it was not a shop at all; it was done by orders by post and by travellers and so forth) had ever heard of the plaintiffs or ever heard that they put on the market an economiser. That, to my mind, matters not one bit when it is realised that those customers were coming with the intention of getting goods from a particular source, namely, the same source as those from which the satisfied customers had got their goods".

The principle applied in that case seems to me to be well applicable to the facts alleged by the plaintiffs. Custom Built, by their misrepresentation, were seeking to induce customers to purchase conservatories from them in order to get a conservatory from the commercial source which had designed and constructed the conservatories shown in the photographs. That was the purpose of Custom Built in showing the photographs and in claiming to have designed and made the conservatories there shown. If a customer ordered a conservatory from Custom Built in response to the misrepresentation—as it was the intention of Custom Built that he should—Custom Built would supply conservatories not of the stated commercial source but of their own manufacture. Lord Greene thought that would be passing off. With respect, so do I.

Ralph Gibson L.J. also dismissed an argument by the defendants that the only forms of actionable passing off were the "classic" form and the extended form established in the "Champagne" and "Sherry" cases and approved in the Advocaat case (see 5.1.1.4 and 5.1.3.4):

I see no reason to hold that their Lordships in the *Warnink* case expressly or by implication ruled that the tort of passing off outside the extended form approved and established by the actual decision in the *Warnink* case should be limited to the classic form of a trader representing his own goods as the goods of somebody else....

I am unable to accept that Lord Diplock, or their Lordships who agreed with him, can be taken to have intended to exclude from the protection of the law a trader injured by the sort of dishonest trading alleged or proved in such cases as *Samuelson*, or the *Plomien Fuel Economiser* case, or in this case. Nor do I think that Lord Fraser is to be taken as having intended to lay down essential requirements which would exclude from the ambit of the tort such cases which were not under consideration in the *Warnink* case itself.

5.1.2.5   *Hodgkinson & Corby Ltd v Wards Mobility Services Ltd* [1995] F.S.R. 169, Jacob J.

Under the trade mark "Roho" the plaintiff sold a cushion for use on wheelchairs, specially designed to prevent or aid in the cure of pressure sores. It was dis-

tinguished by a striking and memorable shape. The defendant proposed to sell a "lookalike" product under the trade mark "Flo'tair". The plaintiff claimed that sales of the defendant's copy would inevitably involve confusion and passing off and sought an injunction to prevent this. After setting out the facts Jacob J. continued:

I turn to consider the law and begin by identifying what is not the law. There is no tort of copying. There is no tort of taking a man's market or customers. Neither the market nor the customers are the plaintiff's to own. There is no tort of making use of another's goodwill as such. There is no tort of competition. I say this because at times the plaintiffs seemed close to relying on such torts. For instance, [counsel for the plaintiff] reminded me of the old adage "Anything worth copying is worth protecting".

At the heart of passing off lies deception or its likelihood, deception of the ultimate consumer in particular. Over the years passing off has developed from the classic case of the defendant selling his goods as and for those of the plaintiff to cover other kinds of deception, *e.g.* that the defendant's goods are the same as those of the plaintiff when they are not, *e.g. Combe International Ltd v Scholl (U.K.) Ltd* [1980] R.P.C. 1; or that the defendant's goods are the same as goods sold by a class of persons of which the plaintiff is a member when they are not, *e.g. Warnink (Erven) Besloten Vennootschap v J. Townend & Sons Ltd* [1980] R.P.C. 29; [above, 5.1.1.4]. Never has the tort shown even a slight tendency to stray beyond cases of deception. Were it to do so it would enter the field of honest competition, declared unlawful for some reason other than deceptiveness. Why there should be any such reason I cannot imagine. It would serve only to stifle competition.

The foundation of the plaintiff's case here must, therefore, lie in deception.

Now the ingredients of passing off are the "classical trinity" (*per* Nourse L.J. in the "*Parma Ham*" case, *Consorzio del Prosciutto di Parma v Marks & Spencer* [1991] R.P.C. 351, . . . namely (1) goodwill of the plaintiff, (2) misrepresentation by the defendant, (3) consequent damage. The plaintiff's problem of proof when there is no manifest badge of trade origin such as a trade mark becomes hard. This is so in the case of a descriptive or semi-descriptive word such as "Camel Hair". It is perhaps even more so where one is concerned simply with the appearance of the article with no self-evident trade origin frill or embellishment. For people are likely to buy the article because of what it is, not *in reliance* on any belief of any particular trade origin. This is so whether they buy it for its eye-appeal (*e.g.* glass dogs) or for what it does (*e.g.* the copy Rubik cube of *Polytechnika, etc. v Dallas Print Transfers Ltd* [1982] F.S.R. 529).

The plaintiff's problem of proof lies in relation to the first two items of the trinity, which are related. It is not good enough for him to show that his article is widely recognised—has a "reputation" in that general sense. The "Louis furniture" of *Jarman & Platt v Barget* [1977] F.S.R. 260 had virtually "captured the market" but that did not:

> begin to prove that a substantial number of the members of the public who buy those goods do so because they know of, or have any interest in, the particular source of the goods; or that they are attracted to buy those goods because of their knowledge or belief that they emanate from a particular maker: *per* Megaw L.J. (at 273).

Exactly the same thought is so clearly expressed by Judge Learned Hand in *Crescent Tool v Kilborn & Bishop* (1917) 247 F. 299, a case about a copy of an adjustable wrench widely sold and trade marked "Crescent." He said, after finding that no adjustable wrench of precisely the same character had ever appeared upon the market:

... all of these (*i.e.* cases where a secondary meaning has been shown) presuppose that the appearance of the article like its descriptive title in the true cases of "secondary" meaning has become associated in the public mind with the first comer as manufacturer or source, and, if a second comer imitates the article exactly, that the public will believe his goods have come from the first, and will buy, in part, at least, because of that deception. Therefore it is apparent that it is an absolute condition to any relief whatever that the plaintiff show that the appearance of his wares has in fact come to mean that some particular person—the plaintiff may not be individually known—makes them, and the public cares who does make them, and not merely for their appearance and structure. It will not be enough only to show how pleasing they are, because all the features of beauty or utility which commend them to the public are by hypothesis already in the public domain....

... The critical question of fact at the outset always is whether the public is moved in any degree to buy the article because of its source and what are the features by which it distinguishes that source. Unless the plaintiff can answer this question he can take no step forward. No degree of imitation of detail is actionable in its absence...

... It is not enough to show the wrench became popular under the name "Crescent"; the plaintiff must prove that before 1910 the public had already established the habit of buying it, not solely because they wanted that kind of wrench, but because they also wanted a Crescent and thought that all such wrenches were Crescents...

I believe that exactly encapsulates what must be shown when the plaintiff is complaining, in a passing off action, about a copy of his product as such. Is the public "moved to buy by source"?

It is, I think, precisely because the difficulties of proof are so great that successful cases of passing off based on the shape of the goods are so rare. ...

The evidence establishes, as I have said, that these cushions are expensive. They are not bought casually. They are far removed from the "penny packets" of the *Dolly Blue* or the cheap plastic lemons of *Jif*. This sort of cushioning is invariably bought at the instance of and fitted by a healthcare professional. It is true that there may be occasional instances where one user may ask another about what cushion that other has. But even where that happens and the user would like to try a ROHO, the process of supply will intimately involve a healthcare professional. Not only will the make of cushion be determined by the healthcare professional, but the precise model will also be determined. Moreover the cushion, once obtained, will be adjusted by a healthcare professional.

Further it seems abundantly clear that Ward's will not be able to sell the FLO'TAIR unless and until it has been evaluated and tested to the satisfaction of the healthcare professionals of its various potential customers. No doubt its salesmen will at least say it is as good as the ROHO (probably they will say it is better), but such is the care taken, that healthcare professionals will not prescribe it until they are satisfied themselves of its effectiveness.

Now all the healthcare professionals I heard struck me particularly as not only caring but also careful people. Not one of them (and I heard from healthcare professionals called by both sides) suggested they would themselves be deceived. The process of ordering itself rules deception out. The main customer is the National Health Service, although, of course, there are also private customers such as charities and private hospitals and nursing homes. There are variations between the ways things are done between regions of the NHS and as to how private purchasers buy. None of this matters. Always it is a healthcare professional who initiates a purchase. Once such a professional decides a particular type of ROHO is needed, he or she puts in a written requisition. That must identify the particular type of

ROHO wanted. If it does not, then the ordering department cannot move and must go back to the prescriber. Most orders mention ROHO by name (for instance the Welsh form requires the name of the maker). In some instances no name is used, but simply the model number. Those responsible for ordering (who are, of course, responsible for ordering a vast range of other things too) then process the order.

In those circumstances the likelihood of deception seems to me to be non-existent. . . .

In the result the action fails.

5.1.3   Passing Off: Defendant's Misrepresentation

5.1.3.1   *Reckitt & Colman v Borden* **[1990] R.P.C. 341, HL**

The plaintiff sold lemon juice in a yellow plastic lemon-shaped container. "Jif" was embossed on the side and printed on a neck-label. There was strong evidence that the purchasing public would think that they were buying a "Jif lemon" if confronted with the defendants' lemon juice in similar packaging. Walton J. and the Court of Appeal found the defendants' proposed get-up to amount to a threat of passing off against which a quia timet *injunction should be granted. The House of Lords agreed, Lord Oliver of Aylmerton dealing with the defendants' arguments thus:*

There is, to my mind, a fallacy in the argument which begins by identifying the contents with the container and is summarised in the central proposition that "you cannot claim a monopoly in selling plastic lemons". Well, of course you cannot any more than you can claim a monopoly in the sale of dimpled bottles. The deception alleged lies not in the sale of the plastic lemons or the dimpled bottles, but in the sale of lemon juice or whisky, as the case may be, in containers so fashioned as to suggest that the juice or the whisky emanates from the source with which the containers of those particular configurations have become associated in the public mind: see *John Haig & Co Ltd v Forth Blending Co Ltd* (1953) 70 R.P.C. 259. It is, no doubt, true that the plastic lemon-shaped container serves, as indeed does a bottle of any design, a functional purpose in the sale of lemon juice. Apart from being a container simpliciter, it is a convenient size; it is capable of convenient use by squeezing; and it is so designed as conveniently to suggest the nature of its contents without the necessity for further labelling or other identification. But those purposes are capable of being and indeed are served by a variety of distinctive containers of configurations other than those of a lemon-sized lemon. Neither the appellants nor the respondents are in the business of selling plastic lemons. Both are makers and vendors of lemon juice and the only question is whether the respondents, having acquired a public reputation for Jif juice by selling it for many years in containers of a particular shape and design which, on the evidence, has become associated with their produce, can legitimately complain of the sale by the appellants of similar produce in containers of similar, though not identical, size, shape and colouring.

[...]

Then it is said—and again there is no disagreement as to this—that the mere fact that the produce of the appellants and that of the respondents may be confused by members of the public is not of itself sufficient. There is no "property" in the accepted sense of the word in a get-up. Confusion resulting from the lawful right of another trader to employ as indicative of the nature of his goods terms which are common to the trade gives rise to no cause of action. The application by a trader to his goods of an accepted trade description or of ordinary English terms may give rise to confusion. It probably will do so where previously another trader was the only person in the market dealing in those goods, for a public which knows only of A will be prone to assume that any similar goods emanate from A. But there can be no cause of action in passing off simply because there will have been no mis-representation. So the application to the defendants' goods of ordinary English terms such as "cellular clothing" (*Cellular Clothing Co Ltd v Maxton and Murray* (1899) 16 R.P.C. 397), or "Office Cleaning" (*Office Cleaning Services Ltd v Westminster Window and General Cleaners Ltd* (1946) 63 R.P.C. 39) or the use of descriptive expressions or slogans in general use such as "Chicago Pizza" (*My Kinda Town Ltd v Soll* [1983] R.P.C. 407) cannot entitle a plaintiff to relief simply because he has used the same or similar terms as descriptive of his own goods and has been the only person previously to employ that description.

[...]

Every case depends upon its own peculiar facts. For instance, even a purely descriptive term consisting of perfectly ordinary English words may, by a course of dealing over many years, become so associated with a particular trader that it acquires a secondary meaning such that it may properly be said to be descriptive of that trader's goods and of his goods alone, as in *Reddaway v Banham* [1896] A.C. 199. In the instant case, what is said is that there was nothing particularly original in marketing lemon juice in plastic containers made to resemble lemons. The respondents were not the first to think of it even though they have managed over the past 30 years to establish a virtual monopoly in the United Kingdom. It is, in fact, a selling device widely employed outside the United Kingdom. It is a natural, convenient and familiar technique—familiar at least to those acquainted with retail marketing methods in Europe and the United States. If and so far as this particular selling device has become associated in the mind of the purchasing public with the respondents' Jif lemon juice, that is simply because the respondents have been the only people in the market selling lemon juice in this particular format. Because there has been in fact a monopoly of this sale of this particular article, the public is led to make erroneous assumption that a similar article brought to the market for the first time must emanate from the same source. This has been referred to in the argument as "the monopoly assumption". The likelihood of confusion was admitted by the appellants themselves in the course of their evidence, but it is argued that the erroneous public belief which causes the product to be confused arises simply from the existing monopoly and not from any deception by the appellants in making use of what they claim to be a normal, ordinary and generally available selling technique.

The difficulty about this argument is that it starts by assuming the only basis upon which it can succeed, that is to say, that the selling device which the appellants wish to adopt is ordinary and generally available or, as it is expressed in some of the cases, "common to the trade": see, *e.g. Payton & Co Ltd v Snelling, Lampard & Co Ltd* (1899) 17 R.P.C. 48. In one sense, the monopoly assumption is the basis of every passing off action. The deceit practised on the public when one trader adopts a get-up associated with another succeeds only because the latter has previously been the only trader using that particular get-up. But the so called "monopoly assumption" demonstrates nothing in itself. As a defence to a passing off claim it can succeed only if that which is claimed by the plaintiff as distinctive of his goods and his goods alone consists of something either so ordinary or in such common use that it would be unreasonable that he should claim it as applicable solely to his goods, as for instance where it consists simply of a description of the goods sold. Here the mere fact that he has previously been the only trader dealing in goods of that type and so described may lead members of the public to believe that all such goods must emanate from him simply because they know of no other. To succeed in such a case he must demonstrate more than simply the sole use of the descriptive term. He must demonstrate that it has become so closely associated with his goods as to acquire the secondary meaning not simply of goods of that description but specifically of goods of which he and he alone is the source ...

The trial judge here has found as a fact that the natural size squeeze pack in the form of a lemon has become so associated with Jif lemon juice that the introduction of the appellants' juice in any of the proposed get-ups will be bound to result in many housewives purchasing that juice in the belief that they are obtaining Jif juice. I cannot interpret that as anything other than a finding that the plastic lemon-shaped container has acquired, as it were, a secondary significance. It indicates not merely lemon juice but specifically Jif lemon juice.

Lord Oliver rejected the proposition that likelihood of deception should be judged only in relation to the literate and careful purchaser. He concluded:

It is pointed out that recent decisions of this House in, for instance, British Leyland Motor Corp Ltd v Armstrong Patents Co Ltd [1986] A.C. 577 and In re Coca Cola Co [1986] 1 W.L.R. 695 have stressed the suspicion with which this House regards any attempt to extend or perpetuate a monopoly and it is suggested again that, because it is not easy in the circumstances of this market effectively to distinguish the appellants' products from the respondents' except at considerable expense, the respondents are achieving, in effect, a perpetual monopoly in the sale of lemon juice in lemon-shaped squeeze packs. I do not accept at all that this is so, but in any event the principle that no man is entitled to steal another's trade by deceit is one of at least equal importance. The facts as found here establish that, unless the injunction is continued, that is what the appellants will be doing and it is not necessary for them to do so in order to establish their own competing business for there is nothing in the nature of the product sold which inherently requires it to be sold in the particular format which the appellants have chosen to adopt. I would dismiss the appeal.

Lord Bridge and Lord Jauncey delivered concurring speeches; Lord Brandon and Lord Goff concurred.

5.1.3.2 *Parker Knoll v Knoll International* [1962] R.P.C. 265, HL

Parker Knoll, the English furniture makers, acquired their name and mark when in the 1930s Frederick Parker & Sons adopted a form of springing for chairs invented by Wilhelm Knoll of Stuttgart. A nephew of Wilhelm, Hans, went to the US and with his wife developed the modern furniture firm, Knoll International, which built up an international business. In 1957, the latter sought to enter the British market marking their own furniture "Knoll International". Parker Knoll sought an injunction to restrain the American company from passing off their goods as those of the plaintiffs.

Lord Morris of Borth-y-Gest:

My Lords, in the interests of fair trading and in the interests of all who may wish to buy or to sell goods the law recognises that certain limitations upon freedom of action are necessary and desirable. In some situations the law has had to resolve what might at first appear to be conflicts between competing rights. In solving the problems which have arisen there has been no need to resort to any abstruse principles but rather, I think, to the straightforward principle that trading must not only be honest but must not even unintentionally be unfair.

The present case is concerned with the selling of goods under a mark or name. The respondents fear that if the appellants, whose honesty is not in any way impugned, are allowed to sell furniture in the way that they desire to do, a great many people would buy furniture in the belief that they were buying the respondents' furniture whereas they would in reality be buying the appellants' furniture.

In approaching the facts of the case I propose to state a few propositions, which, though they are by no means exhaustive, seem to me to apply to such a case as the present.

    1. No one has any right to represent his goods as being the goods of someone else

(*Reddaway v Banham* [1896] A.C. 199 (above 5.1.1.1); *Joseph Rodgers & Sons Limited v W. N. Rodgers & Co* (1924) 41 R.P.C. 277).

2. The court will restrain the making of any such representation even though it is not made fraudulently (see *John Brinsmead & Sons Ltd v Brinsmead* (1913) 30 R.P.C. 493). If A represents his goods as being the goods of B, then B is likely to suffer and is entitled to be protected whether A makes the representation innocently or fraudulently. If there is room for doubt as to whether A has represented his goods as the goods of B, then if there is evidence that A deliberately intended to and set out to make such a representation that evidence will in some cases assist to prove that there was in fact such a representation.

3. A name may be used as a mark under which a person's goods are sold so that the name comes to denote goods made by that person and not the goods made by anyone else or even made by anyone else who has the same name. So also a mark under which a person's goods are sold may come to denote goods made by that person. The name or the mark will have acquired a secondary meaning (see *Chivers v Chivers* (1900) 17 R.P.C. 420).

4. It follows that someone may, even by using his own name and using it innocently, make a representation that is untrue, that is a representation that goods which in fact are his are the goods of someone else (see *Reddaway v Banham* [1896] A.C. 199).

In *Joseph Rodgers & Sons Limited v W. N. Rodgers & Co* (1924) 41 R.P.C. 277, Romer J. (at 29) said that no man is entitled so to describe or mark his goods as to represent that the goods are the goods of another, and further said at 292 that to the rule as so stated there is no exception at all (see also *Baume v Moore* [1958] Ch. 137). In *Marengo v Daily Sketch and Sunday Graphic Limited* (1948) 65 R.P.C. 242, Lord Simonds said at 251: "It is an unassailable general proposition that the interests alike of honest traders and of the public require that the goods of A should not be confused with the goods of B. But that proposition is subject to the qualification that a man must be allowed to trade in his own name and, if some confusion results, that is a lesser evil than that a man should be deprived of what would appear to be a natural and inherent right. But ... it is a fantastic gloss upon this well-established qualification to say that it justifies a trader in placing upon his goods a mark which, however much he may intend it to signify his name, is yet liable to suggest to reasonable men the name of another". Having regard to this passage, I think that some observations made by Lord Greene M.R., in *Wright, Layman & Umney Ltd v Wright* (1949) 66 R.P.C. 149 at 152, must be regarded as incomplete.

5. It is a question of fact, to be decided on the evidence, whether it is proved that a name or a mark has acquired a secondary meaning so that it denotes or has come to mean goods made by a particular person and not goods made by any other person even though such other person may have the same name.

6. If it is proved on behalf of a plaintiff that a name or a mark has acquired such a secondary meaning, then it is a question for the court whether a defendant, whatever may be his intention, is so describing his goods that there is a likelihood that a substantial section of the purchasing public will be misled into believing that his goods are the goods of the plaintiff (see *Chivers & Sons v S. Chivers & Co Ltd* (1900) 17 R.P.C. 420). In arriving at a decision the court must not surrender in favour of any witness its own independent judgment (see *per* Lord Macnaghten in *Payton & Co Limited v Snelling, Lampard & Co Limited* [1901] A.C. 308 at 311; *Spalding v Gamage* (above, 5.1.1.2); *George Ballantine & Son Limited v Ballantyne Stewart & Co Limited* [1959] R.P.C. 273 at 280).

Deriving such assistance as the evidence afforded, Lord Morris concluded that marketing of the defendant's furniture as "Knoll International" would not avoid passing off; and that accordingly the plaintiff was entitled to an injunction qualified by the phrase, "without clearly distinguishing from the goods of the plaintiffs". Lords Hodson and Devlin delivered concurring speeches. Lord Denning dissented, applying Lord Greene's dictum without qualification.

5.1.3.3   *United Biscuits (UK) Ltd v Asda Stores* [1997] R.P.C. 513, Walker J.

The plaintiffs' "Penguin" chocolate-coated sandwich biscuits, were sold in predominantly red packaging with a horizontal yellow band, featuring PENGUIN in a black or dark blue capital lettering together with at least one picture of a penguin. They owned various trade marks including the word mark PENGUIN and various pictorial marks that were used on the packaging at various times until 1988. The defendants produced the "brand-beating" "Puffin" chocolate sandwich biscuit, which they sold in similar packaging with the word PUFFIN in black capital lettering and a cartoon depiction of a puffin. The defendant's biscuits were sold in supermarkets at a cheaper price.

The plaintiffs' action for trade mark infringement failed (save for two incidents of isolated use), primarily due to the court's revocation of its pictorial marks on findings of non-use. Its claim for passing off succeeded, Walker J. identifying three points for consideration: (i) the subjective intention of the defendant; (ii) the quality of the suggestion (conveyed by the get-up of the defendant's goods) of association or connection with the plaintiff's goods; and (iii) the degree to which it is necessary for the plaintiff's name to be known to the general public as the owner of the business whose goodwill and reputation are threatened by any misrepresentation.

On the first point, Walker J. concluded that, while the defendants aimed to avoid what the law would characterise as deception, they were taking a conscious decision to live dangerously, and this could not be disregarded:

... plainly they had that risk in mind, and in my judgment they miscalculated the degree of "challenge" or "matching" or "parody" that was tolerable without the product being actually deceptive (in the material sense).

As to the suggestion conveyed by the defendant's goods, Walker J. said:

Is it sufficient for a substantial part of the general public to be led to suppose, or assume, or guess at such a connection? In *Ewing* (1917) 34 R.P.C. 232 at 238 Warrington L.J. put it in terms of what a customer "might well think" and went on to say:

> "It seems to me that the plaintiff has proved enough. He has proved that the defendants have adopted such name as may lead people who have dealings with the plaintiff to believe that the defendants' business is a branch of or associated with the plaintiff's business."

In *Ravenhead Brick Co Ltd v Ruabon Brick & Terra Cotta Co Ltd* (1937) 54 R.P.C. 341 (the

Rus/Sanrus brick case) it was put in terms of a trade customer saying to himself "This is, or may be, a name used to describe an article of the plaintiff's manufacture." In *Wagamama* [1995] F.S.R. 713, witnesses had been asked by telephone to give their immediate reaction and first thought on hearing of the opening of a restaurant called Rajamama and some of their reactions and first thoughts are recorded in the judgment. These replies are expressed, naturally enough, in terms of what the witness thought, assumed, or took to be suggested. Bearing in mind that those witnesses (whose occupations are recorded) were probably of above-average articulacy, their reactions are not to my mind very different from those of witnesses in the present case. In *Wagamama* Laddie J. held passing off (as well as trade mark infringement) to have been established.

Mr Pollock points out that the *"Ravenhead Brick Co* and *Wagamama* cases were both concerned with artificial and meaningless names, and that is a point of distinction. Moreover, in the bricks case the customers were typically knowledgeable tradesmen, and in the restaurants case the likelihood of word-of-mouth recommendation made the sound of names particularly important. Penguin and Puffin, by contrast, are words denoting real creatures, and they appear on packing designed for self-service shopping in a supermarket. However, they are artificial or "fancy" names in the sense that an unpalatable seabird has no obvious connection with a chocolate-coated sandwich biscuit; and Puffin is, as a word, not wholly dissimilar from Penguin. It was to the seabird, and the names in black lettering, that almost all the witnesses referred in their explanations (some more articulate than others) of why they had been led to suppose, or assume, or guess at a common manufacturer.

As to knowledge of the plaintiff's actual name, Walker J. said:

There is authority that a customer need not know or care about the name of the manufacturer who owns the goodwill, provided that the customer knows that there is such a person and cares that goods which he buys are made by that person. This point was clearly expressed by a famous American judge, Learned Hand J., in a passage in *Crescent Tool Co v Kilborn & Bishop Co* (1917) 247 F.290 at 300 quoted by Jacob J. in *Hogkinson & Corby Ltd v Wards Mobility Services Ltd* [1994] 1 W.L.R. 1564 at 1573,

> "It is an absolute condition to any relief whatever that the plaintiff in such cases show that the appearance of his wares has in fact come to mean that some particular person—the plaintiff may not be individually known—makes them, and the public cares who does make them."

That was said in the special context of the appearance of a product, but the point is of more general application....

Walker J. formed the overall conclusion:

My impression of the Puffin packaging (in all four colours and varieties) is that it would cause a substantial number of members of the public to suppose that there was a connection between the Puffin biscuit and the Penguin biscuit. Despite the evidence of isolated mistakes, I do not consider that a substantial number would believe that the Asda Puffin is the McVities Penguin. But many would believe that the two must be made by the same manufacturer.

5.1.3.4   *Vine Products v Mackenzie* **[1969] R.P.C. 1, Cross J.**

This action—the Sherry *case—was initially brought by the producers of "British Sherry", "South African Sherry", etc. for a declaration that they were entitled to describe their wines by these geographical-cum-descriptive names.*

The case was an outcome of the Spanish Champagne *case [1961] R.P.C. 116. Both are referred to in* Advocaat *(above, 5.1.1.4) on the question of the title of a group of producers to exclusive rights in a word descriptive of their product. In* Champagne *and* Sherry *a further point arose out of the addition of a national adjective by the initiator to the descriptive word.*

Cross J. said of the earlier Champagne *case:*

The evidence established that the word "champagne" meant in England wine produced in the Champagne district of France by the plaintiffs and the other growers and shippers of that district. The defendants argued that nevertheless the addition of the word "Spanish" showed that their produce was not a wine produced in France, and that accordingly the description "Spanish Champagne" could mislead no-one. The judge described this as "a fairly specious argument" (see at 120, line 41) but he rejected it. In doing so he drew a distinction between those who were knowledgeable and those who were ignorant in matters of wine. The former would know that Champagne came exclusively from France, and so would realise if they bought a bottle labelled "Spanish Champagne" that they were not buying real Champagne but a Spanish sparkling wine. But according to the evidence given in that case—which was to the same effect as that given in this case—many people in this country are today drinking wine who were not brought up to this habit and know little or nothing of the various types of wine and their countries of origin. Such people, the judge thought, might well be deceived by a bottle labelled "Spanish Champagne". But how would they be deceived? Counsel for the plaintiffs, if I understand his argument correctly, suggested that Danckwerts J. meant that they would think that the wine which they were buying came from France in the same way as those who purchased from the defendants in the *Pilsbury Washburn* case (1898) 86 Fed. R. 608, would have thought that the flour which they were buying came from Minnesota. That I am sure does far less than justice to the judge's reasoning. A man who does not know where Champagne comes from can have not the slightest reason for thinking that a bottle labelled "Spanish Champagne" contains a wine produced in France. But what he may very well think is that he is buying the genuine article—real Champagne—and that, I have no doubt, was the sort of deception which the judge had in mind. He thought, as I read his judgment, that if people were allowed to call sparkling wine not produced in Champagne "Champagne" even though preceded by an adjective denoting the country of origin, the distinction between genuine Champagne and "champagne type" wines produced elsewhere would become blurred; that the word "Champagne" would come gradually to mean no more than "sparkling wine" and that the part of the plaintiffs' goodwill which consisted in the name would be diluted and gradually destroyed. If I may say so without impertinence I agree entirely with the decision in the *Spanish Champagne* case—but as I see it it uncovered a piece of common law or equity which had till then escaped notice—for in such a case there is not, in any ordinary sense, any representation that the goods of the defendant are the goods of the plaintiffs, and evidence that no-one has been confused or deceived in that way is quite beside the mark. In truth the decision went beyond the well-trodden paths of passing off into the unmapped area of "unfair trading" or "unlawful competition".

Cross J. proceeded to find on the evidence that "Sherry" did properly mean a wine from the Jerez district of Spain, and not a type of wine that may be produced anywhere and in any way. He also held that failure to object to the use of "British Sherry", "South African Sherry" etc, over a very long period raised a defence of acquiescence in those usages.

5.1.3.5 *British Telecommunications v One in a Million* [1999] F.S.R. 1, CA

The defendant registered Internet addresses, using top level domain names, such as <.com>, <.org> and <.co.uk> and attaching to them site names associated with well-known British companies: as in <bt.org> and <marks and spencer.com>. Their intention was not to use these domain names themselves, but to sell them at substantial prices to the company concerned. In proceedings for passing off, Aldous L.J. (for the Court) reviewed the case law concerning the liability of defendants who equipped themselves or another with instruments of fraud. He then concluded:

The judge considered first the action brought by Marks & Spencer Plc and then went on to deal with the other actions. I will adopt the same approach as the Marks & Spencer case raises slightly different issues to those raised in the other cases.

It is accepted that the name Marks & Spencer denotes Marks & Spencer Plc and nobody else. Thus anybody seeing or hearing the name realises that what is being referred to is the business of Marks & spencer Plc. It follows that registration by the appellants of a domain name including the name Marks & Spencer makes a false representation that they are associated or connected with Marks & Spencer Plc. This can be demonstrated by considering the reaction of a person who taps into his computer the domain name marksandspencer.co.uk. and presses a button to execute a "whois" search. He will be told that the registrant is One In A Million Limited. A substantial number of persons will conclude that One In A Million Limited must be connected or associated with Marks & Spencer Plc. That amounts to a false representation which constitutes passing off.

Mr Wilson submitted that mere registration did not amount to passing off. Further, Marks & Spencer Plc had not established any damage or likelihood of damage. I cannot accept those submissions. The placing on a register of a distinctive name such as marksandspencer makes a representation to persons who consult the register that the registrant is connected or associated with the name registered and thus the owner of the goodwill in the name. Such persons would not know of One In A Million Limited and would believe that they were connected or associated with the owner of the goodwill in the domain name they had registered. Further, registration of the domain name including the words Marks & Spencer is an erosion of the exclusive goodwill in the name which damages or is likely to damage Marks & Spencer Plc.

Mr Wilson also submitted that it was not right to conclude that there was any threat by the appellants to use or dispose of any domain name including the words Marks & Spencer. He submitted that the appellants, Mr Conway and Mr Nicholson, were two rather silly young men who hoped to make money from the likes of the respondents by selling domain names to them for as much as they could get. They may be silly, but their letters and activities make it clear that they intended to do more than just retain the names. Their purpose was to threaten use and disposal sometimes explicitly and on other occasions implicitly. The judge was right to grant *quia timet* relief to prevent the threat becoming reality.

I also believe that domain names comprising the name Marks & Spencer are instruments of fraud. Any unrealistic use of them as domain names would result in passing off and there was ample evidence to justify the injunctive relief granted by the judge to prevent them being used for a fraudulent purpose and to prevent them being transferred to others.

The other cases are slightly different. Mr Wilson pointed to the fact that there are people called Sainsbury and Ladbroke and companies, other than Virgin Enterpises Ltd, who have as part of their name the word Virgin and also people or firms whose initials would be BT. He went on to submit that it followed that the domain names which the appellants had registered were not inherently deceptive. They were not instruments of fraud. Further there had been no passing off and none was threatened and a transfer to a third party would not result in the appellants becoming joint tortfeasors in any passing off carried out by the person to whom the registrations were transferred. Thus, he submitted, there was no foundation for the injunctive relief in the actions brought by four of the respondents.

I believe that, for the same reasons I have expressed in relation to the Marks & Spencer Plc action, passing off and threatened passing off has been demonstrated. The judge was right to conclude (at 273):

> "The history of the defendants' activities shows a deliberate practice followed over a substantial period of time of registering domain names which are chosen to resemble the names and marks of other people and are plainly intended to deceive. The threat of passing-off and trade mark infringement, and the likelihood of confusion arising from the infringement of the mark are made out beyond argument in this case, even if it is possible to imagine other cases in which the issue would be more nicely balanced."

I also believe that the names registered by the appellants were instruments of fraud and that injunctive relief was appropriate upon this basis as well. The trade names were well-known "household names" denoting in ordinary usage the respective respondent. The appellants registered them without any distinguishing word because of the goodwill attaching to those names. It was the value of that goodwill, not the fact that they could perhaps be used in some way by a third party without deception, which caused them to register the names. The motive of the appellants was to use that goodwill and threaten to sell it to another who might use it for passing off to obtain money from the respondents. The value of the names lay in the threat that they would be used in a fraudulent way. The registrations were made with the purpose of appropriating the respondents' property, their goodwill, and with an intention of threatening dishonest use by them or another. The registrations were instruments of fraud and injunctive relief was appropriate just a much as it was in those cases where persons registered company names for a similar purpose.

The plaintiffs also proceeded for infringement of registered trademarks. Aldous L.J. confirmed the finding at first instance that there was infringement of rights in the marks in relation to goods or services which were not similar (Trade Marks Act 1994, s.10(3); see below, para. 5.2.7.1). The Court upheld the order to transfer the domain names to the mark owners.

5.1.4   Passing Off: Likely Damage

5.1.4.1   *Henderson v Radio Corporation* (1960) [1969] R.P.C. 218, Full SC, N.S.W.

The plaintiffs, well-known professional ballroom dancers, commenced pro-ceedings against the defendant record company for the unauthorised use of photographs of them on a record cover. The trial judge granted an injunction but refused an inquiry as to damages.

Evatt C.J. and Myers J.:

The respondents have contended that the acts of the appellant were likely to lead to the belief that the business of the appellant was connected with the business of the respondents because, it was said, the picture of the respondents on the record cover would lead buyers of the record to believe that the respondents recommended the record as providing good music for ballroom dancing.

Four witnesses were called on this issue on behalf of the respondents. They were the president of an association of dancing teachers, the secretary of another such association, a theatrical agent and the assistant secretary of the trade union to which the professional dancers belong. Each said in substance that when he saw the record he recognised either Henderson or Henderson and his wife and gathered from the fact that their pictures were on the cover, that they had sponsored, that is recommended or approved, the record, or were associated in some way with it. The appellant called no evidence on this aspect. His Honour did not express any adverse view of these witnesses but he did not accept the view that buyers of the record would come to the same conclusion as the witnesses.

However, the facts relevant to this issue, including the evidence to which we have referred, are not in dispute. The only question is the proper inference to be drawn from them, and in those circumstances we are entitled to form our own opinion, *Benmax v Austin Motor Co Ltd* [1955] A.C. 370.

Unaided by evidence, one might consider that the dancing figures merely indicate the type of music on the record and that it is not possible to come to the conclusion for which the respondents contend. But one is not unaided by evidence and, having regard to the fact that the record was primarily intended for professional dancing teachers, and to the uncon-tradicted evidence of four experts in that field, we are of opinion that the proper finding is that the class of persons for whom the record was primarily intended would probably believe that the picture of the respondents on the cover indicated their recommendation or approval of the record. The only rational purpose of the wrongful use of the respondents' photograph on the disc container was to assist the sale of the disc it contained.

This false representation was not only made by the appellant, but would almost inevitably lead to a similar false representation on the part of every shopkeeper who might buy the records from the appellant and sell them or display them for sale. It still remains to be considered whether that finding established the necessary element of deception, namely, that the business of the appellant was connected with the business of the respondents. In our opinion it does.

The representation that the respondents recommended the record is an inducement to buy it. The recommendation can only be attributed to the respondents in their capacity of professional dancers, that is, a recommendation made in the course of their professional activities, and means that as professional dancers they have associated themselves with the appellant in promoting sales of the record, and that amounts to a connection, in respect of the marketing of the record, between the business of the respondents and the business of the appellant.

The point is not without authority. In *British Medical Association v Marsh* (1931) 48 R.P.C. 565 at 574, Maugham J. referring to the professional cases on passing off, said that they did not establish the proposition that if a tradesman puts forward a remedy as having been prescribed by, or sold for the benefit, or with the approval of a medical man, the latter would have no remedy. "What it is necessary in such a case to prove is, either positive injury, or in a *quia timet* action, a reasonable probability of injury, and if that is done, I, for my part, see no reason why such an action should not succeed".

In our opinion the evidence established a passing off by the appellant and, subject to proof of injury, as to which we will have something to say later, the respondents were entitled to relief by way of injunction.

It has been contended, however, that the court has no jurisdiction to grant an injunction unless there is what has been called a common field of activity and in the case, it is said, there is none. The argument is based on a statement by Wynn Parry J. in *McCulloch v Lewis A. May (Produce Distributors) Ltd* (1947) 65 R.P.C. 58 at 66, 67.

"I am satisfied", he said, "that there is discoverable in all those (cases) in which the Court has intervened this factor, namely, that there was a common field of activity in which, however remotely, both the plaintiff and the defendant were engaged and that it was the presence of that factor that accounted for the jurisdiction of the court."

This principle was accepted by Sugerman J., who found a common field of activity in the capacity of the respondents to place their approval upon a record of ballroom dance music, which, he said, might be regarded as appurtenant or potentially appurtenant to the profession or business of ballroom dancing.

We have some difficulty in accepting the proposition stated in *McCulloch's* case. If deception and damages are proved, it is not easy to see the justification for introducing another factor as a condition of the court's power to intervene.

The physician whose name is attached by the maker to a quack remedy has no business in publicly recommending any remedy at all. It would be improper on his part if he had. The British Medical Association in *British Medical Association v Marsh* (1931) 48 R.P.C. 565 had no business in approving proprietary medicines and it was contrary to the principles of the association to do so. It seems to us to be quite unreal to say that there is a common field of activity in such cases because, whether self-imposed or not, there is an actual restraint on the injured person entering the common field at all. In our opinion, the representation in such cases that the plaintiff recommended or approved the product is, having regard to the nature of his business, equivalent to a representation that he did so in the course of it. It associates both businesses with the sale of the product, the manufacturer in making and selling it and the plaintiff in assisting in its sale by making it attractive by his professional recommendation.

In *McCulloch's* case, the plaintiff had been widely and favourably known as a broadcaster for many years in the "Children's Hour" programme of the British Broadcasting Corporation. He used the name "Uncle Mac" and was well-known by that name. He had written books for children, delivered lectures to them and given away prizes at prizegivings and was clearly a popular and well-known figure.

The defendant placed on the market a cereal which it called "Uncle Mac's Puffed Wheat". It was packed in cartons containing a number of references to "Uncle Mac", associating him with children. One was in these words, "Uncle Mac loves children—and children love Uncle Mac". There was evidence that some witnesses believed that the plaintiff had put his name to a poor or low venture and a well-known broadcaster thought that the plaintiff had been forced to lend his name to the venture through financial difficulties.

An injunction was refused because, there being no "common field of activity", there was no passing off. "Upon the postulate that the plaintiff is not engaged in any degree in producing or marketing puffed wheat, how can the defendant, in using the fancy name used by the plaintiff, be said to be passing off the goods or the business of the plaintiff? I am utterly unable to see any element of passing off in this case" *per* Wynn-Parry J. at 69.

We find it impossible to accept this view without some qualification. The remedy in passing off is necessarily only available where the parties are engaged in business, using that expression in its widest sense to include professions and callings. If they do there does not seem to be any reason why it should also be necessary that there be an area, actual or potential, in which their activities conflict. If it were so, then, object only to the law of defamation, any businessman might falsely represent that his goods were produced by another provided that other was not engaged, or not reasonably likely to be engaged, in producing similar goods. This does not seem to be a sound general principle.

The present case provides an illustration of the unjust consequences of such a principle. For the purposes of this part of its argument, the appellant concedes that it is falsely representing that the respondents recommend, favour or support its dance music record, but it claims that because the respondents are not engaged or likely to be engaged in making or selling gramophone records, it is entitled to appropriate their names and reputations for its own commercial advantage and that the court has no power to prevent it doing so. It would be a grave defect in the law if this were so.

In our view, once it is proved that A is falsely representing his goods as the goods of B, or his business to be the same as or connected with the business of B, the wrong of passing off has been established and B is entitled to relief.

While *McCulloch's* case is open to strong criticism, in actual fact the respondents here are in a real sense competing in the special area of providing gramophone records specially adapted to dancing and dancing teaching. Their activities are competitive in a broad sense. If so, *McCulloch's* case provides no obstacle to the plaintiff's success in the suit.

We now turn to the question of damage and, in view of certain submissions by counsel for the respondents, desire to make a few general remarks on the subject.

Passing off is a wrong and is actionable at law. In such an action damage is presumed on proof of passing off and therefore a nominal sum by way of damages follows as a matter of course. General damages may, however, only be awarded if there is evidence of damage. Instead of proceeding at law a plaintiff may sue in equity for an injunction, as may be done in respect of other wrongful acts of a different nature. If he sees in equity, he takes advantage of the equitable principle that the court will interfere by injunction to restrain irreparable injury to property: *per* Romer L.J. in *Samuelson v Producers Distributing Co Limited* (above, 5.1.1.3) and therefore he must go further than he need at law. He must show irreparable injury, that is that he has suffered injury which cannot be properly compensated by damages, or that he will probably suffer such injury.

If a plaintiff in equity succeeds in having the defendant enjoined, he may also have an account of profits or an inquiry as to damages. Formerly, he could only have had an account, because that was equity's only remedy, but since Lord Cairns' Act, he may have damages. If he elects to take an inquiry as to damages, he takes a common law remedy and his damages will be ascertained in the same way as they would have been ascertained at law.

In a judgment to the same effect, Manning J. said:

Today we find leading amateur sportsmen lending their names for reward to recommendations for a variety of goods and articles, and not merely those which, in the course of their amateur sporting activities, they come to know and appreciate. Indeed, from what I have myself read and observed I believe it to be the fact that at least one prominent amateur sportsman has formed a proprietary company for the exploitation of his name and reputation so that he may sell his recommendations in the advertising market and yet, so I assume, attract a minimum of taxes. In making this comment I do not wish it to be thought that I desire for one moment to criticise amateur sportsmen who have indulged in this activity. The new and altered standards must be accepted by the courts once it is apparent that they have been accepted by the community.

The point which seems to emerge with clarity is that one's conception of the status of an amateur sportsman 30 years ago is quite different to what is accepted today. The development in the advertising of products to which I have referred has opened up a new field of gainful employment for many persons who, by reason not only of their sporting, but of their social, artistic or other activities, which have attracted notoriety, have found themselves in a position to earn substantial sums of money by lending their recommendation or sponsorship to an almost infinite variety of commodities.

To meet changes in the manner of conducting commercial enterprises, I would prefer in considering cases of this kind to propound as the test the one to which I have referred above, namely, whether the plaintiff has suffered a financial detriment and such detriment flows from or arises as a result of the defendant's act, rather than to ask whether the defendant's act caused financial loss to the plaintiff.

The plaintiffs in this case had acquired a reputation which doubtless placed them in a position to earn a fee for any recommendation which they might be disposed to give to aid the sale of recorded dance music of the type in question. I have referred to those engaged in sporting activities because of the facts in *Tolley's* case [1931] A.C. 333, but the position of the plaintiffs is better compared with that of a well-known actress or model. I can see no distinction in any such cases provided, as has been established in this case, that the activity of the party concerned has resulted in their recommendation becoming a saleable commodity.

The result of the defendant's action was to give the defendant the benefit of the plaintiffs' recommendation and the value of such recommendation and to deprive the plaintiffs of the fee or remuneration they would have earned if they had been asked for their authority to do what was done. The publication of the cover amounted to a misrepresentation of the type which will give rise to the tort of passing off, as there was implied in the acts of the defendant an assertion that the plaintiffs had "sponsored" the record.

No evidence was given as to what fee or remuneration would have been payable in circumstances such as these and the major part of the argument was directed rather to the submission that damage would flow because the plaintiffs would be less likely to secure some reward for "sponsoring" some other record or records. In my view damage of the latter type is too remote.

However, I am satisfied that the unauthorised use by the defendant of the commercially valuable reputation of the plaintiffs justifies the intervention of the court. I would have thought that the relief to which the plaintiffs were entitled was an inquiry as to damages, an injunction to restrain the defendant from disposing of any further record covers bearing a visual representation of the plaintiffs and an order for delivery up for destruction of the unsold covers, but the only order made was for an injunction and there is no cross-appeal. I am therefore of opinion that this appeal should be dismissed with costs.

5.1.4.2   *Hogan v Pacific Dunlop* (1989) 12 I.P.R. 225, FC, Australia.

Pacific Dunlop marketed shoes by using the ideas of the famous "knife scene" from the film "Crocodile Dundee", of which the applicants were copyright owners and distributors. The latter accordingly sued for passing off and under ss.52 and 53(c) of the Australian Trade Practices Act 1974. They alleged that the defendant had created an erroneous association between their rights in the image and character of Mick "Crocodile" Dundee in the film and the images portrayed by the respondent in advertising its shoes.

Gummow J. (First Instance):

Within the action for passing off as presently understood in Australia, there are accommodated and adjusted *inter se* three sets of interests. There is the plaintiff's interest in protecting his skill, effort and investment, the interests of the defendant in freedom to attract purchasers for his goods and services, and the interest of consumers in having available a range of competitive goods and services for selection by consumers without the practice upon them of misrepresentations. Any monopoly right so created is limited in duration to the persistence of the plaintiff's reputation and goodwill; if that evaporates, the cause of action in passing off goes with it (the authorities are collected in *10th Cantanae Pty Ltd v Shoshana Pty Ltd* (1987) 79 A.L.R. 299 at 317; 11 I.P.R. 249.

Further, the ability of the plaintiff to take unto himself exclusively striking images otherwise part of the general fund referred to by Mr Pendleton is limited by the nature of the passing off action. As I have stated earlier in these reasons, the action is concerned with misrepresentation, and with a particular type of misrepresentation involving use of the image or indicium in question to convey a representation of a commercial connection between the plaintiff and the goods or services of the defendant, which connection does not exist. This case, like *10th Cantanae Pty Ltd v Shoshana Pty Ltd*, above, is concerned with what will satisfy the requirement of commercial connection. Again, it is not all representations made in commerce, as to connection between the plaintiff and the goods or services of the defendant which will suffice.

These concerns are drawn together in the following passage from the judgment of Goff L.J. in *H. P. Bulmer Ltd & Showerings Ltd v J. Bollinger SA* [1978] R.P.C. 79 at 117:

> "Not every kind of connection claimed will amount to passing off; for example if one says that one's goods are very suitable to be used in connection with the plaintiff's. On the other hand in my view there can be a passing off of goods without representing that they are actually the well-known goods which the plaintiff produces or a new line which he is supposed to have started. It is sufficient in my view if what is done represents the defendant's goods to be connected with the plaintiff's in such a way as would lead people to accept them on the faith of the plaintiff's reputation. Thus for example it would be sufficient if they were taken to be made under licence, or under some trading arrangement which would give the plaintiff some control over them. . . ."

The misrepresentation may be actionable as passing off even though the effect thereof is not to divert sales to the public of goods or services from the defendant to the plaintiff. This is because the effect of the misrepresentation complained of may be to misappropriate the plaintiff's business goodwill. (Examples are given in *10th Cantanae Pty Ltd v Shoshana Pty Ltd* (1987) 79 A.L.R. at 318.) However, in each case, the damage to the goodwill of the plaintiff is actionable only because of apprehended or actual deception of the relevant section of the public by the defendant's conduct.

Gummow J. proceeded to find a case of passing off to have been made out. This judgment was upheld by a majority of the Full Federal Court. On the general issue of misrepresentation Burchett J. said:

To ask whether the consumer reasons that Mr Hogan authorised the advertisement is therefore to ask a question which is a mere side issue, and far from the full impact of the advertisement. The consumer is moved by a desire to wear something belonging in some sense to Crocodile Dundee (who is perceived as a persona, almost an avatar, of Mr Hogan). The arousal of that feeling by Mr Hogan himself could not be regarded as misleading, for then the value he promises the product will have is not in its leather, but in its association with himself. When, however, an advertisement he did not authorise makes the same suggestion, it is misleading; for the product sold by that advertisement really lacks the one feature the advertisement attributes to it.

On the argument that the respondent's advertisement was merely a parody of the film, Beaumont J. commented:

As in *Tolley v Fry*, there is a real distinction to be drawn between a "mere" caricature on the one hand and a caricature "embedded" in an advertisement on the other. The former is innocent because viewers would receive the impression that the person caricatured would not have agreed. The latter carries with it a different impression, favourable to the subject of the caricature, in which he or she is perceived as endorsing the object of the advertising. The distinction between the "mere" caricature and one "embedded" in the advertising is of critical significance. If it were appropriate to divide the advertisement into two discrete parts, one part devoted to a parody of the Dundee figure and the other a sales promotion, it may be that no relevant misrepresentation could be made out. But such a division of the advertising is not possible. The Dundee figure, albeit a variant of the original image, is seen as sponsoring the appellant's shoes. The advertising is not a "mere" caricature.

5.1.4.3 *Tavener Rutledge v Trexapalm* [1977] R.P.C. 275, Walton J.

"Kojak" was the title of a well-known television series in which the eponymous detective-hero sucked lollipops. The plaintiff, without any licence from the promoters of the series, Universal City Studios, launched a "Kojakpop" lolly on the British market with considerable success. The defendant, claiming to be licensed by the promoters, then began selling "Kojak Lollies", which were found to be poor value for money in comparison with the plaintiff's product.

In granting the plaintiff an interlocutory injunction against passing off, Walton J. said:

When one is dealing, as one would here be dealing, in the field of passing off it is not sufficient undoubtedly to refer only to the actual fields of activities of the two parties concerned, one has to look and see what ordinary, reasonable people, the man in the street, would consider to be within the relevant fields of activities.

Walton J. quoted from Annabel's v Shock *[1972] R.P.C. 838 at 844, per Russell L.J., and continued:*

Applying those principles to the present case, as I say, the first step is that there is no risk of confusion or possibility of confusion between the actual lines of activity of the licensors and the plaintiffs; but, says Mr Morcom, that is too simple a view. The business of what he calls character merchandising has become very well known in our present times and everybody who has a character, whether real or fictional, to exploit, does so by the grant of licences to people who wish to use the name of the real or fictional character. I think one must leave real persons out of it because, when one deals with a real person, one has a real person with real qualities and, therefore, his endorsement or the use of his name undoubtedly suggest, or may suggest in proper circumstances, an endorsement which may or may not exist; but, when one has a fictional character such as Kojak, obviously Kojak in that sense does not exist and nobody would imagine that the lollipops put out by the plaintiff company have been actually endorsed by Kojak, still less by the actor who plays the fictional character.

What Mr Morcom says is that, because of this growth of merchandising, what now happens is that the owner of the rights in a series, such as "Kojak" here, licenses a large number of people to use the name "Kojak" in connection with products and members of the public would take it that, if one uses the word "Kojakpops", the right to use that name has been licensed by whoever are the owners of the rights in the series "Kojak", that moreover they have insisted upon a certain standard of quality and that, therefore, anybody who uses the word "Kojakpops" is to some extent taking advantage of the good name of the owner of the copyright.

I regret to say that I am wholly unimpressed by any such argument. Certainly it is not established by the evidence that it has yet arisen and I think that it is a good long way off, if in fact it ever does arise, but there may come a time when the system of character merchandising will have become so well known to the man in the street that immediately he sees "Kojakpops" he will say to himself: "They must have a licence from the person who owns the rights in the television series"; but that, by itself, so far as I can see would not be of any assistance to Mr Morcom at all, because that does not carry him home at all. What he would have to go on to show is that it had also become so well known that people in the situation of licensors of these names exercised quality control over any product bearing their name, so that as soon as anybody in the street came to the conclusion that a product was licensed by the owners of some series, such as the "Kojak" series, he would say to himself not only, "This must have been licensed by them", but also: "and that is a guarantee of its quality". That point we are miles away from reaching and there is not really a shred of evidence in front of me to that effect.

5.1.4.4   *Lego System v Lego M. Lemelstrich* **[1983] F.S.R. 155, Falconer J.**

The Lego Group (of which the parent company and British subsidiary were plaintiffs) manufactured and distributed the well-known construction-kit toys in the UK and much of the world under the mark "Lego". The defendant Israeli company had manufactured irrigation equipment under the mark "Lego" since 1927. Its business had expanded to cover 40 countries and it was about to launch sales in the UK

Falconer J. found that the plaintiff's mark was a household word with such a reputation that the public would be likely to think, despite the difference in character, that the defendant's products were the goods of the plaintiffs or connected with them. On this he accepted evidence collected by a properly conducted opinion survey.

After reviewing the principles of passing off stated by Lords Diplock and Fraser in the "Advocaat" case (above, 5.1.1.4) he continued:

However, as I have indicated, the defendants' case is essentially that the parties are in very different fields and the respective goods of the plaintiffs (toys such as construction sets and building bricks) and those of the defendants (irrigation equipment, particularly for gardens) are so far apart that there could be no misrepresentation, *i.e.* actionable misrepresentation, or any damage or likelihood of damage by the defendants' use of Lego on their goods.

Mr Morcom, for the defendants, submitted that, if the plaintiffs were to succeed in this case, then such a decision would be breaking new ground in extending passing off further than it has ever been extended on the cases in a situation where, as here, there is no evidence of fraudulent intention. I am not impressed with that submission—as the recent *Advocaat* case, extending further the striking development in the *Champagne* case of passing off as a cause of action, clearly demonstrates, the law as to passing off, which is concerned with unfair trading, is constantly being developed to meet changing conditions and practices in trade. Moreover, all those earlier cases now have to be seen in the light of the authoritative statement of the law as to passing off enunciated by the House of Lords in the *Advocaat* case.

After referring to McCulloch v May *and the criticisms of it in* Henderson v Radio Corp. *(above, 5.1.4.1), he concluded:*

However, I respectfully agree with the observation of Oliver J. in the *Abba* case: *Lyngstad v Anabas Products Ltd* [1977] F.S.R. 62

> "I think, if I may say so with respect, that the Australian case to which I have referred is to some extent based on a misconception of what Wynn-Parry J. was saying in *McCulloch v May*. The expression 'common field of activity' is not, I think, a term of art, but merely a convenient shorthand term for indicating what the High Court of New South Wales itself recognised, that is to say, the need for a real possibility of confusion, which is the basis of the action."

That observation is justified by a reference to an earlier part of the judgment of Wynn-Parry J. in 65 R.P.C. at 64, lines 19–35.

Although Mr Morcom contended strongly that the respective fields of the plaintiffs and the defendants, toys such as construction sets and building bricks on the one hand, and irrigation equipment, particularly for gardens, on the other, are too far apart from the defendants' use of LEGO to amount to misrepresentation and, indeed, as I have indicated, went so far as to submit that a decision in this case in favour of the plaintiffs would be extending passing off further than it has hitherto been extended in the absence of fraudulent intention, nevertheless he conceded that, in the light of all the cases including the *Advocaat* case, he could not submit that as a matter of law (my emphasis) passing off could never be established when the respective activities of the plaintiff and the defendant were completely unrelated. In my judgment, he was right in making that concession. Of course, that is not to say that the proximity of a defendant's field of activity to that of the plaintiff will not be relevant to whether the defendant's acts complained of amount to a mis-representation in any particular case—plainly it will, at least in most cases. But, in my judgment, there is much force in Mr Aldous's submission, based on the extent of the plaintiffs' reputation in their mark LEGO, that if, as he contended was this case, the plaintiffs' mark has become part of the English language in the sense that everybody associates LEGO with a particular company, namely, the manufacturers of the LEGO toy construction sets and building bricks, then the misrepresentation by the defendants' use of the mark is easier to assume and to prove; on the other hand, if the mark or name concerned has only a limited field of recognition it is obviously more difficult to establish its understanding as denoting the plaintiff's goods in a field which is not directly comparable with the field of that plaintiff's goods.

Whether or not the acts of a defendant complained of in a passing off action amount to a misrepresentation must be a question of fact and, in the end, that was common ground between Mr Aldous and Mr Morcom. I think Mr Morcom expressed it correctly when, at the conclusion of that part of his argument dealing with misrepresentation, he submitted that what has to be established by a plaintiff is that there is a real risk that a substantial number of persons among the relevant section of the public will in fact believe that there is a business connection between the plaintiff and the defendant. That, as I have found, has been established by the plaintiffs in this case.

On the question of likelihood of damage to the plaintiff, Falconer J. said:

However, Mr Morcom's main submission, as I understood his argument, was that the plaintiffs' and the defendants' respective goods are so far apart that the plaintiffs have not established that injury to the business or goodwill they have built up is a reasonably foreseeable consequence of the defendants' use of the mark, as required by characteristic (4) in Lord Diplock's formulation in the *Advocaat* case. Developing that submission he argued that the plaintiffs are and always have been in a very specific field which, so he argued, is where their goodwill lies and the plaintiffs had not given any evidence of any intention to diversify or franchise. It is the fact that the plaintiffs' business has been in the toy and construction kit field, with some diversification into promotional goods such as I have mentioned earlier, and that they have not up to now operated in the area of garden equipment. It is also correct that there was no evidence of a present intention on their part to enter the garden equipment field, although Mr Skovmose, a member of the Danish bar, who is secretary to the management of the Lego Group and a co-director, *inter alia*, of the second plaintiffs, stated in evidence that "there is no reason why that should not come at a later stage". But, as to the plaintiffs' goodwill being only in a very specific field, I do not accept that submission—their reputation in their mark LEGO, to which their goodwill is attached, is such that it extends beyond the field in which they have hitherto been engaged and, as I have held, has been demonstrated to be so extensive that its use by the defendants on goods such as their coloured plastic garden sprinklers would mislead a very substantial number of persons who would think such use denoted the plaintiffs' goods or some association or connection with the plaintiffs. Mr Morcom further argued, in support of his main submission on damage, that, in the absence of any common field of activity, actual or potential, *i.e.* potential, as he explained, in the sense of a natural extension of the field of the plaintiffs' existing trade, there is no basis on which any injury to the business or goodwill of the plaintiff can be foreseen, apart from exceptional cases where some dishonest activity facilitates the finding that such injury is reasonably foreseeable. It seems to me that that argument cannot be right; as I have already pointed out, in Lord Diplock's formulation of the necessary characteristics to found a cause of action in passing off, there is no limitation as to the relation of the field of activity of the defendant to that of the plaintiff and, indeed, as I have also mentioned, Mr Morcom conceded, rightly in my view, that he could not submit that, as a matter of law, passing off could never be established when the respective activities of the plaintiff and the defendant were completely unrelated. If passing off can be established in a case where the respective activities of plaintiff and defendant are completely unrelated, it must follow that in such a case injury to the plaintiffs' business or goodwill must be reasonably foreseeable, notwithstanding the absence of any common field of activity, actual or potential, in Mr Morcom's narrow sense.

In the result, in my judgment, the plaintiffs have established their case of passing off against the defendants and the action succeeds.

5.1.4.5 *Stringfellow v McCain Foods* [1984] R.P.C. 501, CA

The first plaintiff set up a nightclub, "Stringfellows", in St Martin's Lane, London in 1980. It soon established considerable éclat as a haunt of the young and trendy. The defendant company, having built a considerable business in oven chips—frozen chips needing to be heated only under the grill or in the oven— decided to launch a new line of long and thin oven chips using the name "Stringfellows". The name was found to have been honestly chosen without the least expectation that any benefit could be derived from any association with the plaintiff's club. The first television advertising for the chips, however, gave the appearance of a disco to a domestic kitchen and involved disco dancing by a boy and his two sisters. It was this advertisement in particular which caused the first plaintiff to seek relief against passing off, alleging that damage to his reputation would flow from a supposed association between the chips and his club. The plaintiffs had a public opinion survey conducted upon under- standings of the word "Stringfellows", which was subject to a degree of criticism but not rejected out of hand as evidence by the Court of Appeal. Neither this evidence nor that of other witnesses served to convince the Court of Appeal that there had been any misrepresentation of the relevant kind up to the appearance of the television advertisement.

On the question of overlap of fields which formed part of this discussion, Slade L.J. remarked:

The only tenuous overlap between the respective fields of activities of the plaintiff and of McCain is that McCain market foodstuffs while the plaintiffs sell food in the restaurant at their night club. But frozen foods and potato chips are some of the last kinds of food which would be readily associated in the minds of the public with a high-class, "up-market" restaurant, so that the relevant overlap is very small. The answers to R.S.G.B.'s ques- tionnaires show that a fair proportion of the public (22 per cent of the sample) associate the word "Stringfellows" with a club, night-club or discotheque. But, as Walton J. pointed out in his judgment on the motion, the word is far from being a household word as was, for example, the word "Lego" which fell to be considered by Falconer J. in *Lego Systems A/S v Lego M. Lemelstrich Limited* [1983] F.S.R. 155. The word "Stringfellow", unlike "Lego", is an ordinary surname which, at least in certain parts of the country, is not uncommon. McCain, on the other hand, have a national reputation as purveyors of frozen foods, with their products bought and consumed by very large numbers of the population, as I have already indicated. A member of the public (albeit one already acquainted with the name of the Club), on simply seeing a packet of frozen potato chips clearly marked with the words "McCain Stringfellows Long Thin Oven Ready Fries" (not just "Stringfellows Long Thin Oven Ready Fries") would, in my opinion, be most unlikely to draw the inference that there was any connection at all between the chips and Mr Peter Stringfellow or the club. If he were to draw that inference, it would in my opinion be an unreasonable one, which was not justified by the form in which the product had been presented to him. The reasonable inference would be that this was another frozen food product put on the market by McCain, to which they had chosen to attach the name Stringfellows because the chips in question were "long and thin".

The advertisement was, however, found unwittingly to involve a degree of misrepresentation. Even so, following Lord Diplock's speech in the Advocaat *case, it was necessary to establish damage or a likelihood of damage ensuing to the plaintiffs. After rejecting the one piece of evidence proffered to show actual refusal to deal with the plaintiff because of his supposed connection with the chips, the court considered whether there was sufficient likelihood of damage. It rejected as "little more than speculation based on no solid evidence" the trial judge's view that there would be a likely loss of bookings at the club. Slade L.J. proceeded:*

I now turn to the remaining suggested head of likely damage. Mr Jones, Mr Patrick and Mr Townley, in what in the course of the proceedings have been referred to as "expert reports", gave evidence in regard to modern practices in relation to intellectual property licences. Mr Jones, for example, described in a little detail how licensing of such right can take the form of (*inter alia*) "franchising", "merchandising", "sponsorship" and "endorsement". All these three witnesses expressed the opinion, albeit in rather different words, that any association of the club with an oven-baked chip product would be likely to damage the image of the club and to prejudice the plaintiffs' chances of valuable exploitation of the goodwill attached to the name "Stringfellows".

The status of the evidence of these three witnesses is by no means clear to me, but no objection has been taken to its admissibility. The Judge, having referred to this evidence, said (p.24) that it established that:

"the grant of merchandising rights of this character is now a matter of frequent occurrence, although with the exception of a possible inference that might be drawn from the registration of a trade mark by a club and the example of the Playboy Club backed up of course by the Playboy magazine, they could point to no other cases concerned with the grant of merchandising rights by an organization such as the plaintiffs".

He went on to say (*ibid.*):

"It does plainly emerge that this was thought to be an activity in which the plaintiffs might reasonably want to indulge and that if the impression got around that rights of this character were being granted by the plaintiffs to manufacturers of frozen chips, then it was unlikely to prove attractive to persons who might want to use the name in the luxury goods field".

Much later in his judgment, having referred to the possible loss of customers for special functions, he said (at 38–39):

"The same reasoning may apply so far as other potential sponsors are concerned, at least other potential sponsors selling products in what might be described as the high quality trade or at least expensive products ... Experience in these courts alone has shown that in recent years there has been a vast extension in the field of franchising. The grant of rights of user by the owners of well known names in connection with products other than the original owners' products or business, is a commonplace of today".

Mr Jacob [for the Defendant], while not disputing that the practice of licensing merchandising rights is a common one and has indeed existed for many years, pointed out that the plaintiffs have not achieved a registration of the name "Stringfellows" under the Trade Marks Act 1938. He submitted that they could not grant a licence for the use of this name which would have any legal validity; he referred us to *Star Industrial Co Ltd v Yap Kwee Kor* [1976] F.S.R. 256.

For the purposes of this present appeal, I do not find it necessary to explore any of the niceties of the law relating to the grant of merchandising rights in respect of a name which has not been registered as a trade mark. For such purposes I am quite prepared to assume, without deciding that in many instances a person carrying on a business under a particular name (albeit not registered as a trade mark) to which a valuable goodwill is attached, may be able in practice to exploit that name to great profit in one or more of the ways suggested by Mr Jones, Mr Patrick or Mr Townley.

I do not, however, regard the evidence of these witnesses or any other witnesses in this case as having established either:

    (i) that, but for the television advertisement, the plaintiffs would have been able profitably to exploit merchandising rights in the name "Stringfellows"; or

    (ii) that the showing of the television advertisement has prejudiced or is really likely to prejudice such chances of profitable exploitation of this nature as they may possess.

(If I am right, it is only the television advertisement which has involved any misrepresentation.) As to (i), presumably in view of their fears of tarnishing their image, the plaintiffs would only wish to grant licences (if at all) in connection with goods of a luxury or "up-market" variety, such as clothes or jewellery. But how many, if any, persons marketing goods of this nature would expect to derive any potential benefit from the use of the name of a night club, albeit a celebrated night club? The name "Stringfellows" is not a fancy name. It is a surname which, at least in some parts of the country, is not an uncommon one. Nor is it a name connected with a person, such as a sportsman who has a particular expertise and for the purpose of his job requires particular equipment, the quality of which he can endorse by lending his name. So far as the evidence shows, the plaintiffs possess no relevant copyright (save perhaps their logo) in connection with which they can grant licences. In all the circumstances I do not think it surprising that Mr Stringfellow for all his business acumen, had never contemplated the exploitation of the name in this manner until the present dispute arose. When it was put to him in crossexamination that he had never done anything about franchising the use of his name, he replied with characteristic frankness: "No, sir. The honest truth of that is that McCain's advert has woken me up that I should have been making moves. They jumped the gun on me". But, since the evidence does not show that McCain itself has derived, or is likely to derive, any benefit at all from any association of its product with the club, McCain itself presumably would not have been in the market as a potential franchise. In my opinion, the evidence as a whole gives no solid basis for inferring that, but for the television advertisement, the plaintiffs would have been in a position profitably to exploit merchandising rights in the name "Stringfellows".

5.1.4.6 *Mirage Studios v Counter-feat Clothing Co* **[1991] F.S.R. 145, Browne-Wilkinson V.C.**

The first plaintiffs owned the copyright in cartoon characters called "Teenage Mutant Ninja Turtles". They sold cartoons, films and videos of these characters and also licensed their use on goods, including clothing, by others. The defendants employed an artist to create similar turtle figures, which they licensed to manufacturers of T-shirts and jogging bottoms. The defendants' turtles differed from those of the plaintiff in detail but conveyed the same idea and concept, and there was evidence that members of the public believed them to be the same. The plaintiffs sought an interlocutory injunction for breach of copyright and passing off. On the application of the law of passing off to character merchandising Browne-Wilkinson V.C. referred to the five requirements of passing off identified by Lord Diplock in Warnink v Townend *(above, 5.1.1.4) and continued:*

Applying those requirements to the present case, first, has there been a misrepresentation? The critical evidence in this case is that a substantial number of the buying public now expect and know that where a famous cartoon or television character is reproduced on goods, that reproduction is the result of a licence granted by the owner of the copyright or owner of other rights in that character. Mr Smith, the defendant, accepted that evidence subject to this: he said that was only true where the reproduced matter was an exact reproduction of the character in the cartoon or television show, whereas in his case the defendants' turtles were different. I cannot accept that. If, as the evidence here shows, the public mistake the defendants' turtles for those which might be called genuine plaintiffs' Turtles, once they have made that mistake they will assume that the product in question has been licensed to use the Turtles on it. That is to say, they will connect what they mistakenly think to be the plaintiffs' Turtles with the plaintiffs. To put on the market goods which the public mistake for the genuine article necessarily involves a misrepresentation to the public that they are genuine. On the evidence in this case, the belief that the goods are genuine involves a further misrepresentation, namely that they are licensed.

The second of Lord Diplock's requirements was that the representation must be made by the trader in the course of his trade. Plainly that is so in the present case since the representation of the defendants' turtles on goods licensed by them must be made by or with the authority of the defendants. Similarly, as to Lord Diplock's third requirement it is self-evident that the representation is made to prospective customers of the defendants because they are being presented for sale to such customers.

The fourth requirement is that the misrepresentation must be calculated to injure the business or goodwill of another trader in the sense that that is a reasonably foreseeable consequence. In my judgment, that is the critical question in the present case. What is the plaintiffs' business or goodwill? Mirage Studios are plainly in business as the creators and marketers of cartoons, videos and films of their characters, the Ninja Turtles. But the evidence is quite clear that that is only part of their business: their business also includes the turning to profit of those characters by licensing the reproduction of them on goods sold by other people. A major part of their business income arises from royalties to be received from such licensing enterprise. In relation to the drawings of Ninja Turtles as they appear in cartoons, etc., there is a copyright which can be infringed. If one wishes to take advantage of the Ninja character it is necessary to reproduce the Ninja Turtle and thereby the concept, bizarre and unusual as it is, of the Teenage Mutant Turtle becomes a marketable commodity. It is in that business that the plaintiffs are engaged.

That dual nature of the plaintiffs' business (namely both the creation and exploitation of the cartoons and films themselves and the licensing of the right to use those creations) is in my judgment important. As I have said, if others are able to reproduce or apparently reproduce the Turtles without paying licence royalties to the plaintiffs, they will lose the royalties. Since the public associates the goods with the creator of the characters, the depreciation of the image by fixing the Turtle picture to inferior goods and inferior materials may seriously reduce the value of the licensing right. This damage to an important part of the plaintiffs' business is therefore plainly foreseeable.

The fifth of Lord Diplock's requirements is that that foreseen damage actually occurs, or will probably do so. Again, in my judgment that is manifestly clear in the present case.

Therefore, on that analysis, the five essential elements to a passing off action as laid down by Lord Diplock are present. However, he gives a warning that those are minimum requirements; it does not follow that if those requirements are satisfied, there is necessarily a claim in passing off. This is a case where that is particularly true. In the ordinary case, a passing off action applies to goods which have been manufactured or marketed by the plaintiff. Here the plaintiffs have no part in either manufacturing or marketing the goods; they are neither makers nor sellers. The goods, the T-shirts, the jogging bottoms and so on are manufactured by others. The plaintiffs' only connection with the marketing of those goods is by the affixing of their characters, the Turtles, on to the merchandise of others. But, crucially, the evidence shows that the public is aware that the Turtle characters would not normally appear without the licence of the plaintiffs, *i.e.* they connect the Turtles with the plaintiffs. The question is whether that link between the goods being sold and the plaintiffs is sufficient to found a case in passing off. In my judgment, it should be.

It has been held to be a sufficient link in Australia. In *Children's Television Workshop Inc v Woolworths* (*New South Wales*) *Limited* [1981] R.P.C. 187 (*The Muppet case*) the Chief Justice in Equity of the Supreme Court of New South Wales held that the owners of the copyright and merchandising rights in Australia of the Muppets were entitled to inter- locutory relief against other persons seeking to use Muppet characters in conjunction with the marketing of goods in New South Wales. The evidence there, as it is here, is that the public would know of a link between the appearance of the Muppet characters on goods and the existence of a licence to use those characters granted by the creator of the Muppets. The learned Judge held that by the unlicensed use of Muppet characters on the goods, the defendants were misrepresenting that they had a connection with the owner of the copy- right and were licensee of rights in the Muppets.

Similarly, in *Fido Dido Inc v Venture Stores* (*Retailers*) *Pty Limited* 16 I.P.R. 365, Foster J. in the Federal Court of Australia held that the creator of the character Fido Dido and his licensees in Australia had a cause of action in passing off against somebody seeking to use the character known as Fido Dido there without their licence. Although the injunction was refused on the facts of that case, the learned judge held that it was sufficient that there should be a public awareness that the character, Fido Dido, would have been created and licensed by someone who had a business interest in putting them on the market.

In my judgment, the law as developed in Australia is sound. There is no reason why a remedy in passing off should be limited to those who market or sell the goods themselves. If the public is misled in a relevant way as to a feature or quality of the goods as sold, that is sufficient to found a cause of action in passing off brought by those people with whom the public associate that feature or that quality which has been misrepresented. Miss Vitoria submitted that the Australian law, however good in principle, was not the law of this country and reminded me firmly and correctly that my job is to apply the law of this country and not the law of Australia.

She relies in particular on three cases. The first concerned The Wombles: *Wombles Limited v Womble Skips Limited* [1977] R.P.C. 99. The Wombles were well-known fictitious characters then highly popular amongst children, who had been the subject of a television series and had been otherwise commercially exploited. The defendant chose to call his company Womble Skips Limited and printed Wombles on the side of the skips; but apart from that made no use of any representation of The Wombles or any character in it. Walton J. held that the plaintiffs had no arguable case to found a claim for an interlocutory injunction. His ground for the decision was that there was no common field of activity in which the plaintiffs and the defendants were operating. Secondly, he relied on the fact that there was only the taking of the name "Wombles"; there was no other use of any Wombles character or representation of any copyright material. Miss Vitoria accepts that the so-called requirement of law that there should be a common field of activity is now discredited. As to the other ground (namely that there was only the use of the name) the decision may still be good law. There is no copyright in a name. If Wombles be a name, as the judge thought it was, then it is hard to see what business the plaintiffs could have been carrying on in licensing the copyright in the name and the name alone. Here, on the contrary, the plaintiffs are carrying on the business of licensing the copyright in the drawings of the Ninja Turtles in which copyright does exist.

The second decision is also by Walton J.: *Tavener Rutledge Limited v Trexapalm Limited* [1975] F.S.R. 179. It related to lollipops called in one form or another "Kojak Lollies" or "Kojak Pops", both drawing on the name of the well-known fictitious television character "Kojak", who is much given to sucking lollies. A claim to interlocutory relief by those entitled to what they said were the rights in the name Kojak failed before Walton J. again on the ground that there was no common field of activity. It is interesting to note that at line 40 on p.280, Walton J. said it was not established on the evidence (and he would have been very surprised if it had been) that the system of character merchandising was known to the man on the street. That is contrary to the position as it exists on the evidence before me where, as I say, the evidence clearly establishes that it now is known to the man in the street. After all, 13 years have passed since the decision in that case. Moreover, it is to be noted in *Tavener Rutledge* that the matter at issue was again simply a name, Kojak, in which under copyright law there can be no copyright. Therefore, the defendants could not have been interfering with the business of the plaintiffs in licensing the copyright in the name. Walton J. made certain remarks about the need to show an awareness in the public that licensors of characters were concerned to uphold the quality of the goods on which the characters appear. At the moment I am afraid I do not understand why that is an essential characteristic of passing off: he made the remark in the context of finding that there was no field of common activity.

The third case is the *Abba* case, a decision of Oliver J., as he then was: *Lyngstad v Anabas Products Limited* [1977] F.S.R. 62. The pop group, Abba, sought to restrain the defendants from applying their name to clothing, pillow slips and T-shirts. Therefore, it was another case in which the name only was being copied. Was there any property in the name alone which could be protected under English law? That was the point relied on by Oliver J. at 68 when he stressed the fact that there was no copyright in the name. In addition, in that case, there was no evidence of substantial exploitation by Abba of any licensing rights in this country. In those circumstances, the judge was unimpressed by the strength of the plaintiff's case, and refused an interlocutory injunction on the grounds of balance of convenience. I do not find anything in that case inconsistent with the Australian cases. Again, it was concerned with licensing rights in a name as opposed to licensing rights in what is undoubtedly copyright material. It may be that different factors apply in such a case, though those cases may, given the change in trading habits, require reconsideration on a future occasion if the evidence before the court is different.

In my judgment the three English cases do not touch on a case such as the present where the plaintiff clearly has copyright in the drawings and is in business on a large scale in this country in licensing the use of the copyright in those drawings. The defendant is misrepresenting to the public that his drawings are the drawings of the plaintiffs or are licensed by the plaintiffs. I can see no reason why, in those circumstances, the defendants should be allowed to misrepresent his goods in that way. I therefore consider that if the case went to trial, the plaintiffs' case in passing off would succeed. ...

The second point taken by Miss Vitoria was that the plaintiffs had to prove by evidence that the public in purchasing T-shirts or other clothing carrying Turtle pictures on them would rely on the misrepresentation, namely that the picture of the Turtles was one licensed by the plaintiffs. That is to say, would the public decline to buy T-shirts if they knew that what they were buying were the defendants' counterfeits as opposed to the plaintiffs' genuine Turtles? For that purpose she relied on *Politechnika Ipari Szovetkezet v Dallas Print Transfers Ltd* [1982] F.S.R. 529. In my judgment, that case does not support the proposition. That case was purely concerned with establishing that the plaintiff in a passing off case had to show a reputation which he enjoyed in the goods, which reputation was being interfered with. It does not, as I see it, come anywhere near requiring affirmative evidence that the public will rely on the misrepresentation in acquiring the goods. In my judgment, if the misrepresentation is made there is no requirement of law for further evidence to show that the misrepresentation was the cause of the public buying the goods in question. In general, the public expect to buy what they think they are getting, namely the genuine article. So, here, a teenage child wishing to buy a Mutant Turtle as part of the craze would wish to get a genuine Turtle, one which was indeed a Teenage Mutant Ninja Turtle. In the absence of evidence, the court must infer that if the child in the present case, or the customer in any case, were aware that the object he is buying is not genuine, he would not buy it but would seek the real object.

5.1.4.7   *Taittinger SA v Allbev Ltd* [1993] F.S.R. 641, CA

The defendants produced and sold a non-alcoholic carbonated drink called "Elderflower Champagne". The plaintiffs, acting as representatives of all wine producers of the Champagne region of France with sales in England, issued proceedings for passing off. The trial judge found that the first four characteristics of passing off in Lord Diplock's formulation of the law in Warnink v Townend *(above, 5.1.1.4) were satisfied but that the plaintiffs failed to satisfy the fifth characteristic because there was no likelihood that they would suffer any damage from the defendants' misrepresentation. The plaintiffs appealed.*

In the Court of Appeal Glidewell L.J. found that there was sufficient deception of members of the public to satisfy the requirement of damage, and then continued:

But in my judgment the real injury to the champagne houses' goodwill comes under a different head and although the judge refers to Mr Sparrow putting the point in argument, he does not deal with it specifically or give a reason for its undoubted rejection by him. Mr Sparrow had argued that if the defendants continued to market their product, there would take place a blurring or erosion of the uniqueness that now attends the word "champagne", so that the exclusive reputation of the champagne houses would be debased. He put this even more forcefully before us. He submitted that if the defendants are allowed to continue to call their product "Elderflower Champagne", the effect would be to demolish the distinctiveness of the word champagne, and that would inevitably damage the goodwill of the champagne houses.

In the *Advocaat* case [1980] R.P.C. 31 at 52 Goulding J. held that one type of damage was "a more gradual damage to the plaintiffs' business through depreciation of the reputation that their goods enjoy". He continued: "Damage of [this] type can rarely be susceptible of positive proof. In my judgment, it is likely to occur if the word 'Advocaat' is permitted to be used of alcoholic egg drinks generally or of the defendants' product in particular." In the House of Lords in that case Lord Diplock referred to that type of damage to goodwill as relevant damage, which he described as caused "indirectly in the debasement of the reputation attaching to the name 'advocaat'..." (See [1979] 2 All E.R. 927 at 930–931; [1979] A.C. 731 at 740.)

In *Vine Products Ltd v Mackenzie & Co Ltd* [1969] R.P.C. 1 at 23 Cross J., commenting with approval on the decision of Danckwerts J. in *J. Bollinger v Costa Brava Wine Co Ltd* (*No. 2*), said:

> "[Danckwerts J.] thought, as I read his judgment, that if people were allowed to call sparkling wine not produced in Champagne 'Champagne', even though preceded by an adjective denoting the country of origin, the distinction between genuine Champagne and 'champagne type' wines produced elsewhere would become blurred; that the word 'Champagne' would come gradually to mean no more than 'sparkling wine'; and that the part of the plaintiffs' goodwill which consisted in the name would be diluted and gradually destroyed."

That passage was referred to approvingly by Gault J. in *Wineworths Group Ltd v Comité Interprofessionel du Vin de Champagne* [1992] 2 N.Z.L.R. 327 at 341. In that case the sale of Australian sparkling wine under the name champagne was held to constitute passing off. The New Zealand Court of Appeal upheld the decision of Jeffries J., who had held ([1991] 2 N.Z.L.R. 432 at 450): "By using the word champagne on the label the defendant is deceptively encroaching on the reputation and goodwill of the plaintiffs." Jeffries J. had no doubt that if relief was not granted the plaintiffs would most certainly suffer damage if the word was used on all or any sparkling wine sold in New Zealand. He thought the ordinary purchaser in New Zealand without special knowledge on wines was likely to be misled. Gault J., after agreeing with Jeffries J. on deception, said ([1992] 2 N.Z.L.R. 327 at 343):

> "I find the issue of damage or likely damage to the goodwill with which the name 'Champagne' is associated equally obvious in light of the finding that there is in fact an established goodwill in New Zealand. I have no doubt that erosion of the distinctiveness of a name or mark is a form of damage to the goodwill of the business with which the name is connected. There is no clearer example of this than the debasing of the name 'Champagne' in Australia as a result of its use by local wine makers."

By parity of reasoning it seems to me no less obvious that erosion of the distinctiveness of the name champagne in this country is a form of damage to the goodwill of the business of the champagne houses. There are undoubtedly factual points of distinction between the New Zealand case and the present case, as Mr Isaacs has pointed out, and he placed particular reliance on the fact that in the New Zealand case as well as in *J. Bollinger v Costa Brava Wine Co Ltd* (*No. 2*), the court held that there was a deliberate attempt to take advantage of the name champagne, whereas in the present case the judge found no such specific intention. In general it is no doubt easier to infer damage when a fraudulent intention is established. But that fact does not appear to have played any part in the reasoning on this particular point either of Jeffries J. or of Sir Robin Cooke P., who thought the case exemplified the principle that a tendency to impair distinctiveness might lead to an inference of damage to goodwill (see [1992] 2 N.Z.L.R. 327 at 332), or of Gault J.; nor in logic can I see why it should. It seems to me inevitable that if the defendants, with their not insignificant trade as a supplier of drinks to Sainsbury and other retail outlets, are permitted to use the name "Elderflower Champagne", the goodwill in the distinctive name champagne will be eroded with serious adverse consequences for the champagne houses.

In my judgment therefore the fifth characteristic identified in the *Advocaat* case is established.

Sir Thomas Bingham M.R. found that the defendants' use of the name "Elderflower Champagne" would not reduce the plaintiffs' sales in any significant or direct way but that the requirement of damage was nevertheless satisfied:

The first plaintiffs' reputation and goodwill in the description "Champagne" derive not only from the quality of their wine and its glamorous associations, but also from the very singularity and exclusiveness of the description, the absence of qualifying epithets and imitative descriptions. Any product which is not Champagne but is allowed to describe itself as such must inevitably, in my view, erode the singularity and exclusiveness of the description "Champagne" and so cause the first plaintiffs damage of an insidious but serious kind. The amount of damage which the defendants' product would cause would of course depend on the size of the defendants' operation. That is not negligible now, and it could become much bigger. But I cannot see, despite the defendants' argument to the contrary, any rational basis upon which, if the defendants' product were allowed to be marketed under its present description, any other fruit cordial diluted with carbonated water could not be similarly marketed so as to incorporate the description "champagne". The damage to the first plaintiffs would then be incalculable but severe.

I would allow the plaintiffs' appeal and grant appropriate injunctive relief. This conclusion is not in my view offensive to the common sense or the fairness of the situation. The defendants are plainly very anxious to describe their product as "Elderflower Champagne" rather than as "Elderflower" (the description used while the interlocutory injunction was in force) or some variant such as "Elderflower Sparkling Drink". Why? Because a reference to champagne imports nuances of quality and celebration, a sense of something privileged and special. But this is the reputation which the Champagne houses have built up over the years, and in which they have a property right. It is not in my view unfair to deny the defendants the opportunity to exploit, share or (in the vernacular) cash in on that reputation, which they have done nothing to establish. It would be very unfair to allow them to do so if the consequence was, as I am satisfied it would be, to debase and cheapen that very reputation.

Mann L.J. agreed with the judgment of Peter Gibson L.J.

5.1.4.8   *Irvine v Talksport* [2002] F.S.R. 943, Laddie J.

Eddie Irvine became a well-known Formula 1 racing driver. In 1999, he drove for the Ferrari team and came second in the World Championship. Although it had acquired the radio broadcasting rights for the races, Talk Radio (later Talksport) had no contact with Irvine to endorse its programs. Notwithstanding this it manipulated a photograph of Irvine so that it appeared that he was using a radio with "Talk Radio" on it. The use of this photograph in a promotional brochure was held to constitute passing off.

Laddie J. referred to a line of cases that was critical of, or inconsistent with, the view that passing off required that the parties share a "common field of activity" (Wynn-Parry J., McCulloch v May (1948) 65 R.P.C. 58). He concluded:

38. In my view these cases illustrate that the law of passing off now is of greater width than as applied by Wynn-Parry J. in *McCulloch v May*. If someone acquires a valuable reputation or goodwill, the law of passing off will protect it from unlicensed use by other parties. Such use will frequently be damaging in the direct sense that it will involve selling inferior goods or services under the guise that they are from the claimant. But the action is not restricted to protecting against that sort of damage. The law will vindicate the claimant's exclusive right to the reputation or goodwill. It will not allow others to so use goodwill as to reduce, blur or diminish its exclusivity. It follows that it is not necessary to show that the claimant and the defendant share a common field of activity or that sales of products or services will be diminished either substantially or directly, at least in the short term. Of course there is still a need to demonstrate a misrepresentation because it is that misrepresentation which enables the defendant to make use or take advantage of the claimant's reputation.

39. Not only has the law of passing off expanded over the years, but the commercial environment in which it operates is in a constant state of flux. Even without the evidence given at the trial in this action, the court can take judicial notice of the fact that it is common for famous people to exploit their names and images by way of endorsement. They do it not only in their own field of expertise but, depending on the extent of their fame or notoriety, wider afield also. It is common knowledge that for many sportsman, for example, income received from endorsing a variety of products and services represent a very substantial part of their total income. The reason large sums are paid for endorsement is because, no matter how irrational it may seem to a lawyer, those in business have reason to believe that the lustre of a famous personality, if attached to their goods or services, will enhance the attractiveness of those goods or services to their target market. In this respect, the endorsee is taking the benefit of the attractive force which is the reputation or goodwill of the famous person.

40. This was supported by the evidence at the trial. Mr Bleakley, who gave evidence on behalf of the defendant, summed the position up neatly in his witness statement:

> "Endorsement arrangements by sports stars are often entered into with a view to influencing the target audience's choice." (Witness Statement paragraph 39)

43. Manufacturers and retailers recognise the realities of the market place when they pay for well known personalities to endorse their goods. The law of passing off should do likewise. There appears to be no good reason why the law of passing off in its modern form and in modern trade circumstances should not apply to cases of false endorsement. Indeed, it seems to me that this is not a novel proposition in this country. The *British Medical Association* case and similar trade association cases are all ones in which passing off was used to prevent false endorsement. The most recent case which stands against this is *McCullough v May* which, as explained above, is discredited.

44. In my view nothing said above touches on the quite separate issues which may arise in character merchandising cases, a considerable number of which were cited to me during the trial. In those cases, the defendant's activities do not imply any endorsement. For example, although it was a trade mark registration case, in *ELVIS PRESLEY Trade Marks* (below, 5.2.3.4) much of the argument turned on whether the appellant had merchandising rights in the name Elvis Presley or in his image. It wanted to prevent third parties from selling products such as bars of soap and drinking mugs bearing the name of the performer and photographs of him. There could be no question of the performer endorsing anything since he had been dead for many years. So the argument being advanced was one which amounted to an attempt to create a quasi-copyright in the name and images. The Court of Appeal's rejection of that is, with respect, consistent with a long line of authority. As Robert Walker L.J. said in *ELVIS PRESLEY Trade Marks*:

"However this appeal is not an appropriate occasion on which to attempt to define precisely how far the law of passing off has developed in response to the growth of character merchandising, still less to express views as to how much further it should develop or in what direction."

45. The same point can be made here. Whether such a new right may be created either by development of the common law or as a result of the passing of the Human Rights Act, is not relevant to this action.

46. It follows from the views expressed above that there is nothing which prevents an action for passing off succeeding in a false endorsement case. However to succeed, the burden on the claimant includes a need to prove at least two, interrelated facts. First that at the time of the acts complained of he had a significant reputation or goodwill. Second that the actions of the defendant gave rise to a false message which would be understood by a not insignificant section of his market that his goods have been endorsed, recommended or are approved of by the claimant. I shall turn to those two issues.

Laddie J. found both these elements to be made out on the facts.

5.1.5   Injurious Falsehood

5.1.5.1   *Wilts United Dairies v Robinson* [1957] R.P.C. 220; [1958] R.P.C. 94, Stable J.

The plaintiffs were well-known manufacturers of condensed milk under the brand "British Maid". The Ministry of Food acquired a stock of it. When it became too old for ordinary use, it was sold off on condition that it be used only in manufacturing, for animal feed or for export. The defendant company indirectly purchased large quantities of this, in circumstances where (it was held) it must have known that milk was old stock purchased from the Ministry. It resold at considerable profit. It was found that this conduct amounted to passing off.

On the issue of injurious falsehood, the question arose whether the defendant had been shown to have acted maliciously, given that it did not intend to injure the plaintiff.

Stable J.:

There are three authorities I should like to refer to. The first is *Mogul Steamship Co Ltd v MacGregor, Gow & Co*, the well-known case reported at [1892] A.C. 25, and more particularly the passage from Lord Field's speech at 52. He says: "It follows therefore from this authority, and is undoubted law not only that it is not every act causing damage to another in his trade, nor even every intentional act of such damage, which is actionable, but also that acts done by a trader in the lawful way of his business, although by the necessary results of effective competition interfering injuriously with the trade of another, are not the subject of any action. Of course it is otherwise, as pointed out by Lord Holt, if the acts complained of, although done in the way and under the guise of competition or other lawful right, are in themselves violent or purely malicious, or have for their ultimate object injury to another from ill-will to him, and not the pursuit of lawful rights".

Pausing there, Lord Field says, "It follows ... and is undoubted law not only that it is not every act causing damage to another actionable, but also that acts done by a trader in the lawful way of his business, although by the necessary results of effective competition interfering injuriously with the trade of another are not the subject of any action". It seems to me that the difficulty there is to decide whether the acts done by the trader in the way of his business were lawful or not.

Then Lord Field goes on: "No doubt, also, there have been cases in which agreements to do acts injurious to others have been held to be indictable as amounting to conspiracy, the ultimate object or the means being unlawful, although if done by an individual no such consequence would have followed". Then this is the important part in relation to the present case: "... but I think that in all such cases it will be found that there existed either an ultimate object of malice, or wrong, or wrongful means of execution involving elements of injury to the public, or, at least, negativing the pursuit of a lawful object". He is saying: "... in all such cases it will be found that there existed either an ultimate object of malice, or wrong, or wrongful means of execution involving elements of injury".

The next case which I think has a very strong bearing on the problem is that of *Greers Ltd v Pearman & Corder Ltd* (1922) 39 R.P.C. 406 at 412 and 417. That is an interesting case, because that was an appeal to the Court of Appeal from a decision arrived at the trial of the case before Bray J. and a jury. It is quite obvious, from reading the report and Bray J.'s summing-up, that in the Judge's view the action should have failed: but the matter was left to the jury, the jury found malice, and the Court of Appeal refused to interfere with that finding because they said that there was evidence from which the jury did infer malice, although I think they pretty clearly indicated, as did the learned Judge, that if it had been left to them or him no such inference would have been drawn.

The assistance to be derived from that case in the present one is partly in the direction in the summing-up which tacitly was approved by the Court of Appeal, and the observations, in particular, of Scrutton L.J. What Bray J. said to the jury at 412 was this: "Members of the jury, it is a question for you, only I impress upon you that it is for the plaintiffs to satisfy you that this man knew he had no right, in which case undoubtedly he would be actuated by malice, but if he acted bona fide, fairly believing, though wrongly believing, that they had the right to the protection of this name, having used it ever since 1905—if you think he bona fide believed that—and it is not for the defendants to prove it, but for the plaintiffs to prove the contrary, then I do not see what evidence of malice there is about it". The judge is directing the jury there that if a man says something that he knows to be untrue, it is malicious *ipso facto*, because he has said something that is false and something that he knows to be false, regardless of whether his object in making the false statement was his own advantage or the detriment of someone else.

Lord Justice Scrutton, at 417, says: "The action is one for a form of what is called slander of title—for slander of goods, for making defamatory statements about a man's goods which are actionable if they are untrue, and cause him special damage and are made maliciously". We can eliminate the special damage now because the law has changed. "The only question in this case is—is there evidence on which the jury could find that the statements were made maliciously? 'Maliciously', not in the sense of illegally, but in the sense of being made with some indirect or dishonest motive. Honest belief in an unfounded claim is not malice: but the nature of the unfounded claim may be evidence that there was not an honest belief in it. It may be so unfounded that the particular fact that is put forward may be evidence that it is not honestly believed".

The Lord Justice there apparently is agreeing with the direction that the judge gave the jury, namely, that quite apart from what object you had in mind, if you state something which is defamatory of somebody else's goods and you know what you say is untrue then (although your object and your only object may be your own benefit, although you have no intentional wish or desire to harm) the mere uttering of the untrue statement with knowledge that it is untrue is malice.

Balden v Shorter [1933] 1 Ch. 427 was an action for injurious falsehood. It was a case in which what the defendant had said was wholly inaccurate: it was injurious to the plaintiff. Lord Maugham—Maugham J. as he then was—decided that the man acted in food faith and honestly believed the truth of what he had said. What Lord Maugham said, at 429 was this: "If I could properly conclude that the story told in the witness box by Mr Bensted was untrue and that he knew that the plaintiff was not employed by the defendants, I should have little difficulty in determining the action in the plaintiff's favour because, if Mr Bensted said that knowing it to be untrue, I should draw the inference that he did it from a dishonest motive and maliciously. But I cannot come to that conclusion". Of course, it may be that the learned Judge meant this: "If I come to the conclusion that what Mr Bensted said was untrue and that he knew it was untrue, it would be a fair inference that he did that with the object of harming the plaintiff". That passage taken literally means no more than this—that knowledge of the falsity is evidence of improper motive, therefore of malice, which is very different from saying that to utter a statement known to be false in such a context is malice irrespective of the motive with which the falsehood is uttered. Looking at the judgment as a whole I do not think the learned Judge intended to give such a restricted meaning to malice.

Then at 430 Lord Maugham says this: "The meaning of 'malice' in connection with injurious falsehood is dealt with in Salmond on Torts (7th ed.), pp.582–583, in the following passage, which I accept as correct". Then, quoting from "Salmond": "What is meant by malice in this connection? Lord Davey, in the passage already cited—*Royal Baking Powder Co v Wright, Crossley & Co* (1901) 18 R.P.C. 95 at 99—defines it as meaning the absence of just cause or excuse. It is to be observed, however, that this is not one of the recognised meanings of the term malice in other connections; an act done without just cause or excuse is wrongful but not necessarily malicious: for example, a trespass by mistake on another man's land, or the conversion of his chattels under an erroneous claim of right. Notwithstanding Lord Davey's dictum, it is now apparently settled that malice in the law of slander of title and other forms of injurious falsehood means some dishonest or otherwise improper motive". Then these are the words that I think are important: "A bone fide assertion of title, however mistaken, if made for the protection of one's own interest or for some other proper purpose, is not 'malicious'". I emphasise the words "bona fide".

Lord Maugham proceeds: "In *Greers Ltd v Pearman & Corder Ltd* (1922) 39 R.P.C. 406 Lord Justice Bankes said that 'maliciously' for the purpose which the court was considering meant 'with some indirect object', and Lord Justice Scrutton remarked that the only question in the case was whether there was evidence on which the jury could find that the statements were made maliciously 'in the sense of being made with some indirect or dishonest motive'".

So much for the authorities. As I understand the law it is this, that if you publish a defamatory statement about a man's goods which is injurious to him, honestly believing that it is true, your object being your own advantage and no detriment to him, you obviously are not liable. If you publish a statement which turns out to be false but which you honestly believe to be true, but you publish that statement not for the purpose of protecting your own interests and achieving some advantage to yourself but for the purpose of doing him harm, and it transpires, contrary to your belief, that the statement that you believed to be true has turned out to be false, notwithstanding the bona fides of your belief because the object that you had in mind was to injure him and not to advantage yourself, you would be liable for an injurious falsehood.

The third proposition which I derive from the cases is this, that if you publish an injurious falsehood which you know to be false, albeit that your only object is your own advantage and with no intention or desire to injure the person in relation to whose goods the falsehood is published then provided that it is clear from the nature of the falsehood that it is intrinsically injurious—I say "intrinsically", meaning not deliberately aimed with intent to injure but as being inherent in the statement itself, the defendant is responsible, the malice consisting in the fact that what he published he knew to be false.

To summarise, I have come to the conclusion here that the representation was that this was what I may call the plaintiffs' current milk, which the defendants knew perfectly well that it was not: that their intention or object in selling the milk, making the representations and all the rest of it, was their own advantage and nothing else and own advantage, profit or gain; but the fact that they knew what they were saying was intrinsically injurious and they knew it was not true constitutes malice and therefore they are liable at the suit of the plaintiff under the heading of injurious falsehood.

5.1.5.2   *White v Mellin* [1895] A.C. 156, HL

The defendant, Timothy White, the retail chemist, sold Mellin's infant food, attaching to it a label proclaiming the virtues of Vance's infant food. Mellin sought an injunction to prevent this practice on the ground of injurious false-hood.

Lord Herschell:

Now, my Lords, the only statement made by the defendant by means of the advertisement is this: that Vance's food was the most healthful and nutritious for infants and invalids that had been offered to the public. The statement was perfectly general, and would apply in its terms not only to the respondent's infants' food but to all others that were offered to the public. I will take it as sufficiently pointed at the plaintiff's food by reason of its being affixed to a bottle of the plaintiff's food when sold, and that it does disparage the plaintiff's goods by asserting that they are not as healthful and as nutritious as those recommended by the defendant. The question then arises, has it been proved on the plaintiff's own evidence that that was a false disparagement of the plaintiff's goods?

I will state what I understand to be the result of the plaintiff's evidence. Mellin's food for infants and invalids is a preparation of such a nature that the food is said to be predigested, and therefore not to make that call upon the digestion which food ordinarily does; that as regards children under six months of age Mellin's food is the only one which could be suitably used in the place of the ordinary means of nourishment, the mother's milk, and that any farinaceous food would at that age be not only not nutritious but prejudicial. And so far, accepting the plaintiff's evidence for this purpose, there being no evidence to the contrary, the plaintiff, I think, establishes that his food was specially meritorious for that class of cases, and that it would not be correct to say that as regards these children of very tender age Vance's food or any other farinaceous food would be not only more healthful and nutritious, but as healthful and nutritious. But then it appears that when a child has passed the age up to which nutrition at the breast may ordinarily be said to continue, the use of some farinaceous food is not only not prejudicial but desirable, and that if the child were to be always brought up upon a food which would be suitable during the very earliest weeks or months, its digestion would be likely to suffer rather than benefit, and there would be not more, but less nourishment. After 12 months, as I understand the evidence, the farinaceous food would be distinctly better for the purposes of nutrition and health than this pre-digested food.

Why is it to be supposed that any one buying this bottle at the chemist's would be led to believe that Mellin's food which he has bought was not a good article or not as good an article as another, merely because a person who obviously was seeking to push a rival article said that his article was better? My Lords, why should people give such a special weight to this anonymous puff of Vance's food, obviously the work of someone who wanted to sell it, as that it should lead him to determine to buy it instead of Mellin's foods, which was said to be recommended by the faculty as the best for infants and invalids? I confess I do not wonder that the plaintiff did not insist that he had sustained injury by what the defendant had done. There is an entire absence of any evidence that the statement complained of either had injured or was calculated to injure the plaintiff. If so, then the case is not brought even within the definition of the law which Lindley L.J. gives.

Lopes L.J. adds the word "maliciously", that "it is actionable to publish maliciously without lawful occasion a false statement disparaging the goods of another person". By that it may be intended to indicate that the object of the publication must be to injure another person, and that the advertisement is not published bona fide merely to sell the advertiser's own goods, or at all events, that he published it with a knowledge of its falsity. One or other of those elements, it seems to me must be intended by the addition of the word "maliciously". Both those are certainly absent here. There is nothing to show that the object of the defendant was other than to puff his own goods and so sell them, nor is there anything to show that he did not believe that his food was better than any other.

Lord Herschell then reviewed Western Counties v Lawes Chemical *((1874) L.R. 9 Ex. 218);* Evans v Harlow *((1844) 5 Q.B. 624); and* Canham v Jones *(2 V. & B. 218). He continued:*

But, My Lords, I cannot help saying that I entertain very grave doubts whether any action could be maintained for an alleged disparagement of another's goods, merely on the allegation that the goods sold by the party who is alleged to have disparaged his competitor's goods are better either generally or in this or that particular respect than his competitor's are. Of course, I put aside the question (it is not necessary to consider it) whether where a person intending to injure another, and not in the exercise of his own trade and vaunting his own goods, has maliciously and falsely disparaged the goods of another, an action will lie; I am dealing with the class of cases which is now before us where the only disparagement consists in vaunting the superiority of the defendant's own goods. In *Evans v Harlow* Lord Denman expressed himself thus: "The gist of the complaint is the defendant's telling the world that the lubricators sold by the plaintiff were not good for their purpose, but wasted the tallow. A tradesman offering goods for sale exposes himself to observations of this kind, and it is not by averring them to be 'false, scandalous, malicious and defamatory' that the plaintiff can found a charge of libel upon them. To decide so would open a very wide door to litigation, and might expose every man who said his goods were better than another's to the risk of an action". My Lords, those observations seem to me to be replete with good sense. It is to be observed that *Evans v Harlow* does not appear to have been decided on the ground merely that there was no allegation of special damage. The only judge who alludes to the absence of such an allegation is Patteson J. No reference to it is to be found either in the judgment of Lord Denman or in the judgment of Wightman J., the other two judges who took part in that decision; and I think it is impossible not to see that, as Lord Denman says, a very wide door indeed would be opened to litigation and that the courts might be constantly employed in trying the relative merits of rival productions, if an action of this kind were allowed.

Mr Moulton sought to distinguish the present case by saying that all that Lord Denman referred to was one tradesman saying that his goods were better than his rival's. That, he said, is a matter of opinion, but whether they are more healthful and more nutritious is a question of fact. My Lords, I do not think it is possible to draw such a distinction. The allegation of a tradesman that his goods are better than his neighbour's very often involves only the consideration whether they possess one or two qualities superior to the other. Of course "better" means better as regards the purpose for which they are intended, and the question of better or worse in many cases depends simply upon one or two or three issues of fact. If an action will not lie because a man says that his goods are better than his neighbour's, it seems to me impossible to say that it will lie because he says that they are better in this or that or the other respect. Just consider what a door would be opened if this were permitted. That this sort of puffing advertisement is in use is notorious; and we see rival cures advertised for particular ailments. The court would then be bound to inquire, in an action brought, whether this ointment or this pill better cured the disease which it was alleged to cure—whether a particular article of food was in this respect or that better than another. Indeed, the courts of law would be turned into a machinery for advertising rival productions by obtaining a judicial determination which of the two was the better. As I said, advertisements and announcements of that description have been common enough; but the case of *Evans v Harlow* was decided in the year 1844, somewhat over half a century ago, and the fact that no such action—unless it be *Western Counties Manure Co v Lawes Chemical Manure Co*—has ever been maintained in the Courts of Justice is very strong indeed to show that it is not maintainable. It is, indeed, unnecessary to decide the point in order to dispose of the present appeal.

For the reasons which I have given I have come to the conclusion that the judgment of the court below cannot be sustained, even assuming the law to be as stated by the learned judges; but inasmuch as the case is one of the great importance and some additional colour would be lent to the idea that an action of this description was maintainable by the observations in the court below, I have thought it only right to express my grave doubts whether any such action could be maintained even if the facts brought the case within the law there laid down.

Upon the whole, therefore, I think that the judgment of Romer J. was right and ought to be restored and that this appeal should be allowed, with the usual result as to costs; and I so move your Lordships.

5.1.5.3 *De Beers v International General Electric* [1975] F.S.R. 323, Walton J.

Both plaintiffs and defendants manufactured and distributed abrasives made from diamonds. The plaintiffs' abrasives were made from natural diamonds, whereas those of the defendants' were made from synthetic diamonds. The second defendant caused to be circulated among prospective purchasers of such abrasives, a pamphlet which purported to show the results of comparative scientific tests on the products of the plaintiffs and defendants, carried out by the "Application Laboratory". This comparison purported to show that the plaintiffs' abrasives were distinctly inferior to those of the defendants. The plaintiffs, alleging that the pamphlet contained a number of mis-statements and was misleading, issued a writ claiming damages and an injunction restraining the defendants from publishing this pamphlet or any document containing mis-statements reflecting adversely on the plaintiffs' abrasives. Their claim was put on the two alternative bases of defamation of goods, and of unlawful inference and/or unfair competition in trade. The defendants applied for the statement of claim to be struck out on the ground, inter alia, *that it disclosed no reasonable cause of action.*

Walton J.:

What precisely is the law on this point? It is a blinding glimpse of the obvious to say that there must be a dividing line between statements that are actionable and those which are not; and the sole question of a dry point of law such as we are discussing there is: where does that line lie? On the one hand, it appears to me that the law is that any trader is entitled to puff his own goods, even though such puff must, as a matter of pure logic, involve the denigration of his rival's goods. Thus in the well-known case of the three adjoining tailors who put notices in their respective windows reading: "The best tailor in the world", "The best tailor in this town", and "The best tailor in this street" none of the three committed an actionable offence.

This is, I think, a proposition which extends to a much wider field than the slander of goods; for example, I think it extends to other vague commendatory statements about goods or services on offer. Principal among its application has been the case of auctioneers, who, within limits, have always been allowed to use language which is strictly perhaps not literally true; thus, for example, to take note of one instance, in *Hope v Walter* [1900] 1 Ch.D. 257 Lindley L.J., as he then was, stated "I do not attach any importance to the word 'eligible': it is the ordinary auctioneer's language". In other words, in the kind of situation when one expects, as a matter of ordinary common experience, a person to use a certain amount of hyperbole in the description of goods, property or services, the courts will do what any ordinary reasonable man would do, namely, take it with a large pinch of salt.

Where, however, the situation is not that the trader is puffing his own goods, but turns to denigrate those of his rival, then, in my opinion, the situation is not so clear cut. Obviously the statement: "My goods are better than X's" is only a more dramatic presentation of what is implicit in the statement: "My goods are the best in the world". Accordingly, I do not think such a statement would be actionable. At the other end of the scale, if what is said is: "My goods are better than X's, because X's are absolute rubbish", then it is established by dicta of Lord Shand in the House of Lords in *White v Mellin* [above, 5.1.5.2] which were accepted by Mr Walton as stating the law, the statement would be actionable.

Between these two kinds of statements there is obviously still an extremely wide field; and it appears to me that, in order to draw the line, one must apply this test, namely, whether a reasonable man would take the claim being made as being a serious claim or not.

There then followed *White v Mellin*. This was a case where one product was wrapped in a wrapper advertising another's goods as being superior, but without any direct disparagement of the goods of the first. There was, I think, a considerable diversity of opinion in the House upon that case, and it is very hard to find a completely satisfactory short statement of the law; the speeches cover a very great deal of ground. But I think that what has emerged as being the general approach of the courts is to be found in the speech of Lord Watson at 167, where he said "In order to constitute disparagement which is, in the sense of law, injurious, it must be shown that the defendant's representations were made of and concerning the plaintiff's goods; that they were in disparagement of his goods and untrue; and that they have occasioned special damage to the plaintiff. Unless each and all of these three things be established, it must be held that the defendant has acted within his rights and that the plaintiff has not suffered any legal injuria". Of course, the third matter—that they have occasioned special damage to the plaintiff—is now no longer required.

The next case is *Linotype Co Limited v British Empire Type-Setting Machine Co Limited* (1899) 81 L.T. 331 which went to the House of Lords; but that was a case of libel beyond any question, where the attack shifted from the goods purveyed to the purveyor of the goods; and, in my view, the headnote correctly reflects the decision. It says: "If the only meaning which can be reasonably attached to a writing is that it is a criticism upon the goods or manufacture of a trader, it cannot be the subject of an action for libel, but an imputation upon a man in the way of his trade is properly the subject of an action without proof of special damage ... Whether in any particular case the words complained of are susceptible of a defamatory meaning, or are simply a disparagement of goods, is for the jury".

In a sense, that case was the converse of the case of *Evans v Harlow* (1844) 5 Q.B. 624. It is true that the Lord Chancellor therein uses some language which might be thought, if taken at face value, to endorse the proposition that no reflection upon the plaintiffs' goods or machines could ever form the subject matter of an action; but, as it stands, it is obviously far too wide and I do not think he intended it to be taken in that sense in any event.

The next case was *Hubbuck & Sons Limited v Wilkinson, Heywood & Clark Limited* [1899] 1 Q.B. 86. In this case, the defendant bruited abroad what purported to be the results of a comparison test of some description between his paint and the plaintiffs' paint. If, however, one first gets rid of a certain flavour—and the Court of Appeal got rid of the flavour—which was imparted to the case by the use of the word "genuine" as applied to the defendants' paint as not in fact meaning that the plaintiffs' paint was other than genuine, the test became a rather simple one; and, so far as I can see, of a purely subjective nature. The conclusion of it was that, for all practical purposes, the two paints could be regarded as equal. The sting, of course, was that the defendants' paint was much cheaper.

The facts of this case bear some faint similarity to the facts of the present case, in that there was or purported to be a test of some description; but I do not think that a test ending up with such a statement (that is, that the two paints can be regarded as equal) can really be regarded as something which any reasonable man can be expected to take very seriously. There was in any event no real disparagement or untrue statement made about the plaintiffs' paint. It is hard to distinguish the whole affair from the statement "Our paint is as good as anybody else's", when a stronger statement still could obviously have been made with impunity.

The next case was *Alcott v Millar's Karri and Jarrah Forests Limited* (1904) 91 L.T. 722. Here a letter was written to a third party in terms which that third party must have taken seriously, to the effect that the plaintiff's wooden road blocks would only last 18 months. I think that was an extreme case, and I do not think that anybody would be surprised that the action laid there accordingly.

The next case is *Lyne v Nicholls* (1906) 23 T.L.R. 86. Unfortunately, there was no plea of special damage, so that this action failed; but it was in substance held by Swinfen-Eady J. that the statement that the circulation of a particular newspaper was "twenty to one of any other weekly paper in the district", and that, "where others count by the dozen, we count by the hundred", were not merely puffs, but were to be taken seriously. Mr Walton submitted that this case was plainly at variance with the earlier cases. On the contrary, I find it fully in line with them, properly understood.

The last case is *London Ferro-Concrete Co Limited v Justicz* (1951) 68 R.P.C. 65. In this case the defendant did not content himself with saying that his methods were better than the plaintiffs'; he said that the plaintiffs' methods were inadequate. Again, that was a statement which any outside third party would be likely to take seriously.

After this brief review of the relevant authorities I see no inconsistency between any of them; and I therefore now proceed to ask the question: can I be so certain that nobody would have taken the results of Tech-Data/1 seriously that I should grant the relief sought by the defendants and strike out the statement of claim? I do not feel able to do so in any way at all. It appears to me that, where the interested parties are presented with what purports to be a proper scientific test, properly carried out by the "Application Laboratory" (whatever that is) they must be intended by the persons who furnished them with this information to take it all very seriously indeed. Such a report framed as the present report is so framed cannot be dismissed in any way as a mere idle puff. It may well of course be that that is all in fact it is; but, if so, then the defendants have only themselves to blame for having dressed up a stupid old moke as a thoroughbred Arabian stallion.

If traders take the time and trouble to dress up their advertising material in this manner, then I think they must stand by it; and, if it contains, as in the case here, statements in disparagement of the plaintiffs' goods and if, further, on investigation those statements prove to be false and the plaintiff can show malice, the precise constituents of which for present purposes I think it is better not to investigate, it appears to me that they must answer for it.

Mr Walton in substance submitted that such a conclusion would mean that the courts would be used as a forum for advertising the plaintiffs' wares by means of a judicial decision that their goods were better than the defendants'. Nothing, I think, is further from the truth. All the courts will decide is whether a specific statement, which may of course be express or implied, made concerning the plaintiffs' goods or services is or is not untrue. This appears to me to be a task which the courts are well fitted to perform; which they have on numerous occasions in the past performed; and which they will continue to perform as and when necessary.

This conclusion renders it strictly unnecessary for me to deal with Mr Dillon's second point on the question of unlawful interference and/or unfair competition; and in fact I do not propose to deal with it. Whilst I am indebted to both Mr Dillon and Mr Walton for very interesting arguments on these branches of the law, it must be recognised that there are now very rapidly developing branches of it; and, that being so, I think it is unwise for any judge before whom the suggestion that there is unlawful interference or unfair competition comes to express any views on the matter unless it becomes absolutely necessary. Therefore, I am not going to deal with those questions at all, but I wish to make it perfectly plain that I intend thereby no disrespect whatsoever to the respective arguments which on both sides were very compelling indeed.

5.1.5.4 *Kaye v Robertson* **[1991] F.S.R. 62, CA**

The plaintiff, a well-known actor, was seriously injured in an accident. Robertson was the editor of a tabloid called The Sunday Sport *who sent a journalist and a photographer to interview the plaintiff in his private hospital room. The plaintiff agreed to talk to them but medical evidence showed that at the time he was in no condition to be interviewed or to give any informed consent to be interviewed. The article that* The Sunday Sport *proposed to publish claimed that the plaintiff had agreed to be interviewed and photographed. The plaintiff, through a representative, sought an injunction on the grounds of libel, malicious falsehood, trespass to the person and passing off. Glidewell L.J. noted that English law recognised no general right of action for breach of a person's privacy, and then dealt with the plaintiff's claims in this manner:*

1. Libel

The basis of the plaintiff's case under this head is that the article as originally written clearly implied that Mr Kaye consented to give the first "exclusive" interview to *The Sunday Sport* and to be photographed by their photographer. This was untrue: Mr Kaye was in no fit condition to give any informed consent, and such consent as he may appear to have given was, and should have been known by *The Sunday Sport's* representative to be, of no effect. The implication in the article would have the effect of lowering Mr Kaye in the esteem of right-thinking people, and was thus defamatory.

The plaintiff's case is based on the well-known decision in *Tolley v J.S. Fry & Sons Ltd* [1931] A.C. 333. Mr Tolley was a well-known amateur golfer. Without his consent, Fry published an advertisement which consisted of a caricature of the plaintiff with a caddie, each with a packet of Fry's chocolate protruding from his pocket. The caricature was accompanied by doggerel verse which used Mr Tolley's name and extolled the virtues of the chocolate. The plaintiff alleged that the advertisement implied that he had received payment for the advertisement, which would damage his reputation as an amateur player. The judge at the trial ruled that the advertisement was capable of being defamatory, and on appeal the House of Lords upheld this ruling.

It seems that an analogy with *Tolley v Fry* was the main plank of Potter J.'s decision to grant injunctions in this case.

Mr Milmo for the defendants submits that, assuming that the article was capable of having the meaning alleged, this would not be a sufficient basis for interlocutory relief. In *William Coulson & Sons v James Coulson & Co* (1887) 3 T.L.R. 46, this court held that, though the High Court has jurisdiction to grant an interim injunction before the trial of a libel action, it is a jurisdiction to be exercised only sparingly....

This is still the rule in actions for defamation, despite the decision of the House of Lords in *American Cyanamid Co v Ethicon Ltd.* [1975] A.C. 396 in relation to interim injunctions generally. This court so decided in *Herbage v Times Newspapers Limited*, unreported but decided on April 30, 1981.

Mr Milmo submits that on the evidence we cannot be confident that any jury would inevitably decide that the implication that Mr Kaye had consented to give his first interview to *The Sunday Sport* was libellous. Accordingly, we ought not to grant interlocutory relief on this ground.

It is in my view certainly arguable that the intended article would be libellous, on the authority of *Tolley v Fry*. I think that a jury would probably find that Mr Kaye had been libelled, but I cannot say that such a conclusion is inevitable. It follows that I agree with Mr Milmo's submission and in this respect I disagree with the learned judge; I therefore would not base an injunction on a right of action for libel.

2. Malicious Falsehood

The essentials of this tort are that the defendant has published about the plaintiff words which are false, that they were published maliciously, and that special damage has followed as the direct and natural result of their publication. As to special damage, the effect of section 3(1) of the Defamation Act 1952 is that it is sufficient if the words published in writing are calculated to cause pecuniary damage to the plaintiff. Malice will be inferred if it be proved that the words were calculated to produce damage and that the defendant knew when he published the words that they were false or was reckless as to whether they were false or not.

The test in *Coulson v Coulson* (above) applies to interlocutory injunctions in actions for malicious falsehood as it does in actions for defamation. However, in relation to this action, the test applies only to the requirement that the plaintiff must show that the words were false. In the present case I have no doubt that any jury which did not find that the clear implication from the words contained in the defendants' draft article were false would be making a totally unreasonable finding. Thus the test is satisfied in relation to this cause of action.

As to malice I equally have no doubt from the evidence, including the transcript of the tape-recording of the "interview" with Mr Kaye in his hospital room which we have read, that it was quite apparent to the reporter and photographer from *The Sunday Sport* that Mr Kaye was in no condition to give any informed consent to their interviewing or photographing him. Moreover, even if the journalists had been in any doubt about Mr Kaye's fitness to give his consent. Mr Robertson could not have entertained any such doubt after he read the affidavit sworn on behalf of Mr Kaye in these proceedings. Any subsequent publication of the falsehood would therefore inevitably be malicious.

As to damage, I have already recorded that Mr Robertson appreciated that Mr Kaye's story was one for which other newspapers would be willing to pay "large sums of money." It needs little imagination to appreciate that whichever journal secured the first interview with Mr Kaye would be willing to pay the most. Mr Kaye thus has a potentially valuable right to sell the story of his accident and his recovery when he is fit enough to tell it. If the defendants are able to publish the article they proposed, or one anything like it, the value of this right would in my view be seriously lessened, and Mr Kaye's story thereafter be worth must less to him.

I have considered whether damages would be an adequate remedy in these circumstances. They would inevitably be difficult to calculate, would also follow some time after the event, and in my view would in no way be adequate. It thus follows that in my opinion all the preconditions to the grant of an interlocutory injunction in respect of this cause of action are made out. I will return later to what I consider to be the appropriate form of injunction.

3. Trespass to the person

It is strictly unnecessary to consider this cause of action in the light of the view I have expressed about malicious falsehood. However, I will set out my view shortly. The plaintiff's case in relation to this cause of action is that the taking of the flashlight photographs may well have caused distress to Mr Kaye and set back his recovery, and thus caused him injury. In this sense it can be said to be a battery. Mr Caldecott, for Mr Kaye, could not refer us to any authority in which the taking of a photograph or indeed the flashing of a light had been held to be a battery. Nevertheless I am prepared to accept that it may well be the case that if a bright light is deliberately shone into another person's eyes and injures his sight, or damages him in some other way, this may be in law a battery. But in my view the necessary effects are not established by the evidence in this case. Though there must have been an obvious risk that any disturbance to Mr Kaye would set back his recovery, there is no evidence that the taking of the photographs did in fact cause him any damage.

Moreover, the injunction sought in relation to this head of action would not be intended to prevent another anticipated battery, since none was anticipated. The intention here is to prevent the defendants from profiting from the taking of the photographs, *i.e.* from their own trespass. Attractive though this argument may appear to be, I cannot find as a matter of law that an injunction should be granted in these circumstances. Accordingly I would not base an injunction on this cause of action.

4. Passing off

Mr Caldecott submits (though in this case not with any great vigour) that the essentials of the tort of passing off, as laid down by the speeches in the House of Lords in *E. Warnink BV v J. Townend & Sons (Hull) Ltd* [1979] A.C. 731, are satisfied here. I only need say shortly that in my view they are not. I think that the plaintiff is not in the position of a trader in relation to his interest in his story about his accident and his recovery, and thus fails from the start to have a right of action under this head.

5.2   Registered Trade Marks

5.2.1   Basic Matters

5.2.1.1   Note on Trade Marks Act 1994

The 1994 Act introduced new systems of trade mark registration to the UK. It allows for application to be made to the British Trade Mark Registry (with extension to other countries through the international registrations under the Madrid Agreement Protocol: ss.53, 54). The governing law implements the EC Directive on the Approximation of Trade Mark Laws (89/104). At the same time, a Community Trade Mark, giving unified rights throughout the EC, is becoming available through the CTM Office in Alicante, Spain, by virtue of Regulation (EC) 40/94. The 1994 Act provides for various consequences in national law: ss.51, 52).

For the most part the Regulation contains coordinate provisions to the Directive and hence the new British law. The statutory texts given here are from the 1994 Act and so concern the British law. However, the provisions of the Regulation and Directive from which they derive are noted, using the abbreviations, "CTM Reg." and "TM Dir."

While the overall purpose and content of registration is not changing, the new law departs in detail at many points from the former British system under the Trade Marks Act 1938. Previous case law can therefore be regarded as sug-gestive, rather than authoritative. It is upon that understanding that a limited number of earlier decisions is included here. Given the European derivation of the new law, precedents from the former laws of other EC states will also be influential. The ECJ will have ultimate authority to interpret the new law at most crucial points.

5.2.1.2   Trade Marks Act 1994, s.2: Relation to Common Law Rights

S.2. Registered trade marks (*cf.* CTM Reg. Art. 14(2), TM Dir. Recital 6)

(1) A registered trade mark is a property right obtained by the registration of the trade mark under this Act and the proprietor of a registered trade mark has the rights and remedies provided by this Act.

(2) No proceedings lie to prevent or recover damages for the infringement of an unre-gistered trade mark as such; but nothing in this Act affects the law relating to passing off.

5.2.1.3   Trade Marks Act 1994, s.1: Definitions

S.1 Trade marks (*cf.* CTM Reg. Art. 4, TM Dir. Art. 2)

(1) In this Act a "trade mark" means any sign capable of being represented graphically which is capable of distinguishing goods or services of one undertaking from those of other undertakings.

A trade mark may, in particular, consist of words (including personal names), designs, letters, numerals or the shape of goods or their packaging.

(2) References in this Act to a trade mark include, unless the context otherwise requires, references to a collective mark (see section 49) or certification mark (see section 50).

5.2.2 Registration

5.2.2.1 Trade Marks Act 1994, ss.32, 34, 37, 8, 13, 38, 42 (*cf.* generally, CTM Reg., Titles III, IV)

S.32 Application for registration

(1) An application for registration of a trade mark shall be made to the registrar.

(2) The application shall contain—

    (a) a request for registration of a trade mark,
    (b) the name and address of the applicant,
    (c) a statement of the goods or services in relation to which it is sought to register the trade mark, and
    (d) a representation of the trade mark.

(3) The application shall state that the trade mark is being used, by the applicant or with his consent, in relation to those goods or services, or that he has a *bona fide* intention that it should be so used.

(4) The application shall be subject to the payment of the application fee and such class fees as may be appropriate.

Section 33 concerns the date of filing an application, which is considered the date of application: see further, s.40(3).

S.34 Classification of trade marks

(1) Goods and services shall be classified for the purposes of the registration of trade marks according to a prescribed system of classification.

(2) Any question arising as to the class within which any goods or services fall shall be determined by the registrar, whose decision shall be final.

Section 35 provides for a right of priority of registration under the Act on the basis of a previous application within a Paris Convention country. Section 36 establishes a right of priority on the basis of overseas applications in some other circumstances.

S.37 Examination of application

(1) The registrar shall examine whether an application for registration of a trade mark satisfies the requirements of this Act (including any requirements imposed by rules).

(2) For that purpose he shall carry out a search, to such extent as he considers necessary, of earlier trade marks.

(3) If it appears to the registrar that the requirements for registration are not met, he shall inform the applicant and give him an opportunity, within such period as the registrar may specify, to make representations or to amend the application.

(4) If the applicant fails to satisfy the registrar that those requirements are met, or to amend the application so as to meet them, or fails to respond before the end of the specified period, the registrar shall refuse to accept the application.

(5) If it appears to the registrar that the requirements for registration are met, he shall accept the application.

S.8 Power to require that relative grounds be raised in opposition proceedings

(1) The Secretary of State may by order provide that in any case a trade mark shall not be refused registration on a ground mentioned in section 5 (relative grounds for refusal) unless objection on that ground is raised in opposition proceedings by the proprietor of the earlier trade mark or other earlier right.

(2) The order may make such consequential provision as appears to the Secretary of State appropriate

    (a) with respect to the carrying out by the registrar of searches of earlier trade marks, and

    (b) as to the persons by whom an application for a declaration of invalidity may be made on the grounds specified in section 47(2) (relative grounds).

(3) An order making such provision as is mentioned in subsection (2)(a) may direct that so much of section 37 (examination of application) as requires a search to be carried out shall cease to have effect.

(4) An order making such provision as is mentioned in subsection (2)(b) may provide that so much of section 47(3) as provides that any person may make an application for a declaration of invalidity shall have effect subject to the provisions of the order.

(5) An order under this section shall be made by statutory instrument, and no order shall be made unless a draft of it has been laid before and approved by a resolution of each House of Parliament.

No such draft of an order making such provision as is mentioned in subsection (1) shall be laid before Parliament until after the end of the period of ten years beginning with the day on which applications for Community trade marks may first be filed in pursuance of the Community Trade Mark Regulation.

(6) An order under this section may contain such transitional provisions as appear to the Secretary of State to be appropriate.

S.13 Registration subject to disclaimer or limitation

(1) An applicant for registration of a trade mark, or the proprietor of a registered trade mark, may—

    (a) disclaim any right to the exclusive use of any specified element of the trade mark, or

    (b) agree that the rights conferred by the registration shall be subject to a specified territorial or other limitation;

and where the registration of a trade mark is subject to a disclaimer or limitation, the rights conferred by section 9 (rights conferred by registered trade mark) are restricted accordingly.

(2) Provision shall be made by rules as to the publication and entry in the register of a disclaimer or limitation.

S.38 Publication, opposition proceedings and observations

(1) When an application for registration has been accepted, the registrar shall cause the application to be published in the prescribed manner.

(2) Any person may, within the prescribed time from the date of the publication of the application, give notice to the registrar of opposition to the registration.

The notice shall be given in writing in the prescribed manner, and shall include a statement of the grounds of opposition.

(3) Where an application has been published, any person may, at any time before the registration of the trade mark, make observations in writing to the registrar as to whether the trade mark should be registered; and the registrar shall inform the applicant of any such observations.

A person who makes observations does not thereby become a party to the proceedings on the application.

Section 39 enables the applicant to restrict or withdraw an application and in limited circumstances to correct it. Section 40 provides for the registration of a trade mark where the application is acceptable to the registrar and any opposition proceedings have been disposed of in the applicant's favour. By s.40(3) the date of registration shall be the date of filing of the application. Section 41 provides for the division of an application into several applications, for the merging of separate applications, and for the registration of a number of substantially identical trade marks as a series of trade marks.

S.42 Duration of registration (*cf.* CTM Reg. Arts 46, 47)

(1) A trade mark shall be registered for a period of ten years from the date of registration.

(2) Registration may be renewed in accordance with section 43 for further periods of ten years.

Section 43 sets out the procedure for the renewal of a registration. By section 43(5) a registration not renewed shall be removed from the register. Section 44 provides that a registered trade mark shall not be altered in the register except for details of the proprietor's name or address where this does not substantially affect the identity of the mark. Section 45 provides for the surrender of a registered trade mark.

5.2.3   Absolute Grounds for Refusal of Registration

5.2.3.1   Trade Marks Act 1994, s.3: the Absolute Grounds

S.3 Absolute grounds for refusal of registration (*cf.* CTM Reg. Art. 7, TM Dir. Art. 3)

   (1) The following shall not be registered—

      (a) signs which do not satisfy the requirements of section 1(1),
      (b) trade marks which are devoid of any distinctive character,
      (c) trade marks which consist exclusively of signs or indications which may serve, in trade, to designate the kind, quality, quantity, intended purpose, value, geographical origin, the time of production of goods or of rendering of services, or other characteristics of goods or services,
      (d) trade marks which consist exclusively of signs or indications which have become customary in the current language or in the bona fide and established practices of the trade:

    Provided that, a trade mark shall not be refused registration by virtue of paragraph (b), (c) or (d) above if, before the date of application for registration, it has in fact acquired a distinctive character as a result of the use made of it.

   (2) A sign shall not be registered as a trade mark if it consists exclusively of—

      (a) the shape which results from the nature of the goods themselves,
      (b) the shape of goods which is necessary to obtain a technical result, or
      (c) the shape which gives substantial value to the goods.

   (3) A trade mark shall not be registered if it is—

      (a) contrary to public policy or to accepted principles of morality, or
      (b) of such a nature as to deceive the public (for instance as to the nature, quality or geographical origin of the goods or service).

   (4) A trade mark shall not be registered if or to the extent that its use is prohibited in the United Kingdom by any enactment or rule of law or by any provision of Community law.

   (5) A trade mark shall not be registered in the cases specified, or referred to, in section 4 (specially protected emblems).

   (6) A trade mark shall not be registered if or to the extent that the application is made in bad faith.

Section 4 concerns specially protected emblems such as national flags, insignia of Royalty and international organisations, and coats of arms.

5.2.3.2   *British Sugar v James Robertson* [1996] R.P.C. 281, Jacob J.

British Sugar produces a large range of sugar-related products under the general mark, "Silver Spoon". Among them is a syrup topping for ice cream and other desserts which they market as "Silver Spoon Treat" (in toffee and other flavours). They registered "Treat" for dessert sauces and syrups in Class 30 in 1992 (originally this was in Part B, which under the 1994 Act became a general registration). The basis for the registration was a short declaration of use to that date (showing an annual turnover of £1.8 million).

James Robertson, the well-known jam manufacturer, produced a toffee-fla-voured spread which it sold as "Robertson's Toffee Treat". In four months' selling no evidence was produced of confusion between the products and passing off was not alleged. Jacob J. thought that this use caused the plaintiff no harm because "by and large one is not in practice a substitute for the other". He found that the defendants were not infringing the mark and that the registration was in any case invalid, on the basis of the following considerations:

(a) Does the Robertson product fall within the specification of goods for which the mark is registered?

Is the Robertson product a "dessert sauce or syrup"? British Sugar say it is. The small print on the back of the jar says:

"Toffee Treat is delicious at breakfast, with desserts or as a snack anytime. Spread Toffee Treat on bread, toast or biscuits, spoon it over yoghurt or ice-cream or use as a filling for cakes".

So, say British Sugar, the product can not only be used on a dessert, but Robertson's positively suggest this. Thus, even if the product has other uses, it is, *inter alia*, used on desserts. Moreover when so used it is a sauce—see the dictionary definition of "sauce", *viz*:

"Any preparation, usually liquid or soft, intended to be eaten with food as a relish."

It does not matter if those other uses are much commoner: the fact that the product can be used as a dessert sauce means it is one.

I reject this argument. Notwithstanding what is said on the label, the use of the spread with a dessert is in practice likely to be slight. Mr Lloyd Jones, Robertson's Marketing Director, thought that all potential uses of the product, other than as a spread, amounted to less than five per cent of volume. The product comes in a jam jar because it is like a jam. No-one would describe a jam as a "dessert sauce" in ordinary parlance, yet it too can be used on a dessert and everyone knows and sometimes does that. Supermarkets regard the product as a spread. The jam jar invites use as a spread. When it comes to construing a word used in a trade mark specification, one is concerned with how the product is, as a practical matter, regarded for the purposes of trade. After all a trade mark specification is concerned with use in trade. The Robertson product is not, for the purpose of trade, a dessert sauce.

In the alternative, Jacob J. held that the limitation in the registration, "included in Class 30," had the effect of preventing the registration from extending to jams and jellies (which are in Class 29).

(b) Must the defendant use the mark as a trade mark to fall within section 10(1) or (2)?

Jacob J. referred to the 1994 Act, ss.9(1) and 10(1)–(2). He continued:

Both of these provisions (and section 10(3), with which I am not concerned) begin with the words:

"A person infringes a registered trade mark if he uses in the course of trade a *sign* which ..."

It was argued on behalf of Robertson's that there is a gloss which must be read into all the provisions, namely that the sign must be used as a trade mark (I think either for the defendant's or plaintiff's goods). Here it was said, Robertson's do not use "Treat" as a trade mark and so there could be no infringement within section 10. I will return to that point on the facts. For the present assume a use which is plainly not trade mark use, as for example in the phrase "give your child a treat, give it Robertson's marmalade." Does a non-trade mark use fall within any of the provisions of section 10?

The argument depends on a departure from the language of section 10 which refers only to the use of a *sign*. The argument runs something like this: section 9(1) says that exclusive rights in a trade mark are infringed *by the use of the trade mark* without consent. The contrast is made between *trade mark* in section 9(1) and *sign* in section 10. It is said that section 9(1), in providing in general terms for infringement, also is providing an overriding requirement that there be trade mark use. In that respect it is said to be like the 1938 Act, section 4(1) which specifically, by section 4(1)(a), provided that the use as a trade mark (in effect for the defendant's goods) or a use which referred to the plaintiff or his goods (section 4(1)(b)).

I can see no reason so to limit the provisions of section 10. That is not to say a purely descriptive use is an infringement. It is not, but not because it does not fall within section 10 but because it falls within section 11(2). I see no need to put any gloss upon the language of section 10. It merely requires the court to see whether the sign registered as a trade mark is used in the course of trade and then to consider whether that use falls within one of the three defining subsections. Section 9(1) is really no more than a chatty introduction to the details set out in section 10, itself adding no more than that the acts concerned must be done without consent.

Consideration of the Directive upon which the Act is based supports this conclusion. The infringement provisions are supposed to be implementing Article 5. For reasons which baffle me, our Parliamentary draftsman did not simply copy this. He set about re-writing it. So section 9(1) has no exact equivalent in Article 5. Article 5(1) reads:

"The registered trade mark shall confer on the proprietor exclusive rights therein. The proprietor shall be entitled to prevent all third parties not having his consent from using in the course of trade ... [there then follows language for practical purposes identical to ss.10(1) and 10(2).

The words in section 9(1), *by the use of the trade mark*, are not in the Directive. The suggested gloss, which depends on these words, could not apply to the Directive. So the argument based on section 9(1) involves a departure from the Directive. This is wholly improbable. I reject it.

More generally Mr Shipley relied upon *Bravado Merchandising Services v Mainstream Publishing* [1996] F.S.R. 205. There Lord McClusky had to consider whether the owner of the trade mark *Wet Wet Wet*, registered for books, could stop the use of the title *A Sweet Little Mystery—Wet Wet Wet—The Inside Story* for a book about the pop group *Wet Wet Wet*. Lord McCluskey accepted a concession of counsel that use, to fall within section 10(1)—and the point would be the same for section 10(2)—must be use in a trade mark sense. He referred to what was said by the responsible Minister in Parliament. Counsel did not object to the reference being made.

I have some difficulty with the reference to what was said in Parliament. The language is taken directly from Article 5 of the Directive and must be intended to have the same meaning. *Pepper v Hart* allows reference to *Hansard* to find out the meaning of Parliament in certain limited cases where a statutory intention is ambiguous. But in the case of a provision intended to implement a Directive, I cannot think that the *Pepper* principle can apply. The intention of Parliament is to implement whatever the directive means. Views expressed in Parliament about the meaning, even by Ministers, cannot assist in resolving any ambiguity which stems from the Directive itself. Neither the courts of any other country whose trade marks laws are supposed to implement the Directive, or the European Court of Justice in interpreting it, would refer to what a British Minister said in Parliament in the course of implementation here. It would be irrelevant. What matters is the language of the Directive. That is why it is so important that those responsible for this kind of legislation make serious efforts to be clear. If they are not then the process of litigation imposed on industry will ensure an ultimate cost to the public of the Union.

Mr Young suggested that rather than look at what was said in Parliament I should look at the White Paper published before the Bill leading to the 1994 Act was introduced. But for exactly the same reasons as *Hansard* is irrelevant to construction of those parts of the Act implementing the directive, so is the White Paper. All that can relevantly say (and does say) is that the intention is to implement the directive. Anything else said is merely opinion on the meaning of the directive and not part of any *travail preparatoire*.

Lord McCluskey also referred to the language of the Directive, from which he derived the central theme that a trade mark is intended to guarantee the origin of goods. This is indeed so, but it by no means follows that Article 5 (the basis of section 10) is so limited. The same result can be, and I think is, achieved by section 11(2) to which I shall come.

From what I have said, there was an unnecessary concession by counsel for the defendant in *Wet Wet Wet*. It was conceded that:

> "for there to be infringement the registered traded mark had to be used by the infringer 'in a trade mark sense' but that was exactly what the respondent was doing".

I do not see why the concession was made and it seems to have led to a muddle. One would have thought that *Wet Wet Wet* was used in the title simply to refer to the pop group. So it was not being used *in relation to* goods covered by the registration (section 10(1)) or to similar goods or services (section 10(2)). Whilst added matter or other surrounding circumstances is irrelevant to the question of confusion, it must be relevant to decide in relation to what goods or services the sign is being used.

In the result Lord McCluskey found for the defendants, basing himself on section 11(2). To this I shall return. However I have no doubt that the learned judge reached the right result. It would be fantastic if the new trade mark legislation had the effect of enabling a quasi-censorship of books about people or companies just because those people or companies had registered their names as trade marks for books.

(c) Is there infringement pursuant to s.10(1)?

Jacob J. concluded that, if he was wrong on the issue of classification ((a) above), the defendant's use was within s.10(1).

(d) Is there infringement pursuant to s.10(2)?

British Sugar seek to elide the questions of confusion and similarity. Their skeleton argument contends that there is "use in relation to a product so similar to a dessert sauce that there exists a likelihood of confusion because the product may or will be used for identical purposes." I do not think it is legitimate to elide the question in this way. The sub-section does not merely ask "will there be confusion?": it asks "is there similarity of goods?", if so, "is there a likelihood of confusion?" The point is important. For if one elides the two questions then a "strong" mark would get protection for a greater range of goods than a "weak" mark. For instance "Kodak" for socks or bicycles might well cause confusion, yet these goods are plainly dissimilar from films or cameras. I think the question of similarity of goods is wholly independent of the particular mark the subject of registration or the defendant's sign.

Jacob J. referred to the language of s.10(2)(a) and to the relevant Recitals in the Trade Marks Directive. Of the latter he remarked:

It is not saying that goods are similar if there is confusion, no matter how dissimilar the goods may be. That is a matter for Article 5(2) (which is the basis of our section 10(3)). Then the trade mark owner must go on to show that:

"the mark has a reputation in the U.K. and the use of the sign, being without due cause, takes unfair advantage of, or is detrimental to, the distinctive character or the repute of the mark."

The construction of this phrase I leave for another day. I only note that it might cater for the case where the goods were vastly different but the marks the same or similar and the proprietor could show that the repute of his mark was likely to be affected. The sort of circumstances of the Dutch case of *Claeryn/Klarein Benelux Court of Justice*, March 1, 1975 N.J. 1975, 472 (mark for gin infringed by identical sounding mark for detergent, damage to the gin mark image), may fall within this kind of infringement, even though they do not fall within section 10(2) because there is no likelihood of confusion as to trade origin, see *Wagamama* [1995] F.S.R. 513.

How then is the court to approach the question of similarity? Neither the Act nor Directive (save in the case of the latter for the somewhat cryptic recital I have quoted) provide assistance. Given that is so, I think I must consider the matter as a matter of principle. First it should be noted that the wider the scope of the concept, the wider the absolute scope of protection of a mark may be. In effect a registration covers the goods of the specification plus similar goods. No one may use the registered mark or a similar mark for any of those goods unless he has some other defence. This suggests caution. Otherwise, however narrow a specification, the actual protection will be wide. In particular this would be so in the important sort of case where a mark owner only got registration on the basis of actual distinctiveness for a narrow class of goods. It would surely be wrong that he should then in practice get protection for a wide range of goods. If a man wants wide protection he can always ask for it and will get it only if his claim is justified. The old rule that you could not infringe if your goods were even just outside a specification was too rigid. It meant (to use a classic example of Mr T.A. Blanco White Q.C.) that a registration of a mark for "3-holed razor blades imported from Venezuala" could not be infringed by use of the mark on a 2-holed razor blade so imported. But I do not think the introduction of infringement for similar goods has vastly widened the scope of potential protection.

Under the old U.K. Act there was a conception going by the words *goods of the same description* as those of the registered mark. It was important when the registrar was considering whether there was a prior conflicting registration, 1938 Act ss.1, 12(1), in considering whether a mark which had not been used might nonetheless stay on the register by reason of use for such goods, s.26, and for several other purposes. The phrase depended on judicial gloss for its interpretation, and, as time went on, a body of examples on one side or the other built up by which people could go. See *Daiquiri Rum TM* [1969] R.P.C. 600, HL approving lists of past decisions. I believe that *similar goods* is the same sort of phrase. It not only appears in section 10(2) but is also an important matter for the Registrar in considering registration. Section 5(2) forbids registration of a mark when there is an earlier identical or similar mark registered for similar goods. Actually the language of the section says "similar to those for which the earlier mark is protected". Whether that means the registrar should consider two lots of similarity (*i.e.* what goods are similar to those of the prior registration, because it *protects* use of the mark for such goods, and what goods are similar to the specification of the application) is also to be left for another day.

I think the sort of considerations the court must have in mind are similar to those arising under the old Act in relation to *goods of the same description.* I do not say this because I believe there is any intention to take over that conception directly. There plainly is not. But the purpose of the conception in the old Act was to prevent marks from conflicting not only for their respective actual goods, but for a penumbra also. And the purpose of *similar goods* in the Directive and Act is to provide protection and separation for a similar sort of penumbra. Thus, I think the following factors must be relevant in considering whether there is or is not similarity:

(a) The respective uses of the respective goods or services;

(b) The respective users of the respective goods or services;

(c) The physical nature of the goods or acts of service;

(d) The respective trade channels through which the goods or services reach the market;

(e) In the case of self-serve consumer items, where in practice they are respectively found or likely to be found in supermarkets and in particular whether they are, or are likely to be, found on the same or different shelves;

(f) The extent to which the respective goods or services are competitive. This inquiry may take into account how those in trade classify goods, for instance whether market research companies, who of course act for industry, put the goods or services in the same or different sectors.

Turning to the present case, the two products to some extent have the same use, but broadly in practice have different uses. They are hardly in direct competition and consumers will find them in different places in supermarkets. Their physical nature is somewhat different, the Robertson produce being hardly pourable and really needing spooning out of the jar whereas the British Sugar product is meant to be poured out of the small hole in the plastic top. Moreover it seems that the purposes of market research the two products are regarded as falling within different sectors. Taking all these things together, I think the spread is not be regarded as *similar* to the dessert sauces and syrups of the registration. I therefore think there is no infringement.

(e) Is there, in any case, a defence under s.11(2)?

Jacob J. referred to the provision, and to the Directive, Art.6 from which it derives. He continued:

There is no recital to the Directive which throws any direct light on the purpose of Article 6. But it is noteworthy that the Directive notes the function of a trade mark is:

"in particular to guarantee the trade mark as an indication of origin"

No other purpose is mentioned. I think this sole purpose permeates the whole Directive and hence our 1994 Act. If there is doubt as to the meaning of any particular provision, regard should be had to this purpose. I propose so to do in construing section 11(2).

The parties began with a dispute of law. It was now Mr Young's turn to say that a gloss should be put upon the provision. He said it could not apply if the defendant was using the mark in a trade mark sense. You have to have pure descriptive use, he said. He drew my attention to cases under the UK 1905 and 1938 Act, *De Cordova v Vick* (1951) 68 R.P.C. 103 and *Mars v Cadbury* (1987) R.P.C. 387. I cannot think these these can be of assistance in dealing with a provision whose provenance has nothing whatever to do with the earlier UK Acts. I propose to approach the problem from first principles.

First, I think, unlike section 10, one must here look at the whole context of the use. You cannot tell whether the use is descriptive or not from the use of the sign alone. I think so much is implicitly conceded by British Sugar when they concede that their registration could not stop use of a phrase such as "An irresistible toffee spread for a treat on any occasion!"

Second, I think one must distinguish between a use of the mark by way of an honest comparison and other uses. I see no reason why the provision does not permit a fair comparison between a trade mark owner's goods and those of the defendant. The comparison would have to be honest, but provided it was and was part of a genuine indication of, for instance, quality or price, I think it would be within the provision. Such honest comparative use might well upset the mark proprietor (proprietors particularly do not like price comparisons, even if they are true) but would in no way affect his mark as an indication of trade origin. Indeed the defendant would be using the proprietor's mark precisely for its proper purpose, namely to refer to his goods. I can see nothing in the stated purpose of the Directive indicating that a trade mark monopoly should extend to the point of enabling a proprietor to suppress competition by use of his trade mark in this way.

In saying this, I am of course aware that the UK Act also has its own "home-grown" (to use Laddie J.'s phrase in *Barclays Bank v RBS Advanta* [1996] R.P.C. 307) provision enabling comparative advertising, namely section 10(6). But it is manifest that one cannot use that provision to construe section 11(2) which comes from the Directive. If there is overlap between the two provisions there is, and no matter. Their origins are different and one should not be surprised by any overlap.

Thirdly there is the question of use of the sign for the defendant's goods. I considered the question of comparative advertising first to test the proposition that the sign can only be used as a "pure descriptor". I reject that because it can be used as part of a description when used for the plaintiff's goods. But use of the sign for the defendant's goods is something different. That seems to me to be inconsistent with the mark being used as a description or performing any of the other functions. If a mark is used as a trade mark for the defendant's goods, then it is not used as a description. This conclusion may have important implications where a semi-descriptive mark is validly registered. In particular if the defendant's mark is descriptive to some, but has trade mark significant to others, he will not be within the section.

Before turning to the facts here, I must return to *Wet Wet Wet*. Lord McCluskey held that section 11(2) provided a defence. This was because the use of the sign was a reference to the pop group and was an honest use. This is another example of a kind of trade mark use protected by the section, though the use was not by the defendant to denote the provenance of his goods.

I am, of course, concerned with the word "Treat" alone. I cannot see even a hint that anyone regarded this alone as a trade mark. Mr Young says no matter, once it is incorporated into a phrase which has trade mark significance, *i.e.* "Toffee Treat" that is enough. If I accept that the whole phrase is indeed a trade mark, I think Mr Young must be right. Section 11(2) does not cover the case where a word, outside the context of the use, is decriptive if, in context, it is part of trade mark use for the defendant's goods.

I turn to consider how the word "Treat" is used here. I have no evidence from the public in relation to this question. I have some evidence of internal thinking at Robertson's, but the most important thing of all must be my own impression from the label and all the surrounding circumstances. Looking at the label I think the average customer would not see "Treat" used as a trade mark. It is true that it is written as part of a phrase "Toffee Treat" but this is done in a context where the maker's name is plain. It is of course the case that you can have two trade marks used together ("Ford Prefect"), but whether the secondary word is used as a trade mark is a question of fact. If it is a fancy word, then obviously it is a trade mark because it could not be taken as anything else. But where it is highly descriptive I see no reason why a member of the public should take the mark as a badge of origin. And that is particularly so where the product is a new sort of product, as here. The public are apt to take the name of a novel product as a description rather than a trade mark, particularly where the name is not fancy but is descriptive or laudatory. I do not think Robertson's use is as a trade mark.

(f) Can the registration be attacked for invalidity under s.47, either:

    (i) as being not for a trade mark; or
    (ii) for its lack of distinctiveness under the criteria of s.3(1)(b)–(d), even when taking account of evidence of use after the date of registration?

Jacob J. reiterated his view that the evidence filed in support of registration was nowhere near enough to support the view that it was at that time distinctive. Of the evidence of more extensive subsequent use, he concluded that the word has since acquired some minor degree of distinctiveness in fact, but that this amounted to 60 per cent was much too high a claim. [A market survey introduced by the plaintiffs was the subject of considerable criticism].

How stands the law on these findings? I begin by considering the "not a trade mark" point. Section 1(1) has two parts, *sign*, and *capable of distinguishing*. *Sign* is not in issue: a word is plainly included within the meaning of *sign* as the remainder of section 1 indicates. But what about *capable of distinguishing*? Does this add any requirement beyond that found in section 3(1)? Section 3(1)(b) bars the registration of a mark which is *devoid of distinctive character* unless it has *in fact acquired a distinctive character*. I cannot see that the closing words of the first sentence of section 1(1) add anything to this. If a mark on its face is non-distinctive (and ordinary descriptive and laudatory words fall into this class) but is shown to have a distinctive character in fact then it must be *capable of distinguishing*. Under section 10 of the old Act, for a mark to be registrable in Part B, it also had to be *capable of distinguishing*. But the Pickwickian position was that some marks, even though 100 per cent distinctive in fact, were not regarded as *capable of distinguishing* within the meaning of that provision. I do not think the Directive and the 1994 Act take this more limited meaning over.

Thus, *capable of distinguishing* means whether the mark can in fact do the job of distinguishing. So the phrase in section 1(1) adds nothing to section 3(1) at least in relation to any sign within 3(1)(b)–(d). The scheme is that if a man tenders for registration a sign of this sort without any evidence of distinctiveness then he cannot have it registered unless he can prove it has a distinctive character. That is all. There is no pre-set bar saying no matter how well it is proved that a mark has become a trade mark, it cannot be registered. That is not to say that there are some signs which cannot in practice be registered. But the reason is simply that the applicant will be unable to prove the mark has become a trade mark in practice—"Soap" for "soap" is an example. The bar (no pun intended) will be factual not legal.

Next, is "Treat" within section 3(1)(b)? What does *devoid of any distinctive character* mean? I think the phrase requires consideration of the mark on its own, assuming no use. Is it the sort of word (or other sign) which cannot do the job of distinguishing without first educating the public that it is a trade mark? A meaningless word or a word inappropriate for the goods concerned ("North Pole" for bananas) can clearly do. But a common laudatory word such as "Treat" is, absent use and recognition as a trade mark, in itself (I hesitate to borrow the word from old Act *inherently*, but the idea is much the same) devoid of any distinctive character. I also think "Treat" falls within section 3(1)(c) because it is a trade mark which consists exclusively of a sign or indication which may serve in trade to perform a number of the purposes there specified, particularly, to designate the kind, quality and intended purpose of the product. The word probably also falls within section 3(1)(d): it is a sign which has become customary in the current language. Lots of people use "Treat" in advertisements and on goods and I have some examples in evidence.

Thus, assuming I am right so far, the question is whether British Sugar have shown that the mark now has a *distinctive character*. Is my finding that to some but not most people "Treat" has some trade mark significance enough? This depends on what is meant by a *distinctive character*. Neither the Directive nor Act throw any light on this. So I have to use what I at least regard as my common sense. Take a very descriptive or laudatory word. Suppose the proprietor can educate 10 per cent of the public into recognising the word as his trade mark. Can that really be enough to say it has a *distinctive character* and so enough to let the proprietor lay claim to the word as a trade mark altogether? The character at this stage is part distinctive, but mainly not. I do not think it would be fair to regard the character of the word as *distinctive* in that state of affairs. But if the matter were the other way round, so that to 90 per cent of people it was taken as a trade mark, then I think it would be fair so to regard it. This all suggests that the question of factual *distinctive character* is one of degree. The proviso really means "has the mark acquired a sufficiently distinctive character that the mark has really become a trade mark." In the case of common or apt descriptive or laudatory words, compelling evidence is needed to establish this. And in particular mere evidence of extensive use is unlikely to be enough on its own. Of course the power of advertising may be able to turn almost anything (save a pure description) into a trade mark, but it must be shown in a case of this sort that the mark has really become accepted by a substantial majority of persons as a trade mark—is or is almost a household word.

My findings on the facts here fall a long way short of this. Indeed even the suggested 60 per cent figure put forward for British Sugar falls short. I do not think the mark has been shown to have a *distinctive character* and accordingly I propose to declare the registration invalid pursuant to the provisions of section 47(1). Apparently, and somewhat oddly, I do not revoke the registration (revocation is dealt with under section 46) but I should like to hear counsel on what I am to do. It seems very odd to leave the mark on the register. This is a matter on which I may need the views of the Registrar.

5.2.3.3 *Windsurfing Chiemsee v Huber and Attenberger* [1999] E.C.R. I-2779, ECJ

The Chiemsee is Bavaria's largest lake, famous for sport and leisure. In its environs the claimant, and later the two defendants sold sportswear using the name, "Chiemsee". The claimant held a German trade mark registration for a composite mark including the word. In conjoined proceedings for infringement against the defendants, the Munich District Court (Landgericht München) referred questions to the ECJ about the permitted scope of registrations including geographical names under the Trade Mark Directive, Arts 3(1)(c) and 3(3) (to which TMA 1994, s.3(1)(c) and the proviso to s.3(1) correspond).

Inter alia, the questions raised the relevance, on the one hand, of the former British doctrine excluding most geographical names from registration because of the need to keep their use free for other traders who might wish to use them; and on the other hand, the German doctrine ("Freiheitsbedürfnis") which restricted the need to keep a geographical name free to cases where there was a real, current and serious need. Between these poles the Court steered the following course:

Questions on Article 3(1)(c) of the Directive

24. It should first of all be observed that Article 3(1)(c) of the Directive provides that registration is to be refused in respect of descriptive marks, that is to say marks composed exclusively of signs or indications which may serve to designate the characteristics of the categories of goods or services in respect of which registration is applied for.

25. However, Article 3(1)(c) of the Directive pursues an aim which is in the public interest, namely that descriptive signs or indications relating to the categories of goods or services in respect of which registration is applied for may be freely used by all, including as collective marks or as part of complex or graphic marks. Article 3(1)(c) therefore prevents such signs and indications from being reserved to one undertaking alone because they have been registered as trade marks.

26. As regards, more particularly, signs or indications which may serve to designate the geographical origin of the categories of goods in relation to which registration of the mark is applied for, especially geographical names, it is in the public interest that they remain available, not least because they may be an indication of the quality and other characteristics of the categories of goods concerned, and may also, in various ways, influence consumer tastes by, for instance, associating the goods with a place that may give rise to a favourable response.

27. The public interest underlying the provision which the national court has asked the Court to interpret is also evident in the fact that it is open to the Member States, under Article 15(2) of the Directive, to provide, by way of derogation from Article 3(1)(c), that signs or indications which may serve to designate the geographical origin of the goods may constitute collective marks.

28. In addition, Article 6(1)(b) of the Directive, to which the national court refers in its questions, does not run counter to what has been stated as to the objective of Article 3(1)(c), nor does it have a decisive bearing on the interpretation of that provision. Indeed, Article 6(1)(b), which aims, inter alia, to resolve the problems posed by registration of a mark consisting wholly or partly of a geographical name, does not confer on third parties the right to use the name as a trade mark but merely guarantees their right to use it descriptively, that is to say, as an indication of geographical origin, provided that it is used in accordance with honest practices in industrial and commercial matters.

29. Article 3(1)(c) of the Directive is not confined to prohibiting the registration of geographical names as trade marks solely where they designate specified geographical locations which are already famous, or are know for the category of goods concerned, and which are therefore associated with those goods in the mind of the relevant class of persons, that is to say in the trade and amongst average consumers of that category of goods in the territory in respect of which registration is applied for.

30. Indeed, it is clear from the actual wording of Article 3(1)(c), which refers to "... indications which may serve ... to designate ... geographical origin", that geographical names which are liable to be used by undertakings must remain available to such undertakings as indications of the geographical origin of the category of goods concerned.

31. Thus, under Article 3(1)(c) of the Directive, the competent authority must assess whether a geographical name in respect of which application for registration as a trade mark is made designates a place which is currently associated in the mind of the relevant class of persons with the category of goods concerned, or whether it is reasonable to assume that such an association may be established in the future.

32. In the latter case, when assessing whether the geographical name is capable, in the mind of the relevant class of persons, of designating the origin of the category of goods in question, regard must be had more particularly to the degree of familiarity amongst such persons with that name, with the characteristics of the place designated by the name, and with the category of goods concerned.

33. In that connection, Article 3(1)(c) of the Directive does not in principle preclude the registration of geographical names which are unknown to the relevant class of persons—or at least unknown as the designation of a geographical location—or of names in respect of which, because of the type of place they designate (say, a mountain or lake), such persons are unlikely to believe that the category of goods concerned originates there.

34. However, it cannot be ruled out that the name of a lake may serve to designate geographical origin within the meaning of Article 3(1)(c), even for goods such as those in the main proceedings, provided that the name could be understood by the relevant class of persons to include the shores of the lake or the surrounding area.

35. It follows from the foregoing that the application of Article 3(1)(c) of the Directive does not depend on there being a real, current or serious need to leave a sign or indication free ("Freihaltebedürfnis") under German case-law, as outlined in the third indent of paragraph 16 of this judgment.

36. Finally, it is important to note that, whilst an indication of the geographical origin of goods to which Article 3(1)(c) of the Directive applies usually indicates the place where the goods were or could be manufactured, the connection between a category of goods and a geographical location might depend on other ties, such as the fact that the goods were conceived and designed in the geographical location concerned.

Questions on the first sentence of Article 3(3) of the Directive

44. The first point to note is that Article 3(3) of the Directive provides that a sign may, through use, acquire a distinctive character which it initially lacked and thus be registered as a trade mark. It is therefore through the use made of it that the sign acquires the distinctive character which is a prerequisite for its registration.

45. Article 3(3) therefore constitutes a major exception to the rule laid down in Articles

3(1)(b), (c) and (d), whereby registration is to be refused in relation to trade marks which are devoid of any distinctive character, descriptive marks, and marks which consist exclusively of indications which have become customary in the current language or in the bona fide and established practices of the trade.

46. Secondly, just as distinctive character is one of the general conditions for registering a trade mark under Article 3(1)(b), distinctive character acquired through use means that the mark must serve to identify the product in respect of which registration is applied for as originating from a particular undertaking, and thus to distinguish that product from goods of other undertakings.

47. It follows that a geographical name may be registered as a trade mark if, following the use which has been made of it, it has come to identify the product in respect of which registration is applied for as originating from a particular undertaking and thus to distinguish that product from goods of other undertakings. Where that is the case, the geographical designation has gained a new significance and its connotation, no longer purely descriptive, justifies its registration as a trade mark.

48. Windsurfing, Chiemsee and the Commission are therefore right to assert that Article 3(3) does not permit any differentiation as regards distinctiveness by reference to the perceived importance of keeping the geographical name available for use by other undertakings.

49. In determining whether a mark has acquired distinctive character following the use made of it, the competent authority must make an overall assessment of the evidence that the mark has come to identify the product concerned as originating from a particular undertaking, and thus to distinguish that product from goods of other undertakings.

50. In that connection, regard must be had in particular to the specific nature of the geographical name in question. Indeed, where a geographical name is very well known, it can acquire distinctive character under Article 3(3) of the Directive only if there has been long-standing and intensive use of the mark by the undertaking applying for registration. *A fortiori*, where a name is already familiar as an indication of geographical origin in relation to a certain category of goods, an undertaking applying for registration of the name in respect of goods in that category must show that the use of the mark—both long-standing and intensive—is particularly well established.

51. In assessing the distinctive character of a mark in respect of which registration has been applied for, the following may also be taken into account: the market share held by the mark; how intensive, geographically widespread and long-standing use of the mark has been; the amount invested by the undertaking in promoting the mark; the proportion of the relevant class of persons who, because of the mark, identify goods as originating from a particular undertaking; and statements from chambers of commerce and industry or other trade and professional associations.

52. If, on the basis of those factors, the competent authority finds that the relevant class of persons, or at least a significant proportion thereof, identify goods as originating from a particular undertaking because of the trade mark, it must hold that the requirement for registering the mark laid down in Article 3(3) of the Directive is satisfied. However, the circumstances in which that requirement may be regarded as satisfied cannot be shown to exist solely by reference to general, abstract data such as predetermined percentages.

53. As regards the method to be used to assess the distinctive character of a mark in respect of which registration is applied for, Community law does not preclude the competent authority, where it has particular difficulty in that connection, from having recourse, under

the conditions laid down by its own national law, t an opinion poll as guidance for its judgment (see, to that effect, Case C–210/96 *Gut Springenheide and Tusky* [1998] E.C.R. I-4657, paragraph 37).

5.2.3.4   *Elvis Presley Trade Marks* **[1999] R.P.C. 567, CA.**

Elvis Presley Enterprises applied to register the following trade marks under the 1938 Act: (i) a manuscript/signature version of the name "ELVIS A PRESLEY"; (ii) "ELVIS" simpliciter; and (iii) "ELVIS PRESLEY" simpliciter. All three marks were successfully opposed by Sid David Shaw, who traded under the name "ELVISLY YOURS" and who had registered that mark in the same class of goods for which the present application was sought. The case fell to be decided under the Trade Marks Act 1938, ss.9–12, which together deal with lack of distinctiveness and deceptiveness. The Court of Appeal's judgment is nonetheless directly relevant to interpretation of the 1994 Act.

Concerning the "ELVIS" mark the Court agreed with Laddie J.'s judgment at first instance.

Robert Walker L.J.

[Laddie J.] concluded that none of the marks merited registration because all were lacking in sufficient inherent distinctiveness to succeed without evidence of factual distinctiveness (which, as Mr Prescott concedes, was not there). The judge did not discuss sections 11 and 12 in relation to the ELVIS and ELVIS PRESLEY marks beyond the brief comment that he would have difficulty seeing how Mr Shaw's extensive use of his registered mark could fail to give rise to an objection. He did consider sections 11 and 12 in relation to the signature mark and concluded that its similarity to Mr Shaw's mark would be likely to give rise to deception or confusion and so constituted a further obstacle to registration.

In my judgment the judge was right to conclude that the ELVIS mark has very little inherent distinctiveness. That conclusion was reached by a number of intermediate steps, one of which was the judge's finding that members of the public purchase Elvis Presley merchandise not because it comes from a particular source but because it carries the name or image of Elvis Presley. Indeed the judge came close to finding (although he did not in terms find) that for goods of the sort advertised by Elvisly Yours (or by Enterprises in the United States) the commemoration of the late Elvis Presley *is* the product, and the article on which his name or image appears (whether a poster, a pennant, a mug or a piece of soap) is little more than a vehicle. I consider that the judge was right to treat all these goods as memorabilia or mementoes, and not to treat some as being in a different class of consumable commercial goods. (On any view, of course, these categories cut across the statutory classes of goods.) Given that conclusion, and given that the TARZAN decision ([1970] R.P.C. 450) was binding on him (as it is on this court) the judge's final conclusion as to very low inherent distinctiveness followed almost inevitably, and factual distinctiveness is no longer asserted.

The Court reached a similar conclusion as to the lack of distinctiveness relevant to the "Elvis Presley" mark. Doubts were expressed about whether there was real danger of confusion with Mr Shaw's mark. The signature mark was allowed to proceed to registration.

Finally the judge considered the signature mark (without, as I have noted, reaching any conclusion as to its authenticity). He set out and discussed the structure of section 9(1) of the 1938 Act and said:

> "Although the Registry and the court must start from the premise that signatures are prima facie distinctive, they are not inevitably so ... Someone ... may adopt a signature which consists of his surname spelt out in precise capitals or in a perfect script which is indistinguishable from, say, Times Roman font. Such writings, though signatures, would be indistinguishable from the printed form of the name and, it seems to me, would not be distinctive."

The presumption mentioned at the beginning of that passage is in line with what Tomlin J. said, and this court seems to have approved, in *Fanfold.* But the example given by the judge is a very extreme case—so extreme that the court might simply decline to treat the mark as a signature at all. The "Elvis A. Presley" signature mark is miles away from that and I consider that the judge was wrong, especially in the light of *Fanfold,* to conclude that the signature mark was not distinctive under section 9(1)(b).

However I agree with the judge's alternative ground of decision under sections 11 and 12. Mr Shaw's registered ELVISLY YOURS mark is in a cursive script with a Greek E which (while more regular and more florid) bears at least some resemblance to the Greek E at the beginning of the Elvis A. Presley signature. The test as explained in *Pianotist Co's Application* (1906) 23 R.P.C. and *Smith, Hayden & Co Application* (1946) 63 R.P.C. 97 is whether, if the two rival marks are used in a fair and normal manner, the court is satisfied that there is no reasonable likelihood of deception or confusion being caused to a substantial numbers of members of the public. For this purpose the public is to be regarded as ordinary persons, neither specially careful nor specially careless, who would be in the market as possible purchaser of the goods in question. The burden of proof is on the applicant for the later registration.

5.2.3.5　*Philips Electronics NV v Remington Consumer Products Ltd* [2002] ECJ

Philips owned a registered trade mark for the depiction of the face of its three-headed rotary electric shaver, which it had manufactured and sold since 1966 under the mark "Philishave". In 1995 the defendant introduced a three-headed shaver under its "Remington" mark ("DT 55"). Philips alleged infringement of its registered trade mark, and further claimed that the head of its shaver was a well-known trade mark protected under section 56 of the Trade Marks Act 1994 (giving effect to Article 6bis Paris Convention); Remington counterclaimed for revocation of the trade mark registered by Philips.

Jacob J. allowed the counterclaim and ordered revocation of the registration of the trade mark on the ground that the sign relied on by Philips was incapable of distinguishing the goods concerned from those of other undertakings and was devoid of any distinctive character. He also held that the trade mark consisted exclusively of a sign which served in trade to designate the intended purpose of the goods and of a shape which was necessary to obtain a technical result and which gave substantial value to the goods He held that, even had the trade mark been valid, it would not have been infringed.

Philips appealed to the Court of Appeal, which referred a number of questions to the ECJ for a preliminary ruling. The first issue was

> 1. *Whether there is a special category of marks which is not excluded from registration by Art.3(1)(b), (c) and (d) and Art.3(3) of Council Directive 89/104/EEC which is nonetheless excluded from registration by Art.3(1)(a) of the Directive, as being incapable of distinguishing the goods of the proprietor from those of other undertakings.*

The ECJ reiterated its view that the purpose of trade mark protection is to guarantee the mark as an indicator of origin, and to guarantee the identity of that origin to the consumer or end-user. It ruled that there was no such special class of marks, stating:

36. It is true that Article 3(1)(a) of the Directive provides that signs which cannot constitute a trade mark are to be refused registration or if registered are liable to be declared invalid.

37. However, it is clear from the wording of Article 3(1)(a) and the structure of the Directive that that provision is intended essentially to exclude from registration signs which are not generally capable of being a trade mark and thus cannot be represented graphically and/or are not capable of distinguishing the goods or services of one undertaking from those of other undertakings.

38. Accordingly, Article 3(1)(a) of the Directive, like the rule laid down by Article 3(1)(b), (c) and (d), precludes the registration of signs or indications which do not meet one of the two conditions imposed by Article 2 of the Directive, that is to say, the condition requiring such signs to be capable of distinguishing the goods or services of one undertaking from those of other undertakings.

39. It follows that there is no class of marks having a distinctive character by their nature or by the use made of them which is not capable of distinguishing goods or services within the meaning of Article 2 of the Directive.

The second issue which the Court considered was:

> 2. *Is the shape of an article, or part thereof, only capable of distinguishing for the purposes of Art.2 if it contains some capricious addition (an embellishment with no functional purpose) to the shape of the article?*

The court found that no such addition was necessary:

49. In particular, the Directive in no way requires that the shape of the article in respect of which the sign is registered must include some capricious addition. Under Article 2 of the Directive, the shape in question must simply be capable of distinguishing the product of the proprietor of the trade mark from those of other undertakings and thus fulfil its essential purpose of guaranteeing the origin of the product.

50. .... the shape of the article in respect of which the sign is registered does not require any capricious addition, such as an embellishment which has no functional purpose.

Thirdly, the court assessed the following question:

3. *Where a trader has been the only supplier of particular goods to the market, is extensive use of a sign, which consists of the shape (or part of the shape) of those goods and which does not include any capricious addition, sufficient to give the sign a distinctive character for the purposes of Art.3(3), in circumstances where as a result of that use a substantial portion of the relevant public*

    (a) *associate the shape with that trader and no other undertaking, and*

    (b) *believe that goods of that shape come from that trader absent a statement to the contrary?*

The Court found that such extensive use was sufficient to ground a finding of distinctiveness:

62. However, it must first be pointed out that the Court has made clear that the circumstances in which the requirement under Article 3(3) of the Directive may be regarded as satisfied cannot be shown to exist solely by reference to general, abstract data, such as predetermined percentages (*Windsurfing Chiemsee*, paragraph 52).

63. Second, the distinctive character of a sign consisting in the shape of a product, even that acquired by the use made of it, must be assessed in the light of the presumed expectations of an average consumer of the category of goods or services in question, who is reasonably well-informed and reasonably observant and circumspect (see, to that effect, the judgment in Case C–210/96 *Gut Springenheide and Tusky* 1998 ECR I-4657, paragraph 31).

64. Finally, the identification, by the relevant class of persons, of the product as originating from a given undertaking must be as a result of the use of the mark as a trade mark and thus as a result of the nature and effect of it, which make it capable of distinguishing the product concerned from those of other undertakings.

65. In the light of those considerations, the answer to the third question must be that, where a trader has been the only supplier of particular goods to the market, extensive use of a sign which consists of the shape of those goods may be sufficient to give the sign a distinctive character for the purposes of Article 3(3) of the Directive in circumstances where, as a result of that use, a substantial proportion of the relevant class of persons associates that shape with that trader and no other undertaking or believes that goods of that shape come from that trader. However, it is for the national court to verify that the circumstances in which the requirement under that provision is satisfied are shown to exist on the basis of specific and reliable data, that the presumed expectations of an average consumer of the category of goods or services in question, who is reasonably well-informed and reasonably observant and circumspect, are taken into account and that the identification, by the relevant class of persons, of the product as originating from a given undertaking is as a result of the use of the mark as a trade mark.

Fourthly, the ECJ considered the following:

    4. (a) *Can the restriction imposed by the words "if it consists exclusively of the shape of goods which is necessary to achieve a technical result" appearing in Art.3(1)(e)(ii) be overcome by establishing that there are other shapes which can obtain the same technical result, or*

    (b) *is the shape unregistrable by virtue thereof if it is shown that the essential features of the shape are attributable only to the technical result, or*

(c) *is some other and, if so, what test appropriate for determining whether the restriction applies?*

Philips argued that the purpose of that provision of the Directive was to prevent the obtaining of a monopoly in a particular technical result by means of trade mark protection. However, the registration of a mark consisting of a shape which has a technical result imposes no unreasonable restraint on industry and innovation if that technical result can be obtained by other shapes which are readily available to competitors According to Philips, there were many alternatives to the shape at issue which would achieve the same technical result in shaving terms at an equivalent cost to that of its products, and so the trade mark conferred no such monopoly.

Remington, on the other hand, claimed that Philips' construction of the provision was against the public interest and would render the exclusion so narrow as to be useless; the clear meaning of the provision was rather that a shape that is necessary to achieve a technical result, whether or not it is the only shape that can achieve that function, must be excluded from registration.

The ECJ observed that the grounds for refusal to register signs consisting of the shape of a product are expressly listed in Art.3(1)(e) of the Directive, and that this list is exhaustive. While a sign which is refused registration on the basis of Art.3(1)(b), (c) or (d) may acquire distinctiveness through use for the purposes of Art.3(3), a sign which is refused registration under Art.3(1)(e) can never acquire a distinctive character in this manner for the purposes of Art.3(3). In interpreting Art.3(1)(e) the court found it necessary to do so in light of the public interest underlying each of the factors mentioned. It concluded:

78. The rationale of the grounds for refusal of registration laid down in Article 3(l)(e) of the Directive is to prevent trade mark protection from granting its proprietor a monopoly on technical solutions or functional characteristics of a product which a user is likely to seek in the products of competitors. Article 3(1)(e) is thus intended to prevent the protection conferred by the trade mark right from being extended, beyond signs which serve to distinguish a product or service from those offered by competitors, so as to form an obstacle preventing competitors from freely offering for sale products incorporating such technical solutions or functional characteristics in competition with the proprietor of the trade mark.

79. As regards, in particular, signs consisting exclusively of the shape of the product necessary to obtain a technical result, listed in Article 3(1)(e), second indent, of the Directive, that provision is intended to preclude the registration of shapes whose essential characteristics perform a technical function, with the result that the exclusivity inherent in the trade mark right would limit the possibility of competitors supplying a product incorporating such a function or at least limit their freedom of choice in regard to the technical solution they wish to adopt in order to incorporate such a function in their product.

80. As Article 3(l)(e) of the Directive pursues an aim which is in the public interest, namely

that a shape whose essential characteristics perform a technical function and were chosen to fulfil that function may be freely used by all, that provision prevents such signs and indications from being reserved to one undertaking alone because they have been registered as trade marks (see, to that effect, *Windsurfing Chiemsee*, paragraph 25).

81. As to the question whether the establishment that there are other shapes which could achieve the same technical result can overcome the ground for refusal or invalidity contained in Article 3(1)(e), second indent, there is nothing in the wording of that provision to allow such a conclusion.

82. In refusing registration of such signs, Article 3(1)(e), second indent, of the Directive reflects the legitimate aim of not allowing individuals to use registration of a mark in order to acquire or perpetuate exclusive rights relating to technical solutions.

83. Where the essential functional characteristics of the shape of a product are attributable solely to the technical result, Article 3(1)(e), second indent, precludes registration of a sign consisting of that shape, even if that technical result can be achieved by other shapes.

84. In the light of those considerations, the answer to the fourth question must be that Article 3(1)(e), second indent, of the Directive must be interpreted to mean that a sign consisting exclusively of the shape of a product is unregistrable by virtue thereof if it is established that the essential functional features of that shape are attributable only to the technical result. Moreover, the ground for refusal or invalidity of registration imposed by that provision cannot be overcome by establishing that there are other shapes which allow the same technical result to be obtained.

5.2.4   Relative Grounds for Refusal of Registration

5.2.4.1   Trade Marks Act 1994, ss.5, 6: the Relative Grounds

S.5 Relative grounds for refusal of registration (*cf.* CTM Reg. Art. 8, TM Dir., Art. 4)

(1) A trade mark shall not be registered if it is identical with an earlier trade mark and the goods or services for which the trade mark is applied for are identical with the goods or services for which the earlier trade mark is protected.

(2) A trade mark shall not be registered if because—

   (a) it is identical with an earlier trade mark and is to be registered for goods or services similar to those for which the earlier trade mark is protected, or
   (b) it is similar to an earlier trade mark and is to be registered for goods or services identical with or similar to those for which the earlier trade mark is protected,

   there exists a likelihood of confusion on the part of the public, which includes the likelihood of association with the earlier trade mark.

(3) A trade mark which—

   (a) is identical with or similar to an earlier trade mark, and
   (b) is to be registered for goods or services which are not similar to those for which the earlier trade mark is protected,

   shall not be registered if, or to the extent that, the earlier trade mark has a reputation in the United Kingdom (or, in the case of a Community trade mark, in the European Community) and the use of the later mark without due cause would take unfair advantage of, or be detrimental to, the distinctive character or the repute of the earlier trade mark.

(4) A trade mark shall not be registered if, or to the extent that, its use in the United Kingdom is liable to be prevented—

   (a) by virtue of any rule of law (in particular, the law of passing off) protecting an unregistered trade mark or other sign used in the course of trade, or
   (b) by virtue of an earlier right other than those referred to in subsections (1) to (3) or paragraph (a) above, in particular by virtue of the law of copyright, design right or registered designs.

   A person thus entitled to prevent the use of a trade mark is referred to in this Act as the proprietor of an "earlier right" in relation to the trade mark.

(5) Nothing in this section prevents the registration of a trade mark where the proprietor of the earlier trade mark; or other earlier right consents to the registration.

S.6 Meaning of "earlier trade mark"

(1) In this Act an "earlier trade mark" means—

   (a) a registered trade mark, international trade mark (UK) or Community trade mark which has a date of application for registration earlier than that of the trade mark in question, taking account (where appropriate) of the priorities claimed in respect of the trade marks,
   (b) a Community trade mark which has a valid claim to seniority from an earlier registered trade mark or international trade mark (UK), or

(c) a trade mark which, at the date of application for registration of the trade mark in question or (where appropriate) of the priority claimed in respect of the application, was entitled to protection under the Paris Convention as a well known trade mark.

(2) References in this Act to an earlier trade mark include a trade mark in respect of which an application for registration has been made and which, if registered, would be an earlier trade mark by virtue of subsection (1)(a) or (b), subject to its being so registered.

(3) A trade mark within subsection (1)(a) or (b) whose registration expires shall continue to be taken into account in determining the registrability of a later mark or a period of one year after the expiry unless the registrar is satisfied that there was no bona fide use of the mark during the two years immediately preceding the expiry.

Section 7 provides that, notwithstanding the relative grounds of refusal in s.5(1)–5(4), a trade mark may be registered where there has been honest concurrent use of the applicant's mark and the earlier trade mark. Section 7(3) provides that "honest concurrent use" has the same meaning as it formerly did for the purposes of s.12(2) of the Trade Marks Act 1938. An objection on a relative ground raised by a third party opponent, however, overrides honest concurrent use: s.7(2).

5.2.4.2 *Sabel BV v Puma AG* [1998] R.P.C. 199, ECJ

Sabel applied to register a device mark depicting a bounding cheetah and the word SABEL for leather and clothing products in Germany. These applications were opposed by Puma on the ground that it owned an earlier trade mark which showed a bounding Puma. Article 4(1)(b) of the Trade Marks Directive 89/104/EEC provides that a trade mark shall not be registered or, if registered, shall be liable to be declared invalid "if because of its identity with, or similarity to, the earlier trade mark and the identity or similarity of the goods or services covered by the trade marks, there exists a likelihood of confusion on the part of the public, which includes the likelihood of association with the earlier trade mark." The German Supreme Court referred the following question to the European Court of Justice, to clarify the scope of Art.4(1)(b):

"With reference to the interpretation of Article 4(1)(b) of the First Council Directive of December 21, 1988 to approximate the laws of the Member States relating to trade marks, is it sufficient for a finding that there is a likelihood of confusion between a sign composed of text and picture and a sign consisting merely of a picture, which is registered for identical and similar goods and is not especially well known to the public, that the two signs coincide as to their semantic content (in this case, a bounding feline)?"

The Benelux governments argued that Art.4(1)(b) applied to three situations: (i) where the public confused the sign and the mark in question (direct confusion); (ii) where the public made a connection between the proprietors of the sign and those of the mark and confused them (likelihood of indirect confusion or association); and (iii) where the public considered the sign to be similar to the *mark and perception of the sign called to mind the memory of the mark although the two were not confused (likelihood of association in the strict sense). The inclusion of (iii) was contested by the United Kingdom Government and the Commission; the ECJ accepted their argument:*

... it is to be remembered that Article 4(1)(b) of the Directive is designed to apply only if, by reason of the identity or similarity both of the marks and of the goods or services which they designate, "there exists a likelihood of confusion on the part of the public, which includes the likelihood of association with the earlier trade mark." It follows from that wording that the concept of likelihood of association is not an alternative to that of likelihood of confusion, but serves to define its scope. The terms of the provision itself exclude its application where there is no likelihood of confusion on the part of the public.

The tenth recital in the preamble to the Directive, according to which "the likelihood of confusion ... constitutes the specific condition for such protection", also confirms that interpretation.

The interpretation given in ... this judgment is not inconsistent with Article 4(3) and 4(a) and Article 5(2) of the Directive, which permit the proprietor of a trade mark which has a reputation to prohibit the use without due cause of signs identical with or similar to his mark and do not require proof of likelihood of confusion, even where there is no similarity between the goods in question.

... Article 4(1)(b) of the Directive does not apply when there is no likelihood of confusion on the part of the public. In that respect, it is clear from the tenth recital in the preamble to the Directive that the appreciation of the likelihood of confusion "depends on numerous elements and, in particular, on the recognition of the trade mark on the market, of the association which can be made with the used or registered sign, of the degree of similarity between the trade mark and the sign and between the goods or services identified." The likelihood of confusion must therefore be appreciated globally, taking into account all factors relevant to the circumstances of the case.

That global appreciation of the visual, aural or conceptual similarity of the marks in question, must be based on the overall impression given by the marks, bearing in mind, in particular, their distinctive and dominant components. The wording of Article 4(1)(b) of the Directive ... shows that the perception of marks in the mind of the average consumer of the type of goods or services in question plays a decisive role in the global appreciation of the likelihood of confusion. The average consumer normally perceives a mark as a whole and does not proceed to analyse its various details.

In that perspective, the more distinctive the earlier mark, the greater will be the likelihood of confusion. It is therefore not impossible that the conceptual similarity resulting from the fact that two marks use images with analogous semantic content may give rise to a likelihood of confusion where the earlier mark has particularly distinctive character, either *per se* or because of the reputation it enjoys with the public.

... Article 4(1)(b) ... is to be interpreted as meaning that the mere association which the public might make between two trade marks as a result of their analogous semantic content is not in itself a sufficient ground for concluding that there is a likelihood of confusion within the meaning of that provision.

In that respect, it is sufficient to note that, unlike Article 4(1)(b), those provisions apply exclusively to marks which have a reputation and on condition that use of the third party's mark without due cause takes unfair advantage of, or is detrimental to, the distinctive character or the repute of the trade mark.

5.2.4.3   *Marca Mode v Adidas* [2000] E.C.R. I-4861, ECJ

Adidas, the well-known manufacturer of sports clothes and articles, uses three parallel stripes as a prominent part of its branding and holds Benelux trade mark registrations for it in the relevant classes. Marca Mode marketed a T-shirt bearing three vertical stripes as part of a more elaborate design. Courts in the Netherlands considered that the case would be one of association but not necessarily of confusion between similar marks on goods within the registration. The Dutch Supreme Court accordingly addressed a question to the ECJ which asked: when the registered mark has a particularly distinctive character, is there a presumption from the association that confusion cannot be ruled out; and from that presumption an infringement of the exclusive right required by the Trade Marks Directive, Art.5(1)(b) (TMA 1994, s.10(2)). This was intended to secure a qualification upon the Court's decision in Sabel *(above, 5.2.4.2), but the Court refused to take the step. It reiterated its position in that case and stated:*

36. The interpretation is not inconsistent with Article 5(2) of the Directive which establishes, for the benefit of well-known trade marks, a form of protection whose implementation does not require the existence of a likelihood of confusion. That provision applies to situations in which the specific condition of the protection consists of a use of the sign in question without due cause which takes unfair advantage of, or is detrimental to, the distinctive character or the repute of the trade mark.

37. Adidas cannot effectively rely on paragraph 24 of *Sabel*.

38. In that paragraph, the Court noted that the more distinctive the earlier mark, the greater will be the likelihood of confusion, adding that it is therefore not impossible that the conceptual similarity resulting from the fact that two marks use images with analogous semantic content may give rise to a likelihood of confusion where the earlier mark has a particularly distinctive character, either *per se* or because of the reputation it enjoys with the public.

39. The Court thus stated that the particularly distinctive character of the earlier mark may increase the likelihood of confusion and that, where there is a conceptual similarity between the mark and the sign, that character may contribute to the creation of such a likelihood. The negative formulation it is therefore not impossible which is used in paragraph 24 of *Sabel* simply underlines the possibility that a likelihood may arise from the conjunction of the two factors analysed. It in no way implies a presumption of likelihood of confusion resulting from the existence of a likelihood of association in the strict sense. By such wording, the Court referred by implication to the assessment of evidence which the national court must undertake in each case pending before it. It did not excuse the national court from the necessary positive finding of the existence of a likelihood of confusion which constitutes the matter to be proved.

40. In this connection, it must be noted that the likelihood of confusion must be appreciated globally, taking into account all factors relevant to the circumstances of the case (*Sabel*, paragraph 22). A global assessment implies some interdependence between the relevant factors (*Canon*, paragraph 17). For example, a likelihood of confusion may be found, despite a lesser degree of similarity between the goods or services covered, where the

marks are very similar and the earlier mark, in particular its reputation, is highly distinctive (*Canon*, paragraph 19).

41. The reputation of a mark, where it is demonstrated, is thus an element which, amongst others, may have a certain importance. To this end, it may be observed that marks with a highly distinctive character, in particular because of their reputation, enjoy broader protection than marks with a less distinctive character (*Canon*, paragraph 18). Nevertheless, the reputation of a mark does not give grounds for presuming the existence of a likelihood of confusion simply because of the existence of a likelihood of association in the strict sense.

5.2.4.4 *Canon Kabushiki Kaisha v Metro-Goldwyn Meyer* [1999] E.T.M.R. 1, ECJ

Canon brought proceedings in the German Courts opposing MGM's registration of the word trade mark "Cannon", to be applied on, inter alia, video film cassettes. Canon argued that MGM's mark infringed its earlier trade mark ("Canon"), registered in Germany in respect of, inter alia, video recorders. The courts determined, on the evidence, that the two signs in question were phonetically equivalent, the "Canon" mark had a reputation and the goods by both organisations were not perceived by the public to come from the same manufacturer. In deciding the scope of similarity of the trade marks and the goods to which they were applied under Article 4(1)(b) Trade Marks Directive (see 5.2.4.1), the Bundersgerichtshof referred the following question to the Court of Justice:

> *"May account be taken, when assessing the similarity of the goods or services covered by the two marks, of the distinctive character, in particular the reputation of the mark with earlier priority (on the date which determines the seniority of the later mark) so that, in particular, likelihood of confusion within the meaning of Article 4(1)(b) of Directive 89/104/EEC must be taken to exist even if the public attributes the goods and/or services to different places of origin?"*

The European Court of Justice divided the discussion into two parts:

> *(1) Whether the reputation of an earlier trade mark must be taken into account when determining whether the similarity between the goods or services covered by the two trade marks is sufficient to give rise to the likelihood of confusion:*

16. ... the Court has held that the likelihood of confusion on the part of the public, in the absence of which Article 4(1)(b) of the Directive does not apply, must be appreciated globally, taking into account all factors relevant to the circumstances of the case (Case C–251/95 *Sabel v Puma* [1997] E.C.R. I-6191, paragraph 22).

17 A global assessment of the likelihood of confusion implies some interdependence between the relevant factors, and, in particular, a similarity between the trade marks and between these goods and services. Accordingly, a lesser degree of similarity between these goods or services may be offset by a greater degree of similarity between the marks, and

vice versa. The interdependence of these factors is expressly mentioned in the tenth recital of the preamble to the Directive, which states that it is indispensable to give an interpretation of the concept of similarity in relation to the likelihood of confusion, the appreciation of which depends, in particular, on the recognition of the trade mark on the market and the degree of similarity between the mark and the sign and between the goods or services identified.

18 Furthermore, according to the case-law of the Court, the more distinctive the earlier mark, the greater the risk of confusion (*Sabel*, paragraph 24). Since protection of a trade mark depends, in accordance with Article 4(1)(b) of the Directive, on there being a likelihood of confusion, marks with a highly distinctive character, either *per se* or because of the reputation they possess on the market, enjoy broader protection than marks with a less distinctive character.

19 It follows that, for the purposes of Article 4(1)(b) of the Directive, registration of a trade mark may have to be refused, despite a lesser degree of similarity between the goods or services covered, where the marks are very similar and the earlier mark, in particular, its reputation, is highly distinctive.

20 Against that interpretation, MGM and the United Kingdom Government have argued that to take into account the distinctiveness of the earlier mark when assessing the similarity of the goods or services involves the danger of prolonging the registration procedure. However, the French Government has stated that in its experience consideration of that factor when assessing the similarity of the goods or services covered did not have the effect of unduly lengthening or complicating the registration procedure.

21 In this context, it is important to note that even if the suggested interpretation makes the registration procedure much lengthier, that cannot be decisive for the interpretation of Article 4(1)(b) of the Directive. In any event, for reasons of legal certainty and proper administration, it is necessary to ensure that trade marks whose use could successfully be challenged before the courts are not registered.

22 It is, however, important to stress that, for the purposes of applying Article 4(1)(b), even where a mark is identical to another with a highly distinctive character, it is still necessary to adduce evidence of similarity between the goods or services covered. In contrast to Article 4(4)(a), which expressly refers to the situation in which the goods or services are not similar, Article 4(1)(b) provides that the likelihood of confusion presupposes that the goods or services covered are identical or similar.

23 In assessing the similarity of the goods or services concerned, as the French and United Kingdom Governments and the Commission have pointed out, all the relevant factors relating to those goods or services themselves should be taken into account. Those factors include, *inter alia*, their nature, their end users and their method of use and whether they are in competition with each other or are complementary.

24 In the light of the foregoing, the answer to be given to the first part of the question must be that, on a proper construction of Article 4(1)(b) of the Directive, the distinctive character of the earlier trade mark, and, in particular, its reputation, must be taken into account when determining whether the similarity between the goods or services covered by the two trade marks is sufficient to give rise to the likelihood of confusion.

(2) Whether there can be a likelihood of confusion within the meaning of Art.4(1)(b) of the Directive where the public perception is that goods or services have different places of origin:

27 ... Article 2 of the Directive provides that a trade mark must be capable of distinguishing the goods or services of one undertaking from those of other undertakings, while the tenth recital in the preamble to the Directive states that the function of the protection conferred by the mark is primarily to guarantee the indication of origin.

28 Moreover, according to the settled case-law of the Court, the essential function of the trade mark is to guarantee the identity of the origin of the marked product to the consumer or end user by enabling him, without any possibility of confusion, to distinguish the product or service from others which have another origin. For the trade mark to be able to fulfil its essential role in the system of undistorted competition which the Treaty seeks to establish, it must offer a guarantee that all the goods or services bearing it have originated under the control of a single undertaking which is responsible for their quality (see, in particular, Case C–10/89 *Hag GF (Hag II)* [1990] E.C.R. I-3711, paragraphs 14 and 13).

29 Accordingly, the risk that the public might believe that the goods or services in question come from the same undertaking or, as the case may be, from economically-linked undertakings, constitutes a likelihood of confusion within the meaning of Article 4(1)(b) of the Directive (see *Sabel*, paragraphs 16 to 18). Consequently, as the Advocate General states at point 30 of his Opinion, in order to demonstrate that there is no likelihood of confusion, it is not sufficient to show simply that there is no likelihood of the public being confused as to the place of production of the goods or services.

30 The answer to be given to the second part of the question must therefore be that there may be a likelihood of confusion within the meaning of Article 4(1)(b) of the Directive even where the public perception is that the goods or services have different places of production. By contrast, there can be no such likelihood where it does not appear that the public could believe that the goods or services come from the same undertaking or, as the case may be, from economically-linked undertakings.

5.2.4.5 *Davidoff & Cie v Gofkid* (Case C-292/00), ECJ (Judgment, January 9, 2003)

In Germany the Claimant held registrations for the trade mark, "Davidoff", for men's items, including cosmetics, cognac, ties, spectacle frames, plus tobacco products, pipes and smoking accessories and it had similar registrations internationally as part of its well-established business in these luxury goods. It actually used its mark in script with an emphasis on the formation of the "D" and the "ff". Gofkid subsequently registered "Durffee" in Germany for jewellery, tableware, table items, watches, precious metals and stones, cigarette cases and the like. It used its mark on such goods, in a similar script and with the same formation of the "D" and "ff", in the course of importing them (apparently from China) and marketing them in Germany. The two specifications accordingly covered many goods that were similar. The action in Germany sought an order to stop this use on the Defendant's goods and to secure annulment of the registrations of "Durffee". [In the UK, the issue might well have been treated as a question of passing off because of the imitation of the "D" and "ff", which were not registered as such.]

The lower German courts found no likelihood of confusion of the Defendant's mark with "Davidoff". The German Supreme Court proposed to refer this issue for further consideration by a lower court. But first it directed a question to the

ECJ concerning the Trade Mark Directive, Articles 4(4) and 5(2), which permit Member States to extend the range of trade mark protection in their national law where there is a senior mark with a "reputation". The law may then provide an objection to registration of a junior mark, and a ground of infringement against a sign used later, which is identical or similar to the senior mark but which is for dissimilar goods. It has however to be shown that the latter use without due course would take unfair advantage of, or be detrimental to, the distinctive character or the repute of the senior mark. The question referred asked whether it is permissible in national law to provide similar objections to registration and infringement where the goods are similar, rather than dissimilar. In answering the question in the affirmative, the ECJ stated:

24. The Court observes that Article 5(2) of the Directive must not be interpreted solely on the basis of its wording, but also in the light of the overall scheme and objectives of the system of which it is a part.

25. Having regard to the latter aspects, that article cannot be given an interpretation which would lead to marks with a reputation having less protection where a sign is used for identical or similar goods or services than where a sign is used for non-similar goods or services.

26. On this point, it has not been seriously disputed before the Court that, where a sign is used for identical or similar goods or services, a mark with a reputation must enjoy protection which is at least as extensive as where a sign is used for non-similar goods and services.

27. The question debated before the Court was essentially whether protection of a mark with a reputation against the use of a sign for identical or similar goods or services which is detrimental to the distinctive character or repute of the mark cannot already be obtained under Article 5(1) of the Directive, so that it is not necessary to seek it under Article 5(2).

28. Although, in the light of the 10th recital of the Directive, the protection conferred under Article 5(1) is an absolute right when the use affects or is liable to affect one of the functions of the mark (see Case C-206/01 *Arsenal Football Club* [2002] ECR I-0000, paragraphs 50 and 51), the application of Article 5(1)(b) depends on there being a likelihood of confusion (see Case C-425/98 *Marca Mode* [2000] ECR I-4861, paragraph 34). The Court points out that in *SABEL*, cited above (paragraphs 20 and 21) , it has already excluded a broad interpretation of Article 4(1)(b) of the Directive, which is, in substance, identical to Article 5(1)(b), an interpretation which had been suggested to it on the ground, *inter alia*, that Article 5(2) of the Directive, on its wording, applies only where a sign is used for non-similar goods or services.

29. Accordingly, where there is no likelihood of confusion, Article 5(1)(b) of the Directive could not be relied on by the proprietor of a mark with a reputation to protect himself against impairment of the distinctive character or repute of the mark.

30. In those circumstances, the answer to the first question must be that Articles 4(4)(a) and 5(2) of the Directive are to be interpreted as entitling the Member States to provide specific protection for registered trade marks with a reputation in cases where a later mark or sign, which is identical with or similar to the registered mark, is intended to be used or is used for goods or services identical with or similar to those covered by the registered mark.

5.2.5   Revocation and Invalidity of Registered Marks

5.2.5.1   Trade Marks Act 1994, ss.46–48: Grounds and Limitations

S.46 Revocation of registration (*cf.* CTM Reg., Art. 50, TM Dir. Art. 12)

(1) The registration of a trade mark may be revoked on any of the following grounds—

    (a) that within the period of five years following the date of completion of the registration procedure it has not been put to genuine use in the United Kingdom, by the proprietor or with his consent in relation to the goods or services for which it is registered, and there are no proper reasons for non-use;

    (b) that such use has been suspended for an uninterrupted period of five years, and there are no proper reasons for non-use;

    (c) that in consequence of acts or inactivity of the proprietor, it has become the common name in the trade for a product or service for which it is registered;

    (d) that in consequence of the use made of it by the proprietor or with his consent in relation to the goods or services for which it is registered it is liable to mislead the public, particularly as to the nature, quality or geographical origin of those goods or services.

(2) For the purposes of subsection (1) use of a trade mark includes use in a form differing in elements which do not alter the distinctive character of the mark in the form in which it was registered, and use in the United Kingdom includes affixing the trade mark to goods or to the packaging of goods in the United Kingdom solely for export purposes.

(3) The registration of a trade mark shall not be revoked on the ground mentioned in subsection (1)(a) or (b) if such use as is referred to in that paragraph is commenced or resumed after the expiry of the five year period and before the application for revocation is made:

Provided that any such commencement or resumption of use after the expiry of the five year period but within the period of three months before the making of the application shall be disregarded unless preparations for the commencement or resumption began before the proprietor became aware that the application might be made.

(4) An application for revocation may be made by any person, and may be made either to the registrar or to the court, except that—

    (a) if proceedings concerning the trade mark in question are pending in the court, the application must be made to the court; and

    (b) if in any other case the application is made to the registrar, he may at any stage of the proceedings refer the application to the court.

(5) Where grounds for revocation exist in respect of only some of the goods or services for which the trade mark is registered, revocation shall relate to those goods or services only.

(6) Where the registration of a trade mark is revoked to any extent, the rights of the proprietor shall be deemed to have ceased to that extent as from—

    (a) the date of the application for revocation, or

    (b) if the registrar or court is satisfied that the grounds for revocation existed at an earlier date, that date.

S.47 Grounds for invalidity of registration (*cf.* CTM Reg. Art. 51, TM Dir. Arts 3, 4)

(1) The registration of a trade mark may be declared invalid on the ground that the trade mark was registered in breach of section 3 or any of the provisions referred to in that section (absolute grounds for refusal of registration).

Where the trade mark was registered in breach of subsection (1)(b), (c) or (d) of that section, it shall not be declared invalid if, in consequence of the use which has been made of it, it has after registration acquired a distinctive character in relation to the goods or services for which it is registered.

(2) The registration of a trade mark may be declared invalid on the ground—

   (a) that there is an earlier trade mark in relation to which the conditions set out in section 5(1), (2) or (3) obtain, or
   (b) that there is an earlier right in relation to which the condition set out in section 5(4) is satisfied,

   unless the proprietor of that earlier trade mark or other earlier right has consented to the registration.

(3) An application for a declaration of invalidity may be made by any person, and may be made either to the registrar or to the court, except that—

   (a) if proceedings concerning the trade mark in question are pending in the court, the application must be made to the court; and
   (b) if in any other case the application is made to the registrar, he may, at any stage of the proceedings, refer the application to the court.

(4) In the case of bad faith in the registration of a trade mark, the registrar himself may apply to the court for a declaration of the invalidity of the registration.

(5) Where the grounds of invalidity exist in respect of only some of the goods or services for which the trade mark is registered, the trade mark shall be declared invalid as regards those goods or services only.

(6) Where the registration of a trade mark is declared invalid to any extent, the registration shall to that extent be deemed never to have been made:

   Provided that this shall not affect transactions past and closed.

S.48 Effect of acquiescence (*cf.* CTM Reg. Art. 53, TM Dir. Art. 9)

(1) Where the proprietor of an earlier trade mark or other earlier right has acquiesced for a continuous period of five years in the use of a registered trade mark in the United Kingdom, being aware of that use, there shall cease to be any entitlement on the basis of that earlier trade mark or other right—

   (a) to apply for a declaration that the registration of the later trade mark is invalid, or
   (b) to oppose the use of the later trade mark in relation to the goods or services in relation to which it has been so used,

   unless the registration of the later trade mark was applied for in bad faith.

(2) Where subsection (1) applies, the proprietor of the later trade mark is not entitled to oppose the use of the earlier trade mark or, as the case may be, the exploitation of the earlier right, notwithstanding that the earlier trade mark or right may no longer be invoked against his later trade mark.

5.2.5.2   *"Daiquiri Rum" Trade Mark* [1969] R.P.C. 600, HL

Section 15 of the Trade Marks Act 1938, an elaborate provision, in essence allowed the court to expunge a registration if the mark was shown to have acquired a well-known and established use as a description for an article or substance by persons trading therein and the article or substance was either within the registration or constituted "goods of the same description". (A separate version was later enacted for service marks.) It was in this respect wider than the 1994 Act, s.46(1)(c), while at the same time giving a right which was infringed only in relation to goods within the registration and not (as under the 1994 Act, s.10) in relation to similar or even dissimilar goods or services. The facts and decision deserve comparison with the new Act.

United Rum Merchants owned the mark "Daiquiri Rum" for rum, originally registered in 1922 by a predecessor in title. At about that time "Daiquiri" was becoming used as the name of a cocktail, combining light rum, lime, sugar and ice. The applicants to remove the mark by virtue of s.15 were the agents importing "Bacardi" rum.

The House of Lords considered that rum cocktails and rum were "goods of the same description".

On the proprietor's argument, that the section must be construed narrowly so as to apply only when the descriptive use was on goods within the registration, Lord Wilberforce (for the House) stated:

What, then, does a fair reading of the section require? The words are general; as they stand they do not, if accepted, produce absurdity. To read them at their face value may seem to press hardly on some registered proprietors, who may see a use developing which they cannot stop and which may deprive them of their mark. On the other hand, they may have acted unwisely or unluckily in their choice of the mark and there is certainly a public interest in preventing the appropriation of common words and in avoiding confusion. Indeed, the usefulness of the wider meaning is well exemplified by the present case for, without imputing anything discreditable to the proprietors, there would be little merit in permitting them to secure monopoly rights in a mark containing a word which, in relation to related goods, had acquired an independent trade reputation, which mark they could never have successfully registered (as I think they could not) at the date when they acquired it. On the other side, the proprietors' counsel were not able to give a convincing actual or hypothetical example of injustice or even anomaly if the general meaning were accepted.

In my opinion, no good reason exists why the general unrestricted meaning should not be accepted and, if this is so, the initial portion of section 15 fits the facts because it has been proved that there is a well-known and established use of the word "Daiquiri" which the trade mark contains as the name or description of an article or substance, *viz.*, a Daiquiri cocktail.

5.2.5.3   *General Electric Co v General Electric Co Ltd* **[1970] R.P.C. 339, CA; [1973] R.P.C. 297, HL**

The American (appellant) and English (respondent) companies had originally adopted their very similar names honestly and each had built very large businesses in the UK and elsewhere. The English company applied to expunge the American company's mark—G.E. decoratively written in a rondel—which had been registered for various electrical goods since 1907, at which time the English company was only four years old. Until 1965 the American company made little use of its mark on the British market but then began to use it substantially in combination with other word marks. Both companies had recognised the possibility of confusion and had an understanding that they would do what they could to minimise it. The principal ground for expunction in the House of Lords was that subsequent to registration the mark had become likely to cause confusion with the English company so that the mark was one wrongly remaining on the register by virtue of the Trade Marks Act 1938, s.32(1).

Lord Diplock:

The likelihood of confusion

Where the question of the likelihood of deception or confusion arises on an application to expunge a registered mark which has already been the subject of substantial use, the absence of evidence of actual confusion having occurred is a potent factor in determining whether or not the court should exercise its discretion to expunge the mark from the register. But it does not decide the relevant hypothetical question which must be answered in the affirmative before any question of discretion to expunge the mark arises: would any normal and fair future use of the mark in the course of trade be likely to cause deception or confusion? If actual confusion in the past is proved, this is a strong indication that continued confusion is likely; but the absence of evidence of past confusion may be accounted for by the small extent to which the mark has been used or by special circumstances affecting its past use which may not continue to operate to prevent confusion in the future.

After characterising the case as "a jury question" he continued:

It was also submitted by the American company that if the source of the confusion as to the origin of the goods which resulted from the use of the trade mark was due to the similarity of the names of two different manufacturers either of whom might be associated with the mark in the mind of a potential buyer of the goods, this was confusion "between name and name", not confusion "between mark and mark"; and that only the latter was relevant "confusion" within the meaning of that expression in section 11 of the Act. I am unable to accept this argument. The essence of a trade mark is the association that it bears in the mind of a potential buyer of the goods to which it is applied. I can see no reason for differentiating between cases where the confusion arises because the trade mark is associated with the name of a manufacturer to which some other manufacturer's name is similar, and cases where it is associated with a design or with descriptive words and the confusion arises because some other manufacturer uses a similar design or similar descriptive words to indicate the origin of his goods. In my view, section 11 is wide enough to embrace "confusion" resulting from any of these kinds of association.

*Lord Diplock concurred with the Court of Appeal's view that there was a like-
lihood of confusion on the facts.*

*It was then necessary to consider what the ground of objection was which
would justify removal of the mark. This involved an elaborate investigation of the
1938 Act and its antecedents. For the purpose of comparison with the jurisdiction conferred by the 1994 Act, s.46(1)(d), the essence of the House of
Lords' conclusion should be noted, particularly in relation to the apparent
discretion given by the new section. The House held that the 1938 Act, s.11,
provided a ground for removing a mark which, since its registration, had
become liable to confuse when it was "disentitled to protection in a court of
justice". This was held to arise when the confusion was the result of blameworthy conduct by the registered proprietor.It was claimed that there was an
understanding between the British and American companies that they would
minimise the risk of confusion between the two marks and names, but that this
still assumed that the public could be misled.*

The question whether the American company is entitled to succeed on the main ground of
appeal thus depends on whether the likelihood that the use of the rondel mark *simpliciter*
on electrical goods would cause confusion on July 20, 1967, the date of the application to
expunge, resulted from some blameworthy act of the American company. On the findings
of Graham J., which in my opinion are amply justified, as to the nature of the understanding between the two companies such as it was, it seems to me to be impossible to hold
there was any such blameworthy conduct by the American company as would amount to
an equitable ground for disentitling them to protection for the use of the mark. There is
therefore no ground in law for expunging the mark and no question of the exercise of
discretion of the court can arise.

*The case also raised a question of "muddying the mark" which was important
on the question of unregistered licensing, as it was dealt with by the Court of
Appeal [1970] R.P.C. 339. The point is explained in the judgment of Cross L.J.:*

This sufficed to dispose of the appeal but as the matter may be taken to the House of Lords,
I ought, perhaps, to say something about some grounds of appeal looming very large in the
particulars of objection which do not depend on any possible confusion between G.E. and
G.E.C. They relate to the dealings of G.E. with the mark and would be just as strong or
weak if no such company as G.E.C. had ever existed.

The facts which are alleged to be relevant in this connection are (1) that G.E. has
authorised its wholly owned subsidiary "Housewares" to use the mark in combination with
the word MONOGRAM in the form MONO-GE-GRAM otherwise than under a
"registered user" agreement under section 28 of the Act; (2) that the registered user
agreement entered into with Simplex G.E. extends to user of the mark on goods outside the
scope of its registration; (3) that Simplex G.E. has in fact used the mark on goods not
within the registration; (4) that the registered user agreement contained a clause which on
its true construction precluded Simplex G.E. from using the G.E. mark in combination
with the word Simplex and that they have in fact done so, and (5) that the user of the G.E.
mark in combination with the words SIMPLEX and MONOGRAM has, to use the
appellants' phrase, so "muddied" the mark that it ought to be expunged.

In order to estimate the strength of weakness of this line of attack one must, as I see it, view the matter historically.

When it was established—in the days before the first Trade Mark Act—that a trade mark was an item of property which could be assigned, it was also laid down that it could only be assigned together with the business in the goods to which the mark was affixed. This principle was given statutory force with regard to registered trade marks by section 2 of the 1875 Act and section 70 of the 1883 Act (see the judgment of Fry L.J. in *Pinto v Badman* (1891) 8 R.P.C. 181 at 194, 195). By 1905 the conception of a trade mark had extended to include, as well as marks indicating the manufacturer of the goods, marks indicating other connections between the goods and the owner of the mark. This is shown by the definition of a "trade mark" in section 3 of the 1905 Act, which ran as follows:

> "A 'trade mark' shall mean a mark used or proposed to be used upon or in connection with goods for the purpose of indicating that they are the goods of the proprietor of such trade mark by virtue of manufacture, selection, certification, dealing with, or offering for sale".

But this prohibition against assignment "in gross" was continued by section 22 of the Act.

In the *Bowden* case (1913) 30 R.P.C. 580 and (1914) 31 R.P.C. 385 the wire company had purported to grant to the brake company (over whose methods of manufacture it had no control), together with a licence of patent rights, a licence to use a trade mark of which they were the registered proprietors. It was held that this purported licence offended against section 22 of the 1905 Act (as being a partial assignment of the mark) and had taken the mark outside the statutory definition of a trade mark since it was no longer used for the purpose of indicating that the goods in question were the goods of the proprietor in any of the senses included in the definition. Consequently the court ordered the mark to be taken off the register.

In *"Radiation" Trade Mark* (1930) 47 R.P.C. 37 a company which was applying for registration of a mark did not itself manufacture or sell the goods in question which were made and sold by companies associated with it. The applicant, however, controlled the policy of these associated companies decided whether or not a particular article should be produced and sold maintained its own testing establishment and a staff to inspect the work of the associated companies and ensure that standards of manufacture which it approved were maintained. It was urged by those opposing the registration, on the authority of the *Bowden* case (above), that the applicants by licensing the associated companies to use the mark had deprived it of the quality of a trade mark and any right to protection in a court of law. The Comptroller General, however, distinguished the *Bowden* case on the ground that there the two companies were independent of each other so far as the manufacture and marketing of the goods was concerned and further expressed the view that the connection of the applicants with the goods fell within the words "selection" and "dealing with" in the definition in section 3 of the 1905 Act.

It is common ground between the parties that the 1938 Act to some extent relaxed the previous rules as to the assignment and licensing of registered marks. The question at issue—or, rather, one of the questions at issue—on this branch of the case is how far that relaxation went and what effect (if any) it had on the position of unregistered marks.

Cross L.J. set out the 1938 Act, s.22 (assignment), s.28 (registered user agreements) and the definition of "trade mark" (s.68).

In *"Radiation" Trade Mark* it was held that "quality control" fell within the definition of the 1905 Act, and whether or not that was right, I think that a right to control the standards to be maintained in the manufacture of goods could, in the absence of some special context, be fairly described as a "connection in the course of trade" between the goods and the person having that right.

This view appears to me to be supported by what was said by Lord Macmillan in *Aristoc Ltd v Rysta Ltd* (1945) 62 R.P.C. 65 at 80. It was held in that case that there could be no "connection in the course of trade" between the goods and the owner of the mark after the goods had been sold to the consumer, but Lord Macmillan remarked that the wording of the 1938 Act was wider than that of the 1905 Act and covered any association with the goods in the course of their production and preparation for the market.

Further it is clear that the existence or non-existence of adequate "quality control" is one of the matters which the Registrar is to have in mind in deciding whether or not to permit the registration of registered user agreement. Apart, therefore, from an argument based on the inclusion of the words "or as registered user" in the new definition, to which I will advert in a moment, I would have little hesitation in agreeing with the view of the effect of the 1938 Act on the licensing of marks expressed by Lloyd Jacob J. in *"Bostitch" Trade Mark* [1964] R.P.C. 183. This was, in substance, that, provided that "quality control" was maintained, licensing of a mark—whether registered or unregistered—did not deprive it of protection in a court of law or, if it was registered, afford a ground for its removal; that it was not necessary for the proprietor of a registered mark to avail himself of section 28 in order to grant a valid licence of it; but that if he chose to make use of the section (which was merely permissive) he would obtain certain advantages, for example the advantage of the Registrar's decision that the measure of "quality control" which he would retain was adequate to support the licence to use the mark.

The appellants, however, contended that "quality control", though it would justify the Registrar in sanctioning a registered user agreement, was not a "connection in the course of trade" within the definition in section 68 and that the grant of a licence to use a mark, even if accompanied by "quality control", still had the result, even after the Act of depriving the mark of the character of a trade mark unless it was embodied in a registered user agreement under section 28.

In support of this contention the appellants relied strongly on the words in the definition "some person having the right either as proprietor or registered user to use the mark". If the respondents were right in saying that "quality control" was a connection in the course of trade between the goods and the proprietor of the mark, the definition would have said "a connection in the course of trade between the goods and the proprietor of the mark". It was just because "quality control"—though sufficient to support a registered user agreement—was not a connection in the course of trade that the definition referred to the right to use the mark possessed either by a proprietor who had not parted with his right to use it or by a registered owner who was the one person to whom the proprietor could grant a licence to use without destroying the character of the mark.

This argument is ingenious but, to my mind, it reads too much into the wording of the definition. The draftsman may well have said to himself "A mark on the register will cease to be a 'trade mark' if there is in fact no connection in the course of trade between the goods to which it is affixed and someone appearing on the register as having an interest in the mark, and now that the Act is providing for registered users as well as registered owners we had better mention them in the definition too".

On the whole, therefore, I see no sufficient reason for retracting the approval of what Lloyd-Jacob J. said in *"Bostitch" Trade Mark* which I expressed in *British Petroleum Co Ltd v European Petroleum Distributors Limited* [1968] R.P.C. 54 though the point was not argued then as fully as it has been on this appeal. I would add that in saying, as they did, in *Oertli AG v Bowman* (1950) 67 R.P.C.1 that the grant of the licence had destroyed the validity of the mark, Lord Simonds and Lord Jenkins were clearly only recording what had been conceded in argument and not expressing considered views of their own.

Applying this conclusion to the facts of the case, I am of opinion, first, that the authority given by G.E. to the Housewares company to use the G.E. rondel was open to no objection (a) because as Housewares is a wholly owned subsidiary of G.E., the user might fairly be considered as user by G.E. itself, as in *"Radiation" Trade Mark* (above), and (b) because the licensing of a mark, whether registered or unregistered, does not deprive it of the character of a trade mark providing that the owner of the mark retains a sufficient connection in the course of trade with the relevant goods, which connection can be maintained.

Secondly, I am of opinion that even if Simplex G.E. has been using the G.E. mark on goods which do not fall within the registration, that fact in no way invalidates the mark since G.E. has in fact, as is indeed admitted, "quality control". The licensing agreement certainly envisaged that some of the goods on which the mark might be used might not be covered by the registration. Whether the switchgear, to which this question relates, was or was not in 1907 electrical apparatus included in class 6 (*i.e.* was machinery other than agricultural or horticultural machinery), is to my mind a question which hardly admits of an answer since apparatus of this sort was probably unknown in 1907. If I am right on the general point as to licensing, the question does not arise, I would say, however, that assuming that I am wrong on the general question of licensing, I am not satisfied that the inclusion in the licensing agreement and the user of the mark in relation to goods not covered by the registration would invalidate the registered mark.

. . .

That leaves only the question of the so-called "muddying" of the mark. The respondents could not succeed under this head unless the use of the G.E. rondel in combination with Simplex in the form SIMPLEX G.E. or in combination with Monogram in the form MONO-GE-GRAM caused confusion within the meaning of section 11. If one puts out of the way—as one must, for the purposes of this argument—confusion with G.E.C., then I do not think that any confusion such as is envisaged by section 11 is likely to arise. It is possible that some people looking at the marks may not get the message which G.E. intends them to get, but that would not, as I see it, invalidate the G.E. mark.

In the House of Lords Lord Diplock dealt with the whole issue summarily:

There is, in my view, no logical ground for holding that the right of a proprietor to use a registered mark in respect of goods for which it is registered can be affected by his losing the right to use the same mark as an unregistered mark in respect of other goods. Since he would lose it in any event at common law by disuse, it would follow from this proposition that the owner of a mark registered in respect of a particular class of goods would lose his right as the proprietor of such mark if he failed to continue to use the mark as an unregistered mark in respect of any other class of goods for which he was using it at the time of first registration. This has only to be stated to be rejected.

5.2.6   Ownership, Assignment and Licensing

5.2.6.1   Trade Marks Act 1994, ss.22–24, 28.

S.22 Nature of registered trade mark (*cf.* CTM Reg. Art. 16)

A registered trade mark is personal property (in Scotland, incorporeal moveable property).

S.23 Co-ownership of registered trade mark

(1) Where a registered trade mark is granted to two or more persons jointly each of them is entitled, subject to any agreement to the contrary, to an equal undivided share in the registered trade mark.

(2) The following provisions apply where two or more persons are co-proprietors of a registered trade mark, by virtue of subsection (1) or otherwise.

(3) Subject to any agreement to the contrary, each co-proprietor is entitled by himself or his agents, to do for his own benefit and without the consent of or the need to account to the other or others, any act which would otherwise amount to an infringement of the registered trade mark.

(4) One co-proprietor may not without the consent of the other or others—

   (a) grant a licence to use the registered trade mark, or
   (b) assign or charge his share in the registered trade mark (or, in Scotland cause or permit security to be granted over it).

(5) Infringement proceedings may be brought by any co-proprietor, but he may not, without the leave of the court, proceed with the action unless the other, or each of the others is either joined as a plaintiff or added as a defendant.

A co-proprietor who is thus added as a defendant shall not be made liable for any costs in the action unless he takes part in the proceedings.
Nothing in this subsection affects the granting of interlocutory relief on the application of a single co-proprietor.

(6) Nothing in this section affects the mutual rights and obligations of trustees or personal representatives, or their rights and obligations as such.

S.24 Assignment, &c. of registered trade mark (*cf.* CTM Reg. Art. 17)

(1) A registered trade mark is transmissible by assignment, testamentary disposition or operation of law in the same way as other personal or moveable property.

It is so transmissible either in connection with the goodwill of a business or independently.

(2) An assignment or other transmission of a registered trade mark may be partial, that is, limited so as to apply—

   (a) in relation to some but not all of the goods or services for which the trade mark is registered, or
   (b) in relation to use of the trade mark in a particular manner or a particular locality.

(3) An assignment of a registered trade mark, or an assent relating to a registered trade

mark, is not effective unless it is in writing signed by or on behalf of the assignor or, as the case may be, a personal representative.

Except in Scotland, this requirement may be satisfied in a case where the assignor or personal representative is a body corporate by the affixing of its seal.

(4) The above provisions apply to assignment by way of security as in relation to any other assignment.

(5) A registered trade mark may be the subject of a charge (in Scotland security) in the same way as other personal or moveable property.

(6) Nothing in this Act shall be construed as affecting the assignment or other transmission of an unregistered trade mark as part of the goodwill of a business.

Section 25 provides for the registration of transactions affecting registered trade marks, including assignments and the granting of licences and security interests in trade marks, and the consequences of the failure to register such transactions. Section 26 relates to trusts and equities affecting registered trade marks. Section 27 states that the provisions of ss.22–26 apply, with some modifications, in relation to the application for the registration of a trade mark as in relation to a registered trade mark.

S.28 Licensing of registered trade mark (*cf.* CTM Reg. Arts 22, 23; TM Dir. Art. 7)

(1) A licence to use a registered trade mark may be general or limited. A limited licence may, in particular, apply—

   (a) in relation to some but not all of the goods or services for which the trade mark is registered, or
   (b) in relation to use of the trade mark in a particular manner or a particular locality.

(2) A licence is not effective unless it is in writing signed by or on behalf of the grantor.

Except in Scotland, this requirement may be satisfied in a case where the grantor is a body corporate by the affixing of its seal.

(3) Unless the licence provides otherwise, it is binding on a successor in title to the grantor's interest.

References in this Act to doing anything with, or without, the consent of the proprietor of a registered trade mark shall be construed accordingly.

(4) Where the licence so provides, a sub-licence may be granted by the licensee; and references in this Act to a licence or licensee include a sub-licence or sub-licensee.

Section 29(1) defines an "exclusive licence". Section 29(2) and s.31 respectively provide for the rights of an exclusive licensee against a successor in title of the grantor and against infringers of the trade mark in certain circumstances. The rights of a non-exclusive licensee, and an exclusive licensee not covered by s.31, in cases of infringement are governed by s.30.

5.2.6.2   *Scandecor Development AB v Scandecor Marketing AB* [2002]

In 1967 two Swedish students set up Scandecor International A, to sell art posters and related products. The company became one of the largest poster businesses in the world. Local subsidiary companies were set up in each country to act as distributors, and they each used the word Scandecor as part of their names. The UK company was Scandecor Ltd and two trade marks were registered for the word and for a logo mark incorporating the word "Scandecor". The word mark was registered in the name of Scandecor Ltd and the logo mark in the name of the parent company, Scandecor International. The word mark was later assigned to Scandecor International.

The two founders eventually fell out. Scandecor International was wound up in 1994, and in 1997 the final contractual ties between the pair were severed. Proceedings arose in several jurisdictions concerning the continued use of the word "Scandecor". In the UK, Scandecor Development, which had acquired Scandecor International's assets upon its insolvency, objected to Scandecor Ltd continuing to use the word "Scandecor" in connection with the sale of its own posters and commenced infringement proceedings. Scandecor Ltd counter-claimed for revocation of the marks on the basis that they had ceased to be distinctive.

Lloyd J. declined to revoke the registration of either mark, but held that Scandecor Ltd was entitled to continue to carry out its business under its existing name. Both parties appealed to the Court of Appeal, which ordered that the two trade marks should be revoked. Scandecor Development then appealed to the House of Lords.

Lord Nicholls noted that the present case raised a fundamental question about the application of the 1994 Act to the licensing of trade marks, a form of business activity which is now widely used. He traced the history of assignment and licensing of trade marks before the 1994 Act, with particular reference to "bare" licences under which the licensor has no control over the quality of the goods sold by the licensee. Traditionally, a bare licence would usually not suffice: McGregor Trade Mark *[1979] R.P.C. 36, 53;* Re American Greetings Corp's Application *[1984] 1 All E.R. 426. He then examined the situation since 1994:*

33. The Trade Marks Act 1994 has brought about substantial changes in the registered trade mark law of the United Kingdom. The primary purpose of the Act, as set out in its long title, is "to make new provision for registered trade marks", implementing the Trade Marks Directive. Among other changes the Act has swept away the remaining restrictions on assignment and licensing. Section 1(1) defines a trade mark in the following terms:

> "a 'trade mark' means any sign capable of being represented graphically which is capable of distinguishing goods or services of one undertaking from those of other undertakings"

Inherent in this definition is the notion that distinctiveness as to business source (the "goods of one undertaking") is the essential function of a trade mark today.

34. Under s.24 of the 1994 Act a registered trade mark may be assigned in the same way as other personal property and either with the goodwill of a business or independently. The obligation under the 1938 Act to advertise an assignment of a trade mark when the assignment was unaccompanied by the goodwill of the assignor's business has been abolished. This requirement was thought to be of little practical effect as a safeguard to the public. Now it is up to the assignee of the mark, if he does not also acquire the assignor's business, to make with the assignor whatever arrangements may be necessary to ensure that the mark will continue to be indicative exclusively of one source, *viz.*, after the assignment, the assignee. That is now the responsibility of the assignee, because the abolition of the statutory prohibition on assignment has not altered the fundamental principle of trade mark law that a trade mark which ceases to be distinctive is no longer fulfilling the essential functions of a trade mark and therefore, if registered, should not remain on the register.

35. As to licences, ss.28 to 31 make provision for the grant of licences, either exclusive or non-exclusive, general or limited. Licences are registrable transactions. This wide power to grant licences is drawn directly from Art.8(1) of the Trade Marks Directive. The Directive provides simply that a trade mark "may be licensed for some or all of the goods or services for which it is registered".

Bare licences

36. Against this background I turn to the question whether the use of a mark by a licensee under a bare licence is objectionable as inherently likely to deceive. I shall confine my observations to exclusive licences. What is the message which a trade mark conveys today? What does a trade mark denote? It denotes that goods bearing the mark come from one business source: the goods of one undertaking, in the words of s.1(1) of the 1994 Act. That much is clear. But what does the mark denote about that source? Must the source be the proprietor of the trade mark? On this the Act is silent. But so to read the Act would accord ill with the statutory power to grant licences. And this interpretation would turn the clock the back to 1905. Even under the 1938 Act the source was not so confined. Under the 1938 Act the source could be a registered user.

37. Or is the business source the person who is for the time being entitled to use the mark, whether as proprietor or exclusive licensee? I prefer this view. The commercial background has changed greatly since 1938, and even more so since 1905. The present position was well summarised in a paper, *Reform of Trade Marks Law*, issued by the Department of Trade and Industry in September 1990 (Cm.1203). Para 4.36 reads:

> "Whatever may have been the position in 1938, the public is now accustomed to goods or services being supplied under licence from the trade mark owner. For example there has been the growth of franchise operations. The potential for deception is therefore less. Moreover the strongest guarantee that a proprietor will maintain control over the way in which his trade mark is used is that it is in his own interest to do so. A trade mark is a valuable piece of property, in terms both of its power to attract customers and of the royalties which can be demanded from licensees. Its value is however ultimately dependent on its reputation with the public. If the proprietor tolerates uncontrolled use of his trade mark the value of this property will be diminished. In an extreme case the registration of the mark may become liable to be revoked if it has become deceptive or generic through such use. It is however the responsibility of the proprietor, not the Registrar, to prevent the devaluation of his own property."

38. Thus, the wider interpretation, according to which the source may be either the pro-

prietor or an exclusive licensee, would not be at variance with customers' perceptions. Customers are well used to the practice of licensing of trade marks. When they see goods to which a mark has been affixed, they understand that the goods have been produced either by the owner of the mark or by someone else acting with his consent.

39. Nor does the wider interpretation undermine the protection which a trade mark is intended to afford customers. For their quality assurance customers rely on the self-interest of the owner. They assume that if a licence has been granted the owner can be expected to have chosen a suitable licensee and imposed suitable terms. They also assume that during the currency of any licence the licensee, as well as the owner, is likely to have an interest in maintaining the value of the brand name. Customers are not to be taken to rely on the protection supposedly afforded by a legal requirement that the proprietor must always retain and exercise an inherently imprecise degree of control over the licensee's activities.

40. Some of those who have spent their professional lives under the regime of the 1938 Act, may consider that this view of the matter is distressingly heretical. They would be mistaken. It is no more than the consequence flowing from the 1994 Act having freed the law of registered trade marks from the straitjacket imposed by the statutory definitions of a trade mark in the 1905 Act and then the 1938 Act. Freed from that constraint, the law can now catch up with business practice.

41. Accordingly, I cannot accept Mr Young's "golden thread" submission. From 1984 Scandecor Marketing and Scandecor Ltd were selling their own goods under the Scandecor marks. They were doing so, until 1994 when it was terminated, under a bare licence. This does not of itself mean that from 1984 onwards these marks had become liable to mislead.

Practical implications

42. Before proceeding further I must mention some of the practical implications of the view expressed above, starting with the position which exists while an exclusive licence is in operation. The mere fact that, during this period, some customers may associate the trade mark with the exclusive licensee does not mean that it has become deceptive or that it lacks distinctiveness. During the licence period the goods come from only one source, namely the licensee, and the mark is distinctive of that source.

43. The position after the licence has ended is different. Then the right to use the mark reverts to the proprietor of the mark. He can then apply the mark to his goods. The position is, indeed, comparable to the position which arises when a trade mark is assigned without any assignment of the assignor's business. Whether this change in the person entitled to use the mark gives rise to deception will depend primarily on what then happens to the erstwhile licensee's business. If the former licensee ceases to carry on the business in which he used the mark, no question of deception due to lack of distinctiveness will normally arise. Henceforward the mark will be distinctive of one source, namely the proprietor of the mark. This will be a different source from the source during the licence period, but this change in the source is not itself inherently deceptive. Such a change occurs whenever a trade mark changes hands.

44. What happens if, after the licence has ended, the former licensee continues to carry on the same business as he did during the licence period? Suppose he continues to manufacture the same goods and deal with the same customers, but without using the licensed mark. In such a case there may be scope for confusion and deception. Any customers who were aware of the identity of the source during the licence period may continue to associate goods bearing the mark with the former licensee and his continuing business. When that is

the position, the mark may no longer be distinctive of one business source. Whether that is so will depend on the facts of the case...

49. The claim in these proceedings is that, in consequence of the use made of the marks by Scandecor Marketing and Scandecor Ltd with the consent of Scandecor International, the marks are "liable to mislead the public". That is essentially a question of fact. That question of fact must be answered having regard to matters as they now are, not as they were at some time in the past. In deciding this issue of fact the court must have due regard, as I have been at pains to emphasise, to the message which a trade mark conveys. But since the question is whether the marks are currently liable to mislead, the message which is relevant is the message which use of the marks conveys today, not the message it would have conveyed to the public in the past.

The court then noted that before applying the views they had expressed to the facts of this case, an authoritative ruling from the ECJ was needed on inter-preting the relevant provisions of the Trade Marks Directive of 1988, as it was vital that a uniform view be taken throughout the Community on this matter. Accordingly, Lord Nicholls stated, the House should refer a question to the ECJ as to whether a trade mark is to be regarded as liable to mislead the public, within the meaning of Art.12(2)(b), if the origin of the goods denoted by the mark is a bare exclusive licensee. Other issues which the ECJ should also be asked to consider were (i) the meaning of "undertaking" in Art.2 of the Direc-tive, given the overlapping nature of some of the Scandecor companies; (ii) the validity of the "own name" defence; and (iii) whether s.46(1), implementing the provision in Art.12 of the Directive that a trade mark shall be "'liable" to revo-cation in specified circumstances, has mandatory effect or whether the court retains any discretion. However, the court refused to refer a further question to the ECJ concerning the correct interpretation of Art.10(3) of the Directive.

Lord Nicholls:

56. For completeness I mention a contention of Mr Rosen Q.C. based on Art.10(3) of the Directive. Art.10 makes provision regarding the non-use of trade marks. Art.10(3) provides that "Use of the trade mark with the consent of the proprietor shall be deemed to constitute use by the proprietor". Mr Rosen submitted that the proper interpretation of this article is that use with consent constitutes deemed use by the proprietor for all purposes. Accord-ingly, the use of the marks by Scandecor Marketing and Scandecor Ltd on their goods was not likely to "mislead the public". Their use is deemed to be use by the proprietor of the marks, Scandecor International. The 1994 Act should be construed accordingly.

57. I cannot accept this. I agree with Lloyd J. that the context of Art.10(3) makes clear that Art.10(3) is directed at the non-use provisions of Arts 10 and 11. It is not applicable to the revocation provisions in Art.12(2)(b). Those are the provisions carried into s.46(1)(d) of the Act. The Act incorporates the effect of Art.10(3) into s.46(1)(a). A mark may be revoked if, for a period of five years, it has not been put to genuine use "by the proprietor or with his consent". I consider this is *acte clair*. The Court of Justice should not be burdened with this further point. That court is burdened enough without being asked questions to which the answer is obvious.

The parties, however, did not proceed with the reference to the ECJ.

5.2.7 Infringement

5.2.7.1 Trade Marks Act 1994, ss.9–12: Grounds and Exceptions

S.9 Rights conferred by registered trade mark (*cf.* CTM Reg. Art. 9; TM Dir. Art. 5)

(1) The proprietor of a registered trade mark has exclusive rights in the trade mark which are infringed by use of the trade mark in the United Kingdom without his consent.

The acts amounting to infringement, if done without the consent of the proprietor, are specified in section 10.

(2) References in this Act to the infringement of a registered trade mark are to any such infringement of the rights of the proprietor.

(3) The rights of the proprietor have effect from the date of registration (which in accordance with section 40(3) is the date of filing of the application for registration):

Provided that—

(a) no infringement proceedings may be begun before the date on which the trade mark is in fact registered; and

(b) no offence under section 92 (unauthorised use of trade mark, &c. in relation to goods) is committed by anything done before the date of publication of the registration.

S.10 Infringement of registered trade mark (*cf.* CTM Reg. Art. 9, TM Dir. Art. 5)

(1) A person infringes a registered trade mark if he uses in the course of trade a sign which is identical with the trade mark in relation to goods or services which are identical with those for which it is registered.

(2) A person infringes a registered trade mark if he uses in the course of trade a sign where because—

   (a) the sign is identical with the trade mark and is used in relation to goods or services similar to those for which the trade mark is registered, or

   (b) the sign is similar to the trade mark and is used in relation to goods or services identical with or similar to those for which the trade mark is registered, there exists a likelihood of confusion on the part of the public, which includes the likelihood of association with the trade mark.

(3) A person infringes a registered trade mark if he uses in the course of trade a sign which—

   (a) is identical with or similar to the trade mark, and

   (b) is used in relation to goods or services which are not similar to those for which the trade mark is registered,

where the trade mark has a reputation in the United Kingdom and the use of the sign, being without due cause, takes unfair advantage of, or is detrimental to, the distinctive character or the repute of the trade mark.

(4) For the purposes of this section a person uses a sign if, in particular, he—

   (a) affixes it to goods or the packaging thereof,

   (b) offers or exposes goods for sale, puts them on the market or stocks them for those purposes under the, sign, or offers or supplies services under the sign;

(c) imports or exports goods under the sign; or

(d) uses the sign on business papers or in advertising.

(5) A person who applies a registered trade mark to material intended to be used for labelling or packaging goods, as a business paper, or for advertising goods or services, shall be treated as a party to any use of the material which infringes the registered trade mark if when he applied the mark he knew or had reason to believe that the application of the mark was not duly authorised by the proprietor or a licensee.

(6) Nothing in the preceding provisions of this section shall be construed as preventing the use of a registered trade mark by any person for the purpose of identifying goods or services as those of the proprietor or a licensee.

But any such use otherwise than in accordance with honest practices in industrial or commercial matters shall be treated as infringing the registered trade mark if the use without due cause takes unfair advantage of, or is detrimental to, the distinctive character or repute of the trade mark.

S.11 Limits on effect of registered trade mark (*cf.* CTM Reg. Art. 12, TM Dir. Art. 6)

(1) A registered trade mark is not infringed by the use of another registered trade mark in relation to goods or services for which the latter is registered (but see section 47(6) (effect of declaration of invalidity of registration)).

(2) A registered trade mark is not infringed by—

(a) the use by a person of his own name or address,

(b) the use of indications concerning the kind, quality, quantity, intended purpose, value, geographical origin, the time of production of goods or of rendering of services, or other characteristics of goods or services, or

(c) the use of the trade mark where it is necessary to indicate the intended purpose of a product or service (in particular, as accessories or spare parts),

provided the use is in accordance with honest practices in industrial or commercial matters.

(3) A registered trade mark is not infringed by the use in the course of trade in a particular locality of an earlier right which applies only in that locality.

For this purpose an 'earlier right' means an unregistered trade mark or other sign continuously used in relation to goods or services by a person or a predecessor in title of his from a date prior to whichever is the earlier of—

(a) the use of the first-mentioned trade mark in relation to those goods or services by the proprietor or a predecessor in title of his, or

(b) the registration of the first-mentioned trade mark in respect of those goods or services in the name of the proprietor or a predecessor in title of his;

and an earlier right shall be regarded as applying in a locality if, or to the extent that, its use in that locality is protected by virtue of any rule of law (in particular the law of passing off).

S.12 Exhaustion of rights conferred by registered trade mark (*cf.* CTM Reg. Art. 12, TM Dir. Art. 7)

(1) A registered trade mark is not infringed by the use of the trade mark in relation to

goods which have been put on the market in the European Economic Area under that trade mark by the proprietor or with his consent.

(2) Subsection (1) does not apply where there exist legitimate reasons for the proprietor to oppose further dealings in the goods (in particular, where the condition of the goods has been changed or impaired after they have been put on the market).

Sections 14–21 relate to infringement proceedings, and include provision for the remedies of erasure or removal of offending signs (s.15), and the delivery up (ss.16 and 18) and disposal (s.19) of infringing goods, materials or articles. Section 17 defines "infringing goods, materials or articles". Section 21 concerns groundless threats of infringement proceedings (see below, 7.1.3.1).

5.2.7.2   *Wagamama v City Centre Restaurants* [1995] F.S.R. 713, Laddie J.

The plaintiffs ran a successful Japanese restaurant under the name, "Wagamama," which it held as a registered mark. The defendant opened an Indian restaurant using the name "Rajamama" (later, "Raja Mama"). On the facts this was held likely to cause confusion among customers, so as to amount both to passing off and to infringement of the mark.

As to the latter, the plaintiff argued that, thanks to the introduction into s.10(2) of the Trade Marks Act 1994 of the expression, "likelihood of confusion on the part of the public, which includes the likelihood of association with the trade mark", a much broader form of infringement than under the 1938 Act had been introduced into the law, which would cover a case where a customer, on seeing the defendant's mark, would call to mind the plaintiff's mark, without any misapprehension as to the origin of the goods or services—infringement by "mere association".

The new expression comes from the Trade Marks Directive, Art. 5 (89/104) and a confidential Minute of the EC Council and Commission recorded that "'likelihood of association' is a concept which in particular has been developed by Benelux case-law". Laddie J. refused (following three precedents) to refer to the Minute because of its non-public nature.

In addition, he heard evidence from a Benelux law expert to the effect that that system had adopted a broad meaning for "likelihood of association" and that courts there took the view that the directive had done the same.

One of the documents to which [the expert] referred in his evidence was an article entitled "*Scope of Protection of the Trade Mark in the Benelux Countries and EEC-Harmonization*" written by Fürstner and Geuze. The authors were part of the Benelux delegation at the discussions which eventually gave birth to Article 5 of the 1989 Directive. It is a fascinating account, from the perspective of one delegation only, of the manoeuvering which preceded the acceptance of the final version of the directive. Before considering what the article says it is useful to have in mind that it was under Article 13(A) of the Benelux Trademark Act, 1971 that the case law relating to "association", and non-origin association in particular, was developed. ...

It appears to me that any popular belief, fuelled by articles in legal publications, that Article 5 of the 1988 directive was intended to ensure that the domestic law of trade mark infringement in all member states changed to that already adopted by the Benelux countries is open to question. If Fürstner and Geuze's article is correct, all but the Benelux countries were firmly opposed to any such move. Fürstner and Geuze's article is not admissible to help construe the directive. On the other hand it would be wrong to approach construction of the 1988 directive and the 1994 Act on unverifiable rumours or [the expert's] certainty as to what was intended.

The purpose of the 1989 Directive was to ensure a measure of uniformity between the trade mark laws of member states of the European Union. For that reason it is right that British courts should pay regard to decisions in the courts of other member states on equivalent provisions in their law. However it is apparent from the expert evidence that the Benelux courts have simply assumed that the directive made no alteration to their domestic law. The contents of the Fürstner and Geuze article suggests that this assumption may well have been wrong. In any event, the obligation of the English court is to decide what the proper construction is. If that construction differs from that adopted in the Benelux countries, one, at least, is wrong. It would not be right for an English court to follow the route adopted by the courts of another member state if it is firmly of a different view simply because the other court expressed a view first. The scope of European legislation is too important to be decided on a first past the post basis.

Since none of the arguments on construction put forward by the plaintiff is acceptable, it is necessary to approach the directive and the 1994 Act from first principles.

Monopolies are the antithesis of competition. Intellectual property rights such as patents, trade marks and copyright can create barriers to trade within a country. They can create barriers to trade between countries. Differences between the laws of member states of the European Union may add further obstructions to inter-state trade because what is permissible under the law of one member state may be prohibited under the law of its neighbour. However both at the domestic level and at the international level monopolies can be tolerated or even encouraged if they assist the development of commerce in some other way. Patent monopolies are the classic example. A valid patent may prevent competitors from entering a given field of commerce for up to 20 years. But this is a price which society, through its legislators, has agreed to pay to secure the increased investment in research and development which it is hoped patent monopolies will encourage. The important factor to bear in mind is that what justifies the monopoly is not the monopoly itself but the extent to which it gives, or is hoped to give, a benefit to commerce which compensates for the temporary restraint on competition. The monopoly is an adjunct to, and is designed to promote, commerce. This is central to the western system of commerce. Monopolies are the exception, not the rule (*Marsden v Saville Street Co* (1878) LR 3 Ex. D. 204). They need to be justified. As long ago as 1615 in this country it was said that the effect of an unjustified monopoly was "to take away free trade, which is the birthright of every subject".

Laddie J. referred to a number of authorities which treated the primary function of trade marks as being to indicate the origin of goods or services, notably the decisions of the ECJ in Hag II *(below, 6.2.3.2) and* Quattro *(below, 6.2.1.7.). He concluded:*

As mentioned above, there are two possible constructions which may be placed on Article 5 of the 1988 directive and section 10(2) of the 1994 Act. The rights of the proprietor against alleged infringers may be limited to classic infringement which includes association as to origin or, following the Benelux route, it could cover not only classic infringement but also non-origin association. In my view, the former construction is to be preferred. If the broader scope were to be adopted, the directive and our Act would be creating a new type of monopoly not related to the proprietor's trade but in the trade mark itself. Such a monopoly could be likened to a quasi-copyright in the mark. However, unlike copyright, there would be no fixed duration for the right and it would be a true monopoly effective against copyist and non-copyist alike. I can see nothing in the terms of the directive (or our Act), or in any secondary material which I could legitimately take into account, which would lead me to assume that this was its objective. On the contrary, the preamble to the directive seems to point in the opposite direction since it states:

> "Whereas the protection afforded by the registered trade mark, the function of which is in particular to guarantee the trade mark as an indication of origin, ..."

Furthermore there appears to be little commercial justification for any such extension of trade mark rights. If it had been the intention to make the directive identical with Benelux law on this important issue it could have said so. Indeed, in view of the fact that to have done so would have been significantly to expand trade mark rights and thereby significantly restrict the freedom of traders to compete, I would have expected any such expansion to have been stated in clear and unambiguous words so that traders throughout the European Union would be able to appreciate that their legislators had created a new broad monopoly. As it is, no such clear and unambiguous words have been used and the language of the directive and the 1994 Act is consistent with the rights being restricted to classical infringement.

Assessing likelihood of confusion on "classical grounds", Laddie J. said:

The approach the court should adopt to infringement under section 10 was recently set out by Jacob J. in *Origins Natural Resources Inc v Origin Clothing Limited* [1995] F.S.R. 280 in which at p.284 he said:

> "Section 10 of the Trade Marks Act presupposes that the plaintiff's mark is in use or will come into use. It requires the court to assume the mark of the plaintiff is used in a normal and fair manner in relation to the goods for which it is registered and then to assess the likelihood of confusion in relation to the way the defendant uses its mark, discounting external added matter or circumstances. The comparison is mark for mark."

A judge brings to the assessment of marks his own, perhaps idiosyncratic, pronunciation and view or understanding of them. Although the issue of infringement is one eventually for the judge alone, in assessing the marks he must bear in mind the impact the marks make or are likely to make on the minds of those persons who are likely to be customers for goods or services under the marks. Not all customers are the same. It is therefore sometimes of assistance for the court to hear evidence from witnesses who will help him to assess the variety of ways in which members of the target market will pronounce the marks and what, to them, will be the visual or phonetic impact of the marks. When considering infringement it is also necessary to bear in mind the possible impact of imperfect recollection on the part of members of the target market. ...

I have come to the conclusion that the defendant's mark, in either form, is so similar to the plaintiff's registered mark that in use there exists a substantial likelihood of confusion on the part of the relevant public. That confusion is likely to take the form that some members of the public as a result of imperfect recollection will think the marks are the same while others will think that they are associated in the sense that one is an extension of the other (*cf.* the *"Rus"*/*"Sanrus"* case; or otherwise derived from the same source. It follows that the plaintiff succeeds on the issue of trade mark infringement.

See also Sabel v Puma, above, 5.2.4.2.

5.2.7.3   *General Motors v Yplon* [1999] E.C.R. I-5429, ECJ

General Motors was registered owner of the Benelux mark "Chevy" for motor vehicles in five Classes and used it particularly on vans. Yplon held the Benelux registration of "Chevy" for detergents and other cleaning products in three other Classes. General Motors sought to restrain Yplon from using its mark on its products. It asserted that Yplon's use amounted to a dilution of the General Motors mark on dissimilar goods under the Benelux Trade Mark Law's implementation of Art.5(2) of the Trade Mark Directive (equivalent to TMA 1994, s.10(3)). The question put by the Dutch court raised the issue: what degree of reputation must a claimant show in order to fall within the Directive Art.5(2)? The Court of Justice examined the different linguistic versions of that Article:

21. The German, Dutch and Swedish versions use words signifying that the trade mark must be "known" without indicating the extent of knowledge required, whereas the other language versions use the term "reputation" or expressions implying, like that term, at a quantitative level a certain degree of knowledge amongst the public.

22. That nuance, which does not entail any real contradiction, is due to the greater neutrality of the terms used in the German, Dutch and Swedish versions. Despite that nuance, it cannot be denied that, in the context of a uniform interpretation of Community law, a knowledge threshold requirement emerges from a comparison of all the language versions of the Directive.

23. Such a requirement is also indicated by the general scheme and purpose of the Directive. In so far as Article 5(2) of the Directive, unlike Article 5(1), protects trade marks registered for non-similar products or services, its first condition implies a certain degree of knowledge of the earlier trade mark among the public. It is only where there is a sufficient degree of knowledge of that mark that the public, when confronted by the later trade mark, may possibly make an association between the two trade marks, even when used for non-similar products or services, and that the earlier trade mark may consequently be damaged.

24. The public amongst which the earlier trade mark must have acquired a reputation is that concerned by that trade mark, that is to say, depending on the product or service marketed, either the public at large or a more specialised public, for example traders in a specific sector.

25. It cannot be inferred from either the letter or the spirit of Article 5(2) of the Directive that the trade mark must be known by a given percentage of the public so defined.

26. The degree of knowledge required must be considered to be reached when the earlier mark is known by a significant part of the public concerned by the products or services covered by that trade mark.

27. In examining whether this condition is fulfilled, the national court must take into consideration all the relevant facts of the case, in particular the market share held by the

trade mark, the intensity, geographical extent and duration of its use, and the size of the investment made by the undertaking in promoting it.

28. Territorially, the condition is fulfilled when, in the terms of Article 5(2) of the Directive, the trade mark has a reputation "in the Member State". In the absence of any definition of the Community provision in this respect, a trade mark cannot be required to have a reputation "throughout" the territory of the Member State. It is sufficient for it to exist in a substantial part of it.

29. As far as trade marks registered at the Benelux Trade Mark Office are concerned, the Benelux territory must be treated like the territory of a Member State, since Article 1 of the Directive regards Benelux trade marks as trade marks registered in a Member State. Article 5(2) must therefore be understood as meaning a reputation acquired "in" the Benelux territory. For the same reasons as those relating to the condition as to the existence of a reputation in a Member State, a Benelux trade mark cannot therefore be required to have a reputation throughout the Benelux territory. It is sufficient for a Benelux trade mark to have a reputation in a substantial part of the Benelux territory, which part may consist of a part of one of the Benelux countries.

30. If, at the end of its examination, the national court decides that the condition as to the existence of a reputation is fulfilled, as regards both the public concerned and the territory in question, it must then go on to examine the second condition laid down in Article 5(2) of the Directive, which is that the earlier trade mark must be detrimentally affected without due cause. Here it should be observed that the stronger the earlier mark's distinctive character and reputation the easier it will be to accept that detriment has been caused to it.

5.2.7.4 *Parfums Christian Dior SA v Evora BV* [1998] R.P.C. 166, ECJ

The plaintiff produced luxury perfumes and other cosmetic products, distributed through a selective system. It had registererd a number of Benelux trade marks comprising illustrations of the packaging in which the bottles containing its product were sold. It also owned copyright in respect of the packaging and the bottles of certain of its products. The defendants obtained quantities of the plaintiff's products by parallel importation (the legality of which was not in dispute) and proceeded to advertise the goods by distributing promotional leaflets depicting the bottles and packaging of some of those products. The plaintiff objected to these forms of advertising and trade mark use, since in its view they were liable to damage the luxurious and prestigious image of the plaintiff's trade marks. It began proceedings against the defendants in Netherlands for trade mark and copyright infringement.

The Dutch Supreme Court (Hoge Raad) referred a number of questions to the Court of Justice for consideration, which, inter alia, *included:*

(1) Is it in keeping with Arts 5, 6, 7 of the Council Directive 89/104 to assume that, where it is a question of the resale of goods which have been put on the market in the Community under a trade mark by the trade mark proprietor or with his consent, the reseller is also free to use that trade mark for the purposes of bringing such further commercialisation to the attention of the public? If so, do exceptions exist to that rule?

(2) *If so, is there room for an exception where the advertising function of the mark is endangered by the fact that, as a result of the manner in which the reseller uses the mark in order to attract public attraction in that way, he damages the luxurious and prestigious image of the trade mark?*

(3) *Is there an exception, where, as a result of the way the reseller advertises the goods, their "mental" condition, that is to say the allure, prestigious image and aura of luxury which they have as a result of the manner in which the trade mark owner has chosen to present and advertise the goods using his trade mark, is changed or impaired?*

(4) *Whether Arts 30 and 36 of the EC Treaty preclude the owner of a trade mark or the holder of a copyright, relating to the bottles and packaging which he used for his goods, from using those rights to prevent a retailer from advertising the further commercialisation of those goods in a manner customary to retailers in the relevant sector?*

(5) *If so, is this also the case where the reseller's advertising material damages the luxurious and prestigious image of the trade mark or where the publication or reproduction of the trade mark takes place in circumstances liable to damage the owner of copyright?*

In answer to Question (1), the Court stated:

33 ... it is necessary first of all to consider the relevant provisions of the Directive to which the Hoge Raad refers.

34 On the one hand, Article 5 of the Directive, which determines the rights conferred by trade mark, provides, in paragraph (1), that the proprietor is to be entitled to prevent all third parties from using his trade mark in the course of trade and, in paragraph (3)(d), that he may prohibit all third parties from using the trade mark in advertising.

35 On the other hand, Article 7(1) of the Directive, which concerns the exhaustion of the rights conferred by a trade mark, provides that a trade mark is not to entitle its proprietor to prohibit its use in relation to goods which have been put on the market in the Community under that trade mark by its proprietor or with his consent.

36 If the right to prohibit the use of his trade mark in relation to goods, conferred on the proprietor of a trade mark under Article 5 of the Directive, is exhausted once the goods have been put on the market by himself or with his consent, the same applies as regards the right to use the trade mark for the purpose of bringing to the public's attention the further commercialisation of those goods.

37 It follows from the case law of the court that Article 7 of the Directive is to be interpreted in the light of the rules of the Treaty relating to the free movement of goods, in particular, Article 36 (Joined Cases C–427/93, C–249/93 and C–436/93 *Bristol-Myers Squibb v Paranova* [1996] E.C.R. I-3457, paragraph 27) and that the purpose of the "exhaustion of rights" rule is to prevent owners of trade marks from being allowed to partition national markets and thus facilitate the maintenance of price differences which may exist between Member States (see *Bristol Myers Squibb*, cited above, paragraph 46). Even if the right to make use of a trade mark in order to attract attention to further commercialisation were not exhausted in the same way as the right of resale, the latter would be made considerably more difficult and the purpose of the "exhaustion of rights" rule laid down in Article 7 would thus be undermined.

38 It follows that the answer to be given to the ... question must be that, on a proper

interpretation of Articles 5 and 7 of the Directive, when trade marked goods have been put on the Community market by the proprietor of the trade mark or with his consent, a reseller, besides being free to resell those goods, is also free to make use of the trade mark in order to bring to the public's attention the further commercialisation of those goods.

In answer to Questions (2) and (3), the Court stated:

44   ... where a reseller makes use of a trade mark in order to bring the public's attention to further commercialisation of trade marked goods, a balance must be struck between the legitimate interest of the trade mark owner in being protected against resellers using his trade mark for advertising in a manner which could damage the reputation of the trade mark and the reseller's legitimate interest in being able to resell the goods in question by using advertising methods which are customary in his sector of trade.

45   As regards the instant case, which concerns prestigious, luxury goods, the reseller must not act unfairly in relation to the legitimate interests of the trade mark owner. He must therefore endeavour to prevent his advertising from affecting the value of the trade mark by detracting from the allure and prestigious image of the goods in question and from their aura of luxury.

46   However, the fact that a reseller, who habitually markets articles of the same kind but not necessarily of the same quality, uses for trade marked goods the modes of advertising which are customary in his trade sector, even if they are not the same as those used by the trade mark owner himself or by his approved retailers, does not constitute a legitimate reason, within the meaning of Article 7(2) of the Directive, allowing the owner to oppose that advertising, unless it is established that, given the specific circumstances of the case, the use of the trade mark in the reseller's advertising seriously damages the reputation of the trade mark.

47   For example, such damage could occur if, in an advertising leaflet distributed by him, the reseller did not take care to avoid putting the trade mark in a context which might seriously detract from the image which the trade mark owner has succeeded in creating around his trade mark.

48   In view of the foregoing, ... the proprietor of a trade mark may not rely on Article 7(2) of the Directive to oppose the use of the trade mark, by a reseller who habitually markets articles of the same kind, but not necessarily of the same quality, as the trade-marked goods, in ways customary in the reseller's sector of trade, for the purpose of bringing to the public's attention the further commercialisation of those goods, unless it is established that, given the specific circumstances of the case, the use of the trade mark for this purpose seriously damages the reputation of the trade mark.

In answer to Question (4), the Court stated:

52   The question therefore is whether a prohibition such as that sought in the main proceedings may be allowed under Article 36 of the Treaty, according to which the provisions of Articles 30 to 34 are not to preclude prohibitions or restrictions on imports justified on the grounds of the protection of industrial and commercial property, provided that they do not constitute a means of arbitrary discrimination or a disguised restriction on trade between Member States.

53   As regards the question relating to trade mark rights, it is to be remembered that, according to the case law of the court, Article 36 of the Treaty and Article 7 of the Directive are to be interpreted in the same way (*Bristol Myers Squibb*, cited above, paragraph 40).

54   Consequently, ... on a proper interpretation of Articles 30 and 36 of the Treaty, the proprietor of a trade mark may not oppose the use of the trade mark, by a reseller who habitually markets articles on the same kind, but not necessarily of the same quality,

as the trademarked goods, in ways customary in the reseller's sector of trade, for the purpose of bringing the further commercialisation of those to the public's attention, unless it is established that, given the specific circumstances, the use of the trade mark for this purpose seriously damages the reputation of the trade mark.

In response to Question (5), the Court concluded with the view that a similar principle applied to a copyright owner, holding that the protection conferred by copyright as regards the reproduction of protected works in a reseller's advertising may not, in any event, be broader than that which is conferred on a trade mark owner in the same circumstances.

5.2.7.5 *Bayerische Motorenwerke (BMW) v Deenik* [1999] E.C.R. I-905, ECJ

The motor manufacturer, BMW, holds "BMW" for motor vehicles in the Benelux Trade Mark Registry, as elsewhere. Mr Deenik had considerable experience with BMWs and advertised his business in Dutch as being for "Repairs and Maintenance of BMWs" and, since he also sold secondhand vehicles, "Specialist in BMWs". He was not, however, an authorised BMW agent. The Dutch Supreme Court (Hoge Raad) referred questions to the ECJ, including whether these uses of "BMW" constituted acts within the Trade Marks Directive, Art.5(1)(a) (to which TMA 1994, s.5(1) corresponds); and if so, having regard to Arts 5–7 of the Directive (TMA 1994, ss.10–12), the uses constituted infringement.

The ECJ found that both uses were of the identical mark for goods for which it was registered and within Art.5(1)(a). In regard to the limitations upon in infringement, the Court stated:

44. The court is asked to rule, in particular, on the question whether the trade mark proprietor may prevent such use only where the advertiser creates the impression that his undertaking is affiliated to the trade mark proprietor's distribution network, or whether he may also prevent such use where, because of the manner in which the trade mark is used in the advertisements, there is a good chance that the public might be given the impression that the advertiser is using the trade mark in that regard to an appreciable extent for the purpose of advertising his own business as such, by creating a specific suggestion of quality.

The advertisements for the sale of second-hand BMW cars

47. As regards the advertisements for the sale of second-hand BMW cars put on the market under that trade mark by the trade mark proprietor or with his consent, the case law of the Court should be borne in mind concerning the use of a trade mark to inform the public of the resale of goods covered by a trade mark.

48. In Case C–337/95 *Parfums Christian Dior v Evora* [1997] E.C.R. I-6013, the Court first held, at paragraph 38, that on a proper interpretation of Articles 5 and 7 of the directive, when trade marked goods have been put on the Community market by the proprietor of the trade mark or with his consent, a reseller, besides being free to resell those goods, is also free to make use of the trade mark in order to bring to the public's attention the further commercialisation of those goods.

49. In the same judgment, the Court then found, at paragraph 43, that damage done to the reputation of a trade mark may, in principle, be a legitimate reason, within the meaning of Article 7(2) of the directive, allowing the proprietor to oppose the use of his trade mark for further commercialisation of goods put on the Community market by him or with his consent. As regards prestige goods, the Court stated, at paragraph 45, that the reseller must not act unfairly in relation to the legitimate interests of the trade mark owner, but must endeavour to prevent his advertising from affecting the value of the trade mark by detracting from the prestigious image of the goods in question. At paragraph 48, the Court concluded that the proprietor of a trade mark may not rely on Article 7(2) to opposed the use of the trade mark, in ways customary in the reseller's sector of trade, for the purpose of bringing to the public's attention the further commercialisation of the trade marked goods, unless it is established that such use seriously damages the reputation of the trade mark.

50. In the context of the present case, the consequence of that decision is that it is contrary to Article 7 of the directive for the proprietor of the BMW mark to prohibit the use of its mark by another person for the purpose of informing the public that he has specialised or is a specialist in the sale of second-hand BMW cars, provided that the advertising concerns cars which have been put on the Community market under that mark by the proprietor or with its consent and that the way in which the mark is used in that advertising does not constitute a legitimate reason, within the meaning of Article 7(2), for the proprietor's opposition.

51. The fact that the trade mark is used in a reseller's advertising in such a way that it may give rise to the impression that there is a commercial connection between the reseller and the trade mark proprietor, and in particular that the reseller's business is affiliated to the trade mark proprietor's distribution network or that there is a special relationship between the two undertakings, may constitute a legitimate reason within the meaning of Article 7(2) of the directive.

52. Such advertising is not essential to the further commercialisation of goods put on the Community market under the trade mark by its proprietor or with his consent or, therefore, to the purpose of the exhaustion rule laid down in Article 7 of the directive. Moreover, it is contrary to the obligation to act fairly in relation to the legitimate interests of the trade mark owner and it affects the value of the trade mark by taking unfair advantage of its distinctive character or repute. It is also incompatible with the specific object of a trade mark which is, according to the case law of the Court, to protect the proprietor against competitors wishing to take advantage of the status and reputation of the trade mark (see, *inter alia*, Case C–10/89 *Hag GF* [1990] E.C.R. I-3711, "*Hag II*", paragraph 14).

53. If, on the other hand, there is no risk that the public will be led to believe that there is a commercial connection between the reseller and the trade mark proprietor, the mere fact that the reseller derives an advantage from using the trade mark in that advertisements for sale of goods covered by the mark, which are in other respects honest and fair, lend an aura of quality to his own business does not constitute a legitimate reason within the meaning of Article 7(2) of the directive.

54. In that connection, it is sufficient to state that a reseller who sells second-hand BMW cars and who genuinely has specialised or is a specialist in the sale of those vehicles cannot in practice communicate such information to his customers without using the BMW mark. In consequence, such an informative use of the BMW mark is necessary to guarantee the right of resale under Article 7 of the directive and does not take unfair advantage of the distinctive character or repute of that trade mark.

55. Whether advertising may create the impression that there is a commercial connection

between the reseller and the trade mark proprietor is a question of fact for the national court to decide in the light of the circumstances of each case.

The advertisements relating to repair and maintenance of BMW cars

56. First, the Court finds that the rule concerning exhaustion of the rights conferred by a trade mark laid down in Article 7 of the directive is not applicable to the advertisements relating to repair and maintenance of BMW cars.

57. Article 7 is intended to reconcile the interests of trade mark protection and those of free movement of goods within the Community by making the further commercialisation of a product bearing a trade mark possible and preventing opposition by the proprietor of the mark (see, to that effect, *Parfums Christian Dior*, paragraphs 37 and 38). Advertisements relating to car repair and maintenance do not affect further commercialistion of the goods in question.

58. Nonetheless, so far as those advertisements are concerned, it is still necessary to consider whether use of the trade mark may be legitimate in the light of the rule laid down in Article 6(1)(C) of the directive, that the proprietor may not prohibit a third party from using the trade mark to indicate the intended purpose of a product or service, in particular as accessories or spare parts, provided that the use is necessary to indicate that purpose and is in accordance with honest practices in industrial or commercial matters.

59. In that regard, as the United Kingdom Government has observed, the use of the trade mark to inform the public that the advertiser repairs and maintains trade marked goods must be held to constitute use indicating the intended purposes of the service within the meaning of Article 6(1)(c). Like the use of a trade mark intended to identify the vehicles which a non-original spare part will fit, the use in question is intended to identify the goods in respect of which the service is provided.

60. Furthermore, the use concerned must be held to be necessary to indicate the intended purpose of the service. It is sufficient to note, as the Advocate General did at point 54 of his Opinion, that if an independent trader carries out the maintenance and repair of BMW cars or is in fact a specialist in that field, that fact cannot in practice be communicated to his customers without using the BMW mark.

61. Lastly, the condition requiring use of the trade mark to be made in accordance with honest practices in industrial or commercial matters must be regarded as constituting in substance the expression of a duty to act fairly in relation to the legitimate interests of the trade mark owner, similar to that imposed on the reseller where he uses another's trade mark to advertise the resale of products covered by that mark.

62. Just like Article 7, Article 6 seeks to reconcile the fundamental interests of trade mark protection with those of free movement of goods and freedom to provide services in the common market in such a way that trade mark rights are able to fulfil their essential role in the system of undistorted competition which the Treaty seeks to establish and maintain (see, in particular, *Hag II*, paragraph 13).

63. Consequently, for the reasons set out in paragraphs 51 to 54 of this judgment, which apply *mutatis mutandis*, the use of another's trade mark for the purpose of:

> "informing the public of the repair and maintenance of goods covered by that mark is authorised on the same conditions as those applying where the mark is used for the purpose of informing the public of the resale of goods covered by that mark."

5.2.7.6   *Marks and Spencer v One in a Million* [1998] F.S.R. 265, Sumption Q.C.

This case on domain name pre-emption has already been considered in respect of the CA's finding of passing off (see above, 5.1.3.5). At first instance, liability was placed primarily on the ground of infringement of the Trade Marks Act 1994, s.10(3). The CA agreed with this approach.

Sumption Q.C.:

What then are the issues which the defendants say should go to trial under this head? There appear to be two: (i) they deny that their use of it has been "in the course of trade"; and (ii) they contend that it is an implicit requirement of section 10(3) that there should have been a likelihood of confusion on the part of the public, and there has been none.

The first of these points can be shortly dealt with. Use "in the course of trade" means use by way of business. It does not mean use as a trade mark: *British Sugar Plc v James Robertson & Sons Ltd* [1996] R.P.C. 281 at 290–292. The use of a trade mark in the course of the business of a professional dealer for the purpose of making domain names more valuable and extracting money from the trade mark owner is a use in the course of trade.

Turning to the second point, there is at the moment some uncertainty about whether it is the law that an infringing sign must for the purposes of section 10(3) be such as is likely to cause confusion. Some questions of law can appropriately be decided on an application for summary judgment. This one is, however, rather different. It is on the face of it strange that the likelihood of confusion should be required (as it expressly is) where the infringement consists in the use of an identical sign with similar goods or services, or a similar sign with identical or similar goods or services, but not where it consists of its use with goods which are not even similar. For substantially this reason, it has been decided on at least two occasions in England that section 10(3) does require proof that the use was such as was likely to cause confusion: see *BASF Plc v CEP (UK) Plc* ([1996] E.T.M.R. 51) and *Baywatch Production Co Inc v Home Video Channel* [1997] F.S.R. 22. On the other hand, in a passing dictum in Case C–251/95 *Sabel BV v Puma AG* [above, 5.2.4.2], the European Court of Justice has remarked that under the provision of the directive which permits Member States to include a provision such as section 10(3), no likelihood of confusion is required. This seems to me to be less than conclusive of an issue which raises important questions of principle, requires more fuller argment than can be appropriate on an application for summary judgment, and may ultimately require a reference to the European Court. I do not propose to resolve the question now. Nor do I need to, because even on the footintg that the plaintiffs must demonstrate a likelihood of confusion, they have done so. The test in this context depends not on the way the sign has been used but on whether a comparison between the sign and the trade mark shows an inherent propensity to confuse. There can, as it seems to me, be no doubt that this is the effect of the use by someone else of the domain name *marksandspencer*. The only basis on which the contrary has been suggested is that internet users must be assumed to access sites by using search methods which will disclose their true owners. I am conscious of the heavy burden which lies on a plaintiff seeking summary judgment when a question of fact is raised, but I regard this point as unarguable. Some people might access a site in that way. Plainly many would not. If the defendants' submission had anything in it, they would not have thought it worth their while to register these names and attempt to sell them at a premium.

In the four other cases, the facts relevant to both causes of action are substantially the same in all relevant respects save one. The difference is that in the other four cases it is somewhat less absurd for the defendants to suggest the names which they have registered have an innocent use. It is impossible to imagine any unconnected party using the phrase "Marks and Spencer" in his name or address if not to deceive, and the same may well be true of Cellnet. But the possibility is not so far-fetched in the case of the words "Sainsbury", "Ladbroke", "Virgin" or "BT". The defendants also say that in some cases the suffix (for example, *.org* in the case of BT), serves to differentiate them from the trade marks. The defendants make much of this point, but I am not impressed by it for the simple reason that although the words are probably capable of an innocent use, that is not the use that these defendants intend. The history of the defendants' activities shows a deliberate practice followed over a substantial period of time of registering domain names which are chosen to resemble the names and marks of other people and are plainly intended to deceive. The threat of passing off and trade mark infringement, and the likelihood of confusion arising from the infringement of the mark are made out beyond argument in this case, even in which it is possible to imagine other cases in which the issue would be more nicely balanced.

5.2.7.7   *Barclays Bank v RBS Advanta* **[1996] R.P.C. 307, Laddie J.**

The plaintiff bank has "Barclaycard" registered for credit services and "Barclay" for financial services. Its Barclaycard service provides a "Visa" card, as do various other services.

The defendant, a joint venture between the Royal Bank of Scotland and Advanta, a US corporation, was launching a "RBS Advanta Visa Card" with a pilot campaign. The literature for this included a leaflet which listed "15 ways the RBS Advanta Visa card is a better credit card all round" and a brochure with a table comparing the new card with eight other card services, including "Barclaycard". The comparison was of annual fee, APR on purchases and on advances, and the monthly rate per cent.

In proceedings for an interlocutory injunction, the use of the plaintiff's marks was attacked under the Trade Marks Act 1994, s.10(6). After noting the strict terms of s.10(1), Laddie J. continued:

Under the Trade Marks Act 1938 it was held that comparative advertising in which one trader made express reference to the registered trade mark of a competitor constituted an infringement (see *Bismag v Amblins (Chemists) Ltd* (1940) 57 R.P.C. 209, CA). This was thought to be undesirable. As Lord Strathclyde, the responsible government minister, stated during the passage of the Trade Marks Bill through the House of Lords in 1994:

> "The government have been persuaded that there is no harm in comparative advertising ... provided that it makes fair use of a registered mark for the purpose of informing the public. As foreshadowed in the White Paper, the Bill seeks to chart a middle course; allowing comparative advertising but providing safeguards for the owner of a registered trade mark". (*Hansard*, H.L. Public Bill Committee, col. 42, January 18, 1994)

The provision which seeks to provide this middle course is section 10(6) of the 1994 Act:

> "Nothing in the preceding provisions of this section shall be construed as preventing the use of a registered tade mark by any person for the purpose of identifying the goods or services as those of the proprietor or a licensee.

> But any such use otherwise than in accordance with honest practices in industrial or commercial matters shall be treated as infringing the registered mark if the use without

due cause takes unfair advantage of, or is detrimental to, the distinctive character or repute of the trade mark."

Both Mr Young Q.C. who appeared before me on behalf of the plaintiff and Mr Silverleaf who appeared for the defendant were united in criticising the draughting of this provision. It is a mess. The first half of the subsection allows comparative advertising. Its meaning is clear. However, the second half, beginning with the words "But any such use ..." is a qualifying proviso and its meaning is far from clear.

The origin of the wording in section 10(6)

Section 10(6) is not derived directly either from the EEC Trade Mark Directive 89/104 ("the directive") or from the Paris Convention, neither of which expressly exempts comparative advertising from infringement. The result is that the first half of section 10(6) is home-grown. However the first half of the proviso can be traced back to Article $10^{bis}(2)$ of the Paris Convention, dealing with unfair competition and from there to Article 6(1) of the directive. The latter has been adopted, with minor and, for present purposes, irrelevant changes in wording as section 11(2) of the Act which is as follows:

"A registered trade mark is not infringed by:

    (a) the use by a person of his own name or address;

    (b) the use of indications concerning the kind, quality, quantity, intended purpose, value, geographical origin, the time of production of goods or rendering of services, or other characteristics of goods or services; or

    (c) the use of the trade mark where it is necessary to indicate the intended purpose of a product or service (in particular, as accessories or spare parts);

provided the use is *in accordance with honest practices in industrial or commercial matters*." (emphasis added).

The same language is also to be found in Article 15(2) of the directive and, from there, in Schedule 1(2) of the Act in relation to collective marks.

The language used in the second part of the proviso is to be found in Articles 4(3), 4(4) and 5(2) of the directive and in section 10(3) of the Act which provides:

"A person infringes a registered trade mark if he uses in the course of trade a sign which:

    (a) is identical with or similar to the trade mark; and

    (b) is used in relation to goods or services which are not similar to those for which the trade mark is registered;

where the trade mark has a reputation in the United Kingdom and the use of the sign, *being without due cause, takes unfair advantage of, or is detrimental to, the distinctive character or repute of the trade mark.*" (emphasis added).

Mr Young [for the plaintiff] suggested that the two halves of the proviso to section 10(6) for most purposes meant the same thing. Thus, a use of a competitor's trade mark in comparative advertising without due cause so as to take unfair advantage of the character or repute of that mark would not be in accordance with honest practices. In other words the proviso is tautologous. There is much force in this submission. However, this would produce a very strange result. It would mean that the proviso to section 10(6) would mean the same as the provisos to sections 10(3) and 11(2) even though the language used in each is different.

Mr Silverleaf [for the defendant] on the other hand adopted a more orthodox approach to construction. He said that before use of a registered trade mark in comparative advertising could be held to infringe it needed to be proved by the plaintiff (a) that the use was otherwise than in accordance with honest practices in industrial or commercial matters and (b) was made without due cause so as to take unfair advantage of or to be detrimental to the distinctive character or repute of the trade mark. He accepted that any such use which took unfair advantage of the registered mark would almost inevitably be not honest. On the other hand he said that it was possible to envisage a use which was not in accordance with honest practices, but which did not take unfair advantage of or was not detrimental to the registered mark and therefore was not rendered an infringement by operation of the proviso. The example he put forward was where the comparative advertising was untruthfully flattering about the qualities of both the competitor's and the registered proprietor's goods. He said that such advertising was not honest, but would not constitute an infringement because it was neither harmful nor unfair to the registered mark. I am not convinced that this is right. What the proviso requires is that "such use", *i.e.* use of the registered mark, is not in accordance with honest practices. In my view unjustified flattery neither takes unfair advantage of the registered mark nor is it outside honest practices. Furthermore, it is difficult to believe that the draughtsman drafted the proviso in this way to exclude this type of behaviour from the ambit of infringement. After all, it is most unlikely that any trade mark proprietor would allege infringement by a competitor who overflatters the proprietor's goods or services.

It is difficult to formulate any construction of the proviso to section 10(6) which affords every word in it a distinct function and which also is consistent with sections 10(3) and 11(2). In my view it is necessary to face up to the difficulties of draughting and to consider section 10(6) alone without deciding whether precisely the same construction of the wording used is appropriate for the other subsections.

Construction of section 10(6)

As a general proposition, it seems to me that Mr Silverleaf is right when he says that the primary objective of section 10(6) is to allow comparative advertising. As long as the use of the competitor's mark is "honest", then there is nothing wrong with telling the public of the relative merits of competing goods or services and using registered trade marks to identify them. The proviso should not be construed in a way which effectively prohibits all comparative advertising.

First, Mr Silverleaf argued that if it is to be brought into operation, the onus is on the registered propreitor to show that the factors indicated in the proviso exist. I did not understand Mr Young to dispute this and, in my view, Mr Silverleaf is right.

Secondly, there will be no infringement unless the use of the registered mark is not in accordance with honest practices. Both counsel agreed, rightly in my view, that this test is objective. This part of the proviso simply means that if the use is considered honest by members of a reasonable audience, it will not infringe. The fact that the advertising pokes fun at the proprietor's goods or services and emphasises the benefits of the defendant's is a normal incidence of comparative advertising. Its aim will be to divert customers from the proprietor. No reasonable observer would expect one trader to point to all the advantages of its competitor's business and failure to do so does not *per se* take the advertising outside what reasonable people would regard as "honest". Thus mere trade puffery, even if uncomfortable to the registered proprietor, does not bring the advertising within the scope of trade mark infringement. Much advertising copy is recognised by the public as hyperbole. The Act does not impose on the courts an obligation to try to enforce, through the back door of trade mark legislation, a more puritanical standard. If, on the other hand, a reasonable reader is likely to say, on being given the full facts, that the advertisement is not honest, for example because it is significantly misleading, then the protection from trade mark infringement is removed.

Mr Young suggestsed, at least in relation to section 11(2)(b), that if the registered mark is used in a trade mark sense in the comparative advertising it cannot be honest. I do not agree. Whether the mark is being used in that way has nothing to do with whether that use is honest. In any event the first half of section 10(6) exempts from infringement use of registered trade marks for the purpose of identifying goods or services as those of the proprietor or a licensee. Such use will almost invariably be use in a trade mark sense. If Mr Young's submission as to the scope of the proviso in section 11(2)(b) is correct, and applicable to the section 10(6) defence, then that defence would cease to exist, since the immunity given by the first half of the subsection would be removed by the equal, but opposite effect of the proviso. This cannot be right.

Thirdly, to come within the proviso the use must be otherwise than in accordance with honest practices in "industrial and commercial matters". It was suggested during the motion that this means that the court should look to statutory or industry-agreed codes of conduct to determine whether the advertisement is honest. That approach resulted, in this case, in much of the evidence on this motion being directed to the issue of whether the defendant's advertising met the specific requirements of the 1974 Act and the 1989 Reg-ulations. If this approach to the proviso is correct, it would follow that in some trades where there are very detailed and restrictive codes of practice in relation to advertising, it would be easier to breach the code and, therefore, harder to avoid infringement of regis-tered trade mark. I do not believe that this is the correct way to assess honesty for the purposes of section 10(6).

No doubt the nature of the products or services will affect the degree of hyperbole acceptable. What is tolerable in advertisements for second-hand cars may well not be thought honest if used to encourage the use of powerful medicines. The nature of the goods or services may, therefore, affect the reasonable perception of what advertising is honest. But it is quite another thing to say that statutory or industry imposed codes of advertising conduct define honesty for the purposes of section 10(6) of the 1994 Act. Although most such codes are concerned to ensure probity, they frequently cover other matters as well. Breach of such a code, therefore, does not necessarily mean that the advertisement is other than honest. It follows that the provisons of the 1974 Act and 1989 Regulations [both on consumer credit] are of little direct relevance to the isssue of trade mark infringement. Honesty has to be gauged against what is reasonably to be expected by the relevant public of advertisements for the goods or services in issue.

Fourthly, it seems to me that the final words of the proviso:

> "if the use without due cause takes unfair advantage of, or is detrimental to, the distinctive character or repute of the trade mark",

in most cases adds nothing of significance to the first part of the proviso. An advertisement which makes use of a registered mark in a way which is not honest will almost always take unfair advantage of it and vice versa. At the most these final words emphasise that the use of the mark must take advantage of it or be detrimental to it. In other words the use must either give some advantage to the defendant or inflict some harm on the character or repute of the registered mark which is above the level of *de minimis*.

Applying this construction to the facts, Laddie J. refused interlocutory relief. He found both that the plaintiff's case was, on the affidavit evidence, very weak and that this and a number of other factors put the balance of convenience against intervention. The plaintiff alleged dishonesty (i) in failing to point out that its own service had ancillary advantages not being offered by the defendant; and (ii) in suggesting that the 15 ways were each unique to its new card. Of these allegations the judge concluded:

... the advertisement does not say, and I think it unlikely that a reasonable reader would take it to mean, that there are no features of the plaintiff's service which are better than the defendant's. The advertisement merely picks out the features taken together which are being promoted as making the defendant's product a good package.

5.2.7.8   *British Airways v Ryanair* [2001] F.S.R. 307, Jacob J.

The claimant airline, BA, sued the defendant airline for trade mark infringement and malicious falsehood in respect of two comparative advertisements placed in various newspapers in 1999. Both advertisements included detailed price comparisons, one carried the headline "EXPENSIVE BA....DS!" and the other the headline "EXPENSIVE BA". BA had a registered trade mark consisting of the letters BA for air travel and related services.

Ryanair accepted that in both advertisements it used the exact registered trade mark, but argued that there nevertheless was no infringement. Its advertisements relied on the public knowing that BA denoted the plaintiff. Ryanair claimed that the defences provided by s.10(6) and s.11(2)(b) should apply. BA argued that neither of these sections protected the use of a trade mark as a trade mark by a third party, but only the right to use the marks descriptively; thus honest comparative advertising using a rival's trade mark was not protected. The court rejected this argument.

Jacob J:

19... Mr. Hobbs' submission is startling in its effect. If right, it would mean that no-one in trade is permitted to describe their goods or services perfectly honestly by reference to another's trade mark. In ordinary life consumers regularly do this. Some may say "Bisto" is as tasty as "Oxo", others may say "Bisto" tastes stronger than "Oxo". In neither case is either trade mark being misused. One is being used as a comparator for the other—to describe the other. Likewise traders are apt to describe each other's prices, using their respective trade marks to do so. In all these cases the trade mark is being used as an indication of the characteristics of goods....

BA's argument that the defence of use as a description does not include use of a description by way of use of a trade mark to describe goods was roundly rejected by Jacob J.

BA also unsuccessfully argued that s.10(6) was now to be read in light of the Comparative Advertising Directive (97/55):

24. I turn to Mr. Hobbs' next submission, namely that our s.10(6) should now be construed in light of the Comparative Advertising Directive. He says that s.10(6) should be treated as providing a defence only if there is compliance with the conditions for comparative advertising laid down in the Directive. They read as follows:

"(a) it is not misleading according to Articles 2(2), 3 and 7(1);
(b) it compares goods or services meeting the same needs or intended for the same purpose;
(c) it objectively compares one or more material, relevant, verifiable and representative features of those goods and services, which may include price;
(d) it does not create confusion in the market place between the advertiser and a competitor or between the advertiser's trade marks, trade names, other distinguishing marks, goods or services and those of a competitor;
(e) it does not discredit or denigrate the trade marks, trade names, other distinguishing marks, goods, services, activities, or circumstances of a competitor;
(f) for products with designation of origin, it relates in each case to products with the same designation;
(g) it does not take unfair advantage of the reputation of a trade mark, trade name or other distinguishing marks of a competitor or of the designation of origin of competing products;
(h) it does not present goods or services as imitations or replicas of goods or services bearing a protected trade mark or trade name."

25. Compliance with most of these conditions will obviously be necessary to comply with s.10(6). But there is one significant extra—"denigration". You can be offensive about another's trade mark or name without being dishonest. The Bastards headline does just that. I think Mr Hobbs' elaborate submission about s.10(6) is designed principally to catch that use. Mr Meade (for Ryanair) accurately summarised Mr Hobbs' arguments as follows:

(a) The 1994 was passed to give effect to the trade Marks Directive;

(b) Section 10(6) is, however a "home-grown" add on;

(c) The Community has also legislated about misleading and comparative advertising;

(d) The Comparative Advertising Directive was not promulgated until after the passage of the 1994 Act and was not implemented in the UK until after the acts complained of;

(e) The Comparative Advertising Directive amended the earlier Misleading Advertising Directive, which had force in the UK through the Control of Misleading Advertisement Regulations 1998 (SI 1988/915) made pursuant to s.22(2) of the European Communities Act 1972 to implement Directive 84/450/EEC;

(f) By virtue of the *Marleasing* principle, the 1994 Act must be interpreted in accordance with the Misleading Advertising and Comparative Advertising Directives even though it came before them.

26. This elaborate and ingenious argument breaks down at a number of points. Firstly, I have already indicated that in my view the Comparative Advertising Directive was not intended to amend the Trade Mark Directive. It would follow it is not intended to amend of affect the interpretation of any national law passed to implement the Trade Mark Directive. It is especially difficult to see how it could affect the interpretation of a national law which did not have its own home-grown equivalent of s.10(6). What provisions of the Trade Mark Directive as implemented in national law could be "amended" (*i.e.* interpreted by the *Marleasing* principle) by the Comparative Advertising Directive?

27. Next, the Comparative Advertising Directive says that it may be implemented in a manner chosen by each of the Member States. Recital 11 reads:

"Whereas the conditions of comparative advertising should be cumulative and respected in their entirety; whereas, in accordance with the Treaty, the choice of forms and methods for the implementation of these conditions shall be left to the Member States, insofar as those forms and methods are not already determined by this Directive."

Leaving the method of implementation to the Member States is a far cry from requiring Member States to amend their trade mark laws to permit comparative advertising only in accordance with the Directive. It is an even further cry from requiring Member States to confer or extend private rights such as those given by registration of a trade mark. Actually, in the UK implementation has been achieved by the Control of Misleading Advertisements (Amendment) Regulations 2000 (SI 2000/914). These amend the 1988 Regulations. The amended regulations provide a machinery of complaint in respect of comparative advertising which does not comply with the Regulations. You go to the Director of Fair Trading who can, if necessary, apply to the court to prevent breaches of the code. No private rights are conferred or extended.

28. It should be remembered that the control of misleading advertising is a much wider subject that trade mark infringement, or indeed comparative advertising. Generally such controls do not require the creation of private rights. That is indeed explicit in the case of the 1988 Regulation as amended in relation to comparative advertising. Regulation 4(a)(3) reads:

"The provisions of this regulation shall not be construed as:

(a) conferring a right of action on any civil proceedings in respect of any contravention of this regulation (save as provided for in these Regulations); or
(b) derogating from any right of action or other remedy (whether civil or criminal) in proceedings instituted otherwise than by virtue of these Regulations."

29. There is also the formidable difficulty in the way of Mr Hobbs to the effect the Art.3 of the 1997 Directive required Member States to bring into force the laws, regulations and administrative provisions necessary to comply with it at the latest thirty months after its publication in the OJC. So implementation was not required until after the time of publication of the advertisements in this case. Mr Hobbs seeks to get over that by submitting that the *Marleasing* Principle (Case 106/89 [1990] E.C.R. I-4135) requires one to construe a national law in accordance with a subsequent Directive from the moment of its publication, even though the Directive itself requires implementation later. No authority supports that. Mr Hobbs relied upon the judgment of the court in *Inter-Environmental Wallonie v Region Wallone* (Case C–129/96 [1997] E.C.R. I-7411). But all that case says is that during the period before compliance with a Directive is required, a Member State must refrain from taking any measures liable to compromise the result prescribed. In plain language if you have to do a thing by a certain time you must not put it out of your power to do just that. That is miles from this case.

30. In the result I do not think there is anything in Mr Hobbs' reliance upon the Comparative Advertising Directive. The interpretation of s.10(6) is unqualified by it. In *Cable and Wireless,* I, borrowing from and adding to Mr Crystal Q.C. in *British Telecommunications plc v AT & T Communications (UK) Ltd,* summarised the position:

"(1) The primary objective of section 10(6) of the 1996 Act is to permit comparative advertising (see *Advanta* at 312–313 and 315, and *Vodafone* at 4–5 of the transcript of the judgment);

(2) As long as the use of a competitor's mark is honest, there is nothing wrong in telling the public of the relative merits of competing goods or services and using registered trade marks to identify them (see *Advanta* at 315, *Vodafone* at 4);

(3) The onus is on the registered proprietor to show that the factors indicated in the proviso to section 10(6) exist (see *Advanta* at 315, *Vodafone* at 4);

(4) There will be no trade mark infringement unless the use of the registered mark is not in accordance with honest practices (see *Advanta* at 315);

(5) The test is objective: would a reasonable reader be likely to say, upon being given the full facts, that the advertisement is not honest? (see *Advanta* at 315, *Vodafone* at 4);

(6) Statutory or industry agreed codes of conduct are not a helpful guide as whether an advertisement is honest for the purposes of section 10(6). Honesty has to be gauged against what is reasonably to be expected by the relevant public of advertisements for the goods of services in issue. (see *Advanta* at 316);

(7) It should be borne in mind that the general public are used to the ways of advertisers and expect hyperbole (see *Advanta at* 315 *cf. Vodafone* at 3–4);

(8) The 1994 Act does not impose on the courts an obligation to try and enforce through the back door of trade mark legislation a more puritanical standard than the general public would expect from advertising copy (see *Advanta* at 315, *Vodafone* at 4);

(9) An advertisement which is significantly misleading is not honest for the purposes of section 10(6) (see *Advanta* at 316, *Vodafone* at 4–5). I venture with diffidence to make a number of additional observations.

(10) The advertisement must be considered as a whole (*cf. Advanta* at 316–318);

(11) As a purpose of the 1994 Act is positively to permit comparative advertising, the court should not hold words used in the advertisement to be seriously misleading for interlocutory purposes unless on a fair reading of them in their context and against the background of the advertisement as a whole they can really be said to justify that description;

(12) A minute textual examination is not something upon which the reasonable reader of an advertisement would embark;

(13) The court should therefore not encourage a microscopic approach to the construction of a comparative advertisement on a motion for interlocutory relief."

Those are the principles I intend to apply here.

The court then discussed the appropriate test to be applied in assessing whether a particular description, trade mark or promotional statement is misleading. Counsel for BA argued for a uniform test using the "presumed expectations of an average consumer who is reasonably well-informed and reasonably observant and circumspect", derived from the Estee Lauder Cosmetics *case (case C–220/98 [2000] I.P.&T. 380). Jacob J. did not see this as a departure from the traditional approach of the UK courts in passing off and trade mark infringement cases. His Lordship was critical of what he viewed as too low a standard for confusion in German unfair competition law, as it protects "even the stupid or careless", and instead he advocated an "average consumer" test which accepted that consumers now tend to be somewhat cynical and media-savvy:*

32. It is of course the case that the average consumer has been exposed from birth to

advertising. People get case hardened by it. They expect hyperbole and puff. One can say no advertisement is complete without them....

Jacob J. applied the same average consumer test to the malicious falsehood claim. He outlined the three necessary elements of a successful claim.

  (i) the words complained of were false;

  (ii) they were published maliciously;

  (iii) they were calculated to cause the claimant (BA, in this case) pecuniary damage.

According to the court, BA fell at the first hurdle as it had not shown the information in the advertisements to be false. Jacob J. accepted that there were some ambiguities in the information provided, but that the average consumer would know that the comparisons drawn were the most favourable Ryanair could reasonably make, as this is what advertisers tend to do. The malicious falsehood claim therefore failed.

5.2.7.9   *DaimlerChrysler AG v Javid Alavi (t/a Merc)* **[2001] R.P.C. 813, Pamfrey J**

The claimant was the proprieter of six UK registered trade marks, registered between 1903 and 1985, including MERCEDES and MERCEDES-BENZ for vehicles and clothing, and of Community trade marks MERCEDES-BENZ for all goods and MERC for vehicles The defendant traded in clothes and shoes, some of which were marked MERC, and some of which were sold in his London store named MERC; he had been trading since 1967.

The claimant failed to establish passing off. Nor did it succeed in respect of trade mark infringement of the UK clothing marks, under the Trade Marks Act 1994, s.10(2)(b). As to alleged infringement of the UK vehicle marks under s.10(3), derived from the Trade Marks Directive, Art.5(2), Pumfrey J. considered General Motors Corp v Yplon SA; [1999] ECR I-5421 (the Chevy case):

Pumfrey J:

86... As Jacobs A.G. pointed out in *Chevy*, Article 4(4)(a) (and hence also Article 5(2)) does not require confusion because it is providing a different test of infringement, available only in respect of marks which have a reputation. In *Chevy*, the Court of Justice avoided interpreting the whole provision, [but] it was considered in some detail by Jacobs A.G. He identifies the three key features of Article 5(2) as: (1) protection is provided only for marks with a reputation; (2) protection is provided only in respect of goods and services which are not similar to those in respect of which the mark is registered; and (3) the type of harm to the trade mark is specified. This area of law is bedevilled by the nuances of different national approaches to trade marks and the associated difficulties in translation, but Jacobs A.G. emphasises that the provision is not to be used to give marks "an unduly extensive protection", emphasising that there is no question of a risk of unfair advantage or detriment. But, for this to happen, there must be some sort of connection formed (I avoid the word association) between the sign used by the defendant and the mark and its associated reputation.

Having examined Neuberger J's approach to s.10(3) in the TYPHOON *case (*Premier Brands v Typhoon Europe *[2000] F.S.R. 767), Pumfrey J. concluded:*

88. In my view, the best approach is just to follow the section, remembering Jacobs A.G.'s warning that it is concerned with actual effects, not risks or likelihoods. The inquiry is as follows. (1) Does the proprieter's mark have a reputation? If so, (2) is the defendant's sign sufficiently similar to it that the public are either deceived into the belief that the goods are associated with the proprieter so that the use of the sign takes unfair advantage of the mark, or alternatively causes detriment in their minds to either (a) the repute or (b) the distinctive character of the mark, or (3) even if they are not confused, does the use of the sign nevertheless have this effect, and (4) is the use complained of nonetheless with due cause. Detriment can take the form either of making the mark less attractive (tarnishing, to use Neuberger J.'s word) or less distinctive (blurring).

Pumfrey J. found that the marks were not similar, and moreover, even if they were similar, there was no infringement. He accepted that the word MERC on its own, divorced from any commercial context, might be recognised by some people simply as an abbreviation of the DaimlerChrysler marks with which they are familiar. However, he found there to be no evidence whatsoever of any advantage derived from this recognition by the defendants' use of the sign MERC on their clothing; any advantage he viewed as so minor as to be negligible:

89. ... If the public say, "That is the word which means Mercedes to me, but it is not a Mercedes product", and they do not perceive it as possessing high quality, or as making such a claim, then there is no case for infringement.

The main attack made by the claimant, however, had been on the basis of detriment to the marks. It was argued that the defendant's business was heavily concerned with Mods and Skinheads, who were not people with whom the claimant wished to see the MERC mark being used, and the defendant's website contained links to distasteful Skinhead sites which would adversely affect the marks' image. Pumfrey J. rejected this argument:

91. So far as detriment to the repute of the DaimlerChrysler marks is concerned, there was no evidence that any member of the public would associate the use of the mark MERC on the website with DaimlerChrysler's marks. The kind of detriment with which one is concerned here is perhaps the detriment one can identify in painting the well-known eau de Cologne mark "4711") on the side of a liquid manure tanker (see Kur, "*Well-Known Marks, Highly Renowned Marks and Marks Having a (High) Reputation—What's it all about?*" (1992) 23 I.I.C. 218 at 227, n.26 and also referred to Mostert, *Famous and Well-Known Marks* at p.59, n.29. Here, to those of sensitive disposition the juxtaposition of the mark and the tanker can be said to be detrimental to the repute of the mark. The decision of the Benelux Court of Justice in *Lucas Bols v Colgate-Palmolive* (1976) 7 I.I.C. 420 (CLAERYN/ KLAREIN) for Bols' all purpose cleaner is a well-known further example. There are a number of condom cases: apart from VISA itself, Mr Hobbs Q.C. refers to one in the Bundesgerichtshof (1995) 26 I.I.C. 282 (1995), case number I ZR 79/92, which was concerned with little folding boxes, like matchbooks, made to look like a Mars bar and bearing the registered trade mark MARS, which held a condom. These were joke products. Here the lower court had considered that an appreciable number of the public would consider that the little boxes were advertisements for Mars products, that they would consider them in poor taste or at least an overdone advertising gimmick. This is a finding of

infringement of the advertising right in German trade mark law. But the court went on to consider an allegation of unfair competition, and in so doing discussed the concept of detriment to trade mark, albeit in terms which seem to assume confusion as to the source of the goods in question:

> "If marks, whose reputation was established by the plaintiff only in connection with confectionery, in particular a candy-bar, and which marks have great advertising value for these goods are used—as on the part of the defendant—for labelling of contraceptive wrappers, then this circumstance alone suffices to impair the advertising power in regard to the original goods and, moreover, to ruin their positive image at least as far as part of the public is concerned ... for, by their very purpose, contraceptives evoke certain associations (sexual relations, AIDS prevention, etc.) which significant portions of the addressed public would certainly rather do without when it comes to buying candy, and with which reputable candy manufacturers, in particular, rightly do not wish to be identified because, as a rule, contraceptives do not appear to promote the sale or image of their products. Impairment of the marks' owner [*sc.* in using the mark as it seems fit], and the disparagement of its good name, cannot be ruled out on the basis that the gag item lacks any reference to the marks' owner, so there is no way it could be associated with the latter. For, in the case at issue, the plaintiffs' marks, nearly identical in word and appearance are used directly on the defendant's product in the manner of a trademark, *i.e.* as an identifier. As the court of appeals rightfully established, they consequently also fulfil the mark's function as an indicator of product origin, *i.e.* they point to the plaintiff unless and until the consumer notices the inconspicuous, second reference to the origin of the defendant's company on the back of the package. Accordingly, association with the product 'contraceptives as promotional gifts' with the plaintiffs company appears quite conceivable in this case..."

This passage is not particularly helpful on what is meant by disparagement when there is no confusion, if it is not something along the lines of the *4711* case, or just use of the mark in a non-confusing way in association with what is considered to be a product not consonant with the general reputation of the mark, such as in *VISA* itself. It should be noted that the word "repute" as used in the subsection is apt to include a reference to the proprieter of the mark and his products.

92. The words "detriment to the distinctive character" also give difficulty. Mr Hobbs Q.C. and Neuberger J. discuss them. I find the concept to which they refer somewhat fugitive. The presence of two similar marks where there was only one before seems to me to be detrimental to the distinctive character of the first. I am satisfied that this is not what the words are talking about. Mr Hobbs Q.C. deals with the matter as arising out of deception and confusion, which is logical. But Jacobs A.G. says that Article 5(2) covers cases where there is no deception: what are they? I think, with respect, that the interpretation placed on these words inferentially by Neuberger J. when he refers to blurring and quotes the following passage from Mostert, *Famous and Well-Known Marks* (1997) at 58–59 is no more satisfactory:

> "Obviously, the more a trademark is used on a wide variety of goods becoming saturated in the process, the less a particular mark will call to mind and focus the public's attention on the plaintiffs particular product. If, for example, the TIFFANY mark has become well-known in connection with jewellery, and it used on a multiplicity of other goods such as chocolates, clothing, a motion picture house, and a restaurant, the likelihood that the TIFFANY mark will still exclusively call to mind the owner's jewellery products becomes increasingly diminished."

93. Read literally, this is simply a suggestion that once a mark acquires a reputation one can throw the specification of goods away. Any use of another mark will potentially have

this effect if any member of the relevant public becomes aware of the second mark. Here, the point was not pressed, emphasis being placed on the element of detriment to the repute of the mark, and I prefer to come to no conclusion on it. It raises difficult conceptual problems.

94. In my judgment, no objection to the defendant's use of the sign MERC can be made out on this ground. I consider that in order to succeed under Article 5(2) and section 10(3) it must be shown that there is established in the mind of the relevant public a connection between the mark with which they are familiar and the disparaging use. Thus, it is not sufficient to see the word MERC, note that this is the word which one uses to refer to Mercedes cars, see the disagreeable website and register it as disagreeable, if nothing actually rubs off on the sign MERC itself or on MERCEDES, or on DaimlerChrysler. I was not satisfied that this was the case here, and so this allegation of infringement fails.

6   EEC LAW AND INTELLECTUAL PROPERTY

6.1   Treaty and Convention Provisions

6.1.1   Treaty Establishing the European Community ("EC Treaty")

The numbering of the Articles is that introduced by the Amsterdam version of the Treaty. Earlier numbering is indicated by (ex-nn)

6.1.1.1   EC Treaty, Arts 2, 3, 12 (*ex-2, 3, 6*): Basic Principles

Art. 2

The Community shall have as its task, by establishing a common market and an economic and monetary union and by implementing the common policies of activities referred to in Articles 3 and 3a, to promote throughout the Community a harmonious and balanced development of economic activities, sustainable and non-inflationary growth respecting the environment, a high degree of convergence of economic performance, a high level of employment and of social protection, the raising of the standard of living and quality of life, and economic and social cohesion and solidarity among Member States.

Art. 3

For the purposes set out in Article 2, the activities of the Community shall include, as provided in this Treaty and in accordance with the timetable set out therein:

(a) the elimination, as between Member States, of customs duties and quantitative restrictions on the import and export of goods, and of all other measures having equivalent effect;

(b) a common commercial policy;

(c) an internal market characterised by the abolition, as between Member States, of obstacles to the free movement of goods, persons, services and capital;

(d) measures concerning the entry and movement of persons in the internal market as provided for in Article 100c;

(e) a common policy in the sphere of agriculture and fisheries;

(f) a common policy in the sphere of transport;

(g) a system ensuring that competition in the internal market is not distorted;

(h) the approximation of the laws of Member States to the extent required for the functioning of the common market.

(i) a policy in the social sphere comprising a European Social Fund;

   (j) *the strengthening of economic and social cohesion;*

   (k) *a policy in the sphere of the environment;*

   (l) *the strengthening of the competitiveness of Community industry;*

  (m) *the promotion of research and technological development;*

  (n) *encouragement for the establishment and development of trans-European networks;*

  (o) *a contribution to the attainment of a high level of health protection;*

  (p) *a contribution to education and training of quality and to the flowering of the cultures of the Member States;*

  (q) *a policy in the sphere of development cooperation;*

  (r) *the association of the overseas countries and territories in order to increase trade and promote jointly economic and social development;*

  (s) *a contribution to the strengthening of consumer protection;*

  (t) *measures in the spheres of energy, civil protection and tourism.*

Art. 12

Within the scope of application of this Treaty, and without prejudice to any special provisions contained therein, any discrimination on grounds of nationality shall be prohibited.

The Council, acting in accordance with the procedure referred to in Article 189c, may adopt rules designed to prohibit such discrimination.

6.1.1.2   EC Treaty, Arts 28, 30 (*ex-30, 36*): Elimination of Quantitative Restrictions

Art. 28 Quantitative restrictions on imports and all measures having equivalent effect shall, without prejudice to the following provisions, be prohibited as between Member States.

Art. 30 The provisions of Articles 28 and 29 inclusive shall not preclude prohibitions or restrictions on imports, exports or goods in transit justified on the grounds of public morality; public policy (ordre public); public safety or security; the protection of health and life of humans, animals or plants; the protection of national treasures possessing artistic, historic or archaeological value; or the protection of industrial and commercial property. Such prohibitions or restrictions shall not, however, amount to a means of arbitrary discrimination nor to a disguised restriction on trade between Member States.

6.1.1.3   EC Treaty, Art. 49 (*ex-59*): Freedom to Provide Services

Art. 49 Within the framework of the provisions set out below, restrictions on freedom to provide services within the Community shall be progressively abolished during the transitional period in respect of nationals of Member States who are established in a State of the Community rather than that of the person for whom the services are intended. The Council, acting unanimously, on a proposal from the Commission, may extend the benefit of the provisions of the chapter to nationals of a third country who render services who are established within the Community.

6.1.1.4   EC Treaty, Arts 81, 82 (*ex-85, 86*): Rules of Competition

Art. 81(1) The following practices shall be prohibited as incompatible with the common market: all agreements between undertakings, all decisions by associations of undertakings and all concerted practices, which may affect trade between Member States and the object or effect of which is to prevent, restrict or distort competition within the common market, and in particular those which amount to:

(a) the direct or indirect fixing of purchase or selling prices or of any other trading conditions;

(b) the limiting or controlling of production, markets, technical development or capital investment;

(c) the sharing of markets or sources of supply;

(d) applying, in relation to customers in the trade unequal conditions in respect of equivalent transactions, placing them thereby at a competitive disadvantage;

(e) making the conclusion of contracts subject to acceptance by the other parties of supplementary obligations, which, by their nature or according to commercial practice, have no connection with the subject of such contracts.

(2) Any agreements or decisions prohibited pursuant to this article shall automatically be null and void.

(3) The provisions of paragraph 1 may, however, be declared inapplicable in the case of:

any agreement or category of agreements between undertakings, any decision or category of decisions of associations of undertakings, and any concerted practice or category of concerted practices, which contribute to improve the production or distribution of goods or to promote technical or economic progress, whilst allowing consumers a fair share of the resulting benefit and which does not:

(a) impose on the undertakings concerned restrictions which are not indispensable to the achievement of the above objectives;

(b) afford such undertakings the possibility of eliminating competition in respect of a substantial part of the products in question.

Art. 82 It shall be incompatible with the common market and prohibited, in so far as trade between Member States is liable to be effected by it, for one or more undertakings to exploit in an improper manner a dominant position within the common market or within a substantial part of it. Such improper practices, may, in particular, consist in:

(a) the direct or indirect imposition of unfair purchase or selling prices or of other unfair conditions;

(b) the limitation of production, markets or technical development to the prejudice of consumers;

(c) applying in relation to like parties unequal conditions in respect of like transactions, placing them thereby at a competitive disadvantage;

(d) making the conclusion of contracts subject to agreement by the other parties to make additional payments, which, by their nature or according to commercial practice, have no connection with the subject of such contracts.

6.1.1.5   EC Treaty, Arts 226, 230, 234, 295 (*ex-169, 173, 177, 222*): Community Institutions

Art. 226 If the Commission considers that a Member State has failed to fulfil any of its obligations under this Treaty, it shall issue a reasoned opinion on the matter after giving the

State concerned the opportunity to submit its comments. If the State does not comply with the terms of such opinion within the period laid down by the Commission, the latter may bring the matter before the Court of Justice.

Art. 230 Supervision of the legality of acts taken by the Council and the Commission other than recommendations or opinions shall be a matter for the Court of Justice. It shall for this purpose have jurisdiction in proceedings instituted by a Member State, the Council or the Commission, on the grounds of lack of jurisdiction, infringements of important procedural rules, infringement of this Treaty or of any rule of law relating to its application, or misuse of powers.

Any natural or legal person may, subject to the same conditions, have recourse against a decision directed to him or it or against a decision which, although in the form of a regulation or a decision directed to another person, is of direct and individual concern to him or to it.

The proceedings provided for in this article shall be instituted within a period of two months, dating, as the case may be, either from the publication of the act concerned or from its notification to the complainant or, in default thereof, from the day on which the latter learnt of it.

Art. 234 The Court of Justice shall have jurisdiction to give preliminary rulings concerning:

(a) the interpretation of this Treaty;

(b) the validity and interpretation of acts of the institutions of the Community and of the ECB;

(c) the interpretation of the statutes of bodies established by an act of the Council, where those statutes so provide.

Where such a question is raised before any court or tribunal of a Member State, that court or tribunal may, if it considers that a decision on the question is necessary to enable it to give judgment, request the Court of Justice to give a ruling thereon.

Where any such question is raised in a case pending before a court or tribunal of a Member State against whose decisions there is no judicial remedy under national law, that court or tribunal shall bring the matter before the Court of Justice.

Art. 295 This Treaty shall in no way prejudice the rules in Member States governing the system of property ownership.

6.1.2   Community Patent Convention (1975), Arts 28, 45, 46, 76: Exhaustion of Rights, Compulsory Licences

Art. 28 The rights conferred by a Community patent shall not extend to acts concerning a product covered by that patent which are done within the territories of the Contracting States after that product has been put on the market in one of these States by the proprietor of the patent or with his express consent, unless there are grounds which, under Community law, would justify the extension to such acts of the rights conferred by the patent.

Art. 45(1) Any provisions in the law of a Contracting State for the grant of compulsory licences in respect of national patents shall be applicable to Community patents. The extent and effect of compulsory licences granted in respect of Community patents shall be restricted to the territory of the State concerned. Article 28 shall not apply.

(2) Each Contracting State shall, at least in respect of compensation under a compulsory licence, provide for a final appeal to a court of law.

(3) As far as practicable national authorities shall notify the European Patent Office of the grant of any compulsory licence in respect of a Community patent.

(4) For the purposes of this Convention, the term "compulsory licences" shall be construed as including official licences and any right to use patented inventions in the public interest.

Art. 46 A compulsory licence may not be granted in respect of a Community patent on the ground of lack or insufficiency of exploitation if the product covered by the patent, which is manufactured in a Contracting State, is put on the market in the territory of any other Contracting State, for which such a licence has been requested, in sufficient quantity to satisfy needs in the territory of that other Contracting State. This provision shall not apply to compulsory licences granted in the public interest.

Art. 76(1) The rights conferred by a national patent in a Contracting State shall not extend to acts concerning a product covered by that patent which are done within the territory of that Contracting State after that product has been put on the market in any Contracting State by the proprietor of the patent or with his express consent, unless there are grounds which, under Community law, would justify the extension to such acts of the rights conferred by the patent.

(2) Paragraph 1 shall also apply with regard to a product put on the market by the proprietor of a national patent, granted for the same invention in another Contracting State, who has economic connections with the proprietor of the patent referred to in paragraph 1. For the purpose of this paragraph, two persons shall be deemed to have economic connections where one of them is in a position to exert a decisive influence on the other, directly or indirectly, with regard to the exploitation of a patent, or where a third party is in a position to exercise such an influence on both persons.

(3) The preceding paragraphs shall not apply in the case of a product put on the market under a compulsory licence.

6.1.3   *Collins v Imtrat* [1993] 1 E.C.R. 545, ECJ

A performance in the US by the British singer, Phil Collins was "bootlegged" and copies of the unauthorised recording were sold in Germany. Under the German Copyright Act, the right accorded to performers against such recording was given to German nationals wherever they performed. But non-nationals, including citizens of other EC states, acquired the right only under the condition prescribed by the Rome Convention of 1961, i.e. when the performance took place in a Contracting State to that Convention. The US was not a Rome Convention state, and Collins' claim to the right would have failed but for his successful plea that the German law discriminated against him on ground of nationality, contrary to the Treaty of Rome, Art. 12 (EC Treaty version, Art. 7; see above, 6.1.1.1). In accepting this argument, the court said:

In the present state of Community law, and in the absence of Community measures or the harmonisation of national law, it is for the Member States to specify the conditions and rules for the protection of literary and artistic property, subject to complying with the relevant international agreements: Case 341/87, *EMI Electrola.*

The specific purpose of these rights, as governed by national law, is to protect the moral and economic rights of their owners. The protection of moral rights enables authors and artists to resist any distortion, mutilation or other alteration of the work which would be prejudicial to their honour or reputation. Copyright and related rights also have economic characteristics in that they provide for the possibility of commercially exploiting the marketing of the protected work, particularly in the form of licences granted in return for the payment of royalties: Cases 55 & 57/80, *Musik-Vertrieb Membran.*

As the court observed in the last-mentioned judgment, while the commercial exploitation of copyright is a source of remuneration for the owner it also constitutes a form of control on marketing exercisable by the owner, the copyright management societies acting in his name and the grantees of licences. From this viewpoint the commercial exploitation of copyright raises the same problems as that of any other industrial or commercial property right.

The court has consistently held that Article 7 does not apply to differences in treatment and distortions which affect persons and enterprises under the jurisdiction of the Community and which may arise from differences in the laws of the Member States if such differences affect all persons to whom they apply, according to objective criteria and without regard to nationality: Case 14/68, *Wilhelm.*

By prohibiting "any discrimination on grounds of nationality," EEC Article 7 requires that persons in a situation governed by Community law be placed on a completely equal footing with nationals of the Member State: Case 186/87, *Cowan.* Where this principle applies, it precludes a Member State from making the grant of an exclusive right subject to the condition of being a national of that State.

Consequently the reply to the question must be that EEC Article 7(1) must be interpreted as meaning that it prevents the law of a Member State from refusing, under certain circumstances, authors and performing artists of other Member States and their successors in title the right, which is granted by the same law to nationals, to prohibit the marketing in national territory of a phonogram made without their consent, if the performance in question was given outside national territory.

6.1.4 *Spain v EU Council* [1996] F.S.R. 73, ECJ

Spain brought proceedings, supported by Greece, against the Council for the annulment of Regulation (EEC) No. 1768/92, which created supplementary protection certificates to extend the effective life of pharmaceutical patents in the EU The Regulation was passed by the Council under Art.95 (ex-100a) of the EC Treaty.

Spain challenged the Regulation's validity on two bases. First, it argued that the Community does not have competence to legislate and regulate a new patent right (under Arts 295 and 30); and secondly, that Art.100a EEC was not the correct legal basis for passing the Regulation, since it was not a harmonising measure and does not promote the objectives of the internal market.

The European Court of Justice dimissed the application for annulment, after addressing each Spanish objection in turn:

Community Powers:

13   ... Spain argues that the Community has no power to regulate substantive patent law, and may harmonise only those aspects relating to the exercise of industrial property rights which are capable of having an effect upon the achievement of the general objectives laid down in the Treaty. Such action may not take the form of a new industrial right which, by its nature, content and effects, alters the basic concept in force under the national legal systems of each of the Member States. The duration of a patent is its most important feature, since it intrinsically affects the balance in time between the rights and obligations of its holder, whether legal or economic in character.

14   The Council ... argues that the purpose of Article 36 of the Treaty is not to reserve certain matters for the exclusive competence of Member States. As for Article 222 of the Treaty, its purpose is to allow general freedom to Member States in the organisation of their property regimes, but it cannot completely prohibit Community intervention in the property rights of individuals, without paralysing the powers of the Community.

15   The case law has not excluded the possibility of the Community determining by legislation the conditions and rules regarding the protection conferred by industrial property rights, should such action prove necessary in pursuing its objectives. In any event, the creation of the supplementary certificate does not in any way affect the substance of the rights of the holder of the basic patent. It is a mechanism for correcting the short-comings of the system for protecting pharmaceutical research, which arise from the need to obtain marketing authorisation in order to make use of the innovation.

16   ... the Court must examine whether Articles 222 and 36 of the EEC Treaty reserve the power to regulate substantive patent for the national legislature, thereby excluding any Community action in the matter.

17   In that respect, the Court held in its judgment in *Commission v United Kingdom* ([1992] E.C.R. I-829, paragraphs 16 and 17), that, as Community law stands, the provision on patents have not yet been the subject of unification at Community level or in the context of approximation of laws, and that, in those circumstances, it is for the national legislature to determine the conditions and rules regarding the protection conferred by patents.

18   However, it added that the provisions of the Treaty—and, in particular, Article 222, which provides that the Treaty does not in any way prejudice the rules in Member States governing the system of property ownership—cannot be interpreted as reserving

to the national legislature, in relation to industrial and commercial property, the power to adopt measures which would adversely affect the principle of free movement of goods within the common market as provided for and regulated by the Treaty (paragraph 18 of the same judgment)....

20 The Court follows similar reasoning in relation to Article 36 of the Treaty. That provides, in particular, that the provisions of Articles 30 to 34 shall not preclude prohibitions or restrictions justified on grounds of the protection of industrial and commercial property, but that such prohibitions or restrictions shall not constitute a means of arbitrary discrimination for a disguised restriction on trade between Member States.

21 In its judgment in Case 35/76 *Simmenthal v Italian Minister for Finance* [1976] E.C.R. 1871, paragraph 14, the Court held that Article 36 is not designed to reserve certain matters to the exclusive jurisdiction of Member States but permits national laws to derogate from the principle of the free movement of goods to the extent to which derogation is and continues to be justified for the attainment of the objectives referred to in that article.

22 It follows that neither Article 222 nor Article 36 of the Treaty reserves a power to regulate substantive patent law to the national legislature, to the exclusion of any Community action in the matter.

Article 95 (ex-100a) was the correct basis for the Council to pass the Regulation:

32 ... In its judgment in Case C–300/89 *Commission v Council* [1991] E.C.R. I-2867, paragraph 15, the Court held that, in order to give effect to the fundamental freedoms mentioned in Article 8a, harmonising measures are necessary to deal with disparities between the laws of the Member States in areas where such disparities are liable to create or maintain distorted conditions of competition. For that reason, Article 100a empowers the Community to adopt measures for the approximation of the provisions laid down by law, regulation or administrative action in Member States and lays down the procedure to be followed for that purpose....

34 In this case, the Council has pointed out that, at the time the contested Regulation was adopted, provisions concerning the creation of a supplementary protection certificate for medicinal products existed in two Member States and were at the draft stage in another State. The contested regulation is intended precisely to establish a uniform Community approach by creating a supplementary certificate which may be obtained by the holder of a national or European patent under the same conditions in each Member State, and providing, in particular, for a uniform duration of protection (Article 13).

35 The Regulation thus aims to prevent the heterogeneous development of national laws leading to further disparities which would be likely to create obstacles to the free movement of medicinal products within the Community and thus directly affect the establishment and the functioning of the internal market (sixth recital).

36 The Council rightly emphasises that differences in the protection given in the Community to one and the same medicine would give rise to a fragmentation of the market, whereby the medicine would still be protected in some national markets but no longer protected in others. Such differences in protection would mean that the marketing conditions for the medicines would themselves be different in each of the Member States.

37 ... the Regulation recognises the necessity, in a sector as complex as the pharmaceutical sector, to take all the interests at stake into account, including those of public health (ninth recital). In that regard, Article 13(2) of the regulation provides that the certificate may not be issued for a period longer than five years.

40 ... It follows from the above that the regulation was validly adopted on the basis of

Article 100a of the Treaty, and did not therefore have to be adopted on the basis of Article 100 or Article 235.

6.2 Free Movement of Goods and Intellectual Property

6.2.1 General

6.2.1.1 *Consten and Grundig v EC Commission* [1966] E.C.R. 299; [1966] C.M.L.R. 418, ECJ

The German electrical goods manufacturer, Grundig, appointed the French company, Consten, as its exclusive distributor in France. It likewise appointed other companies as national exclusive distributors in other countries of the Common Market and elsewhere. In support of this exclusivity, Grundig labelled its products not only with its own name but also with the mark, "Gint". It agreed with Consten that the latter would apply for registration of "Gint" in France, upon the understanding that, on termination of the distributorship, the mark would be assigned to Grundig. A parallel importer began importing Grundig products into France from elsewhere in the EC and was sued for unfair competition and trade mark infringement by Consten.

In Art.81 (ex-85) proceedings, the EC Commission issued a decision that the entire exclusive distributorship agreement was void and refused to grant exemption under Art.85(3). The decision also enjoined Consten from using its trade mark right to obstruct parallel imports from another E.C. country.

In a path-breaking decision, the European Court of Justice agreed with the substance of the Commission's view of exclusive distributorships and Article 85. It only criticised the lower decision for declaring the entire agreement void, rather than just the provisions which offended Art.81(1); and over its approach in some respects to the application of Art.81(3).

On the basic issue, it held that Art.81 makes no distinction between horizontal and vertical agreements and may accordingly apply to an agreement between a manufacturer and its own distributor. Although the two are not themselves in competition, the agreement might have an adverse effect on competition between one of them and a third party (in this case, Consten and any other distributor of Grundig products in France). Thus it is distortive of competition to make agreements designed to insulate national markets within the Community for a widespread brand of products. Once this distortion is shown, it is not necessarily an answer that the improvement in the distribution of Grundig products, which the agreement would promote, would lead to an increase in competition with similar products of other producers.

On the question of Consten's use of its right to the "Gint" trade mark, the court agreed with the Commission:

Consten's right under the contract to the exclusive user in France of the "GINT" trade mark, which may be used in a similar manner in other countries, is intended to make it possible to keep under surveillance and to place an obstacle in the way of parallel imports. Thus, the agreement by which Grundig, as the holder of the trade mark by virtue of an international registration, authorised Consten to register it in France in its own name tends to restrict competition.

Although Consten is, by virtue of the registration of the "GINT" trade mark, regarded under French law as the original holder of the rights relating to that trade mark, the fact nevertheless remains that it was by virtue of an agreement with Grundig that it was able to effect the registration.

That agreement therefore is one which may be caught by the prohibition in Article 85(1). The prohibition would be ineffective if Consten could continue to use the trade mark to achieve the same object as that pursued by the agreement which has been held to be unlawful.

Articles 36, 222 and 234 of the Treaty relied upon by the applicants do not exclude any influence whatever of Community law on the exercise of national industrial property rights.

Article 36, which limits the scope of the rules on the liberalisation of trade contained in Title I, Chap. 2, of the Treaty, cannot limit the field of application of Article 85. Article 222 confines itself to stating that the "Treaty shall in no way prejudice the rules in Member States governing the system of property ownership". The injunction contained in Article 3 of the operative part of the contested decision to refrain from using rights under national trade-mark law in order to set an obstacle in the way of parallel imports does not affect the grant of those rights but only limits their exercise to the extent necessary to give effect to the prohibition under Article 85(1). The power of the Commission to issue such an injunction for which provision is made in Article 3 of Regulation No. 17/62 of the council is in harmony with the nature of the Community rules on competition which have immediate effect and are directly binding on individuals.

Such a body of rules, by reason of its nature described above and its function, does not allow the improper use of rights under any national trade-mark law in order to frustrate the Community's law on cartels.

Article 234 which has the aim of protecting the rights of third countries is not applicable in the present instance.

6.2.1.2 *Deutsche Grammophon v Metro-SB-Grossmarkte* **[1971] E.C.R. 487; [1971] C.M.L.R. 631, ECJ**

At the time in question, resale prices could be maintained under German law provided that no retail selling below the set minimum price occurred. "Polydor" records, manufactured by Deutsche Grammophon or its subsidiaries, were subject to this r.p.m.; in West Germany their retail price was approximately double that in France, where there was no r.p.m. In addition, in West Germany, the manufacturer of sound recordings had a neighbouring right covering their making and distribution under the Copyright Law of 1965, Art.85 (cf. Copyright, Designs and Patents Act 1988 (UK), s.5). There was no equivalent right in

French law, though it may have been possible at that period to proceed against a record pirate under unfair competition law (subsequent legislation has strengthened the record companies' position in France).

Records originally manufactured by Deutsche Grammophon were marketed through its French subsidiary in France. They were apparently bought by a Swiss enterprise, then by a Hamburg wholesaler and finally by the defendant which retailed them in a Hamburg supermarket at cut price. In proceedings for infringement of Art.81 (ex-85), the Hanseatische Obergericht, Hamburg, considered that the right under that Article had not been exhausted by the authorised sale in France, so that by German law the sale of the records by the defendant constituted infringement.

Under the Treaty of Rome, Art.234 (ex-177), the court raised two questions before the European Court of Justice. The first question asked whether this operation of the German copyright law was in conflict with Art.81(1) (ex-85(1)) of the Treaty. After referring to those Articles, the European Court of Justice for the first time drew attention in this context to the terms of Art.36. It proceeded:

If a right related to copyright is relied upon to prevent the marketing in a Member State of products distributed by the holder of the right or with his consent on the territory of another Member State on the sole ground that such distribution did not take place on the national territory, such a prohibition, which would legitimise the isolation of national markets, would be repugnant to the essential purpose of the Treaty, which is to unite national markets into a single market.

That purpose could not be attained if, under the various legal systems of the Member States, nationals of those States were able to partition the market and bring about arbitrary discrimination or disguised restrictions on trade between Member States.

Consequently, it would be in conflict with the provisions prescribing the free movement of products within the common market for a manufacturer of sound recordings to exercise the exclusive right to distribute the protected articles, conferred upon him by the legislation of a Member State, in such a way as to prohibit the sale in that State of products placed on the market by him or with his consent in another Member State solely because such distribution did not occur within the territory of the first Member State.

The second question was treated asking whether an abuse of dominant position within Art.82 (ex-86) arose from the facts (i) that the price differential for the same records existed in different EC countries, and (ii) that the recording company had exclusive contracts with its performing artists. In answer, the European Court of Justice stated:

For it to fall within Article 86 a dominant position must further be abused. The difference between the controlled price and the price of the product reimported from another Member State does not necessarily suffice to disclose such an abuse; it may, however, if unjustified by any objective criteria and if it is particularly marked, be a determining factor in such abuse.

6.2.1.3   *Centrafarm v Sterling Drug; Centrafarm v Winthrop* [1974] E.C.R. 1147, 1183; [1974] 2 C.M.L.R. 480, ECJ

The American parent of the Sterling Winthrop group, Sterling Drug, owned a patent for a urinary infection drug in a number of countries, including the UK and the Netherlands. In those two countries, the mark under which it was sold— "Negram"—was owned by a local marketing subsidiary of the group: in the UK, Sterling Winthrop Group Ltd; in the Netherlands, Winthrop BV.

Centrafarm obtained supplies of "Negram" in the UK and exported them for sale in the Netherlands, but was met by proceedings for infringement of the Dutch patent and trade mark. The Hoge Raad referred a number of interrelated questions to the European Court of Justice under Art.234 (ex-177). In each case the first of these concerned the compatibility of the intellectual property rights asserted with the rules concerning the free movement of goods.

In respect of the case concerning the patent, the court stated:

As regards question I(a):

4   This question requires the court to state whether, under the conditions postulated, the rules in the EEC Treaty concerning the free movement of goods prevent the patentee from ensuring that the product protected by the patent is not marketed by others.

5   As a result of the provisions in the Treaty relating to the free movement of goods and in particular of Article 30, quantitative restrictions on imports and all measures having equivalent effect are prohibited between Member States.

6   By Article 36 these provisions shall nevertheless not include prohibitions or restrictions on imports justified on grounds of the protection of industrial or commercial property.

7   Nevertheless, it is clear from this same Article, in particular its second sentence, as well as from the context, that whilst the Treaty does not affect the existence of rights recognised by the legislation of a Member State in matters of industrial and commercial property, yet the exercise of these rights may nevertheless, depending on the circumstances, be affected by the prohibitions in the Treaty.

8   Inasmuch as it provides an exception to one of the fundamental principles of the Common Market, Article 36 in fact only admits of derogations from the free movement of goods where such derogations are justified for the purpose of safeguarding rights which constitute the specific subject matter of this property.

9   In relation to patents, the specific subject matter of the industrial property is the guarantee that the patentee, to reward the creative effort of the inventor, has the exclusive right to use an invention with a view to manufacturing industrial products and putting them into circulation for the first time, either directly or by the grant of licences to third parties, as well as the right to oppose infringements.

10 An obstacle to the free movement of goods may arise out of the existence, within a national legislation concerning industrial and commercial property, of provisions laying down that a patentee's right is not exhausted when the product protected by the patent is marketed in another Member State, with the result that the patentee can prevent importation of the product into his own Member State when it has been marketed in another State.

11 Whereas an obstacle to the free movement of goods of this kind may be justified on the ground of protection of industrial property where such protection is invoked against a product coming from a Member State where it is not patentable and has been man-

ufactured by third parties without the consent of the patentee and in cases where there exist patents, the original proprietors of which are legally and economically independent, a derogation from the principle of the free movement of goods is not, however, justified where the product has been put onto the market in a legal manner, by the patentee himself or with his consent, in the Member State from which it has been imported, in particular in the case of a proprietor of parallel patents.

12   In fact, if a patentee could prevent the import of protected products marketed by him or with his consent in another Member State, he would be able to partition off national markets and thereby restrict trade between Member States, in a situation where no such restriction was necessary to guarantee the essence of the exclusive rights flowing from the parallel patents.

13   The plaintiff in the main action claims, in this connection, that by reason by divergences between national legislations and practice, truly identical or parallel patents can hardly be said to exist.

14   It should be noted here that, in spite of the divergences which remain in the absence of any unification of national rules concerning industrial property, the identity of the protected invention is clearly the essential element of the concept of parallel patents which it is for the courts to assess.

15   The question referred should therefore be answered to the effect that the exercise, by a patentee, of the right which he enjoys under the legislation of a Member State to prohibit the sale, in that State, of a product protected by the patent which has been marketed in another Member State by the patentee or with his consent is incompatible with the rules of the EEC Treaty concerning the free movement of goods within the Common Market.

In respect of the case concerning the trade mark, the court repeated its general statement of the operation of Arts 28 and 30 (ex-30 and 36), and proceeded:

8   In relation to trade marks, the specific subject-matter of the industrial property is the guarantee that the owner of the trade mark has the exclusive right to use that trade mark, for the purpose of putting products protected by the trade mark into circulation for the first time, and is therefore intended to protect him against competitors wishing to take advantage of the status and reputation of the trade mark by selling products illegally bearing that trade mark.

9   An obstacle to the free movement of goods may arise out of the existence, within a national legislation concerning industrial and commercial property, of provisions laying down that a trade mark owner's right is not exhausted when the product protected by the trade mark is marketed in another Member State, with the result that the trade mark owner can prevent importation of the product into his own Member State when it has been marketed in another Member State.

10   Such an obstacle is not justified when the product has been put onto the market in a legal manner in the Member State from which it has been imported, by the trade mark owner himself or with his consent, so that there can be no question of abuse or infringement of the trade mark.

11   In fact, if a trade mark owner could prevent the import of protected products marketed by him or with his consent in another Member State, he would be able to partition off national markets and thereby restrict trade between Member States, in a situation where no such restriction was necessary to guarantee the essence of the exclusive right flowing from the trade mark.

12   The question referred should therefore be answered to the effect that the exercise, by the owner of a trade mark, of the right which he enjoys under the legislation of a Member State to prohibit the sale, in that State, of a product which has been marketed under the trade mark in another Member State by the trade mark owner or with his consent is incompatible with the rules of the EEC Treaty concerning the free movement of goods within the Common Market.

The court also ruled as follows:

1. The applicable test for determining whether the Treaty provisions override a national intellectual property right is whether the goods have been placed on some part of the common market with the consent of the patentee or trade mark proprietor, not whether the right-owner and a licensee belong to the same group or not.

2. The applicable test applies even when the following further factors are present:

(a) price differences for the product exist because for price control measures taken by public authorities in the exporting country. (In the circumstances of the case, this arose because the Department of Health and Social Security in Britain could rely upon its Crown use powers under the Patents Act in negotiating favourable prices with the pharmaceutical companies. These powers allowed it, if it wished, to procure the drug from an alternative source and pay "reasonable" compensation to the patentee).

(b) in order to protect the public from the risk of receiving defective products, the right-owner needed to be able to control the distribution of a product between different countries.

6.2.1.4 *Merck v Stephar* [1981] E.C.R. 2063; [1981] 3 C.M.L.R. 463, ECJ

Merck held patents in all EC States save Luxembourg and Italy for a hypertension drug, "Moduretic". It marketed the product in Italy and Stephar purchased supplies there for importation into the Netherlands, where infringement proceedings were in consequence launched. On reference of the issue by the Arrondissementsrechtbank Rotterdam, the European Court of Justice quoted its own definition of the "specific subject-matter" of a patent right (see Centrafarm v Sterling Drug, above, 6.2.1.3), and continued:

7 Stephar and the Commission conclude that once the proprietor of the patent has himself placed the product in question on the open market in a Member State in which it is not patentable, the importation of such goods into the Member State in which the product is protected may not be prohibited because the proprietor of the patent has placed it on the market of his own free will.

8 In contrast Merck, supported by the French Government and the Government of the United Kingdom, maintains that the purpose of the patent, which is to reward the inventor, is not safeguarded if owing to the fact that the patent right is not recognised by law in the country in which the proprietor of the patent has marketed his product he is unable to collect the reward for his creative effort because he does not enjoy a monopoly in first placing the product on the market.

9 In the light of that conflict of views, it must be stated that in accordance with the definition of the specific purpose of the patent, which has been described above, the substance of a patent right lies essentially in according the inventor an exclusive right of first placing the product on the market.

10 That right of first placing a product on the market enables the inventor, by allowing

him a monopoly in exploiting his product, to obtain the reward for his creative effort without, however, guaranteeing that he will obtain such a reward in all circumstances.

11   It is for the proprietor of the patent to decide, in the light of all the circumstances, under what conditions he will market his product, including the possibility of marketing it in a Member State where the law does not provide patent protection for the product in question. If he decides to do so he must then accept the consequences of his choice as regards the free movement of the product within the Common Market, which is a fundamental principle forming part of the legal and economic circumstances which must be taken into account by the proprietor of the patent in determining the manner in which his exclusive right will be exercised.

12   That is borne out, moreover, by the statements of the Court in its judgments of June 22, 1976 (*Terrapin*, Case 119/75 [1976] E.C.R. 1039, below, 6.2.3.4) and January 20, 1981 (*Musik-Vertrieb Membran and K-tel*, Joined Cases 55 and 57/80, below, 6.2.2.2) inasmuch as "the proprietor of an industrial or commercial property right protected by the law of a Member State cannot rely on that law to prevent the importation of a product which has been lawfully marketed in another Member State by the proprietor himself or with his consent".

13   Under those conditions to permit an inventor, or one claiming under him, to invoke a patent held by him in one Member State in order to prevent the importation of the product freely marketed by him in another Member State where that product is not patentable would bring about a partitioning of the national markets which would be contrary to the aims of the Treaty.

6.2.1.5   *Keurkoop v Nancy Kean Gifts* [1982] E.C.R. 2853; [1983] 2 C.M.L.R. 47, ECJ

A handbag, which was the subject of a US design patent, had been marketed in the US during the late 1970s. Nancy Kean Gifts, the Dutch subsidiary of an international group, purchased quantities of the bag through a Swiss enterprise from Taiwan. The bags were sent direct from Taiwan to the Netherlands for marketing there. Before launching them, Nancy Kean Gifts registered the design under the Benelux Designs Law of 1966, even though (as was alleged) it had no entitlement deriving from the American designer or his associates.

Keurkoop also procured a supply of Taiwanese bags to virtually the same design. The Dutch court hearing design infringement proceedings was led to consider the impact of the Treaty of Rome if these bags were produced by the defendant in another Community country where the plaintiff had no protection for the design.

The Dutch court raised two questions under Art.234 (ex-177) before the European Court of Justice:

(1) Whether it is compatible with the Rome Treaty provisions on free movement of goods for a regional Designs Law to confer a right on an applicant for that right without permitting others to challenge his entitlement by relying on the fact that he is not the author of the design or the person commissioning it or employing the author?

To this question the Court answered:

... national legislation having the characteristics of the Uniform Benelux Law on Designs falls within the scope of the provisions of Article 36 of the Treaty on the protection of industrial and commercial property. In the present state of its development Community law does not prevent the adoption of national provisions of the kind contained in the Uniform Benelux Law, as described by the national court.

(2) Whether the Dutch court could enjoin the marketing of products within a Benelux registered design, if they were obtained by the defendant in another Common Market country where the Benelux design-owner has no equivalent right?

After referring to its earlier interpretation of Art.30 (ex-36), the Court answered:

... the proprietor of a right to a design acquired under the legislation of a Member State may oppose the importation of products from another Member State which are identical in appearance to the design which has been filed, provided that the products in question have not been put into circulation in the other Member State by, or with the consent of, the proprietor of the right or a person legally or economically dependent on him, that as between the natural or legal persons in question there is no kind of agreement or concerted practice in restraint of competition and finally that the respective rights of the proprietors of the right to the design in the various Member States were created independently of one another.

6.2.1.6   *EMI Electrola v Patricia* **[1989] E.C.R. 79; [1989] 2 C.M.L.R. 544, ECJ**

Sound recording right in recordings of songs by Cliff Richard had expired in Denmark but not in West Germany, because the pertinent period in each case was in the circumstances calculated from a different date.

The defendant company, Patricia, manufactured the recordings in question in West Germany for a Danish company which imported them to Denmark. Patricia then re-purchased them in Denmark and re-imported them for marketing there. No assent to this conduct had been given by EMI or its German subsidiary (which as assignee of the German sound recording rights was plaintiff in the action for infringement of the rights). The Landgericht Hamburg referred the question whether enforcement of the rights would be compatible with Articles 28 and 30 (ex-30 and 36).

The European Court of Justice stated:

7   Pursuant to Article 36 of the Treaty, the provisions of Article 30 prohibiting all measures having an equivalent effect to quantitative restrictions on imports between member-States do not preclude prohibitions or restrictions on imports justified on grounds of the protection of industrial and commercial property. Such protection covers the protection of literary and artistic property including copy-right, if it is exploited commercially. Therefore it also covers protection for exclusive rights of reproduction and distribution of sound recordings, if that is treated in the same way as copyright by the relevant national law.

8   Therefore, the object of Articles 30 and 36 is to reconcile the requirements of the free movement of goods with upholding the lawful exercise of exclusive rights in literary and artistic property. In particular, that reconciliation means that protection must be

refused to any improper exercise of those rights which would be likely to maintain or create artificial partitioning in the Common Market.

9   From this the Court's case law has inferred that a copyright owner cannot rely on the exclusive exploitation right conferred by his copyright to prevent or restrict the importation of sound recordings which have been lawfully marketed in another member-State by the owner himself or with his consent (*Musik-Vertrieb Membran*, Cases 55 and 57/80.)

10   However, that situation differs from the situation envisaged by the national court. The question before the Court shows that the fact that sound recordings were marketed lawfully in the market of another member-State is due, not to an act or consent of the copyright owner or his licensee, but to expiry of the protection period granted by the legislation of that member-State. Therefore the problem arises from the disparity between legislation of different countries regarding the protection period given by copyright and by similar rights. The disparity lies either in the duration of protection itself or the details or protection, such as the time when the protection period begins to run.

11   In this connection it should be observed that, in the present state of Community law, which is characterised by the absence of harmonisation or approximation of legislation on the protection of literary and artistic property, it is for national legislatures to specify the conditions and rules for such protection.

12   To the extent that the disparity between national laws is likely to create restrictions on sound recordings in the Community, such restrictions are justified by Article 36 of the Treaty if they arise from the difference in arrangements relating to the duration of protection and if the protection period is inseparably linked with the existence of the exclusive rights themselves.

13   There would be no justification if the restrictions on trade imposed or allowed by the national legislation on which the owner of exclusive rights or his licensee rely were such as to constitute a means of arbitrary discrimination or a disguised measure for restricting trade. However, there is nothing in the file which would permit the presumption that this situation could arise in a case such as the present.

6.2.1.7 *Deutsche Renault AG v Audi AG* **[1995] 1 C.M.L.R. 461, ECJ**

Audi owned the German trade mark for a single number in Italian, "Quattro", on which they brought infringement proceedings against Renault for importing the "Espace Quadro". Renault challenged both the registration and the finding of infringement, in so far as they inhibited inter-state trade in the European Community, for failure to satisfy the conditions of the Art.30 (ex-36) proviso. The court rejected this challenge:

(1) Establishment of the right to the designation "Quattro"

20   As the Court decided in the judgments in *Keurkoop BV v Nancy Kean Gifts*, [above, 6.2.1.5], and in *Volvo AB v Veng*, [below, 6.2.2.9], with regard to designs and in *Thetford v Fiamma SA*, [1988] [below, 6.2.2.5], with regard to patents, in the present state of Community law and in the absence of Community standardisation or harmonisation of laws, the conditions and procedures for the protection of an intellectual property right are a matter for national law.

21   Consequently, the conditions for the protection of a designation such as "Quattro" are, subject to the limits imposed by the second sentence of Article 36, a matter for national law.

22   The first point to be made in this regard is that the national legislation at issue, in the

interpretation given by the court making the reference, lays down very strict conditions for the protection under trade mark law of a designation such as "Quattro".

23 Apart from the statutory limitations on the registration of a numeral as a trade mark ..., an unregistered trade mark is in general protected only if it has gained acceptance in trade, that is, if the mark is perceived by the German public as an indication that the goods to which it is applied come from a particular undertaking. That is the position only if the great majority of consumers have that impression.

24 This degree of recognition, which is called for by the court making the reference, must be all the higher if, as with the figure 4 in the automobile sector, the symbol is one which ought to remain available for use. In view of the importance of keeping the symbol available, the court making the reference regards the degree of recognition hitherto demonstrated as insufficient.

25 In addition, these rules also apply where the numeral is represented by a word in a foreign language, in so far as the language concerned is sufficiently well known in Germany.

26 Finally, it can be seen from section 16 of the [German Unfair Competition Law]— which is also applicable by analogy to the right to a get-up (*Ausstattungsrecht*)—that a competitor is not prevented by the protection of the mark from applying to his goods indications of their properties on condition that they are not used by way of a trade mark. The same rules apply to descriptive designations in foreign languages. However, the courts which had to decide the dispute in the main proceedings did not regard the use of the designation "Quadra" as descriptive.

27 Secondly, it should be noted that it does not appear from the documents before the Court that a manufacturer from another Member State is precluded from claiming under the same conditions the protection granted under German law to a registered or unregistered trade mark or that such protection varies according to whether or not the goods bearing that trade mark are of national or foreign origin.

28 It follows that national legal provisions such as those at issue in the main proceedings, which permit the establishment under the aforementioned conditions of an exclusive right to the use of a designation such as "Quattro", represent neither arbitrary discrimination nor a disguised restriction on intra-Community trade.

(2) Risk of confusion between the designations "Quattro" and "Quadra".

29 With regard to the exercise of the right, the Commission states that the concept of actual risk of confusion must be strictly interpreted in order to avoid obstructing the free movement of goods further than is necessary for the protection of trade marks. As an exception to a basic principle of the common market Article 36 allows restrictions to the free movement of goods only in so far as they are justified by the protection of the rights which constitute the specific subject-matter of the industrial or commercial property at issue.

30 In view of that argument it should be noted, first, that the specific subject-matter of trade mark rights consists in protecting the proprietor of the mark against a risk of confusion such as to allow third persons to take unlawful advantage of the reputation of the proprietor's goods.

31 Further, the adoption of criteria for a finding of risk of confusion forms part of the detailed rules for trade mark protection which, as already stated, are a matter for national law. A trade mark right as an exclusive right and protection against marks giving rise to risk of confusion are in reality, as the Advocate General rightly emphasises in section 21 of his Opinion, two sides of the same coin: reducing or extending the scope of protection against the risk of confusion simply reduces or extends the scope of the right itself. Both aspects must accordingly be governed by a single, homogeneous source of law—that is, at present, by national law.

32 Community law does not therefore lay down any strict interpretative criterion for the concept of risk of confusion.

33 However, national law is subject to the restrictions set out in the second sentence of EEC Article 36. As it is, there is nothing in the documents before the court to indicate that those restrictions have been exceeded. In particular, there is nothing to suggest that the German courts interpret the concept of confusion broadly where the protection of the trade mark of a German producer is at issue, but interpret the same concept strictly where the protection of the trade mark of a producer established in another Member State is concerned.

34 In these circumstances, national laws such as those in question here, under which an exclusive right to use a designation such as "Quattro" may be exercised in order to prevent the use of a designation such as "Quadra", which is assumed to be capable of creating a risk of confusion with the former designation, constitute neither arbitrary discrimination nor a disguised restriction on intra-Community trade.

35 The Commission further contends that, in order to appraise the risk of confusion, composite trade marks must be regarded in their entirety, so that in this case account must be taken of the fact that the vehicles in question are marketed under the designation "Espace Quadra" and "AUDI Quattro".

36 According to German law, there is a risk of confusion between two trade marks not only when the trade concerned might mistakenly assume that the goods concerned come from one and the same undertaking (direct risk of confusion) but also when the mistaken assumption relates to the existence of an organisational or economic link between the undertakings concerned, such as a licensing agreement under which one undertaking is authorised to manufacture a product with the same properties as the product of the other (risk of confusion in the broader sense).

37 No exception can be taken under Community law to the protection granted by a national law against this last-mentioned risk of confusion since it corresponds to the specific subject-matter of the trade mark right which, as stated above, consists in protecting the proprietor against the risk of confusion.

38 It is for the national court to decide whether the use of the words "Quattro" and "Quadra" in composite designations such as "AUDI Quattro" and "Espace Quadra" is sufficient to exclude the risk of confusion, even if it be established that the designation "Quattro" has achieved a high degree of recognition.

6.2.1.8 *EMI Records v CBS UK* **[1976] E.C.R. 811; [1976] 2 C.M.L.R. 235, ECJ**

The trade mark "Columbia" for records was originally used by the American Graphophone Co, predecessors of the CBS Group, in the US, UK and other countries. The marks passed to various companies, but ultimately in 1922, ownership of the US and UK marks was separated because there no longer existed any business connection between the Columbia undertakings in the two countries. Subsequently the British marks passed to EMI Records Ltd It (or another EMI subsidiary) owned the "Columbia" mark for all countries of the EEC.

In the Americas, "Columbia" continued to be the principal trade mark of the CBS group, but in Europe it sold its records under different marks. Both CBS subsidiaries and independent retailers on occasion imported CBS "Columbia" records from America and some of these were then sold without changing the labelling to a different mark. Actions for trade mark infringement were in consequence commenced by EMI in England, Denmark and West Germany, which led to Art.177 proceedings from all three countries. The various questions from the national courts raised issues under both Arts 28 and 30, and 81 (ex-30, 36, 85).

With regard to the free movement of goods, the European Court of Justice said:

9   Within the framework of the provisions of the Treaty relating to the free movement of goods and in accordance with Article 3(a), Article 30 *et seq.* on the elimination of quantitative restrictions and measures having equivalent effect expressly provide that such restrictions and measures shall be prohibited "between Member States".

10 Article 36, in particular, after stipulating that Articles 30 to 34 shall not preclude restrictions on imports, exports or goods in transit justified *inter alia* on grounds of the protection of industrial and commercial property, states that such restrictions shall in no instance constitute a means of arbitrary discrimination or disguised restriction on trade "between Member States".
Consequently the exercise of a trade-mark right in order to prevent the marketing of products coming from a third country under an identical mark, even if this constitutes a measure having an effect equivalent to a quantitative restriction, does not affect the free movement of goods between Member States and thus does not come under the prohibitions set out in Article 30 *et seq.* of the Treaty.

11 In such circumstances the exercise of a trade-mark right does not in fact jeopardise the unity of the common market which Article 30 *et seq.* are intended to ensure.

With regard to competition, the court said:

26 A trade-mark right, as a legal entity, does not possess those elements of contract or concerted practice referred to in Article 86(1).

27 Nevertheless, the exercise of that right might fall within the ambit of the prohibitions contained in the Treaty if it were to manifest itself as the subject, the means, or the consequence of a restrictive practice.

28 A restrictive agreement between traders within the common market and competitors in third countries that would bring about an isolation of the common market as a whole which, in the territory of the Community, would reduce the supply of products originating in third countries and similar to those protected by a mark within the Community, might be of such a nature as to affect adversely the conditions of competition within the common market.

29 In particular if the proprietor of the mark in dispute in the third country has within the Community various subsidiaries established in different Member States which are in a position to market the products at issue within the common market such isolation may also affect trade between Member States.

30 For Article 85 to apply to a case, such as the present one, of agreements which are no longer in force it is sufficient that such agreements continue to produce their effects after they have formally ceased to be in force.

31 An agreement is only regarded as continuing to produce its effects if from the behaviour of the persons concerned there may be inferred the existence of elements of concerted practice and of co-ordination peculiar to the agreement and producing the same result as that envisaged by the agreement.

32 This is not so when the said effects do not exceed those flowing from the mere exercise of the national trade mark rights.

33 Furthermore it is clear from the file that the foreign trader can obtain access to the common market without availing himself of the mark in dispute.

34 In those circumstances the requirement that the proprietor of the identical mark in a third country must, for the purposes of his exports to the protected market, obliterate this mark on the products concerned and perhaps apply a different mark forms part of the permissible consequences flowing from the protection of the mark.

6.2.1.9 *Polydor v Harlequin Records* [1982] E.C.R. 329; [1982] 1 C.M.L.R. 677, ECJ

The plaintiffs were the owner and the exclusive licensee of the UK sound recording right in a recording made by the Bee-Gees. Copies of the recording made and sold in Portugal by companies associated with the plaintiffs, were imported by the defendants into the UK. In an action for this secondary infringement the defendants relied upon provisions in the Agreement between the EC and Portugal (itself an implementation of the GATT), equivalent to Arts 28 and 30 (ex-30, 36) of the Treaty of Rome. These Arts (14(2), 23) were said to have the same effect upon imports from Portugal as Arts 28 and 30 have upon trade between Member States of the Community.

This argument was referred by the English Court of Appeal under Art. 177. The European Court of Justice stated:

The considerations which led to that interpretation of Articles 30 and 36 of the Treaty do not apply in the context of the relations between the Community and Portugal as defined by the Agreement. It is apparent from an examination of the Agreement that although it makes provision for the unconditional abolition of certain restrictions on trade between the Community and Portugal, such as quantitative restrictions and measures having equivalent effect, it does not have the same purpose as the EEC Treaty, inasmuch as the latter, as has been stated above, seeks to create a single market reproducing as closely as possible the conditions of a domestic market.

It follows that in the context of the Agreement restrictions on trade in goods may be considered to be justified on the ground of the production of industrial and commercial property in a situation in which their justification would not be possible within the Community.

In the present case such a distinction is all the more necessary inasmuch as the instruments which the Community has at its disposal in order to achieve the uniform application of Community law and the progressive abolition of legislative disparities within the common market have no equivalent in the context of the relations between the Community and Portugal.

It follows from the foregoing that a prohibition on the importation into the Community of a product originating in Portugal based on the protection of copyright is justified in the framework of the free-trade arrangements established by the Agreement by virtue of the first sentence of Article 23. The findings of the national court do not disclose any factor which would permit the conclusion that the enforcement of copyright in a case such as the present constitutes a means of arbitrary discrimination or a disguised restriction on trade within the meaning of the second sentence of that Article.

6.2.2   Application to Patents, Designs, Copyright and Other Rights against Misappropriation

6.2.2.1   *Dansk Supermarked v Imerco* [1981] E.C.R. 181; [1981] 3 C.M.L.R. 587, ECJ

With a view to celebrating its fiftieth anniversary, the Danish hardware firm, Imerco, ordered from a British manufacturer, Broadhurst, a number of china services depicting Danish castles and referring to the Imerco anniversary. Very strict quality standards were prescribed by Imerco and Broadhurst was left with some 1,000 sub-standard sets, which Broadhurst was permitted to sell only outside Denmark. Nevertheless 300 of them found their way via a parallel importer from the UK to Dansk Supermarked, which retailed them in its stores.

Imerco sought relief against infringement of its Danish copyright and trade mark, and against conduct contrary to approved market usage (by virtue of the Danish Marketing Act of 1974). Under Art.177, the Danish court referred the question whether those Danish provisions could be applied, having regard to provisions of the Treaty of Rome. The European Court of Justice referred to its Terrapin *decision (below, 6.2.3.4) and continued:*

12   The first part of the reply to the question submitted must therefore be that Articles 30 and 36 of the EEC Treaty must be interpreted to mean that the judicial authorities of a Member State may not prohibit, on the basis of a copyright or of a trade mark, the marketing on the territory of that State of a product to which one of those rights applies if that product has been lawfully marketed on the territory of another Member State by the proprietor of such rights or with his consent.

13   The Danish Law of June 14, 1974 upon which Imerco relies, requires undertakings in their dealings to comply with the requirements of approved marketing usage. It authorises the competent courts to issue injunctions prohibiting all acts in breach of the provisions of the law and prescribed penalties for breach of such injunctions. As the Danish Government has explained, that Law is comparable in certain respects to the legislation in force in other Member States against unfair competition, but it has in addition other objectives in that sphere, in particular the protection of consumers.

14   The question submitted by the Højesteret is intended to establish whether it is possible to consider as contrary to approved marketing usage the sale in Denmark of goods marketed in another Member State with the agreement of a Danish undertaking but subject to the condition that the goods must not be exported to Denmark so as to compete there with goods marketed exclusively by the undertaking concerned.

15   In order to reply to that question it must first of all be remarked that Community law does not in principle have the effect of preventing the application in a Member State to goods imported from other Member States of the provisions on marketing in force in the State of importation. It follows that the marketing of imported goods may be prohibited if the conditions on which they are sold constitutes an infringement of the marketing usages considered proper and fair in the Member State of importation.

16   It must nevertheless be emphasised, as the Court of Justice has stressed in another context in its judgment of November 25, 1971 (*Béguelin*, Case 22/71, [1971] ECR 949), that the actual fact of the importation of goods which have been lawfully marketed in another Member State cannot be considered as an improper or unfair act since that

description may be attached only to offer or exposure for sale on the basis of circumstances distinct from the importation itself.

17   It must furthermore be remarked that it is impossible in any circumstances for agreements between individuals to derogate from the mandatory provisions of the Treaty on the free movement of goods. It follows that an agreement involving a prohibition on the importation into a Member State of goods lawfully marketed in another Member State may not be relied upon or taken into consideration in order to classify the marketing of such goods as an improper or unfair commercial practice.

18   The second part of the reply to the question submitted must thus be that Article 30 of the Treaty must be interpreted as meaning that the importation into a Member State of goods lawfully marketed in another Member State cannot as such be classified as an improper or unfair commercial practice, without prejudice however to the possible application of legislation of the State of importation against such practices on the ground of the circumstance or methods of offering such goods for sale as distinct from the actual fact of importation; and

That an agreement between individuals intended to prohibit the importation of such goods may not be relied upon or taken into consideration in order to classify the marketing of such goods as an improper or unfair commercial practice.

6.2.2.2   *Musik Vertrieb Membran v GEMA* [1981] E.C.R. 147; [1981] 2 C.M.L.R. 44, ECJ

The GEMA, as well as being the performing right society of West Germany, licenses the mechanical recording rights of music in its repertoire. In the UK, this function is carried out for music copyright owners (mainly individual publishers) by an agency, the Mechanical Copyright Society (MCPS). Where MCPS licensed the production of records of copyright music in the UK its royalty was 6.25 per cent of the net retail selling price, the level set in the Copyright Act 1956, s.8, for the statutory licence there conferred (a provision of the law abandoned in the Copyright, Designs and Patents Act 1988). On records exported from the UK to Germany, MCPS failed to secure payment of an additional royalty representing the difference between the royalty obtained there by the GEMA (over 8 per cent) and 6.25 per cent. GEMA accordingly sought to use its rights under German law to prevent the importation of such records into Germany. The importers' reliance on the free movement of goods Articles of the Treaty of Rome led the German Supreme Court to refer this issue under Art.234 (ex-177).

The European Court of Justice stated:

10   It is apparent from the well-established case-law of the Court and most recently from the judgment of June 22, 1976 in *Terrapin*, (below, 6.2.3.4), that the proprietor of an industrial or commercial property right protected by the law of a Member State cannot rely on that law to prevent the importation of a product which has been lawfully marketed in another Member State by the proprietor himself or with his consent.

11   In the proceedings before the Court the French Government has argued that that case-law cannot be applied to copyright, which comprises *inter alia* the right of an author to claim authorship of the work and to object to any distortion, mutilation or other alteration thereof, or any other action in relation to the said work which would be prejudicial to his honour or reputation. It is contended that, in thus conferring extended protection, copyright is not comparable to other industrial and commercial property rights such as patents or trade-marks.

12 It is true that copyright comprises moral rights of the kind indicated by the French Government. However, it also comprises other rights, notably the right to exploit commercially the marketing of the protected work, particularly in the form of licences granted in return for payment of royalties. It is this economic aspect of copyright which is the subject of the question submitted by the national court and, in this regard, in the application of Article 36 of the Treaty there is no reason to make a distinction between copyright and other industrial and commercial property rights.

13 While the commercial exploitation of copyright is a source of remuneration for the owner it also constitutes a form of control on marketing exercisable by the owner, the copyright management societies acting in his name and the grantees of licences. From this point of view commercial exploitation of copyright raises the same issues as that of any other industrial or commercial property right.

14 The argument put to the Court by the Belgian and Italian Governments that in the absence of harmonisation in this sector the principle of the territoriality of copyright laws always prevails over the principle of freedom of movement of goods within the Common Market cannot be accepted. Indeed, the essential purpose of the Treaty, which is to unite national markets into a single market, could not be attained if, under the various legal systems of the Member States, nationals of those Member States were able to partition the market and bring about arbitrary discrimination or disguised restrictions on trade between Member States.

15 It follows from the foregoing considerations that neither the copyright owner or his licensee, nor a copyright management society acting in the owner's or licensee's name, may rely on the exclusive exploitation right conferred by copyright to prevent or restrict the importation of sound recordings which have been lawfully marketed in another Member State by the owner himself or with his consent.

16 GEMA has argued that such an interpretation of Articles 30 and 36 of the Treaty is not sufficient to resolve the problem facing the national court since GEMA's application to the German courts is not for the prohibition or restriction of the marketing of the gramophone records and tape cassettes in question on German territory but for equality in the royalties paid for any distribution of those sound recordings on the German market. The owner of a copyright in a recorded musical work has a legitimate interest in receiving and retaining the benefit of his intellectual or artistic effort regardless of the degree to which his work is distributed and consequently it is maintained that he should not lose the right to claim royalties equal to those paid in the country in which the recorded work is marketed.

17 It should first be observed that the question put by the national court is concerned with the legal consequences of infringement of copyright. GEMA seeks damages for that infringement pursuant to the applicable national legislation and it is immaterial whether the *quantum* of damages which it seeks is calculated according to the difference between the rate of royalty payable to distribution in the national market and the rate of royalty paid in the country of manufacture or in any other manner. On any view its claims are in fact founded on the copyright owner's exclusive right of exploitation, which enables him to prohibit or restrict the free movement of the products incorporating the protected musical work.

18 It should be observed next that no provision of national legislation may permit an undertaking which is responsible for the management of copyrights and has a monopoly on the territory of a Member State by virtue of that management to charge a levy on products imported from another Member State where they were put into circulation by or with the consent of the copyright owner and thereby cause the Common Market to be partitioned. Such a practice would amount to allowing a private undertaking to impose a charge on the importation of sound recordings which are already in free circulation in the Common Market on account of their crossing a frontier; it would therefore have the effect of entrenching the isolation of national markets which the Treaty seeks to abolish.

19 It follows from those considerations that this argument must be rejected as being

incompatible with the operation of the Common Market and with the aims of the Treaty.

On the effect of the UK Act, s.8, the court stated:

24 As the Court held in another context in its judgment of October 31, 1974 in *Centrafarm v Sterling Drug* [1974] E.C.R. 1147, the existence of a disparity between national laws which is capable of distorting competition between Member States cannot justify a Member State's giving legal protection to practices of a private body which are incompatible with the rules concerning free movement of goods.

25 It should further be observed that in a common market distinguished by free movement of goods and freedom to provide services an author, acting directly or through his publisher, is free to choose the place, in any of the Member States, in which to put his work into circulation. He may make that choice according to his best interests, which involve not only the level of remuneration provided in the Member State in question but other factors such as, for example, the opportunities for distributing his work and the marketing facilities which are further enhanced by virtue of the free movement of goods within the Community. In those circumstances, a copyright management society may not be permitted to claim, on the importation of sound recordings into another Member State, payment of additional fees based on the difference in the rates of remuneration existing in the various Member States.

26 It follows from the foregoing considerations that the disparities which continue to exist in the absence of any harmonisation of national rules on the commercial exploitation of copyrights may not be used to impede the free movement of goods in the Common Market.

The answer to the question put by the Bundesgerichtshof should therefore be that Articles 30 and 36 of the Treaty must be interpreted as precluding the application of national legislation under which a copyright management society empowered to exercise the copyrights of composers of musical work reproduced on gramophone records or other sound recordings in another Member State is permitted to invoke those rights where those sound recordings are distributed on the national market after having been put into circulation in that other Member State by or with the consent of the owners of those copyrights, in order to claim payment of a fee equal to the royalties ordinarily paid for marketing on the national market less the lower royalties paid in the Member State of manufacture.

6.2.2.3 *Pharmon v Hoechst* [1985] E.C.R. 2281; [1985] 3 C.M.L.R. 775, ECJ

Hoechst held patents in the UK and the Netherlands for the drug, frusemide. Under the former compulsory licensing provision of UK law, relating specifically to food and medicine patents (Patents Act 1949, s.41; repealed in 1977), DDSA obtained authority to manufacture and sell frusemide in the UK; but the compulsory licence was subject to a prohibition against export. Despite this limitation, DDSA exported batches of frusemide to Pharmon in the Netherlands, claiming the right to do so under Art.28 (ex-30) of the Rome Treaty. On reference of questions by the Dutch Supreme Court, the European Court of Justice held as follows:

14 The Hoge Raad's first question asks in substance whether Articles 30 and 36 of the EEC Treaty preclude the application of legal provisions of a Member State which give a patent proprietor the right to prevent the marketing in that State of a product which has been manufactured in another Member State by the holder of a compulsory licence granted in respect of a parallel patent held by the same proprietor.

22 It must be recalled that the court has consistently held that Articles 30 and 36 of the EEC Treaty preclude the application of national provisions which enable a patent proprietor to prevent the importation and marketing of a product which has been lawfully marketed in another Member State by the patent proprietor himself, with his consent, or by a person economically or legally dependent on him.

23 If a patent proprietor could preclude the importation of protected products marketed in another Member State by him or with his consent, he would be able to partition the national markets and thus restrict trade between the Member States, although such a restriction is not necessary to protect the substance of his exclusive rights under the parallel patents.

24 The Hoge Raad's question is therefore essentially intended to establish whether the same rules apply where the product imported and offered for sale has been manufactured in the exporting Member State by the holder of a compulsory licence granted in respect of a parallel patent held by the proprietor of the patent in the importing Member State.

25 It is necessary to point out that where, as in this instance, the competent authorities of a Member State grant a third party a compulsory licence which allows him to carry out manufacturing and marketing operations which the patentee would normally have the right to prevent, the patentee cannot be deemed to have consented to the operation of that third party. Such a measure deprives the patent proprietor of his right to determine freely the conditions under which he markets his products.

26 As the Court held most recently in its judgment of July 14, 1981 (*Merck v Stephar*), the substance of a patent right lies essentially in according the inventor an exclusive right of first placing the product on the market so as to allow him to obtain the reward for his creative effort. It is therefore necessary to allow the patent proprietor to prevent the importation and marketing of products manufactured under a compulsory licence in order to protect the substance of his exclusive rights under his patent.

27 Consequently, in reply to Question 1 it must be stated that Articles 30 and 36 of the EEC Treaty do not preclude the application of legal provisions of a Member State which gives a patent proprietor the right to prevent the marketing in that state of a product which has been manufactured in another Member State by the holder of a compulsory licence granted in respect of a parallel patent held by the same proprietor.

28 Questions 2 and 3 ask essentially whether the reply to Question 1 depends, in the first place, on whether the authorities of the Member State which granted the compulsory licence have attached to it a prohibition on exportation and secondly, on whether the compulsory licence provides for a system of royalties for the patentee and whether he has actually accepted or received such royalties.

29 It is sufficient to state that the limits referred to above imposed by Community law on the application of the law of the importing Member State in no way depend on the conditions attached by the competent authorities of the exporting Member State to the grant of the compulsory licence.

30 It follows that in reply to Question 2 and 3 it must be stated that it makes no difference to the reply to Question 1 whether a prohibition on exportation is attached to the compulsory licence, whether that licence fixes royalties payable to the patentee or whether the patentee has accepted or refused such royalties.

6.2.2.4   *Allen & Hanburys v Generics* **[1988] E.C.R. 1245; [1988] 1 C.M.L.R. 701, ECJ**

Under the Patents Act 1977, certain pre-1978 patents would have their terms extended from 16 to 20 years. However, during the additional four years they would be endorsed "licences of right" and a competitor seeking such a licence could have its terms set, if necessary, by the Comptroller-General of Patents, in accordance with s.46. Allen & Hanburys held such a patent for an asthma treatment drug and Generics sought a licence of right under it. While applying to the Comptroller, Generics informed Allen & Hanburys of its intention to import the drug from Italy where it was unpatented; and this led to infringement proceedings.

Section 46(3) provided that if an alleged infringer undertook to obtain a licence of right under an endorsed patent no injunction against infringement should be granted; and any damages should be limited to at most double the amount payable under the licence. This however did not apply to an infringement by importation.

The principal question referred by the House of Lords to the European Court of Justice concerned the double distinction drawn by s.46(3) between the infringing acts of a competitor in the U.K. and those of a competitor importing from another Common Market country. As to this the European Court of Justice stated:

14   In those circumstances it must be considered that the power of national courts to prohibit the importation of the product in question may be justified under the provisions of Article 36 on the protection of industrial and commercial property only if that prohibition is necessary in order to ensure that the proprietor of such a patent has, *vis-à-vis* importers, the same rights as he enjoys as against producers who manufacture the product in the national territory, that is to say the right to a fair return from his patent.

15   That is therefore the test which must be applied in examining the merits of a number of arguments raised before the court, both by Allen & Hanburys and by the United Kingdom, in order to justify an injunction prohibiting imports granted against an importer-infringer.

16   It has been observed in the first place that an importer may have no substantial presence in the importing member state, in particular where his assets and employees are not subject to the jurisdiction of that state. An injunction prohibiting him from importing the product is then justified until the patent proprietor has been guaranteed actual payment of the sums due to him.

17   However, that argument cannot be accepted in the case of a member state where, under the relevant legislation, the fact that manufacturers based in its territory do not have adequate assets cannot justify the grant of an injunction against them until they have offered guarantees of payment. For a manufacturer based in the territory of a member state as well as for an importer such guarantees of payment can only be included among the terms fixed in the licensing agreement or, in default of an agreement, by the competent national authority.

18   It has also been maintained that an injunction prohibiting imports may be justified by the difficulty of carrying out checks on the origin and quantities of goods imported, on the basis of which the royalties payable to the patent proprietor must be calculated.

19   However, it should be pointed out that it may also be difficult to check the quantity of goods marketed even when they are manufactured within the national territory and yet no injunction or interdict is possible in those circumstances. It is therefore a matter for the licensing agreement alone or, in default of agreement, for the competent national authority to lay down detailed rules to enable the patent proprietor to check the supporting documents produced by the importer regarding the purchase, import and sale of the product.

20   Finally, it has been maintained that an injunction prohibiting imports may be justified

in order to enable the patent proprietor to check on the quality of an imported medicine in the interests of public health.

21   It must be observed, however, that that consideration has nothing to do with protection of the exclusive rights of the patent proprietor and, therefore, may not be relied on in order to justify, on grounds of protection of industrial and commercial property, a restriction on trade between member states.

22   It must therefore be concluded that an injunction issued against an importer-infringer in the circumstances described by the national court would constitute arbitrary discrimination prohibited by Article 36 of the Treaty and could not be justified on grounds of the protection of industrial and commercial property.

In response to further questions from the House of Lords the European Court of Justice also ruled:

(a) *that Arts 28 and 30 (ex-30, 36) prohibited the Comptroller from restricting a licence of right so as to exclude importation from another Member State;*

(b) *that it was irrelevant that the patented product was a pharmaceutical drug and that it came from a state where it was not patentable;*

(c) *that there were no imperative grounds of consumer protection or fair trading which could justify any exception being admitted under Art.30 itself in the distinction between domestic and imported products created by s.46.*

6.2.2.5   *Thetford v Fiamma* [1988] E.C.R. 3585; [1989] 3 C.M.L.R. 549, ECJ

Under the Patents Act 1949, the novelty and inventiveness of a patent was to be judged against a state of the art which excluded the content of UK and other patent specifications published more than 50 years before the priority date in issue (s.50(1)—a provision which does not affect patents governed by the 1977 Act).

Thetford owned a patent for portable lavatories, which was arguably anticipated in seven citations which were excluded from consideration by s.50(1) in the UK even though they would have been a proper basis of objection in most other Community States.

Fiamma imported infringing lavatories from Italy. When sued it sought inter alia to plead that it was not liable to an injunction because s.50(1) operated in a manner which could not be justified under Art.36 of the Rome Treaty.

The English Court of Appeal first asked whether a UK patent which would have been anticipated but for the provisions of s.50(1) constituted "industrial or commercial property" entitled to protection under Art.36.

After referring in general terms to Arts 28 and 30 (ex-30, 36), the European Court of Justice continued:

11   Fiamma argues that the derogation provided for in Article 36 can apply only if a

patent right granted pursuant to national legislation fulfils certain fundamental conditions. In particular, a patent granted in the absence of novelty or an inventive step cannot be regarded as being covered by the expression "protection of industrial and commercial property".

12 In that regard, it must be observed, as the court held in *Keurkoop BV v Nancy Kean Gifts BV*, [above, 6.2.1.5], on the protection of designs, that—
> "in the present state of Community law and in the absence of Community standardisation or of a harmonisation of laws the determination of the conditions and procedures under which protection . . . is granted is a matter for national rules . . ."

13 However, Fiamma contends that the court's case law on designs may not be transposed to the field of patents in view of the higher degree of harmonisation of national legislation which has already been achieved in that field and the existence of international conventions based on the principle of absolute novelty.

14 That argument cannot be upheld. First, no harmonisation of the patents legislation of the member states has yet been effected by virtue of measures of Community law. Secondly, none of the international conventions in force on patents is capable of supporting Fiamma's argument. The entry into force of the Convention on the Grant of European Patents (the European Patent Convention) (Munich, October 5, 1973; TS 20 (1978); Cmnd. 7090), which is based on the principle of absolute novelty, did not affect the existence of national legislation on the granting of patents. Article 2(2) of that convention expressly provides that "The European patent shall, in each of the Contracting States for which it is granted, have the effect of and be subject to the same conditions as a national patent granted by that State". As for the Convention on the Unification of Certain Points of Substantive Law on Patents for Invention (Strasbourg, November 27, 1963; TS 70 (1980); Cmnd. 8002), it must be pointed out that, since that convention entered into force after the patent in question had been granted, it cannot serve as a determining factor for the purposes of the interpretation of Community law. The only instrument the provisions of which might afford support for Fiamma's point of view with regard to the recognition in the Community legal order of the principle of absolute novelty is the Convention for the Patent for the Common Market (the Community Patent Convention) (Luxembourg, December 15, 1975; (1976) E.C. 18; Cmnd. 6553), which has close links with the aforementioned Munich Convention but which has not yet entered into force.

15 It follows that, as the court held in *Parke Davis & Co v Probel* Case 24/67 [1968] E.C.R. 55, since the existence of patent rights is at present a matter solely of national law, a member state's patents legislation, such as the legislation at issue, is covered in principle by the derogations from Article 30 which are provided for in Article 36.

16 It must next be considered whether the application of the principle at issue may not constitute a means of arbitrary discrimination or a disguised restriction on trade between member states within the meaning of the second sentence of Article 36.

17 As regards the first possibility, namely whether a means of arbitrary discrimination is involved, it is sufficient, in order to refute that argument, to point out that before the court the agent of the United Kingdom stated, without being contradicted by the other parties, that the application of section 50(1) of the Patents Act 1949 does not give rise to any discrimination. On the one hand, that rule prevents consideration from being given to a specification disclosing an invention whether it was filed in the United Kingdom or in another state; secondly, there is no discrimination based on the nationality of applicants for patents: foreign nationals applying for patents in the United Kingdom have the same rights as United Kingdom nationals.

18 It must further be considered whether the application of the principle in question may not give rise to a disguised restriction on trade between member states.

19 In that regard, the justification for the rule of relative novelty, as given in the documents before the court, disclose that the objective pursued by the United Kingdom legislature in introducing the "50-year rule" in 1902 was to foster creative activity on

the part of inventors in the interest of industry. To that end, the "50-year rule" aimed to make it possible to give a reward, in the form of the grant of a patent, even in cases in which an "old" invention was "rediscovered". In such cases the United Kingdom legislation was designed to prevent the existence of a former patent specification which had never been utilised or published from constituting a ground for revoking a patent which had been validly issued.

20   Consequently, a rule such as the "50-year rule" cannot be regarded as constituting a disguised restriction on trade between member states.

21   In view of the foregoing considerations, the answer to the national court's first question must be that, in the present state of Community law, Article 36 must be interpreted as not precluding the application of a member state's legislation on patents which provides that a patent granted for an invention may not be declared invalid by reason only of the fact that the invention in question appears in a patent specification filed more than 50 years previously.

The question was also raised whether under Art.36 it was permissible only to award monetary compensation but not to enjoin importation of infringing pro- ducts from another Member State.

23   Fiamma maintains in that connection that the "rule of proportionality" as defined in the case law of the court and, in particular, by *de Peijper* Case 104/75 [1976] E.C.R. 613 should also be applied in the field of industrial and commercial property. In particular, in view of the particular features of the case at issue, in which the protection conferred by Article 36 relates to a patent obtained by virtue of the rule of relative novelty, the specific subject matter of the patent is already adequately protected by conferring on the proprietor of the patent the right to obtain reward for the marketing of the patented article without going so far as to give him the right to obtain an injunction.

24   However, it must be observed in that connection that according to the case law of the court (most recently in *Pharmon BV v Hoechst AG* Case 19/84 [1985] E.C.R. 2281) the right of the proprietor of a patent to prevent the importation and marketing of pro- ducts manufactured under a compulsory licence is part of the substance of patents law. There is all the more reason for that conclusion to apply in a case such as this where no licence has been granted by the proprietor of the patent in the country of manufacture.

6.2.2.6   *Warner Brothers v Christiansen* [1988] E.C.R. 2605, ECJ

Warner Brothers assigned their Danish copyright in the film, "Never Say Never Again", to an associate company. Together they sued the defendant for hiring out a video of the film contrary to the rental right which formed part of the copyright in Danish law. The defendant had bought the video in the UK at a time when there was no equivalent rental right in that country and when copies could not be purchased or hired in Denmark. The defendant claimed that enforce- ment of the Danish right offended Arts 28 and 30 (ex-30, 36) of the Rome Treaty.

The E.C.J. held:

9   It should be noted that, unlike the national copyright legislation which gave rise to the judgment of 20 January 1981 in Joined Cases 55 and 57/80 (*Musik-Vertrieb Membran v GEMA* [1981] E.C.R. 147), the legislation which gives rise to the present preliminary question does not enable the author to collect an additional fee on the actual importation of recordings of protected works which are marketed with his consent in

another Member State, or to set up any further obstacle whatsoever to importation or resale. The rights and powers conferred on the author by the national legislation in question comes into operation only after importation has been carried out.

10   None the less, it must be observed that the commercial distribution of video-cassettes takes the form not only of sale but also, and increasingly, that of hiring-out to individuals who possess video-tape recorders. The right to prohibit such hiring-out in a Member State is therefore liable to influence trade in video-cassettes in that State and hence, indirectly, to affect intra-Community trade in those products. Legislation of the kind which gave rise to the main proceedings must therefore, in the light of established case-law, be regarded as a measure having an effect equivalent to a quantitative restriction on imports, which is prohibited by Article 30 of the Treaty.

11   Consideration should therefore be given to whether such legislation may be considered justified on grounds of the protection of industrial and commercial property within the meaning of Article 36—a term which was held by the Court, in its judgment of 6 October 1982 in Case 262/81 (*Coditel v Ciné-Vog* [1982] E.C.R. 3381), to include literary and artistic property.

12   In that connection it should first be noted that the Danish legislation applies without distinction to video-cassettes produced *in situ* and video-cassettes imported from another Member State. The determining factor for the purposes of its application is the type of transaction in video-cassettes which is in question, not the origin of those video-cassettes. Such legislation does not therefore, in itself, operate any arbitrary discrimination in trade between Member States.

13   It should further be pointed out that literary and artistic works may be the subject of commercial exploitation, whether by way of public performance or of the reproduction and marketing of the recordings made of them, and this is true in particular of cinematographic works. The two essential rights of the author, namely the exclusive right of performance and the exclusive right of reproduction, are not called in question by the rules of the Treaty.

14   Lastly, consideration must be given to the emergence, demonstrated by the Commission, of a specific market for the hiring-out of such recordings, as distinct from their sale. The existence of that market was made possible by various factors such as the improvement of manufacturing methods for video-cassettes which increased their strength and life in use, the growing awareness amongst viewers that they watch only occasionally the video-cassettes which they have bought and, lastly, their relatively high purchase price. The market for the hiring-out of video-cassettes reaches a wider public than the market for their sale and, at present, offers great potential as a source of revenue for makers of films.

15   However, it is apparent that, by authorizing the collection of royalties only on sales to private individuals and to persons hiring out video-cassettes, it is impossible to guarantee to makers of films a remuneration which reflects the number of occasions on which the video-cassettes are actually hired out and which secures for them a satisfactory share of the rental market. That explains why, as the Commission points out in its observations, certain national laws have recently provided specific protection of the right to hire out video-cassettes.

16   Laws of that kind are therefore clearly justified on grounds of the protection of industrial and commercial property pursuant to Article 36 of the Treaty.

17   However, the defendant in the main proceedings, relying on the judgments of 22 January 1981 in Case 58/80 (*Dansk Supermarked v Imerco* [1981] E.C.R. 181) and of 20 January 1981 (*Musik-Vertrieb Membran v GEMA*, cited above), contends that the author is at liberty to choose the Member State in which he will market his work. The defendant in the main proceedings emphasizes that the author makes his choice according to his own interests and must, in particular, take into consideration the fact that the legislation of certain Member States, unlike that of certain others, confers on him an exclusive right enabling him to restrain the hiring-out of the recording of the work even when that work has been offered for sale with his consent. That being so, a

maker of a film who has offered the video-cassette of that film for sale in a Member State whose legislation confers on him no exclusive right of hiring it out (as in the main proceedings) must accept the consequences of his choice and the exhaustion of his right to restrain the hiring-out of that video-cassette in any other Member State.

18   That objection cannot be upheld. It follows from the foregoing consideration that, where national legislation confers on authors a specific right to hire out video-cassettes, that right would be rendered worthless if its owner were not in a position to authorize the operations for doing so. It cannot therefore be accepted that the marketing by a film-maker of a video-cassette containing one of his works, in a Member State which does not provide specific protection for the right to hire it out, should have repercussions on the right conferred on that same film-maker by the legislation of another Member State to restrain, in that State, the hiring-out of that video-cassette.

6.2.2.7   *Basset v SACEM* [1987] E.C.R. 1747; [1987] 3 C.M.L.R. 173, ECJ

The French Copyright Law of 1957, Art. 31, requires that, upon the transfer of a copy of a copyright work, the extent and purpose of its use should be defined. From this has grown the practice of selling recordings for private use only, the object being to require a separate, supplementary fee under the reproduction right (the so-called droit de destination) for public performance or broadcasting of the recording of the work in addition to a licence fee under the performing right in respect of the same use. Only in Belgium is there a similar practice. Thus the French collecting society for composers, SACEM, demanded of discothèque owners a licence fee of 8.25 per cent of receipts, comprising 6.6 per cent performance fee and 1.65 per cent supplementary mechanical reproduction fee. This applied equally to legitimate recordings purchased in other EC countries and imported into France.

The Cour de Cassation raised the legitimacy of the second charge in relation to Arts 28 and 30 (ex-30, 36) of the Rome Treaty before the European Court of Justice which held:

12   It appears from the judgment of the national court that the "supplementary mechanical reproduction fee" with which the preliminary questions are concerned is charged not on the importation or marketing of records or other sound recordings but by reason of their public use, for example by a radio station, in a discothèque or in a device such as a juke-box installed in a public place. The problem raised by the national court lies in the fact that in such circumstances that royalty is charged in addition to a performance royalty.

13   The national court asks whether Articles 30 and 36 or Article 86 of the Treaty prohibits the charging of such an aggregate fee where the sound recordings were manufactured and marketed in a Member State where there is no such aggregation of fees and only a performance royalty is charged on the public use of a recorded work. That is the hypothesis that must be examined.

14   It is undisputed that, as is normally the case with regard to copyright management, on the basis of the applicable international conventions, the aggregation of a performance fee and a supplementary mechanical reproduction fee charged on the public use in France of a recorded musical work takes place whether the records are of French origin or are manufactured or marketed in another Member State. It is true that public use in another Member State may give rise only to the collection of a performance royalty in favour of the author and the record manufacturer, but that circumstance does not imply that the amount of the royalty charged or its function are different from those of the royalties charged in France on such use.

15 In other words, disregarding the concepts used by French legislation and practice, the supplementary mechanical reproduction fee may thus be analysed as constituting part of the payment for an author's rights over the public performance of a recorded musical work. Moreover, the amount of that royalty, like that of the performance fee strictly so called, is calculated on the basis of the discothèque's turnover and not the number of records bought or played.

16 It follows that, even if the charging of the fee in question were to be capable of having a restrictive effect on imports, it does not constitute a measure having equivalent effect prohibited under Article 30 of the Treaty inasmuch as it must be regarded as a normal exploitation of copyright and does not constitute a means of arbitrary discrimination or a disguised restriction on trade between Member States for the purposes of Article 36 of the Treaty.

The court proceeded to hold that the act of charging the second fee did not of itself amount to an abuse of SACEM's dominant position as the sole French collecting society for composers.

6.2.2.8 *Industrie Diensten Groep v Beele* [1982] E.C.R. 707; [1982] 3 C.M.L.R. 102, ECJ

Beele was the sole importer into the Netherlands of a cable-duct system, MCT, produced by a Swedish firm and until 1975 protected by patent. After that year, a German firm began to produce a rival product, SVT, which was virtually identical in all aspects, including appearance. This was imported to the Netherlands by Industrie Diensten Groep, against whom Beele instituted proceedings for unfair competition based on a slavish imitation of products which would mislead purchasers as to source. The Court of Appeal of the Hague raised the question whether an injunction against such conduct under Dutch law was compatible with the rules on free movement of goods in the Rome Treaty.

The European Court of Justice stated:

2 The question was raised in the context of an action between a Netherlands undertaking, the sole importer of cable ducts manufactured in Sweden which have been marketed in the Netherlands since 1963, and another Netherlands undertaking which since 1978 has marketed in the Netherlands cable ducts manufactured in the Federal Republic of Germany. The case file shows that the Swedish cable ducts were previously protected by patent rights in the Federal Republic of Germany, the Netherlands and elsewhere, and that the German cable ducts were first made and imported into the Netherlands after the period of validity of those patents had expired.

3 The first-mentioned undertaking applied to the President of the Arrondissementsrechtbank [District Court], The Hague, for interlocutory relief against the second undertaking on the ground that the German cable ducts were a precise imitation of the Swedish cable ducts and sought an order from him restraining the defendant from marketing the German cable ducts or causing them to be marketed in the Netherlands.

4 The President of the Arrondissementsrechtbank granted the application whereupon the second undertaking appealed to the Gerechtshof, The Hague. According to the judgment making the reference for a preliminary ruling, that court arrived at the provisional view that the German manufacturer could have designed a cable-duct system different from the Swedish system without impairing the quality of its product economically or technically and by not doing so had caused the two products to be

confused. The Gerechtshof accordingly considers that the President of the Arrondis-sementsrechtbank rightly decided that under Netherlands law the German product is a precise imitation of the Swedish cable ducts. Since the appellant claimed that the cable ducts which it sold were lawfully marketed in another Member State and that the respondent's action was therefore contrary to Articles 30 to 36 of the EEC Treaty, the Gerechtshof decided to ask the Court the following question:
"Assuming that:

    (a) A trader, A, markets products in the Netherlands which are no longer covered by any patent and which for no compelling reason are practically identical with products which have been marketed for a considerable period of time in the Netherlands by another trader, B, and which are different from similar kinds of articles, and in so doing trader A needlessly causes confusion:

    (b) Under Netherlands law trader A is thereby competing unfairly with trader B and acting unlawfully;

    (c) Netherlands law gives trader B the right to obtain an injunction on that ground restraining trader A from continuing to market the products in the Netherlands;

    (d) The products of trader B are manufactured in Sweden and those of trader A in the Federal Republic of Germany;

    (e) Trader A imports his products from the Federal Republic of Germany in which those products are lawfully put on the market by someone other than trader B, the Swedish manufacturer, someone who is associated with one of them or by someone who is authorised to do so by one of them,

do the rules contained in the EEC Treaty on the free movement of goods, notwith-standing the provisions of Article 36 thereof, then prevent trader B from obtaining such an injunction against trader A?"

5   The case-file shows that, just like protection against precise imitation in the law of most other Member States, the rule of Netherlands law to which the question refers has been developed chiefly by the courts. As the Commission has pointed out, no effort has been made hitherto at Community level to harmonise national rules against precise imitation. Therefore an examination of the question whether such protection accords with the rules of the Treaty on the free movement of goods should be confined to the way in which that protection is provided in Netherlands law, as described in the judgment of the Gerechtshof.

6   That judgment shows that, subject to the answer to be given to the question raised, the Gerechtshof is prepared to uphold the injunction against the marketing in the Neth-erlands of products which it presumes have been lawfully marketed in another Member State.

7   Such an injunction constitutes an obstacle to the free movement of goods between the Member States and in principle is caught by Article 30 which prohibits all measures having an effect equivalent to quantitative restrictions on imports. However, the Court has repeatedly held (for example, in the judgment of February 20, 1979 in Case 120/1978, the *Cassis de Dijon* case, [1979] E.C.R. 649 and in the judgment of June 17, 1981 in Case 113/80 *Commission v Ireland* [1981] E.C.R. 1625) that in the absence of common rules relating to the production and marketing of products, obstacles to movement within the Community resulting from disparities between national legis-lation must be accepted in so far as such legislation, applying without discrimination to both domestic and imported products, may be justified as being necessary in order to satisfy mandatory requirements relating in particular to the protection of con-sumers and fairness in commercial transactions. Therefore the protection against imitation provided in the way described in the judgment making the reference for a preliminary ruling must be examined to determine whether it meets those conditions.

8   Although the main action concerns the protection of a product manufactured in a non-member country against the marketing of a product manufactured in a Member

State, according to the national court the application of case-law does not depend on country of origin of the product imitated and country of origin of the imitation. What is more, there is nothing in the judgment of the national court from which it may be inferred that that case-law is applied in a manner adapted to the specific needs of national products thereby putting imported products at a disadvantage. Therefore it must be assumed that the case-law referred to by the national court applies without distinction to national and imported products.

9   National case-law prohibiting the precise imitation of someone else's product which is likely to cause confusion may indeed protect consumers and promote fair trading; these are general interests which, according to the decisions of the Court cited above, may justify the existence of obstacles to movement within the Community resulting from disparities between national laws relating to the marketing of products. That such a rule does meet mandatory requirements is moreover borne out by the fact that it accords with the principle underlying Article 10 bis of the Paris Convention for the Protection of Industrial Property, as last revised on July 14, 1967 at Stockholm, which prohibits *inter alia* all acts of such a nature as to create confusion with the goods of a competitor, and by the fact that this rule is recognised in principle in the case-law of most Member States.

10   In order to answer the question whether case-law such as that described in the judgment of the Gerechtshof is necessary to achieve the aforesaid objectives, or whether it goes beyond the limit which they may justify, the manner in which that case-law is applied, as described in the judgment, should be scrutinised.

11   As to that, the very wording of the question submitted shows first that in the provisional view of the national court the products which it intends to prohibit from being marketed are for no compelling reason practically identical to the products imitated and that the appellant in the main action thereby needlessly causes confusion. Furthermore, the judgment of the national court shows that the question whether or not such imitation is necessary was considered not only from the technical point of view, but also from the economic and commercial point of view.

12   Secondly, it is apparent from the wording of the question submitted and from the case-file that there is no indication of an agreement or of dependence between the Swedish manufacturer of the original product and the German manufacturer of the product which is supposed to be an imitation thereof and the marketing of which in the Netherlands is in dispute.

13   Where the circumstances mentioned by the national court are met a body of case-law prohibiting precise imitation of someone else's product may not be regarded as exceeding the scope of the mandatory requirements which the protection of consumers and the fairness of commercial transactions constitute.

14   The appellant in the main action has raised before the Court the question of spare parts. It points out that the cable ducts are installed not only in buildings but also in ships and an injunction against the marketing of the German product in the Netherlands would make it necessary to carry out repairs on ships in the Netherlands using spare parts for the Swedish product, even if the ship is fitted with German cable ducts. Since this question has not been raised by the national court and the respondent in the main action has indicated during the procedure before the Court that the injunction which it seeks does not relate to spare parts for the repair of the German cable ducts, it is not necessary to resolve this question for which the foregoing considerations are not necessarily conclusive.

6.2.2.9   *Volvo v Veng* [1988] E.C.R. 6211, ECJ

Volvo, the proprietor in the UK of a registered design for the front wings of Volvo series 200 cars, instituted proceedings against Veng before the High Court of Justice for infringement of its sole and exclusive rights. Veng imported the same

*body panels, manufactured without authority from Volvo, and marketed them in
the UK. By way of defence, Veng alleged that this assertion of right constituted
on abuse of dominant position contrary to Art.82 (ex-86).*

*Of three questions put to the European Court of Justice under Art.234 (ex-177),
the court found it necessary to answer the second:*

[Assuming that Volvo was in a dominant position], Is it prima facie *an abuse of
such dominant position for such a manufacturer to refuse to license others to
supply such body panels, even where they are willing to pay a reasonable
royalty for all articles sold under the licence (such royalty to represent an award
which is just and equitable having regard to the merits of the design and all the
surrounding circumstances, and to be determined by arbitration or in such
other manner as the national court shall direct)?*

The European Court of Justice stated:

7   It must first be observed, as the court held in its judgment of September 14, 1982 [in
     Case 144/81, *Keurkoop v Nancy Kean Gifts*, above, 6.2.1.5], with respect to the pro-
     tection of designs and models, that, as Community law stands at present and in the
     absence of Community standardisation or harmonisation of laws, the determination
     of the conditions and procedures under which protection of designs and models is
     granted is a matter for national rules. It is thus for the national legislatures to
     determine which products are to benefit from protection, even where they form part of
     a unit which is already protected as such.

8   It must also be emphasised that the right of the proprietor of a protected design to
     prevent third parties from manufacturing and selling or importing, without its consent,
     products incorporating the design constitutes the very subject-matter of his exclusive
     right. It follows that an obligation imposed upon the proprietor of a protected design
     to grant to third parties, even in return for a reasonable royalty, a licence for the
     supply of products incorporating the design would lead to the proprietor thereof being
     deprived of the substance of his exclusive right, and that a refusal to grant such a
     licence cannot in itself constitute an abuse of a dominant position.

9   It must however be noted that the exercise of an exclusive right by the proprietor of a
     registered design in respect of car body panels may be prohibited by Article 86 if it
     involves, on the part of an undertaking holding a dominant position, certain abusive
     conduct such as the arbitrary refusal to supply spare parts to independent repairers, the
     fixing of prices for spare parts at an unfair level or a decision no longer to produce
     spare parts for a particular model even though many cars of that model are still in
     circulation, provided that such conduct is liable to affect trade between Member States.

10   In the present case no instance of any such conduct has been mentioned by the
     national court.

Note that in the similar case, CICRA v Renault *[1988] E.C.R. 6039, the court
held, as in previous decisions, that:*

With regard more particularly to the difference in price between the components sold by
the car manufacturer and those sold by independent producers ... the fact that the price of
the former was higher than that of the latter did not necessarily constitute an abuse, since
the proprietor of protected rights in respect of an ornamental design could legitimately
claim to be entitled to remuneration for the costs which he had incurred in perfecting the
registered design.

6.2.3   Application to Trade Mark and Related Cases

6.2.3.1   *Sirena v Eda* [1971] E.C.R. 69; [1971] C.M.L.R. 260, ECJ

Mark Allen, an American company, developed and built up an international market in "Prep" shaving cream before the second world war. In Italy it registered the mark in 1933 and in 1937 by agreement assigned it to Sirena. Thereafter, Sirena manufactured and marketed its own product under the mark, without receiving technical know-how from Mark Allen.

In Germany, Mark Allen apparently licensed use of the mark to a German company, whose products were exported to Italy by an import-export business, Novimpex. When they appeared on the Italian market. Sirena sued for infringement of its "Prep" marks. The questions submitted to the European Court of Justice by the Tribunale Civile e Penale di Milano referred to interpretation of Arts 81 and 82 (ex-85, 86) of the EEC Treaty. Concerning Art.81 (ex-85) the court stated:

5   In the sphere of provisions relating to the free movement of products, prohibitions and restrictions on imports justified on the grounds of protection of industrial and commercial property are allowed by Article 36, subject to the express condition that they "shall not, however, constitute a means of arbitrary discrimination or a disguised restriction on trade between Member States". Article 36, although it appears in the Chapter of the Treaty dealing with quantitative restrictions on trade between Member States, is based on a principle equally applicable to the question of competition, in the sense that even if the rights recognised by the legislation of a Member State on the subject of industrial and commercial property are not affected, so far as their existence is concerned, by Articles 85 and 86 of the Treaty, their exercise may still fall under the prohibitions imposed by those provisions.

The court referred to provisions concerning trade mark use in the Commission Regulation 67/67 (Exclusive Distribution Agreement Block Exemption), and continued:

7   The exercise of a trade-mark right is particularly apt to lead to a partitioning of markets, and thus to impair the free movement of goods between States which is essential to the Common Market. Moreover, a trade-mark right is distinguishable in this context from other rights of industrial and commercial property, inasmuch as the interests protected by the latter are usually more important, and merit a higher degree of protection, than the interests protected by an ordinary trade-mark.

8   The request for interpretation is primarily directed to ascertaining in what circumstances the exercise of trade-mark rights may constitute infringement of the prohibition imposed by Article 85(1).

9   By virtue of this provision, "all agreements between undertakings, decisions by association of undertakings, and concerted practices" which may affect trade between Member States, and which have as their object or effect the distortion of competition, are prohibited as incompatible with the Common Market. A trade-mark right, as a legal entity, does not in itself possess those elements of contract or concerted practice referred to in Article 85(1). Nevertheless, the exercise of that right might fall within the ambit of the prohibitions contained in the Treaty each time it manifests itself as the subject, the means or the result of a restrictive practice. When a trade-mark right is

exercised by virtue of assignments to users in one or more Member States, it is thus necessary to establish in each case whether such use leads to a situation falling under the prohibitions of Article 85.

10   Such situations may in particular arise from restrictive agreements between proprietors of trade-marks or their successors in title enabling them to prevent imports from other Member States. If the combination of assignments to different users of national trade-marks protecting the same product has the result of re-enacting impenetrable frontiers between the Member States, such practice may well affect trade between States, and distort competition in the Common Market. The matter would be different if, in order to avoid any partitioning of the market, the agreements concerning the use of national rights in respect of the same trade-mark were to be effected in such conditions as to make the general use of trade-mark rights at Community level compatible with the observance of the conditions of competition and unity of the market which are so essential to the Common Market that failure to observe them is penalised by Article 85 by a declaration that they are automatically void.

11   Article 85, therefore, is applicable to the extent to which trade-mark rights are invoked so as to prevent imports of products which originate in different Member States, which bear the same trade-mark by virtue of the fact that the proprietors have acquired it, or the right to use it, whether by agreements between themselves or by agreements with third parties. Article 85 is not precluded from applying merely because, under national legislation trade-mark rights may originate in legal or factual circumstances other than the abovementioned agreements, such as registration of the trade-mark, or its undisturbed use.

12   If the restrictive practices arose before the Treaty entered into force, it is both necessary and sufficient that they continue to produce their effects after that date.

13   Before restrictive practice can come under Article 85(1) it must affect trade between Member States to an appreciable extent, and restrict competition within the Common Market.

Concerning Art.86, the court stated:

15   It is clear from the wording of this provision that what it prohibits is a combination of three elements: the existence of a dominant position, its abuse, and the possibility that trade between Member States may thereby be affected.

16   It should first be observed that the proprietor of a trade-mark does not enjoy a "dominant position" within the meaning of Article 86 merely because he is in a position to prevent third parties from putting into circulation, on the territory of a Member State, products bearing the same trade-mark. Since the article requires that the position in question should extend to at least a "substantial part" of the Common Market, it is also necessary that the proprietor should have power to impede the maintenance of effective competition over a considerable part of the relevant market, having regard in particular to the existence and position of any producers or distributors who may be marketing similar goods or goods which may be substituted for them.

17   As regards the abuse of a dominant position, although the price level of the product may not of itself necessarily suffice to disclose such an abuse, it may, however, if unjustified by any objective criteria, and if it is particularly high, be a determining factor.

6.2.3.2   *C.N.L.-Sucal v Hag* [1990] 1 E.C.R. 3711 ("Hag II"), ECJ

The German company, Hag AG developed a successful business in dec-affeinated coffee early in this century, originally using a patented process. In 1927, it formed a Belgian subsidiary to supply the Belgian and Luxembourg markets and in 1934 transferred to it its "Hag" trade marks for those countries.

In 1946, the Belgian government administration which had taken over the subsidiary as enemy property, sold it to an unrelated buyer by an act of sequestration. Subsequently the business and marks were assigned to Van Zuylen.

Hag AG sought to enter these markets with the brand, "Decofa", but was not successful. In 1972, it then secured the sale of "Hag" brand coffee in Luxembourg through an agent there. Trade mark infringement proceedings were launched against it, to which it pleaded a right of access under Arts 30–36 and 85 of the Treaty of Rome.

The European Court of Justice held (Van Zuylen v Hag [1974] E.C.R. 731 ("Hag I")) that the Benelux owner could not use its mark to preclude the importing of German "Hag" coffee either directly or through an intermediate buyer. The nub of its decision at that time was:

11   The exercise of a trade mark right tends to contribute to the partitioning off of the markets and thus to affect the free movement of goods between Member States, all the more so since—unlike other rights of industrial and commercial property—it is not subject to limitations in point of time.

12   Accordingly, one cannot allow the holder of a trade mark to rely upon the exclusiveness of a trade mark right—which may be the consequence of the territorial limitation of national legislations—with a view to prohibiting the marketing in a Member State of goods legally produced in another Member State under an identical trade mark having the same origin.

13   Such a prohibition, which would legitimise the isolation of national markets, would collide with one of the essential objects of the Treaty, which is to unite national markets in a single market.

14   Whilst in such a market the indication of origin of a product covered by a trade mark is useful, information to consumers on this point may be ensured by means other than such as would affect the free movement of goods.

However, in "Hag II", the court had to consider the obverse situation between effectively the same parties: could the Belgian owners export their "Hag" coffee to Germany, the country where the mark originated and where it had never been transferred away from its first owner? The court chose to reverse its ruling in "Hag I", announcing that the only applicable rule of Community law went to parallel importing of goods initially marketed by the right-owner or with his consent. It now held:

13   With regard to trade mark rights, it should be observed that such rights constitute an essential element of the system of undistorted competition which the Treaty aims to establish and maintain. In such a system enterprises must be able to gain customers by the quality of their products or services, which can be done only by virtue of the existence of distinctive signs permitting identification of those products and services. For a trade mark to be able to play this part, it must constitute a guarantee that all the products bearing it have been manufactured under the supervision of a single enterprise to which responsibility for their quality may be attributed.

14   Consequently, as the Court has stated on many occasions, the specific subject-matter of a trade mark right is to grant the owner the right to use the mark for the first marketing of a product and, in this way, to protect him against competitors who

would like to abuse the position and reputation of the mark by selling products to which the mark has been improperly affixed. To determine the exact effect of this exclusive right which is granted to the owner of the mark, it is necessary to take account of the essential function of the mark, which is to give the consumer or final user a guarantee of the identity of the origin of the marked product by enabling him to distinguish, without any possible confusion, that product from others of a different provenance: see Case 102/77, *Hoffmann-La Roche* and Case 3/78, *Centrafarm v American Home Products.*

15 In assessing in the light of the foregoing considerations a situation such as that described by the national court, the decisive fact is the absence of any element of consent, on the part of the owner of the trade mark right protected by national legislation, to the marketing in another Member State, under a mark which is identical or may cause confusion, of a similar product manufactured and marketed by an enterprise which has no tie of legal or economic dependence with that owner.

16 Under these circumstances the essential function of the mark would be compromised if the owner of the right could not exercise his option under national law to prevent the importation of the similar product under a name likely to be confused with his own mark because, in this situation, consumers would no longer be able to identify with certainty the origin of the marked product and the bad quality of a product for which he is in no way responsible could be attributed to the owner of the right.

17 This conclusion cannot be altered by the fact that the mark protected by national legislation and the similar mark borne by the imported product pursuant to the legislation of the member-State of provenance originally belonged to the same owner, which was dispossessed of one of the marks as a result of expropriation by one of the two States in question before the Community was established.

18 In fact, since the date of expropriation and in spite of their common origin, each of the marks has independently fulfilled, within its own territorial limits, its function of guaranteeing that the marked products come from a single source.

19 It follows from what has been said that, in a situation like the present, where the mark originally had one owner and where single ownership ended as a result of expropriation, each of the owners of the trade mark right must be able to prevent the importation and marketing, in the member-State where the mark belongs to him, of products originating from the other owner, if they are similar products bearing a mark which is identical or which may cause confusion.

6.2.3.3 *IHT v Ideal Standard* [1994] 1 E.C.R. 2789, ECJ

In 1984, the French subsidiary of the American Standard Group voluntarily assigned the French mark, "Ideal Standard", to an independent French company, but only as to heating equipment and not as to sanitary fittings. The French assignee used the mark on its heating equipment, and through a subsidiary exported it to Germany. In Germany, the German subsidiary of American Standard was using the mark only on sanitary fittings, but secured a judgment that its mark for those goods was infringed by the French heating equipment, because potential purchasers might conclude that the latter came from it.

The European Court of Justice ruled that its "Hag II" judgment also covered cases where the division of ownership of a mark resulted from a voluntary assignment. The court stressed the territorial scope of trade mark rights and their independent existence. It summarised its remarks in "Hag II" on the nature of trade mark rights (above, 6.2.3.2, Judgment, 13–16). It continued:

47   [The defendant] in particular has submitted that the owner of a trade mark who assigns the trade mark in one Member State, while retaining it in others, must accept the consequences of the weakening of the identifying function of the trade mark flowing from that assignment. By a territorially limited assignment, the owner voluntarily renounces his position as the only person marketing goods bearing the trade mark in question in the Community.

48   That argument must be rejected. It fails to take account of the fact that, since trade marks are territorial, the function of the trade mark is to be assessed by reference to a particular territory (paragraph 18 of *HAG II*).

49   IHT has further argued that the French subsidiary, Ideal-Standard SA, has adjusted itself in France to a situation where products (such as heating equipment and sanitary fittings) from different sources may be marketed under the same trade mark on the same national territory. The conduct of the German subsidiary of the same group which opposes the marketing of the heating equipment in Germany under the trade mark "Ideal Standard" is therefore abusive.

50   That argument cannot be upheld either.

51   First of all, the assignment was made only for France. The effect of that argument, if it were accepted, would, as the German Government points out, be that assignment of the right for France would entail permission to use the device in Germany, whereas assignments and licences always relate, having regard to the territorial nature of national trade-mark rights, to a specified territory.

52   Moreover, and most importantly, French law, which governs the assignment in question here, permits assignments of trade marks confined to certain products, with the result that similar products from different sources may be in circulation on French territory under the same trade mark, whereas German law, by prohibiting assignments of trade marks confined to certain products, seeks to prevent such co-existence. The effect of IHT's argument, if it were accepted, would be to extend to the importing State whose law opposes such co-existence the solution prevailing in the exporting State despite the territorial nature of the rights in question.

The court noted that both the Uniform Benelux Trade Mark Law and the Community Trade Mark Regulation provided for a unified mark which could not be assigned for part only of the respective territories. Nonetheless it declined to impose an equivalent rule on the national systems of member states.

57   That sanction cannot be introduced through case law. To hold that the national laws are measures having equivalent effect which fall under Article 30 and are not justified by Article 36, in that, given the independence of national rights (see paragraphs 25 to 32 above), they do not, at present, make the validity of assignments for the territories to which they apply conditional on the concomitant assignment of the trade mark for the other States of the Community, would have the effect of imposing on the State a positive obligation, namely to embody in their laws a rule rendering void assignments of national trade marks made for part only of the Community.

58   It is for the Community legislature to impose such an obligation on the Member States by a directive adopted under Article 100a of the EEC Treaty, elimination of the obstacles arising from the territoriality of national trade marks being necessary for the establishment and functioning of the internal market, or itself to enact that rule directly by a regulation adopted under the same provision.

59   It should be added that, where undertakings independent of each other make trade-mark assignments following a market-sharing agreement, the prohibition of anti-competitive agreements under Article 85 applies and assignments which give effect to that agreement are consequently void. However, as the United Kingdom rightly pointed out, that rule and the accompanying sanction cannot be applied mechanically to every assignment. Before a trade-mark assignment can be treated as giving effect to

an agreement prohibited under Article 85, it is necessary to analyse the context, the commitments underlying the assignment, the intention of the parties and the consideration for the assignment.

6.2.3.4 *Terrapin (Overseas) v Terranova Industrie* [1976] E.C.R. 1039; [1976] 2 C.M.L.R. 482, ECJ

The German manufacturer, Terranova, was the registered proprietor in West Germany of trade marks, which included, "Terra" and "Terranova", for its well-known business in finished plaster for facades and other construction materials. The English company, Terrapin, manufactured prefabricated houses and components for their construction under its name. Terrapin was denied registration of its mark, and was sued for trade mark infringement by Terranova. In the latter proceedings the Oberlandesgericht, Munich, found infringement. In a subsequent appeal, the Bundesgerichtshof referred to the European Court of Justice the following question:

"Is it compatible with the provisions relating to the free movement of goods (Articles 30 and 36 of the EEC Treaty) that an undertaking established in Member State A, by using its commercial name and trade-mark rights existing there, should prevent the import of similar goods of an undertaking established in Member State B if these goods have been lawfully given a distinguishing name which may be confused with the commercial name and trade-mark which are protected in State A for the undertaking established there, if there are no relations between the two undertakings, if their national trade-mark rights arose autonomously and independently of one another (no common origin) and at the present time there exist no economic or legal relations of any kind other than those appertaining to trade-marks between the undertakings?"

The European Court of Justice held:

It is for the court of first instance, after considering the similarity of the products and the risk of confusion, to enquire further in the context of this last provision whether the exercise in a particular case of industrial and commercial property rights may or may not constitute a means of arbitrary discrimination or a disguised restriction on trade between Member States. It is for the national court in this respect to ascertain in particular whether the rights in question are in fact exercised by the proprietor with the same strictness whatever the national origin of any possible infringer.

The court then referred to its interpretation of Arts 28 and 30, and continued:

6   It follows from the above that the proprietor of an industrial or commercial property right protected by the law of a Member State cannot rely on that law to prevent the importation of a product which has lawfully been marketed in another Member State by the proprietor himself or with his consent. It is the same when the right relied on is the result of the subdivision, either by voluntary act or as a result of public constraint, of a trade-mark right which originally belonged to one and the same proprietor. In these cases the basic function of the trade-mark to guarantee to consumers that the product has the same origin is already undermined by the subdivision of the original right. Even where the rights in question belong to different proprietors the protection

given to industrial and commercial property by national law may not be relied on when the exercise of those rights is the purpose, the means or the result of an agreement prohibited by the Treaty. In all these cases the effect of invoking the territorial nature of national laws protecting industrial and commercial property is to legitimise the insulation of national markets without this partitioning within the common market being justified by the protection of a legitimate interest on the part of the proprietor of the trade-mark or business name.

7   On the other hand in the present state of Community law an industrial or commercial property right legally acquired in a Member State may legally be used to prevent under the first sentence of Article 36 of the Treaty the import of products marketed under a name giving rise to confusion where the rights in question have been acquired by different and independent proprietors under different national laws. If in such a case the principle of the free movement of goods were to prevail over the protection given by the respective national laws, the specific objective of industrial and commercial property rights would be undermined. In the particular situation the requirements of the free movement of goods and the safeguarding of industrial and commercial property rights must be so reconciled that protection is ensured for the legitimate use of the rights conferred by national laws, coming within the prohibitions on imports "justified" within the meaning of Article 36 of the Treaty, but denied on the other hand in respect of any improper exercise of the same rights of such a nature as to maintain or effect artificial partitions within the common market.

6.2.3.5   *Mag Instrument v CTC* [1998] 1 C.M.L.R. 331, EFTA Court

The EFTA Court rendered an advisory opinion on whether Art.7(1) of the Trade Mark Directive operated in favour of international exhaustion. This arose out of trade mark litigation commenced by Mag against CTC for purchasing genuine "Maglites" in the US and then importing them into Norway without Mag's consent. Mag argued that exhaustion only took place when goods were placed into the EEA by or with the consent of the trade mark owner, and not when the same products were put on the market of a third country, prior to importation into an EEA country.

The Court advised that Art.7(1) of the Directive, as reflected in point 4(c) of Annex XVII to the EEA Agreement, only covered regional exhaustion. It was for EFTA states to determine for themselves whether to introduce or maintain international exhaustion of trade mark rights for goods which originate from non-EEA countries:

. . .

[24] Further, the main argument of the Government of France, the Federal Government of Germany, the Government of the United Kingdom and the E.C. Commission against interpreting Article 7 of the Trade Mark Directive in favour of international exhaustion is that if individual States are allowed to determine freely whether holders of rights are able to object to imports from third countries, it could lead to a situation where the same products may be subject to parallel imports into one State, but not into another. This could lead to internal disparities in the market. Therefore, they submit that the principle of free movement of goods must be the same in all Member States and that the principle must also apply for the EEA.

[25] This argumentation has to be rejected in so far as it concerns the EFTA States. Unlike the E.C. Treaty, the EEA Agreement does not establish a customs union. The purpose

and the scope of the E.C. Treaty and the EEA Agreement are different (see Opinion 1/91 of the European Court regarding the Draft Agreement between the Community, on the one hand, and the countries of the European Free Trade Association, on the other, relating to the creation of the European Economic Area[1]). Thus, the EEA Agreement does not establish a customs union, but a free trade area.

[26] The abovementioned differences between the Community and the EEA will have to be reflected in the application of the principle of exhaustion of trade mark rights. According to Article 8 EEA, the principle of free movement of goods as laid down in Articles 11 to 13 EEA applies only to goods originating in the EEA, while in the Community a product is in free circulation once it has been lawfully placed on the market in a Member State. In general, the latter applies in the context of the EEA only in respect of products originating in the EEA. In the case at hand, the product was manufactured in the United States and imported into Norway. Accordingly, it is not subject to the principle of the free movement of goods within the EEA.

[27] Additionally, the EEA Agreement does not entail a common commercial policy towards third countries (see, in particular, Article 113 E.C.). The EFTA States have not transferred their respective treaty-making powers to any kind of supranational organs. They remain free to conclude treaties and agreements with third countries in relation to foreign trade (see Articles 5 and 6 of Protocol 28 EEA). Requiring Article 7(1) to be interpreted in the EEA context as obliging the EFTA Member States to apply the principle of Community-wide exhaustion would impose restraints on the EFTA States in their third-country trade relations. Such a result would not be in keeping with the aim of the EA Agreement, which is to create a fundamentally improved free trade area but no customs union with a uniform foreign trade policy.

[28] In the light of these considerations, the EFTA Court notes that it is for the EFTA States, *i.e.* their legislators or courts, to decide whether they wish to introduce or maintain the principle of international exhaustion of rights conferred by a trade mark with regard to goods originating from outside the EEA.

6.2.3.6   *Silhouette International v Hartlauer* [1998] F.S.R. 729, ECJ

Silhouette, the manufacturer and seller of expensive spectacle frames, sold a consignment of outdated spectacle frames which came into the hands of a third party in Bulgaria on the basis that resale would take place only in Bulgaria and within the Soviet Bloc. Hartlauer, the defendant, imported large quantities of the plaintiff's product from Bulgaria for resale in Austria in its "down-market" shops. Silhouette sued them for infringement of its Austrian trade mark, arguing that the doctrine of exhaustion as set out in Art.7(1) Trade Mark Directive only applied to goods placed on the market within the EEA by the trade mark proprietor or with his consent and did not apply to the importation of goods from territories outside the EEA. The European Court of Justice addressed two questions referred to it by the Oberster Gerichtshof (Austria). The first question was:

"Is Article 7(1) of the First Council Directive 89/104/EEC of December 21, 1988 to approximate the laws of Member States relating to trademarks ([1989] O.J. L40/1) to be interpreted as meaning that the trade mark entitles its proprietor to prohibit a third party from using the mark for goods which have been put on the market under that mark in a State which is not a Contacting State?"

[1] [1991] E.C.R. I-6079.

. . .

15   By its first question the Oberster Gerichtshof is in substance asking whether national rules providing for exhaustion of trade mark rights in respect of products put on the market outside the EEA under that mark by the proprietor or with his consent are contrary to Article 7(1) of the Directive.

16   It is to be noted at the outset that Article 5 of the Directive defines "rights conferred by a trade mark" and Article 7 contains the rule concerning "exhaustion of the rights conferred by a trade mark".

17   According to Article 5(1) of the Directive, the registered trade mark confers on the proprietor exclusive rights therein. In addition, Article 5(1)(a) provides that those exclusive rights entitle the proprietor to prevent all third parties not having his consent from use in the course of trade of, *inter alia*, any sign identical with the trade mark in relation to goods or services which are identical to those for which the trade mark is registered. Article 5(3) sets out a non-exhaustive list of the kinds of practice which the proprietor is entitled to prohibit under paragraph 1, including, in particular, importing or exporting goods under the trade mark concerned.

18   Like the rules laid down in Article 6 of the Directive, which set certain limits to the effects of a trade mark, Article 7 states that, in the circumstances which it specifies, the exclusive rights conferred by the trade mark are exhausted, with the result that the proprietor is no longer entitled to prohibit use of the mark. Exhaustion is subject first of all to the condition that the goods have been put on the market by the proprietor or with his consent. According to the text of the Directive itself, exhaustion occurs only where the products have been put on the market in the Community (in the EEA since the EEA Agreement came into force).

. . .

20   . . . Hartlauer and the Swedish Government have maintained that the Directive left the Member States free to provide in their national law for exhaustion, not only in respect of products put on the market in the EEA but also of those put on the market in non-member countries.

21   The interpretation of the Directive proposed by Hartlauer and the Swedish Government assumes, having regard to the wording of Article 7, that the Directive, like the Court's case law concerning Articles 30 and 36 of the E.C. Treaty, is limited to requiring the Member States to provide for exhaustion within the Community, but that Article 7 does not comprehensively resolve the question of exhaustion of rights conferred by the trade mark, thus leaving it open to the Member States to adopt rules on exhaustion going further than those explicitly laid down in Article 7 of the Directive.

22   As Silhouette, the Austrian, French, German, Italian and United Kingdom Governments and the Commission have all argued, such an interpretation is contrary to the wording of Article 7 and to the scheme and purpose of the rules of the Directive concerning the rights which a trade mark confers on its proprietor.

23   In that respect, although the third recital in the preamble to the Directive states that "it does not appear to be necessary at present to undertake full scale approximation of the trade mark laws of the Member States", the Directive nonetheless provides for harmonisation in relation to substantive rules of central importance in this sphere, that is to say, according to that same recital, the rules concerning those provisions of national law which most directly affect the functioning of the internal market, and that that recital does not preclude the harmonisation relating to those rules from being complete.

24   The first recital in the preamble to the Directive notes that the trade mark laws applicable in the Member States contain disparities which may impede the free movement of goods and freedom to provide services and may distort competition within the common market, so that it is necessary, in view of the establishment and functioning of the internal market, to approximate the laws of Member States. The

ninth recital emphasises that it is fundamental, in order to facilitate the free movement of goods and services, to ensure that registered trade marks enjoy the same protection under the legal systems of all the Member States, but that this should not prevent Member States from granting at their option more extensive protection to those trade marks which have a reputation.

25   In the light of those recitals, Articles 5 to 7 of the Directive must be construed as embodying a complete harmonisation of the rules relating to the rights conferred by a trade mark. That interpretation, it may be added, is borne out by the fact that Article 5 expressly leaves it open to the Member States to maintain or introduce certain rules specifically defined by the Community legislature. Thus, in accordance with Article 5(2), to which the ninth recital refers, the Member States have the option to grant more extensive protection to trade marks with a reputation.

26   Accordingly, the Directive cannot be interpreted as leaving it open to the Member States to provide in their domestic law for exhaustion of the rights conferred by a trade mark in respect of products put on the market in non-member countries.

27   This, moreover, is the only interpretation which is fully capable of ensuring that the purpose of the Directive is achieved, namely to safeguard the functioning of the internal market. A situation in which some Member States could provide for internal exhaustion while others provided for Community exhaustion only would inevitably give rise to barriers to the free movement of goods and the freedom to provide services.

Accordingly, the Court of Justice ruled that national laws of Member States providing for the exhaustion of trade mark rights in respect of products put on the market outside the EEA by or with the consent of the proprietor are contrary to Art.7(1) of the Directive. The Court went on to address the second question:

"May the proprietor of the trade mark on the basis of Article 7(1) of the Trade Marks Directive alone seek an order that the third party cease using the trade mark for goods which have been put on the market under that mark in a State which is not a Contracting State?"

...

34   Under the scheme of the Directive, the rights conferred by a trade mark are defined by Article 5, while Article 7 contains an important qualification with respect to that definition, in that it provides that the rights conferred by Article 5 do not entitle the proprietor to prohibit the use of the trade mark where the conditions laid down in that provision are satisfied.

35   Accordingly, while it is undeniable that the Directive requires Member States to implement provisions on the basis of which the proprietor of a trade mark, when his rights are infringed, must be able to obtain an order restraining third parties from making use of his mark, that requirement is imposed, not by Article 7, but by Article 5 of the Directive.

36   That being so, it is to be remembered, first, that, according to settled case law of the Court, a directive cannot of itself impose obligations on an individual and cannot therefore be relied upon as such against an individual. Secondly, according to the same case law, when applying domestic law, whether adopted before or after the Directive, the national court that has to interpret that law must do so, as far as possible, in the light of the wording and the purpose of the directive so as to achieve the result it has in view and thereby comply with the third paragraph of Article 189 of the Treaty (see, *inter alia*, Case C–106/89 *Marleasing v La Comercial Internacional de Alimentaciæn* [1990] E.C.R. I-4135, paragraphs 6 and 8, and Case C–91/92 *Faccini Dori v Recreb* [1994] E.C.R. I-3325, paragraphs 20 and 26).

37   The answer to be given to the second question must therefore be that, subject to the national court's duty to interpret, so far as possible, domestic law in conformity with Community law, Article 7(1) of the Directive cannot be interpreted as meaning that the proprietor of a trade mark is entitled, on the basis of that provision alone, to obtain an order restraining a third party from using his trade mark for products which have been put on the market outside the EEA under that mark by the proprietor or with his consent.

6.2.3.7   *Hoffmann-La Roche v Centrafarm* [1978] E.C.R. 1139; [1979] 3 C.M.L.R. 217, ECJ

Hoffmann-La Roche sold their well-known tranquilliser, "Valium", in Britain in packets of 100 or 500 tablets. In Germany its packaging was in lots of 20 or 50 for individual use and 100 or 250 for hospitals. The British price was substantially lower than the German. Centrafarm accordingly purchased British supplies and repackaged them in batches of 1000, which were acceptable for the German market, before reselling them there. It marked its own packages "Valium" and "Roche"—and stated its identity as the firm marketing the drug. This practice constituted an infringement of German trade mark law. The issue was whether it was nonetheless permissible under Arts 30–36.

The European Court of Justice held:

7   In relation to trade-marks, the specific subject-matter is in particular to guarantee to the proprietor of the trade-mark that he has the exclusive right to use that trade-mark for the purpose of putting a product into circulation for the first time and therefore to protect him against competitors wishing to take advantage of the status and reputation of the trade-mark by selling products illegally bearing that trade-mark. In order to answer the question whether that exclusive right involves the right to prevent the trade-mark being affixed by a third person after the product has been repackaged, regard must be had to the essential function of the trade-mark, which is to guarantee the identity of the origin of the trade-marked product to the consumer or ultimate user, by enabling him without any possibility of confusion to distinguish that product from products which have another origin. This guarantee of origin means that the consumer or ultimate user can be certain that a trade-marked product which is sold to him has not been subject at a previous stage of marketing to interference by a third person, without the authorisation of the proprietor of the trade-mark, such as to affect the original condition of the product. The right attributed to the proprietor of preventing any use of the trade-mark which is likely to impair the guarantee of origin so understood is therefore part of the specific subject-matter of the trade-mark right.

8   It is accordingly justified under the first sentence of Article 36 to recognise that the proprietor of a trade-mark is entitled to prevent an importer of a trade-mark product, following repackaging of that product, from affixing the trade-mark to the new packaging without the authorisation of the proprietor.

9   It is, however, necessary to consider whether the exercise of such a right may constitute a "disguised restriction on trade between Member States" within the meaning of the second sentence of Article 36. Such a restriction might arise, *inter alia*, from the proprietor of the trade-mark putting onto the market in various Member States an identical product in various packages while availing himself of the rights inherent in the trade-mark to prevent repackaging by a third person even if it were done in such a way that the identity of origin of the trade-marked product and its original condition could not be affected. The question, therefore, in the present case is whether the

repackaging of a trade-marked product such as that undertaken by Centrafarm is capable of affecting the original condition of the product.

10   In this respect the answer must vary according to the circumstances and in particular according to the nature of the product and the method of repackaging. Depending on the nature of the product repackaging in many cases inevitably affects its condition, while in others repackaging involves a more or less obvious risk that the product might be interfered with or its original condition otherwise affected. Nevertheless, it is possible to conceive of the repackaging being undertaken in such a way that the original condition of the product cannot be affected. This may be so where, for example, the proprietor of the trade-mark has marketed the product in a double packaging and the repackaging affects only the external packaging, leaving the internal packaging intact, or where the repackaging is inspected by a public authority for the purpose of ensuring that the product is not adversely affected. Where the essential function of the trade-mark to guarantee the origin of the product is thus protected, the exercise of his rights by the proprietor of the trade-mark in order to fetter the free movement of goods between Member States may constitute a disguised restriction within the meaning of the second sentence of Article 36 of the Treaty if it is established that the use of the trade-mark right by the proprietor, having regard to the marketing system which he has adopted, will contribute to the artificial partitioning of the markets between Member States.

11   Although this conclusion is unavoidable in the interests of freedom of trade, it amounts to giving the trader, who sells the imported product with the trademark affixed to the new packaging without the authorisation of the proprietor, a certain licence which in normal circumstances is reserved to the proprietor himself. In the interests of the proprietor as trade-mark owner and to protect him against any abuse it is therefore right to allow such licence only where it is shown that the repackaging cannot adversely affect the original condition of the product.

12   Since it is in the proprietor's interest that the consumer should not be misled as to the origin of the product, it is moreover right to allow the trader to sell the imported product with the trade-mark affixed to the new packaging only on condition that he gives the proprietor of the mark prior notice and that he states on the new packaging that the product has been repackaged by him.

13   It follows from what has been stated above that, subject to consideration of the facts of a particular case, it is irrelevant in answering the legal question raised regarding the substance of trade-mark law that the question referred by the national court is exclusively concerned with medicinal products.

14   The first question must therefore be answered to the effect that:

(a)   The proprietor of a trade-mark right which is protected in two Member States at the same time is justified pursuant to the first sentence of Article 36 of the EEC Treaty in preventing a product to which the trade-mark has lawfully been applied in one of those States from being marketed in the other Member State after it has been repacked in new packaging to which the trade-mark has been affixed by a third party.

(b)   However, such prevention of marketing constitutes a disguised restriction on trade between Member States within the meaning of the second sentence of Article 36 where:

—   It is established that the use of the trade-mark right by the proprietor, having regard to the marketing system which he had adopted, will contribute to the artificial partitioning of the markets between Member States;

—   It is shown that the repackaging cannot adversely affect the original condition of the product;

—   The proprietor of the mark receives prior notice of the marketing of the repackaged product; and

—   It is stated on the new packaging by whom the product has been repackaged.

The court also held that there was no abuse of dominant position under Art.86.

Note that in Pfizer v Eurim-Pharm *[1981] E.C.R. 2913; [1982] 1 C.M.L.R. 406,* the court considered the application of this judgment to a case where the parallel importer repackaged the 5-capsule blister strips put out by the manufacturer of a drug into larger packets; these were transparent so that the manufacturer's name and trade mark for the drug could be seen within, the name and address of manufacturer and repacker were clearly stated and a leaflet to comply with German law was included. The court stated:

10   No use of the trade mark in a manner liable to impair the guarantee of origin takes place in a case such as the one in point where, according to the findings of the national court and the terms of the question submitted by it, a parallel importer has re-packaged a pharmaceutical product merely by replacing the outer wrapping without touching the internal packaging and by making the trade mark affixed by the manufacturer on the internal packaging visible through the new external wrapping.

11   In such circumstances the re-packaging in fact involves no risk of exposing the product to interference or influences which might affect its original condition and the consumer or final user of the product is not liable to be misled as to the origin of the product, above all where, as in this case, the parallel importer has clearly indicated on the external wrapping that the product was manufactured by a subsidiary of the proprietor of the trade mark and has been re-packaged by the importer.

12   The fact that the parallel importer inserted in the external packaging a leaflet containing information relating to the medicinal product—a fact which is not even mentioned in the question submitted—does not affect this conclusion.

6.2.3.8   *American Home Products v Centrafarm* **[1978] E.C.R. 1823; [1979] 1 C.M.L.R. 326, ECJ**

American Home Products marketed a drug containing the tranquillising constituent, oxazepamum, for which it had patents in the Netherlands and the UK. In the Netherlands, it used the registered Benelux mark, "Seresta" and in the UK the registered mark, "Serenid D". The two products had identical therapeutic effects, though they were not quite the same, differing particularly in taste. Centrafarm purchased supplies of "Serenid D" in the UK and marketed them as "Seresta" in the Netherlands, giving its own name in addition to this latter mark.

In infringement proceedings upon the Benelux registration, the Rotterdam court referred the question to the European Court of Justice , whether a finding of infringement in these circumstances would be consistent with the Rome Treaty rules concerning the free movement of goods.

After referring to its interpretation of Arts 28 and 30 (ex-30, 36) in relation to intellectual property rights, the court stated:

11   In relation to trade-marks, the specific subject-matter is in particular the guarantee to the proprietor of the trade-mark that he has the exclusive right to use that trade-mark for the purpose of putting a product into circulation for the first time and therefore his protection against competitors wishing to take advantage of the status and reputation of the mark by selling products illegally bearing that trade-mark.

12 In order to establish in exceptional circumstances the precise scope of that exclusive right granted to the proprietor of the mark regard must be had to the essential function of the trade-mark, which is to guarantee the identity of the origin of the trade-marked product to the consumer or ultimate user.

13 This guarantee of origin means that only the proprietor may confer an identity upon the product by affixing the mark.

14 The guarantee of origin would in fact be jeopardised if it were permissible for a third party to affix the mark to the product, even to an original product.

15 It is thus in accordance with the essential function of the mark that national legislation, even where the manufacturer or distributor is the proprietor of two different marks for the same product, prevents an unauthorised third party from usurping the right to affix one or other mark to any part whatsoever of the production or to change the marks affixed by the proprietor to different parts of the production.

16 The guarantee of the origin of the product requires that the exclusive right of the proprietor should be protected in the same manner where the different parts of the production, bearing different marks, come from two different Member States.

17 The right granted to the proprietor to prohibit any unauthorised affixing of his mark to his product accordingly comes within the specific subject-matter of the trade-mark.

18 The proprietor of a trade-mark which is protected in one Member State is accordingly justified pursuant to the first sentence of Article 36 in preventing a product from being marketed by a third party in that Member State under the mark in question even if previously that product has been lawfully marketed in another Member State under another mark held in the latter State by the same proprietor.

19 Nevertheless it is still necessary to consider whether the exercise of that right may constitute a "disguised restriction on trade between Member States" within the meaning of the second sentence of Article 36.

20 In this connexion it should be observed that it may be lawful for the manufacturer of a product to use in different Member States different marks for the same product.

21 Nevertheless it is possible for such a practice to be followed by the proprietor of the marks as part of a system of marketing intended to partition the markets artificially.

22 In such a case the prohibition by the proprietor of the unauthorized affixing of the mark by a third party constitutes a disguised restriction on intra-Community trade for the purposes of the above-mentioned provision.

23 It is for the national court to settle in each particular case whether the proprietor has followed the practice of using different marks for the same product for the purpose of partitioning the markets.

6.2.3.9   *Bristol-Myers Squibb v Paranova* **[1997] F.S.R. 102, ECJ**

In the light of the Trade Marks Directive, Art.7, the Court of Justice considered the extent to which a trade mark owner may oppose the importation and sale of pharmaceutical products bearing its trade mark, where such products had been sold in another member state with its consent, in circumstances where the parallel importer subsequently repackaged the goods or simply reaffixed the trade mark to goods without altering the packaging

The trade mark owners argued unsuccessfully that the principle of exhaustion under Art.7(1) cannot apply if the importer has repackaged and reaffixed the trade marks in question. The Court of Justice ruled:

. . .

35 To accept the argument that the principle of exhaustion under Article 7(1) cannot

apply if the importer has repackaged the product and reaffixed the trade mark would therefore imply a major alteration to the principles flowing from Articles 30 and 36 of the Treaty.

36   There is nothing to suggest that Article 7 of the Directive is intended to restrict the scope of that case law. Nor would such an effect be permissible, since a Directive cannot justify obstacles to intra-Community trade save within the bounds set by the Treaty rules. The Court's case law shows that the prohibition on quantitative restrictions and measures having equivalent effect applies not only to national measures but also to those emanating from Community institutions (see, most recently, Case C-51/93 *Meyhui v Schott Zwiesel Glaswerke* [1994] E.C.R. I-3879, paragraph 11).

37   ... Article 7(1) of the Directive precludes the owner of a trade mark from relying on his rights as owner to prevent an importer from marketing a product which was put on the market in another Member State by the owner or with his consent, even if that importer repackaged the product and reaffixed the trade mark to it without the owner's authorisation.

The Court then outlined the circumstances under Art.7(2) in which a trade mark owner can object to repackaging by a parallel importer, where the goods in question have been put on the market of another Member State by or with his consent. Applying Hoffmann-La Roche v Centrafarm *[1978] F.S.R. 598 and* Pfizer v Eurim-Pharm *[1981] E.C.R. 2913 (above, para. 6.2.3.7), the Court continued:*

. . .

52   Reliance on trade mark rights by their owner in order to oppose marketing under that trade mark of products repackaged by a third party would contribute to the partitioning of markets between Member States, in particular, where the owner has placed an identical pharmaceutical product on the market in several Member States in various forms of packaging, and the product may not, in the condition in which it has been marketed by the trade mark owner in one Member State, be imported and put on the market in another Member State by a parallel importer.

53   The trade mark owner cannot, therefore, oppose the repackaging of the product in new external packaging when the size of packet used by the owner in the Member State where the importer purchased the product cannot be marketed in the member State of importation by reason, in particular, of a rule authorising packaging only of a certain size or a national practice to the same effect, sickness insurance rules making the reimbursement of medical expenses depend on the size of the packaging, or well-established medical expenses depend on the size of the packaging, or well-established medical prescription practices based, *inter alia*, on standard sizes recommended by professional groups and sickness insurance institutions.

54   Where, in accordance with the rules and practices in force in the Member State of importation, the trade mark owner uses many different sizes of packaging in that State, the finding that one of those sizes is also marketed in the Member State of exportation is not enough to justify the conclusion that repackaging is unnecessary. Partitioning of the markets would exist if the importer were able to sell the product in only part of his market.

55   The owner may, on the other hand, oppose the repackaging of the product in new external packaging where the importer is able to achieve packaging which may be marketed in the Member State of importation by, for example, affixing to the original external or inner packaging new labels in the language of the Member State of importation, or by adding new user instructions or information in the language of the Member State of importation, or by replacing an additional article not capable of

gaining approval in the Member State of importation with a similar article that has obtained such approval.

56 The power of the owner of trade mark rights protected in a Member State to oppose the marketing of repackaged products under the trade mark should be limited only in so far as the repackaging undertaken by the importer is necessary in order to market the product in the Member State of importation.

On the issue of whether the original condition of the product is adversely affected, the Court stated:

. . .

58 . . . it should be clarified at the outset that the concept of adverse effects on the original condition of the product refers to the condition of the product inside the packaging.

59 The trade mark owner may therefore oppose any repackaging involving a risk of the product inside the package being exposed to tampering or to influences affecting its original condition. To determine whether that applies account must be taken, as the Court held in paragraph 10 of the *Hoffmann-La Roche* judgment, of the nature of the product and the method of repackaging.

60 As regards pharmaceutical products, it follows from the same paragraph in *Hoffmann-La Roche* that repackaging must be regarded as having been carried out in circumstances not capable of affecting the original condition of the product where, for example, the trade mark owner has placed the product on the market in double packaging and the repackaging affects only the external layer, leaving the inner packaging intact, or where the repackaging is carried out under the supervision of a public authority in order to ensure that the product remains intact.

61 It follows from that case law that the mere removal of blister packs, flasks, phials, ampoules or inhalers from their original external packaging and their replacement in new external packaging cannot affect the original condition of the product inside the packaging.

. . .

64 As for operations consisting in the fixing of self-stick labels to flasks, phials, ampoules or inhalers, the addition to the packaging of new user instructions or information in the language of the Member State of importation, or the insertion of an extra article, such as a spray, from a source other than the trade mark owner, there is nothing to suggest that the original condition of the product inside the packaging is directly affected thereby.

65 It should be recognised, however, that the original condition of the product inside the packaging might be indirectly affected where, for example:

- the external or inner packaging of the repackaged product, or a new set of user instructions or information, omits certain important information or gives inaccurate information concerning the nature, composition, effect, use or storage of the product; or

- an extra article inserted into the packaging by the importer and designed for the ingestion and dosage of the product does not comply with the method of use and the doses envisaged by the manufacturer.

66 It is for the national court to assess whether that is so, in particular, by making a comparison with the product marketed by the trade mark owner in the Member State of importation. The possibility of the importer providing certain additional information should not be excluded, however, provided that information does not

contradict the information provided by the trade mark owner in the Member State of importation, that condition being met in particular in the case of different information resulting from the packaging used by the owner in the Member State of exportation.

As to other requirements to be met by the parallel importer, the Court stated:

...

70   Since it is in the trade mark owner's interest that the consumer or end user should not be led to believe that the owner is responsible for the repackaging, an indication must be given on the packaging of who repackaged the product.

71   As the Court has already stated, that indication must be clearly shown on the external packaging of the repackaged product (*Hoffmann-La Roche*, paragraph 12, and *Pfizer*, paragraph 11). That implies ... that the national court must assess whether it is printed in such a way as to be understood by a person with normal eyesight, exercising a normal degree of attentiveness.

72   It is, however, not necessary to require that the further express statement be made on the packaging that the repackaging was carried out without the authorisation of the trade mark owner, since such a statement could be taken to imply ... that the repackaged product is not entirely legitimate.

73   However, where the parallel importer has added to the packaging an extra article from a source other than the trade mark owner, he must ensure that the origin of the extra article is indicated in such a way as to dispel any impression that the trade mark owner is responsible for it.

74   Similarly, ... a clear indication may be required on the external packaging as to who manufactured the product, since it may indeed be in the manufacturer's interest that the consumer or end user should not be led to believe that the importer is the owner of the trade mark, and that the product was manufactured under his supervision.

75   Even if the person who carried out the repackaging is indicated on the packaging of the product, there remains the possibility that the reputation of the trade mark, and thus of its owner, may nevertheless suffer from an inappropriate presentation of the repackaged product. In such a case, the trade mark owner has a legitimate interest, related to the specific subject matter of the trade mark right, in being able to oppose the marketing of the product. In assessing whether the presentation of the repackaged product is liable to damage the reputation of the trade mark, account must be taken of the nature of the product and the market for which it is intended.

76   In the case of pharmaceutical products, that is certainly a sensitive area in which the public is particularly demanding as to the quality and integrity of the product, and the presentation of the product may indeed be capable of inspiring public confidence in that regard. It follows that defective, poor quality or untidy packaging could damage the trade mark's reputation.

77   However, the requirements to be met by the presentation of a repackaged pharmaceutical product vary according to whether the product is sold to hospitals or through pharmacies to consumers. In the former case, the products are administered to patients by professionals, for whom the presentation of the product is of little importance. In the latter case, the presentation of the product is of greater importance for the consumer, even if the fact that the products in question are subject to prescription by a doctor may in itself give consumers some degree of confidence in the quality of the product.

78   Finally, ... the trade mark owner must be given advance notice of the repackaged product being put on sale. The owner may also require the importer to supply him with a specimen of the repackaged product before it goes on sale, to enable him to check that the repackaging is not carried out in such a way as directly or indirectly to affect the original condition of the product and that the presentation after repackaging

is not likely to damage the reputation of the trade mark. Similarly, such a requirement affords the trade mark owner a better possibility of protecting himself against counterfeiting.

6.2.3.10 *Boehringer Ingelheim v Swingward* [2002] F.S.R. 970, ECJ

In rather similar circumstances to Bristol-Myers Squibb v Paranova *(above 6.2.3.9), Laddie J referred eight questions to the ECJ concerning the effect of Art.30 on trade mark rights over goods which has been purchased in one EC state and then repackaged for marketing in another. The Court's answers to two issues thereby raised are given here.*

As to the question whether the right to object to repackaging fell within the specific subject-matter of a trade mark:

28   Although it is possible to derogate from the fundamental principle of free movement of goods where the proprietor of a mark relies on the mark to oppose the repackaging of pharmaceutical products imported in parallel, that is only to the extent necessary to enable the proprietor to safeguard rights which form part of the specific subject-matter of the mark, as understood in the light of its essential function.

29   It is not in dispute that the specific subject-matter of a mark is to guarantee the origin of the product bearing that mark and that repackaging of that product by a third party without the authorisation of the proprietor is likely to create real risks for that guarantee of origin.

30   Thus, in paragraphs 7 and 8 of *Hoffmann-La Roche*, the Court considered that the proprietor's right to oppose the repackaging of pharmaceutical products bearing its mark is, having regard to that risk to the guarantee of origin, related to the specific subject-matter of the mark. According to that case law, it is the repackaging of the trade-marked pharmaceutical products in itself which is prejudicial to the specific subject-matter of the mark, and it is not necessary in that context to assess the actual effects of the repackaging by the parallel importer.

31   However, it is clear from paragraph 9 of *Hoffmann-La Roche* that the derogation from free movement of goods which is the consequence of the trade mark proprietor's opposition to repackaging cannot be accepted if the proprietor's exercise of that right constitutes a disguised restriction on trade between Member States within the meaning of the second sentence of Article 30 EC.

32   A disguised restriction within the meaning of that provision will exist where the exercise by a trade mark proprietor of its right to oppose repackaging contributes to artificial partitioning of the markets between Member States and where, in addition, the repackaging is done in such a way that the legitimate interests of the proprietor are respected. This means, in particular, that the repackaging must not adversely affect the original condition of the product and must not be such as to harm the reputation of the mark.

33   As was recalled in paragraph 15 above, the Court has found that a trade mark proprietor's opposition to repackaging of pharmaceutical products must be regarded as contributing to artificial partitioning of the markets between Member States where the repackaging is necessary in order to enable the product imported in parallel to be marketed in the importing State.

34   Thus it is clear from settled case law that the change brought about by any repackaging of a trade-marked pharmaceutical product—creating by its very nature the risk of interference with the original condition of the product—may be prohibited by the trade mark proprietor unless the repackaging is necessary in order to enable the marketing of the products imported in parallel and the legitimate interests of the

proprietor are also safeguarded (see, to that effect, *Bristol-Myers Squibb*, paragraph 57).

35 The answer to the first, second, fourth and eighth questions must therefore be that Article 7(2) of the Directive must be interpreted as meaning that a trade mark proprietor may rely on its trade mark rights in order to prevent a parallel importer from repackaging pharmaceutical products unless the exercise of those rights contributes to artificial partitioning of the markets between Member States.

As to the circumstances which nevertheless justify repackaging in order to ensure the effective operation of Art.28 (ex-30):

45 According to the Court's case law, where a trade mark proprietor relies on its trade mark rights to prevent a parallel importer from repackaging where that is necessary for the pharmaceutical products concerned to be marketed in the importing State, that contributes to artificial partitioning of the markets between Member States, contrary to Community law.

46 The Court has found in that respect that it is necessary to take account of the circumstances prevailing at the time of marketing in the importing Member State which make repackaging objectively necessary in order that the pharmaceutical product can be placed on the market in that State by the parallel importer. The trade mark proprietor's opposition to the repackaging is not justified if it hinders effective access of the imported product to the market of that State (see, to that effect, *Upjohn*, paragraph 43).

47 Such an impediment exists, for example, where pharmaceutical products purchased by the parallel importer cannot be placed on the market in the Member State of importation in their original packaging by reason of national rules or practices relating to packaging, or where sickness insurance rules make reimbursement of medical expenses depend on a certain packaging or where well-established medical prescription practices are based, *inter alia*, on standard sizes recommended by professional groups and sickness insurance institutions. In that regard, it is sufficient for there to be an impediment in respect of one type of packaging used by the trade mark proprietor in the Member State of importation (see *Bristol-Myers Squibb*, paragraphs 53 and 54).

48 In contrast, the trade mark proprietor may oppose the repackaging if it is based solely on the parallel importer's attempt to secure a commercial advantage (see, to that effect, *Upjohn*, paragraph 44).

49 In that context, it has also been held that the trade mark proprietor may oppose replacement packaging where the parallel importer is able to reuse the original packaging for the purpose of marketing in the Member State of importation by affixing labels to that packaging (see *Bristol-Myers Squibb*, paragraph 55).

50 Thus, while the trade mark proprietor may oppose the parallel importer's use of replacement packaging, that is conditional on the relabelled pharmaceutical product being able to have effective access to the market concerned.

51 Resistance to relabelled pharmaceutical products does not always constitute an impediment to effective market access such as to make replacement packaging necessary, within the meaning of the Court's case law.

52 However, there may exist on a market, or on a substantial part of it, such strong resistance from a significant proportion of consumers to relabelled pharmaceutical products that there must be held to be a hindrance to effective market access. In those circumstances, repackaging of the pharmaceutical products would not be explicable solely by the attempt to secure a commercial advantage. The purpose would be to achieve effective market access.

53 It is for the national court to determine whether that is the case.

54 The answer to the third question must therefore be that replacement packaging of pharmaceutical products is objectively necessary within the meaning of the Court's

case law if, without such repackaging, effective access to the market concerned, or to a substantial part of that market, must be considered to be hindered as the result of strong resistance from a significant proportion of consumers to relabelled pharmaceutical products.

The court also considered the question whether prior notice to the trade mark owner is necessary in cases where the specific subject-matter is not prejudiced by the repackaging. It found that notice was needed in all cases.

6.2.3.11   *Loendersloot v George Ballantine* [1998] 1 C.M.L.R. 1015, ECJ

Ballantine, the whisky producer, marketed their product in bottles to which labels and identification numbers were affixed. It sued its distributors, Loendersloot, for trade mark infringement, claiming that they had relabelled the bottles, removing the word "pure", the name of their approved importers and identification numbers from their packaging. The Netherlands Supreme Court (Hoge Raad) found infringement against Loendersloot, and referred, inter alia, the following questions to the European Court of Justice: whether the specific subject matter of a trade mark included the possibility of opposing the removal and reaffixing of labels by a third party; whether the use of trade mark rights against the relabelling constituted a disguised restriction on trade between States, and what significance was to be placed on the fact that identifying marks had been affixed for the purposes of controlling product safety or combatting counterfeiting.

In considering the circumstances in which a trade mark owner was entitled to object to the removal and affixing of labels carrying its trade mark, the Court affirmed the principles stated in Bristol-Myers Squibb v Paranova *(see 6.2.3.9):*

[29] It follows that under Article 36 of the Treaty the owner of trade marks rights may rely on those rights to prevent a third party from removing and then reaffixing or replacing labels bearing the trade mark, unless:

(a) it is established that the use of the trade mark rights by the owner to oppose the marketing of the relabelled products under that trade mark would contribute to the artificial partitioning of the markets between Member States;

(b) it is shown that the repackaging cannot affect the original condition of the product; and

(c) the presentation of the relabelled product is not such as to be liable to damage the reputation of the trade mark and its owner.

[30] According to the Court's case law a person who repackages pharmaceutical products is also required to inform the trade mark owner of the repackaging, to supply him, on demand, with a specimen of the repackaged product, and to state on the repackaged product the person responsible for the repackaging (see in particular, *Bristol-Myers Squibb*).

The Court formed the view that the use of a trade mark to prevent the removal of identification numbers (which were applied for legitimate purposes in the first place) in the course of repackaging did not fall foul of Art.36:

[39] With respect to the removal and reaffixing or replacing of labels in order to remove the identification numbers, Ballantine and others observe that that removal is not necessary to enable the products in question to be marketed on the markets of the various Member States in accordance with the rules in force there.

[40] It should be observed that, while that statement is correct, removal of the identification numbers might nevertheless prove necessary, as Loendersloot has observed, to prevent artificial partitioning of the markets between Member States caused by difficulties for persons involved in parallel trade in obtaining supplies from distributors of Ballantine and others for fear of sanctions being imposed by the producers in the event of sales to such persons. Even if, as Ballantine and others state, such conduct on the part of the producers would be in breach of the Treaty rules on competition, it cannot be excluded that identification numbers have been placed on products by producers to enable them to reconstruct the itinerary of their products, with the purpose of preventing their dealers from supplying persons carrying on parallel trade.

[41] It must also be acknowledged, however, that for the producer's application of identification numbers may be necessary to comply with a legal obligation, in particular, under Council Directive 89/396 on indications or marks identifying the lot to which a foodstuff belongs, or to realise other important objectives which are legitimate from the point of view of Community law, such as the recall of faulty products and measures to combat counterfeiting.

[42] In those circumstances, where identification numbers have been applied for purposes such as those mentioned in the preceding paragraph, the fact that an owner of trade mark rights makes use of those rights to prevent a third party from removing and then reaffixing or replacing labels bearing his trade mark in order to eliminate those numbers does not contribute to artificial partitioning of the markets between Member States. In such situations there is no reason to limit the rights which the trade mark owner may rely on under Article 36 of the Treaty.

[43] Where it is established that the identification numbers have been applied for purposes which are legitimate from the point of view of Community law, but are also used by the trade mark owner to enable him to detect weaknesses in his sales organisation and thus combat parallel trade in his products, it is under the Treaty provisions on competition that those engaged in parallel trade should seek protection against action of the latter type.

Removal of the word "pure" and the name of the approved importer from original labels:

The Court of Justice ruled that where the marketing of the product would be prevented in the Member State of destination but for the relabelling (e.g. because such labelling was contrary to the law in that State), use of a trade mark in these circumstances to prevent such relabelling would fall foul of Art.36 since it contributing to an artificial partitioning of markets:

. . .

[45] On this point, it must be stated that use by Ballantine and others of their trade mark rights to prevent relabelling for the purposes mentioned by Loendersloot would contribute to artificial partitioning of the markets between Member States if it were established that the use of the English word "pure" and the name of the approved importer on the original labels would prevent the products in question from being

marketed in the Member State of destination because it was contrary to the rules on labelling in force in that State. In such situation, relabelling would be necessary for the product to be marketed in that State.

[46] The person carrying out the relabelling must, however, use means which make parallel trade feasible while causing as little prejudice as possible to the specific subject matter of the trade mark right. Thus, if the statements on the original labels comply with the rules on labelling in force in the Member State of destination, but those rules require additional information to be given, it is not necessary to remove and reaffix or replace the original labels, since the mere application to the bottles in question of a sticker with the additional information may suffice.

6.2.3.12   *Pall v Dahlhausen* [1989] E.C.R. 4827, ECJ

Dahlhausen produced blood filters in Italy using its Italian mark "Miropore" and indicating registration of the mark there by the symbol ®. The mark was not registered in Germany and a competitor there objected that the ® would therefore mislead German consumers, contrary to the Unfair Competition Law of 1909, Art. 3. The Landgericht München referred to the European Court of Justice the question of whether a finding against Dahlhausen would be compatible with Art.28 (ex-30) of the Rome Treaty.

Holding that it would not be compatible, the court said:

...

12   The Court has ... consistently held that obstacles to intra-Community trade resulting from disparities between provisions of national law must be accepted in so far as such provisions, applicable to domestic and to imported products without distinction, may be justified as *necessary in order to satisfy imperative requirements relating, inter alia, to consumer protection and fair trading*. However, in order to be permissible, such provisions must be *proportionate to the objective* pursued and that objective must *not be capable of being achieved by measures* which are less restrictive of intra-Community trade (see, in particular, the judgment in Case 120/78 *Rewe v Bundesmonopolverwaltung* [1979] E.C.R. 649 ("*Cassis de Dijon*"))

13   A prohibition such as the one at issue in this case is capable of impeding intra-Community trade because it can force the proprietor of a trade mark that has been registered in only one Member State to change the presentation of his products according to the place where it is proposed to market them and to set up separate distribution channels in order to ensure that products bearing the symbol ® are not in circulation in the territory of Member States which have imposed the prohibition at issue.

14   Moreover, such a prohibition is applicable to domestic and to imported products without distinction. It seeks to prevent the risk of error as to the place in which the trade mark of the product is registered and protected, and the question whether the product is of national or foreign origin is of no relevance whatsoever in that regard.

15   Consideration must therefore be given to the question whether such a prohibition can be justified by the abovementioned imperative requirements.

16   It has been argued that the prohibition is justified because the use of the symbol ®, which indicates that a trade mark is registered, misleads consumers if the trade mark is not registered in the country in which the goods are marketed.

17   That argument cannot be upheld.

18   Firstly, it has not been established that in practice the symbol ® is generally used and

understood as indicating that the trade mark is registered in the country in which the product is marketed.

19   Secondly, even assuming that consumers, or some of them, might be misled on that point, such a risk cannot justify so considerable an obstacle to the free movement of goods, since consumers are more interested in the qualities of a product than in the place of registration of the trade mark.

The Court also rejected arguments (i) that competitors would be unfairly disadvantaged if Dahlhausen could choose to register in the least demanding country and then use the ®; and (ii) that the Directive 84/450 on the approximation of misleading advertising required prohibition of the symbol.

6.2.3.13   *Verband Sozialer Wettbewerb v Clinique Laboratories* [1992] 1 E.C.R. 317, ECJ

Estée Lauder marketed a line of cosmetics under the mark "Clinique", save in Germany where an unfair competition objection was raised: this mark might lead an appreciable proportion of consumers into thinking the products had medical qualities. The firm, obliged instead to use "Linique", objected to the cost of the separate packaging which this entailed and secured a reference concerning compatibility with Art.28 (ex-30). After referring to its decision in Pall v Dahlhausen *(above, 6.2.3.12) the court concluded:*

19   The prohibition also under paragraph 3 of the UWG of the distribution within the Federal Republic of Germany of cosmetic products under the same name as that under which they are marketed in the other Member States constitutes in principle such an obstacle to intra-Community trade. The fact that by reason of that prohibition the undertaking in question is obliged in that Member State alone to market its products under a different name and to bear additional packaging and advertising costs demonstrates that this measure does affect free trade.

20   In order to determine whether, in preventing a product being attributed with characteristics which it does not have, the prohibition of the use of the name "Clinique" for the marketing of cosmetic products in the Federal Republic of Germany can be justified by the objective of protecting consumers or the health of humans, it is necessary to take into account the information set out in the order of reference.

21   In particular, it is apparent from that information that the range of cosmetic products manufactured by the Estée Lauder company is sold in the Federal Republic of Germany exclusively in perfumeries and cosmetic departments of large stores, and therefore none of those products is available in pharmacies. It is not disputed that those products are presented as cosmetic products and not as medicinal products. It is not suggested that, apart from the name of the products, this presentation does not comply with the rules applicable to cosmetic products. Finally, according to the very wording of the question referred, these products are ordinarily marketed in other countries under the name "Clinique" and the use of that name apparently does not mislead consumers.

22   In the light of these facts, the prohibition of the use of that name in the Federal Republic of Germany does not appear necessary to satisfy the requirements of consumer protection and the health of humans.

23   The clinical or medical connotations of the word "Clinique" are not sufficient to make that word so misleading as to justify the prohibition of its use on products marketed in the aforesaid circumstances.

6.2.3.14   *Keck and Mithouard* [1995] 1 C.M.L.R. 101, ECJ

The French Finance Act 1963 prohibited a trader from reselling at a loss. This law, which applied equally to importers and to domestic sellers, was challenged by two French supermarket owners who brought products across the Alsatian border from Germany, subsequently sold them at a loss, and were prosecuted under the law. In refusing to apply Art.28 (ex-30) against the provision the court warned:

[14] In view of the increasing tendency of traders to invoke Article 30 of the Treaty as a means of challenging any rules whose effect is to limit their commercial freedom even where such rules are not aimed at products from other Member States, the court considers it necessary to re-examine and clarify its case law on this matter.

[15] It is established by the case law beginning with *"Cassis de Dijon"* [1979] E.C.R. 649; [1979] 3 C.M.L.R. 494, that, in the absence of harmonisation of legislation, obstacles to free movement of goods which are the consequence of applying, to goods coming from other Member States where they are lawfully manufactured and marketed, rules that lay down requirements to be met by such goods (such as those relating to designation, form, size, weight, composition, presentation, labelling, packaging) constitute measures of equivalent effect prohibited by Article 30. This is so even if those rules apply without distinction to all products unless their application can be justified by a public-interest objective taking precedence over the free movement of goods.

[16] By contrast, contrary to what has previously been decided, the application to products from other Member States of national provisions restricting or prohibiting certain selling arrangements is not such as to hinder directly or indirectly, actually or potentially, trade between Member States within the meaning of *Dassonville* [1974] E.C.R. 837, [1974] 2 C.M.L.R. 436, so long as those provisions apply to all relevant traders operating within the national territory and so long as they affect in the same manner, in law and in fact, the marketing of domestic products and of those from other Member States.

[17] Provided that those conditions are fulfilled, the application of such rules to the sale of products from another Member State meeting the requirements laid down by that State is not by nature such as to prevent their access to the market or to impede access any more than it impedes the access of domestic products. Such rules therefore fall outside the scope of Article 30 of the Treaty.

6.3   Free Provision of Services and Intellectual Property

6.3.1   *Coditel v Ciné Vog (No. 1)* [1980] E.C.R. 881; [1981] 2 C.M.L.R. 362, ECJ

The copyright owner of the film "Le Boucher" granted the exclusive performing rights in Belgium (including the right of television transmission) to Ciné Vog for a period of seven years. By another licence, the German television channel, ARD, broadcast a German version of the film which the Coditel companies received off air in Belgium and transmitted to their cable subscribers. This amounted to a breach of Ciné Vog rights for which they sued for damages. Coditel pleaded in defence that such a result would prejudice the free provision of services guaranteed by the Rome Treaty, Art.49 (ex-59) (see above, 6.1.1) and this issue was referred to the European Court of Justice by two questions of which the court found it necessary to answer only the second:

12   A cinematographic film belongs to the category of literary and artistic works made available to the public by performances which may be infinitely repeated. In this respect the problems involved in the observance of copyright in relation to the requirements of the Treaty are not the same as those which arise in connection with literary and artistic works the placing of which at the disposal of the public is inseparable from the circulation of the material form of the works, as in the case of books or records.

13   In these circumstances the owner of the copyright in a film and his assigns have a legitimate interest in calculating the fees due in respect of the authorisation to exhibit the film on the basis of the actual or probable number of performances and in authorising a television broadcast of the film only after it has been exhibited in cinemas for a certain period of time. It appears from the file on the present case that the contract made between Les Films la Boétie and Ciné Vog stipulated that the exclusive right which was assigned included the right to exhibit the film "Le Boucheur" publicly in Belgium by way of projection in cinemas and on television but that the right to have the film diffused by Belgian television could not be exercised until 40 months after the first showing of the film in Belgium.

14   These facts are important in two regards. On the one hand, they highlight the fact that the right of a copyright owner and his assigns to require fees for any showing of a film is part of the essential function of copyright in this type of literary and artistic work. On the other hand, they demonstrate that the exploitation of copyright in films and the fees attaching thereto cannot be regulated without regard being had to the possibility of television broadcasts of those films. The question whether an assignment of copyright limited to the territory of a Member State is capable of constituting a restriction on freedom to provide services must be examined in this context.

15   Whilst Article 59 of the Treaty prohibits restrictions upon freedom to provide services, it does not thereby encompass limits upon the exercise of certain economic activities which have their origin in the application of national legislation for the protection of intellectual property, save where such application constitutes a means of arbitrary discrimination or a disguised restriction on trade between Member States. Such would

be the case if that application enabled parties to an assignment of copyright to create artificial barriers to trade between Member States.

16   The effect of this is that, whilst copyright entails the right to demand fees for any showing or performance, the rules of the Treaty cannot in principle constitute an obstacle to the geographical limits which the parties to a contract of assignment have agreed upon in order to protect the author and his assigns in this regard. The mere fact that those geographical limits may coincide with national frontiers does not point to a different solution in a situation where television is organised in the Member States largely on the basis of legal broadcasting monopolies, which indicates that a limitation other than the geographical field of application of an assignment is often impracticable.

17   The exclusive assignee of the performing right in a film for the whole of a Member State may therefore rely upon his right against cable television diffusion companies which have transmitted that film on their diffusion network having received it from a television broadcasting station established in another Member State, without thereby infringing Community law.

18   Consequently the answer to the second question referred to the Court by the Cour d'Appel, Brussels, should be that the provisions of the Treaty relating to the freedom to provide services do not preclude an assignee of the performing right in a cinematographic film in a Member State from relying upon his right to prohibit the exhibition of that film in that State, without his authority, by means of cable diffusion if the film so exhibited is picked up and transmitted after being broadcast in another Member State by a third party with the consent of the original owner of the right.

Subsequently, a second issue was referred to the European Court of Justice by the Cour d'Appel, Brussels: the right to show the film in Belgium had been licensed exclusively to Ciné Vog, subject to the condition that it would not be televised there within 40 months of its cinema release. This was alleged to constitute a contravention of Art.85, which would also amount to a defence to the copyright infringement proceedings against Coditel.

The European Court of Justice ruled that it was for the national court to ascertain whether, in a given case, the manner in which such an exclusive right conferred by contract is exercised is subject to a situation in the economic or legal sphere the object or effect of which is to prevent or restrict the distribution of films or to distort competition on the cinematographic market, regard being had to the specific characteristics of the market: Coditel v Ciné Vog (No. 2) [1982] E.C.R. 3381.

6.4　Application of Rules of Competition to Intellectual Property

6.4.1　*RTE and ITP v EC Commission* [1995] 4 C.M.L.R. 718; [1995] F.S.R. 530, ECJ

In the UK and Ireland, the listed programmes of television channels are copyright (given the limited concept of originality in their laws). Public television broadcasting being restricted to the licensed channels of the BBC and ITV (UK) and RTE (Ireland, these organisations each published weekly magazines listing their own output. At the same time, they obtained injunctions against independent publishers, who sought to produce a single weekly listing all their programmes. (They also restricted newspapers to a daily or weekend listing.)

Magill, a Dublin company put out publication for both Ireland and Northern Ireland, which would list channels received in most Irish households and 30–40 per cent of households in Northern Ireland; but it was immediately enjoined for copyright infringement. It complained to the Commission, which found the conduct of RTE and ITP to be an abuse of dominant position under the Rome Treaty, Art.82 (ex-86), and ordered them to supply all third parties with weekly listings in advance (on a non-discriminatory basis, but, if they chose, subject to a reasonable royalty). This was upheld by the European Court of Justice.

For the channels, it was argued in particular:

(i) *That the exercise by an owner of intellectual property rights of his exclusive rights, in particular his refusal to grant a licence, cannot in itself be regarded as an abuse of dominant position (relying on* Volvo v Veng, *above, 6.2.2.9);*

(ii) *that copyright was by its nature beneficial to competition, being restricted to the protection of expression and not idea;*

(iii) *that there had been no analysis below of the economic power in the marketplace exerted by the television organisations, but instead an assumption that this followed from the holding of copyrights;*

(iv) *that the conduct in any case had no appreciable effect on trade between the two member states concerned, principally because of the very small sales of RTE's current magazine in Northern Ireland.*

(v) *that the order conflicted with the obligation of all member states, as parties the Berne Convention, to offer the reproduction right over literary works to non-national authors, subject only to such limits as they might introduce under the terms of the Convention's Art.9(2), which were said not in this case to be met.*

The court held:

(a) Existence of a dominant position

46   So far as dominant position is concerned, it is to be remembered at the outset that mere ownership of an intellectual property right cannot confer such a position.

47   However, the basic information as to the channel, day, time and title of programmes is the necessary result of programming by television stations, which are thus the only source of such information for an undertaking, like Magill, which wishes to publish it together with commentaries or pictures. By force of circumstance, RTE and ITP, as the agent of ITV, enjoy, along with the BBC, a *de facto* monopoly over the information used to compile listings for the television programmes received in most households in Ireland and 30 per cent to 40 per cent of households in Northern Ireland. The appellants are thus in a position to prevent effective competition on the market in weekly television magazines. The Court of First Instance was therefore right in confirming the Commission's assessment that the appellant occupied a dominant position (see the judgment in Case 322/81 *Michelin*, cited above, paragraph 30).

(b) Existence of abuse

48   With regard to the issue of abuse, the arrangements of the appellant and IPO wrongly presuppose that where the conduct of an undertaking in a dominant position consists of the exercise of a right classified by national law as "copyright", such conduct can never be reviewed in relation to Article 86 of the Treaty.

49   Admittedly, in the absence of Community standardization or harmonization of laws, determination of the conditions and procedures for granting protection of an intellectual property right is a matter for national rules. Further, the exclusive right of reproduction forms part of the author's rights, so that refusal to grant a licence, even if it is the act of an undertaking holding a dominant position, cannot in itself constitute abuse of a dominant position (judgment in Case 238/87 *Volvo*, cited above, paragraphs 7 and 8).

50   However, it is also clear from that judgment (paragraph 9) that the exercise of an exclusive right by the proprietor may, in exceptional circumstances, involve abusive conduct.

51   In the present case, the conduct objected to is the appellant's reliance on copyright conferred by national legislation so as to prevent Magill—or any other undertaking having the same intention—from publishing on a weekly basis information (channel, day, time and title of programmes) together with commentaries and pictures obtained independently of the appellants.

52   Only weekly television guides containing comprehensive listings for the week ahead would enable users to decide in advance which programmes they wished to follow and arrange their leisure activities for the week accordingly. The Court of First Instance also established that there was a specific, constant and regular potential demand on the part of consumers (see the *RTE* judgment, paragraph 62, and the *ITP* judgment, paragraph 48).

53   Thus the appellants—who were, by force of circumstance, the only sources of the basic information on programme scheduling which is the indispensable raw material for compiling a weekly television guide—gave viewers wishing to obtain information on the choice of programmes for the week ahead no choice but to buy the weekly guides for each station and draw from each of them the information they needed to make comparisons.

54 The appellants' refusal to provide basic information by relying on national copyright provisions thus prevented the appearance of a new product, a comprehensive weekly guide to television programmes, which the appellants did not offer and for which there was a potential consumer demand. Such refusal constitutes an abuse under heading (b) of the second paragraph of Article 86 of the Treaty.

55 Second, there was no justification for such refusal either in the activity of television broadcasting or in that of publishing television magazines.

56 Third, and finally, as the Court of First Instance also held, the appellants, by their conduct, reserved to themselves the secondary market of weekly television guides by excluding all competition on that market (see the judgment in Joined Cases 6/74 and 7/74 *Commercial Solvents v Commission* [1974] ECR 223, paragraph 25) since they denied access to the basic information which is the raw material indispensable for the compilation of such a guide.

(c) Trade between Member States

69 In order to satisfy the condition that trade between Member States must be affected, it is not necessary that the conduct in question should in fact have substantially affected that trade. It is sufficient to establish that the conduct is capable of having such an effect (judgments in Case 322/81 *Michelin v Commission*, cited above, paragraph 104, and in Case C–41/90 *Höfner and Elser v Macrotron* [1991] ECR I–1979, paragraph 32).

70 In this case, the Court of First Instance found that the applicant had excluded all potential competitors on the geographical market consisting of one Member State (Ireland) and had thus modified the structure of competition on that market, thereby affecting potential commercial exchanges between Ireland and the United Kingdom. From this the Court of First Instance drew the proper conclusion that the condition that trade between Member States must be affected had been satisfied.

(d) Berne Convention

83 It is appropriate to observe at the outset, as the Court of First Instance did, that the Community is not a party to the Convention for the Protection of Literary and Artistic Works.

84 Next, so far as the United Kingdom and Ireland are concerned, it is true that they were already parties to the Convention when they acceded to the Community and that Article 234 of the Treaty therefore applies to that Convention, in accordance with Article 5 of the Act of Accession. It is, however, settled case-law that the provisions of an agreement concluded prior to entry into force of the Treaty or prior to a Member State's accession cannot be relied on in intra-Community relations if, as in the present case, the rights of non-member countries are not involved (see, in particular, the judgment in Case 286/86 *Ministère Public v Deserbais* [1988] E.C.R. 4907, paragraph 18).

85 Finally, the Paris Act, which amended Article 9(1) and (2) of the Convention (the provisions relied on by RTE), was ratified by the United Kingdom only after its accession to the Community and has still not been ratified by Ireland.

6.4.1.1 *Nungesser and Eisele v EC Commission* [1982] E.C.R. 2015; [1983] 1 C.M.L.R. 278, ECJ

A French governmental research station, INRA, developed a new variety of maize seed and obtained plant variety rights for it in France. These it licensed in that country to a number of seed producers.

By a set of contractual arrangements INRA in effect granted an exclusive licence of the equivalent rights in West Germany to Eisele and his company,

Nungesser. Parallel imports of seed produced in France were in consequence hindered by actions which included legal proceedings by Eisele against one particular parallel importer. In consequence complaints were lodged with the EC Commission, which investigated and decided that the contractual arrangements according Eisele his exclusive position on the German market contravened Art.85(1) and were not capable of exemption under Art.85(3). On the central issues in the decision, the West German Licensee appealed to the European Court of Justice.

The court found that plant variety rights were not distinguishable in basic character from other intellectual property:

43   It is therefore not correct to consider that breeders' rights are a species of commercial or industrial property right with characteristics of so special a nature as to require, in relation to the competition rules, a different treatment from other commercial or industrial property rights. That conclusion does not affect the need to take into consideration, for the purposes of the rules on competition, the specific nature of the products which form the subject-matter of breeders' rights.

Accordingly in relation to the exclusive licensing of plant variety rights, the court proceeded to distinguish between two categories of obligation, even though the Commission had held that both these categories constituted infractions of Art.85(1). These were the "open" and the "exclusive" elements in the contractual arrangements:

53   ... The first case concerns a so-called open exclusive licence or assignment and the exclusivity of the licence relates solely to the contractual relationship between the owner of the right and the licensee, whereby the owner merely undertakes not to grant other licences in respect of the same territory and not to compete himself with the licensee on that territory. On the other hand, the second case involves an exclusive licence or assignment with absolute territorial protection, under which the parties to the contract propose, as regards the products and the territory in question, to eliminate all competition from third parties, such as parallel importers or licensees for other territories.

In the contractual arrangements before the court, the "open" aspects comprised INRA's obligation (and the obligations of those deriving rights from INRA) to refrain from producing or selling seeds in West Germany, or having them produced or sold by another licensee there. The "exclusive" aspects consisted of the obligations on INRA (and those deriving rights from it) to prevent third parties from exploiting the seeds to West Germany without Eisele's authority for use or sale there, and Eisele's concurrent use of his contractual rights and plant breeder's rights to prevent all imports into Germany or exports from there to other Member States.

Of the "open" aspects, the court, disagreeing with the Commission, held:

56   An exclusive licence which forms the subject-matter of the contested decision concerns the cultivation and marketing of hybrid maize seeds which were developed by INRA after years of research and experimentation and were unknown to German farmers at

the time when the cooperation between INRA and the applicants were taking shape. For that reason the concern shown by the interveners as regards the protection of new technology is justified.

57   In fact in the case of a licence of breeders' rights over hybrid maize seeds so developed in one Member State, an undertaking established in another Member State which was not certain that it would not encounter competition from other licensees for the territory granted to it, or from the owner of the right himself, might be deterred from accepting the risk of cultivating and marketing that product; such a result would be damaging to the dissemination of a new technology and would prejudice competition in the Community between the new product and similar existing products.

58   Having regard to the species nature of the products in question, the Court concludes that, in a case such as the present, the grant of an open exclusive licence, that is to say a licence which does not affect the position of third parties, such as parallel importers and licensees for other territories, is not in fact incompatible with Article 85(1) of the Treaty.

Of the "exclusive" aspects, the court, accepting the view of the Commission, held:

60   As regard to the position of third parties, the Commission in essence criticises the parties to the contract for having extended the definition of exclusivity to importers who are not bound to the contract, in particular parallel importers. Parallel importers or exporters, such as Louis David K.G. in Germany and Robert Bomberault in France who offered INRA seed for sale to German buyers, had found themselves subjected to pressure and legal proceedings by INRA, Frasema and the applicants, the purpose of which was to maintain the exclusive position of the applicants on the German market.

61   The Court has consistently held (*cf.* Joined Cases 56 and 58/64 *Consten and Grundig v Commission* [1966] E.C.R. 299) that absolute territorial protection granted to a licensee in order to enable parallel imports to be controlled and prevented results in the artificial maintenance of separate national markets, contrary to the Treaty.

The court also agreed with the Commission that, while the contracting parties sought to maintain these "exclusive" aspects of the arrangements, there could be no exemption under Art.81(3) (ex-85(3)):

74   [In the view of the Caisse de Gestion des Licences Végétales], the territorial protection enjoyed by the licensee in the present case was rather a relative protection on account of the presence on the market of numerous varieties of maize seed which could be substituted for INRA varieties and which could thus enter into direct competition with those varieties.

75   The Commission rightly stated in reply that the view ... concerns the problem of the demarcation of the market; that is a problem which arises when the Commission has to examine whether an agreement affords "the possibility of eliminating competition in respect of a substantial part of the products in question" (Article 85(3)(b)) but which is not relevant to the question whether an agreement is capable of improving the production or distribution of goods.

76   It must be remembered that under the terms of Article 85(3) of the Treaty an exemption from the prohibition contained in Article 85(1) may be granted in the case of any agreement between undertakings which contributes to improving the production or distribution of goods or to promoting technical progress, and which does not impose on the undertakings concerned restrictions which are not indispensable to the attainment of those objectives.

77   It was a question of seeds intended to be used by a large number of farmers in the production of maize, which is an important product for human and animal foodstuffs,

absolute territorial protection manifestly goes beyond what is indispensable for the improvement of production or distribution or the promotion of technical progress, as is demonstrated in particular in the present case by the prohibition, agreed to by both parties to the agreement, of any parallel imports of INRA maize seeds into Germany even if those seeds were bred by INRA itself and marketed in France.

78   It follows that the absolute territorial protection conferred on the licensee, as established to exist by the contested decision, constituted a sufficient reason for refusing to grant an exemption under Article 85(3) of the Treaty. It is therefore no longer necessary to examine the other grounds set out in the decision for refusing to grant such an exemption.

6.4.2 EC Regulation 240/1996 Application of Art.81(3) *(ex-85(3))* to certain Technology Transfer Agreements

The Preamble to the regulation has been omitted; but its 21 Recitals contain statements concerning the objectives of the regulation which are relevant to the interpretation of the substantive Articles. They should accordingly be referred to in making any complete analysis of the provisions.

Article 1

1. Pursuant to Article 85(3) of the Treaty and subject to the conditions and limitations set out below, it is hereby declared that Article 85(1) of the Treaty shall not apply to pure patent licensing or know-how licensing agreements and to mixed patent and know-how licensing agreements, including those agreements containing ancillary provisions relating to intellectual property rights other than patents, to which only two undertakings are party and which include one or more of the following obligations:

(1) an obligation on the licensor not to license other undertakings to exploit the licensed technology in the licensed territory;

(2) an obligation on the licensor not to exploit the licensed technology in the licensed territory himself;

(3) an obligation on the licensee not to exploit the licensed technology in territories within the common market which are reserved for the licensor;

(4) an obligation on the licensee not to manufacture or use the licensed product, or use the licensed process, in territories within the common market which are licensed to other licensees;

(5) an obligation on the licensee not to pursue an active policy of putting the licensed product on the market in the territories within the common market which are licensed to other licensees, and in particular not to engage in advertising specifically aimed at those territories or to establish any branch or maintain any distribution depot there;

(6) an obligation on the licensee not to put the licensed product on the market in the territories licensed to other licensees within the common market in response to unsolicited orders;

(7) an obligation on the licensee to use only the licensor's trade mark or get up to distinguish the licensed product during the term of the agreement, provided that the licensee is not prevented from identifying himself as the manufacturer of the licensed products;

(8) an obligation on the licensee to limit his production of the licensed product to the quantities he requires in manufacturing his own products and to sell the licensed product only as an integral part of or a replacement part for his own products or otherwise in connection with the sale of his own products, provided that such quantities are freely determined by the licensee.

2. Where the agreement is a pure patent licensing agreement, the exemption of the obligations referred to in paragraph 1 is granted only to the extent that and for as long as the licensed product is protected by parallel patents, in the territories respectively of the licensee (points 1, 2, 7 and 8), the licensor (point 3) and other licensees (points 4 ad 5). The exemption of the obligation referred to in paragraph 1(6) is granted for a period not exceeding five years from the date when the product is first put on the market within the common market by one of the

licensees, in as much and for as long as, in these territories, this product is protected by parallel patents.

3. Where the agreement is a pure know-how licensing agreement, the period for which the exemption of the obligations referred to in paragraph 1(1) to (5) is granted may not exceed ten years from the date when the licensed product is first put on the market in the Community by one of the licensees.

The exemption of the obligation referred to in paragraph 1(6) is granted for a period not exceeding five years from the date when the product is first put on the market within the common market by one of the licensees.

The obligations referred to in paragraph 1(7) and (8) are exempted for the lifetime of the agreement.

However, the exemption in paragraph 1 shall apply only where the parties have identified in any appropriate form the initial know-how and any subsequent improvements to it, which become available to one party and are communicated to the other party pursuant to the terms of the agreement and for the purpose thereof, and only for as long as the know-how remains secret and substantial.

4. Where the agreement is a mixed patent and know-how licensing agreement, the exemption of the obligations referred to in paragraph 1(1) to (5) shall apply in Member States in which the licensed technology is protected by necessary patents for as long as the licensed product or process is protected in those Member States by such patents if the duration of such protection exceeds the periods specified in paragraph 3.

The duration of the exemption provided under paragraph 1(6) cannot exceed the five year period.

However, these agreements qualify for the exemption in paragraph 1 only for as long as the patents remain in force and provided the know-how is identified and for as long as it remains secret and substantial.

5. When the parties are competing manufacturers, the exemption in paragraph 1(1) of the obligation on the licensor not to grant other licences shall apply only provided that the licensee's market share does not exceed 40%.

6. When the parties are competing manufacturers, the exemption of the obligations referred to in paragraph 1(2)–(6) shall apply only where the party which is protected by such obligations holds a market share of no more than 40%.

7. The exemption provided for in paragraph 1 shall also apply where in a particular agreement the parties undertake obligations of the types referred to in that paragraph but with a more limited scope than is permitted by that paragraph.

Article 2

1. Article 1 shall apply notwithstanding the presence in particular of any of the following clauses, which are generally not restrictive of competition.

   (1) an obligation on the licensee not to divulge the know-how communicated by the licensor, the licensee may be held to this obligation after the agreement has expired;

   (2) an obligation on the licensee not to grant sublicences or assign the licence;

   (3) an obligation on the licensee not to exploit the licensed know-how or patents after

termination of the agreement in so far and as long as the know-how is still secret or the patents are still in force;

(4) an obligation on the licensee to grant to the licensor a licence in respect of his own improvements to or his new applications of the licensed technology, provided:

— that such a licence is not exclusive, so that the licensee is free to use his own improvements or to license them to third parties, in so far as that does not disclose the know-how communicated by the licensor that is still secret;

— and that the licensor undertakes to grant an exclusive or non-exclusive licence of his own improvements to the licensee, and accepts an obligation to pay appropriate royalties to the licensee when his right to use the licensee's improvements is of a longer duration than the licensee's right to use the licensed technology.

(5) an obligation on the licensee to observe minimum quality specifications for the licensed product or to procure goods or services from the licensor or from an undertaking designated by the licensor, in so far as these quality specifications, products or services contribute to:

(i) a technically satisfactory exploitation of the licensed technology, or

(ii) ensuring that the product of the licensee conforms to the quality standards that are respected by the licensor and other licensees,

and allow the licensor to carry out related checks;

(6) obligations:

(a) to inform the licensor of misappropriation of the know-how or of infringements of the licensed patents, or

(b) to take or to assist the licensor in taking legal action against such misappropriation or infringements;

(7) an obligation on the licensee, in the event of the know-how becoming publicly known or the patents prematurely losing their validity other than by action of the licensor, to continue paying the royalties until the end of the agreement or the regular expiry of the patents, in the amounts, for the periods and according to the methods freely determined by the parties, without prejudice to the payment of any additional damages in the event of the know-how becoming publicly known or the patents losing their validity by the action of the licensee in breach of the agreement; this provision does not prevent royalties for the use of the licensed technology being spread, in order to facilitate payment, over a period going beyond the duration of the licensed patents or the entry of know-how into the public domain;

(8) an obligation on the licensee to restrict his exploitation of the licensed technology to one or more technical fields of application covered by the licensed technology or to one or more product markets;

(9) an obligation on the licensee to pay a minimum royalty or to produce a minimum quantity of the licensed product or to carry out a minimum number of operations exploiting the licensed technology;

(10) an obligation on the licensor to grant the licensee any more favourable terms that the licensor may grant to another undertaking after the agreement is entered into;

(11) an obligation on the licensee to mark the licensed product with an indication of the licensor's name of the licensed patent;

(12) an obligation on the licensee not to use the licensor's know-how to construct facilities for third parties; this is without prejudice to the right of the licensee to increase the capacity of his facilities or to set up additional facilities for his own use on normal commercial terms, including the payment of additional royalties;

(13) an obligation on the licensee to supply only a limited quantity of the licensed product to a particular customer, where the licence was granted so that the licensee might have a second supplier inside the licensed territory; this provision shall also apply where the customer is the licensee, and the licence which was granted in order to provide a second source of supply provides that the customer is himself to manufacture the licensed products or to have them manufactured by a subcontractor.

(14) a reservation by the licensor of the right to exercise the rights conferred by the patent to oppose the exploitation of the technology by the licensee outside the licensed territory;

(15) a reservation by the licensor of the right to terminate the agreement if the licensee contests the secrecy of the licensed know-how or challenges the validity of licensed patents within the common market belonging to the licensor or undertakings connected with him.

2. In the event that, because of particular circumstances, the clauses referred to in paragraph 1 fall within the scope of Article 85(1), they shall also be exempted even if they are not accompanied by any of the obligations exempted by Article 1.

3. The exemption in paragraph 2 shall also apply where an agreement contains clauses of the types referred to in paragraph 1 but with a more limited scope than is permitted by that paragraph.

Article 3

Articles 1 and 2(2) shall not apply where:

(1) on party is restricted in the determination of prices, components of prices or discounts for the licensed products;

(2) one party is restricted from competing within the common market with the other party, with undertakings connected with the other party or with other undertakings in respect of research and development, production, use or distribution of competing products without prejudice to an obligation on the licensee to use his best endeavours to exploit the licensed technology and without prejudice to the right of the licensor to terminate the exclusivity granted to the licensee and to stop communicating improvements to him when the licensee enters into such competition, and to require the licensee to prove that the licensed know-how is not being used for the production of products and services other than those licensed:

(3) one or both of the parties are required without any objectively justified reason:

   (a) to refuse to meet demand from users or resellers in their respective territories who would market products in other territories within the common market;
   (b) to make it difficult for users or resellers to obtain the products from other resellers within the common market, and in particular to exercise intellectual property rights or take measures so as to prevent users or resellers from obtaining outside, or from putting on the market in the licensed territory products which have been lawfully put on the market within the common market by the licensor or with his consent;

   or do so as a result of a concerted practice between them;

(4) the parties were already competing manufacturers before the grant of the licence and one of them is restricted within the same technological field of use or within the same product market as to the customers he may serve, in particular by being prohibited from supplying certain classes of user, employing certain forms of distribution or, with

the aim of sharing customers, using certain types of packaging for the products, save as provided in Article 1(1)(7) and Article 2(1)(13);

(5) the quantity of the licensed products one party may manufacture or sell or the number of operations exploiting the licensed technology he may carry out are subject to limitations, save as provided in Article 1(1)(8) and Article 2(1)(13).

(6) the licensee is obliged to assign in whole or in part to the licensor rights to improvements to or new applications of the licensed technology.

(7) the licensor is required, albeit in separate agreements, for a period exceeding that permitted under Article 1(2) and (3) not to license other undertakings to exploit the same technology in the licensed territory, or a party is required for periods exceeding those permitted under Articles 1(2) and (3) or Article 1(4) not to exploit the same technology in the territory of the other party or of other licensees;

Article 4

(1) The exemption provided for in Articles 1 and 2 shall also apply to agreements containing obligations restrictive of competition which are not covered by those Articles and do not fall within the scope of Article 3, on condition that the agreements in question are notified to the Commission in accordance with the provisions of Commission Regulation No. 3385/94 and that the Commission does not oppose such exemption within a period of four months.

(2) Paragraph 1 shall apply in particular where:

    (a) the licensee is obliged at the time the agreement is entered into to accept quality specifications or further licences or to procure goods or services which are not necessary for a technically satisfactory exploitation of the licensed technology or for ensuring that the production of the licensee conforms to the quality standards that are respected by the licensor and other licensees;

    (b) the licensee is prohibited from contesting the secrecy of the licensed know-how or from challenging the validity of patents licensed within the common market belonging to the licensor or undertakings connected with him.

Article 4(3)–(9) contain further provisions relating to the opposition procedure.

Article 5

This Regulation shall not apply to:

(1) agreements between members of a patent or know-how pool which relate to the pooled technologies;

(2) licensing agreements between competing undertakings which hold interests in a joint venture, or between one of them and the joint venture, if the licensing agreements relate to the activities of the joint venture;

(3) agreements under which one party grants the other a patent and/or know-how licence and the other party, albeit in separate agreements or through connected undertakings, grants the first party a patent, trade mark or know-how licence or exclusive sales rights, where the parties are competitors in relation to the products covered by those agreements;

(4) licensing agreements of intellectual property rights other than patents except where these licences enable the better achievement of the object of the licensed technology and contain only ancillary provisions.

This Regulation shall nevertheless apply:

(1) to agreements to which paragraph 1(2) applies, under which a parent undertaking grants the joint venture a patent or know-how licence, provided that the licensed products and the other goods and services of the participating undertakings which are considered by users to be equivalent in view of their characteristics, price and intended use represent:

— in case of a licence limited to production not more than 20%, and
— in case of a licence covering production and distribution not more than 10%

of the market for the licensed products and all equivalent goods and services in the common market or a substantial part thereof;

(2) to agreements to which paragraph 1(1) applies and to reciprocal licences within the meaning of paragraph 1(3), provided the parties are not subject to any territorial restriction within the common market with regard to the manufacture, use or putting on the market of the licensed products or on the use of the licensed or pooled technologies.

Article 6

This Regulation shall also apply to:

(1) agreements where the licensor is not the holder of the know-how or the patentee, but is authorized by the holder or the patentee to grant a licence;

(2) assignments of know-how, patents or both where the risk associated with exploitation remains with the assignor, in particular where the sum payable in consideration of the assignment is dependent on the turnover obtained by the assignee in respect of products made using the know-how or the patents, the quantity of such products manufactured or the number of operations carried out employing the know-how or the patents;

(3) licensing agreements in which rights or obligations of the licensor or the licensee are assumed by undertakings connected with them.

Article 7

The Commission may withdraw the benefit of this Regulation, pursuant to Article 7 of Regulation No. 19/65/EEC, where it finds in a particular case that an agreement exempted by this Regulation nevertheless has certain effects which are incompatible with the conditions laid down in Article 85(3) of the Treaty, and in particular where:

(1) the effect of the agreement is to prevent the licensed products from being exposed to effective competition in the licensed territory from identical products or products considered by users as equivalent in view of their characteristics, price and intended use;

(2) without prejudice to Article 1(1)(6), the licensee refuses, without valid reason, to meet unsolicited demand from users or resellers in the territory of other licensees;

(3) the parties;

(a) without any objectively justified reason refuse to meet demand from users or resellers in their respective territories who would market the products in other territories within the common market; or

(b) make it difficult for users or resellers to obtain the products from other resellers within the common market, and in particular where they exercise intellectual property rights or take measures so as to prevent resellers or users from obtaining outside, or from putting on the market in the licensed territory products which have been lawfully put on the market within the common market by the licensor or with his consent;

(4) the parties were already competing manufacturers before the grant of the licence and obligations on the licensee to produce a minimum quantity or to use his best endeavours as referred to in Article 2(1)(9) and Article 3(2) have the effect of preventing the licensee from using competing technologies.

(5) the licensor does not have the right to terminate the exclusivity granted to the licensee at the latest five from the date the agreement was entered into and at least annually thereafter if, without legitimate reason, the licensee fails to exploit the patent or to do so adequately.

Article 8

1. For purposes of this Regulation:

(a) patent applications,

(b) utility models,

(c) applications for registration of utility models,

(d) *certificats d'utilité* and *certificats d'addition* under French law,

(e) applications for *certificats d'utilité* and *certificats d'addition* under French law, and

(f) supplementary protection certificates for medicinal products or other products for which such supplementary protection certificates may be obtained

shall be deemed to be patents.

2. This Regulation shall also apply to agreements relating to the exploitation of an invention if an application within the meaning of paragraph 1 is made in respect of the invention for a licensed territory within one year from the date when the agreement was entered into.

3. This Regulation shall furthermore apply to pure patent or know-how licensing agreements or to mixed agreements whose initial duration is automatically prolonged by the inclusion of any new improvements, whether patented or not, communicated by the licensor, provided that the licensee has the right to refuse such improvements or each party has the right to terminate the agreement at the expiry of the initial term of the agreement and at least every three years thereafter.

Article 9

For purposes of this Regulation the following terms shall have the following meanings:

(1) "*know-how*" means a body of technical information that is secret, substantial and identified in any appropriate form;

(2) the term "*secret*" means that the know-how package as a body or in the precise configuration and assembly of its components is not generally known or easily accessible, so that part of its value consists in the lead which the licensee gains when it is communicated to him; it is not limited to the narrow sense that each individual

component of the know-how should be totally unknown or unobtainable outside the licensor's business;

(3) the term *"substantial"* means that the know-how includes information which is of importance for the whole or a significant part of

    (i) a manufacturing process or
    (ii) a product or service, or
    (iii) for the development thereof

and excludes information which is trivial; such know-how must thus be useful, i.e. can reasonably be expected at the date of conclusion of the agreement to be capable of improving the competitive position of the licensee, for example by helping him to enter a new market or giving him an advantage in competition with other manufacturers or providers of services who do not have access to the licensed secret know-how or other comparable secret know-how;

(4) the term *"identified"* means that the know-how is described or recorded in such a manner as to make it possible to verify that it fulfils the criteria of secrecy and substantiality and to ensure that the licensee is not unduly restricted in his exploitation of his own technology; to be identified the know-how can either be set out in the licence agreement or in a separate document or recorded in any other appropriate form at the latest when the know-how is transferred or shortly thereafter, provided that the separate document or other record can be made available if the need arises;

(5) *"necessary patents"* are patents the licensing of which is necessary for the putting into effect of the licensed technology insofar as, in their absence, the realisation of the licensed technology would not be possible or would only be possible to a lesser extent or in more difficult or costly conditions. These patents must therefore be of technical, legal or economic interest to the licensee;

(6) the term *"licensed technology"* means the initial know-how or the necessary patents, or both, existing at the time the first licensing agreement is concluded, and improvements subsequently made to the know-how or patents, irrespective of whether and to what extent they are exploited by the parties or by other licensees;

(7) *"the licensed products"* are goods or services the production or provision of which requires the use of the licensed technology;

(8) *"market share"* means the proportion which the licensed products and other goods or services provided by the licensor or the licensee which are considered by users to be equivalent in view of their characteristics, price and intended use represent of the market for the licensed products and all other equivalent goods and services in the common market or a substantial part of it;

(9) the term *"exploitation"* refers to any use of the licensed technology in particular in the production, active or passive sales in a territory even if not coupled with manufacture in that territory, or leasing of the licensed products;

(10) *"the licensed territory"* is the territory covering all or at least part of the common market where the licensee is entitled to exploit the licensed technology;

(11) *"territory reserved for the licensor"* means territories in which the licensor has not granted any licences for patents he holds there or for his know-how;

(12) *"parallel patents"* means patents for the same invention as the term has been used by the Court of Justice;

(13) *"connected undertakings"* means:

    (a) undertakings in which a party to the agreement directly or indirectly:
       — owns more than half the capital or business assets, or

— has the power to exercise more than half the voting rights, or

— has the power to appoint more than half the members of the supervisory board, board of directors or bodies legally representing the undertaking, or

— has the right to manage the affairs of the undertaking;

(b) undertakings which directly or indirectly have in or over a party to the agreement the rights or powers listed in (a);

(c) undertakings in which an undertaking referred to in (b) directly or indirectly has the rights or powers listed in (a);

(d) undertakings in which the parties to the agreement or undertakings connected with them jointly have the rights or powers listed in (a): such jointly controlled undertakings are considered to be connected with each of the parties to the agreement.

(14) *"ancillary provisions"* are provisions relating to the exploitation of intellectual property rights other than patents, where there are no obligations restrictive or competition other than those also attached to the licensed know-how or patents and exempted under the present Regulation.

Article 10 contains transitional provisions.

7 ENFORCEMENT PROCEDURES

7.1 Civil Actions

7.1.1 Interim Injunction

7.1.1.1 *American Cyanamid v Ethicon* [1975] R.P.C. 513, HL

In an action for infringement of a patent for surgical sutures, the defendant denied that its product fell within the claims of the patent and contested validity on grounds of obviousness, lack of fair basis, ambiguity and inutility (under the 1949 Act). In interlocutory proceedings for an injunction, the Court of Appeal refused relief. It required first to be satisfied that if the case went to trial upon no other evidence than was before the court at the hearing of the application the plaintiff would be entitled to judgment for a permanent injunction in the same terms as that being sought; only after this could it consider the balance of convenience. On appeal as to the correctness of this approach, Lord Diplock stated:

Your Lordships should in my view take this opportunity of declaring that there is no such rule. The use of such expressions as "a probability", "a prima facie case", or "a strong prima facie case" in the context of the exercise of a discretionary power to grant an interlocutory injunction leads to confusion as to the object sought to be achieved by this form of temporary relief. The court no doubt must be satisfied that the claim is not frivolous or vexatious; in other words, that there is a serious question to be tried.

It is no part of the court's function at this stage of the litigation to try to resolve conflicts of evidence on affidavit as to facts on which the claims of either party may ultimately depend nor to decide difficult questions of law which call for detailed argument and mature considerations. These are matters to be dealt with at the trial. One of the reasons for the introduction of the practice of requiring an undertaking as to damages upon the grant of an interlocutory injunction was that "it aided the court in doing that which was its great object, *viz.* abstaining from expressing any opinion, upon the merits of the case until the hearing" (*Wakefield v Duke of Buccleugh* (1865) 12 L.T. N.S. 628 at 629). So unless the material available to the court at the hearing of the application for an interlocutory injunction fails to disclose that the plaintiff has any real prospect of succeeding in his claim for a permanent injunction at the trial, the court should go on to consider whether the balance of convenience lies in favour of granting or refusing the interlocutory relief that is sought.

As to that, the governing principle is that the court should first consider whether if the plaintiff were to succeed at the trial in establishing his right to a permanent injunction he would be adequately compensated by an award of damages for the loss he would have sustained as a result of the defendant's continuing to do what was sought to be enjoined between the time of the application and the time of the trial. If damages in the measure recoverable at common law would be an adequate remedy and the defendant would be in a financial position to pay them, no interlocutory injunction should normally be granted, however strong the plaintiff's claim appeared to be at that stage. If, on the other hand, damages would not provide an adequate remedy for the plaintiff in the event of his succeeding at the trial, the court should then consider whether, on the contrary hypothesis that the defendant were to succeed at the trial in establishing his right to do that which was sought to be enjoined, he would be adequately compensated under the plaintiff's undertaking as to damages for the loss he would have sustained by being prevented from doing so between the time of the application and the time of the trial. If damages in the measure recoverable under such an undertaking would be an adequate remedy and the plaintiff would be in a financial position to pay them, there would be no reason upon this ground to refuse an interlocutory injunction.

It is where there is doubt as to the adequacy of the respective remedies in damages available to either party or to both, that the question of balance of convenience arises. It would be unwise to attempt even to list all the various matters which may need to be taken into consideration in deciding where the balance lies, let alone to suggest the relative weight to be attached to them. These will vary from case to case.

Where other factors appear to be evenly balanced it is a counsel of prudence to take such measures as are calculated to preserve the status quo. If the defendant is enjoined temporarily from doing something that he has not done before, the only effect of the interlocutory injunction in the event of his succeeding at the trial is to postpone the date at which he is able to embark upon a course of action which he has not previously found it necessary to undertake; whereas to interrupt him in the conduct of an established enterprise would cause much greater inconvenience to him since he would have to start again to establish it in the event of his succeeding at the trial.

Save in the simplest cases, the decision to grant or to refuse an interlocutory injunction will cause to whichever party is unsuccessful on the application some disadvantages which his ultimate success at the trial may show he ought to have been spared and the disadvantages may be such that the recovery of damages to which he would then be entitled either in the action or under the plaintiff's undertaking would not be sufficient to compensate him fully for all of them. The extent to which the disadvantages to each party would be incapable of being compensated in damages in the event of his succeeding at the trial is always a significant factor in assessing where the balance of convenience lies; and if the extent of the uncompensatable disadvantage to each party would not differ widely, it may not be improper to take into account in tipping the balance the relative strength of each party's case as revealed by the affidavit evidence adduced on the hearing of the application. This, however, should be done only where it is apparent upon the facts disclosed by evidence as to which there is no credible dispute that the strength of one party's case is disproportionate to that of the other party. The court is not justified in embarking upon anything resembling a trial of the action upon conflicting affidavits in order to evaluate the strength of either party's case.

I would reiterate that, in addition to those to which I have referred, there may be many other special factors to be taken into consideration in the particular circumstances of individual cases.

As to the fact that the proceedings concerned patent infringement, Lord Diplock said:

The instant appeal arises in a patent case. Historically there was undoubtedly a time when in an action for infringement of a patent that was not already "well established", whatever that may have meant, an interlocutory injunction to restrain infringement would not be granted if counsel for the defendant stated that it was intended to attack the validity of the patent.

Relics of this reluctance to enforce a monopoly that was challenged, even though the alleged grounds of invalidity were weak, are to be found in the judgment of Scrutton L.J. as late as 1924 in *Smith v Grigg Limited* [1924] 1 K.B. 655; but the elaborate procedure for the examination of patent specifications by expert examiners before a patent is granted, the opportunity for opposition at that stage and the provisions for appeal to the Patent Appeal Tribunal in the person of a patent judge of the High Court, make the grant of a patent nowadays a good prima facie reason, in the true sense of that term, for supposing the patent to be valid, and have rendered obsolete the former rule of practice as respects interlocutory injunctions in infringement actions. In my view the grant of interlocutory injunctions in actions for infringement of patents is governed by the same principles as in other actions.

7.1.1.2　*BBC v Talbot* [1981] F.S.R. 228, Megarry V.C.

The BBC was developing a traffic information system for cars under the name "Carfax". Although not yet on the market, it had been exhibited and had received considerable publicity. The corporation accordingly sought to restrain the defendant from using "Carfax" for a vehicle spare parts service. In interlocutory proceedings, Megarry V.C. referred to the legal elements needed to show passing off, and continued:

One other matter that I should mention at this stage is that this appears to be one of those cases in which, in applying the principles laid down in *American Cyanamid Co v Ethicon Ltd* [1975] A.C. 396, an important additional factor to be brought into considering the balance of convenience is the judge's estimation of the prospects of success that the plaintiff would have had if the case had gone to trial; for like so many passing off motions, this motion is one which may well prove decisive in one way or the other, without it being possible to go to trial. See generally *NWL Ltd v Woods* [1979] 1 W.L.R. 1294 at 1306, 1307; *Newsweek Inc v The British Broadcasting Corporation* [1979] R.P.C. 441. Here, the decision on the motion is going to produce one of two immediate results, it is said. If the BBC win, Talbot will have to call off the proposed launching of its "Carfax" parts scheme in the middle of next January, and then, if they can surmount all the difficulties of obtaining the necessary funds, find another name, get all the requisite trade mark clearances for it, re-design all the publicity equipment and materials so as to use the new name, and get everything produced according to the new design. This, they say, will postpone the launching of their scheme for some six months, a period which Mr Morritt says is far longer than is necessary. If Talbot win, then the BBC, says Mr Morritt, will lose their only prospect of financial support and their scheme will be dead, a prospect which Mr Yorke controverts. At all events, the decision on the motion is going to have an immediate and serious effect on one side or the other. For either Talbot or the BBC, there is bound to be much wasted expenditure. I shall not attempt to analyse that expenditure, especially as I feel little doubt that there has been some degree of exaggeration on each side: but after all, these are proceedings for passing off.

Megarry V.C. explored the evidence on motion, the assertions about its effects. He concluded in favour of granting an interlocutory injunction to preserve the status quo.

7.1.1.3   *Belfast Ropework v Pixdane* [1976] R.P.C. 337, CA

The defendant in an action for infringement of a patent for synthetic agricultural twine was beginning to import its product from Portugal. In interlocutory proceedings, the substantial issue concerned the balance of convenience.

Buckley L.J.:

The defendants are not manufacturers. They have no large capital sums tied up in plant or buildings, which would be sterilised by the grant of an injunction. They are merchants in agricultural equipment. It may be that at the present time their activities are substantially confined to the sale of baler twine. They have dealt in some other goods, although apparently not to any very substantial extent. But there seems to be no particular reason why they should not diversify their business into other goods. It is suggested in the evidence that if the injunction is granted, the defendant company will really have no alternative to going out of business. I am not altogether persuaded that that is a wholly justified view. But, even if it is so, their business has only been recently established, if it can yet be properly described as established at all, and it was initiated in circumstances in which the defendant company can I think reasonably be said to have been courting litigation. They may, of course, succeed in their counterclaim for the revocation of the patent, which would vindicate their conduct, and it is not for us at this stage to form any concluded opinion about that one way or the other. But, unless and until they do so, I do not think that they can feel aggrieved at being restrained until after the trial from continuing to pursue this newly and contentiously established business. If they are victorious in the outcome, they will be entitled to damages under the plaintiffs' undertaking, which will be a concomitant of the granting of an interlocutory injunction.

Mr Young has contended that the damage that the defendant company would suffer would be irretrievable damage and that they would never be able to re-establish themselves in this market. I do not think that that view is really justified on the evidence. I see no reason why a delay of one year or 18 months, or even two years, in the establishment of this new business should be regarded as something which will eventually shut them out of this market altogether. Nor do I see why, as has been suggested, if the injunction is granted, there will really be no alternative to the defendant company going into liquidation. It is said that if the injunction is granted, the defendant company will be unable to finance the defence of the action and that the action will go unfought. If that is the position, it is perhaps a misfortune which attends starting a venture of this kind in the circumstances in which this venture was started, knowing that it would almost inevitably involve the defendant company in litigation.

In these circumstances, will the trial judge, if and when the action comes to be tried, be better able to do justice as between the parties, whichever party wins, if the injunction is granted or if it is refused? If the injunction is refused, the plaintiffs will be at risk of having suffered damage to their established business considerably in excess of the sum of £15,000, which can I think be regarded as the only sum available to meet any claim for damages that they may have against the defendant company. If it is granted, the defendants will be at risk of having suffered damage by having been prevented from continuing for the time being in this infant business. But, whatever the measure of that damage may be, there is not I think any reason to suppose that the plaintiff company will not be of sufficient financial substance to meet it.

In these circumstances, in my judgment, the balance of convenience is clearly on the side of granting the injunction. Accordingly, I would allow this appeal and reverse the learned judge's decision.

The other members of the Court of Appeal agreed.

7.1.1.4 *Catnic Components v Stressline* [1976] F.S.R. 157, CA

The plaintiffs' main business was in the patented steel lintel which was the subject of litigation elsewhere digested (see 1.2.1.4, 1.3.1.6). At the date of these proceedings it had a gross annual turnover of £6m. The defendants were introducing, as a small part of a similar business, a product which allegedly infringed the plaintiffs' patent. On the balance of convenience in interlocutory proceedings, Buckley L.J. said:

I take it to be the basis of the views expressed by the House of Lords in the *American Cyanamid* case that the function of an interlocutory junction is to ensure that the court, when the day comes to do final justice between the parties, will not find that something has happened in the meantime which puts it outside the power of the court then to do justice. However, on the facts of this case, if the plaintiffs succeed, it is unlikely that anything that happens between the present time and the trial of the action would so damage the plaintiffs as to make it impractical to compensate them by giving them damages. I can understand that, if the facts of the case are such that improper competition with an inventor in the exploitation of his invention would severely restrict his ability to lay the foundations of his own business in exploiting his invention and would stunt the expansion of that business, you might find that those circumstances were likely permanently to damage the plaintiff in the exploitation of his invention throughout the life of the patent because the early or formative years or even months of a business may be very important to the way in which the business will develop throughout its whole life. ...

When I turn to consider the facts of the present case, with deference to the learned judge below, I find it difficult to believe that anything done by the defendant company in the way of selling metal lintels during the period—and I again repeat that it is likely to be a relatively short period—between now and the trial of this action could have so drastic an effect upon the plaintiffs' business in the exploitation of their metal lintels as to make damages an inadequate remedy. Any loss of business that the plaintiffs suffer as a result of competition by the defendants pending trial will be adequately compensated by damages calculated in relation to the number of lintels sold by the defendants; and, if it can then be shown that the plaintiffs have suffered in any respect in connection with their goodwill as a result of the defendants' action, I apprehend that that would be a perfectly proper head of damage to take into account in awarding damages to the plaintiffs for infringement down to the trial. I have not been satisfied that there is any likelihood in the present case of the plaintiff company's suffering any more drastic or far-reaching damage or that any damage which the plaintiff company is likely to suffer will be damage of a kind which could not be adequately recompensed in quantifiable damages.

7.1.1.5 *Series 5 Software Limited v Philip Clarke* [1996] F.S.R. 273, Laddie J.

The plaintiff sought, inter alia, interim injunctions against three former employees restraining them from contacting customers and/or using or disclosing alleged trade secrets relating to its computer source codes. At the interlocutory stage, the dispute centred on the weight that should be given (if at all) to the relative strength of the parties' cases in deciding whether to grant interim relief. Laddie J. considered the following passage from American Cyanamid:

The supposed problem with *American Cyanamid* centres on the statement:

> "[Assessing the relative strength of the parties' cases], however, should be done only where it is apparent upon the facts disclosed by evidence as to which there is no credible dispute that the strength of one party's case is disproportionate to that of the other party. ([1975] A.C. 409C)"

If this means that the court *cannot* take into account its view of the strength of each party's case if there is any dispute on the evidence, as suggested by the use of the words "only" and "no credible dispute", then a new inflexible rule has been introduced ... For example, all a defendant would have to do is raise a non-demurrable dispute as to relevant facts in his affidavit evidence and then he could invite the court to ignore the apparent strength of the plaintiff's case. This would be inconsistent with the flexible approach suggested in *Hubbard v Vosper* which was cited with approval earlier in the *American Cyanamid* decision. Furthermore, it would be somewhat strange since *American Cyanamid* directs courts to assess the adequacy of damages and the balance of convenience yet these too are topics which will almost always be the subject of unresolved conflicts in the affidavit evidence.

In my view Lord Diplock did not intend by the last quoted passage to exclude consideration of the strength of the cases in most applications for interlocutory relief. It appears to me that what is intended is that the court should not attempt to resolve difficult issues of fact or law on an application for interlocutory relief. If, on the other hand, the court is able to come to a view as to the strength of the parties' cases on the credible evidence then it can do so. In fact, as any lawyer who has experience of interlocutory proceedings will know, it is frequently the case that it is easy to determine who is most likely to win the trial on the basis of the affidavit evidence and any exhibited contemporaneous documents. If it is apparent from that material that one party's case is much stronger than the other's then that is a matter the court should not ignore. To suggest otherwise would be to exclude from consideration an important factor and such exclusion would fly in the face of the flexibility advocated earlier in *American Cyanamid*. As Lord Diplock pointed in *Roche*[1] one of the purposes of the cross undertaking in damages is to safeguard the defendant if this preliminary view of the strength of the plaintiff's case proves to be wrong.

After a review of the authorities, Laddie J. listed the following principles:

It follows that it appears to me that in deciding whether to grant interlocutory relief, the court should bear the following matters in mind:

(1) The grant of an interlocutory injunction is a matter of discretion and depends on all the facts of the case.

(2) There are no fixed rules as to when an injunction should or should not be granted. The relief must be kept flexible.

(3) Because of the practice adopted on the hearing of applications for interlocutory relief, the court should rarely attempt to resolve complex issues of disputed fact or law.

(4) Major factors the court can bear in mind are (a) the extent to which damages are likely to be an adequate remedy for each party and the ability of the other party to pay, (b) the balance of convenience, (c) the maintenance of the status quo, (d) any clear view the court may reach as to the relative strength of the parties' cases.

---

[1] *Hoffman-La Roche & Co Att.-Gen. v Secretary of State for Trade and Industry* [1975] A.C. 295.

In coming to this conclusion I am encouraged by the following considerations:

(1) The House of Lords in *American Cyanamid* did not suggest that it was changing the basis upon which most courts had approached the exercise of the discretion in this important area.

(2) The only issue which it was expressly addressing was the existence of the inflexible "rule of law" which had been applied as a mandatory condition by the Court of Appeal.

(3) It would mean that there was no significant inconsistency between the *Roche* and *American Cyanamid* decisions.

(4) It would be consistent with the approval given by the House of Lords to the decision in *Hubbard v Vosper*[2] and, implicitly, the decision to the same effect in *Evans Marshall & Co v Bertola SA*[3] (a decision of Lord Edmund-Davies when in the Court of Appeal).

(5) It would preserve what was one of the great values of interlocutory proceedings, namely an early, though non-binding, view of the merits from a judge. Before *American Cyanamid* a decision at the interlocutory stage would be a major ingredient leading to the parties resolving their differences without the need for a trial. There is nothing inherently unsatisfactory in this. Most clients ask for and receive advice on prospects from their lawyers well before there has been cross-examination. In most cases the lawyers have little difficulty giving such advice. It should also be remembered that in many jurisdictions on the continent trials are conducted without discovery or cross-examination. There is nothing inherently unfair in a court here expressing at least a preliminary view based on written evidence. After all it is what the courts managed to do for a century and a half.

(6) Allowing parties to come to an earlier view on prospects would assist in reducing the costs of litigation. This is an issue to which much attention is being given at the moment.

(7) It would mean that the approach of the courts in England and Wales to the grant of interlocutory relief would be the same as that followed in Scotland. In *NWL v Woods* [1979] 3 All E.R. 614, Lord Fraser of Tullybelton commented on the practice in Scotland and compared it with what he understood to be the English practice since *American Cyanamid*, namely that the court is prevented from considering the strength of the parties' cases. He said:

> "In Scotland the practice is otherwise, and the court is used to have regard to the relative strength of the cases put forward in averment and argument by each party at the interlocutory stage as one of the many factors that may go to make up the balance of convenience. That is certainly in accordance with my own experience as Lord Ordinary, and I believe the practice of other judges in the Court of Session was the same. Whether the likelihood of success should be regarded as one of the elements of the balance of convenience or as a separate matter seems to me an academic question of no real importance, but my inclination is in favour of the former alternative. It seems to make good sense: if the pursuer or petitioner appears very likely to succeed at the end of the day, it will tend to be convenient to grant interim interdict and thus prevent the defender or respondent from infringing his rights, but if the defender or respondent appears very likely to succeed at the end of the day it will tend to be

---

[2] [1972] 2 Q.B. 84 at 96 (Lord Denning).
[3] [1973] 1 W.L.R. 349.

convenient to refuse interim interdict because an interim interdict would probably only delay the exercise of the defender's legal activities (page 628f–h)."

Applying these principles to the facts, Laddie J. refused to grant the injunctive relief sought.

7.1.2   Order to Obtain Discovery and Preserve Evidence and Assets

7.1.2.1   *Anton Piller v Manufacturing Processes* [1976] R.P.C. 719, CA

The plaintiff, a German company, sued the first defendant, its British agents and others for infringement of copyright, passing off and breach of confidence in respect of the design of sophisticated electrical components. On the basis of evidence that the first defendant was passing the plaintiff's drawings and other confidential material to third parties without authority, the plaintiff sought an order, ex parte *and in* camera, *that it be permitted to enter the first defendant's premises in order to inspect documents and remove them or copies of them.*

Lord Denning M.R.:

Let me say at once that no court in this land has any power to issue a search warrant to enter a man's house so as to see if there are papers or documents there which are of an incriminating nature, whether libels or infringements of copyright or anything else of the kind. No constable or bailiff can knock at the door and demand entry so as to inspect papers or documents. The householder can shut the door in his face and say "Get out". That was established in the leading case of *Entick v Carrington* (1765) 2 Wils. 275. None of us would wish to whittle down that principle in the slightest. But the order sought in this case is not a search warrant. It does not authorise the plaintiff's solicitors or anyone else to enter the defendant's premises against his will. It does not authorise the breaking down of any doors, nor the slipping in by a back door, nor getting in by an open door or window. It only authorises entry and inspection by the permission of the defendant. The plaintiff must get the defendant's permission. But it does do this: it brings pressure on the defendant to give permission. It does more. It actually orders him to give permission—with, I suppose, the result that if he does not give permission, he is guilty of contempt of court.

This may seem to be a search warrant in disguise. But it was fully considered in the House of Lords 150 years ago and held to be legitimate. The case is *East India Co v Kynaston* (1821) 3 Bli. 153. Lord Redesdale said at p.163:

> "The arguments for the appellants at the Bar are founded upon the supposition that the court has directed a forcible inspection. This is an erroneous view of the case. The order is to permit; and if the East India Company should refuse to permit inspection, they will be guilty of a contempt of the court ... It is an order operating on the person requiring the defendants to permit inspection, not giving authority of force, or to break open the doors of their warehouse".

That case was not, however, concerned with papers or things. It was only as to the value of a warehouse; and that could not be obtained without an inspection. But the distinction drawn by Lord Redesdale affords ground for thinking that there is jurisdiction to make an order that the defendant "do permit" when it is necessary in the interests of justice.

Accepting such to be the case, the question is in what circumstances ought such an order to be made. If the defendant is given notice beforehand and is able to argue the pros and cons, it is warranted by that case in the House of Lords and by Order 29, r.2(1) and (5), of the Rules of the Supreme Court. But it is a far stronger thing to make such an order *ex parte* without giving him notice. This is not covered by the Rules of Court and must be based on the inherent jurisdiction of the court. There are one or two old precedents which give some colour for it, *Hennessey v Bohmann* [1877] W.N. 14, and *Morris v Howell* (1888) 22 L.R. Ir.

77, an Irish case. But they do not go very far. So it falls to us to consider it on principle. It seems to me that such an order can be made by a judge *ex p.*, but it should only be made where it is essential that the plaintiff should have inspection so that justice can be done between the parties: and when, if the defendant were forewarned, there is a grave danger that vital evidence will be destroyed, the papers will be burnt or lost or hidden, or taken beyond the jurisdiction, and so the ends of justice be defeated: and when the inspection would do no real harm to the defendant or his case.

Nevertheless, in the enforcement of this order, the plaintiffs must act with due circumspection. On the service of it, the plaintiffs should be attended by their solicitor, who is an officer of the court. They should give the defendant an opportunity of considering it and of consulting his own solicitor. If he wishes to apply to discharge the order as having been improperly obtained, he must be allowed to do so. If the defendant refuses permission to enter or to inspect, they must not force their way in. They must accept his refusal, and bring it to the notice of the court afterwards, if need be on an application to commit.

You might think that with all these safeguards against abuse, it would be of little use to make such an order. But it can be effective in this way: it serves to tell the defendant that, on the evidence put before it, the court is of opinion that he ought to permit inspection—nay, it orders him to permit—and that he refuses as his peril. It puts him in peril not only of proceedings for contempt, but also of adverse inferences being drawn against him; so much so that his own solicitor may often advise him to comply. We are told that in two at least of the cases such an order has been effective. We are prepared, therefore, to sanction its continuance but only in an extreme case where there is grave danger of property being smuggled away or of vital evidence being destroyed.

Ormrod L.J.:

There are three essential pre-conditions for the making of such an order, in my judgment. First, there must be an extremely strong prima facie case. Secondly, the damage, potential or actual, must be very serious for the applicant. Thirdly, there must be clear evidence that the defendants have in their possession incriminating documents or things, and that there is a real possibility that they may destroy such material before any application *inter partes* can be made.

The form of the order makes it plain that the court is not ordering or granting anything equivalent to a search warrant. The order is an order on the defendant *in personam* to permit inspection. It is therefore open to him to refuse to comply with such an order, but at his peril either of further proceedings for contempt of court—in which case, of course, the court will have the widest discretion as to how to deal with it, and if it turns out that the order was made improperly in the first place, the contempt will be dealt with accordingly—but more important, of course, the refusal to comply may be the most damning evidence against the defendant at the subsequent trial. Great responsibility clearly rests on the solicitors for the applicant to ensure that the carrying out of such an order is meticulously, carefully done with the fullest respect for the defendant's rights, as my Lord has said, of applying to the court, should he feel it necessary to do so, before permitting the inspection.

Shaw L.J. agreed and the order was made, subject to a cross-undertaking in damages, supported in the circumstances by a bond of £10,000.

7.1.2.2 *Columbia Picture Industries v Robinson* [1986] F.S.R. 367, Scott J.

The plaintiffs secured an Anton Piller *search order and* Mareva *freezing injunction against Robinson and his company on the basis of evidence impli-*

cating him in illicit taping of films for hire to the public. On a subsequent application to discharge these, heard in conjunction with trial of the action, Scott J. dealt at length with the nature of the Anton Piller *search order:*

It is a fundamental principle of civil jurisprudence in this country that citizens are not to be deprived of their property by judicial or quasi-judicial order without a fair hearing. *Audi alterem partem* is one of the principles of natural justice and contemplates a hearing at which the defendant can, if so advised, be represented and heard. As was said by Slade L.J. in *Bank Mellat v Nikpour* [1985] F.S.R. 87 and cited by Whitford J. in *Jeffrey Rogers Knitwear Productions Limited v Vinola Knitwear Manufacturing Co* [1985] F.S.R. 184:

> "There is a primary precept governing the administration of justice, that no man is to be condemned unheard and, therefore, as a general rule, no order should be made to the prejudice of a party unless he has the opportunity of being heard in defence".

What is to be said of the *Anton Piller* procedure which, on a regular and institutionalised basis, is depriving citizens of their property and closing down their businesses by orders made *ex parte*, on applications of which they know nothing and at which they cannot be heard, by orders which they are forced, on pain of committal, to obey, even if wrongly made?

There are some possible answers to this criticism of *Anton Piller* orders and their effect. One is that every *Anton Piller* order records an undertaking by the applicants who have obtained it to compensate the respondent for any damage caused to him by the order and for which the court thinks the plaintiff ought to pay. This is theoretically a valuable safeguard. In the present case the defendants are seeking compensation under just such an undertaking. But, in my judgment, it does not meet the main objection to *Anton Piller* procedure. The main objection to the procedure is that the orders made produce for the respondents damaging and irreversible consequences without any hearing at which they can be heard. The respondents may lack the means or the strength of purpose to pursue the applicants for relief under the undertaking in damages. And even villains ought not to be deprived of their property by proceedings at which they cannot be heard.

The second comment is that which Mr Cumberland gave in the course of his cross-examination. *Anton Piller* orders, he said, are not sought by his firm against innocent persons. Mr Hoffman, too, emphasised in his evidence the care with which Hamlins satisfy themselves that the proposed objects of *Anton Piller* procedure were engaged in piratical activities before applying for *Anton Piller* orders. This comment serves, in my opinion, not to mitigate but to underline the dangers inherent in *ex parte* procedure and, *a fortiori, ex parte* procedure where the object is to obtain a mandatory order intended for immediate execution. ...

The draconian and essentially unfair nature of *Anton Piller* orders from the point of view of respondents against whom they are made requires, in my view, that they do so drawn as to extend no further than the minimum extent necessary to achieve the purpose for which they are granted, namely, the preservation of documents or articles which might otherwise be destroyed or concealed. Anything beyond that is, in my judgment, impossible to justify. For example, I do not understand how an order can be justified that allows the plaintiff's solicitors to take and retain all relevant documentary material and correspondence. Once the plaintiffs' solicitors have satisfied themselves what material exists and have had an opportunity to take copies thereof, the material ought, in my opinion, to be returned to its owner. The material need be retained no more than a relatively short period of time for that purpose.

Secondly, I would think it essential that a detailed record of the material taken should always be required to be made by the solicitors who execute the order before the material is removed from the respondent's premises. So far as possible, disputes as to what material was taken, the resolution of which depends on the oral testimony and credibility of the solicitors on the one hand and the respondent on the other hand, ought to be avoided. In the absence of any corroboration of a respondent's allegation that particular material (for instance, divorce papers) was taken, a solicitor's sworn and apparently credible denial is likely always to be preferred. This state of affairs is unfair to respondents. It ought to be avoided so far as it can be.

Thirdly, no material should, in my judgment be taken from the respondent's premises by the executing solicitors unless it is clearly covered by the terms of the order. In particular, I find it wholly unacceptable that a practice should have grown up whereby the respondent to the order is procured by the executing solicitors to give consent to additional material being removed. In view of the circumstances in which *Anton Piller* orders are customarily executed (the execution is often aptly called "a raid"), I would not, for my part, be prepared to accept that an apparent consent by a respondent had been freely and effectively given unless the respondent's solicitor had been present to confirm and ensure that the consent was a free and informed one.

Fourthly, I find it inappropriate that seized material the ownership of which is in dispute, such as allegedly pirate tapes, should be retained by the plaintiffs' solicitors pending the trial. Although officers of the court, the main role of solicitors for plaintiffs is to act for the plaintiffs. If the proper administration of justice requires that material taken under an *Anton Piller* order from defendants should, pending trial, be kept from the defendants, then those responsible for the administration of justice might reasonably be expected to provide a neutral officer of the court charged with the custody of the material. In lieu of any such officer, and there is none at present, the plaintiffs' solicitors ought, in my view, as soon as solicitors for the defendants are on the record, be required to deliver the material to the defendants' solicitors on their undertaking for its safe custody and production, if required, in court.

Finally, the nature of *Anton Piller* orders requires that the affidavits in support of applicants for them ought to err on the side of excessive disclosure. In the case of material falling into the grey area of possible relevance, the judge, not the plaintiffs' solicitors, should be the judge of relevance. Whitford J., whose experience in these matters probably exceeds that of any other first instance judge, has recently drawn attention to the particular importance of full disclosure on *Anton Piller* applications. In the *Jeffrey Rogers Knitwear* case the learned judge said this at 189:

> "I wholly reject the suggestion ... that when seeking an *Anton Piller* order, there is no need to investigate the question whether or not in the absence of an order there is a real possibility that infringing material or evidence will be done away with. Any plaintiff seeking an *Anton Piller* order must place before the court all the information they have relating to the circumstances of the defendant which they can suggest points to the probability that in the absence of an *Anton Piller* order material which should be available will disappear".

Scott J. proceeded to find that the plaintiff's solicitors had permitted infractions to occur under each of his five criteria. While he found substantially for the plaintiffs in trial of the action, he also found that the preliminary orders had been improperly obtained. He accordingly awarded £10,000 compensatory and aggravated damages to the defendants on the plaintiffs' cross-undertaking.

7.1.2.3   Supreme Court Act 1981, s.72: Withdrawal of privilege against incrimination of self or spouse in certain proceedings

S.72(1) In any proceedings to which this subsection applies a person shall not be excused, by reason that to do so would tend to expose that person, or his or her spouse, to proceedings for a related offence or for the recovery of a related penalty—

(a) from answering any question put to that person in the first-mentioned proceedings; or

(b) from complying with any order made in those proceedings.

(2) Subsection (1) applies to the following civil proceedings in the High Court, namely—

(a) proceedings for infringement of rights pertaining to any intellectual property or for passing off;

(b) proceedings brought to obtain disclosure of information relating to any infringement of such rights or to any passing off; and

(c) proceedings brought to prevent any apprehended infringement of such rights or any apprehended passing off.

(3) Subject to subsection (4), no statement or admission made by a person—

(a) in answering a question put to him in any proceedings to which subsection (1) applies; or

(b) in complying with any order made in any such proceedings,

shall, in proceedings for any related offence or for the recovery of any related penalty, be admissible in evidence against that person or (unless they married after the making of the statement or admission) against the spouse of that person.

(4) Nothing in subsection (3) shall render any statement or admission made by a person as there mentioned inadmissible in evidence against that person in proceedings for perjury or contempt of court.

(5) In this section—

"intellectual property" means any patent, trade mark, copyright, registered design, technical or commercial information or other intellectual property;

"related offence", in relation to any proceedings to which subsection (1) applies means—

(a) in the case of proceedings within subsection (2)(a) or (b)—

(i) any offence committed by or in the course of the infringement or passing off to which those proceedings relate; or

(ii) any offence not within sub-paragraph (i) committed in connection with that infringement or passing off, being an offence involving fraud or dishonesty;

(b) in the case of proceedings within subsection (2)(c), any offence revealed by the facts on which the plaintiff relies in those proceedings;

"related penalty", in relation to any proceedings to which subsection (1) applies means—

(a) in the case of proceedings within subsection (2)(a) or (b), any penalty incurred in respect of anything done or omitted in connection with the infringement or passing off to which those proceedings relate;

(b) in the case of proceedings within subsection (2)(c), any penalty incurred in respect of any act or omission revealed by the facts on which the plaintiff relies in those proceedings.

(6) Any reference in this section to civil proceedings in the High Court of any description includes a reference to proceedings on appeal arising out of civil proceedings in the High Court of that description.

7.1.2.4 *Chappell v United Kingdom* [1989] 1 F.S.R. 617, ECHR

Chappell operated a video exchange club. A substantial number of the videos distributed by him had been made in breach of copyright. Two film companies and two film industry associations ("the plaintiffs") obtained an Anton Piller *search order against Chappell's business which they executed, by arrangement with the police, at the same time as the police executed a search and seizure order relating to pornographic material at Chappell's premises. Chappell claimed that the* Anton Piller *order had been improperly obtained, served and executed, but the High Court and Court of Appeal dismissed these claims and he was refused leave to appeal to the House of Lords. He then took proceedings under Art.8 of the European Human Rights Convention, which provides:*

1. Everyone has the right to respect for his private and family life, his home and his correspondence.

2. There shall be no interference by a public authority with the exercise of this right such as is in accordance with the law and is necessary in a democratic society in the interests of national security, public safety or the economic well-being of the country, for the prevention of disorder or crime, for the protection of health or morals, or for the protection of the rights and freedoms of others.

The European Human Rights Commission found no violation of Art.8, a finding upheld by the European Court of Human Rights which said:

53. The applicant submitted that the grant and the execution of the *Anton Piller* order in his case were not "in accordance with the law" since they did not comply with English law. In support of his submission, which was accepted by a minority of the Commission, he relied on the following factors:

(a) the inadequate disclosure to Whitford J., when the order was originally sought, of the arrangements between the plaintiffs and the police;

(b) the manner in which the plaintiffs gained admission to the premises on March 2, 1981, which in effect denied him his right to refuse entry;

(c) the fact that the searches of the premises by the plaintiffs and the police were conducted simultaneously and by a total of 16 or 17 people, and the adverse effects of this on Mr Chappell's ability to supervise the operations;

(d) the absence from the *Anton Piller* order of the usual undertaking to inform the person served on his right to obtain legal advice and the alleged fact that Mr Chappell did not receive proper legal advice before the plaintiffs' search was effected;

(e)   the fact that no inventory of the material seized was prepared;

(f)   the removal of a number of private papers unconnected with the copyright action;

(g)   the plaintiffs' access, after their search of Mr Chappell's premises, to other documents of his at Bath police station.

The Court found that these factors were not sufficient to establish that the Anton Piller *order was not in accordance with English law and continued:*

56.   It remains to consider whether the future requirements which the Court has identified as flowing from the phrase "in accordance with the law" were satisfied. ...
      As regards "foreseeability," ... the applicant maintained that the granting of *Anton Piller* orders and, in particular, their terms were largely matters of discretionary practice and that the state of the law was too "amorphous" for it to constitute "law" for the purposes of Article 8(2).
      The Court does not share this view. Since 1974 a substantial body of case law has restated and refined the principles followed by the English courts as regards *Anton Piller* orders. It is true that some variations may occur as between the content of individual orders. Nevertheless, the basic terms and conditions for the grant of this relief were, at the relevant time, laid down with sufficient precision for the "foreseeability" criterion to be regarded as satisfied.

57.   In its report, the Commission examined whether the legal basis for the interference at issue satisfied the further criterion of showing respect for the applicants' rights, and concluded that it did. In so doing—the Delegate explained at the hearing—the Commission had had in mind *dicta* of the Court exemplified by the following passage from its *Olsson* judgment of March 24 1988 (Series A No. 130, page 30, paragraph 61(b)):

> "The phrase 'in accordance with the law' does not merely refer back to domestic law but also relates to the quality of the law, requiring it to be compatible with the rule of law; it thus implies that there must be a measure of protection in domestic law against arbitrary interferences by public authorities with the rights safeguarded by, *inter alia* paragraph 1 of Article 8 ..."

      An *Anton Piller* order is granted without the defendant's being notified or heard and is capable of giving rise to damaging and irreversible consequences for him. For these reasons it is essential that this measure should be accompanied by adequate and effective safeguards against arbitrary interference and abuse. In point of fact, the order made against Mr Chappell and his company was coupled with a number of safeguards of various kinds. ...

58.   Mr Chappell did not allege that the grant of the *Anton Piller* order in his case, as such, was not "necessary in a democratic society." However, as regards its terms, he questioned the adequacy of the safeguards incorporated in and the remedies available to him in respect of the order, especially in view of the irreversible consequences of its implementation. Above all, he directed his submissions to the manner in which the measure had been executed: adverting to the factors set out at (b) to (g) in paragraph 53 above, he contended that the interference with his rights was not proportionate to the legitimate aim pursued. A minority of the Commission agreed with this conclusion.

The Court rejected Chappell's submissions relating to the grant and terms of the order and then turned to its execution:

62.   There remains the question whether the actual execution of the order can be regarded as "necessary" and, in particular, as proportionate to the legitimate aim pursued.
      The Court, first of all, finds itself unable to accept that factors (d), (e), (f) and (g) set out in paragraph 53 above justify the applicant's allegation in this respect. Factor (f)

relates to a matter which the Commission declared inadmissible. The other three ...
are not in its opinion of sufficient weight to warrant a finding of disproportionality.

63. Of more consequence are the remaining factors relied on, namely the manner in which the plaintiffs gained entry to the applicant's premises and the fact that the latter were searched, simultaneously, by 16 or 17 people.

The Court would agree with the criticisms of these aspects of the case made by the Court of Appeal, which described what happened as "disturbing" and "unfortunate and regrettable."

64. Mr Chappell was admittedly not afforded a proper opportunity to refuse the plaintiffs entry to his premises at the door, since members of their party entered together with Detective Chief Inspector A.

However, the applicant subsequently raised no objection on this score. Indeed, rather than exercising his right of asking the plaintiffs to leave, he acquiesced, after receiving legal advice, in their search operations. Moreover, it was not until such advice had been tendered that those operations were put in hand.

65. Manifestly the simultaneous searches by the police and the plaintiffs must have been distracting for Mr Chappell and must have created difficulties for him, as regards to his solicitor. Indeed, Warner J. recognised that this circumstance made the execution of the *Anton Piller* order "more oppressive than it should have been."

Against this have to be weighed the following factors. Firstly, it is clear that the two searches concerned at least partly the same materials. Secondly, the applicant made no request for one of the searches to be deferred until the other had been completed. Thirdly, the domestic courts—after hearing first-hand evidence—found that in fact Mr Chappell was able to look after his interests whilst the order was being implemented. Finally, Warner J. found that "there was nothing inherently wrong with the mode of execution" of the order and the Court of Appeal concluded that it was not necessary to set the order aside for the purpose of doing justice to Mr Chappell.

66. In the light of the above, the Court is of the opinion that the shortcomings in the procedure followed—which, by its very nature, was bound to cause some difficulties for the applicant—were not so serious that the execution of the order can, in the circumstances of this case, be regarded as disproportionate to the legitimate aim pursued.

7.1.2.5   *Universal Thermosensors Ltd v Hibben* [1992] F.S.R. 361, Nicholls V.C.

The plaintiff company manufactured temperature-measuring equipment. Two of its employees and a former employee (Mrs Hibben) decided to set up a competing business (TPL), but before doing so took and used confidential information (including the "item 3" and "item 4" lists) from the plaintiff. The plaintiff, through its managing director and major shareholder (James), commenced proceedings against them, and obtained an Anton Piller *search order which was executed both at their private homes and at the premises of their new business. At the trial the defendants claimed damages against the plaintiff and the plaintiff's solicitor based on the mode of execution of the* Anton Piller *order. This claim was settled during the trial (by payments to the defendants) and Nicholls V.C., at the conclusion of his judgment, made the following observations about* Anton Piller *orders:*

Anton Piller orders

This case furnishes an illustration of both the virtues and vices of *Anton Piller* orders. The virtue was that the plaintiff was enabled to recover the item 3 list, the item 4 list and other documents, which, I strongly suspect, would never have seen the light of day if less draconian steps, such as an order for delivery up of all documents containing confidential information regarding the plaintiff's customer contacts, had been the limit of the relief granted to the plaintiff. In all probability, incriminating evidence of that nature would simply have been destroyed.

But this result was achieved at a very high price. As I have said, the defendants' claims arising out of the faulty execution of the *Anton Piller* order were disposed of by an agreement reached between the parties during the course of the trial. It would, therefore, be quite wrong for me to say anything which might be understood as criticism of the conduct of those, and in particular the solicitors, who were responsible for the execution of the *Anton Piller* order in this action. Nevertheless, from the undisputed facts which emerged before me certain lessons are to be learned. I draw attention to these points, in the hope that thereby these problems will not arise again. The *Anton Piller* procedure lends itself all too readily to abuse. This has been highlighted more than once: see the powerful judgments of Scott J. in *Columbia Picture Industries Inc v Robinson* [1987] Ch. 38 and Hoffmann J. in *Lock International plc v Beswick* [1989] 1 W.L.R. 1268. My impression is that these warning signals have been heeded, and that *Anton Piller* orders are, rightly, made much more sparingly than previously. But arising out of the history of what occurred in the present case, the following points may be noted:

(1) *Anton Piller* orders normally contain a term that before complying with the order, the defendant may obtain legal advice, provided this is done forthwith. This is an important safeguard for defendants, not least because *Anton Piller* orders tend to be long and complicated, and many defendants cannot be expected to understand much of what they are told by the solicitor serving the order. But such a term, if it is to be of use, requires that in general, *Anton Piller* orders should be permitted to be executed only on working days in office hours, when a solicitor can be expected to be available. In the present case Mrs Hibben was alone in her house, with her children in bed. She was brought to the door in her night attire at 7.15 am, and told by a stranger knocking on the door that he had a court order requiring her to permit him to enter, that she could take legal advice forthwith, but otherwise she was not permitted to speak to anyone else at all. But how could she get legal advice at that time in the morning? She rang her solicitor's office but, predictably, there was no response.

(2) There is a further feature of the situation to which I have just alluded which must never be allowed to occur again. If the order is to be executed at a private house, and it is at all likely that a woman may be in the house alone, the solicitor serving the order must be, or must be accompanied by, a woman. A woman should not be subjected to the alarm of being confronted without warning by a solitary, strange man, with no recognisable means of identification, waving some unfamiliar papers and claiming an entitlement to enter her house and, what is more, telling her she is not allowed to get in touch with anyone (except a lawyer) about what is happening.

(3) In the present case a dispute arose about which documents were taken away, and from which of the premises visited. Understandably, those who execute these orders are concerned to search and seize and then get away as quickly as possible so as to minimise the risk of confrontation and physical violence. Nevertheless, in general *Anton Piller* orders should expressly provide that, unless this is seriously impracticable, a detailed list of the items being removed should be prepared at the premises before they are removed, and that the defendant should be given an opportunity to check this list at the time.

(4) *Anton Piller* orders frequently contain an injunction retraining those on whom they are served from informing others of the existence of the order for a limited period. This is to prevent one defendant from alerting others to what is happening. There is an exception for

communication with a lawyer for the purpose of seeking legal advice. In the present case that injunction was expressed to last for a whole week; that is far too long. I suspect something went awry with the drafting of the order in this case.

(5) In the present case there was no officer or employee of TPL or Emco present when their offices and workshops were searched and documents and components taken away. This is intolerable. Orders should provide that, unless there is good reason for doing otherwise, the order should not be executed at business premises save in the presence of a responsible officer or representative of the company or trader in question.

(6) The making of an *Anton Piller* order in this case can be seen to be justified by what was discovered. But it is important not to lose sight of the fact that one thing which happened was that Mr James carried out a thorough search of all the documents of a competitor company. This is most unsatisfactory. When *Anton Piller* orders are made in this type of case consideration should be given to devising some means, appropriate to the facts of the case, by which this situation can be avoided.

(7) *Anton Piller* orders invariably provide for service to be effected by a solicitor. The court relies heavily on the solicitor, as an officer of the court. to see that the order is properly executed. Unhappily, the history in the present case, and what has happened in other cases, show that this safeguard is inadequate. The solicitor may be young and have little or no experience of *Anton Piller* orders. Frequently he is the solicitor acting for the plaintiff in the action, and however diligent and fair minded he may be, he is not the right person to be given a task which to some extent involves protecting the interests of the defendant. I think there is force in some of the criticisms set out in the invaluable article by Professor Dockray and Mr Hugh Laddie Q.C. in *"Piller Problems"* in (1990) 106 L.Q.R. 601. It seems to me that the way ahead here, pursuing one of the suggestions made in that article, is that when making *Anton Piller* orders, judges should give serious consideration to the desirability of providing, by suitable undertakings and otherwise, (a) that the order should be served, and its execution should be supervised, by a solicitor other than a member of the firm of solicitors acting for the plaintiff in the action, (b) that he or she would be an experienced solicitor having some familiarity with the workings of *Anton Piller* orders, and with judicial observations on this subject (*e.g.* as summarised in the notes to RSC, Ord.29, r.3 in S.C.P.), (c) that the solicitor should prepare a written report on what occurred when the order was executed, (d) that a copy of the report should be served on the defendants, and (e) that in any event and within the next few days the plaintiff must return to the court and present that report at an *inter partes* hearing, preferably to the judge who made the order. As to (b), I can see advantages in the plaintiff being required to include in his evidence, put to the judge in support of his application for an *Anton Piller* order, details of the name of the solicitor and of his experience.

Of course this procedure would add considerably to the cost of executing an *Anton Piller* order. The plaintiff would have to be responsible for paying the fees of the solicitor in question, without prejudice to a decision by the court on whether ultimately those costs should be borne in whole or in part by the defendant. But it must be appreciated, and certainly it is my view, that *in suitable and strictly limited cases, Anton Piller* orders furnish courts with a valuable aid in their efforts to do justice between two parties. Especially is this so in blatant cases of fraud. It is important therefore that these orders should not be allowed to fall into disrepute. If further steps are necessary to prevent this happening, they should be taken. If plaintiffs wish to take advantage of this truly draconian type of order, they must be prepared to pay for the safeguards which experience has shown are necessary if the interests of defendants are fairly to be protected.

7.1.2.6 *Practice Direction: Mareva Injunctions and Anton Piller Orders* [1994] R.P.C. 617

1. The granting of a *Mareva* injunction or *Anton Piller* order is a matter for the discretion of the judge hearing the application. However, it is desirable that a consistent approach should in general be adopted in relation to the form and carrying out of such orders, since they represent serious restrictions on the rights of those persons subjected to them imposed after hearing only the applicant's case on an *ex parte* application. This practice direction set out guidelines for the assistance of judges and those who apply for these orders.

2. Attached to this practice direction are new standard forms of the following orders: Annex 1—*Anton Piller* order; Annex 2—worldwide *Mareva* injunction; Annex 3—*Mareva* injunction limited to assets within the jurisdiction. These forms, inevitably, are complicated, but their language and layout are intended to make it easier for persons served with these orders to understand what they mean. These forms of order should be used save to the extent that the judge hearing a particular application considers there is a good reason for adopting a different form.

3. The following matters should be borne in mind in relation to an *ex parte* application for any of these orders.

(A) On an application for either a Mareva or an Anton Piller order

(1) Where practicable the papers to be used on the application should be lodged with the judge at least two hours before the hearing.

(2) An applicant should be required, in an appropriate case, to support his cross-undertaking in damages by a payment into court or the provision of a bond by an insurance company. Alternatively, the judge may order a payment by way of such security to the applicant's solicitor to be held by the solicitor as an officer of the court pending further order.

(3) So far as practicable, any application for the discharge or variation of the order should be dealt with effectively on the return date.

(B) On an application for an Anton Piller order

(1)(a) As suggested in *Universal Thermosensors Ltd v Hibben* [1992] 1 W.L.R. 840, 861 (above, 7.1.2.5) the specimen order provides for it to be served by a supervising solicitor and carried out in his presence and under his supervision. The supervising solicitor should be an experienced solicitor, having some familiarity with the operation of *Anton Piller* orders, who is not a member or employee of the firm acting for the applicant. The evidence in support of the application should include the identity and experience of the proposed supervising solicitor. (b) If in any particular case the judge does not think it appropriate to provide for the order to be served by a supervising solicitor, his reasons should be expressed in the order itself.

(2) Where the premises are likely to be occupied by an unaccompanied woman and the supervising solicitor is a man, at least one of the persons attending on the service of the order should be a woman.

(3) Where the nature of the items removed under the order makes this appropriate, the applicant should be required to insure them.

(4) The applicant should undertake not to inform any third party of the proceedings until after the return date.

(5) In future, applications in the Queen's Bench Division will no longer be heard by the judge in chambers. In both Chancery and Queen's Bench Division, wherever practicable, applications will be listed before a judge in such a manner as to ensure that he has sufficient time to read and consider the paper in advance.

(6) On circuit, applications will be listed before a High Court judge or a circuit judge, sitting as a judge of the High Court specially designated by the presiding judge to hear such applications.

4. If an *Anton Piller* order or *Mareva* injunction is discharged on the return date, the judge should always consider whether it is appropriate that he should assess damages at once and direct immediate payment by the applicant.

5. This practice direction is made by the Lord Chief Justice with the concurrence of the President of the Family Division and the Vice-Chancellor. It applies to all divisions of the High Court.

7.1.2.7 *CBS United Kingdom v Lambert* [1983] F.S.R. 123, CA

In copyright infringement proceedings against two large-scale distributors of private tapes, plaintiffs representing the British Phonographic Industry Ltd sought an Anton Piller *search order coupled with a* Mareva *freezing injunction. The defendants appeared to have no assets from which judgment could be satisfied other than a number of expensive cars and one object of the order was to identify these and have them seized pending the outcome of the proceedings.*

The Mareva *injunctions were permitted by the Court to Appeal to stand part of the order on the particular facts, in accordance with the following guidelines:*

Lawton L.J.:

First, there should be clear evidence that the defendant is likely, unless restrained by order, to dispose of or otherwise deal with his chattels in order to deprive the plaintiff of the fruits of any judgment he may obtain. Moreover, the court should be slow to order the delivery up of property belonging to the defendant unless there is some evidence or inference that the property has been acquired by the defendant as a result of his alleged wrongdoing. In the present case, for example, the inference is that the motor vehicles which the defendants own could only have been purchased out of the proceeds of sale by the defendants of articles which infringe the plaintiff's copyright. The inference is also that, if the defendants are forewarned or left in possession of the motor vehicles, those vehicles will be sold on and the proceeds of sale dissipated or hidden so that the plaintiffs would be deprived not only of damages but also of the proceeds of sale of infringing articles which belong to the plaintiffs.

Second, no order should be made for the delivery up of a defendant's wearing apparel, bedding, furnishings, tools of his trade, farm implements, live stock or any machines (including motor vehicles) or other goods such as materials or stock in trade, which it is likely he uses for the purposes of a lawful business. Sometimes furnishings may consist of objets d'art of great value. If the evidence is clear that such objects were bought for the purposes of frustrating judgment creditors they could be included in an order.

Third, all orders should specify as clearly as possible what chattels or classes of chattels are to be delivered up. A plaintiff's inability to identify what he wants delivered up and why is an indication that no order should be made.

Fourth, the order must not authorise the plaintiff to enter on the defendant's premises or to seize the defendant's property save by permission of the defendant. In *Anton Piller KG v Manufacturing Processes Ltd* and others [1976] Ch. 55 at 60, Lord Denning emphasised that the order in that case:

> "... does not authorise the plaintiffs' solicitors or anyone else to enter the defendants' premises against their will ... It only authorises entry and inspection by the permission of the defendants. The plaintiffs must get the defendants' permission. But it does do this: It brings pressure on the defendants to give permission. It does more. It actually orders them to give permission—with, I suppose, the result that if they do not give permission, they are guilty of contempt of court".

The order in the present case was in the same form.

Fifth, no order should be made for delivery up to anyone other than the plaintiff's solicitor or a receiver appointed by the High Court. The court should appoint a receiver to take possession of the chattels unless satisfied that the plaintiffs solicitor has, or can arrange, suitable safe custody for what is delivered to him.

Sixth, the court should follow the guidelines set out in the *Z Ltd* case insofar as they are applicable to chattels in the possession, custody or control of third parties.

Finally, provision should always be made for liberty to apply to stay, vary or discharge the order.

Guidelines are guidelines; they are not Rules of Court and the spirit of them and not the letter should be kept in mind.

Costs reserved to the trial of the action.

7.1.2.8   *Norwich Pharmacal v Commissioners of Customs and Excise* [1974] R.P.C. 101, HL

The first plaintiff, patentee of the drug, furazolidone, learned that it was being imported by unauthorised persons. Since the Customs held records of who those persons were, the plaintiff applied to know the names but their request was refused. The plaintiff accordingly brought an action, inter alia, for discovery of the names and inspection of the relevant documents.

Lord Reid:

Discovery as a remedy in equity has a very long history. The chief occasion for its being ordered was to assist a party in an existing litigation. But this was extended at an early date to assist a person who contemplated litigation against the person from whom discovery was sought, if for various reasons it was just and necessary that he should have discovery at that stage. Such discovery might disclose the identity of others who might be joined as defendants with the person from whom discovery was sought.Indeed in some cases it would seem that the main object in seeking discovery was to find the identity of possible other defendants. It is not clear to me whether in all these cases the plaintiff had to undertake in some way to proceed against the person from whom he sought discovery if he found on discovery being ordered that it would suit him better to drop his complaint against that person and concentrate on his cause of action against those whose identity was disclosed by the discovery. But I would think that he was entitled to do this if he chose.

But it is argued for the respondents that it was an indispensable condition for the ordering of discovery that the person seeking discovery should have a cause of action against the person from whom it was sought. Otherwise it was said the case would come within the "mere witness" rule.

I think that there has been a good deal of misunderstanding about this rule. It has been clear at least since the time of Lord Hardwicke that information cannot be obtained by discovery from a person who will in due course be compellable to give that information either by oral testimony as a witness or on a *subpoena duces tecum*. Whether the reasons justifying that rule are good or bad it is much too late to enquire: the rule is settled. But the foundation of the rule is the assumption that eventually the testimony will be available either in an action already in progress or in an action which will be brought later. It appears to me to have no application to a case like the present case. Here if the information in the possession of the respondents cannot be made available by discovery now, no action can ever be begun because the appellants do not know who are the wrongdoers who have infringed their patent. So the appellants can never get the information.

To apply the mere witness rule to a case like this would be to divorce it entirely from its proper sphere. Its purpose is not to prevent but to postpone the recovery of the information sought. It may sometimes have been misapplied in the past but I see no reason why we should continue to do so.

But that does not mean, as the appellants contend, that the discovery will be ordered against anyone who can give information as to the identity of a wrongdoer. There is absolutely no authority for that. A person injured in a road accident might know that a bystander had taken the number of the car which ran him down and have no other means of tracing the driver. Or a person might know that a particular person is in possession of a libellous letter which he has good reason to believe defames him but the author of which he cannot discover. I am satisfied that it would not be proper in either case to order discovery in order that the person who has suffered damage might be able to find and sue the wrongdoer. Neither authority, principle nor public policy would justify that.

So discovery to find the identity of a wrongdoer is available against anyone against whom the plaintiff has a cause of action in relation to the same wrong. It is not available against a person who has no other connection with the wrong than that he was a spectator or has some document relating to it in his possession. But the respondents are in an intermediate position. Their conduct was entirely innocent; it was in execution of their statutory duty. But without certain action on their part the infringements could never have been committed. Does this involvement in the matter make a difference?

On the view which I take of the case I need not set out in detail the powers and duties of the respondents with regard to imported goods. From the moment when they enter the port until the time when the consignee obtains clearance and removes the goods, they are under the control of the Customs in the sense that the Customs authorities can prevent their movement or specify the places where they are to be put, and in the event of their having any suspicions they have full powers to examine or test the goods. When they are satisfied and the appropriate duty has been paid the consignee or his agent is authorised to remove the goods. No doubt the respondents are never in possession of the goods, but they do have considerable control of them during the period from entry into the port until removal by the consignee. And the goods cannot get into the hands of the consignee until the respondents have taken a number of steps and have released them.

My noble and learned friends, Lord Cross of Chelsea and Lord Kilbrandon, have dealt with the authorities. They are not very satisfactory, not always easy to reconcile and in the end inconclusive. On the whole I think they favour the appellants, and I am particularly impressed by the views expressed by Lord Romilly and Lord Hatherley in *Upmann v Elkan* (1871) 12 Eq. 140; 7 Ch. App. 130. They seem to me to point to a very reasonable principle that if through no fault of his own a person gets mixed up in the tortious acts of others so as to facilitate their wrongdoing he may incur no personal liability but he comes under a duty to assist the person who has been wronged by giving him full information and disclosing the identity of the wrongdoers. I do not think that it matters whether he became so mixed up by voluntary action on his part or because it was his duty to do what he did. It may be that if this causes him expense the person seeking the information ought to reimburse him. But justice requires that he should co-operate in righting the wrong if he unwittingly facilitated its perpetration.

I am the more inclined to reach this result because it is clear that if the person mixed up in the affair has to any extent incurred any liability to the person wronged, he must make full disclosure even though the person wronged has no intention of proceeding against him. It would I think be quite illogical to make his obligation to disclose the identity of the real offenders depend on whether or not he has himself incurred some minor liability. I would therefore hold that the respondents must disclose the information now sought unless there is some consideration of public policy which prevents that.

Apart from public policy the respondents say that they are prevented by law from making this disclosure. I agree with your Lordships that that is not so. If it were they could not even disclose such information in a serious criminal case, but their counsel were, quite rightly, not prepared to press their argument so far as that.

So we have to weigh the requirements of justice to the appellants against the considerations put forward by the respondents as justifying non-disclosure. They are twofold. First it is said that to make such disclosures would or might impair or hamper the efficient conduct of their important statutory duties. And secondly it is said that such disclosure would or might be prejudicial to those whose identity would be disclosed.

There is nothing secret or confidential in the information sought or in the documents which came into the hands of the respondents containing that information. Those documents are ordinary commercial documents which pass through many different hands. But it is said that those who do not wish to have their names disclosed might concoct false documents and thereby hamper the work of the Customs. That would require at least a conspiracy between the foreign consignor and the importer and it seems to me to be in the highest degree improbable. It appears that there are already arrangements in operation by the respondents restricting the disclosure of certain matters if the importers do not wish them to be disclosed. It may be that the knowledge that a court might order discovery in certain cases would cause somewhat greater use to be made of these arrangements. But it was not suggested in argument that that is a matter of any vital importance. The only other point was that such disclosure might cause resentment and impair good relations with other traders: but I find it impossible to believe that honest traders would resent failure to protect wrongdoers.

Protection of traders from having their names disclosed is a more difficult matter. If we could be sure that those whose names are sought are all tort feasors, they do not deserve any protection. In the present case the possibility that any are not is so remote that I think it can be neglected. The only possible way in which any of these imports could be legitimate and not an infringement would seem to be that someone might have exported some fur-azolidone from this country and then whoever owned it abroad might have sent it back here. Then there would be no infringement. But again that seems most unlikely.

But there may be other cases where there is much more doubt. The validity of the patent may be doubtful and there could well be other doubts. If the respondents have any doubts in any future case about the propriety of making disclosures they are well entitled to require the matter to be submitted to the court at the expense of the person seeking the disclosure. The court will then only order discovery if satisfied that there is no substantial chance of injustice being done.

Lords Morris, Dilhorne, Cross and Kilbrandon delivered concurring speeches.

7.1.2.9   *British Steel v Granada Television* [1981] A.C. 1096, HL

Granada obtaining access to secret documents of the plaintiff, which related to important facts affecting a current, much discussed strike by the British Steel workforce. The documents were revealed by a source within British Steel without solicitation or payment, but on condition that the source's identity would not be revealed. Granada used the documents in order to confront the Chairman of British Steel in a broadcast. In response to an order for delivery up, it returned the documents but took steps to remove any indication of who the source was. An order was accordingly sought to compel Granada to reveal the name. Against this Granada sought to establish a public interest immunity in favour of journalists and other media workers.

Lord Wilberforce reviewed case law which established that journalists in general enjoy no privilege against disclosure in litigation. He then considered whether a Norwich Pharmacal *order could be made against a journalist or similar worker:*

But Mr Neill Q.C., for Granada, argued that the remedy of, in effect, a bill of discovery ought not to be applied to a case such as the present. His grounds were, I think, as follows. Historically there is no case of such an action having been brought against a newspaper, or in a breach of confidence case. Yet, in the eighteenth to nineteenth centuries many opportunities must have arisen for doing so, if the action lay. The press was, then as now, eager to publish any information, the more sensational the better, which it had obtained from confidential sources, and, then as now, breaches of confidence or leaks were of common occurrence. The failure or abstinence to invoke such proceedings must, it is said, be taken to reflect an *opinio juris* that no such proceedings could be brought.

Lord Wilberforce reviewed cases and the Newspaper Stamp Act 1836, which (it was argued) gave support to this contention. He continued:

But in the end I am not persuaded that we ought to deny the plaintiffs their remedy. The cases are indecisive and only support an argument *a silentio*: the statute of 1836 seems to have been passed for a different purpose. Abstinence from using this weapon hitherto can be explained by the fact that it is only exceptionally that the aggrieved person would have, and could demonstrate, a real interest in suing the source. If the present is such a case (and I think it is), it is to that extent exceptional and decision on it would not open floodgates to actions against newspapers, still less support any general argument that the confidence existing between journalists and their sources is something which the courts will not respect, still less stifle investigation. To succeed in proceedings aimed at compelling disclosure the plaintiff will always have to satisfy the court that he has a real grievance, even after suing the newspaper, which, in the interest of justice, he ought to be allowed to pursue, and that this ought, in the particular case, to outweigh whatever public interest there may be in preserving the confidence. It is possible that, if the plaintiff succeeds here, fewer "leaks" will occur, though that must be speculation. But I do think that judicially we are able to place a value on this. "Leaks" may vary all the way from mere gossip or scandal to matters of national or international importance. A general proposition that leaks should be encouraged, or at least not discouraged, cannot be made without weighing the detriments in loss of mutual confidence and co-operation which they involve. The public interest involved in individual leaks can be taken account of and weighed by the court in deciding whether to grant the remedy in a particular case.

Lord Wilberforce also held that the order should be granted even though British Steel's primary objective may have been to be able to dismiss the source. He refused to find sufficient countervailing public interest in the information given to the public to justify protecting the source by not making the order. Lords Dilhorne, Fraser and Russell gave concurring speeches; Lord Salmon dissented.

7.1.3   Threats to Sue

7.1.3.1   Patents Act 1977, s.70: Groundless threats of infringement proceedings

S.70(1) Where a person (whether or not the proprietor of, or entitled to any right in, a patent) by circulars, advertisements or otherwise threatens another person with proceedings for any infringement of a patent, a person aggrieved by the threats (whether or not he is the person to whom the threats are made) may, subject to subsection (4) below, bring proceedings in the court against the person making the threats, claiming any relief mentioned in subsection (3) below.

(2) In any such proceedings the plaintiff or pursuer shall, if he proves that the threats were so made and satisfies the court that he is a person aggrieved by them, be entitled to the relief claimed unless—

- **(a) the defendant or defender proves that the acts in respect of which proceedings were threatened constitute or, if done, would constitute an infringement of a patent; and**

- **(b) the patent alleged to be infringed is not shown by the plaintiff or pursuer to be invalid in a relevant respect.**

(3) The said relief is—

- **(a) a declaration or declarator to the effect that the threats are unjustifiable;**

- **(b) an injunction or interdict against the continuance of the threats; and**

- **(c) damages in respect of any loss which the plaintiff or pursuer has sustained by the threats.**

(4) Proceedings may not be brought under this section for a threat to bring proceedings for an infringement alleged to consist of making or importing a product for disposal or of using a process.

(5) It is hereby declared that a mere notification of the existence of a patent does not constitute a threat of proceedings within the meaning of this section.

The Registered Designs Act 1949, s.26, the Copyright Designs and Patents Act 1988, s.253, and the Trade Marks Act 1994, s.21, provide a threats action in generally similar terms, respectively concerning registered designs, (unregistered) design rights and registered marks. There is no equivalent statutory action in respect of other intellectual property.

7.1.3.2   *Granby Marketing Services v Interlego* **[1984] R.P.C. 209, Vinelott J.**

The plaintiff operated as an agent for the promotion of products, including Kellogg's cereals. For a Kellogg's campaign, the plaintiff undertook to procure kits of toy bricks from an Australian supplier. These were to be distributed in the promotion but Interlego wrote claiming that the bricks infringed copyright in their drawings for "Lego" bricks and threatening proceedings. In consequence, Kellogg's refused to take delivery of their bricks and ended their contract with the plaintiff by a small ex gratia payment.

Even on the assumption that the plaintiff could demonstrate that Interlego's action was intended to induce Kellogg to break its contract with the plaintiff, the defendant asserted that no cause of action had been disclosed and applied to strike out.

Vinelott J.:

It appears that there is no clear decision, at least of the English courts, whether a defendant who in good faith asserts a legal right which he claims would be infringed by the performance of a contract between the plaintiff and a third party, intending that the contract be not performed, can be made liable in an action brought by the plaintiff for unjustified interference with his contractual relationship with the third party. Mr Hoffman submits that, although there is no clear decision that no such action will lie, it has been assumed *sub silentio* in a very long series of cases that it will not.

Vinelott J. referred to Pitt v Donovan *(1813) 1 M & S 639;* Green v Button *(1835) 2 Cromp. M & R 707 and* Wren v Weild *(1869) L.R. 4 Q.B. 730. He continued:*

Mr Lightman points out that that case was decided not long after the decision in *Lumley v Gye* when the limits of the tort of wrongful interference with contractual relations were perhaps imperfectly defined. That cannot however be said of *Halsey v Brotherhood* (1880) 15 Ch. D. 514, another case concerning a patent. The plaintiff and the defendant both manufactured steam engines. The defendant owned certain patents and claimed that the plaintiff's engines infringed them. He told customers of the plaintiff what he genuinely believed to be true; that is, that the plaintiff's engines infringed his patent and that, if they dealt with the defendant, he would obtain an injunction. Sir George Jessel M.R. said at 517:

> "The defendant alleges that the plaintiff is making and selling engines which are infringements of his patent. It is said that he is not entitled to tell persons buying the plaintiff's engines that they are infringements and that those persons are liable to an action; and that he is not entitled even to give a notice that these engines are infringements of his patent rights unless he follows up that notice by some legal proceedings. I must entirely dissent from that proposition. There is, as far as I am aware, no law in this country compelling a man to assert his legal right by action. He may, if he thinks fit, give notice to persons, the notices being given bona fide, that they are infringing his legal rights: in many cases it is his duty to do so before bringing an action, and in some cases the legislature has compelled him to do so before bringing an action. Take, for example, those cases of infringement of copyrights and designs, and so on, where the seller is only liable if he knows that the right has been infringed; there you must let him know before bringing an action, or your action would fail".

Then, after observing that in many contexts a person who proposes to assert a legal right is bound not by law but by propriety to give notice of his intention to assert it, he said at 518:

> "If a man, with a view to preventing another man from carrying on his business, knowing he himself has no patent, or knowing that he has an invalid patent, or knowing that the thing manufactured by the other man is not an infringement for the purpose of injuring the other man in his trade, threatens the purchasers or advertises that the thing is an infringement, of course he is liable like any other person who makes a false assertion to the injury of another in his trade, because it is an untrue assertion and not made bona fide. The mere fact of a man mentioning he has a right, and that something is an infringement of it, does not *per se* give a ground of action. It

is obvious that such a course of conduct, adopted bona fide, does not constitute a case in which an action could be maintained, for the essence of the case is the falsity of the assertion and the want of good faith in making it. That is, the assertion is made, not for the purpose of preserving the alleged legal right, but for a different purpose, and has injured the plaintiff in his trade".

That decision was affirmed in the Court of Appeal: see (1884) 19 Ch. D. 386.

Vinelott J. referred to the consequent change introduced for patents and designs in 1883 by the creation of the special "threats action"; to the restricted scope of this provision revealed in Ellis v Pogson *(1923) 40 R.P.C. 62 which was dealt with by statutory amendment in 1932; and to the restrictive general rule at common law to which this development was an admitted exception. He referred for the same approach to* James v Commonwealth *(1939) 62 C.L.R. 339 at 367, per* Dixon J.; *and to the Second US Restatement of Law of Torts, s.773. He continued:*

However, Mr Lightman founds his submission on a passage in the judgment of Whitford J. in *Jaybeam Limited v Abru Aluminium Limited* [1976] R.P.C. 308. In that case, the defendant owned a copyright in drawings relating to a lightweight step-ladder and a registered design relating to it. The plaintiff manufactured a similar step-ladder. The defendant's solicitors wrote to a customer of the plaintiff making certain demands. Implicit in the letter was a claim that the defendant owned the copyright in drawings for their step-ladder which was infringed by the plaintiff's step-ladder. They added:

"Notwithstanding the above and as a separate matter we would also draw your attention to the fact that Abru are registered proprietors of registered design number 940,140".

As regards the claim to be the proprietor of a registered design, the case fell within the threats section in the 1949 Act. As to that, Whitford J. said at 314 that:

"the plaintiffs are undoubtedly entitled to relief in respect of the issue of the threat, more particularly because, although I am prepared to accept for present purposes that there may be an arguable case or possibly an arguable case that what the IPC were selling and what the plaintiffs were making is an infringement of the registered design, the ground of justification is not so thoroughly made out that relief pending the trial should be withheld. Threats of this kind are of tremendous potential damage. Nobody wants to be involved in litigation, let alone litigation about registered designs and patents, which is no doubt why provisions of this sort have been specifically enacted".

He then went on to deal with the copyright claim in a passage which I shall read in full. He said:

"The copyright position is in an entirely different position. So far as threats of proceedings on registered designs are concerned, there is specific statutory provision, a prohibition against threats. So far as copyright is concerned, there is no such statutory provision. The importance of that has perhaps not been quite so acute until in recent years people have come to realise, as the defendants have, that under the provisions of the existing Act manufactured articles which could previously have only been protected under a registered design can confidently be asserted to be an infringement of copyright in drawings. The penalties which may be secured under the Act, particularly by way of damages for conversion, are enormous and threat of proceedings in respect of infringement of copyright may in the end be even more persuasive than the threat of proceedings in respect of infringement of patents or registered designs. However that may be, counsel for the plaintiffs quite rightly accepted there is no statutory provision prohibiting threats and that if he is to succeed in this action he has to succeed on some other basis. That is why he advances the alternative bases of malicious falsehood on the one hand or interference with business relations—possibly interference with contractual relations—on the other".

I do not think I need read the next paragraph, but he continues:

"Let me assume for the moment that the case so far as infringement of copyright is concerned when the action comes may go the one way or the other. Can the plaintiffs succeed in restraining the sending out of letters of this character on the basis of malicious falsehood or some sort of interference with business relations? Once again counsel for the defendants did not argue that it was impossible that the plaintiffs should succeed on one or other of these heads. I myself take the view that it is indeed possible that they may succeed on one or other of these heads. Counsel for the defendants accepts that at the trial of the action the plaintiffs might be entitled to some sort of relief of the kind which they seek in this motion, though he said for interlocutory purposes the relief sought goes much too wide".

That passage seems to me to afford flimsy support for Mr Lightman's submission. Whitford J. clearly thought that the plaintiff might succeed at the trial in establishing that the threats were made maliciously. Moreover the ground on which he thought the plaintiff might, even in the absence of malice, succeed on the other of the heads he mentions namely interference with business relations, referred to earlier as including "possibly interference with contractual relations", is not examined, no doubt because it was conceded in argument that the plaintiff's case in inducing breach of contract was arguable but not strong. None of the relevant authorities were cited to him. I do not therefore feel constrained by the respect which is due to a decision of Whitford J. on a matter relating to copyright law to hold that the facts relied on in the statement of claim can found a possible cause of action.

7.1.3.3 *Mentmore v Fomento* (1955) 72 R.P.C. 157, CA

The defendant sued another enterprise for patent infringement and succeeded before the Court of Appeal, which however stayed the injunction and order for delivery up pending further appeal to the House of Lords. The defendants' legal representative (a solicitor) allegedly said to a buyer from Selfridge's that the decision applied equally to Mentmore pens and that she had until Friday to remove them from the shelves if there were not to be "a little court job again": it was also claimed that he said nothing about suspension of the order. Mentmore then sued the defendants for threats concerning patent infringement and for injurious falsehood. On the latter basis alone, Roxburgh J. made an interlocutory order restraining the defendants from making misleading statements of the kind alleged.

Evershed M.R.:

I have said that the amendment of the writ had been such as to raise the cause of action known as "injurious falsehood"; and, in order that such an action may succeed, it appears that two characteristics must be established, namely, first, that representations have been made which are false and, second, that the representations were not only false but made as it is said, maliciously. The precise significance of the word "maliciously" in that context may be a subject which hereafter will have to be further considered and debated. According to the language of Scrutton L.J. which was quoted by Roxburgh J. himself in an earlier case of *Joyce v Motor Surveys Ltd* [1948] Ch. 252 at 255, "'Maliciously' (is used), not in the sense of illegality, but in the sense of being made with some indirect or dishonest motive. Honest belief in an unfounded claim is not malice; but the nature of the unfounded claim may be evidence that there was not an honest belief in it".

Without pursuing the matter further, if it is eventually found, when all the witnesses have been heard, that a statement here was made which was not only false but was put forward by or on behalf of the defendants not honestly believing it to be true, and with the primary object of damaging the defendants' rivals in business, it would appear to me, prima facie, that a case of injurious falsehood has been established.

Accordingly the Court of Appeal refused to interfere with the judge's order.

7.2   Criminal Offences

7.2.1   Trade Descriptions Act 1968, ss.1(1), 2(1), 14(1), 34

S.1(1) Prohibition of false trade descriptions
Any person who, in the course of a trade or business—

    (a) applies a false trade description to any goods; or

    (b) supplies or offers to supply any goods to which a false trade description is applied;

shall, subject to the provisions of this Act, be guilty of an offence.

S.2(1) Trade Description
A trade description is an indication, direct or indirect, and by whatever means given of any of the following matters with respect to any goods or parts of goods, that is to say—

    (a) quantity, size or gauge;

    (b) method of manufacture, production, processing or reconditioning;

    (c) composition;

    (d) fitness for purpose, strength, performance, behaviour or accuracy;

    (e) any physical characteristics not included in the preceding paragraphs;

    (f) testing by any person and results thereof;

    (g) approval by any person or conformity with a type approved by any person;

    (h) place or date of manufacture, production, processing or reconditioning;

    (i) person by whom manufactured, produced, processed or reconditioned;

    (j) other history, including previous ownership or use.

Section 2(2)–(5) contain a variety of definitions relating to s.2(1).

Section 3 further defines broadly the concept of a false trade description; s.4 likewise defines what constitutes applying a trade description to goods; s.5 deals with case where the description is applied in an advertisement; s.6 gives broad meaning to "offering to supply".

S.14(1) False or misleading statements as to services, etc.
It shall be an offence for any person in the course of any trade or business—

    (a) to make a statement which he knows to be false; or

    (b) recklessly to make a statement which is false; as to any of the following matters, that is to say—

(i) **the provision in the course of any trade or business of any services, accommodation or facilities;**

(ii) **the nature of any services, accommodation or facilities provided in the course of any trade or business;**

(iii) **the time at which, manner in which or persons by whom any services, accommodation or facilities are so provided;**

(iv) **the examination, approval or evaluation by any person of any services, accommodation or facilities so provided; or**

(v) **the location or amenities of any accommodation so provided.**

Section 14(2)–(4) provide definitions, notably of what constitutes "falsity". Section 23 makes it an offence to cause another to commit an offence under the Act; s.24 gives a defence relating to mistake, reliance on information from another and accident which a defendant may rely upon if he can show that he exercised all due diligence to avoid commission.

S.34 Trade marks containing trade descriptions

The fact that a trade description is a trade mark, or part of a trade mark, within the meaning of the Trade Marks Act 1938 does not prevent it from being a false trade description when applied to any goods, except where the following conditions are satisfied, that is to say—

(a) **that it could have been lawfully applied to the goods if this Act had not been passed; and**

(b) **that on the day this Act is passed the trade mark either is registered under the Trade Marks Act 1938 or is in use to indicate a connection in the course of trade between such goods and the proprietor of the trade mark; and**

(c) **that the trade mark as applied is used to indicate such a connection between the goods and the proprietor of the trade mark or a person registered under section 28 of the Trade Marks Act 1938 as a registered user of the trade mark; and**

(d) **that the person who is the proprietor of the trade mark is the same person as, or a successor in title of, the proprietor on the day this Act is passed.**

7.2.2   *Bulmer v Bollinger* [1978] R.P.C. 79, CA

Two British drink manufacturers sought a declaration that they were entitled to call products "Champagne Cider" and "Champagne Perry". Amongst the objections raised by the French champagne producers was a claim that under the Trade Descriptions Act 1968, s.1 they had a civil cause of action against the British manufacturers. On this aspect of the case, Buckley L.J. stated:

I now come to the claim under the Trade Descriptions Act 1968. Section 1 of that Act makes it a criminal offence for any person to apply a false trade description to any goods or to supply or offer to supply any goods to which a false trade description is applied. There is no provision in the Act expressly conferring upon anyone a civil right of action in relation to a false trade description. Mr Sparrow contends, however, that by implication the Act is capable of giving rise to a civil cause of action. In *Cutler v Wandsworth Stadium Ltd* [1949] A.C. 398, Lord Simonds pointed out at 407 that it is often a difficult question whether, where a statutory obligation is placed on A, B who conceives himself to be damnified by A's breach of it has a right of action against him. Lord Simonds went on to say: "The only rule which in all circumstances is valid is that the answer must depend on a consideration of the whole Act and the circumstance, including the pre-existing law, in which it was enacted" Lord Simonds then proceeded to consider certain authorities, including *Black v Fife Coal Co Ltd* [1912] A.C. 149, where Lord Kinnear said at 165: "We are to consider the scope and purpose of the Statute and in particular for whose benefit it is intended. Now the object of the present Statute is plain. It was intended to compel mine owners to make due provision for the safety of the men working in their mines, and the persons for whose benefit all these Rules are to be enforced are the persons exposed to danger. But when a duty of this kind is imposed for the benefit of particular persons, there arises at common law a correlative right in those persons who may be injured by its contravention". So we have to consider whether the defendants can successfully assert that the Trade Descriptions Act 1968 was intended for the protection of the Champagne Houses or of any class of which the Champagne Houses form part.

A similar question arose in respect of the Merchandise Marks Act 1887 to 1953 in the *Spanish Champagne Case* in which Danckwerts J. reached the conclusion that it was impossible to regard those Acts as giving civil rights of action to rival traders [1960] R.P.C. 16 at 34, line 7. Mr Sparrow has placed reliance upon an observation of Lord Goddard C.J., in *Kat v Diment* [1951] 1 K.B. 34 at 42 where he said: "It should be borne in mind that this Act" (The Merchandising Marks Act 1887) "is intended to protect not only the public or traders who may purchase the goods, but also the proprietors of trade marks and those who manufacture and deal in the genuine article". Lord Goddard was not in that case concerned with any question about civil liability, but in any case his language seems to me to be directed to emphasising the wide and general nature of the protection afforded by the Act and not to any suggestion that the Act was intended to protect any particular class of the public. In my judgment, there is no sound basis for suggesting that the Trade Descriptions Act 1968 was passed for the protection of any particular class of the public, and accordingly I think that it cannot give rise to any civil cause of action. Nor, in my opinion, have the defendants established any ground for relief by way of injunction upon any such principle as is adumbrated by Lord Denning M.R. in *Acrow Ltd v Rex Chainbelt Inc* [1971] 1 W.L.R. 1676 at 1682 G.

The other members of the court agreed.

7.2.3   *Scott v Metropolitan Police Commissioner* **[1975] A.C. 819, HL**

The defendant temporarily obtained copies of films from cinema staff in order to make and distribute copies in infringement of copyright. He was charged inter alia *with conspiracy to defraud at common law. No deceit was involved and it was argued (relying on Buckley J.,* Re London and Globe Finance *[1903] 1 Ch. 728 at 732) that this was a necessary element of the offence.*

Viscount Dilhorne reviewed a number of cases which he considered to be inconsistent with this proposition and continued:

What conclusions are to be drawn from the cases to which I have referred? I think they are these:

1. There is no separate and distinct class of criminal conspiracy called conspiracy to effect a public mischief.

2. That description has in the past been applied to a number of cases which might have been regarded as coming within well-known heads of conspiracy, *e.g.* conspiracy to defraud, to pervert the course of justice, etc.: see *Brailsford* [1905] 2 K.B. 730; *Porter* [1910]

1 K.B. 369; *Bassey* 22 Cr.App.R. 160; *Young* 30 Cr.App.R.57; *Newland* [1954] 1 Q.B. 158 and *Bailey* [1956] N.I. 15.

3. It is far too late to hold that a conspiracy of the kind that occurred in those cases was not criminal and Lord Goddard C.J.'s observations in *Newland* should be understood in that sense.

4. The judges have no power to create new offences.

5. Where a charge of conspiracy to effect a public mischief has been preferred, the question to be considered is whether the objects or means of the conspiracy are in substance of such a quality or kind as has already been recognised by the law as criminal.

6. If there are, then one has to go on to consider, on an appeal, whether the course the trial took in consequence of the reference to public mischief was such as to vitiate the conviction.

Relating these conclusions to this appeal, it may be that, if the references to public mischief had been omitted from counts 1 and 2 of the indictment, the case might have proceeded on the basis that the conspiracy charged in each count was conspiracy to defraud, and if the accused had been then convicted, that by applying the reasoning of Lord Radcliffe in *Welham v Director of Public Prosecutions* [1961] A.C. 103, 123 *et seq.* and the dictum of Lord Tucker in *Board of Trade v Owen* [1957] A.C. 602, 621, which I have cited, the convictions could have been upheld.

I express no firm opinion on this though at one time I thought that it might become necessary to do so in order to determine whether or not this appeal should be dismissed on the ground that no miscarriage of justice had actually occurred: Criminal Appeal Act 1968, s.2(1).

7.2.4   *DPP v Withers* [1975] A.C. 852, HL

The defendants, operating an investigation agency, deceived banks, building societies and government agencies into providing personal information about customers, etc., by representing themselves as other branches or agencies. They were charged on two counts of conspiracy to effect a public mischief.

Viscount Dilhorne reviewed the line of cases which allowed charges to be preferred on this basis. He continued:

In *Welham v Director of Public Prosecutions* [1961] A.C. 103 this House had to consider the meaning of "intent to defraud" in relation to forgery. In the course of his speech Lord Radcliffe said, at 123, 124:

> "Now, I think that there are one or two things that can be said with confidence about the meaning of this word 'defraud'. It requires a person as its object: that is, defrauding involves doing something to someone. Although in the nature of things it is almost invariably associated with the obtaining of an advantage for the person who commits the fraud, it is the effect upon the person who is the object of the fraud that ultimately determines its meaning. ... Secondly, popular speech does not give, and I do not think ever has given, any sure guide as to the limits of what is meant by 'to defraud'. It may mean to cheat someone. It may mean to practise a fraud upon

someone. It may mean to deprive someone by deceit of something which is regarded as belonging to him or, though not belonging to him, as due to him or his right".

Later, Lord Radcliffe said, at 126, that he was unable to accept Buckley J.'s observations in *In Re London and Globe Finance Corp Ltd* [1903] 1 Ch. 728, which he said were *obiter*, as an authoritative exposition of words employed in a subsequent statute.

While the meaning to be given to words may be affected by their context and Lord Radcliffe was only considering the meaning of intent to defraud in section 4 of the Forgery Act 1913, the passages which I have cited from his speech are, I think, of general application; and certainly those passages and his speech lend no support to the contention that there cannot be a conspiracy to defraud which does not involve deceit.

In the course of delivering the judgment of the Court of Appeal in *R. v Sinclair* [1968] 1 W.L.R. 1246, where the defendants had been convicted of conspiracy to cheat and defraud a company, its shareholders and creditors by fraudulently using its assets for purposes other than those of the company and by fraudulently concealing such use, James J. said, at 1250: "To cheat and defraud is to act with deliberate dishonesty to the prejudice of another person's proprietary right". Again, one finds in this case no support for the view that in order to defraud a person that person must be deceived.

One must not confuse the object of a conspiracy with the means by which it is intended to be carried out. In the light of the cases to which I have referred, I have come to the conclusion that Mr Blom-Cooper's main contention must be rejected. I have not the temerity to attempt an exhaustive definition of the meaning of "defraud". As I have said, words take colour from the context in which they are used, but the words "fraudulently" and "defraud" must ordinarily have a very similar meaning. If, as I think, and as the Criminal Law Revision Committee appears to have thought, "fraudulently" means "dishonestly", then "to defraud" ordinarily means, in my opinion, to deprive a person dishonestly of something which is his or of something to which he is or would or might but for the perpetration of the fraud be entitled.

The other members of the House agreed that the convictions should be quashed.

7.3 Customs Authorities

7.3.1 Trade Marks Act 1994, ss.89, 91: Restrictions on importation of goods bearing infringing trade marks

S.89(1) The proprietor of a registered trade mark, or a licensee, may give notice in writing to the Commissioners of Customs and Excise—

    (a) that he is the proprietor or, as the case may be, a licensee of the trade mark

    (b) that, at a time and place specified in the notice, goods which are, in relation to that registered trade mark, infringing goods, material or articles are expected to arrive in the United Kingdom—

        (i) from outside the European Economic Area, or
        (ii) from within that Area but not having been entered for free circulation,

    and

    (c) that he requests the Commissioners to treat them as prohibited goods.

(2) When a notice is in force under this section the importation of the goods to which the notice relates, otherwise than by a person for his private and domestic use, is prohibited; but a person is not by reason of the prohibition liable to any penalty other that forfeiture of the goods.

(3) This section does not apply to goods entered, or expected to be entered, for free circulation in respect of which the proprietor of the registered trade mark, or a licensee, is entitled to lodge an application under Article 3(1) of Council Regulation (EEC) No 3842/86 laying down measures to prohibit the release for free circulation of counterfeit goods.

Section 90 gives the power by which the Trade Marks (Customs) Regulations (SI 1994/2625) have been made.

S.91 Where information relating to infringing goods, material or articles has been obtained by the Commissioners of Customs and Excise for the purposes of, or in connection with, the exercise of their functions in relation to imported goods, the Commissioners may authorise the disclosure of that information for the purpose of facilitating the exercise by any person of any function in connection with the investigation or prosecution of an offence under section 92 below (unauthorised use of trade mark, &c. in relation to goods) or under the Trade Descriptions Act 1968.

Note that a similar provision to s.89 operates in respect of infringing copies of literary, dramatic and musical works, sound recordings and films which are the subject of copyright: Copyright, Designs and Patents Act 1988, ss.111, 112. Other intellectual property is not so treated.

INDEX